P9-AGE-616

# THE SCIENCE OF PSYCHOLOGY 5

## An Appreciative View

**LAURA A. KING**
University of Missouri, Columbia

THE SCIENCE OF PSYCHOLOGY: AN APPRECIATIVE VIEW, FIFTH EDITION
Published by McGraw-Hill Education, 2 Penn Plaza, New York, NY 10121. 

This book is printed on acid-free paper.

1 2 3 4 5 6 7 8 9 LWI 24 23 22 21 20 19

ISBN 978-1-260-50052-3 (bound edition)
MHID 1-260-50052-7 (bound edition)

ISBN 978-1-260-04171-2 (loose-leaf edition)
MHID 1-260-04171-9 (loose-leaf edition)

Senior Portfolio Manager: Nancy Welcher
Senior Product Developer: Cara Labell
Executive Marketing Manager: Augustine Laferrera
Marketing Manager: Olivia Kaiser
Lead Content Project Managers: Jodi Banowetz; Sandy Wille
Senior Buyer: Laura Fuller
Lead Designer: David W. Hash
Senior Content Licensing Specialist: Ann Marie Jannette
Cover Image: ©Creative Crop/Getty Images
Compositor: Lumina Datamatics, Inc.



**Library of Congress Cataloging-in-Publication Data**

Names: King, Laura A. (Laura Ann), author.
Title: The science of psychology: an appreciative view / Laura A. King, University of Missouri, Columbia.
Description: Fifth edition. | New York, NY: McGraw-Hill Education, [2020]
Identifiers: LCCN 2019018566 | ISBN 9781260500523 (alk. paper)
Subjects: LCSH: Psychology–Study and teaching.
Classification: LCC BF77 .K53 2020 | DDC 150.76–dc23 LC record available at https://lccn.loc.gov/2019018566



mheducation.com/highered

**for** *Sam*

## about *the author*

©Lisa Jensen

## LAURA A. KING

Laura King did her undergraduate work at Kenyon College, where, already an English major, she declared a second major in psychology during the second semester of her junior year. She completed her AB in English with high honors and distinction and in psychology with distinction in 1986. Laura then did graduate work at Michigan State University and the University of California, Davis, receiving her PhD in personality psychology in 1991.

Laura began her career at Southern Methodist University in Dallas, moving to the University of Missouri in 2001, where she is now a Curators' Professor of Psychological Science. In addition to seminars in the development of character, social psychology, and personality psychology, she has taught undergraduate lecture courses in introductory psychology, introduction to personality psychology, and social psychology. At SMU, she received six different teaching awards, including the "M" award for "sustained excellence" in 1999. At the University of Missouri, she received the Chancellor's Award for Outstanding Research and Creative Activity in 2004.

Her research, which has been funded by the National Institute of Mental Health and the National Science Foundation, has focused on a variety of topics relevant to the question of what it is that makes for a good life. She has studied goals, life stories, happiness, well-being, and meaning in life. In general, her work reflects an enduring interest in studying what is good and healthy in people. In 2001, she earned recognition for her research accomplishments with a Templeton Prize in Positive Psychology. In 2011, she received the Ed and Carol Diener Award for Distinguished Contributions to Personality Psychology. In 2015, she received the Society for Personality and Social Psychology Award for service to the field, in part for her efforts in bringing the science of psychology to students. In 2019, she received the Jack Block Award for distinguished contributions to personality psychology. Laura's research (often in collaboration with undergraduate and graduate students) has been published in *American Psychologist,* the *Journal of Personality and Social Psychology, Psychological Bulletin,* and *Psychological Science.*

Laura has held numerous editorial positions. She is currently the editor of *Perspectives on Psychological Science*. She was editor-in-chief of the Personality and Individual Differences section of the *Journal of Personality and Social Psychology* and the *Journal of Research in Personality* and associate editor for the *Journal of Personality and Social Psychology* and *Personality and Social Psychology Bulletin,* as well as on numerous grant panels. She has edited or coedited special sections of the *Journal of Personality* and *American Psychologist*.

In "real life," Laura is an accomplished cook and enjoys hosting lavish dinner parties, listening to music (mostly jazz vocalists and singer-songwriters), running with her faithful dogs Bill and John, and swimming and debating with her son Sam.

# BRIEF CONTENTS

# CONTENTS

# 3 Biological Foundations of Behavior 58

# 4 Sensation and Perception 98

# 5 States of Consciousness 138

# 8 Thinking, Intelligence, and Language 246

# 9 Human Development 284

# 10 Motivation and Emotion 322

# 11 Gender, Sex, and Sexuality 352

# 12 Personality 390

# 17 Health Psychology 560

# PREFACE

# When Things Go Right for Students... Things Go Right for Instructors

Focusing on why things go right, *The Science of Psychology: An Appreciative View,* Fifth Edition, helps students understand and appreciate psychology as a science and as an integrated whole. Informed by student data, the fifth edition's program extends these themes and enhances their pedagogical value by supporting student understanding of the topics they find the most challenging and then offering learning resources to help students master them.

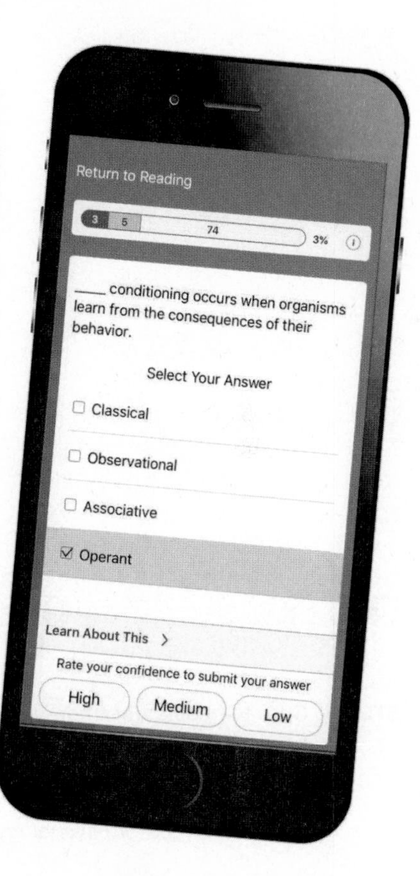


## Appreciating Student Learning

Students today are as different from the learners of the last generation as the current discipline of psychology is from the field 40 years ago. Students now learn in multiple modalities; rather than sitting down and reading traditional printed chapters from beginning to end, their work preferences tend to be more visual and interactive. They like to access information in multiple ways and expect their course material to be engaging and personalized. *The Science of Psychology: An Appreciative View* supports learning by presenting content clearly with engaging examples, presenting key concepts in various ways, providing assignable assessments through Connect Psychology®, and showing students what they know and do not know through the SmartBook 2.0® adaptive reading experience.

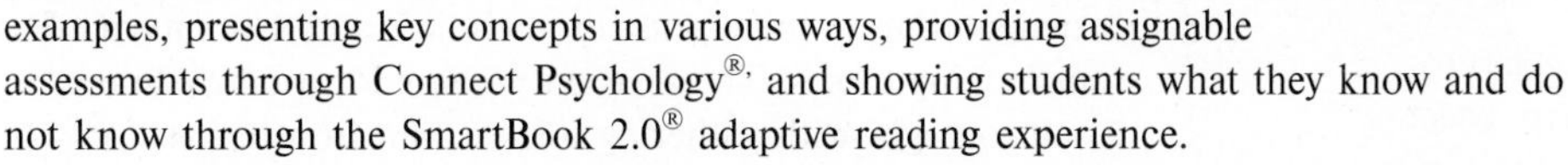

McGraw-Hill Education Connect is a digital assignment and assessment platform that strengthens the link between faculty, students, and coursework, helping everyone accomplish more in less time. Connect Psychology includes assignable and assessable videos, quizzes, exercises, and interactivities, all associated with learning objectives for *The Science of Psychology: An Appreciative View.* Interactive assignments and videos allow students to experience and apply their understanding of psychology to the world with fun and stimulating activities.

### A Personalized Experience that Leads to Improved Learning and Results

Students study more effectively with Connect and SmartBook 2.0. How many students think they know everything about introductory psychology, but struggle on the first exam?

SmartBook helps students study more efficiently by highlighting what to focus on in the chapter, asking review questions, and directing them to resources until they understand. SmartBook creates a personalized study path customized to individual student needs, continually adapting to pinpoint knowledge gaps and focus learning on concepts requiring additional study. By taking the guesswork out of what to study, SmartBook fosters more productive learning and helps students better prepare for class.

Connect reports deliver information regarding performance, study behavior, and effort so instructors can quickly identify students who are having issues or focus on material that the class hasn't mastered.

More than nine years ago, backed by the belief that we could unlock the potential of every type of student with the power of learning science, we embarked on a journey to create a unique educational experience. Spanning over 90+ disciplines and serving multiple educational markets around the world, SmartBook has emerged as the leader in adaptive learning.

Today, SmartBook 2.0 builds on our market-leading technology with enhanced capabilities that deliver a more personalized, efficient, and accessible learning experience for students and instructors. Some of the enhancements include:

- **Mobile and offline reading**–SmartBook 2.0 is available for mobile use on smart devices using McGraw-Hill's ReadAnywhere App. Content can also be downloaded so students and instructors can access their materials anytime and anywhere, whether online or offline.
- **Greater flexibility**–With SmartBook 2.0, instructors can now assign readings down to the sub-topic level (rather than only to the topic level). This provides even greater control and alignment with their syllabus.
- **Accessibility**–SmartBook 2.0 was built from the ground up with accessibility in mind to account for appropriate color contrast, keyboard navigation, and screen reader usability, better supporting students with accessibility needs.

## THE HEAT MAP STORY

### APPRECIATING THE POWER OF STUDENT DATA

**STEP 1.** Over the course of three years, data points showing concepts that caused students the most difficulty were anonymously collected from Connect Psychology's SmartBook for *The Science of Psychology*, 4e.

**STEP 2.** The data from ***SmartBook*** was provided to the author in the form of a **Heat Map**, which graphically illustrated "hot spots" in the text that impacted student learning.

**STEP 3.** Laura King used the ***Heat Map*** data to refine the content and reinforce student comprehension in the new edition. Additional quiz questions and assignable activities were created for use in Connect Psychology to further support student success.

**RESULT:** With empirically-based feedback at the paragraph and even sentence level, Laura King developed the new edition using precise student data to pinpoint concepts that caused students to struggle.

## Better Data, Smarter Revision, Improved Results

For this new edition, data were analyzed to identify the concepts students found to be the most difficult, allowing for expansion upon the discussion, practice, and assessment of challenging topics. The revision process for a new edition used to begin with gathering information from instructors about what they would change and what they would keep. Experts in the field were asked to provide comments that pointed out new material to add and dated material to review. Using all these reviews, authors would revise the material. But today a new tool has revolutionized that model.

McGraw-Hill Education authors now have access to student performance data to analyze and inform their revisions. These data are anonymously collected from the many students who use SmartBook, the adaptive learning system that provides students with individualized assessment of their own progress. Because virtually every text paragraph is tied to several questions that students answer while using SmartBook, the specific concepts with which students are having the most difficulty are easily pinpointed through empirical data in the form of a "heat map" report.

## Powerful Reporting

Whether a class is face-to-face, hybrid, or entirely online, McGraw-Hill Connect provides the tools needed to reduce the amount of time and energy instructors spend administering their courses. Easy-to-use course management tools allow instructors to spend less time administering and more time teaching, while reports allow students to monitor their progress and optimize their study time.

- The **At-Risk Student Report** provides instructors with one-click access to a dashboard that identifies students who are at risk of dropping out of the course due to low engagement levels.
- The **Category Analysis Report** details student performance relative to specific learning objectives and goals, including APA learning goals and outcomes and levels of Bloom's taxonomy.
- **Connect Insight** is a one-of-a-kind visual analytics dashboard—now available for both instructors and student—that provides at-a-glance information regarding student performance.
- **The SmartBook 2.0 Reports** allow instructors and students to easily monitor progress and poinpoint areas of weakness, giving each student a personalized study plan to achieve success.

Expand each category to see scores.

| | Questions | Students submitted | Category score (*Best assignment attempt*) |
|---|---|---|---|
| Bloom's | | | |
| Analyze | 38 | 30/35 | 78% |
| Apply | 214 | 32/35 | 87% |
| Create | 8 | 29/35 | 86% |
| Evaluate | 24 | 31/35 | 92% |
| Remember | 257 | 35/35 | 93% |
| Understand | 238 | 34/35 | 89% |

Expand each category to see scores.

| | Questions | Students submitted | Category score (*Best assignment attempt*) |
|---|---|---|---|
| APA Outcome | | | |
| 1.1: Describe key concepts, principles, and overarching themes in psychology | 315 | 34/35 | 89.15% |
| 1.2: Develop a working knowledge of psychology's content domains | 459 | 33/35 | 88.75% |
| .3: Describe applications of sychology | 132 | 35/35 | 90.5% |
| 1: Use scientific reasoning to erpret psychological enomena | 299 | 28/35 | 78.9% |
| Demonstrate psychology rmation literacy | 304 | 34/35 | 83.5% |
| 2.3: Engage in innovative and integrative thinking and problem solving | 1 | 35/35 | 85.5% |
| 2.4: Interpret, design, and conduct basic psychological research | 16 | 34/35 | 81.7% |
| 3.1: Apply ethical standards to evaluate psychological science and practice | 6 | 33/35 | 92.5% |
| 5.1: Apply psychological content and skills to career goals | 35 | 29/35 | 73.8% |
| 5.2: Exhibit self-efficacy and self-regulation | 24 | 33/35 | 81.6% |

## Informing and Engaging Students on Psychological Concepts

Using Connect Psychology, students can learn the course material more deeply and study more effectively than ever before.

At the Remember and Understand levels of Bloom's taxonomy, **Concept Clips**, help students break down key themes and difficult concepts in psychology. Using easy-to-understand analogies, visual cues, and colorful animation, Concept Clips make psychology meaningful to everyday life. New Concept Clips in the fifth edition include Attraction, Sexual Attraction and Mate Selection, and Replication of Research.



At the Understand and Apply levels of Bloom's taxonomy, **Interactivities**, assignable through Connect, engage students with content through experiential activities. New activities include Sexually Transmitted Infections, Sexual Anatomy, Explicit and Implicit Biases, Cognitive Dissonance, Heuristics, Gardner's Theory of Multiple Intelligences, Personality Assessment, and First Impressions and Attraction.

At the Understand and Apply levels of Bloom's taxonomy, **NewsFlash** exercises, powered by Connect, tie current news stories to key psychological principles and learning objectives. After interacting with a contemporary news story, students are assessed on their ability to make the connection between real life and research findings.

At the Apply level of Bloom's taxonomy, new **Application-Based Activities** provide a means for experiential learning. These are highly interactive, automatically graded, online learn-by-doing exercises that offer students a safe space to apply their knowledge and problem-solving skills to real-world scenarios. Each scenario addresses key concepts and skills that students must use to work through and solve course-specific problems, resulting in improved critical thinking and development of relevant workplace skills.

At the Apply and Analyze levels of Bloom's taxonomy, **Power of Process** guides students through the process of critical reading and analysis. Faculty can select or upload content, such as journal articles, and assign guiding questions to gain insight into students' understanding of the scientific method while helping them improve upon their information literacy skills.

At the Apply and Analyze levels of Bloom's taxonomy, **Scientific Reasoning Exercises** offer in-depth arguments to sharpen students' critical thinking skills and prepare them to be more discerning consumers of psychology in their everyday lives. For each chapter, there are multiple sets of arguments accompanied by auto-graded assessments requiring students to think critically about claims presented as facts. These exercises can also be used in Connect as group activities or for discussion.

## Connecting Anatomy and Physiology to the Science of Psychology

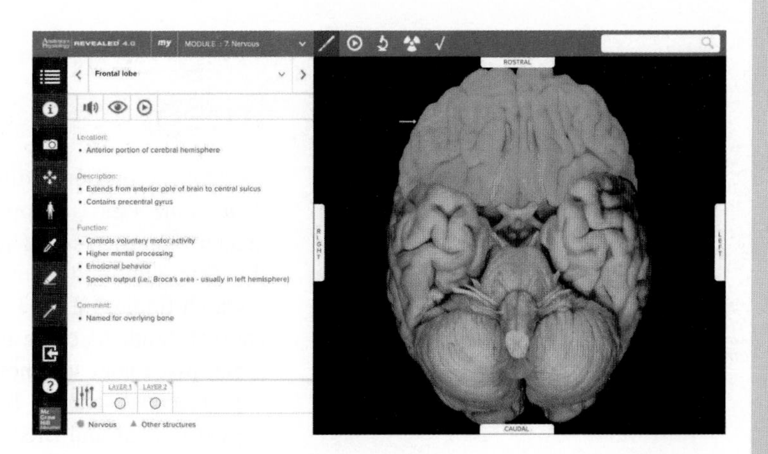


Two interactive tools allow for the exploration of the connection between biology and behavior.

**Lab Activities**: McGraw Hill presents assignments in Connect that walk students through topic-based, real-life scenarios that relate behavior to biology, with illustrated animations, real-life imagery of the nervous system, cells, CT scans, X-ray imaging and histology.

**Touring the Brain and Touring the Senses**: Two digital components, **Touring the Brain and Nervous System** and **Touring the Senses,** offer detailed digital overlays of key structures. These tours provide students with practice in grasping key biological structures and processes that are essential to an appreciation of the role of science in psychology and success in the course. These are available with the instructor's resources and embedded in the ebooks.

# Appreciating Why Things Go Right

*The Science of Psychology: An Appreciative View* continues to emphasize function before dysfunction. Rather than focusing on why things go wrong, the focus is first on *why things go right.*

One of the challenges of this alternative focus is that it goes against human nature. Research in psychology itself tells us that the negative captures our attention more readily than the positive. There is no question that bad news makes headlines. A terrorist attack, a global recession, disturbing climate changes, political scandals, and the everyday demands of juggling work, family, and finances—these and other issues loom large for us all. We strive and struggle to find balance and to sculpt a happy life. The science of psychology has much to offer in terms of helping us understand the choices we make and the implications of these choices for ourselves and for others around the world.

*The Science of Psychology: An Appreciative View* communicates the nature and breadth of psychology—and its value as a science—with an appreciative perspective. Its primary goal is to help students think like psychological scientists.

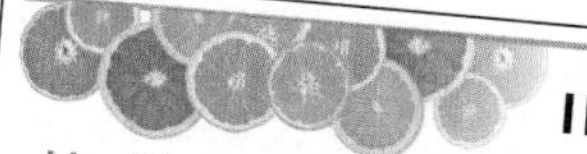

**INTERSECTION**

**Health Psychology and Social Psychology: Can Difference-oriented Interventions Buffer the Stress of Coming to College?**

Do I belong here? Do I have what it takes to succeed? The way new college students answer these questions can have important implications not only for their academic success but also their psychological and physical health (Adelman & others, 2017; Jury & others, 2017). Coming to college can be especially challenging for first-generation college students (those whose parents never attended college). These students can experience a mix of emotions—from excitement and pride to homesickness and worry (Fisher, O'Donnell, & Oyserman, 2017). If people feel that they differ in important ways from everyone around them, they can begin to feel uncertain about their answers to that question, "Do I belong here?" (Destin, Rheinschmidt-Same, & Richeson, 2017). Sometimes, such concerns lead students to dedicate themselves to academic success while sacrificing their physical health (Destin, 2018). Is there a way to succeed academically without harming physical health?

*How do you answer the question "Do I belong here?"*

Many universities have instituted orientation programs to ease the transition to college for first-generation students (Harackiewicz & Priniski, 2018; Zuo & others, 2018). At one school, new students listened for an hour as seniors shared stories about coming to college and learning how to be successful. In this "difference-education" program, the stories highlighted students' diverse backgrounds and how these experiences influenced their college life, both as weaknesses and as strengths. Sounds inspiring, but can something as minor as an hour in an orientation program really have an impact on how students adjust to college over the long haul?

A team of psychologists decided to answer this question. Two years after this orientation experience, the researchers recruited students who had taken part in the difference-education experience as well as students who had participated in an orientation program that addressed the transition to college but did not highlight diverse backgrounds (Stephens & others, 2015). The students came to the lab and were asked to complete a series of stressful tasks, including giving a speech about themselves and completing standardized tests. Their bodily responses to the stressful tasks were measured, and the results of the study were striking: Even two years later, participants who had received the difference-education orientation were more likely to talk about their own diverse backgrounds as strengths in their speeches. In addition, first-generation students who had received difference education were more physiologically balanced during the stressful tasks. The difference-education orientation experience led their bodies to respond better under stress. These results speak to the enduring power of a simple experience to help students recognize that they do have what it takes to succeed in college.

©Hero Images/Getty Images

Certainly, for all of us, entering a new and unfamiliar situation can lead us to feel uncertain about our skills, abilities, and even our very identities. Our expectations for others and ourselves, our identities, roles, and group memberships can influence us in profound ways throughout our lives. Our answers to the question, "Do I belong here?" guide us in and out of situations every day, and we always take our bodies with us.

# Appreciating Psychology as an Integrated Whole

As with the previous editions, the continuing goal of *The Science of Psychology: An Appreciative View* is to present psychology as an integrated field in which the whole is greater than the sum of its parts, but the parts are essential to the whole. Accordingly, this fifth edition illuminates many areas where specialized subfields overlap and where research findings in one subfield support important studies and exciting discoveries in another. Students come to appreciate, for example, how neuroscientific findings inform social psychology and how discoveries in personality psychology relate to leadership in organizational settings. **Intersection** features showcase research at the crossroads of at least two areas and shed light on these intriguing connections.

The fifth edition includes many new Intersections showing the influence of work in one field of psychology on another. For example, the Intersection in the chapter "Health Psychology" links work in personality psychology with health psychology and social psychology to explore the topic "Can Economic Stress Age the Immune System?"

# Appreciating Psychology as a Science

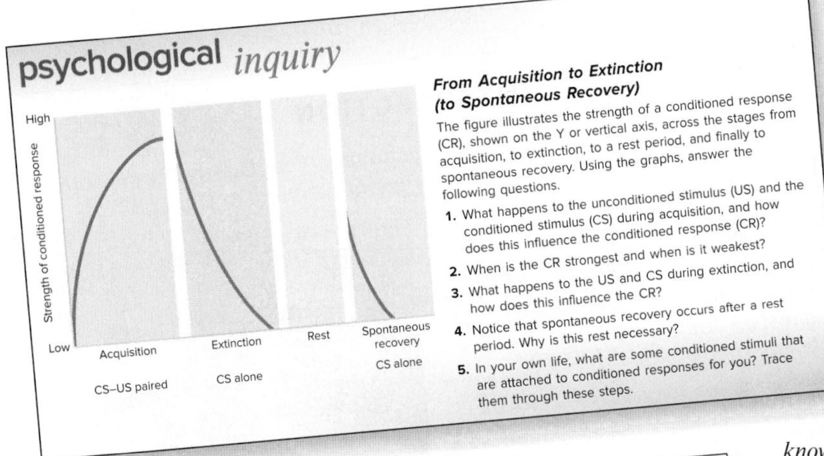

psychological inquiry
High
Strength of conditioned response
Low
Acquisition
CS–US paired
Extinction
CS alone
Rest
Spontaneous recovery
CS alone
From Acquisition to Extinction (to Spontaneous Recovery)
The figure illustrates the strength of a conditioned response (CR), shown on the Y or vertical axis, across the stages from acquisition, to extinction, to a rest period, and finally to spontaneous recovery. Using the graphs, answer the following questions.
1. What happens to the unconditioned stimulus (US) and the conditioned stimulus (CS) during acquisition, and how does this influence the conditioned response (CR)?
2. When is the CR strongest and when is it weakest?
3. What happens to the US and CS during extinction, and how does this influence the CR?
4. Notice that spontaneous recovery occurs after a rest period. Why is this rest necessary?
5. In your own life, what are some conditioned stimuli that are attached to conditioned responses for you? Trace them through these steps.


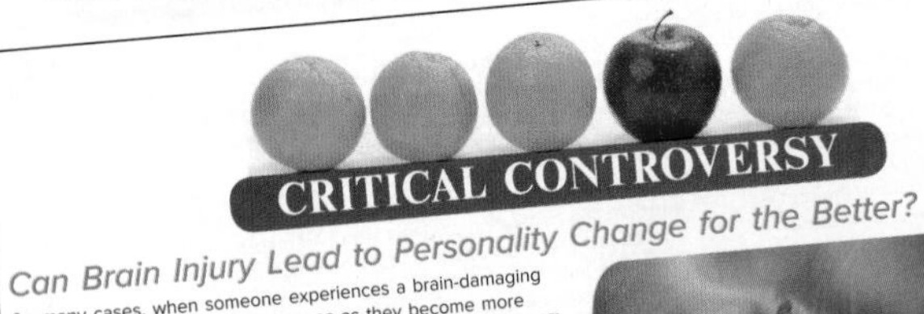

CRITICAL CONTROVERSY
Can Brain Injury Lead to Personality Change for the Better?
In many cases, when someone experiences a brain-damaging
event their very personality changes as they become more
moody, withdrawn, or socially inappropriate (King & others, 2018).
Research on personality change following strokes, surgery, or
brain injuries typically focuses on negative changes. But isn't it
possible that some people become better after these events?
Consider Jason Padgett. As a young man he worked as a clerk
at a futon store. He was brutally attacked by muggers one night,
suffering a concussion. During his recovery, Jason, who had never
been interested in math, suddenly began seeing the world as
made up of intricate, mathematical patterns. He discovered that
he had a special talent for creating artwork based on the
arithmetic laws he saw everywhere. Jason's brain had unlocked
capacities he had never known before (Karlinsky & Frost, 2012).
Jason is now a published author, successful artist, and public
speaker. His case is striking but also quite unusual. Is it possible
for less dramatic positive changes to occur after brain injury?
Some studies do show improvements in people's personalities
following brain injury (Kapur, 1996). Is it possible that such
benefits are linked to the particular brain areas affected?
Recently, a team of scientists (King & others, 2018) studied
97 patients who were rated by a family member or close friend
on personality and behavior before and after a brain-damaging

*The Science of Psychology: An Appreciative View* communicates the nature and breadth of psychology and its value as a science from an appreciative perspective. Its primary goal is to help students think like psychological scientists, which includes asking them questions about their own life experiences. Throughout, students' curiosity is nurtured through timely, applied examples and a focus on what psychological science means for people going about their daily lives.

The fifth edition's attention to function before dysfunction, up-to-date coverage, and broad scope reflect the field of psychology *today*. These qualities underscore psychology's vital and ongoing role as a *science that ever advances knowledge* about ourselves and our interactions in the world. Psychology is a vigorous young science and one that changes quickly. The text narrative interweaves the most current research with classic findings to give students an appreciation of this vitality. In the chapter "Social Psychology", for instance, the treatment of Milgram's classic study on obedience is complemented by an analysis of Burger's more recent attempts to recreate the study.

The **Psychological Inquiry** feature stimulates students' analytical thinking about psychology's practical applications. The selections reinforce student understanding of central aspects of research design, such as the difference between correlational and experimental studies and the concepts of independent and dependent variables. The selections in each chapter guide students' analysis of a figure, graph, or other illustration and include a set of critical thinking questions. For example, one of the Psychological Inquiry features in the chapter "Learning" prompts students to analyze graphical schedules of reinforcement and different patterns of responding to them.

In conjunction with creating current and contemporary course materials, *The Science of Psychology: An Appreciative View* includes citations that bring the most important recent and ongoing research into the text. These updated references give students and instructors the very latest that psychology has to offer on each topic.

Appreciating science also means appreciating disagreements in the field. Each chapter contains a **Critical Controversy** feature highlighting current psychological debates and posing thought-provoking questions that encourage students to examine the evidence on both sides. For example, the Critical Controversy in the chapter "Psychology's Scientific Method" examines how we know research participants are who they say they are, and this feature in the chapter "Learning" explores whether machines can *truly* learn.

©David Lees/Getty Images

## Appreciating Psychology in the Workplace

Because *The Science of Psychology: An Appreciative View* is dedicated to connecting the science of psychology to students' everyday lives and their aspirations, it is only natural to include a chapter on the psychology of work. Nearly all students—some 95 percent—will one day hold a job. Sharing what psychologists have learned about practical matters—such as where employers find new hires, how employees can be fairly evaluated, and the place of work in the good life—is an opportunity that should not be missed. In this fifth edition, the chapter "Industrial and Organizational Psychology" has been updated with new features, including a Critical Controversy on the challenge of work-life balance.

Psychology at Work videos, assignable and assessable within McGraw-Hill Connect, highlight careers in which knowledge of psychology is beneficial. Each video introduces a person at work in his or her job, who specifies how knowledge gained from taking introductory psychology in college is applied to the work environment.

## Appreciating Psychology's Role in Health and Wellness

This fifth edition of *The Science of Psychology: An Appreciative View* continues to emphasize the relevance of psychology to the health and well-being of students and the people in their lives. As in prior editions, substantial discussion and examples focus on the scientific understanding of human strengths and capacities, health, and wellness in order to cultivate students' appreciation for how extensively psychology applies to their lives. These sections are crafted around the idea that although we sometimes think of "health behaviors" as a separate category of activities associated with physical and psychological wellness, the truth is that our bodies and minds are always intertwined, and all of our behaviors are relevant to our capacity to function.

# Appreciating the Course You Want to Teach

## Supporting Instructors with Technology

With McGraw-Hill Education, you can develop and tailor the course you want to teach.

**MCGRAW-HILL CAMPUS** McGraw-Hill Campus (www.mhcampus.com) provides faculty with true single sign-on access to all of McGraw-Hill's course content, digital tools, and other high-quality learning resources from any learning management system. This innovative offering allows for secure and deep integration enabling seamless access for faculty and students to any of McGraw-Hill's course solutions such as McGraw-Hill Connect (all-digital teaching and learning platform), McGraw-Hill Create (state-of-the-art custom-publishing platform), McGraw-Hill LearnSmart (online adaptive study tool), and Tegrity (a fully searchable lecture-capture service).

McGraw-Hill Campus includes access to McGraw-Hill's entire content library, including eBooks, assessment tools, presentation slides, and multimedia content, among other resources, providing faculty with open, unlimited access to prepare for class, create tests/quizzes, develop lecture material, integrate interactive content, and more.

**TEGRITY** With Tegrity, you can capture lessons and lectures in a searchable format and use them in traditional, hybrid, "flipped classes," and online courses. With Tegrity's personalized learning features, you can make study time efficient. Its ability to affordably scale brings this benefit to every student on campus. Patented search technology and real-time learning management system (LMS) integrations make Tegrity the market-leading solution and service.

**CREATE** Easily rearrange chapters, combine material from other content sources, and quickly upload content you have written, such as your course syllabus or teaching notes, using McGraw-Hill Education's Create. Find the content you need by searching through thousands of leading McGraw-Hill Education textbooks. Arrange your book to fit your teaching style. Create even allows you to personalize your book's appearance by selecting the cover and adding your name, school, and course information. Order a Create book and you will receive a complimentary print review copy in three to five business days or a complimentary electronic review copy via e-mail in about an hour. Experience how McGraw-Hill Education empowers you to teach *your* students *your* way. http://create.mheducation.com

## Trusted Service and Support

McGraw-Hill Education's Connect offers comprehensive service, support, and training throughout every phase of your implementation. If you're looking for some guidance on how to use Connect or want to learn tips and tricks from super users, you can find tutorials as you work. Our Digital Faculty Consultants and Student Ambassadors offer insight into how to achieve the results you want with Connect.

## Integration with Your Learning Management System

McGraw-Hill integrates your digital products from McGraw-Hill Education with your school LMS for quick and easy access to best-in-class content and learning tools. Build an effective digital course, enroll students with ease, and discover how powerful digital teaching can be.

Available with Connect, integration is a pairing between an institution's learning management system (LMS) and Connect at the assignment level. It shares assignment information, grades, and calendar items from Connect into the LMS automatically, creating an easy-to-manage course for instructors and simple navigation for students. Our assignment-level integration is available with **Blackboard Learn**, **Canvas by Instructure**, and **Brightspace by D2L**, giving you access to registration, attendance, assignments, grades, and course resources in real time, at one location.

## Instructor Supplements

**INSTRUCTOR'S MANUAL** The Instructor's Manual provides a wide variety of tools and resources for presenting the course, including learning objectives, ideas for lectures and discussions, and handouts.

**TEST BANK** By increasing the rigor of the Test Bank development process, McGraw-Hill Education has raised the bar for student assessment. A coordinated team of subject-matter experts prepared over 3,000 questions. The team methodically vetted each question and set of possible answers for accuracy, clarity, effectiveness, and accessibility; each question has been annotated for level of difficulty, Bloom's taxonomy, APA learning outcomes, and corresponding coverage in the text. Organized by chapter, the questions are designed to test factual, conceptual, and applied understanding. All test questions are available within Test Builder. Test Builder, available in Connect, is a cloud-based tool that enables instructors to format tests that can be printed or administered within a LMS.

**POWERPOINT PRESENTATIONS** The PowerPoint Presentations, available in dynamic, lecture-ready, and accessible WCAG-compliant versions, highlight the key points of the chapter and include supporting visuals. All of the slides can be modified to meet individual needs.

**IMAGE GALLERY** The Image Gallery features the complete set of downloadable figures and tables from the text. These can be easily embedded by instructors into their own PowerPoint slides.

# Appreciating Our Dynamic Field: Chapter-by-Chapter Changes

The fifth edition was revised in response to student "heat map" data that pinpointed the topics and concepts where students struggled the most. Based on this information, feedback from instructors, and changes in the field, the following content revisions have been made.

### CHAPTER 1: WHAT IS PSYCHOLOGY?

- New Critical Controversy: Does Birth Order Matter to Personality?
- New coverage of Mary Whiton Calkin's contribution to the field of psychology
- New coverage of Charles Henry Turner's contribution to the field of psychology
- New Intersection: Health Psychology and Social Psychology: Can Difference-Oriented Interventions Buffer the Stress of Coming to College?

### CHAPTER 2: PSYCHOLOGY'S SCIENTIFIC METHOD

- New metanalysis example on random acts of kindness
- New Intersection: Emotion and Social Psychology: Why Not Say "Thanks"?
- New examples of quasi-experiments
- Expanded discussion of experimenter bias
- New Critical Controversy: How Do We Know Participants Are Who They Say They Are?
- New coverage of the replication crisis
- New coverage of p-hacking in relation to the replication crisis

### CHAPTER 3: BIOLOGICAL FOUNDATIONS OF BEHAVIOR

- Revised coverage of plasticity
- Expanded explanation of action potential
- Revised coverage of glial cells
- Expanded coverage of face processing
- New Critical Controversy: Can Brain Injury Lead to Personality Change for the Better?
- New Intersection: Neuroscience and Language: What Is a Word to a Dog?

### CHAPTER 4: SENSATION AND PERCEPTION

- New explanation and examples of how senses interact
- New Intersection: Sensation and Neuroscience: How Does the Brain Respond when Senses Disagree?
- Expanded coverage of how the brain processes sensory signals
- New research examples on the influence of texting on driving safety
- Expanded discussion of parallel processing and serial processing
- New Critical Controversy: Can We Read Two Words at Once?
- Revised coverage of the primate retina
- Expanded discussion of gender differences in pain

### CHAPTER 5: STATES OF CONSCIOUSNESS

- Expanded discussion of the brain and consciousness
- New Intersection: Consciousness and Comparative Cognition: Do Marmosets Recognize the Minds of Others?
- Expanded coverage of opioids
- Expanded coverage of the impact of THC on the brain
- Expanded coverage of marijuana
- Critical Controversy: Does Legalized Medical Marijuana Reduce Opioid Abuse and Overdoses?

### CHAPTER 6: LEARNING

- New coverage of AI and machine learning
- New Critical Controversy: Can Machines *Truly* Learn?
- New coverage of conditioned immune responses in transplant patients
- New Intersection: Psychology of Learning and Rehabilitation: Can Limbs Relearn Reflexes After Spinal Cord Injury?

### CHAPTER 7: MEMORY

- Updated coverage of the brain and memory
- New Critical Controversy: When Is Your First Memory?
- Expanded exploration of elaboration
- New Intersection: Neuroscience, Cognition, and Emotion: How Can We Explain Déjà Vu?
- Removed emphasis on behavioral priming studies

### CHAPTER 8: THINKING, INTELLIGENCE, AND LANGUAGE

- Revised presentation of the Cognitive Revolution in Psychology
- Expanded explanation of loss aversion
- New Intersection: Cognitive Psychology and Developmental Psychology: Can Young Children Be More Rational than Adults?
- New Critical Controversy: How Does Open-Minded Thinking Relate to Views of Climate Change?
- Revised discussion of heritability and intelligence
- Revised discussion of environmental influences on childhood IQ
- New discussion of intellectual disability as involving functional impairment
- New extended example of child to demonstrate role of environment in language development
- New critical analysis of classic study on the influence of environment on language acquisition

## CHAPTER 9: HUMAN DEVELOPMENT

- New Critical Controversy: Can an Unpredictable Childhood Predict Better Cognitive Function?
- New Intersection: Developmental Psychology and Cognitive Neuroscience: Are Brain Differences the Cause or Effect of Developmental Dyslexia?
- New research on replicability of sticky mittens study

## CHAPTER 10: MOTIVATION AND EMOTION

- Removed coverage of questionable research on eating
- New Intersection: Perception and Eating: Can Portion Information Affect Eating?
- New discussion of controversy around Maslow's hierarchy of needs related to its original source
- New Critical Controversy: Does It Matter How Long a Child Waits for That Second Marshmallow?
- New coverage of the Family Tree Model of Positive Emotion

## CHAPTER 11: GENDER, SEX, AND SEXUALITY

- Updated coverage of Gender Identity
- New Critical Controversy: Isn't Gender "Really" Binary?
- New coverage of Transitioning as a Transgender Person
- Revised coverage of Gender Roles
- Revised coverage of Cognitive Ability
- New Intersection: Psychology of Gender and Social Psychology: Do You "Match" the Scientist Category?
- New cover of the Gender Similarity Hypothesis
- New coverage of Pansexuality
- New coverage of Asexuality
- New coverage of Intersectionality
- New discussion of Frequency of Sexual Activity
- Revised coverage of Pedophilic Disorder
- Revised and expanded coverage of Types and Causes of Sexually Transmitted Infections

## CHAPTER 12: PERSONALITY

- Expanded coverage of Reaction Formation
- Expanded description of the Big Five traits
- New Intersection: Personality and Sleep Science: Are You a Morning Person or an Evening Person - and Does It Matter?
- New Critical Controversy: Are There Personality Types?

## CHAPTER 13: SOCIAL PSCYHOLOGY

- Expanded coverage of Fundamental Attribution Error
- Revised coverage of Altruism
- New Intersection: Social Psychology and Neuroscience: What Can the Brain Reveal About Empathy and Extraordinary Altruism?
- New coverage of Personality as a Factor in Prosocial Behavior
- Revised coverage of Neurobiological Factors and Aggression
- Updated coverage on Video Game Exposure and Aggression
- Revised coverage of Biological Factors in Conformity
- New Critical Controversy: What Happened in the Stanford Prison Experiment?
- Expanded coverage of Explicit and Implicit Prejudice
- Expanded coverage of Social Isolation and Loneliness

## CHAPTER 14: INDUSTRIAL AND ORGANIZATIONAL PSYCHOLOGY

- Updated coverage of Interviews
- New Critical Controversy: Are the Extremely Rich Happier than Those Who Are Very Rich?
- New Intersection: Psychology of Consciousness and I/O Psychology: How Does Leader Mindfulness Affect Employee Well-Being?
- Updated coverage of Transformational Leadership

## CHAPTER 15: PSYCHOLOGICAL DISORDERS

- New section discussing common terms in abnormal psychology
- New major section on Neurodevelopmental Disorders (ASD and ADHD)
- New Critical Controversy: Could Birth Month Predict ADHD Diagnosis?
- Post-Traumatic Stress Disorder and Dissociative Disorders moved to the section on Trauma and Stress-Related Disorders
- Revised discussion of Biological Factors of Depression including evaluation of the role of the serotonin transporter gene
- Expanded treatment of psychosis and first psychotic episode
- Revised discussion of Antisocial Personality Disorder
- Revised coverage of Death by Suicide
- New Intersection: Clinical Psychology and Social Psychology: How Does the Stigma of Mental Illness Affect Social Interactions?

## CHAPTER 16: THERAPIES

- Updated coverage of prescription privileges
- Expanded coverage of the Therapeutic Alliance
- New coverage of cultural humility
- New Intersection: Clinical Psychology and Neuroscience: How Does Dialectic Behavior Therapy Affect the Brain?
- New Critical Controversy: Who Should Decide What Treatment Is Best for a Person?

## CHAPTER 17: HEALTH PSYCHOLOGY

- New table that lists Health Psychology-related topics covered in previous chapters
- Revised presentation of Motivation in relation to resources for effective life change
- New Intersection: Health Psychology and Social Psychology: Can Economic Stress Age the Immune System?
- Revised Critical Controversy: How Powerful Is the Power of Positive Thinking?
- New coverage of Vaping

# ACKNOWLEDGMENTS


## APPRECIATING VALUABLE INSTRUCTOR AND STUDENT FEEDBACK

The quality of *The Science of Psychology: An Appreciative View,* Fifth Edition, is a testament to the skills and abilities of so many people, and I am tremendously grateful to the following individuals for their insightful contributions during the project's development and production.

Adviye Tolunay-Ryan, *Moreno Valley College*
Benjamin Clark, *Florida State College–Jacksonville*
Brandy Young, *Cypress College*
Dan Bellack, *Trident Technical College–Main Campus*
Diana Ciesko, *Valencia College East*
Doug Peterson, *University of South Dakota*
Gabriela Martorell, *Virginia Wesleyan University*
Heather Merchant, *Kirtland Community College*
Jeffrey Armstrong, *Northampton Community College*
Jennifer Engler, *York College of Pennsylvania*
Jennifer Hughes, *Agnes Scott College*
Jerry Green, *Tarrant County College*
Deacon Joe Ferrari, *DePaul University*
John Terrell, *Reedley College*
Johnathan Forbey, *Ball State University*
Joyce Bateman Jones, *Central Texas College*
Kelly Bordner, *Southern Connecticut State University*
Lauren Coursey, *University of Texas–Arlington*
Leslie Kelley, *Collin College*
Marion Perlmutter, *University of Michigan–Ann Arbor*
Nathan Gandy, *Crowder College*
Rene Hernandez, *North Central Texas College*
Richard Sheridan, *William Carey University*
Terry Booth, *Horry-Georgetown Technical College*

Since the publication of the first edition, I have met hundreds of faculty members across the country, and I continue to be awestruck by the hard work, dedication, and enthusiasm of introductory psychology instructors. So, I wanted to say thank you. You all continue to inspire me–to be a better teacher myself, to develop the best learning solutions for the introductory psychology course, and to make our field relevant, accessible, and fun to today's students. I appreciate you!

Thanks as well to the manuscript reviewers whom I have not met in person. Your critical and thoughtful appraisals of the book will benefit students in innumerable ways. I thank you for sharing your expertise with me.

©ESB Professional/Shutterstock


## PERSONAL ACKNOWLEDGMENTS

I would like to extend my deepest appreciation to the many energetic and talented individuals at McGraw-Hill who have contributed so much to this work. Certainly, I owe a debt of gratitude to the amazing sales representatives whose hard work allowed the previous editions of *The Science of Psychology* to be such successes. In addition, I thank Nancy Welcher and Mike Ryan for their encouragement throughout the process of this fifth edition. Thanks also to Dawn Groundwater for wonderful ideas and contributions along the way, as well as to A. J. Laferrera and Olivia Kaiser for finding ways to "let me be me" in the service of the book.

Readers of this fifth edition will benefit from the conscientious efforts of senior product developer Cara Labell, who added her personal energies and gifts to make this edition a special and exciting new introduction to psychology. Cara was extraordinarily helpful in navigating the data from the LearnSmart heat maps, identifying places where the students needed more or different material. It allowed me to "hear" students' needs in a way that was truly invaluable. A very special thanks to copyeditor Janet Tilden for her attention to detail. Her thoughtfulness, her "ear" for the written word, and her willingness to take on responsibilities have been incredible. This fifth edition is better for her efforts. And I am grateful to Content Project Manager Sandy Wille for her deep well of professionalism and skill. Thanks also to Designer David Hash, Content Licensing Specialists Ann Marie Jannette, and Buyer Laura Fuller for their hard work on this project.

Thanks as well to my graduate students, Jake Womick and Chris Sanders. I appreciate how they have patiently managed to build scholarly careers while their advisor has juggled her writing, editing, and teaching.

Finally, I thank my family for their love, support, patience, and encouragement. The last few years have not been easy, but I have been fortunate beyond words to have you on my side.


**Design elements:** brief contents/preface orange ©McGraw-Hill Education/Mark Dierker, photographer; preface orange: ©John Foxx/Imagestate; running heads icon: ©Cre8tive Studios/Alamy

# CHAPTER 1

## CHAPTER OUTLINE

1. Defining Psychology
2. Psychology in Historical Perspective
3. Contemporary Approaches to Psychology
4. What Psychologists Do
5. The Science of Psychology and Health and Wellness

©visualspace/E+/Getty Images

# What Is Psychology?

## Unlocking the Secrets of Heroism

**In a restaurant in Olathe, Kansas, in February of 2017, two men, Srinivas Kuchibhotla and Alok Madasani, both engineers and immigrants to the U.S. from India, were enjoying their regular after-work hangout.** A man began harassing the friends with ethnic slurs, telling them they did not belong in America. The man was asked to leave the restaurant but soon returned with a gun. He opened fire on the two men, killing Srinivas and injuring Alok. Twenty-four-year-old Ian Grillot was in the restaurant that evening and took action. Thinking the gunman had run out of bullets, he rushed toward him to prevent his escape. However, Ian had miscalculated and was shot himself, through the chest and hand. The entire nation of India hailed Ian Grillot as a hero. The Indian community in Kansas, though heartbroken over the loss of life, took up a collection for the young hero and presented him with $100,000 (Victor, 2017). After accepting the check, Ian said he could not have lived with himself if he had not taken action.

As you reflect on this incident, many questions may come to mind. How can we understand such courageous behavior? Why did others in the restaurant not intervene? What motivated the gunman to open fire on two strangers? How can a person be so motivated by hate? These are the kinds of questions psychologists might ask about this remarkable act of heroism.

Although psychologists are interested in extraordinary moments like this one, they are also interested in everyday experiences. The science of psychology is about *all* of human behavior. In fact, ordinary human behavior can become extraordinary when viewed in the right light, with a close lens. Scientists, including psychologists, look at the world with just such a lens. Right now, dedicated scientists are studying things about you that you might never have considered, like how your eyes adjust to a sunny day. There is not a single thing about you that is not fascinating to some psychologist somewhere. Psychologists are passionate about what they study—and what they study is you. ●

# PREVIEW

This introductory chapter begins by formally defining psychology and then gives context to that definition by reviewing the history and the intellectual underpinnings of the field. We next examine a number of contemporary approaches to the subject. We explore what psychologists do—including research, teaching, and therapeutic practice—and consider the areas of specialization within psychology. Our introduction to this dynamic field closes with a look at how understanding and applying psychological findings can positively influence human health and wellness.

● **psychology** The scientific study of behavior and mental processes.

● **science** The use of systematic methods to observe the natural world and to draw conclusions.

# 1. DEFINING PSYCHOLOGY

When you think of the word *psychology,* what first comes to mind? Formally defined, **psychology** is the scientific study of behavior and mental processes. Let's consider the three key terms in this definition: *science, behavior,* and *mental processes.*

As a **science**, psychology uses systematic methods to observe human behavior and draw conclusions. The goals of psychological science are to describe, predict, and explain behavior. In addition, psychologists are often interested in controlling or changing behavior. They use scientific methods to examine interventions that might help–for example, techniques that might reduce violence or promote happiness.

Researchers might be interested in knowing whether individuals will help a stranger who has fallen down. The investigators could devise a study in which they observe people walking past a person who needs help. Through many observations, the researchers could come to *describe* helping behavior by counting how many times it occurs in particular circumstances. They may also try to *predict* who will help, and when, by examining characteristics of the individuals studied. Are happy people more likely to help? Are women or men more likely to help? After psychologists have analyzed their data, they also will want to *explain* why helping behavior occurred when it did. Finally, these investigators might be interested in changing helping behavior by devising strategies to increase helping.

**Behavior** is everything we do that can be directly observed–two people kissing, a baby crying, a college student riding a motorcycle to campus. **Mental processes** are the thoughts, feelings, and motives that each of us experiences privately but that cannot be observed directly. Although we cannot see thoughts and feelings, they are nonetheless real. They include *thinking* about kissing someone, a baby's *feelings* when its mother leaves the room, and a student's *memory* of a motorcycle trip.

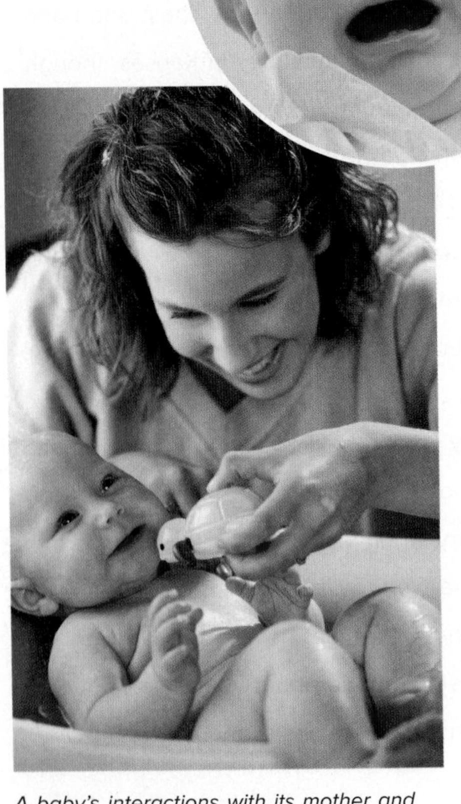

*A baby's interactions with its mother and the infant's crying are examples of behavior because they are observable. The feelings underlying the baby's crying are an example of a mental process that is not observable.*

(first) ©GlowImages/Alamy Stock Photo; (second) ©Brand X Pictures/PunchStock

## The Psychological Frame of Mind

What makes for a good job, a good marriage, or a good life? Although there are a variety of ways to answer the big questions of life, psychologists approach these questions as scientists. This scientific approach means that psychologists test assumptions and rely on objective evidence to solve these puzzles. Psychologists conduct research and rely on that research to provide the bases for their conclusions. They examine the available evidence about some aspect of mind and behavior, evaluate how strongly the data (information) support their hunches, analyze disconfirming evidence, and carefully consider whether they have explored all of the possible factors and explanations. At the core of this scientific approach are four attitudes: critical thinking, skepticism, objectivity, and curiosity.

Like all scientists, psychologists are critical thinkers. **Critical thinking** is the process of reflecting deeply and actively, asking questions, and evaluating the evidence (Lanagan-Leitzel & Diller, 2018). Thinking critically means asking ourselves *how* we know something. Critical thinkers question and test what some people say are facts. They examine research to see if it soundly supports an idea (Kozak, 2018; Shrout & Rodgers, 2018).

Critical thinking reduces the likelihood that conclusions will be based on unreliable personal beliefs, opinions, and emotions. Thinking critically will be very important as you read *The Science of Psychology*. Some of the things you read will fit with your current beliefs, and some will challenge you to reconsider your assumptions. Actively engaging in critical thinking is vital to making the most of psychology. As you read, think about how what you are learning relates to your life experiences and to your assumptions about others.

- **behavior** Everything we do that can be directly observed.
- **mental processes** The thoughts, feelings, and motives that each of us experiences privately but that cannot be observed directly.
- **critical thinking** The process of reflecting deeply and actively, asking questions, and evaluating the evidence.

In addition, scientists are characterized by *skepticism*. Skeptical people challenge whether a supposed fact is really true. Being skeptical can mean questioning what "everybody knows." There was a time when "everybody knew" that women were morally inferior to men, that race could influence a person's IQ, and that the earth was flat. Psychologists, like all scientists, look at such assumptions in new and questioning ways and with a skeptical eye. You might use scientific skepticism the next time you encounter an infomercial about the latest diet craze that promises to help you lose weight "without diet or exercise." A skeptic knows that if something sounds too good to be true, it probably is.

Related to critical thinking and skepticism is the distinction between science and pseudoscience. *Pseudo* means "fake," and *pseudoscience* refers to information that is couched in scientific terminology but is not supported by sound scientific research. Astrology is an example of a pseudoscience. Although astrologers may present detailed information about an individual, supposedly based on when that person was born, no scientific evidence supports these assumptions and predictions. One way to tell that an explanation is pseudoscientific rather than scientific is to look at how readily proponents of the explanation will accept evidence to the contrary.

Being open to the evidence means thinking *objectively*. To achieve this goal, scientists apply the empirical method to learn about the world. Using the **empirical method** means gaining knowledge through the observation of events, the collection of data, and logical reasoning. Being objective involves seeing things as they really are, *not as we would like them to be*. Objectivity means waiting to see what the evidence tells us rather than going with our hunches. Does the latest herbal supplement truly help relieve depression? An objective thinker knows that we must have sound evidence before answering that question.

- **empirical method** Gaining knowledge through the observation of events, the collection of data, and logical reasoning.

Last, scientists are *curious*. Scientists notice things in the world (a star in the sky, an insect, a hero in a bar) and want to know what it is and why it is that way. Science involves asking questions, even very big questions, such as where did the earth come from, and how does love between two people endure for 50 years? Thinking like a psychologist means opening your mind and imagination to wondering why things are the way they are. Once you begin to think like a psychologist, you might notice that the world looks like a different place. Easy answers and simple assumptions will not do.

As you can probably imagine, psychologists have many different opinions about many different things, and psychology, like any science, is filled with debate and controversy. Throughout this book, we will survey areas of debate in psychology in a feature called Critical Controversy. As the first example, check out this chapter's Critical Controversy concerning the relationship between birth order and personality.

Debate and controversy are a natural part of thinking like a psychologist. Psychology has advanced as a field *because* psychologists do not always agree with one another about why the mind and behavior work as they do. Psychologists have reached a more accurate understanding of human behavior *because* psychology fosters controversies and *because* psychologists think deeply and reflectively and examine the evidence on all sides. A good place to try out your critical thinking skills is by revisiting the definition of psychology.

## Psychology as the Science of All Human Behavior

As you consider the definition of psychology as the science of human behavior, you might be thinking, okay, where's the couch? Where's the mental illness? Psychology certainly does include the study of therapy and psychological disorders. *Clinical*

CRITICAL CONTROVERSY

## Does Birth Order Matter to Personality?

When you think of all the experiences siblings share, it may seem odd that people have been fascinated by the potential effects of one difference among them: their birth order. Yet, common beliefs tell us that being born first, second, or last in our family matters in important ways to who we are as people. There is no question that when we find out someone is, say, the baby of the family, we often think we know some things about that person. Is there evidence for birth order's effects on personality?

Impressive contemporary research examining the relationship between birth order and personality characteristics has surveyed very large samples: nearly 400,000 U.S. teenagers (Damian & Roberts, 2015a), as well as over 5,000 U.S. adults, nearly 5,000 British adults, and over 10,000 German teens and adults (Rohrer, Egloff, & Schmukle, 2015). In each study, participants rated their personality characteristics. Additional information was collected about birth order, family size, socioeconomic status, and a range of other things that might matter to their personalities. In addition, the studies compared individuals across different families (for example, comparing all firstborns to all secondborns) as well as within families (comparing siblings to each other).

Because the research used very large samples, accounted for a number of factors that might affect the relationship between birth order and personality, and employed the most sophisticated analytical tools, the investigators were very well positioned to find links between birth order and personality, if those links existed. The results? For all of the samples, the relationship between birth order and personality was, essentially, zero. Birth order was unrelated to personality characteristics. For example, firstborns were no more likely to have leadership traits than their younger siblings were, nor were they more responsible (Damian & Roberts, 2015a; Rohrer, Egloff, & Schmukle, 2015). The lack of associations held as well across genders: Whether older brothers or sisters were compared to younger brothers and sisters, no systematic differences in personality characteristics were found.

©Natalia Lebedinskaia/Shutterstock

These studies tell us that birth order has very little to do with personality. There might be some characteristics that are related to birth order, and psychologists have continued to examine a range of these in explaining important life outcomes, ranging from sexual orientation (Bailey, 2018; Bartlett & Hurd, 2018) to managerial skill (Black, Grönqvist, & Öckert, 2018). Nevertheless, the bulk of evidence indicates that birth order is not as influential as common beliefs might hold. Perhaps a more interesting question might be why we have those common beliefs in the first place.

**WHAT DO YOU THINK?**

- Are you convinced that birth order bears no relationship to personality? Why or why not?
- Where do your beliefs about personality and birth order originate?

*psychologists* in particular specialize in studying and treating psychological disorders. By definition, though, psychology is a much more *general* science. Surely, psychological disorders are very interesting, and the media often portray psychologists as therapists. Yet the view of psychology as the science of what is wrong with people started long before television was invented. So how did we end up with the idea that psychology is only about mental illness?

When they think about psychology, many people think of Sigmund Freud (1856–1939). Freud believed that most of human behavior is caused by dark, unpleasant, unconscious impulses clamoring for expression. For Freud, even the average person on the street is a mysterious well of unconscious desires. Certainly, Freud's theories have had a lasting impact on psychology and on society. You have probably heard of a "Freudian slip." A Freudian slip means someone makes an error in speech that seems to be full of unintentional meaning (like wanting to say "Sigmund Freud" and instead saying "Sigmund

Fraud"). Consider, though, that Freud based his ideas about human nature on the patients whom he saw in his clinical practice–individuals who were struggling with psychological problems. His experiences with these clients, as well as his analysis of himself, colored his outlook on all of humanity. Freud once wrote, "I have found little that is 'good' about human beings on the whole. In my experience most of them are trash" (Freud, [1918] 1963).

Freud's view of human nature has crept into general perceptions of what psychology is all about. Imagine, for example, that you are seated on a plane, having a pleasant conversation with a stranger sitting next to you. At some point you ask your seatmate what she does for a living, and she informs you she is a psychologist. You might think to yourself, "Uh oh. What have I already told this person? What secrets does she know about me that I don't know about myself? Has she been analyzing me this whole time?" Would you be surprised to discover that this psychologist studies happiness? Or intelligence? Or the processes related to the experience of vision? The study of psychological disorders is a very important aspect of psychology, but it represents only one part of the science of psychology.

It is very likely that you yourself have thought about a number of the puzzles of life that interest psychologists. For example, have you ever wondered if having siblings or being an only child can affect a person's personality? Many people have opinions on this issue. Think of all the common beliefs people hold about birth order: Firstborns are natural leaders; "babies of the family" are indulged; middle children are neglected (like Jan Brady). Ask yourself, what is the typical firstborn, middle, or youngest child like? Chances are, if you have siblings (and even if you do not), you have some ideas about the way birth order relates to personality. Do these naive theories have a kernel of truth? The answer to that question might surprise you. The Critical Controversy takes a look at what scientists have to say about this topic.

Psychology seeks to understand the truths of human life in *all* its dimensions, including people's best and worst experiences. Psychologists acknowledge that sometimes an individual's best moments emerge amid the most difficult circumstances. Research on the human capacity for forgiveness demonstrates this point (Riek & DeWit, 2018). Forgiveness is the act of letting go of our anger and resentment toward someone who has harmed us. Through forgiveness we cease seeking revenge or avoiding the person who did us harm, and we might even wish that person well.

One such example is a tragic event from October 2006. Charles Carl Roberts held 10 young Amish girls hostage in a one-room schoolhouse in Pennsylvania, eventually murdering 5 of them and wounding 5 others before killing himself. The grief-stricken Amish community focused not on hatred and revenge but on forgiveness. In addition to raising money for the victims' families, the Amish insisted on establishing a fund for the murderer's family. As they prepared simple funerals for the dead girls, the community invited the killer's wife to attend. The science of psychology has much to offer in expanding our understanding of not only the perpetrator's violence but also the victims' capacity for forgiveness.

The willingness of the Amish community to forgive this horrible crime is both remarkable and puzzling. Can we scientifically understand the human ability to forgive even what might seem to be unforgivable? Psychologists have taken up the topic of forgiveness in research and clinical practice (Akhtar & Barlow, 2018; Wade & others, 2018). Researchers have explored the relationship between religious commitment and forgiveness (Braun & others, 2018), how forgiveness affects memory (Robertson & Swickert, 2018), the cognitive skills required for forgiveness (Karremans, Pronk, & van der Wal, 2015), and the potential dark side of forgiveness, which might emerge, for example, when forgiveness leads an abusive spouse to feel free to continue a harmful behavior (McNulty, 2011). Recent research has examined how individuals can come to forgive themselves (Cornish & others, 2018).

Some argue that psychology has focused too much on the negative while neglecting qualities that reflect the best of humanity (Seligman & Csikszentmihalyi, 2000). From these criticisms positive psychology has emerged. **Positive psychology** is a branch of psychology that emphasizes human strengths. Research in positive psychology centers on

● **positive psychology** A branch of psychology that emphasizes human strengths.

### test yourself

1. What makes psychology a science? What are the goals of psychological scientists?
2. What four attitudes are at the core of the scientific approach?
3. Which particular Freudian views of human nature have influenced general perceptions of what psychology is all about?

topics such as hope, optimism, happiness, and gratitude (Brazeau & Davis, 2018; Kushlev & others, 2018; Rostalski, Muehlan, & Schmidt, 2018). One goal of positive psychology is to bring a greater balance to the field by moving beyond focusing on how and why things go wrong in life to understanding how and why things go right (Dunn, 2018). Positive psychology is not without its own critics, though. Indeed, some psychologists insist that human weaknesses are the most important topics to study (Lazarus, 2003; Lee, 2018).

To be a truly general science of human behavior, psychology must address *all* sides of human experience. Surely, controversy–such as that concerning positive psychology–is a part of any science. The healthy debate that characterizes the field of psychology can give rise to new psychological perspectives, and this is a sign of a lively discipline.

# 2. PSYCHOLOGY IN HISTORICAL PERSPECTIVE

Psychology seeks to answer questions that people have been asking for thousands of years–for example:

- How do we learn?
- What is memory?
- Why does one person grow and flourish while another struggles?

It is a relatively new idea that such questions might be answered through scientific inquiry. From the time human language included the word *why* and became rich enough to enable people to talk about the past, people have created folklore to explain why things are the way they are. Ancient myths attributed most important events to the pleasure or displeasure of the gods. When a volcano erupted, the gods were angry; if two people fell in love, they had been struck by Cupid's arrows. Gradually, myths gave way to *philosophy*–the rational investigation of the underlying principles of being and knowledge–and people began trying to explain events in terms of natural rather than supernatural causes.

Western philosophy came of age in ancient Greece in the fifth and fourth centuries B.C.E. Socrates, Plato, Aristotle, and others debated the nature of thought and behavior, including the possible link between the mind and the body. Later philosophers, especially René Descartes, argued that the mind and body were completely separate, and they focused their attention on the mind. Psychology grew out of this tradition of thinking about the mind and body. The influence of philosophy on contemporary psychology persists today, as researchers who study emotion still talk about Descartes, and scientists who study happiness often refer to Aristotle (Homan, 2018; Schmitter, 2017).

In addition to philosophy, psychology also has roots in the natural sciences of biology and physiology. Read on to trace how the modern field of psychology developed.

**Wilhelm Wundt (1832–1920)** *Wundt founded the first psychology laboratory (with his coworkers) in 1879 at the University of Leipzig.*



## Wundt's Structuralism and James's Functionalism

Wilhelm Wundt (1832–1920), a German philosopher-physician, integrated philosophy and the natural sciences to create the academic discipline of psychology. Some historians say that modern psychology was born in December 1879 at the University of Leipzig when Wundt and his students performed an experiment to measure the time lag between the instant a person heard a sound and the moment he or she pressed a telegraph key to signal having heard it. What was so special about this experiment? Wundt's study was about the workings of the brain: he was trying to measure the time it took the human brain and nervous system to translate information into action. At the heart of this experiment was the idea that mental processes could be measured. This notion ushered in the new science of psychology.

Wundt and his collaborators concentrated on discovering the basic elements, or "structures," of mental processes. Their approach was thus called **structuralism** because it focused on identifying the structures of the human mind. These structures were explored through *introspection,* a process of looking inside our own minds by focusing on our own thoughts (literally, "looking inside"). For this type of research, a person in Wundt's lab would be asked to think (introspect) about what was going on mentally as various events took place. For example, the individual might be subjected to a sharp, repetitive clicking sound and then asked to report whatever conscious thoughts and feelings the clicking produced. Introspection relies entirely on the person's conscious reflection. What made this method scientific was the systematic, detailed self-report required of the person in the controlled laboratory setting.

Although Wundt is most often regarded as the founding father of modern psychology, it was psychologist and philosopher William James (1842–1910), perhaps more than anyone else, who gave the field an American stamp. From James's perspective, the key question for psychology is not so much what the mind *is* (that is, its structures) as what it *is for* (its purposes or functions). James's view was eventually named *functionalism.*

In contrast to structuralism, which emphasized the components of the mind, **functionalism** probed the functions and purposes of the mind and behavior in the individual's adaptation to the environment. Whereas structuralists were looking inside the mind and searching for its structures, functionalists focused on human interactions with the outside world and the purpose of thoughts. If structuralism is about the "what" of the mind, functionalism is about the "why." Unlike Wundt, James did not believe in the existence of rigid structures in the mind. Instead, James saw the mind as flexible and fluid, characterized by constant change in response to a continuous flow of information from the world. James called this natural flow of thought a "stream of consciousness."

A core question in functionalism is "Why is human thought *adaptive*—that is, why are people better off because they can think than they would be otherwise?" When we talk about whether a characteristic is adaptive, we are focusing on how it makes an organism better able to survive. As we will see next, functionalism fit well with the theory of evolution through natural selection proposed by British naturalist Charles Darwin (1809–1882).

**William James (1842–1910)** *James's approach became known as functionalism.*



● **structuralism** Wundt's approach to discovering the basic elements, or structures, of mental processes; so called because of its focus on identifying the structures of the human mind.

● **functionalism** James's approach to mental processes, emphasizing the functions and purposes of the mind and behavior in the individual's adaptation to the environment.

## Darwin's Natural Selection

In 1859, Darwin published his ideas in *On the Origin of Species* (1979). A centerpiece of his theory was the principle of **natural selection**, an evolutionary process in which organisms that are better adapted to their environment will survive and, importantly, produce more offspring.

● **natural selection** Darwin's principle of an evolutionary process in which organisms that are better adapted to their environment will survive and produce more offspring.

Darwin noted that the members of any species are often locked in competition for scarce resources such as food and shelter. Natural selection is the process by which the environment determines who wins that competition. Darwin asserted that organisms with biological features that led to survival and reproduction would be better represented in subsequent generations. Over many generations, organisms with these characteristics would constitute a larger percentage of the population. Eventually, this process could change an entire species.

Importantly, a characteristic cannot be passed from one generation to the next unless it is recorded in the *genes,* those collections of molecules that are responsible for heredity. Genetic characteristics that are associated with survival and reproduction are passed down over generations. According to evolutionary theory, species change through random genetic mutation. That means that, essentially by accident, some members of a species are born with genetic characteristics that make them different from other members. If these changes are adaptive (if they help those members compete for food, survive, and reproduce), they become more common in the species. If environmental conditions were to change, however, other characteristics might become favored by natural selection, moving the process in a different direction.

Evolutionary theory implies that the way we are, at least in part, is the way that is best suited to survival in our environment. The Psychological Inquiry feature lets you critically apply the principles of Darwin's theory of evolution.

## psychological *inquiry*

©Pyty/Shutterstock

### *Explore Evolution from Giraffes to Human Beings*

Evolution through natural selection and genetic mutation is a slow process. Darwin developed his theory of evolution by observing the tremendous variety of natural phenomena in the world.

Let's take a look at one of these creatures—the giraffe. Giraffes are the tallest mammals on earth, with some reaching a soaring height of 19 feet. Much of that height comes from the giraffe's very long neck. That neck poses a mystery that fascinates scientists: Why does the giraffe have such a long neck? Critically explore some possible reasons below, and answer the questions that accompany each explanation.

1. An evolutionary explanation for the giraffe's neck would begin by assuming that, ages ago, some giraffes were genetically predisposed to have longer necks, and others were genetically predisposed to have shorter necks. Take this evolutionary argument one step further: Why do we now see *only* giraffes with long necks?
2. You might reasonably guess that giraffes have long necks in order to reach leaves growing on tall trees—in other words, so that they can eat and survive. However, giraffes often prefer to eat from bushes and relatively low tree branches. Instead, male giraffes use their long necks in fights with other giraffes as they compete over mates. The males that win the fights are more likely to reproduce. Over time, were the winners those with the longer necks or the shorter necks? Explain.
3. The process of evolution sheds light on why members of a particular species share common characteristics. If you were to apply evolutionary theory to human beings, what kinds of characteristics would you focus on and why? Choose one human characteristic and apply the same kinds of questions you considered about the giraffe's long neck. Why are we humans the way we are?

Darwin's theory continues to influence psychologists today because it is strongly supported by observation. We can make such observations every day. Right now, for example, in your kitchen sink, various bacteria are locked in competition for scarce resources in the form of those tempting food particles from your last meal. When you use an antibacterial cleaner, you are playing a role in natural selection, because you are effectively killing off the bacteria that cannot survive the cleaning agents. However, you are also letting the bacteria that are genetically adapted to survive that cleanser to take over the sink. The same principle applies to taking an antibiotic medication at the first sign of a sore throat or an earache. By killing off the bacteria that may be causing the illness, you are creating an environment in which their competitors (so-called antibiotic-resistant bacteria) may flourish. These observations powerfully demonstrate Darwinian selection in action.

If structuralism won the battle to be the birthplace of psychology, functionalism won the war. To this day, psychologists continue to talk about the adaptive nature of human characteristics, although they have branched out to study more aspects of human behavior than Wundt and James would ever have imagined.

**Mary Whiton Calkins (1863–1930)** *Calkins was the first female president in the American Psychological Association*

Wundt and James are rightfully recognized as the twin founders of psychological science. Everyone who holds a PhD in psychology today can trace his or her intellectual family tree back to one of these two men. However, it is important to bear in mind that women and people of color also contributed to psychology, despite facing great discrimination as they sought to pursue the science of human behavior. For example, Mary Whiton Calkins studied psychology with William James at Harvard. She completed all the degree requirements for a PhD but Harvard refused to award her the degree because she was a woman. Nevertheless, she contributed to the early science of psychology, writing four books and over a hundred scholarly articles in her career. She also became the first female president of the American Psychological Association in 1905 (APA, 2018). Racism prevented many talented people of color from contributing to psychology in its early days. Charles Henry Turner, who received a PhD in zoology in 1907, is often recognized as the first African American to conduct psychological research. He was interested in insect behavior and learning, especially the perceptual capacities of honey bees. He published 70 scholarly articles (Abramson, 2009). Sadly, this brilliant scholar was never able to secure a faculty position in a research-oriented university. Creating a truly diverse and representative science is a continuing goal in psychology. Because psychologists are interested in complex, difficult questions, it is vital that everyone with something to contribute–regardless of gender, gender identity, race/ethnicity, disability, or sexual orientation–has a place at the table. Everyone has something to offer to psychology.

Since the early days of psychology, the field has defined itself as the science of human behavior. The question of what exactly counts as human behavior, however, has fueled debate throughout the history of the field. For some psychologists, behavior has meant only observable actions; for others, it has included thoughts and feelings; for still others, unconscious processes have been the focal point. Traces of this debate can be seen today in the various contemporary approaches to the science of psychology that we will consider next.

**Charles Henry Turner (1867–1923)** *Turner is often recognized as the first African American to conduct psychological research.*
©Walter Oleksy/Alamy Stock Photo

# 3. CONTEMPORARY APPROACHES TO PSYCHOLOGY

In this section we survey seven different approaches that represent the intellectual backdrop of psychological science: biological, behavioral, psychodynamic, humanistic, cognitive, evolutionary, and sociocultural.

### test yourself

1. What is structuralism? How does functionalism contrast with structuralism?
2. What is meant when we say that a particular characteristic of an organism is adaptive?
3. In what ways is Darwin's work relevant to psychology?

## The Biological Approach

Some psychologists examine behavior and mental processes through the **biological approach**, which focuses on the body, especially the brain and nervous system. For example, researchers might investigate the way your heart races when you are afraid or how your hands sweat when you tell a lie. Although a number of physiological systems may be involved in thoughts and feelings, the emergence of neuroscience has perhaps contributed the most to physiological psychology (Cacioppo, Cacioppo, & Petty, 2018; Shallice & Cipolotti, 2018).

- **biological approach** An approach to psychology focusing on the body, especially the brain and nervous system.

- **neuroscience** The scientific study of the structure, function, development, genetics, and biochemistry of the nervous system, emphasizing that the brain and nervous system are central to understanding behavior, thought, and emotion.

**Neuroscience** is the scientific study of the structure, function, development, genetics, and biochemistry of the nervous system. Neuroscience emphasizes that the brain and nervous system are central to understanding behavior, thought, and emotion. Neuroscientists believe that thoughts and emotions have a physical basis in the brain. Electrical impulses zoom throughout the brain's cells, releasing chemical substances that enable us to think, feel, and behave. Our remarkable human capabilities would not be possible without the brain and nervous system, which constitute the most complex, intricate, and elegant system imaginable.

Although neuroscience is perhaps most often linked with research on human thought, it has spread to many research areas. Today, psychologists from diverse perspectives study topics such as behavioral neuroscience, developmental neuroscience, social neuroscience, and so forth. Although biological approaches might sometimes seem to reduce complex human experience to simple physical structures, developments in neuroscience have allowed psychologists to understand the brain as an amazingly complex organ, perhaps just as complex as the psychological processes linked to its functioning (Brascamp & others, 2018; Le Bihan, 2016).

*B. F. Skinner was a tinkerer who liked to make new gadgets. Deborah, the younger of his two daughters, was raised in Skinner's enclosed Air-Crib. Some critics accused Skinner of monstrous experimentation with his children; however, the early controlled environment has not had any noticeable harmful effects. Deborah, shown here as a child with her parents, is today a successful artist whose work strongly reflects her unique early childhood experience.*

©AP Images

## The Behavioral Approach

The **behavioral approach** emphasizes the scientific study of observable behavioral responses and their environmental determinants. It focuses on an organism's visible interactions with the environment–that is, behaviors, not thoughts or feelings. The principles of the behavioral approach have been widely applied to help people change their behavior for the better (Baum, 2017; Larson & others, 2018; Moore, 2017). The psychologists who adopt this approach are called *behaviorists*. Under the intellectual leadership of John B. Watson (1878–1958) and B. F. Skinner (1904–1990), behaviorism dominated psychological research during the first half of the twentieth century.

Skinner (1938) emphasized that psychology should be about what people do–their actions and behaviors–and should not concern itself with things that cannot be seen, such as thoughts, feelings, and goals. He believed that rewards and punishments determine our behavior. For example, a child might behave in a well-mannered fashion because her parents have previously rewarded this behavior. We do the things we do, behaviorists say, because of the environmental conditions we have experienced and continue to experience.

Contemporary behaviorists still emphasize the importance of observing behavior to gain understanding of an individual, and they use rigorous methods advocated by Watson and Skinner (Kettering & others, 2018; Miller & Grace, 2013). However, not every behaviorist today accepts the earlier behaviorists' rejection of thought processes, which are often called *cognition*.

## The Psychodynamic Approach

The **psychodynamic approach** emphasizes unconscious thought, the conflict between biological drives (such as the drive for sex) and society's demands, and early childhood family experiences (Barber & Sharpless, 2015; Guntrip, 2018; Marmor, 2018). Practitioners of this approach believe that sexual and aggressive impulses buried deep within the unconscious mind influence the way people think, feel, and behave.

Sigmund Freud, the founding father of the psychodynamic approach, theorized that early relationships with parents shape an individual's personality. Freud's (1924) theory was the basis for the therapeutic technique that he called *psychoanalysis,* which involves an analyst's unlocking a person's unconscious conflicts by talking with the individual about his or her childhood memories, as well as the individual's dreams, thoughts, and feelings. Certainly, Freud's views have been controversial, but they remain a part of contemporary psychology. Today's psychodynamic theories tend to place less emphasis on sexual drives and more on cultural and social experiences as determinants of behavior.

**Sigmund Freud (1856–1939)** *Freud was the founding father of the psychodynamic approach.*

©Ingram Publishing

● **behavioral approach** An approach to psychology focusing on the scientific study of observable behavioral responses and their environmental determinants.

## The Humanistic Approach

The **humanistic approach** emphasizes a person's positive qualities, the capacity for positive growth, and the freedom to choose one's destiny. Humanistic psychologists stress that people have the ability to control their lives and are not simply controlled by the environment (Maslow, 1971; Rogers, 1961). They theorize that rather than being driven by unconscious impulses (as the psychodynamic approach dictates) or by external rewards (as the behavioral approach emphasizes), people can choose to live by higher human values such as *altruism*–unselfish concern for other people's well-being–and free will. Many aspects of this optimistic approach appear in research on motivation, emotion, health, and personality psychology (Anderson, 2018; Hancox & others, 2018; Vansteenkiste & others, 2018).

## The Cognitive Approach

According to cognitive psychologists, the human brain houses a "mind" whose mental processes allow us to remember, make decisions, plan, set goals, and be creative (Dai, Pleskac, & Pachur, 2018; Engle, 2018; Fox & Christoff, 2018). The **cognitive approach**, then, emphasizes the mental processes involved in knowing: how we direct our attention, perceive, remember, think, and solve problems. Many scientists who adopt this approach focus on *information processing,* the ways that the human mind interprets incoming information, weighs it, stores it, and applies it to decision making. Cognitive psychologists seek answers to questions such as how we solve math problems, why we remember some things for only a short time but others for a lifetime, and how we use our imagination to plan for the future.

Cognitive psychologists view the mind as an active and aware problem-solving system (Pezzuti & others, 2014). This view contrasts with the behavioral view, which portrays behavior as governed by external environmental forces. In the cognitive view, an individual's mental processes control behavior through memories, perceptions, images, and thinking.

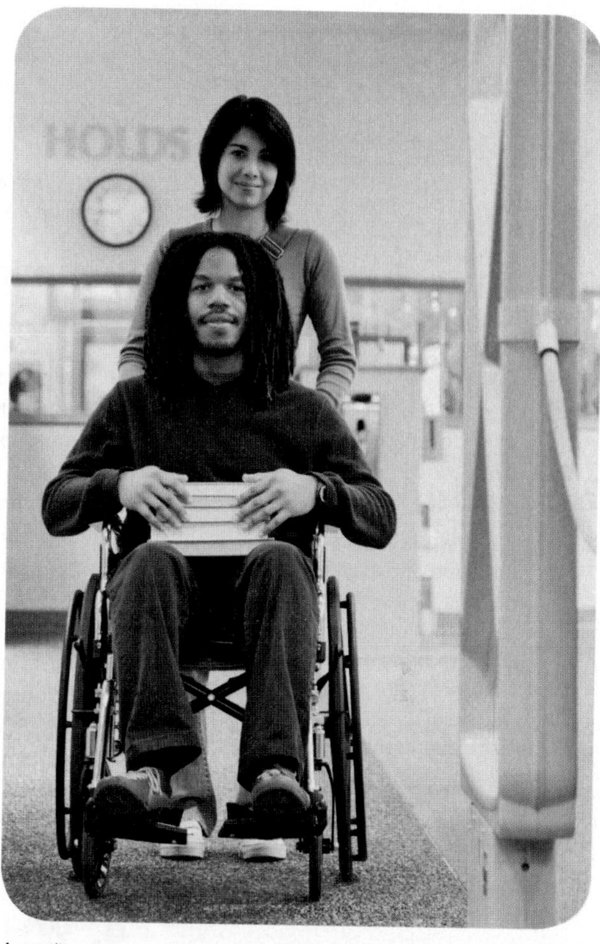

*According to humanistic psychologists, warm, supportive behavior toward others helps us to realize our capacity for self-understanding.*
©Andersen Ross/Blend Images

## The Evolutionary Approach

Although arguably all of psychology emerges out of evolutionary theory, some psychologists emphasize an **evolutionary approach** that uses evolutionary ideas such as adaptation, reproduction, and natural selection as the basis for explaining specific human behaviors. Evolutionary inquiries sometimes involve examining the behavior of nonhuman primates to look for clues for the origins of human behavior (Masterton & others, 2018). David Buss (2015; 2018; Lewis & others, 2017) argues that just as evolution molds our physical features, such as body shape, it also influences our decision making, level of aggressiveness, fears, and mating patterns. Thus, evolutionary psychologists argue, the way we adapt is traceable to problems early humans faced in adapting to their environment (McDermott & Hatemi, 2018).

Evolutionary psychologists believe their approach provides an umbrella that unifies the diverse fields of psychology (Frankenhuis & Tiokhin, 2018; Jost, Sapolsky, & Nam, 2018; Saad, 2017). Not all psychologists agree with this conclusion, however. For example, some critics stress that the evolutionary approach inaccurately explains why men and women have different social roles and does not adequately account for cultural diversity and experiences (Bosak & others, 2018; Eagly & Wood, 2013; 2017). Yet, even psychologists who disagree with applying the evolutionary approach to psychological characteristics still agree with the general principles of evolutionary theory.

## The Sociocultural Approach

The **sociocultural approach** examines the ways in which social and cultural environments influence behavior. Socioculturalists argue that understanding a person's behavior requires knowing about the cultural context in which the behavior occurs (Matsumoto & Juang, 2017; Ott & Michailova, 2018; Steel & others, 2018b). Researchers who focus on sociocultural influences might compare people from different cultures to see whether they are similar or different in important ways.

The sociocultural view focuses not only on comparisons of behavior across countries but also on the behavior of individuals from different ethnic and cultural groups within a country. Rising cultural diversity in the United States in recent years has prompted increasing interest in the lives of ethnic minority groups, especially the factors that have

- **psychodynamic approach** An approach to psychology focusing on unconscious thought, the conflict between biological drives (such as the drive for sex) and society's demands, and early childhood family experiences.
- **humanistic approach** An approach to psychology focusing on a person's positive qualities, the capacity for positive growth, and the freedom to choose one's destiny.
- **cognitive approach** An approach to psychology focusing on the mental processes involved in knowing: how we direct our attention, perceive, remember, think, and solve problems.
- **evolutionary approach** An approach to psychology focusing on evolutionary ideas such as adaptation, reproduction, and natural selection as the basis for explaining specific human behaviors.
- **sociocultural approach** An approach to psychology focusing on the ways in which social and cultural environments influence behavior.

restricted or enhanced their ability to adapt and cope with living in a predominantly non-Latino White society. Further, as the nations of the world grow increasingly economically interdependent, it becomes especially important to understand cultural influences on human interaction. For example, psychologists are interested in studying how psychological characteristics may help or hinder negotiations among individuals from different cultures (Adler & Aycan, 2018).

## Summing Up the Seven Contemporary Approaches

These seven psychological approaches provide different views of the same behavior, and all of them may offer valuable insights that the other perspectives miss. Think about the simple experience of seeing a cute puppy. Looking at that puppy involves physical processes in the eyes, nervous system, and brain—the focus of the biological approach to psychology. The moment you spot that puppy, though, you might smile without thinking and reach down to pet the little guy. That reaction might be a response based on your past learning with your own dog (behavioral perspective), or on unconscious memories of a childhood dog (psychodynamic perspective), or on conscious memories that you especially like this dog breed (cognitive perspective), or even on evolutionary processes that promoted cuteness to help offspring survive (evolutionary approach). You might find yourself striking up a conversation with the puppy's owner, based on your shared love of dogs (humanistic perspective). Further, sociocultural factors might play a role in your decision about whether to ask the owner if you could touch the puppy, whether you share those warm feelings about the puppy with others, or whether the puppy is likely to be viewed as a family member, a worker, or nuisance.

### *test yourself*

1. What are two differences between the cognitive and psychodynamic approaches to psychology?
2. How are the biological and evolutionary perspectives on psychology similar and how are they different?
3. What specific ideas did B. F. Skinner's behaviorist approach emphasize?

# 4. WHAT PSYCHOLOGISTS DO

People who think of themselves as psychologists work in a wide range of settings and engage in many different activities. Figure 1 shows the various settings in which psychologists practice their profession. In this section we look at what psychologists do, and then we zoom in on the areas of specialization.

## Careers in Psychology

Individuals with undergraduate training in psychology might use their expertise in occupations ranging from human resources and business consulting to doing casework for individuals struggling with psychological disorders. Those with graduate training in psychology might work as therapists and counselors, researchers and teachers in universities, or as business consultants or marketing researchers.

Individuals who are primarily engaged in helping others are often called *practitioners* of psychology. They spend most of their time in clinical practice, seeing clients and offering them guidance as they work through problems. However, even psychologists who are primarily concerned with clinical practice pay attention to scientific research. For these individuals, rigorous research guides their therapeutic practice and their efforts to make improvements in the lives of their patients. Increasingly, psychologists who primarily provide therapy engage in *evidence-based practice*—that is, they use therapeutic tools whose effectiveness is supported by empirical research (Dobson & Dobson, 2018).

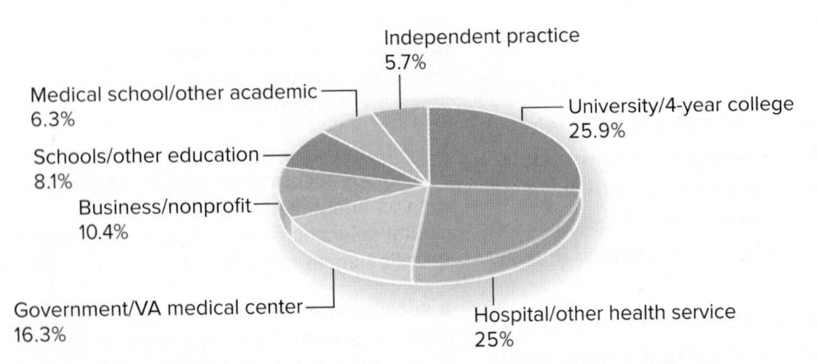


**FIGURE 1 Settings in Which Psychologists Work** This figure shows where individuals who have recent Ph.D.s in psychology work. As you can see, many are employed in higher education and medical contexts. Source: Michalski, Kohout, Wicherski, & Hart (2011).

An important distinction that is often not well understood is the difference between a clinical psychologist and a psychiatrist. A clinical psychologist typically has a doctoral degree in psychology, which requires approximately four to five years of graduate work and one year of internship in a mental health facility. In contrast, a psychiatrist is a physician with a medical degree who subsequently specializes in abnormal behavior and psychotherapy. Another difference between a clinical psychologist and a psychiatrist is that a psychiatrist can prescribe drugs, whereas a clinical psychologist generally cannot. Despite these differences, clinical psychologists and psychiatrists are alike in sharing an interest in improving the lives of people with mental health problems.

Many psychologists who are employed at universities divide their time between teaching and doing research. Research in psychology creates the knowledge that is presented in this book and that you will be learning about in your introductory psychology course.

Human behavior is a vast, complex topic. Most psychologists specialize in a particular area of study, as we consider next.

*Richard J. Davidson of the University of Wisconsin, Madison, shown with the Dalai Lama, is a leading researcher in behavioral neuroscience.*



## Areas of Specialization

Psychology has many areas of specialization. Currently, there are 56 divisions in the American Psychological Association, each focusing on a specific subfield of psychology. Division 1, the Society for General Psychology, seeks to provide a coherent integration of the vast science of psychology. Division 2, the Society for the Teaching of Psychology, is dedicated to devising the best ways to help students learn about this fascinating science. The other main specializations in the field of psychology include the following.

**Physiological Psychology and Behavioral Neuroscience** Researchers who study *physiological psychology* are interested in the physical processes that underlie mental operations such as thinking and memory. Physiological psychologists may use animal models (that is, they may employ animals, such as rats, to study processes that are difficult or impossible to study in the same way in humans) to examine such topics as the development of the nervous system. The field of *behavioral neuroscience* focuses on biological processes, especially the brain's role in behavior. Researchers are engaging in behavioral neuroscience when they track how brain processes reflect behavior. In the chapter "Biological Foundations of Behavior", we will examine the many ways that physiological processes relate to psychological experience.

**Sensation and Perception** Researchers who study *sensation and perception* focus on the physical systems and psychological processes that allow us to experience the world—to listen to a favorite song and to see the beauty of a sunset. These complex processes are the subject of the chapter "Sensation and Perception".

**Learning** *Learning* is the intricate process by which behavior changes in response to changing circumstances. Many researchers study the basic principles of learning using animals such as rats and pigeons. Learning has been addressed from behavioral and cognitive perspectives. This topic is covered in the chapter "Learning".

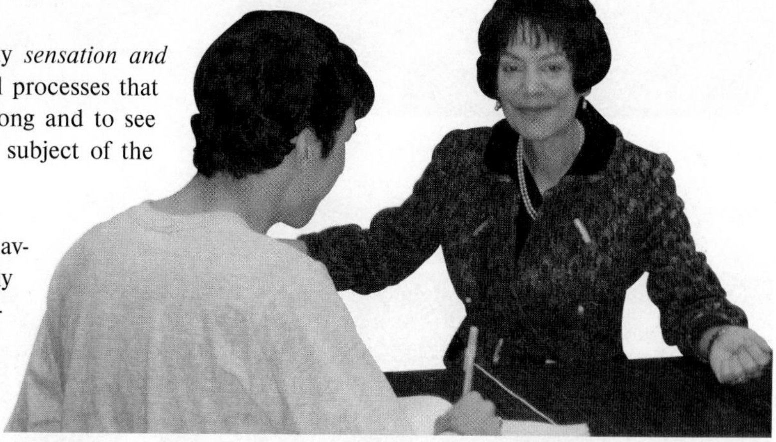

*The research of Carol S. Dweck of Stanford University spans developmental and social psychology. Her influential work looks at how our ideas of self affect our motivation, self-regulation, and achievement.*

Courtesy of Carol S. Dweck, Stanford University

**Cognitive Psychology** *Cognitive psychology* (explored in the chapter "Memory" and the chapter "Thinking, Intelligence, and Language") is the broad name given to the field of psychology that examines attention, consciousness, information processing, and memory. Cognitive psychologists are also interested in skills and abilities such as problem solving, decision making, expertise, and intelligence, topics covered in the chapter "Thinking, Intelligence, and Language". Researchers in cognitive psychology and sensation perception are sometimes called *experimental psychologists.*

**Developmental Psychology** *Developmental psychology* is concerned with how people become who they are, from conception to death. In particular, developmental psychologists concentrate on the biological and environmental factors that contribute to human development. Developmentalists study child development but also adult development and aging. Their inquiries span the biological, cognitive, and social domains of life. The chapter "Human Development" reviews the key findings in this fascinating area.

**Motivation and Emotion** Researchers from a variety of specializations are interested in *motivation and emotion,* two important aspects of experience. Scientists who study motivation address research questions such as how individuals persist to attain a difficult goal and how rewards affect the experience of motivation. Emotion researchers delve into topics including the physiological and brain processes that underlie emotional experience, the role of emotional expression in health, and the possibility that emotions are universal. These fascinating questions are examined in the chapter "Motivation and Emotion".

**Psychology of Women and Gender** Researchers who study the *psychology of women* consider the psychological, social, and cultural influences on women's development and behavior. This field stresses the integration of information about women with current psychological knowledge and beliefs and applies that information to society and its institutions. Psychologists are also interested in understanding the broad topic of *gender* and the way in which our biological sex influences our ideas about ourselves as men and women. We consider these important topics in the chapter "Gender, Sex, and Sexuality".

*Social psychologists explore the powerful influence of groups (such as, clockwise, Chinese Americans, members of motorcycle clubs, gay Americans, inner-city youths, and military families) on individuals' attitudes, thinking, and behavior.*

**Personality Psychology** *Personality psychology* considers personality, consisting of the relatively enduring characteristics of individuals. Personality psychologists study topics such as traits, goals, motives, genetics, personality development, and well-being. Researchers in personality psychology are interested in those aspects of your psychological makeup that make you uniquely you. The field of personality is explored fully in the chapter "Personality".

**Social Psychology** *Social psychology* deals with people's interactions with one another, relationships, social perceptions, social cognition, and attitudes. Social psychologists are interested in the influence of groups on our thinking and behavior and in the ways that the groups to which we belong influence our attitudes. Their research focuses on topics such as understanding and working to reduce racial prejudice, determining whether two heads really are better than one, and exploring how the presence of others influences performance. The chapter "Social Psychology" reviews the major research findings of social psychology.

**Industrial and Organizational Psychology** *Industrial and organizational psychology (I-O psychology)* centers on the workplace–both the workers and the organizations that employ them. I-O psychology is often divided into *industrial psychology* and *organizational psychology*. Among the main concerns of industrial psychology are personnel matters and human resource management. Thus, industrial psychology is increasingly referred to as *personnel psychology*. *Organizational psychology* examines the social influences in organizations, as well as organizational leadership. The chapter "Industrial and Organizational Psychology" investigates the key concerns and findings of I-O psychology.

**Clinical and Counseling Psychology** *Clinical and counseling psychology* is the most widely practiced specialization in psychology. Clinical and counseling psychologists diagnose and treat people with psychological problems. Counseling psychologists sometimes work with people to help solve practical problems in life. For example, counseling psychologists may work with students, advising them about personal problems and career planning. Clinical psychologists are interested in **psychopathology**–the scientific study of psychological disorders and the development of diagnostic categories and treatments for those disorders. The chapters "Psychological Disorders" and "Therapies" explore the intriguing world of psychological disorders and therapies.

● **psychopathology** The scientific study of psychological disorders and the development of diagnostic categories and treatments for those disorders.

**Health Psychology** *Health psychology* is a multidimensional approach to human health that emphasizes psychological factors, lifestyle, and the nature of the healthcare delivery system. Many health psychologists study the roles of stress and coping in people's lives. Health psychologists may work in physical or mental health areas. Some are members of multidisciplinary teams that conduct research or provide clinical services. Health psychology is examined in the chapter "Health Psychology".

This list of specialties cannot convey the extraordinarily rich knowledge you will gain as a student in introductory psychology. To whet your appetite for what is to come, check out the Psychological Inquiry feature and try answering some of the questions that fascinate psychologists.

The specialties that we have discussed so far are the main areas of psychology that we cover in this book. However, they do not represent an exhaustive list of the interests of the field. Other specializations in psychology include the following.

**Community Psychology** *Community psychology* concentrates on improving the quality of relationships among individuals, their community, and society at large. Community psychologists are practitioner scientists who provide accessible care for people with psychological problems. Community-based mental health centers are one means of delivering services such as outreach programs to people in need, especially those who traditionally have been underserved by mental health professionals.

## psychological *inquiry*

### *Questions That Psychology Specialists Ask*

This table identifies the chapter topics we will investigate in this book (column 1). For each topic, a question is posed that the chapter will answer (column 2). What do you think the research will show about each of these questions?

| Chapter Topic | Question | Your Hunch |
|---|---|---|
| Psychology's Scientific Method | How is deception used in psychological research? | 2. |
| Biological Foundations of Behavior | How does behavior change the brain? | 3. |
| Sensation and Perception | Is there evidence for the existence of ESP? | 4. |
| States of Consciousness | What do dreams mean? | 5. |
| Learning | How do pop quizzes influence studying? | 6. |
| Memory | Are you likely to remember what you've learned in intro psychology this year, 50 years from now? | 7. |
| Thinking, Intelligence, and Language | If you know you are fighting a losing battle, does it make sense to quit or keep trying? | 8. |
| Human Development | What kind of parenting is associated with children who are responsible and kind? | 9. |
| Motivation and Emotion | Does pursuing happiness make people happier? | 10. |
| Gender, Sex, and Sexuality | Where does sexual orientation come from? | 11. |
| Personality | Are personality characteristics genetically determined? | 12. |
| Social Psychology | How can we best combat racial prejudice? | 13. |
| Industrial and Organizational Psychology | What kind of leadership leads to success? | 14. |
| Psychological Disorders | What role do genes play in psychological disorders? | 15. |
| Therapies | Does psychotherapy work? | 16. |
| Health Psychology | What is the role of religion and spirituality in influencing healthy choices? | 17. |

Community psychologists strive to create communities that are more supportive of their residents by pinpointing needs, providing services, and teaching people how to access resources that are already available. Community psychologists are also concerned with prevention. That is, they try to prevent mental health problems by identifying high-risk groups and then intervene by connecting individuals with appropriate services and resources in the community.

Feeling lost, lonely, desperate?
When it seems like there's
no hope, there is help.
If you feel trapped...If you feel you have no one to turn to...If you've been feeling down for a while and you're not exactly sure why...
It's important to talk to someone. You can talk to someone right now by calling the Lifeline. Help is available at any time of the day or night—and it's completely free and confidential. We're here to listen and to help you find your way back to a happier, healthier life.
If you or someone you know is thinking about suicide, call the National Suicide Prevention Lifeline:
1-800-273-TALK (8255)
With help comes hope.

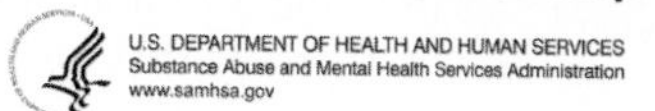


*Community psychologists provide accessible care to local populations, often through efforts such as the suicide-prevention program advertised in this poster.*

Source: U.S. Department of Health and Human Services

**School and Educational Psychology** *School and educational psychology* focuses children's learning and adjustment in school. School psychologists in elementary and secondary school systems test children, make recommendations about educational placement, and collaborate on educational planning teams. Educational psychologists work at colleges and universities, teach classes, and do research on teaching and learning.

**Environmental Psychology** *Environmental psychology* is the study of the interactions between people and their physical environment. Environmental psychologists explore the effects of physical settings in most major areas of psychology, including perception, cognition, learning, development, abnormal behavior, and social relations. Topics that an environmental psychologist might study range from how different arrangements of buildings and rooms influence behavior to what strategies might be used to reduce human behavior that harms the environment (Steg, 2015).

**Forensic Psychology** *Forensic psychology* is the field of psychology that applies psychological concepts to the legal system. Social and cognitive psychologists increasingly conduct research on topics related to psychology and law. Forensic psychologists are hired by legal teams to provide input about many aspects of trials, such as jury selection. Forensic psychologists who have clinical training may also testify as experts in trials, such as when they are asked to evaluate whether a person is likely to be a danger to society.

**Sport Psychology** *Sport psychology* applies psychology's principles to improving sport performance and enjoying sport participation. Sport psychology is a relatively new field, but it is rapidly gaining acceptance. It is now common to hear about elite athletes working with a sport psychologist to improve their performance.

**Cross-Cultural Psychology** Cross-cultural psychology is the study of cultural influences on behavior, thought, and emotion. Cross-cultural psychologists compare the nature of psychological processes in different cultures with a particular focus on whether psychological phenomena are universal or culture specific. Comparing different cultures can provide a way to answer some of the most fascinating questions that psychologists in other areas puzzle over.

Keep in mind that psychology is a collaborative science in which psychologists work together to examine a wide range of research questions. It is common for scholars from different specialties within psychology to join forces to study some aspect of human behavior. *The Science of Psychology* has features called Intersections that show how areas of psychology come together to address important questions. You will read one later in this chapter.

### test yourself

1. What are some career options for a person with an undergraduate degree in psychology? What careers might someone with a graduate degree in psychology pursue?
2. What are the important distinctions between a clinical psychologist and a psychiatrist?
3. Name five areas of specialization in psychology and describe the primary concerns of each.

# 5. THE SCIENCE OF PSYCHOLOGY AND HEALTH AND WELLNESS

We have reviewed a variety of ways that psychologists approach human behavior, and psychologists have learned much about behavior that is relevant to you and your life. By tying research in psychology to your physical health and psychological wellness, in *The Science of Psychology* we seek to answer the question "What does psychology say about *you?*" At the close of each chapter, we will consider how the topics covered matter to your mind and your physical body. This link between the mind and the body has fascinated philosophers for centuries. Psychology occupies the very spot where the mind and body meet.

## How the Mind Impacts the Body

When you think about psychology, your first thought might be about the mind and the complex feelings–such as love, gratitude, hate, and anger–that emanate from it. Psychologists have come to recognize more and more the degree to which the mind is intricately connected to the body. As you will see when we examine neuroscience in the chapter "Biological Foundations of Behavior", observations of the brain at work reveal that when mental processes change, so do physical processes.

Health psychologists view health behavior as a subset of behaviors that are relevant to physical health. These behaviors might include eating well, exercising, not smoking, performing testicular and breast self-exams, and getting enough sleep. But think about it: Is there ever a time when your behavior is *not* relevant to your body and therefore to your health? Is there ever a time when you are doing something–thinking, feeling, walking, running, singing–when your physical body is not present? As long as your body is there–with your heart, lungs, blood, and brain activated–your health is affected. In short, *everything* we do, see, think, and feel is potentially important to our health and well-being.

The way we think can have important implications for our physical health. To read about research showing the ways that students think about how much they fit in at college can affect their experience of stress, see the Intersection.

*The skills of tennis great Sloane Stephens combine psychological and physical processes.*

©jctabb/Shutterstock

## How the Body Impacts the Mind

Similarly, the body can influence the mind in dramatic ways. Consider your fuzzy morning thinking after a late night on the town and how much easier it is to solve life's problems when you have had a good night's sleep. Also recall your outlook on the first day of true recovery from a nagging cold: Everything just seems better, and your mood and your work improve. Clearly, physical states such as illness and health influence the way we think.

The relationship between body and mind is illustrated in a major question that psychologists regularly encounter: What is the relative impact of nature (genetic heritage) versus nurture (social experience) on a person's psychological characteristics? The influence of genetics on a variety of psychological features and the ways that genetic endowments can themselves be altered by social experience will be addressed in many of the main topics in this book, from development (in the chapter "Human Development") to personality (in the chapter "Personality") to psychological

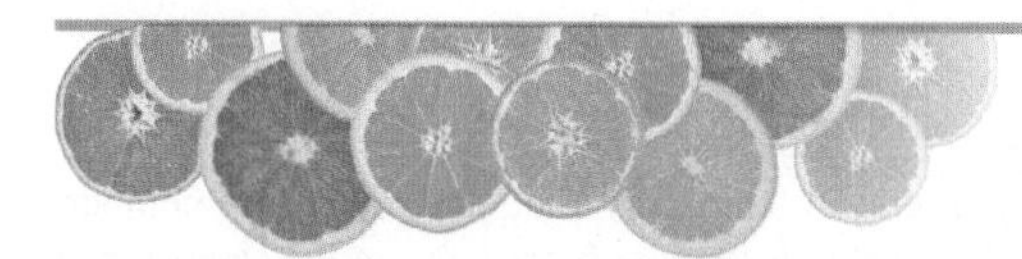

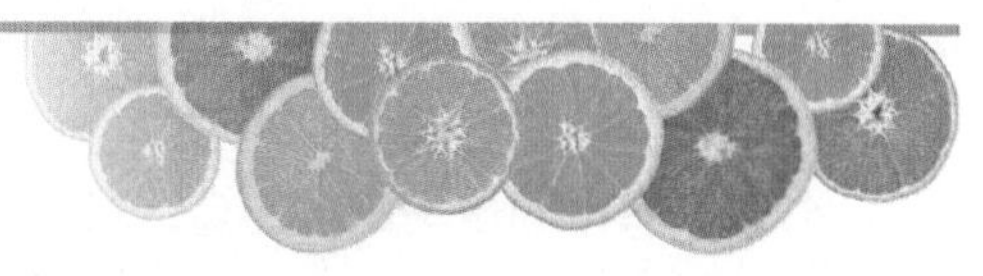

# INTERSECTION

## Health Psychology and Social Psychology: Can Difference-oriented Interventions Buffer the Stress of Coming to College?

Do I belong here? Do I have what it takes to succeed? The way new college students answer these questions can have important implications not only for their academic success but also their psychological and physical health (Adelman & others, 2017; Jury & others, 2017). Coming to college can be especially challenging for first-generation college students (those whose parents never attended college). These students can experience a mix of emotions—from excitement and pride to homesickness and worry (Fisher, O'Donnell, & Oyserman, 2017). If people feel that they differ in important ways from everyone around them, they can begin to feel uncertain about their answers to that question, "Do I belong here?" (Destin, Rheinschmidt-Same, & Richeson, 2017). Sometimes, such concerns lead students to dedicate themselves to academic success while sacrificing their physical health (Destin, 2018). Is there a way to succeed academically without harming physical health?

*How do you answer the question "Do I belong here?"*

Many universities have instituted orientation programs to ease the transition to college for first-generation students (Harackiewicz & Priniski, 2018; Zuo & others, 2018). At one school, new students listened for an hour as seniors shared stories about coming to college and learning how to be successful. In this "difference-education" program, the stories highlighted students' diverse backgrounds and how these experiences influenced their college life, both as weaknesses and as strengths. Sounds inspiring, but can something as minor as an hour in an orientation program really have an impact on how students adjust to college over the long haul?

A team of psychologists decided to answer this question. Two years after this orientation experience, the researchers recruited students who had taken part in the difference-education experience as well as students who had participated in an orientation program that addressed the transition to college but did not highlight diverse backgrounds (Stephens & others, 2015). The students came to the lab and were asked to complete a series of stressful tasks, including giving a speech about themselves and completing standardized tests. Their bodily responses to the stressful tasks were measured, and the results of the study were striking: Even two years later, participants who had received the difference-education orientation were more likely to talk about their own diverse backgrounds as strengths in their speeches. In addition, first-generation students who had received difference education were more physiologically balanced during the stressful tasks. The difference-education orientation experience led their bodies to respond better under stress. These results speak to the enduring power of a simple experience to help students recognize that they do have what it takes to succeed in college.

©Hero Images/Getty Images

Certainly, for all of us, entering a new and unfamiliar situation can lead us to feel uncertain about our skills, abilities, and even our very identities. Our expectations for others and ourselves, our identities, roles, and group memberships can influence us in profound ways throughout our lives. Our answers to the question, "Do I belong here?" guide us in and out of situations every day, and we always take our bodies with us.

disorders (in the chapter "Psychological Disorders"). You will see that your physical and mental selves are intertwined in ways you may have never considered.

Throughout *The Science of Psychology*, we investigate the ways that the various approaches to psychology matter to your life. Psychology is crucially about *you*—essential to your understanding of your life, your goals, and the ways that you can use the insights of thousands of scientists to make your life healthier and happier. In taking introductory psychology, you have an amazing opportunity. You will learn a great deal about human beings, especially one particular human being: you. Whether the psychological research presented is about emotions and motivation or the structures of the nervous system, it is still essentially about the mystery that is you.

### test yourself

1. What has psychology increasingly come to recognize about the relationship between the mind and the body?
2. What are some mental processes that might be involved in efforts to change your physical body, as through diet or exercise?
3. What is some real-life evidence of the body's impact on the mind? Give examples that are different from those in the text.

# SUMMARY

## 1. DEFINING PSYCHOLOGY

Psychology is the scientific study of human behavior and mental processes. Psychologists approach human behavior as scientists who think critically and are curious, skeptical, and objective. Behavior includes everything organisms do that can be observed. Mental processes are thoughts, feelings, and motives.

As a truly general science, psychology addresses all sides of human experience–positive and negative, strengths and weaknesses. Psychology is characterized by controversy and debate, and new psychological perspectives sometimes arise when some scientists question the views of others.

## 2. PSYCHOLOGY IN HISTORICAL PERSPECTIVE

Psychology emerged as a science from the fields of philosophy and physiology. Two founders of the science of psychology are Wilhelm Wundt and William James. Wundt's structuralism emphasized the conscious mind and its structures. James's functionalism focused on the functions of the mind in human adaptation to the environment. The functionalist emphasis on the mind's adaptive character fit well with the new understandings that came from Charles Darwin's theory of evolution.

## 3. CONTEMPORARY APPROACHES TO PSYCHOLOGY

Different approaches to psychology include biological, behavioral, psychodynamic, humanistic, cognitive, evolutionary, and sociocultural views. All of these consider important questions about human behavior from different but complementary perspectives.

The biological approach focuses on the body, especially the brain and nervous system. Technological advances in brain imaging have allowed researchers to examine the brain in all its complexity. The behavioral approach emphasizes the scientific study of observable behavioral responses and their environmental determinants. John B. Watson and B. F. Skinner were important early behaviorists. The psychodynamic approach emphasizes unconscious thought, the conflict between biological instincts and society's demands, and early childhood family experiences. Sigmund Freud was the founding father of the psychodynamic approach. The humanistic approach emphasizes human beings' capacity for positive growth, freedom to choose their destiny, and positive qualities. The cognitive approach emphasizes the mental processes involved in knowing. Cognitive psychologists study attention, thinking, problem solving, remembering, and learning. The evolutionary approach stresses the importance of adaptation, reproduction, and "survival of the fittest." The sociocultural approach focuses on the social and cultural determinants of behavior and encourages us to attend to the ways that our behavior and mental processes are embedded in a social context.

## 4. WHAT PSYCHOLOGISTS DO

Psychologists work in a wide range of settings and engage in many different activities. Individuals with undergraduate training in psychology hold occupations ranging from human resources and business consulting to doing casework for individuals struggling with psychological disorders. Those with graduate training in psychology might work as therapists and counselors, researchers and teachers in universities, or as business consultants or marketing researchers.

A clinical psychologist typically has a doctoral degree in psychology, whereas a psychiatrist is a medical doctor who specializes in treating people with abnormal behavior. A psychiatrist treats patients with psychotherapy and can prescribe drugs; a clinical psychologist generally cannot prescribe medication.

Main areas of specialization in psychology include physiological psychology and behavioral neuroscience, developmental psychology, sensation and perception, cognitive psychology, learning, motivation and emotion, personality psychology, social psychology, industrial and organizational psychology, clinical and counseling psychology, and health psychology. Other specialties include community psychology, school and educational psychology, environmental psychology, the psychology of women, forensic psychology, sport psychology, and cross-cultural psychology.

## 5. THE SCIENCE OF PSYCHOLOGY AND HEALTH AND WELLNESS

Psychologists recognize that the mind and the body are intricately related. The mind can influence the body. The way we think has implications for our nervous system and brain. Our motives and goals can influence our bodies as we strive to be physically fit and eat well. In turn, the body can have an impact on the mind. We think differently when our bodies are rested versus tired, healthy versus unhealthy.

Plan to make the most of your experience in taking introductory psychology by applying your learning to your life. Psychology is, after all, the scientific study of you–your behavior, thoughts, goals, and well-being.

## key *terms*

behavior
behavioral approach
biological approach
cognitive approach
critical thinking
empirical method
evolutionary approach
functionalism
humanistic approach
mental processes
natural selection
neuroscience
positive psychology
psychodynamic approach
psychology
psychopathology
science
sociocultural approach
structuralism

# apply your *knowledge*

1. Ask 10 friends and family members to tell you the first thing that comes to mind when they think of psychology or a psychologist. After hearing their answers, share with them the broad definition of psychology given in this chapter. How do they react?

2. Visit the website of a major book retailer (such as Amazon) and enter "psychology" as a search term. Read the descriptions of five to seven of the most popular psychology books listed. How well do the themes covered in these books represent your perceptions of what psychology is? How well do they represent the approaches to psychology discussed in the text? Are any perspectives over- or underrepresented? If so, why do you think that is?

3. In the directory for your school (or for another institution), look up the psychology faculty. Select several faculty members and see what the areas of specialization are for each person (be careful: their specialty areas may not be the same as the classes they teach). How do you think their areas of academic training might affect the way they teach their classes?

4. Human beings evolved long ago in a very different environment than we occupy today. The survivors were those who were most able to endure extremely difficult circumstances, struggling to find food, avoid predators, and create social groups. What do you think were the most adaptive traits for these early humans? Are those traits still adaptive? To what specific environments are humans adapting today?

5. Adopt Wilhelm Wundt's approach to understanding the human mind and behavior. Invite three friends to listen to a piece of music, and then ask them to reflect on the experience. Examine what each of them say about various aspects of the music. What does this exercise tell you about the subjectivity of introspection? In what ways do you think the method is worthwhile and in what ways is it limited?

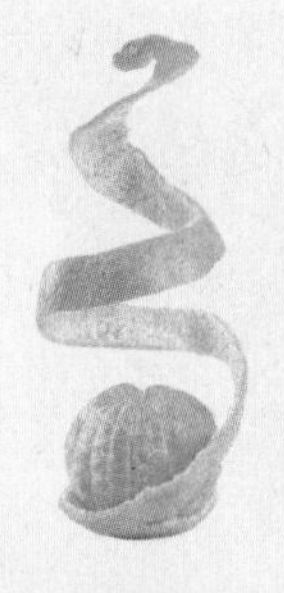

# CHAPTER 2

## CHAPTER OUTLINE

1 Psychology's Scientific Method
2 Types of Psychological Research
3 Research Samples and Settings
4 Analyzing and Interpreting Data
5 Conducting Ethical Research
6 Thinking Critically About Psychological Research
7 The Scientific Method and Health and Wellness

# Psychology's Scientific Method

## Growing Up to Be a "Laser Jock"

**In October 2018, Donna Strickland became the third woman in history (and the first in 55 years) to receive the Nobel Prize in physics.** Strickland, a self-described "laser jock," and her co-inventor were recognized for their discovery of ways to enhance the intensity of lasers (Bryner, 2018). Their work affects many aspects of everyday life, because lasers are used in surgery, manufacturing, drilling, and cutting. Donna Strickland faced barriers throughout her career. Women and people of color are sorely underrepresented among the group of people who call themselves scientists. Not everybody grows up with the idea that they can or should think the way a scientist thinks. Thinking like a scientist means looking at the world with a particular mindset and the goal of understanding why things are the way they are and how they might be changed for the better. Science provides us with solutions to problems by showing us what works and what doesn't. Leaders, policymakers, and concerned people might come up with various ideas to fix a problem, but finding out whether a proposed solution will work requires scientific observation. Psychologists are scientists who examine behavior in all its forms. In a sense, psychologists are children who grow up to become "behavior jocks." ●

# PREVIEW

Being a psychologist means being a scientist who studies psychology. In this chapter, we review the scientific method. You will read about the ways psychologists have applied this general method and about the steps that are involved in recognizing research questions, developing methods to test them, and using statistical techniques to understand the results. Later in the chapter we will consider some of the ethical issues involved in scientific inquiry. Psychology shares a great deal with other sciences, but as you will see, topics that psychologists study sometimes require special methodological and ethical consideration. At the end of the chapter we will examine the role of psychological research in health and wellness.

## 1. PSYCHOLOGY'S SCIENTIFIC METHOD

Science is defined not by *what* it studies but by *how* it does so. Whether you want to study butterflies, Saturn's moons, or happiness, the *way* you study your question of interest determines whether your approach is scientific. The scientific method allows psychologists to gain knowledge about mind and behavior.

Using the scientific method makes psychology a science. Indeed, most of the studies published in psychological research journals follow the scientific method, which comprises these five steps (Figure 1):

1. Observing some phenomenon
2. Formulating hypotheses and predictions
3. Testing through empirical research
4. Drawing conclusions
5. Evaluating the theory

*Science is defined not by what it studies but by how it investigates. Butterflies and happiness can be studied in a scientific manner.*

(first) ©elenathewise/123RF; (second) ©Sam Edwards/Glow Images

### Step 1. Observing Some Phenomenon

The first step in conducting a scientific inquiry involves observing a specific phenomenon. The curious, critically thinking psychologist sees something and wants to know why or how it is the way it is. Examples of moments that might inspire a scientific inquiry include the following:

- Current events, such as public protests of various policies
- Social issues, like the divorce rate
- Personal experiences, such as an interaction with a child

● **theory** A broad idea or set of closely related ideas that attempts to explain observations and to make predictions about future observations.

As scientists consider such issues, they often develop theories. A **theory** is a broad idea or set of closely related ideas that attempts to explain observations. Theories tell us about the relationships between variables on a conceptual level. They seek to explain why certain things have happened and can be used to make predictions about future observations. Theories provide a logical basis for aspects of research studies, from predictions to designs.

It can be difficult to fully grasp what a theory is or why theories are important. A theory is a testable set of propositions that describe something important about the world and allow scientists to make predictions. Psychologists have proposed theories that describe human behavior and lead to specific predictions about that behavior. For instance, some psychologists theorize that the most important human need is to belong to a social group (Baumeister & Leary, 2000). From this theory we might come up with a variety of predictions. For example, we might expect that people will be highly motivated to fit in and feel especially distressed when they are not accepted by others (Verhagen, Lodder, & Baumeister, 2018). This theory might also lead to the prediction that being rejected by others would be a very distressing experience (Antico & others, 2018). Theories make sense of some aspect of human behavior and allow us to extrapolate into different circumstances and domains to

**1**
**Observing Some Phenomenon**
We feel good when we give someone a gift. However, do we genuinely feel better giving something away than we might feel if we could keep it? Elizabeth Dunn, Lara Aknin, and Michael Norton (2008) decided to test this question.

**2**
**Formulating Hypotheses and Predictions**
These researchers hypothesized that spending money on other people would lead to greater happiness than spending money on oneself.

**3**
**Testing Through Empirical Research**
In an experiment designed to examine this prediction, the researchers randomly assigned undergraduate participants to receive money ($5 or $20) that the students had to spend either on themselves or on someone else by 5 p.m. that day. Those who spent the money on *someone else* reported greater happiness that night.

**4**
**Drawing Conclusions**
The experiment supported the hypothesis that spending money on others can be a strong predictor of happiness. Money might not buy happiness, the researchers concluded, but spending money in a particular way—that is, on other people—may enhance happiness.

**5**
**Evaluating the Theory**
The experimental results were published in the prestigious journal *Science*. Now that the findings are public, other researchers might investigate related topics and questions inspired by this work, and their experiments might shed further light on the original conclusions.

**FIGURE 1 Steps in the Scientific Method: Is It Better to Give Than to Receive?** This figure shows how the steps in the scientific method were applied in a research experiment examining how spending money on ourselves or others can influence happiness.
(first photo) ©C Squared Studios/Photodisc/Getty Images; (third photo) ©Jupiter Images/Brand X Pictures/Alamy Stock Photo

think about what we should expect. Those expectations are hypotheses and predictions. Theories are useful because they guide scientists in designing their research.

## Step 2. Formulating Hypotheses and Predictions

The second step in the scientific method is stating a hypothesis. A **hypothesis** is an educated guess that derives logically from a theory. It is an expectation that can be tested. A theory can generate many hypotheses. If more and more hypotheses related to a theory turn out to be true, the theory gains in credibility. For example, a researcher who believes that social belonging is the most important aspect of human functioning might predict that people who belong to social groups will be happier than those who do not. Another hypothesis from the theory that belonging to a group is important to human functioning might be that individuals who have been socially excluded will feel less happy than those who have been socially included. These general hypotheses can be tested in different studies. A **prediction** is a specific expectation for the outcome of a study.

- **hypothesis** An educated guess that derives logically from a theory; a prediction that can be tested.

- **prediction** A statement about the specific expectation for the outcome of a study.

## Step 3. Testing Through Empirical Research

The next step in the scientific method is to test the hypothesis by conducting empirical research. The **empirical method**, as discussed in the "What Is Psychology?" chapter, means gaining knowledge by observing objective evidence. In empirical research, we learn about the world by conducting systematic inquiries, collecting data, and analyzing the information. During this step in the scientific process, it is time to design a study that will test predictions that are based on the theory. To do so, a researcher first needs to find a concrete way to measure the variables of interest. Empirical researchers gain knowledge by observing objective evidence, not by relying on beliefs or theories. The person who designed the research described in Figure 1 probably believed that spending on others would lead to higher happiness than spending on oneself. But science requires empirical research to determine whether this is true.

- **empirical method** Gaining knowledge through the observation of events, the collection of data, and logical reasoning.

topic. For a meta-analysis, a researcher tries to find all of the studies that have been done on the topic of interest. The researcher then compares results from all the studies. A meta-analysis allows researchers to determine whether a result is consistent in the literature and to estimate the size of the relationship between variables or the effect of an intervention (Gurevitch & others, 2018). Meta-analytic results are more powerful than those of any single study because they combine many findings in the literature.

For example, you have probably heard of people engaging in "random acts of kindness" like putting coins in an expired parking meter or anonymously paying for the next car in a drive-thru. Such behaviors are thought to boost the mood of the person doing them. Do they work? A recent meta-analysis addressed this question (Curry & others, 2018). The researchers gathered studies in which people who had engaged in kind behaviors were compared with others to find out whether kindness boosted well-being. From 27 studies employing over 4,000 people, the researchers concluded that yes, doing nice things for others does lead to a small but consistent increase in happiness.

The research community maintains an active conversation about what scientists know, and this dialogue constantly questions conclusions. From published studies, a scholar may come up with a new idea that will eventually change the established thinking on a particular topic. Steps 3, 4, and 5 in the scientific method are part of an ongoing process. That is, researchers go back and do more research, revise their theories, hone their methods, draw conclusions, and evaluate their revised theories. Think of science as an ongoing conversation. Published papers tell us what we know, right now. But conclusions are always open to revision.

### *test yourself*

1. What are the five steps in the scientific method?
2. What is an operational definition, and what is its value in a study?
3. What is a meta-analysis? Why do researchers use this procedure?

**descriptive research** Research that determines the basic dimensions of a phenomenon—defining what it is, how often it occurs, and so on.

## 2. TYPES OF PSYCHOLOGICAL RESEARCH

Psychologists commonly use three types of research. *Descriptive research* involves finding out about the basic dimensions of some variable (for example, what the average level of happiness is for men in the United States). *Correlational research* seeks to discover relationships among variables (for instance, whether being married predicts greater happiness for men). *Experimental research* concerns establishing causal relationships between variables (such as, whether women perceive men as more attractive if the men are smiling). In this section, we examine each of these types of research.

### Descriptive Research

Just as its name suggests, **descriptive research** is about describing some phenomenon—determining its basic dimensions and defining what this thing is, how often it occurs, and so on. Descriptive research can help identify problems, such as the spread of a disease or the frequency of negative outcomes, such as violent crime. By itself, descriptive research cannot prove what causes some phenomenon, but it can reveal important information about people's behaviors and attitudes. Descriptive research methods include observation, surveys and interviews, and case studies.

©McGraw-Hill Education/John Flournoy, photographer

#### OBSERVATION

Imagine that you are going to conduct a study on how children who are playing together resolve conflicts that arise. The data that interest you concern conflict resolution. As a first step, you might go to a playground and simply observe what the children do—how often you see conflict resolution occur and how it unfolds. You would likely keep careful notes of what you observe.

This type of scientific observation requires important skills. Unless you are a trained observer and practice your skills regularly, you might not know what to look for, you might not remember what you saw, you might not realize that what you are looking for is changing from one moment to the next, and you might not document and communicate your observations effectively. Furthermore, you might not realize the value of

**1**
**Observing Some Phenomenon**
We feel good when we give someone a gift. However, do we genuinely feel better giving something away than we might feel if we could keep it? Elizabeth Dunn, Lara Aknin, and Michael Norton (2008) decided to test this question.

**2**
**Formulating Hypotheses and Predictions**
These researchers hypothesized that spending money on other people would lead to greater happiness than spending money on oneself.

**3**
**Testing Through Empirical Research**
In an experiment designed to examine this prediction, the researchers randomly assigned undergraduate participants to receive money ($5 or $20) that the students had to spend either on themselves or on someone else by 5 p.m. that day. Those who spent the money on *someone else* reported greater happiness that night.

**4**
**Drawing Conclusions**
The experiment supported the hypothesis that spending money on others can be a strong predictor of happiness. Money might not buy happiness, the researchers concluded, but spending money in a particular way—that is, on other people—may enhance happiness.

**5**
**Evaluating the Theory**
The experimental results were published in the prestigious journal *Science*. Now that the findings are public, other researchers might investigate related topics and questions inspired by this work, and their experiments might shed further light on the original conclusions.

**FIGURE 1** **Steps in the Scientific Method: Is It Better to Give Than to Receive?** This figure shows how the steps in the scientific method were applied in a research experiment examining how spending money on ourselves or others can influence happiness.


think about what we should expect. Those expectations are hypotheses and predictions. Theories are useful because they guide scientists in designing their research.

## Step 2. Formulating Hypotheses and Predictions

The second step in the scientific method is stating a hypothesis. A **hypothesis** is an educated guess that derives logically from a theory. It is an expectation that can be tested. A theory can generate many hypotheses. If more and more hypotheses related to a theory turn out to be true, the theory gains in credibility. For example, a researcher who believes that social belonging is the most important aspect of human functioning might predict that people who belong to social groups will be happier than those who do not. Another hypothesis from the theory that belonging to a group is important to human functioning might be that individuals who have been socially excluded will feel less happy than those who have been socially included. These general hypotheses can be tested in different studies. A **prediction** is a specific expectation for the outcome of a study.

• **hypothesis** An educated guess that derives logically from a theory; a prediction that can be tested.

• **prediction** A statement about the specific expectation for the outcome of a study.

## Step 3. Testing Through Empirical Research

The next step in the scientific method is to test the hypothesis by conducting empirical research. The **empirical method**, as discussed in the "What Is Psychology?" chapter, means gaining knowledge by observing objective evidence. In empirical research, we learn about the world by conducting systematic inquiries, collecting data, and analyzing the information. During this step in the scientific process, it is time to design a study that will test predictions that are based on the theory. To do so, a researcher first needs to find a concrete way to measure the variables of interest. Empirical researchers gain knowledge by observing objective evidence, not by relying on beliefs or theories. The person who designed the research described in Figure 1 probably believed that spending on others would lead to higher happiness than spending on oneself. But science requires empirical research to determine whether this is true.

• **empirical method** Gaining knowledge through the observation of events, the collection of data, and logical reasoning.

● **variable** Anything that can change.

● **operational definition** A definition that provides an objective description of how a variable is going to be measured and observed in a particular study.

The phenomena that scientists study are called *variables*, a word related to the verb *to vary*. A **variable** is anything that can change. All the different things psychologists study are variables, including experiences like happiness, gratitude, aggression, belongingness, conformity, and so forth. An **operational definition** provides an objective description of how a variable is going to be measured and observed in a particular study. Operational definitions eliminate the fuzziness that might creep into thinking about a problem. Imagine, for instance, that everyone in your psychology class is asked to observe a group of children and to keep track of kind behaviors. Do you think that all your classmates will define "kind behaviors" in the same way? Establishing an operational definition ensures that everyone agrees on what a variable means.

To measure personal happiness, for example, prominent psychologist Ed Diener and his students (1985) devised a self-report questionnaire that measures how satisfied a person is with his or her life, called the Satisfaction with Life Scale. (You will get a chance to complete the questionnaire later in this chapter.) Scores on this questionnaire are then used as measures of happiness. Research using this scale and others like it has shown that certain specific factors–marriage, religious faith, purpose in life, and good health–are strongly related to being happy (Diener, 1999, 2012b).

Importantly, there is not just one operational definition for any variable. Although Diener and his colleagues used a questionnaire, researchers have used diverse operational definitions for this variable–in this case, happiness. For instance, in a study of the relationship between happiness and important life outcomes, researchers used the facial expressions displayed by women in their college yearbook pictures as a measure of happiness. The women in the pictures had graduated 30 years prior. The researchers coded the photographs for the appearance of *Duchenne smiling* (Harker & Keltner, 2001). This type of smiling is genuine smiling–the kind that creates little wrinkles around the outer corner of the eyes–and it has been shown to be a sign of true happiness (Danvers & Shiota, 2018). (If you want to see whether someone in a photograph is smiling genuinely, cover the bottom of the person's face. Can you still tell that he or she is smiling? A genuine smile is evident in the eyes, not just the mouth.) In addition to coding those photos, the researchers followed up on the women's life experiences since graduating and found that happiness, as displayed in yearbook pictures, predicted positive life outcomes, such as successful marriages and satisfying lives, some 30 years later (Harker & Keltner, 2001).

So, in Diener's research, happiness was operationally defined as a score on a questionnaire; however, in this second study, happiness was operationally defined as Duchenne smiling. These definitions are just two among the many ways that psychologists have operationalized happiness. Another way to operationally define happiness is to *make* people happy, for example, by giving them an unexpected treat like candy or cookies or having them watch an amusing video or listen to happy music.

Devising effective operational definitions for the variables in a study is a crucial step in designing psychological research. To study anything, we must have a way to see it or measure it. Clearly, to establish an operational definition for any variable, we first have to agree on what we are trying to measure. If we think of happiness as something that people know about themselves, then a questionnaire score might be a good operational definition of the variable. If we think that people might not be aware of how happy they are (or aren't), then a facial expression might be a better operational definition. In other words, our definition of a variable must be set out clearly before we operationally define it. You might try your hand at operationally defining the following variables: generosity, love, maturity, exhaustion, and physical attractiveness. What are some things that *you* find interesting? How might you operationally define these variables?

Because operational definitions allow for the measurement of variables, researchers have a lot of numbers to deal with once they have conducted a study. A key aspect of the process of testing hypotheses is data analysis. *Data* are all the information (all those numbers) researchers collect in a study–say, the questionnaire scores or the behaviors observed. Data analysis means "crunching" those numbers mathematically to find out whether they support predictions. We will cover some of the basics of data analysis later in this chapter.

*Researchers have identified Duchenne smiling (notice the wrinkles) as a sign of genuine happiness.*

©Mirko Iannace/AGE Fotostock/Getty Images

Let's consider an example that demonstrates the first three steps in the scientific method. One theory of well-being is *self-determination theory* (Rigby & Ryan, 2018; Ryan & Deci, 2017). According to this theory, people are likely to feel fulfilled when their lives meet three important needs: relatedness (warm relationships with others), autonomy (independence), and competence (mastering new skills).

One hypothesis that follows logically from this theory is that people who value money, material possessions, prestige, and physical appearance (that is, *extrinsic rewards*) over relatedness, autonomy, and competence (*intrinsic rewards*) should be less fulfilled, less happy, and less well adjusted (Sortheix & Schwartz, 2017). In a series of studies entitled "The Dark Side of the American Dream," researchers Timothy Kasser and Richard Ryan asked participants to complete self-report measures of values and of psychological and physical functioning (Dittmar & others, 2014; Kasser & Ryan, 1996; Kasser & others, 2004). Thus, the operational definitions of values and psychological functioning were questionnaire scores. The researchers found that individuals who value material rewards over more intrinsic rewards do indeed tend to suffer as predicted.

## Step 4. Drawing Conclusions

Based on the results of the data analyses, scientists then draw conclusions from their research. Do the data support the predictions or not? What do the findings tell us about the theory that guided the study? Psychologists write articles presenting those findings. The articles are submitted for publication in scientific journals where they undergo rigorous review by other scientists who evaluate the work for its scientific merit. If the research is judged to be of sufficiently high quality, the paper is published for all to see and read.

## Step 5. Evaluating the Theory

The final step in the scientific method is one that never really ends. Once a paper is published, the community of scientists continues to evaluate it in light of other research. When many studies have been conducted on the same topic, scholars go back and consider the theory that started it all. Do the studies really support the theory? It is important to keep in mind that usually a theory is revised only after a number of studies produce similar results.

A key step after a study is published is **replication**. Replicating a study means repeating it and getting the same results. Scientific conclusions rely on showing that the results remain the same, regardless of the specific scientist who conducts the study or the specific group of people who were studied. *Direct replication* means doing the study precisely as it was conducted in its original form. *Conceptual replication* means doing the study with different methods or different types of samples. For instance, a researcher might want to know if a particular strategy to enhance social skills works not only for college students but for older adults. If a research finding is shown again and again–that is, if it is *replicated*–across different researchers and different specific methods–it is considered *reliable*. It is a result on which we can depend.

• **replication** Repeating a study in a new sample to see if results are the same as in previous work. A direct replication employs the very same methods as the original study. A conceptual replication employs different methods to test the same prediction.

Recently, many fields of science, including psychology, have confronted what has become known as a "replication crisis" (Nosek & Errington, 2017). When other investigators have tried to reproduce results from many studies they have not found the same results (Shrout & Rodgers, 2018). In response to this issue, two important principles have emerged to guide researchers. First, scientists should use large numbers of participants in their studies and should pool data across labs when a single lab can only collect a small number of participants (for instance, in infant research). Second, researchers should be transparent and thorough in reporting methods so that their work can be replicated correctly. Contemporary researchers often provide public access to their original data so that others can repeat the statistical analyses used. In addition, many psychologists have begun to *preregister* their hypotheses, predictions, and methods prior to running their studies. These scientists publicly report exactly what they predict and how they plan to test those predictions in advance (Rusz, Bijleveld, & Kompier, 2018).

A special type of study is called a meta-analysis. **Meta-analysis** is a statistical procedure that summarizes a large body of evidence from the research literature on a particular

• **meta-analysis** A statistical procedure that summarizes a large body of evidence from the research literature on a particular topic, allowing the researcher to assess the strength of the relationship between the variables.

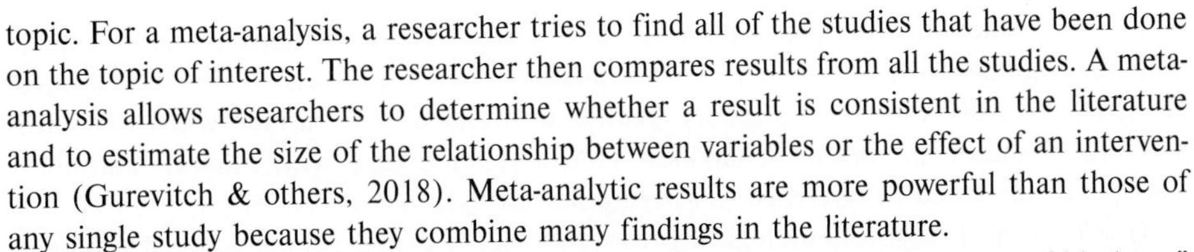

topic. For a meta-analysis, a researcher tries to find all of the studies that have been done on the topic of interest. The researcher then compares results from all the studies. A meta-analysis allows researchers to determine whether a result is consistent in the literature and to estimate the size of the relationship between variables or the effect of an intervention (Gurevitch & others, 2018). Meta-analytic results are more powerful than those of any single study because they combine many findings in the literature.

For example, you have probably heard of people engaging in "random acts of kindness" like putting coins in an expired parking meter or anonymously paying for the next car in a drive-thru. Such behaviors are thought to boost the mood of the person doing them. Do they work? A recent meta-analysis addressed this question (Curry & others, 2018). The researchers gathered studies in which people who had engaged in kind behaviors were compared with others to find out whether kindness boosted well-being. From 27 studies employing over 4,000 people, the researchers concluded that yes, doing nice things for others does lead to a small but consistent increase in happiness.

The research community maintains an active conversation about what scientists know, and this dialogue constantly questions conclusions. From published studies, a scholar may come up with a new idea that will eventually change the established thinking on a particular topic. Steps 3, 4, and 5 in the scientific method are part of an ongoing process. That is, researchers go back and do more research, revise their theories, hone their methods, draw conclusions, and evaluate their revised theories. Think of science as an ongoing conversation. Published papers tell us what we know, right now. But conclusions are always open to revision.

### test yourself

1. What are the five steps in the scientific method?
2. What is an operational definition, and what is its value in a study?
3. What is a meta-analysis? Why do researchers use this procedure?

# 2. TYPES OF PSYCHOLOGICAL RESEARCH

Psychologists commonly use three types of research. *Descriptive research* involves finding out about the basic dimensions of some variable (for example, what the average level of happiness is for men in the United States). *Correlational research* seeks to discover relationships among variables (for instance, whether being married predicts greater happiness for men). *Experimental research* concerns establishing causal relationships between variables (such as, whether women perceive men as more attractive if the men are smiling). In this section, we examine each of these types of research.

**descriptive research** Research that determines the basic dimensions of a phenomenon—defining what it is, how often it occurs, and so on.

## Descriptive Research

Just as its name suggests, **descriptive research** is about describing some phenomenon—determining its basic dimensions and defining what this thing is, how often it occurs, and so on. Descriptive research can help identify problems, such as the spread of a disease or the frequency of negative outcomes, such as violent crime. By itself, descriptive research cannot prove what causes some phenomenon, but it can reveal important information about people's behaviors and attitudes. Descriptive research methods include observation, surveys and interviews, and case studies.

©McGraw-Hill Education/John Flournoy, photographer

### OBSERVATION

Imagine that you are going to conduct a study on how children who are playing together resolve conflicts that arise. The data that interest you concern conflict resolution. As a first step, you might go to a playground and simply observe what the children do—how often you see conflict resolution occur and how it unfolds. You would likely keep careful notes of what you observe.

This type of scientific observation requires important skills. Unless you are a trained observer and practice your skills regularly, you might not know what to look for, you might not remember what you saw, you might not realize that what you are looking for is changing from one moment to the next, and you might not document and communicate your observations effectively. Furthermore, you might not realize the value of

having one or more others do the observations as well, so that you develop a sense of the accuracy of your observations. In short, for observations to be effective, they must be systematic. You must know whom you are observing, when and where you will observe, and how you will make the observations. Also, you need to know in advance how you will document your observations: in writing, by sound recording, or by video.

## SURVEYS AND INTERVIEWS

Sometimes the best and quickest way to get information about people is to ask them for it. One technique is to interview people directly. A related method that is especially useful when you need information from many people is a *survey,* or questionnaire. A survey presents a standard set of questions, or *items,* to obtain people's self-reported attitudes or beliefs about a particular topic.

Surveys can be a straightforward way to measure psychological variables but constructing them requires care. For example, surveys can measure only what people think about themselves. Thus, if we are interested in studying a variable that we believe is unconscious, such as a psychodynamic drive, we cannot use a survey. Furthermore, people do not always know the truth about themselves. If you were answering a survey that asked, "Are you a generous person?" how might your answer compare with that of a friend who is asked to make that same rating about you? One particular problem with surveys and interviews is the tendency of participants to answer questions in a way that will make them look good rather than in a way that communicates what they truly think or feel. This problem is called "*socially desirable responding.*"

Another challenge in survey construction is that when a questionnaire is used to define variables operationally, it is crucial that the items clearly measure the specific topic of interest and not some other characteristic. Therefore, the language used in a survey must be clear and understandable if the responses are to reflect participants' actual feelings.

Surveys and interviews can examine a wide range of topics, from personality traits to sexual habits to attitudes about a host of issues. Some survey and interview questions are unstructured and open-ended, such as "How fulfilling would you say your marriage is?" Such questions allow for unique responses from each person surveyed. Other survey and interview questions are more structured and ask about specific things. For example, a structured question might ask, "How many times have you talked with your partner about a personal problem in the past month: 0, 1–2, 3–5, 6–10, 11–30, every day?"

Questionnaires often use rating scales as a way for participants to indicate their agreement with a statement. Such scales, sometimes called *Likert scales* (after their inventor, Rensis Likert) usually involve the person selecting a number that indicates their level of agreement with a statement. For example, in response to the item, "I am outgoing and sociable," the respondent might be asked to select a number from 1 (indicating "not at all") to 7 (indicating "very much"). Later in this chapter, you will complete a questionnaire that uses such a scale.

● **case study or case history** An in-depth look at a single individual.

## CASE STUDIES

A **case study or case history** is an in-depth look at a single individual. Case studies are performed mainly by clinical psychologists when, for either practical or ethical reasons, the unique aspects of an individual's life cannot be duplicated and tested with other individuals. A case study provides information about one person's goals, hopes, fantasies, fears, traumatic experiences, family relationships, health, and anything else that helps the psychologist understand the person's mind and behavior. Case studies can also involve in-depth explorations of particular families or social groups.

An example of a case study is the analysis of India's spiritual leader Mahatma Gandhi (1869–1948) by psychodynamic theorist Erik Erikson (1969). Erikson studied Gandhi's life in great depth to discover how his positive spiritual identity developed, especially during his youth. In piecing together Gandhi's identity development, Erikson described the contributions of culture, history, family, and various other factors that might affect the way people form an identity.

*Mahatma Gandhi was India's spiritual leader in the mid-twentieth century. Erik Erikson conducted an extensive case study of Gandhi's life to determine what factors contributed to his identity development.*



A case history provides a detailed portrait of a person's life, but we must be cautious about applying what we learn from one person's life to others. The subject of a case study is unique, with a genetic makeup and personal history that no one else shares. Case studies can be valuable as the first step of the scientific method, in that they often provide observations that can then be tested in other ways through psychological research. However, an in-depth study of a single case may not be generalizable to the wider population. A case study may tell us a great deal about the person being studied but not very much about people in general.

## THE VALUE OF DESCRIPTIVE RESEARCH

Descriptive research allows researchers to get a sense of a subject of interest, but it cannot answer questions about how and why things are the way they are. Nevertheless, descriptive research does explore intriguing topics, such as the experience of happiness in different cultures. Before reading about and considering the value of that research, complete the measure below. Specifically, using the 7-point scale, indicate your agreement with each item that follows the scale.

| 1 | 2 | 3 | 4 | 5 | 6 | 7 |
|---|---|---|---|---|---|---|
| Strongly Disagree | Disagree | Slightly Disagree | Neither Agree nor Disagree | Slightly Agree | Agree | Strongly Agree |

**1.** In most ways my life is close to my ideal.

**2.** The conditions of my life are excellent.

**3.** I am satisfied with my life.

**4.** So far I have gotten the important things I want in life.

**5.** If I could live my life over, I would change almost nothing.

You have just completed the Satisfaction with Life Scale (Diener & others, 1985), one operational definition of happiness. To find out your score, add up your ratings and divide by 5. This average rating could be considered your level of general happiness. Many different kinds of studies from many different countries have used this scale and others like it to measure happiness levels. Based on such research, Ed and Carol Diener (1996) concluded that most people are pretty happy because the average score is 4, which is the midpoint on the scale you just completed. However, research on happiness in various cultures has generally centered on developed countries. Can these results be generalized to include developing societies that are not as prosperous?

One study examined levels of happiness in groups of people who have not generally been included in psychological studies (Biswas-Diener, Vittersø, & Diener, 2005). The research assessed three groups: the Inughuits (Inuits) of Greenland, the Maasai of southern Kenya, and the American Old Order Amish. All three groups completed measures that were essentially the same as the one you just did.

The Inughuits live at 79 degrees latitude (very far north), in the harshest climate inhabited by a traditional human society. Rocks, glaciers, and the sea dominate the landscape. Farming is impossible. The Inughuits have some modern conveniences, but they generally adhere to a traditional hunting culture. It is not uncommon to find an Inughuit hunter butchering a seal or caribou on the kitchen floor while children watch TV in the next room. Most of us might feel a little blue in the winter months when gloomy weather seems to stretch on, day after day. For the Inughuits, however, the sun never rises at all throughout the winter months, and in the summer, it never sets. How happy could an individual be in such a difficult setting? Pretty happy, it turns out, as the Inughuits averaged a 5.0 on the Satisfaction with Life Scale.

The Maasai are an indigenous (native) African nomadic group who live in villages of about 20 people, with little exposure to the West. Maasai are fierce warriors, and their culture has many traditional ceremonies built around a boy's passage from childhood to manhood. Boys are circumcised between the ages of 15 and 22, and they are forbidden from moving or making a sound during the procedure. Girls are also circumcised as they enter puberty, in a controversial ritual that involves the removal of the clitoris and makes childbirth extremely difficult. The Maasai practice child marriage and polygamy. Maasai women have very little power and are generally expected to do most of the work. How happy could an individual be in this context? Maasai men and women who completed the measure orally in their native tongue, Maa, averaged a 5.4 on the Satisfaction with Life Scale (Biswas-Diener, Vittersø, & Diener, 2005).

Finally, the Old Order Amish of the midwestern and northeastern United States belong to a strict religious sect that explicitly rejects modern aspects of life. The Amish separate themselves from mainstream society and travel by horse and buggy. The women wear bonnets, and the men sport beards, dark clothes, and dark, brimmed hats. They do not use modern farming equipment or other technology such as washing machines, cars, computers, TVs, iPads, and smartphones. Still, the Amish are relatively happy, averaging 4.4 on the 7-point happiness scale (Biswas-Diener, Vittersø, & Diener, 2005).

Like a host of other studies conducted in developed nations, these results indicate that most individuals are pretty happy. Such descriptive findings provide researchers who study well-being with a valuable foundation. These studies cannot tell us why the differences exist or what processes are making people happy. If researchers wanted to extend these findings to investigate predictors of happiness in different cultures, they would then turn to a correlational design.

## Correlational Research

We have seen that descriptive research tells us about the basic dimensions of a variable. In contrast, **correlational research** tells us about the relation between two or more variables. The purpose of correlational research is to examine whether and how two variables *change together*. That is, correlational research looks at a *co*-relation: If one of the variables increases, what happens to the other one? When two variables change together, we can predict one from the other, and we say that the variables are correlated. Correlational studies involve systematically observing variables and determining whether and how they change together.

● **correlational research** Research that examines the relationship between variables in order to find out whether and how two variables change together.

The key feature of a correlational study is that the factors of interest are measured or observed to see how they relate. If we want to know whether shy people are happy, we might give the same people two questionnaires–one that measures shyness and another that assesses happiness. For each person we would have two scores, and we would then see whether shyness and happiness relate to each other in a systematic way.

The degree of relation between two variables is expressed as a numerical value called a *correlation coefficient,* most commonly represented by the letter *r*. The value of a correlation always falls between −1.00 and +1.00. The correlation coefficient is a statistic that tells us two things about the relationship between two variables–its strength and its direction. The number or size of the correlation tells us about the *strength* of the relationship. The closer the number is to ±1.00, the stronger the relationship. The sign (+ or −) tells us the *direction* of the relation between the variables. A positive sign means that as one variable increases, the other also increases. A negative sign means that as one variable increases, the other decreases. A zero correlation means that there is no relation between the variables.

Examples of scatter plots (a type of graph that plots scores on the two variables) showing positive and negative correlations appear in Figure 2. Note that every dot in this figure represents both scores for one person.

### CORRELATION IS NOT CAUSATION

Look at the terms in bold type in the following newspaper headlines:

Researchers **Link** Coffee Consumption to Cancer of Pancreas

Brain Size Is **Associated** with Gender

Psychologists Discover **Relationship** Between Religious Faith and Good Health

Reading these headlines, one might conclude that coffee causes pancreatic cancer, gender causes differences in brain size, and religious faith causes good health. The boldface words are synonymous only with correlation, however, not with causality.

*Correlation does not equal causation.* Remember, correlation means only that two variables change together. Being able to predict one event based on the occurrence of another event does not tell us anything about the cause of either event. At times some other

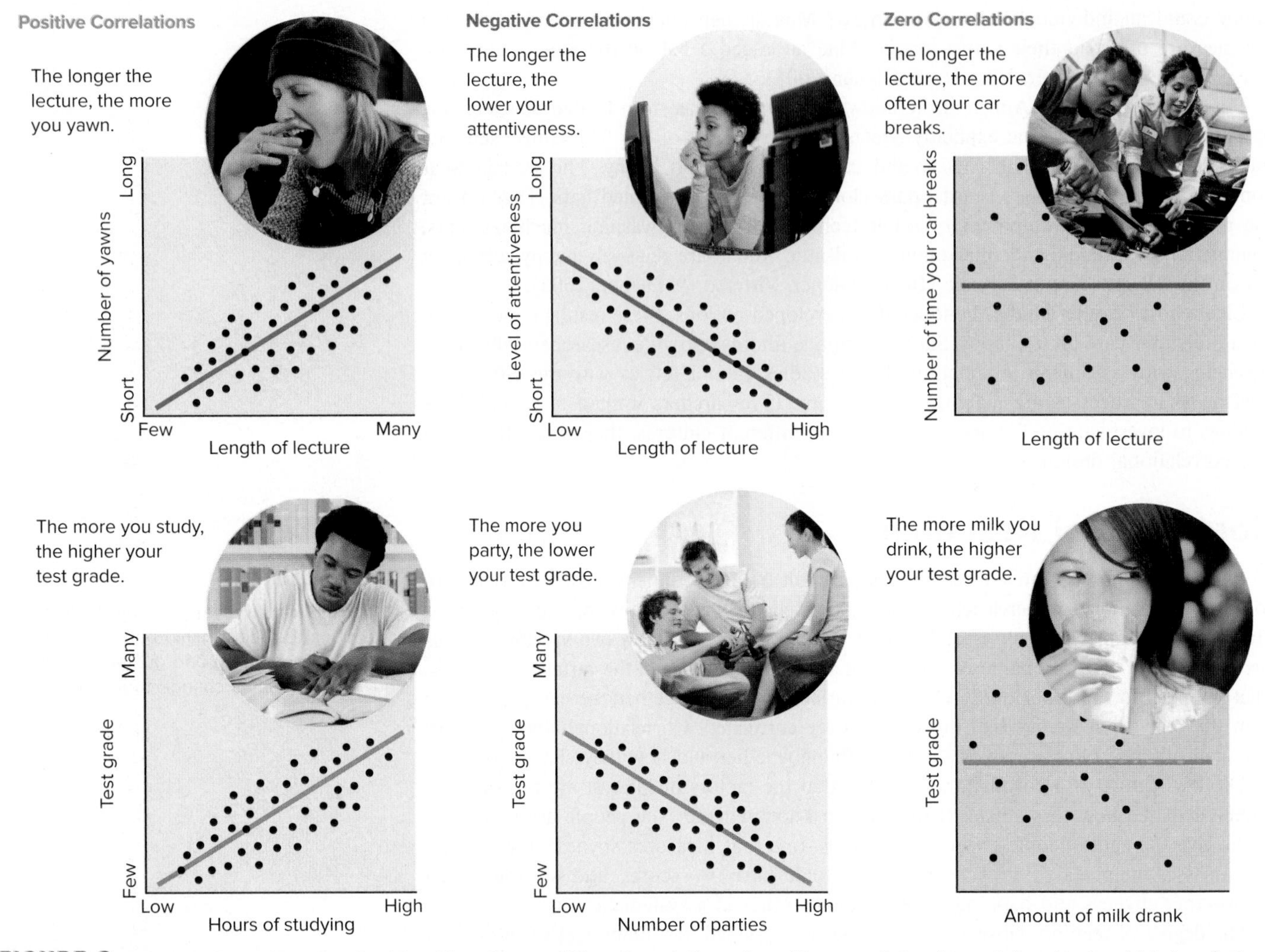


**FIGURE 2** **Scatter Plots Showing Positive, Negative, and Zero Correlations** A positive correlation is a relationship in which two factors vary in the same direction, as shown in the two scatter plots on the left. A negative correlation is a relationship in which two factors vary in opposite directions, as shown in the two scatter plots in the middle. A zero correlation is illustrated by the scatter plots on the right.
(first photo) ©Doug Menuez/Getty Images; (second photo) ©Ariel Skelley/Blend Images; (third photo) ©ColorBlind Images/Getty Images; (fourth photo) ©andreypopov/123RF; (fifth photo) ©Stockbyte/Punchstock; (sixth photo) ©JGI/Blend Images

variable that has not been measured accounts for the relationship between two others. Researchers refer to this circumstance as the **third variable problem**.

● **third variable problem** The circumstance in which a variable that has not been measured accounts for the relationship between two other variables. Third variables are also known as confounds.

To understand the third variable problem, consider this example. A researcher measures two variables: the number of ice cream cones sold in a town and the number of violent crimes that occur in that town throughout the year. The researcher finds that ice cream cone sales and violent crimes are positively correlated, to the magnitude of +.50. This high positive correlation indicates that as ice cream sales increase, so do violent crimes. Would it be reasonable for the local paper to run the headline "Ice Cream Consumption Leads to Violence"? Should concerned citizens gather outside the local Frosty Freeze to stop the madness? Probably not. Perhaps you have already thought of the third variable that might explain this correlation–heat. Indeed, when it is hot outside, people are more likely both to purchase ice cream and to act aggressively (Rinderu, Bushman, & Van Lange, 2018; Younan & others, 2018).

Consider that interesting study on smiling in college yearbook pictures and happy marriages. What are some third variables that might explain that association? If we think about the reasons women might not be smiling in those yearbook pictures, we might come up with a few possibilities. Perhaps those women experienced parental divorce during their college years. Perhaps they experienced a recent romantic breakup. Perhaps they were having trouble with their coursework, leading them to less successful occupations. Even very compelling correlational studies might be open to alternative explanations.

Further, if a causal link did exist between two variables, a correlation between them cannot tell us about the *direction* of that link. A correlation cannot tell us which variable is the cause and which is the effect. Imagine a study showing that happiness and physical health are positively correlated in a group of elderly people. We cannot tell, based on that positive correlation, whether greater happiness leads to better health or better health leads to greater happiness.

This example also illustrates a specific type of correlational study known as a cross-sectional design. A **cross-sectional design** is a type of correlational study in which variables are measured at a single point in time. Observations from this single measurement are then compared.

● **cross-sectional design** A type of correlational study in which variables are measured at a single point in time.

## THE VALUE OF CORRELATIONAL RESEARCH

Given the potential problems with third variables and the difficulty in drawing causal conclusions, why do researchers bother to conduct correlational studies? There are several very good reasons. Although correlational studies cannot show a causal connection between variables, they do allow us to use one variable to predict a person's score on another. This is the reasoning behind tests such as the SAT and ACT, which are used to predict performance in college. Also, some important questions can be investigated only through correlational studies. Such questions may involve variables that can *only* be measured or observed, such as biological sex, personality traits, genetic factors, and ethnic background. When researchers are interested in variables that cannot be manipulated, they conduct correlational research.

Another reason researchers conduct correlational studies is that sometimes the variables of interest are real-world events, such as hurricanes or earthquakes, that influence people's lives. Researchers might compare individuals who have been exposed to a natural disaster to a similar group who have not been exposed. Important research questions, such as the relationship between the #MeToo movement and the frequency of reports of sexual harassment, can only be addressed using correlational research.

Correlational research is also valuable in cases where it would not be ethical to do the research in any other way. For example, it would be unethical for an experimenter to direct expectant mothers to smoke varying numbers of cigarettes in order to see how cigarette smoke affects infant development. It is unethical for researchers to randomly assign people to harmful experiences like smoking or using illicit drugs. In these cases, correlational research can provide insight.

Although we have focused mainly on relations between just two variables, researchers often include many variables in their studies. In this way, they can assess whether a connection between two variables is explained by a third (or fourth or fifth) variable. An interesting question that researchers have examined in this way is, "Do happy people live longer?" In one study, 2,000 Mexican Americans age 65 and older were interviewed twice over the course of two years (Ostir & others, 2000). In the first assessment, participants completed measures of happiness but also reported about potential third variables such as diet, physical health, smoking, marital status, and distress. Two years later, the researchers contacted the participants again to see who was still alive. Even with these many potential third variables taken into account, happiness predicted who was still living two years later.

*Correlational research is useful for studying the impact on people's lives of events such as Hurricane Michael in 2018.*

©Terry Kelly/Shutterstock

Correlational studies also are useful when researchers are interested in studying everyday experience. For example, correlational researchers often use reports that track experiences, known as *ecological momentary assessment (EMA),* to assess people in their natural settings (Trull, 2018). In EMA studies, people report on their experiences a few times

## psychological *inquiry*

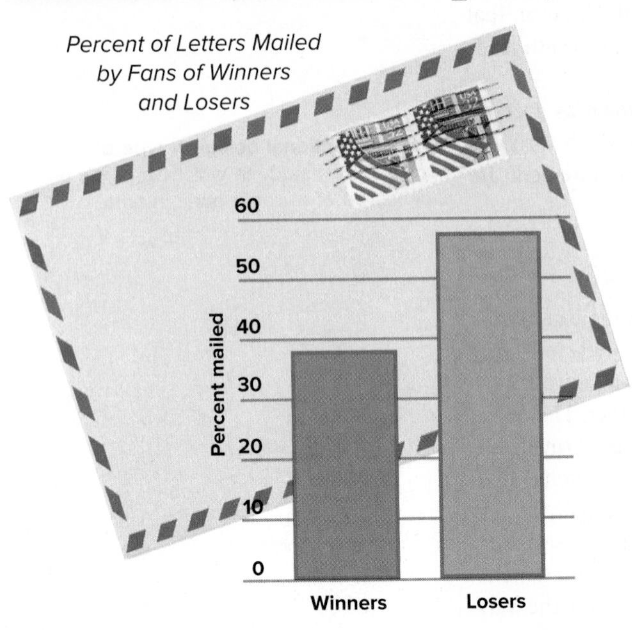


Source: Job (1987); ©goir/iStoc k/Getty Images

### *Miserable but Helpful?*

Many studies have shown that happy individuals are more helpful than people in a negative mood. Social psychologist R. F. Soames Job (1987) was interested in examining how mood relates to helping. In a clever study, he used naturally occurring mood and an unusual measure of helpfulness.

The study took place outside a major rugby match pitting Canterbury-Bankstown against St. George in Sydney, Australia. Rugby is enormously popular in Sydney—more than 40,000 people attended the match.

During the game, the researchers placed 100 stamped letters on the windshields of cars parked around the sporting grounds. The letters were addressed to the same person, and a handwritten note on each letter said, "Found near your car." The researchers identified which cars belonged to supporters of each team by the different colored streamers, team stickers, and posters. Fifty letters were placed on the cars of supporters of each team. The researchers then waited to see which type of fan was most likely to put the letter in the mailbox—fans of the winning team or of the losing team.

The figure shows the results. Try your hand at the questions below.

1. What were the variables of interest in this study?
2. How did the study operationally define these variables?
3. Why is this a correlational study?
4. Job concluded that these data support the notion that negative mood relates to helping. Is this conclusion justified, in your opinion? Why or why not?
5. Identify at least one third variable that might explain the results of this study.

a day or whenever they are prompted to do so (typically by a smartphone) (Soriano & others, 2018). Increasingly, participants use their smartphones and download an app to participate in EMA studies. A similar method, *event-contingent responding,* asks participants to complete a report each time they engage in a particular behavior, such as drinking alcohol, dealing with conflict in a family, or experiencing violence (Chaix, 2018; Roman, Klein, & Wolff, 2017). Such methods of collecting data allow researchers to get close to real life as it happens.

Although the correlation coefficient is often used to express the relation between two variables, it is important to keep in mind that what makes a study correlational is not the statistic researchers use to analyze the data. Rather, a study is correlational when it involves measuring variables to see how they are related. To get a sense of this distinction and learn about some clever ways in which psychologists have operationalized variables, check out the Psychological Inquiry above.

### LONGITUDINAL DESIGNS

One way that correlational researchers can deal with the issue of causation is to employ a special kind of systematic observation called a **longitudinal design**. Longitudinal research involves obtaining measures of the variables of interest in multiple waves over time. (Note that longitudinal designs differ from cross-sectional designs in that cross-sectional designs measure the variables only once.) Longitudinal research can suggest potential causal relationships because if one variable is thought to cause changes in another, it should at least come before that variable in time.

• **longitudinal design** A special kind of systematic observation, used by correlational researchers, that involves obtaining measures of the variables of interest in multiple waves over time.

One intriguing longitudinal study is the Nun Study (Grossi & others, 2007; Mortimer, Snowdon, & Markesbery, 2009; Weinstein & others, 2018). The study began in 1986 and has followed a sample of 678 School Sisters of Notre Dame ever since. Ranging in age from 75 to 103 when the study began, the nuns complete a variety of psychological and physical measures annually. This sample is unique in many respects. However, certain characteristics render the participants an excellent group for correlational research. For one thing, many potential extraneous third variables are relatively identical for all the women in the group: Their biological sex, living conditions, diet, activity levels, marital status, and religious participation are essentially held constant. So, there is little chance that differences would arise in these variables that might explain the study's results.

Researchers assessed the link between happiness and longevity using this rich data set. All of the nuns were asked to write a spiritual autobiography when they entered the convent (for some, up to 80 years prior). These documents were used as indicators of happiness earlier in life by counting the number of positive emotions expressed in the autobiographies (note that here we have yet another operational definition of happiness) (Danner, Snowdon, & Friesen, 2001). Higher levels of positive emotion expressed in autobiographies written at an average age of 22 were associated with a 2.5-fold difference in risk of mortality when the nuns were in their 80s and 90s. That is, women who included positive emotion in their autobiographies when they were in their early 20s were 2.5 times more likely to survive some 60 years later. Interestingly, other researchers replicated this finding using autobiographies of 88 famous psychologists. They found that when the psychologists used more active positive emotion words (such as *lively* and *excited*) to describe their life, they lived longer (Pressman & Cohen, 2012).

Longitudinal designs help correlational researchers attempt to demonstrate causal relations among variables. Still, even in longitudinal studies, causal relationships are not completely clear. An excellent longitudinal study still cannot prove causation. For example, the nuns who wrote happier autobiographies may have had happier childhood experiences that might be influencing their longevity, or a particular genetic factor might explain both their happiness and their survival.

As you read about correlational research studies throughout this book, do so critically and with a modicum of skepticism; consider that even the brightest scientist may not have thought of all of the potential third variables that could have explained the results. It is easy to assume causality when two events or characteristics are merely correlated. Remember those innocent ice cream cones, and critically evaluate conclusions that may be drawn from simple observation.

## Experimental Research

To determine whether a causal relationship exists between variables, researchers must use experimental methods. An **experiment** is a carefully regulated procedure in which the researcher manipulates one or more variables that are believed to influence some other variable. Imagine, for example, that a researcher notices that people who listen to classical music seem to be of above-average intelligence. A correlational study on this question would not tell us whether listening to classical music *causes* increases in intelligence. In order to demonstrate causation, the researcher would have to manipulate whether or not people listen to classical music. He or she might create two groups: one that listens to classical music and one that does not. To test for differences in intelligence, the researcher would then measure intelligence.

● **experiment** A carefully regulated procedure in which the researcher manipulates one or more variables believed to influence some other variable.

If that manipulation led to differences between the two groups on intelligence, we could say that the manipulated variable *caused* those differences: The experiment has demonstrated cause and effect. This notion that experiments can demonstrate causation is based on the idea that if participants are *randomly assigned* to groups, the only systematic difference between them must be the manipulated variable. **Random assignment** means that researchers assign participants to groups *by chance*. Random assignment is an essential aspect of experimental research because it allows psychologists to assume that there are no preexisting differences between groups.

● **random assignment** The assignment of participants to experimental groups by chance, to reduce the likelihood that a study's results will be due to preexisting differences between groups.

The logic of random assignment is this: If participants in an experiment are assigned to each group only by chance, the potential differences between the groups will cancel out over the long run. So, for instance, in the example of classical music and intelligence, we might wonder if it is possible that the groups differed on intelligence to begin with. Because participants were randomly assigned, we assume that intelligence is spread across the groups evenly.

Random assignment does not always produce equivalent groups. One way to improve its effectiveness is to start with a large pool of people. Let's say you decided to do that study—examining whether listening to classical music (as compared to no music) prior to taking an intelligence test leads to higher scores on the test. Although you wisely use random assignment, you begin with just 10 people. Unbeknownst to you, there are two geniuses (people with extraordinarily high IQs) in that small pool of participants. Each person in the pool has a 50–50 chance of ending up in either group, so there is a 25 percent chance that the two geniuses will both end up in the classical music group and a 25 percent chance they will both end up in the control group. In other words, there is a 50 percent chance that your groups will differ systematically in intelligence before you even start the study.

In contrast, if your study had begun with, say, 100 people, intelligence scores would likely be more evenly distributed throughout the overall pool. When these individuals are randomly assigned to groups, differences in intelligence would be much more likely to cancel out across the two groups. That is why it is important that random assignment is allowed to work its magic on a larger pool of people.

*In laboratory experiments by King and her colleagues (Hicks & others, 2012; King & others, 2006), participants who listened to happy music rated their lives as more meaningful than those who listened to neutral music.*

©Fuse/Getty Images

To get a sense of what experimental studies, as compared with correlational studies, can reveal, consider the following example. Experiencing one's life as meaningful is an important aspect of psychological well-being (Frankl, [1946] 2006; Steger, 2012). Because surveys that measure well-being and meaning in life correlate positively (that is, the more meaningful your life, the happier you are), the assumption has been that experiencing meaning in life causes greater happiness. However, because studies exploring this relationship have been correlational, the causal direction is unclear. Meaning in life may lead people to be happier, but the reverse might also be true: Happiness might make people feel that their lives are more meaningful.

To address this issue, Laura King and her colleagues (Hicks & others, 2012; King & others, 2006) conducted a series of laboratory experiments. In one study, the researchers put some participants in a positive mood by having them listen to happy music. Other participants listened to neutral music. Then they all rated their meaning in life. The results showed that participants who listened to happy music rated their lives as more meaningful than did individuals who listened to neutral music. In this case happiness was operationally defined by the type of music participants heard, and meaning in life was operationally defined by ratings on a questionnaire. Because participants were randomly assigned to the two conditions, we can assume that the only systematic difference between the two groups was the type of music they heard. As a result, we can say that the happy music caused the increase in meaning in life.

## INDEPENDENT AND DEPENDENT VARIABLES

● **independent variable** A manipulated experimental factor; the variable that the experimenter changes to see what its effects are.

● **dependent variable** The outcome; the variable that may change in an experiment in response to changes in the independent variable.

Experiments have two types of variables: independent and dependent. An **independent variable** is a manipulated experimental factor. The independent variable is the variable that the experimenter changes to see what its effects are; it is a potential cause. In the example of listening to classical music and intelligence, the independent variable is whether participants listened to music. In the study of positive mood and meaning in life, the independent variable is mood (positive versus neutral), operationally defined by the type of music participants heard.

A **dependent variable** is the variable that may change as a result of manipulation of the independent variable. It is the outcome (effect) in an experiment. Researchers manipulate the independent variable and measure the dependent variable to test for the effect of the manipulation. In the example of listening to classical music and intelligence, the dependent variable is intelligence test scores. In the study of positive mood and meaning in life, meaning in life is the dependent variable.

Any experiment may include several independent variables, or factors, that are manipulated to determine their effect on the outcome. Similarly, many experiments include more than one dependent variable as well, to examine the effects of manipulations on a number of outcomes.

Independent and dependent variables are two of the most important concepts in psychological research. Despite their similar names, they are very different. Remember that the independent variable is the *cause,* and the dependent variable is the *effect*. The independent variable is the one that is manipulated, and the dependent variable is the outcome.

Independent and dependent variables can be operationalized in many ways. Sometimes the independent variable involves an individual's social context. Social psychologists often manipulate the social context with the help of a confederate. A **confederate** is a person who is given a role to play in a study so that the social context can be manipulated. The confederate may pretend to be just another participant in a study, but he or she is actually working with the experimenter to help manipulate the situation.

● **confederate** A person who is given a role to play in an experiment so that the social context can be manipulated.

Let's consider one more example to review the process of experimental research step-by-step. Imagine that you are reminiscing about a past vacation with two family members, a grandparent and a cousin who is your age. If one of these individuals mentions something you are pretty sure never happened on that vacation, are you likely to incorporate that information (even if it is false) into your own memory of the vacation? And does it matter if the false information is coming from your grandparent or your cousin? A recent study (Numbers & others, 2018) examined this question. The study used a procedure called the contagious false memory paradigm. In the paradigm, two people (one a participant; the other a confederate) are asked to memorize the items in a series of pictures. The pictures have been carefully created so that some details that would generally be part of a scene have been left out. For example, there is no toothbrush in the bathroom. Then, the pair is asked to work together to recall everything they can from the pictures. During this shared recall session, the confederate either mentions those missing items—the ones that were definitely not in the pictures—or does not. Thus, for some participants in this study the confederate spread false memories. In addition, the age of the confederate was manipulated so that half of the participants (who were all traditional-aged college students) were paired with a similar-aged confederate and the other half were paired with an older adult. Later all participants were asked to recall, alone, what they remembered from the pictures. The results showed that participants paired with confederates who shared false information did incorporate that information into their memories of the scenes. The age of the confederate did not matter. So, you are likely to incorporate false information about that family vacation regardless of whether it comes from Grandpa or your cousin Frank.

Let's review the concepts covered so far in the context of this example. First, this study involved a confederate—a person working with the experimenter—so that the researchers could manipulate exposure to false information. In addition, this study involved two independent variables. First, the age of the confederate (older versus younger) was manipulated to see whether people might be more likely to discount false information from an older person. This independent variable did not affect the dependent variable, which was the amount of false information recalled by participants. The second independent variable was whether the confederate shared false information. One group was exposed to false information and the other was not. Why did the researchers need *both* of these groups? They were only interested in how exposure to false information influences memory, so why did they have a group that was not exposed to false information? Note that if they did not have that second group, they would have nothing with which to compare their results—no way to determine whether participants might have remembered false information on their own. This is the logic behind the concepts of experimental and control groups, our next topic.

## EXPERIMENTAL AND CONTROL GROUPS

Experiments involve comparing different groups exposed to differing versions of the independent variable. These groups have names. An **experimental group** consists of the participants in an experiment who are exposed to *the change* that the independent variable represents. A **control group** in an experiment is as much like the experimental group as possible and is treated in every way like the experimental group *except for that change.* The control group provides a comparison against which the researcher can test the effects of the independent variable.

● **experimental group** The participants in an experiment who receive the drug or other treatment under study; those who are exposed to the change that the independent variable represents.

● **control group** The participants in an experiment who are as much like the experimental group as possible and who are treated in every way like the experimental group except for a manipulated factor, the independent variable.

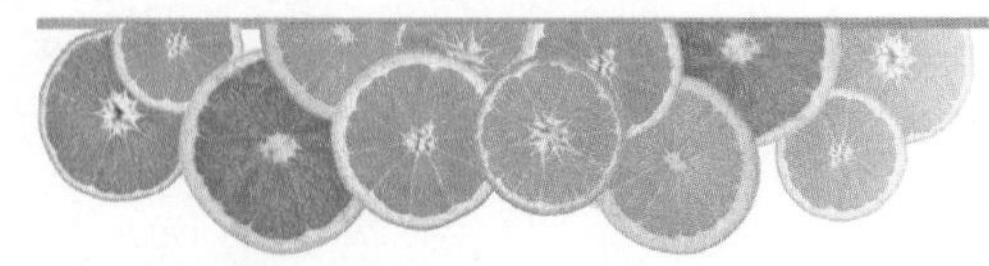
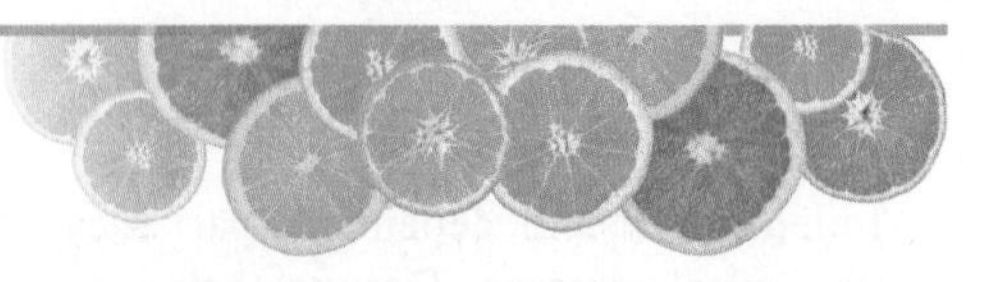

## INTERSECTION

### Emotion and Social Psychology: Why Not Just Say "Thanks"?

Correlational studies consistently show that people who are highly grateful report higher well-being (Wood, Froh, & Geraghty, 2010): there is a positive correlation between gratitude and well-being. Considering that correlation, you might think, "It makes sense that feeling grateful should lead to higher well-being." But remember, correlation does not imply causation. Perhaps happy people have more things to be grateful for. Experiments are the only way to establish a causal relationship between gratitude and well-being. Gratitude intervention experiments involve randomly assigning people to feeling grateful (or not) and then comparing their well-being. Such studies show that inducing a sense of gratitude (for instance by having people write about things they are grateful for) leads to higher well-being compared to control groups (Davis & others, 2016; Gilbert, Foulk, & Bono, 2018; Wong & others, 2018). In fact, experiments show that gratitude interventions lead to many benefits, including better sleep (Jackowska & others, 2016), higher job satisfaction (Stegen & Wankier, 2018), helping others more (Moieni & others, 2018), and even less aggression in prison populations (Deng & others, 2019).

With these benefits in mind, we might ask why people don't always express gratitude to those who behave kindly toward them. Psychologists Amit Kumar and Nick Epley (2018) reasoned that people might not express their gratitude for two reasons. First, they might assume the person already knows they are grateful. Second, they might underestimate how nice it is to have someone say "thank you." The researchers probed these possibilities in a fascinating study. Participants wrote gratitude letters to individuals who had helped them in meaningful ways. Then those "gratitude expressers" rated how surprised, happy, and awkward the recipient would feel if they read the letter. Next (with the permission of the expressers), the researchers sent the letters to the targets of gratitude. After reading the letters, recipients rated their feelings of surprise, happiness, and awkwardness. The results? Recipients consistently felt more surprised, more happy, and less awkward than expressers expected.

Note the strengths and weaknesses of correlational and experimental research. Without correlational studies showing a relationship between gratitude and well-being, we might question whether a naturally occurring sense of gratitude would have the same effect as an experimental manipulation. Without experiments, we could not say that gratitude causes higher well-being. Finally, without that last correlational study, we would not know about people's faulty assumptions about the effects of receiving thanks.

*Think of all the people who have helped you in meaningful ways. Have you taken the opportunity to thank them?*

©Atstock Productions/Shutterstock

We now have reviewed three examples of experimental and control groups:

- In our imaginary study of music and intelligence, the experimental group is the group that listened to classical music; the no-music group is the control group.
- In the study of happiness and meaning in life, participants who listened to happy music are the experimental group; those who heard neutral music are the control group.
- In the study of false memory contagion, participants who interacted with a confederate who shared false information are the experimental group; those who interacted with a confederate who did not share false information are the control group.

Many questions can be addressed both through experimental and correlational research. For example, gratitude is the experience of appreciative thankfulness for someone's kindness. To see how correlational and experimental research can work together, check out the Intersection on the experience of gratitude.

### QUASI-EXPERIMENTAL DESIGNS

Another approach to research is a *quasi-experimental design*. As the prefix *quasi-* ("as if") suggests, this type of design is similar to an experiment, but it is not quite the same thing.

The key difference is that a quasi-experimental design does not randomly assign participants to conditions because such assignment is either impossible or unethical.

Quasi-experimental designs might be used to study groups that already exist—say, soldiers who have seen combat versus those who have not or children whose school was destroyed by a tornado versus those in a neighboring town where the school was not affected. In a quasi-experimental design, researchers examine participants in varying groups, but group assignment is not determined randomly. It might be determined by natural events or by participants placing themselves in groups of interest. For example, a recent study used a quasi-experimental design to examine how exposure to an Ebola outbreak affected parents and guardians of young children (Green & others, 2018); another included divorced parents seeking help in raising their children (Becher & others, 2018).

Quasi-experimental designs have important pitfalls. Let's say a researcher is interested in the influence of using online learning tools on performance in introductory psychology. She might compare students from two different sections of a class—one that uses online tools and one that does not. Because students typically choose which section of a course they take, the experimenter cannot randomly assign them to sections. Assessing differences between the groups might provide information about the merits of online learning tools. However, there might be confounding factors (whether students are morning people or not, for example) that could account for differences between the groups. Although quasi-experimental designs are common, they do not allow for the strong causal conclusions that can be drawn from true experiments that employ random assignment (Roman, Klein, & Wolff, 2017).

## SOME CAUTIONS ABOUT EXPERIMENTAL RESEARCH

Earlier we noted that psychologists are interested in drawing conclusions not just from a single study but from a whole body of research on a given topic. We discussed the idea that if a finding is replicated (that is, repeated again and again), it is considered *reliable;* we would expect that this finding will stand the test of time. However, even a reliable finding may not be *valid.*

*Validity* refers to the soundness of the conclusions that a researcher draws from an experiment. In experimental designs, there are two broad types of validity that matter. The first is **external validity**, which refers to the degree to which an experimental design actually reflects the real-world issues it is supposed to address. Often, operationalizing variables in the lab involves creating analogues to real-world experiences. External validity is concerned with how well those analogues represent the real-world contexts they are meant to represent. In other words, the researcher assesses external validity to see whether the experimental methods and the results *generalize*—whether they apply—to the real world.

- **external validity** The degree to which an experimental design actually reflects the real-world issues it is supposed to address.

Imagine, for example, that a researcher is interested in the influence of stress (the independent variable) on creative problem solving (the dependent variable). The researcher randomly assigns individuals to be blasted with loud noises at random times during the session (the high-stress or experimental group) or to complete the task in relative quiet (the control group). As the task, the researcher gives all participants a chance to be creative by asking them to list every use they can think of for a cardboard box. Counting up the number of uses that people list, the researcher discovers that those in the high-stress group generated fewer uses of the box. This finding might seem to indicate that stress reduces creativity. In considering the external validity of this study, however, we might ask some questions: How similar are the blasts of loud, random noises to the stresses people experience every day? Is listing uses for a cardboard box really an indicator of creativity? Even if a large number of laboratory studies demonstrated this effect, we would still need to consider whether this result generalizes to the real world. External validity means asking if operational definitions do a good job of reflecting the real-world processes they are supposed to represent.

The second type of validity is **internal validity**, which refers to the degree to which changes in the dependent variable are genuinely due to the manipulation of the independent variable. In the case of internal validity, we want to know whether the experimental methods are free from biases and logical errors that may render the results suspect. Although experimental research is a powerful tool, it requires safeguards. Expectations and biases can tarnish results, as we now consider.

- **internal validity** The degree to which changes in the dependent variable are due to the manipulation of the independent variable.

● **experimenter bias** The influence of the experimenter's expectations on the outcome of the research.

● **demand characteristic** Any aspect of a study that communicates to the participants how the experimenter wants them to behave.

**Experimenter Bias** Experimenters may subtly (and often unknowingly) influence research participants. **Experimenter bias** occurs when the experimenter's expectations influence the outcome of the research. No one designs an experiment without wanting meaningful results. Consequently, experimenters can sometimes subtly communicate to participants what they want the participants to do. A **demand characteristic** is any aspect of a study that communicates to participants how the experimenter wants them to behave. The influence of experimenter expectations can be very difficult to avoid.

In a classic study, Robert Rosenthal (1966) turned college students into experimenters. He randomly assigned the participants rats from the same litter. Half of the students were told that their rats were "maze bright," whereas the other half were told that their rats were "maze dull." The students then conducted experiments to test their rats' ability to navigate mazes. The results were stunning. The so-called maze-bright rats were more successful than the maze-dull rats at running the mazes. The only explanation for the results is that the college students' expectations, conveyed in their behaviors, affected the rats' performance.

Often the participants in psychological studies are not rats but people. Imagine that you are an experimenter, and you know that a participant is going to be exposed to disgusting pictures in a study. Is it possible that you might treat the person differently than you would if you were about to show him photos of cute kittens? The reason experimenter bias is important is that it introduces systematic differences between the experimental group and the control groups; this means that we cannot know if those who looked at disgusting pictures were more, say, upset because of the pictures or because of different treatment by the experimenter. Whenever the person interacting with participants is aware of a study's hypotheses and which group participants have been assigned to, experimenter bias may affect results. Experimenter bias has been implicated in some studies that have failed to replicate past research (Doyen & others, 2012; Lane & others, 2015).

These systematic biases are called *confounds*. In experimental research, confounds are factors that "ride along" with the experimental manipulation, systematically and undesirably influencing the dependent variable. Experimenter bias, demand characteristics, and confounds may all lead to biased results.

● **research participant bias** In an experiment, the influence of participants' expectations, and of their thoughts on how they should behave, on their behavior.

● **placebo effect** A phenomenon in which the expectation of the participants, rather than actual treatment, produces an outcome.

● **placebo** In a drug study, a harmless substance that has no physiological effect, given to participants in a control group so that they are treated identically to the experimental group except for the active agent.

**Research Participant Bias and the Placebo Effect** Like experimenters, research participants may have expectations about what they are supposed to do and how they should behave, and these expectations may affect the results of experiments. **Research participant bias** occurs when the behavior of research participants during the experiment is influenced by how they think they are supposed to behave or by their expectations about what is happening to them.

One example of the power of participant expectations is the placebo effect. The **placebo effect** occurs when participants' expectations, rather than the experimental treatment, produce a particular outcome. Participants in a drug study might be assigned to an experimental group that receives a pill containing an actual painkiller or to a control group that receives a placebo pill. A **placebo** is a harmless substance that has no physiological effect. This placebo is given to participants in a control group so that they are treated identically to the experimental group except for the active agent—in this case, the painkiller. Giving individuals in the control group a placebo pill allows researchers to determine whether changes in the experimental group are due to the active drug agent and not simply to participants' expectations.

*Advertisements for prescription drugs usually describe not only the side effects on people taking the actual drug but also the effects experienced by individuals receiving a placebo.*

Image Courtesy of The Advertising Archives

# psychological *inquiry*

*Target Employee Helping as a Function of Mood Condition*

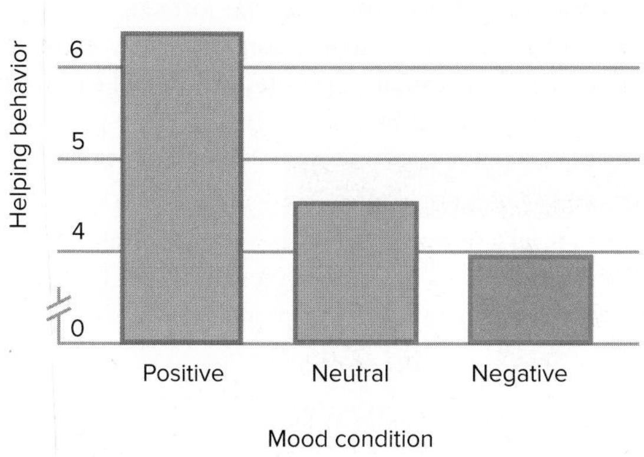


Source: Adapted from Forgas, Dunn, & Granland, (2008).

©Ted S. Warren/AP Images

## *Experimentation in a Natural Setting*

A team of social psychologists was interested in studying how mood influences helping behavior in the real world (Forgas, Dunn, & Granland, 2008). They hypothesized that, especially among the less-experienced members of a sales staff, mood would guide behavior, so that happy salespeople would be more helpful to customers and unhappy salespeople less so. The researchers conducted an experiment in a Target department store, as follows.

First, the experimenters trained two confederates. The first confederate was in charge of manipulating the employees' mood across three conditions:

- In the *positive mood condition,* the confederate said, "I just wanted to let someone know that I am so impressed with the service at this store! The store looks great, and the staff is so nice. I was able to get what I wanted and will be coming back to this store again."
- In the *negative mood condition,* the confederate said, "I just wanted to let someone know that I am so disappointed with the service at this store. The store looks terrible, and the staff is rude. I couldn't get anything I wanted and won't be coming back here again."
- In the *neutral mood condition,* the confederate simply observed, "Interesting, I have been coming here quite regularly, and this store seems always the same; nothing much changes."

Employees were chosen randomly by the confederate and were randomly assigned to the conditions.

Then, after the first confederate interacted with the employees, the second confederate, who was blind to the mood procedure (meaning unaware of the mood condition for each participant), approached the employees individually and asked, "Excuse me, could you tell me where I could find the book *The White Bear*?" This second confederate surreptitiously recorded (1) the number of helpful responses, (2) the number of actual attempts to help, and (3) the time spent helping. These three values were averaged to create an overall helpfulness score. (If the salesperson saw the confederate jotting things down, the confederate pretended to be checking a shopping list.) The researchers were also interested in how workers' experience level influenced the results.

The figure shows the results for the less-experienced sales staff. As you can see, those in a positive mood were most helpful. The researchers concluded that mood caused these differences. Now, answer these questions to see how much you remember about experimental design.

1. Despite the natural setting, this was an experiment. Why?
2. What was the independent variable, and what was its operational definition?
3. What was the dependent variable, and what was its operational definition?
4. Why is it important that the second confederate was "blind" to the mood condition?
5. Why were the employees assigned to mood condition randomly?
6. The store management was aware of the study, but the employees were not. Do you think the experiment was ethical? Why or why not?

## MEASURES OF CENTRAL TENDENCY

A *measure of central tendency* is a single number that indicates the overall characteristics of a set of data. The three measures of central tendency are the mean, the median, and the mode.

● **mean** A measure of central tendency that is the average for a sample.

Most quantitative techniques in psychological science begin with the mean. The **mean** is what people often call the average. The mean is calculated by adding all the scores in a set of scores and then dividing by the number of scores. As a good indicator of the central tendency for a group of scores, the mean is the measure that is used most often. When your instructors provide students with their exam grades, they might mention the test mean, because this average gives the class a general idea of how the group performed.

The mean is not so helpful, however, when a group of scores contains a few extreme scores, especially if the number of cases in the group is small. Consider the annual earnings for the two groups of five people shown in the table below.

| Group 1 | Group 2 |
|---|---|
| $19,000 | $ 19,000 |
| 19,000 | 19,000 |
| 23,000 | 23,000 |
| 24,000 | 24,000 |
| 25,000 | 45,000,000 |
| Mean $22,000 | Mean $9,017,000 |
| Median $23,000 | Median $ 23,000 |
| Mode $19,000 | Mode $ 19,000 |

Group 1 lists the earnings of five ordinary people. Group 2 is composed of the earnings of four ordinary people plus the approximate earnings of movie director Steven Spielberg. Now look at the means that have been calculated for the two groups. The vast difference between them is due to the one extreme score. In such a situation, one of the other two measures of central tendency, the median or the mode, would give a more accurate picture of the data overall.

● **median** A measure of central tendency that is the middle score in a sample.

The **median** is the score that falls exactly in the middle of the distribution of scores after they have been arranged (or ranked) from highest to lowest. When you have an odd number of scores (say, five or seven), the median is the score with the same number of scores above it as below it. In the table above, each group has a median income of $23,000. Notice that, unlike the mean, the median is unaffected by extreme scores. The medians are the same for both groups ($23,000), but their means are extremely different ($22,000 versus $9,017,000). Of course, if there is an even number of scores, there is no "middle" score. This problem is dealt with by averaging the scores that share the middle location.

● **mode** A measure of central tendency that is the most common score in a sample.

The **mode** is the score that occurs most often in a dataset. In our earnings example, the mode is $19,000, which occurs twice in each group. All of the other annual incomes occur only once. The mode is the least-used measure of central tendency. Yet the mode can be particularly useful in certain circumstances: for example, when information is desired about preference or popularity. Consider a teacher who wants to know which child is the most popular or the least popular in her classroom. She might create a questionnaire and ask students which of their classmates they like the most or the least. The most frequently nominated child would be the mode in these instances.

Although the mode and the median can provide useful information, the most commonly used measure of central tendency in psychological research is the mean. As you will see, the mean is also a key component of calculating other important descriptive statistics–measures of dispersion.

## MEASURES OF DISPERSION

In addition to revealing the central characteristics of a sample, descriptive statistics can also give us *measures of dispersion,* which describe how much the scores in a sample differ from one another. That is, these measures give us a sense of the spread of scores, or how much variability exists in the data. Like measures of central tendency, measures of dispersion involve a single number that characterizes a dataset. But although measures of central tendency involve numbers that tell us about the scores in that dataset, measures of dispersion tell us about the differences among those scores. Let's look at some common ways that researchers measure dispersion.

To begin, suppose that four students rate their positive mood on a scale from 1 (not at all positive) to 7 (extremely positive), as follows:

**Positive Mood**

| | |
|---|---|
| Sarah | 7 |
| Sun Mee | 6 |
| Josh | 2 |
| Rodney | 5 |

(You might note that the mean for these data is 20/4, or 5.) One common measure of dispersion is the **range**, which is the distance between the highest and the lowest scores. In the example above, the range in positive mood is 5 (that is, the highest score, 7, minus the lowest score, 2). Generally speaking, the range is a rather simplistic estimate of the variability within a group of scores. Because the range takes into account only the lowest and highest scores, it can produce a misleading picture of how different the scores in the dataset actually are. Note that for positive mood, most people in the example have fairly similar scores, but using the range alone gives the impression that scores are widely dispersed.

A more informative measure of dispersion, and the one most commonly used in psychological research, is the standard deviation. The **standard deviation** measures how much scores vary, on average, around the mean of the sample. There is a little hitch, however. One of the mathematical properties of the mean is that if you add up each person's difference from the mean, the sum will always be 0. So, calculating the average difference (or deviation) from the mean does not produce a meaningful answer.

To get around this problem, we take each person's difference from the mean and multiply it by itself (or square it). This removes the negative numbers, and the sum of these differences will no longer equal 0. We add these squared deviations together and then divide by the number of cases (minus 1). Finally, we take the square root of that number (to get rid of the squaring we did earlier). Essentially, then, the standard deviation is the square root of the average squared deviation from the mean. The smaller the standard deviation, the less variability in the dataset. A small standard deviation indicates that, on average, scores are close to the mean.

The following table presents the information needed to calculate the standard deviation for the positive mood ratings given above.

| | A | B | C |
|---|---|---|---|
| Participant | Rating | Difference from the mean (5) | *Squared* difference from the mean (5) |
| **Sarah** | 7 | 2 | 4 |
| **Sun Mee** | 6 | 1 | 1 |
| **Josh** | 2 | -3 | 9 |
| **Rodney** | 5 | 0 | 0 |
| MEAN $= \frac{(7 + 6 + 2 + 5)}{4} =$ **5.0** | | Sum of this column = 0 | Sum of these differences = 4 + 1 + 9 + 0 = 14 |

Column A presents the ratings by each participant. Column B shows the differences of these scores from the mean (5). Notice that if we add up column B, the answer is 0. Column C shows the squared deviations from the mean for each participant. Adding up those squared differences, we get 14. Next, we divide 14 by the number of participants minus 1, in this case 14 divided by 3, which is 4.67, and then we take the square root of that number, which is 2.16. This is the standard deviation of our sample, which, compared to the range of 5, tells us that the group is actually fairly closely arranged around the mean.

©Cyberstock/Alamy Stock Photo

● **range** A measure of dispersion that is the difference between the highest and lowest scores.

● **standard deviation** A measure of dispersion that indicates how much the scores in a sample differ from the mean in the sample.

The mean and standard deviation together yield a lot of information about a sample. Indeed, given the raw scores, the means, and the standard deviations of two variables, we can calculate the correlation coefficient in no time. The correlation coefficient is not a descriptive statistic but rather an inferential statistic, our next topic.

## Inferential Statistics

Imagine that, inspired by the research on college yearbook pictures (discussed earlier in this chapter), you conduct a study on the relationship between expressions of positive emotion and interpersonal success. In your study, you videotape job candidate interviews, code the videos for Duchenne smiling by the candidates, and document which of the job seekers were called back for a second interview. Let's say you calculate that the mean number of smiles for candidates who were not called back is 3.5, and the mean number of smiles for candidates who were called back is 6.5. So, those who were called back generated, on average, 3 more smiles than those who were not called back. Does that difference matter? It seems pretty big, but is it big enough? Could we have obtained the same difference simply by chance?

To draw conclusions about differences we observe in studies, we want to know that the difference is likely to be one that can be replicated or found consistently in a variety of studies. Inferential statistics are the tools that help us to state whether a difference is unlikely to be the result of chance. More specifically, **inferential statistics** are the mathematical methods used to indicate whether the data sufficiently support a research hypothesis. A psychologist conducting a study would certainly calculate the means and standard deviations to describe the sample, but in order to *test predictions* about that sample, the researcher needs inferential statistics.

● **inferential statistics** Mathematical methods that are used to indicate whether the data sufficiently support a research hypothesis.

The logic behind inferential statistics is relatively simple. Inferential statistics give us a statement of probability about the differences observed between two or more groups or the size of an association between two or more variables; this probability statement gives the odds that the observed differences or associations were due simply to chance. Traditionally, in psychological research, the standard has been that if the odds are 5 out of 100 (or .05) or less that the differences are due to chance, the results are considered *statistically significant.* In statistical language, this is referred to as the .05 level of statistical significance. In published articles, researchers report the inferential statistic followed by a statement about the probability of obtaining the results by chance; for instance, $p < .05$.

The .05 level of statistical significance was long considered the minimum level of probability that scientists would accept to conclude that observed effects are real. Now, this standard has been questioned. In response to the replication crisis, a group of 72 scientists argued that .05 is insufficient and researchers must show that results are *very* unlikely to have occurred by chance. They asserted that the standard should be changed from .05 to .005 (Benjamin & others, 2018)–in other words, the results would be expected to occur by chance just 5 times in 1000.

Why do *p*-values matter to the replication crisis? It is extremely difficult to publish studies that do not produce statistically significant results. And, publishing original science is the key way that people are hired and promoted at universities. So, researchers are strongly motivated to produce results that are statistically significant. This motivation can lead to behavior called *p-hacking. P*-hacking refers to questionable data analytic practices. If researchers know their results must have a *p*-value below a specific standard, they might try to reduce the *p*-value for a test, by, for instance, dropping participants, not including conditions that were in an experiment in analyses, or statistically controlling for variables in ways that were not specified in advance. *P*-hacked results are unlikely to replicate because the analyses that produced them are tailored to particular samples. *P*-hacking is one reason many researchers now *preregister* their planned data analyses so that concerns with this practice are removed.

Recall that although we study a sample, we typically wish to generalize our findings to a population. Inferential statistics are the bridge between a sample and a population, because they tell us the likelihood that the results we found with a sample reflect differences in the larger population. It makes sense that the larger our sample is, the more likely it is to represent that population. Thus, significance tests are based in part on the number of cases in a sample. The higher the number of cases, the easier it is to get statistical significance. As a result, with a very large sample, even very small differences may be significant. However, statistical significance is not the same thing as real-world significance. Even if a difference is found to be statistically significant, its real-world value remains to be evaluated by critically thinking scientists. Indeed, even very low *p*-values are no substitute for thinking. No matter whether the results are statistically significant or not, scientists must think about their data and results critically.

### test yourself

1. What is meant by a measure of central tendency? Name three measures of central tendency.
2. What do measures of dispersion describe?
3. What does standard deviation measure?

# 5. CONDUCTING ETHICAL RESEARCH

Ethics is a crucial consideration for all science. This fact came to the fore in the aftermath of World War II, for example, when it became apparent that Nazi doctors had forced concentration camp prisoners to participate in experiments. These atrocities spurred scientists to develop a code of appropriate behavior–a set of principles about the rights of research participants. In general, ethical principles of research focus on balancing the rights of the participants with the rights of scientists to ask research questions.

The issue of ethics in psychological research may affect you personally if at some point you participate in a study. In that event, you need to know your rights as a participant and the researchers' responsibilities in ensuring that these rights are safeguarded. Experiences in research can have unforeseen effects on people's lives.

Consider, for instance, that many researchers who are interested in close relationships might ask romantic couples to keep diaries tracking the quality of their interactions (Hsueh & others, 2018; Soriano & others, 2018). Might just paying close attention to this variable influence it?

Other researchers have couples come into the lab and discuss a topic that is a source of conflict in that relationship (Taylor & others, 2018). Such procedures are important in measuring how couples handle conflicts. But, could such interactions influence the couple long after the study is over? Researchers have a responsibility to anticipate the any problems their study might cause and, at least, to inform the participants of the possible fallout.

*Being part of a research study can potentially lead to unintended consequences for the participants.*
©Sam Edwards/Glow Images

Ethics comes into play in every psychological study. Even smart, conscientious students sometimes think that members of their church, athletes in the Special Olympics, or residents of the local nursing home present great samples for psychological research. Without proper permission, though, the most well-meaning and considerate researchers still violate the rights of the participants. It is also important to keep in mind that risks to participants must be balanced against the scientific merit of any study. If a study is not scientifically sound, even the slightest risk to participants is not ethically justifiable.

## Ethics Guidelines

A number of guidelines have been developed to ensure that research is conducted ethically. The foundation of these guidelines is the notion that people participating in psychological research should be no worse off coming out of the study than they were going in.

Today colleges and universities have a board, typically called the *institutional review board (IRB),* that evaluates the ethical nature of research conducted at their institutions. Proposed research plans must pass the scrutiny of a research ethics committee before the study can be initiated. In addition, the American Psychological Association (APA) has developed ethics guidelines for its members. The code of ethics instructs psychologists to protect their participants from mental and physical harm. The participants' best interests must be kept foremost in the researcher's mind. The APA's guidelines address four important issues:

- *Informed consent:* All participants must know what their participation will involve and what risks might develop. For example, participants in a study on dating should be told beforehand that a questionnaire might stimulate thoughts about issues in their relationships that they have not considered. Participants also should be informed that in some instances a discussion of the issues might improve their relationships but that in others it might worsen the relationships and even end them. Even after informed consent is given, participants must retain the right to withdraw from the study at any time and for any reason.

- *Confidentiality:* Researchers are responsible for keeping all of the data they gather on individuals completely confidential and, when possible, completely anonymous. Confidential data are not the same as anonymous. When data are confidential, it is possible to link a participant's identity to his or her data.
- *Debriefing:* After the study has been completed, the researchers should inform the participants of its purpose and the methods they used. In most cases, the experimenters also can inform participants in a general manner beforehand about the purpose of the research without leading the participants to behave in a way that matches what they think the experimenters are expecting. When preliminary information about the study is likely to affect the results, participants can at least be debriefed after the study's completion.
- *Deception:* In some circumstances, telling the participants beforehand what the research study is about would substantially alter the participants' behavior, thereby invalidating the researcher's study. Recall the study of false memory contagion. The participants were not told that the person they interacted with was a confederate following a script. Had the psychologist informed the participants beforehand that this was the case, the whole study would have been ruined. Thus, the researcher deceived participants about the purpose of the study and the nature of their relationship with the interaction partner.

©sidsnapper/Getty Images

In all cases of deception, the psychologist must ensure that the deception will not harm the participants and that the participants will be told the true nature of the study (will be debriefed) as soon as possible after the study is completed. Researchers can never deceive participants about actual harms that may occur in a study. Researchers should use deception only when their research question could not be answered in any other way. Note that when a study uses deception, the principle of informed consent is violated. This is why participants in studies involving deception should have the option of withdrawing consent after they find out what the study is actually about.

The federal government also takes a role in ensuring that research involving human participants is conducted ethically. The Office for Human Research Protections is devoted to ensuring the well-being of participants in research. Over the years, the office has dealt with many challenging and controversial issues–among them, informed consent rules for research on mental disorders, regulations governing research on pregnant women and fetuses, and ethical issues regarding AIDS vaccine research.

## Ethical Treatment of Research Animals

For generations, psychologists have used animals in some research. Animal studies have provided a better understanding of and solutions for many human problems (Capitanio, 2017; Keehn, 2018). Research using nonhuman animals has produced important benefits to human life, ranging from psychotherapeutic treatments to medications (Herzog & others, 2018; Stevenson & others, 2018). Certainly using nonhuman animals, who cannot provide consent, poses an ethical dilemma (Davies & others, 2018).

About 5 percent of APA members use nonhuman animals in their research. Rats and mice account for 90 percent of all psychological research with animals. It is true that researchers sometimes use procedures with animals that would be unethical with humans, but these scientists are guided by standards for housing, feeding, and maintaining the psychological and physical well-being of their animal subjects. Researchers are required to weigh potential benefits of the research against possible harm to the animal and to avoid inflicting unnecessary pain. In short, researchers must follow stringent ethical guidelines, whether studies involve animals or humans.

### *test yourself*

1. What two things do the ethical principles used in research seek to balance?
2. With respect to the participants in a study, what do the various ethical guidelines covering research all fundamentally seek to protect?
3. What four key issues do the APA's ethics guidelines address?

# 6. THINKING CRITICALLY ABOUT PSYCHOLOGICAL RESEARCH

Not all psychological information presented for public consumption comes from the most reliable sources. Because journalists, television reporters, online bloggers, and other media personnel are not usually trained in psychological research, they often have trouble sorting through the widely varying material they find and making sound decisions about the best information to present to the public. In addition, the media often focus on sensationalistic psychological findings to capture public attention.

Even when the media present the results of excellent research, they sometimes have trouble accurately informing people about the findings and their implications. *The Science of Psychology* is dedicated to carefully introducing, defining, and elaborating on key concepts and issues, research, and clinical findings. The media, however, do not have the luxury of devoting time and space to details or describing the limitations or qualifications of research. In the end, *you* must take responsibility for evaluating media reports on psychological research. To put it another way, you have to consume psychological information critically and wisely. Five guidelines follow.

## Avoid Overgeneralizing Based on Little Information

Media reports of psychological information often leave out details about the nature of the sample used in a given study. Without information about sample characteristics—such as the number of participants, their sex, or their ethnic representation—it is wise to take research results with a grain of salt. For example, research that demonstrated the classic "fight or flight" response to stress has had great impact on how we understand the body's response to threatening situations. Yet the original work on this topic included only men (Taylor, 2011). The implications of the lack of women in these studies will be explored in the chapter "Biological Foundations of Behavior".

## Distinguish Between Group Results and Individual Needs

Just as we cannot generalize from a small group to all people, we also cannot apply conclusions from a group to an individual. When you learn about psychological research through the media, you might try to apply the results to your life. It is important to keep in mind that statistics about a group do not necessarily represent each individual in the group equally well. Imagine, taking a test in a class and being told that the class average was 75 percent, but you got 98 percent. It is unlikely that you would want the instructor to apply the group average to your score.

Sometimes consumers of psychological research can get the wrong idea about whether their own experience is "normal" if it does not match group statistics. New parents often face this issue. They read about developmental milestones that supposedly characterize an entire age group of children; one such milestone might be that most 2-year-olds are conversing with their parents. However, this group information does not necessarily characterize *all* children who are developing normally. Albert Einstein did not start talking until he was the ripe old age of 3.

## Look for Answers Beyond a Single Study

The media might identify an interesting piece of research and claim that its conclusions are phenomenal, with far-reaching implications. Such pivotal studies do occur but they are rare. It is safer to assume that no single study will provide conclusive answers to

*Wherever you encounter psychological research keep a critical mindset.*

©Jamie Grill/Blend Images/Getty Images

an important question, especially answers that apply to all people. In fact, for psychological issues that prompt many investigations, conflicting results are common. Answers to questions in research usually emerge after many scientists have conducted similar investigations that yield similar conclusions. Remember that you should not take one research study as the absolute, final answer to a problem, no matter how compelling the findings.

## Avoid Attributing Causes Where None Have Been Found

Drawing causal conclusions from correlational studies is one of the most common mistakes the media make. For example, the results of the Nun Study described earlier suggest that happy people live longer. However, we cannot state that happiness *caused* them to live longer. Remember from the discussion of correlation earlier in the chapter that causal interpretations cannot be made when two or more factors are simply correlated. We cannot say that one causes the other. When you hear about correlational studies, be skeptical of words indicating causation until you know more about the research.

## Consider the Source of Psychological Information

Studies conducted by psychologists are not automatically accepted by the rest of the research community. The researchers usually must submit their findings to an academic journal for review by their colleagues, who make a decision about whether to publish the paper, depending on its scientific merit. Although the quality of research and findings is not uniform among all psychology journals, in most cases journals submit the findings to far greater scrutiny than do the popular media.

Within the media, though, you can usually draw a distinction. The reports of psychological research in respected newspapers such as the *New York Times* and the *Washington Post,* as well as in credible magazines such as *Time* and the *Atlantic Monthly,* are far more trustworthy than reports in tabloids such as the *National Enquirer* or online bloggers without scientific credentials. Yet, whatever the source–serious publication, tabloid, blog, or even academic journal–you are responsible for reading the details behind the reported findings and for analyzing the study's credibility.

### test yourself

1. For what reasons are media reports on psychological studies often problematic?
2. Why is it wise to look beyond the conclusions of just one research study?
3. How does the submission of research findings to a respectable academic journal aid both researchers and the public?

# 7. THE SCIENTIFIC METHOD AND HEALTH AND WELLNESS

Throughout this book we examine many ways that psychological research has implications for health and wellness. Here, we focus on a research topic in which the scientific method has played a particularly important role in the conclusions drawn–the power of expressive writing to enhance health and wellness.

James Pennebaker has conducted a number of studies that converge on the same conclusion: that writing about one's deepest thoughts and feelings concerning one's most traumatic life event leads to a number of health and well-being benefits (Pennebaker & Evans, 2014). This research began with a correlational study comparing two groups of individuals–those who had lost a spouse to suicide and those who had lost a spouse to an accident (Pennebaker & O'Heeron, 1984). The results showed that survivors of spousal suicide were more likely to have gotten sick in the months after the death, compared to those whose spouses had died from an accident. Importantly, the difference was explained by the fact that individuals whose spouses had died by suicide were much less likely to talk about their loss, compared with the other participants.

These correlational findings led Pennebaker to wonder whether it might be possible to manipulate expressing one's thoughts and feelings about a traumatic event *experimentally* and thereby to receive the benefits of socially sharing the trauma. So, in subsequent studies, participants were randomly assigned to write about one of two topics–either the individual's most traumatic life event (the experimental group) or a relatively uninteresting topic (the control group).

Participants wrote about the same topic on three or four consecutive days for about 20 minutes each day. Weeks or months after writing, the trauma writing group had better physical health than the control group. Since the first traumatic writing study, a host of researchers have replicated these effects, showing that writing about trauma is associated with superior immune function, better response to a vaccine, higher psychological well-being, better adjustment to starting college, reduced depression, and better coping with a variety of stressful events including cancer, military combat, and parenting a child on the autism spectrum (Da Paz, Wallander, & Tiemensma, 2018; Lepore & Smyth, 2002; Lu & others, 2018; Pennebaker, 2016; Pennebaker & Smyth, 2016; Reinhold, Bürkner, & Holling, 2018; Sayer & others, 2015; Sloan & Marx, 2018). Thus, we might conclude that documenting one's deepest thoughts and feelings about traumatic life events is necessary to attain the health benefits of writing.

*The research of James Pennebaker of the University of Texas, Austin, explores the connections among traumatic life experience, expressive writing, physical and mental health, and work performance.*

Courtesy of James W. Pennebaker, University of Texas. Photo by Marsha Miller.

Note that the participants in the trauma group were documenting an important personal experience. Thinking about these results in terms of the internal validity of the conclusions, we might ask if focusing on a trauma is the key ingredient in producing health benefits. Might there be other, less negative aspects of life that are equally meaningful and that might promote good health when they are the subject of personal writing? Indeed, subsequent research has shown that health benefits can emerge from writing about a variety of topics, including how one has grown from a negative experience (King & Miner, 2000; Low, Stanton, & Danoff-Burg, 2006), one's life dreams (King, 2001), and one's most intensely positive experiences (Burton & King, 2004, 2009). In one study, participants who wrote about either a traumatic life event or an extremely positive event for just 2 minutes a day over two days reported fewer illnesses a month later (Burton & King, 2008).

The body of evidence for the effects of expressive writing on health is substantial and has been subjected to two meta-analyses. These meta-analyses indicate that individuals who write over a period of days that are spaced apart tend to benefit most from writing and that feeling distressed while writing is not necessary to enjoy these benefits (Frattaroli, 2006; Smyth, 1998).

If you would like to explore the benefits of writing in your own life, use the simple guidelines below:

*Even writing about peak experiences and personal accomplishments can lead to health and well-being benefits.*

©Olga Danylenko/Shutterstock

- Find a quiet place to write.
- Pick just one topic to explore through writing.
- Dedicate yourself to a few minutes of writing each day, perhaps writing once a week for a few weeks.
- While writing, do not worry about punctuation, grammar, or spelling–just let yourself go and write about all of the thoughts, emotions, and feelings associated with the experience you are documenting.
- If you feel that writing about something negative is not for you, try writing about your most positive life experiences, the people you care about, or all the things for which you feel grateful.

The long and growing literature on the effects of expressive writing on health demonstrates how the process of scientific research builds from one study to the next. This literature also demonstrates how psychological research is relevant to the daily life of everyone with a story to write–and how an individual can benefit from writing that story.

## test yourself

1. Briefly describe Pennebaker's initial correlational study comparing two groups of individuals who had lost a spouse.
2. What did Pennebaker's subsequent experimental research show?
3. What does the accumulated body of evidence indicate about the effects of expressive writing on health?

SUMMARY

## 1. PSYCHOLOGY'S SCIENTIFIC METHOD

Psychologists use the scientific method to address research questions. This method involves starting with a theory and then making observations, formulating hypotheses, testing these through empirical research, drawing conclusions, and evaluating the theory.

## 2. TYPES OF PSYCHOLOGICAL RESEARCH

Three types of research commonly used in psychology are descriptive research (finding out about the basic dimensions of some variable), correlational research (finding out if and how two variables change together), and experimental research (determining the causal relationship between variables). Descriptive research includes observation, surveys, interviews, and case studies. Correlational research often includes surveys and interviews as well as observation. Experimental research often occurs in a lab but can also be done in a natural setting.

In an experiment, the independent variable is manipulated to see if it produces changes in the dependent variable. An experiment involves comparing two groups: the experimental group (the one that receives the treatment or manipulation of the independent variable) and the control group (the comparison group or baseline that is equal to the experimental group in every way except for the independent variable). Experimental research relies on random assignment to ensure that the groups are roughly equivalent before the manipulation of the independent variable.

## 3. RESEARCH SAMPLES AND SETTINGS

Researchers must decide whom to study and where to study them. A sample is the group that participates in a study; a population is the group to which the researcher wishes to generalize the results. A random sample is the best way of ensuring that the sample reflects the population.

Research settings include both the laboratory and real-world, naturalistic contexts. The laboratory allows a great deal of control, but naturalistic settings may give a truer sense of natural behavior.

## 4. ANALYZING AND INTERPRETING DATA

Descriptive statistics are used to describe and summarize samples of data in a meaningful way. Two types of descriptive statistics are measures of central tendency and measures of variability. Measures of central tendency are the mean (or the mathematical average), the median (the middle score), and the mode (the most common score). Measures of variability include the range (the difference between the highest and lowest scores) and the standard deviation (the square root of the average squared deviation from the mean).

Inferential statistics are used to draw conclusions about data. Inferential statistics aim to uncover statistical significance, which means that the differences observed between groups (or the correlation between variables) are unlikely to be the result of chance. Previously psychologists thought that findings were likely to be "real" if the odds of finding them by chance was 5 in 100 but currently many scientists are questioning whether .05 is sufficiently rigorous.

## 5. CONDUCTING ETHICAL RESEARCH

For all kinds of research, ethical treatment of participants is crucial. Participants should leave a psychological study no worse off than they were when they entered. Some guiding principles for ethical research in psychology include informed consent, confidentiality, debriefing (participants should be fully informed about the purpose of a study once it is over), and explaining the use of deception in a study. Researchers must follow stringent ethical guidelines, whether animals or humans are the subjects in their studies.

## 6. THINKING CRITICALLY ABOUT PSYCHOLOGICAL RESEARCH

In your everyday life and in introductory psychology, you will be exposed to psychological research findings. In approaching psychological research in the media, you should adopt the attitude of a scientist and critically evaluate the research presented. This means being careful to avoid overgeneralizing based on little information, realizing that group results may not apply to every individual, looking for answers beyond a single study, and avoiding attributing causation when none has been found. Finally, it is important to consider the source when you encounter research in the popular media.

## 7. THE SCIENTIFIC METHOD AND HEALTH AND WELLNESS

A great deal of psychological research has relevance to health and wellness. An example is research by James Pennebaker on the effects of expressive writing on health and well-being. This research has shown that individuals who are randomly assigned to write about a traumatic life event for a few minutes a day over three or four days show a host of health and well-being benefits compared with those in a control condition. Subsequent research has shown that these health benefits can be obtained by writing about positive life experiences and even just writing for a couple of minutes.

This research demonstrates how a research question can begin as a correlational study and then move to the laboratory to demonstrate causation. When many studies have been done on a topic, a meta-analysis can provide a sense of the overall importance of the results. This example also shows how psychological research can have important implications for everyday life.

# key *terms*

case study or case history
confederate
control group
correlational research
cross-sectional design
demand characteristic
dependent variable
descriptive research
descriptive statistics
double-blind experiment
empirical method
experiment
experimental group
experimenter bias
external validity
hypothesis
independent variable
inferential statistics
internal validity
longitudinal design
mean
median
meta-analysis
mode
naturalistic observation
operational definition
placebo
placebo effect
population
prediction
random assignment
random sample
range
replication
research participant bias
sample
standard deviation
theory
third variable problem
variable

# apply your *knowledge*

1. It's time to get out those old photos from the prom, wedding, or family reunion and see just how happy people were (or weren't). Look at some pictures from your own life and see who was genuinely smiling and who was faking it. Just cover the mouths with your finger—you can see who is happy from their eyes.
2. Is an old diary of yours hanging around somewhere? Pull it out and take a look at what you wrote. Count up your positive emotion words or negative emotion words. Are there themes in your diary from years ago that are still relevant to your life today? Does looking at your own diary change the way you might think about the results of the Nun Study? Explain.
3. What are some positive and negative correlations that you have observed in your own experience? What are some third variables that might explain these relationships? Do you think these relationships may be causal? How would you design an experiment to test that possibility?
4. In the next few days, look through several newspapers and magazines for reports about psychological research. Also notice what you find on the Internet and on television about psychology. Apply the guidelines for being a wise consumer of information about psychology to these media reports.
5. The opening of this chapter presented research on a difference-education program for college students. Design a replication of this work using a different population of participants. How might you study this phenomenon among middle-aged adults, elderly individuals, or children?
6. Pick a topic of interest to you and define the variables. Then list as many ways to operationalize the variables as you can. Come up with at least one behavioral measure of the variable. Would your topic be best studied using a correlational or an experimental method? How would you conduct the study?

**Design elements:** Preview icon: ©Jiang Hongyan; Intersection box icon: ©D. Hurst/Alamy, ©Creative Crop/Getty Images, ©Dimitris66/Getty Images, ©Savany/Getty Images; Critical Controversy box icon: ©Ultrashock; running heads icon: ©Cre8tive Studios/Alamy; Summary icon: ©Vadarshop

# CHAPTER 3

## CHAPTER OUTLINE

©Jamie Grill/JGI/Getty Images

# Biological Foundations of Behavior

## "The Things I'm Seeing Are Really Strange"

**Milena Canning was 30 years old when, 18 years ago, she suffered a severe infection that led to several major strokes.** After 8 weeks in a coma, she emerged completely blind. Months after the coma, she started noticing strange images, like sparkles bubbling into sight. Eventually, she found that she could see some objects, sometimes. She could see the steam rising out of her coffee (but not the cup of coffee itself). She could see her daughter's ponytail bobbing behind her as she walked (but not her daughter's face). She could see and catch a ball thrown to her (but not see the ball sitting still). She could see many things, *but only when they were moving* (University of Western Ontario, 2018). Recently, neuroscientists were able to find out what might explain Milena's very rare condition, known as *Riddoch phenomenon* (the ability to see things only when they are moving) (Arcaro & others, 2018). Using brain imaging, the researchers found that Milena's brain was missing an apple-sized portion at the back—the area responsible for processing visual experience. But the damage wrought by the strokes was not the end of the road for Milena's brain. Over time, her brain developed a "workaround" using what remained of her visual system, including the area responsible for seeing motion. Essentially, Milena's brain rewired itself to make the most of what she had, allowing her to develop a surprisingly rich visual life. She no longer sees as she did before her illness. She now sees a world of motion.

This example illuminates the brain's role in precious human experience, its amazing capacity to adapt itself to change, and its sometimes mysterious nature. Imagine: This intricate 3-pound structure that you are reading about is the engine that is doing the work of reading itself. The brain is at once the object of study and the reason we are able to study it. ●

# PREVIEW

In this chapter, our focus is the biological foundations of human behavior. We review the essentials of what we know about the nervous system and its command center—the brain. We then look at how genetic processes influence who we are as individuals and how we behave. Finally, we explore the role of the brain and nervous system in the experience of stress and consider ways to unlock the brain's unique resources to better meet life's challenges and maintain health and well-being.

# 1. THE NERVOUS SYSTEM

● **nervous system** The body's electrochemical communication circuitry.

The **nervous system** is the body's electrochemical communication circuitry. The field that studies the nervous system is called *neuroscience.* The human nervous system is made up of billions of communicating nerve cells, and it is likely the most intricately organized aggregate of matter on the planet. A single cubic centimeter (the size of a snack cube of cheese) of the human brain contains over 50 million nerve cells, each of which communicates with many other nerve cells in information-processing networks that make the most elaborate computer seem primitive.

## Characteristics of the Nervous System

The brain and nervous system guide our interactions with the world around us, move our bodies through the world, and direct our adaptation to the environment. Several extraordinary characteristics allow the nervous system to direct our behavior: complexity, integration, adaptability, and electrochemical transmission.

### COMPLEXITY

The human brain and nervous system are enormously complex. This complexity is demonstrated in the orchestration of the billions of nerve cells in the brain—to allow you to talk, write, sing, dance, and think. This capacity is awe-inspiring. Right now as you read, your brain is carrying out a multitude of functions, including seeing, reading, learning, and (we hope) breathing. Extensive assemblies of nerve cells participate in each of these activities, all at once (Teoh & others, 2018).

*As we dance, write, play sports, talk, think, and connect with the world in countless other ways, the brain and the nervous system guide our every interaction, movement, and adaptation.*

(first) ©Paul Bradbury/Getty Images; (second) ©Digital Vision/Getty Images

### INTEGRATION

The brain does an amazing job of pulling information together. Think of everything going on around you right now, as well as a number of processes happening in your body—like breathing, the digestion of your last meal, the healing of a cut (Klingseisen & Lyons, 2018; Veiga-Fernandes & Artis, 2018). Somehow, you need to make sense of all of these various stimuli. Similarly, the shapes on this page are not simply splashes of ink but letters, and those letters compose words that make sense. It is your brain that draws your experiences together into a coherent whole. Sounds, sights, touches, tastes, and smells—the brain integrates all of these sensory inputs so that you can function in the world (Nummenmaa & others, 2018; Vastano & others, 2018).

The nervous system has different levels and many different parts. Brain activity is integrated across these levels through countless interconnections of brain cells and extensive

pathways that link different parts of the brain and body. Each nerve cell communicates, on average, with 10,000 others, making an astronomical number of connections. The complexity of connections in the brain is one of its key features (Avena-Koenigsberger, Misic, & Sporns, 2018). The evidence for these connections is observable, for example, when a loved one takes your hand. How does your brain know, and tell you, what has happened? Bundles of interconnected nerve cells relay information about the sensation in your hand through the nervous system in a very orderly fashion, all the way to the areas of the brain involved in recognizing that someone you love is holding your hand. Then the brain might send a reply and prompt your hand to give your loved one's hand a little squeeze.

### ADAPTABILITY

Think about all the different places human beings live or could live someday. People inhabit blazing deserts and frozen tundra. People live in bustling cities and small rural towns. They hunt and farm and work online. Yet, in all these different places, people possess the same amazing engine, the brain, that helps them solve the problems of survival. If we send people to live on Mars, that same organ will be required to figure out how to exist there. Human beings need a brain that is ready to meet these varied challenges. To survive, we must adapt to new conditions. The brain and nervous system together serve as our agent for adapting to the world. Nerve cells are not unchanging structures. They have a hereditary, biological foundation, but they are constantly adapting to changes in the body and the environment.

The term **plasticity** refers to the brain's special physical capacity for change. The description of Milena Canning at the opening of this chapter provides a great example of this plasticity. Her brain rewired connections, optimizing the functional areas of her visual system, allowing her to see more and more of her environment. Less dramatic examples of plasticity occur in all of us. Because of the brain's plasticity, it can change in response to experience. For example, you might believe that thinking is a mental process, not a physical one. Yet thinking *is* a physical event, because every thought you have is reflected in physical activity in the brain.

• **plasticity** The brain's special physical capacity for change.

Importantly, the brain can be changed by experience. London cab drivers who have developed a familiarity with the city show increases in the brain region that is thought to be responsible for reading maps (Maguire & others, 2000; Peng & others, 2018). Think about that: When you change the way you think, you are *literally* changing the brain's physical processes and even its shape. Our daily experiences contribute to the wiring or rewiring of our brains, just as do the experiences of those London cab drivers (Starrett & Ekstrom, 2018).

### ELECTROCHEMICAL TRANSMISSION

The brain and nervous system function as an information-processing system powered by electrical impulses and chemical messengers. When an impulse travels down a nerve cell, or *neuron,* it does so through electrical charges. When that impulse gets to the end of the line, it communicates with the next neuron using chemicals, as we will consider later in this chapter. Throughout the nervous system, information is conveyed in one of these two ways–electrically or chemically.

## Pathways in the Nervous System

As we interact with and adapt to the world, the brain and the nervous system receive and transmit sensory input (like sounds, smells, and flavors), integrate the information taken in from the environment, and direct the body's motor activities. Information

flows into the brain through input from our senses, and the brain makes sense of that information, pulling it together and giving it meaning. In turn, information moves out of the brain to the rest of the body, directing all of the things we do.

The nervous system has specialized pathways that are adapted for different functions. These pathways are made up of afferent nerves, efferent nerves, and neural networks (discussed later in the chapter). **Afferent nerves or sensory nerves** carry information *to* the brain and spinal cord. These sensory pathways communicate information about the external environment (for example, the sight of a sunrise) and internal conditions (for example, fatigue or hunger) from sensory receptors to the brain and spinal cord. **Efferent nerves or motor nerves** carry information *out of* the brain and spinal cord–that is, they carry the nervous system's output. These motor pathways communicate information from the brain and spinal cord to other areas of the body, including muscles and glands, instructing them, in a sense, to get busy. Notice that the fact that we have separate afferent and efferent nerves tells us something interesting about neurons: Each neuron is a one-way street in the nervous system.

These terms can be hard to remember because they are so similar. Remember that sensory nerves are afferent nerves. They bring the brain and spinal cord information about the world. Motor nerves are efferent nerves that send information out from the brain and spinal cord. Note that *a*fferent nerves *a*rrive at the brain and spinal cord, and *e*fferent nerves *e*xit these components of the nervous system.

● **afferent nerves or sensory nerves** Nerves that carry information about the external environment *to* the brain and spinal cord via sensory receptors.

● **efferent nerves or motor nerves** Nerves that carry information *out of* the brain and spinal cord to other areas of the body.

## Divisions of the Nervous System

This elegant system is highly ordered and organized for effective function. Figure 1 shows the two primary divisions of the human nervous system: the central nervous system and the peripheral nervous system.

The **central nervous system (CNS)** is made up of the brain and spinal cord. More than 99 percent of all nerve cells in our body are located in the CNS. The **peripheral nervous system (PNS)** is the network of nerves that connects the brain and spinal cord to other parts of the body. The functions of the peripheral nervous system are to bring information to and from the brain and spinal cord and to carry out the commands of the CNS to execute various muscular and glandular activities.

The peripheral nervous system has two major divisions: the somatic nervous system and the autonomic nervous system. The **somatic nervous system** consists of sensory nerves, whose function is to convey information from the skin and muscles to the CNS about conditions such as pain and temperature, and motor nerves, whose function is to tell the muscles what to do. The function of the **autonomic nervous system** is to take messages to and from the body's internal organs, monitoring such processes as breathing, heart rate, and digestion.

The autonomic nervous system also is divided into two parts. One part, the **sympathetic nervous system**, arouses the body to mobilize it for action, while the other, the **parasympathetic nervous system**, calms the body. The sympathetic nervous system is involved in the "fight or flight" response, the body's reaction to a threat (an incident to which you can respond either by staying to fight or by running away). When you feel your heart pounding and your hands sweating under stress, those experiences reveal the sympathetic nervous system in action. In an emergency, the sympathetic nervous system triggers the body's release of stress hormones that allow you to focus attention on what needs to be done *now*. For example, in an emergency, people sometimes report feeling strangely calm and doing what has to be done, like calling 911. Such experiences reveal the benefits of stress hormones in times of acute emergency (Robinson & Leach, 2018).

The parasympathetic nervous system is responsible for the ways you calm down once you have escaped the danger. While the sympathetic nervous system is associated with "fight or flight," the parasympathetic nervous system might be thought of as the system that "rests and digests."

● **central nervous system (CNS)** The brain and spinal cord.

● **peripheral nervous system (PNS)** The network of nerves that connects the brain and spinal cord to other parts of the body.

● **somatic nervous system** The body system consisting of the sensory nerves, whose function is to convey information from the skin and muscles to the CNS about conditions such as pain and temperature, and the motor nerves, whose function is to tell muscles what to do.

● **autonomic nervous system** The body system that takes messages to and from the body's internal organs, monitoring such processes as breathing, heart rate, and digestion.

● **sympathetic nervous system** The part of the autonomic nervous system that arouses the body to mobilize it for action and thus is involved in the experience of stress.

● **parasympathetic nervous system** The part of the autonomic nervous system that calms the body.

### *test yourself*

1. Name and explain four characteristics that allow the nervous system to direct human behavior.
2. What is the difference between afferent and efferent nerves?
3. What are the two main parts of the autonomic nervous system, and what is the function of each?

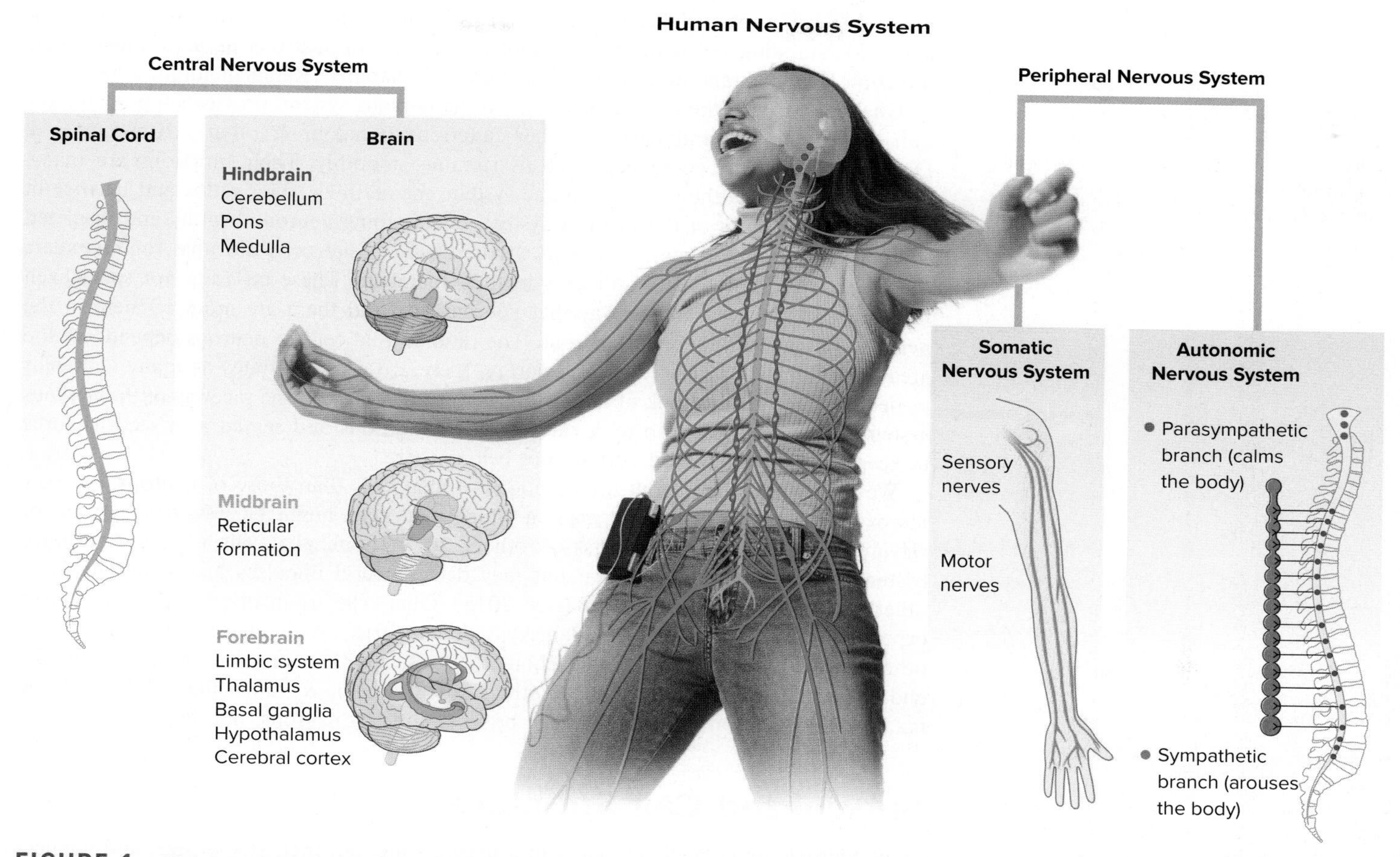


**FIGURE 1** **Major Divisions of the Human Nervous System** The nervous system has two main divisions. One is the *central nervous system* (*left*), which comprises the brain and the spinal cord. The nervous system's other main division is the *peripheral nervous system* (*right*), which itself has two parts—the *somatic nervous system*, which controls sensory and motor neurons, and the *autonomic nervous system*, which monitors processes such as breathing, heart rate, and digestion. These complex systems work together to help us successfully navigate the world. ©RubberBall Productions

## 2. NEURONS

Within each division of the nervous system, much is happening at the cellular level. Nerve cells, chemicals, and electrical impulses work together to transmit information at speeds of up to 330 miles per hour. As a result, information can travel from your brain to your hands (or vice versa) in a matter of milliseconds. Just how fast is 330 miles per hour? The NASCAR speed record is about 213 miles per hour.

There are two types of cells in the nervous system: neurons and glial cells. **Neurons** are the nerve cells that handle information processing; we will generally concentrate on neurons in this chapter. The human brain contains about 100 billion neurons. The average neuron is a complex structure with as many as 10,000 physical connections with other cells.

One particularly interesting type of neuron are **mirror neurons**. Mirror neurons are activated (in human and nonhuman primates) both when we perform an action and when we watch someone else perform that same activity. Why that is such a big deal? Remember, neurons are specialized: Motor neurons do not respond to sensory information, and sensory neurons do not respond to motor information. Yet, mirror neurons appear to respond to both kinds of information–doing and seeing. This responsiveness to two different kinds of input is one characteristic that makes mirror neurons so fascinating. The discovery of mirror neurons led to provocative predictions about the function of these

• **neurons** One of two types of cells in the nervous system; neurons are the type of nerve cell that handles the information-processing function.

• **mirror neurons** Nerve cells in the brain that are activated (in human and nonhuman primates) both when an action is performed and when the organism observes the action being performed by another.

neurons in imitation, social cognition (that is, thinking about oneself and others), empathy, and understanding behavior. Some scholars hail mirror neurons as a promising new direction in understanding the origins of human sociability (Ramachandran, 2000).

**glial cells or glia** The second of two types of cells in the nervous system; glial cells provide support, nutritional benefits, and other functions and keep neurons running smoothly.

**Glial cells or glia**, the other type of cell in the nervous system, provide support, bestow nutritional benefits, and perform other functions (Chalour & others, 2018; Jäkel & Dimou, 2017). Glial cells keep neurons running smoothly. Their functions are many, including serving as the brain's immune system, maintaining water ratios and balance in the chemical aspects of the nervous system, and keeping neurons healthy and insulated so they can communicate (Rankin & Artis, 2018). Glial cells are able to repopulate themselves and reproduce to fill gaps in their members. These cells are not specialized to process information in the way that neurons are, and there are more of them in the nervous system than there are neurons. The ratio of glial cells to neurons depends on the area of the brain considered. In the cortex, there are nearly 4 times as many glial cells as neurons. You might think of the glial cells as the pit crew in the raceway of the nervous system–if that pit crew also took care of road conditions and served as a security force to keep people off the road who do not belong there.

We know much less about the functions of glial cells than those of neurons, but new discoveries have shed light on ways in which glial cells might be involved in behavior (Hyung & others, 2018; Verkhratsky & others, 2018). Some glial cells are not just passive bystanders to neural transmission but may detect neural impulses and send signals to other glial cells (Fields, Woo, & Basser, 2015). Glial cells are involved important human experiences, including memory (Adamsky & others, 2018); Alzheimer disease (Mecocci & others, 2018; Lin & others, 2018; Zhou & others, 2018); pain (Song & others, 2018); and psychological disorders (Rash & others, 2018; Tanabe & Yamashita, 2018). Still, by far, most information processing in the brain is done by neurons, not glia.

## Specialized Cell Structure

Most neurons are created very early in a person's life, but their shape, size, and connections can change throughout life. The way neurons function reflects the major characteristic of the nervous system described at the beginning of the chapter: plasticity. That is, neurons can and do change.

**cell body** The part of the neuron that contains the nucleus, which directs the manufacture of substances that the neuron needs for growth and maintenance.

Neurons are specialized to handle different functions but all neurons have some common features. Every neuron has a cell body, dendrites, and an axon (Figure 2). The **cell body**

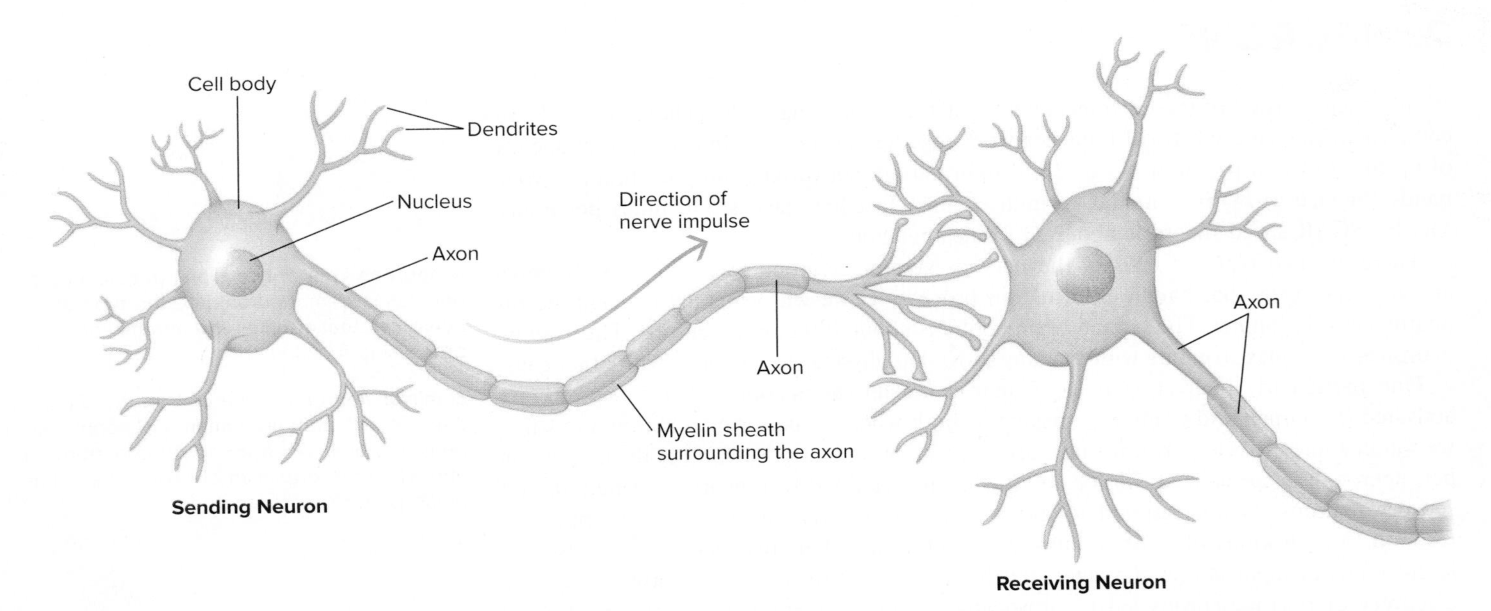


**FIGURE 2** **The Neuron** The drawing shows the parts of a neuron and the connection between one neuron and another. Note the cell body, the branching of dendrites, and the axon with a myelin sheath.

contains the *nucleus,* which directs the manufacture of substances that the neuron needs for growth and maintenance. **Dendrites**, treelike fibers projecting from a neuron, receive information and orient it toward the neuron's cell body. Most neurons have numerous dendrites, allowing each neuron to receive input from many others. The **axon** is the part of the neuron that carries information away from the cell body toward other cells. (Remember that *axon* and *away* both start with the letter *a*). Although extremely thin (1/10,000th of an inch–a human hair by comparison is 1/1000th of an inch), axons can be very long and possess many branches. In fact, some extend more than 3 feet–all the way from the top of the brain to the base of the spinal cord. Finally, covering all surfaces of the neurons, including the dendrites and axons, is a very thin cellular membrane.

- **dendrites** Treelike fibers projecting from a neuron, which receive information and orient it toward the neuron's cell body.
- **axon** The part of the neuron that carries information away from the cell body toward other cells.
- **myelin sheath** A layer of fat cells that encases and insulates most axons.

A **myelin sheath**, a layer of cells containing fat, encases and insulates most axons (Stassart & others, 2018). By insulating the axons, myelin sheaths speed up transmission of nerve impulses (Baraban, Koudelka, & Lyons, 2018). The myelin sheath developed as the nervous system evolved. As brain size increased, it became necessary for information to travel over longer distances in the nervous system. Axons without myelin sheaths are not great conductors of electricity. However, with the insulation of myelin sheaths, axons transmit electrical impulses and convey information rapidly. We can compare the myelin sheath's development to the evolution of interstate highways as cities grew: Highways keep fast-moving, long-distance traffic from being impeded by slow, local traffic.

Numerous disorders are associated with problems in either creation or maintenance of myelin (Shaharabani & others, 2018). For example multiple sclerosis (MS) is a degenerative disease of the nervous system in which scar tissue replaces the myelin sheath, disrupting neuronal communication. Symptoms of MS include blurry and double vision, tingling sensations throughout the body, and weakness.

*Actor Selma Blair recently shared her struggles with multiple sclerosis (MS) on social media.*

©Dfree/Shutterstock

## The Neural Impulse

To transmit information to other neurons, a neuron sends brief electrical impulses (let's call them "blips") through its axon. As you reach to turn a page, hundreds of such impulses stream down the axons in your arm to tell your muscles when to flex and how quickly. By changing the rate of the signals, or blips, the neuron can vary its message. Those impulses traveling down the axon are electrical. How does a neuron–a living cell–generate electricity? To answer this question, let's take a moment to examine the axon and the cellular membrane that surrounds it.

The axon is a tube encased in a membrane. There are fluids both inside and outside the axon. Floating in those fluids are electrically charged particles called *ions.* Some of these ions, notably sodium and potassium, carry positive charges. Negatively charged ions of chlorine and other elements also are present. The membrane surrounding the axon prevents negative and positive ions from randomly flowing in and out. That membrane has thousands of tiny gates in it. These gates are generally closed, but they can open. We call the membrane *semipermeable* because fluids and ions can sometimes flow into and out of it. The neuron creates electrical signals by moving positive and negative ions back and forth through its outer membrane.

Normally, when the neuron is resting–not transmitting information–the tiny gates in the membrane, called *ion channels,* are closed, and a slight negative charge is present inside the cell membrane. On the outside of the cell membrane, the charge is positive. Because of the difference in charge, the membrane of the resting neuron is said to be *polarized,* with most negatively charged ions on the inside and most positively charged ions on the outside. This polarization creates a voltage between the inside and outside of the axon wall (Figure 3). That voltage, called the neuron's **resting potential**, is between −60 and −75 millivolts. A millivolt (mV) is 1/1000th of a volt.

- **resting potential** The stable, negative charge of an inactive neuron.

How does the movement of ions occur across the membrane? When an impulse causes a neuron to fire, those ion channels open and close to let the ions pass into and out of the cell. For ions, it is true that opposites attract. The negatively charged ions on the

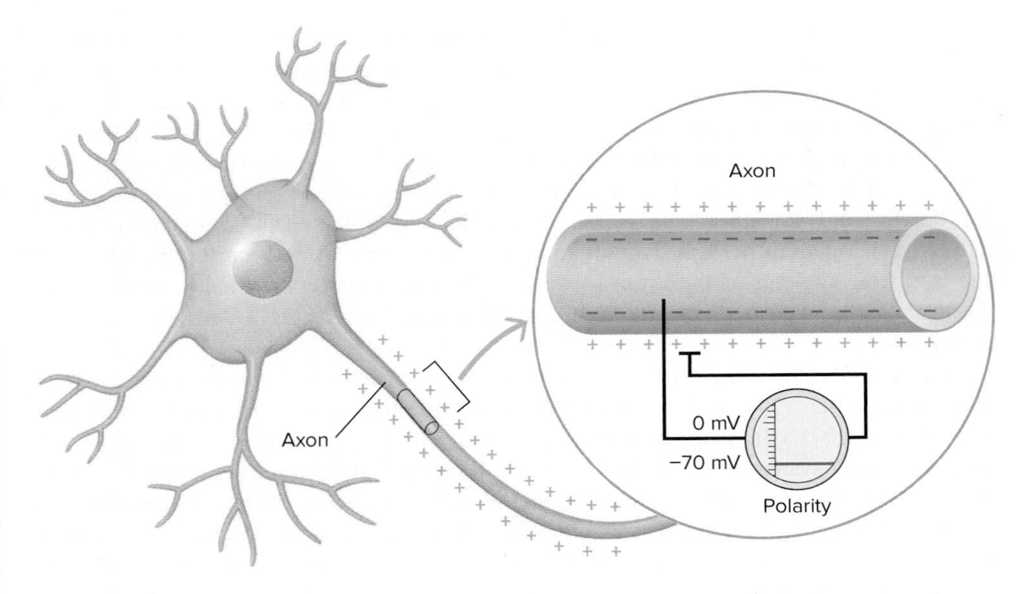


**FIGURE 3** **The Resting Potential** An oscilloscope measures the difference in electrical potential between two electrodes. When one electrode is placed inside an axon at rest and one is placed outside, the electrical potential inside the cell is −70 millivolts (mV) relative to the outside. This difference is due to the separation of positive (+) and negative (−) charges along the membrane.

inside of the membrane and the positively charged ions on the outside of the membrane rush to each other if given the chance. Impulses that travel down the neuron do so by opening and closing ion channels, allowing the ions to flow in and out.

A neuron becomes activated when an incoming impulse—a reaction to, say, a pinprick—raises the neuron's voltage, and the sodium gates at the base of the axon open briefly. This action allows positively charged sodium ions to flow into the neuron, creating a more positively charged neuron and *depolarizing* the membrane by decreasing the charge difference between the fluids inside and outside of the neuron. Then potassium channels open, and positively charged potassium ions move out through the neuron's semipermeable membrane. This outflow returns the neuron to a negative charge. Some of the channels then pump the sodium out of the neuron so that the cell returns to its resting potential. The same process occurs as the next group of channels flips open briefly.

So it goes all the way down the axon, like a long row of cabinet doors opening and closing in sequence. It is hard to imagine, but this system of opening and closing tiny doors is responsible for the beautiful fluid movements of a ballet dancer and the flying fingers of a pianist playing a concerto.

● **action potential** The brief wave of positive electrical charge that sweeps down the axon.

The term **action potential** describes the brief wave of positive electrical charge that sweeps down the axon (Figure 4). An action potential lasts only about 1/1000th of a second, because the sodium channels can stay open for only a very brief time. They quickly close again and become reset for the next action potential. When a neuron sends an action potential, it is commonly said to be "firing."

Let's review the steps shown in Figures 3 and 4 so you can appreciate the electrical part of electrochemical transmission. Keep mind that these steps occur all along the axon, in a very short amount of time.

- First, at rest, the neuron has a mild negative charge, because negatively charged ions are on the inside of the membrane and positively charged ions are on the outside of the membrane. At this stage the neuron is polarized and said to have a resting potential.
- When the neuron fires, the tiny gates (or channels) open and positively charged sodium ions rush into the neuron. So many sodium ions rush in that for a brief moment the neuron has a *positive charge*. This activity sweeps down the axon as the channels open and then close. This is called the action potential.
- After firing, the sodium channels close and potassium channels open, moving positively charged potassium ions out of the neuron and returning it to its previous negative charge. Some of the channels then pump sodium out of the neuron, returning it to its negative polarized resting potential.

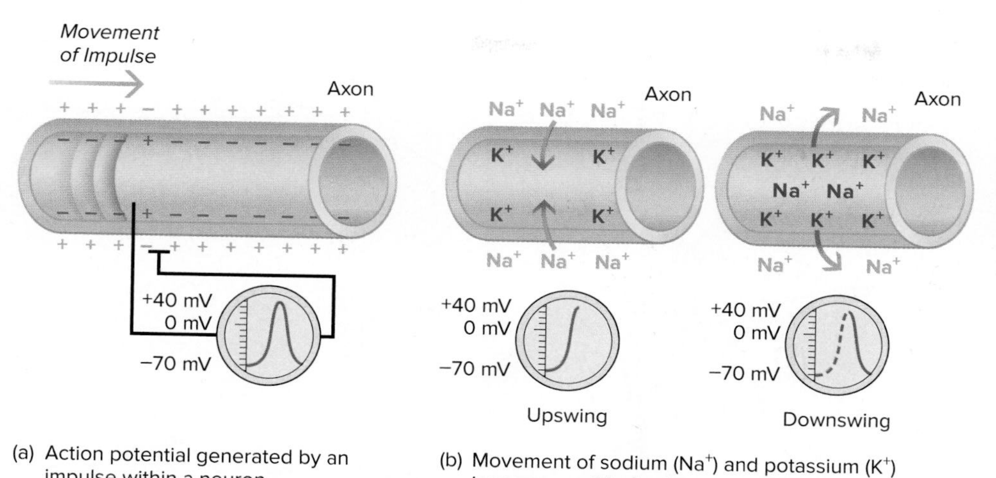


(a) Action potential generated by an impulse within a neuron

(b) Movement of sodium ($Na^+$) and potassium ($K^+$) ions responsible for the action potential

**FIGURE 4 The Action Potential** An action potential is a brief wave of positive electrical charge that sweeps down the axon as the sodium channels in the axon membrane open and close. (*a*) The action potential causes a change in electrical potential as it moves along the axon. (*b*) The movements of sodium ions ($Na^+$) and potassium ions ($K^+$) into and out of the axon cause the electrical changes.

The action potential abides by the **all-or-nothing principle**, meaning that once the electrical impulse reaches a certain level of intensity, called its *threshold,* it fires and moves all the way down the axon without losing any of its intensity. The impulse traveling down an axon is comparable to the burning fuse of a firecracker. Whether you use a match or a blowtorch to light the fuse, once the fuse has been lit, the spark travels quickly and with the same intensity down the fuse. So, the intensity of the impulse is communicated by the rate (not the intensity) of the blips coming down the axon.

● **all-or-nothing principle** The principle that once the electrical impulse reaches a certain level of intensity (its threshold), it fires and moves all the way down the axon without losing any intensity.

## Synapses and Neurotransmitters

The movement of an impulse down an axon may be compared to a crowd doing "the wave" in a stadium. With the wave, there is a problem, however–the aisles. How does the wave get across the aisle? A similar problem arises for neurons, because they do not touch one another directly, and electricity cannot cross the space between them. Yet neurons do communicate.

Here is where the chemical part of electro*chemical* transmission comes in. Neurons communicate with one another through chemicals that carry messages across the space. This connection between one neuron and another is one of the most intriguing areas of contemporary neuroscience. Figure 5 gives an overview of how this connection between neurons takes place.

### SYNAPTIC TRANSMISSION

**Synapses** are tiny spaces (the aisle in our stadium analogy) between neurons, and the space between neurons that the synapses create is referred to as the *synaptic gap.* Most synapses lie between the axon of one neuron and the dendrites or cell body of another neuron. Before an impulse can cross the synaptic gap, it must be converted from an electrical signal to a chemical signal.

● **synapses** Tiny spaces between neurons; the gaps between neurons are referred to as synaptic gaps.

Each axon branches out into numerous fibers that end in structures called *terminal buttons.* Stored in very tiny synaptic vesicles (*sacs*) within the terminal buttons are chemicals called **neurotransmitters**. As their name suggests, neurotransmitters transmit, or carry, information across the synaptic gap to the next neuron. When an impulse reaches the terminal button, it triggers the release of neurotransmitter molecules from the synaptic vesicles. The neurotransmitter molecules flood the synaptic gap. Their movements are random, but some of them bump into receptor sites in the next neuron.

● **neurotransmitters** Chemical substances that are stored in very tiny sacs within the terminal buttons and involved in transmitting information across a synaptic gap to the next neuron.

The neurotransmitters are like pieces of a puzzle, and the receptor sites on the next neuron are differently shaped spaces. If the shape of a receptor site corresponds to the shape of a neurotransmitter molecule, the neurotransmitter fits into the space opening

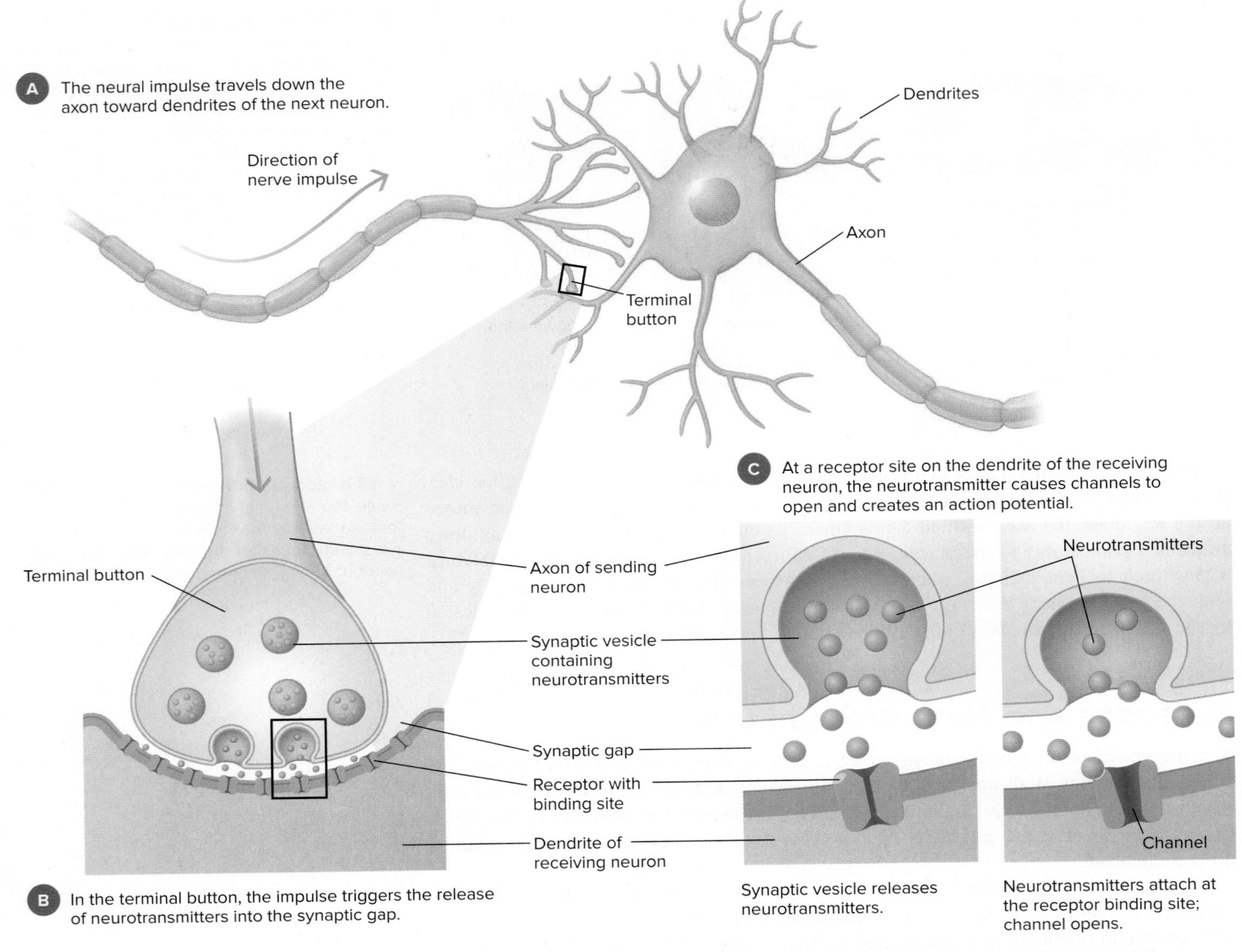
A The neural impulse travels down the axon toward dendrites of the next neuron.
Direction of nerve impulse
Dendrites
Axon
Terminal button
C At a receptor site on the dendrite of the receiving neuron, the neurotransmitter causes channels to open and creates an action potential.
Terminal button
Axon of sending neuron
Neurotransmitters
Synaptic vesicle containing neurotransmitters
Synaptic gap
Receptor with binding site
Dendrite of receiving neuron
Channel
Synaptic vesicle releases neurotransmitters.
Neurotransmitters attach at the receptor binding site; channel opens.
B In the terminal button, the impulse triggers the release of neurotransmitters into the synaptic gap.

**FIGURE 5** **How Synapses and Neurotransmitters Work** (A) The axon of the presynaptic (sending) neuron meets dendrites of the postsynaptic (receiving) neuron. (B) This is an enlargement of one synapse, showing the synaptic gap between the two neurons, the terminal buttons, and the synaptic vesicles containing a neurotransmitter. (C) This is an enlargement of the receptor site. Note how the neurotransmitter opens the channel on the receptor site, triggering the neuron to fire.

the receptor site, so that the neuron receives the signals coming from the previous neuron. You might think of the receptor site as a keyhole in a lock and the neurotransmitter as the key that fits that lock. After delivering its message, some of the neurotransmitter is used up in the production of energy, and some of it is reabsorbed by the axon that released it to await the next neural impulse. This reabsorption is called *reuptake*.

## NEUROCHEMICAL MESSENGERS

There are many different neurotransmitters. Each plays a specific role and functions in a specific pathway. Some neurotransmitters stimulate or excite neurons to fire; others can inhibit neurons from firing. Some neurotransmitters are both excitatory *and* inhibitory.

Most neurons secrete only one type of neurotransmitter, but often many different neurons are simultaneously secreting different neurotransmitters into the synaptic gaps of a single neuron. At any given time, a neuron is receiving a mixture of messages from the neurotransmitters. At the neuron's receptor sites, the chemical molecules bind to the membrane and either excite the neuron, bringing it closer to the threshold at which it will fire, or inhibit the neuron from firing. Triggering an action potential often requires a number of neurons sending excitatory messages simultaneously, or fewer neurons sending rapid-fire excitatory messages.

Scientists do not know exactly how many neurotransmitters exist, and more are discovered every year. In organisms ranging from snails to whales, neuroscientists have found the same neurotransmitter molecules that our own brains use. To get a better sense of what neurotransmitters do, let's consider eight that have major effects on behavior.

**Acetylcholine** *Acetylcholine (ACh)* usually stimulates the firing of neurons and is involved in muscle action, learning, and memory (Zucca, Zucca, & Wickens, 2018). ACh is found throughout the central and peripheral nervous systems. The venom from the bite of the black widow spider causes ACh to gush out of the synapses between the spinal cord and skeletal muscles, producing violent muscle spasms. The role of ACh in muscle function also comes to light in the working of Botox, a brand-name product made from botulin. A bacterial poison, botulin destroys ACh, so that when someone gets an injection of Botox, the person's facial muscles—which are activated by ACh—are prevented from moving, with the result that wrinkles do not form.

Individuals with Alzheimer disease, a degenerative brain disorder that gradually destroys memory, have an ACh deficiency (Polverino & others, 2018). Some drugs used to treat Alzheimer symptoms do so by compensating for the loss of the brain's supply of ACh.

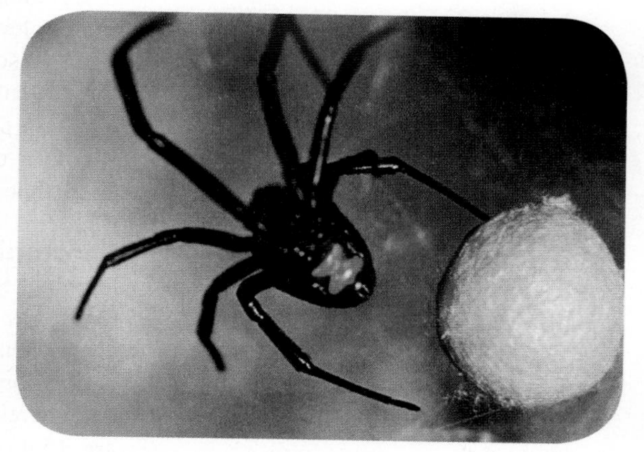

*The neurotransmitter-like venom of the black widow spider does its harm by disturbing neurotransmission.*
Source: Centers for Disease Control

**GABA** *GABA (gamma aminobutyric acid)* is found throughout the central nervous system. It is believed to be present in as many as one-third of the brain's synapses. GABA plays a key function in the brain by inhibiting many neurons from firing (Biscocho & others, 2018); indeed, GABA is the brain's brake pedal, helping to regulate neuron firing and control the precision of the signal being carried from one neuron to the next. Low levels of GABA are linked with anxiety (Lowery-Gionta & others, 2018; Savage & others, 2018). Valium and other antianxiety drugs increase the inhibiting effects of GABA.

**Glutamate** *Glutamate* is the most prevalent neurotransmitter. If GABA is the brain's brake pedal, glutamate is the accelerator. Glutamate has a key role in exciting many neurons to fire and is especially involved in learning and memory (Kim & Baik, 2019). Glutamate is also thought to be a factor in anxiety, depression, schizophrenia, Alzheimer disease, and Parkinson disease (Bagga & others, 2018). Too much glutamate can overstimulate the brain and trigger migraine headaches or even seizures (Hoffmann & Charles, 2018). Because of the widespread expression of glutamate in the brain, glutamate receptors have increasingly become the targets of drug treatment for a number of neurological and psychological disorders (Hoffmann & Charles, 2018).

**Norepinephrine** Stress stimulates the release of the neurotransmitter *norepinephrine* (Rankin & Artis, 2018). When we respond to stress, multiple things must happen at once, and so it is not surprising that norepinephrine (also called *noradrenaline*) has a number of effects on the body. If you think of all the things your body does when you are experiencing extreme fear, for instance, you might be able to guess some of the ways norepinephrine affects your body. It *inhibits* the firing of neurons in the central nervous system, but it simultaneously *excites* the heart muscle, intestines, and urogenital tract.

Norepinephrine also helps to control alertness. Too much norepinephrine triggers agitation or jumpiness. For example, amphetamines and cocaine cause hyperactive, manic states of behavior by rapidly increasing norepinephrine levels in the brain (Lichstein & others, 2018). However, too little norepinephrine is associated with depression (Sindhu & others, 2018).

**Dopamine** *Dopamine* helps to control voluntary movement and affects sleep, mood, attention, learning, and the ability to recognize opportunities for rewarding experiences in the environment (Coddington & Dudman, 2018). Stimulant drugs such as cocaine and amphetamines produce excitement, alertness, elevated mood, and decreased fatigue mainly by activating dopamine receptors (Gannon & others, 2018). Dopamine is related to the personality trait of extraversion (being outgoing and gregarious) (Dang & others, 2018), as we will see in the chapter "Personality". Problems in regulating dopamine are associated with a variety of psychological disorders, especially schizophrenia (Weinstein & others, 2018), a severe disorder we examine in the chapter "Psychological Disorders".

Low levels of dopamine are associated with Parkinson disease, a degenerative neurological disorder in which a person develops jerky physical movements and a tremor and has difficulty with speech and walking (Tinaz & others, 2018). This disease affects about a million people in the United States (Parkinson Foundation, 2018); actor Michael J. Fox has been diagnosed with this disease. Parkinson impairs coordinated movement to the point that just walking across a room can be a major ordeal.

**Serotonin** *Serotonin* is involved in the regulation of sleep, mood, attention, and learning. Serotonin's role in mood regulation has been an important focus of research (Moran & others, 2018). One prominent theory maintains that lower levels of serotonin are associated with depression (Schneider & others, 2018). Medications used to treat depression often act upon serotonin, slowing down its reuptake into terminal buttons and thereby increasing brain levels of serotonin (Little, Zhang, & Cook, 2006). There are 15 known types of serotonin receptors in the brain (Hoyer, Hannon, & Martin, 2002), and each type of antidepressant drug has its effects on different receptors. It is important to bear in mind that the hypothesized role of serotonin in depression is not without its critics (Healy, 2015; Katakam & others, 2018). Figure 6 shows the brain pathways for serotonin.

Recall from the beginning of the chapter that one of the most important characteristics of the brain and nervous system is integration. In the case of neurotransmitters, they may work in teams of two or more. For example, in regulating states of sleep and wakefulness, serotonin teams with acetylcholine and norepinephrine.

**Endorphins** *Endorphins* are natural opiates—substances that depress nervous system activity and eliminate pain—that mainly stimulate the firing of neurons. As opiates, endorphins shield the body from pain and elevate feelings of pleasure. A long-distance runner, a woman giving birth, and a person in shock after a car wreck all have elevated levels of endorphins (Valentino & Volkow, 2018).

**Oxytocin** *Oxytocin* is a hormone and neurotransmitter that plays an important role in the experience of love and social bonding. A powerful surge of oxytocin is released in mothers who have just given birth, and oxytocin is related to the onset of lactation (milk production) and breastfeeding (Mustoe, Taylor, & French, 2018). Oxytocin, however, is involved in more than a mother's ability to provide nourishment for her baby. It is also a factor in the experience of parents who find themselves "in love at first sight" with their newborn (Olazábal, 2018).

Oxytocin is released as part of sexual orgasm and is thought to play a role in the human experience of pleasure during orgasm and emotional bonds with romantic partners (Khajehei & Behroozpour, 2018). One study found that a higher level of oxytocin was present in new lovers and persisted at a higher level six months later compared with oxytocin levels in non-attached single young adults (Schneiderman & others, 2012). In this study, higher oxytocin levels were associated with positive mood, affectionate touch, and preoccupation with one's partner and the relationship.

Provocative research also has linked oxytocin to the way that some individuals respond to stress. According to Shelley Taylor (2011), women under stress do not experience the classic "fight or flight" response—rather, the influx of oxytocin they experience suggests that women may seek bonds with others when under stress. This response, which has

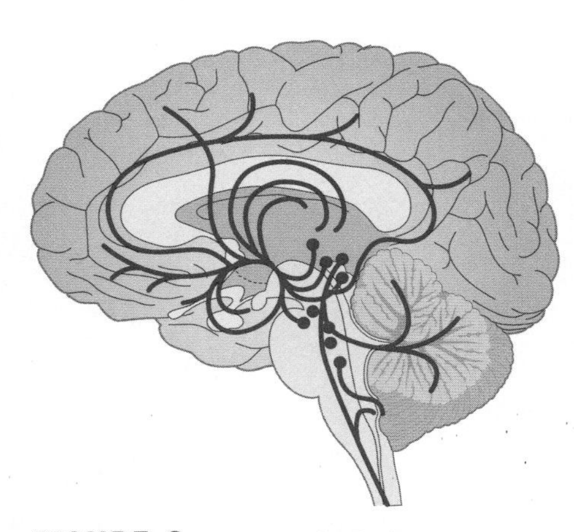

**FIGURE 6 Serotonin Pathways** Each of the neurotransmitters in the brain has specific pathways in which it functions. Shown here are the pathways for serotonin. Source: Healy (2015).

been labeled "tend and befriend," is believed to more accurately represent the stress response of women (Nickels, Kubicki, & Maestripieri, 2017; von Dawans & others, 2019).

### DRUGS AND NEUROTRANSMITTERS

Recall that neurotransmitters fit into the receptor sites like keys in keyholes. Other substances, such as drugs, can sometimes fit into those receptor sites as well, producing a variety of effects. Many animal venoms, such as that of the black widow spider mentioned above, act by disturbing neurotransmission. Similarly, most drugs that influence behavior do so mainly by interfering with the work of neurotransmitters.

Drugs can mimic or increase the effects of a neurotransmitter, or they can block those effects. For example, the drug morphine mimics the actions of endorphins by stimulating receptors in the brain and spinal cord associated with pleasure and pain, producing feelings of pleasure (Hauser & Knapp, 2018). Other drugs can block a neurotransmitter's action by preventing it from getting into the receptor site. Drugs used to treat schizophrenia, for example, interfere with the activity of dopamine.

## Neural Networks

● **neural networks** Networks of nerve cells that integrate sensory input and motor output.

So far, we have focused mainly on how a single neuron functions and on how a nerve impulse travels from one neuron to another. Now let's look at how large numbers of neurons work together to integrate incoming information and coordinate outgoing information.

Most information processing occurs when information moves through **neural networks**–interconnected pathways of nerve cells that integrate sensory input and motor output. As you read your class notes, the input from your eyes is transmitted to your brain and then passed through many neural networks, which translate the characters on the page into neural codes for letters, words, associations, and meanings. Some of the information is stored in the neural networks, and, if you read aloud, some is passed on as messages to your lips and tongue.

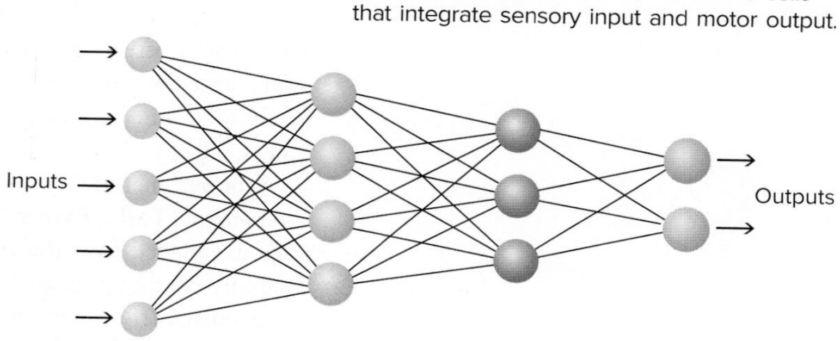

Inputs

Outputs

**FIGURE 7 An Example of a Neural Network** *Inputs* (information from the environment and from sensory receptors, such as the details of a person's face) become embedded in extensive connections between neurons in the brain. This embedding process leads to *outputs* such as remembering the person's face.

Neural networks can take years to develop and make up most of the brain. Working in networks allows neurons to amplify the brain's computing power. Figure 7 shows a simplified drawing of a neural network and gives you an idea of how the activity of one neuron is linked with that of many others.

Some neurons have short axons and communicate with other nearby neurons. Other neurons have long axons and communicate with circuits of neurons some distance away. These neural networks are not static. They can be altered through changes in the strength of synaptic connections. Connections are strengthened when they are used and weaken when they are not.

Any piece of information, such as a name, might be embedded in hundreds or even thousands of connections between neurons. In this way, human activities such as being attentive, memorizing, and thinking are distributed over a wide range of connected neurons. Differences in these neural networks are responsible for the brain differences observed in the London cab drivers discussed earlier in this chapter.

### *test yourself*

1. What are neurons, and what are their three parts?
2. What is meant by the neuron's action potential? How does the all-or-nothing principle apply to it?
3. What do neurotransmitters do? Name four specific neurotransmitters and describe the role each plays.

# 3. STRUCTURES OF THE BRAIN AND THEIR FUNCTIONS

The intricate networks of neurons in the living brain are invisible to the naked eye. In this section, we first review techniques used to form pictures of the structure and function of the brain. Then, we consider what these tools reveal about the brain's structures and functions, with special attention to the cerebral cortex.

## How Researchers Study the Brain and Nervous System

Early knowledge of the human brain came mostly from studies of individuals who had suffered brain damage from injury or disease. Modern discoveries typically rely, instead, on technology that enables researchers to "look inside" the brain while it is at work. Increasingly, researchers have begun to combine multiple techniques in one study to fully capture the brain and its activity (Chen & others, 2018). Let's examine some of these techniques.

### BRAIN LESIONING

*Brain lesioning* is an abnormal disruption in the tissue of the brain resulting from injury or disease. In a lab setting, neuroscientists produce lesions in laboratory animals to determine the effects on the animal's behavior (Cenci & Crossman, 2018). They create lesions by surgically removing brain tissue, destroying tissue with a laser, or eliminating tissue by injecting it with a drug. Examining the person or animal that has the lesion gives the researchers a sense of the function of the part of the brain that has been damaged.

Do you know anyone who has experienced a stroke or brain-damaging head injury? These events create lesions in the brain. Identifying the areas affected by a stroke or brain injury and then observing how a person is affected by the injury can allow researchers to identify the kinds of functions associated with specific brain areas (Arcaro & others, 2018).

A newer method based on the same logic as brain lesioning is *transcranial magnetic stimulation* (TMS; Barker, Jalinous, & Freeston, 1985). In the TMS procedure, magnetic coils are placed over the person's head and directed at a particular brain area. TMS uses a rapidly changing magnetic field to induce brief electrical current pulses in the brain, and these pulses trigger action potentials in neurons (Gordon & others, 2018). Immediately following this burst of action potentials, activity in the targeted brain area is inhibited, causing a *virtual lesion*. Completely painless, this technique allows scientists to identify the functions of brain regions. TMS is often combined with brain-imaging techniques to establish causal links between brain activity and behavior, to examine neuronal functioning following brain-injuring events, and to treat some eurological and psychological disorders (Hammoud & Milad, 2018).

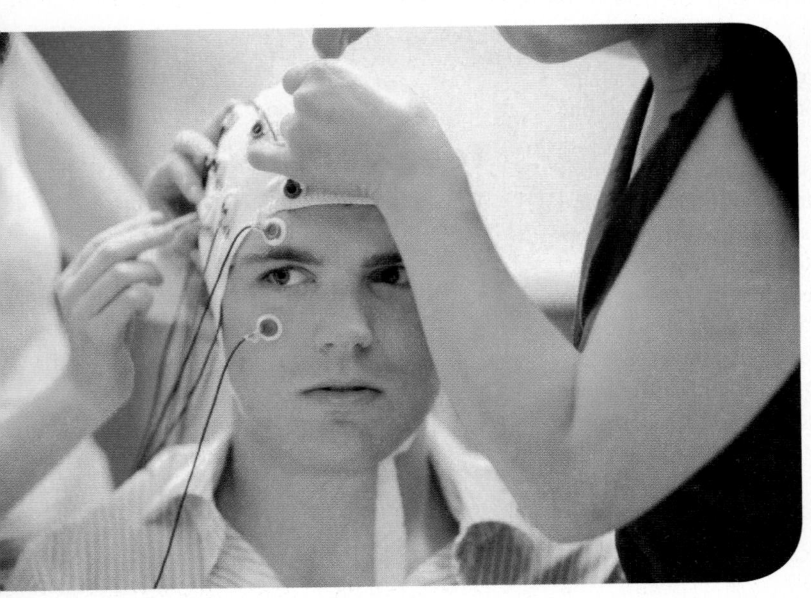

**FIGURE 8** **An EEG Recording** The electroencephalograph (EEG) is widely used in sleep research. The device has led to some major breakthroughs in understanding sleep by showing how the brain's electrical activity changes during sleep. ©annedde/E+/Getty Images

### ELECTRICAL RECORDING

An *electroencephalograph (EEG)* records the brain's electrical activity. Electrodes placed on the scalp detect brain-wave activity, which is recorded on a chart known as an *electroencephalogram* (Figure 8). EEG can assess brain damage, seizure disorder, and other problems.

In research, EEG has been used to examine the brain and happiness. Paul Ekman, Richard Davidson, and Wallace Friesen (1990) measured EEG activity during emotional experiences evoked by watching film clips. Participants watched amusing clips (a puppy playing with flowers) as well as clips likely to provoke fear or disgust (a leg amputation) How did the brain respond to such stimuli? EEG showed that while watching the amusing clips, people tended to exhibit more left than right activity in the very front of the brain (the prefrontal area). In contrast, when the participants viewed the unpleasant or fear-provoking films, the right prefrontal area was generally more active than the left. The left hemisphere was more active for pleasant stimuli and the right hemisphere was more active for the unpleasant stimuli.

Do these differences generalize to overall differences in feelings of happiness? They might. Heather Urry and her colleagues (2004) found that people who have relatively more left than right prefrontal activity, or *prefrontal asymmetry,* tend to rate themselves higher on measures of well-being. Keep in mind that behavior can change the brain, so it is possible that being happy and engaged in life leads to this asymmetry rather than being caused by it (Reznik & Allen, 2018).

Another technique that measures electrical activity is called *single unit recording.* In single-unit recording, a thin probe is inserted in or near an individual neuron. The probe transmits that neuron's electrical activity to an amplifier so that researchers can "see" the activity (Sakai, 2018).

*Important experiences, such as learning to play a musical instrument can affect brain structure and function.*

©Imgorthand/iStock/Getty Images

## BRAIN IMAGING

Four techniques that allow scientists to get a picture of the brain are CAT, PET, MRI, and fMRI. Let's take a brief look at each of these.

First, *computerized axial tomography* (*CAT scan* or *CT scan*) produces a three-dimensional image obtained from X rays of the head that are assembled into a composite image by a computer. The CT scan provides valuable information about the location and extent of damage involving stroke, language disorder, or loss of memory (Sau & Saha, 2018). CT scans provide information about structure but not activity.

*Positron-emission tomography (PET scan)* is based on metabolic changes in the brain related to activity. PET provides information about brain activity, tracking the amount of glucose in areas of the brain and sends this information to a computer for analysis. Neurons use glucose for energy, so glucose levels vary with the levels of activity throughout the brain. Tracing the amounts of glucose generates a picture of brain activity. PET scans can be used to examine the amount of neurotransmitters waiting to be released into the synaptic gap in brain neurons (Jabbi & others, 2013). PET scans are also used to diagnose diseases such as Alzheimer's (Fantoni & others, 2018).

Another technique psychologists use to image the brain is *magnetic resonance imaging (MRI).* MRI involves creating a strong magnetic field around a person's body and using radio waves to construct images. The magnetic field used to create an MRI image is over 50,000 times more powerful than the earth's magnetic field (Parry & Matthews, 2002). MRI takes advantage of the fact that the human brain contains a great deal of water and neurons have more water in them than do other brain tissues. Each water molecule contains hydrogen atoms (remember, water is $H_2O$). When these hydrogen atoms encounter a very strong magnetic field, they act like tiny magnets and align themselves with it. The contrast between neurons and other brain tissues provides the nuanced brain images that MRI produces.

MRI generates very clear pictures of the brain's interior, does not require injecting the brain with a substance, and (unlike X rays) does not pose a problem of radiation overexposure. In fact, there are no known side effects of MRI. Getting an MRI scan involves lying still in a large metal tunnel, similar to a barrel. MRI scans provide an excellent picture of the architecture of the brain and allow researchers to see if and how experience affects brain structure.

Katrin Amunts and her colleagues (1997; Gärtner & others, 2013) used MRI to document the link between the number of years a person has practiced musical skills (playing the piano or violin, for example) and the size of the brain region that is responsible for controlling hand movements. The brain structures of individuals who have practiced a musical instrument differ from those who have not. Note that these brain changes reflect, as well, the development of neural networks (Puschmann, Baillet, & Zatorre, 2018).

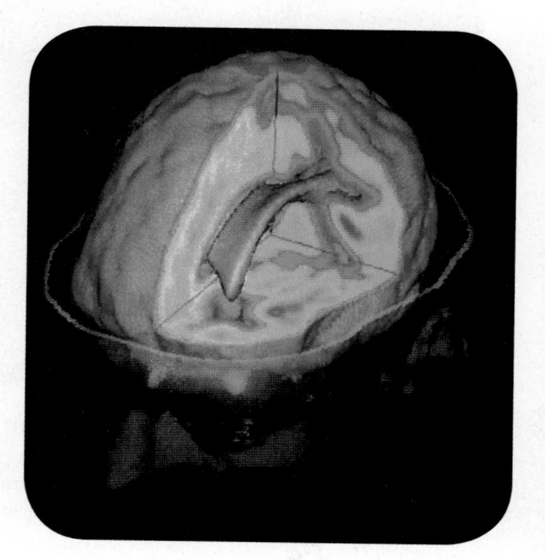

**FIGURE 9 Functional Magnetic Resonance Imaging (fMRI)** Through fMRI, scientists can literally see what areas of the brain are active during a task by monitoring oxygenated blood levels. ©Peter Arnold, Inc./Stegerphoto/Getty Images

Although MRI scans can reveal considerable information about brain *structure,* they do not show brain *function.* Other techniques can serve as a window to the brain in action. One such method, *functional magnetic resonance imaging,* or *fMRI,* allows scientists literally to see what is happening in the brain while it is working (Abidi & others, 2018) (Figure 9).

Like the PET scan, fMRI rests on the idea that mental activity is associated with changes in the brain. PET relies on the use of glucose as fuel for thinking. In contrast, fMRI exploits changes in blood oxygen that occur in association with brain activity. When part of the brain is working, oxygenated blood rushes into the area. This oxygen, however, is more than is needed. In a sense, fMRI is based on the fact that thinking is like running sprints. When you run the 100-yard dash, blood rushes to the muscles in your legs, carrying oxygen. Right after you stop, you might feel a tightness in your legs, because the oxygen has not all been used. Similarly, if an area of the brain is hard at work—for example, solving a math problem—the increased activity leads to a surplus of oxygenated blood. This "extra" oxygen allows the brain activity to be imaged.

Getting an fMRI involves reclining in the same large metal barrel as does an MRI, but for fMRI the person is actively doing things during the procedure. The individual may be listening to audio signals sent by the researcher through headphones or watching visual images on a screen mounted overhead. During these procedures, pictures of the brain are taken, both while the brain is at rest and while it is engaging in an activity such as listening to music, looking at a picture, or making a decision. By comparing the at-rest picture to the activity picture, fMRI tells us what specific brain activity is associated with the mental experience being studied.

Note that saying that fMRI tells us about the brain activity *associated* with a mental experience is a *correlational* statement. As we saw in the chapter "Psychology's Scientific Method," correlations show *associations* between variables, not to the causal link between them. For example, although identifying a picture as a cat may relate to activation in a particular brain area, we do not know whether recognizing the cat *caused* the brain activity (Dien, 2009). Still, fMRI is used in experiments in very interesting ways, bolstering what people say about themselves with evidence directly from the brain.

Functional MRI is used not only to establish links between brain areas and behaviors but also to understand the links among different brain areas. *Functional connectivity* refers to the correlation between different brain areas or the degree to which their operation is dependent on each other. Studies of functional connectivity are important because they can tell us about how the brain operates, as a whole, in accomplishing the many complex tasks that it performs (Sahib & others, 2018).

Functional MRI is especially useful for examining cognitive activity in organisms that cannot tell us what they are thinking or feeling. For example, fMRI can be used with infants (Ellis & Turk-Browne, 2018) who are too young to tell us about their experiences. Similarly, fMRI can be used to reveal what is going on in the heads of nonhuman animals. The Intersection reviews interesting recent research using fMRI with dogs.

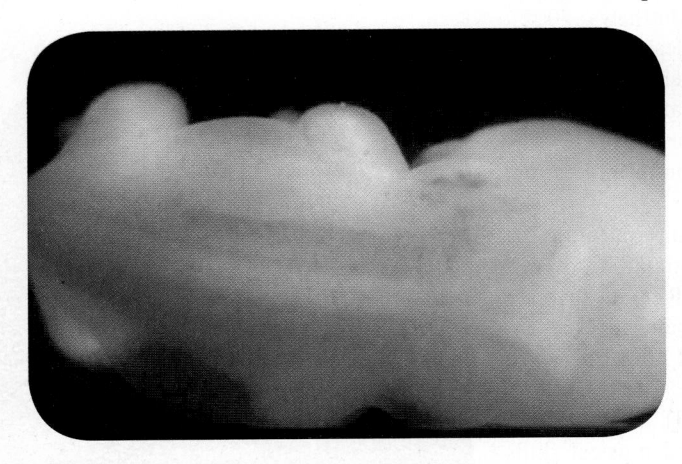

**FIGURE 10 Embryological Development of the Nervous System** The photograph shows the primitive tubular appearance of the nervous system in the human embryo six weeks after conception. ©Petit Format/Science Source

## How the Brain Is Organized

As a human embryo develops prenatally the nervous system begins forming as a long, hollow tube on the embryo's back called the *neural tube*. At three weeks or so after conception, cells making up the neural tube develop into a mass of neurons, most of which then develop into three major regions of the brain: the hindbrain, the very base of next to the top part of the spinal cord; the midbrain, which rises above the hindbrain; and the forebrain, which is the uppermost region of the brain (Figure 10).

### HINDBRAIN

● **hindbrain** Located at the skull's rear, the lowest portion of the brain, consisting of the medulla, cerebellum, and pons.

The **hindbrain**, located at the skull's rear, is the lowest portion of the brain. The three main parts of the hindbrain are the medulla oblongata, cerebellum, and pons. Figure 11 locates these brain structures.

The *medulla* begins where the spinal cord enters the skull. The medulla controls many vital functions, such as breathing and heart rate, and regulates reflexes. The *pons* is

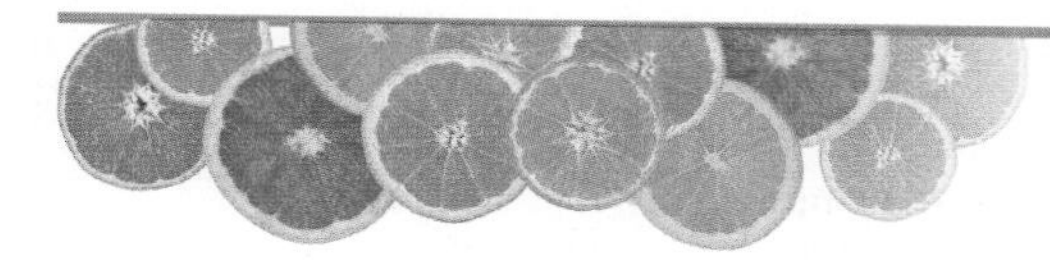

## INTERSECTION

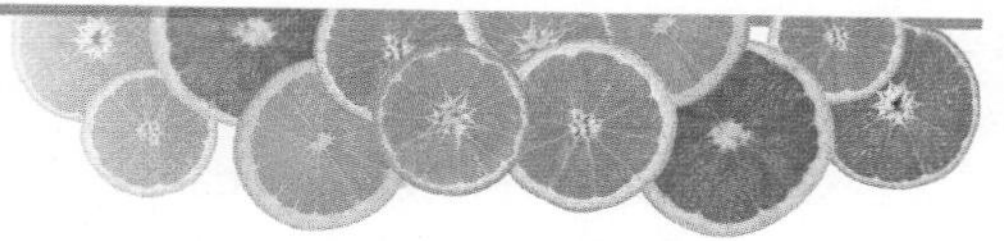

### Neuroscience and Language: What Is a Word to a Dog?

Dogs learn to respond to many different verbal labels. Ask a family dog if he or she wants a treat, a ride, or a walk and you will likely see a great deal of enthusiasm. But does a dog "know" that the words "treat," "ride," or "walk" refer to different things? If an owner said "dance" with the same intonation would the dog be just as eager? A recent study used fMRI to find out (Prichard & others, 2018).

The participants were 12 pet dogs (with names like Ninja, Eddie, and Truffles). The dogs were a variety of sizes and breeds. All of the dogs had been trained previously to lie still in an fMRI machine. This is important because imaging requires the subject to be very still while being tested. Also, the scanner makes loud noises, so it was important that the dogs were accustomed to those noises. In the weeks prior to the study the dogs were trained to associate two words with two different toys. Owners played fetch and tug-of-war with the objects and their dogs, always saying the object names during the training. For example, Ninja's two objects were a block (called "block") and a toy monkey (called "monkey"). Ninja was trained to fetch each of the objects when its name was called by her owner. Before the scanning session, the dogs had to show that they were able to fetch each object in response to its name.

The dogs laid on their bellies in the scanner, with heads toward the opening. While their brains were scanned, the dogs experienced different types of trials. On some trials, owners (who stood just outside the barrel of the magnet) said one of the two object names five times and then showed the dog that object. On other trials, the owner said a completely fake word that was new to the dog (such as, "doba," or "bobbu") and showed the dog a new object. Finally, to keep the dogs engaged, some trials just involved the dogs getting treats for being such good dogs and remaining still for so long. Brain activity was compared to see how the dogs' brains responded to the known versus unknown words.

*What other questions might be addressed using fMRI with nonhuman animals?*

The results? The dogs' brains showed stronger activation to the unknown, fake words that preceded the new objects. This result differs from what would be expected in humans, who are relatively more responsive to real (versus fake) words (Prichard & others, 2018). The researchers surmised that this difference was likely due to dogs' increased processing in the context of learning the association between the new word and the new object that followed it. Dogs, it seems, are especially motivated to learn new things. Interestingly, in half the dogs, the area activated by the new words was analogous to the area in the human brain that processes word meanings. Overall, the results show that dogs *do* have neural representations of words.

This study shows that a dog's capacity to learn words goes beyond simply being rewarded for their responses. Comedian Groucho Marx once quipped, "Outside of a dog, a book is a man's best friend. Inside of a dog, it's too dark to read." This study sheds some light on what goes on inside of a dog.

©Image Source

a bridge in the hindbrain that connects the cerebellum and the brain stem. It contains several clusters of fibers involved in sleep and arousal.

Collectively, the medulla, pons, and much of the hindbrain (as well as the midbrain, discussed below) are called the **brain stem**. Embedded deep within the brain, the brain stem connects with the spinal cord at its lower end and then extends upward to encase the reticular formation in the midbrain. The most ancient part of the brain, the brain stem evolved more than 500 million years ago when organisms needed to breathe out of water (Hagadorn & Seilacher, 2009). Clumps of cells in the brain stem determine alertness and regulate basic survival functions such as breathing, heartbeat, and blood pressure. Interestingly, just as musical training can influence other areas of the brain, it relates to differences in the brain stem as well (Tichko & Skoe, 2018).

● **brain stem** The stemlike brain area that includes much of the hindbrain (excluding the cerebellum) and the midbrain; it connects with the spinal cord at its lower end and then extends upward to encase the reticular formation in the midbrain.

The *cerebellum* consists of two rounded structures that extend from the rear of the hindbrain. It plays important roles in motor coordination (Stoodley & Schmahmann, 2018).

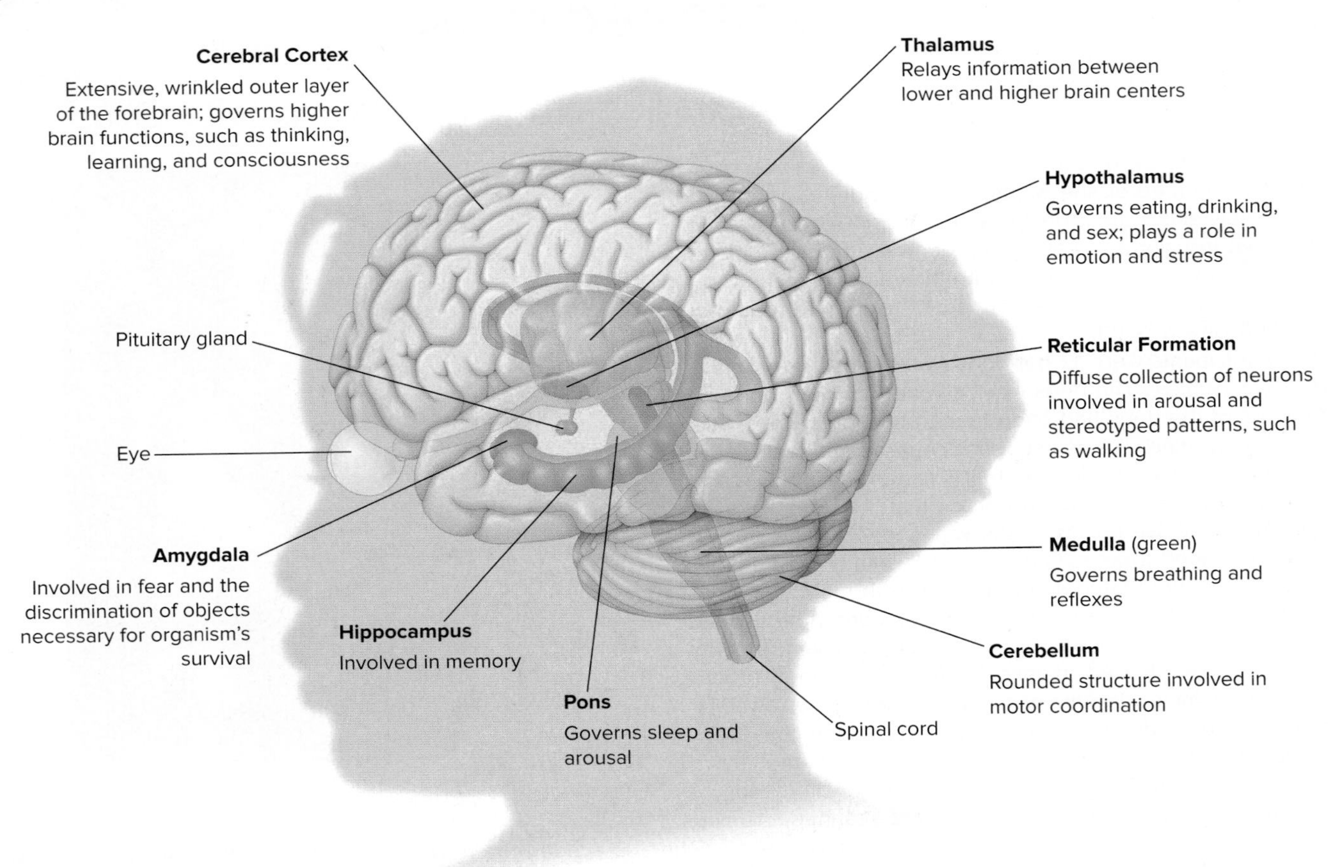
Cerebral Cortex
Extensive, wrinkled outer layer of the forebrain; governs higher brain functions, such as thinking, learning, and consciousness
Thalamus
Relays information between lower and higher brain centers
Hypothalamus
Governs eating, drinking, and sex; plays a role in emotion and stress
Pituitary gland
Reticular Formation
Diffuse collection of neurons involved in arousal and stereotyped patterns, such as walking
Eye
Amygdala
Involved in fear and the discrimination of objects necessary for organism's survival
Medulla (green)
Governs breathing and reflexes
Hippocampus
Involved in memory
Cerebellum
Rounded structure involved in motor coordination
Pons
Governs sleep and arousal
Spinal cord

**FIGURE 11** **Structure and Regions in the Human Brain** To get a feel for where these structures are in your own brain, use the eye (*pictured on the left in the figure*) as a landmark. Note that structures such as the thalamus, hypothalamus, amygdala, pituitary gland, pons, and reticular formation reside deep within the brain.

The cerebellum coordinates leg and arm movements; for example, when we walk, play golf, or practice the piano, the cerebellum is hard at work. Damage to the cerebellum can lead to awkward and jerky movements. Extensive damage to the cerebellum makes it impossible to stand up.

## MIDBRAIN

- **midbrain** Located between the hindbrain and forebrain, an area in which many nerve-fiber systems ascend and descend to connect the higher and lower portions of the brain; in particular, the midbrain relays information between the brain and the eyes and ears.

The **midbrain**, located between the hindbrain and forebrain, is an area in which many nerve-fiber systems ascend and descend to connect the higher and lower portions of the brain (Saddoris & others, 2018). In particular, the midbrain relays information between the brain and the eyes and ears. Two important structures in the midbrain are the substantia nigra and the reticular formation.

The *substantia nigra* contains a large number of dopamine-producing neurons. This part of the midbrain feeds dopamine into the *striatum,* the central input station for the basal ganglia, to which we will turn our attention in a moment. The midbrain, which is rich in dopamine receptors, is especially involved in reward experiences, pleasure, and also addiction (Saddoris & others, 2018). Parkinson disease damages a section near the bottom of the midbrain called the *substantia nigra* (Grünblatt & others, 2018), causing deterioration in body movement, rigidity, and tremors.

- **reticular formation** A system in the midbrain comprising a diffuse collection of neurons involved in stereotyped patterns of behavior such as walking, sleeping, and turning to attend to a sudden noise.

Another part of the midbrain is the **reticular formation**—a diffuse collection of neurons involved in stereotyped patterns of behavior such as walking, sleeping, and turning to attend to a sudden noise (Satpute & others, 2018) (see Figure 11).

## psychological *inquiry*

### *The Brain in Different Species*

The illustration compares the brain of a rat, a cat, a chimpanzee, and a human. In examining the figure, keep in mind that each species has adapted to deal with specific environmental challenges.

1. In what ways is each brain well suited to the challenges faced by its particular species?
2. What structures are similar across all the species? Why do you think certain brain structures are common for these various species? What challenges do all of these species face that would account for the common features of their brains?
3. Note how much larger the cerebral cortex becomes as we go from the brain of a rat to the brain of a human. Why don't rats have a large cerebral cortex?
4. We often think of the human brain as an amazing accomplishment of nature. How might life be different for a rat or a cat with a human brain?

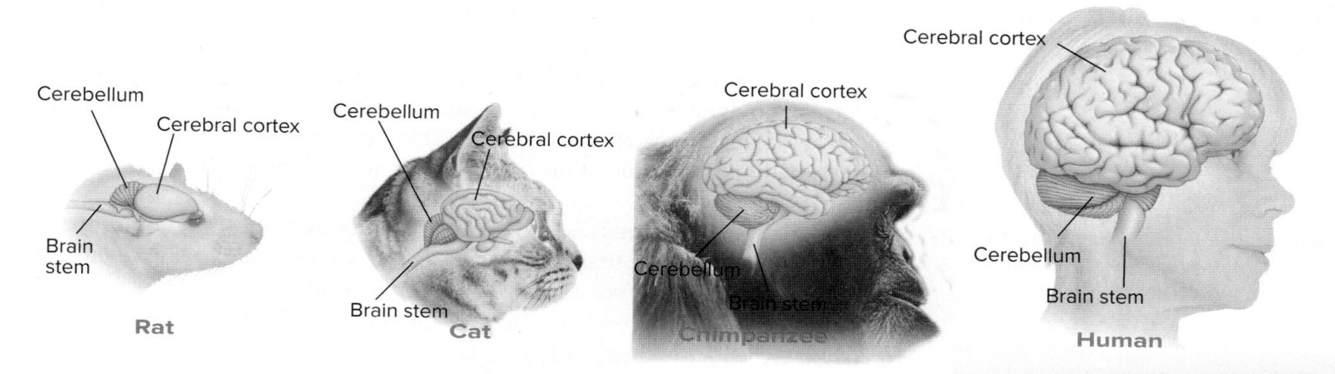




## FOREBRAIN

You try to understand what all of these terms and parts of the brain mean. You talk with friends and plan a party for this weekend. You remember that it has been six months since you went to the dentist. All of these experiences and millions more would not be possible without the **forebrain**—the brain's largest division and its most forward part.

Before we explore the structures and function of the forebrain, let's stop for a moment and examine how the brain evolved. The brains of the earliest vertebrates were smaller and simpler than those of later animals. Genetic changes during the evolutionary process were responsible for the development of more complex brains with additional parts and interconnections (Heide, Huttner, & Mora-Bermúdez, 2018).

The Psychological Inquiry above compares the brains of a rat, a cat, a chimpanzee, and a human. In both the chimpanzee's brain and (especially) the human's brain, the hindbrain and midbrain structures are covered by a forebrain structure called the *cerebral cortex.* The human hindbrain and midbrain are similar to those of other animals, so it is the relative size of the forebrain that mainly differentiates the human brain from the brains of animals such as rats, cats, and chimps. The human forebrain's most important structures are the limbic system, thalamus, basal ganglia, hypothalamus, and cerebral cortex.

● **forebrain** The brain's largest division and its most forward part.

**Limbic System** The **limbic system**, a loosely connected network of structures under the cerebral cortex, is important in both memory and emotion. Its two principal structures are the amygdala and the hippocampus (see Figure 11).

● **limbic system** A loosely connected network of structures under the cerebral cortex, important in both memory and emotion. Its two principal structures are the amygdala and the hippocampus.

**amygdala** An almond-shaped structure within the base of the temporal lobe that is involved in the discrimination of objects that are necessary for the organism's survival, such as appropriate food, mates, and social rivals. There is one amygdala in each hemisphere of the brain.

The **amygdala** is an almond-shaped structure located inside the brain toward the base. In fact, there is an amygdala (the plural is *amygdalae*) on each side of the brain. The amygdala is involved in the detection of objects that are necessary for the organism's survival, such as food and mates. Neurons in the amygdala often fire selectively at the sight of such stimuli, and lesions in the amygdala can cause animals to engage in incorrect behavior such as attempting to eat, fight, or even mate with an object like a chair.

In both humans and animals, the amygdala is active in response to unpredictable stimuli (Herry & others, 2007; Roquet & others, 2018). In humans, damage to the amygdala can result in an inability to recognize facial expressions of distress (Adolphs, 2009). The amygdala is involved in emotional awareness and expression through its many connections with a variety of brain areas. One study showed that individuals who are particularly good at regulating their emotions had greater functional connectivity between the amygdalae and the area of the brain that is just behind the forehead (Rohr & others, 2015). This area, called the *prefrontal cortex,* is associated with planning, self-control, and decision making. Interestingly, the size of both the left and right amygdalae is linked to the size of a person's social network (Von Der Heide, Vyas, & Olson, 2014). Throughout this book you will encounter the amygdalae whenever we turn to discussions of intense emotions.

**hippocampus** The structure in the limbic system that has a special role in the storage of memories.

The **hippocampus** has a special role in memory (Jeffrey, 2018). Individuals who suffer extensive hippocampal damage cannot retain any new conscious memories after the damage. However, memories are not stored "in" the limbic system. Instead, the limbic system seems to determine what parts of the information passing through the cortex should be "printed" into durable, lasting neural traces in the cortex. The hippocampus helps us recall things by waking up the areas of the brain that were used when we originally encountered the information–reinstating a previous brain state for memory (Lohnas & others, 2018).

**thalamus** The forebrain structure that sits at the top of the brain stem in the brain's central core and serves as an important relay station.

### Thalamus

The **thalamus** is a forebrain structure that sits at the top of the brain stem in the central core of the brain (see Figure 11). It serves as a very important relay station, functioning much like a server in a computer network. The thalamus sorts information and sends it to the appropriate places in the forebrain for further integration and interpretation (Koenig & others, 2018). In fact, most neural input to the cerebral cortex goes through the thalamus. One area of the thalamus works to orient information from the sense receptors (hearing, seeing, and so on), another region seems to be involved in sleep and wakefulness, having ties with the reticular formation, and yet another receives information from the cerebellum and projects it to the motor area of the cerebral cortex.

**basal ganglia** Large neuron clusters located above the thalamus and under the cerebral cortex that work with the cerebellum and the cerebral cortex to control and coordinate voluntary movements.

### Basal Ganglia

Surrounding the thalamus are large clusters, or *ganglia,* of neurons called **basal ganglia**. The basal ganglia work with the cerebellum and the cerebral cortex to control and coordinate voluntary movements. Basal ganglia enable people to engage in habitual activities such as riding a bicycle and vacuuming a carpet. Individuals with damage to basal ganglia suffer from either unwanted movement, such as constant writhing or jerking of limbs, or too little movement, as in the slow and deliberate movements of people with Parkinson disease (Bostan & Strick, 2018).

**hypothalamus** A small forebrain structure, located just below the thalamus, that monitors three pleasurable activities—eating, drinking, and sex—as well as emotion, stress, and reward.

### Hypothalamus

The **hypothalamus**, a small forebrain structure just below the thalamus, monitors three rewarding activities–eating, drinking, and sex–as well as emotion, stress, and reward (see Figure 11 for the location of the hypothalamus). As we will see later, the hypothalamus also helps direct the endocrine system.

Perhaps the best way to describe the function of the hypothalamus is as a regulator of the body's internal state. It is sensitive to changes in the blood and neural input, and it responds by influencing the secretion of hormones and neural outputs. If the temperature of circulating blood near the hypothalamus is increased by just one or two degrees, cells in the hypothalamus start increasing their rate of firing, setting a chain of events in motion. Increased circulation through the skin and sweat glands occurs immediately to release this heat from the body. The cooled blood circulating to the hypothalamus slows down the activity of some of the neurons there, stopping the process when the temperature is just right–37.1 degrees Celsius (98.6 degrees Fahrenheit). These temperature-sensitive neurons function like a finely tuned thermostat.

The functions of the hypothalamus go far beyond serving as a thermostat, however (Alvarez-Bolado, Grinevich, & Puelles, 2015). The hypothalamus also is involved in emotional states and stress, playing an important role as an integrative location for handling stress. Much of this integration is accomplished through the hypothalamus's action on the pituitary gland—an important endocrine gland located just below it.

If certain areas of the hypothalamus are electrically stimulated, a feeling of pleasure results. In a classic experiment, James Olds and Peter Milner (1954) implanted an electrode in the hypothalamus of a rat's brain. When the rat ran to a corner of an enclosed area, a mild electric current was delivered to its hypothalamus. The researchers thought the electric current would cause the rat to avoid the corner. Much to their surprise, the rat kept returning to the corner. Olds and Milner believed they had discovered a pleasure center in the hypothalamus. Olds (1958) conducted further experiments and found that rats would press bars until they dropped over from exhaustion just to continue to receive a mild electric shock to their hypothalamus. One rat pressed a bar more than 2,000 times an hour for a period of 24 hours to receive the stimulation to its hypothalamus (Figure 12).

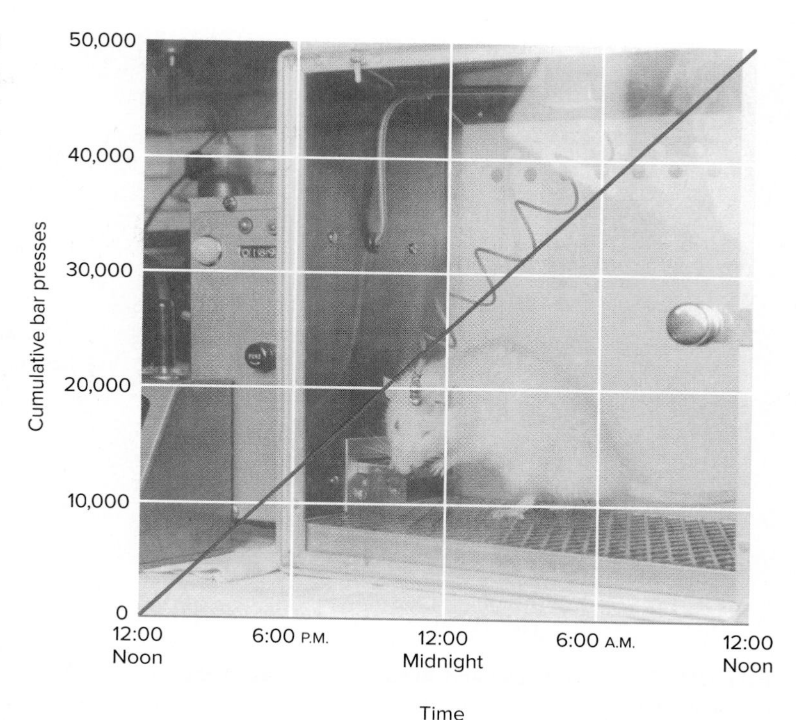


**FIGURE 12 Results of the Experiment on the Role of the Hypothalamus in Pleasure** The graphed results for one rat show that it pressed the bar more than 2,000 times an hour for a period of 24 hours to receive stimulation to its hypothalamus. A rat is shown here pressing a similar bar. Source: Olds (1958); ©Science Source

Today researchers agree that the hypothalamus is involved in pleasurable feelings, but they have found that other brain areas, such as the limbic system and two other structures—the nucleus accumbens and the ventral tegmental area, to be discussed in the chapter "States of Consciousness"—also play important roles in the link between the brain and pleasure (Castro, Cole, & Berridge, 2015). Certainly, the Olds studies have implications for drug addiction. We will explore the effects of drugs on the reward centers of the brain in the chapter "States of Consciousness".

- **cerebral cortex** Part of the forebrain, the outer layer of the brain, responsible for the most complex mental functions, such as thinking and planning.
- **neocortex** The outermost part of the cerebral cortex, making up 80 percent of the cortex in the human brain.

## The Cerebral Cortex

The **cerebral cortex** is part of the forebrain and is the most recently developed part of the brain in the evolutionary scheme. The word *cortex* means "bark" (as in tree bark) in Latin, and the cerebral cortex is in fact the outer layer of the brain. It is in the cerebral cortex that the most complex mental functions, such as thinking and planning, take place.

The **neocortex** (or "new bark") is the outermost part of the cerebral cortex. In humans, this area makes up 80 percent of the cortex (compared with just 30 to 40 percent in most other mammals). The size of the neocortex in mammals is strongly related to the size of the social group in which the organisms live. Some scientists theorize that this part of the human brain, which is responsible for high-level thinking, evolved so that human beings could make sense of one another (Dunbar, 2014).

The neural tissue that makes up the cerebral cortex covers the lower portions of the brain like a sheet that is laid over the brain's surface. In humans, the cerebral cortex has many grooves and bulges, and these considerably enlarge its surface area (compared to a brain with a smooth surface). The cerebral cortex is highly connected with other parts of the brain. Millions of axons connect the neurons of the cerebral cortex with those located elsewhere in the brain.

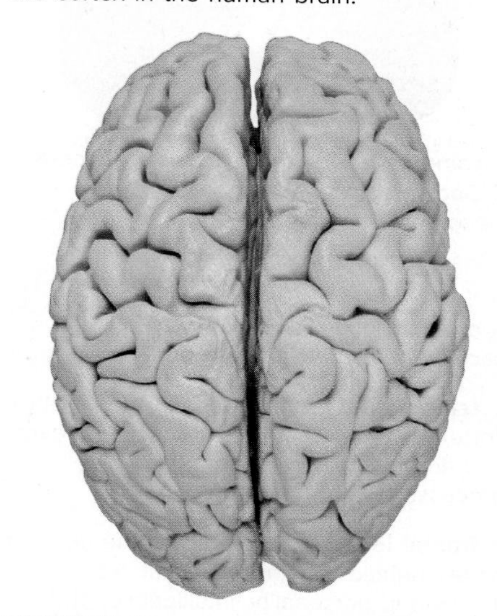

**FIGURE 13 The Hemispheres of the Human Brain** The two halves (hemispheres) of the human brain can be seen clearly in this photograph. ©McGraw-Hill Education/ Christine Eckel, photographer

### LOBES

The wrinkled surface of the cerebral cortex is divided into two halves called *hemispheres* (Figure 13). Each hemisphere is subdivided into four regions, or *lobes*—occipital, temporal, frontal, and parietal (Figure 14).

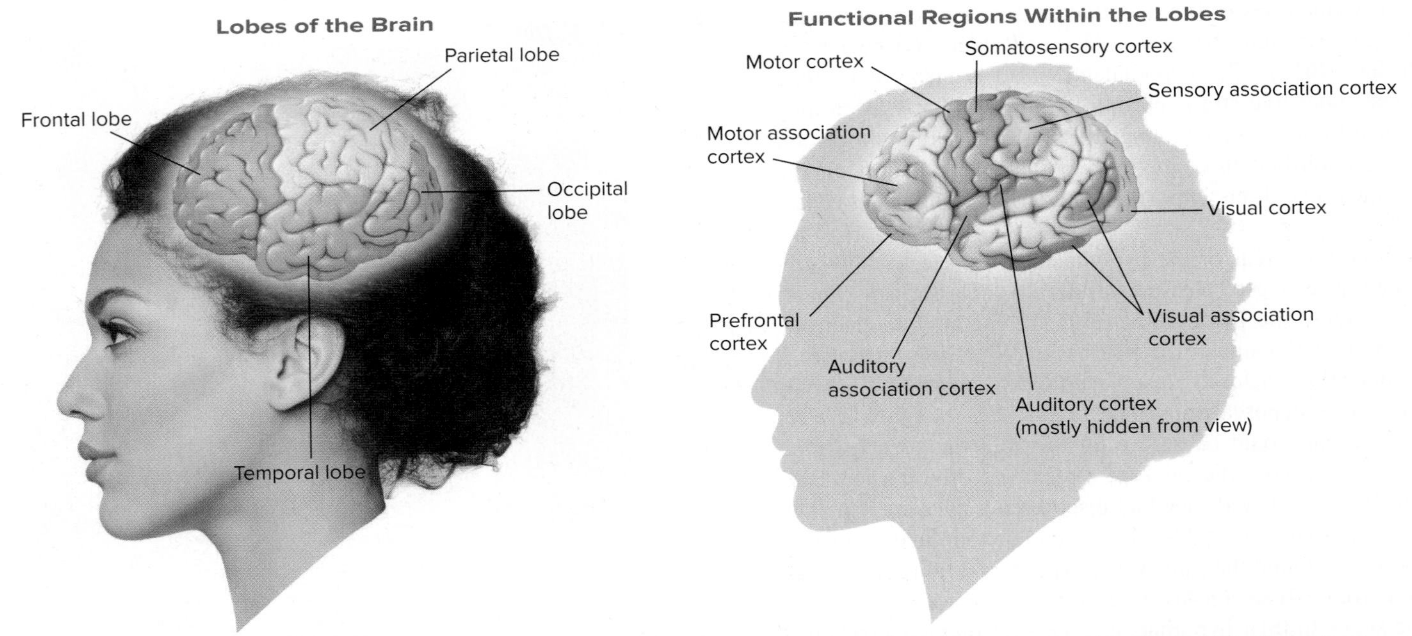


**FIGURE 14** **The Lobes and Association Areas of the Cerebral Cortex** The cerebral cortex (*left*) is roughly divided into four lobes: occipital, temporal, frontal, and parietal. The cerebral cortex (*right*) also consists of the motor cortex and somatosensory cortex. Further, the cerebral cortex includes association areas, such as the visual association cortex, auditory association cortex, and sensory association cortex. ©Paffy69/iStock/Getty Images

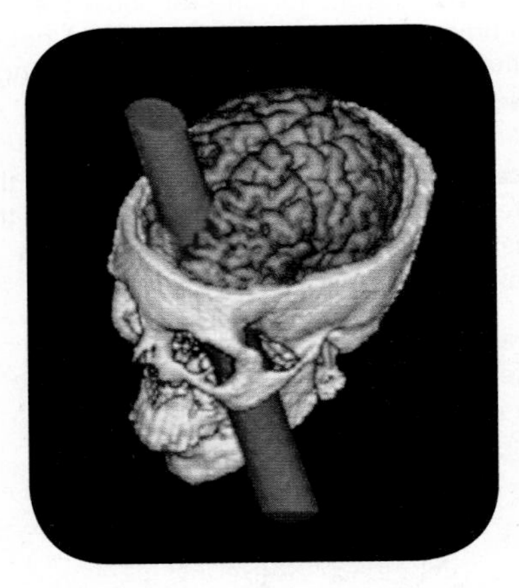

*A computerized reconstruction of Phineas T. Gage's accident, based on measurements taken of his skull.*
©Patrick Landmann/Science Source

The **occipital lobes**, located at the back of the head, respond to visual stimuli. Connections among various areas of the occipital lobes allow for the processing of aspects of visual stimuli such as color, shape, and motion (Arcaro & others, 2018). The eyes can only detect and transport information; they cannot interpret it. Even with perfectly functioning eyes, the occipital lobes are needed in order for the viewer to "see" the world. As described in the example at the beginning of this chapter, a stroke or a wound in the occipital lobe can lead to blindness or wipe out a portion of the person's visual field.

The **temporal lobes**, the part of the cerebral cortex just above the ears, are involved in hearing, language processing, and memory. The temporal lobes have a number of connections to the limbic system. For this reason, people with damage to the temporal lobes cannot retain long-term memory (Berron & others, 2018).

The **frontal lobes** are the portions of the cerebral cortex behind the forehead that are involved in personality, intelligence. and the control of voluntary muscles. A fascinating case study illustrates the effects of damage to the frontal lobes. Phineas T. Gage, a 25-year-old foreman who worked for the Rutland and Burlington Railroad, was the victim of a terrible accident in 1848. The crew drilled holes in the rock and gravel, poured in the blasting powder, and then tamped down the powder with an iron rod. While Phineas was still tamping it down, the powder exploded, driving the iron rod up through the left side of his face and out through the top of his head. Although the wound healed in a matter of weeks, Phineas had become a different person. Previously he had been mild-mannered, hardworking, and emotionally calm. Afterward, he was stubborn, hot-tempered, aggressive, and unreliable. Damage to the frontal lobe area of his brain had dramatically altered Phineas's personality and his ability to engage in self-control.

An important part of the frontal lobes is the *prefrontal cortex,* which is at the front of the motor cortex (see Figure 14). The prefrontal cortex is involved in cognitive functions such as planning, reasoning, and self-control (Barrash & others, 2018; Domenech & Koechlin, 2015).

The **parietal lobes**, located at the top and toward the rear of the head, are involved in registering spatial location, attention, and motor control (Parvizi & Wagner, 2018; Sheremata, Somers, & Shomstein, 2018). Thus, the parietal lobes are at work when you are judging how far you have to throw a ball to get it to someone else. Parietal lobes are also involved in our perception of numerical information (Parvizi & Wagner, 2018).

- **occipital lobes** Structures located at the back of the head that respond to visual stimuli.
- **temporal lobes** Structures in the cerebral cortex that are located just above the ears and are involved in hearing, language processing, and memory.
- **frontal lobes** The portions of the cerebral cortex behind the forehead that are involved in personality, intelligence, and the control of voluntary muscles.
- **parietal lobes** Structures at the top and toward the rear of the head that are involved in registering spatial location, attention, and motor control.

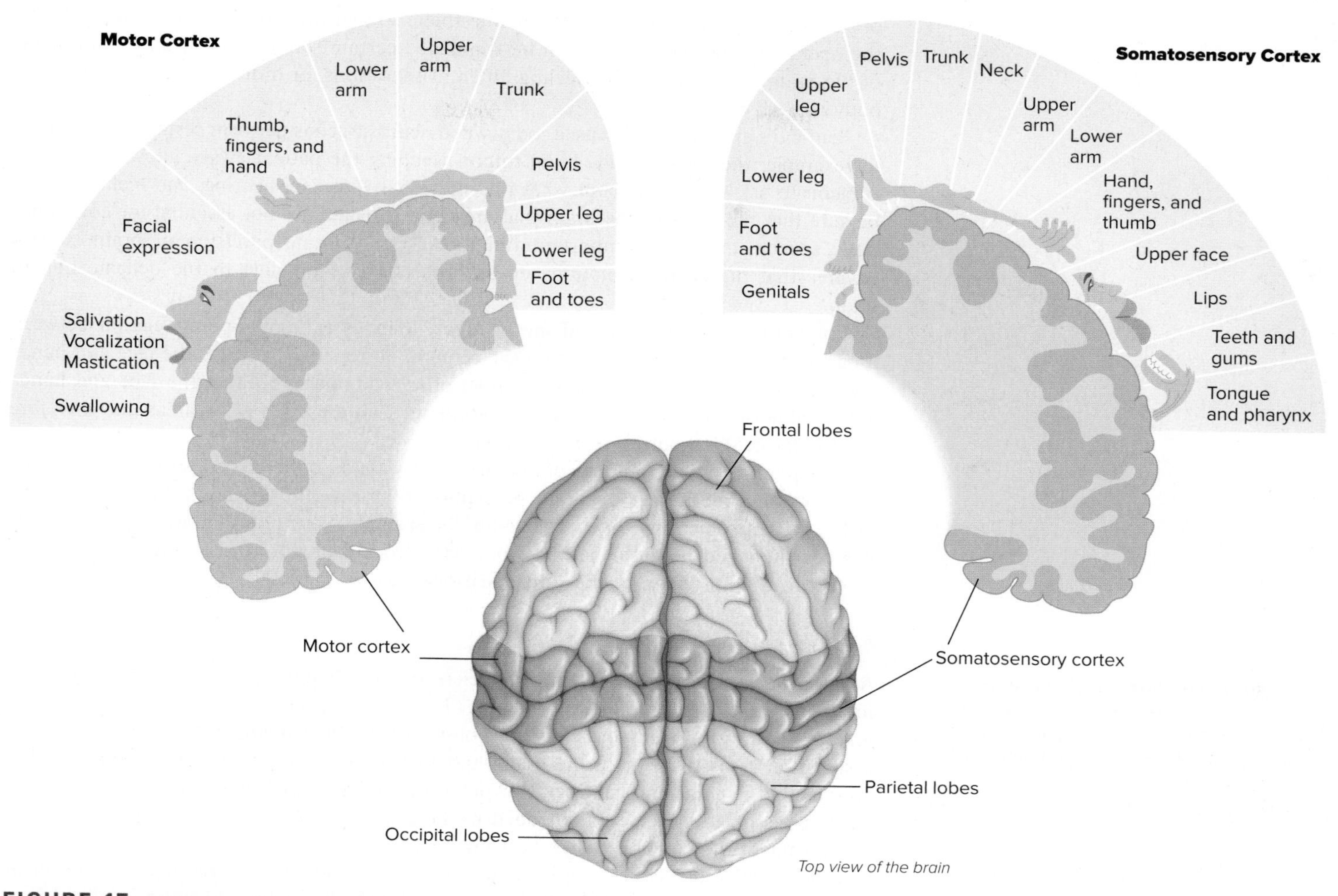


**FIGURE 15** **Disproportionate Representation of Body Parts in the Motor and Somatosensory Areas of the Cortex** The amount of cortex allotted to a body part is not proportionate to the body part's size. Instead, the brain has more space for body parts that require precision and control. Thus, the thumb, fingers, and hand require more brain tissue than does the arm. Source: Penfield (1947).

The brilliant physicist Albert Einstein said that his reasoning often was best when he imagined objects in space. It turns out that his parietal lobes were 15 percent larger than average (Witelson, Kigar, & Harvey, 1999).

A word of caution is in order about going too far in localizing function within a particular lobe. Although this discussion has attributed specific functions to a specific lobe (such as vision in the occipital lobe), considerable integration and connection occur between any two or more lobes and between lobes and other parts of the brain.

## SOMATOSENSORY CORTEX AND MOTOR CORTEX

Two other important regions of the cerebral cortex are the somatosensory cortex and the motor cortex (see Figure 14). The **somatosensory cortex** processes information about body sensations. It is located at the front of the parietal lobes. The **motor cortex**, at the rear of the frontal lobes, processes information about voluntary movement.

The map in Figure 15 shows which parts of the somatosensory and motor cortexes are associated with various parts of the body. It is based on research done by Wilder Penfield (1947), a neurosurgeon at the Montreal Neurological Institute. He worked with patients who had severe epilepsy, and he often performed surgery to remove portions of the epileptic patients' brains. However, he was concerned that removing a portion of the brain might impair some of the individuals' functions. Penfield's solution was to map the cortex during surgery by stimulating different cortical areas and observing the responses

- **somatosensory cortex** A region in the cerebral cortex that processes information about body sensations, located at the front of the parietal lobes.
- **motor cortex** A region in the cerebral cortex that processes information about voluntary movement, located just behind the frontal lobes.

of the patients, who were given a local anesthetic so that they would remain awake during the operation. He found that when he stimulated certain somatosensory and motor areas of the brain, patients reported feeling different sensations, or different parts of a patient's body moved.

Penfield's approach is still used today when neurosurgeons perform certain procedures–for example, the removal of a brain tumor. Keeping the patient awake allows the neurosurgeon to ask questions about what the individual is seeing, hearing, and feeling and to be sure that the parts of the brain that are being affected are not essential for consciousness, speech, and other important functions. The extreme precision of brain surgery ensures that life-saving operations do as little harm as possible to the delicate human brain.

For both somatosensory and motor areas, there is a point-to-point relation between a part of the body and a location on the cerebral cortex. In Figure 15, the face and hands are given proportionately more space than other body parts because the face and hands are capable of finer perceptions and movements than are other body areas and therefore need more cerebral cortex representation.

The point-to-point mapping of somatosensory fields onto the cortex's surface is the basis of our orderly and accurate perception of the world (Hsiao & Gomez-Ramirez, 2013). When something touches your lip, for example, your brain knows what body part has been touched because the nerve pathways from your lip are the only pathways that project to the lip region of the somatosensory cortex.

### ASSOCIATION CORTEX

● **association cortex or association area** The region of the cerebral cortex that is the site of the highest intellectual functions, such as thinking and problem solving.

**Association cortex or association area** refers to the regions of the cerebral cortex that integrate sensory and motor information. (The term *association cortex* applies to cortical material that is not somatosensory or motor cortex–but it is not filler space.) There are association areas throughout the brain, and each sensory system has its own association area in the cerebral cortex. Cognitive processes, such as thinking and problem solving, occur in association cortex. Embedded in the brain's lobes, association cortex makes up 75 percent of the cerebral cortex (see Figure 14).

Interestingly, damage to a specific part of association cortex often does not result in a specific loss of function. With the exception of language areas, which are localized, loss of function seems to depend more on the extent of damage to association cortex than on the location of the damage.

The largest portion of association cortex is located in the frontal lobes, directly behind the forehead. Damage to this area does not lead to somatosensory or motor loss but rather to problems in planning and problem solving, or what are called *executive functions*. Recall the misfortune of Phineas Gage, whose personality and self-control radically changed after he experienced frontal lobe damage.

## The Cerebral Hemispheres and Split-Brain Research

The cerebral cortex is divided into two halves–left and right (see Figure 13). Do these hemispheres have different functions? A discovery by French surgeon Paul Broca provided early evidence that they do.

In 1861 Broca saw a patient who had received an injury to the left side of his brain some 30 years earlier. The patient was known as Tan because *tan* was the only word he could say. Tan suffered from *expressive aphasia* (also called *Broca's aphasia*), a language disorder that involves the inability to produce language. Tan died several days after Broca evaluated him, and an autopsy revealed that the injury was to a precise area of the left hemisphere. Today we refer to this area of the brain as *Broca's area,* and we know that it plays an important role in the production of speech.

● **corpus callosum** The large bundle of axons that connects the brain's two hemispheres, responsible for relaying information between the two sides.

Another area of the left hemisphere that has an important role in language is *Wernicke's area.* This area is named for Carl Wernicke, a German neurologist who noticed in 1874 that individuals with injuries in the left hemisphere had difficulties in understanding language. Damage to this region causes problems in comprehending language; although an individual with an injury to Wernicke's area can produce words, he or she may not be able to understand what others are saying. Figure 16 shows the locations of Broca's area and Wernicke's area. It is easy to confuse Broca's area (associated with speech production) and Wernicke's area (associated with language comprehension). You might remember that Broca's famous patient was called Tan because that was the only word he could produce, so Broca's area is about speech production.

Scientists continue to study the degree to which the brain's left hemisphere or right hemisphere is involved in various aspects of thinking, feeling, and behavior (Fuertinger & others, 2018; Volz & others, 2018). For many years, scientists speculated that the **corpus callosum**, the large bundle of axons that connects the brain's two hemispheres, has something to do with relaying information between the two sides (Figure 17).

Roger Sperry (1974) confirmed this hypothesis in an experiment in which he cut the corpus callosum in cats. He also severed nerves leading from the eyes to the brain. After the operation, Sperry trained the cats to solve a series of visual problems with one eye blindfolded. After a cat learned the task—say, with only its left eye uncovered—its other eye was blindfolded, and the animal was tested again. The "split-brain" cat behaved as if it had never learned the task. In these cats, memory was stored only in the left hemisphere, which could no longer communicate directly with the right hemisphere.

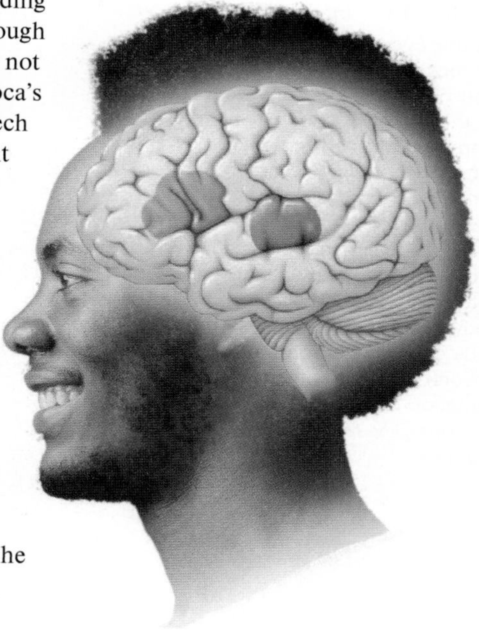

**FIGURE 16 Broca's Area and Wernicke's Area** Broca's area is located in the brain's left hemisphere and is involved in the control of speech. Individuals with damage to Broca's area have problems saying words correctly. Also shown is Wernicke's area, the portion of the left hemisphere that is involved in understanding language. Individuals with damage to this area cannot comprehend words; they hear the words but do not know what they mean. ©Ranta Images/iStock/Getty Images

Further evidence of the corpus callosum's function has come from studies of patients with severe seizure disorders. Seizures are electrical "brainstorms" that can flash uncontrollably across the corpus callosum. In one famous case, neurosurgeons severed the corpus callosum of an epileptic patient now known as W. J. in a final attempt to alleviate his unbearable seizures. Sperry (1968) examined W. J. and found that the corpus callosum functions the same in humans as in animals—cutting the corpus callosum seemed to leave the patient with "two separate minds" that learned and operated independently (Volz & others, 2018).

As it turns out, the right hemisphere receives information only from the left side of the body, and the left hemisphere receives information only from the right side of the body. When you hold an object in your left hand, for example, only the right hemisphere of your brain detects the object. When you hold an object in your right hand, only the left hemisphere of the brain detects it (Figure 18). In individuals with a normally functioning corpus callosum, both hemispheres receive this information eventually, as it travels between the hemispheres through the corpus callosum.

You can appreciate how well the corpus callosum rapidly integrates your experience by considering how hard it is to do two things at once (Stirling, 2002). Maybe as a child you tried to pat your head and rub your stomach at the same time. Even with two separate hands controlled by two separate hemispheres, such dual activity is hard.

In people with intact brains, hemispheric specialization of function occurs in some areas. Researchers have uncovered evidence for hemispheric differences in function by sending different information to each ear. Remember that the left hemisphere gets its information (first) from the right ear, and the right hemisphere hears what is going on (first) in the left ear. Such research has shown that the brain tends to divide its functioning into one hemisphere or the other, as we now consider.

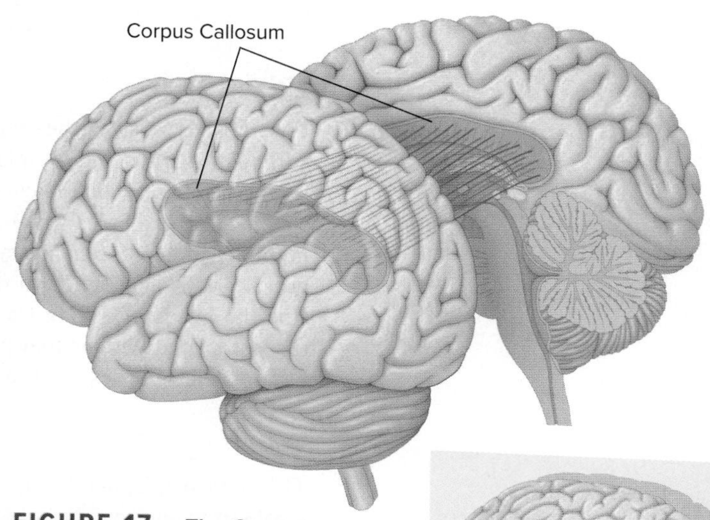


**FIGURE 17 The Corpus Callosum** The corpus callosum is a thick bundle of fibers (essentially axons) that connects the brain cells in one hemisphere to those in the other. In healthy brains, the two sides engage in a continuous flow of information via this neural bridge. Source: Fuertinger & others (2018); Volz & others (2018).

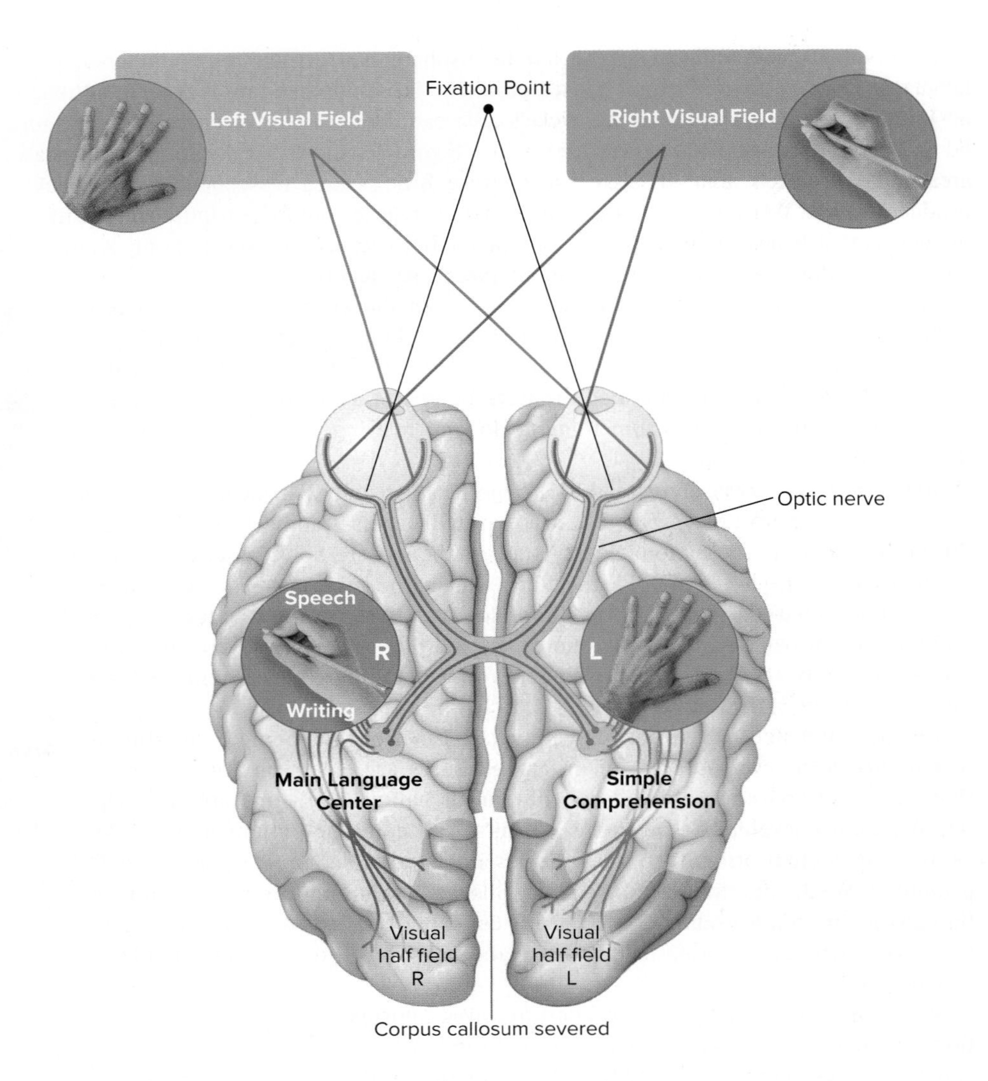


**FIGURE 18 Information Pathways from the Eyes to the Brain** Each of our eyes receives sensory input from both our left and our right field of vision. Information from the left half of our visual field goes to the brain's right hemisphere (which is responsible for simple comprehension), and information from the right half of our visual field goes to the brain's left hemisphere (the brain's main language center, which controls speech and writing). The input received in either hemisphere passes quickly to the other hemisphere across the corpus callosum. When the corpus callosum is severed, however, this transmission of information cannot occur. (top left) ©Hanis/E+/Getty Images; (top right) ©GooDween123/Shutterstock

## LEFT HEMISPHERE FUNCTION

The most extensive research on the brain's two hemispheres has focused on language. Although it is a common misconception that *all* language processing occurs in the brain's left hemisphere, *much* language processing and production does take place in this hemisphere. For example, when we are reading, the left hemisphere recognizes words and numbers and comprehends syntax (rules for forming phrases and sentences) and grammar, but the right hemisphere does not. The left hemisphere is also keenly involved when we sing the words of a song (Whitehead & Armony, 2018). In addition, although not generally associated with spatial perception, the left hemisphere can direct us in solving some basic spatial puzzles, such as identifying whether an object is inside or outside a box.

## RIGHT HEMISPHERE FUNCTION

The right hemisphere is not as verbally oriented as the left hemisphere, but it does play a role in language. The reason we know that the right hemisphere is the source of some human verbal abilities is that people with split brains can draw (with their left hand) pictures of things that are communicated to them in words that are spoken to them (in their left ear). Also, researchers have found increasing evidence that following damage to the left hemisphere, especially early in development, the right hemisphere can take over some language functions (Schlaug, 2018). Moreover, the right hemisphere is adept at picking up the meanings of stories and the intonations of voices, and it excels at recognizing song melodies (Whitehead & Armony, 2018). Furthermore, the right hemisphere is involved in conversation processing (Alexandrou & others, 2017).

The real strength of the right hemisphere, however, appears to lie in the processing of nonverbal information such as spatial perception, visual recognition, and emotion (Kensinger & Choi, 2009). With respect to interpreting spatial information, the right hemisphere is involved in our ability to tell if something is on top of something else, how far apart two objects are, and whether two objects moving in space might crash.

The right hemisphere is the one mainly at work when we process information about people's faces (Caspers & others, 2015; Haeger & others, 2018; Kanwisher, 2006). How do we know this is true? One way we know is that researchers have asked people to watch images on a computer screen and to press a button with either their right or left hand if they recognize a face. Even right-handed people are faster to recognize faces with their left hand because the information goes directly from the part of the brain that recognizes faces (the right hemisphere) to the left hand (Gillihan & Farah, 2005).

Research by Nancy Kanwisher and her colleagues has provided evidence for the role of a specialized area in the right hemisphere for processing faces (Kanwisher & Yovel, 2010; McKone, Crookes, & Kanwisher, 2010; Pitcher & others, 2012). This area, located in the fusiform gyrus in the right temporal lobe, is called the *fusiform face area (FFA)*. The FFA is a dime-size spot just behind your right ear. Using fMRI, researchers have shown that the FFA is especially active when a person is viewing a face–a human face, a cat's face, or a cartoon face (Tong & others, 2000). The FFA and an area of the right occipital lobe called the *occipital face area* (Powell, Kosakowski, & Saxe, 2018) appear to be responsible for the right hemisphere's skill at processing faces. Interestingly, a recent study with children showed that the area of left hemisphere that corresponds to the FFA on the right hemisphere is taken up with learning about letters and words (Centanni & others, 2018).

The right hemisphere may be more involved than the left hemisphere in processing information about emotions–both when we express emotions ourselves and when we interpret others' emotions (Carmona, Holland, & Harrison, 2009). People are more likely to remember emotion words if they hear them in the left ear. As well, much of our sense of humor resides in the right hemisphere (Sidtis & Sidtis, 2018). If you want to be sure that someone laughs at your joke, tell it to the person's left ear!

### RIGHT-BRAINED VERSUS LEFT-BRAINED

People commonly use the terms *left-brained* (meaning logical and rational) and *right-brained* (meaning creative or artistic) as a way of categorizing different brain functioning in themselves and others. Such generalizations have little scientific basis, however–and that is a good thing. We have both hemispheres for a reason: We use them both. For most complex human activities, there is interplay between the brain's two hemispheres.

## Integration of Function in the Brain

How do all of the regions of the brain cooperate to produce the wondrous complexity of thought and behavior that characterizes humans? Neuroscience still does not have answers to questions such as how the brain solves a murder mystery or composes an essay. Even so, we can get a sense of integrative brain function by using a real-world scenario, such as the act of escaping from a burning building.

Imagine that you are sitting at your computer, writing an e-mail, when a fire breaks out behind you. The sound of crackling flames is relayed from your ear through the thalamus, to the auditory cortex, and on to the auditory association cortex. At each stage, the stimulus is processed to extract information, and at some stage, probably at the association cortex level, the sounds are finally matched with something like a neural memory representing sounds of fires you have heard previously.

The association "fire" sets new machinery in motion. Your attention (guided in part by the reticular formation) shifts to the auditory signal being held in your association cortex and on to your auditory association cortex, and simultaneously (again guided by reticular systems) your head turns toward the noise.

Now your visual association cortex reports in: "Objects matching flames are present." In other regions of the association cortex, the visual and auditory reports are synthesized

### test yourself

1. Describe three techniques that allow researchers to examine the brain while it is working.
2. What specific part of the brain is responsible for directing our most complex mental functions, such as thinking and planning, and where is it located?
3. In what ways are the brain's left and right hemispheres specialized in terms of their functioning?

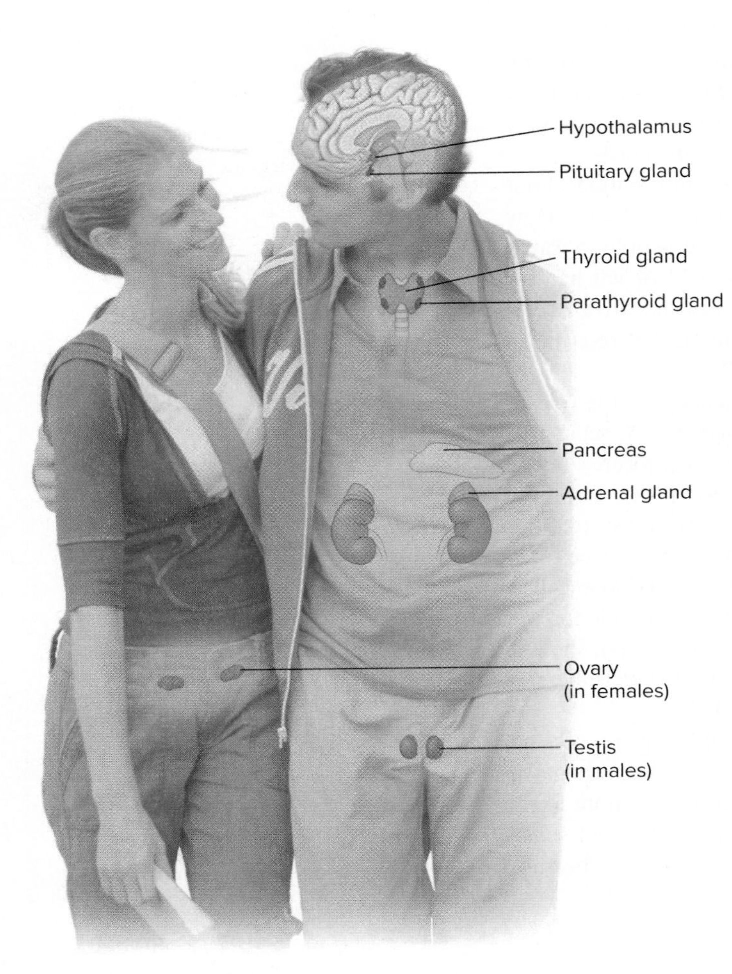


**FIGURE 19** **The Major Endocrine Glands** The pituitary gland releases hormones that regulate the hormone secretions of the other glands. The pituitary gland is regulated by the hypothalamus.
©PhotoAlto/PunchStock

("We have things that look and sound like fire"), and neural associations representing potential actions ("flee") are activated. However, firing the neurons that code the plan to flee will not get you out of the chair. For that task, the basal ganglia must become engaged, and from there the commands will arise to set the brain stem, motor cortex, and cerebellum to the work of transporting you out of the room. All of this happens in mere seconds.

So, which part of your brain did you use to escape? Virtually all systems had a role. By the way, you would probably remember this event because your limbic circuitry would likely have started memory formation when the association "fire" was triggered. The next time the sounds of crackling flames reach your auditory association cortex, the associations triggered would include this most recent escape. In sum, considerable integration of function takes place in the brain. All of the parts of the nervous system work together as a team to keep you safe and sound.

## 4. THE ENDOCRINE SYSTEM

The nervous system works closely with another bodily system–the endocrine system. The **endocrine system** is a set of glands that regulate the activities of certain organs by releasing their chemical products into the bloodstream. **Glands** are organs or tissues in the body that produce chemicals that control many bodily functions. The endocrine glands consist of the pituitary gland, the thyroid and parathyroid glands, the adrenal glands, the pancreas, the ovaries in females, and the testes in males (Figure 19). The chemical messengers produced by these glands are called **hormones**. The bloodstream carries hormones to all parts of the body, and the membrane of every cell has receptors for one or more hormones. Let's take a closer look at the function of some of the main endocrine glands.

The **pituitary gland**, a pea-sized gland just beneath the hypothalamus, controls growth and regulates other glands (Figure 20). The anterior (front) part of the pituitary is known as the *master gland* because almost all of its hormones direct the activity of target glands elsewhere in the body. In turn, the anterior pituitary gland is controlled by the hypothalamus.

The **adrenal glands**, located at the top of each kidney, regulate mood, energy level, and the ability to cope with stress. Each adrenal gland secretes epinephrine (also called *adrenaline*) and norepinephrine (also called *noradrenaline*). You may remember that norepinephrine functions as a neurotransmitter when it is released by neurons. In the adrenal glands, norepinephrine is released as a hormone. In both instances, norepinephrine conveys information–in the first case, to neurons; in the second case, to glands (Sun & others, 2018). Unlike most hormones, epinephrine and norepinephrine act quickly. Epinephrine helps a person get ready for an emergency by acting on smooth muscles, the heart, stomach, intestines, and sweat glands. In addition, epinephrine stimulates the reticular formation, which in turn arouses the sympathetic nervous system, and this system subsequently excites the adrenal glands to produce more epinephrine. The activation of the adrenal glands plays an important role in dealing with stress and maintaining physical health, as we will see at the end of this chapter.

The **pancreas**, located under the stomach, is a dual-purpose gland that performs both digestive and endocrine functions. The part of the pancreas that serves endocrine functions produces a number of hormones, including insulin. This part of the pancreas, the *islets of Langerhans,* busily turns out hormones like a little factory. Insulin is an essential hormone that controls glucose (blood sugar) levels in the body and is related to metabolism, body weight, and obesity.

● **endocrine system** The body system consisting of a set of glands that regulate the activities of certain organs by releasing their chemical products into the bloodstream.

● **glands** Organs or tissues in the body that create chemicals that control many bodily functions.

● **hormones** Chemical messengers that are produced by the endocrine glands and carried by the bloodstream to all parts of the body.

● **pituitary gland** A pea-sized gland just beneath the hypothalamus that controls growth and regulates other glands.

● **adrenal glands** Glands at the top of each kidney that are responsible for regulating mood, energy level, and the ability to cope with stress.

● **pancreas** A dual-purpose gland under the stomach that performs both digestive and endocrine functions.

The **ovaries**, located in the pelvis on either sides of the uterus in females, and **testes**, located in the scrotum in males, are the sex-related endocrine glands that produce hormones involved in sexual development and reproduction. These glands and the hormones they produce play important roles in the development of sexual characteristics, as we will discover in the chapter "Gender, Sex, and Sexuality". They are also involved in other characteristics and behaviors, as we will see throughout this book.

The nervous system and endocrine system are intricately interconnected (Pillinger & others, 2018). The brain's hypothalamus connects the nervous system and the endocrine system and that the two systems work together to control the body's activities. Recall from earlier in the chapter that the autonomic nervous system regulates processes such as respiration, heart rate, and digestion. The autonomic nervous system acts on the endocrine glands to produce a number of important physiological reactions to strong emotions, such as rage and fear.

The endocrine system differs significantly from the nervous system in at least two ways. First, as you saw in Figure 19, the parts of the endocrine system are not all connected in the way that the parts of the nervous system are. Second, the endocrine system works more slowly than the nervous system does, because hormones are transported in our blood through the circulatory system. Our hearts do a mind-boggling job of pumping blood throughout the body, but blood moves far more slowly than the neural impulses do in the nervous system's superhighway.

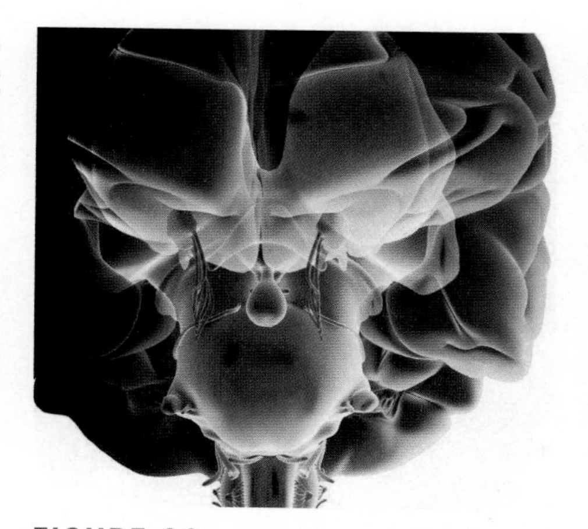

**FIGURE 20** **The Pituitary Gland** The pituitary gland, which hangs by a short stalk from the hypothalamus, regulates the hormone production of many of the body's endocrine glands. Here it is enlarged 30 times. ©MedicalRF.com

- **ovaries** Sex-related endocrine glands that produce hormones involved in female sexual development and reproduction.

- **testes** Sex-related endocrine glands in the scrotum that produce hormones involved in male sexual development and reproduction.

### test yourself

1. What is the endocrine system's function, and what role do hormones play in it?
2. What two adrenal gland secretions prepare the body to react quickly to emergencies, and what specifically do they do?
3. Through what brain structure are the nervous and the endocrine systems connected, and what do the two systems work together to control?

# 5. BRAIN DAMAGE, PLASTICITY, AND REPAIR

An important aspect of the brain is its remarkable plasticity. Neuroscientists have studied plasticity, especially following brain damage, charting the brain's ability to repair itself. Brain damage can produce horrific effects, including paralysis, sensory loss, memory loss, and personality deterioration. When such damage occurs, can the brain recover some or all of its functions? The capacity to recover from brain damage varies considerably, depending on the age of the individual and the extent of the damage (Keenan & others, 2018; Vasquez & others, 2018).

## The Brain's Plasticity and Capacity for Repair

The human brain shows the most plasticity in young children, before the functions of the cortical regions become localized (DiFrancesco & others, 2018). For example, if the speech areas in an infant's left hemisphere are damaged, the right hemisphere assumes much of this language function. However, after age 5, damage to the left hemisphere can permanently disrupt language ability. We examine the brain's plasticity further in the chapter "Sensation and Perception" and the chapter "Human Development".

A key factor in recovery is whether some or all of the neurons in an affected area are just damaged versus whether they are destroyed (Huang & Chang, 2009). If the neurons have not been destroyed, brain function often is restored over time. There are three ways in which repair of the damaged brain might take place:

- *Collateral sprouting,* the process by which axons of some healthy neurons adjacent to damaged cells grow new branches.
- *Substitution of function,* the process by which the damaged region's function is taken over by another area or areas of the brain.
- *Neurogenesis,* the process by which new neurons are generated.

Researchers have found that neurogenesis occurs in mammals such as mice. In mice, exercise increases neurogenesis, while social isolation decreases it (Clemenson, Deng, & Gage, 2015; Gil-Mohapel & others, 2011; Leasure & Decker, 2009). Neurogenesis can

*This fluorescent micrograph shows glial stem cells. Like other stem cells, these have the capacity to develop into a wide range of other cells.*



occur in humans (Göritz & Frisén, 2012; Inta & Gass, 2015; Mahar & Cavalli, 2018; Sun, 2016). However, to date, the presence of new neurons has been documented only in the hippocampus, which is involved in memory, and the olfactory bulb, which is involved in the sense of smell (Anacker, Denny, & Hen, 2015; Xu & others, 2013). Researchers are exploring how grafting neural stem cells to various regions of the brain, such as the hypothalamus, might increase neurogenesis (Dadwal & others, 2015; Decimo & others, 2012). If researchers can discover how new neurons are generated, that information might be used to fight degenerative diseases of the brain such as Alzheimer and Parkinson disease.

Damage to the brain can be devastating. Recall the plight of Phineas Gage who went from being a reliable, mild-mannered worker to an impatient man with a fiery temper. However, the effects of brain injury may not always be negative. To read about this possibility, see the Critical Controversy.

## Brain Tissue Implants

The brain naturally recovers some, but not all, functions that are lost following damage. Is it possible to help nature along? *Brain grafts* are implants of healthy tissue into damaged brains. Brain grafts have greater potential success when the brain tissue used is from the fetal stage—an early stage in prenatal development (L'Episcopo & others, 2018; Thomas & others, 2009). Fetal neurons are still growing and have a much higher probability of making connections with other neurons than does mature brain tissue. In a number of studies, researchers have damaged part of an adult rat's brain, waited until the animal recovered as much as possible by itself, and assessed its behavioral deficits. They then took the corresponding area of a fetal rat's brain and transplanted it into the damaged brain of the adult rat. In these studies, the rats that received the brain transplants demonstrated considerable behavioral recovery (Reyes, Tajiri, & Borlongan, 2015; Shetty, Rao, & Hattiangady, 2008).

Might such grafts be successful in humans suffering from brain damage? The research results are promising, but finding donors is a problem (Glaw & others, 2009). Although using brain tissue from aborted fetuses is a possibility, there are ethical concerns about that practice.

Perhaps one of the most heated debates in recent years has concerned the use of human embryonic stem cells in research and treatment. **Stem cells** are unique because they are primitive cells that have the capacity to develop into most types of human cells.

● **stem cells** Unique primitive cells that have the capacity to develop into most types of human cells.

Because of their amazing plasticity, stem cells might replace damaged cells in the human body, including cells involved in spinal cord injury and brain damage.

Typically, researchers have harvested the stem cells from frozen embryos left over from *in vitro fertilization* procedures. In these procedures, a number of eggs, or *ova,* are collected from a woman's ovaries in order to be fertilized in a lab. In successful in vitro fertilization, the ova are brought together with sperm, producing human embryos. Because the procedure is difficult, doctors typically fertilize a large number of eggs in the hope that some will survive when implanted in the woman's uterus. Typically, there are leftover embryos. These embryos are in the *blastocyst* stage, which occurs five days after conception. At this stage the embryo has not yet attached to the uterus and has no brain and no central nervous system—it is an undifferentiated ball of cells.

Some supporters of stem cell technology emphasize that using these cells for research and treatment might relieve a great deal of human suffering. Opponents of abortion disapprove of the use of stem cells in research or treatment on the grounds that the embryos die when the stem cells are removed. (In fact, leftover embryos are likely to be destroyed in any case.) In 2009, President Barack Obama removed restrictions on stem cell research.

One possible use of stem cells is in the treatment of spinal cord injuries. A spinal cord injury can lead to impaired motor function and paralysis. The extent of a person's ability to move after spinal cord injury depends on the location of the damage. Generally,

### *test yourself*

1. Describe three ways in which a damaged brain may repair itself.
2. What specific discovery have researchers made about neurogenesis in human beings? For what kinds of disease might knowledge about the process lead to promising treatment?
3. What are brain grafts, and why does the use of fetal tissue in grafts often lead to successful results?

## Can Brain Injury Lead to Personality Change for the Better?

In many cases, when someone experiences a brain-damaging event their very personality changes as they become more moody, withdrawn, or socially inappropriate (King & others, 2018). Research on personality change following strokes, surgery, or brain injuries typically focuses on negative changes. But isn't it possible that some people become *better* after these events?

Consider Jason Padgett. As a young man he worked as a clerk at a futon store. He was brutally attacked by muggers one night, suffering a concussion. During his recovery, Jason, who had never been interested in math, suddenly began seeing the world as made up of intricate, mathematical patterns. He discovered that he had a special talent for creating artwork based on the arithmetic laws he saw everywhere. Jason's brain had unlocked capacities he had never known before (Karlinsky & Frost, 2012). Jason is now a published author, successful artist, and public speaker. His case is striking but also quite unusual. Is it possible for less dramatic positive changes to occur after brain injury?

Some studies do show improvements in people's personalities following brain injury (Kapur, 1996). Is it possible that such benefits are linked to the particular brain areas affected? Recently, a team of scientists (King & others, 2018) studied 97 patients who were rated by a family member or close friend on personality and behavior before and after a brain-damaging event. They found that 22 of the patients were viewed as improving in personality and behavior; 21 showed no change; and the rest showed impairment. Those who improved were rated as less irritable, more outgoing, and generally happier than they had been before their brain injury (King & others, 2018). Compared with those who showed impairment, the patients who showed improvement were more likely to have lesions in the front of the brain, across both hemispheres, with damage extending to the right side of the brain.

These provocative results suggest that it might be possible to improve a person's personality by changing the brain. The use of surgery to alter a person's behavior has a controversial history (as we will see later). However, problems with connections between the prefrontal cortex and other brain areas have been implicated in many psychological disorders. Interestingly, this study showed that those who were rated as improving also were rated as having more difficult personalities prior to the brain injury, being socially withdrawn and moody before their brain injury. Might these individuals have *chosen* to change their brains if they could have?

©Steve Allen/Brand X Pictures/Getty Images

**WHAT DO YOU THINK?**

- If you could have surgery to change your personality, would you do it? Why or why not?
- If someone's personality changes drastically after a brain-damaging event, do you think they are still the same person?

the higher on the spinal cord the damage occurs, the less motor function a person will retain. Recent research shows that treatment in which intermittent electrical current is generated through an implant might help individuals regain motor function, although this work is still at a very early stage (Capogrosso & others, 2018; Wagner & others, 2018).

● **chromosomes** In the human cell, threadlike structures that come in 23 pairs, one member of each pair originating from each parent, and that contain the remarkable substance DNA.

● **deoxyribonucleic acid (DNA)** A complex molecule in the cell's chromosomes that carries genetic information.

● **genes** The units of hereditary information, consisting of short segments of chromosomes composed of DNA.

# 6. GENETICS AND BEHAVIOR

In addition to the brain and nervous system, other aspects of our physiology also have consequences for psychological processes. Genes, the focal point of this section, are an essential contributor to these processes. As noted in the "What Is Psychology?" chapter, the influence of nature (our genetic endowment) and nurture (our experience) on psychological characteristics has long fascinated psychologists. We begin by examining some basic facts about the central internal agent of human differences: our genes.

## Chromosomes, Genes, and DNA

Within the human body are literally trillions of cells. The nucleus of each human cell contains 46 **chromosomes**, threadlike structures that come in 23 pairs, with one member of each pair from each biological parent. Chromosomes contain the remarkable substance **deoxyribonucleic acid (DNA)**, a complex molecule that carries genetic information. **Genes**, the units of hereditary information, are short chromosome segments composed of DNA. The relationship among cells, chromosomes, genes, and DNA is illustrated in Figure 21.

Genes hold the code for creating proteins out of amino acids forming the bases for everything our bodies do. Specifically, genes direct and regulate the production of proteins out of amino acids. Every cell in our body contains a full complement of our genes but different genes are active in each cell. Many genes encode proteins that are unique to a particular cell and give the cell its identity. Will it be a neuron or a bone cell? The activation of our genes holds the key to this question. Some genes are involved in the development of the embryo and then are turned off for the rest of life. Genes do not operate independently but work with one another and in collaboration with hormones and the environment to direct the body's function (Mlecnik, Galon, & Bindea, 2018).

*A positive result of mapping the entire human genome. Shortly after Andrew Gobea was born, his cells were genetically altered to prevent his immune system from failing.*



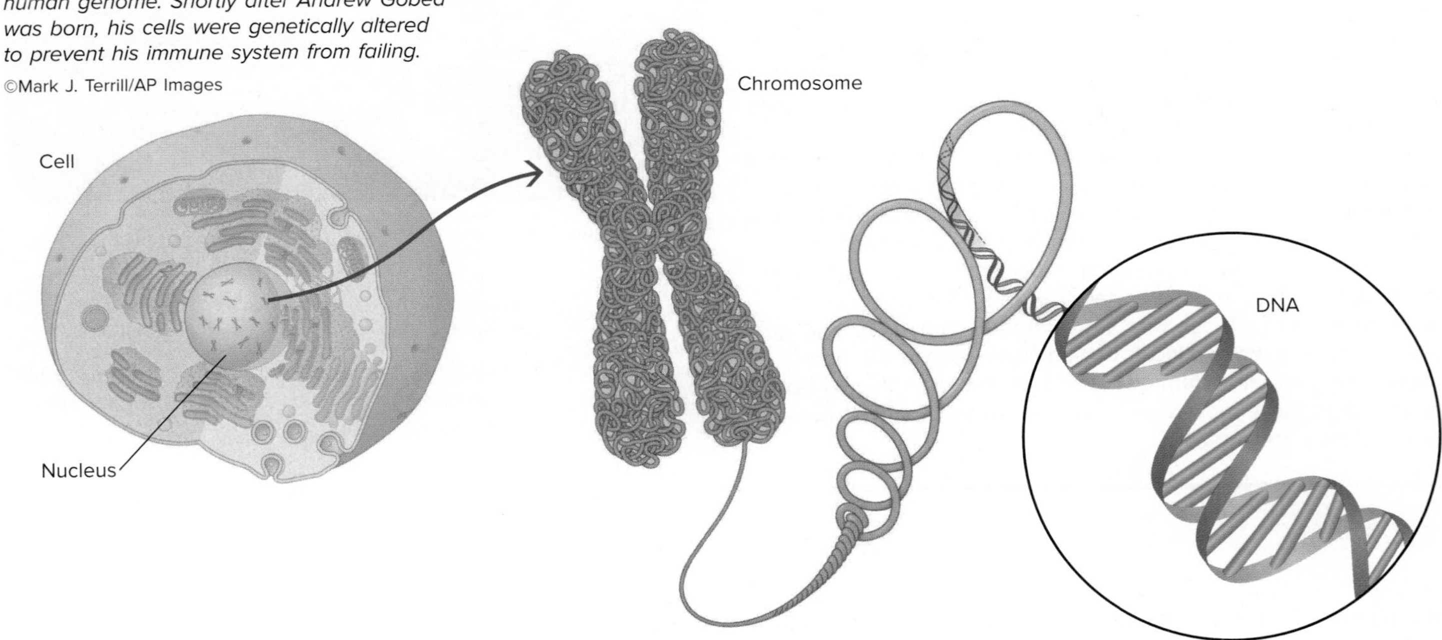


**FIGURE 21** **Cells, Chromosomes, Genes, and DNA** (*left*) The body houses trillions of cells, which are the basic structural units of life. Each cell contains a central structure, the nucleus. (*middle*) Chromosomes and genes are located in the nucleus of the cell. Chromosomes are made up of threadlike structures composed mainly of DNA molecules. Note that inside the chromosome are the genes. (*right*) A gene is a segment of DNA that contains the hereditary code. The structure of DNA resembles a spiral ladder.

*Genome* refers to an organism's complete genetic material. The exact number of genes on the human genome continues to be debated (Willyard, 2018). Current estimates suggest there are 19,000 to 30,000 genes, each producing 3 proteins (NIH, 2018). Although scientists are still a long way from unraveling all the mysteries about the way genes work, some aspects of this process are well understood, starting with the fact that multiple genes interact to give rise to observable characteristics.

## The Study of Genetics

The relatively young science of genetics traces its roots to the mid-nineteenth century, when an Austrian monk, Gregor Mendel, studied heredity in generations of pea plants. By crossbreeding plants with different characteristics and noting the characteristics of the offspring, Mendel discovered predictable patterns of heredity and thereby laid the foundation for modern genetics.

Mendel noticed that some genes seem to be more likely than others to show up in the physical characteristics of an organism. In some gene pairs, one gene is dominant over the other. If one gene of a pair is dominant and one is recessive, the **dominant-recessive genes principle** applies, meaning that the dominant gene overrides the recessive gene—that is, it prevents the recessive gene from expressing its instructions. The recessive gene exerts its influence only if *both* genes of a pair are recessive. If you inherit a recessive gene from only one biological parent, you may never know you carry the gene.

● **dominant-recessive genes principle** The principle that, if one gene of a pair is dominant and one is recessive, the dominant gene overrides the recessive gene. A recessive gene exerts its influence only if both genes of a pair are recessive.

In the world of dominant-recessive genes, brown eyes, farsightedness, and dimples rule over blue eyes, nearsightedness, and freckles. If, however, you inherit a recessive gene for a trait from *both* of your biological parents, you will show the trait. That is why two brown-haired parents can have a child with red hair: Each parent would have dominant genes for brown hair and recessive genes for red hair. Because dominant genes override recessive genes, the parents have brown hair. However, the child can inherit recessive genes for red hair from each biological parent. With no dominant genes to override them, the recessive genes make the child's hair red.

Yet the relationship between genes and characteristics is complex. Even simple traits such as eye color and hair color are likely the product of *multiple* genes. Moreover, many different genes probably influence complex human characteristics such as personality and intelligence. Scientists use the term *polygenic inheritance* to describe the influences of multiple genes on behavior. As we will see throughout our study of psychology, many important characteristics, like intelligence or kindness, are thought to be at least partially explained by polygenic inheritance (Plomin & von Stumm, 2018; Rosenson & others, 2018).

We next survey four ways in which scientists investigate our genetic heritage: molecular genetics, selective breeding, genome-wide association studies, and behavior genetics.

### MOLECULAR GENETICS

The field of *molecular genetics* involves the manipulation of genes using technology to determine their effect on behavior. There is currently a great deal of enthusiasm about the use of molecular genetics to discover the specific locations on genes that determine an individual's susceptibility to many diseases and other aspects of health and well-being (Plomin & von Stumm, 2018; Rosenson & others, 2018).

### SELECTIVE BREEDING

*Selective breeding* is a genetic method in which organisms are chosen for reproduction based on how much of a particular trait they display. Mendel developed this technique in his studies of pea plants. A more recent example involving behavior is the classic selective breeding study conducted by Robert Tryon (1940). He chose to study maze-running ability

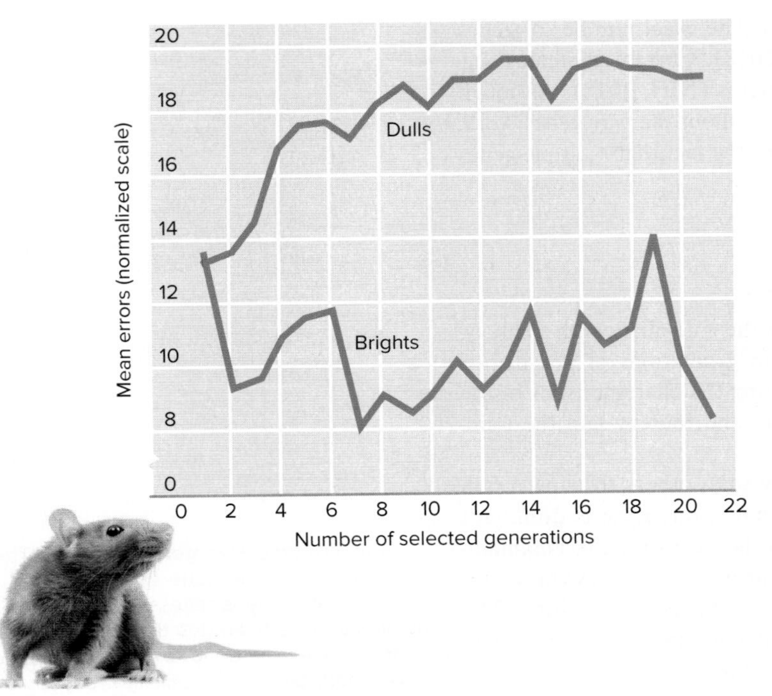


**FIGURE 22 Results of Tryon's Selective Breeding Experiment with Maze-Bright and Maze-Dull Rats** These results demonstrate genetic influences on behavior. Source: Tryon (1940); ©Sonsedska Yuliia/Shutterstock

in rats. After he trained a large number of rats to run a complex maze, he then mated the rats that were the best at maze running ("maze bright") with each other and the ones that were the worst ("maze dull") with each other. He continued this process with 21 generations of rats. As Figure 22 shows, after several generations, the maze-bright rats significantly outperformed the maze-dull rats.

Selective breeding studies demonstrate that genes are an important influence on behavior, but this does not mean experience is unimportant. For example, in another study, maze-bright and maze-dull rats were reared in one of two environments: (1) an impoverished environment that consisted of a barren wire-mesh group cage or (2) an enriched environment that contained tunnels, ramps, visual displays, and other stimulating objects (Cooper & Zubeck, 1958). When they reached maturity, only the maze-dull rats that had been reared in an impoverished environment made more maze-learning errors than the maze-bright rats.

It is unethical to conduct selective breeding studies with human beings. (*Eugenics* refers to the application of selective breeding to humans; Adolf Hitler notoriously espoused this practice in Nazi Germany.) In humans, researchers generally examine the influence of genetics on psychological characteristics by using behavior genetics.

## GENOME-WIDE ASSOCIATION METHOD

*The genome-wide association method* has been used to identify genetic variations linked to particular diseases, such as cancer, cardiovascular disease, or Alzheimer disease (Duncan & others, 2018; Lahm & others, 2018; Marioni & others, 2018). To conduct a genome-wide association study, researchers obtain DNA from individuals who have the disease under study and from those who do not. Then, each participant's complete set of DNA, or genome, is purified and scanned on machines to determine markers of genetic variation. If the genetic variations occur more frequently in people who have the disease, the variations point to the region in the human genome where the disease-causing problem exists.

Genes that are close to one another in our DNA are more likely to be inherited together. This link between genes is used in what is called *linkage analysis.* This analysis may help identify the location of certain genes by referring to other genes whose position is already known. This strategy is often used to search for genes associated with a disease. Gene linkage studies are now being conducted on a wide variety of disorders and health issues (Zheutlin & Ross, 2018).

A key challenge in genome-wide association studies, as well as genetic linkage studies, is replication. Recall that replicating a research finding means repeating it. If a genetic characteristic is associated with a particular disorder, disease, or characteristic in one sample of participants, this association should emerge as well in another sample. Unfortunately, many early findings using genome-wide analyses did not replicate; that is, genes that were associated with a particular characteristic in one sample did not show the same association in later studies. As a result, scientists who use these tools have become increasingly cautious about drawing conclusions (Jannot, Ehret, & Perneger, 2015).

## BEHAVIOR GENETICS

*Behavior genetics* is the study of the degree and nature of heredity's influence on behavior. Behavior genetics is less invasive than the other types of genetic investigation. Using methods such as *twin studies,* behavior geneticists examine the extent to which individuals are shaped by their heredity and their environmental experiences (Boomsma & others, 2018; Moberg & others, 2018).

In the most common type of twin study, researchers compare the behavioral similarity of identical twins with the behavioral similarity of fraternal twins. *Identical twins* develop from a single fertilized egg that splits into two genetically identical embryos, each of which becomes a person. *Fraternal twins* develop from separate eggs and separate sperm, and so they are genetically no more similar than non-twin siblings. They may even be of different sexes. Comparing the differences in similarity between these groups allows researchers to gauge how much having 100 percent similarity in genes affects similarity on other characteristics, such as intelligence, extraversion, or happiness. For example, in one study, 428 identical and fraternal twin pairs in Italy were compared with respect to their levels of self-esteem, life satisfaction, and optimism for the future (Caprara & others, 2009). The identical twins were much more similar than the fraternal twins on these measures.

In another type of twin study, researchers evaluate identical twins who were reared in separate environments. If their behavior is similar, the assumption is that heredity has played an important role in shaping their behavior. This strategy is the basis for the Minnesota Study of Twins Reared Apart, directed by Thomas Bouchard and his colleagues (1996). The researchers bring identical twins who have been reared apart to Minneapolis from all over the world to study their behavior. The twins answer thousands of questions about their family, childhood, interests, and values. Researchers obtain detailed medical histories with information about diet, smoking, and exercise habits. However, drawing strong conclusions about genetics from twins reared apart has been criticized for various reasons. First, some of the separated twins in the Minnesota study had been together several months prior to their adoption and some had been reunited prior to testing (in certain cases, for a number of years). In addition, adoption agencies often put identical twins in similar homes. Finally, even strangers (of exactly the same age) are likely to have some coincidental similarities (Joseph, 2006).

You have probably heard of instances of twins who were separated at birth and who, upon being reunited later in life, found themselves strikingly similar to each other. To think critically about such cases, consider the Psychological Inquiry.

## psychological *inquiry*

©Kenneth Sponsler/Getty Images

### *Identical Twins*

We've all heard stories about identical twins who were separated at birth. When these twins meet up in adulthood, people often find the similarities between them to be uncanny. Are these similarities evidence of the extraordinary power of genes? Let's take a closer look.

1. Imagine that you did not see this photo of twins and were simply asked how similar two people of the same gender, ethnicity, and age might be. In what ways might such people be alike?
2. How might such individuals, even growing up in very different environments, evoke similar responses from others?
3. Do you think that people of this same gender, age, and ethnicity might enjoy similar hobbies? Have similar jobs?
4. What does this Psychological Inquiry tell you about the power of vivid and unusual cases in the conclusions we reach?

*Our height depends significantly on the genes we inherit. However, even if we have genes that call for the stature of a basketball center, we may not reach that "genetically programmed" height if we lack good nutrition, adequate shelter, and medical care.*



## Genes and the Environment

So far, we have focused a lot on genes, and you are probably getting the picture that genes are a powerful force in an organism. The role of genetics in some characteristics may seem obvious; for instance, how tall you are depends to a large degree on how tall your parents are. However, imagine a person growing up in an environment with poor nutrition, inadequate shelter, little or no medical care. This individual may have genes that call for the height of an NBA or WNBA center, but without environmental support for this genetic capacity, he or she may never reach that genetically programmed height.

The relationship between an individual's genes and the actual person we see before us is not a perfect one-to-one correspondence. Even for a characteristic such as height, genes do not fully determine where a person will stand on this variable. We need to account for the role of nurture, or environmental factors, in the characteristics we see in the fully grown person.

If the environment matters for an apparently simple characteristic such as height, imagine the role it might play in a complex psychological characteristic such as being outgoing or intelligent. For such a trait, genes are, again, not directly reflected in the characteristics of the person. Indeed, genes cannot tell us exactly what a person will be like. Genes are simply related to some of the characteristics we see in a person.

- **genotype** An individual's genetic heritage; one's actual genetic material.

- **phenotype** An individual's observable characteristics.

To account for this gap between genes and actual observable characteristics, scientists distinguish between a genotype and a phenotype. A **genotype** is an individual's genetic heritage, the actual genetic material present in every cell in the person's body. A **phenotype** is the individual's observable characteristics. The relationship between a genotype and phenotype is not always obvious. Recall that some genetic characteristics are dominant and others are recessive. Seeing that a person has brown eyes (his or her phenotype) tells us nothing about whether the person might also have a gene for blue eyes (his or her genotype) hiding out as well. The phenotype is influenced both by the genotype and by environmental factors.

The word *phenotype* applies to both physical *and* psychological characteristics. Consider a trait such as extraversion–the tendency to be outgoing and sociable. Even if we knew the exact genetic recipe for extraversion, we still could not perfectly predict a person's level of (phenotypic) extraversion from his or her genes, because at least some of this trait comes from the person's experience. We will revisit the concepts of genotype and phenotype throughout this book–for example, when we look at intelligence, when we explore human development, and when we examine personality.

Whether a gene is "turned on"–that is, directing cells to assemble proteins–is a matter of collaboration between hereditary and environmental factors. *Genetic expression,* a term that refers to gene activity that affects the body's cells, is influenced by the genes' environment (Gottlieb, 2007). For example, hormones that circulate in the blood make their way into the cell, where they can turn genes on and off. This flow of hormones can be affected by external environmental conditions such as the amount of light, the length of the day, nutrition, and behavior. Another factor that can influence DNA synthesis is stress, a powerful factor in health and wellness that we will consider next.

### test yourself

1. What is the relationship among chromosomes, genes, and DNA?
2. According to the dominant-recessive genes principle, how could two brown-haired parents have a blonde-haired child?
3. What term refers to our genetic makeup, and what term refers to the observable physical expression of that genetic makeup?

# 7. PSYCHOLOGY'S BIOLOGICAL FOUNDATIONS AND HEALTH AND WELLNESS

- **stress** The responses of individuals to environmental stressors.

- **stressors** Circumstances and events that threaten individuals and tax their coping abilities and that cause physiological changes to ready the body to handle the assault of stress.

The components of the nervous system play an essential role in our health and wellness.

**Stress** is the response of individuals to **stressors**, which are the circumstances and events that threaten them and tax their coping abilities. You know what stress feels like.

Imagine that you show up for class one morning, and it looks as if everyone else knows that there is a test that day. You hear others talking about how much they have studied, and you nervously ask yourself: "Test? What test?" You might start to sweat, and your heart might thump fast and hard in your chest. Sure enough, the instructor shows up with a stack of exams. You are about to be tested on material you have not even thought about, much less studied.

As we have seen, stress begins with a "fight or flight" response sparked by the sympathetic nervous system. This reaction quickly mobilizes the body's physiological resources to deal with threats to survival. An unexpected exam is not literally a threat to your survival, but the human stress response is such that it can occur in reaction to *anything* that threatens personally important motives (Sapolsky, 2004).

*Acute stress* is the stress that occurs in response to an immediate perceived threat. When the stressful situation ends, so does acute stress. Acute stress is adaptive, because it allows us to do the things we need to do in an emergency. Once the danger passes, the parasympathetic nervous system can calm us down and focus on body maintenance. However, we are not in a live-or-die situation most of the time when we experience stress. Indeed, we can even "stress ourselves out" just by thinking.

*Chronic stress*–stress that goes on continuously–may lead to persistent autonomic nervous system arousal (Bergamini & others, 2018; Mellman & others, 2018). While the sympathetic nervous system is working to meet the demands of whatever is stressing us out, the parasympathetic nervous system is not getting a chance to do its job of maintenance and repair, of digesting food, and of keeping our organs in good working order. Furthermore, in chronic stress, the stress hormones adrenaline and norepinephrine are produced by the endocrine system and constantly circulated in the body, eventually causing a breakdown of the immune system (Davis & Maney, 2018; Sapolsky, 2004). In other words, over time, chronic autonomic nervous system activity can bring about an immune system collapse, leaving the person vulnerable to disease (Kirschman, Crespi, & Warne, 2018; Prather & others, 2018).

Chronic stress is clearly best avoided. The brain, a structure that is itself powerfully affected by chronic stress, can be our ally in helping us avoid such continuous stress. Consider that when we face a challenging situation, we can exploit the brain's abilities and interpret the experience in a way that is not so stressful. For example, maybe we can approach an upcoming audition for a play not so much as a stressor but as an opportunity to shine. Changing the way people think about their life challenges and experiences can help them live less stressfully and maintain good health.

At the beginning of this chapter, we considered how changing the way we think leads to physical changes in the brain and its operations. In light of this remarkable capacity, it is reasonable to conclude that we can use our brain's powers to change how we look at life experiences–and maybe even to deploy the brain as a defense against stress.

The biological foundations of psychology are in evidence across the entire nervous system, including the brain, the intricately working neurotransmitters, the endocrine system, and our genes. These physical realities of our body work in concert to produce our behavior, thoughts, and feelings. The activities you perform every day are all signs of the success of this physical system. Your mastery of the material in this chapter is only one reflection of the extraordinary capabilities of this biological achievement.

### test yourself

1. Define *stress* and *stressors*.
2. What part of the nervous system sets off the "fight or flight" reaction, and how does this reaction affect the body?
3. What is the difference between acute stress and chronic stress?

SUMMARY

## 1. THE NERVOUS SYSTEM

The nervous system is the body's electrochemical communication circuitry. Four important characteristics of the brain and nervous system are complexity, integration, adaptability, and electrochemical transmission. The brain's special ability to adapt and change is called *plasticity*.

Decision making in the nervous system occurs in specialized pathways of nerve cells. These pathways involve sensory input, motor output, and neural networks.

The nervous system is divided into two main parts: central (CNS) and peripheral (PNS). The CNS consists of the brain and spinal cord. The PNS has two major divisions: somatic and autonomic. The autonomic nervous system consists of two main divisions: sympathetic and parasympathetic. The sympathetic nervous system drives our body's response to threatening circumstances, while the parasympathetic nervous system is involved in maintaining the body, digesting food, and healing wounds.

## 2. NEURONS

Neurons are cells that specialize in processing information. They make up the communication network of the nervous system. The three main parts of the neuron are the cell body, dendrite (receiving part), and axon (sending part). A myelin sheath encases and insulates most axons and speeds up transmission of neural impulses.

Impulses are sent from a neuron along its axon in the form of brief electrical impulses. Resting potential is the stable, slightly negative charge of an inactive neuron. The brief wave of electrical charge that sweeps down the axon, called the action potential, is an all-or-nothing response. The synapse is the space between neurons. At the synapse, neurotransmitters are released from the sending neuron, and some of these attach to receptor sites on the receiving neuron, where they stimulate another electrical impulse. Neurotransmitters include acetylcholine, GABA, glutamate, norepinephrine, dopamine, serotonin, endorphins, and oxytocin. Neural networks are clusters of neurons that are interconnected and are developed through experience.

## 3. STRUCTURES OF THE BRAIN AND THEIR FUNCTIONS

The main techniques used to study the brain are brain lesioning, electrical recording, and brain imaging. These methods have revealed a great deal about the three major divisions of the brain—the hindbrain, midbrain, and forebrain.

The cerebral cortex makes up most of the outer layer of the brain, and it is here that higher mental functions such as thinking and planning take place. The wrinkled surface of the cerebral cortex is divided into hemispheres, each with four lobes: occipital, temporal, frontal, and parietal. There is considerable integration and connection among the brain's lobes.

The brain has two hemispheres. Two areas in the left hemisphere that involve specific language functions are Broca's area (speech) and Wernicke's area (language comprehension). The corpus callosum is a large bundle of fibers that connects the two hemispheres. Research suggests that the left brain is more dominant in processing verbal information (such as language) and the right brain in processing nonverbal information (such as spatial perception, visual recognition, faces, and emotion). Nonetheless, in a person whose corpus callosum is intact, both hemispheres of the cerebral cortex are involved in most complex human functioning.

## 4. THE ENDOCRINE SYSTEM

The endocrine glands release hormones directly into the bloodstream for distribution throughout the body. The pituitary gland is the master endocrine gland. The adrenal glands play important roles in moods, energy levels, and ability to cope with stress. Other parts of the endocrine system include the pancreas, which produces insulin, and the ovaries and testes, which produce sex hormones.

## 5. BRAIN DAMAGE, PLASTICITY, AND REPAIR

The brain has considerable plasticity. Its ability to adapt and change is greater in young children than later in development. Three ways in which a damaged brain might repair itself are collateral sprouting, substitution of function, and neurogenesis. Brain grafts are implants of healthy tissue into damaged brains. Brain grafts are more successful when fetal tissue is used. Stem cell research may allow for novel treatments for damaged nervous systems.

## 6. GENETICS AND BEHAVIOR

Chromosomes are threadlike structures that occur in 23 pairs, with one member of each pair coming from each biological parent. Chromosomes contain the genetic substance deoxyribonucleic acid (DNA). Genes, the units of hereditary information, are short segments of chromosomes composed of DNA. According to the dominant-recessive genes principle, if one gene of a pair is dominant and one is recessive, the dominant gene overrides the recessive gene.

Different ways of studying heredity's influence are molecular genetics, selective breeding, genome-wide association method, and behavior genetics.

Two important concepts in the study of genetics are the genotype and phenotype. The genotype is an individual's actual genetic material. The phenotype is the observable characteristics of the person.

Both genes and environment play a role in determining the phenotype of an individual. Even for characteristics in which genes play a large role (such as height and eye color), the environment also is a factor.

## 7. PSYCHOLOGY'S BIOLOGICAL FOUNDATIONS AND HEALTH AND WELLNESS

Stress is the body's response to changes in the environment. Stressors are the circumstances and events that threaten the organism. The body's stress response is largely a function of sympathetic nervous system activation that prepares us for action in the face of a threat. The stress response involves slowing down maintenance processes (such as immune function and digestion) in favor of rapid action. Acute stress is an adaptive response, but chronic stress can have negative consequences for our health. Although stress may be inevitable, our reaction to a stressful event is largely a function of how we think about it.

# key *terms*

- action potential
- adrenal glands
- afferent nerves or sensory nerves
- all-or-nothing principle
- amygdala
- association cortex or association area
- autonomic nervous system
- axon
- basal ganglia
- brain stem
- cell body
- central nervous system (CNS)
- cerebral cortex
- chromosomes
- corpus callosum
- dendrites
- deoxyribonucleic acid (DNA)
- dominant-recessive genes principle
- efferent nerves or motor nerves
- endocrine system
- forebrain
- frontal lobes
- genes
- genotype
- glands
- glial cells or glia
- hindbrain
- hippocampus
- hormones
- hypothalamus
- limbic system
- midbrain
- mirror neurons
- motor cortex
- myelin sheath
- neocortex
- nervous system
- neural networks
- neurons
- neurotransmitters
- occipital lobes
- ovaries
- pancreas
- parasympathetic nervous system
- parietal lobes
- peripheral nervous system (PNS)
- phenotype
- pituitary gland
- plasticity
- resting potential
- reticular formation
- somatic nervous system
- somatosensory cortex
- stem cells
- stress
- stressors
- sympathetic nervous system
- synapses
- temporal lobes
- testes
- thalamus

# apply your *knowledge*

1. Consider the four characteristics of the nervous system discussed in this chapter. Suppose you had to do without one of them. Which would you choose, and what would be the consequences of your decision for your behavior?
2. Do an Internet search for "nutrition" and "the brain." Examine the claims made by one or more of the websites. In light of what you have learned about the nervous system in this chapter, how could nutrition affect brain function? Based on your scientific knowledge, how believable are the claims on the site? Explain.
3. Imagine that you could make one part of your brain twice as big as it is now. Which part would it be, and how do you think your behavior would change as a result? What if you had to make another part of your brain half its current size? Which part would you choose to shrink, and what would the effects be?
4. Search the Internet for information about a worry gene. How would you evaluate research on such a gene, given what you have read so far in this book? What (if anything) would the existence of such a gene mean for your well-being?
5. Do you know anyone who has experienced a brain-damaging event, such as a stroke or head injury? If you feel comfortable doing so, ask the person about the experience and the life changes it may have caused. Based on your interview, which areas of the individual's brain might have been affected?

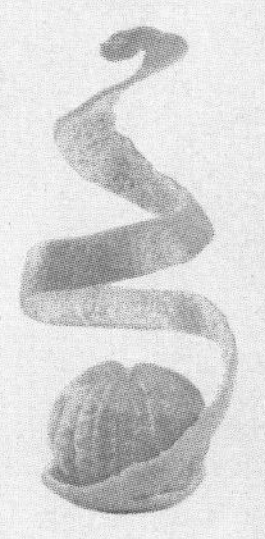

# CHAPTER 4

## CHAPTER OUTLINE

# Sensation and Perception

## A Sightseeing Bucket List

**Imagine that you found out you would lose your vision in a few months.** What sorts of sights would you savor? Thinking of all the wondrous sights in the world—the Grand Canyon, your loved ones' faces—which would you hope to lock into memory forever? Or consider finding out you would lose your sense of taste. What kinds of flavors would you seek out? What would end up on your sensation bucket list? At age 2, Cailee Herrell was diagnosed with *familial exudative vitreoretinopathy*, a rare genetic disorder that would slowly, inevitably rob her of vision (Pittman, 2016). When Cailee was 6 years old, her mother set out to give her images of the world she could savor even once she could no longer see. For Cailee, that meant a chance to see the Disney princesses as well as the beach. Cailee and her mother traveled the United States collecting up memories of all the amazing images in the world before she could no longer see them.

Our senses give us access to the world, with all of its delights and challenges. The things we see, hear, taste, and feel provide the raw ingredients of a lifetime of memories. And, through memory, we are able to conjure even sensory experiences that are no longer part of our world—the sight of our first puppy in our mind's eye or the sound of our grandmother's voice in our mind's ear. Our senses link us to the world, laying a foundation for our behavior and our mental life. ●

# PREVIEW

In this chapter we explore sensation and perception, the vital processes by which we connect with and function in the world. We first examine vision, the sense about which scientists know the most. We then investigate the nature of hearing, the skin senses, taste, smell, and the kinesthetic and vestibular senses. Finally, we trace the connections between our senses and health and wellness.

# 1. HOW WE SENSE AND PERCEIVE THE WORLD

Sensation and perception researchers come from a broad range of specialties, including *ophthalmology,* the study of the eye's structure, function, and diseases; *audiology,* the science of hearing; *neurology/neuroscience,* the study of the nervous system; and many others. To understand sensation and perception, we have to understand the physical properties of the objects of our perception–light, sound, texture, and so on. Psychologists approach these processes by studying the physical structures and functions of the sense organs, and the brain's conversion of information from these organs into experience.

## The Processes and Purposes of Sensation and Perception

Our world is alive with stimuli–everything that surrounds us. We do not actually experience these stimuli directly; rather, our senses allow us to get information about our environment, and we then take that information and form a perception of the world. Sensation and perception are intertwined but also separable. **Sensation** is the process of receiving stimulus energies from the external environment and transforming those energies into neural energy. **Perception** is the process of organizing and interpreting sensory information so that it makes sense. Sensation detects the raw materials of experience. Perception is the experience itself (what the brain does with those raw materials).

● **sensation** The process of receiving stimulus energies from the external environment and transforming those energies into neural energy.

● **perception** The process of organizing and interpreting sensory information so that it makes sense.

In sensation, specialized receptor cells in the sense organs–the eyes, ears, skin, nose, and tongue–detect physical energy, such as light, sound, and heat. When the receptor cells register a stimulus, the energy is converted to an electrochemical impulse that relays information about the stimulus through the nervous system to the brain (Ripp & others, 2018). When it reaches the brain, the information travels to the appropriate area of the cerebral cortex (Huang & others, 2018; Kundu & others, 2018). There, the brain produces perception. Receptor cells in our eyes detect a sleek silver object in the sky, but they do not "see" a jet plane. Recognizing that silver object as a plane is perception.

Our senses provide us with a unified experience of the world and they can affect each other. For instance, the shape and size of a cup can affect perceptions of the aroma and taste of the coffee in that cup (Carvalho & Spence, 2018). Sometimes our senses provide us with conflicting information. For example, the color of foods can create expectations about how those foods will taste (Zellner & others, 2018). Some foods do not taste the way one might expect. Children who have learned through experience with strawberries, cherries, and red candies to expect red food to taste sweet might be shocked when they first try red beets. Many contemporary chefs play with this idea, creating, for example, desserts that look like tacos or a bundle of asparagus. How does the brain respond when two senses produce conflicting information? To read about research examining this question, see the Intersection.

### BOTTOM-UP AND TOP-DOWN PROCESSING

● **bottom-up processing** The operation in sensation and perception in which sensory receptors register information about the external environment and send it up to the brain for interpretation.

Psychologists distinguish between bottom-up and top-down processing in sensation and perception. In **bottom-up processing**, sensory receptors register information about the external environment and send it up to the brain for interpretation. Bottom-up processing

## INTERSECTION

### Sensation and Neuroscience: How Does the Brain Respond when Senses Disagree?

Cross-modal conflict happens when two senses provide conflicting information. When sensory modalities match, cognitive processing is faster and more accurate than when our senses conflict (Hart & others, 2010). A recent study examined how the brain responds when unpleasant or delicious tastes were paired with images of sour or sweet foods. Participants first put sweet (sugar) or sour (a pure vitamin C tablet) substances on their tongues (Xiao & others, 2018). FMRI scanned their brains while they indicated, as quickly as possible, whether images of sweet (such as chocolate cake) or sour (such as a lemon) foods matched the flavor on their tongue. Prior to the scanning sessions, all participants agreed that the sugar was tasty and the vitamin C tablet was disgusting. On some trials, the taste on the tongue matched the visual image (for example, sweet flavor matched with ice cream or sour taste matched with a lemon). On other trials the taste and image conflicted: the sweet taste was paired with a sour image or the sour taste with a sweet image.

As in past research, participants were faster and more accurate at detecting sensory matches than mismatches. It took them longer to recognize that a sour taste did not match with ice cream, for instance.

How did the brain respond to mismatches in sensory information? Sour tastes paired with sweet (versus sour) images evoked greater activation in three specific brain areas (Xiao & others, 2018). First, the right middle frontal gyrus or MFG (an area that stretches from the front to the back of the middle of the frontal lobe) is known to be associated with controlling conflicting information. Activity in this area suggests the brain was working to make sense of the mismatched pair. Second, the lingual gyrus (located in the occipital lobe) is associated with vision and detecting novel information. This result suggests that the sour taste set up an expectation that was violated by the sweet images. Finally, the postcentral gyrus (the area we have reviewed as the somatosensory cortex behind the motor cortex) is an area of the brain associated with taste perception. It is possible that this area was more activated because of the contrast between the sour taste and the sweet images (like drinking orange juice after brushing your teeth).

(first) ©M. Unal Ozmen/Shutterstock; (second) ©Christian Jung/Shutterstock

Interestingly, the brain did not respond more strongly to sour images when sugar was on the tongue. Why? A first possibility is that sweet tastes can evoke positive emotions (Wang & Chen, 2018). Positive emotion, in turn, can increase cognitive flexibility (Nelson & Simm, 2014). Perhaps the feelings produced by the sweet taste allowed the brain to easily process the conflicting image. It is also possible that the lack of findings for sweet tastes shows a well-established bias in human information processing toward negative information (March, Gaertner, & Olson, 2018). Detecting threats is important for survival. Perhaps that bad taste was a stronger experience than the sweet one.

This study shows how brain imaging can help to illuminate the processes of sensation and perception. It tells us that not all sensory conflicts are equally problematic for the brain—bad tastes appear to concern the brain much more than good ones (Wabnegger, Schwab, & Schienle, 2018).

*If your favorite dessert was presented to look exactly like sushi, would you still like it?*

means taking in information and trying to make sense of it. In contrast, **top-down processing** starts with cognitive processing in the brain. In top-down processing, we begin with some sense of what is happening and apply that framework to incoming information (Brauchli & others, 2018; de Lange, Heilbron, & Kok, 2018).

- **top-down processing** The operation in sensation and perception, launched by cognitive processing at the brain's higher levels, that allows the organism to sense what is happening and to apply that framework to information from the world.

To understand the difference between bottom-up and top-down processing, think about how you experience a song you have never heard before versus that same song when you have heard it many times (Figure 1). The first time you hear the song, you listen carefully to get a "feel" for it. That is bottom-up processing: taking the incoming information of the music and relying on that external experience. Once you have a good feel for the song, you listen to it in a different way. You have expectations and know what comes next. That is top-down processing. You might even sing along with the song when it comes on the radio or is played at a club. In top-down processing, we start with an idea of what a particular stimulus is; in bottom-up processing we piece together information to make that idea.

**FIGURE 1 Top-Down and Bottom-Up Processes in Perception** When you listen to a song for the first time, bottom-up processing allows you to get a feel for the tune. Once you know the song well, you can create a perceptual experience in your mind's ear by "playing" it in your head. That's top-down processing.

Top-Down Processing
Thinking about the music...
...creates a perceptual experience in the mind's ear.
...that the brain interprets as music.
Taking in the sounds...
Bottom-Up Processing

Top-down processing can happen even in the absence of any stimulus at all. You can experience top-down processing by "listening" to your favorite song in your head. As you "hear" the song in your mind's ear, you are engaged in a perceptual experience produced by top-down processing.

Bottom-up and top-down processing work together to allow us to function. For example, by themselves our ears provide only incoming information about sound in the environment. Only when we consider both what the ears hear (bottom-up processing) and what the brain interprets (top-down processing) can we fully understand sound perception. In fact, in everyday life, the two processes of sensation and perception are essentially inseparable. So, sensation and perception operate as a unified information-processing system (Xiao & others, 2018).

Have you ever begged a friend to listen to try your favorite food, only to be disappointed when he or she reacted to it with a shrug? If so, you might note that although both tongues register the same information, perception is a *subjective* interpretation of that information. Check out the Psychological Inquiry feature for further perspective on the difference between sensation and perception.

*Most predatory animals have eyes at the front of their face; most animals that are prey have eyes on the sides of their head. Through these adaptations, predators perceive their prey accurately, and prey gain a measure of safety from their panoramic view of their environment. Which of these creatures is trying to avoid being the other's lunch?*

(first) ©Ondrej Prosicky/Shutterstock; (second) ©Drew Horne/Shutterstock

## THE PURPOSE OF SENSATION AND PERCEPTION

From an evolutionary perspective, the purpose of sensation and perception is adaptation that improves a species' chances for survival. An organism must be able to sense and respond quickly and accurately to events in the environment, such as the approach of a predator, the presence of prey, or the appearance of a potential mate.

Not surprisingly, therefore, most animals–from goldfish to gorillas to humans–have eyes, ears, and sensitivities to touch and chemicals. A close comparison of sensory systems in animals reveals that each species is exquisitely adapted to the habitat in which it evolved. Animals that are primarily predators (such as owls and hawks) generally have their eyes at the front of their face so that they can perceive their prey. In contrast, animals that are more likely to be someone else's lunch (such as rabbits and elk) have their eyes on the sides of their head, giving them a wide view of their surroundings at all times.

The crucial role of the senses in survival is reflected in the beautiful match between those survival needs and an animal's sense organs. A shark relies so heavily on the sense of smell to detect prey that two-thirds of its brain is wired for smell. An albatross must detect the smell of its prey beneath the surface of water. To accomplish this feat, this waterfowl has a very large nose at the top of its beak allowing it to capture food even in the dark. Look in a mirror and consider the evidence you find there of the important ways that humans' sense organs are adapted for survival.

## psychological *inquiry*

Source: Library of Congress [LC-DIG-ds-00175]

### *Old Woman or Young Woman?*

Study the illustration and analyze your perceptions by answering these questions.

1. What do you see? If you see an old woman, can you see a young woman as well? (*Hint:* The old woman's nose is the young woman's jawline.) If you see a young woman, can you see an old woman as well? (*Hint:* The young woman's chin is the tip of the old woman's nose.)
2. How many pictures do you sense visually in the illustration? Notice that for each of *two* possible perceptions, just *one image* is sensed.
3. What do you think determined your first response to this picture? Explain.

## Sensory Receptors and the Brain

Sensation begins with **sensory receptors**, specialized cells that detect stimuli and transmit information to sensory (*afferent*) nerves. Afferent nerves bring information to the brain from the world. Sensory receptors are the openings through which the brain and nervous system experience the world. Figure 2 shows the human sensory receptors for vision, hearing, touch, smell, and taste.

● **sensory receptors** Specialized cells that detect stimulus information and transmit it to sensory (afferent) nerves and the brain.

Figure 3 shows the flow of information from the environment to the brain. As you can see, perception involves three steps. Energy from the environment triggers sensory

| | Vision | Hearing | Touch | Smell | Taste |
|---|---|---|---|---|---|
| Sensory Receptor Cells | 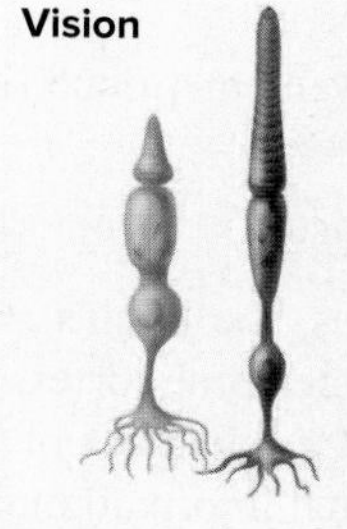 | 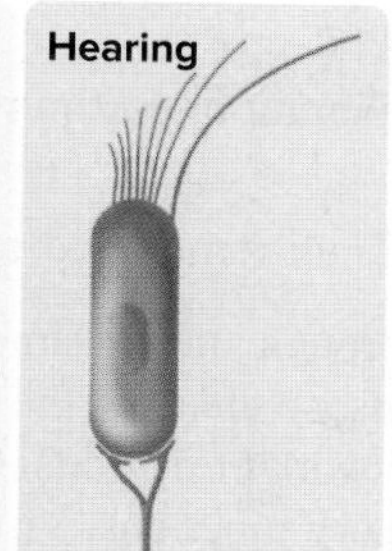 |  | 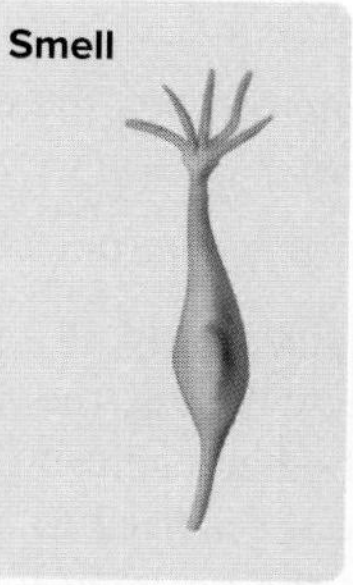 | 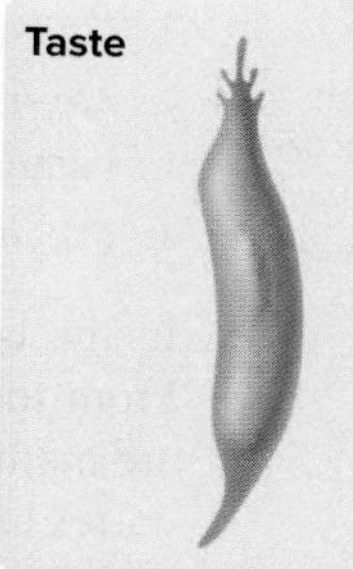 |
| Type of Energy Reception | Photoreception: detection of light, perceived as sight | Mechano-reception: detection of vibration, perceived as hearing | Mechano-reception: detection of pressure, perceived as touch | Chemoreception: detection of chemical stimuli, perceived as smell | Chemoreception: detection of chemical stimuli, perceived as taste |
| Sense Organ |  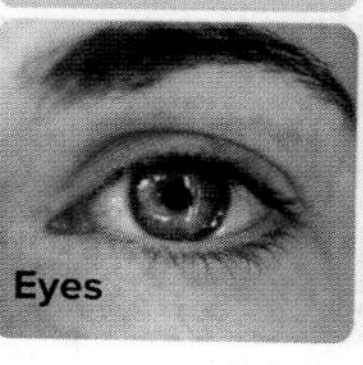 Eyes | Ears | 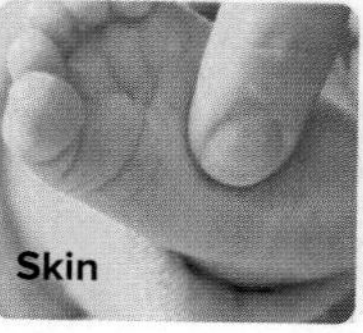 Skin |  Nose |   Tong |

**FIGURE 2 Human Senses: Organs, Energy Stimuli, and Sensory Receptors** The receptor cells for each sense are specialized to receive particular types of energy stimuli. (eye) ©Barbara Penoyar/Getty Images; (ear) ©Geoff du Feu/Alamy Stock Photo; (skin) ©McGraw-Hill Education/Jill Braaten, photographer; (nose) ©ZenShui/Sigrid Olsson/Getty Images; (tongue) ©fStop Images GmbH/Alamy Stock Photo

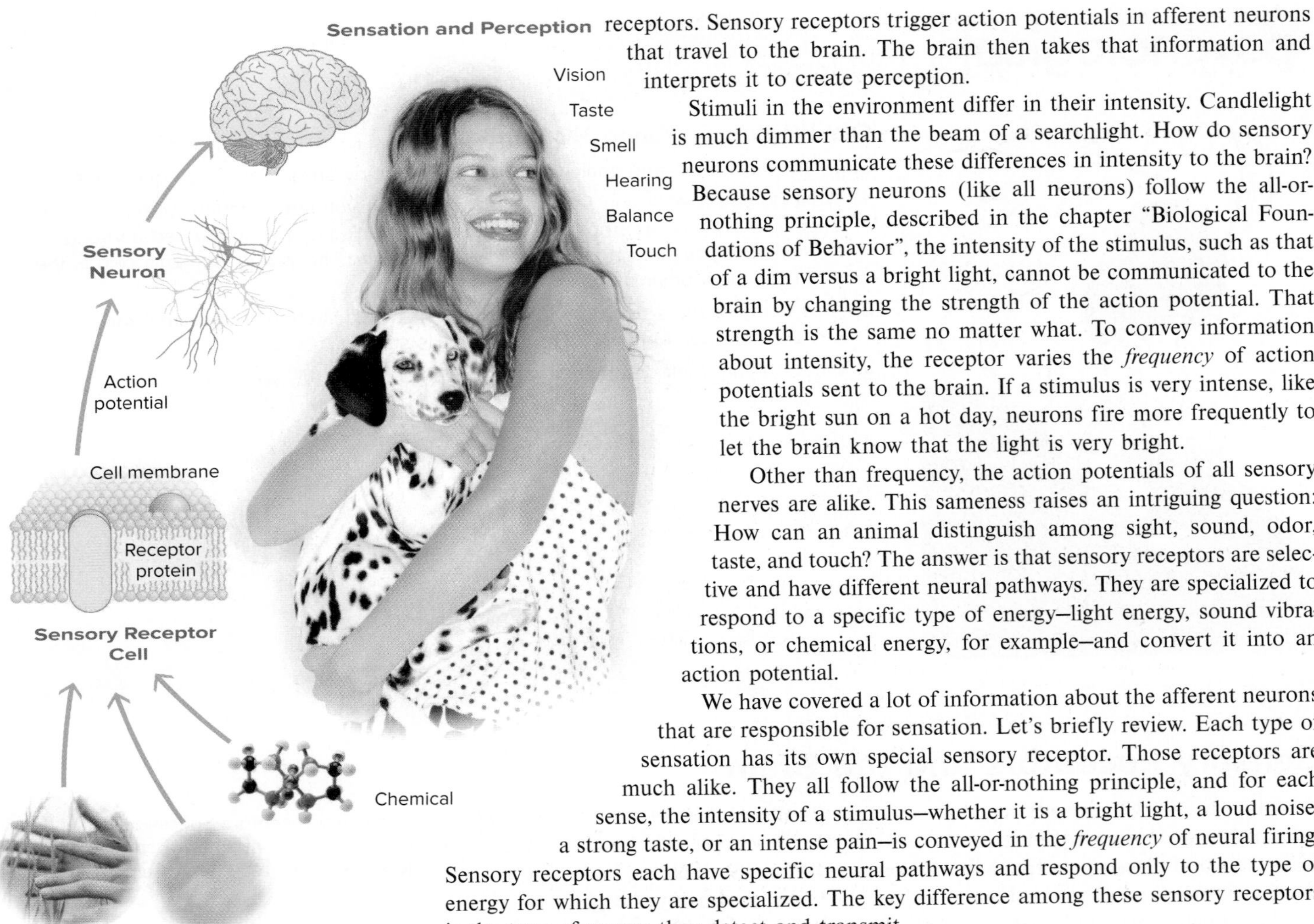


**FIGURE 3 Information Flow in Senses** The diagram shows a general flow of sensory information from energy stimulus to sensory receptor cell to sensory neuron to sensation and perception. (girl) ©Stockbyte/PunchStock; (hands) ©Brand X Pictures/Getty Images; (chemical) ©AndrUa/Shutterstock

receptors. Sensory receptors trigger action potentials in afferent neurons that travel to the brain. The brain then takes that information and interprets it to create perception.

Stimuli in the environment differ in their intensity. Candlelight is much dimmer than the beam of a searchlight. How do sensory neurons communicate these differences in intensity to the brain? Because sensory neurons (like all neurons) follow the all-or-nothing principle, described in the chapter "Biological Foundations of Behavior", the intensity of the stimulus, such as that of a dim versus a bright light, cannot be communicated to the brain by changing the strength of the action potential. That strength is the same no matter what. To convey information about intensity, the receptor varies the *frequency* of action potentials sent to the brain. If a stimulus is very intense, like the bright sun on a hot day, neurons fire more frequently to let the brain know that the light is very bright.

Other than frequency, the action potentials of all sensory nerves are alike. This sameness raises an intriguing question: How can an animal distinguish among sight, sound, odor, taste, and touch? The answer is that sensory receptors are selective and have different neural pathways. They are specialized to respond to a specific type of energy—light energy, sound vibrations, or chemical energy, for example—and convert it into an action potential.

We have covered a lot of information about the afferent neurons that are responsible for sensation. Let's briefly review. Each type of sensation has its own special sensory receptor. Those receptors are much alike. They all follow the all-or-nothing principle, and for each sense, the intensity of a stimulus—whether it is a bright light, a loud noise, a strong taste, or an intense pain—is conveyed in the *frequency* of neural firing. Sensory receptors each have specific neural pathways and respond only to the type of energy for which they are specialized. The key difference among these sensory receptors is the type of energy they detect and transmit.

Sensation involves detecting and transmitting information about different kinds of energy. The sense organs and sensory receptors fall into classes based on the type of energy that is detected, including

- *Photoreception:* detection of light (sight)
- *Mechanoreception:* detection of pressure, vibration, and movement (touch, hearing, balance)
- *Chemoreception:* detection of chemical stimuli (smell and taste)

In the brain, nearly all sensory signals go through the thalamus, the brain's relay station. From the thalamus, the signals go to the sensory areas of the cerebral cortex, where they are modified and spread throughout a vast network of neurons. Certain areas of the cerebral cortex are specialized to handle different sensory functions. Visual information is processed mainly in the occipital lobes (the back of the hemispheres); hearing in the temporal lobes (the areas around your ears); and pain, touch, and temperature in the parietal lobes (the top of the brain). Keep in mind, however, that the interactions and pathways of sensory information are complex, and the brain often must coordinate extensive information and interpret it. So, afferent neurons for each sense detect the type of energy that neuron is specialized to detect. Then, the information is typically sent to the thalamus and from there to the relevant area of the brain. In the brain, this information is integrated with many other impulses to create experience (Kim & Frank, 2018).

The process of sensation and perception is complex but elegant, with each type of afferent neuron responding to its particular type of energy and engaging corresponding brain processes. There are rare cases, however, in which the senses can become confused. The term *synaesthesia* describes an experience in which one sense (say, sight) induces an experience in another sense (say, hearing) (Ward & others, 2018). For example, a person might "see" music or "taste" a color. One woman was able to taste sounds, so that a piece of music, to her, tasted like tuna fish (Beeli, Esslen, & Jäncke, 2005). Neuroscientists are exploring the neurological bases of synaesthesia, especially in the connections among the various sensory regions of the cerebral cortex (Curwen, 2018; Ward, Schnakenberg, & Banissy, 2018).

*Phantom limb pain* is another example of confused senses. Among individuals who have lost an arm or a leg, as many as 80 percent of them report alarming and puzzling pain in the amputated limb (Fuchs, Flor, & Bekrater-Bodmann, 2018). Although the limb that contains the sensory receptors is gone, the areas of the brain and nervous system that received information from those receptors are still there, causing confusion (Andoh & others, 2018; Collins & others, 2018; Kikkert & others, 2018; Philip & others, 2017).

In one treatment for phantom limb pain, individuals place a mirror in front of their existing limb and move the limb around while watching the mirror. For example, if a person's left leg has been amputated, the mirror is placed so that the right leg is seen moving in the mirror where the left leg would be if it had not been amputated. Similar types of treatment include having people "see" their missing limb using virtual reality glasses (Ambron & others, 2018) or on a TV screen (De Nunzio, Farina, & Falla, 2017). These procedures seem to trick the brain into perceiving the missing limb as still there, allowing it to make sense of incoming sensation (Griffin & others, 2017). Such treatments are still being studied and their effectiveness is still being evaluated (Collins & others, 2018). However, note that the very existence of these therapies demonstrates how our senses cooperate to produce experience—how the bottom-up processes (the incoming messages from the missing limb) and the top-down processes (the brain's efforts to make sense of these messages) work together.

The principles you have read about so far apply to all of the senses. The senses are about detecting different energies. They all have specialized receptor cells and areas of the brain that serve their functions. You have probably heard about a "sixth" sense—*extrasensory perception,* or *ESP.* ESP means that a person can detect information from the world without receiving concrete sensory input—like reading someone's mind or sensing future events. Do human beings have a sixth sense? Although some psychologists remain open to the possibility (Schooler, Baumgart, & Franklin, 2018), most psychologists answer that question with a resounding "No" (Fiedler & Krueger, 2013; R. Hyman, 2010; Rouder, Morey, & Province, 2013). Consider ESP in the context of the processes we have discussed. What is the afferent neuron for ESP, and what sort of energy conveys these messages? The success of gambling casinos, daily experiences with surprise, and scientific evidence (Barušs & Rabier, 2014; Rabeyron, 2014) suggest that there is, in fact, no "Sixth Sense."

## Thresholds

Any sensory system must be able to detect varying degrees of energy in the form of light, sound, chemical, or mechanical stimulation. How much of a stimulus is necessary for you to see, hear, taste, smell, or feel something? How low can the stimulation go and still be detected?

### ABSOLUTE THRESHOLD

One way to think about the lowest limits of perception is to assume that there is an **absolute threshold**, or minimum amount of stimulus energy that a person can detect (Kellen & Klauer, 2018). When the energy of a stimulus falls below this absolute threshold, we cannot detect it; when the energy of the stimulus rises above the absolute threshold, we can detect it. As an example, find a clock that ticks; put it on a table and walk far enough away that you no longer hear it. Then gradually move toward the clock. At some point, you will begin to hear it ticking. Hold your position and notice that occasionally the ticking fades, and you may have to move forward to reach the threshold; at other times, it may become loud, and you can move backward.

• **absolute threshold** The minimum amount of stimulus energy that a person can detect.

In this experiment, if you measure your absolute threshold several times, you likely will record several different distances for detecting the ticking. The first time you try it,

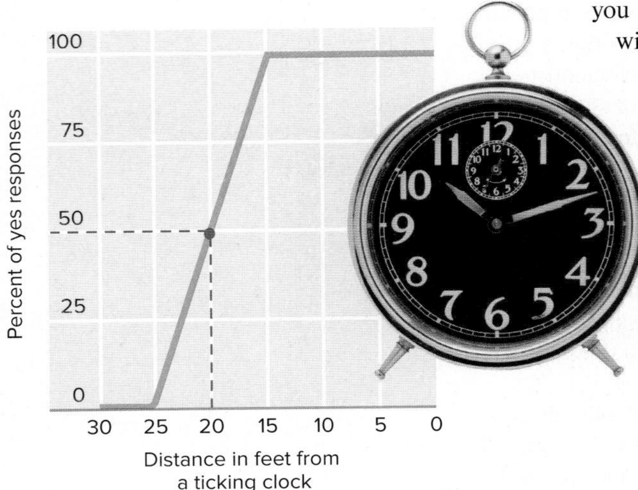

100
75
50
25
0
Percent of yes responses
30 25 20 15 10 5 0
Distance in feet from a ticking clock

**FIGURE 4** **Measuring Absolute Threshold** Absolute threshold is the minimum amount of energy we can detect. To measure absolute threshold, psychologists have arbitrarily decided to use the criterion of detecting the stimulus 50 percent of the time. In this graph, the person's absolute threshold for detecting the ticking clock is at a distance of 20 feet. ©Yuri Kevhiev/Alamy Stock Photo

you might hear the ticking at 25 feet from the clock. However, you probably will not hear it every time at 25 feet. Maybe you hear it only 38 percent of the time at this distance, but you hear it 50 percent of the time at 20 feet away and 65 percent of the time at 15 feet. Figure 4 shows one person's measured absolute threshold for detecting a clock's ticking. Psychologists have arbitrarily decided that the absolute threshold is the point at which the individual detects the stimulus 50 percent of the time—in this case, 20 feet away. Using the same clock, different person might have different thresholds.

People have different thresholds. Some have better hearing than others, and some have better vision. Figure 5 lists the approximate absolute thresholds of five senses.

Under ideal circumstances, our senses have very low absolute thresholds, so we can be very good at detecting small amounts of stimulus energy. You might be surprised to learn that the human eye can see a candle flame at 30 miles on a dark, clear night. However, our environment seldom gives us ideal conditions with which to detect stimuli. If the night were cloudy, for example, you would have to be closer to see the flame. In addition, other lights on the horizon—car or house lights—would hinder your ability to detect the candle's flicker. **Noise** is the term given to irrelevant and competing stimuli—not just sounds but any distracting stimuli (Gregory, 2015; van Ede & others, 2018). In perception, any stimulus that interferes with the perception of another is considered noise—whether it is the din of a crowded restaurant drowning out a conversation, or the bright lights of big city drowning out the lights of distant stars.

- **noise** Irrelevant and competing stimuli—not only sounds but also any distracting stimuli for the senses.

## DIFFERENCE THRESHOLD

Psychologists also investigate the degree of *difference* that must exist between two stimuli before the difference is detected. This is the **difference threshold**, or *just noticeable difference* (Jakhetiya & others, 2018; Kellen & Klauer, 2018). An artist might detect the difference between two similar shades of color. A fashion designer might notice a difference in the texture of two fabrics. How different must the colors and textures be for someone to say, "These are different"? Like the absolute threshold, the difference threshold is the smallest difference in stimulation required to discriminate one stimulus from another 50 percent of the time.

- **difference threshold** The degree of difference that must exist between two stimuli before the difference is detected.

What determines whether we can detect the difference between two stimuli? Difference thresholds increase as a stimulus becomes stronger. That means that at very low levels of stimulation, small changes can be detected, but at very high levels, small changes are less noticeable. If you are carrying one heavy book in your backpack, you might notice the

**Vision** A candle flame at 30 miles on a dark, clear night
**Hearing** A ticking clock at 20 feet under quiet conditions
**Smell** One drop of perfume diffused throughout three rooms
**Taste** A teaspoon of sugar in 2 gallons of water
**Touch** The wing of a fly falling on your neck from a distance of 1 centimeter

**FIGURE 5** **Approximate Absolute Thresholds for Five Senses** These thresholds show the amazing power of our senses to detect even very slight variations in the environment. ©Image Source Plus/Alamy Stock Photo

addition of a smaller volume. But, if you are carrying two heavy books, you might not even notice the additional weight of that slim volume.

E. H. Weber made an important discovery about the difference threshold more than 150 years ago. **Weber's law** is the principle that two stimuli must differ by a constant proportion to be perceived as different. For example, we add 1 candle to 20 candles and notice a difference in the brightness of the candles; we add 1 candle to 120 candles and do not notice a difference, but we would notice the difference if we added 6 candles to 120 candles. Although there are some exceptions to the rule (Löwenkamp & others, 2015), Weber's law generally holds true (Anobile & others, 2015).

● **Weber's law** The principle that two stimuli must differ by a constant minimum percentage (rather than a constant amount) to be perceived as different.

### SUBLIMINAL PERCEPTION

Can sensations that occur below our absolute threshold affect us without our being aware of them? **Subliminal perception** refers to the detection of information below the level of conscious awareness. In 1957, James Vicary, an advertising executive, announced that he was able to increase popcorn and soft drink sales by secretly flashing the words "EAT POPCORN" and "DRINK COKE" on a movie screen in a local theater (Weir, 1984). Vicary's claims were a hoax, but people have continued to wonder whether behavior can be influenced by stimuli that are presented so quickly that we cannot perceive them. The brain responds to information that is presented below the conscious threshold (Hudac, 2018; Sperdin & others, 2015) and such information can influence behavior, although often very weakly (Weingarten & others, 2016).

● **subliminal perception** The detection of information below the level of conscious awareness.

In one experiment, researchers asked participants to come to the study having not had anything to drink for at least three hours prior (Strahan, Spencer, & Zanna, 2002). The participants were randomly assigned to words related to being thirsty (such as *dry* and *thirst*) or words unrelated to thirst (such as *won* and *pirate*) flashed on a computer screen for 16 milliseconds while they performed an unrelated task. None of the participants reported seeing the flashed words. After this subliminal exposure to thirst or non-thirst words, participants were allowed to drink a beverage. When given a chance to drink afterward, those who had seen thirst-related words drank more. The Psychological Inquiry feature explores the results of the study.

The notion that stimuli we do not consciously perceive can influence our behavior challenges the usefulness of the idea of thresholds. If stimuli that fall below the threshold can have an impact on us, what do thresholds really tell us? Further, the definition of absolute threshold is not absolute. It refers to the intensity of stimulation detected *50 percent of the time*. How can something absolute change from one trial to the next?

If you tried the ticking clock experiment described earlier, you might have found yourself making judgment calls. Sometimes you felt very sure you could hear the clock, but other times you were uncertain and probably took a guess. Sometimes you guessed right, and other times you were mistaken. Now, imagine that someone offered to pay you $50 for every correct answer you gave–would that incentive change your judgments? Alternatively, what if you were charged $50 for every time you said you heard the clock and it was not ticking? Perception is often about making such judgment calls.

An alternative approach to the question of whether a stimulus is detected acknowledges the *decision* that is involved in saying (or not saying) "Yes, I hear that ticking." This approach is called signal detection theory.

## Signal Detection Theory

**Signal detection theory** focuses on decision making about stimuli under conditions of uncertainty. In signal detection theory, detection of sensory stimuli depends on a variety of factors besides the physical intensity of the stimulus and the sensory abilities of the person (Kellen & Klauer, 2018). These factors include individual and contextual variations such as fatigue, expectations, and the urgency of the moment.

● **signal detection theory** An approach to perception that focuses on decision making about stimuli under conditions of uncertainty.

To grasp how signal detection theory works, consider this scenario. Your cousin is getting married in a week, and you are looking for someone to accompany you to the wedding. Studying at the library, you see a potential candidate, someone with whom you have exchanged

## psychological *inquiry*

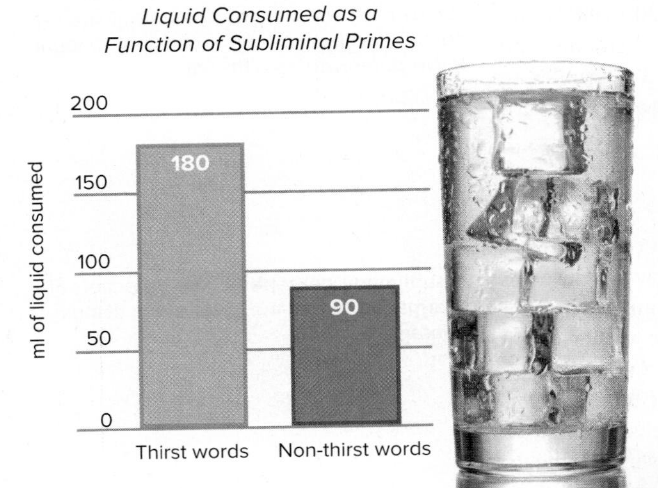


Source: Strahan, Spencer, & Zanna (2002); ©Africa Studio/Shutterstock

### *Subliminal Perception: Working Up a Thirst*

This graph is adapted from the results of the study by Erin Strahan, Steven Spencer, and Mark Zanna (2002) described in the text. The dependent variable is represented on the vertical, or Y, axis. The columns represent the results of the study for each of the two groups—those who were exposed to "thirst words" and those who saw "non-thirst words." Answer the following questions.

1. What was the independent variable in this study? Explain.
2. Which group would be considered the experimental group? Which is the control group?
3. Why were the participants randomly assigned to conditions?

glances before. Now you face a decision: Should you ask this person out? Is the signal present (that is, is the person a good date for the wedding)? You scan your library acquaintance for indications of availability (no wedding or engagement ring) and interest (didn't he or she smile at you as you passed by earlier?). You consider other information as well: Do you find the person attractive? Does he or she seem friendly? Based on these factors, you decide that (1) yes, you will ask the person to the wedding (because you have determined that the signal is present) or (2) no, you will keep looking (the signal is not present). These decisions might be correct or incorrect, leading to four possible outcomes (Figure 6):

- Hit: You ask, and he or she says yes.
- Miss: He or she would have said yes, but you do not ask.
- False alarm: You think the individual seemed interested, but your offer is politely declined–ouch.
- Correct rejection: You do not ask the person out, and he or she would have said no–phew.

Decision making in signal detection theory has two main components: information acquisition and criterion. *Information acquisition* refers to the gathering of relevant indicators. *Criterion* refers to the standards that will be used to make a decision. In terms of information acquisition, for our example, the questions might be "What information is your potential date communicating? Is the person available? Attractive?" and so on. The criterion component of signal detection theory is the basis for making a judgment from the available information. The criterion is the decision maker's assessment of the stakes involved in each possible outcome. Is a miss (not asking out someone who would have said yes) or a false alarm (getting turned down) a worse outcome? Is getting a "hit" worth surviving some false alarms? So, in addition to relying on the characteristics of your potential wedding date, you might also be feeling desperate, because your family is always giving you a hard time about never having a date. Maybe getting a lot of rejections (false alarms) is not as bad as missing an opportunity to keep them quiet. Alternatively, you may feel that rejections are just too upsetting and prefer to experience "misses" even if it means going stag to your cousin's wedding.

| | Observer's Response | |
|---|---|---|
| | *"Yes, I see the signal."* | *"No, I don't see the signal."* |
| **Signal Present** | Hit (correct) | Miss (mistake) |
| **Signal Absent** | False alarm (mistake) | Correct rejection (correct) |

**FIGURE 6 Four Outcomes in Signal Detection** Signal detection research helps to explain when and how perceptual judgments are correct or mistaken.

Let's return now to the domain of sensation and perception. Can you see how signal detection theory might provide a way to examine the processes that underlie our judgments about whether we perceive a stimulus or not? By presenting stimuli of varying intensities (and trials when no stimulus is presented), and asking a participant to report on his or her detection of the sound or sight of interest, a researcher can use signal detection theory to understand the data. Importantly, signal detection theory allows us to consider the mistakes a perceiver might make—and the reasons behind those errors.

## Perceiving Sensory Stimuli

As we just saw, perception of stimuli is influenced by more than the characteristics of the environmental stimuli themselves. Two important factors in perceiving sensory stimuli are attention and perceptual set.

### ATTENTION

**Attention** is the process of focusing awareness on a narrow aspect of the environment. The world holds a lot of information to perceive. At this moment you are perceiving the letters and words that make up this sentence. Now gaze around you and fix your eyes on something else. Then, curl up the toes on your right foot. In each of these activities, you engaged in **selective attention**, which involves focusing on a specific aspect of experience while ignoring others. A familiar example of selective attention is the ability to concentrate on one voice among many in a noisy crowd. Psychologists call this common occurrence the *cocktail party effect* (Kuyper, 1972).

● **attention** The process of focusing awareness on a narrow aspect of the environment.

● **selective attention** The act of focusing on a specific aspect of experience while ignoring others.

Highly practiced and familiar stimuli, like your own name and hometown, often are perceived so automatically that it is almost impossible to ignore them. The *Stroop effect,* named for John Ridley Stroop (1935), who first showed the effect, refers to the way that automatically reading a color name can make it difficult to name the color in which the word is printed. To experience the Stroop effect, see Figure 7. Most of the time, the highly practiced and almost automatic perception of word meaning makes reading easier. However, this automaticity makes it hard to ignore the meaning of the words for colors (such as *blue*) when they are printed in a different color (such as orange). Thus, the Stroop effect represents a failure of selective attention.

Attention is not only selective but also is *shiftable*. For example, you might be paying close attention to your instructor's lecture, but if the person next to you starts texting, you might look to see what is going on over there. The fact that we can attend selectively

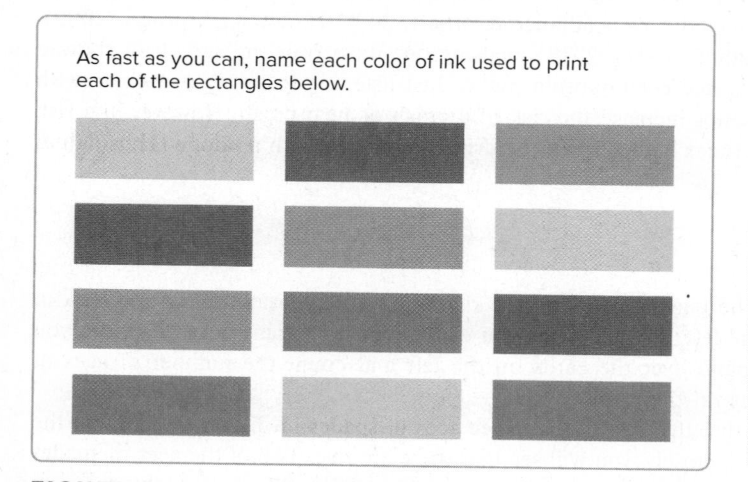

As fast as you can, name each color of ink used to print each of the rectangles below.


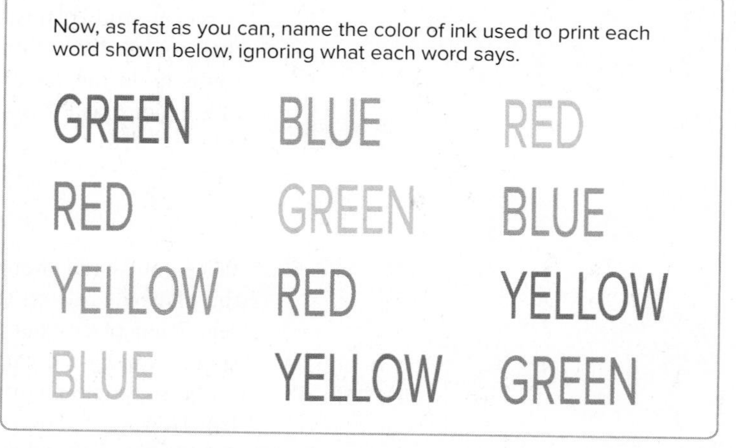

Now, as fast as you can, name the color of ink used to print each word shown below, ignoring what each word says.
GREEN BLUE RED
RED GREEN BLUE
YELLOW RED YELLOW
BLUE YELLOW GREEN


**FIGURE 7** **The Stroop Effect** Before reading further, read the instructions above and complete the tasks. You probably had little or no difficulty naming the colors of the rectangles in the set on the left. However, you likely stumbled more when you were asked to name the color of ink used to print each word in the set on the right. This automaticity in perception is the Stroop effect. Source: Stroop (1935).

to one stimulus and shift readily to another indicates that we must be monitoring many things at once.

Certain features of stimuli draw attention to them (Cunningham & Egeth, 2018). *Novel stimuli* (those that are new, different, or unusual) often attract our attention. *Size, color, and movement* also influence our attention; we are more likely to attend to large, vividly colored, or moving stimuli than to things that are small, dull-colored, or stationary. In addition, *emotional stimuli* can influence attention and therefore perception.

In the case of emotional stimuli, here is how the process works. An emotionally laden stimulus, such as the word *torture,* captures our attention. As a result, we are often quicker and more accurate at identifying an emotional stimulus than a neutral one. This advantage for emotional stimuli may come at a cost to other stimuli we experience. The term *emotion-induced blindness* refers to the fact that when we encounter an emotionally charged stimulus, we often fail to recognize a stimulus that is presented immediately after it (Kennedy & Most, 2015; Zhao & Most, 2018). Imagine that you are driving along a highway, and an ambulance, with sirens screaming and lights flashing, whizzes by. You might not notice the other cars around you or a road sign because you are preoccupied by the ambulance.

Sometimes, especially if our attention is otherwise occupied, we miss even very interesting stimuli. *Inattentional blindness* refers to the failure to detect unexpected events when our attention is engaged by a task. For instance, when we are focusing intently on a task, such as finding a seat in a packed movie theater, we might not detect an unexpected stimulus such as a friend waving to us in the crowd.

Researchers Daniel Simons and Christopher Chabris (1999) found a striking example of inattentional blindness. They asked participants to watch a video of two teams playing basketball. Participants were instructed to closely count the number of passes thrown by each team. During the video, a small woman dressed in a gorilla suit walked through the action and was clearly visible for five seconds. Surprisingly, over half of the participants (who were apparently deeply engaged in the counting task) never noticed the "gorilla." When they later saw the video without having to count passes, many of the participants could not believe they had missed a gorilla in their midst (Chabris & Simons, 2010). Inattentional blindness is more likely to occur when a task is difficult and occupying (Macdonald & Lavie, 2008; Murphy & Greene, 2015) and when the distracting stimulus is very different from stimuli that are relevant to the task at hand (Wiemer, Gerdes, & Pauli, 2013).

Emotion-induced blindness and inattentional blindness have important implications for driving safety. Engaging in a task such as talking on a phone or sending text messages can so occupy attention that little is left over for the important task of piloting a motor vehicle. In a fascinating study, cameras continuously observed drivers for more than 6 million miles of driving. The results showed that texting drew the drivers' eyes away from the road long enough for the vehicle to travel the length of a football field at 55 miles an hour. Individuals who texted others while driving faced 23 times the risk of a crash or near-crash compared with nondistracted drivers (Blanco & others, 2009; Hanowski & others, 2009). A recent study (Huisingh & others, 2018) focusing on adults over the age of 70 showed that not all distractions were equally problematic. Just listening to music or talking with someone in the car did not increase the risk of a crash or near crash. However, the risk of a major crash was 4 times higher when the driver interacted with a phone (Huisingh & others, 2018).

## PERCEPTUAL SET

Place your hand over the playing cards on the right in the illustration below and look at the playing cards on the left. As quickly as you can, count how many aces of spades you see. Then place your hand over the cards on the left and count the number of aces of spades among the cards on the right.

Most people report that they see two or three aces of spades in the set of cards on the left. However, if you look closely, you will see that there are five. Two of the aces of spades are black and three are red. When people look at the set of cards on the right, they are more likely to count five aces of spades. Why do we perceive the two sets of cards differently? We expect the ace of spades to be black because it is always black in a regular deck

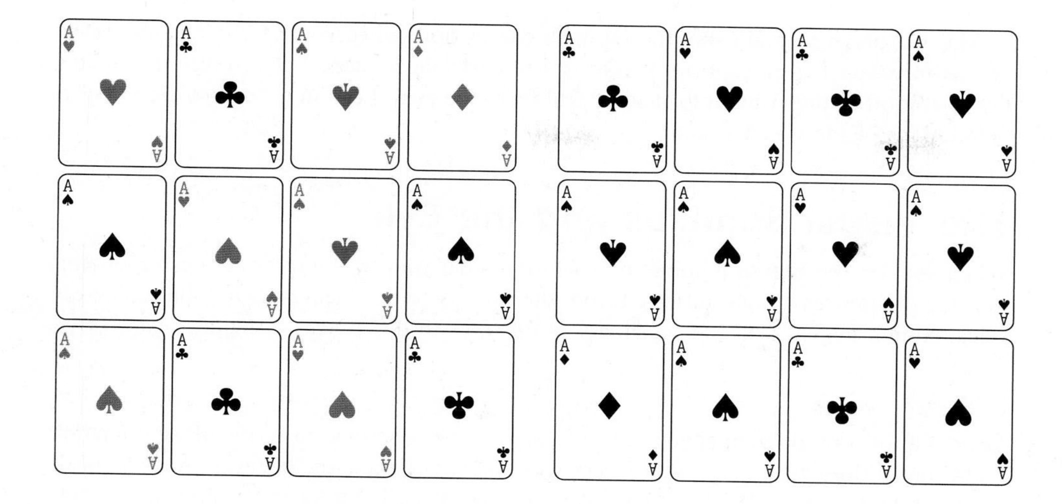

of cards. We do not expect red spades, so we skip right over the red ones: Expectations influence perceptions.

Psychologists refer to a predisposition or readiness to perceive something in a particular way as a **perceptual set**. Perceptual sets, which reflect top-down influences on perception, act as psychological filters in processing information about the environment (Jones, Crozier, & Strange, 2017). Interestingly, young children are more accurate than adults at the task involving the ace of spades because they have not built up the perceptual set that the ace of spades is black.

● **perceptual set** A predisposition or readiness to perceive something in a particular way.

## Sensory Adaptation

Turning out the lights in your bedroom at night, you stumble across the room to your bed, blind to the objects around you. Gradually the objects become clearer. The ability of the visual system to adjust to a darkened room is an example of **sensory adaptation**—a change in the responsiveness of the sensory system based on the average level of surrounding stimulation.

● **sensory adaptation** A change in the responsiveness of the sensory system based on the average level of surrounding stimulation.

You have experienced sensory adaptation countless times. For example, you adjust to the water in an initially "freezing" swimming pool. You turn on your windshield wipers while driving in the rain, and shortly you are unaware of their rhythmic sweeping back and forth. You enter a room and are at first bothered by the air conditioner's hum, but after a while you get used to it. All of these experiences represent sensory adaptation.

In the example of adapting to the dark, when you turn out the lights, everything at first is black. Conversely, when you step out into the bright sunshine after spending time in a dark basement, light floods your eyes and everything appears light. These momentary blips in sensation arise because adaptation takes time.

### test yourself

1. What are sensation and perception? How are they linked?
2. Compare and contrast top-down and bottom-up processing.
3. What is meant by the terms *absolute threshold* and *difference threshold?* What is *subliminal perception?*

# 2. THE VISUAL SYSTEM

When Michael May was 3 years old, an accident left him visually impaired, with only the ability to perceive the difference between night and day. His life was rich. He married, had kids, founded a successful company, and became an expert skier. Twenty-five years passed before doctors transplanted stem cells into May's right eye, giving him partial sight (Kurson, 2007). After the operation, May could see; his right eye is functional, allowing him to detect color and negotiate the world without using a cane or relying on his guide dog. His visual experience remains unusual, though, even more than 10 years after the operation (Huber & others, 2015). May sees the world as an abstract painting. He can catch a ball thrown to him by his sons, but he cannot recognize his wife's face. His brain has to work at interpreting the new information that his right eye is providing.

May's experience highlights the intimate connection between the brain and the sense organs in producing perception. Vision is a remarkable process that involves the brain's interpretation of the visual information sent from the eyes. Let's now explore the physical foundations of the visual system.

## The Visual Stimulus and the Eye

When you see the beautiful colors of a fall day, what your eyes and brain are responding to is the differences in light reflected from the various colorful leaves. Our ability to detect visual stimuli depends on the sensitivity of our eyes to differences in light.

### LIGHT

*Light* is a form of electromagnetic energy that can be described in terms of wavelengths. Light travels through space in waves. The *wavelength* of light is the distance from the peak of one wave to the peak of the next. Wavelengths of visible light range from about 400 to 700 nanometers (a nanometer is 1 billionth of a meter and is abbreviated nm). The wavelength of light that is reflected from a stimulus determines its *hue* or color.

Outside the range of visible light are longer radio and infrared radiation waves and shorter ultraviolet and X rays (Figure 8). These other forms of electromagnetic energy continually bombard us, but we do not see them.

We can also describe waves of light in terms of their height, or *amplitude.* The amplitude of the wavelength determines the *brightness* of the stimulus (Figure 9). Finally, the *purity* of the wavelengths—whether they are all the same or a mix of waves—determines the perceived *saturation,* or richness, of a visual stimulus. The color tree shown in Figure 10 can help you to understand saturation. Colors that are very pure have no white light in

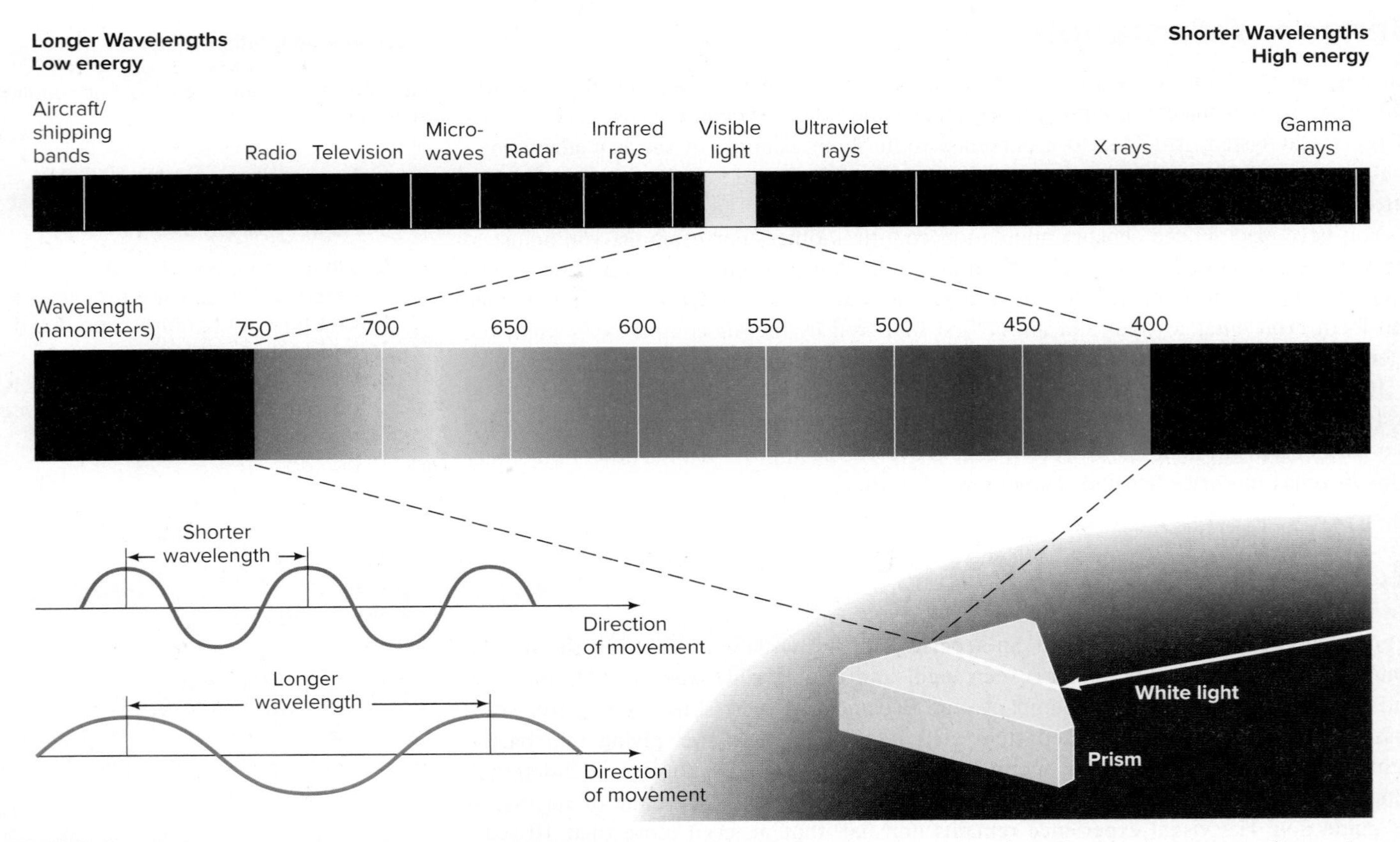


**FIGURE 8 The Electromagnetic Spectrum and Visible Light** (*top*) Visible light is only a narrow band in the electromagnetic spectrum. Visible light wavelengths range from about 400 to 700 nm. X rays are much shorter; radio waves, much longer. (*bottom*) The two graphs show how waves vary in length between successive peaks. Shorter wavelengths are higher in frequency, as reflected in blue colors; longer wavelengths are lower in frequency, as reflected in red colors.

them. They are located on the outside of the color tree. Notice how the closer we get to the center of the color tree, the more white light has been added to the single wavelength of a particular color. In other words, the deep colors at the edge fade into pastel colors toward the center.

Light waves of greater amplitude make up brighter light.

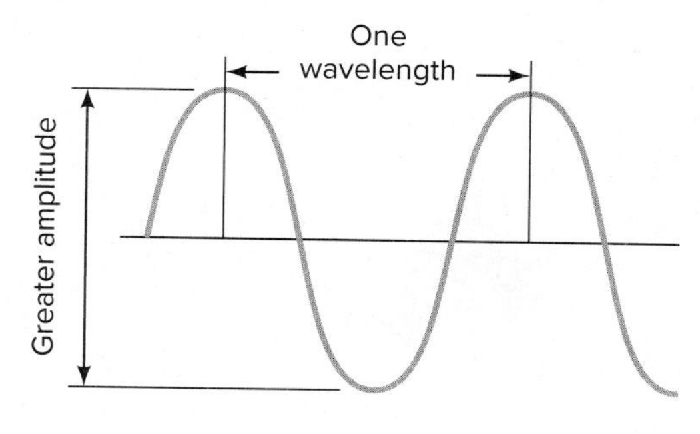


Light waves of smaller amplitude make up dimmer light.

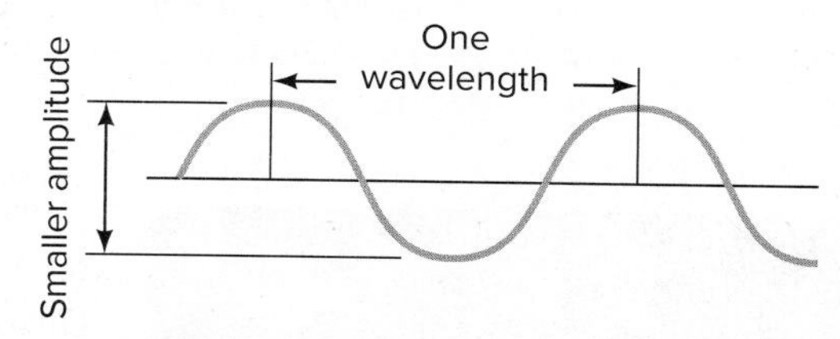


**FIGURE 9** **Light Waves of Varying Amplitude** The top graph might suggest a spotlight on a concert stage; the bottom might represent a candlelit dinner.

## THE STRUCTURE OF THE EYE

The eye, like a camera, is constructed to get the best possible picture of the world. An accurate picture is in focus, is not too dark or too light, and has good contrast between the dark and light parts. Several structures in the eye plays an important role in this process.

Looking closely at your eyes in a mirror, you will see three parts–the sclera, iris, and pupil (Figure 11). The *sclera* is the white, outer part of the eye that helps to maintain the shape of the eye and to protect it from injury. The *iris* is the colored part of the eye. The *pupil,* which appears black, is the opening in the center of the iris. The iris contains muscles that control the size of the pupil and, hence, the amount of light that gets into the eye. To get a good picture of the world, the eye needs to be able to adjust the amount of light that enters. In darkness, the pupil opens to take in more light; in bright light it closes to let in less light.

Two structures bring the image into focus: the *cornea,* a clear membrane in front of the eye, and the *lens,* a transparent and somewhat flexible, disklike structure filled with a gelatinous material. Both of these structures bend the light falling on the surface of the eye just enough to focus it at the back. The curved surface of the cornea does most of this bending, while the lens fine-tunes things. When you are looking at faraway objects, the lens has a relatively flat shape because the light reaching the eye from faraway objects is parallel, and the bending power of the cornea is sufficient to keep things in focus. However, the light reaching the eye from objects that are close is more scattered, so more bending of the light is required to achieve focus.

Without this ability of the lens to change its curvature, the eye would have a tough time focusing on close objects such as reading material. As we get older, the lens loses its flexibility and hence its ability to change from its normal flattened shape to the rounder shape needed to bring close objects into focus. That is why many people with normal vision throughout their young adult lives require reading glasses as they age.

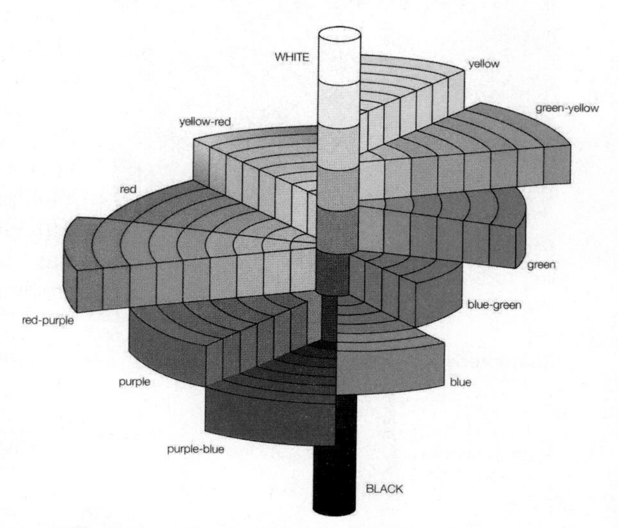


**FIGURE 10** **A Color Tree Showing Color's Three Dimensions: Hue, Saturation, and Brightness** Hue is represented around the color tree—saturation horizontally and brightness vertically. ©Universal Images Group/Getty Images

The parts of the eye we have considered so far work together to give us the sharpest picture of the world. They take the light energy and concentrate it onto the back of the eye–where the light energy is transformed into something we see. That structure at the back of the eye is like the film in a camera. Photographic film is made of a material that responds to light. The eye's "film" is the multilayered **retina**. The retina is the light-sensitive surface that records electromagnetic energy and converts it into neural impulses for processing in the brain. The analogy between the retina and film goes only so far, however. The retina is amazingly complex and elegantly designed. The retina is, in fact, the primary mechanism of sight. Even after decades of intense study, the full marvel of this structure is far from understood (Burns & others, 2019; Dedania & others, 2018; Lombardo & others, 2018).

The human retina has about 126 million receptor cells. They turn the electromagnetic energy of light into a form of energy the nervous system can process. There are two kinds of visual receptor cells: rods and cones. Rods and cones differ both in how they respond to light and in their patterns of distribution on the surface of the retina. **Rods** are receptors in the retina that are sensitive to light but not very useful for color vision. Rods function well with little light; they are hard at work at night. Humans have about 120 million rods. **Cones** are the receptors that we use for color perception. Cones are light-sensitive but they require a larger amount of light to respond than the rods do. They operate best in bright light. There are about 6 million cone cells in the retina. Figure 12 shows what rods and cones look like.

- **retina** The multilayered, light-sensitive surface in the eye that records electromagnetic energy and converts it to neural impulses for processing in the brain.
- **rods** The receptor cells in the retina that are sensitive to light but not very useful for color vision.
- **cones** The receptor cells in the retina that allow for color perception.

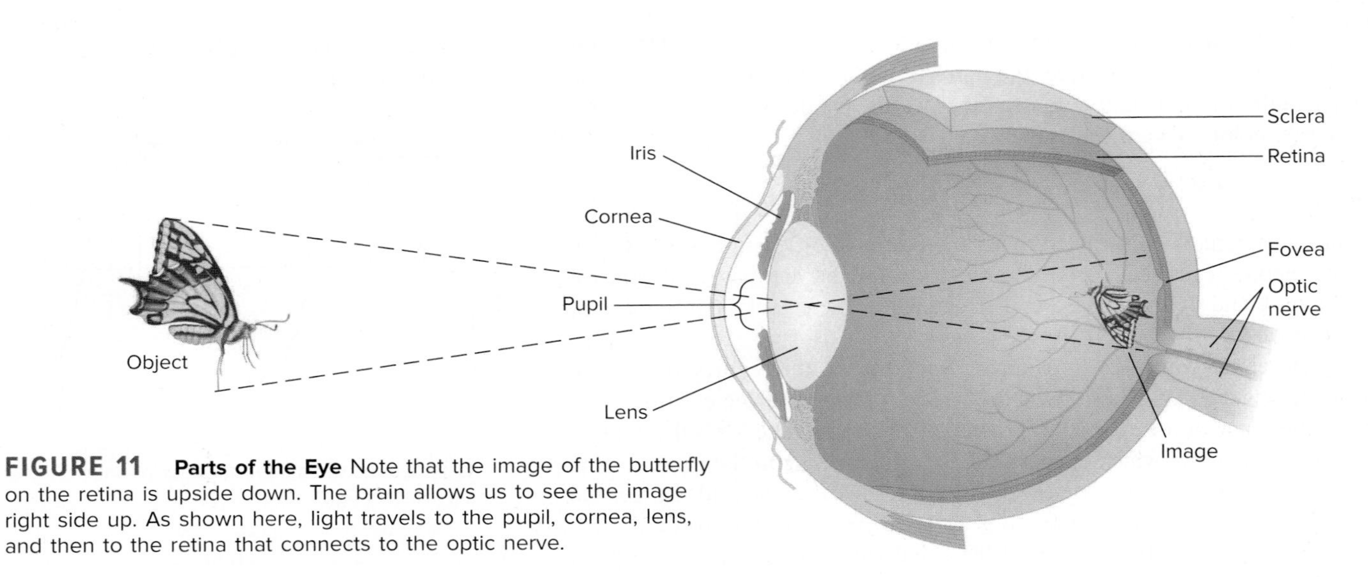


**FIGURE 11** **Parts of the Eye** Note that the image of the butterfly on the retina is upside down. The brain allows us to see the image right side up. As shown here, light travels to the pupil, cornea, lens, and then to the retina that connects to the optic nerve.

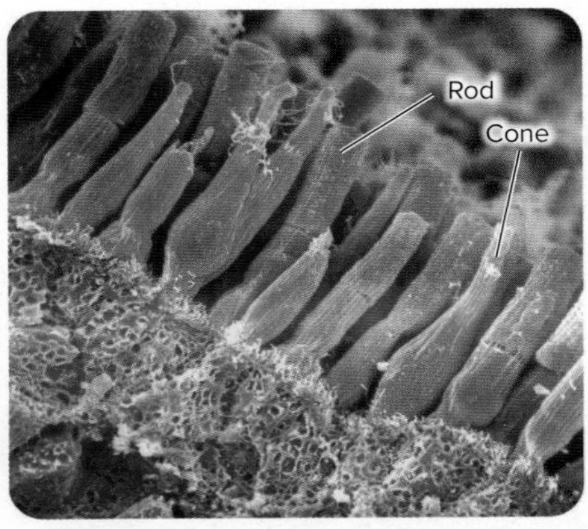


**FIGURE 12** **Rods and Cones** In real life, rods and cones look somewhat like stumps and corncobs. ©Science Source

The most important part of the retina is the *fovea,* a tiny area in the center of the retina at which vision is at its best (see Figure 11). The fovea contains only cones (Bringmann & others, 2018). To get a sense of how well the cones in the fovea work, try reading out of the corner of your eye. The task is difficult because the fovea is not getting to "see" the page. Rods are found almost everywhere on the retina except in the fovea. Rods give us the ability to detect fainter spots of light on the peripheral retina than at the fovea. If you want to see a very faint star, gaze slightly away from it, to allow your rods to do their work. Figure 13 summarizes the characteristics of rods and cones.

Figure 14 shows how the rods and cones convert light into electrochemical impulses. There are three layers of cells in the retina. The first layer are the rods and cones. They communicate with *bipolar cells* which make up the second layer. Finally, the impulse moves to the third layer: specialized cells called *ganglion cells* (Manookin, Patterson, & Linehan, 2018; Puller & others, 2015). The axons of the ganglion cells make up the **optic nerve**, which carries the visual information to the brain for further processing.

| Characteristics | Rods | Cones |
|---|---|---|
| Type of vision | Black and white | Color |
| Responses to light conditions | Dimly lit | Well lit |
| Shape | Thin and long | Short and fat |
| Distribution | Not on fovea | On fovea and scattered outside of fovea |

**FIGURE 13** **Characteristics of Rods and Cones** Rods and cones differ in shape, location, and function.

One place on the retina contains neither rods nor cones. This area, the *blind spot,* is the place on the retina where the optic nerve leaves the eye on its way to the brain (see Figure 14). We cannot see anything that reaches only this part of the retina. To prove to yourself that you have a blind spot, look at Figure 15. Once you have seen the yellow pepper disappear, you have probably noticed it took a while to succeed at this task. Now shut one eye and look around. You see a perfectly continuous picture of the world around you; there is no blind spot. This is a great example of top-down processing and a demonstration of the constructive aspect of perception. Your brain fills in the gap for you (the one that ought to be left by your blind spot) with a pretty good guess about what must be in that spot, like a creative artist painting in the blind spot.

## Visual Processing in the Brain

The next step in visual perception occurs when neural impulses generated in the retina are sent to the brain for analysis and integration (Gayet, Paffen, & Van der Stigchel, 2018; Gregory, 2015).

The optic nerve leaves the eye, carrying information about light toward the brain. Light travels in a straight line; therefore, stimuli in

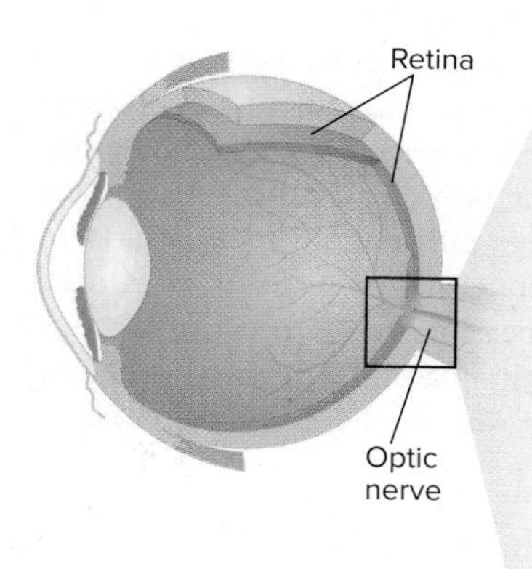


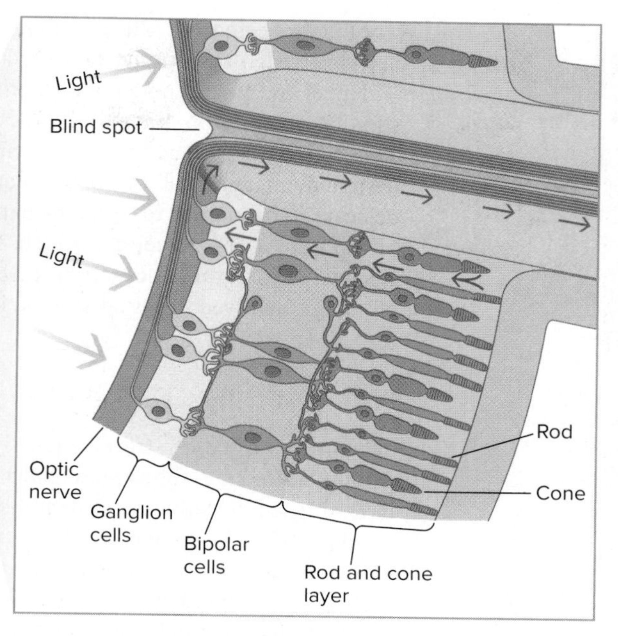


**FIGURE 14 Direction of Light in the Retina** After light passes through the cornea, pupil, and lens, it falls on the retina. Three layers of specialized cells in the retina convert the image into a neural signal that can be transmitted to the brain. First, light triggers a reaction in the rods and cones at the back of the retina, transducing light energy into electrochemical neural impulses. The neural impulses activate the bipolar cells, which in turn activate the ganglion cells. Then light information is transmitted to the optic nerve, which conveys it to the brain. The arrows indicate the sequence in which light information moves in the retina. Source: Manookin, Patterson, & Linehan (2018); Puller, Manookin, Neitz, Rieke, & Neitz (2015).

the left visual field are registered in the right half of the retina in both eyes, and stimuli in the right visual field are registered in the left half of the retina in both eyes (Figure 16). In the brain, at a point called the *optic chiasm,* the optic nerve fibers divide, and approximately half of the nerve fibers cross over the midline of the brain. As a result, the visual information originating in the right halves of the two retinas is transmitted to the right side of the occipital lobe and the visual information coming from the left halves of the retinas is transmitted to the left side of the occipital lobe. These crossings mean that what we see in the left side of our visual field is registered in the right side of the brain, and what we see in the right visual field is registered in the left side of the brain (see Figure 16).

● **optic nerve** The structure at the back of the eye, made up of axons of the ganglion cells, that carries visual information to the brain for further processing.

This crossing of information can be confusing. Think of the retina as divided in half, vertically. Information that hits the half that is on the "nose" side crosses over. Information that hits the outer half stays on the same side. This information is processed and combined into a recognizable object or scene in the visual cortex.

● **feature detectors** Neurons in the brain's visual system that respond to particular features of a stimulus.

## THE VISUAL CORTEX

The *visual cortex,* located in the occipital lobe at the back of the brain, is the part of the cerebral cortex involved in vision. Most visual information travels to the primary visual cortex, where it is processed, before moving to other visual areas for further analysis (Gregory, 2015).

An important aspect of visual information processing is the specialization of neurons. Many cells in the primary visual cortex are highly specialized. **Feature detectors** are individual neurons or groups of neurons in the brain's visual system that respond to particular features of stimuli. These neurons might respond to the edges of an object or stimulus, or to its movement.

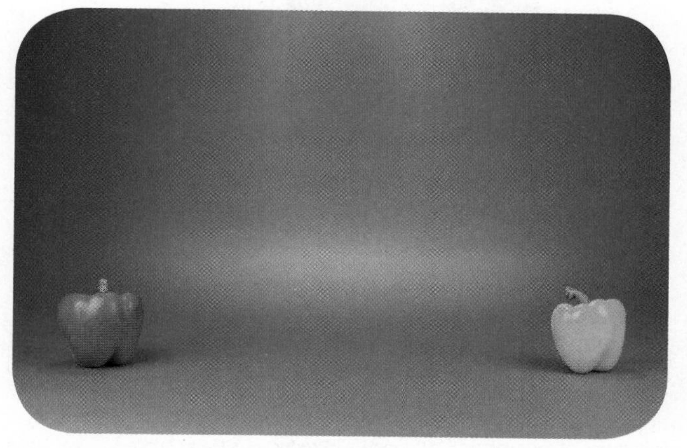

**FIGURE 15 The Eye's Blind Spot** There is a normal blind spot in your eye, a small area where the optic nerve leads to the brain. To find your blind spot, hold this book at arm's length, cover your left eye, and stare at the red pepper on the left with your right eye. Move the book slowly toward you until the yellow pepper disappears. To find the blind spot in your left eye, cover your right eye, stare at the yellow pepper, and adjust the book until the red pepper disappears. ©Editorial Image, LLC/Alamy Stock Photo

David Hubel and Torsten Wiesel (1963) won a Nobel Prize for their research on feature detectors. By recording the activity of a *single* neuron in a cat while it looked at patterns that varied in size, shape, color, and movement, they found that the visual cortex has neurons that are individually sensitive to different types of lines and angles. One neuron might show a sudden burst of activity when stimulated by lines of a particular angle; another neuron might fire only when moving stimuli appear; yet another neuron might be stimulated when the object in the visual field has a combination of certain angles, sizes, and shapes. In a

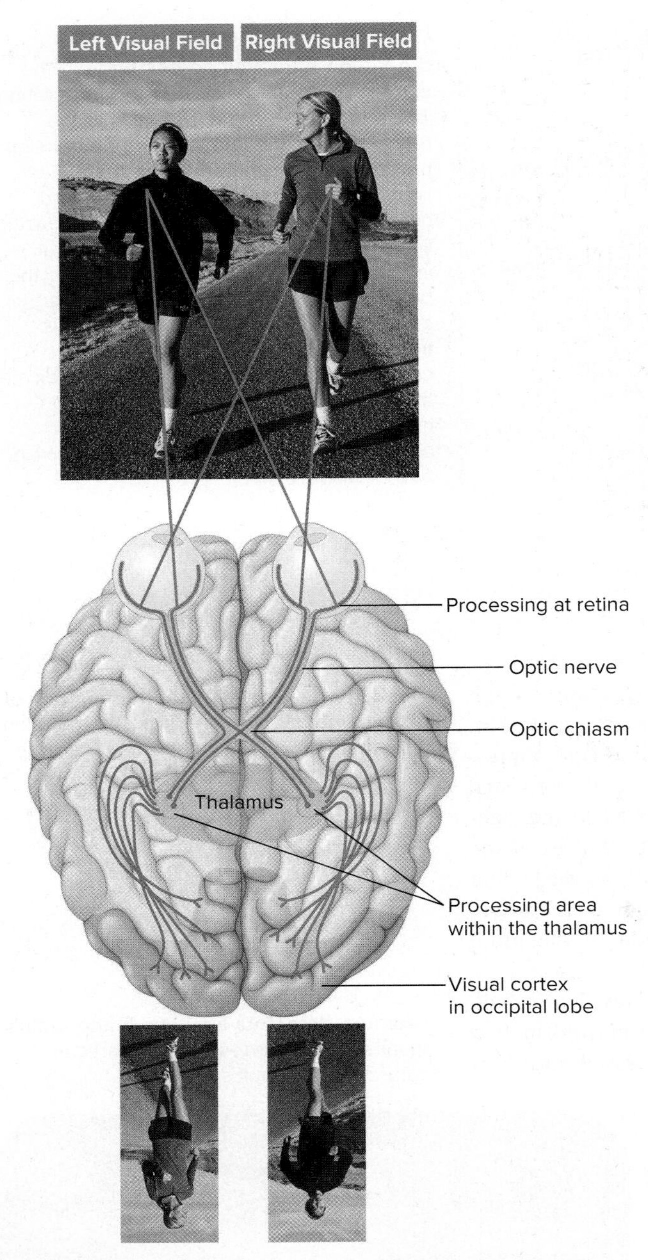


**FIGURE 16** **Visual Pathways to and Through the Brain** Light from each side of the visual field falls on the opposite side of each eye's retina. Visual information then travels along the optic nerve to the optic chiasm, where most of the visual information crosses over to the other side of the brain. From there visual information goes to the occipital lobe at the rear of the brain. All these crossings mean that what we see in the left side of our visual field (here, the shorter, dark-haired woman) is registered in the right side of our brain, and what we see in the right visual field (the taller, blonde woman) is registered in the left side of our brain. ©RubberBall Productions/Getty Images

● **parallel processing** The simultaneous distribution of information across different neural pathways.

● **binding** In the sense of vision, the bringing together and integration of what is processed by different neural pathways or cells.

way, then, seeing a "whole" stimulus is the work of various feature detectors, each responding to a specific aspect of that stimulus.

Hubel and Wiesel noted that when deprived of certain types of visual stimulation early on, kittens lost the ability to perceive these patterns. This finding suggested that there might be a critical period in visual development and that the brain requires stimulation in its efforts to delegate its resources to different perceptual tasks. In other words, the brain "learns" to perceive through experience. This process explains Michael May's experience (from the beginning of this section), whereby his brain, deprived of visual stimulation early in life, has redeployed its resources to other tasks.

## PARALLEL PROCESSING

Sensory information travels quickly through the brain because of **parallel processing**, the simultaneous distribution of information across different neural pathways (Kuchibhotla & Bathellier, 2018; Marcar & Jäncke, 2018; White, Palmer, & Boynton, 2018). A system designed to process information about stimulus features on at a time (such as processing first shape then color, then location) would be too slow to allow us to handle our rapidly changing world. To function in the world, we need to "see" all of the characteristics at once. Parallel processing means that we can perceive the all of them at once. In the visual system, parallel processing occurs from the beginning, as the retina captures a host of information from the world. Parallel processing may also occurs for other sensory systems as well (Kuchibhotla & others, 2017; Oxenham, 2018).

Why is parallel processing so important? Consider the alternative, *serial processing*. Processing features in a serial fashion would mean that you might detect the shape of your date's face, the color of their hair, their facial expression, one at a time, one after the other. The problem with serial processing is that it sets up a bottleneck in perception with the perceiver waiting for all the features to be processed prior to putting them together in a meaningful way. The visual system's capacity for parallel processing puts a typical multi-tasker to shame.

One activity we do with our vision is read. In the science of reading, there is debate about how you are reading right now. Is it best understood as resulting from parallel processing (that is, taking in many different pieces of information simultaneously) or from serial processing (that is, reading each word one at a time in sequence)? You probably recognize that even just glancing at a line of text, you are reading much of it, almost automatically. As we read the visual system processes the features of letters in parallel (Grainger, Dufau, & Ziegler, 2016). But how much of reading is characterized as parallel processing? To read about clever research examining this issue, see the Critical Controversy.

## BINDING

Neurons respond to different features of stimulus, however there is still just one stimulus. How does the brain know that features, communicated by different neurons, all belong to the same object of perception?

**Binding** is the bringing together and integration of what is processed by different pathways or cells (Schneegans & Bays, 2017), coupling of the activity of various cells and pathways. Through binding, we integrate information about a stimulus so that it is "one thing." Precisely how binding occurs is a puzzle that fascinates neuroscientists (Cecere & others, 2017). All the neurons throughout pathways that are activated

## Can We Read Two Words at Once?

To find out if the act of reading is best characterized by parallel or serial processing, researchers designed a simple but elegant experiment (White, Palmer & Boynton, 2018). Participants focused their eyes on a cross (or *fixation point*) in the middle of a computer screen and completed a few simple tasks. Words flashed on either side of the fixation point. Sometimes just one word flashed (on one side only) and sometimes there were two words—one on each side of the fixation point. Participants were asked to either identify the color in which the word (or words) was printed (red or gray) or to identify the words. Comparing performance for just one vs. two words, the researchers were able to gauge whether the color or word judgments were the result of parallel or serial processing. Parallel processing would be indicated by little or no difference between the one-word and two-word trials—because parallel processing would allow for two words to be processed at once. Serial processing would be indicated if two-word trials led to much worse performance than one-word trials.

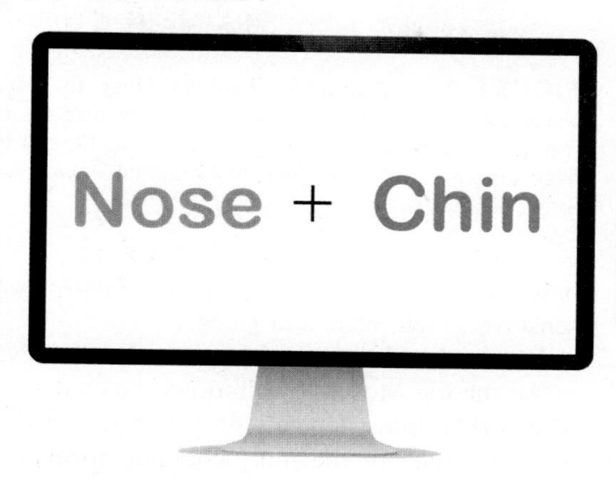

©Can Yesil/Shutterstock

They found two different, consistent results. First, accurately identifying colors was a snap. Even when two words were flashed at once, participants were accurate at identifying the colors of *both* words. However, for reading the words, performance was much worse when participants had to identified two words compared to one. In fact, during the two-word trials, if they got one word right, they typically did not recognize the other at all, a sure sign that the words were being processed *one at a time*. These results show two different processes: parallel processing of colors but serial processing of semantic meaning.

Some components of reading may be processed in parallel. Generally all participants tended to get words presented on the *right* side of the fixation point correct (White, Palmer, & Boynton, 2018), suggesting that in reading, we might automatically process the word that is just to the right of a particular word. As we read one word, we might also be processing the very next one. A final fun fact about this work is that in one of the studies (as noted by the researchers), one of the researchers was also a participant.

**WHAT DO YOU THINK?**

- Why would words presented on the right be processed more accurately overall?
- Do you think it is appropriate for a scientist to be a participant in his or her own study? Why or why not?

---

by a visual object pulse together at the same frequency (Engel & Singer, 2001) and within the vast network of cells in the cerebral cortex, this set of neurons appears to *bind* together all the features of the objects into a unified perception (Hayworth, 2012).

## Color Vision

Flowers and sunsets would lose much of their beauty if we could not see their rich hues. The process of color perception starts in the retina, the eyes' film. Interestingly, theories about how the retina processes color were developed long before methods existed to study the anatomical and neurophysiological bases of color perception. Instead, psychologists made some amazingly accurate guesses about how color vision occurs in the retina by observing how people see. The two main theories proposed were the trichromatic theory and opponent-process theory. Both turned out to be correct.

The **trichromatic theory**, proposed by Thomas Young (1802) and extended by Hermann von Helmholtz (1852), states that color perception is produced by three types of cone receptors in the retina that are particularly sensitive to different, but overlapping, ranges of wavelengths. The theory is based on experiments showing that a person with normal vision can match any color in the spectrum by combining three other wavelengths. Young and Helmholtz reasoned that if the combination of any three wavelengths of different intensities is indistinguishable from any single pure wavelength, the visual system must

- **trichromatic theory** Theory stating that color perception is produced by three types of cone receptors in the retina that are particularly sensitive to different, but overlapping, ranges of wavelengths.

*If you have seen The Wizard of Oz, you might remember that goose bumps moment when Dorothy steps out of her house and the black-and-white of Kansas gives way to the Technicolor glory of Oz.*

©Silver Screen/Hulton Archives/Getty Images

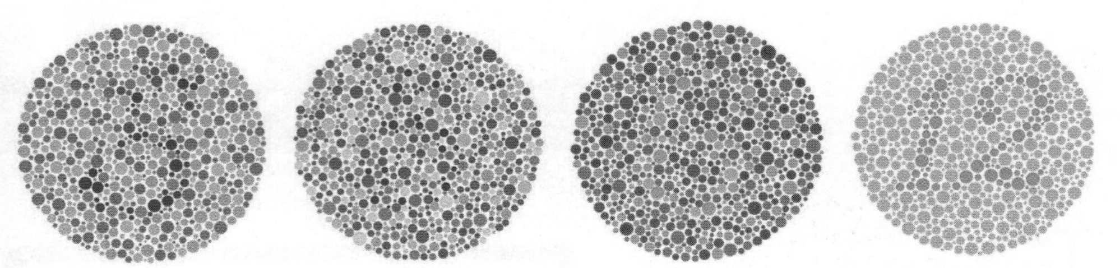

**FIGURE 17 Examples of Stimuli Used to Test for Colorblindness** People with normal vision see the number 12 in the left circle and the number 5 in the right circle. People with red-green colorblindness may see just the 12, just the 5, or neither. A complete colorblindness assessment involves the use of 15 stimuli. ©Alexander Kaludov/Alamy Stock Photo

base its perception of color on the relative responses of three receptor systems—cones sensitive to red, blue, and green.

The study of atypical color vision, or *colorblindness* (Figure 17) supports the trichromatic theory. Most colorblind people can see some colors but not others. The nature of colorblindness depends on which of the three kinds of cones (red, blue, or green) is inoperative. In the most common form of colorblindness, the green cone system malfunctions, rendering green indistinguishable from certain combinations of blue and red.

In 1878, German physiologist Ewald Hering noticed that some colors cannot exist together, whereas others can. For example, it is easy to imagine a greenish blue but not a reddish green. Hering also noted that trichromatic theory could not adequately explain *afterimages*—sensations that remain after a stimulus is removed. Color afterimages involve specific color pairs. If you look at red long enough, a green afterimage will appear. If you look at yellow long enough, a blue afterimage will appear. (Figure 18 gives you a chance to experience an afterimage.)

Hering's observations led him to propose that there were not three types of color receptor cones (as trichromatic theory proposed) but four, organized into complementary

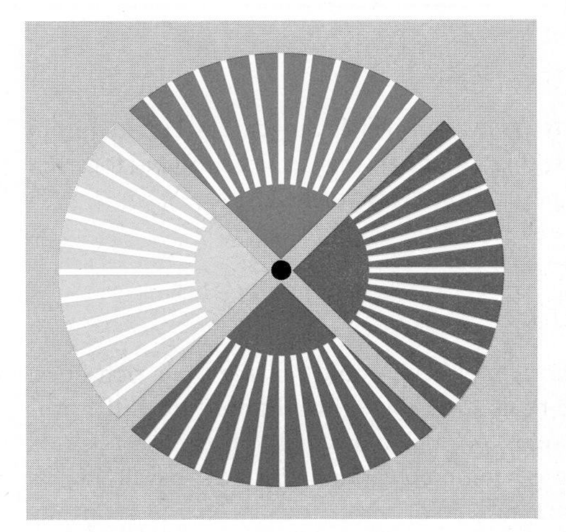

**FIGURE 18 Negative Afterimage—Complementary Colors** If you gaze steadily at the dot in the colored panel on the left for a few moments, then shift your gaze to the gray box on the right, you will see the original hues' complementary colors. The blue appears as yellow, the red as green, the green as red, and the yellow as blue. This pairing of colors occurs because color receptors in the eye are apparently sensitive as pairs: When one color is turned off (when you stop staring at the panel), the other color in the receptor is briefly turned on. The afterimage effect is especially noticeable with bright colors.
Source: Hering (1878).

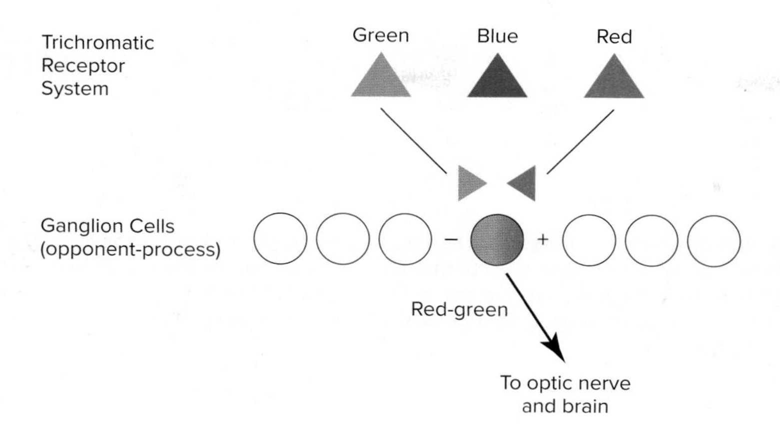


**FIGURE 19 Trichromatic and Opponent-Process Theories: Transmission of Color Information in the Retina** Cones responsive to green, blue, or red light form a trichromatic receptor system in the retina. As information is transmitted to the retina's ganglion cells, opponent-process cells are activated. As shown here, a retinal ganglion cell is inhibited by a green cone (–) and excited by a red cone (+), producing red-green color information.

pairs: red-green and blue-yellow. Hering's view, **opponent-process theory**, states that cells in the visual system respond to red-green and blue-yellow colors. A given cell might be excited by red and inhibited by green; another cell might be excited by yellow and inhibited by blue. Opponent-process theory explains afterimages. If you stare at red, your red-green system seems to "tire," and when you look away, it rebounds, giving you a green afterimage.

How can these two approaches to color vision both be true? The answer is that the red, blue, and green cones in the retina (recognized by trichromatic theory) are connected to retinal ganglion cells in such a way that the three-color code is immediately translated into the opponent-process code (Figure 19). For example, a green cone might inhibit and a red cone might excite a particular ganglion cell. Thus, *both* the trichromatic and opponent-process theories are correct–the eye and the brain use both methods to code colors.

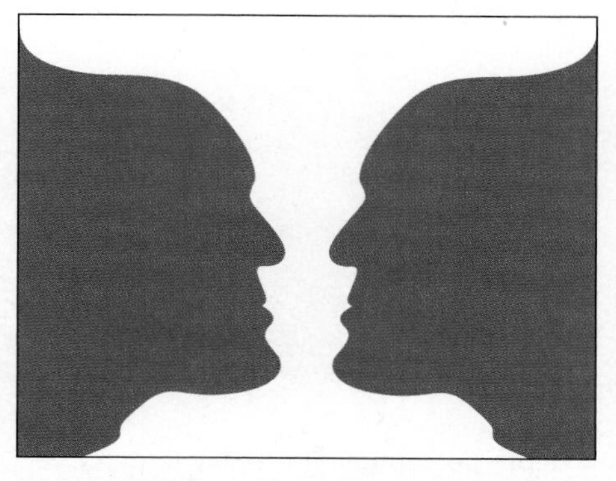

**FIGURE 20 Reversible Figure-Ground Pattern** Do you see the silhouette of a goblet or a pair of faces in profile?

● **opponent-process theory** Theory stating that cells in the visual system respond to complementary pairs of red-green and blue-yellow colors; a given cell might be excited by red and inhibited by green, whereas another cell might be excited by yellow and inhibited by blue.

## Perceiving Shape, Depth, Motion, and Constancy

Information about the dimensions of what we are seeing is critical to visual perception. Among these dimensions are shape, depth, motion, and constancy.

### SHAPE

Think about the visible world and its shapes–buildings against the sky, boats on the horizon. We see these shapes because they are marked off from the rest of what we see by *contour,* a location at which a sudden change of brightness occurs.

Now think about the letters on this page. Looking at the page, you see letters, which are shapes or figures, in a field or background–the white page. The **figure-ground relationship** is the principle by which we organize the perceptual field into stimuli that stand out (*figure*) and those that are left over (*background,* or *ground*). Generally this principle works well for us, but some figure-ground relationships are ambiguous, and it may be difficult to tell what is figure and what is ground. Figure 20 shows a well-known ambiguous figure-ground relationship. As you look at the figure, your perception is likely to shift from seeing two faces to seeing a single goblet.

● **figure-ground relationship** The principle by which we organize the perceptual field into stimuli that stand out (figure) and those that are left over (ground).

The figure-ground relationship is a gestalt principle (Figure 21 shows others). *Gestalt* is German for "configuration" or "form," and **gestalt psychology** is a school of thought interested in how people naturally organize their perceptions by certain patterns. One of gestalt psychology's main principles is that the whole is different from the sum of its parts. For example, thousands of tiny pixels make up an image (whole) on a computer screen.

● **gestalt psychology** A school of thought interested in how people naturally organize their perceptions according to certain patterns.

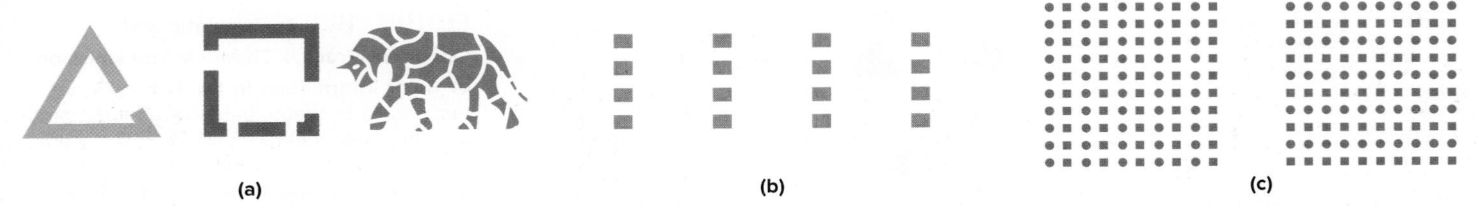


**FIGURE 21** **Gestalt Principles of Closure, Proximity, and Similarity** (*a*) *Closure:* When we see disconnected or incomplete figures, we fill in the spaces and see them as complete figures. (*b*) *Proximity:* When we see objects that are near each other, they tend to be seen as a unit. You are likely to perceive the grouping as four columns of four squares, not one set of 16 squares. (*c*) *Similarity:* When we see objects that are similar to each other, they tend to be seen as a unit. Here, you are likely to see vertical columns of circles and squares in the left box but horizontal rows of circles and squares in the right box.

The principles of gestalt are closure, proximity, and similarity:

- *Closure*: When we see disconnected or incomplete figures, we fill in the spaces and see them as complete figures.
- *Proximity*: When we see objects that are near each other, they tend to be seen as a unit.
- *Similarity*: When we see objects that are similar to each other, they tend to be seen as a unit.

Each of these concepts is about how, when we look at the pieces of something, we "get" the big picture. See how these principles are illustrated in Figure 21.

## DEPTH PERCEPTION

● **depth perception** The ability to perceive objects three-dimensionally.

Images appear on the retina in two-dimensions. Yet we see a three-dimensional world. **Depth perception** is the ability to perceive objects three-dimensionally. Look around you. Are your surroundings flat? No, you see some objects farther away, some closer. Some objects overlap each other. The scene and objects that you are looking at have depth. How do you see depth? To perceive a world of depth, we use two kinds of information, or cues—binocular and monocular. As the names imply, binocular cues are rooted in the fact that we have two eyes and monocular cues are aspects of stimuli that suggest depth even for one eye.

● **binocular cues** Depth cues that depend on the combination of the images in the left and right eye and on the way the two eyes work together.

Because we have two eyes, we get two views of the world. The pictures are slightly different because the eyes are in different positions. **Binocular cues** are depth cues that depend on the combination of the images in the left and right eyes and on the way the two eyes work together. Hold your hand a few inches from your face and open and close each eye so that only one eye is open at a time. The image of your hand will appear to jump back and forth, because the image is in a slightly different place on the left and right retinas. The *disparity,* or difference, between the images in the two eyes is the binocular cue the brain uses to determine the depth, or distance, of an object. The combination of the two images in the brain, and the disparity between them in the eyes, give us information about the three-dimensional world. Those 3-D glasses that you wear for viewing some movies give you a sense of depth by creating visual disparity. The coloring of the lenses presents a different image to each eye. Your eyes then compete with each other, and your brain makes sense of the conflict by creating the perception of three dimensions.

● **convergence** A binocular cue to depth and distance in which the muscle movements in an individual's two eyes provide information about how deep and/or far away something is.

**Convergence** is another binocular cue to depth and distance. When we use our two eyes to look at something, they are focused on the same object. If the object is near us, our eyes converge, or move together, almost crossing. If the object is farther away, we can focus on it without pulling our eyes together. The muscle movements involved in convergence provide information about how far away or how deep something is.

● **monocular cues** Powerful depth cues available from the image in one eye, either the right or the left.

In addition to using binocular cues depth is conveyed by a number of **monocular cues**, or depth cues, available from the image in one eye. Monocular cues are features of the

**FIGURE 22** **An Artist's Use of the Monocular Cue of Linear Perspective** Source: National Gallery of Art

visual world that provide information about depth. These cues are the features that give paintings and photographs a sense of depth. Here are some examples of monocular cues:

- *Familiar size:* This cue to the depth and distance of objects is based on what we have learned from experience about the standard sizes of objects. We know how large oranges tend to be, so we can tell how far away an orange is likely to be by the size of its image on the retina.
- *Height in the field of view:* All other things being equal, objects positioned higher in a picture are seen as farther away.
- *Linear perspective and relative size:* Objects that are farther away take up less space on the retina. So, things that appear smaller are perceived to be farther away. As Figure 22 shows, as an object recedes into the distance, parallel lines in the scene appear to converge.
- *Overlap:* We perceive an object that partially conceals or overlaps another object as closer.
- *Shading:* This cue involves changes in perception due to the position of the light and the position of the viewer. Consider an egg under a desk lamp. If you walk around the desk, you will see different shading patterns on the egg.
- *Texture gradient:* Texture becomes denser and finer the farther away it is from the viewer (Figure 23).

**FIGURE 23** **Texture Gradient** The gradients of texture create an impression of depth on a flat surface.

Depth perception is quite complex. Individuals with only one functioning eye cannot see depth the way that those with two eyes can. The late Oliver Sacks (2006) described the case of Susan Barry, who was born with crossed eyes. Corrective surgery left her cosmetically fine, but unable to perceive depth. As an adult, she was determined to see depth. With a doctor's aid, she found special glasses and undertook eye muscle exercises to improve her chances of perceiving in three dimensions. One day she noticed things starting to "stick out" at her—as you might experience when watching a 3-D film. Although Barry had successfully adapted to life in a flat visual world, she realized that relying on monocular cues was not the same as experiencing a rich, binocular, visual world. She described flowers as suddenly appearing "inflated." She noted how "ordinary things looked extraordinary" as she saw the leaves of a tree, an empty chair, and her office door projecting out from the background.

**FIGURE 24** **Size Constancy** Even though our retinal images of the hot air balloons vary, we still realize the balloons are approximately the same size. This illustrates the principle of size constancy. ©Thitisan/Shutterstock

**FIGURE 25** **Shape Constancy** The various projected images from an opening door are quite different, yet you perceive a rectangular door.

## MOTION PERCEPTION

Motion perception plays an important role in the lives of many species (Leo & others, 2018; Paeye & others, 2018; Rosa-Salva & others, 2018). For some animals, motion perception is critical for survival. Predators and their prey depend on being able to detect motion quickly. Frogs and some other simple vertebrates may not even see an object unless it is moving. For example, if a dead fly is dangled motionlessly in front of a frog, the frog cannot sense its winged meal. The bug-detecting cells in the frog's retinas are wired only to sense movement.

Scientists once believed that primate retinas did not detect motion (Bach & Hoffman, 2000). In fact, the saying was, "The smarter the animal, the dumber the retina," suggesting a trade-off between the retina and the brain. In humans and other primates, the perception of motion was thought to occur later in visual processing and involve the brain (Murphy-Baum & Awatramani, 2018). Recently, however, scientists have discovered that the primate retina *does* have neurons that detect motion (Kuo, Schwartz & Rieke, 2016; Manookin, Patterson, & Linehan, 2018). These neurons, called *parasol ganglion cells*, are sensitive to motion. The human retina, it turns out, is not so dumb after all.

The retina is just the first step in motion perception. In addition to neurons that are specialized to detect motion, feedback from our body tells us whether we are moving or whether someone or some object is moving; for example, you move your eye muscles as you watch a ball coming toward you.

In addition, the environment is rich in cues that give us information about movement.

Psychologists are interested in both real movement and **apparent movement**, which occurs when we perceive a stationary object as moving. You can experience apparent movement at IMAX movie theaters. In watching a film of a climb of Mount Everest, you may find yourself feeling breathless as your visual field floods with startling images. In theaters without seats, viewers of these films are often warned to hold the handrail because perceived movement is so realistic that they might fall.

● **apparent movement** The perception that a stationary object is moving.

## PERCEPTUAL CONSTANCY

Retinal images change constantly. Yet even though the stimuli that fall on our retinas change as we move closer to or farther away from objects or as we look at objects from different orientations, our perception of them remains stable. **Perceptual constancy** is the recognition that objects are constant and unchanging even though sensory input about them is changing (Cronin & Irwin, 2018).

● **perceptual constancy** The recognition that objects are constant and unchanging even though sensory input about them is changing.

We experience three types of perceptual constancy–for size, shape, and color–as follows:

- *Size constancy* means an object remains the same size even though the retinal image of the object changes (Figure 24). Experience is important to size perception: No matter how far away you are from your car, you know how large it is.
- *Shape constancy* means an object retains the same shape even though its orientation to you changes. If you walk around the room, you see objects from different sides and angles. Even though the retinal image of the object changes as you walk, you still perceive the objects as having the same shape (Figure 25).

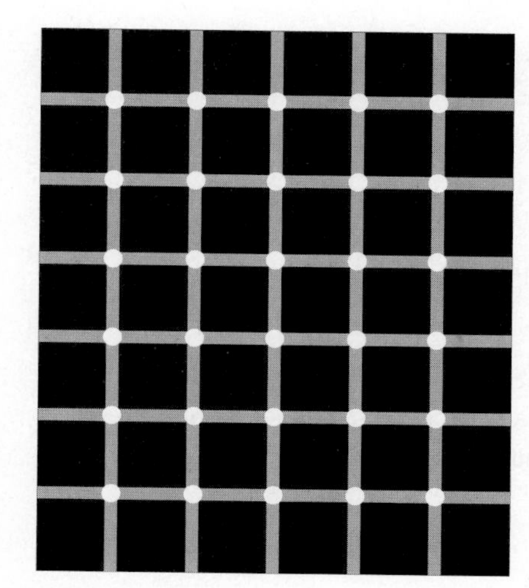

**Blinking Effect Illusion**
Stare at the white circles and notice the intermittent blinking effect. Your eyes make the static figure seem dynamic, attempting to fill in the white circle intersections with the black of the background.

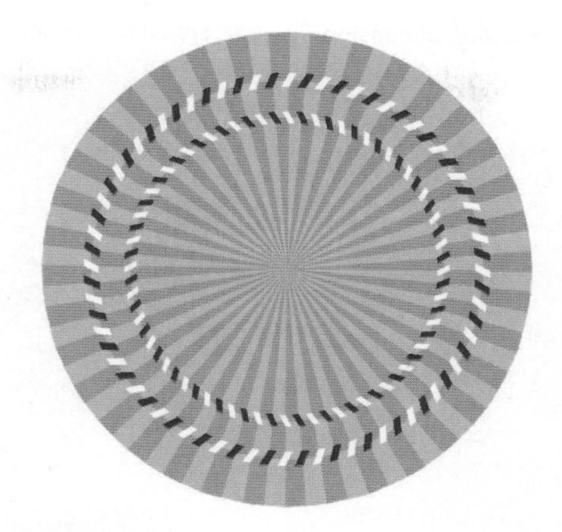

**Rotational Illusion**
The two rings appear to rotate in different directions when we approach or move away from this figure while fixing our eyes on the center.

**Pattern Recognition**
Although the diagram contains no actual triangles, your brain "sees" two overlapping triangles. The explanation is that the notched circles and angled lines merely suggest gaps in which complete objects should be. The brain fills in the missing information.

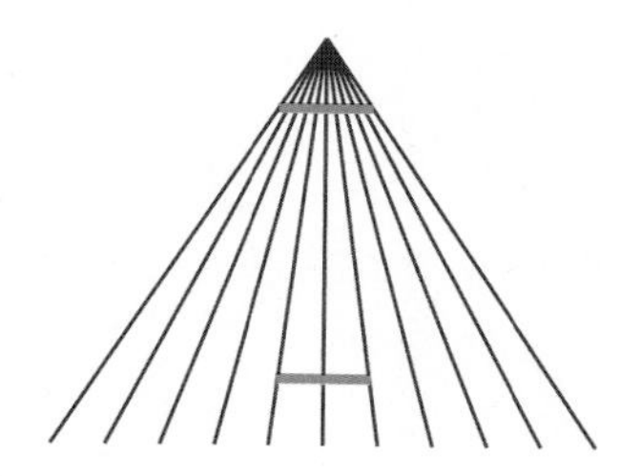

**Ponzo Illusion**
The top line looks much longer than the bottom, but they are the same length.

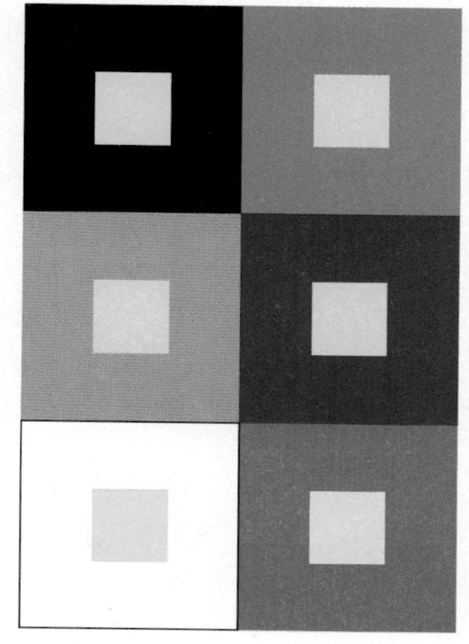

**Induction Illusion**
The yellow patches are identical, but they look different and seem to take on the characteristics of their surroundings when they appear against different-color backgrounds.

**FIGURE 26** **Perceptual Illusions** These illusions show how adaptive perceptual cues can lead to errors when taken out of context. These mind-challenging images are definitely fun, but keep in mind that these illusions are based on processes that are quite adaptive in real life.

- *Color constancy* means an object retains the same color even though different amounts of light fall on it. If you are reaching for a green Granny Smith apple, it looks green to you whether you are having it for lunch, in the bright noon sun, or as an evening snack in the pale pink of sunset.

Perceptual constancy tells us about the crucial role of interpretation in perception: We *interpret* sensation. We perceive objects as having particular characteristics regardless of the retinal image detected by our eyes. Images may flow across the retina, but experiences are made sensible through perception. The many cues we use to visually perceive the real world can lead to optical illusions when they are taken out of that real-world context, as you can experience for yourself in Figure 26.

### test yourself

1. What is light? What are some terms scientists use to describe it?
2. What are rods and cones, and what are their functions in the eye?
3. What are the main principles of trichromatic theory? How does this theory explain color vision and colorblindness?

## 3. THE AUDITORY SYSTEM

Sounds provide information about the environment. They tell us about the presence of a person behind us, the approach of an oncoming car, or the mischief of a 2-year-old. Perhaps most important, sounds allow us to communicate through language and music.

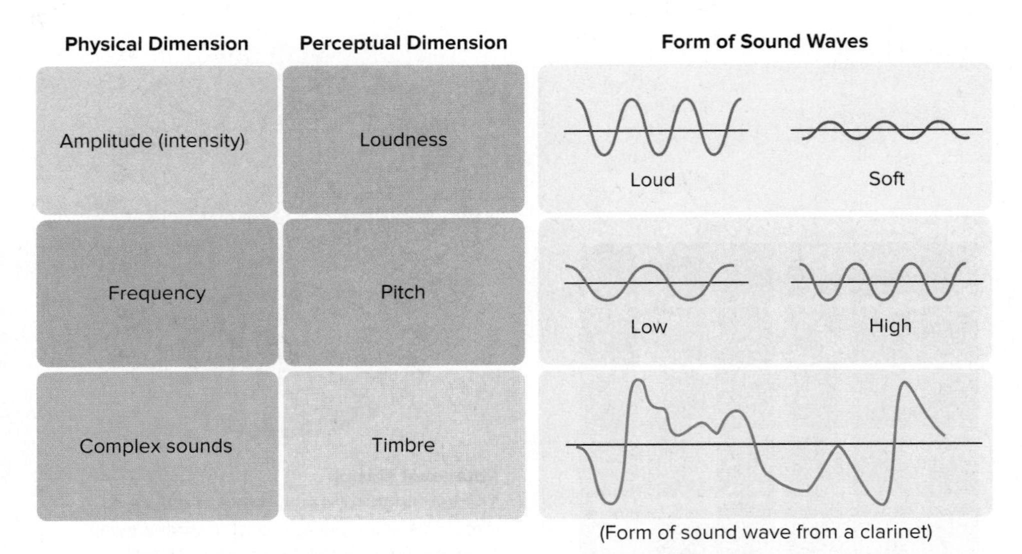


**FIGURE 27 Physical Difference in Sound Waves and the Qualities of Sound They Produce** Here we can see how the input of sound stimuli requires our ears and brain to attend to varying characteristics of the rich sensory information that is sound.

## The Nature of Sound and How We Experience It

At a fireworks show, you may feel the loud boom of an explosion in your chest. At a concert, you might sense that the air around you is vibrating. How does sound generate these sensations? Sound waves are vibrations in the air that are processed by the *auditory* system. Sounds waves are like waves in the ocean moving toward the beach of your ears.

Sound waves vary in length. The wavelength determines the sound wave's *frequency*–that is, the number of cycles (full wavelengths) that pass through a point in a given time interval. *Pitch* is the perception of that frequency. High-frequency sounds (a soprano's voice) have a high pitch and low-frequency sounds (a bass voice) have a low pitch. Human sensitivity is limited to a range of sound frequencies. In contrast, dogs can hear higher frequencies than we can. The full range of the human capacity for hearing pitch, however is remarkable. The auditory system's capacity to perceive pitch is *ten times* that of the visual system's perception of color (Oxenham, 2018).

Sound waves also vary in amplitude. A sound wave's *amplitude,* measured in decibels (dB), is the amount of pressure the it produces relative to a standard. The typical standard–0 decibels–is the weakest sound the human ear can detect. *Loudness* is the perception of the sound wave's amplitude. In general, the higher the amplitude (or the higher the decibel level), the louder a sound is perceived to be. Loud noises come from air pressing forcibly against you and your ears.

So far we have been describing a sound wave with just one frequency. Most sounds, including those of speech and music, are *complex sounds,* those in which numerous frequencies of sound blend together. *Timbre* is the tone saturation, or the perceptual quality, of a sound. If two musicians play a note of the same pitch (let's say a high C), even though the pitch is the same, the tones will sound different. Timbre is responsible for this perceptual difference, as well as for the quality differences we hear in human voices. Figure 27 illustrates the physical differences in sound waves that produce the different qualities of sounds.

## Structures and Functions of the Ear

Sitting in a park talking to a friend, you hear many different things going on–the chatter of children playing, the conversation of passersby, or the roar of a passing bus. All of

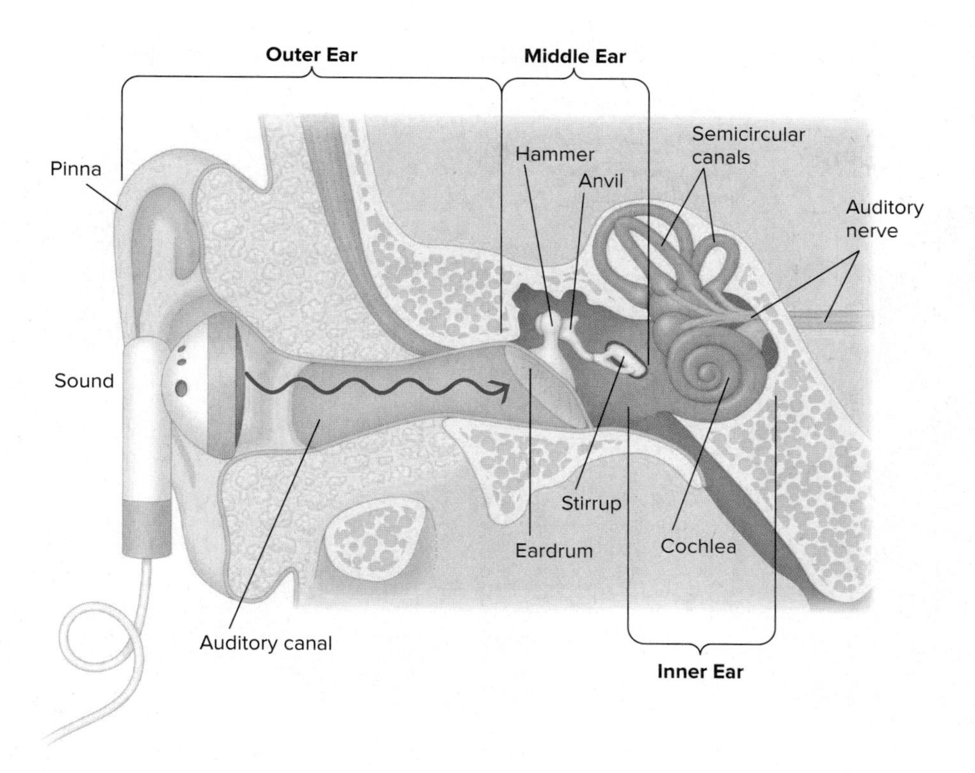


**FIGURE 28 The Outer, Middle, and Inner Ear** On entering the outer ear, sound waves travel through the auditory canal, where they generate vibrations in the eardrum. These vibrations are transferred via the hammer, anvil, and stirrup to the fluid-filled cochlea in the inner ear. There the mechanical vibrations are converted to an electrochemical signal that the brain will recognize as sound.

those sounds are part of a single sound wave that crashes into your ears. The auditory system takes that sound wave and turns it into the experience of the afternoon at the park. How do various structures of the ear transform sound waves into signals that the brain will recognize as sound?

Like the eye in the visual system, the ear serves the purpose of transmitting a high-fidelity version of sounds to the brain for analysis and interpretation. Just as an image requires focus and sufficient brightness for the brain to interpret it, a sound needs to be transmitted in a way that preserves information about its location, its frequency, and its timbre. The ear is divided into three parts: outer ear, middle ear, and inner ear (Figure 28).

## OUTER EAR

The **outer ear** consists of the pinna and the external auditory canal. The funnel-shaped *pinna* (plural, *pinnae*) is the outer, visible part of the ear. (Elephants have very large pinnae.) The pinna collects sounds and channels them into the interior of the ear. The pinnae of many animals, such as cats, are movable and serve a more important role in sound localization than do the pinnae of humans.

- **outer ear** The outermost part of the ear, consisting of the pinna and the external auditory canal.

## MIDDLE EAR

After passing the pinna, sound waves move through the auditory canal to the middle ear. The **middle ear** channels the sound through the *eardrum* (or tympanic membrane), hammer, anvil, and stirrup to the inner ear. The tympanic membrane separates the outer ear from the middle ear. It is the first structure that sound touches in the middle ear. It vibrates in response to sound. The eardrums are continuously responding to changes in sound pressure. The *hammer, anvil,* and *stirrup* are an intricately connected chain of the three smallest bones in the human body. When they vibrate, they transmit sound waves to the fluid-filled inner ear. The muscles that operate these tiny bones take the vibration of the eardrum and transmit it to the oval window, the opening of the inner ear.

- **middle ear** The part of the ear that channels sound through the eardrum, hammer, anvil, and stirrup to the inner ear.

Sound travels far more easily in air than in water. Sound waves entering the ear travel in air until they reach the inner ear. At the border between the middle and the inner ear—which, as we will see below, is a border between air and fluid—sound meets the same

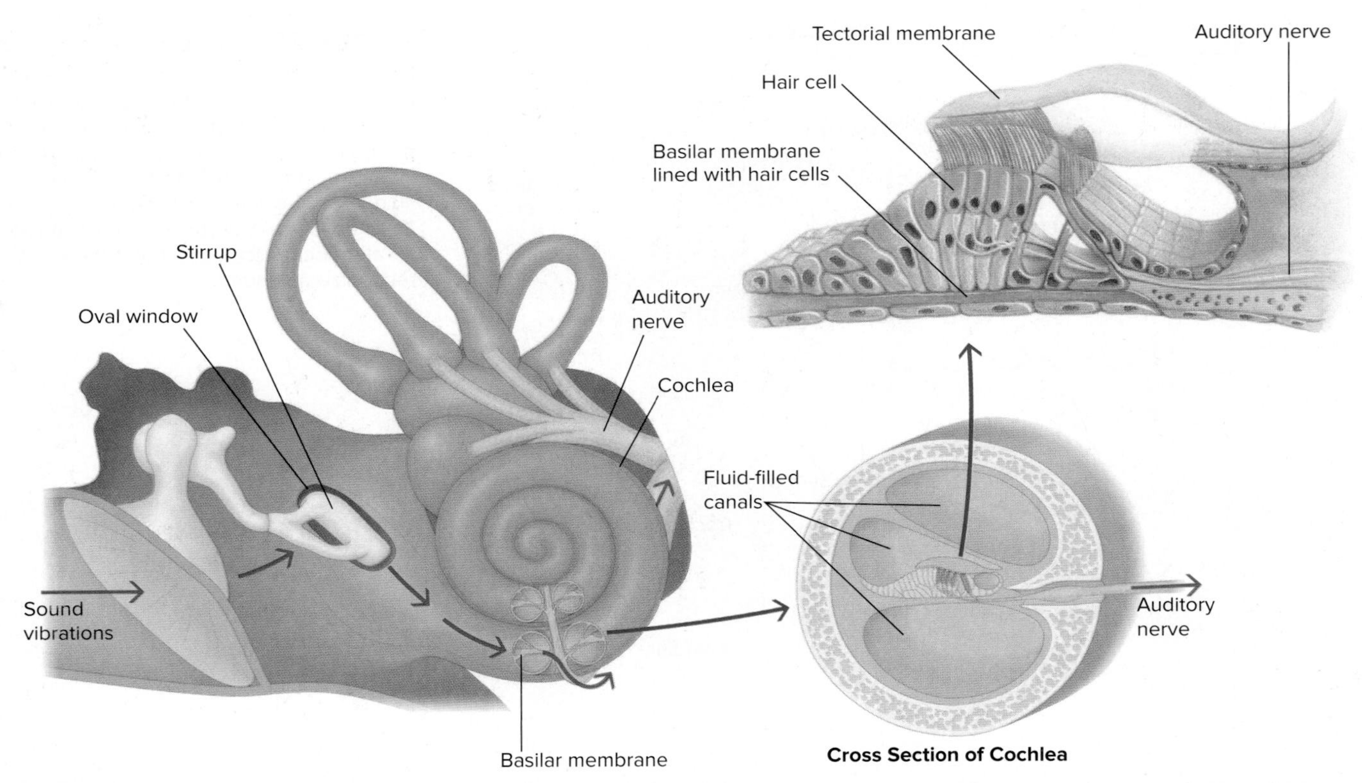


**FIGURE 29** **The Cochlea** The cochlea is a spiral structure consisting of fluid-filled canals. When the stirrup vibrates against the oval window, the fluid in the canals vibrates. Vibrations along portions of the basilar membrane correspond to different sound frequencies. The vibrations exert pressure on the hair cells (between the basilar and tectorial membranes); the hair cells in turn push against the tectorial membrane, and this pressure bends the hairs. This sequence of events triggers an action potential in the auditory nerve.

kind of resistance encountered by shouts directed at an underwater swimmer when the shouts hit the surface of the water. To compensate, the muscles of the middle ear can maneuver the hammer, anvil, and stirrup to amplify the sound waves. These muscles can also work to decrease the intensity of sound waves, if necessary, to protect the inner ear.

## INNER EAR

● **inner ear** The part of the ear that includes the oval window, cochlea, and basilar membrane and whose function is to convert sound waves into neural impulses and send them to the brain.

The function of the **inner ear**, which includes the oval window, cochlea, and basilar membrane, is to fine tune sound waves and convert them into neural impulses that are sent to the brain (Oxenham, 2018). The stirrup is connected to the membranous *oval window,* which transmits sound waves to the cochlea. The *cochlea* is a tubular, fluid-filled structure that is coiled up like a snail shell (Figure 29). The *basilar membrane* lines the inner wall of the cochlea and runs its entire length. It is narrow and rigid at the base of the cochlea but widens and becomes more flexible at the top. The variation in width and flexibility allows different areas of the basilar membrane to vibrate more intensely when exposed to different sound frequencies (Oxenham, 2018).

In humans and other mammals, hair cells line the basilar membrane (see Figure 29). These *hair cells* are the ear's sensory receptors. They are called hair cells because of the tufts of fine bristles, or *cilia,* that sprout from the top of them. The movement of the hair cells against the *tectorial membrane,* a jellylike flap above them, generates impulses that the brain interprets as sound. Hair cells are so delicate that exposure to loud noise can destroy them, leading to hearing impairment. Once lost, hair cells cannot regenerate. The cochlear hair cells sharply tune the sound wave and providing the raw ingredient of auditory perception. This means that the information that comes from the cochlea determines our perceptual ability (Oxenham, 2018).

Cochlear implants are devices developed to replace damaged hair cells. A *cochlear implant*—a small electronic device that is surgically implanted in the ear and head—allows individuals who are deaf or have significantly impaired hearing to detect sound. The implant works by using electronic impulses to directly stimulate any working auditory nerves that the recipient has in his or her cochlea (Vavatzanidis & others, 2018). Cochlear implants have been remarkably successful, but note that they substitute 12 to 24 electrodes for the approximately 3,500 hair cells in the cochlea (Oxenham, 2018). As such, they do not fully restore typical hearing. Worldwide, over 300,000 individuals have received cochlear implants (National Institute on Deafness and Other Communication Disorders, 2017).

## Theories of Hearing

A mystery of the auditory system is how the inner ear registers the frequency of sound: How do we hear a high-pitched piccolo versus the low tones of a cello? This issue remains a source of controversy (Oxenham, 2018). Two theories aim to explain this mystery: place theory and frequency theory.

**Place theory** states that each frequency produces vibrations at a particular spot on the basilar membrane. Georg von Békésy (1960) studied the effects of vibration applied at the oval window on the basilar membrane of human cadavers. Through a microscope, he saw that this stimulation produced a traveling wave on the basilar membrane. A traveling wave is like the ripples that appear in a pond when you throw a stone into the water. However, because the cochlea is a long tube, the ripples travel in only one direction—from the oval window at one end of the cochlea to the far tip of the cochlea. High-frequency vibrations create traveling waves that maximally displace, or move, the area of the basilar membrane closest to the oval window; low-frequency vibrations maximally displace areas of the membrane closer to the tip of the cochlea. So, the high-pitched tinkle of a little bell stimulates the narrow region of the basilar membrane at the base of the cochlea, whereas the low-pitched tones of a tuba stimulate the wide end.

• **place theory** Theory regarding how the inner ear registers the frequency of sound, stating that each frequency produces vibrations at a particular spot on the basilar membrane.

Place theory adequately explains high-frequency but not low-frequency sounds (Oxenham, 2018; Plack, 2018). A high-frequency sound—like the screech of a referee's whistle—stimulates a precise area on the basilar membrane, just as place theory suggests. However, a low-frequency sound—like the tone of a tuba—causes a large part of the basilar membrane to be displaced, making it hard to identify an exact location on the membrane that is associated with hearing this kind of sound. Looking only at the movement of the basilar membrane, you would get the impression that humans are probably not very good at hearing low-frequency sounds, and yet we are. Therefore, some other factors must be at play in low-frequency hearing.

**Frequency theory** gets at these other influences by stating that the perception of a sound's frequency depends on how *often* the auditory nerve fires (Plack, 2018). Higher-frequency sounds cause the auditory nerve to fire more often than do lower-frequency sounds. One limitation of frequency theory, however, is that a single neuron has a maximum firing rate of about 1,000 times per second. Therefore, frequency theory cannot explain tones that would require a neuron to fire more rapidly.

• **frequency theory** Theory regarding how the inner ear registers the frequency of sound, stating that the perception of a sound's frequency depends on how often the auditory nerve fires.

To deal with this limitation of frequency theory, researchers developed the **volley principle**, which states that a cluster of nerve cells can fire neural impulses in rapid succession, producing a volley of impulses. Individual neurons cannot fire faster than 1,000 times per second, but if the neurons team up and alternate their neural firing, they can attain a combined frequency above that rate.

• **volley principle** Modification of frequency theory stating that a cluster of nerve cells can fire neural impulses in rapid succession, producing a volley of impulses.

To get a sense for how the volley principle works, imagine a troop of soldiers who are all armed with guns that can fire only one round at a time and that take time to reload. If all the soldiers fire at the same time, the frequency of firing is limited and cannot go any faster than it takes to reload those guns. If, however, the soldiers are coordinated as a group and fire at different times, some of them can fire while others are reloading, leading to a greater frequency of firing.

Frequency theory better explains the perception of sounds below 1,000 times per second. However, a combination of frequency and place theory is needed for sounds above 1,000 times per second.

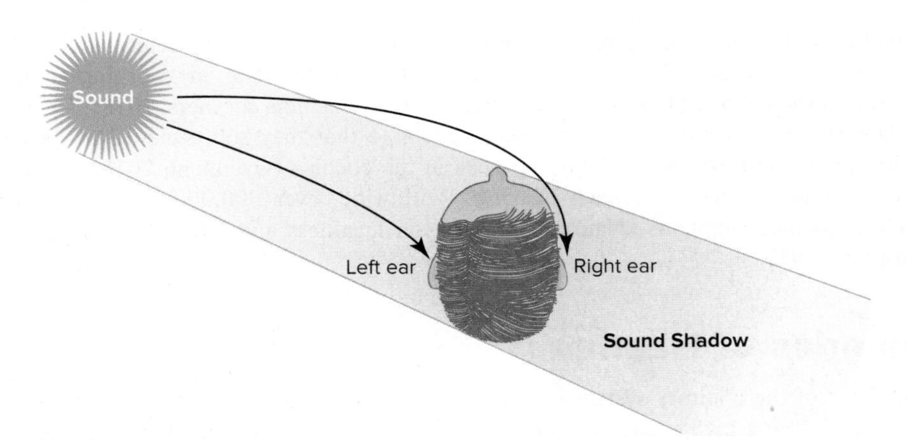


**FIGURE 30** **The Sound Shadow** The sound shadow is caused by the listener's head, which forms a barrier that reduces the sound's intensity. Here the sound is to the person's left, so the sound shadow will reduce the intensity of the sound that reaches the right ear.

## Auditory Processing in the Brain

As we considered in the discussion of the visual system, the responses of the rod and cone receptors feed into ganglion cells and leave the eye via the optic nerve. In the auditory system, information about sound moves from the hair cells of the inner ear to the **auditory nerve**, which carries neural impulses to the brain's auditory areas. The auditory nerve extends from the cochlea to the brain stem. Remember that it is the movement of the hair cells that transforms the physical stimulation of sound waves into the action potential of neural impulses.

● **auditory nerve** The nerve structure that receives information about sound from the hair cells of the inner ear and carries these neural impulses to the brain's auditory areas.

Auditory information moves up the auditory pathway via electrochemical transmission in a more complex manner than does visual information in the visual pathway. Many synapses occur in the ascending auditory pathway, with most fibers crossing over the midline between the hemispheres of the cerebral cortex, although some proceed directly to the hemisphere on the same side as the ear of reception (Oxenham, 2018). This means that most of the auditory information from the left ear goes to the right side of the brain, but some also stays on the left side. The cortical destination of most of these impulses is the temporal lobes of the brain. As in the case of visual information, features are extracted from auditory information and transmitted along parallel pathways in the brain (Huggins, 2017; Kopp-Scheinpflug, Sinclair, & Linden, 2018).

## Localizing Sound

When we hear the bark of a dog, how do we know where the sound is coming from? The basilar membrane gives us information about the frequency, pitch, and complexity of a sound, but it does not tell us where a sound is located.

Earlier in the chapter we saw that because our two eyes see slightly different images, we can determine how near or far away an object is. Similarly, having two ears helps us to localize a sound because each receives somewhat different stimuli from the sound source. A sound coming from the left has to travel different distances to the two ears, so if a barking dog is to your left, your left ear receives the sound sooner than your right ear. Also, your left ear will receive a slightly more intense sound than your right ear in this case. The sound reaching one ear is more intense than the sound reaching the other ear for two reasons: (1) it has traveled less distance, and (2) the other ear is in what is called the *sound shadow* of the listener's head, which provides a barrier that reduces the sound's intensity (Figure 30).

Thus, differences in both the *timing* and the *intensity* help us to localize a sound (Yost, 2018). We have difficulty localizing sounds coming from a source that is directly in front of us, above our heads, or directly behind us, because that sound reaches both ears simultaneously.

### test yourself

1. When you hear the pitch of a voice or an instrument, what quality of sound are you perceiving? When you hear the loudness of music, what characteristic of sound are you perceiving?
2. When you hear any sound, what vibrates, and how are the vibrations then transferred to the inner ear?
3. What is the pinna? What role does it play in hearing?

# 4. OTHER SENSES

We turn now to the body's other sensory systems. These include the skin senses and the chemical senses (smell and taste), as well as the kinesthetic and vestibular senses (systems that allow us to stay upright and to coordinate our movements).

## The Skin Senses

Many of us think of our skin as a painter's canvas: We color it with cosmetics, dyes, and tattoos. In fact, the skin is our largest sensory system, draped over the body with receptors for touch, temperature, and pain. These three kinds of receptors form the *cutaneous senses.*

### TOUCH

Touch is one of the senses that we most often take for granted, yet our ability to respond to touch is astounding. What do we detect when we feel "touch"? What kind of energy does our sense of touch pick up from our external environment?

In touch we detect *mechanical energy*, or pressure against the skin. The lifting of a single hair causes pressure on the skin around the shaft of hair. This tiny bit of mechanical pressure at the base of the hair is sufficient for us to feel the touch of a pencil point. More commonly we detect the mechanical energy of the pressure of a car seat against our buttocks or of a pencil in our hand. Is this energy so different from the kind of energy we detect in vision or hearing? Sometimes the only difference is one of intensity–the sound of a rock band playing softly is an auditory stimulus, but at the high volumes that make a concert hall reverberate, this auditory stimulus is also *felt* as mechanical energy pressing against our skin.

How does information about touch travel from the skin through the nervous system? Sensory fibers arising from receptors in the skin first enter the spinal cord. From the spinal cord, the information travels to the brain stem, where most fibers from each side of the body cross over to the opposite side of the brain. Next, the information moves on to the thalamus, which serves as a relay station. The thalamus then projects the map of the body's surface onto the somatosensory areas of the parietal lobes in the cerebral cortex (Aktar & others, 2017).

Just as the visual system is more sensitive to images on the fovea than to images in the peripheral retina, our sensitivity to touch is not equally good across all areas of the skin. Human toolmakers need excellent touch discrimination in their hands, but they require much less touch discrimination in other parts of the body, such as the torso and legs. The brain devotes more space to analyzing touch signals coming from the hands than from the legs.

The sense of touch is one of the ways we connect with each other. Patting a friend on the shoulder during a difficult time or giving someone a much-needed hug are just two of the ways interpersonal touch communicates our feelings. The human capacity for empathy, the ability to feel what others are feeling, lies at the heart of compassion and caring. For some people with a rare condition called *mirror-touch synaesthesia* (MTS), the feeling of empathy takes on a very different character. MTS means that a person experiences tactile sensations when the person sees someone else being touched (Ward, Schnakenberg, & Banissy, 2018). Interestingly, MTS appears to be linked to empathy and recognizing the emotions that others are feeling.

### TEMPERATURE

We not only feel the warmth of a comforting hand on our own, we also can feel the warmth or coolness of a room. To maintain our body temperature, we have to be able to detect temperature. **Thermoreceptors**, sensory nerve endings under the skin, respond to changes in temperature at or near the skin's surface and provide input to keep the body's temperature at 98.6 degrees Fahrenheit. There are two types of thermoreceptors: warm and cold. Warm thermoreceptors respond to the warming of the skin, and cold

● **thermoreceptors** Sensory nerve endings under the skin that respond to changes in temperature at or near the skin's surface and provide input to keep the body's temperature at 98.6 degrees Fahrenheit.

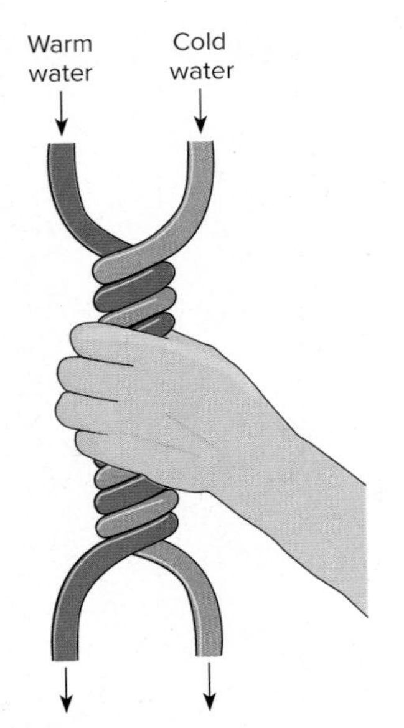


**FIGURE 31** **A "Hot" Experience** When two pipes, one containing cold water and the other warm water, are braided together, a person touching the pipes feels a sensation of "hot." The perceived heat coming from the pipes is so intense that the individual cannot touch them for longer than a couple of seconds.

● **pain** The sensation that warns an individual of damage to the body.

thermoreceptors respond to the cooling of the skin. When warm and cold receptors that are close to each other in the skin are stimulated simultaneously, we experience the sensation of hotness. Figure 31 illustrates this "hot" experience.

## PAIN

**Pain** is the sensation that warns us of damage to the body. When contact with the skin takes the form of a sharp pinch, our sensation of mechanical pressure changes from touch to pain. When a pot handle is so hot that it burns our hand, our sensation of temperature becomes one of pain. Intense stimulation of any one of the senses can produce pain—too much light, very loud sounds, or too many habanero peppers, for example.

Our ability to sense pain is vital for our survival as a species. In other words, this ability is adaptive. Individuals who cannot perceive pain often have serious difficulty navigating the world. They might not notice that they need to move away from a danger such as a hot burner on a stove, or they may be unaware that they have seriously injured themselves. Pain functions as a quick-acting messenger that tells the brain's motor systems that they must act quickly to eliminate or minimize damage.

Pain receptors are dispersed widely throughout the body—in the skin, in the sheath tissue surrounding muscles, in internal organs, and in the membranes around bone. Although all pain receptors are anatomically similar, they differ in the type of physical stimuli to which they most readily react. Mechanical pain receptors respond mainly to pressure, such as when we encounter a sharp object. Heat pain receptors respond primarily to strong heat that is capable of burning the tissue in which the receptors are embedded. Other pain receptors have a mixed function, responding to both types of painful stimuli. Many pain receptors are chemically sensitive and respond to a range of pain-producing substances (Hachisuka, Chiang, & Ross, 2018; Yam & others, 2018).

Pain receptors have a much higher threshold for firing than receptors for temperature and touch. This means that pain receptors require a higher level of stimulation to be activated. Pain receptors react mainly to physical stimuli that distort them or to chemical stimuli that irritate them into action. Inflamed joints or sore, torn muscles produce *prostaglandins,* which stimulate the receptors and cause the experience of pain. Drugs such as aspirin likely reduce the feeling of pain by reducing prostaglandin production.

Two different neural pathways transmit pain messages to the brain: a fast pathway and a slow pathway (Dunne & others, 2018). In the *fast pathway,* fibers connect directly with the thalamus and then to the motor and sensory areas of the cerebral cortex. This pathway transmits information about sharp, localized pain, like a cut to skin. The fast pathway may serve as a warning system, providing immediate information about an injury; it takes less than a second for the information in this pathway to reach the cerebral cortex. In the *slow pathway,* pain information travels through the limbic system, a detour that delays the arrival of information at the cerebral cortex by seconds. The unpleasant, nagging pain that characterizes the slow pathway may function to remind the brain that an injury has occurred and that we need to restrict normal activity and monitor the pain (Koch, Acton, & Goulding, 2018).

Many neuroscientists believe that the brain actually generates the experience of pain (Woolf, 2018). There is evidence that turning pain signals on and off is a chemical process that probably involves *endorphins* (Corder, Castro, Bruchas, & Scherrer, 2018). Recall from the chapter "Biological Foundations of Behavior" that endorphins are neurotransmitters that function as natural opiates in producing pleasure and pain. Endorphins are believed to be released mainly in the synapses of the slow pathway (Chen, Taché, & Marvizón, 2018).

Perception of pain is complex and often varies from one person to the next (Furman & others, 2018; Woolf, 2018). Some people rarely feel pain; others seem to be in great pain if they experience a minor bump or bruise. To some degree, these individual variations may be physiological. A person who experiences considerable pain even with a minor injury may have a neurotransmitter system that is deficient in endorphin production. Chronic pain shares genetic features with depression (Dunne & others, 2018; van Hecke & others, 2017). However, perception of pain goes beyond physiology. Although it is true that motivation, expectation, and other related decision factors affect all sensations, the perception of pain is especially susceptible to these factors (Watson & others, 2006). Cultural and ethnic contexts also influence the degree to which an individual experiences or reports pain (Kim & others, 2017).

Some studies show that women report greater pain than men (Abraham & others, 2018; Madsen & others, 2018). Research on newborns suggests that some of the difference may be biological—although baby boys and girls both cry in response to a painful stimulus, the female infant brain shows wider spreading of activation (Verriotis & others, 2018). However, a review of studies from 1998 to 2008 of laboratory-induced pain in nonclinical participants found no sex differences in perception of pain intensity and unpleasantness and no sex differences in many types of pain (Racine & others, 2012a, 2012b). A meta-analysis of lab-induced pain in adolescents also showed no gender difference (Boerner & others, 2014).

An important factor to consider in the realm of gender differences in pain is the important role of cultural expectations (Berke & others, 2017). One study showed that men were particularly likely to show high pain tolerance when the experimenter was a woman, and especially if she was an attractive woman (Levine & De Simone, 1991). In addition, a recent study showed that men who scored higher on measures of stereotypical masculinity and aggression were more likely to volunteer to participate in a pain study (Feijó & others, 2018). Women showed no such association. This suggests that gender comparisons in pain studies may not reflect real gender differences in the world.

Before we leave the topic of pain, let's revisit the importance of the experience of pain. Pain provides us with information about what is happening to us (Koch, Acton, & Goulding, 2018). This feeling, like all of our other senses, connects us to the external world. A pain-free existence might sound nice, but in fact pain is an important sensation. Consider the situation of Ashlyn Blocker, age 18. She was born without the ability to sense pain. Ashlyn was a baby who did not cry—even when stinging eye drops were put in her eyes, even when she had a terrible diaper rash (Agresz, 2017).

Researchers have studied Ashlyn, and other children like her, to understand not only the cause of her condition but the nature of pain itself (Marchi & others, 2018; Schon, Parker, & Woods, 2018). It turns out that Ashlyn has a genetic mutation that short-circuits the pain signals in her brain. Without pain, she has missed some of life's "warning signals," suffering severe burns as well as two broken ankles before age 20. She has to remind herself that the sight of blood coming from a cut means that something is wrong. Cases like Ashlyn's remind us that pain plays an important role in allowing us to navigate the world (Sexton & others, 2018).

## The Chemical Senses

The information processed through our senses comes in many diverse forms: electromagnetic energy in vision, sound waves in hearing, and mechanical pressure and temperature in the skin senses. The two senses we now consider, smell and taste, are responsible for processing chemicals in our environment (Spence & Wang, 2018). Through smell, we detect airborne chemicals, and through taste we detect chemicals that have been dissolved in saliva. Smell and taste are frequently stimulated simultaneously. We notice the strong links between the two senses when a nasty cold with lots of nasal congestion takes the pleasure out of eating. Our favorite foods become "tasteless" without their characteristic smells. Despite this link, taste and smell are two distinct systems.

### TASTE

Think of your favorite food. Imagine that food without its flavor—would there still be pleasure in eating it?

How does taste happen? To get at this question, try this. Take a drink of milk and allow it to coat your tongue. Then go to a mirror, stick out your tongue, and look carefully at its surface. You should be able to see rounded bumps above the surface. Those bumps, called **papillae**, contain *taste buds*, the receptors for taste. Your tongue houses about

• **papillae** Rounded bumps above the tongue's surface that contain the taste buds, the receptors for taste.

10,000 taste buds, which are replaced about every two weeks (Bartoshuk, 2018). As with all of the other sensory systems we have studied, the information picked up by these taste receptors is transmitted to the brain for analysis and, when necessary, for a response (spitting something out, for example). With age, the replacement process is not as efficient, and an older individual may have just 5,000 working taste buds at any given moment.

Traditionally, tastes were categorized as sweet, sour, bitter, and salty. However, today scientists believe that the breakdown into those categories far underestimates the complexity of taste. The taste fibers leading from a taste bud to the brain often respond strongly to a range of chemicals spanning *multiple* taste elements, such as salty *and* sour. The brain processes these incoming signals and integrates them into a perception of taste (Cook & others, 2018; Fondberg & others, 2018).

Researchers and chefs now recognize a taste called *umami* (Han & others, 2018). *Umami* is the Japanese word for "delicious" or "yummy." The taste of umami is the flavor of L-glutamate. What is that taste? Umami is a savory flavor that is present in many seafoods as well as soy sauce, parmesan and mozzarella cheese, anchovies, mushrooms, and hearty meat broths. A recent candidate for yet another taste is *fat*. Some sensory receptors on the tongue respond selectively to the taste of fat (Besnard, Passilly-Degrace, & Khan, 2016; Keast & Costanzo, 2015; Liu & others, 2018). What does fat taste like? Not surprisingly, perhaps, an excellent example of this taste is *butter*.

Culture certainly influences the experience of taste. Any American who has watched the Japanese version of *Iron Chef* or *Bizarre Foods* on television quickly notices that some people enjoy the flavor of sea urchin or raw meat, while others just do not get the appeal. In some cultures, food that is so spicy as to be practically inedible for the outsider may be viewed as quite delicious. The culture in which we live can influence the foods we are exposed to and our sense of what tastes good.

## SMELL

*Dogs have an especially powerful olfactory sense. Watson, a Labrador retriever, reliably paws his owner, who has epilepsy, 45 minutes before her seizures begin, giving her time to move to a safe place. How does Watson know to do so? The best hypothesis is that the dog smells the chemical changes that precede epileptic seizures.*



Why do we have a sense of smell? One way to appreciate the importance of smell is to think about animals with a more sophisticated sense of smell than our own. A dog, for example, can use smell to find its way back from a long stroll, to distinguish friend from foe, and even (with practice) to detect illegal drugs concealed in a suitcase. In fact, dogs can detect odors in concentrations 100 times lower than those detectable by humans.

What do humans use smell for? For one thing, humans need the sense of smell to decide what to eat. We can distinguish rotten food from fresh food. The smell of a food that has previously made us sick is often by itself enough to make us feel nauseated. Also, although tracking is a function of smell that we often associate only with animals, humans are competent odor trackers. We can follow the odor of gas to a leak, the smell of smoke to a fire, and the aroma of freshly baked cookies to a kitchen. Our noses tell us if something dangerous or appealing is nearby.

What physical equipment do we use to process odor information? Just as the eyes scan the visual field for objects of interest, the nose is an active instrument. We actively sniff when we are trying to track down the source of a fire or an unfamiliar chemical odor. The **olfactory epithelium** lining the roof of the nasal cavity contains a sheet of receptor cells for smell (Figure 32), so sniffing maximizes the chances of detecting an odor. The receptor cells are covered with millions of minute, hairlike antennae that project through the mucus in the top of the nasal cavity and make contact with air on its way to the throat and lungs (Linster, 2018). Interestingly, unlike the neurons of most sensory systems, the neurons in the olfactory epithelium tend to replace themselves after injury and with age (Chang & Glezer, 2018; Child & others, 2018).

• **olfactory epithelium** The lining of the roof of the nasal cavity, containing a sheet of receptor cells for smell.

What is the neural pathway for information about smell? Although all other sensory pathways pass through the thalamus, the pathway for smell does not. In smell, the neural pathway first goes to the olfactory areas in the temporal lobes and then projects to various

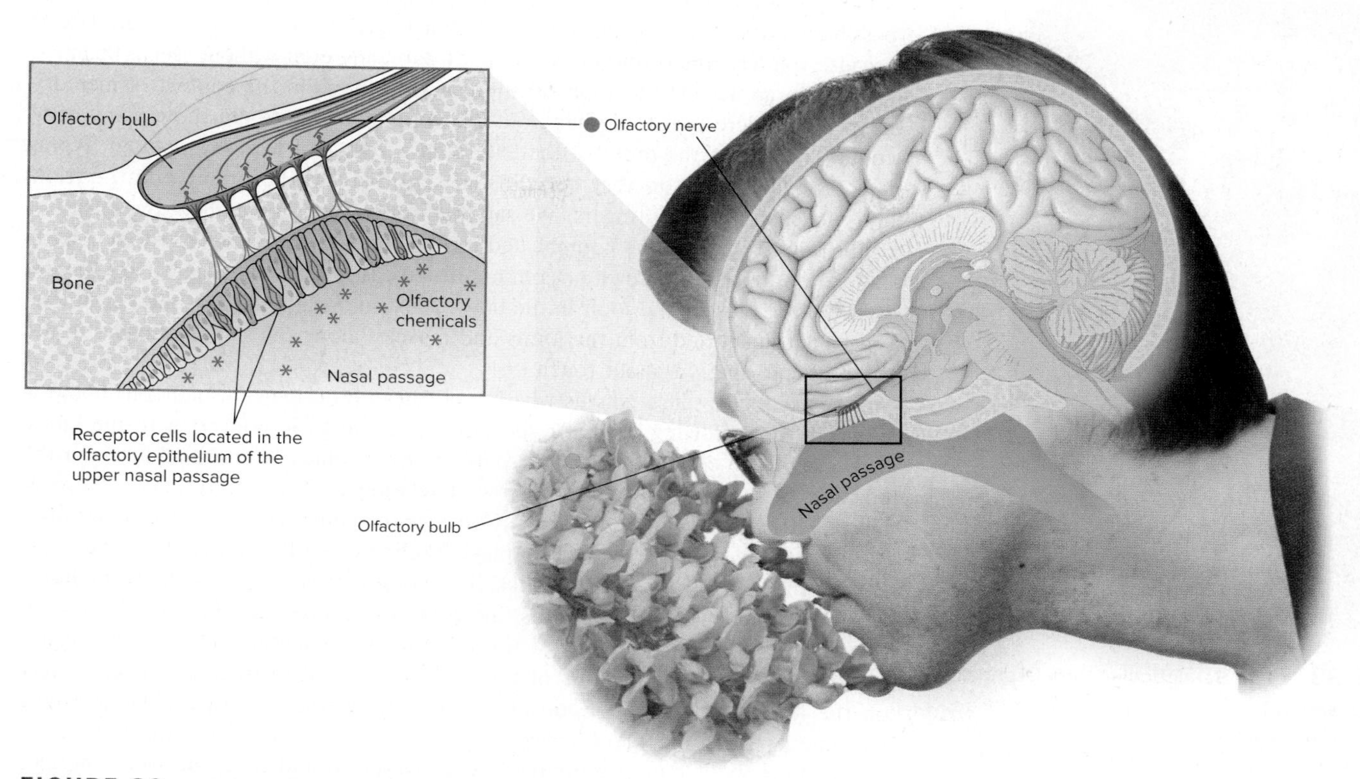


**FIGURE 32** **The Olfactory Sense** Airborne molecules of an odor reach tiny receptor cells in the roof of the nasal cavity. The receptor cells form a mucus-covered membrane called the olfactory epithelium. Then the olfactory nerve carries information about the odor to the brain for further processing. ©Directphoto.org/Alamy Stock Photo

brain regions, especially the limbic system, which is involved in emotion and memory. Unlike the other senses, smells take a superhighway to emotion and memory.

Smell might have a role to play in the chemistry of interpersonal attraction (Wu & others, 2018). From an evolutionary perspective, the goal of human mating is to find someone with whom to produce the healthiest offspring (Buss, 2015). Mates with differing sets of genes (known as the *major histocompatibility complex,* or *MHC*) produce healthier offspring with the broadest immune systems (Garamszegi & others, 2018). How do we find these people, short of taking a blood test? We may smell them (Wu & others, 2018). Research on humans and other primates suggests that female members of the species can identify males with advantageous MHC from their smell (Holy, 2018; Huchard & Pechouskova, 2014). So, the eye may be the window to the soul, but the nose might be the gateway to love.

## The Kinesthetic and Vestibular Senses

You know the difference between walking and running and between lying down and sitting up. To perform even the simplest act of motor coordination, such as getting up out of a chair, the brain must constantly receive and coordinate information from every part of the body. Your body has two kinds of senses that give you information about your movement and orientation in space, as well as helping you maintain balance. The **kinesthetic senses** provide information about movement, posture, and orientation. The **vestibular sense** provides information about balance and movement.

- **kinesthetic senses** Senses that provide information about movement, posture, and orientation.
- **vestibular sense** Sense that provides information about balance and movement.

No specific organ contains the kinesthetic senses. Instead, they are embedded in muscle fibers and joints (Ivanenko & Gurfinkel, 2018). As we stretch and move, these receptors signal the state of the muscle. *Kinesthesia* is a sense that you often do not even notice until it is gone. Try walking when your leg is "asleep" or smiling when you have just come from a dentist's

**FIGURE 33** **The Semicircular Canals and the Vestibular Sense** The semicircular canals provide feedback to the gymnast's brain as her head and body tilt in different directions. Any angle of head rotation is registered by hair cells in one or more semicircular canals in both ears. (*Inset*) The semicircular canals. (photo) ©Thomas Coex/AFP/Getty Images; (inset) ©MedicalRF/Getty Images

● **semicircular canals** Three fluid-filled circular tubes in the inner ear containing the sensory receptors that detect head motion caused when an individual tilts or moves the head and/or the body.

office and are still under the effects of Novocain. The kinesthetic senses make it possible for you to touch your nose with your fingertip even if your eyes are closed, because you feel where your body and body parts are, even without seeing them.

We can appreciate the sophistication of kinesthesis in the context of memory. Even a mediocre typist can bang out 20 words per minute—but how many of us could write down the order of the letters on a keyboard without looking? Typing is a skill that relies on very coordinated sensitivity to the orientation, position, and movements of our fingers. We say that our fingers "remember" the positions of the keys. Likewise, the complicated movements a pitcher uses to throw a baseball cannot be written down or communicated easily using language. They involve nearly every muscle and joint in the body. Most information about the kinesthetic senses is transmitted from the joints and muscles along the same pathways to the brain as information about touch.

The vestibular sense tells us whether our head (and hence usually our body) is tilted, moving, slowing down, or speeding up. It works in concert with the kinesthetic senses to coordinate *proprioceptive feedback,* which is information about the position of our limbs and body parts in relation to other body parts (Moro & Harris, 2018; Ono & others, 2018). Consider the combination of sensory abilities involved in the motion of a hockey player skating down the ice, cradling the puck, and pushing it forward with the stick. The hockey player is responding simultaneously to a multitude of sensations, including those produced by the slickness of the ice, the position of the puck, the speed and momentum of the forward progression, and the requirements of the play to turn and to track the other players on the ice. Proprioceptive feedback is not only relevant to large, obvious bodily movements, like playing hockey. It also functions when we are talking—as information about mouth movements is conveyed to and from the facial muscles (Ding & others, 2018).

The **semicircular canals** of the inner ear contain the sensory receptors that detect head motion caused when we tilt or move our head and/or body (Figure 33). These canals consist of three fluid-filled, circular tubes that lie in the three planes of the body—right-left, front-back, and up-down. We can picture these as three intersecting hula hoops. As you move your head, the fluid of the semicircular canals flows in different directions and at different speeds (depending on the force of the head movement). Our perception of head movement and position is determined by the movements of these receptor cells (Jones & others, 2018).

This ingenious system of using the motion of fluid in tubes to sense head position is similar to the auditory system of the inner ear. However, the fluid movement in the cochlea results from the pressure sound exerts on the oval window, whereas the movements in the semicircular canals reflect physical movements of the head and body. Vestibular sacs in the semicircular canals contain hair cells embedded in a gelatinous mass. Just as the hair cells in the cochlea trigger hearing impulses in the brain, the hair cells in the semicircular canals transmit information about balance and movement.

Unlike other sensory information, vestibular information is more likely to impinge on many aspects of the brain. The brain pathways for the vestibular sense begin in the auditory nerve, which contains both the cochlear nerve (with information about sound) and the vestibular nerve (which has information about balance and movement). Most of the axons of the vestibular nerve connect with the medulla, although some go directly to the cerebellum (Woo & others, 2018). Vestibular information is also processed in the parietal lobe (Dieterich & Brandt, 2018).

Information from the sense of vision supplements the combination of kinesthetic and vestibular senses (Caudron & others, 2018). This principle causes a motorist to slam on the brakes in his tiny sports car when the big truck next to him starts to move forward. When everything in our visual field appears to be moving, it is generally because *we* are moving. Consider as well how people behave when they try out virtual reality or augmented reality goggles. Out in the "real world" we can get a laugh watching them moving in the world they are seeing—as if that world were real (Nilsson & others, 2018).

### *test yourself*

1. What three kinds of receptors form the cutaneous senses?
2. Describe how and why pain is adaptive.
3. What information about the body do the kinesthetic senses and the vestibular sense provide?

# 5. SENSATION, PERCEPTION, AND HEALTH AND WELLNESS

Our senses connect us to the world and we should not take them for granted. Ensuring the health of our senses means caring for our precious sensory organs—for example, by getting vision and hearing screenings and noting changes that might occur in our sensory experiences.

Taking care of your eyes means avoiding high-fat food, not smoking, and eating a diet rich in vitamins A, E, and C, zinc, and beta carotene. This means consuming a wide variety of fruits and vegetables (including spinach). It also means reading with appropriate lighting (three times brighter than the rest of the room light) and with your work at eye level—about 16 inches away—and wearing sunglasses that protect your eyes from UVA and UVB, the sun's damaging rays. Some common causes of blindness are preventable. A glaucoma test is especially important after the age of 60. Staying active and eating healthy are important for avoiding another cause of blindness: diabetic retinopathy.

For hearing, perhaps the most dangerous threat comes from loud noise. A special concern is hearing damage that can be caused by loud noise during leisure activities. Dance clubs and concerts often feature music that is very, very loud. You may have had the experience of leaving a loud venue and feeling your ears ringing for quite some time after. One way to aid our ears in recovery from loud music is to take brief breaks (Helleman & Dreschler, 2015). Just as we may need to step outside for some fresh air, stepping into a quiet space can help our ears return to normal faster.

Another potential risk for our ears is listening to music through earphones, whether earbuds or Beats. Research suggests that a typical person could safely listen to an iPod for nearly five hours at 70 percent volume (Portnuff, Fligor, & Arehart, 2011). Those who like their tunes louder should not listen as long; if you listen at 90 percent volume, for example, keep yourself plugged in for no more than 90 minutes. One important issue is the environment in which the person is listening. People are more likely to pump up the volume if they are listening to their iPods in environments that are already noisy. Effects on hearing do not depend on choice of music. So, whether it is Drake, Adele, or Mozart, sensible listening is wise.

Throughout this chapter we have viewed sensation and perception as our connections to the world. How about treating your senses by taking them outside? Few things engage all of our senses like being outside in a natural environment. And experiences with the natural world have been shown to improve overall physical and psychological well-being (Hyvönen & others, 2018; Pasanen, Neuvonen, & Korpela, 2018; Swami, Barron, & Furnham, 2018). Hospital patients recover more quickly if they have a window that looks out onto trees, sky, and plants (Ulrich & others, 1991). Taking a walk outside is an excellent way to get exercise as well as to open up your senses to the world. While you are walking, remember to stop and smell the flowers—literally. Flowers are visually pleasant and they smell good, so they are a natural mood booster for both men and women (Haviland-Jones & others, 2005).

Our senses allow us to experience the world in all its vibrancy. Sue Berry, who achieved the ability to perceive depth only after a long, arduous effort, described her encounter with nature on a snowy day. "I felt myself within the snowfall, among the snowflakes. . . . I was overcome with a sense of joy. A snowfall can be quite beautiful—especially when you see it for the first time" (Sacks, 2006, p. 73). Recall the example of Michael May who was able to see after 25 years of blindness. One night, with his seeing-eye dog Josh at his side, he decided to go look at the sky. Lying on the grass in a field, he opened his eyes. He thought he was "seeing stars"—in the metaphorical sense. He thought that the thousands of white lights in the sky could not possibly be real, but they were. As he remarked in his vision diary: "How sweet it is" (May, 2003; Stein, 2003).

### test yourself

1. What are several strategies individuals can use to protect and preserve their vision?
2. What factor poses the most serious threat to hearing?
3. How do portable media players such as iPods impact hearing, and what can consumers do to reduce the potential harm from using them?

SUMMARY

## 1. HOW WE SENSE AND PERCEIVE THE WORLD

Sensation is the process of receiving stimulus energies from the environment. Perception is the process of organizing and interpreting sensory information to give it meaning. All sensation begins with sensory receptors, specialized cells that detect and transmit information about a stimulus to sensory neurons and the brain. Sensory receptors are selective and have different neural pathways.

Absolute threshold refers to the minimum amount of energy that people can detect. The difference threshold, or just noticeable difference, is the smallest difference in stimulation required to discriminate one stimulus from another 50 percent of the time.

Signal detection theory focuses on decision making about stimuli in the presence of uncertainty. In this theory, detection of sensory stimuli depends on many factors other than the physical properties of the stimuli, and differences in these other factors may lead different people to make different decisions about identical stimuli.

Perception is influenced by attention, beliefs, and expectations. Sensory adaptation is a change in the responsiveness of the sensory system based on the average level of surrounding stimulation, essentially the ways that our senses start to ignore a particular stimulus once it is around long enough.

## 2. THE VISUAL SYSTEM

Light is the stimulus that is sensed by the visual system. Light can be described in terms of wavelengths. Three characteristics of light waves determine our experience: wavelength (hue), amplitude (brightness), and purity (saturation).

In sensation, light passes through the cornea and lens to the retina, the light-sensitive surface in the back of the eye that houses light receptors called rods (which function in low illumination) and cones (which react to color). The fovea of the retina contains only cones and sharpens detail in an image. The optic nerve transmits neural impulses to the brain. There it diverges at the optic chiasm, so that what we see in the left visual field is registered in the right side of the brain and vice versa. In the occipital lobes of the cerebral cortex, the information is integrated.

The trichromatic theory of color perception holds that three types of color receptors in the retina allow us to perceive three colors (green, red, and blue). The opponent-process theory states that cells in the visual system respond to red-green and blue-yellow colors. The eye and the brain likely use both methods to code colors.

Shape perception is the ability to distinguish objects from their background. Depth perception is the ability to perceive objects three-dimensionally and depends on binocular (two-eye) cues and monocular (one-eye) cues. Motion perception by humans depends on specialized neurons, feedback from the body, and environmental cues. Perceptual constancy is the recognition that objects are stable despite changes in the way we see them.

## 3. THE AUDITORY SYSTEM

Sound waves are vibrations in the air that are processed by the auditory system. These waves vary in ways that influence what we hear. Pitch (how high or low in tone a sound is) is the perceptual interpretation of wavelength frequency. Amplitude of wavelengths, measured in decibels, is perceived as loudness. Complex sounds involve a blending of frequencies. Timbre is the tone saturation, or perceptual quality, of a sound.

The outer ear consists of the pinna and external auditory canal and acts to funnel sound to the middle ear. In the middle ear, the eardrum, hammer, anvil, and stirrup vibrate in response to sound and transfer the vibrations to the inner ear. Important parts of the fluid-filled inner ear are the oval window, cochlea, and basilar membrane. The movement of hair cells between the basilar membrane and the tectorial membrane generates nerve impulses.

Place theory states that each frequency produces vibrations at a particular spot on the basilar membrane. Place theory adequately explains high-frequency sounds but not low-frequency sounds. Frequency theory holds that the perception of a sound's frequency depends on how often the auditory nerve fires. The volley principle states that a cluster of neurons can fire impulses in rapid succession, producing a volley of impulses.

Information about sound moves from the hair cells to the auditory nerve, which carries information to the brain's auditory areas. The cortical destination of most fibers is the temporal lobes of the cerebral cortex. Localizing sound involves both the timing of the sound and the intensity of the sound arriving at each ear.

## 4. OTHER SENSES

The skin senses include touch, temperature, and pain. Touch is the detection of mechanical energy, or pressure, against the skin. Touch information travels through the spinal cord, brain stem, and thalamus and on to the somatosensory areas of the parietal lobes. Thermoreceptors under the skin respond to increases and decreases in temperature. Pain is the sensation that warns us about damage to the body.

The chemical senses of taste and smell enable us to detect and process chemicals in the environment. Papillae are bumps on the tongue that contain taste buds, the receptors for taste. The olfactory epithelium contains a sheet of receptor cells for smell in the roof of the nose.

The kinesthetic senses provide information about movement, posture, and orientation. The vestibular sense gives us information about balance and movement. Receptors for the kinesthetic senses are embedded in muscle fibers and joints. The semicircular canals in the inner ear contain the sensory receptors that detect head motion.

## 5. SENSATION, PERCEPTION, AND HEALTH AND WELLNESS

Senses connect us to the world. Taking care of your precious sense organs means adopting healthy practices such as eating a low-fat diet rich in vitamins and beta carotene. Caring for your eyes means wearing protective lenses when you are in the bright sun. Protecting your hearing requires avoiding dangerously loud noises. Noise at 80 decibels or higher, if heard for prolonged periods, can damage hearing. Experiences in nature have been shown to reduce stress and enhance well-being.

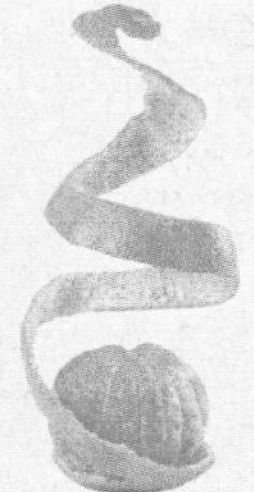

# key *terms*

absolute threshold
apparent movement
attention
auditory nerve
binding
binocular cues
bottom-up processing
cones
convergence
depth perception
difference threshold
feature detectors
figure-ground relationship
frequency theory
gestalt psychology
inner ear
kinesthetic senses
middle ear
monocular cues
noise
olfactory epithelium
opponent-process theory
optic nerve
outer ear
pain
papillae
parallel processing
perception
perceptual constancy
perceptual set
place theory
retina
rods
selective attention
semicircular canals
sensation
sensory adaptation
sensory receptors
signal detection theory
subliminal perception
thermoreceptors
top-down processing
trichromatic theory
vestibular sense
volley principle
Weber's law

# apply your *knowledge*

1. Find a partner and test your absolute threshold for sugar. Have your partner set up the following sugar-and-water mixtures. Mix 2 teaspoons of sugar in 4 cups of water. Label this solution ("solution X," for example). Take 2 cups of solution X, add 2 cups of water, and give this solution a second label ("solution D," for example). Then take 2 cups of solution D, add 2 cups of water, and give this a third label ("solution Q"). Continue taking 2 cups from each successive solution until you have a total of eight solutions, making sure to keep track of which solution is which. When you are done, the concentration of the solutions should be equivalent to 1 teaspoon in each of the following amounts of water: 1 pint (2 cups), 1 quart, 1 half-gallon, 1 gallon, 2 gallons, 4 gallons, and 8 gallons. Your partner should place a sample of one of the solutions in a cup and a sample of plain water in another, identical cup. You should taste the solution in each cup and decide which one is the sugar solution. Do this with all of the solutions until you can decide what your absolute threshold is according to the text's definition. Do you think your absolute threshold would vary depending on what you had recently eaten? Why or why not?

2. If you found the example of inattentional blindness in this chapter interesting, check out this website where you will find a video so that you can see for yourself:

   www.theinvisiblegorilla.com

3. If you found the example of mirror-touch synaesthesia interesting, you might be interested in checking out the Entanglement episode of the Invisibilia Podcast, hosted by Lulu Miller and Alix Spiegel:

   www.npr.org/podcasts/510307/invisibilia

4. Create a gestalt moment. Use the corners of the pages of a book or notebook. Draw a series of small, simple pictures, sketching one on the lower right-hand corner of each page. How about a stick figure–standing still, and then moving its arm, and then waving? Each successive picture should be as close to the one before it as possible but changing slightly to reflect the movement. Then, using your thumb, quickly allow the pages to flip rapidly in front of you. You have created a cartoon.

5. If you have a few minutes and a strong stomach, give your vestibular system a workout. Spin around quickly and repeatedly for a minute, either in a swivel chair or standing in the center of a room (be careful of sharp edges nearby). When you stop, you will feel dizzy. Here's what is happening. The fluid in the semicircular canals moves slowly and is even slower to change direction. When we spin for a while, the fluid eventually catches up with our rate of motion and starts moving in the same direction. When we stop moving, however, the slow-moving fluid keeps on moving. It tells the hair cells in the vestibular canals (which in turn tell the brain), "We are still spinning"–and we feel as if we are.

6. Jot down all the foods you have eaten today. Search the web for the nutritional information on these–and evaluate how good you have been to your eyes today.

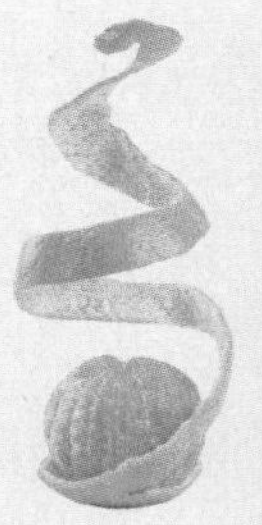

**Design elements:** Preview icon: ©Jiang Hongyan; Intersection box icon: ©D. Hurst/Alamy, ©Creative Crop/Getty Images, ©Dimitris66/Getty Images, ©Savany/Getty Images; Critical Controversy box icon: ©Ultrashock; running heads icon: ©Cre8tive Studios/Alamy; Summary icon: ©Vadarshop

# CHAPTER 5

## CHAPTER OUTLINE

# States of Consciousness

## Locked-In

**Mia Austin was an active 21-year-old working as a travel agent when her life changed forever.** One day in 2009, she went to her job and then headed to the gym afterwards for her usual workout. She came home, took a bath, and passed out in the bathroom. Her parents called an ambulance that took her to a hospital where she lost consciousness again. Later, she awoke to find herself living a completely different life (Simon, 2018). She had suffered a stroke. After weeks in the hospital, her family believed there was no hope left and were prepared to remove her from life support. Just then, her eyes opened and she looked around. Mia's doctors realized that she was conscious and could see, hear, and think. Mia's diagnosis was a rare and permanent condition called *locked-in syndrome*. A person with locked-in syndrome is immobile but has normal cognitive and emotional function. Mia cannot move or speak. She can feel an itch on her face but cannot reach up to scratch it. She can use her eyes (the only muscles over which she has control) to communicate, using a letter board and a specialized computer that tracks eye movements. In the nine years since the stroke, with the help of family, friends, and doctors, Mia has gone to college, bungee jumped, and climbed mountains (Jeffay, 2017). She has even written a book about her experiences (Simon, 2018). Despite all the limitations in her life, Mia has one important thing left: her mind.

You might be surprised to learn that patients with locked-in syndrome feel like "themselves" and report high quality of life (Iyer, Finch, & Kalu, 2018; Vidal, 2018). Imagine living as a mind literally locked inside an immobile body. To some, it might sound like a nightmare. Yet patients with locked-in syndrome and the scientists dedicated to helping them connect with the world demonstrate a simple truth: A conscious mind, even if it is locked in a body that cannot move, is still a person very much worth reaching. Such is the power of consciousness.

# PREVIEW

In this chapter, we review various states of consciousness, as well as the world of sleep and dreams. We also survey two channels of altered states of consciousness—psychoactive drugs and hypnosis. Finally, we consider the positive effects on health and well-being that come from achieving a meditative state of consciousness.

## 1. THE NATURE OF CONSCIOUSNESS

Conscious awareness represents that private inner mind where we think, feel, plan, wish, pray, imagine, and quietly relive experiences. In 1890, psychology pioneer William James described the mind as a **stream of consciousness**, a continuous flow of changing sensations, images, thoughts, and feelings (James, 1950). The content of our awareness changes from moment to moment. Information moves rapidly in and out of consciousness. Our minds can race from one topic to the next—from the person approaching us to the café where we will have lunch to our plan for a test tomorrow.

● **stream of consciousness** Term used by William James to describe the mind as a continuous flow of changing sensations, images, thoughts, and feelings.

In his description of the stream of consciousness, James included aspects of our awareness that he described as on the "fringe" of the conscious stream. This fringe includes all of the thoughts and feelings that we have *about* our thoughts. We are aware not only of those things that take center stage in our mental life, those shiny fish in the stream of consciousness, but also of all the thoughts and feelings that surround those fish.

Today, the term *metacognition* describes the processes by which we think about thinking. This term includes our awareness of the fringe of consciousness. When we read a text, for instance, the difficulty or ease with which we comprehend what is written can influence how we feel about what we read (Huang & others, 2018). When something is easy to read, we are more likely to think that it is true and accurate (Schwarz, 2018).

Metacognitive ease affects our thought processes in surprising ways. Consider the two items below, taken from a scale that measures meaning in life (Steger & others, 2006). The top one is printed in a difficult-to-read combination of fonts, the bottom one in a clear, easy-to-read font:

I HAVE found a really significant meaning in my life.
I have found a really significant meaning in my life.

One study found that participants rated their meaning in life to be lower when the scale was printed in the difficult-to-read format (Trent, Lavelock, & King, 2013).

● **consciousness** An individual's awareness of external events and internal sensations under a condition of arousal, including awareness of the self and thoughts about one's experiences.

Other research has shown that when youth experienced metacognitive difficulty in thinking about their life goals, they were less likely to believe they could reach those goals (Oyserman, Elmore, & Smith, 2012). The logic behind such results is that youth might reason, "If it is this hard for me to even imagine myself pursuing these goals, they must not be very possible."

During much of the twentieth century, psychologists focused less on the study of mental processes and more on the study of observable behavior. More recently, the study of consciousness has compelled widespread interest in psychology. Scientists from many different fields are interested in consciousness (Dehaene, Lau, & Kouider, 2017; Friedman & Jack, 2018; Hassabis & others, 2017).

### Defining Consciousness

We define consciousness in terms of its two parts: awareness and arousal. **Consciousness** is an individual's awareness of external events and internal sensations under a condition of arousal. *Awareness* includes awareness of the self and thoughts about one's experiences. Consider that on an autumn afternoon, when you see a beautiful tree, vibrant with color, you do not simply see the colors; you are *aware* that you are seeing them.

©vasabii/Shutterstock

The second part of consciousness is *arousal*, the physiological state of being engaged with the environment. Thus, a sleeping person is not conscious in the same way that he or she would be while awake.

## Consciousness and the Brain

Recently, theoretical and research interest in understanding how the brain functions to produce consciousness has greatly increased. Scientists have sought to identify what happens in the brain when we feel that we are conscious of our experience (Pantani, Tagini, & Raffone, 2018). This task is quite important. For instance, it is very difficult to tell if a person with locked-in syndrome is conscious or unconscious from a brain scan (Barttfeld & others, 2015; Kirschner, 2018).

We know the two aspects of consciousness, awareness and arousal, are associated with different parts of the brain. First, let's consider brain areas and processes associated with *awareness*—the subjective state of being conscious of what is going on. Awareness is a feeling we have about our experiences. This feeling is associated with many parts of the brain working in synchrony (Babiloni & others, 2016). It appears that the subjective feeling of awareness occurs in a *global brain workspace* that involves various brain areas working in parallel (Dehaene, 2018; Dehaene & Changeux, 2011; Michel, 2017). These locations include the front-most part of the brain—the prefrontal cortex—as well as the anterior cingulate (an area associated with acts of will) and association areas (Fu & others, 2017; Mashour & Hudetz, 2017). This wide-reaching brain workspace is an assembly of neurons that are thought to work in cooperation to produce the subjective sense of consciousness. Areas of the prefrontal cortex appear to be especially involved in the ways that awareness goes beyond the input of sensory information. For instance, these areas of the brain are active when we taste complex flavors and they track the subjective pleasure that accompanies rewarding experiences (Kringelbach, 2005). Still, scientists still do not know many of the details that link consciousness with brain states (Jerath & Beveridge, 2018; Tsuchiya & others, 2015), and studies have challenged even the idea that many areas of the brain working together account for the feeling of awareness (Scott & others, 2018).

The second part of consciousness, *arousal,* is a physiological state determined by a system of brain structures, the reticular activating system. The **reticular activating system**, includes the brain stem, medulla, and thalamus. These structures work together to determine your sense of wakefulness. Arousal is the way awareness is regulated: If we are in danger, we might need to be on "high alert," but if we are in a safe environment with no immediate demands, we can relax, and arousal may be low.

● **reticular activating system** A network of structures including the brain stem, medulla, and thalamus that are involved in the experience of arousal and engagement with the environment.

You might think of consciousness as the mind—that part of yourself that contains your private thoughts and feelings. It might seem obvious that other people have private thoughts and feelings too, but the human ability to recognize the subjective experience of another is a true developmental accomplishment (Johansson Nolaker & others, 2018). **Theory of mind** refers to a person's understanding that others think, feel, perceive, and have private experiences (Prochazkova & others, 2018). Previous research suggested that theory of mind was likely to emerge around the age of 4, but more recent studies show that if the tasks used to measure theory of mind are simplified, even younger children demonstrate a capacity to understand that other people have their own perspective on things (Carr & others, 2018; Rubio-Fernández & Geurts, 2013).

● **theory of mind** Individuals' understanding that they and others think, feel, perceive, and have private experiences.

Theory of mind is essential to many social capacities, like empathy and sympathy (Carr & others, 2018; Prochazkova & others, 2018; Reniers & others, 2012; Sebastian & others, 2012). Simon Baron-Cohen (1995, 2008, 2011) is an expert on *autism spectrum disorder,* a disorder that affects communication, social interaction, and behavior. He has proposed that the emergence of theory of mind is so central to human functioning that evolution would not leave it up to chance. Baron-Cohen suggests that we are born with a brain mechanism that is ready to develop a theory of mind; he hypothesizes that autistic individuals lack a well-developed theory of mind, a condition that would explain their unique social deficits. In studies, children and adolescents with autism spectrum disorder do show lower performance on theory of mind tasks (Jones & others, 2018).

Theory of mind may seem like a uniquely human attribute, and in its fullest form it may be. But other primates also show some indications of awareness that the inhabitants of their social world have minds of their own. To read about research examining this issue, see the Intersection.

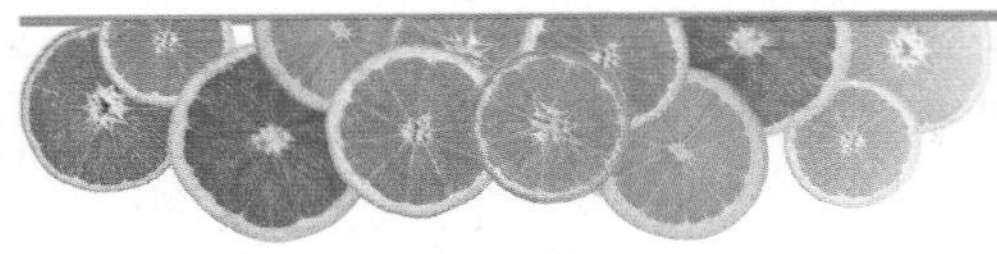

# INTERSECTION

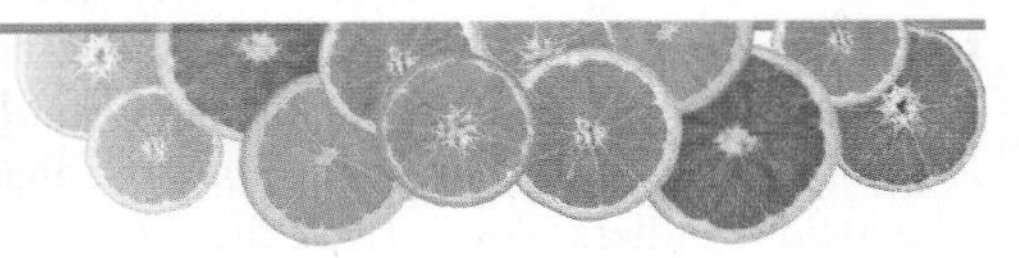

## Consciousness and Comparative Cognition: Do Marmosets Recognize the Minds of Others?

Marmosets are very social primates. These small monkeys usually live high in the trees of the South American rain forest. Monogamous, they live in small social groups (Marini & others, 2018). Baby marmosets are carried by adults in the group, and moving an infant from one adult to another requires cooperation (Miss & Burkart, 2018). Marmosets are a good context in which to explore the possibility that nonhuman primates, even if they lack a full theory of mind, do have a sense that other members of their group may have subjective experiences.

To study this possibility, marmosets first had to learn the Simon Task, which is a little tricky. In humans, the Simon Task involves a person sitting at a computer, wearing earphones, and hearing tones that signal which of two buttons to press. The pitch of the tone indicates whether the participant should press a button on the left or the right. So, a high pitch might mean to press the left button and a low pitch might mean to press the right button. The tones are presented to either the left or right ear—but the location of the tone is irrelevant to the task. Interestingly, people are faster to press the button when the tone is heard in the ear on the side that needs to be pressed. In other words, if a high-pitched tone means "press the left button," people are faster if that tone is heard in the left ear rather than the right ear. This bias is the Simon effect. In the *joint* Simon task, participants work in pairs. In this case, although both hear the sounds on different sides, they are each responsible for only one side. You might think having two heads work on this task would wipe out the Simon effect but it does not. Rather, when paired with another person, people act as if they are engaging in both sides. In humans, this tendency is thought to show that we are mentally representing the partner's job. Is it possible that marmosets would show this same, joint Simon effect?

To answer this question, researchers trained marmosets to complete the Simon Task (Miss & Burkart, 2018). In their version, marmosets learned to open a left- or right-side drawer to get treats in response to different sounds (presented on a loudspeaker on either side of the cage). When the marmosets opened the correct drawer, they were given a treat (nuts, crickets, or sweet fruits). Just like humans working alone, the marmosets showed the Simon effect—they were better at pulling the correct drawer when the sides of the sound and the drawer matched.

To test whether they represent a partner's mental state, the marmosets were tested in pairs. Each monkey was responsible for pulling the drawer on its own side. The drawer to open was signaled by a sound on either side of the cage. When a member of the pair pulled the correct drawer, they both got a treat. Remember, in humans, such a joint task produces a Simon effect: Each person is better at pressing the button on their own side when the right pitched sound is heard in that ear. Results showed that marmosets are much like humans. They showed the joint Simon effect: They did mentally represent their partner's task (not just their own). Marmosets also showed another indication of this representation: they looked over at their partner when they needed to pull the drawer, as if to say, "Your turn."

These results indicate that organisms do not require a fully formed theory of mind to hold a mental representation of another's mental state. For marmosets, working together is required for survival. Consider what fully formed theory of mind tells us about its adaptive function for humans: We need to know each other to survive.

*What does theory of mind tell us about the human species?*

| Level of Awareness | Description | Examples |
|---|---|---|
| **Higher-Level Consciousness** | Involves controlled processing, in which individuals actively focus their efforts on attaining a goal; the most alert state of consciousness | Doing a math or science problem; preparing for a debate; taking an at-bat in a baseball game |
| **Lower-Level Consciousness** | Includes automatic processing that requires little attention, as well as daydreaming | Punching in a number on a cell phone; typing on a keyboard when one is an expert; gazing at a sunset |
| **Altered States of Consciousness** | Can be produced by drugs, trauma, fatigue, possibly hypnosis, and sensory deprivation | Feeling the effects of having taken alcohol or psychedelic drugs; undergoing hypnosis to quit smoking or lose weight |
| **Subconscious Awareness** | Can occur when people are awake, as well as when they are sleeping and dreaming | Sleeping and dreaming |
| **No Awareness** | Freud's belief that some unconscious thoughts are too laden with anxiety and other negative emotions for consciousness to admit them | Having unconscious thoughts; being knocked out by a blow or anesthetized |

**FIGURE 1** **Levels of Awareness** Each level of awareness has its time and place in human life.

## Levels of Awareness

The flow of sensations, images, thoughts, and feelings that William James spoke of can occur at different levels of awareness. There are shades of awareness, just as there are shades of perception in signal detection theory, as discussed in the chapter "Sensation and Perception". Here we consider five levels of awareness: higher-level consciousness, lower-level consciousness, altered states of consciousness, subconscious awareness, and no awareness (Figure 1).

### HIGHER-LEVEL CONSCIOUSNESS

In **controlled processes**, the most alert states of human consciousness, individuals actively focus their efforts toward a goal. For example, watch a classmate as he struggles to master the unfamiliar buttons on his new smartphone. He does not hear you humming or notice the intriguing shadow on the wall. His state of focused awareness illustrates the idea of controlled processes. Controlled processes require selective attention (see the chapter "Sensation and Perception"): the ability to concentrate on a specific aspect of experience while ignoring others. Controlled processes are slower than automatic processes and are more likely to involve the prefrontal cortex (Kragel & others, 2018). Often, after we have practiced an activity a great deal, we no longer have to think about it while doing it. It becomes automatic and faster.

• **controlled processes** The most alert states of human consciousness, during which individuals actively focus their efforts toward a goal.

A key aspect of controlled processing is executive function. **Executive function** refers to higher-order, complex cognitive processes, like thinking, planning, and problem solving. These cognitive processes are linked to the functioning of the brain's prefrontal cortex (Lawson, Hook, & Farah, 2018; Weiss, Meltzoff, & Marshall, 2018). Executive function is the person's capacity to harness consciousness, focusing on specific thoughts and ignoring others. This aspect of executive function is called *cognitive control;* it is the ability to maintain attention by reducing interfering thoughts and being cognitively flexible (Meltzer, 2018). From managing finances to achieving emotional and social well-being, it is hard to imagine a domain of life in which executive function is not valuable.

• **executive function** Higher-order, complex cognitive processes, including thinking, planning, and problem solving.

## LOWER-LEVEL CONSCIOUSNESS

Beneath the level of controlled processes are lower levels of conscious awareness, including automatic processes and daydreaming.

**Automatic Processes** A few weeks after acquiring his smartphone, a classmate sends a text message in the middle of a conversation with you. He does not have to concentrate on the keys and hardly seems aware of the device as he continues to talk to you while finishing his lunch. Using his phone has reached the point of automatic processing.

● **automatic processes** States of consciousness that require little attention and do not interfere with other ongoing activities.

**Automatic processes** are states of consciousness that require little attention and do not interfere with other ongoing activities. Automatic processes require less conscious effort than controlled processes. When we are awake, our automatic behaviors occur at a lower level of awareness than controlled processes, but they are still conscious behaviors. Your classmate pushed the right buttons, so at some level he apparently was aware of what he was doing. This kind of automatic behavior suggests that we can be aware of stimuli on some level without paying attention to them.

**Daydreaming** Another state of consciousness that involves a low level of conscious effort is *daydreaming,* which lies between active consciousness and dreaming while asleep. It is a little like dreaming while we are awake (Domhoff, 2018). Daydreams usually begin spontaneously when we are doing something that requires less than our full attention.

Mind wandering is probably the most obvious type of daydreaming (Smallwood & Schooler, 2015; Zedelius & Schooler, 2018). We regularly take brief side trips into our own private kingdoms of imagery and memory while reading, listening, or working. When we daydream, we drift into a world of fantasy. We might imagine ourselves on a date, at a party, on television, in a faraway place, or at another time in our life. Sometimes daydreams are about everyday events, such as paying rent, going to the dentist, and meeting with someone at school or work. Mind wandering can lead to negative outcomes when a person, for example, "zones out" in the middle of a lecture (Franklin & others, 2016). But mind wandering can also be a way to regulate boredom, improve mood, and enhance creativity (Seli & others, 2018; Welz & others, 2018; Williams & others, 2018). Daydreaming keeps our minds active, helping us to cope, create, and fantasize.

## ALTERED STATES OF CONSCIOUSNESS

*Altered states of consciousness* or *awareness* are mental states that are noticeably different from normal awareness. Altered states of consciousness can range from losing one's sense of self-consciousness to hallucinating. Such states can be produced by trauma, fever, fatigue, sensory deprivation, meditation, hypnosis, and psychological disorders. Drug use can also induce altered states of consciousness, as we will consider later in this chapter.

## SUBCONSCIOUS AWARENESS

In the chapter "Biological Foundations of Behavior", we saw that a great deal of brain activity occurs without impinging on awareness. Right now you are unaware of many things your brain is doing to keep your body functioning or even the many stimuli in the environment to which your brain is responding. Your brain is processing information without you noticing it. Psychologists are increasingly interested in the subconscious processing of information, which can occur while we are awake or asleep (Borsook & others, 2018; L. Chen & others, 2018).

**Waking Subconscious Awareness** When we are awake, processes are going on just below the surface of our awareness (Almeida & others, 2013; Williams & others, 2018). For example, while we are grappling with a problem, the solution may pop into our head. Such insights can occur when a subconscious connection between ideas is so strong that it rises into awareness.

*Incubation* refers to subconscious processing that leads to a solution after a break from conscious thought about the problem. Incubation is interesting because it suggests that even as you have stopped actively thinking about a problem, on some level your brain is still working on finding a solution. Interestingly, successful incubation requires that we first expend effort thinking carefully about the problem (Sio & Ormerod, 2015). So, although subconscious processing can ultimately lead to a solution, it first requires that the appropriate information be thoughtfully considered. What we do while we are incubating can influence the creativity of our problem solving. One study showed that people who took a break and enjoyed humorous videos produced more creative solutions to problems than did those who worked continuously or who were shown sad videos (Hao & others, 2015).

Recall from the chapter "Sensation and Perception" the idea of parallel processing. Subconscious information processing also can occur simultaneously in a distributed manner along many parallel tracks. For instance, when you see a dog running down the street, you are consciously aware of the event but not of your subconscious processing of the object's identity (a dog), its color (black), and its movement (fast). In contrast, conscious processing occurs in sequence and is slower than much subconscious processing. The various levels of awareness often work together. You rely on controlled processing when memorizing material for class, but later the answers on a test just pop into your head as a result of automatic or subconscious processing.

**Subconscious Awareness During Sleep and Dreams** When we sleep and dream, our level of awareness is lower than when we daydream, but sleep and dreams are not the *absence* of consciousness; rather, they are *low levels* of consciousness.

Researchers have found that when people are asleep, they remain aware of external stimuli to some degree. In sleep laboratories, when people are clearly asleep (as determined by physiological monitoring devices), they are able to respond to faint tones by pressing a handheld button (Ogilvie & Wilkinson, 1988). In one study, the presentation of pure auditory tones to sleeping people activated auditory regions of the brain, whereas participants' names activated language areas, the amygdalae, and the prefrontal cortex (Stickgold, 2001). We will return to the topics of sleep and dreams in the next section.

### NO AWARENESS

The term *unconscious* generally applies to someone who has been knocked out by a blow, anesthetized, or who has fallen into a deep, prolonged unconscious state. However, Sigmund Freud (1924) used the term *unconscious* in a different way. **Unconscious thought**, said Freud, is a reservoir of unacceptable wishes, feelings, and thoughts that are beyond conscious awareness. In other words, Freud's interpretation viewed the unconscious as a storehouse for vile, animalistic impulses. He believed that some aspects of our experience remain unconscious for good reason, as if we are better off not knowing about them. From Freud's perspective, the mind is full of disturbing impulses such as a desire to have sex with our parents. For Freud, the conscious mind was needed to keep the wild beast of the unconscious in check.

Although Freud's view remains controversial, psychologists now widely accept that unconscious processes do exist. Many mental processes (thoughts, emotions, and perceptions) can occur outside of awareness. These unconscious processes can have a substantial impact on behavior. In the chapter "Sensation and Perception", we saw how stimuli presented outside of awareness can influence thoughts and behaviors; in the chapter "Learning", we will see that many forms of learning operate without the need for awareness.

• **unconscious thought** According to Freud, a reservoir of unacceptable wishes, feelings, and thoughts that are beyond conscious awareness.

#### test yourself

1. Describe the global brain workspace approach to consciousness and our experience of consciousness.
2. What are controlled processes and automatic processes? In what level or levels of consciousness is each involved?
3. What is daydreaming, according to the text discussion?

## 2. SLEEP AND DREAMS

You have had quite a bit of experience with sleep. You already know that sleep involves a decrease in body movement and (typically) having one's eyes closed. We define **sleep** as a natural state of rest for the body and mind that involves the reversible loss of consciousness. Surely, sleep must be important, because it comprises a third of our life, taking up more time than anything else we do. But *why* is sleep so important? Before tackling this question, let's consider the biological underpinnings of sleep.

• **sleep** A natural state of rest for the body and mind that involves the reversible loss of consciousness.

## Biological Rhythms and Sleep

**biological rhythms** Periodic physiological fluctuations in the body, such as the rise and fall of hormones and accelerated and decelerated cycles of brain activity, that can influence behavior.

**Biological rhythms** are periodic physiological fluctuations in the body. These rhythms are controlled by biological clocks, which include annual or seasonal cycles, like those involving the migration of birds and the hibernation of bears. Humans are unaware of most rhythms, such as the rise and fall of hormones and accelerated and decelerated cycles of brain activity, but they can influence our behavior. The 24-hour cycles like the sleep/wake cycle and temperature changes in the human body are types of biological rhythms. Let's further explore the body's 24-hour cycles.

### CIRCADIAN RHYTHMS

**circadian rhythms** Daily behavioral or physiological cycles that involve the sleep/wake cycle, body temperature, blood pressure, and blood sugar level.

**suprachiasmatic nucleus (SCN)** A small brain structure that uses input from the retina to synchronize its own rhythm with the daily cycle of light and dark; the body's way of monitoring the change from day to night.

**Circadian rhythms** are daily behavioral or physiological cycles. Daily circadian rhythms involve the sleep/wake cycle, body temperature, blood pressure, and blood-sugar level (Cooper, Abrahamsson, & Prosser, 2018). For example, body temperature fluctuates about 3 degrees Fahrenheit in a 24-hour day, peaking in the afternoon and dropping to its lowest point between 2 A.M. and 5 A.M.

Researchers have discovered that the body monitors the change from day to night by means of the **suprachiasmatic nucleus (SCN)**, a small brain structure that uses input from the retina to synchronize its own rhythm with the daily cycle of light and dark (Cheng & others, 2018). The SCN sends information to the hypothalamus and pineal gland to regulate daily rhythms such as temperature, hunger, and the release of hormones such as melatonin. The SCN also communicates with the reticular formation to regulate daily rhythms of sleep and wakefulness (Figure 2). Although a number of biological clocks seem to be involved in regulating circadian rhythms, the SCN is critical (Hastings, Maywood, & Brancaccio, 2018; Patton & Hastings, 2018).

Our capacity to sleep, then, is embedded in the world we live in, a world that has daylight and nighttime (Malkani & others, 2018). The SCN is guided by the information it receives from the retina to tell us it is time to go to sleep. Many individuals who are totally blind experience sleep problems because their retinas cannot detect light. They may suffer from a condition called non-24-hour sleep/wake disorder because their circadian rhythms often do not follow a 24-hour cycle (Aubin & others, 2018).

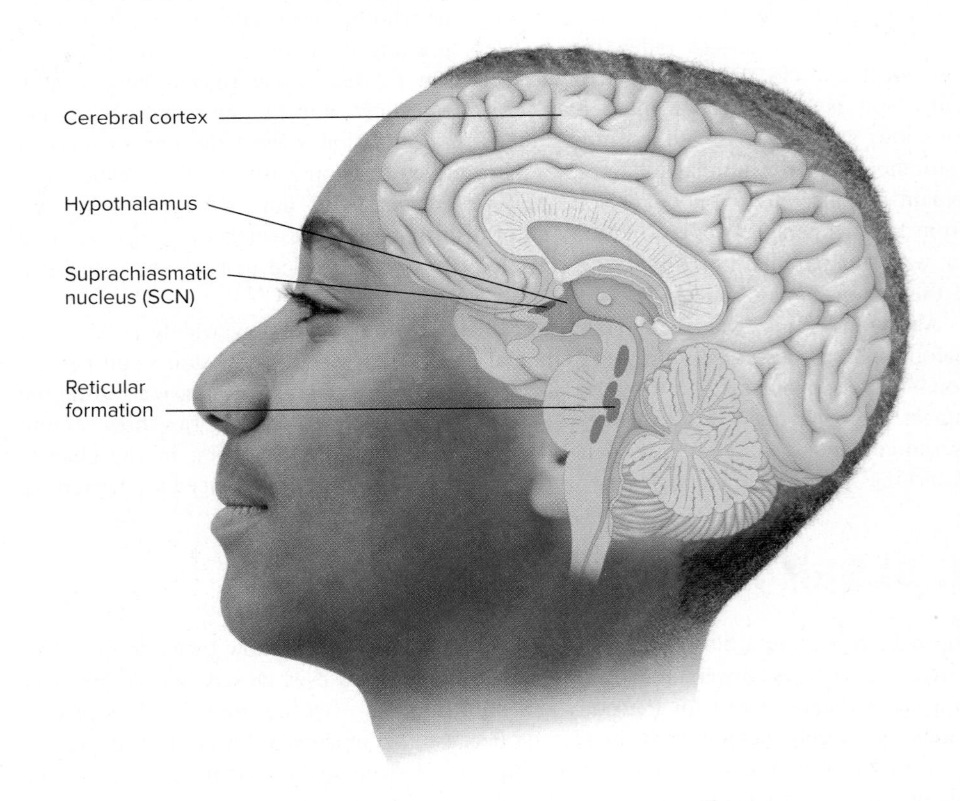


**FIGURE 2** **Suprachiasmatic Nucleus** The suprachiasmatic nucleus (SCN) plays an important role in keeping our biological clock running on time. The SCN is located in the hypothalamus. It receives information from the retina about light, which is the external stimulus that synchronizes the SCN. Output from the SCN is distributed to the rest of the hypothalamus and to the reticular formation. ©Image Source/Alamy Stock Photo

### DESYNCHRONIZING THE BIOLOGICAL CLOCK

Biological clocks can become *desynchronized,* or thrown off their regular schedules. If you fly from Los Angeles to New York and then go to bed at 11 P.M. Eastern time, you may have trouble falling asleep because your body is still on Pacific time. Even if you sleep for 8 hours that night, you may have a hard time waking up at 7 A.M. Eastern time because your body thinks it is 4 A.M. If you stay in New York for several days, your body will adjust to this new schedule.

The jet lag you experience when you fly from Los Angeles to New York occurs because your body time is out of phase, or synchronization, with clock time. Jet lag is the result of two or more body rhythms being out of sync. You usually go to bed when your body temperature begins to drop, but in your new location, you might be trying to go to sleep when it is rising. In the morning, your adrenal glands release large doses of the hormone cortisol to help you wake up. In your new geographic time zone, the glands may be releasing this chemical just as you are getting ready for bed at night.

Circadian rhythms may also become desynchronized when shift workers change their work hours. A number of near accidents in air travel have been associated with pilots who have not yet become synchronized to their new shifts and are not working as efficiently as usual (Powell, Spencer, & Petrie, 2011). Shift-work problems most often affect night-shift workers who never fully adjust to sleeping in the daytime after they get off work. Not only might these individuals struggle to stay awake at work, but they may face a heightened risk of illness, kidney disease, gastrointestinal disorders, obesity, and impaired immune system functioning (Codoñer-Franch & Gombert, 2018; Sasaki & others, 2018; Seixas & others, 2018; Sun & others, 2018).

*Changing to a night-shift job can desynchronize one's biological clock and affect circadian rhythms and performance.*



### RESETTING THE BIOLOGICAL CLOCK

If your biological clock for sleeping and waking becomes desynchronized, how can you reset it? With regard to jet lag, if you take a transoceanic flight and arrive at your destination during the day, it is a good idea to spend as much time as possible outside in the daylight. Bright light during the day, especially in the morning, increases wakefulness, whereas bright light at night delays sleep. In a few days, jet lag typically resolves. Melatonin supplements are another common treatment for jet lag (Arendt, 2018). Melatonin, a hormone that increases at night, can help reduce jet lag by advancing the circadian clock.

Jet lag is not just a drag for vacationers. Airline pilots, flight crews, members of the military, and international athletes must be able to adapt quickly to new time zones. Research shows that very intense light, administered through the ear canals, can speed recovery from jet lag (Cingi, Emre, & Muluk, 2018).

## Why Do We Need Sleep?

All animals require sleep. Furthermore, the human body regulates sleep, as it does eating and drinking–a fact that suggests sleep may be just as essential for survival. Yet why we need sleep remains a bit of a mystery (Neligan, 2018).

### THEORIES ON THE NEED FOR SLEEP

A variety of theories have been proposed for the need for sleep. First, from an evolutionary perspective, sleep may have developed because animals needed to protect themselves at night. The idea is that it makes sense for animals to be inactive when it is dark, because nocturnal inactivity helps them to avoid both becoming other animals' prey and injuring themselves due to poor visibility.

A second possibility is that sleep is a way to conserve energy (Schmidt, 2014). Spending a large chunk of any day sleeping allows animals to conserve their calories, especially when food is scarce (Siegel, 2005). For some animals, the search for food and water is easier and safer when the sun is up. When it is dark, it is adaptive for these animals to save their energy. Animals that are likely to serve as someone else's food sleep the least. Figure 3 illustrates the average amount of sleep per day of various animals.

A third explanation for the need for sleep is that sleep is restorative (Neligan, 2018). Sleep restores, replenishes, and rebuilds the brain and body, which the day's waking activities can wear out. This idea fits with the feeling of being tired before we go to sleep and restored when we wake up.

In support of the theory of a restorative function of sleep, many of the body's cells show increased production and reduced breakdown of proteins during deep sleep (Vazquez & others, 2008). Protein molecules are the building blocks needed for cell growth and for repair of damage from factors such as stress. Sleep deprivation can affect the body much like stress itself (van Leeuwen & others, 2018).

A final explanation for the need for sleep centers on the role of sleep in brain plasticity. Recall from the chapter "Biological Foundations of Behavior" that the plasticity of the brain refers to its capacity to change in response to experience. Sleep has been recognized as playing an important role in the ways that experiences influence the brain, especially in how sleep affects synaptic connections.

If sleep affects connections in the brain, we might expect it to play a role in consolidating memories. Research supports that conclusion. During sleep, memories are pulled together, resulting in the retention of information, skills, learned associations, and emotional experiences (Antony & others, 2018).

Why does sleep improve memory? One possible reason is that during sleep the cerebral cortex is free to conduct activities that strengthen memory associations, so that memories formed during waking hours can be integrated into long-term memory storage (Picchioni & others, 2018). Lost sleep often results in lost memories (Cross & others, 2018). So, if you are thinking about studying all night for your next test, you might want to think again. Sleep can enhance your memory.

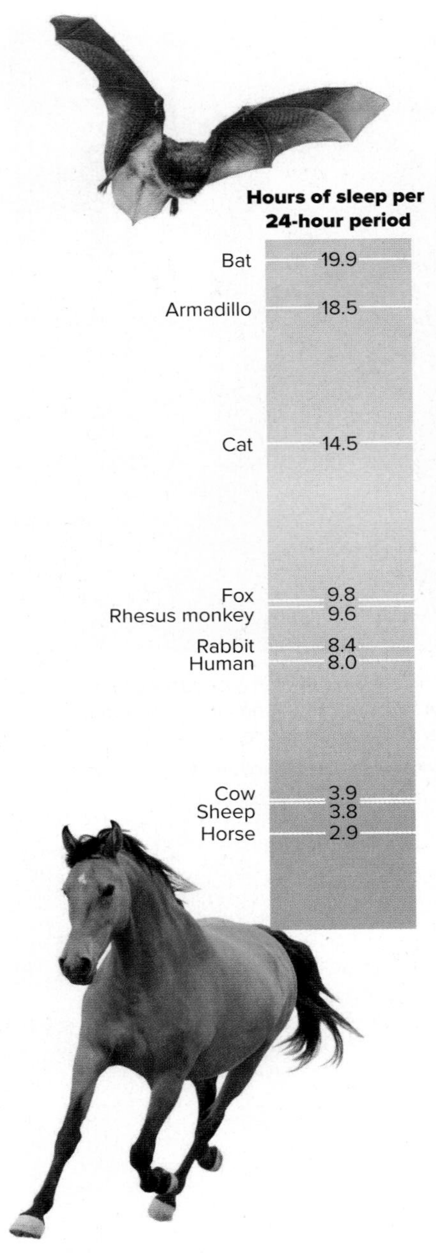


**FIGURE 3 From Bats to Horses: The Wide Range of Sleep in Animals** We might feel envious of bats, which sleep nearly 20 hours a day, and more than a little in awe of horses, still running on just under 3 hours of rest. Source: Siegel (2005); (bat) ©Frank Greenaway/Getty Images; (horse) ©Dewald Kirsten/Shutterstock

## THE EFFECTS OF CHRONIC SLEEP DEPRIVATION

Most people think of 8 hours of sleep as a good night's rest. However, the amount of sleep each person needs may vary from person to person and as a function of age and activities. For example, the optimal amount of sleep for infants is between 14 and 17 hours in a 24-hour period. For an adult, the optimal night's sleep is between 7 and 9 hours.

Lack of sleep is stressful, affecting the brain and the rest of the body. Sleep deprivation lowers the complexity of processing in the brain because it decreases brain activity in the thalamus and the prefrontal cortex (Kilic & others, 2018; Shokri-Kojori, & others, 2018). The thalamus is crucial to receiving and responding to sensory information, and the prefrontal cortex is the brain area associated with thinking and planning. A tired brain must compensate by using different pathways or alternative neural networks (W. H. Chen & others, 2018). Given these effects on the brain, it is not surprising that people who get insufficient sleep have trouble paying attention to tasks and solving problems (Jackson & others, 2011).

The profound effect of sleep deprivation is vividly clear in a very rare disorder known as *fatal familial insomnia (FFI)*. This disorder, caused by a genetic mutation, involves a progressive inability to sleep (Cracco, Appleby, & Gambetti, 2018). Over time, the person sleeps less and less, becomes agitated, engages in strange motor movements, and is confused. The person may hallucinate and enact dreams. FFI has no known cure, and it leads to death, about 18 months after symptoms appear. The disorder can be difficult to diagnose and may be mistaken for other neurological or psychological disorders. Although rare, this unusual condition demonstrates the vital restorative power of sleep. FFI also highlights the role of the thalamus in sleep, because in cases of FFI the thalamus shows enormous damage.

Why do Americans get too little sleep? Pressures at work and school, family responsibilities, and social obligations often lead to long hours of wakefulness and irregular sleep/wake schedules. Not having enough hours to do all that we want or need to do in a day, we cheat on our sleep. As a result we may suffer from a "sleep debt," an accumulated level of exhaustion. Even a small sleep debt can take a toll on well-being. A large-scale study of over 27,000 high school students found that even 1 less hour of sleep predicted higher rates of hopelessness, suicidal thoughts, and substance abuse (Winsler & others, 2015).

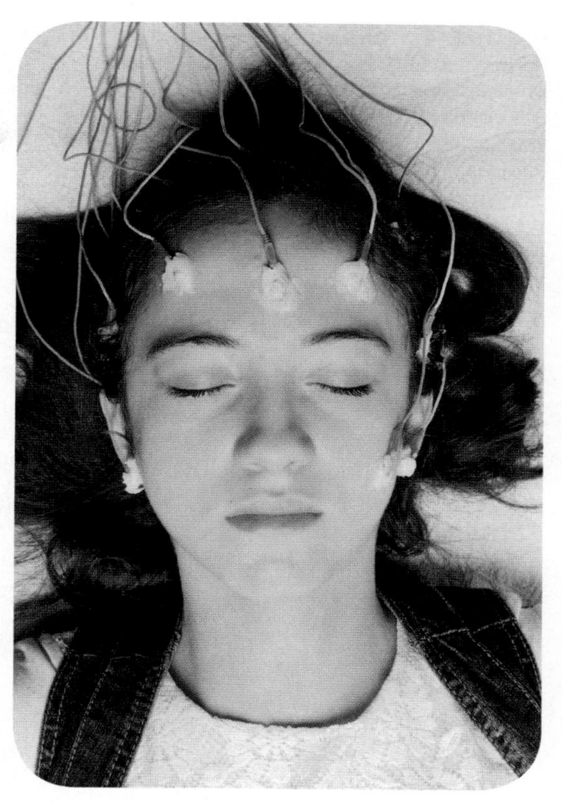

*An individual being monitored by an EEG in a sleep experiment.*

©minemero/Getty Images

## Stages of Wakefulness and Sleep

Have you ever awakened from sleep and been totally disoriented? Or momentarily woken up in the middle of a dream and then gone right back into the dream as if it were a movie running just below the surface of your consciousness? These two experiences reflect two distinct stages in the sleep cycle.

Stages of sleep correspond to massive electrophysiological changes that occur throughout the brain as the fast, irregular, and low-amplitude electrical activity of wakefulness is replaced by the slow, regular, high-amplitude waves of deep sleep. Using the electroencephalograph (EEG) to monitor the brain's electrical activity, as well as electromyography (EMG) to monitor the action of motor neurons, scientists have identified four stages of sleep (Herlan & others, 2018; Müller & others, 2015).

The following stages of wakefulness and sleep are defined by both the brain's activity and muscle tone. The stages are named by letters and numbers that represent what is going on at that stage, including whether the person is awake or asleep and whether they are experiencing rapid eye movement (REM). These stages can be hard to remember, so be sure to review Figure 4 below.

**Stage W** The "W" stands for "wake." During this stage, when a person is awake, EEG patterns exhibit two types of waves: beta and alpha. *Beta waves* reflect concentration and alertness. These waves are the highest in frequency and lowest in amplitude—that is, they go up and down a great deal but do not have very high peaks or very low ebbs. They also are more *desynchronous* than other waves, meaning that they do not form a very consistent pattern because of the great variation in sensory input and activities we experience when awake.

Relaxed but still awake, our brain waves slow down, increase in amplitude, and become more *synchronous,* or regular. These waves, associated with relaxation or drowsiness, are called *alpha waves*.

**Stage N1 (Non-REM1) Sleep** When people are just falling asleep, they enter the first stage of non-REM sleep. The "N" stands for "non-REM," meaning that rapid eye movements do not occur during these stages. Stage N1 is characterized by drowsy sleep. In stage N1, the person may experience sudden muscle movements or *myoclonic jerks*. If you watch someone in a class fighting to stay awake, you might notice his or her head jerking upward. This first stage of sleep often involves the feeling of falling.

EEGs of individuals in stage N1 sleep are characterized by *theta waves,* which are even slower in frequency and greater in amplitude than alpha waves. The difference between being relaxed and being in stage N1 sleep is gradual. Figure 4 shows the EEG pattern of stage N1 sleep, along with the EEG patterns for the other stages of wakefulness and sleep.

**Stage N2 (Non-REM2) Sleep** In stage N2 sleep, muscle activity decreases, and the person is not consciously aware of the environment. Theta waves continue but are interspersed with a defining characteristic of stage N2 sleep: *sleep spindles*. These involve a sudden increase in high-frequency wave bursts (Lechinger & others, 2015). Stages N1 and N2 are both relatively light stages of sleep. If people awaken during one of these stages, they often report not having been asleep at all.

**Stage N3 (Non-REM3) Sleep** Stage N3 sleep is characterized by *delta waves,* the slowest and highest-amplitude brain waves during sleep. Delta sleep is the deepest sleep,

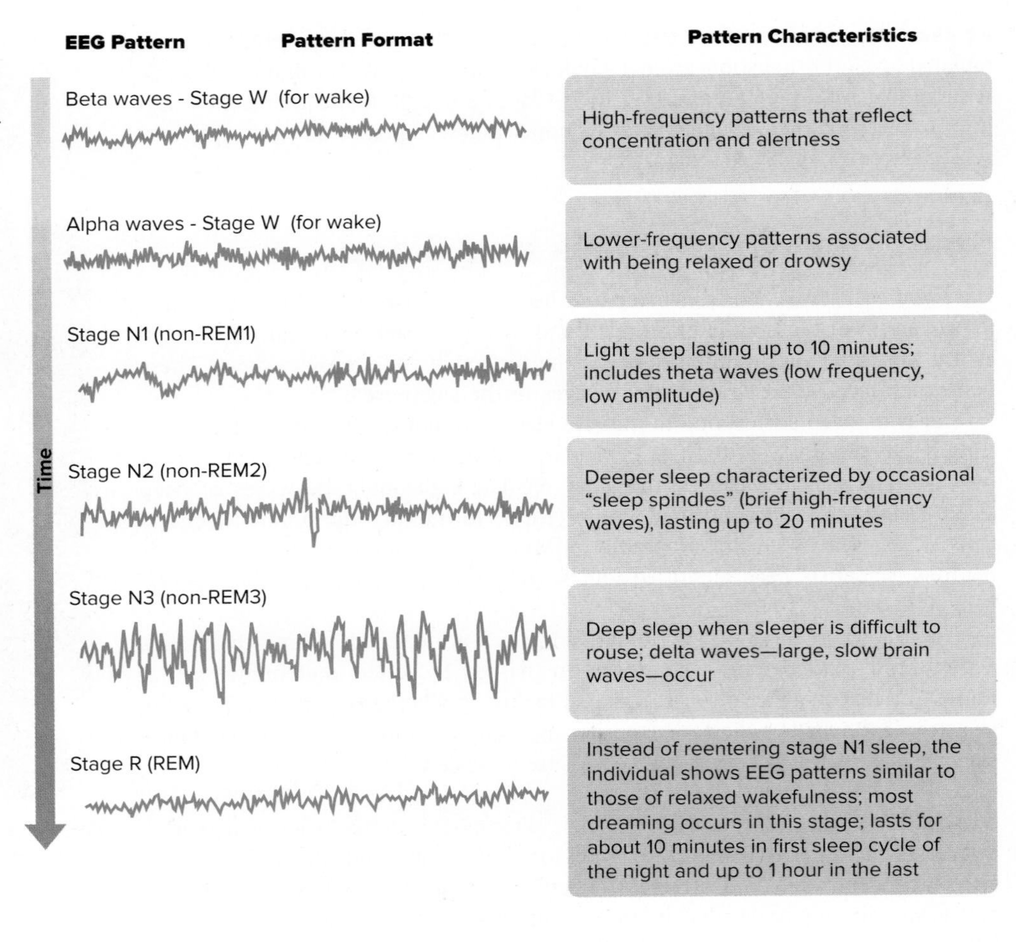

EEG Pattern
Pattern Format
Pattern Characteristics
Time
Beta waves - Stage W (for wake)
High-frequency patterns that reflect concentration and alertness
Alpha waves - Stage W (for wake)
Lower-frequency patterns associated with being relaxed or drowsy
Stage N1 (non-REM1)
Light sleep lasting up to 10 minutes; includes theta waves (low frequency, low amplitude)
Stage N2 (non-REM2)
Deeper sleep characterized by occasional "sleep spindles" (brief high-frequency waves), lasting up to 20 minutes
Stage N3 (non-REM3)
Deep sleep when sleeper is difficult to rouse; delta waves—large, slow brain waves—occur
Stage R (REM)
Instead of reentering stage N1 sleep, the individual shows EEG patterns similar to those of relaxed wakefulness; most dreaming occurs in this stage; lasts for about 10 minutes in first sleep cycle of the night and up to 1 hour in the last


**FIGURE 4 Characteristics and Formats of EEG Recordings During Stages of Wakefulness and Sleep** Even while you are sleeping, your brain is busy. No wonder you sometimes wake up feeling tired.

the time when our brain waves are least like our brain waves while awake. Delta sleep is also called *slow-wave sleep*. This is the stage when bedwetting (in children), sleepwalking, and sleep talking occur. If awakened during this stage, people usually are confused and disoriented.

**Stage R (REM) Sleep** After going through stages N1 to N3, sleepers drift up through the sleep stages toward wakefulness. Instead of reentering stage N1, however, they enter stage R, a different form of sleep called REM (rapid eye movement) sleep (Llewellyn & Hobson, 2015). **REM sleep** is an active stage of sleep during which the most vivid dreaming occurs. The EEG pattern for REM sleep shows fast waves similar to those of relaxed wakefulness, and the sleeper's eyeballs move up and down and from left to right (Figure 5).

● **REM sleep** An active stage of sleep during which dreaming occurs.

A person who is awakened during REM sleep is more likely to report having dreamed compared to other stages. Even those who claim they rarely dream frequently report dreaming when they are awakened during REM sleep. The longer the period of REM sleep, the more likely the person will report dreaming. Dreams also occur during slow-wave or non-REM sleep, but the frequency of dreams in these stages is relatively low (Llewellyn & Hobson, 2015), and we are less likely to remember these dreams. Reports of dreaming by individuals awakened from REM sleep are typically longer, more vivid, more physically active, more emotionally charged, and less related to waking life than reports by those awakened from non-REM sleep.

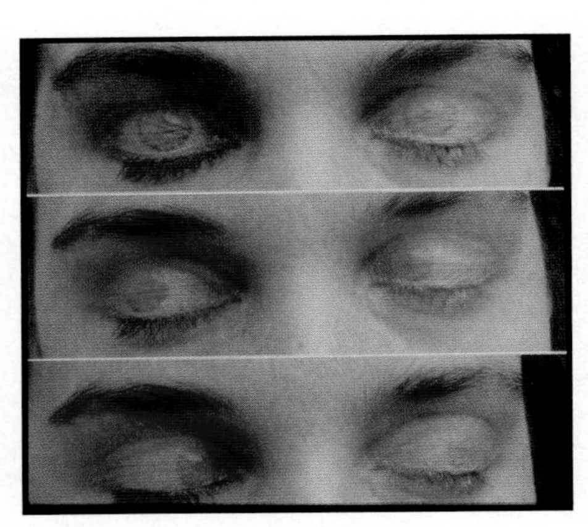

**FIGURE 5 REM Sleep** During REM sleep, your eyes move rapidly. ©Allan Hobson/Science Source

## SLEEP CYCLING THROUGH THE NIGHT

The stages of sleep we have considered make up a normal cycle of sleep. A complete cycle lasts about 90 to 100 minutes. Several cycles occur during the night. The amount of deep, stage N3 sleep is much greater in the first half of a night's sleep than in the

# psychological *inquiry*

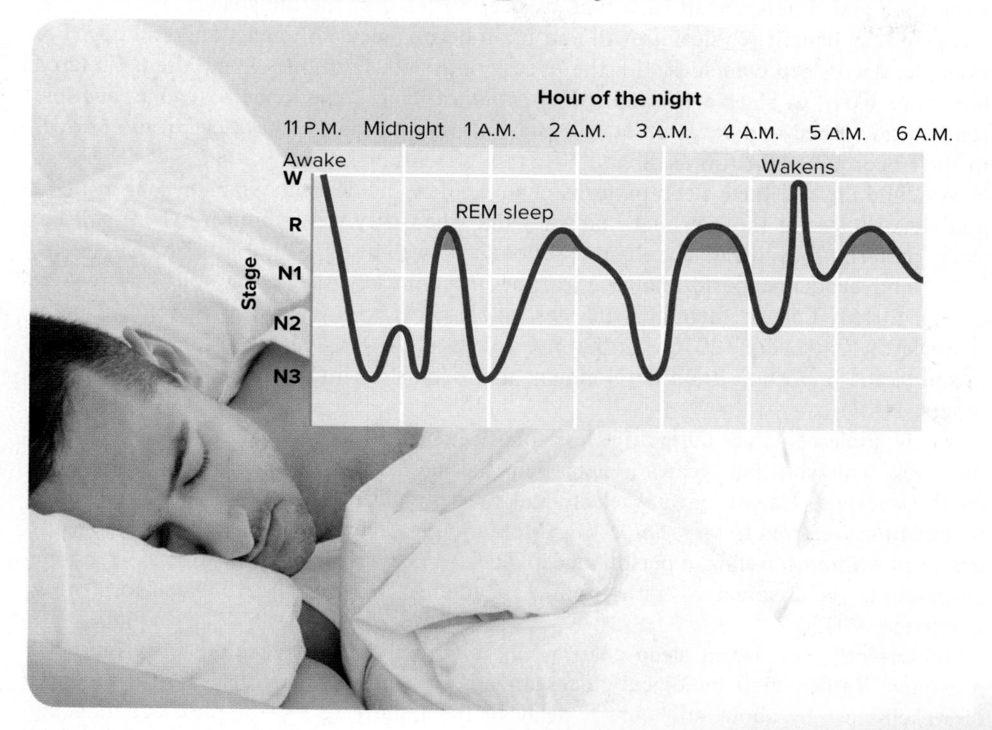


©Robert Nicholas/AGE Fotostock

### *Taking a Ride on the Sleep Cycles*

This graph depicts a night's sleep. During nightly sleep, we go through several cycles. Depth of sleep decreases, and REM sleep (shown in light blue) increases as the night progresses. Look carefully at the graph and answer the following questions.

1. How many sleep cycles are presented?
2. What time does the sleeper wake up?
3. If you woke the sleeper up at 2 A.M., would the sleeper be likely to remember a dream? Explain.
4. How much time is this sleeper spending in slow-wave sleep?
5. Trace the rise and fall of the neurotransmitters acetylcholine, serotonin, and norepinephrine in the sleep cycles depicted.
6. Based on the night's sleep illustrated here, has this sleeper achieved a good night's rest? Why or why not?

second half. Most stage R sleep takes place toward the end of a night's sleep, when REM stages become progressively longer. The night's first REM stage might be only 10 minutes, but the final REM stage might continue for as long as an hour. During a normal night of sleep, individuals will spend about 60 percent of sleep in light sleep (stages N1 and N2), 20 percent in slow-wave or deep sleep (stage N3), and 20 percent in REM sleep (Webb, 2000). So, you can think of your night's sleep as starting out with deep sleep and ending with the big show of the night's REM.

## SLEEP AND THE BRAIN

The sleep stages are associated with distinct patterns of neurotransmitter activity initiated in the reticular formation, the core of the brain stem. In all vertebrates, the reticular formation plays a crucial role in sleep and arousal (see Figure 2). Damage to the reticular formation can result in coma and death.

Three important neurotransmitters involved in sleep are serotonin, norepinephrine, and acetylcholine. As sleep begins, levels of neurotransmitters sent to the forebrain from the reticular formation start dropping, and they continue to fall until they reach their lowest levels during the deepest sleep stage—stage N3. REM sleep is initiated by a rise in acetylcholine (the neurotransmitter that typically gets our bodies moving), which activates the cerebral cortex while the rest of the brain remains relatively inactive.

REM sleep ends when there is a rise in serotonin and norepinephrine, which increase the level of forebrain activity nearly to the awakened state. You are most likely to wake up just after a REM period. If you do not wake up then, the level of the neurotransmitters falls again, and you enter another sleep cycle. To review the sleep cycles, complete the Psychological Inquiry exercise.

## Sleep Throughout the Life Span

Getting sufficient sleep is important throughout human life. Figure 6 shows how total sleep time and time spent in each type of sleep varies over the life span.

Sleep may benefit physical growth and brain development in infants and children. For example, deep sleep coincides with the release of growth hormones in children. Children are more likely to sleep well when they avoid caffeine, experience a regular bedtime routine, go to bed and wake up at consistent times, and do not have electronic devices in their bedrooms (Buxton & others, 2015).

As children age, their sleep patterns change. Many adolescents stay up later at night and sleep longer in the morning than they did when they were younger. These shifting sleep patterns may influence their psychological well-being (Tu, Erath, & El-Sheikh, 2015) and academic performance (Asarnow, McGlinchey, & Harvey, 2014; Titova & others, 2015). Left to their own devices, adolescents will sleep over 9 hours a night (Crowley & Carskadon, 2010; Tarokh & Carskadon, 2010). This need for sleep may be linked to the important brain development that occurs during adolescence (Campbell & others, 2012).

Many adolescents get quite a bit less than 9 hours of sleep a night, especially during the week. This shortfall creates a sleep debt that adolescents often attempt to make up on the weekend. Having one's weekday and weekend sleep schedules drastically at odds is sometimes referred to as *social jet lag* (McMahon & others, 2018). Social jet lag means that even without traveling, a person's sleep clock can be desynchronized. Social jet among adolescents is associated with poorer academic performance (Díaz-Morales & Escribano, 2015).

Importantly, adolescent sleep changes *are not* simply about academic work or social pressures. Rather, their biological clocks undergo a shift with age, delaying their period of wakefulness by about an hour. A delay in the nightly release of the sleep-inducing hormone melatonin seems to underlie this shift. Melatonin is secreted at about 9:30 P.M. in younger adolescents and approximately an hour later in older adolescents (Eckerberg & others, 2012). Based on research on the adolescent sleep cycle, many school districts have

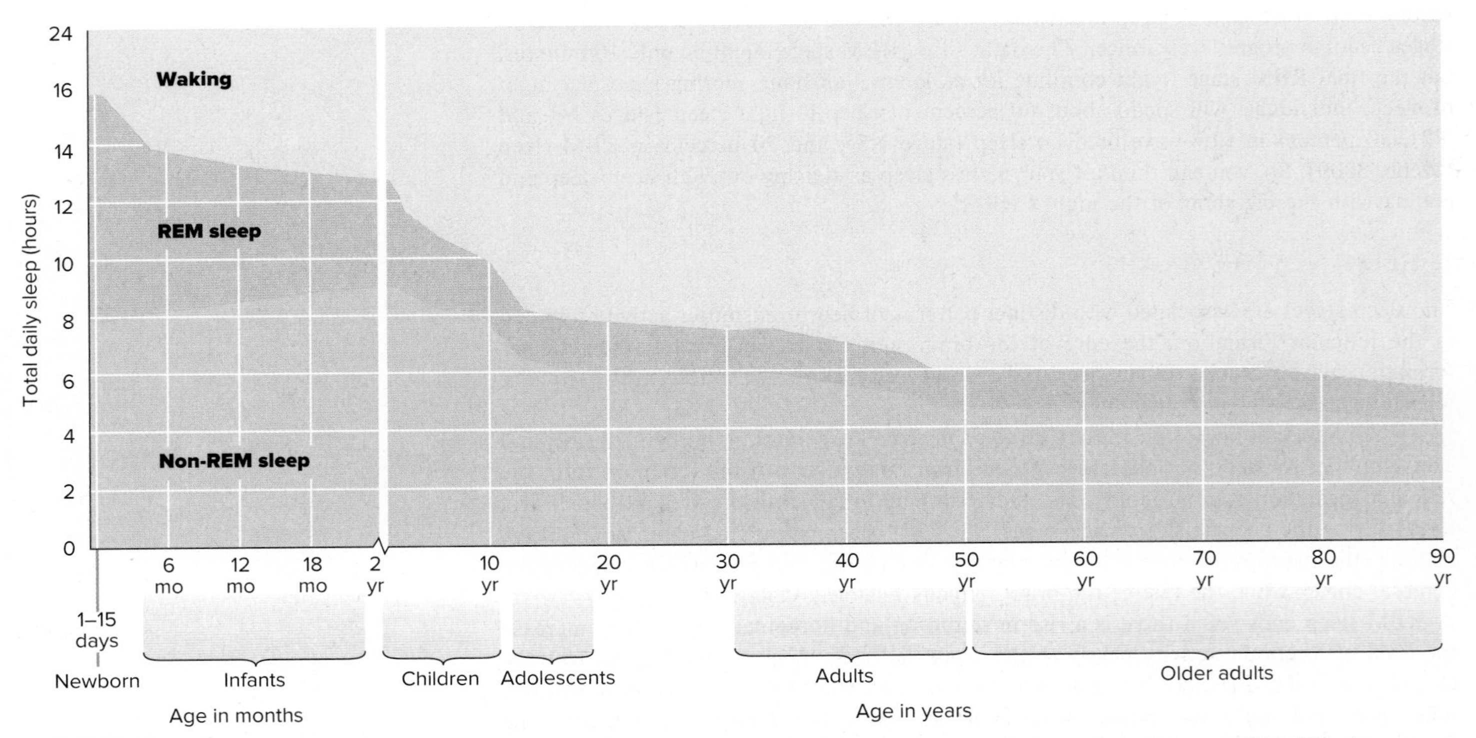


**FIGURE 6** **Sleep Across the Human Life Span** With age, humans require less sleep. Source: Roffwarg, Muzio, & Dement (1966, 29 April).

begun to delay start times for high schools. Research shows that later start times benefit students' well-being and lead to more sleep, less sleepiness at school, and less tardiness (Lo & others, 2018; Minges & Redeker, 2016).

Sleep patterns also change in emerging adulthood (18–25 years of age). In one study, the weekday bedtimes and rise times of first-year college students were approximately 1 hour and 15 minutes later than those of seniors in high school (Lund & others, 2010). However, the first-year college students also had later bedtimes and rise times than third- and fourth-year college students. An important correlate of poorer sleep in young adults (and probably most people) is media use, especially smartphone time in the hours before bed (Orzech & others, 2016; Vernon, Modecki, & Barber, 2018).

©Rubberball/Alamy Stock Photo

Sleep patterns also change as people age through the middle-adult (40s and 50s) and late-adult (60s and older) years (Geiker & others, 2018). Many adults in these age spans go to bed earlier at night and wake up earlier in the morning than they did previously. Beginning in their 40s, people report that they are less likely to sleep through the entire night than they did when they were younger. Middle-aged adults also spend less time in deep sleep than they did before their middle years.

Changes in sleep duration in middle age relate to cognitive abilities such as problem solving and memory (della Monica & others, 2018; Ferrie & others, 2011). Many older adults complain of having difficulty sleeping (Sabeti & others, 2018). Poor sleep is related to poorer cognitive function (Boyle & others, 2018; Seelye & others, 2015). Among adults aged 50 and older, sleeping 7 to 8.5 hours a night is associated with better health (Stenholm & others, 2018).

## Sleep and Disease

Sleep plays a role in many diseases and disorders. Chronic inability to sleep through the night is associated with physical and psychological problems, including diabetes, coronary heart disease, chronic liver disease, dementia, pneumonia, anxiety, and depression (Bertisch & others, 2018; Hung & others, 2018; Li, Starr, & Wray-Lake, 2018; Lin & others, 2018). Lack of sleep is often associated with health problems but sleeping too much may also be a sign of problems (Grossi & others, 2015; Lopez & others, 2017).

Neurons that control sleep interact closely with the immune system (Hahn, Günter, & Autenrieth, 2015; Latorre & others, 2018; Swinbourne & others, 2018). As anyone who has had the flu knows, infectious diseases make us sleepy. The probable reason is that chemicals called *cytokines*, produced by the body's cells while we are fighting an infection, are powerfully sleep-inducing (Besedovsky, Lange, & Born, 2012). Sleep may help the body conserve resources it needs to overcome infection (Irwin & others, 2006). Essentially, lack of sleep is stressful and affects the body just as other stressful experiences do (McEwen & Karatsoreos, 2015).

Sleep problems afflict most people who have psychological and physical disorders. Individuals with depression often awaken in the early hours of the morning and cannot get back to sleep, and they typically spend less time in delta-wave or deep sleep than do individuals who are not depressed (Ashworth & others, 2015). Sleep problems are also common in many medical disorders, such as Alzheimer disease, stroke, and cancer. In some cases, these problems may arise not from the disease itself but from the drugs used to treat the disease.

## Sleep Disorders

Major sleep disorders include insomnia, sleepwalking and sleep talking, nightmares and night terrors, narcolepsy, and sleep apnea.

## INSOMNIA

*Insomnia* is the inability to sleep. Insomnia can involve problems falling asleep, waking up during the night, or waking up too early. A 2018 study showed that 1 in 4 Americans develops insomnia each year, and many individuals who develop insomnia never return to normal sleep patterns (Penn Medicine, 2018). Insomnia is more common among women, older adults, and those with diabetes (Ford & others, 2015; National Sleep Foundation, 2007). Not everyone who thinks they have insomnia actually does. Confirming the actual amount of sleep a person is getting requires a sleep study with physiological measures (Bertisch & others, 2018).

For short-term insomnia, most physicians prescribe sleeping pills. However, most sleeping pills stop working after several weeks and their long-term use can interfere with good sleep. Mild insomnia often can be reduced by practicing good sleep habits, such as always going to bed at the same time, even on weekends, and sleeping in a dark, quiet place. In more serious cases, researchers are experimenting with light therapy, melatonin supplements, and other ways to alter circadian cycles (Tang & others, 2015). Behavioral changes (such as avoiding naps, caffeine, and nicotine, reducing light in the bedroom, and using an alarm to wake up in the morning) can help insomniacs increase their sleep time (Jansson-Fröjmark, Evander, & Alfonsson, 2018).

## SLEEPWALKING AND SLEEP TALKING

*Somnambulism* is the formal term for sleepwalking, which occurs during the deepest stages of sleep . People once believed that somnambulists were acting out their dreams. However, somnambulism takes place during stages N2 and N3, when a person is unlikely to be dreaming (Zadra & Pilon, 2012).

The specific causes of sleepwalking have not been identified, but it is more likely to occur when individuals are sleep deprived or when they have been drinking alcohol. There is nothing abnormal about sleepwalking, and despite superstition, it is safe to awaken sleepwalkers. In fact, they probably should be awakened, as they may harm themselves wandering around in the dark.

Another quirky night behavior is sleep talking, or *somniloquy*. If you interrogate sleep talkers, can you find out what they did, for instance, last Thursday night? Probably not. Although sleep talkers will converse with you and make fairly coherent statements, they are soundly asleep. Thus, even if a sleep talker mumbles a response to your question, do not count on its accuracy.

You may have heard of other strange behaviors occurring while people sleep, especially if they have taken medicine to help them sleep. Individuals who engage in activity while they are asleep may suffer from *rapid eye-movement sleep behavior disorder* (Dauvilliers & others, 2018). This disorder can be a reaction to some sleep aids. Sleep eating and sleep driving have been reported as unusual side effects of these medications (Paulke, Wunder, Toennes, 2015; Popat & Winslade, 2015). Some Ambien users began to notice odd things upon waking up from a much-needed good night's sleep, such as candy wrappers strewn around the room, crumbs in the bed, and food missing from the refrigerator. Ambien users can also notice unusual weight gain (Mitchell, 2014).

The phenomena of sleep eating and sleep driving illustrate that even when we feel fast asleep, we may be "half-awake." In such a state we might put together unusual late-night snacks, like salt sandwiches, or find our car keys and set off on a trip. For people battling persistent insomnia, a drug that provides a good night's rest may be worth the risk of these side effects. No one should abruptly stop taking any medication without consulting a physician.

## NIGHTMARES AND NIGHT TERRORS

A *nightmare* is a frightening dream that awakens a dreamer from REM sleep (Germain, 2012). The nightmare's content invariably involves danger–the dreamer is being chased, robbed, or thrown off a cliff. Nightmares are common (Schredl, 2010); most of us have had them, especially as young children. Reported frequency of nightmares or worsening nightmares are often associated with increased life stressors such as the loss of a job, the death of a loved one, or conflicts with others.

A *night terror* features sudden arousal from sleep and intense fear. Night terrors are accompanied by a number of physiological reactions, such as rapid heart rate and breathing, loud screams, heavy perspiration, and movement (Zadra & Pilon, 2012). Night terrors, which peak at 5 to 7 years of age, are less common than nightmares, and unlike nightmares, they occur during slow-wave stage N3 (non-REM) sleep.

### NARCOLEPSY

*Narcolepsy* involves a sudden, overpowering urge to sleep. This urge is so uncontrollable that the person may fall asleep while talking or standing up. People with narcolepsy immediately enter REM sleep rather than progressing through the first four sleep stages (O'Neill & Nicholls, 2018). Those with narcolepsy are often very tired during the day. Narcolepsy can be triggered by extreme emotional reactions, such as surprise, laughter, excitement, or anger. The disorder appears to involve problems with neurons in the hypothalamus and may have an autoimmune component (Latorre & others, 2018).

### SLEEP APNEA

*Sleep apnea* is a sleep disorder in which individuals stop breathing because the windpipe fails to open or because brain processes involved in respiration fail to work properly. People with sleep apnea experience numerous brief awakenings during the night so that they can breathe better, although they usually are not aware of waking up. During the day, these people may feel sleepy because they were deprived of sleep at night. A common sign of sleep apnea is loud snoring, punctuated by silence (the apnea).

Sleep apnea affects about 4 percent of U.S. adults (Jaradat & Rahhal, 2015). The disorder is most common among infants and adults over the age of 65. Sleep apnea also occurs more frequently among obese people (Koren & others, 2015), men, and people with large necks and recessed chins (Sinnapah & others, 2015). Untreated sleep apnea can cause high blood pressure, stroke, and sexual dysfunction (Parati, Lombardi, & Narkiewicz, 2007; Vitulano & others, 2013). The daytime sleepiness caused by sleep apnea can result in accidents, lost productivity, and relationship problems. Sleep apnea is commonly treated by weight-loss programs, side sleeping, propping the head on a pillow, or wearing a device (called a CPAP, for *continuous positive airway pressure*) that sends pressurized air through a mask to prevent the airway from collapsing.

Sleep apnea may also be a factor in *sudden infant death syndrome (SIDS),* the unexpected sleep-related death of an infant less than 1 year old. It is common for infants to have short pauses in their breathing during sleep, but for some infants frequent sleep apnea may be a sign of problems in regulating arousal (Kato & others, 2003; Lipford & others, 2015). There is evidence that infants who die of SIDS experience multiple episodes of sleep apnea in the days before the fatal event (Cohen & de Chazal, 2015). One possible explanation for SIDS is an abnormality in the brain stem areas responsible for arousal (Lavezzi, Ottaviani, & Matturri, 2015). Such an abnormality may lead to sleep apnea, which in turn might worsen the brain stem damage, ultimately leading to death.

## Dreams

Have you ever dreamed that you left your long-term romantic partner for a former lover? If so, did you tell your partner about that dream? Not likely. However, you probably wondered about the dream's meaning, and if so you would not be alone. The meaning of dreams has eternally fascinated human beings. As early as 5000 B.C.E., Babylonians recorded and interpreted their dreams on clay tablets. Egyptians built temples in honor of Serapis, the god of dreams. Dreams are described at length in more than 70 passages in the Bible. Psychologists have also examined this intriguing topic.

©Thinkstock/Stockbyte/Getty Images

● **manifest content** According to Freud, the surface content of a dream, containing dream symbols that disguise the dream's true meaning.

● **latent content** According to Freud, a dream's hidden content; its unconscious and true meaning.

## FREUD'S PSYCHODYNAMIC APPROACH

Sigmund Freud put great stock in dreams as a key to our unconscious minds. He believed that dreams (even nightmares) symbolize unconscious wishes and that analysis of dream symbols could uncover our hidden desires. Freud distinguished between a dream's manifest content and its latent content. **Manifest content** is the dream's surface content, which contains dream symbols that disguise the dream's true meaning; **latent content** is the dream's hidden content, its unconscious–and true–meaning. For example, if a person had a dream about riding on a train and talking with a friend, the train ride would be the dream's manifest content. The manifest content is simply the dream itself. The latent content is the dream's deeper true meaning.

Freud thought that this manifest content expresses a wish in disguised form. To get to the latent or true meaning of the dream, the person would have to analyze the dream images. In our example, the dreamer would be asked to think of all the things that come to mind when the person thinks of a train, the friend, and so forth. By following these associations to the objects in the manifest content, the latent content of the dream could be brought to light.

More recently, psychologists have considered dreams not as expressions of unconscious wishes but as mental events that come from various sources. Research has revealed a great deal about the nature of dreams (Blagrove & others, 2018; Eichenlaub & others, 2018). A common misconception is that dreams are typically bizarre or strange, but many studies of the content of thousands of dreams, collected from individuals in sleep labs and sleeping at home, have shown that dreams generally are not especially strange. Instead, research shows that dreams are often very similar to waking life (Blagrove & others, 2018).

So, *why* do many of us believe that our dreams are very peculiar? The probable reason is that we are likely to remember our most vividly bizarre dreams and to forget those dreams that are more mundane. Thus, we never realize how commonplace most dreams are. Although some aspects of dreams *are* unusual, dreams often are no more bizarre than a typical fairy tale, TV show episode, or movie plot. However, dreams do generally contain more negative emotion than everyday life; and certainly some unlikely characters, including dead people, sometimes show up in dreams (Rosen, 2018).

There is also no evidence that dreams provide opportunities for problem solving or advice about how to handle life's difficulties. We may dream about a problem we are facing, but we typically find the solution while we are awake and thinking about the problem, not during the dream itself. There is also no evidence that people who remember their dreams are better adjusted psychologically than those who do not (Blagrove & Akehurst, 2000; Blagrove & others, 2018).

So, if the typical dream involves doing ordinary things, what *are* dreams? Two examples of theories that attempt to explain dreams are cognitive theory and activation-synthesis theory.

## COGNITIVE THEORY OF DREAMING

● **cognitive theory of dreaming** Theory proposing that dreaming can be understood by applying the same cognitive concepts used to study the waking mind.

The **cognitive theory of dreaming** proposes that we can understand dreaming by applying the same cognitive concepts we use in studying the waking mind. The theory rests on the idea that dreams are essentially subconscious cognitive processing, arguing that there is continuity between waking thought and dreams (Domhoff, 2018; Domhoff & Fox, 2015). Dreaming involves information processing and memory. Indeed, thinking during dreams appears to be very similar to thinking in waking life (Eichenlaub & others, 2018).

In the cognitive theory of dreaming, there is little or no search for the hidden, symbolic content of dreams that Freud sought. Instead, dreams are viewed as dramatizations of general life concerns that are similar to relaxed daydreams. Even very unusual aspects of dreams–such as odd activities, strange images, and sudden scene shifts–can be understood as metaphorically related to a person's preoccupations while awake (Domhoff, 2018; Zadra & Domhoff, 2011). The cognitive theory also ties the brain activity that occurs during dreams to the activity that occurs during waking life. The term *default network* refers to a collection of neurons that are active during mind wandering and daydreaming, essentially whenever we are not focused on a task. Research suggests that dreaming during sleep may also emerge from the activity of this network (Domhoff, 2018; Domhoff & Fox, 2015).

The cognitive theory of dreaming strongly argues that dreams should be viewed as a kind of mental simulation that is very similar in content to our everyday waking thoughts. The purpose of dreams is to process information, solve problems, and think creatively about the issues we face in our daily lives. This perspective on dreams contrasts with the activation-synthesis theory of dreaming.

### ACTIVATION-SYNTHESIS THEORY OF DREAMING

According to the **activation-synthesis theory of dreaming**, dreaming occurs when the cerebral cortex synthesizes neural signals generated from activity in the lower part of the brain (Schredl, 2018). Dreams result from the brain's attempts to find logic in random brain activity that occurs during sleep (Hobson, 1999; Hobson & Friston, 2012; Hobson & Voss, 2011; Zhang & Zhang, 2018).

● **activation-synthesis theory of dreaming** Theory that dreaming occurs when the cerebral cortex synthesizes neural signals generated from activity in the lower part of the brain and that dreams result from the brain's attempts to find logic in random brain activity that occurs during sleep.

When we are awake and alert, our conscious experience tends to be driven by *external* stimuli–all those things we see, hear, and respond to. During sleep, according to activation-synthesis theory, conscious experience is driven predominantly by internally generated stimuli that have no apparent behavioral consequence. A key source of such internal stimulation is spontaneous neural activity in the brain stem (Hobson, 2000). Of course, some of the neural activity that produces dreams comes from external sensory experiences. If a fire truck with sirens blaring drives past your house, you might find yourself dreaming about an emergency. Many of us have had the experience of incorporating the sound of our phone alarm (or alarm clock) going off in an early morning dream.

Supporters of activation-synthesis theory have suggested that neural networks in other areas of the forebrain play a significant role in dreaming (Hobson, Pace-Schott, & Stickgold, 2000). Specifically, they believe that the same regions of the forebrain that are involved in certain waking behaviors also function in particular aspects of dreaming (Lu & others, 2006). As levels of neurotransmitters rise and fall during the stages of sleep, some neural networks are activated and others shut down.

Random neural firing in various areas of the brain leads to dreams that are the brain's attempts to make sense of the activity. So, firing in the primary motor and sensory areas of the forebrain might be reflected in a dream of running and feeling wind on your face. From the activation-synthesis perspective, our nervous system is cycling through various activities, and our consciousness is simply along for the ride (Hobson, 2004). Dreams are merely a flashy sideshow, not the main event (Hooper & Teresi, 1993). Indeed, one activation-synthesis theorist has referred to dreams as so much "cognitive trash" (Hobson, 2002, p. 23).

#### test yourself

1. Describe how the human body monitors the change from day to night.
2. What happens during each of the five stages of sleep?
3. According to researchers, what functions does sleep play in infants and children? What functions does it play in adolescents?

## 3. PSYCHOACTIVE DRUGS

One way people try to alter their consciousness is through the use of psychoactive drugs. Illicit drug use is a global problem. According to the United Nations Office on Drugs and Crime (UNODC), more than 246 million people between the ages of 15 and 64 worldwide use drugs each year (UNODC, 2018). Among those, approximately 12 million individuals are characterized as problem drug users–individuals whose drug habit interferes with their ability to engage in work and social relationships (UNODC, 2018).

Drug consumption among youth is a special concern because of its links to problems such as unsafe sex, sexually transmitted infections, unplanned pregnancy, depression, and school difficulties (UNODC, 2018). Drug use among U.S. secondary school students declined in the 1980s but began to increase in the early 1990s (Miech & others, 2018). Then in the late 1990s and early 2000s, it again declined.

Drug use by U.S. high school seniors since 1975 and by U.S. eighth- and tenth-graders since 1991 has been tracked in a national survey called Monitoring the Future (Miech & others, 2018). This survey is the focus of the Psychological Inquiry feature. Let's take a look at these trends.

## psychological *inquiry*

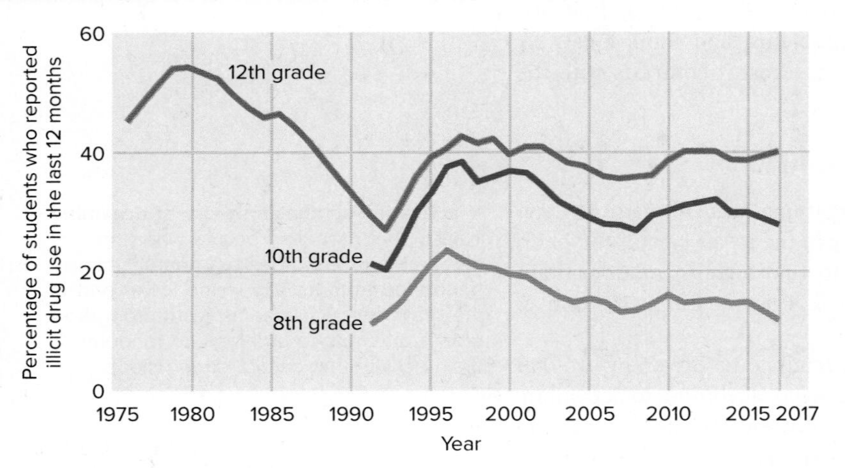


Source: Miech & others (2018).

### *Drug Use by U.S. Teenagers*

This graph shows the percentage of U.S. eighth-, tenth-, and twelfth-grade students who reported having taken any illicit drug in the last 12 months from 1991 to 2017 (for eighth- and tenth-graders) and from 1975 to 2017 (for twelfth-graders) (Miech & others, 2018). The vertical axis shows the percentage of children and adolescents who report using illegal substances. The horizontal axis identifies the year of data collection. The recent increase in illicit drugs use appears to be due to increased use of marijuana. As you examine the data, answer these questions.

1. Do some research to find out about the social and cultural climate in each of the decades represented. Who was president at the time, and what historical events occurred? How does adolescent drug use reflect those times?
2. Data were not collected from eighth- and tenth-graders until 1991. Why do you think these two age groups were added?
3. After the mid-1990s, all age groups showed a similar decline in drug use. Why might this pattern have occurred in all three groups?
4. What are the implications of using self-reports from children and adolescents to track their drug use? Do you think each age group is similarly likely to report honestly, to overreport, or to underreport their drug use? Explain.

## Uses of Psychoactive Drugs

- **psychoactive drugs** Drugs that act on the nervous system to alter consciousness, modify perception, and change mood.

**Psychoactive drugs** act on the nervous system to alter consciousness, modify perception, and change mood. Some people use psychoactive drugs to deal with life's difficulties. Drinking, smoking, and taking drugs reduce tension, relieve boredom and fatigue, and provide a temporary escape from the harsh realities of life. Some people use drugs because they are curious about their effects.

The use of psychoactive drugs, whether it is to cope with problems or just for fun, can carry a high price tag. It can lead to neglected responsibilities, problems in the workplace and in relationships, drug dependence, and increased risk for serious, sometimes fatal diseases (UNODC, 2018). For example, drinking alcohol may initially help people relax and forget about their worries. If, however, they turn more and more to alcohol to escape reality, they may develop a dependence that can destroy their relationships, career, and health. It is also important to realize that illicit drugs such as marijuana and MDMA today are often a great deal stronger—containing higher concentrations of their active ingredients—than they were when they were first introduced to the world (Mounteney & others, 2018). Higher concentrations of drugs means higher risk of overdose.

- **tolerance** The need to take increasing amounts of a drug to get the same effect.
- **physical dependence** The physiological need for a drug that causes unpleasant withdrawal symptoms such as physical pain and a craving for the drug when it is discontinued.
- **psychological dependence** The strong desire to repeat the use of a drug for emotional reasons, such as a feeling of well-being and reduction of stress.
- **addiction** Either a physical or a psychological dependence, or both, on a drug.
- **depressants** Psychoactive drugs that slow down mental and physical activity.

Continued use of these drugs leads to **tolerance**, the need to take increasing amounts of a drug to get the same effect (Rafful & others, 2018). For example, the first time someone takes 5 milligrams of the tranquilizer Valium, the person feels very relaxed. However, after taking the pill every day for six months, the person may need to consume twice as much to achieve the same calming effect.

Ongoing drug use can also result in **physical dependence**, the physiological need for a drug that causes unpleasant withdrawal symptoms such as physical pain and a craving for the drug when it is discontinued. **Psychological dependence** is the strong desire to repeat the use of a drug for emotional reasons, such as a feeling of well-being and reduction of stress. Experts on drug abuse use the term **addiction** to describe either a physical or a psychological dependence, or both, on the drug (DiClemente, 2018).

How does the brain become addicted? Psychoactive drugs increase dopamine levels in the brain's reward pathways (Kringelbach & Berridge, 2018). This reward pathway is located in the *ventral tegmental area (VTA)* and *nucleus accumbens (NAcc)* (Figure 7). Only the limbic and prefrontal areas of the brain are directly activated by dopamine, which comes from the VTA (Beier & others, 2015). Although different drugs have different mechanisms of action, each drug increases the activity of the reward pathway by increasing dopamine transmission. Drugs of addiction have their influence through this common pathway and neurotransmitter.

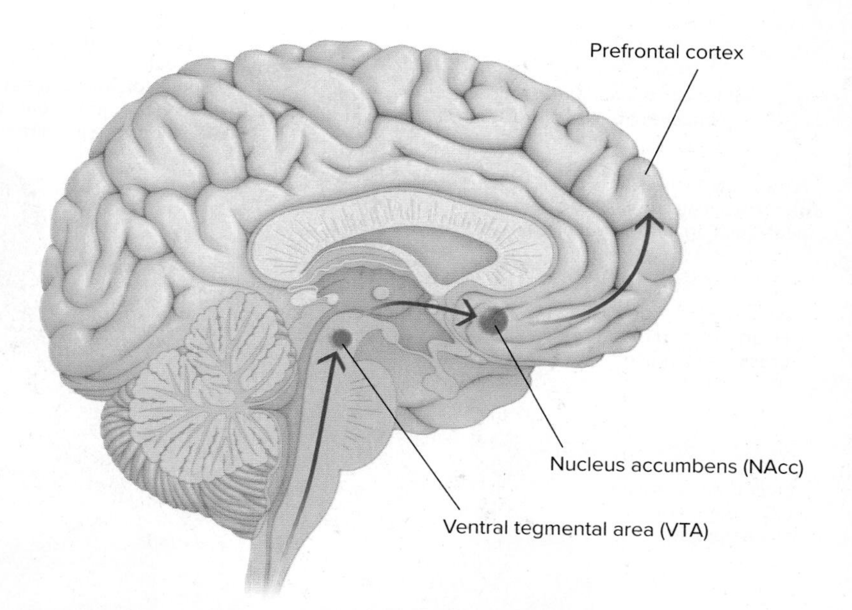


**FIGURE 7** **The Brain's Reward Pathway for Psychoactive Drugs** The ventral tegmental area (VTA) and nucleus accumbens (NAcc) are important locations in the reward pathway for psychoactive drugs (Russo & others, 2010). Information travels from the VTA to the NAcc and then up to the prefrontal cortex. The VTA is located in the midbrain just above the pons, and the NAcc is located in the forebrain just beneath the prefrontal cortex. Source: Russo & others (2010).

## Types of Psychoactive Drugs

Three main categories of psychoactive drugs are depressants, stimulants, and hallucinogens. All have the potential to cause problems involving health, behavior or both. To evaluate whether you abuse drugs, see Figure 8.

### DEPRESSANTS

**Depressants** are psychoactive drugs that slow down mental and physical activity. Among the most widely used depressants are alcohol, barbiturates, tranquilizers, and opioids.

**Alcohol** Alcohol is a powerful drug. It acts on the body primarily as a depressant and slows down the brain's activities. This effect might seem surprising, as people who tend to be inhibited may begin to talk, dance, and socialize after a few drinks. However, people "loosen up" after a few drinks because the brain areas involved in inhibition and judgment slow down. As people drink more, their inhibitions decrease even further, and their judgment becomes increasingly impaired. Activities that require intellectual functioning and motor skills, such as driving, become harder to perform. Eventually the drinker falls asleep. With extreme intoxication, the person may lapse into a coma and die. Figure 9 illustrates alcohol's main effects on the body.

The effects of alcohol vary from person to person. Factors in this variation are body weight, the amount of alcohol consumed, individual differences in the way the body metabolizes alcohol, and the presence or absence of tolerance. Men and women differ in terms of the intoxicating effects of alcohol. Because of differences in body fat as well as stomach enzymes, women are likely to be more strongly affected by alcohol than men.

How does alcohol influence the brain? Like other psychoactive drugs, alcohol goes to the VTA and the NAcc (di Volo & others, 2018). Alcohol also increases the concentration of the neurotransmitter gamma aminobutyric acid (GABA), which is widely distributed in many brain areas, including the cerebral cortex, cerebellum, hippocampus, amygdala, and nucleus accumbens (Lieberman & others, 2018).

Respond yes or no to the following items:

| Yes | No | |
|---|---|---|
| ☐ | ☐ | I have gotten into problems because of using drugs. |
| ☐ | ☐ | Using alcohol or other drugs has made my college life unhappy at times. |
| ☐ | ☐ | Drinking alcohol or taking other drugs has been a factor in my losing a job. |
| ☐ | ☐ | Drinking alcohol or taking other drugs has interfered with my studying for exams. |
| ☐ | ☐ | Drinking alcohol or taking other drugs has jeopardized my academic performance. |
| ☐ | ☐ | My ambition is not as strong since I've been drinking a lot or taking drugs. |
| ☐ | ☐ | Drinking or taking other drugs has caused me to have difficulty sleeping. |
| ☐ | ☐ | I have felt remorse after drinking or taking drugs. |
| ☐ | ☐ | I crave a drink or other drugs at a definite time of the day. |
| ☐ | ☐ | I want a drink or other drug in the morning. |
| ☐ | ☐ | I have had a complete or partial loss of memory as a result of drinking or using other drugs. |
| ☐ | ☐ | Drinking or using other drugs is affecting my reputation. |
| ☐ | ☐ | I have been in the hospital or another institution because of my drinking or taking drugs. |

College students who responded yes to items similar to these on the Rutgers Collegiate Abuse Screening Test were more likely to be substance abusers than those who answered no. If you responded yes to just 1 of the 13 items on this screening test, consider going to your college health or counseling center for further screening.

**FIGURE 8** **Do You Abuse Drugs?** Take this short quiz to see if your use of drugs and alcohol might be a cause for concern.

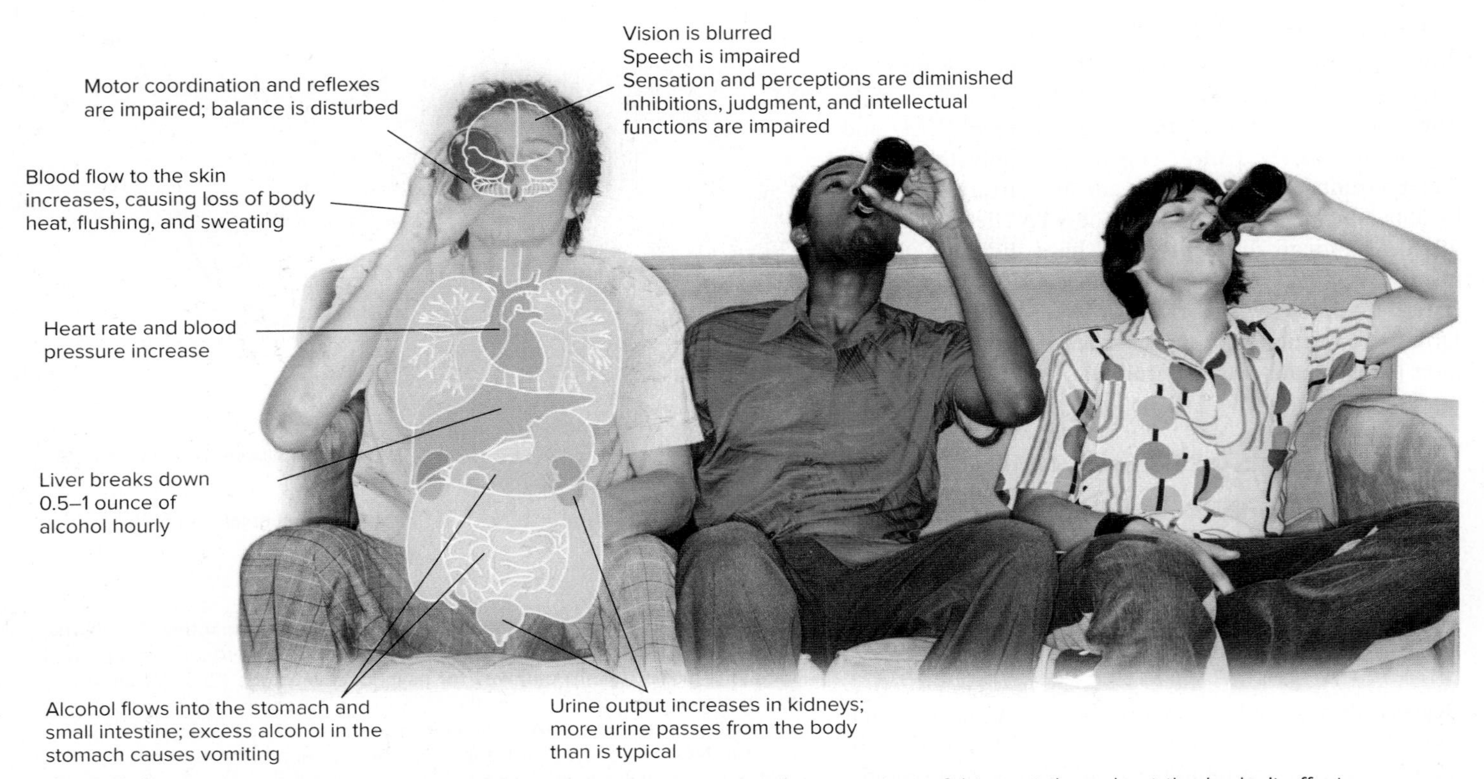
Vision is blurred
Speech is impaired
Sensation and perceptions are diminished
Inhibitions, judgment, and intellectual functions are impaired
Motor coordination and reflexes are impaired; balance is disturbed
Blood flow to the skin increases, causing loss of body heat, flushing, and sweating
Heart rate and blood pressure increase
Liver breaks down 0.5–1 ounce of alcohol hourly
Alcohol flows into the stomach and small intestine; excess alcohol in the stomach causes vomiting
Urine output increases in kidneys; more urine passes from the body than is typical

**FIGURE 9** **The Physiological and Behavioral Effects of Alcohol** Alcohol has a powerful impact throughout the body. It affects everything from the operation of the nervous, circulatory, and digestive systems to sensation, perception, motor coordination, and intellectual functioning. ©George Doyle/Stockbyte/Getty Images

Recall that GABA is the brain's brake pedal, and the increase in GABA has a calming effect. In addition, increases in dopamine in reward areas are associated with the experience of pleasure and a decrease in anxiety (Trantham-Davidson & Chandler, 2015). Alcohol consumption also may affect the areas of the frontal cortex involved in judgment and impulse control (Walters & others, 2018). It is further believed that changes in the basal ganglia, which are involved in compulsive behaviors, may lead to a greater demand for alcohol, regardless of reason and consequences (Renteria, Baltz, & Gremel, 2018).

After caffeine, alcohol is the most widely used drug in the United States. According to the Centers for Disease Control and Prevention (CDC), as many as two-thirds of U.S. adults drink beer, wine, or liquor at least occasionally, and approximately one in six adults reported consuming more than eight drinks at one sitting four times a month (CDC, 2018a). Frequent use of alcohol is related to other serious problems, including death and injury from driving while drinking. In 2016 in the United States, alcohol-impaired driving accounted for over a quarter of all traffic deaths (CDC, 2017). Each day in the United States, 29 people die in alcohol-related car accidents, which amounts to one death every 50 minutes (CDC, 2017).

©Hurst Photo/Shutterstock

Alcohol use is linked to violence and aggression (Denson & others, 2018; Gorman & others, 2018). Over 60 percent of homicides involve alcohol use by the offender or the victim, and 65 percent of aggressive sexual acts against women are associated with alcohol consumption by the offender. Studies have linked substance use to dating violence in adolescents and college students (Collibee & Furman, 2018; Testa & others, 2015). Some people may be especially susceptible to the effects of alcohol on aggressive behavior (Haynes & others, 2018; Miczek & others, 2015).

The percentage of U.S. high school seniors who reported consuming alcohol in the last 30 days dropped from 73 percent in 1980 to 33 percent in 2017 (Miech & others, 2018). Binge drinking (defined as having five or more drinks in a row in the last week) also declined among high school seniors, from 41 percent in 1980 to 16.6 percent in 2017.

©Jim Arbogast/Getty Images

Binge drinking often increases during the first two years of college, peaking at 21 to 22 years of age (Schulenberg & others, 2018). Binge drinking can take a serious toll on students, personally and academically (White, Tapert, & Shukla, 2018). In a national survey of drinking patterns on college campuses, almost half of the binge drinkers reported problems such as missed classes, injuries, trouble with the police, driving after drinking, and unprotected sex (Wechsler & others, 2000, 2002). Intensity of binge drinking in college can predict later problem drinking (Reich & others, 2015; Saitz & others, 2018). Many emerging adults decrease their alcohol use as they assume adult responsibilities–such as a permanent job, marriage or cohabitation, and parenthood–and as they mature psychologically (Lee, Ellingson, & Sher, 2015).

**Alcoholism** is a disorder that involves long-term, repeated, uncontrolled, compulsive, and excessive use of alcoholic beverages and is associated with impairment of the drinker's health and social relationships. According to the National Institute for Alcohol Abuse and Alcoholism (NIAAA, 2018), over 15 million adults aged 18 and older have alcohol use disorder, meaning that alcohol use has severely impaired their ability to function. Those who start drinking alcohol at younger ages are at risk for heavy drinking and alcohol problems (Aiken & others, 2018; Xuan & others, 2015).

- **alcoholism** A disorder that involves long-term, repeated, uncontrolled, compulsive, and excessive use of alcoholic beverages and is associated with impairment of the drinker's health and social relationships.

One in nine people who drink continues down the path to alcoholism. A key risk factor is family history. Family studies consistently find a high frequency of alcoholism in the close biological relatives of alcoholics (Farmer & others, 2018). There may be genetic predispositions to alcohol abuse (Salvatore & others, 2018). These genes may be involved in the regulation and production of dopamine, the neurotransmitter that can make us feel pleasure (Bazov & others, 2018). For these individuals, alcohol may increase dopamine concentration and the resulting pleasure to the point that it leads to addiction.

Like other psychological characteristics, though, alcoholism is not all about nature. Research shows that experience plays a role in alcoholism (Cox & others, 2018; Kendler, Gardner, & Dick, 2011; Pucci & others, 2018). Many alcoholics do not have close relatives who are alcoholics (Duncan & others, 2006), suggesting environmental influences.

What does it take to stop alcoholism? About one-third of alcoholics recover whether they are in a treatment program or not. This finding came from a long-term study of 700 individuals (Vaillant, 2003). George Vaillant followed these individuals for over 60 years, and he formulated the so-called one-third rule for alcoholism: By age 65, one-third are dead or in terrible shape; one-third are still trying to beat their addiction; and one-third are abstinent or drinking only socially. In his extensive research, Vaillant found that recovery from alcoholism was predicted by (1) having a strong negative experience with drinking, such as a serious medical emergency; (2) finding a substitute dependency, such as meditation, exercise, or overeating (although overeating has its own adverse health effects); (3) developing new, positive relationships; and (4) joining a support group such as Alcoholics Anonymous.

**Barbiturates** **Barbiturates**, like Nembutal and Seconal, are depressant drugs that decrease central nervous system activity. Physicians once widely prescribed barbiturates as sleep aids because barbiturates put people to sleep. In heavy dosages, they can lead to impaired memory, poor decision making, and difficulty breathing. When combined with alcohol, barbiturates can be lethal. Heavy doses of barbiturates by themselves can cause death. Abrupt withdrawal can produce seizures. Because of the addictive potential and risk of toxic overdose, barbiturates have largely been replaced by tranquilizers in the treatment of insomnia.

- **barbiturates** Depressant drugs, such as Nembutal and Seconal, that decrease central nervous system activity.

**Tranquilizers** **Tranquilizers**, like Valium and Xanax, are depressant drugs that reduce anxiety and induce relaxation. In small doses tranquilizers can bring on a feeling of calm; higher doses can lead to drowsiness and confusion. Tolerance for tranquilizers can develop within a few weeks of usage, and these drugs are addictive. Widely prescribed in the United States to calm anxious individuals, tranquilizers can produce withdrawal symptoms when use is stopped. Prescription tranquilizers were part of the lethal cocktail of drugs that ended the life of Whitney Houston in 2012.

©Ingram Publishing/SuperStock

● **tranquilizers** Depressant drugs, such as Valium and Xanax, that reduce anxiety and induce relaxation.

● **opioids** A class of drugs that act on the brain's endorphin receptors. These include opium and its natural derivatives (sometimes called opiates) as well as chemicals that do not occur naturally but that have been created to mimic the activity of opium. These drugs (also called narcotics) depress activity in the central nervous system and eliminate pain.

**Opioids** Narcotics, or **opioids**, are a class of drugs that act on the brain's endorphin receptors. They include opium and its natural derivatives (morphine and heroin) as well as synthetic chemicals created to mimic the activity of opium. These drugs depress activity in the central nervous system and eliminate pain.

Opioids are powerful painkillers. They affect synapses in the brain that use endorphins as their neurotransmitter. When they bind to the brain's opioid receptors, they drive up the production of dopamine, producing feelings of pleasure (NIDA, 2016). For several hours after taking an opiate, the person feels euphoric and pain-free and has an increased appetite for food and sex. Opioids are highly addictive, and users experience craving and painful withdrawal when the drug becomes unavailable.

Many people who abuse opioids first encountered them as (legal) prescription pain killers. Fentanyl is a fast-acting opioid prescription pain killer that has been implicated in numerous overdoses, including the death of music legend Prince in 2016. Fentanyl is estimated to be 50 to 100 times more powerful than morphine (NIDA, 2016). In 2016, prescription opioids accounted for more deaths than heroin and cocaine combined (NIDA, 2017).

The availability of prescription opioids is a public health emergency. Because these drugs are prescribed by doctors, people may not realize how powerful and dangerous they are. One healthcare expert cautioned, "Prescription pain pills are similar to having heroin in the medicine cabinet" (Hazelden Betty Ford Foundation, 2015). Children who live in households where adults have prescription drugs are at risk for overdose (Turkewitz, 2017). Research shows that nonopioid anti-inflammatory medications (such as Tylenol or Motrin) can be just as effective as opioids in treating acute pain (Chang & others, 2017; Khan & others, 2018). One study examined the recovery time among patients with broken legs and found no difference between those who took anti-inflammatory pain killers and those who took opioids (Fader & others, 2018).

The risk of death from overdose of opioids is very high. Remember, these drugs work by attaching to receptors for endorphins. Such receptors are present in the brain stem, the region that controls breathing. So, if someone takes too much of an opioid (or an opioid mixed with another drug such as alcohol) they can stop breathing (NIDA, 2016). Naloxone, a drug used to treat opioid overdose, can restore normal breathing. In 2016, an estimated 64,000 people died from opioid overdose, outnumbering those killed in car accidents by more than 20,000 (NIDA, 2017). It is estimated that each day, 90 Americans die of an opioid overdose (Hill & Saxon, 2018). A person does not have to be addicted to opioids to die of an overdose.

Often when a person experiences an overdose, it falls to family and friends to respond. Symptoms of an opioid overdose are pinpoint pupils, unconsciousness, and slowed breathing (WHO, 2018a). If you think someone has overdosed, immediately call 911 for help. Bringing pill bottles to the hospital can help professionals know what to do.

## STIMULANTS

● **stimulants** Psychoactive drugs—including caffeine, nicotine, amphetamines, and cocaine—that increase the central nervous system's activity.

**Stimulants** are psychoactive drugs that increase the central nervous system's activity. The most widely used stimulants are caffeine, nicotine, amphetamines, and cocaine.

**Caffeine** Often overlooked as a drug, caffeine is the world's most widely used psychoactive drug. Caffeine is a stimulant and a natural component of the plants that are the sources of coffee, tea, and cola drinks. Caffeine also is present in chocolate, in many nonprescription medications, and in energy drinks such as Red Bull. People often perceive the stimulating effects of caffeine as beneficial for boosting energy and alertness, but some experience unpleasant side effects.

*Caffeinism* refers to an overindulgence in caffeine. It is characterized by mood changes, anxiety, and sleep disruption. Caffeinism often develops in people who drink five or more cups of coffee (at least 500 milligrams of caffeine) each day. Common symptoms are insomnia, irritability, headaches, ringing ears, dry mouth, increased blood pressure, and digestive problems.

Caffeine affects the brain's pleasure centers, so it is not surprising that it is difficult to kick the caffeine habit. When individuals who regularly consume caffeinated beverages remove caffeine from their diet, they typically experience headaches, lethargy, apathy, and concentration difficulties. These symptoms of withdrawal are usually mild and subside after several days.

**Nicotine** Nicotine is the main psychoactive ingredient in all forms of smoking and smokeless tobacco. Even with all the publicity given to the enormous health risks posed by tobacco, we sometimes overlook the highly addictive nature of nicotine. Nicotine stimulates the brain's reward centers by raising dopamine levels. Behavioral effects of nicotine include improved attention and alertness, reduced anger and anxiety, and pain relief. Figure 10 shows the main effects of nicotine on the body.

Tolerance develops for nicotine both in the long run and on a daily basis, so that cigarettes smoked later in the day have less effect than those smoked earlier. Withdrawal from nicotine often quickly produces strong, unpleasant symptoms such as irritability, cravings, inability to focus, sleep disturbance, and increased appetite. Withdrawal symptoms can persist for months.

Attention and alertness improve
At high levels, muscles become more relaxed; anxiety and anger may be reduced; pleasant feelings induce the individual to smoke more
Circulation to extremities decreases
Heart rate and blood pressure increase
In a pregnant woman, nicotine freely passes through the placenta wall into amniotic fluid
Smoker loses appetite for carbohydrates

**FIGURE 10 The Physiological and Behavioral Effects of Nicotine** Smoking has many physiological and behavioral effects. Highly addictive, nicotine delivers pleasant feelings that encourage more smoking, but tobacco consumption poses very serious health risks in the individual. ©Anton Dotsenko/123RF

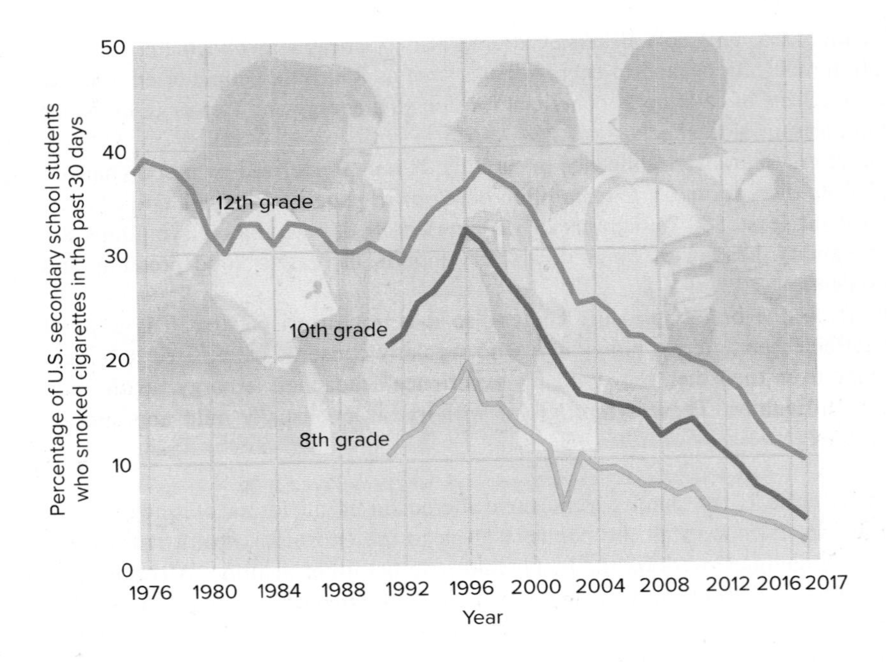


**FIGURE 11** **Trends in Cigarette Smoking by U.S. Secondary School Students** Cigarette smoking by U.S. high school students is on the decline.
Source: Miech & others (2018); ©Digital Vision/PunchStock

Tobacco poses a much larger threat to public health than illegal drugs. According to the CDC, tobacco is involved in one in every five deaths in the United States (CDC, 2018b). That is more than the total number killed by AIDS, alcohol, motor vehicles, homicide, illegal drugs, and suicide combined. Even as smoking rates decline, smoking remains the leading cause of preventable death in the United States. According to the World Health Organization (2018b), there are more than 1 billion smokers globally, and smoking will kill at least half of them.

Cigarette smoking is decreasing among both adolescents and college students. In the national Monitoring the Future survey, the percentage of U.S. adolescents who are current cigarette smokers has declined steeply in the last year, with all age groups showing a significant drop from 2014 to 2017 (Miech & others, 2018) (Figure 11).

The drop in cigarette use by U.S. youth may have several sources, including higher cigarette prices, less tobacco advertising reaching adolescents, more antismoking advertisements, and more negative publicity about the tobacco industry than previously. Increasingly, adolescents report perceiving cigarette smoking as dangerous, disapprove of it, are less accepting of being around smokers, and prefer to date nonsmokers (Miech & others, 2018). Among college students and young adults, smoking has shown a smaller decline than among adolescents and adults (Schulenberg & others, 2018).

In sum, cigarette smoking is generally on the decline. Most smokers recognize the serious health risks of smoking and wish they could quit. The chapter "Health Psychology" explores the difficulty of giving up smoking and describes strategies for quitting.

**Amphetamines** Amphetamines, or uppers, are stimulant drugs that people use to boost energy, stay awake, or lose weight. Often prescribed in the form of diet pills, these drugs increase the release of dopamine, which enhances the user's activity level and pleasurable feelings. Prescription drugs for attention deficit disorder, such as Ritalin, are also stimulants.

Perhaps the most insidious illicit drug for contemporary society is crystal methamphetamine, or crystal meth. Smoked, injected, or swallowed, crystal meth (also called "crank" or "tina") is a synthetic stimulant that causes a powerful feeling of euphoria, particularly the first time it is ingested. Meth is made using household products such as battery acid, cold medicine, drain cleaner, and kitty litter, and its effects have been devastating, notably in rural areas of the United States.

Crystal meth releases enormous amounts of dopamine in the brain, producing intense feelings of pleasure. The drug is highly addictive. The extreme high of crystal meth

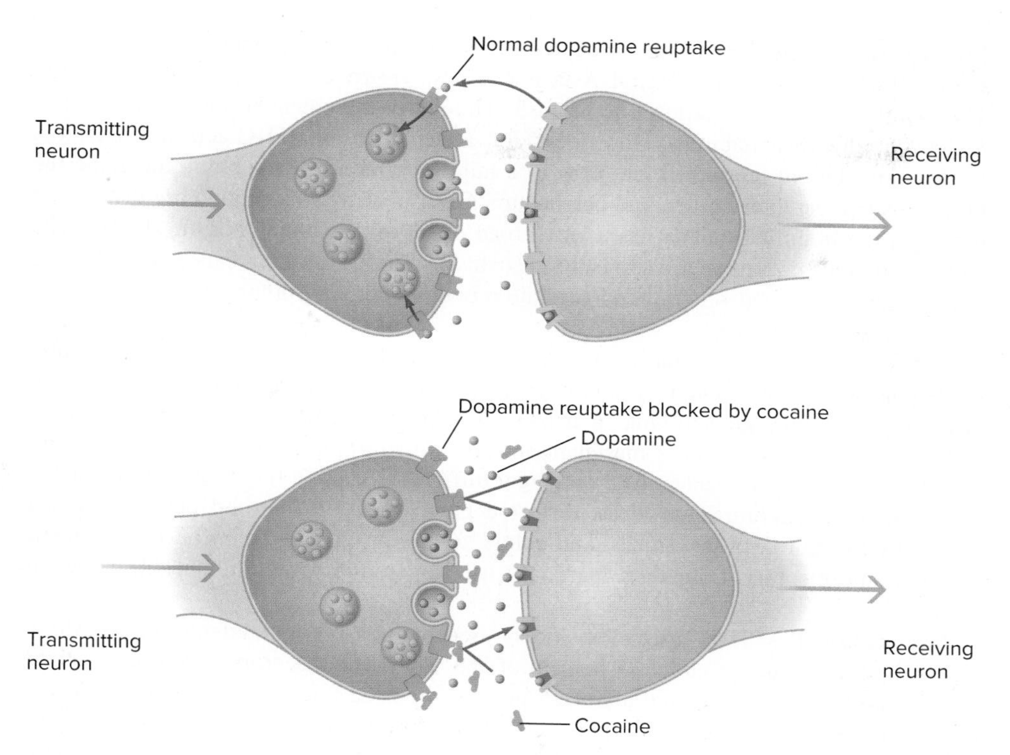


**FIGURE 12 Cocaine and Neurotransmitters** Cocaine concentrates in areas of the brain that are rich in dopamine synapses such as the VTA and the nucleus accumbens (NAcc). (*top*) What happens in normal reuptake: The transmitting neuron releases dopamine, which stimulates the receiving neuron by binding to its receptor sites. After binding occurs, dopamine is carried back into the transmitting neuron for later release. (*bottom*) What happens when cocaine is present in the synapse: Cocaine binds to the uptake pumps and prevents them from removing dopamine from the synapse. The result is that more dopamine collects in the synapse, and more dopamine receptors are activated.

leads to a severe "come down" experience that is associated with strong cravings. Crystal meth also damages dopamine receptors, so that the crystal meth addict is chasing a high that the person's brain can no longer produce. A person's very first experience with crystal meth can lead to ruinous consequences, making it a drug not worth trying even once.

**Cocaine** Cocaine is an illegal drug that comes from the coca plant, native to Bolivia and Peru. Cocaine is either snorted or injected in the form of crystals or powder. Used this way, cocaine floods the bloodstream rapidly, producing a rush of euphoric feelings that lasts for about 15 to 30 minutes. Because the rush depletes the brain's supply of the neurotransmitters dopamine, serotonin, and norepinephrine, an agitated, depressed mood usually follows as the drug's effects decline. Figure 12 shows how cocaine affects dopamine levels in the brain.

Crack is a potent form of cocaine, consisting of chips of pure cocaine that are usually smoked. Scientists believe that crack is one of the most addictive substances known. Treatment of cocaine and crack addiction is difficult (Erickson, 2018).

**MDMA (Ecstasy)** MDMA–called Ecstasy, X, or XTC–is an illegal synthetic drug with both stimulant and hallucinogenic properties (Mounteney & others, 2018). People have called Ecstasy an "empathogen" because under its influence, users tend to feel warm bonds with others. Not surprisingly, then, MDMA is associated with increased sexual risk taking (Glynn & others, 2018). MDMA produces its effects by releasing serotonin, dopamine, and norepinephrine. MDMA impairs memory and cognitive processing (Petschner & others, 2018). In addition, chronic use may impair the serotonin system (Roberts & others, 2018).

## HALLUCINOGENS

**Hallucinogens** are psychoactive drugs that modify a person's perceptual experiences and produce visual images that are not real. Hallucinogens are also called *psychedelic* (from the Greek word that means "mind-revealing") drugs. Marijuana has a mild hallucinogenic effect; LSD, a stronger one.

● **hallucinogens** Psychoactive drugs that modify a person's perceptual experiences and produce visual images that are not real.

**Marijuana** Marijuana is the dried leaves and flowers of the hemp plant *Cannabis sativa,* which originated in Central Asia but is now grown in most parts of the world. The plant's dried resin is known as hashish. The active ingredient in marijuana is THC (delta-9-tetrahydrocannabinol). How does THC affect the brain? THC activates receptors (called cannabinoid receptors) that exist in a number of areas of the brain, including the limbic system, cerebral cortex, and cerebellum. Given that these receptors are distributed widely in the brain, marijuana has a very broad effect on the brain (NIDA, 2018). THC attaches to receptors that are typically used by a neurotransmitter called *anandamide,* a neurotransmitter that functions to regulate mood, eating, and other functions (Ashton, Dowie, & Glass, 2017).

The physical effects of marijuana include increased pulse rate and blood pressure, reddening of the eyes, coughing, and dry mouth. Like tobacco cigarettes and any other drugs ingested through smoking, marijuana smoke can damage the lungs (Mannino, 2015). Psychological effects of marijuana include a mixture of excitatory, depressive, and mildly hallucinatory characteristics, making it difficult to classify the drug. Marijuana can trigger spontaneous unrelated ideas; distorted perceptions of time and place; increased sensitivity to sounds, tastes, smells, and colors; and erratic verbal behavior. It can impair attention and memory. Long-term marijuana use can lead to addiction and difficulties in quitting.

Marijuana is the illegal drug most widely used by high school students. In the Monitoring the Future survey, about 35 percent of U.S. high school seniors said they had tried marijuana in their lifetime, and about 25 percent reported that they had used marijuana in the last 30 days (Miech & others, 2018). One concern about adolescents' use of marijuana is that the drug might be a gateway to the use of more serious illicit substances. Although there is a correlational link between using marijuana and using other illicit drugs, evidence for the notion that using marijuana leads to using other drugs is mixed (Kandel & Kandel, 2015; Tarter & others, 2006).

Marijuana is used in the treatment of a variety of illnesses including AIDS, cancer, and chronic pain (Thompson, 2015). Recently, Canada legalized the use of marijuana for recreational purposes (Bilefsky, 2018). In the United States, 33 states currently allow the medicinal use of marijuana. Importantly, a recent large-scale meta-analysis showed that adolescent use of marijuana was unaffected by these laws (Sarvet & others, 2018). This means that legalizing marijuana for medical use does not appear to encourage young people to abuse the drug.

In addition, 10 states and the District of Columbia have legalized the possession and recreational use of marijuana. However, U.S. federal law continues to treat marijuana as an illegal substance. Recently, large-scale correlational studies have shown that states with legal medical marijuana have lower incidents of opioid use and abuse. Might medical marijuana present a legal alternative to opioids and help in resolving the opioid crisis? To answer this question, let's take a deep dive into the data, in the Critical Controversy.

**LSD** LSD (lysergic acid diethylamide) is a hallucinogen that even in low doses produces striking perceptual changes. Objects change shape and glow; colors become kaleidoscopic, and astonishing images unfold. LSD-induced images are sometimes pleasurable and sometimes grotesque. LSD can also influence a user's sense of time so that brief glances at objects are experienced as deep, penetrating, and lengthy examinations, and minutes turn into hours or even days. A bad LSD trip can trigger extreme anxiety, paranoia, and suicidal or homicidal impulses.

LSD's effects on the body can include dizziness, nausea, and tremors. LSD acts primarily on the neurotransmitter serotonin in the brain, although it also can affect dopamine (González-Maeso & Sealfon, 2009). Emotional and cognitive effects may include rapid mood swings and impaired attention and memory. The use of LSD peaked in the 1960s and 1970s, and its consumption has been decreasing in the twenty-first century (Miech & others, 2018).

Figure 13 summarizes the effects of a variety of other psychoactive drugs.

### test yourself

1. What are psychoactive drugs, and for what reasons do people use them?
2. Describe what stimulants and depressants are, and give three examples of each.
3. What are hallucinogens? What are two common examples of hallucinogens?

# CRITICAL CONTROVERSY

## Does Legalized Medical Marijuana Reduce Opioid Abuse and Overdoses?

Ever since states in the U.S. started legalizing medical marijuana, scientists have been interested in gauging the effects of legalization. A key focus has been the effects of medical marijuana on opioid overdoses. In 2014, a study compared two groups of states: 13 (California, Oregon, Washington, Alaska, Colorado, Hawaii, Maine, Michigan, Montana, Nevada, New Mexico, Rhode Island, and Vermont) that had legalized medical marijuana and 37 states that had not (Bachhuber & others, 2014). It showed that states with legal medical marijuana had nearly 25 percent fewer deaths from opioid overdose. States that legalized medical marijuana also showed 33 percent drops in opioid mortality rates and the declines grew over the years after legalization.

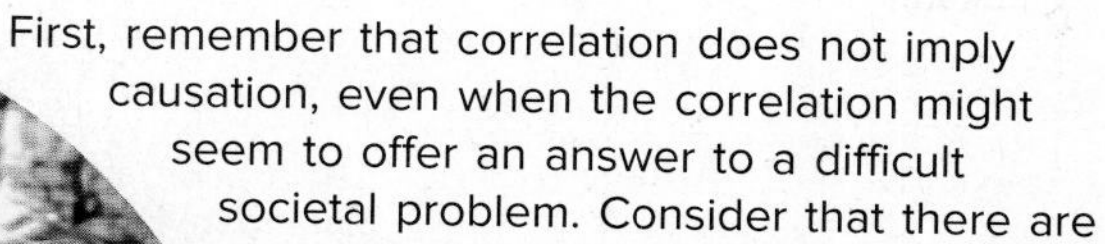

©Soru Epotok/Shutterstock

Since that study, a number of additional studies have examined the association between medical marijuana legalization and opioid overdoses and deaths. Results show that legalization of marijuana is negatively correlated with opioid overdose (Powell, Pacula, & Jacobson, 2018). Fewer studies have examined the potential correlation between the number of opioid-related deaths and legalization of marijuana for recreational, not just medical, use (Shi & others, 2019). A study examining opioid deaths in Colorado after the state legalized medical *and* recreational marijuana showed the laws were linked with just under 1 less death per month (Livingston & others, 2018). Passage of the laws also marked a turning point in the trajectory of opioid-related deaths, which began to decline instead of increase.

Many people first encounter opioids as legally prescribed painkillers. Do medical professionals prescribe fewer opioids when they can turn to marijuana instead? Population-based studies examining opioid prescriptions have shown that these drop by 5 to 7 percent after laws legalizing medical and recreational marijuana go into effect (Wen & Hockenberry, 2018). The change in prescription rates for all opioids amounts to over *3.7 million* fewer daily doses per year following the legalization of medical marijuana (Bradford & others, 2018).

Do these findings indicate that a move to more liberalized marijuana laws is a way to solve the opioid epidemic? Answering this question is more complicated that it might seem. First, remember that correlation does not imply causation, even when the correlation might seem to offer an answer to a difficult societal problem. Consider that there are a multitude of third variables that might account for the negative association between legalized medical marijuana and opioid deaths (Hall & others, 2018). For example, improved economic conditions may play a role in reduced opioid use. Programs that have been in place to combat opioid abuse (which happened at the same time as changes to marijuana laws) may be having an effect. Perhaps growing awareness of opioid addiction has led physicians to reduce their prescriptions or patients to be more careful with their medications. High-profile overdose deaths of celebrities like Prince might also have reduced opioid use.

Large-scale studies cannot tell us about what is going on in specific cases. We might assume that these findings mean individuals are being prescribed marijuana instead of opioids or that those who would have used powerfully addictive opioids are substituting marijuana, but the current data cannot tell us whether this is what is happening. The data are not relevant to those experiences "on the ground."

One recent study demonstrates the complexity of these issues. This large-scale study of the effects of medical marijuana on opioid death rates (Powell, Pacula, & Jacobson, 2018) showed that the availability of medical marijuana was associated with reduced rates of opioid-related deaths. However, and importantly, this effect was only true for states that maintained liberal policies about the distribution of marijuana. When states were more stringent in their regulation of marijuana dispensaries, the negative relation to opioid deaths was weaker. The researchers concluded that legalized marijuana does seem to facilitate substitution of marijuana for more seriously addictive opioids but this benefit is only apparent when states allow access in a fairly liberal fashion. Such nuances may be important as more and more states legalize medical marijuana.

**WHAT DO YOU THINK?**

- Why do you think legalized marijuana is associated with lower opioid prescriptions and overdoses?
- Do you think marijuana should be legalized broadly? Why or why not?

| Drug Classification | Medical Uses | Short-Term Effects | Overdose Effects | Health Risks | Risk of Physical/ Psychological Dependence |
|---|---|---|---|---|---|
| **Depressants** | | | | | |
| Alcohol | Pain relief | Relaxation, depressed brain activity, slowed behavior, reduced inhibitions | Disorientation, loss of consciousness, even death at high blood-alcohol levels | Accidents, brain damage, liver disease, heart disease, ulcers, birth defects | Physical and psychological: moderate |
| Barbiturates | Sleeping pill | Relaxation, sleep | Breathing difficulty, coma, possible death | Accidents, coma, possible death | Physical and psychological: moderate to high |
| Tranquilizers | Anxiety reduction | Relaxation, slowed behavior | Breathing difficulty, coma, possible death | Accidents, coma, possible death | Physical: low to moderate Psychological: moderate to high |
| Opiates (narcotics) | Pain relief | Euphoric feelings, drowsiness, nausea | Convulsions, coma, possible death | Accidents, infectious diseases such as AIDS | Physical: high Psychological: moderate to high |
| **Stimulants** | | | | | |
| Amphetamines | Weight control | Increased alertness, excitability; decreased fatigue, irritability | Extreme irritability, feelings of persecution, convulsions | Insomnia, hypertension, malnutrition, possible death | Physical: possible Psychological: moderate to high |
| Cocaine | Local anesthetic | Increased alertness, excitability, euphoric feelings; decreased fatigue, irritability | Extreme irritability, feelings of persecution, convulsions, cardiac arrest, possible death | Insomnia, hypertension, malnutrition, possible death | Physical: possible Psychological: moderate (oral) to very high (injected or smoked) |
| MDMA (Ecstasy) | None | Mild amphetamine and hallucinogenic effects; high body temperature and dehydration; sense of well-being and social connectedness | Brain damage, especially memory and thinking | Cardiovascular problems; death | Physical: possible Psychological: moderate |
| Caffeine | None | Alertness and sense of well-being followed by fatigue | Nervousness, anxiety, disturbed sleep | Possible cardiovascular problems | Physical and psychological: moderate |
| Nicotine | None | Stimulation, stress reduction, followed by fatigue, anger | Nervousness, disturbed sleep | Cancer and cardiovascular disease | Physical and psychological: high |
| **Hallucinogens** | | | | | |
| LSD | None | Strong hallucinations, distorted time perception | Severe mental disturbance, loss of contact with reality | Accidents | Physical: none Psychological: low |
| Marijuana* | Treatment for glaucoma, cancer, and chronic pain, as well as stimulating appetite and well-being for individuals with conditions such as AIDS | Euphoric feelings, relaxation, mild hallucinations, time distortion, attention and memory impairment | Fatigue, disoriented behavior | Accidents, respiratory disease | Physical: very low Psychological: moderate |

**FIGURE 13** **Categories of Psychoactive Drugs: Depressants, Stimulants, and Hallucinogens** Note that these various drugs have different effects and negative consequences. *Classifying marijuana is difficult because of its diverse effects.

# 4. HYPNOSIS

Shelley Thomas arrived at a London hospital for a 30-minute pelvic surgery. Before the operation, with her hypnotherapist guiding her, Shelley counted backward from 100 and entered a hypnotic trance. Her surgery was performed with no anesthesia (Song, 2006); rather, Shelley relied on hypnosis to harness her mind's powers to overcome pain.

You may have seen a hypnotist on TV or in a nightclub, putting a person into a trance and then perhaps making the individual act like a chicken or pretend to be a contestant on *The Voice* or enact some similarly strange behavior. When we observe someone in such a trance, we might be convinced that hypnosis involves a powerful manipulation of another person's consciousness. What is hypnosis, really? What is going on inside the mind of the person who has been hypnotized? The answer to this question is a source of some debate (Coltheart & others, 2018; Elkins & others, 2015; Lynn & others, 2015).

Some psychologists think of hypnosis as an altered state of consciousness (Pekala, 2015). Others believe that it is simply a product of everyday social cognitive processes, such as focused attention, expectations, and a relationship between two people (Lynn & others, 2015). In fact, both views are reasonable, and we may define **hypnosis** as an altered state of consciousness or as a psychological state of altered attention and expectation in which the individual is unusually receptive to suggestions. People have used basic hypnotic techniques since the beginning of recorded history, in association with religious ceremonies, magic, and the supernatural.

● **hypnosis** An altered state of consciousness or a psychological state of altered attention and expectation in which the individual is unusually receptive to suggestions.

Today, psychology and medicine recognize hypnosis as a legitimate process, although researchers still have much to learn about how it works. In addition, there is continuing debate about whether hypnosis truly is an altered state of consciousness (Elkins & others, 2015).

## The Nature of Hypnosis

When Shelley Thomas was in a hypnotic trance, what exactly was happening in her brain? Patterns of brain activity during the hypnotic state suggest that hypnosis produces a state of consciousness similar to other states of consciousness. For example, individuals in a typical hypnotic state display a predominance of alpha and beta waves, characteristic of people in a relaxed waking state, when monitored by an EEG. In a very deep state of hypnosis the brain can show a predominance of theta waves (Cavallaro & others, 2010; Williams & Gruzelier, 2001). The pattern of brain activation associated with the hypnotic state is not unlike that found when people engage in mental imagery (Faymonville, Boly, & Laureys, 2006). In sum, a hypnotic state is not like being asleep. It is more similar to being relaxed and awake. How does the hypnotist lead people into this state of relaxation and imagery?

### THE FOUR STEPS IN HYPNOSIS

Hypnosis involves four steps. The hypnotist

1. Minimizes distractions and makes the person to be hypnotized comfortable.
2. Tells the person to concentrate on something specific, such as an imagined scene or the ticking of a watch.
3. Informs the person what to expect in the hypnotic state, such as relaxation or a pleasant floating sensation.
4. Suggests certain events or feelings he or she knows will occur or observes occurring, such as "Your eyes are getting tired." When the suggested effects occur, the person interprets them as being caused by the hypnotist's suggestion and accepts them as an indication that something is happening. This increase in the person's expectations that the hypnotist will make things happen in the future makes the person even more suggestible.

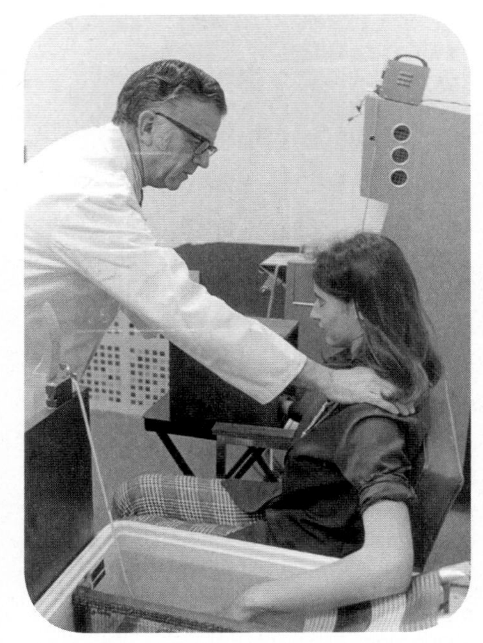

**FIGURE 14 Hilgard's Divided Consciousness Experiment** Ernest Hilgard tests a participant in the study in which he had individuals place one hand in ice-cold water. ©Stanford News Service

### INDIVIDUAL VARIATIONS IN HYPNOSIS

Some people are more easily hypnotized than others, and some are more strongly influenced by hypnotic suggestions. *Hypnotizability* refers to the extent to which a person's responses *are changed* by being hypnotized (Frischholz & others, 2015a; Picerni & others, 2018). If you have the capacity to immerse yourself deeply in an imaginative activity–listening to a favorite piece of music or reading a novel, for example–you might be a likely candidate for hypnosis (Frischholz & others, 2015b).

## Explaining Hypnosis

How does hypnosis have its effects? Contemporary theorists disagree as to whether hypnosis is a divided state of consciousness or simply a learned social behavior (Lynn & others, 2015).

### A DIVIDED STATE OF CONSCIOUSNESS

Ernest Hilgard (1977, 1992), in his **divided consciousness view of hypnosis**, proposed that hypnosis involves a special divided state of consciousness, a splitting of consciousness into separate components. One component follows the hypnotist's commands, while another component acts as a "hidden observer."

● **divided consciousness view of hypnosis** Hilgard's view that hypnosis involves a splitting of consciousness into two separate components: one that follows the hypnotist's commands and the other that acts as a "hidden observer."

Hilgard placed one hand of hypnotized individuals in a bucket of ice-cold water and told them that they would not feel pain but that a part of their mind–a hidden part that would be aware of what was going on–could signal any true pain by pressing a key with the hand that was not submerged (Figure 14). The individuals under hypnosis reported afterward that they had not experienced any pain; yet while their hand had been submerged in the ice-cold water, they had pressed the key with their non-submerged hand, and they had pressed it more frequently the longer their hand was in the cold water. Thus, in Hilgard's view, in hypnosis consciousness has a hidden part that stays in contact with reality and feels pain while another part feels no pain.

Critics of Hilgard's view suggest that the hidden observer simply demonstrates that the hypnotized person is not in an altered state of consciousness at all. From this perspective, the hidden observer is simply the person himself or herself, having been given permission to admit to the pain that he or she was always feeling (Green & others, 2005). This argument is part of the social cognitive behavior view of hypnosis.

### SOCIAL COGNITIVE BEHAVIOR

Some psychologists are skeptical that hypnosis is an altered state of consciousness (Lynn, Laurence, & Kirsch, 2015). In the **social cognitive behavior view of hypnosis**, hypnosis is a normal state in which the hypnotized person behaves the way the individual believes that a hypnotized person should behave. The social cognitive perspective frames the important questions about hypnosis around cognitive factors–the attitudes, expectations, and beliefs of good hypnotic participants–and around the powerful social context in which hypnosis occurs. Individuals being hypnotized surrender their responsibility to the hypnotist and follow the hypnotist's suggestions; and they have expectations about what hypnosis is supposed to be like.

● **social cognitive behavior view of hypnosis** The perspective that hypnosis is a normal state in which the hypnotized person behaves the way the individual believes that a hypnotized person should behave.

Experts continue to debate whether hypnosis is an altered state of consciousness or simply a reaction to a special social situation (Kihlstrom, 2005). There may be no consensus about what hypnosis is, but scientists use hypnosis to explore the brain and its functions, and health professionals have begun to apply it to a number of problems.

## Uses of Hypnosis

As psychologists' interest in studying consciousness has grown, hypnosis has emerged as a useful tool (Tomé-Pires & Miró, 2012). Some researchers employ hypnosis in a way similar to transcranial magnetic stimulation (described in the chapter "Biological Foundations of Behavior"), to experimentally dampen brain processes (Cox & Bryant, 2008).

Combining hypnosis with brain imaging allows researchers to understand both the effects of hypnosis itself and the brain's functioning (Oakley & Halligan, 2011).

Hypnosis has been applied to a variety of problems. In the United States, practitioners of hypnosis use the technique to treat alcoholism, somnambulism, insomnia, depression, suicidal tendencies, post-traumatic stress disorder, overeating, diabetes, smoking, and various types of pain. Whether hypnosis actually works for these diverse problems remains debatable (Brown, 2007; Chamine, Atchley, & Oken, 2018; Krouwel & others, 2018). Hypnosis appears to be most effective when combined with psychotherapy (Rossi, 2009). Psychotherapy, a major focus in the chapter "Therapies", is a form of nonmedical treatment in which a professional seeks to help someone overcome life difficulties.

A long history of research and practice has clearly demonstrated that hypnosis can reduce the experience of pain (Elkins, Johnson, & Fisher, 2012). Brain-imaging studies show that hypnosis appears to have widespread effects on the brain's pain network (Del Casale & others, 2015). A fascinating study examined the pain perceptions of hypnotized individuals, with the goal of changing their pain threshold. In that study, the brains of participants were monitored while they received painful electrical shocks (rated 8 or higher on a 1 to 10 pain scale) (Schulz-Stübner & others, 2004). Those who were hypnotized to find the shocks less painful did rate them as lower in pain (giving them a 3 or less). The brain-scanning results were most interesting: The subcortical brain areas (the brain stem and midbrain) of the hypnotized patients responded the same as those of the patients who were not hypnotized, suggesting that these brain structures recognized the painful stimulation. However, the sensory cortex was not activated in the hypnotized patients, indicating that although they sensed pain on some level, they were never conscious of it. In essence, the "ouch" signal never made it to awareness.

In summary, although the nature of hypnosis remains a mystery, evidence is increasing that hypnosis can play a role in a variety of health contexts, and it can influence the brain in fascinating ways. For psychologists, part of the ambiguity about the definition of hypnosis comes from the fact that it has been studied in specific social contexts involving a hypnotist. It is also possible, however, to experience altered states of consciousness without these special circumstances, as we next consider.

### test yourself

1. What is hypnosis?
2. What are the four steps in hypnosis?
3. Name and describe two different theories about hypnosis.

## 5. CONSCIOUSNESS AND HEALTH AND WELLNESS: MEDITATION

**Meditation** involves attaining a peaceful state of mind in which thoughts are not occupied by worry. The meditator is mindfully present to his or her thoughts and feelings but is not consumed by them.

● **meditation** The attainment of a peaceful state of mind in which thoughts are not occupied by worry; the meditator is mindfully present to his or her thoughts and feelings but is not consumed by them.

There are many types of meditative practice (Kok, Waugh, & Fredrickson, 2013; Lumma, Kok, & Singer, 2015); Nyer & others, 2018). They share at least two characteristics: *focused attention* and *open monitoring*. Focused attention means bringing awareness to one's inner life and attending to one's thoughts; it is being psychologically present as one thinks. Open monitoring refers to the capacity to observe one's thoughts as they happen without getting preoccupied with them. That is, through open monitoring, the person is able to reflect without becoming attached to a particular thought or idea. Let's take a closer look at two types of meditation: mindfulness meditation and lovingkindness meditation.

### Mindfulness Meditation

Melissa Munroe, a Canadian woman diagnosed with Hodgkin lymphoma (a cancer of the immune system), was tormented by excruciating pain (Wijesiri, 2005). Seeking ways to cope with the agony, Munroe enrolled in a meditation program. She was skeptical at first. "What I didn't realize," she said, "is that if people have ever found themselves taking a walk in the countryside or in the forest or on a nice pleasant autumn day . . . and find themselves in a contemplative state, that's a form of meditation."

*Among those practicing meditation are Zen monks who explore the Buddha-nature at the center of their being.*

©Erin Koran

Munroe worked hard to use meditation to control her pain. Interestingly, she found that the way to handle her pain was not by trying to avoid thinking about it; instead, she harnessed the power of her mind to concentrate on the pain.

Using *mindfulness meditation,* a technique practiced by yoga enthusiasts and Buddhist monks, Munroe focused on her pain. By doing so, she was able to isolate the pain from her emotional response to it and to her cancer diagnosis. She grew to see her physical discomfort as bearable.

Munroe's success shows that contrary to what a non-meditator might think, meditation is not about avoiding one's thoughts. Indeed, the effort involved in avoidance steers the person away from the contemplative state. Munroe described her thoughts as like people striding by her on the street, walking in the other direction; she explained, "They come closer and closer, then they pass you by." Her comment reflects the open monitoring that is common to many forms of meditation.

Jon Kabat-Zinn (2006, 2009) has pioneered the use of meditation techniques in medical settings. Research by Kabat-Zinn and colleagues has demonstrated the beneficial effects of mindfulness meditation for a variety of conditions, including depression, panic attacks, and anxiety (Miller, Fletcher, & Kabat-Zinn, 1995), chronic pain (Kabat-Zinn, Lipworth, & Burney, 1985), and stress and the skin condition psoriasis (Kabat-Zinn & others, 1998). Many of these effects are long-lasting.

Richard Davidson and colleagues (including Jon Kabat-Zinn) studied the brain and immune system changes that might underlie the health and wellness effects of meditation (Davidson & others, 2003). They performed MRIs on the brains of individuals who were in a standard eight-week meditation-training program. After the training program they were compared with a control group, and those in the meditation program reported reduced anxiety and fewer negative emotions than the control group did. Furthermore, brain scans revealed that these individuals showed increased activation in the left hemisphere. In addition, the meditators showed better immune system response to a flu vaccine (Davidson & others, 2003; Kabat-Zinn & Davidson, 2012). Still, a great deal more research is needed to identify how mindfulness meditation is reflected in the brain (Tang, Hölzel, & Posner, 2015).

## Lovingkindness Meditation

Another popular form of meditation is called *lovingkindness meditation*. The goal of this meditative practice is the development of loving acceptance of oneself and others. Lovingkindness fosters feelings of warmth, friendliness, compassion, and appreciative joy. At its highest level, the person experiences a sense of equanimity, or a feeling of openness to his or her thoughts and feelings without becoming preoccupied with them (Zeng & others, 2015). In lovingkindness meditation, the meditator begins by developing warm, accepting feelings toward himself or herself. Then, the person moves to meditate about a very close other, such as a family member one loves and respects. Over time, lovingkindness meditation widens to include an ever-broadening circle of people.

Lovingkindness meditation leads to heightened feelings of social connection, positive emotions (Engen & Singer, 2015), and better coping with stress (Hanley, Garland, & Black, 2014).

## The Meditative State of Mind

What actually is the meditative state of mind? As a physiological state, meditation shows qualities of sleep *and* wakefulness, yet it is distinct from both. You may have experienced a state called *hypnagogic reverie*—an overwhelming feeling of wellness right before you fall asleep, the sense that everything is going to work out. Meditation has been compared to this relaxed sense that all is well (Friedman, Myers, & Benson, 1998).

In a study of Zen meditators, researchers examined what happens when people switch from their normal waking state to a meditative state (Ritskes & others, 2003). Using fMRI, the experimenters obtained images of the brain before and after the participants entered the meditative state. They found that the switch to meditation involved, first, initial increases in activation in the basal ganglia and prefrontal cortex (the now familiar area that is often activated during consciousness). However, and interestingly, these initial activations led to *decreases* in the anterior cingulate, the brain area associated with conscious awareness and acts of will. These results provide a picture of the physical events of the brain that are connected with the somewhat paradoxical state of meditation—controlling one's thoughts in order to let go of the need to control.

*Regular meditation can help you to clarify your goals and purpose in life, strengthen your values, and improve your outlook.*
©mheim3011/Getty Images

## Getting Started with Meditation

Would you like to experience the meditative state? If so, you can probably reach that state by following some simple instructions:

- Find a quiet place and a comfortable chair.
- Sit upright in the chair, lower your chin, comfortably toward your chest, and place your arms in your lap. Close your eyes.
- Now focus on your breathing. Every time you inhale and every time you exhale, pay attention to the sensations of air flowing through your body, the feeling of your lungs filling and emptying.
- After you have focused on several breaths, begin to repeat silently to yourself a single word every time you breathe out. You can make a word up, use the word *one*, or try a word associated with an emotion you want to produce, such as *trust, love, patience*, or *happy*. Experiment with several different words to see which one works best for you.
- If you find that thoughts are intruding and you are no longer attending to your breathing, refocus on your breathing and say your chosen word each time you exhale.

After you have practiced this exercise for 10 to 15 minutes, twice a day, every day for two weeks, you will be ready for a shortened version. If you notice that you are experiencing stressful thoughts or circumstances, simply meditate, on the spot, for several minutes. If you are in public, you do not have to close your eyes; just fix your gaze on a nearby object, attend to your breathing, and say your word silently every time you exhale.

Meditation is an age-old practice. Without explicitly mentioning meditation, some religions advocate related practices such as daily prayer and peaceful introspection. Whether the practice involves praying over rosary beads, chanting before a Buddhist shrine, or taking a moment to commune with nature, a contemplative state clearly has broad appeal and may convey benefits (Kabat-Zinn & Davidson, 2012). Of course, meditation is not a miracle cure for all of life's problems (van Dam & others, 2018). However, research on the contemplative state suggests that there are good reasons why human beings have been harnessing its beneficial powers for thousands of years.

### test yourself

1. What does the meditator experience during meditation?
2. Define mindfulness meditation and lovingkindness meditation.
3. On what body process does a meditator focus, and how is that focus maintained?

SUMMARY

## 1. THE NATURE OF CONSCIOUSNESS

Consciousness is the awareness of external events and internal sensations, including awareness of the self and thoughts about experiences. A global brain workspace that includes the association areas and prefrontal lobes is thought to play an important role in consciousness.

William James described the mind as a stream of consciousness. Consciousness occurs at different levels of awareness that include higher-level awareness (controlled processes and selective attention), lower-level awareness (automatic processes and daydreaming), altered states of consciousness (produced by drugs, trauma, fatigue, and other factors), subconscious awareness (waking subconscious awareness, sleep, and dreams), and no awareness (unconscious thought).

Theory of mind (our understanding of other people's consciousness) is important to social capacities such as empathy.

## 2. SLEEP AND DREAMS

The circadian rhythm is the biological rhythm that regulates the daily sleep/wake cycle. The part of the brain that keeps our biological clocks synchronized is the suprachiasmatic nucleus, a small structure in the hypothalamus that registers light. Biological clocks can become desynchronized by jet travel and work shifts; however, there are some helpful strategies for resetting the biological clock.

We need sleep for physical restoration, adaptation, growth, and memory. Research studies increasingly reveal that people do not function optimally when they are sleep-deprived.

Stages of sleep correspond to electrophysiological changes that occur in the brain and that can be assessed by an EEG. The human sleep cycle occurs in stages. In stage W, the person is awake. In the non-REM stages (stages N1 to N3), the person moves from light sleep to deep sleep. Stage N3 is the deepest sleep (also called slow wave sleep). Most dreaming occurs during stage R or REM sleep. Each sleep cycle lasts about 90 to 100 minutes, and several cycles occur during the night. The REM stage lasts longer toward the end of a night's sleep.

The sleep stages are associated with patterns of neurotransmitter activity. Levels of the neurotransmitters serotonin, norepinephrine, and acetylcholine decrease as the sleep cycle progresses from stage N1 through stage N3. Stage R, REM sleep, begins when the reticular formation raises the level of acetylcholine.

Sleep plays a role in a large number of diseases and disorders. Neurons that control sleep interact closely with the immune system, and when our body is fighting infection, our cells produce a substance that makes us sleepy. Individuals with depression often have sleep problems.

Many Americans suffer from chronic, long-term sleep disorders that can impair normal daily functioning. These include insomnia, sleepwalking and sleep talking, nightmares and night terrors, narcolepsy, and sleep apnea.

Contrary to popular belief, most dreams are not bizarre or strange. Freud thought that dreams express unconscious wishes in disguise. Cognitive theory attempts to explain dreaming in terms of the same concepts that are used in studying the waking mind. According to activation-synthesis theory, dreaming occurs when the cerebral cortex synthesizes neural signals emanating from activity in the lower part of the brain. In this view, the rising level of acetylcholine during REM sleep plays a role in neural activity in the brain stem that the cerebral cortex tries to make sense of.

## 3. PSYCHOACTIVE DRUGS

Psychoactive drugs act on the nervous system to alter states of consciousness, modify perceptions, and change moods. Some people are attracted to these drugs because they seem to help them deal with difficult life situations.

Addictive drugs activate the brain's reward system by increasing dopamine concentration. The reward pathway involves the ventral tegmental area and nucleus accumbens. The abuse of psychoactive drugs can lead to tolerance, psychological and physical dependence, and addiction—a pattern of behavior characterized by a preoccupation with using a drug and securing its supply.

Depressants slow down mental and physical activity. Among the most widely used depressants are alcohol, barbiturates, tranquilizers, and opioids.

After caffeine, alcohol is the most widely used drug in the United States. Alcoholism is a disorder that involves long-term, repeated, uncontrolled, compulsive, and excessive use of alcoholic beverages that impairs the drinker's health and work and social relationships.

Stimulants increase the central nervous system's activity and include caffeine, nicotine, amphetamines, cocaine, and MDMA (Ecstasy). Hallucinogens modify a person's perceptual experiences and produce visual images that are not real. Marijuana has a mild hallucinogenic effect; LSD has a strong one.

## 4. HYPNOSIS

Hypnosis is a psychological state or possibly altered attention and awareness in which the individual is unusually receptive to suggestions. The hypnotic state is different from a sleep state, as EEG recordings confirm. Inducing hypnosis involves four basic steps, beginning with minimizing distractions and making the person feel comfortable and ending with the hypnotist's suggesting certain events or feelings that he or she knows will occur or observes occurring.

There are substantial individual variations in people's susceptibility to hypnosis. Two theories have been proposed to explain hypnosis. In Hilgard's divided consciousness view, hypnosis involves a divided state of consciousness, a splitting of consciousness into separate components. One component follows the hypnotist's commands; the other acts as a hidden observer. In the social cognitive behavior view, hypnotized individuals behave the way they believe hypnotized individuals are expected to behave.

## 5. CONSCIOUSNESS AND HEALTH AND WELLNESS: MEDITATION

Meditation refers to a state of quiet reflection; the practice has benefits for a wide range of psychological and physical illnesses. Meditation can also benefit the body's immune system. Mindfulness meditation is a powerful tool for managing life's problems. Lovingkindness meditation has both emotional and social benefits. Research using fMRI suggests that meditation allows an individual to control his or her thoughts in order to "let go" of the need to control. Seeking times of quiet contemplation can have a positive impact on our ability to cope with life's ups and downs.

# key *terms*

activation-synthesis theory of dreaming
addiction
alcoholism
automatic processes
barbiturates
biological rhythms
circadian rhythms
cognitive theory of dreaming
consciousness
controlled processes
depressants
divided consciousness view of hypnosis
executive function
hallucinogens
hypnosis
latent content
manifest content
meditation
opioids
physical dependence
psychoactive drugs
psychological dependence
reticular activating system
REM sleep
sleep
social cognitive behavior view of hypnosis
stimulants
stream of consciousness
suprachiasmatic nucleus (SCN)
theory of mind
tolerance
tranquilizers
unconscious thought

# apply your *knowledge*

1. Take 20 minutes and document your stream of consciousness. Just write whatever comes into your mind for this period. When you have finished, take a close look at what your stream of consciousness reveals. What topics came up that surprised you? Are the thoughts and feelings you wrote down reflective of your daily life? Your important goals and values? What is *not* mentioned in your stream of consciousness that is surprising to you?
2. Keep a sleep journal for several nights. Compare your sleep patterns with those described in the text. Do you have a sleep debt? If so, which stages of sleep are you most likely missing? Does a good night's sleep affect your behavior? Keep a record of your mood and energy levels after a short night's sleep and then after you have had at least 8 hours of sleep in one night. What changes do you notice, and how do they compare with the changes predicted by research on sleep deprivation described in the chapter?
3. Keep a dream diary for a few days. When you wake up in the morning, immediately write down all that you can remember about your dreams. Have you had many bizarre or unusual dreams? Are there themes in your dreams that reflect the concerns of your daily life? Compare the content of your dream diary with the stream-of-consciousness document you produced for question 1 above. Are there similarities in the content of your relaxed, waking mind and your dreams?
4. Go on a caffeine hunt. Check out the ingredients for the beverages, painkillers, and snacks you typically consume. Which contain caffeine? Are you surprised how much caffeine you ingest regularly?
5. Try out mindfulness meditation. Following the guidelines outlined in "Getting Started with Meditation", meditate once a day for a week. Keep track of your mood, health, and behaviors over the course of the week. How did mindfulness meditation work for you?

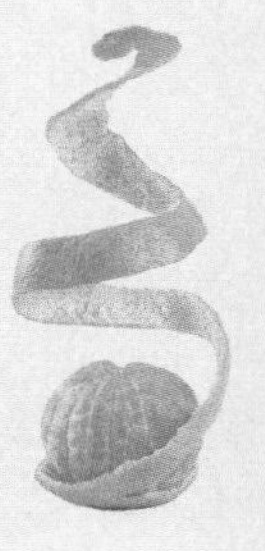

# CHAPTER 6

CHAPTER OUTLINE



©Peathegee Inc/Blend Images/Getty Images

# Learning

## Service Dogs Helping Heroes Heal

**Returning home after serving in combat can be stressful and lonely for many military veterans.** Civilian life may include coping with the wounds of war: physical injury and psychological trauma. Across the United States, nonprofit groups have paired returning military veterans with rescue dogs trained to help them make the transition from military to civilian life. Some dogs provide the simple comfort of a loving pet and help with many tasks of daily living. For example, Healing4Heroes in Atlanta provides dogs that have been through five days of training to live with U.S. military veterans as companion animals (Johnson, 2018). Another service, Pups4Patriots, trains rescued dogs as service animals, especially to assist former military members who suffer from post-traumatic stress disorder (a trauma-related psychological disorder) and traumatic brain injury (Carrozza, 2018). Canine Companions for Independence trains dogs to assist their owners by fetching medications, helping with household tasks, and so forth (Rogers, 2018). All of these services bring together people who need help and dogs who need homes. These services also rely on training that turns rescue dogs into trained professionals.

The hundreds of thousands of service dogs working in the United States are trained to aid people with a variety of disabilities. Their skills are amazing. They provide sound discrimination for the hearing impaired, assist those with limited mobility, and retrieve items that are out of reach; they locate people, bathrooms, elevators, and lost cell phones. They open and close doors, help people dress and undress, flush toilets, and even put clothes in a washer and dryer.

Truly, service dogs are highly skilled professionals. Service dogs are trained to perform these complex acts using the principles that psychologists have uncovered in studying the processes that underlie learning, the focus of this chapter. ●

# PREVIEW

This chapter begins by defining learning and sketching out its main types: associative learning and observational learning. We then turn our attention to two types of associative learning—classical conditioning and operant conditioning—followed by a close look at observational learning. Next, we consider the role of cognitive processes in learning before examining biological, cultural, and psychological constraints on learning. The close of the chapter looks at the role of learning in human health and wellness.

## 1. TYPES OF LEARNING

©Hello Lovely/Blend Images/Getty Images

Learning anything new involves change. Once you learn the alphabet, it does not leave you; it becomes part of a "new you" who has been changed through the process of learning. Similarly, once you learn how to drive a car, you do not have to go through the process again at a later time. When you first arrived on campus at your school, you might have spent a lot of time lost. But once you got the lay of the land, you were able to navigate just fine. And perhaps you avoid eating a particular food because you once ate it and it made you sick.

By way of experience, too, you may have learned that you need to study to do well on a test, that there usually is an opening act at a rock concert, and that there is a technique to playing a guitar chord. Putting these pieces together, we arrive at a definition of **learning**: a systematic, relatively permanent change in behavior that occurs through experience.

● **learning** A systematic, relatively permanent change in behavior that occurs through experience.

● **behaviorism** A theory of learning that focuses solely on observable behaviors, discounting the importance of mental activity such as thinking, wishing, and hoping.

If someone were to ask you what you learned in class today, you might mention new ideas you heard about, lists you memorized, or concepts you mastered. However, how would you define learning if without referring to unobservable mental processes? You might follow the lead of behavioral psychologists. **Behaviorism** is a theory of learning that focuses solely on observable behaviors, discounting the importance of mental activity such as thinking, wishing, and hoping. Psychologists who examine learning from a behavioral perspective define learning as relatively stable, observable changes in behavior. The behavioral approach emphasizes general laws that guide behavior change and make sense of some puzzling aspects of human life (Greenwood, 2015).

Behaviorism maintains that the principles of learning are the same whether we are talking about humans or nonhuman animals. Because of the influence of behaviorism, psychologists' understanding of learning started with studies of rats, cats, pigeons, and even raccoons. A century of research on learning in animals and in humans suggests that many of the principles generated initially in research on animals also apply to humans.

In this chapter we look at two types of learning: associative learning and observational learning. Let's briefly review each of these before getting into the details.

● **associative learning** Learning that occurs when an organism makes a connection, or an association, between two events.

First, **associative learning** occurs when an organism makes a connection, or an association, between two events. *Conditioning* is the process of learning these associations. There are two types of conditioning—classical and operant—both of which have been studied by behaviorists.

In *classical conditioning,* organisms learn the association between two stimuli. As a result of this association, organisms learn to anticipate events. For example, lightning is associated with thunder and regularly precedes it. Thus, when we see lightning, we anticipate that we will hear thunder soon afterward. In *operant conditioning,* organisms learn the association between a behavior and a consequence, such as a reward. As a result of this association, organisms learn to increase behaviors that are followed by rewards and to decrease behaviors that are followed by punishment. For example, children are likely to repeat their good manners if their parents reward them with candy after they have shown good manners. Also, if children's bad manners provoke scolding words and harsh glances by parents, the children are less likely to repeat the bad manners. Figure 1 compares classical and operant conditioning.

Much of what we learn, however, is not a result of direct consequences but rather of exposure to models performing a behavior or skill (Ma & others, 2018; Schoppmann,

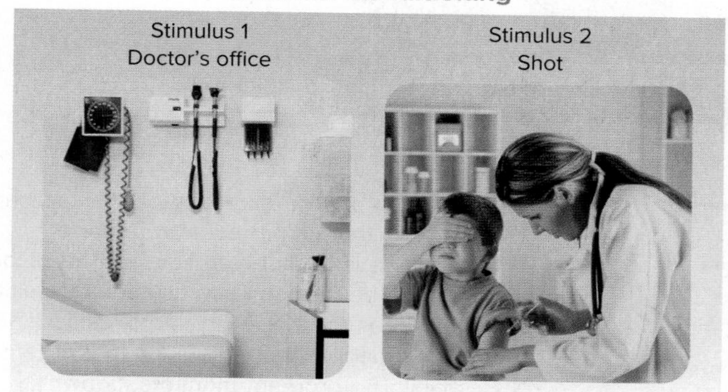

**FIGURE 1** **Associative Learning: Comparing Classical and Operant Conditioning** (*first*) In this example of classical conditioning, a child associates a doctor's office (stimulus 1) with getting a painful injection (stimulus 2). (*second*) In this example of operant conditioning, performing well in a swimming competition (behavior) becomes associated with getting awards (consequences).
(first) ©Punchstock; (second) ©Philip Nealey/Getty Images; (third) ©Ryan McVay/Getty Images; (fourth) ©kali9/Getty Images

Schneider, & Seehagen, 2018). For instance, as you watch someone shoot baskets, you get a sense of how the shots are made. This brings us to our second type of learning: observational learning. **Observational learning** occurs when a person observes and imitates another's behavior. Observational learning is different from the associative learning described by behaviorism because it relies on mental processes: The learner has to pay attention, remember, and reproduce what the model did (Howard, Festa, & Lonsdorf, 2018). Observational learning is especially important to human beings. In fact, watching other people is another way in which human infants acquire skills.

• **observational learning** Learning that involves observing and imitating another's behavior.

Human infants differ from baby monkeys in their strong reliance on imitation (Gerson, Simpson, & Paukner, 2016). After watching an adult model perform a task, a baby monkey will figure out its own way to do it, but a human infant will do exactly what the model did. Imitation may be the human baby's way to solve the huge problem it faces: to learn the vast amount of cultural knowledge that is part of human life. Many of our behaviors are rather arbitrary. Why do we clap to show approval or wave hello or bye-bye? The human infant has a lot to learn and may be well served to follow the old adage, "When in Rome, do as the Romans do."

Learning applies to many areas of acquiring new behaviors, skills, and knowledge. Our focus in this chapter is on the two types of associative learning–classical conditioning and operant conditioning–and on observational learning. Interestingly, the human capacity to learn has inspired computer scientists and engineers who work in the area of *artificial intelligence*. As we will see in the chapter "Thinking, Intelligence, and Language", artificial intelligence involves creating machines capable of performing activities that require intelligence when people do them. *Machine learning* is a branch of artificial intelligence that focuses on creating machines that can change their behavior in response to data without a human being stepping in. Do machines actually learn? To explore this provocative question, see the Critical Controversy.

### test yourself

1. What is associative learning?
2. What is conditioning? What two types of conditioning have behavioral psychologists studied?
3. What is observational learning? Give two examples of it.

## 2. CLASSICAL CONDITIONING

Early one morning, Bob is in the shower. While he showers, his wife enters the bathroom and flushes the toilet. Scalding hot water suddenly bursts down on Bob, causing him to yell in pain. The next day, Bob is back for his morning shower, and once again his wife enters the bathroom and flushes the toilet. Panicked by the sound of the toilet flushing, Bob yelps in fear and jumps out of the shower stream. Bob's panic at the sound of the toilet flushing illustrates the learning process of **classical conditioning**, in which a neutral stimulus (the sound of a toilet flushing) becomes associated with an innately meaningful stimulus (the pain of scalding hot water) and acquires the capacity to elicit a similar response (panic).

• **classical conditioning** Learning process in which a neutral stimulus becomes associated with an innately meaningful stimulus and acquires the capacity to elicit a similar response.

## *Can Machines* Truly *Learn?*

Entering a word in a text box on a smartphone, you have likely noticed the predictive text that appears just above the keyboard, offering suggestions to finish your sentence. You type in "what" and it suggests, "time" or "happened." This is just one example of machine learning, that branch of artificial intelligence in which computers use data to reach conclusions, make decisions, offer suggestions, and so forth. That predictive text is a result of a machine learning about human language and your typical texting behavior. Machine learning occurs when a computer program is able to use data to direct its own actions without the intervention of a human programmer. The first example of machine learning was a program for a checkers game that learned from its successes and failures, invented by Arthur Samuel in 1959. Today across a wide range of contexts, computer scientists "train" computers to rely on ever expanding databases to direct their actions.

The question is, are computers actually *learning*? As you consider this question you might recognize that the answer depends very much on what is meant by *actually learning* (Burgos, 2018). Let's consider the definition offered in the main text above: "a systematic, relatively permanent change in behavior that occurs through experience." Nowhere in this definition does the word "living organism" appear. Does that mean that nonliving entities, such as computers, can learn?

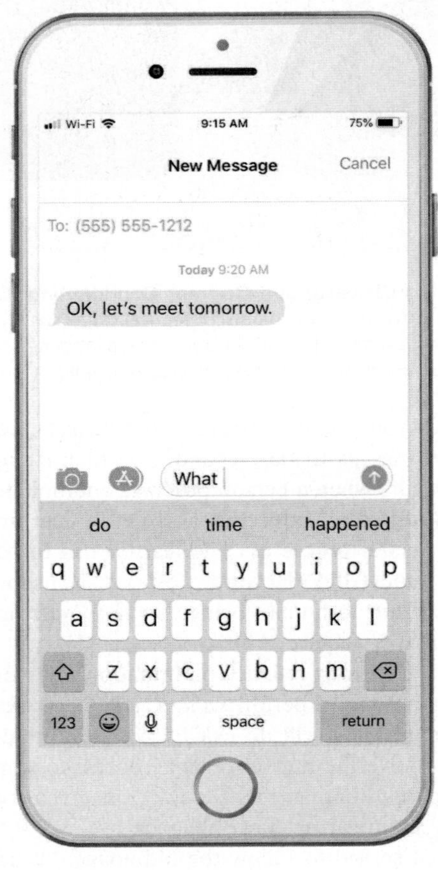


©GreenLandStudio/Shutterstock

Let's apply our definition to an example of machine learning, an email spam filter. Spam emails are unsolicited messages often involving sales or even fraud. For example, someone tells you that they will deposit $1 million into your bank account if you give them your account information. You have likely had an email appear in your inbox with the warning "SUSPECTED SPAM." This warning is the product of machine learning. The spam filter relies on a huge database of all words and phrases that might reveal whether a message is likely being sent with malicious intent. The program searches all incoming messages for these indicators, calculating the probability that any given message is spam. The program monitors its own success or failure in identifying spam and then tinkers with the database—perhaps adding a phrase or deleting another. Over time, it becomes more and more precise at detecting spam emails. Has that program then, *learned*? What separates what it has done from what a dog, a cat, or human has done when learning occurs?

In computer science, *deep learning* refers to modeling computer programs after the human brain, sensory processes, and behavior. We might ask, If computers simply model human behavior, can we say they are *really* learning (Burgos, 2018)? Consider that when this type of program starts processing, it starts changing itself and its behavior based on experience.

Media depictions of artificial intelligence often imply that humans will be in grave danger if intelligent machines begin to think for themselves. Are we all at risk of being enslaved by robot overlords? Probably not, but the feeling that machines might replace us may explain our reluctance to call their relatively permanent change in behavior based on experience true learning. If a computer program alters its own behavior based on experience, might that be considered learning?

**WHAT DO YOU THINK?**

- Other than predictive text and spam filters, what is one example of machine learning you have encountered in your daily life?
- Do you think computers truly *learn*? Why or why not?

## Pavlov's Studies

Even before beginning this course, you might have heard about Pavlov's dogs. The work of the Russian physiologist Ivan Pavlov is well known. Still, it is easy to take its true significance for granted. Importantly, Pavlov demonstrated that neutral aspects of the environment can attain the capacity to evoke responses through pairing with other stimuli and that bodily processes can be influenced by environmental cues.

In the early 1900s, Pavlov was interested in how the body digests food. In his experiments, he routinely placed meat powder in a dog's mouth, causing the dog to salivate. By accident, Pavlov noticed that the meat powder was not the only stimulus that caused the dog to drool. The dog salivated in response to a number of stimuli associated with the food, such as the sight of the food dish, the sight of the individual who brought the food into the room, and the sound of the door closing when the food arrived. Pavlov recognized that the dog's association of these sights and sounds with the food was an important type of learning, which came to be called *classical conditioning.*

Pavlov wanted to know *why* the dog salivated in reaction to various sights and sounds before eating the meat powder. He observed that the dog's behavior included both unlearned and learned components. The unlearned part of classical conditioning is based on the fact that some stimuli automatically produce responses apart from any prior learning; in other words, they are inborn (innate). *Reflexes* are such automatic stimulus-response connections. They include salivation in response to food, nausea in response to spoiled food, shivering in response to low temperature, coughing in response to throat congestion, pupil constriction in response to light, and withdrawal in response to pain.

An **unconditioned stimulus (US)** is a stimulus that produces a response without prior learning; food was the US in Pavlov's experiments. An **unconditioned response (UR)** is an unlearned reaction that is automatically elicited by the US. Unconditioned responses are involuntary; they happen in response to a stimulus without conscious effort. In Pavlov's experiment, drooling in response to food was the UR. In the case of Bob and the flushing toilet, Bob's learning and experience did not cause him to shriek when the hot water hit his body. His cry of pain occurred automatically. The hot water was the US, and Bob's panic was the UR.

- **unconditioned stimulus (US)** A stimulus that produces a response without prior learning.
- **unconditioned response (UR)** An unlearned reaction that is automatically elicited by the unconditioned stimulus.

In classical conditioning, a **conditioned stimulus (CS)** is a previously neutral stimulus that eventually elicits a conditioned response after being paired with the unconditioned stimulus. The **conditioned response (CR)** is the learned response to the conditioned stimulus that occurs after CS–US pairing (Pavlov, 1927). Sometimes conditioned responses are quite similar to unconditioned responses, but typically they are not as strong.

- **conditioned stimulus (CS)** A previously neutral stimulus that eventually elicits a conditioned response after being paired with the unconditioned stimulus.
- **conditioned response (CR)** The learned response to the conditioned stimulus that occurs after conditioned stimulus–unconditioned stimulus pairing.

In studying a dog's response to various stimuli associated with meat powder, Pavlov rang a bell before giving meat powder to the dog. Until then, ringing the bell did not have an effect on the dog, except perhaps to wake the dog from a nap. The bell was a *neutral* stimulus, meaning that in the dog's world, this stimulus did not have any signal value at all. Prior to being paired with the meat powder, the bell was meaningless. However, the dog began to associate the sound of the bell with the food and salivated when it heard

*Pavlov (the white-bearded gentleman in the center) is shown demonstrating the nature of classical conditioning to students at the Military Medical Academy in Russia.*

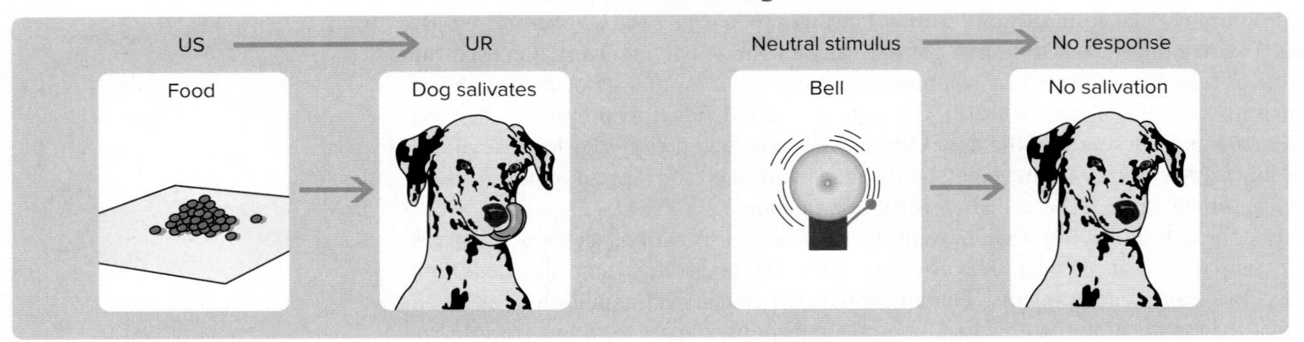


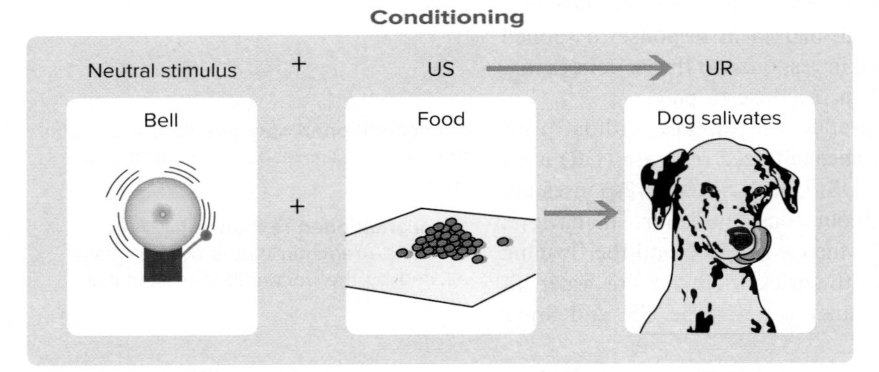


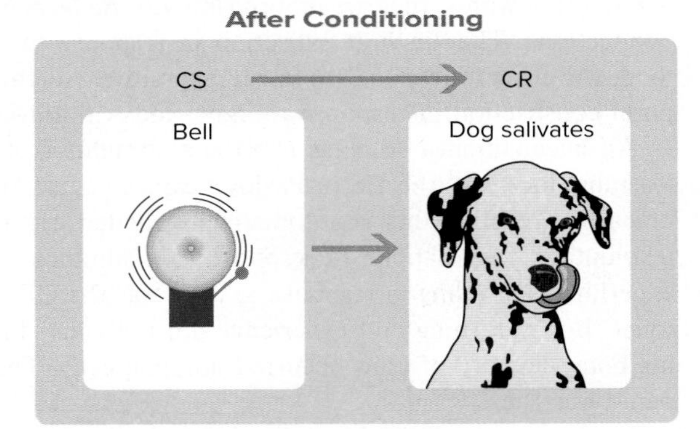


**FIGURE 2** **Pavlov's Classical Conditioning** In one experiment, Pavlov presented a neutral stimulus (bell) just before an unconditioned stimulus (food). The neutral stimulus became a conditioned stimulus by being paired with the unconditioned stimulus. Subsequently, the conditioned stimulus (bell) by itself was able to elicit the dog's salivation.

the bell. The bell had become a conditioned (learned) stimulus (CS), and salivation was now a conditioned response (CR). In the case of Bob's interrupted shower, the sound of the toilet flushing was the CS, and panicking was the CR after the scalding water (US) and the flushing sound (CS) were paired. Figure 2 summarizes how classical conditioning works.

Researchers have shown that salivation can be used as a conditioned response not only in dogs and humans but also in, of all things, cockroaches (Nishino & others, 2015; Watanabe & Mizunami, 2007). These researchers paired the smell of peppermint (the CS, which was applied to the cockroaches' antennae) with sugary water (the US). Cockroaches naturally salivate (the UR) in response to sugary foods, and after repeated pairings between peppermint smell and sugary water, the cockroaches salivated in response to the smell of peppermint (the CR). When they collected and measured the cockroach saliva, the researchers found that the cockroaches had slobbered over that smell for 2 minutes.

To summarize, in classical conditioning, two stimuli are paired repeatedly. The US is the one that evokes an automatic response–including things like food or loud noises. The UR is that automatic response. The CS comes before the US and this stimulus would not evoke a natural response except that it is being paired with the US. The response to the CS is the CR. Classical conditioning involves learning because the organism responds to the CS in a new way, because of the learned association between the CS and the US.

## ACQUISITION

Whether it is human beings, dogs, or cockroaches, the first part of classical conditioning is called acquisition. **Acquisition** is the initial learning of the connection between the US and CS when these two stimuli are paired (as with a bell and food). During acquisition, the CS is repeatedly presented followed by the US. Eventually, the CS will produce a response. Note that classical conditioning is a type of learning that occurs without awareness or effort, based on the presentation of two stimuli together. For this pairing to work, however, two important factors must be present: contiguity and contingency.

● **acquisition** The initial learning of the connection between the unconditioned stimulus and the conditioned stimulus when these two stimuli are paired.

*Contiguity* means that the CS and US are presented very close together in time—even a mere fraction of a second apart. In Pavlov's work, if the bell had rung 20 minutes before the presentation of the food, the dog probably would not have associated the bell with the food because the bell would not have served as a *timely* signal that food was coming.

Pairing the CS and US close together in time is not all that is needed for conditioning to occur. Imagine that the bell not only rings just before the food is delivered, but it also rings many times when the food is not on its way. In such a situation, the dog would not associate the bell with the food, and no learning would occur. Why? Because the CS is not a signal that the US is coming. *Contingency* means that the CS must serve as a reliable indicator that the US is on its way (Rescorla, 1966, 1988, 2009).

To get a sense of the importance of contingency, imagine that the dog in Pavlov's experiment is exposed to a ringing bell at random times all day long. Whenever the dog receives food, the delivery of the food always immediately follows a bell ring. However, in this situation, the dog will not associate the bell with the food, because the bell is not a reliable signal that food is coming: It rings a lot when no food is on the way. Whereas *contiguity* refers to the fact that the CS and US occur close together in time, *contingency* refers to the information value of the CS relative to the US. When contingency is present, the CS provides a systematic signal that the US is on its way (Kringelbach & Berridge, 2015).

## GENERALIZATION AND DISCRIMINATION

Pavlov found that the dog salivated in response not only to the tone of the bell but also to other sounds, such as a whistle. These sounds had not been paired with the unconditioned stimulus of the food. Pavlov discovered that the more similar the noise was to the original sound of the bell, the stronger the dog's salivary flow.

**Generalization** in classical conditioning is the tendency of a new stimulus that is similar to the original conditioned stimulus to elicit a response that is similar to the conditioned response.

● **generalization (in classical conditioning)** The tendency of a new stimulus that is similar to the original conditioned stimulus to elicit a response that is similar to the conditioned response.

Generalization has value in preventing learning from being tied to specific stimuli. Once we learn the association between a given CS (say, flashing police lights behind our car) and a particular US (the dread associated with being pulled over), we do not have to learn it all over again when a similar stimulus presents itself (a police car with its siren howling as it cruises directly behind our car).

Stimulus generalization is not always beneficial. For example, the cat that generalizes from a harmless minnow to a dangerous piranha has a major problem; therefore, it is important to also discriminate among stimuli. **Discrimination** in classical conditioning is the process of learning to respond to certain stimuli and not others. To produce discrimination, Pavlov gave food to the dog only after ringing the bell and not after any other sounds. In this way, the dog learned to distinguish between the bell and other sounds.

● **discrimination (in classical conditioning)** The process of learning to respond to certain stimuli and not others.

## EXTINCTION AND SPONTANEOUS RECOVERY

After conditioning the dog to salivate at the sound of a bell, Pavlov rang the bell repeatedly in a single session and did not give the dog any food. Eventually the dog stopped salivating. This result is **extinction**, which in classical conditioning is the weakening of the conditioned response when the unconditioned stimulus is absent. Without continued association with the unconditioned stimulus (US), the conditioned stimulus (CS) loses its power to produce the conditioned response (CR). You might notice that although extinction weakens the link between the CS and the presence of the US, it can also be thought of as a second type of learning: learning that the CS means the US is *not* coming.

● **extinction (in classical conditioning)** The weakening of the conditioned response when the unconditioned stimulus is absent.

Extinction is not always the end of a conditioned response. The day after Pavlov extinguished the conditioned salivation to the sound of a bell, he took the dog to the laboratory and rang the bell but still did not give the dog any meat powder. The dog salivated, indicating that an extinguished response can spontaneously recur. **Spontaneous recovery** is the process in classical conditioning by which a conditioned response can recur after a time delay, without further conditioning (Monaco & others, 2018; Thompson, McEvoy, & Lipp, 2018).

● **spontaneous recovery** The process in classical conditioning by which a conditioned response can recur after a time delay, without further conditioning.

## psychological *inquiry*

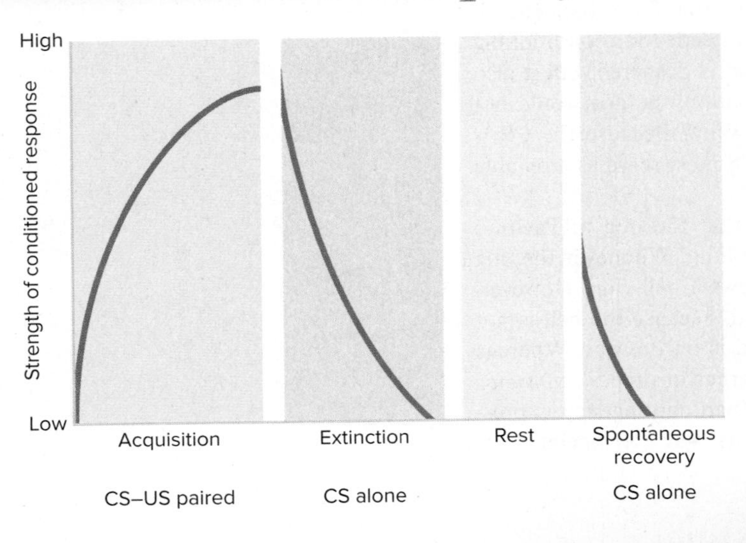


### *From Acquisition to Extinction (to Spontaneous Recovery)*

The figure illustrates the strength of a conditioned response (CR), shown on the Y or vertical axis, across the stages from acquisition, to extinction, to a rest period, and finally to spontaneous recovery. Using the graphs, answer the following questions.

1. What happens to the unconditioned stimulus (US) and the conditioned stimulus (CS) during acquisition, and how does this influence the conditioned response (CR)?
2. When is the CR strongest and when is it weakest?
3. What happens to the US and CS during extinction, and how does this influence the CR?
4. Notice that spontaneous recovery occurs after a rest period. Why is this rest necessary?
5. In your own life, what are some conditioned stimuli that are attached to conditioned responses for you? Trace them through these steps.

Consider an example of spontaneous recovery you may have experienced: You thought that you had forgotten about (extinguished) an old girlfriend or boyfriend, but then you found yourself in a particular context (perhaps the restaurant where you used to dine together), and you suddenly got a mental image of your ex, accompanied by an emotional reaction to him or her from the past (spontaneous recovery).

The steps in classical conditioning are reviewed in the Psychological Inquiry. The figure in the feature shows the sequence of acquisition, extinction, and spontaneous recovery. Spontaneous recovery can occur several times, but as long as the conditioned stimulus is presented alone (that is, without the unconditioned stimulus), spontaneous recovery becomes weaker and eventually ceases.

Not only do extinguished learned associations show spontaneous recovery, but they can be reinstated just by moving the organism to a new setting. **Renewal** refers to the recovery of the conditioned response when the organism is placed in a novel context (Anderson & Petrovich, 2018). Renewal can be a powerful problem to overcome–as it is when a person leaves a drug treatment facility to return to his or her previous living situation (Marchant & others, 2018).

• **renewal** The recovery of the conditioned response when the organism is placed in a novel context.

The processes of acquisition, extinction, spontaneous recovery, and renewal all demonstrate the important role of learned associations for the survival of all creatures. All animals, including humans, are, in some ways, on the look-out for survival-relevant connections, such as learning what cues signal food. Once such connections are made, they are difficult to break entirely as demonstrated in spontaneous recovery. Finally, those connections remain in the organism's repertoire and can pop back up in a new setting.

## Classical Conditioning in Humans

Although the process of classical conditioning has often been studied in nonhuman animals, the human capacity to learn associations is extremely important for our survival. Here we review examples of classical conditioning at work in human life.

### EXPLAINING FEARS

Classical conditioning provides an explanation of fears. John B. Watson (who coined the term *behaviorism*) and Rosalie Rayner (1920) demonstrated classical conditioning's role in the development of fears with an infant named Albert. They showed Albert a white laboratory rat to see whether he was afraid of it. He was not. As Albert played with the rat, the researchers sounded a loud noise behind his head. The noise caused little Albert to cry. After only seven pairings of the loud noise with the white rat, Albert began to fear the rat even when the noise was not sounded. Albert's fear was generalized to a rabbit, a dog, and a sealskin coat.

Let's use Albert's example to review the key concepts of classical conditioning. In the beginning, Albert had no response to the rat. The rat, then, is a neutral stimulus–the conditioned stimulus (or CS). The rat was then paired with a loud noise. The loud noise would startle Albert and make him cry: Loud noises upset babies. That makes the loud noise the unconditioned stimulus (US), because it evokes a response naturally without the need for learning. Albert's reaction to the loud noise is the unconditioned response (or UR). Again, being upset by loud noises is something that babies just do. The white rat (CS) and loud noise (US) were paired together in time, and each time the loud noise would upset little Albert (UR). This pairing is the process of acquisition. Then, the rat (the CS) was presented to Albert without the loud noise (the US), and Albert became alarmed and afraid even without the noise. Poor Albert's enduring fear of the rat is the conditioned response (CR).

Today, Watson and Rayner's (1920) study would violate the ethical guidelines of the American Psychological Association. In any case, Watson correctly concluded that we learn many of our fears through classical conditioning. We might develop fear of the dentist because of a painful experience, fear of driving after having been in a car crash, and fear of dogs after having been bitten by one.

If we can learn fears through classical conditioning, we also can possibly unlearn them through that process. In the chapter "Therapies", for example, we will examine the application of classical conditioning to therapies for treating phobias.

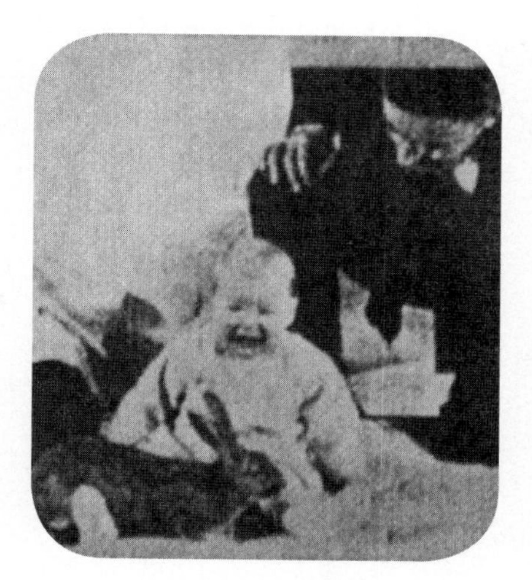

*Watson and Rayner conditioned 11-month-old Albert to fear a white rat by pairing the rat with a loud noise. When little Albert was later presented with other stimuli similar to the white rat, such as the rabbit shown here with Albert, he was afraid of them too. This study illustrates stimulus generalization in classical conditioning.*

Courtesy of Professor Benjamin Harris

## BREAKING HABITS

**Counterconditioning** is a classical conditioning procedure for changing the relationship between a conditioned stimulus and its conditioned response. Therapists have used counterconditioning to break apart the association between certain stimuli and positive feelings (Kang & others, 2018). **Aversive conditioning** is a form of treatment that consists of repeated pairings of a stimulus with a very unpleasant stimulus. Electric shocks, loud noises, and nausea-inducing substances are examples of noxious stimuli that are used in aversive conditioning.

- **counterconditioning** A classical conditioning procedure for changing the relationship between a conditioned stimulus and its conditioned response.
- **aversive conditioning** A form of treatment that consists of repeated pairings of a stimulus with a very unpleasant stimulus.

To reduce drinking, for example, every time a person drinks an alcoholic beverage, he or she also consumes a mixture that induces nausea. In classical conditioning terminology, the alcoholic beverage is the conditioned stimulus, and the nausea-inducing agent is the unconditioned stimulus. Through a repeated pairing of alcohol with the nausea-inducing agent, alcohol becomes the conditioned stimulus that elicits nausea, the conditioned response. As a consequence, alcohol no longer is associated with something pleasant but rather with something highly unpleasant. The effectiveness of Antabuse, a drug that has been used in treating alcoholism since the late 1940s, is based on this association (Ullman, 1952; Williams & others, 2018). When someone takes this drug, ingesting even the smallest amount of alcohol will make the person quite ill, even if the exposure to the alcohol is through mouthwash or cologne. Antabuse continues to be used in treating alcoholism today.

Classical conditioning is likely to be at work whenever we engage in mindless, habitual behavior (Marien, Custers, & Aarts, 2018). Cues in the environment serve as conditioned stimuli, evoking feelings and behaviors without thought. These associations become implicit "if-then" connections: If you are sitting in front of your laptop, then you check your e-mail. These automatic associations can function for good (for instance, you get up every morning and go for a run without even thinking) or ill (you walk into the kitchen and open the fridge for a snack without even thinking).

## CLASSICAL CONDITIONING AND THE PLACEBO EFFECT

The chapter "Psychology's Scientific Method" defined the *placebo effect* as the effect of a substance (such as taking a pill orally) or a procedure (such as using a syringe to inject a substance) that researchers use as a control to identify the actual effects of a treatment. Placebo effects are observable changes (such as a drop in pain) that cannot be explained by the effects of an actual treatment. The principles of classical conditioning can help to explain some of these effects (Colloca, 2019; Tu & others, 2019). In this case, the pill or syringe serves as a CS, and the actual drug is the US. After the experience of pain relief following the consumption of a drug, for instance, the pill or syringe might lead to a CR of reduced pain even in the absence of an actual painkiller. The strongest evidence for the role of classical conditioning on placebo effects comes from research on the immune system and the endocrine system.

## CLASSICAL CONDITIONING AND THE IMMUNE AND ENDOCRINE SYSTEMS

Even the human body's internal organ systems can be classically conditioned. The immune system is the body's natural defense against disease. A number of studies reveal that classical conditioning can produce *immunosuppression,* a decrease in the production of antibodies, which can lower a person's ability to fight disease (Tekampe & others, 2018).

The initial discovery of this link between classical conditioning and immunosuppression came as a surprise. In studying classical conditioning, Robert Ader (1974) was examining how long a conditioned response would last in some laboratory rats. He paired a conditioned stimulus (saccharin solution) with an unconditioned stimulus, a drug called Cytoxan, which induces nausea. Afterward, while giving the rats saccharin-laced water without the accompanying Cytoxan, Ader watched to see how long it would take the rats to forget the association between the two.

Unexpectedly, in the second month of the study, the rats developed a disease and began to die off. In analyzing this unforeseen result, Ader looked into the properties of the nausea-inducing drug he had used. He discovered that one of its side effects was suppressed immune system functioning. It turned out that the rats had been classically conditioned to associate sweet water not only with nausea but also with the shutdown of the immune system. The sweet water apparently had become a conditioned stimulus for immunosuppression.

Researchers have found that conditioned immune responses also occur in humans (Hadamitzky & others, 2018; Tekampe & others, 2018). For example, consider that individuals who receive donated organs must begin a lifetime of immunosuppressing medication. These medicines help to prevent the body from rejecting the donated organ. Could classical conditioning allow individuals to reduce reliance on these medications? A recent study showed that it is possible to use classical conditioning to reduce the immune response in individuals who have received a kidney transplant (Kirchhof & others, 2018). In the study, a particular taste was paired with immunosuppressing drugs in 30 transplant patients. Results showed the taste alone did eventually lead to lowered immune response. This work suggests that classical conditioning might be leveraged to improve the lives of individuals who receive transplants, both by boosting the effectiveness of medications and by reducing dosages.

Classical conditioning effects have also been found for the endocrine system. Recall from the "Biological Foundations of Behavior" chapter that the endocrine system is a loosely organized set of glands that produce and circulate hormones. Research has shown that placebo pills can influence the secretion of hormones if patients had previous experiences with pills containing actual drugs that affected hormone secretion (Piedimonte & Benedetti, 2015). Studies have revealed that the sympathetic nervous system (the part of the autonomic nervous system that responds to stress) plays an important role in the learned associations between conditioned stimuli and immune and endocrine functioning (Tekampe & others, 2018).

## TASTE AVERSION LEARNING

Consider this scenario. Mike goes out for sushi with some friends and eats spicy yellow tail, his favorite dish. He then proceeds to a jazz concert. Several hours later, he becomes very ill with stomach pains and nausea. A few weeks later, he tries to eat spicy yellow tail again but cannot stand it. Importantly, Mike does not experience an aversion to jazz, even though he attended the jazz concert that night before getting sick. Mike's experience exemplifies *taste aversion:* a special kind of classical conditioning involving the learned association between a particular taste and nausea (Garcia, Ervin, & Koelling, 1966; Lavi & others, 2018; Nakajima, 2018; Ward-Fear & others, 2017).

Taste aversion is special because it typically requires only one pairing of a neutral stimulus (a taste) with the unconditioned response of nausea to seal that connection, often for a very long time. As we consider later, it is highly adaptive to learn taste aversion in only one trial. An animal that required multiple pairings of taste with poison likely would not survive the acquisition phase. It is notable, though, that taste aversion can occur even if the "taste" had nothing to do with getting sick—perhaps, in Mike's case, he was simply coming down with a stomach bug. Taste aversion can even occur when a person has been sickened by a completely separate event, such as being spun around in a chair (Klosterhalfen & others, 2000).

*The U.S. Fish and Wildlife Service is trying out taste aversion as a tool to prevent Mexican gray wolves from preying on cattle. To instill taste aversion for beef, the agency is deploying bait made of beef and cowhide that also contains odorless and flavorless substances that induce nausea (Bryant, 2012). The hope is that wolves that are sickened by the bait will no longer prey on cattle and might even rear their pups to enjoy alternative meals.*



Although taste aversion is often considered an exception to the rules of learning, Michael Domjan (2005, 2015) has suggested that this form of learning demonstrates how classical conditioning works in the natural world, where associations matter to survival. Remember, in taste aversion, the taste or flavor is the CS; the agent that made the person sick (it could be a roller-coaster ride or salmonella, for example) is the US; nausea or vomiting is the UR; and taste aversion is the CR.

Taste aversion learning is particularly important in the context of the traditional treatment of some cancers. Chemotherapy for cancer can produce nausea in patients, with the result that individuals sometimes develop strong aversions to foods they ingest prior to treatment (Coa & others, 2015; Davidson & Riley, 2015; Krautbauer & Drossel, 2018). Consequently, they may experience a general tendency to be turned off by food, a situation that can lead to nutritional deficits (Krautbauer & Drossel, 2018).

Researchers have used classical conditioning principles to combat these taste aversions, especially in children, for whom antinausea medication is often ineffective (Skolin & others, 2006) and for whom aversions to protein-rich food are particularly problematic (Ikeda & others, 2006). Early studies demonstrated that giving children a "scapegoat" conditioned stimulus prior to chemotherapy would help contain the taste aversion to only one specific type of food or flavor (Broberg & Bernstein, 1987). For example, children might be given a particular flavor of Life Savers® candy before receiving treatment. For these children, the nausea would be more strongly associated with the Life Savers flavor than with the foods they needed to eat for good nutrition. These results show discrimination in classical conditioning—the kids developed aversions only to the specific scapegoat flavor.

## CLASSICAL CONDITIONING AND ADVERTISING

Classical conditioning provides the foundation for many of the commercials that bombard us daily. (Appropriately, when John Watson, whom you will recall from the baby Albert study, left the field of psychology, he went into advertising.) Think about it: Advertising involves creating an association between a product and pleasant feelings (buy that pumpkin spice latte and be happy). TV advertisers cunningly apply classical conditioning principles to consumers by showing ads that pair something positive—such as a beautiful woman (the US) producing pleasant feelings (the UR)—with a product (the CS) in hopes that you, the viewer, will experience those positive feelings toward the product (the CR).

Even when commercials are not involved, advertisers exploit classical conditioning principles—for instance, through the technique of product placement, or what is known as *embedded marketing*. For example, suppose that while viewing a TV show or movie, you notice that a character is drinking a particular brand of soft drink or eating a particular type of cereal. By placing their products in the context of a show or movie you like, advertisers are hoping that your positive feelings about the show, movie plot, or a character (the UR) rub off on their product (the CS). It may seem like a long shot, but all they need to do is enhance the chances that, say, navigating through a car dealership or a grocery store, you will feel attracted to their product.

The psychoactive drug is an unconditioned stimulus (US) because it naturally produces a response in the body.

Appearance of the drug tablets and the room where the person takes the drug are conditioned stimuli (CS) that are paired with the drug (US).

The body prepares to receive the drug in the room. Repeated pairings of the US and CS have produced a conditioned response (CR).

**FIGURE 3** **Drug Habituation** The figure illustrates how classical conditioning is involved in drug habituation. As a result of conditioning, the drug user will need to take more of the drug to get the same effect as the person did before the conditioning. Moreover, if the user takes the drug without the usual conditioned stimulus or stimuli—represented in the middle panel by the bathroom and the drug tablets—overdosing is more likely.
(first) ©Thinkstock/Jupiterimages; (second) ©McGraw-Hill Education/Jill Braaten, photographer; (third) ©AndreyPopov/iStockphoto/Getty Images

## DRUG HABITUATION

The "States of Consciousness" chapter noted how, over time, a person might develop a tolerance for a psychoactive drug and need a higher and higher dose of the substance to get the same effect. Classical conditioning helps to explain **habituation**, which refers to the decreased responsiveness to a stimulus after repeated presentations. A mind-altering drug is an unconditioned stimulus: It naturally produces a response in the person's body. This unconditioned stimulus is often paired systematically with a previously neutral stimulus (CS). For instance, the physical appearance of the drug in a pill or syringe, and the room where the person takes the drugs, are conditioned stimuli that are paired with the unconditioned stimulus of the drug. These repeated pairings should produce a conditioned response, and they do–but it is different from those we have considered so far.

● **habituation** Decreased responsiveness to a stimulus after repeated presentations.

The conditioned response to a drug can be the body's way of *preparing* for the effects of a drug (Junior & others, 2018; Ettenberg & others, 2015). In this case, the body braces itself for the effects of the drug with a CR that is the opposite of the UR. For instance, if the drug (the US) leads to an increase in heart rate (the UR), the CR might be a drop in heart rate. The CS serves as a warning that the drug is coming, and the conditioned response in this case is the body's compensation for the drug's effects (Figure 3). In this situation the conditioned response works to decrease the effects of the US, making the drug experience less intense. Some drug users try to prevent habituation by varying the physical location where they take the drug.

This aspect of drug use can play a role in deaths caused by drug overdoses. How is classical conditioning involved? A user typically takes a drug in a particular setting, such as a bathroom, and acquires a CR to this location (McClernon & others, 2015; Siegel, 1988). Because of classical conditioning, as soon as the drug user walks into the bathroom, the person's body begins to prepare for and anticipate the drug dose in order to lessen the effect of the drug. Essentially, the context in which the drug is taken (for example, the bathroom) becomes a CS that signals that the drug is coming. However, if the user takes the drug in a location other than the usual one, such as at a rock concert, the drug's effect is greater because no conditioned responses have built up in the new setting, and therefore the body is not prepared for the drug.

When you read about cases of deadly overdoses, note how often the person has taken the drug under unusual circumstances or after a visit to rehab. In these cases, with no CS signal, the body is unprepared for (and tragically overwhelmed by) the drug's effects. After time in rehab, the associative links have been extinguished and the individual is at risk of overdosing (Rafful & others, 2018).

### *test yourself*

1. What is meant by an unconditioned stimulus (US) and an unconditioned response (UR)? In Pavlov's experiments with dogs, what were the US and the UR?
2. What is meant by a conditioned stimulus (CS) and a conditioned response (CR)? In Pavlov's experiments with dogs, what were the CS and the CR?
3. What learning principle is illustrated by the Watson and Rayner study with baby Albert?

# 3. OPERANT CONDITIONING

Recall from early in the chapter that classical conditioning and operant conditioning are forms of associative learning, which involves learning that two events are connected. In classical conditioning, organisms learn the association between two stimuli (US and CS). Classical conditioning is a form of *respondent behavior,* behavior that occurs in automatic response to a stimulus such as a nausea-producing drug and later to a conditioned stimulus such as sweet water that was paired with the drug. Calling a behavior "respondent" means that it happens on auto pilot.

Classical conditioning explains how neutral stimuli become associated with unlearned, *involuntary responses.* Classical conditioning is not as effective, however, in explaining *voluntary behaviors.* Voluntary actions, such as a student studying hard for a test, a gambler playing slot machines in Las Vegas, or a service dog fetching his owner's cell phone on command, are clearly not the product of associating a CS and US. Rather, they must be explained by a different kind of associative learning, operant conditioning. Operant conditioning is usually much better than classical conditioning at explaining such voluntary behaviors. Whereas classical conditioning focuses on the association between stimuli, operant conditioning focuses on the association between behaviors and the stimuli that follow them.

## Defining Operant Conditioning

**Operant conditioning or instrumental conditioning** is a form of associative learning in which the consequences of a behavior change the probability of the behavior's recurrence. The American psychologist B. F. Skinner (1938) chose the term *operant* to describe the behavior of the organism. An operant behavior occurs spontaneously. According to Skinner, the consequences that follow such spontaneous behaviors determine whether the behavior will be repeated.

• **operant conditioning or instrumental conditioning** A form of associative learning in which the consequences of a behavior change the probability of the behavior's recurrence.

Imagine, for example, that you spontaneously decide to take a different route while driving to campus one day. You are more likely to repeat that route on another day if you have a pleasant experience–for instance, arriving at school faster or finding a new coffee place to try–than if you have a lousy experience such as getting stuck in traffic. In either case, the consequences of your spontaneous act influence whether that behavior happens again.

Recall that *contingency* is an important aspect of classical conditioning in which the occurrence of one stimulus can be predicted from the presence of another one. Contingency also plays a key role in operant conditioning. For example, when a rat pushes a lever (behavior) that delivers food, the delivery of food (consequence) is contingent on that behavior. This principle of contingency helps explain why passersby should never praise, pet, or feed a service dog while he is working (at least without asking first). Providing rewards during such times might interfere with the dog's training.

## Thorndike's Law of Effect

Although Skinner emerged as the primary figure in operant conditioning, the experiments of E. L. Thorndike (1898) established the power of consequences in determining voluntary behavior. At about the same time that Pavlov was conducting classical conditioning experiments with salivating dogs, Thorndike, another American psychologist, was studying cats in puzzle boxes. Thorndike put a hungry cat inside a box and placed a piece of fish outside. To escape from the box and obtain the food, the cat had to learn to open the latch inside the box. At first the cat made a number of ineffective responses. It clawed or bit at the bars and thrust its paw through the openings. Eventually the cat accidentally stepped on the lever that released the door bolt. When the cat returned to the box, it went through the same random activity until it stepped on the lever once more. On subsequent trials, the cat made fewer and fewer random movements until finally it immediately stepped on the lever to open the door (Figure 4). Thorndike's resulting **law of effect** states that behaviors followed by pleasant outcomes are strengthened and that behaviors followed by unpleasant outcomes are weakened.

• **law of effect** Thorndike's law stating that behaviors followed by positive outcomes are strengthened and that behaviors followed by negative outcomes are weakened.

The law of effect is profoundly important because it presents the basic idea that the consequences of a behavior influence the likelihood of that behavior's recurrence. Quite simply, a behavior can be followed by something good or something bad, and the probability that a behavior will be repeated depends on these outcomes. As we now explore, Skinner's operant conditioning model expands on this basic idea.

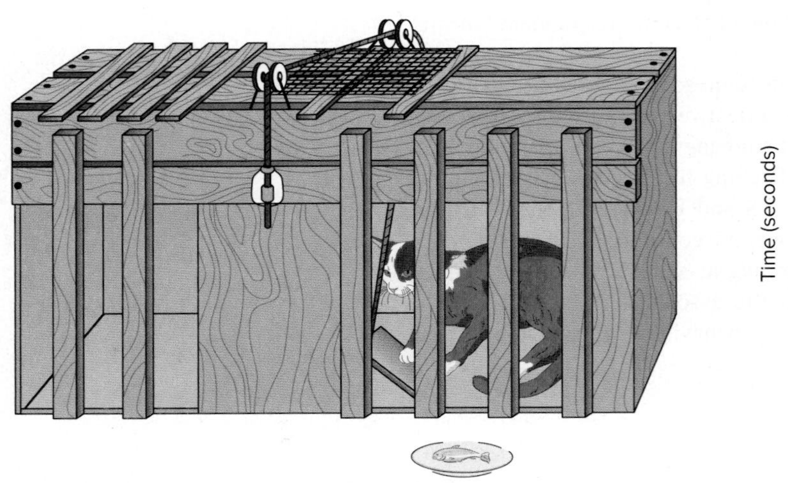

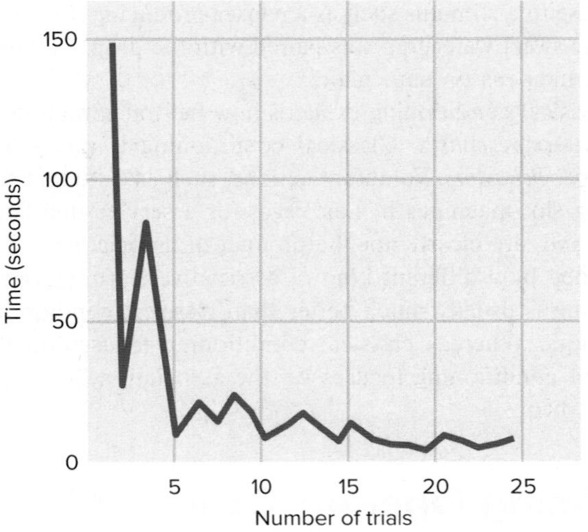


**FIGURE 4** **Thorndike's Puzzle Box and the Law of Effect** (*left*) A box typical of the puzzle boxes Thorndike used in his experiments with cats to study the law of effect. Stepping on the lever released the door bolt; a weight attached to the door then pulled the door open and allowed the cat to escape. After accidentally pressing the lever as it tried to get to the food, the cat learned to press the lever when it wanted to escape the box. (*right*) One cat's learning curve over 24 separate trials. Notice that the cat escaped much more quickly after about five trials. It had learned the consequences of its behavior. Source: Thorndike (1898).

## Skinner's Approach to Operant Conditioning

Skinner believed that the mechanisms of learning are the same for all species. This conviction led him to study animals in the hope that he could discover the components of learning with organisms simpler than humans, including pigeons. During World War II, Skinner trained pigeons to pilot missiles. Naval officials just could not accept pigeons guiding their missiles in a war, but Skinner congratulated himself on the degree of control he was able to exercise over the pigeons (Figure 5).

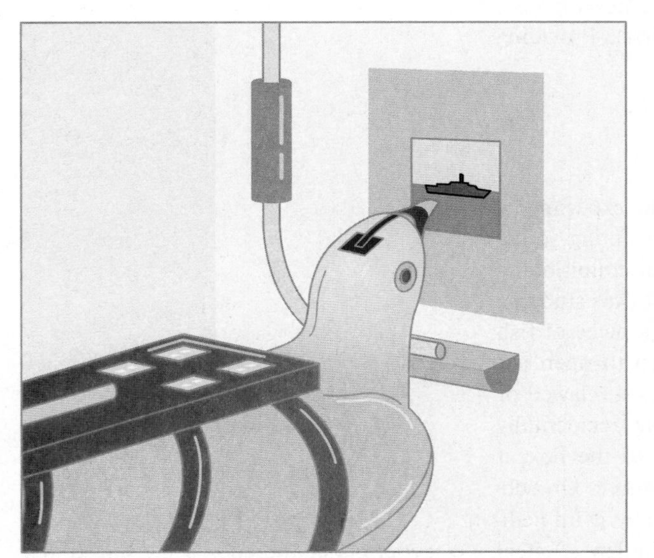

**FIGURE 5** **Skinner's Pigeon-Guided Missile** Skinner wanted to help the military during World War II by using the tracking behavior of pigeons. A gold electrode covered the tip of the pigeons' beaks. Contact with the screen on which the image of the target was projected sent a signal informing the missile's control mechanism of the target's location. A few grains of food occasionally given to the pigeons maintained their tracking behavior.

Skinner and other behaviorists made every effort to study organisms under precisely controlled conditions so that they could examine the connection between the operant behavior and the specific consequences in minute detail. In the 1930s, Skinner created an operant conditioning chamber, sometimes called a "Skinner box," to control experimental conditions (Figure 6). The Skinner box would allow an animal (such a rat) to be conditioned to push a bar to receive a reward with minimal interaction with a person.

A device in the box delivered food pellets into a tray at random. After a rat became accustomed to the box, Skinner installed a lever and observed the rat's behavior. As the hungry rat explored the box, it occasionally pressed the lever, and a food pellet was dispensed. Soon the rat learned that the consequences of pressing the lever were positive: It would be fed. Skinner achieved further control by soundproofing the box to ensure that the experimenter was the only influence on the organism. In many of the experiments, the responses were mechanically recorded, and the food (the consequence) was dispensed automatically. These precautions were aimed at preventing human error.

## Shaping

Imagine trying to teach even a really smart dog how to signal that her owner's blood-glucose level is low—or how to turn on the lights or do the laundry. These challenges might seem insurmountable, as it is unlikely that a dog will spontaneously perform any of these behaviors. You could wait a very long time for such feats to occur. Nevertheless, it *is* possible to train a dog or another animal to perform highly complex tasks through shaping.

**Shaping** refers to rewarding successive approximations of a desired behavior. For example, shaping can be used to train a rat to press a bar to obtain food. When a rat is first placed in a Skinner box, it rarely presses the bar. Thus, the experimenter may start off by giving the rat a food pellet if it is in the same half of the cage as the bar. Then the experimenter might reward the rat's behavior only when it is within 2 inches of the bar, then only when it touches the bar, and finally only when it presses the bar.

Returning to the service dog example, rather than waiting for the dog to spontaneously put the clothes in the washing machine, we might reward the dog for carrying the clothes to the laundry room and for bringing them closer and closer to the washing machine. Finally, we might reward the dog only when it gets the clothes inside the washer. Indeed, trainers use this type of shaping technique extensively in teaching animals to perform tricks. A dolphin that jumps through a hoop held high above the water has been trained to perform this behavior through shaping. Shaping is also used in interventions that help individuals who are coping with neurological disorders to walk (Thompson & others, 2018). To read about this fascinating work, see the Intersection.

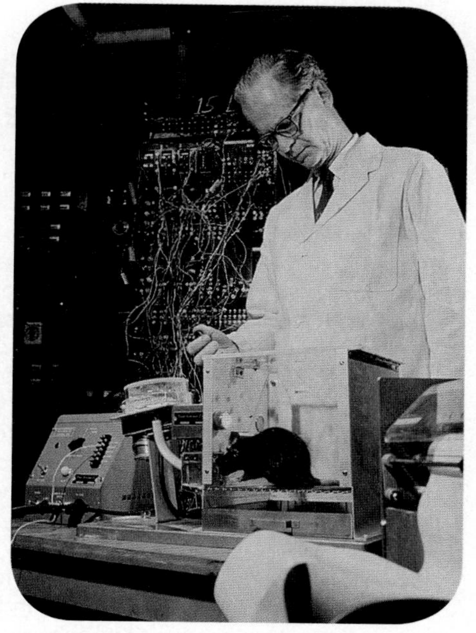

**FIGURE 6 The Skinner Box**
B. F. Skinner conducting an operant conditioning study in his behavioral laboratory. The rat being studied is in an operant conditioning chamber, sometimes referred to as a Skinner box. ©Nina Leen/Time & Life Pictures/Getty Images

## Principles of Reinforcement

We noted earlier that a behavior can be followed by something pleasant or something unpleasant. When behaviors are followed by a desirable outcome, the behaviors are likely to be repeated. When behaviors are followed by an undesirable outcome, they are less likely to occur. Now we can put some labels on these different patterns.

**Reinforcement** is the process by which a stimulus or event (a *reinforcer*) following a particular behavior increases the probability that the behavior will happen again. These desirable (or rewarding) consequences of a behavior fall into two types, called *positive reinforcement* and *negative reinforcement.* Both of these types of consequences are experienced as pleasant, and both increase the frequency of a behavior.

*Through shaping, animals can learn to do amazing things—even ride a wave, like these two canines.*
©dutchmanphotography/iStock/Getty Images

### POSITIVE AND NEGATIVE REINFORCEMENT

In **positive reinforcement** the frequency of a behavior increases because it is followed by a desirable stimulus. For example, if someone you meet smiles at you after you say, "Hello, how are you?" and you keep talking, the smile has reinforced your talking. The same principle of positive reinforcement is at work when you teach a dog to "shake hands" by giving it a piece of food when it lifts its paw.

In contrast, in **negative reinforcement** the frequency of a behavior increases because it is followed by *the removal* of something undesirable. For example, if your father nagged you to clean out the garage and kept nagging until you cleaned out the garage, your response (cleaning out the garage) removed the unpleasant stimulus (your dad's nagging). Taking an aspirin when you have a headache works the same way: A reduction of pain reinforces the act of taking an aspirin. Similarly, if your laptop is making an irritating buzzing sound, you might give it a good smack on the side, and if the buzzing stops, you are more likely to smack it again if the buzzing resumes. Ending the buzzing sound rewards the laptop-smacking.

Notice that both positive and negative reinforcement involve rewarding behavior—but they do so in different ways. Positive reinforcement means following a behavior with the addition of something pleasant, and negative reinforcement means following a behavior with the removal of something unpleasant. So, in this case "positive" and "negative" have nothing to do with "good" and "bad." Rather, they refer to processes in which something is given (positive reinforcement) or removed (negative reinforcement).

- **shaping** Rewarding successive approximations of a desired behavior.
- **reinforcement** The process by which a stimulus or event (a reinforcer) following a particular behavior increases the probability that the behavior will happen again.
- **positive reinforcement** The presentation of a stimulus following a given behavior in order to increase the frequency of that behavior.
- **negative reinforcement** The removal of a stimulus following a given behavior in order to increase the frequency of that behavior.

# INTERSECTION

## Psychology of Learning and Rehabilitation: Can Limbs Relearn Reflexes After Spinal Cord Injury?

Much of our capacity to walk depends on the use of reflexes deploying at precisely the right time, in precisely the right way. Many of these reflexes involve single neurons that activate muscles in our legs. A particularly problematic aspect of walking following a spinal cord injury is that reflexes become dysregulated. Individuals with incomplete spinal cord injury may find that their reflexes are too extreme or not strong enough (Eftekhar & others, 2018). As we have seen, operant conditioning is best suited to voluntary behaviors. Reflexes, of course, are not voluntary—they happen automatically. How can operant conditioning retrain these automatic reflexes? One way is to provide people with feedback about their reflexes so they can change their behavior accordingly (Eftekhar & others, 2018). Here is how it is done. While holding on to a handrail for safety, the person walks in place on a mat that has sensors tracking their gait. Electrodes placed on their legs convey information about their reflexes that are then shown on a monitor that the person watches. The patient can then see if their reflexes are optimal or not and change their behavior accordingly.

*Can operant conditioning be used to shape even automatic behaviors?*

Capitalizing on the plasticity of the nervous system, this type of training can help people retrain their reflexes so that they can walk (Al'bertin, 2018; Eftekhar & others, 2018; Mikolajczyk & others, 2018). Here's something that is especially interesting about this intervention: not only does the training benefit the targeted reflex, it also seems to generalize to other reflexes, providing broader benefits to a person's ability to move (Eftekhar & others, 2018). When a person can monitor even automatic behaviors, they can be brought into the realm of operant conditioning and respond to feedback—rewards and punishments—that shape that behavior. Of course, few things would be more rewarding than being able, at last, to take a walk in the park with family and friends.



Whether it is positive or negative, reinforcement is about increasing a behavior (Eder, Krishna & Van Dessel, 2019). Be sure to review Figure 7, as it provides further examples to help you understand the distinction between positive and negative reinforcement. These processes can be tricky.

A special kind of response to negative reinforcement is avoidance learning. **Avoidance learning** occurs when the organism learns that by making a particular response, a negative stimulus can be avoided. For instance, a student who receives one bad grade might thereafter always study hard in order to avoid the negative outcome of bad grades in the future. Even when the bad grade is no longer present, the behavior pattern sticks. Avoidance learning is very powerful in the sense that the behavior is maintained even in the absence of any aversive stimulus. For example, animals that have been trained to avoid a negative stimulus, such as an electrical shock, by jumping into a safe area may thereafter gravitate toward the safe area, even when the shock is no longer presented.

● **avoidance learning** An organism's learning that it can altogether avoid a negative stimulus by making a particular response.

Experience with unavoidable negative stimuli can lead to a particular deficit in avoidance learning called learned helplessness. In **learned helplessness** the organism has learned that it has no control over negative outcomes. Learned helplessness was first identified by Martin Seligman and his colleagues (Altenor, Volpicelli, & Seligman, 1979; Hannum, Rosellini, & Seligman, 1976). Seligman and his associates found that dogs that were first exposed to inescapable shocks were later unable to learn to avoid those shocks, even when they could avoid them (Seligman & Maier, 1967). This inability to learn to escape was persistent: The dogs would suffer painful shocks hours, days, and even weeks later and never attempt to escape.

● **learned helplessness** An organism's learning through experience with negative stimuli that it has no control over negative outcomes.

Exposure to unavoidable negative circumstances may also set the stage for humans' inability to learn avoidance, such as with the experience of depression and despair (Landgraf & others, 2015; Reznik & others, 2017). Learned helplessness has aided psychologists in understanding a variety of perplexing issues, such as why some victims of domestic violence fail to escape their terrible situation and why some students respond to failure at school by no longer trying to succeed.

Positive Reinforcement

| Behavior | Rewarding Stimulus Provided | Future Behavior |
|---|---|---|
| You turn in homework on time. | Teacher praises your performance. | You increasingly turn in homework on time. |
| You wax your skis. | The skis go faster. | You wax your skis the next time you go skiing. |
| You randomly press a button on the dashboard of a friend's car. | Great music begins to play. | You deliberately press the button again the next time you get into the car. |

Negative Reinforcement

| Behavior | Stimulus Removed | Future Behavior |
|---|---|---|
| You turn in homework on time. | Teacher stops criticizing late homework. | You increasingly turn in homework on time. |
| You wax your skis. | People stop zooming by you on the slopes. | You wax your skis the next time you go skiing. |
| You randomly press a button on the dashboard of a friend's car. | An annoying song shuts off. | You deliberately press the button again the next time the annoying song is on. |

**FIGURE 7** **Positive and Negative Reinforcement** Positive reinforcers involve adding something (generally something rewarding). Negative reinforcers involve taking away something (generally something aversive). Source: Eder, Krishna & Van Dessel (2019).

## TYPES OF REINFORCERS

Psychologists classify positive reinforcers as primary or secondary based on whether the rewarding quality of the consequence is innate or learned. A **primary reinforcer** is innately satisfying; that is, a primary reinforcer does not require any learning on the organism's part to make it pleasurable. Food, water, and sexual satisfaction are primary reinforcers.

A **secondary reinforcer** acquires its positive value through an organism's experience; a secondary reinforcer is a learned or conditioned reinforcer. Secondary reinforcers can be linked to primary reinforcers through classical conditioning. For instance, if someone wanted to train a cat to do tricks, the person might first repeatedly pair the sound of a whistle with food. Once the cat associates the whistle with food, the whistle can be used in training.

● **primary reinforcer** A reinforcer that is innately satisfying; a primary reinforcer does not require any learning on the organism's part to make it pleasurable.

● **secondary reinforcer** A reinforcer that acquires its positive value through an organism's experience; a secondary reinforcer is a learned or conditioned reinforcer.

We encounter hundreds of secondary reinforcers in our lives, such as getting an *A* on a test and a paycheck for a job. Although we might think of these as positive outcomes, they are not innately positive. We learn through experience that *A*'s and paychecks are good. Secondary reinforcers can be used in a system called a *token economy*. In a token economy behaviors are rewarded with tokens (such as poker chips or stars on a chart) that can be exchanged later for desired rewards (such as candy or money).

## GENERALIZATION, DISCRIMINATION, AND EXTINCTION

Not only are generalization, discrimination, and extinction important in classical conditioning, but they are also key principles in operant conditioning.

**Generalization** In operant conditioning, **generalization** means performing a reinforced behavior in a different situation. For example, in one study pigeons were reinforced for pecking at a disk of a particular color (Guttman & Kalish, 1956). To assess stimulus generalization, researchers presented the pigeons with disks of varying colors. As Figure 8 shows, the pigeons were most likely to peck at disks closest in color to the original. When a student who gets excellent grades in a calculus class by studying the course material every night starts to study psychology and history every night as well, generalization is at work.

● **generalization (in operant conditioning)** Performing a reinforced behavior in a different situation.

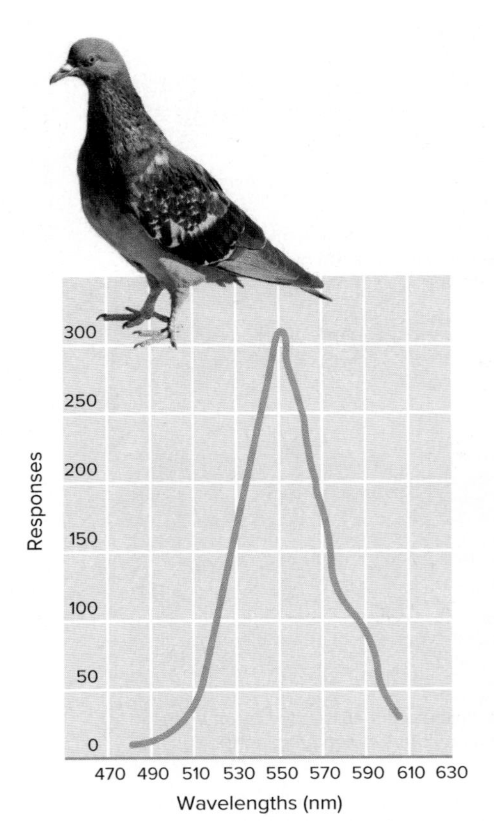


**FIGURE 8 Stimulus Generalization** In the experiment by Norman Guttman and Harry Kalish (1956), pigeons initially pecked at a disk of a particular color (in this graph, a color with a wavelength of 550 nm) after they had been reinforced for this wavelength. Subsequently, when the pigeons were presented with disks of colors with varying wavelengths, they were likelier to peck at those with a similar color to the original disk. Source: Guttman & Kalish (1956); ©s_oleg/Shutterstock

- **discrimination (in classical conditioning)** The process of learning to respond to certain stimuli and not others.

- **extinction (in operant conditioning)** Decreases in the frequency of a behavior when the behavior is no longer reinforced.

- **schedules of reinforcement** Specific patterns that determine when a behavior will be reinforced.

**Discrimination** In operant conditioning, **discrimination** means responding appropriately to stimuli that signal that a behavior will or will not be reinforced. For example, you go to a restaurant that has a "University Student Discount" sign in the front window, and you enthusiastically flash your student ID with the expectation of getting the reward of a reduced-price meal. Without the sign, showing your ID might get you only a puzzled look, not cheap food.

The principle of discrimination helps to explain how a service dog "knows" when she is working. Typically, the dog wears a training harness while on duty but not at other times. Thus, when a service dog is wearing her harness, it is important to treat her like the professional that she is. Similarly, an important aspect of the training of service dogs is the need for selective disobedience. Selective disobedience means that in addition to obeying commands from her human partner, the service dog must at times override such commands if the context provides cues that obedience is not the appropriate response. So, if a guide dog is standing at the street corner with her visually impaired owner, and the person commands her to move forward, the dog might refuse if she sees the "Don't Walk" sign flashing. Stimuli in the environment serve as cues, informing the organism if a particular reinforcement contingency is in effect.

**Extinction** In operant conditioning, **extinction** occurs when a behavior is no longer reinforced and decreases in frequency. If, for example, a soda machine that you frequently use starts "eating" your coins without dispensing soda, you quickly stop inserting more coins. Several weeks later, you might try to use the machine again, hoping that it has been fixed. Such behavior illustrates spontaneous recovery in operant conditioning (Bouton & Schepers, 2015).

## CONTINUOUS REINFORCEMENT, PARTIAL REINFORCEMENT, AND SCHEDULES OF REINFORCEMENT

Most of the examples of reinforcement we have considered so far involve *continuous reinforcement,* in which a behavior is reinforced every time it occurs. When continuous reinforcement takes place, organisms learn rapidly. However, when reinforcement stops, extinction takes place quickly.

A variety of conditioning procedures have been developed that are particularly resistant to extinction. These involve *partial reinforcement,* in which a reinforcer follows a behavior only a portion of the time. Partial reinforcement characterizes most life experiences. For instance, a golfer does not win every tournament she enters; a chess whiz does not win every match she plays; a student does not get a pat on the back each time he solves a problem.

**Schedules of reinforcement** are specific patterns that determine when a behavior will be reinforced. There are four main schedules of partial reinforcement: fixed ratio, variable ratio, fixed interval, and variable interval. With respect to these, *ratio schedules* involve the number of behaviors that must be performed prior to reward, and *interval schedules* refer to the amount of time that must pass before a behavior is rewarded. In a fixed schedule, the number of behaviors or the amount of time is always the same. In a variable schedule, the required number of behaviors or the amount of time that must pass changes and is unpredictable from the perspective of the learner. Let's look concretely at how each of these schedules of reinforcement influences behavior.

A *fixed-ratio schedule* reinforces a behavior after a set number of behaviors. For example, a child might receive a piece of candy or an hour of video-game play not *every* time he practices his piano, but after five days of practicing at least an hour per day. A mail carrier must deliver mail to a fixed number of houses each day before he or she can head home. A factory might require a line worker to produce a certain number of items in order to get paid a particular amount. As you can imagine, fixed-ratio schedules are not very mysterious, especially to human learners.

Consider, for instance, if you were playing the slot machines in Las Vegas, and they were on a fixed-ratio schedule, providing a $5 win every 20th time you put money in the machine. It would not take long to figure out that if you watched someone else play the machine 18 or 19 times, not get any money back, and then walk away, you should step up, insert your coin, and get $5. Of course, if the reward schedule for a slot machine were that easy to figure out, casinos would not be so successful.

What makes gambling so tantalizing is the unpredictability of wins (and losses). Slot machines are on a *variable-ratio schedule,* a timetable in which behaviors are rewarded an average number of times but on an unpredictable basis. For example, a slot machine might pay off at *an average* of every 20th time, but the gambler does not know when this payoff will be. The slot machine might pay off twice in a row and then not again until after 58 coins have been inserted. This averages out to a reward for every 20 behavioral acts, but *when* the reward will be given is unpredictable.

*Slot machines are on a variable-ratio schedule of reinforcement.*



Variable-ratio schedules produce high, steady rates of behavior that are more resistant to extinction than the other three schedules. Clearly, slot machines can make quite a profit. This is because not only are the rewards unpredictable, but they require behavior on the part of the person playing. One cannot simply wait around and then put in a coin after hours of not playing, hoping for a win. The machine requires that a certain *number* of behaviors occur; that is what makes it a *ratio* schedule.

In contrast to ratio schedules of reinforcement, *interval* reinforcement schedules are determined by the *time elapsed* since the last behavior was rewarded. A *fixed-interval schedule* reinforces the first appropriate behavior after a fixed amount of time has passed. If you take a class that has four scheduled exams, you might procrastinate most of the semester and cram just before each test. Fixed-interval schedules of reinforcement are also responsible for the fact that pets seem to be able to "tell time," eagerly sidling up to their food dish at 5 P.M. in anticipation of dinner. On a fixed-interval schedule, the rate of a behavior increases rapidly as the time approaches when the behavior likely will be reinforced. For example, suppose you are baking cookies, and when you put the cookie sheet into the oven, you set a timer. But before the timer goes off, you find yourself checking the cookies, over and over.

A *variable-interval schedule* is a timetable in which a behavior is reinforced after a variable amount of time has elapsed. Pop quizzes occur on a variable-interval schedule. Random drug testing follows a variable-interval schedule as well. So does fishing—you do not know if the fish will bite in the next minute, in a half hour, in an hour, or ever. Because it is difficult to predict when a reward will come, behavior is *slow and consistent* on a variable-interval schedule. This is why pop quizzes lead to more consistent levels of studying, compared with the cramming that might be seen with scheduled tests.

Let's take a closer look at the responses associated with each schedule of reinforcement in the Psychological Inquiry feature.

## PUNISHMENT

We began this section by noting that behaviors can be followed by something good or something bad. So far, we have explored only the good things—reinforcers that are meant to increase behaviors. Sometimes, however, the goal is to decrease a behavior, and in such cases the behavior might be followed by something unpleasant. **Punishment** is a consequence that decreases the likelihood that a behavior will occur. For instance, a child plays with matches and gets burned when he lights one; the child consequently is less likely to play with matches in the future. As another example, a student interrupts the instructor, and the instructor scolds the student. This consequence—the teacher's verbal reprimand—makes the student less likely to interrupt in the future. In punishment, a response decreases because of its unpleasant consequences.

- **punishment** A consequence that decreases the likelihood that a behavior will occur.

Just as the positive–negative distinction applies to reinforcement, it can also apply to punishment. As was the case for reinforcement, "positive" means adding something, and "negative" means taking something away. Thus, in **positive punishment** a behavior decreases when it is followed by the presentation of a stimulus, whereas in **negative punishment** a behavior decreases when a stimulus is removed. Examples of positive punishment include spanking a misbehaving child and scolding a spouse who forgot to call when she was running late at the office; the coach who makes his team run wind sprints after a lackadaisical practice is also using positive punishment. *Time-out* is a form of negative

- **positive punishment** The presentation of a stimulus following a given behavior in order to decrease the frequency of that behavior.

- **negative punishment** The removal of a stimulus following a given behavior in order to decrease the frequency of that behavior.

## psychological *inquiry*

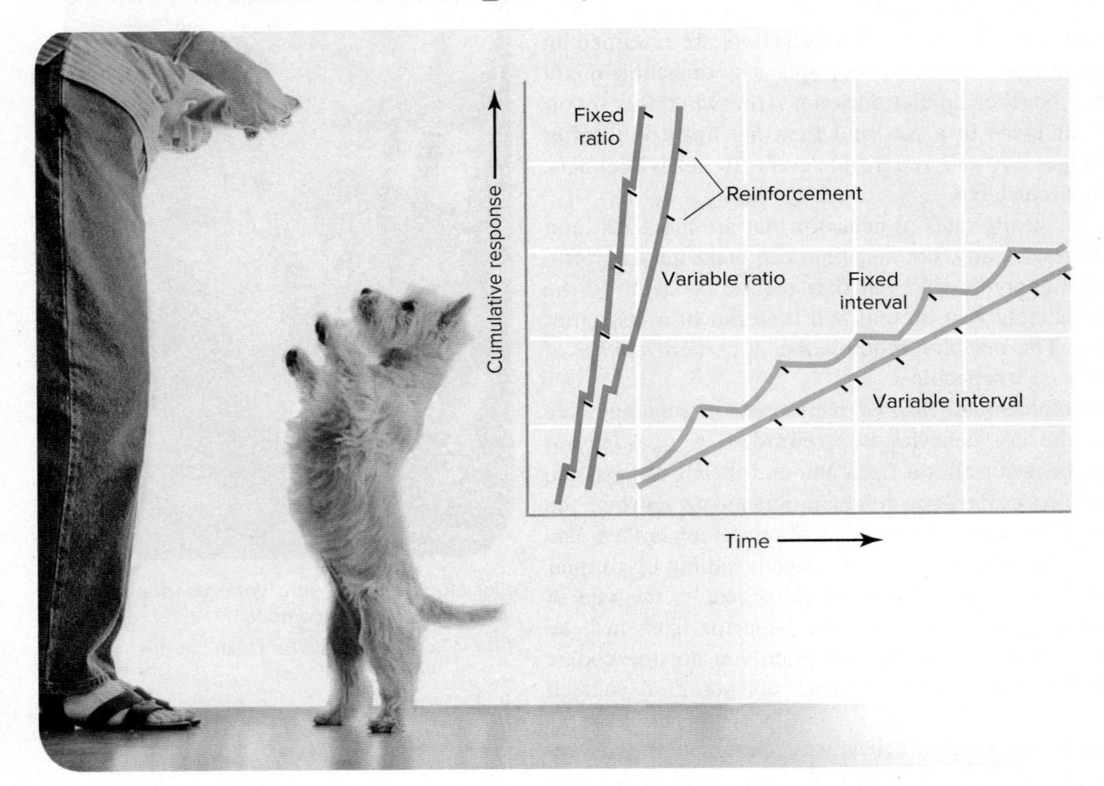


©Corbis VGC/Getty Images

### *Schedules of Reinforcement and Different Patterns of Responding*

This figure shows how the different schedules of reinforcement result in different rates of responding. The X or horizontal axis represents time. The Y or vertical axis represents the cumulative responses. That means that as the line goes up, the total number of responses are building and building. In the figure, each hash mark indicates the delivery of reinforcement. That is, each of those little ticks indicates that a reward is being given.

Look closely at the pattern of responses over time for each schedule of reinforcement. On the fixed-ratio schedule, notice the dropoff in responding after each response; on the variable-ratio schedule, note the high, steady rate of responding. On the fixed-interval schedule, notice the immediate dropoff in responding after reinforcement and the increase in responding just before reinforcement (resulting in a scalloped curve); and on the variable-interval schedule, note the slow, steady rate of responding.

1. Which schedule of reinforcement represents the "most bang for the buck"? That is, which one is associated with the most responses for the least amount of reward?
2. Which schedule of reinforcement is most similar to pop quizzes?
3. Which reinforcement schedule is most similar to regular tests on a course syllabus?
4. Which schedule of reinforcement would be best if you have very little time for training?
5. Which schedule of reinforcement do you think is most common in your own life? Why?

punishment in which a child is removed from a positive reinforcer, such as her toys. Getting grounded is also a form of negative punishment, as it involves taking a teenager away from the fun things in his life. Figure 9 compares positive reinforcement, negative reinforcement, positive punishment, and negative punishment.

## TIMING, REINFORCEMENT, AND PUNISHMENTS

How does the timing of reinforcement and punishment influence behavior? And does it matter whether the reinforcement is small or large?

**Immediate Versus Delayed Reinforcement** As is the case in classical conditioning, in operant conditioning learning is more efficient when the interval between a behavior and its reinforcer is a few seconds rather than minutes or hours, especially in nonhuman animals. If a food reward is delayed for more than 30 seconds after a rat presses a bar, it is virtually ineffective as reinforcement. Humans have the ability to connect their behaviors to delayed reinforcers. We can, for instance, study hard knowing that a test is a few weeks away (as there is the reward of the grade we will earn).

Sometimes important life decisions involve whether to seek and enjoy a small, immediate reinforcer or to wait for a delayed but more highly valued reinforcer (Göllner &

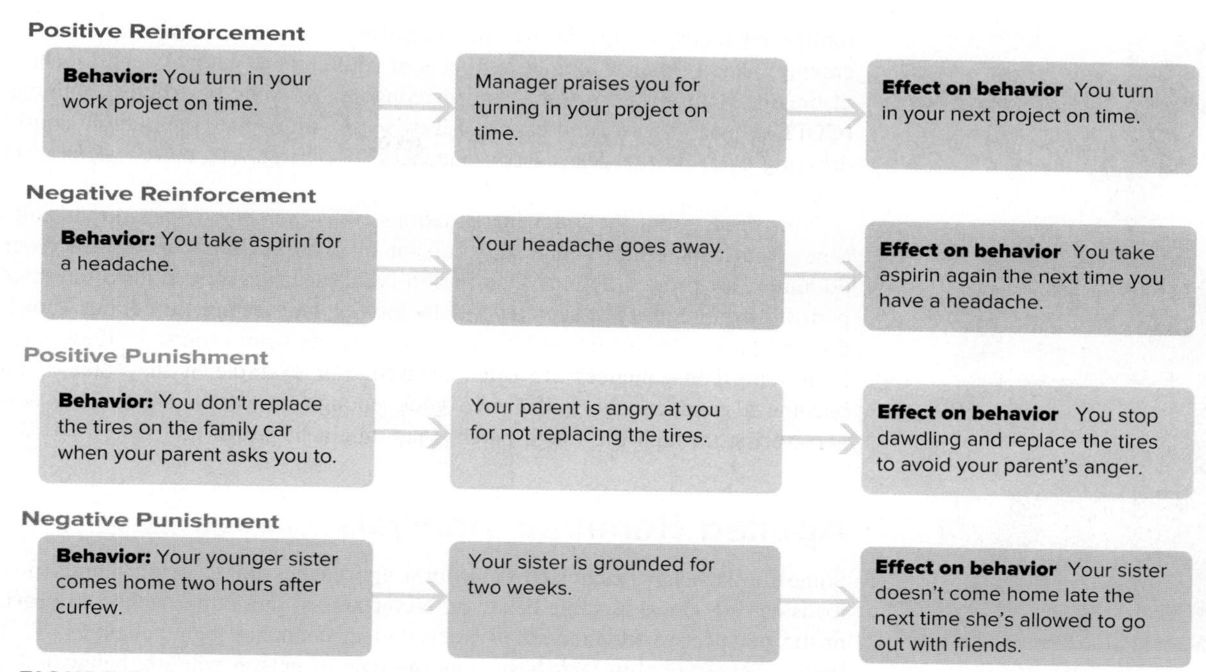


**FIGURE 9 Positive Reinforcement, Negative Reinforcement, Positive Punishment, and Negative Punishment** The fine distinctions here can sometimes be confusing. With respect to reinforcement, note that both types of reinforcement are intended to increase behavior, either by presenting a stimulus (in positive reinforcement) or by taking away a stimulus (in negative reinforcement). Punishment is meant to decrease a behavior either by presenting something (in positive punishment) or by taking away something (in negative punishment). The words *positive* and *negative* mean the same things in both cases.

others, 2018; Watson, & Milfont, 2017). For example, you might spend your money now on clothes, concert tickets, and the latest smartphone, or you might save your money and buy a car later. You might choose to enjoy yourself now in return for immediate small reinforcers, or you might opt to study hard in return for delayed stronger reinforcers like good grades, admission to grad school, and a better job.

**Immediate Versus Delayed Punishment** As with reinforcement, in most instances of research with lower animals, immediate punishment is more effective than delayed punishment in decreasing the occurrence of a behavior. However, also as with reinforcement, delayed punishment can have an effect on human behavior. Not studying at the beginning of a semester can lead to poor grades much later, and humans have the capacity to notice that this early behavior contributed to the negative outcome.

**Immediate Versus Delayed Reinforcement and Punishment** Many daily behaviors revolve around rewards and punishments, both immediate and delayed. We might put off going to the dentist to avoid a small punisher (such as the discomfort that comes with getting a cavity filled). However, this procrastination might contribute to greater pain later (such as the pain of having a tooth pulled). Sometimes life is about enduring a little pain now to avoid a lot of pain later.

How does receiving immediate small reinforcement versus delayed strong punishment affect human behavior? One reason that obesity is such a major health problem is that eating is a behavior with immediate positive consequences—food tastes great and quickly provides a pleasurable, satisfied feeling. Although the potential delayed consequences of overeating are negative (obesity and other possible health risks), the immediate consequences are difficult to override. When the delayed consequences of behavior are punishing and the immediate consequences are reinforcing, the immediate consequences usually win, even when the immediate consequences are minor reinforcers and the delayed consequences are major punishers.

Smoking and drinking follow a similar pattern. The immediate consequences of smoking are reinforcing for most smokers—the powerful combination of positive reinforcement

©Sam Edwards/age fotostock

(enhanced focus, energy boost) and negative reinforcement (tension relief, removal of craving). The primarily long-term effects of smoking are punishing and include shortness of breath, a chronic sore throat and/or coughing, chronic obstructive pulmonary disease (COPD), heart disease, and cancer. Likewise, the immediate pleasurable consequences of drinking override the delayed consequences of a hangover or even alcoholism and liver disease.

Now think about the following situations. Why are some of us so reluctant to take up a new sport, try a new dance step, run for office on campus or in local government, or do almost anything different? One reason is that learning new skills often involves minor punishing consequences, such as initially looking and feeling stupid, not knowing what to do, and having to put up with sarcastic comments from others. In these circumstances, reinforcing consequences are often delayed. For example, it may take a long time to become a good enough golfer or a good enough dancer to enjoy these activities, but persevering through the rough patches just might be worth it.

## Applied Behavior Analysis

Some thinkers have criticized behavioral approaches for ignoring mental processes and focusing only on observable behavior. Nevertheless, these approaches do provide an optimistic perspective for individuals interested in changing their behaviors. That is, rather than concentrating on factors such as the type of person you are, behavioral approaches imply that you can modify even longstanding habits by changing the reward contingencies that maintain those habits.

One real-world application of operant conditioning principles to promote better functioning is applied behavior analysis. **Applied behavior analysis**, also called **behavior modification**, is the use of operant conditioning principles to change human behavior. In applied behavior analysis, the rewards and punishers that exist in a particular setting are carefully analyzed and manipulated to change behaviors. If we can figure out what rewards and punishers are controlling a person's behavior, we can change them—and eventually change the behavior itself.

• **applied behavior analysis or behavior modification** The use of operant conditioning principles to change human behavior.

A manager who rewards staff members with a casual-dress day or a half day off if they meet a particular work goal is employing applied behavior analysis. So are a therapist and a client when they establish clear consequences for the client's behavior in order to reinforce more adaptive actions and discourage less adaptive ones. A teacher who notices that a troublesome student seems to enjoy the attention he receives—even when that attention is scolding—might use applied behavior analysis by changing her responses to the child's behavior, ignoring it instead (an example of negative punishment). These examples show how attending to the consequences of behavior can be used to improve performance in settings such as the workplace or a classroom.

Applied behavior analysis has been effective in a wide range of situations. Practitioners have used it, for example, to treat individuals on the autism spectrum (Makrygianni & others, 2018), children and adolescents with psychological problems (Castillo & others, 2018), and residents of mental health facilities (Buchmeier & others, 2018); to instruct individuals in effective parenting (Pennefather & others, 2018); to enhance environmentally conscious behaviors such as recycling and properly disposing of garbage (Elba & Ivy, 2018); to get people to wear seatbelts (Kidd & others, 2018) and adhere to speed limits (Mullen, Maxwell, & Bédard, 2015); and to promote workplace safety (Gravina, King, & Austin, 2019; Yu & others, 2018).

### test yourself

1. What is operant conditioning?
2. Define shaping and give two examples of it.
3. What is the difference between positive reinforcement and negative reinforcement? Between positive punishment and negative punishment?

# 4. OBSERVATIONAL LEARNING

Would it make sense to teach a 15-year-old girl how to drive with either classical conditioning or operant conditioning procedures? Driving a car is a voluntary behavior, so classical conditioning would not apply. In terms of operant conditioning, we could ask her to try to drive down the road and then reward her positive behaviors. Not many of us would want to be on the road, though, when she makes mistakes. Consider, as well, how many things human beings do that are arbitrary but important. We wave to say hello or goodbye, we eat certain foods for breakfast and not others. These conventions are learned through observational learning (Schoppmann, Schneider, & Seehagen, 2018).

If all of our learning were conducted in such a trial-and-error fashion, learning would be exceedingly tedious and at times hazardous. Although humans do learn through associative conditioning, we also learn in a different way: by observing others. Many complex behaviors are learned by watching competent models perform them (Bandura, 2011a). By observing other people, we can acquire knowledge, skills, rules, strategies, beliefs, and attitudes. The capacity to learn by observation eliminates trial-and-error learning, and often such learning takes less time than operant conditioning.

*Observational learning,* also called *imitation* or *modeling,* is learning that occurs when a person observes and imitates behavior. Perhaps the most famous example of observational learning is the Bobo doll study, conducted by Albert Bandura and his colleagues (Bandura, Ross, & Ross, 1961). In the study, children were randomly assigned to watch an adult either behave aggressively or nonaggressively toward an inflated doll. In the experimental condition, children saw the model hit an inflated Bobo doll with a mallet, kick it in the air, punch it, and throw it, all the while hollering aggressive phrases such as "Hit him!" "Punch him in the nose!" and "Pow!" In the control condition, the model played with Tinkertoys and ignored the Bobo doll. Children who watched the aggressive model were much more likely to engage in aggressive behavior when left alone with Bobo (Bandura, Ross, & Ross, 1961).

Bandura (1986) described four main processes that are involved in observational learning: attention, retention, motor reproduction, and reinforcement. The first process that must occur is *attention* (which we considered in the chapter "Sensation and Perception" due to its crucial role in perception). To reproduce a model's actions, you must attend to what the model is saying or doing. You might not hear what a friend says if music is blaring, and you might miss your instructor's analysis of a problem if you are admiring someone sitting in the next row. As a further example, imagine that you decide to take a class to improve your drawing skills. To succeed, you need to attend to the instructor's words and hand movements. Characteristics of the model can influence whether we pay attention to him or her. Warm, powerful, atypical people, for example, command more attention than do cold, weak, typical people.

*Retention* is the second process required for observational learning to occur. Retention means you must hold the information in memory. To reproduce a model's actions, you must encode the information and keep it in memory so that you can retrieve it. A simple verbal description, or a vivid image of what the model did, assists retention. (Memory is such an important cognitive process that we devote the chapter "Memory" exclusively to it.) In the example of taking a class to sharpen your drawing skills, you will need to remember what the instructor said and did in modeling good drawing skills.

*Motor reproduction,* a third element of observational learning, is the process of imitating the model's actions. People might pay attention to a model and encode what they have seen, but limitations in motor development might make it difficult for them to reproduce the model's action. A 13-year-old might see a professional basketball player do a reverse two-handed dunk but be unable to reproduce the pro's play. Similarly, in your drawing class, if you lack fine motor reproduction skills, you might be unable to follow the instructor's example.

*Reinforcement* is a final component of observational learning. In this case, the question is whether the model's behavior is followed by a consequence. Seeing a model attain a reward for an activity increases the chances that an observer will repeat the behavior—a process called *vicarious reinforcement.* On the other hand, seeing the model punished makes the observer less likely to repeat the behavior—a process called *vicarious punishment.* Unfortunately, vicarious reinforcement and vicarious punishment are often absent in, for example, media portrayals of violence and aggression.

Observational learning has been studied in a variety of contexts. Researchers have explored observational learning, for example, as a means by which gorillas learn from one another about motor skills (Byrne, Hobaiter, & Klailova, 2011). They have also studied it

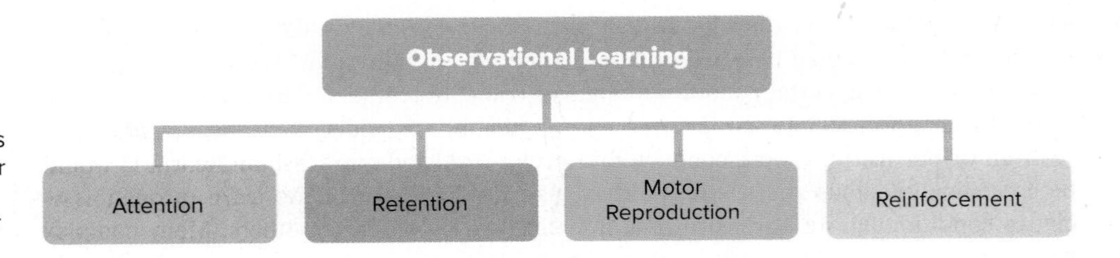


**FIGURE 10 Bandura's Model of Observational Learning** In terms of Bandura's model, if you are learning to ski, you need to attend to the instructor's words and demonstrations. You need to remember what the instructor did and said about how to avoid disasters. You also need the motor abilities to reproduce what the instructor has shown you. Praise from the instructor after you have completed a few moves on the slopes should improve your motivation to continue skiing.

as a process by which people learn whether stimuli are likely to be painful (Helsen & others, 2011) and as a tool individuals use to make economic decisions (Beshears & others, 2015).

Observational learning can be an important factor in the functioning of role models in inspiring people and changing their perceptions. Whether a model is similar to us can influence that model's effectiveness in modifying our behavior. The shortage of role models for women and minorities in science and engineering has often been suggested as a reason for the lack of women and minorities in these fields. After the election of Barack Obama as president of the United States, many commentators noted that for the first time, African American children could see concretely that they might also attain the nation's highest office someday. Figure 10 summarizes Bandura's model of observational learning.

### test yourself

1. What are the four processes involved in observational learning?
2. What are two other names for observational learning?
3. What are vicarious reinforcement and vicarious punishment?

# 5. COGNITIVE FACTORS IN LEARNING

In learning about learning, we have looked at cognitive processes only as they apply in observational learning. Skinner's operant conditioning perspective and Pavlov's classical conditioning approach focus on the environment and observable behavior, not what is going on in the head of the learner. Many contemporary psychologists, including some behaviorists, recognize the importance of cognition and believe that learning involves more than environment-behavior connections. A good starting place for considering cognitive influences on learning is the work of E. C. Tolman.

## Purposive Behavior

E. C. Tolman (1932) emphasized the *purposiveness* of behavior—the idea that much of behavior is goal-directed. Tolman believed that it is necessary to study entire behavioral sequences in order to understand why people engage in particular actions. For example, high school students whose goal is to attend a leading college or university study hard in their classes. If we focused only on their studying, we would miss the purpose of their behavior. The students do not always study hard because they have been reinforced for studying in the past. Rather, studying is a means to intermediate goals (learning, high grades) that in turn improve their likelihood of getting into the college or university of their choice. To understand human behavior, we sometimes need to place it in a larger context.

We can see Tolman's legacy today in the extensive interest in the role of goal setting in human behavior (Kaminer & others, 2018; Nelis & others, 2018). Researchers are especially curious about how people self-regulate and self-monitor their behavior to reach a goal (Reynolds & others, 2018).

### EXPECTANCY LEARNING AND INFORMATION

In studying the purposiveness of behavior, Tolman went beyond the stimuli and responses of Pavlov and Skinner to focus on cognitive mechanisms. Tolman said that when classical conditioning and operant conditioning occur, the organism acquires certain expectations. In classical conditioning, the young boy fears the rabbit because he expects it will hurt him. In operant conditioning, a woman works hard all week because she expects a paycheck on Friday. Expectancies are acquired from people's experiences with their environment. Expectancies influence a variety of human experiences. We set the goals we do because we believe that we can reach them.

Expectancies also play a role in the placebo effect, described earlier. Many painkillers have been shown to be more effective in reducing pain if patients can see the intravenous injection sites (Price, Finniss, & Benedetti, 2008). If patients can observe that they are getting a drug, they can harness their own expectations for pain reduction.

Tolman (1932) emphasized that the information value of the conditioned stimulus is important as a signal or an expectation that an unconditioned stimulus will follow. Anticipating contemporary thinking, Tolman believed that the information that the CS provides is the key to understanding classical conditioning.

One contemporary view of classical conditioning describes an organism as an information seeker, using logical and perceptual relations among events, along with preconceptions, to form a representation of the world (Rescorla, 2003, 2004, 2005, 2006a, 2006b, 2006c, 2009).

A classic experiment conducted by Leon Kamin (1968) illustrates the importance of an organism's history and the information provided by a conditioned stimulus in classical conditioning. Kamin conditioned a rat by repeatedly pairing a tone (CS) and a shock (US) until the tone alone produced fear (CR). Then he continued to pair the tone with the shock, but he turned on a light (a second CS) each time the tone sounded. Even though he repeatedly paired the light (CS) and the shock (US), the rat showed no conditioning to the light (the light by itself produced no CR). Conditioning to the light was blocked, almost as if the rat had not paid attention. The rat apparently used the tone as a signal to predict that a shock would be coming; information about the light's pairing with the shock was redundant with the information already learned about the tone's pairing with the shock. In this experiment, conditioning was governed not by the contiguity of the CS and US but instead by the rat's history and the informational value of the stimuli it encountered. The rat already possessed a good signal for the shock; the additional CS was not useful (Mackintosh, 2018).

### LATENT LEARNING

Experiments on latent learning provide other evidence to support the role of cognition in learning. **Latent learning** or **implicit learning** is unreinforced learning that is not immediately reflected in behavior.

● **latent learning or implicit learning** Unreinforced learning that is not immediately reflected in behavior.

In one study, researchers put two groups of hungry rats in a maze and required them to find their way from a starting point to an end point (Tolman & Honzik, 1930). The first group found food (a reinforcer) at the end point; the second group found nothing there. In the operant conditioning view, the first group should learn the maze better than the second group, which is exactly what happened. However, when the researchers subsequently took some of the rats from the nonreinforced group and gave them food at the end point of the maze, they quickly began to run the maze as effectively as the reinforced group. The nonreinforced rats apparently had learned a great deal about the maze as they roamed around and explored it. However, their learning was *latent,* stored cognitively in their memories but not yet expressed behaviorally. When these rats were given a good reason (reinforcement with food) to run the maze speedily, they called on their latent learning to help them reach the end of the maze more quickly.

Outside a laboratory, latent learning is evident when you walk around a new setting to get "the lay of the land." The first time you visited your college campus, you may have wandered about without a specific destination in mind. Exploring the environment made you better prepared when the time came to find that 8 A.M. class.

## Insight Learning

Like Tolman, the German gestalt psychologist Wolfgang Köhler believed that cognitive factors play a significant role in learning. Köhler spent four months in the Canary Islands during World War I observing the behavior of apes. There he conducted two fascinating

**FIGURE 11** **Insight Learning** Sultan, one of Köhler's brightest chimps, was faced with the problem of reaching a cluster of bananas overhead. He solved the problem by stacking boxes on top of one another to reach the bananas. Köhler called this type of problem solving "insight learning." (first) ©SuperStock; (second) ©SuperStock; (third) ©SuperStock

experiments—the stick problem and the box problem. Although these two experiments are basically the same, the solutions to the problems are different. In both situations, the ape discovers that it cannot reach an alluring piece of fruit, either because the fruit is too high or because it is outside of the ape's cage and beyond reach. To solve the stick problem, the ape has to insert a small stick inside a larger stick to reach the fruit. To master the box problem, the ape must stack several boxes to reach the fruit (Figure 11).

According to Köhler (1925), solving these problems does not involve trial and error or simple connections between stimuli and responses. Rather, when the ape realizes that its customary actions are not going to help it get the fruit, it often sits for a period of time and appears to ponder how to solve the problem. Then it quickly rises, as if it has had a sudden flash of insight, piles the boxes on top of one another, and gets the fruit. **Insight learning** is a form of problem solving in which the organism develops a sudden insight into or understanding of a problem's solution.

● **insight learning** A form of problem solving in which the organism develops a sudden insight into or understanding of a problem's solution.

The idea that insight learning is essentially different from learning through trial and error or through conditioning has always been controversial (Spence, 1938). Insight learning appears to entail both gradual and sudden processes, and understanding how these lead to problem solving continues to fascinate psychologists (Chu & MacGregor, 2011; Weisberg, 2015).

Research has documented that nonhuman primates are capable of remarkable learning that certainly appears to be insightful (Manrique, Völter, & Call, 2013). In one study, researchers observed orangutans trying to figure out a way to get a tempting peanut out of a clear plastic tube (Mendes, Hanus, & Call, 2007). The primates wandered about their enclosures, experimenting with various strategies. Typically, they paused for a moment before finally landing on a solution: Little by little they filled the tube with water that they transferred by mouth from their water dishes to the tube. Once the peanut floated to the top, the clever orangutans had their snack. Other research shows that chimps can solve the floating peanut task through observational learning (Tennie, Call, & Tomasello, 2010).

Insight learning requires that we think "outside the box," setting aside previous expectations and assumptions. One way to enhance insight learning and creativity in human beings is through multicultural experiences (Leung & others, 2008). Correlational studies have shown that time spent living abroad is associated with higher insight learning performance among MBA students (Maddux & Galinsky, 2009). Experimental studies have also demonstrated this effect. In one study, U.S. college students were randomly assigned to view one of two slide shows—one about Chinese and U.S. culture and the other about a control topic. Those who saw the multicultural slide show scored higher on measures of creativity and insight, and these changes persisted for a week (Leung & others, 2008).

Importantly, we can gain the benefits of multicultural exposure even without travel abroad or specific slide shows. One of the most dramatic changes in U.S. higher education is the increasing diversity of the student body. Might this growing diversity benefit students? Research suggests that it does. For instance, in a study of over 53,000 undergraduates at 124 colleges and universities, students' reported interactions with individuals from other racial and ethnic backgrounds predicted a variety of positive outcomes, including academic achievement, intellectual growth, and social competence (Hu & Kuh, 2003).

Many universities recognize that as U.S. society becomes more multiculturally diverse, students must be prepared to interact in a diverse community as they enter the job market. Participation in diversity courses in college is related to cognitive development (Bowman, 2010) and civic involvement (Gurin & others, 2002), with outcomes especially positive for non-Latino White students (Byrd, 2015; Hu & Kuh, 2003). Diverse groups provide broader knowledge and more varied perspectives than do homogeneous groups, to the positive benefit of all group members. As university communities become more diverse, they offer students an ever-greater opportunity to share and to benefit from those differences.

***test yourself***

1. What did Tolman mean by the purposiveness of behavior?
2. How do expectancies develop through classical and operant conditioning?
3. Define latent learning and insight learning and give an example of each.

# 6. BIOLOGICAL, CULTURAL, AND PSYCHOLOGICAL FACTORS IN LEARNING

Albert Einstein had many special talents. He combined enormous creativity with keen analytic ability to develop some of the twentieth century's most important insights into the nature of matter and the universe. Genes obviously endowed Einstein with extraordinary intellectual skills that enabled him to think and reason on a very high plane, but cultural factors also contributed to his genius. Einstein received an excellent, rigorous European education, and later in the United States he experienced the freedom and support believed to be important in creative exploration. Would Einstein have been able to develop his skills fully and to make such brilliant insights if he had grown up in a less advantageous environment? It is unlikely. Clearly, both biological *and* cultural factors contribute to learning.

## Biological Constraints

Human beings cannot breathe under water, fish cannot ski, and cows cannot solve math problems. The structure of an organism's body permits certain kinds of learning and inhibits others. For example, chimpanzees cannot learn to speak human languages because they lack the necessary vocal equipment. In animals, various aspects of their physical makeup can influence what they can learn. Sometimes, species-typical behaviors (or instincts) can override even the best reinforcers, as we now consider.

### INSTINCTIVE DRIFT

Keller and Marion Breland (1961), students of B. F. Skinner, used operant conditioning to train animals to perform at fairs and conventions and in television advertisements. They applied Skinner's techniques to teach pigs to cart large wooden nickels to a piggy bank and deposit them. They also trained raccoons to pick up a coin and drop it into a metal tray.

**FIGURE 12** **Instinctive Drift** This raccoon's skill in using its hands made it an excellent basketball player, but because of instinctive drift, the raccoon had a much more difficult time dropping coins into a tray. Source: Boston Public Library

Although the pigs and raccoons, as well as chickens and other animals, performed most of the tasks well (raccoons became adept basketball players, for example—see Figure 12), some of the animals began acting strangely. Instead of picking up the large wooden nickels and carrying them to the piggy bank, the pigs dropped the nickels on the ground, shoved them with their snouts, tossed them in the air, and then repeated these actions. The raccoons began to hold on to their coins rather than dropping them into the metal tray. When two coins were introduced, the raccoons rubbed them together in a miserly fashion. Somehow these behaviors overwhelmed the strength of the reinforcement. This example of biological influences on learning illustrates **instinctive drift**, the tendency of animals to revert to instinctive behavior that interferes with learning.

● **instinctive drift** The tendency of animals to revert to instinctive behavior that interferes with learning.

Why were the pigs and the raccoons misbehaving? The pigs were rooting, an instinct that is used to uncover edible roots. The raccoons were engaging in an instinctive food-washing response. Their instinctive drift interfered with learning.

### PREPAREDNESS

Some animals learn readily in one situation but have difficulty learning in slightly different circumstances (Garcia & Koelling, 1966, 2009). The difficulty might result not from some aspect of the learning situation but from the organism's biological predisposition (Seligman, 1970). **Preparedness** is the species-specific biological predisposition to learn in certain ways but not others.

● **preparedness** The species-specific biological predisposition to learn in certain ways but not others.

Much evidence for preparedness comes from research on taste aversion (Garcia, 1989; Garcia & Koelling, 2009). Recall that taste aversion involves a single trial of learning the association between a particular taste and nausea. Rats that experience low levels of radiation after eating show a strong aversion to the food they were eating when the radiation made them ill. This aversion can last for as long as 32 days. Such long-term effects cannot be accounted for by classical conditioning, which would argue that a single pairing of the conditioned and unconditioned stimuli would not last that long (Garcia, Ervin, & Koelling, 1966). Taste aversion learning occurs in animals, including humans, that choose their food based on taste and smell. Other species are prepared to learn rapid associations between, for instance, colors of foods and illness.

Another example of preparedness comes from research on conditioning humans and monkeys to associate snakes with fear. Research has demonstrated that snakes have a natural power to evoke fear in many mammals (Åhs & others, 2018; Bertels & others, 2018). Many monkeys and humans fear snakes, and both monkeys and humans are very quick to learn the association between snakes and fear. In classical conditioning studies, when pictures of snakes (CS) are paired with electrical shocks (US), the snakes are likely to quickly and strongly evoke fear (CR). Interestingly, pairing pictures of, say, flowers (CS) with electrical shocks produces much weaker associations. More significantly, pictures of snakes can serve as conditioned stimuli for fearful responses, even when the pictures are presented so rapidly that they cannot be consciously perceived (Öhman & Mineka, 2001).

The link between snakes and fear has been demonstrated not only in classical conditioning paradigms. Monkeys that have been raised in the lab and that have never seen a snake rapidly learn to fear snakes, even entirely by observational learning. Lab monkeys that see a videotape of a monkey expressing fear toward a snake learn to be afraid of snakes faster than monkeys seeing the same fear video spliced so that the feared object is a rabbit, a flower, or a mushroom (Öhman & Mineka, 2003).

Such results seem to demonstrate preparedness among mammals to associate snakes with fear and aversive stimuli. They suggest that this association is related to the amygdala (the part of the limbic system that is related to emotion) and is difficult to modify. Preparedness for fear of snakes might have emerged out of the threat that reptiles likely posed to our evolutionary ancestors.

## Cultural Influences

Traditionally, interest in the cultural context of human learning has been limited, partly because the organisms in those contexts typically were animals. The question arises, how might culture influence human learning? Most psychologists agree that the principles of classical conditioning, operant conditioning, and observational learning are universal and are powerful learning processes in every culture. However, culture can influence the *degree* to which these learning processes are used (Matsumoto & Juang, 2017). For example, Mexican American students may learn more through observational learning, while non-Latino White students may be more accustomed to learn through direct instruction (Martin & others, 2017).

In addition, culture can determine the *content* of learning (Mistry, Contreras, & Dutta, 2013; Zhang & Sternberg, 2013). We cannot learn about something we do not experience. The 4-year-old who grows up among the Bushmen of the Kalahari Desert is unlikely to learn about taking baths and eating with a knife and fork. Similarly, a child growing up in Chicago is unlikely to be skilled at tracking animals and finding water-bearing roots in the desert. Learning often requires practice, and certain behaviors are practiced more often in some cultures than in others. In Bali, many children are skilled dancers by the age of 6, whereas Norwegian children are much more likely to be good skiers and skaters by that age.

*On the Indonesian island of Bali, young children learn traditional dances, whereas in Norway children commonly learn to ski early in life. As cultures vary, so does the content of learning.*

(first) ©Paul Chesley/Stone/Getty Images; (second) ©Paul A. Souders/Getty Images

## Psychological Constraints

Are there psychological constraints on learning? For animals, the answer is probably no. For humans, the answer may well be yes. This section opened with the claim that fish cannot ski. The truth of this statement is clear. Biological circumstances make it impossible. If we put biological considerations aside, we might ask ourselves about times in our lives when we feel like a fish trying to ski—when we feel that we just do not have what it takes to learn a skill or master a task (Talsma & others, 2018).

Some people believe that humans have particular learning styles that make it easier for them to learn in some ways but not others. For example, you may have heard that someone can be a visual learner (he or she learns by seeing), an aural learner (the person learns by listening), or a kinesthetic learner (the individual learns through hands-on experience). Although these labels may be popular, there is no evidence that teaching people in a way that matches their learning style leads to better learning (Pashler & others, 2008; Rohrer & Pashler, 2012). However, our beliefs about learning can affect whether we learn.

Carol Dweck (2006; Gunderson & others, 2018; Rattan & others, 2015) uses the term *mindset* to describe the way our beliefs about ability dictate what goals we set for ourselves, what we think we *can* learn, and ultimately what we *do* learn. Individuals have one of two mindsets: a *fixed mindset,* in which they believe that their qualities are carved in stone and cannot change; or a *growth mindset,* in which they believe their qualities can change and improve through their effort. These two mindsets have implications for the meaning of failure. From a fixed mindset, failure means lack of ability. From a growth mindset, however, failure tells the person what he or she still needs to learn. Your mindset influences whether you will be optimistic or pessimistic, what your goals will be, how hard you will strive to reach those goals, and how successful you are in college and after.

Dweck (2006) studied first-year pre-med majors taking their first chemistry class in college. Students with a growth mindset got higher grades than those with a fixed mindset. Even when they did not do well on a test, the growth-mindset students bounced back on the next test. Fixed-mindset students typically read and re-read the text and class notes or tried to memorize everything verbatim. The fixed-mindset students who did poorly on tests concluded that chemistry and maybe all pre-med courses were not for them. By contrast, growth-mindset students took charge of their motivation and learning, searching for themes and principles in the course and going over mistakes until they understood why they had made them. In Dweck's analysis, "They were studying to learn, not just ace the test. And, actually, this is why they got higher grades—not because they were smarter or had a better background in science" (Dweck, 2006, p. 61).

Dweck and her colleagues have continued to explore ways to improve students' motivation to achieve and succeed (Rattan & others, 2015). In one study, they assigned two groups of students to eight sessions of either (1) study skills instruction or (2) study skills instruction plus information about the importance of developing a growth mindset (called *incremental theory* in the research) (Blackwell, Trzesniewski, & Dweck, 2007). Exercises that increase growth-mindset emphasized that the brain is like a muscle that can change and grow as it is exercised and develops new connections. Students were informed that the more they challenged their brain to learn, the more their brain cells would grow. Prior to the intervention, both groups had a pattern of declining math scores. Following the intervention, the group that received the study skills instruction *plus* the growth-mindset emphasis reversed the downward trend and improved their math achievement.

Here are some effective strategies for developing a growth mindset (Dweck, 2006):

- *Understand that your intelligence and thinking skills are not fixed but can change.* Even if you are extremely bright, with effort you can increase your intelligence.
- *Become passionate about learning and stretch your mind in challenging situations.* It is easy to withdraw into a fixed mindset when the going gets tough. However, as you bump up against obstacles, keep growing, work harder, stay the course, and improve your strategies, you will become a more successful person.
- *Think about the growth mindsets of people you admire.* Possibly you have a hero, someone who has achieved something extraordinary. You may have thought his or her accomplishments came easily because the person is so talented. If you find out more about this person, though, you likely will discover that hard work and effort over a long period of time were responsible for his or her achievements.
- *Begin now.* If you have a fixed mindset, commit to changing now. Think about when, where, and how you will begin using your new growth mindset.

Dweck's work challenges us to consider the limits we place on our own learning. Our beliefs about ability profoundly influence what we try to learn. As any 7-year-old with a growth mindset would tell you, you never know what you can do until you try.

**test yourself**

1. What are two biological constraints on learning?
2. How does culture influence learning?
3. What is the difference between a fixed mindset and a growth mindset?

## 7. LEARNING AND HEALTH AND WELLNESS

In this chapter, we have examined the main psychological approaches to learning. In this final section, we consider specific ways that research on learning has shed light on human health and wellness. We examine in particular the factors that animal learning models have identified as playing an important role in the experience of stress–which, as you will recall from the chapter "Biological Foundations of Behavior", is the organism's response to a threat in the environment. A great deal of research in learning has relied primarily on models of animals, such as rats, to examine the principles that underlie human learning. Research on the stress response in rats provides useful insights into how we humans can deal with stress.

©Tom Merton/Image Source

### STRESS AND PREDICTABILITY

One very powerful aspect of potentially stressful experiences is their predictability. For a rat, predictability might depend on getting a warning buzzer before receiving a shock. Although the rat still experiences the shock, a buzzer-preceded shock causes less stress than a shock that is received with no warning (Abbott, Schoen, & Badia, 1984). Even having *good* experiences on a predictable schedule is less stressful than having good things happen at random times. For example, a rat might do very well receiving its daily chow at specific times during the day, but if the timing is random, the rat experiences stress. Similarly, when you receive a gift on your birthday or a holiday, the experience feels good. However, if someone surprises you with a present out of the blue, you might feel some stress as you wonder, "What is this person up to?"

Also relevant is classic research by Judith Rodin and her colleagues. In this study, nursing home residents showed better adjustment if they experienced a given number of visits at predictable times rather than the same number of visits at random times (Langer & Rodin, 1976).

## STRESS AND CONTROL

Feeling in control may be a key to avoiding feelings of stress over difficulties (Carver & Scheier, 2013). Specifically, once you have experienced control over negative events, you may be "protected" from stress, even during trying times.

Returning to an animal model, suppose that a rat has been trained to avoid a shock by pressing a lever. Over time, even when the lever is no longer related to the shock, the rat presses it during the shock—and experiences less stress. We might imagine the rat thinking, "Gee, it would be worse if I weren't pressing this lever!" Researchers have also found links between having control and experiencing stress in humans. For example, as mentioned above with the nursing home study (Langer & Rodin, 1976), residents are more likely to thrive if they receive visits at times they personally choose. In addition, simply having a plant to take care of is associated with living longer for nursing home residents.

A lack of control over aversive stimuli can be particularly stressful. For example, individuals exposed to uncontrollable loud blasts of noise show lower immune system function (Sieber & others, 1992). One result of exposure to uncontrollable negative events is *learned helplessness,* which we examined earlier in this chapter. In learned helplessness, the organism has learned through experience that outcomes are not controllable. As a result, the organism stops trying to exert control.

Research has shown that, to break the lock of learned helplessness, dogs and rats have to be forcibly moved to escape an aversive shock (Seligman, Rosellini, & Kozak, 1975). From such animal studies, we can appreciate how difficult it may be for individuals who find themselves in situations in which they have little control—for example, women who are victims of domestic violence (Walker, 2009)—to take action. We can also appreciate the helplessness sometimes experienced by students with learning difficulties who withdraw from their coursework because they feel unable to influence outcomes in school (Gwernan-Jones & Burden, 2010).

## STRESS AND IMPROVEMENT

Imagine that you have two rats, both of which are receiving mild electrical shocks. One of them, Jerry, receives 50 shocks every hour, and the other, Chuck-E, receives 10 shocks every hour. The next day both rats are switched to 25 shocks every hour. Which one is more stressed out at the end of the second day? The answer is that even though Jerry has experienced more shocks in general, Chuck-E is more likely to show the wear and tear of stress. In Jerry's world, even with 25 shocks an hour, *things are better*. The perception of improvement, even in a situation that is objectively worse than another, is related to lower stress (Sapolsky, 2004).

## OUTLETS FOR FRUSTRATION

When things are not going well for us, it often feels good to find an outlet, such as going for a run or, perhaps even better, taking a kickboxing class. Likewise, for a rat, having an outlet for life's frustrations is related to lower stress symptoms. Rats that have a wooden post to gnaw on or even a furry little friend to complain to are less stressed out in response to negative circumstances.

Although studies using rats and dogs may seem far afield of our everyday experiences, researchers' observations provide important clues for avoiding stress. When we cultivate predictable environments and take control of circumstances, stress decreases. Further, when we can see improvement, even in difficult times, stress is likely to diminish. Finally, when we have an outlet for our frustrations in life—whether it is physical exercise, writing, or art—we can relieve our stress. When it comes to stress, humans have a lot to learn from rats.

### test yourself

1. Based on research involving animal models, what are four ways in which human beings can reduce stress?
2. What is the main effect of learned helplessness on an organism?
3. Why do individuals who are experiencing domestic violence often have difficulty overcoming their troubles?

SUMMARY

## 1. TYPES OF LEARNING

Learning is a systematic, relatively permanent change in behavior that occurs through experience. Associative learning involves learning by making a connection between two events. Observational learning is learning by watching what other people do. Conditioning is the process by which associative learning occurs. In classical conditioning, organisms learn the association between two stimuli. In operant conditioning, they learn the association between behavior and a consequence.

## 2. CLASSICAL CONDITIONING

Classical conditioning occurs when a neutral stimulus becomes associated with a meaningful stimulus and comes to elicit a similar response. Pavlov discovered that an organism learns the association between an unconditioned stimulus (US) and a conditioned stimulus (CS). The US automatically produces the unconditioned response (UR). After conditioning (CS–US pairing), the CS elicits the conditioned response (CR) by itself. Acquisition in classical conditioning is the initial linking of stimuli and responses, which involves a neutral stimulus being associated with the US so that the CS comes to elicit the CR. Two important aspects of acquisition are contiguity and contingency.

Generalization in classical conditioning is the tendency of a new stimulus that is similar to the original conditioned stimulus to elicit a response that is similar to the conditioned response. Discrimination is the process of learning to respond to certain stimuli and not to others. Extinction is the weakening of the CR in the absence of the US. Spontaneous recovery is the recurrence of a CR after a time delay without further conditioning. Renewal is the occurrence of the CR (even after extinction) when the CS is presented in a novel environment.

In humans, classical conditioning has been applied to eliminating fears, treating addiction, understanding taste aversion, and explaining different experiences such as pleasant emotions and drug overdose.

## 3. OPERANT CONDITIONING

Operant conditioning is a form of learning in which the consequences of behavior produce changes in the probability of the behavior's occurrence. Skinner described the behavior of the organism as operant: The behavior operates on the environment, and the environment in turn operates on the organism. Whereas classical conditioning involves respondent behavior, operant conditioning involves operant behavior. In most instances, operant conditioning is better at explaining voluntary behavior than is classical conditioning.

Thorndike's law of effect states that behaviors followed by pleasant outcomes are strengthened, whereas behaviors followed by unpleasant outcomes are weakened. Skinner built on this idea to develop the notion of operant conditioning.

Shaping is the process of rewarding approximations of desired behavior in order to shorten the learning process. Principles of reinforcement include the distinction between positive reinforcement (the frequency of a behavior increases because it is followed by a rewarding stimulus) and negative reinforcement (the frequency of behavior increases because it is followed by the removal of an aversive, or unpleasant, stimulus). Positive reinforcement can be classified as primary reinforcement (using reinforcers that are innately satisfying) and secondary reinforcement (using reinforcers that acquire positive value through experience).

Reinforcement can also be continuous (a behavior is reinforced every time) or partial (a behavior is reinforced only a portion of the time). Schedules of reinforcement–fixed ratio, variable ratio, fixed interval, and variable interval–determine when a behavior will be reinforced.

Operant, or instrumental, conditioning involves generalization (giving the same response to similar stimuli), discrimination (responding to stimuli that signal that a behavior will or will not be reinforced), and extinction (a decreasing tendency to perform a previously reinforced behavior when reinforcement is stopped).

Punishment is a consequence that decreases the likelihood that a behavior will occur. In positive punishment, a behavior decreases when it is followed by a (typically unpleasant) stimulus. In negative punishment, a behavior decreases when a positive stimulus is removed from it.

Applied behavior analysis, or behavior modification, involves the application of operant conditioning principles to a variety of real-life behaviors.

## 4. OBSERVATIONAL LEARNING

Observational learning occurs when a person observes and imitates someone else's behavior. Bandura identified four main processes in observational learning: attention (paying heed to what someone is saying or doing), retention (encoding that information and keeping it in memory so that you can retrieve it), motor reproduction (imitating the actions of the person being observed), and reinforcement (seeing the person attain a reward for the activity).

## 5. COGNITIVE FACTORS IN LEARNING

Tolman emphasized the purposiveness of behavior. His belief was that much of behavior is goal-directed. In studying purposiveness, Tolman went beyond stimuli and responses to discuss cognitive mechanisms; he believed that expectancies, acquired through experiences with the environment, are an important cognitive mechanism in learning.

Latent learning is unreinforced learning that is not immediately reflected in behavior. Latent learning may occur when a rat or a person roams a particular location and shows knowledge of the area when that knowledge is rewarded.

Köhler developed the concept of insight learning, a form of problem solving in which the organism develops a sudden insight into or understanding of a problem's solution.

## 6. BIOLOGICAL, CULTURAL, AND PSYCHOLOGICAL FACTORS IN LEARNING

Biology restricts what an organism can learn from experience. These constraints include instinctive drift (the tendency of animals to revert to instinctive behavior that interferes with learned behavior), preparedness (the species-specific biological predisposition to learn in certain ways but not in others), and taste aversion (the biological predisposition to avoid foods that have caused sickness in the past).

Although most psychologists agree that the principles of classical conditioning, operant conditioning, and observational learning are universal, cultural customs can influence the degree to which these learning processes are used. Culture also often determines the content of learning.

In addition, what we learn is determined in part by what we believe we can learn. Dweck emphasizes that individuals benefit enormously from having a growth mindset rather than a fixed mindset.

## 7. LEARNING AND HEALTH AND WELLNESS

Research using rats and other animals has demonstrated four important variables involved in the human stress response: predictability, perceived control, perceptions of improvement, and outlets for frustration.

# key *terms*

acquisition
applied behavior analysis or behavior modification
associative learning
aversive conditioning
avoidance learning
behaviorism
classical conditioning
conditioned response (CR)
conditioned stimulus (CS)
counterconditioning
discrimination (in classical conditioning)
discrimination (in operant conditioning)
extinction (in classical conditioning)
extinction (in operant conditioning)
generalization (in classical conditioning)
generalization (in operant conditioning)
habituation
insight learning
instinctive drift
latent learning or implicit learning
law of effect
learned helplessness
learning
negative punishment
negative reinforcement
observational learning
operant conditioning or instrumental conditioning
positive punishment
positive reinforcement
primary reinforcer
punishment
preparedness
reinforcement
renewal
schedules of reinforcement
secondary reinforcer
shaping
spontaneous recovery
unconditioned response (UR)
unconditioned stimulus (US)

# apply your *knowledge*

1. Enlist some of your classmates to play this mind game on your professor. Every time your instructor moves to the right side of the room during lecture, be more attentive, smile, and nod. Start out by shaping—every time he or she moves even a little to the right, give a smile or nod. See how far you can get the instructor to go using this simple reward. In one introductory psychology class, students got their professor to move all the way to the right wall of the classroom, where she leaned, completely clueless.

2. The next time you are alone with a friend, try your best to use shaping and the principles of operant conditioning to get the person to touch the tip of his or her nose. Can you do it?

3. Demonstrate Pavlov's work with your friends. First buy some lemons and slice them. Then gather a group of friends to watch something on TV together, maybe the Academy Awards or the Super Bowl. Pick a conditioned stimulus that you know will come up a lot on the show—for example, someone saying "thank you" during the Oscars or a soft drink or beer ad during the Super Bowl. For the first half hour, everyone has to suck on a lemon slice (the US) when the CS is presented. After the first half hour, take the lemons away. Have everyone report on their salivation levels (the CR) whenever the CS is presented later in the show. What happens?

4. Positive reinforcement and negative reinforcement can be difficult concepts to grasp. The real-world examples and accompanying practice exercises on the following website should help to clarify the distinction:

   http://psych.athabascau.ca/html/prtut/reinpair.htm

5. Imagine that you are about to begin an internship in an organization where you would like to have a permanent position someday. Use the processes of observational learning to describe your strategy for making the most of your internship.

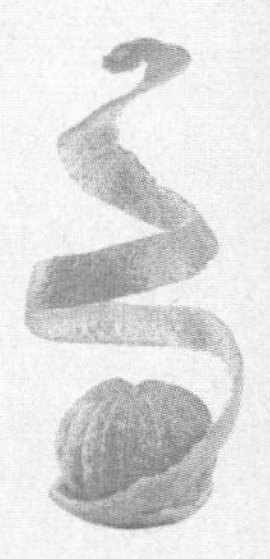

# CHAPTER 7

CHAPTER OUTLINE

1. The Nature of Memory
2. Memory Encoding
3. Memory Storage
4. Memory Retrieval
5. Forgetting
6. Study Tips from the Science of Memory
7. Memory and Health and Wellness

# Memory

## "She Didn't Know Who I Was"

**Jeff Hartung and Angela Sartin-Hartung had been married for 13 years when she was hit by a car as she crossed a street.** Injuries to her brain devastated her memory. When she awoke from a medically induced coma, Angela could walk and talk but had lost all memory of the last 16 years. She thought she was still married to her first husband (who had died years before) and her children (who were now teens) were still toddlers (Thorbecke, 2018). Jeff found that he was a stranger to his wife, who assumed that he was a doctor working on her case. He stayed at her side and wooed her all over again. As she recovered, he took her on long walks triggering occasional memories and giving them a chance to bond for the first time, all over again. Eventually Angela fell in love with her husband as they made new memories together. Their happy ending notwithstanding, Angela grieved her lost memories, especially of watching her children grow up. The memories we share with others are part of the glue that bonds us. Memories are precious because they represent a lasting imprint of our experiences, moments from the past that give our lives meaning. ●

# PREVIEW

Through memory, we weave the past into the present and establish a foundation for the future. In this chapter, we explore key processes of memory, including how information gets into our memory, how it is stored, retrieved, and sometimes forgotten. We probe what the science of memory can teach us about the best way to study and retain course material. In the final section, we look at the link between memory and health and wellness, consider strategies by which to keep memory sharp as we age.

## 1. THE NATURE OF MEMORY

Shining stars, full moon: A beautiful evening is coming to a close. Looking at your significant other you think, "I'll never forget this night." How is it possible that in fact you never do forget it? Years hence, you might tell your children about that special night many years ago, even if you had not thought about it in the years since. How does one perfect night become a part of your enduring memory?

Psychologists define **memory** as the retention of information or experience over time. Memory occurs through three important processes: encoding, storage, and retrieval. For memory to work, we have to take in information (*encode* the sights and sounds of that night), store it or represent it in some manner (*retain* it in some mental storehouse), and then recall it for a later purpose (*retrieve* it when asked, "How did you two end up together?"). In the next three sections, we focus on these phases of memory: encoding, storage, and retrieval (Figure 1).

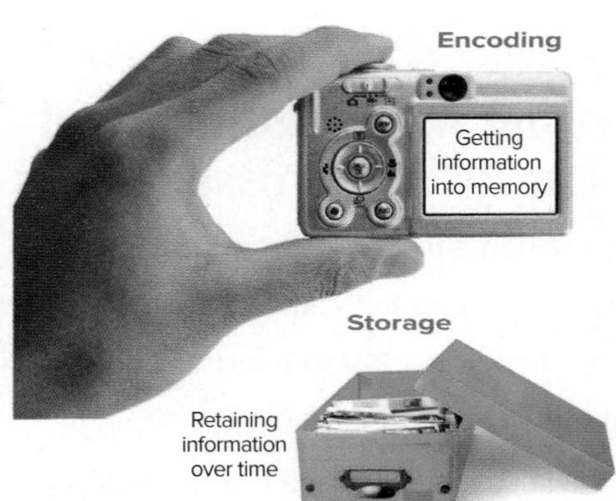

**FIGURE 1 Processing Information in Memory** As you read about the many aspects of memory in this chapter, think about the organization of memory in terms of these three main activities. (top) ©gbautista87/iStock/Getty Images; (middle) ©gvictoria/iStock/Getty Images; (bottom) ©McGraw-Hill Education/Gary He, photographer

- **memory** The retention of information or experience over time as the result of three key processes: encoding, storage, and retrieval.
- **encoding** The first step in memory; the process by which information gets into memory storage.

Except for those occasions when memory fails, you probably do not often consider how much everything you do or say depends on the smooth operation of your memory system. Think of a restaurant server. He has to attend to the orders he gets—who is asking for what and how each person would like the food prepared. To do so, he must encode the information about each customer and each order. He might look at each customer and associate the person's face with the menu items requested. Without writing anything down, he must retain the information, at least until he gets the orders to the kitchen or onto the computer. He might rehearse the orders in his mind as he walks to the back of the restaurant. Delivering the food to the table, he must accurately retrieve the information about who ordered what. Human memory systems are remarkable when we consider how much information we put into our memories and how much we must retrieve to perform life's activities.

### *test yourself*

1. How do psychologists define memory?
2. What three important processes play key roles in memory?
3. Which memory process is centrally involved when we recall information?

## 2. MEMORY ENCODING

The first step in memory is **encoding**, the process by which information gets into memory storage. Listening to a lecture, watching a play, or talking with a friend, you are encoding information into memory. Some information gets into memory virtually automatically, whereas encoding other information takes effort. Here we examine some of the encoding processes that require effort. These include paying attention, processing deeply, elaborating, and using mental imagery.

### Attention

To begin encoding, we have to pay attention to information (Engle, 2018). Recall from the chapter "Sensation and Perception" that *selective attention* involves focusing on a specific aspect of experience while ignoring others. Attention is selective because the brain's resources are limited—they cannot attend to everything. These limitations mean that we must attend selectively to some things and ignore others. So, on that special night with your romantic partner, you never noticed the bus that roared by or the people whom you passed as you strolled along the street. Those aspects of that night did not make it into your enduring memory.

In addition to selective attention, psychologists have described two other ways that attention may be allocated: divided attention and sustained attention. **Divided attention** involves concentrating on more than one activity at the same time (Sahakyan & Malmberg, 2018). If you are checking your phone while you are reading this chapter, you are engaging in divided attention. **Sustained attention** (also called **vigilance**) is the ability to maintain attention to a selected stimulus for a prolonged period of time (Danckert & Merrifield, 2018; Waninger & others, 2018). For example, paying close attention to your notes while studying for an exam is a good application of sustained attention.

Divided attention can be quite detrimental to encoding. *Multitasking,* which involves dividing attention not just between two activities but among three or more, is the ultimate in divided attention. High school and college students often divide their attention among homework, instant messaging, tweeting, and watching YouTube, simultaneously. Multitaskers are often very confident in their multitasking skills (Pattillo, 2010). But, multitasking has negative consequences for memory (Carrier & others, 2015). Listening to a class lecture while also texting or playing a game on your phone is likely to interfere with encoding the lecture.

©Image Source/Corbis

● **divided attention** Concentrating on more than one activity at the same time.

● **sustained attention or vigilance** The ability to maintain attention to a selected stimulus for a prolonged period of time.

## Levels of Processing

Another factor that influences memory is whether we engage with information superficially (shallow processing) or really get into it (deep processing). Fergus Craik and Robert Lockhart (1972) first suggested that encoding can be influenced by levels of processing. The term **levels of processing** refers to a continuum from shallow to intermediate to deep.

● **levels of processing** A continuum of memory processing from shallow to intermediate to deep, with deeper processing producing better memory.

Imagine that you are asked to memorize a list of words, including the word *mom.* Shallow processing means noting the physical features of a stimulus, such as the shapes of the letters in the word *mom.* Intermediate processing involves giving the stimulus a label, as in reading the word *mom.* The deepest level of processing entails thinking about the meaning of a stimulus–for instance, thinking about the meaning of the word *mom,* about your own mother, her face, and her special qualities.

The more deeply we process, the better the memory (Alexander, 2018; Rose & Craik, 2012; Rose, Craik, & Buchsbaum, 2015) (Figure 2). For example, if we encode something meaningful about a face and make associations with it, we are more likely to remember it (Mattarozzi & others, 2018).

| Level of Processing | Process | Examples |
|---|---|---|
| Shallow | Physical and perceptual features are analyzed. | The lines, angles, and contour that make up the physical appearance of an object, such as a car, are detected. |
| Intermediate | Stimulus is recognized and labeled. | The object is recognized as a car. |
| Deep | Semantic, meaningful, symbolic characteristics are used. | Associations connected with car are brought to mind—you think about the Porsche or Ferrari you hope to buy or the fun you and friends had on spring break when you drove a car to the beach. |

Depth of Processing (arrow: Shallow → Deep)

**FIGURE 2** **Depth of Processing** According to the levels of processing principle, deeper processing of stimuli produces better memory of them. Source: Alexander (2018); Rose & Craik (2012); Rose, Craik, & Buchsbaum (2015).

Laptops and tablets can interfere with learning because they distract attention. Yet, even when digital devices are used *only* for notes (not checking social media, or live tweeting an introductory psychology lecture), pen and paper outperform laptops in student memory for material (Mueller & Oppenheimer, 2014). Here's why: Most of us can type far faster than we can write by hand. When we take notes on a keyboard, we become like a court reporter, recording everything that is said verbatim. When we do this, we prevent active, deep encoding. Writing by hand, we have to think about what we are writing down—interacting actively with the material so that we can jot down the most important points. This sort of focused attention during encoding is far more effective than having a lot of notes but no actual memory of the lecture (Ravizza, Uitvlugt, & Fenn, 2017).

## Elaboration

**elaboration** The formation of a number of different connections around a stimulus at any given level of memory encoding.

Another way to improve encoding is through elaboration. **Elaboration** refers to the formation of a number of different connections around a stimulus at any given level of memory encoding. When we elaborate during encoding we develop many mental connections between new information and what we already know.

Elaboration is like creating a big spider web of links between a new piece of information and it can occur at any level of processing. For the word *mom,* a person can elaborate on *mom* even at a shallow level–for example, by thinking of the shapes of the letters and how they relate to the shapes of other letters, say, how an *m* looks like two *n*'s. At a deeper level of processing, a person might elaborate by thinking about various mothers she knows, images of mothers in art, and portrayals of mothers on television. Generally speaking, the more elaborate the processing, the better memory will be. Deep, elaborate processing is a powerful way to remember because it creates paths that we can use for retrieval.

When we elaborate on material, we memorize without trying to memorize. For instance, you might use the process of elaboration in remembering the definition of *memory.* You might weave a complex spider web around the concept of memory by coming up with a real-world example of how information enters your mind, how it is stored, and how you can retrieve it.

Thinking of concrete examples of a concept is a good way to understand it. *Self-reference*–relating material to your own experience–is another highly effective way to elaborate deeply on information, drawing mental links between aspects of your own life and new information (Figure 3) (Gutchess & Kensinger, 2018). When we elaborate on a topic during encoding we are laying a pathway to help us retrieve the information. The more paths we create, the more likely it is that we will remember the information.

The process of elaboration is evident in the physical activity of the brain. Neuroscience research has shown a link between elaboration during encoding and brain activity (Bartsch, Singmann, & Oberauer, 2018). In one study, researchers placed individuals in magnetic resonance imaging (MRI) machines (see section titled "Brain Imaging") and flashed one word every 2 seconds on a screen inside (Wagner & others, 1998). Initially, the individuals simply noted whether the words were in uppercase or lowercase letters. As the study progressed, they were asked to determine whether each word was concrete, such as *chair* or *book,* or abstract, such as *love* or *democracy*. In this study, the participants showed more neural activity in the left frontal lobe of the brain during the concrete/abstract task than they did when they were asked merely to state whether the words were in uppercase or lowercase letters. Further, they demonstrated better memory in the concrete/abstract task. The researchers concluded that greater elaboration of information is linked with neural activity, especially in the brain's left frontal lobe. In addition to the left frontal lobes, the hippocampus is activated when individuals use elaboration during encoding (Staresina, Gray, & Davachi, 2009; Vanlangendonck & others, 2018).

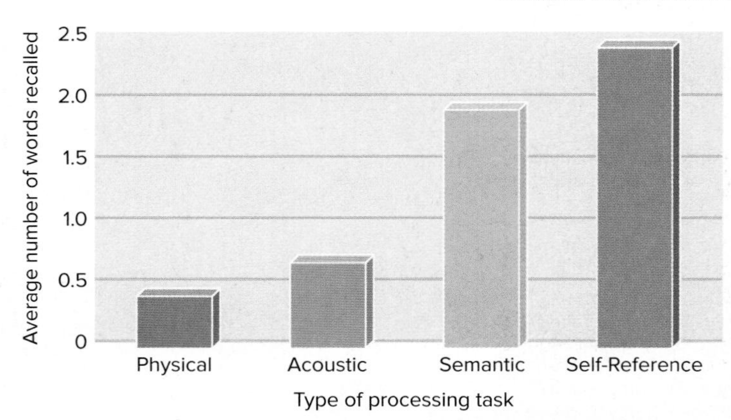


**FIGURE 3** **Self-Reference Improves Memory** In one study, researchers asked participants to remember lists of words according to the words' physical, acoustics (sound), semantic (meaning), or self-referent characteristics. As the figure illustrates, when individuals generated self-references for the words, they remembered them better. Source: Gutchess & Kensinger (2018).

| Memorization of... | Record Holder | Country | Year | Record |
|---|---|---|---|---|
| **Written numbers in 1 minute, no errors** | Gunther Karsten | Germany | 2007 | 102 numbers |
| **Random words in 15 minutes*** | Simon Reinhard | Germany | 2010 | 300 words |
| **Speed to recall a single deck of 52 shuffled playing cards, no errors** | Simon Reinhard | Germany | 2015 | 20.44 seconds |
| **Historic dates in 5 minutes** | Johannes Mallow | Germany | 2011 | 132 dates |
| **Abstract images in 15 minutes** | Johannes Mallow | Germany | 2015 | 495 images |

*Participants view random words in columns of 25 words. Scoring is tabulated by column: one point for each word. One mistake reduces the score for that column by half, and the second mistake reduces the score for that column to zero.

**FIGURE 4 World Champions of Memory** For memorization wizards such as these world record holders, imagery is a powerful encoding tool. Source: Reed (2010).

## Imagery

Mental imagery is a powerful way to remember (Dennis, Astell, & Dritschel, 2012). The use of imagery means that a person conjures up pictures that are associated with each thing that needs to be remembered (Meade, Wammes, & Fernandes, 2018; Morisaki, Bon, & Levitt, 2016). Imagery can help establish even the most complex information in memory. Consider, for instance, Akira Haraguchi, who recited the digits of pi to the first 83,431 decimal places ("Japanese breaks pi memory record," 2005). Think about memorizing a list of over 80,000 numbers. How would you go about it? One way would be to use mental imagery to create a rich visual walk through the digits. To memorize the first eight digits of pi (3.1415926), one might say, "3 is a chubby fellow who walks with a cane (1), up to a take-out window (4), and orders 15 hamburgers. The cook (9), who has very large biceps (2), slips on his way to deliver the burgers (6)." Imagery functions as a powerful encoding tool for all of us (Reed, 2010), including the memory record holders shown in Figure 4.

Mental imagery can come in handy in everyday life. A restaurant server might remember who ordered what by imagining each person eating his or her food. A student might remember last night's reading material by associating it with a figure or photo on the page. You might remember someone's name by imagining how the name relates to the person's face. Not only mental imagery, but creating actual images–by drawing what is to be remembered–can enhance memory (Meade, Wammes, & Fernandes, 2018).

Classic studies by Allan Paivio (1971, 1986, 2007) showed how imagery can improve memory. Paivio argued that memory is stored in one of two ways: as a verbal code (a word or a label) or an image code. Paivio thought that the image code, which is highly detailed and distinctive, produces better memory than the verbal code. His *dual code hypothesis* claims that memory for pictures is better than memory for words because pictures–at least those that can be named–are stored as both image codes and verbal codes (Paivio & Sadoski, 2011; Tian, Zarate, & Poeppel, 2016). Thus, when we use imagery to remember, we have two potential avenues by which we can retrieve information, and information that is stored in pictures and in words is easier to remember. Even those who do not think of themselves as "visual learners" can benefit from using imagery during encoding (Cuevas & Dawson, 2018).

### test yourself

1. What four encoding processes do not happen automatically but instead require effort?
2. How does divided attention differ from selective attention?
3. Explain the process of elaboration and its importance.

# 3. MEMORY STORAGE

In addition to being encoded, a memory must be stored properly. **Storage** encompasses how information is retained over time and how it is represented in memory.

● **storage** The retention of information over time and how this information is represented in memory.

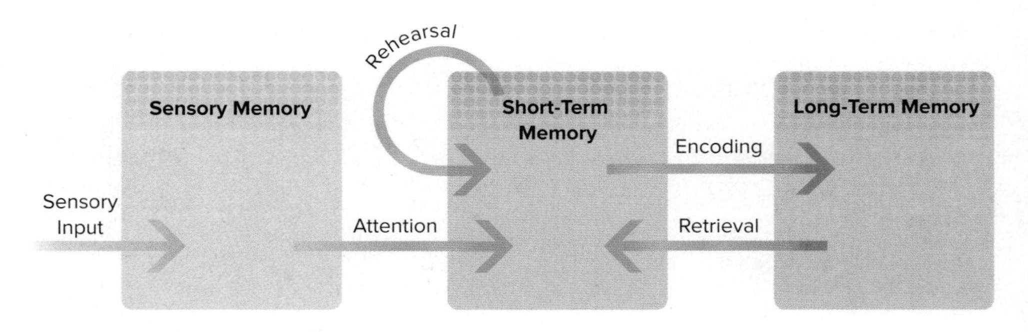


**FIGURE 5 Atkinson and Shiffrin's Theory of Memory** In this model, sensory input goes into sensory memory. Through the process of attention, information moves into short-term memory, where it remains for only up to 30 seconds unless it is rehearsed. When the information goes into long-term memory storage, it can be retrieved over a lifetime. Source: Atkinson & Shiffrin (1968).

We remember some information for less than a second, some for half a minute, and some for minutes, hours, years, or even a lifetime. Richard Atkinson and Richard Shiffrin (1968) formulated an early theory of memory that acknowledged the varying life span of memories (Figure 5). The **Atkinson–Shiffrin theory** states that memory storage involves three systems:

● **Atkinson–Shiffrin theory** Theory stating that memory storage involves three separate systems: sensory memory, short-term memory, and long-term memory.

- *Sensory memory:* time frames of a fraction of a second to several seconds
- *Short-term memory:* time frames up to 30 seconds
- *Long-term memory:* time frames up to a lifetime

Time frame is not the only difference among these memory systems. Each type of memory operates in a distinctive way and has a special purpose.

● **sensory memory** Memory system that involves holding information from the world in its original sensory form for only an instant, not much longer than the brief time it is exposed to the visual, auditory, and other senses.

## Sensory Memory

**Sensory memory** holds information from the world in its original sensory form for only an instant, not much longer than the brief time it is exposed to the visual, auditory, and other senses. Sensory memory, also called our sensory register, is very rich and detailed, but we lose the information in it quickly unless we use strategies that transfer it into short-term or long-term memory.

Think about the sights and sounds you encounter as you walk to class on a typical morning. Literally thousands of stimuli come into your field of vision and hearing—cracks in the sidewalk, chirping birds, the blue sky, faces and voices of hundreds of people. You do not process all of these stimuli, but you do process a number of them. Generally, you process more stimuli at the sensory level than you consciously notice. Sensory memory retains this information from your senses (including a large portion of what you think you ignore), but only for a few moments.

*Echoic memory* (from the word *echo*) refers to auditory sensory memory, which is retained for up to several seconds. Imagine standing in an elevator with a friend who asks, "What was that song?" about the piped-in tune that just ended. If your friend asks the question quickly enough, you just might have a trace of the song left on your sensory registers to answer.

*Iconic memory* (from the word *icon,* which means "image") refers to visual sensory memory, which is retained only for about ¼ of a second (Figure 6). Visual sensory memory is responsible for our ability to "write" in the air using a sparkler on the Fourth of July—the residual iconic memory is what makes a moving point of light appear to be a line. The sensory memory for other senses, such as smell and touch, has received little attention in research studies.

The first study of sensory memory focused on iconic memory. In George Sperling's (1960) classic study, participants viewed patterns of stimuli such as those in Figure 7. Looking at the letters, you have no trouble recognizing them. But, Sperling flashed the letters on a screen for just $^{1}/_{20}$ of a second! Afterward, participants could report only four or five letters. With such a short exposure, reporting all nine letters was impossible.

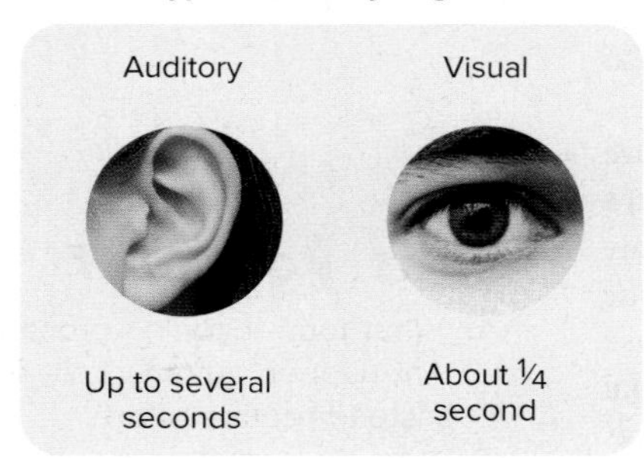


**FIGURE 6 Auditory and Visual Sensory Memory** If you hear this bird's call while walking through the woods, your auditory sensory memory holds the information for several seconds. If you see the bird, your visual sensory memory holds the information for only about ¼ of a second. (bird) ©Manuela Schewe-Behnisch/EyeEm/Getty Images; (ear) ©Geoff du Feu/Alamy Stock Photo; (eye) ©ColorBlind Images/Blend Images

Now, some participants in Sperling's study reported feeling that, for an instant, they *could* see all nine letters even that short span of time. But they ran into trouble when they tried to name all the letters they had seen. Perhaps, Sperling thought, all nine letters were initially processed in the iconic sensory memory—they were all present, briefly. However, forgetting from iconic memory occurred so rapidly that the participants did not have time to transfer all the letters to short-term memory, where they could be named.

Sperling reasoned that if all nine letters are actually in sensory memory, they should all be available for a brief time. To test this hypothesis, Sperling sounded a low, medium, or high tone just after a pattern of letters was shown. Participants were told that the tone was a signal to report only the letters from the bottom, middle, or top row. By giving the participants the signal, Sperling helped them to quickly scan their mental image so that they could find the specific pieces of the information that it contained in various places. Indeed, after the tone, participants performed much better, suggesting remarkably, that the iconic sensory register contained all or most of the available information.

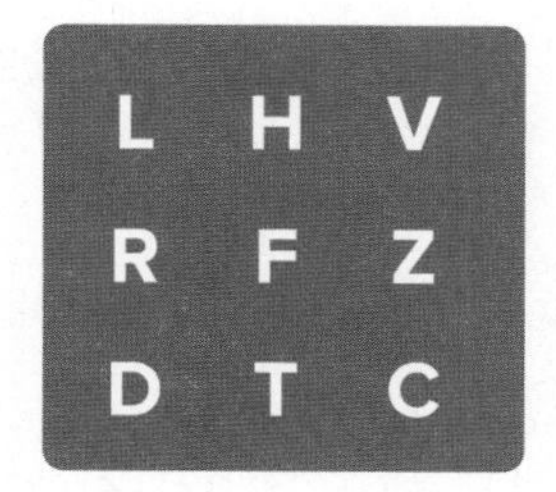


**FIGURE 7** **Sperling's Sensory Memory Experiment** This array of stimuli is similar to those flashed for about $^{1}/_{20}$ of a second to the participants in Sperling's study.
Source: Sperling (1960).

## Short-Term Memory

Much information goes no further than sensory memory stage, retained for only a brief instant. However, some information, especially that to which we pay attention, proceeds into short-term memory. **Short-term memory** is a limited-capacity memory system in which information is usually retained for only as long as 30 seconds unless we use strategies to retain it longer. Compared with sensory memory, short-term memory is limited in capacity, but it can store information for a longer time.

● **short-term memory** Limited-capacity memory system in which information is usually retained for only as long as 30 seconds unless the individual uses strategies to retain it longer.

George Miller examined the limited capacity of short-term memory in the classic paper "The Magical Number Seven, Plus or Minus Two" (Miller, 1956). Miller pointed out that on many tasks, individuals are limited in how much information they can keep track of without external aids. Usually the limit is in the range of 7 ± 2 items. If you think of important numbers in your life (such as phone numbers, student ID numbers, and your Social Security number), you will probably find that they fit into the 7 ± 2 range.

*Memory span* refers to the number of digits an individual can report back, in order, after a single presentation of them. Most college students can remember eight or nine digits without making errors (think about how easy it is to remember a phone number). Longer lists pose problems because they exceed short-term memory capacity. If you rely on short-term memory to retain longer lists, you probably will make errors.

### CHUNKING AND REHEARSAL

Two ways to improve short-term memory are chunking and rehearsal. *Chunking* involves grouping or "packing" information that exceeds the 7 ± 2 memory span into higher-order units that can be remembered as single units. Chunking works by making large amounts of information more manageable (Cowan, 2015; Tanida, Nakayama, & Saito, 2018).

To get a sense of chunking, consider this list: *hot, city, book, forget, tomorrow,* and *smile.* Hold these words in memory for a moment; then write them down. If you recalled the words, you succeeded in holding 30 letters, grouped into six chunks, in memory. This activity shows just how much information you could hold in short-term memory by chunking. Now hold the following list in memory and then write it down:

O LDH ARO LDAN DYO UNGB EN

How did you do? Do not feel bad if you did poorly. This string of letters is very difficult to remember, even though it is arranged in chunks. The problem is the chunks lack meaning. If you re-chunk the letters to form the meaningful words "Old Harold and Young Ben," they become much easier to remember.

Another way to improve short-term memory is *rehearsal,* the conscious repetition of information (Kowialiewski & Majerus, 2018; Morra, 2015). You are likely very familiar with rehearsal already. It simply means repeating the information over and over in your head to keep it in memory. Information stored in short-term memory lasts half a minute or less without rehearsal. However, if rehearsal is not interrupted, information can be retained indefinitely. Rehearsal is often verbal, giving the impression of an inner voice, but it can also be visual or spatial, giving the impression of a private inner eye (Sheremata, Somers, & Shomstein, 2018).

Rehearsal works best when we must briefly remember a list of numbers or items such as entrées from a menu. If we need to remember information for longer periods of time, as when we are studying for a test coming up next week, other strategies usually work better. One reason rehearsal does not work well for retaining information over the long term is that rehearsal often involves mechanically repeating information, without imparting meaning to it. Over the long term, we remember information best when we add meaning to it, demonstrating the importance of deep, elaborate processing.

## WORKING MEMORY

Though useful, Atkinson and Shiffrin's theory of the three time-linked memory systems fails to capture the dynamic way short-term memory functions. Think about the way you use information from your memory. You do not simply store information in short-term memory: You attend to it, manipulate it, and use it to solve problems (Christophel & others, 2018; Kobylecki & others, 2018). How can we understand these processes?

● **working memory** A combination of components, including short-term memory and attention, that allow individuals to hold information temporarily as they perform cognitive tasks; a kind of mental workbench on which the brain manipulates and assembles information to guide understanding, decision making, and problem solving.

The way psychologists have addressed this question is through the key concept of working memory. **Working memory** refers to a combination of components that include short-term memory and attention that allow us to hold information temporarily as we perform cognitive tasks (Adams, Nguyen, & Cowan, 2018; Cowan, 2008; D'Esposito & Postle, 2015; Gosseries & others, 2018). Essentially, working memory is the mental place where thinking occurs.

Working memory is not the same as short-term memory. Short-term memory is a *passive* storehouse that stores information until it moves to long-term memory. Working memory, in contrast, is an *active* memory system. For instance, a person can hold a list of words in short-term memory by rehearsing them over and over. But we cannot solve a problem while we are rehearsing information using short-term memory, and we cannot rehearse information (requiring effort and attention) while we are trying to solve a problem.

Working memory capacity is separable from short-term memory capacity. Because short-term memory capacity can rely on rehearsal, 7 ± 2 chunks are generally manageable. However, in working memory, if the chunks are relatively complex, most young adults can only remember 4 ± 1, that is, 3 to 5 chunks (Cowan, 2010). This might explain why measures of short-term memory capacity are not strongly related to cognitive aptitudes such as intelligence, whereas working memory capacity is (Cowan, 2008).

*Consider the* Lion Man, *an ivory sculpture archaeologists found in a cave in Germany. The 28-centimeter figurine, with the head of a lion and the body of a man, is believed to have been created 32,000 years ago.*



Working memory is like a mental blackboard, a place where we can imagine and visualize. In this sense, working memory is the context for conscious thought (see the chapter "States of Consciousness"). In working memory, the brain assembles and works with information to help us understand, make decisions, and solve problems. If, say, all of the information on the hard drive of your computer is like long-term memory, then working memory is comparable to what you actually have open and active at any given moment. Working memory has a limited capacity, and, to take the computer metaphor further, the capacity of working memory is like RAM.

Anthropologists, archaeologists, and psychologists are interested in understanding how working memory evolved. Some scholars have suggested that working memory lays the foundation for creative culture. Prehistoric tools (Haidle, 2010) and works of art (Laughlin, 2015; Wynn, Coolidge, & Bright, 2009) reveal how (and when) early humans were thinking. Working memory has been proposed as a key difference between Neanderthals and *Homo sapiens* (Wynn & Coolidge, 2010).

Consider the *Lion Man*, an ivory sculpture archaeologists found in a cave in Germany. The 28-centimeter figurine, with the head of a lion and the body of a man, is believed to have been created 32,000 years ago (Balter, 2010). This ancient work of art must have been the product of an individual who had the capacity to see two things and, *in working memory,* ask something like, "What would they look like if I combined them?"

Working memory has helped address practical problems outside the laboratory (Baddeley, 2012). For instance, advances in the understanding of working memory have allowed researchers to identify students at risk for academic underachievement and to improve their memory (Dumontheil & Klingberg, 2012; Gathercole & Alloway, 2008; G. Roberts & others, 2011). Working memory also has been beneficial in the early detection of Alzheimer disease (Kobylecki & others, 2018).

Because working memory is important in problem solving and cognitive function, many have tried to expand the capacity of their working memory by using various exercises. Although early research appeared promising, later studies have produced mixed results (Redick & others, 2015).

How does working memory operate? Cognitive psychologists have proposed models or schematics to help them answer this question, based on the way working memory allows us to hold information temporarily "in mind" as we perform cognitive tasks (D'Esposito & Postle, 2015). Let's take a closer look at one of those models.

British psychologist Alan Baddeley (2017) proposed a three-part model of working memory. The three components of Baddeley's model are the phonological loop, the visuo-spatial sketchpad, and the central executive. You can think of them as two assistants or workers (the phonological loop and the visuo-spatial sketchpad) who work for the same boss (the central executive). Let's take a closer look at these components:

1. The *phonological loop* is specialized to briefly store speech-based information about the sounds of language. The phonological loop contains two separate components: an acoustic code (the sounds we hear), which decays in a few seconds, and rehearsal, which allows us to repeat the words in the phonological store.
2. The *visuo-spatial sketchpad* stores visual and spatial information, including visual imagery. As in the case of the phonological loop, the capacity of the visuo-spatial sketchpad is limited. If we try to put too many items in the visuo-spatial sketchpad, we cannot represent them accurately enough to retrieve them successfully. The phonological loop and the visuo-spatial sketchpad function independently. We can rehearse numbers in the phonological loop while making spatial arrangements of letters in the visuo-spatial sketchpad.
3. The *central executive* integrates information not only from the phonological loop and the visuo-spatial sketchpad but also from long-term memory. In Baddeley's (2010a, 2010b, 2012) view, the central executive plays important roles in attention, planning, and organizing. The central executive acts like a supervisor who monitors which information deserves our attention and which we should ignore. It also selects which strategies to use to process information and solve problems. Like the phonological loop and the visuo-spatial sketchpad, the central executive has a limited capacity. If working memory is like the files you have open on your computer, the central executive is *you*. You pull up information you need, close out other things, and so forth.

Take a closer look at Baddeley's working memory model in the Psychological Inquiry.

Though it is compelling, Baddeley's notion of working memory is a metaphor describing processes in memory. Neuroscientists have only just begun to search for brain areas and activity that might be responsible for these processes. Current evidence shows that there is no one place or structure in the brain that represents the workers in working memory. Rather, areas of the brain associated with the information to be used in cognition are temporarily activated as that information is brought into awareness (Guell, Gabrieli, & Schmahmann, 2018). In addition, the prefrontal cortex plays a key role as attention is deployed to these various aspects of memory. Most recently, the existence of a specialized "visuo-spatial" processing space in working memory has been challenged (Morey, 2018).

# psychological *inquiry*

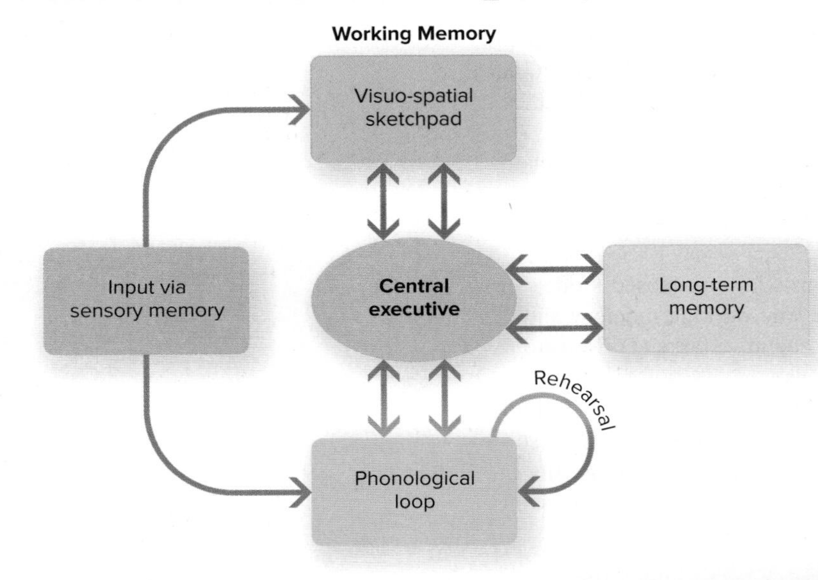


### *The Inner Workings of Working Memory*

This figure represents Baddeley's working memory model. Although the diagram might seem complicated, it will start to make sense if you take a moment to answer the questions that follow.

1. What is the central executive, and why is it in the center of the figure?
2. Can you see where rehearsal takes place? Why would rehearsal fit there?
3. Notice the number of double-headed arrows in this figure. They signify that information flows in both directions. Now look for the single-headed arrows (there are three). Why does that information flow in only one direction?
4. Imagine that you have met a very attractive person whom you would like to get to know better. The individual has just given you his or her phone number. Trace that information along the steps of this figure. How does it flow, and where does it end up? When and how will you take it out and put it to use?

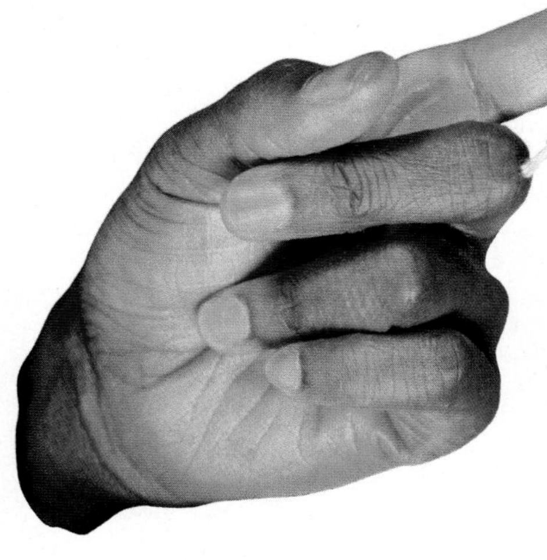

©Ingram Publishing/Alamy Stock Photo

● **long-term memory** A relatively permanent type of memory that stores huge amounts of information for a long time.

## Long-Term Memory

**Long-term memory** is a relatively permanent type of memory that stores huge amounts of information for a long time. The capacity of long-term memory is staggering. John von Neumann (1958), a distinguished mathematician, put the size at $2.8 \times 10^{20}$ (280 quintillion) bits, which in practical terms means that our storage capacity is virtually unlimited. von Neumann assumed that we never forget anything; but even considering that we do forget things, we can hold several billion times more information than a large computer.

An interesting question is how the availability of information on the Internet has influenced memory. If we know we can look something up on the web, why bother storing it in our head? A series of studies by Betsy Sparrow and colleagues (Sparrow, Liu, & Wegner, 2011) demonstrated that when faced with difficult memory tasks, people are likely to think immediately of using their computer to find the answer, rather than doing the hard work of remembering.

### COMPONENTS OF LONG-TERM MEMORY

Long-term memory is complex, as Figure 8 shows. At the top level, it is divided into substructures of explicit memory and implicit memory (Vakil, Wasserman, & Tibon, 2018). Explicit memory can be further subdivided into episodic and semantic memory. Implicit memory includes the systems involved in procedural memory, classical conditioning, and priming.

In simple terms, explicit memory has to do with remembering who, what, where, when, and why; implicit memory has to do with remembering how.

To explore the distinction, let's look at the case of a person known as H. M. To treat severe seizures, H. M. underwent surgery in 1953 that involved removing the hippocampus and a portion of the temporal lobes of both hemispheres in his brain. (We examined the location and functions of these brain areas in the chapter "Biological Foundations of

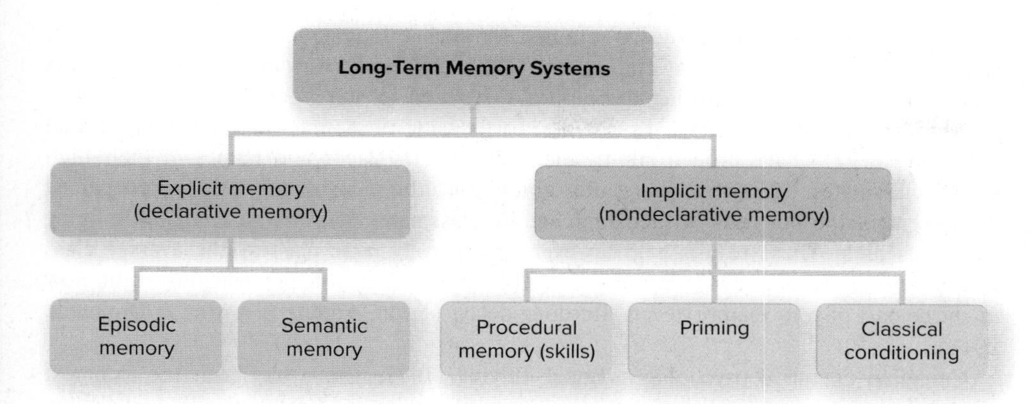


**FIGURE 8 Systems of Long-Term Memory** Long-term memory stores huge amounts of information for long periods of time, much like a computer's hard drive. The hierarchy in the figure shows the division of long-term memory at the top level into explicit memory and implicit memory. Explicit memory can be further divided into episodic and semantic memory; implicit memory includes procedural memory, priming, and classical conditioning.
Source: Vakil, Wasserman, & Tibon (2018).

Behavior".) H. M.'s epilepsy improved, but something devastating happened to his memory (Benjamin & others, 2018; Winter, 2018). Most dramatically, he developed an inability to form new memories that outlive working memory. H. M.'s memory time frame was only a few minutes at most, so he lived, until his death in 2007, in a perpetual present and could not remember past events. In contrast, his memory of *how* to do things was less affected. For example, he could learn new physical tasks, even though he had no memory of how or when he learned them.

H. M.'s situation demonstrates a distinction between explicit memory, which was dramatically impaired in his case, and implicit memory, which was less influenced by his surgery. Let's explore the subsystems of explicit and implicit memory more thoroughly.

**Explicit Memory** **Explicit memory** (also called **declarative memory**) is the conscious recollection of information, such as specific facts and events and, at least in humans, information that can be verbally communicated. Examples of using explicit or declarative memory include recounting the events in a movie you have seen and recalling the names of the justices on the U.S. Supreme Court.

• **explicit memory or declarative memory** The conscious recollection of information, such as specific facts or events and, at least in humans, information that can be verbally communicated.

How long does explicit memory last? Explicit memory includes things you are learning in your classes even now. Will it stay with you? Research by Harry Bahrick has examined this very question. Ohio Wesleyan University, where Bahrick is a professor of psychology, is a small (about 1,800 students) liberal arts school that boasts very loyal alumni who faithfully return to campus for reunions and other events.

Bahrick (1984, 2000) took advantage of this situation to conduct an ingenious study on the retention of course material over time. He gave vocabulary tests to individuals who had taken Spanish in college as well as to a control group of college students who had not taken Spanish in college. The individuals chosen for the study had used Spanish very little since their college courses. Some individuals were tested at the end of an academic year (just after having taken the courses), but others were tested years after graduation—as many as 50 years later. When Bahrick assessed how much the participants had forgotten, he found a striking pattern (Figure 9): Forgetting tended to occur in the first 3 years after taking the classes and then leveled off, so that adults maintained considerable knowledge of Spanish vocabulary words up to 50 years later.

Bahrick (1984) assessed not only how long ago adults had studied Spanish but also how well they had done in Spanish classes during college. Those who had received *A* grades in their courses 50 years earlier remembered more Spanish than adults who had received *C* grades when taking Spanish only 1 year earlier. Thus, how well students had initially learned the material was even more important than how long ago they had studied it.

*Your explicit memory system is activated when you describe events in a movie you have seen.*
©Nestor Rizhniak/Shutterstock

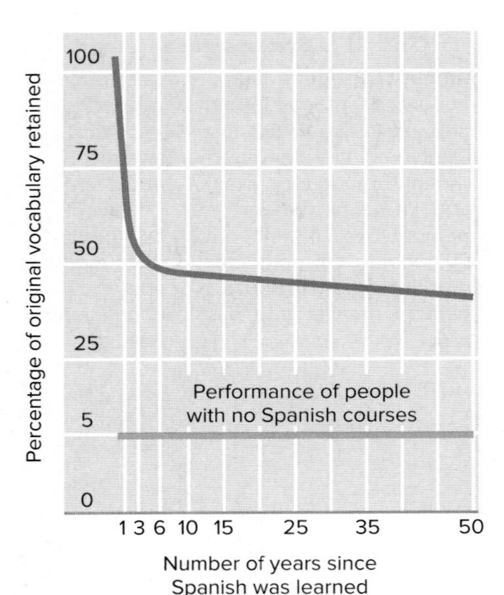


**FIGURE 9 Memory for Spanish Vocabulary as a Function of Years Since Spanish Classes** The first few years after college, individuals had a steep decline in memory for vocabulary learned in Spanish classes. However, there was little dropoff in memory for Spanish vocabulary from 3 years after taking Spanish classes to 50 years after taking them. Even 50 years after taking Spanish classes, individuals still remembered almost 50 percent of the vocabulary. Source: Bahrick (1984); Bahrick (2000).

Bahrick calls information that is retained for such a long time "permastore" content (Bahrick, 2000, 2005; Bahrick, Hall, & Da Costa, 2008). *Permastore memory* represents that portion of original learning that appears destined to stay with the person virtually forever, even without rehearsal. In addition to focusing on course material, Bahrick and colleagues (1974) have probed adults' memories for the faces and names of their high school classmates. Thirty-five years after graduation, the participants visually recognized 90 percent of the portraits of their high school classmates, with name recognition being almost as high. These results held up even in relatively large classes (the average class size in the study was 294). Somewhat surprisingly, what you are learning right now might be part of your memory even after long delays (Yoon, Anders Ericsson, & Donatelli, 2018).

Canadian cognitive psychologist Endel Tulving (1972, 1989) has been the foremost advocate of distinguishing between two subtypes of explicit memory: episodic and semantic. **Episodic memory** is the retention of information about the where, when, and what of life's happenings–basically, how we remember life's episodes. Episodic memory is autobiographical. For example, episodic memory includes the details of where you were when your younger brother or sister was born, what happened on your first date, and what you ate for breakfast this morning.

Episodic memory, then, is essentially about the episodes or stories we collect in our lives. Research has shown that, in the brain, episodic memory involves reinstating activity that occurred when the experience itself took place (Lohnas & others, 2018; Waldhauser, Braun, & Hanslmayr, 2016). Specifically, when we think about past experiences, activation in the hippocampus reinstates activity associated with those memories (Mack & Preston, 2016).

**Semantic memory** is a type of explicit memory pertaining to a person's knowledge about the world. It includes your areas of expertise, general knowledge of the sort you are learning in school, and everyday knowledge about the meanings of words, famous individuals, important places, and common things. For example, semantic memory is involved in a person's knowledge of chess, of geometry, and of who Melania Trump, LeBron James, and Lady Gaga are.

An important aspect of semantic memory is that it appears to be independent of an individual's personal identity with the past. You can access a fact–such as the detail that Lima is the capital of Peru–and have no idea when and where you learned it. Your memory of your first day on campus involves episodic memory. If you take a history class, your memory of the information you need to know to do well on the next test involves semantic memory.

The difference between episodic and semantic memory is also demonstrated in certain cases of amnesia (memory loss). A person with amnesia might forget entirely who she is–her name, family, career, and all other vital information about herself–yet still be able to talk, know what words mean, and have general knowledge about the world, such as what day it is or who currently holds the office of U.S. president (Moscovitch & others, 2016). In such cases, episodic memory is impaired, but semantic memory remains.

Figure 10 summarizes some aspects of the episodic/semantic distinction. The differences listed are controversial. One criticism is that many cases of explicit, or declarative, memory are neither purely episodic nor purely semantic but fall in between. Consider your memory for what you studied last night. You probably added knowledge to your semantic memory–that was, after all, the reason you were studying. You probably remember where you were studying, as well as about when you started and when you stopped. You probably also can remember some minor occurrences, such as a burst of loud laughter from the next room or the coffee you spilled on the desk. Is episodic or semantic memory involved here? Tulving (1983, 2000) argues that semantic and episodic systems often work together in forming new memories. In such cases, the memory that ultimately forms might consist of an autobiographical episode *and* semantic information.

● **episodic memory** The retention of information about the where, when, and what of life's happenings—that is, how individuals remember life's episodes.

● **semantic memory** A person's knowledge about the world, including his or her areas of expertise; general knowledge, such as of things learned in school, and everyday knowledge.

| Characteristic | Episodic Memory | Semantic Memory |
|---|---|---|
| Units | Events, episodes | Facts, ideas, concepts |
| Organization | Time | Concepts |
| Emotion | More important | Less important |
| Retrieval process | Deliberate (effortful) | Automatic |
| Retrieval report | "I remember" | "I know" |
| Education | Irrelevant | Relevant |
| Intelligence | Irrelevant | Relevant |
| Legal testimony | Admissible in court | Inadmissible in court |

**FIGURE 10 Some Differences Between Episodic and Semantic Memory** These characteristics have been proposed as the main ways to differentiate episodic from semantic memory. Source: Tulving (1983, 2000).

**Implicit Memory** Another type of long-term memory is related to non-consciously remembering skills and sensory perceptions rather than consciously remembering facts (Larzabal & others, 2018; Mitchell, Kelly, & Brown, 2018). **Implicit memory** (also called **nondeclarative memory**) is memory in which behavior is affected by prior experience without a conscious recollection of that experience. Implicit memory comes into play, for example, in the skills of playing tennis and snowboarding, or the physical act of text messaging. Another example of implicit memory is the repetition in your mind of a song you heard in the supermarket, even though you did not notice the song playing. Implicit memory explains why you might find yourself knowing all the words to a song you hate. You have heard it so many times that you have memorized it without even trying.

● **implicit memory or nondeclarative memory** Memory in which behavior is affected by prior experience without a conscious recollection of that experience.

Three subsystems of implicit memory are procedural memory, classical conditioning, and priming. All of these subsystems refer to memories that you are not aware of but that influence behavior (Larzabal & others, 2018; Mitchell, Kelly, & Brown, 2018).

**Procedural memory** is an implicit memory process that involves memory for skills (Elsey, Van Ast, & Kindt, 2018; Finn & others, 2016). For example, assuming that you are an expert typist, as you type a paper, you are not conscious of where the keys are for the various letters, but your well-learned, unconscious typing skill allows you to hit the right keys. Similarly, once you have learned to drive a car, you remember how to go about it: You do not have to remember consciously how to drive the car as you put the key in the ignition, turn the steering wheel, depress the gas pedal, and step on the brake pedal. To grasp the distinction between explicit memory and procedural memory, imagine trying to describe to someone in words exactly how to tie a shoe—something you can do successfully in just a few seconds—without having a shoe around.

● **procedural memory** Memory for skills.

Another type of implicit memory involves classical conditioning, a form of learning. Recall that classical conditioning involves the automatic learning of associations between stimuli, so that one comes to evoke the same response as the other. Classically conditioned associations such as this involve non-conscious, implicit memory (Dunsmoor & Kroes, 2019).

A final type of implicit memory process is priming. **Priming** is the activation of information that people already have in storage to help them remember new information better and faster (Geurten, Lloyd, & Willems, 2017; Mitchell, Kelly, & Brown, 2018; McNamara, 2013). In a common demonstration of priming, individuals study a list of words (such as *hope, walk,* and *cake*). Then they are given a standard recognition task to assess explicit memory. They must select all of the words that appeared in the list—for example, "Did you see the word *hope*? Did you see the word *form*?" Then participants perform a stem-completion task, which assesses implicit memory. In this task, they view a list of incomplete words (for example, *ho*__, *wa*__, *ca*__), called word stems, and must fill in the blanks with whatever word comes to mind. The results show that individuals more often fill in the blanks with the previously studied words than would be expected if they were filling in the blanks randomly. For example, they are more likely to complete the stem *ho*__ with *hope* than with *hole*. This result occurs even when individuals do not recognize the words on the earlier recognition task. Because priming takes place even when explicit memory for previous information is not required, it is assumed to be an unconscious process.

● **priming** The activation of information that people already have in storage to help them remember new information better and faster.

Priming occurs when something in the environment evokes a response in memory—such as the activation of a particular concept. Priming a term or concept makes it more available in memory. Could this heightened accessibility of information also influence behavior? This question has been the focus of some controversy in psychology in recent years.

To get a sense for the way priming might influence behavior, let's review an example—a study by social cognitive psychologist John Bargh and his colleagues (2001). The researchers asked students to perform a word-search puzzle. Embedded in the puzzle were either neutral words (*shampoo, robin*) or achievement-related words (*compete, win, achieve*). Participants who were exposed to the achievement-related words did better on a later puzzle task, finding an average of 26 words in other puzzles, whereas those with the neutral primes found only 21.5. The researchers concluded that these implicit cues to achievement led participants to work harder. Recently, these kinds of studies have been criticized because researchers have been unable to reproduce the findings using large samples (O'Donnell & others, 2018; Rohrer, Pashler, & Harris, 2015).

The idea that very subtle primes can influence the way people behave–including how we treat others; whether we work hard; and what we buy, eat, and like–seems almost magical. It is important to bear in mind that priming works through natural memory processes and the associations that have accrued in our everyday experiences. A meta-analysis showed that the effects of primes on behavior are real but likely to be weak (Weingarten & others, 2016).

## HOW MEMORY IS ORGANIZED

Explaining the forms of long-term memory does not address the question of how the different types of memory are organized for storage. The word *organized* is important: Memories are not haphazardly stored but instead are carefully sorted.

Here is a demonstration. Recall the 12 months of the year as quickly as you can. How long did it take you? What was the order of your recall? Chances are, you listed them within a few seconds in chronological order (January, February, March, and so on). Now try to remember the months in alphabetical order. How long did it take you? Did you make any errors? It should be obvious that your memory for the months of the year is organized in a particular way. Indeed, one of memory's most distinctive features is its organization.

Researchers have found that if people are encouraged to organize material simply, their memories of the material improve even if they receive no warning that their memories will be tested (Mandler, 1980). Psychologists have developed a variety of theories of how long-term memory is organized. Let's consider two of these more closely: schemas and connectionist networks.

● **schema** A preexisting mental concept or framework that helps people to organize and interpret information. Schemas from prior encounters with the environment influence the way individuals encode, make inferences about, and retrieve information.

● **script** A schema for an event, often containing information about physical features, people, and typical occurrences.

● **connectionism or parallel distributed processing (PDP)** The theory that memory is stored throughout the brain in connections among neurons, several of which may work together to process a single memory.

**Schemas** You and a friend have taken a long drive to a new town where neither of you has ever been before. You stop at the local diner, have a seat, and look over the menu. You have never been in this diner before, but you know exactly what is going to happen. Why? Because you have a schema for what happens in a restaurant. When we store information in memory, we often fit it into the collection of information that already exists, as you do even in a new experience with a diner. A **schema** is a preexisting mental concept or framework that helps people to organize and interpret information. Schemas from prior encounters with the environment influence the way we handle information–how we encode it, the inferences we make about it, and how we retrieve it.

Schemas can also be at work when we recall information. Schema theory holds that long-term memory is not very exact. We seldom find precisely the memory that we want, or at least not all of what we want; hence, we have to *reconstruct* the rest. Our schemas support the reconstruction process, helping us fill in gaps between our fragmented memories.

We have schemas for lots of situations and experiences–for scenes and spatial layouts (a beach, a bathroom), as well as for common events (playing football, writing a term paper). A **script** is a schema for an event (Schank & Abelson, 1977). Scripts often have information about physical features, people, and typical occurrences. This kind of information is helpful when people need to figure out what is happening around them. For example, if you are enjoying your after-dinner coffee in an upscale restaurant and a man in a tuxedo comes over and puts a piece of paper on the table, your script tells you that the man probably is a waiter who has just given you the check. Scripts help to organize our storage of memories about events.

*Each of us has a schema for what happens in a restaurant.*

©Drazen/E+/Getty Images

**Connectionist Networks** Schema theory has little or nothing to say about the role of the physical brain in memory. Thus, a new theory based on brain research has generated a wave of excitement among psychologists. **Connectionism,** also called **parallel distributed processing (PDP)**, is the theory that memory is stored throughout the brain in connections among neurons, several of which may work together to process a single memory (Cox, Seidenberg, & Rogers, 2015; McClelland, 2011). We initially considered the concept of neural networks in the chapter "Biological Foundations of Behavior" and the idea of parallel sensory processing pathways in the chapter "Sensation and Perception". These concepts also apply to memory.

In the connectionist view, memories are not large knowledge structures (as in schema theories). Instead, memories are more like electrical impulses, organized only to the extent that neurons, the connections among them, and their activity are organized. Any piece of knowledge–such as your dog's name–is embedded in the strengths of hundreds or thousands of connections among neurons and is not limited to a single location.

How does the connectionist process work? A neural activity involving memory, such as remembering your dog's name, is spread across a number of areas of the cerebral cortex. The locations of neural activity, called *nodes,* are interconnected. When a node reaches a critical level of activation, it can affect another node across synapses. We know that the human cerebral cortex contains millions of neurons that are richly interconnected through hundreds of millions of synapses. Because of these synaptic connections, the activity of one neuron can be influenced by many other neurons. Owing to these simple reactions, the connectionist view argues that changes in the strength of synaptic connections are the fundamental bases of memory (Hasson, Chen, & Honey, 2015; McClelland & others, 2010). From the connectionist network perspective, memories are organized sets of neurons that are routinely activated together.

Part of the appeal of the connectionist view is that it is consistent with what we know about brain function and allows psychologists to simulate human memory studies using computers (Morowitz, 2018). Connectionist approaches also help to explain how priming a concept (achievement) can influence behavior (performance).

So far, we have examined the many ways cognitive psychologists think about how information is stored. The question remains, *where?* The puzzle of the physical location of memories has long fascinated psychologists. Although memory may seem to be a mysterious phenomenon, it, like all psychological processes, must occur in a physical place: the brain.

## WHERE MEMORIES ARE STORED

Karl Lashley (1950) spent a lifetime looking for a location in the brain in which memories are stored. He trained rats to discover the correct pathway in a maze and then cut out various portions of the animals' brains and retested their memory of the maze pathway. Experiments with thousands of rats showed that the loss of various cortical areas did not affect rats' ability to remember the pathway, leading Lashley to conclude that memories are not stored in a specific location in the brain. Other researchers, continuing Lashley's quest, agreed that memory storage is diffuse, but they developed additional insights. Canadian psychologist Donald Hebb (1949, 1980) suggested that assemblies of cells, distributed over large areas of the cerebral cortex, work together to represent information, just as the connectionist network perspective would predict.

The neuroscience of memory suggests that rather than being stored in one place in the brain, memories are processes: They are represented as connections throughout the brain and states of brain activity, recreating the brain's function when experiences first took place (Lohnas & others, 2018).

**Neurons and Memory** The collections of connected neurons that make up memory may involve as many as 1,000 neurons (Squire, 1990, 2004, 2007). At the same time, single neurons are also at work in memory (Braun & others, 2012; Squire, 2007). Just as perception involves specific neurons responding to bits and pieces of experience, single neurons may fire in response to faces, eyes, or hair color. Yet, in order for you to recognize your Uncle Albert, individual neurons that provide information about hair color, size, and other characteristics must act together.

Researchers also believe that brain chemicals may be the ink with which memories are written. Remember that neurotransmitters are the chemicals that allow neurons to communicate across the synapse. These chemicals play a crucial role in forging the connections that represent memory.

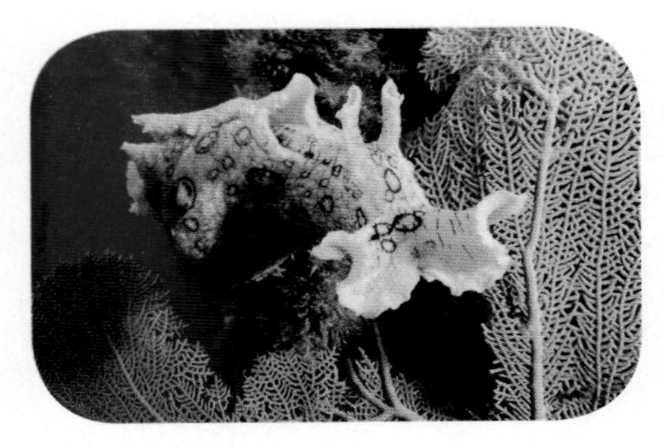

*Species of sea slug similar to that studied by Kandel and Schwartz (1982).*

©Tim Laman/Getty Images

Ironically, some of the answers to complex questions about the neural mechanics of memory come from studies on a very simple experimental animal—the inelegant sea slug. Eric Kandel and James Schwartz (1982) chose this large snail-without-a-shell because of the simple architecture of its nervous system, which consists of only about 10,000 neurons. (You might recall from the chapter "Biological Foundations of Behavior" that the human brain has about 100 billion neurons.)

The sea slug is hardly a quick learner or an animal with a good memory, but it is equipped with a reliable reflex. When anything touches the gill on its back, it quickly withdraws it. First the researchers accustomed the sea slug to having its gill prodded. After a while, the animal ignored the prod and stopped withdrawing its gill. Next the researchers applied an electric shock to its tail when they touched the gill. After many rounds of the shock-accompanied prod, the sea slug violently withdrew its gill at the slightest touch. The researchers found that the sea slug remembered this message for hours or even weeks. They also determined that shocking the sea slug's gill releases the neurotransmitter serotonin at the synapses of its nervous system, and this chemical release basically provides a reminder that the gill was shocked. This "memory" informs the nerve cell to send out chemical commands to retract the gill the next time it is touched. If nature builds complexity out of simplicity, then the mechanism used by the sea slug may work in the human brain as well.

The concept *long-term potentiation* is used to explain how memory functions at the neuron level. In line with connectionist theory, long-term potentiation means that neurons that fire together develop a connection (Lømo, 2018). This means that the connection between them—and thus the memory—is strengthened (Grigoryan, Korkotian, & Segal, 2012). Long-term potentiation has been demonstrated experimentally by administering a drug that increases the flow of information from one neuron to another across the synapse, raising the possibility of someday improving memory through drugs that increase neural connections (Zorumski & Izumi, 2012). The concept of long-term potentiation means that what you experience as a memory is really a collection of well-worn pathways in your brain. In sum, memories are not stored in one spot in the brain. Rather, they are longstanding connections, worn into the brain by experience.

**Brain Structures and Memory Functions** Whereas some neuroscientists are unveiling the cellular basis of memory, others are examining its broad-scale architecture in the brain. Many different parts of the brain and nervous system are involved in the complex process that is memory. The brain structures involved depend in part on what is being remembered: Is it a smell? A sight? A story? Although there is no one memory center in the brain, researchers have demonstrated that specific brain structures are involved in particular aspects of memory. Generally, no matter what a memory might be, it will be linked to activation in the hippocampus, the gateway to memory (Sekeres, Winocur, & Moscovitch, 2018; Thielen & others, 2018).

Figure 11 shows the location of brain structures active in different types of long-term memory. Note that implicit and explicit memory appear to involve different locations in the brain.

- *Explicit memory:* The hippocampus is sometimes called the gateway to memory because it is so vital to explicit memories. In addition to the hippocampus, two other areas of the brain also play important roles in explicit memory: the amygdalae and the temporal lobes in the cerebral cortex (Rolls, 2015). In many aspects of explicit memory, information is transmitted from the hippocampus to the frontal lobes, which are involved in both *retrospective memory*

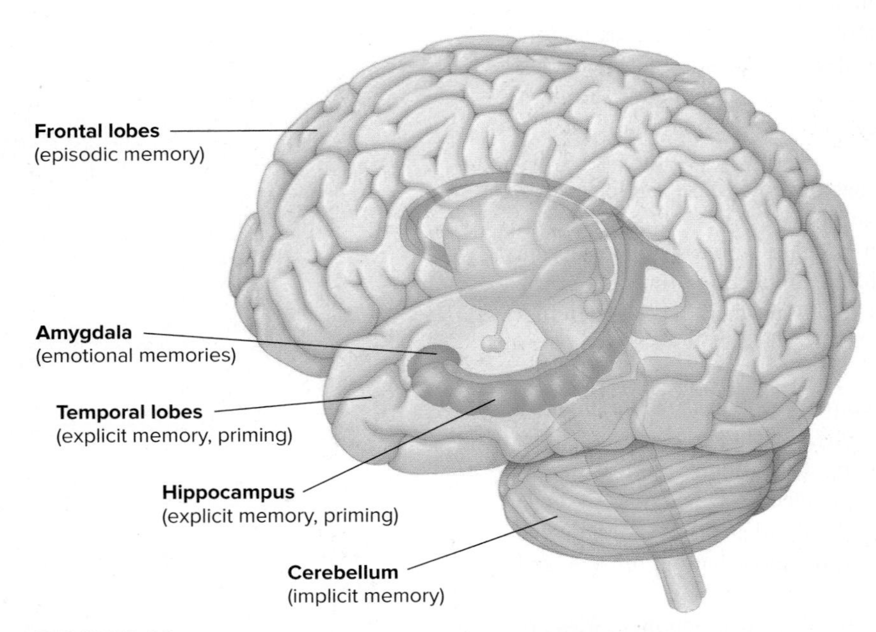


**FIGURE 11 Structures of the Brian Involved in Different Aspects of Long-Term Memory** Note that explicit memory and implicit memory appear to involve different locations in the brain.

(remembering things from the past) and *prospective memory* (remembering things that you need to do in the future) (Peira, Ziaei, & Persson, 2016). The left frontal lobe is especially active when we encode new information into memory; the right frontal lobe is more active when we subsequently retrieve it (Babiloni & others, 2006).

- *Implicit memory:* The hippocampus, again, is important to implicit memory, as are the temporal lobes, especially for priming (Noel, Wallace, & Blake, 2015). Given its role in coordination and balance, it is not surprising that the cerebellum (the structure at the back and toward the bottom of the brain) is active in the implicit memory required to perform skills (Bussy & others, 2011).

**test yourself**

1. How do sensory memory and short-term memory differ in terms of their duration?
2. What two kinds of memory are at the top level of long-term memory, and how is each defined?
3. How do the schema theory of memory and the connectionist network theory of memory differ in terms of their explanation of memories?

# 4. MEMORY RETRIEVAL

Remember that unforgettable night of shining stars with your romantic partner? Let's say the evening has indeed been encoded deeply and elaborately in your memory. Through the years you have thought about the night a great deal and told your best friends about it. The story of that night has become part of the longer story of your life. Fifty years later, your grandson asks, "How did you two end up together?" You share the story you have been saving for just such a question. What are the processes that allow you to do so?

Memory **retrieval** takes place when information that was retained in memory comes out of storage. You might think of long-term memory as a library. You retrieve information in a fashion similar to the process you use to locate and check out a book in an actual library. To retrieve something from your mental data bank, you search your store of memory to find the relevant information.

● **retrieval** The memory process that occurs when information that was retained in memory comes out of storage.

The efficiency with which we retrieve information from memory is impressive. It usually takes only a moment to search through a vast storehouse to find the information. When and where were you born? What is your mother's name? Who developed the first psychology laboratory? You can, of course, answer all of these questions instantly. (The answer to that last one is Wilhelm Wundt.) Yet retrieval of memory is a complex and at times imperfect process (Zhang & others, 2018).

Before examining ways that retrieval may fall short, let's look at some basic concepts that affect the likelihood that information will be accurately encoded, stored, and ultimately retrieved. As we will see, retrieval depends on the circumstances under which a memory was encoded and the way it was retained (Barnacle & others, 2018).

## Serial Position Effect

The **serial position effect** is the tendency to recall the items at the beginning and end of a list more readily than those in the middle. If you are a reality TV fan, you might notice that you always seem to remember the first person to get voted off and the last few survivors. All those people in the middle, however, are a blur. The *primacy effect* refers to better recall for items at the beginning of a list; the *recency effect* refers to better recall for items at the end. Together with the relatively low recall of items from the middle of a list, this pattern makes up the serial position effect (Berry & others, 2018; Peteranderl & Oberauer, 2018). Of course, not every bit of information that is in the middle is likely to be forgotten. If information is extremely vivid or unusual, it will be remembered. You can sharpen your understanding of the serial position effect by completing the exercise in the Psychological Inquiry.

● **serial position effect** The tendency to recall the items at the beginning and end of a list more readily than those in the middle.

Psychologists explain these effects using principles of encoding. For the primacy effect, the first few items in the list are easily remembered because they are rehearsed more or because they receive more elaborate processing than do words later in the list (Atkinson & Shiffrin, 1968; Craik & Tulving, 1975). Working memory is relatively empty when the items enter, so there is little competition for rehearsal time. Moreover, because the items get more rehearsal, they stay in working memory longer and are more likely to be encoded into long-term memory. In contrast, many items from the middle of the list drop out of working memory before being encoded into long-term memory.

## psychological *inquiry*

### *The Serial Position Effect: Lost in Midstream*

This figure shows typical serial position effects. The vertical axis is the probability of an individual's remembering a particular item in a list. The highest value on this axis is 1.0, meaning that the chance of remembering the item is 100 percent. The horizontal axis is the position of the items from first to last (in this case the 20th item). Examine the figure to answer the following questions.

1. What is the probability that the item presented in the 15th position will be remembered? What about the item that was presented first?
2. In this figure, which is stronger—primacy or recency? Explain.
3. When it is time for final exams, which information from your class do you think it would be best to brush up on, and why?
4. Suppose you are going for a job interview, and there are several other candidates there that day for interviews. If you want to make a memorable impression, which position in the sequence of interviews would you prefer, and why?

©Punchstock/Digital Vision

For the recency effect occurs for different reasons. First, when the last few items on a list are recalled, they might still be in working memory. Second, even if these items are not in working memory, the fact that they were just encountered makes them easier to recall.

Students sometimes confuse primacy and recency. One way to remember them to remember that *p* comes before *r* in the alphabet. ***P***rimacy refers to what is encountered first; ***r***ecency refers to what was encountered last.

## Retrieval Cues and the Retrieval Task

Two factors involved in retrieval are the cues that prompt your memory and the retrieval task that you set for yourself. Let's consider each.

Retrieval cues are stimuli that help us remember. The presence of such a cue can trigger memories. For instance, the smell of apple pie baking may remind you of a family dinner. If effective cues for what you are trying to remember are not available, you can create them. For example, if you have a block about remembering a new friend's name, you might go through the alphabet, generating names that begin with each letter. If you manage to stumble across the right name, you will probably recognize it. Imagine trying to write down the names of everyone from your middle school class. How might you do it?

One good strategy is to use different subcategories. For example, write down the names of as many of your classmates as you can remember. When you run out of names, think about the activities you were involved in during those school years, such as math class, lunch, and so on. This set of cues can help you to remember more names.

Your success in retrieving information also depends on the retrieval task you set for yourself. For instance, if you are simply trying to decide whether something seems familiar, retrieval is often a snap. Let's say that you see a short, dark-haired woman walking toward you on the street. You quickly decide that she is someone who shops at the same market as you do. However, remembering her name or a precise detail, such as when you met her, can be harder. Such distinctions have implications for police investigations: A witness might be sure she has previously seen a face, yet she might know whether it was at the crime scene or in a mug shot.

## RECALL AND RECOGNITION

Another factor in retrieval is the demands of the task. *Recall* is a memory task in which the individual has to retrieve previously learned information, as on essay tests. *Recognition* is a memory task in which the individual only has to identify (recognize) learned items, as on multiple-choice tests. Recall tests such as essay tests have poor retrieval cues. You are told to try to recall a certain class of information ("Discuss the factors that caused World War I"). In recognition tests such as multiple-choice tests, you merely judge whether a stimulus is familiar (such as that Archduke Franz Ferdinand was assassinated in 1914).

You probably have heard some people say that they never forget a face. However, recognizing a face is far simpler than recalling a face "from scratch," as law enforcement officers know. In some cases, police bring in an artist to draw a suspect's face from witnesses' descriptions (Figure 12). Recalling faces is difficult, and often artists' sketches of suspects are not detailed or accurate enough to result in apprehension.

## ENCODING SPECIFICITY

Another consideration in understanding retrieval is the *encoding specificity principle,* which states that information present at the time of encoding or learning tends to be effective as a retrieval cue (Unsworth, Brewer, & Spillers, 2011). For instance, you know your instructors when they are in the classroom setting–you see them there all the time. If, however, you run into one of them in an unexpected setting and in more casual attire, such as at the gym in workout clothes, the person's name might escape you. Your memory might fail because the cues you encoded are not available for use.

**FIGURE 12** **Remembering Faces** Ted Kaczynski, also known as the Unabomber, is a serial killer who conducted a sequence of mail bombings targeting universities and airlines beginning in the late 1970s. The drawing of Kaczynski, created by an FBI sketch artist, was based on bits and pieces of observations people had made of the infamous Unabomber. The FBI widely circulated the artist's sketch in the hope that someone would recognize the Unabomber. Now look at the photograph of Kaczynski. Would you have been able to recognize Kaczynski from the artist's sketch? Probably not. Although most people say they are good at remembering faces, they usually are not as good as they think they are.
(first) ©AP Images; (second) ©Ralf-Finn Hestoft/Corbis Historical/Getty Images

©rostislavv/123RF

### CONTEXT AT ENCODING AND RETRIEVAL

One consequence of encoding specificity is that a change in context between encoding and retrieval can cause memory to fail (Boywitt & Meiser, 2012). In many instances, people remember better when they try to recall information in the same context in which they learned it—a process referred to as *context-dependent memory*. This better recollection is believed to occur because they have encoded features of the context in which they learned the information along with the actual information. Such features can then act as retrieval cues (Bridge, Chiao, & Paller, 2010).

In one study, scuba divers learned information on land and under water (Godden & Baddeley, 1975). Later they were asked to recall the information when they were either on land or under water. The divers' recall was much better when the encoding and retrieval contexts matched (both on land or both under water).

## Special Cases of Retrieval

We began this discussion by likening memory retrieval to looking for and finding a book in the library. However, the process of retrieving information from long-term memory is not as precise as the library analogy suggests. When we search through long-term memory, we do not always find the exact "book" we want—or we might find the book but discover that several pages are missing. We have to fill in these gaps somehow.

Our memories are affected by a number of factors, including the pattern of information we remember, schemas and scripts, the situations we associate with memories, and the personal or emotional context. Certainly, everyone has had the experience of remembering a shared situation with a particular individual, only to have him or her tell us, "Oh, that wasn't me!" Such moments provide convincing evidence that memory may be best understood as reconstructive.

*False memories* occur when people remember something that never actually happened. For example, imagine that you want to tell a friend some exciting news. You might think about telling him or her so much that you eventually come to think you actually did so when you did not. We have all had those conversations that include the apologetic, "I thought I told you."

False memories involve an error in distinguishing between two kinds of mental contents: internally generated experience (for instance, your thoughts about telling your friend) and externally generated experience (actually telling your friend) (Hyman & others, 2014; Wang & Bukuan, 2015). Events and experiences that actually happen are assumed to be more vivid in memory than things that we have only thought about, so we can usually tell the difference.

Scientists have devised a clever way to study false memories (Roediger & McDermott, 1995). First, participants are asked to study a list of words that are all related to one concept, but that key concept is not included on the list. For example, a list might include the following words: *drowsy*, *bed*, *night*, and *tired*. Note that the list does not include the crucial word *sleep*. Later, participant memories are tested. If participants say they remember studying the word *sleep*, we know that memory is false. The idea is that all of the other words are so strongly related to the key word that it can create a strong internal activation. This activation can be confused for actually studying the word (Kaplan & others, 2016; Yang & others, 2015).

Sometimes we have memories that we are sure are not true. Déjà vu refers to the feeling of having experienced something before, despite knowing you have not (Brown & Marsh, 2010; Wells, O'Connor, & Moulin, 2018). To see how we can understand this experience in the context of memory, see the Intersection.

Although the factors we have discussed so far relate to the retrieval of generic information, various kinds of special memory retrieval also have generated much research. These memories are notable because of their relevance to the self, their emotional or traumatic character, or their unusually high levels of apparent accuracy (Barry & others, 2018; Piolino & others, 2006). Cognitive psychologists debate whether these memories rely on processes that are different from those already described or are simply extreme cases of typical memory processes (Lane & Schooler, 2004; Schooler & Eich, 2000). We now turn to these special cases of memory.

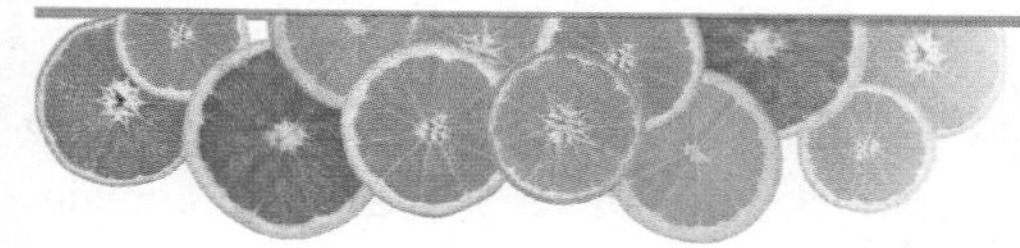
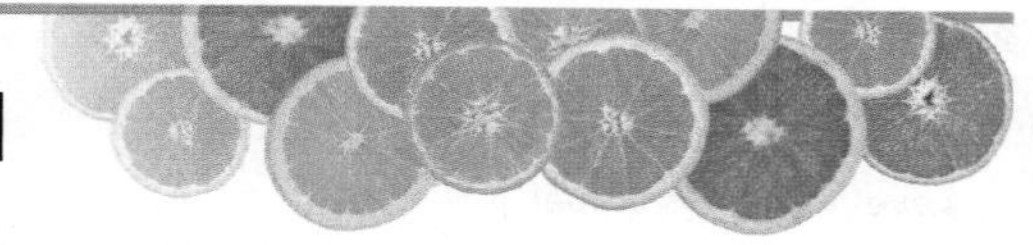

# INTERSECTION

## Neuroscience, Cognition, and Emotion: How Can We Explain Déjà Vu?

Have you ever been in the middle of an activity—maybe talking to a friend—and suddenly had the strong impression that you have done this before—like you distinctly remember aspects of what is happening? Déjà vu is the feeling of having experienced something before despite knowing you have not (Brown & Marsh, 2010). Déjà vu is common. More than 65 percent of young adults report multiple such experiences every year (Brown, 2004). The idea that déjà vu is a type of memory process is supported by brain imaging studies showing involvement of the hippocampus—the gateway to memory—in déjà vu (Pešlová & others, 2018). Déjà vu appears to involve a memory conflict: a strong feeling of familiarity clashing with a strong feeling of knowing that one did not actually experience a particular event (Urquhart & O'Connor, 2014; Urquhart & others, 2018). There is an uncanny, goose-bump quality to déjà vu. Not only do you feel like you have "been here, done this," but you might feel that you know what is about to happen next. Déjà vu is unpredictable and often fades quickly—how could it be studied scientifically? Let's review recent studies to see, first, how déjà vu can be created in the lab and, second, whether that feeling of knowing what is going to happen next has any validity (Spoiler alert: It doesn't).

*When was the last time you experienced déjà vu?*

In a series of studies (Cleary & Claxton, 2018), researchers were able to evoke déjà vu. First, they had people watch and encode 32 brief videos. The videos showed, from a first-person perspective, tours of various scenes. For instance, participants might see themselves walking through a manicured garden as the video led them through the setting. Next, participants were exposed to another set of 32 videos. Half of these featured an unusual quality—the layout of the objects was identical to the layout in some of the videos seen during encoding, but the setting and objects differed. For example, a junkyard might be identical in physical layout to the manicured garden. Instead of shrubs, the yard included piles of discarded wood. Interestingly, participants were more likely to report experiencing déjà vu when watching these videos than when watching the others. The similarity in layout led to that feeling of "having been there before"—even though participants "knew" they had not been there before and they did not recognize the similarity of layouts. This aspect of the study suggests that déjà vu involves a failure of retrieval. Participants *did* have a memory of the layout, but they did not recall that fact (Cleary & Claxton, 2018).

The studies also probed the feeling of knowing what might happen next. The researchers stopped the videos prior to a crucial turn and asked participants which way they should go—right or left? The results showed that participants who had experienced déjà vu felt more sure that they knew which way to go. However, this strong feeling of knowing was not related to accuracy (Cleary & Claxton, 2018).

These studies give us a surprising take on déjà vu. When we experience déjà vu it is not that we are wrong about feeling we have been there before. Rather, we *have* been in a very similar situation before, but we don't recall that fact. Déjà vu, an experience that feels almost magical, is actually a case of retrieval failure. And those feelings of knowing what will happen next that are part of déjà vu? They are best considered illusory (Cleary & Claxton, 2018).

## RETRIEVAL OF AUTOBIOGRAPHICAL MEMORIES

**Autobiographical memory**, a special form of episodic memory, is a person's recollections of their life experiences (Marsh & Roediger, 2013). An intriguing discovery about autobiographical memory is the *reminiscence bump*—the effect that adults remember more events from the second and third decades of life than from other decades (Koppel & Berntsen, 2016).

This reminiscence bump may occur because it is during our teens and 20s that we are forging a sense of identity. It may also be that these are simply the times in our life when a lot of important events happen (Berntsen & Rubin, 2002). In fact, when children describe what they think will happen to them in the future, they anticipate that they will have significant experiences in their early adult years (Bohn & Berntsen, 2011). So, it may be that the reminiscence bump is simply a life event bump.

• **autobiographical memory** A special form of episodic memory, consisting of a person's recollections of his or her life experiences.

| Level | Label | Description |
|---|---|---|
| Level 1 | Life time periods | Long segments of time measured in years and even decades |
| Level 2 | General events | Extended composite episodes measured in days, weeks, or months |
| Level 3 | Event-specific knowledge | Individual episodes measured in seconds, minutes, or hours. |

**FIGURE 13 The Three-Level Hierarchical Structure of Autobiographical Memory** When people relate their life stories, all three levels of information are typically present and intertwined.
Source: Conway & Rubin (1993).

Autobiographical memories are complex and seem to contain unending strings of stories and snapshots, but they can be categorized. For example, based on their research, Martin Conway and David Rubin (1993) sketched a structure of autobiographical memory that has three levels (Figure 13). The most abstract level consists of *life time periods;* for example, you might remember something about your life in high school. The middle level in the hierarchy is made up of *general events,* such as a trip you took with your friends after high school graduation. The most concrete level in the hierarchy is composed of *event-specific knowledge;* for example, from your trip, you might remember the exhilarating experience you had the first time you jet-skied. When people tell their life stories, all three levels of information are usually present and intertwined.

Most autobiographical memories include some reality and some myth. Personality psychologist Dan McAdams (2001, 2006, 2013; McAdams & Guo, 2015) argues that autobiographical memories are less about facts and more about meanings. They provide a reconstructed, embellished telling of the past that connects the past to the present. We will explore McAdams's approach to autobiographical memory in more detail when we look at the chapter "Personality".

## RETRIEVAL OF EMOTIONAL MEMORIES

Memories of life experience are often wrapped in emotion. Emotion affects the encoding and storage of memories and thus shapes the details that are retrieved (Rimmele, Davachi, & Phelps, 2012). The role that emotion plays in memory is of considerable interest to contemporary researchers and is echoed in public life.

● **flashbulb memory** The memory of emotionally significant events that people often recall with more accuracy and vivid imagery than everyday events.

**Flashbulb memory** is the memory of emotionally significant events that people often recall with more accuracy and vivid imagery than everyday events (Roehm, 2016). Previous generations of Americans might have discussed flashbulb memories of the assassination of President John F. Kennedy or the terrorist attacks on the United States on September 11, 2001. More recent examples of flashbulb memories might include the killing of Osama bin Laden on May 2, 2011, the tragic shootings at Sandy Hook Elementary School in Connecticut on December 14, 2012, or the shootings at Stoneman Douglas High school in Florida on February 14, 2018.

An intriguing dimension of flashbulb memories is that several decades later, people often remember where they were and what was going on in their lives at the time of such an emotionally charged event. These memories seem to be part of an adaptive system that fixes in memory the details that accompany important events so that they can be interpreted at a later time. We might say, "I will never forget where I was when I heard about" some important event. Such a statement fits with research showing that we may be more likely to remember our own personal experiences of an event than to recall details of the event itself (Smith, Bibi, & Sheard, 2003).

*Many people have flashbulb memories of where they were and what they were doing when the shooter attacked Sandy Hook Elementary School in Connecticut on December 14, 2012.*
©Jason DeCrow/AP Images

Most people express confidence about the accuracy of their flashbulb memories. However, flashbulb memories probably are not as precisely etched in our brain as we think. One way to gauge the exactness of flashbulb memories is to look at the consistency of the details of these memories over time. Research on memories of the 9/11 terrorist attack shows that the physical proximity of individuals to the event affected the accuracy of memory. For instance, individuals in New York showed greater accuracy than those in Hawaii (Pezdek, 2003).

Researchers have examined the accuracy and persistence of memories of the 9/11 attack, 10 years later (Hirst & others, 2015). In this study, both individuals who reported flashbulb memories and those who did not showed a sharp decline in memory during the first year after the attack. However, forgetting leveled off, such that many aspects of the experience remained in memory 10 years later. Interestingly, even aspects of flashbulb memories were found to change over time. The key

## When Is Your First Memory?

What is the earliest memory you can recall? How old were you when the event happened? Most people report a "first memory" occurring when they were between 3 and 4 years old (Akhtar & others, 2018). This "time stamp" makes sense. That is when children are able to form and share autobiographical memories (Fivush, 2011).

There is little evidence that children can form verbal autobiographical memories of events that happened prior to their being able to speak. Consider a clever experiment in which developmental psychologists staged a very interesting event for children, some of whom were younger than 3. The event involved a "Magic Shrinking Machine." The machine was a large square box with a light on top, an on-and-off lever, and a crank on the side. The researchers brought the box and a suitcase full of toys to the children's homes. Children were told that the machine could shrink things, magically. The child turned on the machine, placed a stuffed toy in the hole on the top, and cranked the crank. Then they opened a door on the bottom. Lo and behold, out popped a toy that was an exact replica but much smaller. For the kids, this was a notable event. They "shrank" a number of other toys during the session. One year later, when the children were old enough to talk, none of them could describe their memory of the magic machine (Simcock & Hayne, 2002). This lack of memories for events early in life is sometimes called *infantile amnesia,* referring to the fact that infants do not have the capacity to encode memories that can be shared later when they have language.

Now, interestingly, you might have answered our opening question with a memory of something that happened before you were 3—like being in a crib or welcoming a new sibling home when you were just 2 or younger. In studies probing first memories, there are always some who claim to have a memory that occurred before age 3 (Akhtar & others, 2018). In a recent study of over 6000 adults, 40 percent reported a first memory that occurred prior to age 3 (Akhtar & others, 2018), including some from the first year of life. The researchers concluded that such memories are likely *fictional*—emerging not out of experiences but from family stories, videos, and photographs. Much of our life story is created with and by the people with whom we share our lives. Even if fictional first memories are not "real" memories, they reflect who we were, even before we had a sense of what that meant. Fictional first memories can be thought of as *episodic memory-like* representations of the self (Akhtar & others, 2018). Actually translating a preverbal experience into an autobiographical memory is much less probable than the alternative of creating a narrative memory around an event.

©Ariel Skelley/Digital Vision/Getty Images

**WHAT DO YOU THINK?**

- Do you think first memories from infancy are fictional? Why or why not?
- What characteristics, other than age, might determine when a person is able to encode and share autobiographical memories?

predictors of memory accuracy were media attention to the event and continuing conversations with others (Hirst & others, 2015). The results of this work suggest that even when we feel like our memories of an event are strong, a reality check may be in order.

Still, on the whole, flashbulb memories do seem more durable and accurate than memories of day-to-day happenings (Davidson, Cook, & Glisky, 2006). One possible explanation is that flashbulb memories are quite likely to be rehearsed in the days following the event. However, it is not just the discussion and rehearsal of information that make flashbulb memories so long-lasting. The emotions triggered by flashbulb events also figure in their durability. Research points to the right amygdala, especially, as playing a role in flashbulb memories (Spanhel & others, 2018).

Although we have focused on negative news events as typical of flashbulb memories, such memories can also occur for positive events. An person's wedding day and the birth of a child are events that may become milestones in personal history and are always remembered (Roehm, 2016). Still, the precise accuracy of these memories may be less important to us than their role in our feelings about our experiences. A similar conclusion may be reached about another interesting class of autobiographical memories, first memories, as described in the Critical Controversy.

*Traumatic memory took center stage in 2018 when cognitive psychologist, Dr. Christine Blasey Ford, testified before the U.S. Senate about her experience of sexual assault as a teenager.*

©Pool/Getty Images

## MEMORY FOR TRAUMATIC EVENTS

In 1890, the American psychologist and philosopher William James said that an experience can be so emotionally arousing that it leaves a kind of scar on the brain. Personal traumas are candidates for such emotionally stirring experiences. Are traumatic events more or less likely to be remembered accurately? Some psychologists argue that memories of emotionally traumatic events are precisely retained, possibly forever, in considerable detail (Langer, 1991).

There is good evidence that memory for traumatic events is usually more accurate than memory for ordinary events (Turner, 2018). Stress-related hormones likely play a role in memories that involve personal trauma. The release of stress-related hormones, signaled by the amygdala (see Figure 11), likely accounts for some of the extraordinary durability and vividness of traumatic memories (Bucherelli & others, 2006; Goosens, 2011). Nevertheless, even traumatic memories can contain errors (Laney & Loftus, 2009; Moore & Zoellner, 2012). Distortions in traumatic memories may arise in the details of the traumatic episode.

## REPRESSED MEMORIES

Can an individual forget, and later recover, memories of traumatic events? There is a great deal of debate surrounding this question (Bruck & Ceci, 2012; Klemfuss & Ceci, 2012a, 2012b; Kuehnle & Connell, 2013). *Repression* is a defense mechanism in which a person is so traumatized by an event that he or she forgets it and then forgets the act of forgetting. According to psychodynamic theory, the main function of repression is to protect the individual from threatening information.

The prevalence of repression is a matter of controversy. Most studies of traumatic memory indicate that a painful life event such as childhood sexual abuse is very likely to be remembered. However, there is also evidence that childhood sexual abuse may not be remembered. Linda Williams and colleagues conducted a number of investigations of memories of childhood abuse (Banyard & Williams, 2007; Liang, Williams, & Siegel, 2006; L. M. Williams, 2003, 2004). One study involved 129 women for whom hospital emergency room records indicated a childhood abuse experience (L. M. Williams, 1995). Seventeen years after the incident, the researchers contacted the women and asked (among other things) whether they had ever been the victim of childhood sexual abuse. Of the 129 women, most reported remembering and never having forgotten the experience; 10 percent of the participants reported having forgotten about the abuse at least for some portion of their lives.

● **motivated forgetting** Forgetting that occurs when something is so painful or anxiety-laden that remembering it is intolerable.

If repression does exist, it can be considered a special case of **motivated forgetting**, which occurs when individuals forget something because it is so painful or anxiety-laden that remembering is intolerable (Fujiwara, Levine, & Anderson, 2008). This type of forgetting may be a consequence of the emotional trauma experienced by victims of rape or physical abuse, war veterans, and survivors of earthquakes, plane crashes, and other terrifying events. These emotional traumas may haunt people for many years unless they can put the details out of mind. Even when people have not experienced trauma, they may use motivated forgetting to protect themselves from memories of painful, stressful, or otherwise unpleasant circumstances (Shu, Gino, & Bazerman, 2011).

Cognitive psychologist Jonathan Schooler suggested that recovered memories are better termed *discovered memories* because, regardless of their accuracy, individuals do experience them as real (Geraerts & others, 2009; Schooler, 2002). Schooler and his colleagues (1997) were able to identify cases in which the perpetrator or some third party could verify a discovered memory. The existence of such cases suggests that it is inappropriate to reject all claims by adults that they were victims of long-forgotten childhood sexual abuse.

How do psychologists interpret these cases? Generally, there is consensus around a few key issues (Knapp & VandeCreek, 2000). First, all agree that child sexual abuse is an important and egregious problem that has been unacknowledged historically. Second, psychologists widely believe that most individuals who were sexually abused as children remember all or part of what happened to them and that these continuous memories are likely to be accurate. Third, there is broad agreement that it is possible for someone who was abused to forget those memories for a long time, and it is also possible to construct memories that are false but that feel very real to an individual. Finally, it is highly difficult to separate accurate from inaccurate memories, especially if methods such as hypnosis have been used in the "recovery" of memories.

What about children's memories for childhood abuse? Are their memories likely to be accurate? Gail Goodman, a cognitive developmental psychologist with expertise in legal issues, has pioneered research examining whether children are easily coerced and whether they are likely to make false claims (Block & others, 2012; Chae & others, 2011; Cordon & others, 2013; Goodman, 1991, 2005, 2006; Goodman & others, 1997). In her studies children undergo relatively traumatic events (for instance, getting vaccinated) or embarrassing experiences (for instance, having a genital exam as part of a physical at the doctor's office). The children are then interviewed about their experiences. The interviews follow procedures that mimic those in legal settings, including the use of anatomically correct dolls, leading questions (such as "Did the doctor touch you here?"), and even criminal lineups where the children are asked to identify the perpetrator of the "crime" ("Who gave you the shot?"). The results demonstrate that children over the age of 4 are very unlikely to falsely report genital touching; only about 8 percent of children give such false reports.

## EYEWITNESS TESTIMONY

By now, you should realize that memory is not a perfect reflection of reality. Understanding the distortions of memory is particularly important when people are called on to report what they saw or heard in relation to a crime. Eyewitness testimonies, like other types of memories, may contain errors (Houston & others, 2013; Wells & Loftus, 2013), but faulty memory in criminal matters has especially serious consequences. When eyewitness testimony is inaccurate, the wrong person might go to jail or even be put to death, or the perpetrator of the crime might not be prosecuted. It is important to note that witnessing a crime is often traumatic for the individual, and so this type of memory typically fits into the larger category of memory for highly emotional events.

Much of the interest in eyewitness testimony focuses on distortion, bias, and inaccuracy in memory (Davis & Loftus, 2018; Wells & Loftus, 2013). One reason for distortion is that, quite simply, memory fades with time. Furthermore, unlike a video, memory can be altered by new information (Simons & Chabris, 2011). In one study, researchers showed students a film of an automobile accident and then asked them how fast the white sports car was going when it passed a barn (Loftus, 1975). Although there was no barn in the film, 17 percent of the students mentioned the barn in their answer.

Bias is also a factor in faulty memory. Studies have shown that people of one ethnic group are less likely to recognize individual differences among people of another ethnic group (Horry, Wright, & Tredoux, 2010). In one experiment, a mugging was shown on a television news program (Loftus, 1993). Immediately afterward, a lineup of six suspects was broadcast and viewers were asked to phone in and identify which one of the six individuals they thought had committed the robbery. Of the 2,000 callers, more than 1,800 identified the wrong person. In addition, even though the robber was a non-Latino White male, one-third of the viewers identified an African American or a Latino suspect as the criminal.

Hundreds of individuals have been harmed by witnesses who have made a mistake. In his book *Convicting the Innocent*, law professor Brandon Garrett (2011) traced the first 250 cases in the United States in which a convicted individual was exonerated—proved to be not guilty—by DNA evidence. Of those cases, 190 (or *76 percent*) involved mistaken eyewitness identification of the accused.

Every year, more than 75,000 individuals are asked to identify suspects, and it is estimated that these identifications are wrong one-third of the time (Pezdek, 2012). TV crime dramas might give the impression that DNA evidence is widely available to protect innocent people from false accusations. However, it is estimated that less than 5 percent of legal cases involving eyewitness identifications include biological evidence to potentially exonerate mistakenly identified convicts (Wells, Steblay, & Dysart, 2011). So, for many crimes, eyewitness identification remains an important piece of evidence—and improving the validity of these identifications is a crucial goal (Smalarz & Wells, 2013).

To reduce the chances that innocent individuals will be accused of crimes, law enforcement officials are applying psychological research to improve the way they conduct criminal lineups. In lineups, a witness views a group of individuals or looks at photos of people, one of whom is the suspect. The witness is asked to identify the perpetrator of the crime if he or she is among those shown.

Psychological research has influenced these procedures in two ways. First, research strongly supports the use of *double-blind* procedures (Brewer & Wells, 2011). Recall that in a double-blind study, neither the participants nor the experimenter knows what condition the participants are in, to reduce the effects of bias on the results. For police lineups this means that no one directly involved in administering the lineup has any of which person is suspected of the crime, thereby removing any bias. Second, research shows that presenting suspects (either pictures or in person) sequentially (that is, one at a time) is less likely to produce erroneous identifications than presenting them all at one time (Steblay, Dysart, & Wells, 2011). A large field study in four jurisdictions in the United States found that double-blind and sequential procedures decreased witness errors in real criminal investigations (Wells, Steblay, & Dysart, 2011).

### test yourself

1. What are the primacy effect and the recency effect, and how do psychologists explain each?
2. What is the difference between recall and recognition?
3. Explain autobiographical memory and the reminiscence bump.

Faulty memory is not just about accusing the wrong person. For example, faulty memories were evident in descriptions of the suspects' vehicle in sniper attacks in 2002 that killed 10 people in and around Washington, DC. Witnesses reported seeing a white truck or van fleeing several of the crime scenes. It appears that a white van may have been near one of the first shootings; media repetition of this information contaminated the memories of witnesses to later attacks, making them more likely to remember a white truck or van. When caught, the snipers were driving a blue car.

Before police even arrive at a crime scene, witnesses talk among themselves, and this dialogue can contaminate memories. This is why, during the DC sniper attacks, law enforcement officials advised any persons who might witness the next attack to write down immediately what they had seen—even on their hands if they did not have a piece of paper.

*Faulty memories complicated the search for the perpetrators in the sniper attacks that killed 10 people in and around Washington, DC, in 2002. Police released photos of the type of white truck or van that witnesses said they saw fleeing some of the crime scenes. In the end, however, the suspects were driving a blue car when law enforcement officials apprehended them.*

# 5. FORGETTING

Human memory is imperfect. It is not unusual for two people to argue about whether something did or did not happen, each supremely confident that their memory is accurate and the other person's is faulty. Missed appointments, misplaced keys, and the failure to recall the name of a familiar face are everyday examples of forgetting. Why do we forget?

The first scientific research on forgetting was conducted by Hermann Ebbinghaus (1850–1909). In 1885, he made up and memorized a list of 13 nonsense syllables (for instance, *xid, lek,* or *riy*). Then he tested how many of them he could remember as time passed. Just one hour later, Ebbinghaus could recall only a few of the nonsense syllables he had memorized. Figure 14 shows Ebbinghaus's forgetting curve for nonsense syllables. Ebbinghaus concluded that most forgetting takes place soon after we learn something.

Fortunately, research has demonstrated that forgetting is not as extensive as Ebbinghaus envisioned (Harris, Sutton, & Barnier, 2010; Yonelinas & Ritchey, 2015). Ebbinghaus studied meaningless nonsense syllables. When we memorize meaningful material—like history or the content of this text—forgetting is neither so rapid nor so extensive. Let's look at some of the key topics related to forgetting.

**Hermann Ebbinghaus (1850–1909)**
*Ebbinghaus was the first psychologist to conduct scientific research on forgetting.*
©Bettmann/Getty Images

## Encoding Failure

Sometimes when people say they have forgotten something, they have not really forgotten it; rather, they never encoded the information in the first place. *Encoding failure* occurs when the information was never entered into long-term memory.

As an example of encoding failure, think about what the U.S. penny looks like. Researchers showed 15 versions of the penny to participants and asked them which one was correct (Nickerson & Adams, 1979). Look at the pennies in Figure 15 (but do not read the caption yet) and see whether you can tell which is the real penny. Most people do not do well on this task. Unless you are a coin collector, it is unlikely you have encoded specific details about pennies. You may have encoded just enough information to distinguish them from other coins (pennies are copper-colored, dimes and nickels are silver-colored; pennies fall between the sizes of dimes and quarters).

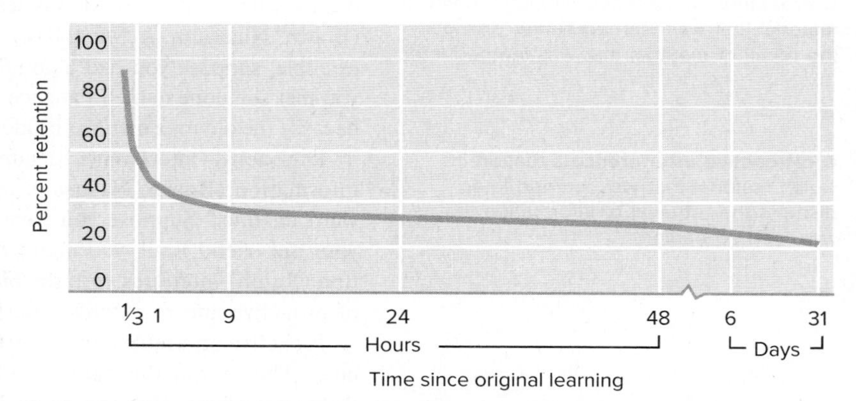


**FIGURE 14** **Ebbinghaus's Forgetting Curve** The figure illustrates Ebbinghaus's conclusion that most forgetting occurs soon after we learn something.

**FIGURE 15** **Which Is a Real U.S. Penny?** In the original experiment, participants viewed 15 versions of pennies; only one version was an actual U.S. penny. This figure shows re-creations of 7 of the 15 versions, and as you likely can tell, the task is still very difficult. Why? By the way, the actual U.S. penny is (C). ©David Tietz/Editorial Image, LLC

The penny exercise illustrates that we encode and enter into long-term memory only a small portion of our experiences. In a sense, then, encoding failures really are not cases of forgetting; they are cases of not remembering.

## Retrieval Failure

You paid attention to the lecture. You studied the material and are certain you know it. Yet, during the exam you simply cannot bring it to mind. That is an example of retrieval failure. Psychologists have theorized that the causes of retrieval failure include problems with the information in storage, the effects of time, personal reasons for remembering or forgetting, and the brain's condition (Barrouillet, De Paepe, & Langerock, 2012; Pica & others, 2018). An interesting fact about retrieval failure is that persistently trying to retrieve information is associated with better learning, even if those attempts are not successful (Kornell, Klein, & Rawson, 2015).

### INTERFERENCE

● **interference theory** The theory that people forget not because memories are lost from storage but because other information gets in the way of what they want to remember.

● **proactive interference** Situation in which material that was learned earlier disrupts the recall of material that was learned later.

● **retroactive interference** Situation in which material that was learned later disrupts the retrieval of information that was learned earlier.

*Interference* is one reason people forget. According to **interference theory**, people forget not because memories are lost from storage but because other information gets in the way of what they want to remember. In other words, memory for one thing fails because memory for something else gets in the way.

There are two kinds of interference: proactive and retroactive. **Proactive interference** occurs when material that was learned earlier disrupts the recall of material learned later (Brawn, Nusbaum, & Margoliash, 2018). Remember that *pro* means "forward in time." For example, suppose you had a good friend 10 years ago named Prudence and then last night you met someone named Patience. You might find yourself calling your new friend Prudence because the old information (Prudence) interferes with retrieval of new information (Patience).

**Retroactive interference** occurs when newer material disrupts the retrieval of older information (Brawn, Nusbaum, & Margoliash, 2018). Remember that *retro* means "backward in time." Suppose you have lately become friends with Ralph. In sending a note to your old friend Raul, you might mistakenly address it to Ralph because the new information (Ralph) interferes with the old information (Raul). Figure 16 depicts another example of proactive and retroactive interference.

Proactive and retroactive interference can both be explained as problems with retrieval cues. The reason the name Prudence interferes with the name Patience and the name Ralph interferes with the name Raul might be that the cue you are using to remember the one name does not distinguish between the two memories. For example, if the cue you are using is "my good friend," it might evoke both names. Retrieval cues (such as "friend" in our example) can become overloaded, and when that happens we are likely to forget or to retrieve incorrectly.

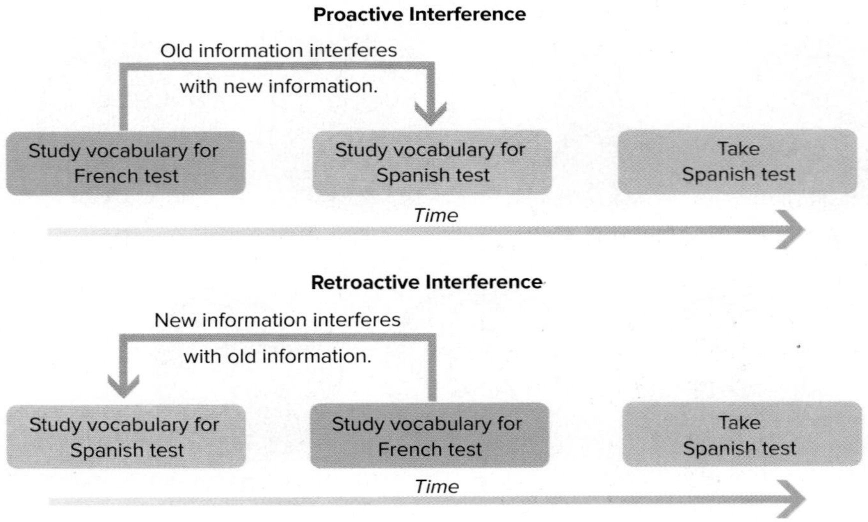

**FIGURE 16 Proactive and Retroactive Interference** *Pro* means "forward"; in proactive interference, old information has a forward influence by getting in the way of new material learned. Retro means "backward"; in retroactive interference, new information has a backward influence by getting in the way of material learned earlier.
Source: Brawn, Nusbaum, & Margoliash (2018).

## DECAY

Another reason for forgetting is the passage of time. According to **decay theory**, when we learn something new, a neurochemical memory trace forms, but over time this trace disintegrates. Decay theory suggests that the passage of time always increases forgetting.

Memories often do fade with the passage of time, but decay alone cannot explain forgetting. For example, under the right retrieval conditions, we can recover memories that we seemed to have forgotten. You might have forgotten the name of someone from high school but when you return to the setting where you knew the person, the name pops into your head. Similarly, you may not have thought about someone from your past for a long time, but when the person "friends" you on Facebook, you remember experiences you shared.

● **decay theory** Theory stating that when an individual learns something new, a neurochemical memory trace forms but then disintegrates over time, suggesting that the passage of time always increases forgetting.

## TIP-OF-THE-TONGUE PHENOMENON

We are all familiar with the retrieval glitch called **tip-of-the-tongue (TOT) phenomenon**—a type of "effortful retrieval" that occurs when we are confident that we know something but cannot quite pull it out of memory (A. S. Brown, 2012; D'Angelo & Humphreys, 2015). In a TOT state, we usually can retrieve characteristics of the word, such as the first letter and the number of syllables, but not the word itself. The TOT phenomenon arises when we can retrieve some of the desired information but not all of it (Schwartz & Metcalfe, 2011).

The TOT phenomenon reveals interesting aspects of memory. For one thing, it demonstrates that we do not store all of the information about a particular topic or experience in one way. If you have ever struggled to think of a specific word, you probably came up with various words that mean the same thing as the word you were looking for, but you still had a nagging feeling that none was quite right. Sometimes you might find the solution in an unexpected way. Imagine you are doing a crossword puzzle with the clue "colorful scarf" for a seven-letter word. You have a feeling you know this word. If you have not thought of the answer yet, say the following word aloud: *banana.* If you were experiencing the TOT phenomenon when doing the crossword, thinking of *banana* might help you come up with the correct answer, *bandana.* Although the meaning of *banana* is unrelated to that of *bandana,* the fact that these words start with the same sounds (and therefore are linked in verbal memory) can lead you to the word *bandana* (Abrams & Rodriguez, 2005). The sounds of words are linked in memory even if their meanings are not (Antón-Méndez & others, 2012; Buján & others, 2012).

● **tip-of-the-tongue (TOT) phenomenon** A type of effortful retrieval associated with a person's feeling that he or she knows something (say, a word or a name) but cannot quite pull it out of memory.

## PROSPECTIVE MEMORY

The main focus of this chapter has been on **retrospective memory**, which is remembering the past. **Prospective memory** involves remembering information about doing something in the future; it includes memory for intentions. Prospective memory includes both *timing*—when we have to do something—and *content*—what we have to do.

We can make a distinction between time-based and event-based prospective memory. *Time-based* prospective memory is our intention to engage in a given behavior after a specified amount of time has gone by, such as an intention to make a phone call to someone in an hour. In *event-based* prospective memory, we engage in the intended behavior when some external event or cue elicits it, as when we give a message to a roommate when we see her. The cues available in event-based prospective memory make it more effective than time-based prospective memory (McDaniel & Einstein, 2007; Smith-Spark, Zięcik, & Sterling, 2016).

Some failures in prospective memory are referred to as "absentmindedness." We are more absentminded when we become preoccupied with something else, are distracted by something, or are under a lot of time pressure. Absentmindedness often involves a breakdown between attention and memory storage (Schacter, 2001). Fortunately, research has shown that our goals are encoded into memory along with the features of situations that would allow us to pursue them. Our memories, then, prepare us to recognize when a situation presents an opportunity to achieve those goals.

● **retrospective memory** Remembering information from the past.

● **prospective memory** Remembering information about doing something in the future; includes memory for intentions.

Older adults perform worse on prospective memory tasks than younger adults do, but typically these differences are true only for artificial lab tasks (Smith, Horn, & Bayen, 2012; Zöllig & others, 2012). In real life, older adults generally perform as well as younger adults in terms of prospective memory (Rendell & Craik, 2000). Generally, prospective memory failure (forgetting to do something) occurs when retrieval is a conscious, effortful (rather than automatic) process (Henry & others, 2004).

### AMNESIA

- **amnesia** The loss of memory.
- **anterograde amnesia** A memory disorder that affects the retention of new information and events.
- **retrograde amnesia** Memory loss for a segment of the past but not for new events.

Recall the case of H. M. in the discussion of explicit and implicit memory. In H. M.'s surgery, the part of his brain responsible for laying down new memories was damaged beyond repair. The result was **amnesia**, the loss of memory.

H. M. suffered from **anterograde amnesia**, a memory disorder that affects the retention of new information and events (*antero* indicates amnesia that moves forward in time). What he learned before the surgery (and thus before the onset of amnesia) was not affected. For example, H. M. could identify his friends, recall their names, and even tell stories about them–*if* he had known them before the surgery. People who met H. M. after the surgery remained strangers, even if they spent thousands of hours with him. H. M.'s postsurgical experiences were rarely encoded in his long-term memory.

Whereas anterograde amnesia involves the inability to make new memories, **retrograde amnesia** involves memory loss for a segment of past events (*retro* indicates amnesia that moves back in time). In contrast with anterograde amnesia, in retrograde amnesia the forgotten information is *old*–it occurred prior to the event that caused the amnesia–and the ability to acquire new memories is not affected. (You can remember that retrograde amnesia involves forgetting old information by keeping in mind the use of the prefix "retro" to describe old things that become, sometimes inexplicably, popular.) Recall Angela Sartin-Hartung from the opening of this chapter. She suffered from retrograde amnesia and forgot her 13-year marriage to her husband. Retrograde amnesia is much more common than anterograde amnesia and frequently occurs when the brain is injured. Sometimes individuals have both anterograde and retrograde amnesia.

### test yourself

1. What is the term for the failure of information to enter long-term memory?
2. Name four factors that, according to psychologists, may be the cause of retrieval failure.
3. What is the tip-of-the-tongue (TOT) phenomenon, and what does it reveal about how we store information?

## 6. STUDY TIPS FROM THE SCIENCE OF MEMORY

How can you apply your new knowledge of memory processes to improving your academic performance? You can sharpen your memory by thinking deeply about the "material" of life and connecting the information to other things you know. The most connected node or most elaborate schema to which you can link new information is the self–what you know and think about yourself. To make something meaningful and to secure its place in memory, make it matter to you.

If you think about memory as a physical event in the brain, you can see that memorizing material is like training a muscle. Repeated recruitment of sets of neurons creates the connection you want available not only at exam time but throughout life.

©Design Pics/Monkey Business

### ORGANIZE

Before you engage the powerful process of memory, the first step in improving your academic performance is to make sure that the information you are studying is accurate and well organized.

#### Tips for Organizing

- *Review your course notes routinely and catch potential errors and ambiguities early.* There is no sense in memorizing inaccurate or incomplete information.
- *Organize the material in a way that will allow you to commit it to memory effectively.* Arrange information, rework material, and give it a structure that will help you to remember it.

- *Experiment with different organizational techniques.* One approach is to use a hierarchy such as an outline. You might create analogies (such as the earlier comparison of retrieval from long-term memory to finding a book in the library) that take advantage of your preexisting schemas. As you begin to organize the information, you might explore possible mnemonics to help you memorize.

## ENCODE

Once you ensure that the material to be remembered is accurate and well organized, it is time to memorize. Although some types of information are encoded automatically, academic learning usually requires effort.

### Tips for Encoding

- *Pay attention.* Remember that staying focused on one thing is crucial. In other words, no divided attention.
- *Process information at an appropriate level.* Think about the material meaningfully and process it deeply.
- *Elaborate on the points to be remembered.* Make associations to your life and to other aspects of the material you want to remember. Take notes by hand, and when you do, think about what you are writing down.
- *Use imagery.* Devise images to help you remember (such as the mental picture of a computer screen to help you recall the concept of working memory); this allows you to "double encode" the information.
- *Use chunking.* Break up the material into chunks to help you get it into memory.
- *Understand that encoding is not simply something that you should do before a test.* Rather, encode early and often. During class, while reading, or in discussing issues, take advantage of opportunities to create associations to your course material.

## REHEARSE

While learning material initially, relate it to your life and attend to examples that help you do so. After class, rehearse the course material over time to solidify it in memory.

### Tips for Rehearsing

- *Rewrite, type, or retype your notes.* Some students find this exercise a good form of rehearsal.
- *Talk to people about what you have learned and how it is important to real life in order to reinforce memory.* You are more likely to remember information over the long term if you understand it and relate it to your world than if you just mechanically rehearse and memorize it. Rehearsal works well for information in short-term memory, but when you need to encode, store, and then retrieve information from long-term memory, it is much less efficient. Thus, for most information, understand it, give it meaning, elaborate on it, and personalize it.
- *Test yourself.* It is not enough to look at your notes and think, "Oh, yes, I know this." Sometimes recognition instills a false sense of knowing. If you have developed mnemonics for material, test your ability to use them effectively. It is not enough to simply know that you have memorized, "Pete LoVeS CatE" to remember the components of Baddeley's model of working memory. You must be able to produce the concepts this mnemonic stands for: Phonological Loop, Visuo-Spatial Sketchpad, and Central Executive. If you look at a definition, and it seems so familiar that you are certain you know it, challenge yourself. What happens when you close the book and try to reconstruct the definition? Compare your personal definition to the technical one in the book. How did you do?
- *While reading and studying, ask yourself questions.* Ask questions such as, "What is the meaning of what I just read?" "Why is this important?" and "What is an example of the concept I just read about?" When you make a concerted effort to ask yourself

questions about what you have read or about an activity in class, you expand the number of associations you make with the information you will need to retrieve later.

- *Treat your brain kindly*. If you are genuinely seeking to improve your memory performance, keep in mind that the brain is a physical organ. Perhaps the best way to promote effective memory storage is to make sure that your brain is able to function at maximum capacity. That means resting it, nourishing it by eating well, and keeping it free of mind-altering substances. A key way we can take care of our memory capacity is to get sufficient sleep.

### RETRIEVE

Let's say you have studied not just hard but deeply, elaborating on important concepts and committing lists to memory. You have slept well and eaten a nutritious breakfast. Now it is exam time. How can you best retrieve the essential information?

#### Tips for Retrieving

- *Use retrieval cues*. Sit in the same seat where you learned the material. Remember that the exam is full of questions about topics that you have thoughtfully encoded. Some of the questions on the test might help jog your memory for answers to others.
- *Sit comfortably, take a deep breath, and stay calm*. Bolster your confidence by recalling that research on long-term memory has shown that material that has been committed to memory is there for a very long time—even among those who may experience a moment of panic when the test is handed out.

Memory is crucial for learning and academic success, but it also serves many other purposes. As we now consider, these include contributing to healthy functioning as we age and giving our life a sense of meaning.

***test yourself***

1. What steps can you take to ensure that your course information is well organized?
2. Give at least three tips for encoding information and at least three tips for rehearsing information.
3. What strategies can help you retrieve essential information when taking an examination?

## 7. MEMORY AND HEALTH AND WELLNESS

Autobiographical memory is a vital part of human life (Fivush, 2011; Prebble, Addis, & Tippett, 2013). It allows us to learn from experience (Pillemer, 1998), storing the lessons we have learned from life. These memories become a resource to which we can turn when faced with life's difficulties.

Autobiographical memory allows us to understand ourselves and provides a source of identity. In studies of self-defining memories, Jefferson Singer and his colleagues maintain that these internalized stories of personal experience serve as signs of the meaning we have created from life events and give our lives coherence (Baddeley & Singer, 2010; Singer & Conway, 2011; Singer, Singer, & Berry, 2013).

Dan McAdams (2006, 2009, 2013, 2018) says autobiographical memories form the core of our personal identity. Research has shown that the stories we tell about our lives have important implications. For instance, McAdams and his colleagues have demonstrated that individuals who describe important life experiences that go from bad to better (*redemptive stories*) are more *generative*—that is, they are the kind of people who make a contribution to future generations, people who leave a legacy that will outlive them (McAdams, 2018). These individuals are also better adjusted than those whose self-defining memories go from good to bad (*contamination stories*). One study showed that individuals in Alcoholics Anonymous who told stories about their last drink that were characterized by redemption were more likely to abstain from alcohol (Dunlop & Tracy, 2013). Clearly, the construction and reconstruction of autobiographical memory may reveal important aspects of how individuals function, grow, and discover meaning in their lives (Cox & McAdams, 2012; King & Hicks, 2007; McAdams, 2013).

Memory matters to us in social ways as well. We apologize if we have forgotten someone's name, even if that forgetting is unintentional. Remembering details such as names is a way we demonstrate that someone matters to us (King & Geise, 2011; Ray & others, 2018).

## Keeping Memory Sharp—and Preserving Brain Function

*Engaging in an intellectually challenging activity such as playing chess seems to offer some protection against the mental decline associated with aging.*

©uniquely india/photosindia/Getty Images

Memory is also an indicator of brain functioning. Preserving memory is of vital importance as we age. A strong message from research on aging and memory is that, as for many things in life, the phrase "Use it or lose it" applies to memory.

Consider the case of Richard Wetherill, a retired lecturer and a very good chess player (Melton, 2005). Wetherill was so skilled that he was able to think eight moves ahead in a chess match. At one point, he noticed that he was having trouble playing chess–he could anticipate only five moves ahead. He was sure that something was seriously wrong with him, despite his wife's assurances that she noticed no changes. A battery of cognitive tests revealed no abnormalities, and a brain scan was similarly reassuring. Two years later, Wetherill was dead, and the autopsy showed a brain ravaged by Alzheimer disease. Such extensive brain damage usually indicates that a person was incapable of coherent thought. Wetherill's symptoms, however, had been limited to a small decline in his skill at playing chess.

Wetherill's case is surprising but also typical. Individuals who lead active intellectual lives seem to be protected against the mental decline generally associated with age. Indeed, research has shown that individuals who are educated, have high IQs, and remain mentally engaged in complex tasks tend to cope better with a variety of assaults to the brain, including Alzheimer disease, stroke, head injury, and even poisoning with neurotoxins (Halliwell, 2018; McAleese & others, 2018; Zammit & others, 2018). It appears that an active mental life in which the person engages in challenging cognitive tasks builds up what is a called a "cognitive store." This cognitive store is like an emergency stash of mental capacity that allows individuals to avoid the negative effects of harm to the brain (Thow & others, 2018).

Yaakov Stern found that among a group of individuals with Alzheimer disease who appeared to be equal in terms of their outward symptoms, those who were more educated were actually suffering from much worse brain damage–yet they were functioning at a level similar to others with relatively less damage (Stern & others, 1992). Stern and his colleagues (2004) have also shown that intellectual pursuits such as playing chess and reading reduce the severity of Alzheimer's symptoms.

Importantly, research demonstrates that although maintaining an active mental life can reduce the speed of cognitive decline associated with Alzheimer disease, it can also be related to more rapid decline once a person is diagnosed (Wilson & others, 2010). Can you see why this might be the case? Individuals who lead active cognitive lives may be diagnosed much later than others because their brains have compensated flexibly for the issues brought on by disease.

A lifetime of mental engagement may produce a cognitive reserve that allows the brain to maintain its ability to recruit new neural networks that compensate for damage. These brains are better able to move to a backup plan to maintain the individual's level of functioning (Andel & others, 2005). In addition to mental activity, staying physically active also seems to play a role in maintaining a sharp mind (Diamond & Savin-Williams, 2013; Halliwell, 2019; Sattler & others, 2012).

## Memory and the Shaping of Meaningful Experiences

Finally, let's consider the role of memory in shaping meaningful experiences in daily life. Think of the most meaningful event of your life. Clearly, that event is one that you remember, among *all* the things you have experienced in your life.

## test yourself

1. What crucial functions does autobiographical memory serve?
2. What did McAdams mean when he described certain individuals as "generative"?
3. What factors are involved in keeping memory sharp as we age?

We all have certain particularly vivid autobiographical memories that stand out as indicators of meaning. In fact, however, everyday life is filled with potentially remarkable moments—a beautiful sunrise, a delicious meal prepared just for you, an unexpected phone call from a friend. Experiencing the richness of everyday life requires us to be attentive and engaged. Sometimes daily chores and problems lead us to feel that we are just going through the motions. This sort of mindless living may be a way to survive, but it is unlikely to be a way to thrive.

The processes of attention and encoding that we have explored in this chapter suggest that actively engaging in life—investing ourselves in the events of the day—can help to ensure that our life stories are rich and nuanced. That way, when someone says, "So, tell me about yourself," we will have a story to tell.

# SUMMARY

## 1. THE NATURE OF MEMORY

Memory is the retention of information over time. The three processes involved in memory are encoding (getting information into storage), storage (retaining information over time), and retrieval (taking information out of storage).

## 2. MEMORY ENCODING

Encoding requires attention, but the attention must be selective. Memory is negatively influenced by divided attention.

According to the theory of levels of processing, information is processed on a continuum from shallow (sensory or physical features are encoded) to intermediate (labels are attached to stimuli) to deep (the meanings of stimuli and their associations with other stimuli are processed). Deeper processing produces better memory. Elaboration—the extensiveness of processing at any given level of memory encoding—improves memory. Using imagery, or mental pictures, as a context for information can improve memory.

## 3. MEMORY STORAGE

The Atkinson–Shiffrin theory describes memory as a three-stage process: sensory memory, short-term memory, and long-term memory.

Sensory memory holds perceptions of the world for only an instant. Visual sensory memory (iconic memory) retains information for about ¼ of a second; auditory sensory memory (echoic memory) preserves information for several seconds.

Short-term memory is a limited-capacity memory system in which information is usually retained for as long as 30 seconds. Short-term memory's limitation is $7 \pm 2$ bits of information. Chunking and rehearsal can benefit short-term memory. Working memory is a combination of short-term memory and attention, a mental workspace where we hold information in mind and solve problems. Because it cannot rely on rehearsal, working memory capacity is estimated to be $4 \pm 1$ chunks of information. Baddeley's model of working memory has three components: a central executive and two assistants (phonological loop and visuo-spatial sketchpad).

Long-term memory is a relatively permanent type of memory that holds huge amounts of information for a long time. Long-term memory has two main subtypes: explicit and implicit memory. Explicit memory is the conscious recollection of information, such as specific facts or events. Implicit memory affects behavior through prior experiences that are not consciously recollected.

Explicit memory has two dimensions. One dimension includes episodic memory and semantic memory. The other dimension includes retrospective memory and prospective memory. Implicit memory is multidimensional too and includes systems for procedural memory, priming, and classical conditioning.

It is important to remember that memories are not stored in single locations in the brain. Instead, memories are best considered as networks of associated neurons that represent well-worn paths and that are activated when we remember. The exact areas of the brain that are active when we remember will depend on what we are remembering.

## 4. MEMORY RETRIEVAL

The serial position effect is the tendency to recall items at the beginning and the end of a list better than the middle items. The primacy effect is the tendency to recall items at the beginning of the list better than the middle items. The recency effect is the tendency to remember the items at the end of a list better than the middle items.

Retrieval is easier when effective cues are present. Another factor in effective retrieval is the nature of the retrieval task. Simple recognition of previously remembered information in the presence of cues is generally easier than recall of the information.

According to the encoding specificity principle, information present at the time of encoding or learning tends to be effective as a retrieval cue, a process referred to as context-dependent memory. Retrieval also benefits from priming, which activates particular connections or associations in memory. The tip-of-the-tongue phenomenon occurs when we cannot quite pull something out of memory.

Special cases of retrieval include autobiographical memory, emotional memory, memory for trauma, repressed memory, and eyewitness testimony. Autobiographical memory is a person's recollections of his or her life experiences. The reminiscence bump refers to the fact that most people have more autobiographical memories for the second and third decades of life. Autobiographical memory has three levels: life time periods, general events, and event-specific knowledge. Biographies of the self connect the past and the present to form our identity.

Emotional memories may be especially vivid and enduring. Particularly significant emotional memories, or flashbulb memories, capture emotionally profound events that people often recall accurately and vividly. Memory for personal trauma also is usually more accurate than memory for ordinary events, but it too is subject to distortion and inaccuracy. People tend to remember the core information about a personal trauma but might distort some of the details. Personal trauma can cause individuals to repress emotionally laden information so that it is not accessible to consciousness.

Repression means forgetting a particularly troubling experience because it would be too upsetting to remember it. Eyewitness testimony may contain errors due to memory decay or bias.

## 5. FORGETTING

Encoding failure is forgetting information that was never entered into long-term memory. Retrieval failure can occur for at least four reasons.

First, interference theory stresses that we forget not because memories are lost from storage but because other information gets in the way of what we want to remember. Interference can be proactive (as occurs when material learned earlier disrupts the recall of material learned later) or retroactive (as occurs when material learned later disrupts the retrieval of information learned earlier).

The second reason for retrieval failure is explained by decay theory, which states that when we learn something new, a neurochemical memory trace forms, but over time this chemical trail disintegrates.

Third, motivated forgetting occurs when we want to forget something. It is common when a memory becomes painful or anxiety-laden, as in the case of emotional traumas such as rape and physical abuse.

Finally, amnesia, the physiologically based loss of memory, can cause retrieval failure. Anterograde amnesia affects the retention of new information or events. Retrograde amnesia affects memories of the past but not memories of new events. Amnesia can be a combination of both types.

## 6. STUDY TIPS FROM THE SCIENCE OF MEMORY

Memory research can be applied to each stage of studying: Organizing the material, encoding, rehearsing, and retrieving it. For each step in preparation, memory research suggests the importance of paying attention and minimizing distractions, understanding the material rather than relying on rote memorization, asking yourself questions, and taking good notes. Research on memory suggests that the best way to remember course material is to relate it to many different aspects of your life.

## 7. MEMORY AND HEALTH AND WELLNESS

Autobiographical memories, particularly self-defining memories, provide a unique source of identity, and sharing those memories with others plays a role in social bonding.

Taking on challenging cognitive tasks throughout life can stave off the effects of age on memory and lessen the effects of Alzheimer disease.

Engaging in everyday life means living memorably. Mindfulness to life events provides a rich reservoir of experiences upon which to build a storehouse of autobiographical memories.

# key *terms*

amnesia
anterograde amnesia
Atkinson-Shiffrin theory
autobiographical memory
connectionism or parallel distributed processing (PDP)
decay theory
divided attention
elaboration
encoding
episodic memory
explicit memory or declarative memory
flashbulb memory
implicit memory or nondeclarative memory
interference theory
levels of processing
long-term memory
memory
motivated forgetting
priming
proactive interference
procedural memory
prospective memory
retrieval
retroactive interference
retrograde amnesia
retrospective memory
schema
script
semantic memory
sensory memory
serial position effect
short-term memory
storage
sustained attention or vigilance
tip-of-the-tongue (TOT) phenomenon
working memory

# apply your *knowledge*

1. Write down a memory that you feel has been especially important in making you who you are. What are some characteristics of this self-defining memory? What do you think the memory says about you? How does it relate to your current goals and aspirations? Do you think of the memory often? You might find that this part of your life story can be inspiring when things are going poorly or when you are feeling down.
2. Become a memory detective and explore the accuracy of your own memory for major events. Think about an event for which you might have a flashbulb memory. You might choose from a major event in recent history, such as the 9/11 attacks, Hurricane Sandy, or the earthquake in Haiti. Then ask yourself some easily verifiable questions about it, such as what day of the week did it happen? What time of day? What were the date and year? How many people were involved? When you have done your best to answer these questions, check your facts online. Were your memories accurate?
3. It is sometimes difficult to believe that our memories are not as accurate as we think. To test your ability to be a good eyewitness, visit one of the following websites:

   www.pbs.org/wgbh/pages/frontline/shows/dna/

   https://public.psych.iastate.edu/glwells/theeyewitnesstest.html

   Did this exercise change your opinion of the accuracy of eyewitness testimony? Explain.

# CHAPTER 8

## CHAPTER OUTLINE

1. The Cognitive Revolution in Psychology
2. Thinking
3. Intelligence
4. Language
5. Thinking, Problem Solving, and Health and Wellness

# Thinking, Intelligence, and Language

## Giving Sight to the Blind

**Think about the way you edit photos on a smartphone.** Stretching with your fingers, you enlarge the image. You might enhance the contrast or focus in on features you especially like. Now, imagine being able to use these techniques to change the way you see the world all the time. The inventors of the eSight3 used technologies like these and others to produce glasses that give sight to the blind. The eSight3, which looks like a lightweight virtual reality headset, produces real-time, high-definition video that enhances the visual input for the wearer. These glasses allow individuals who are legally blind to see. The eSight3 lifts the limits that visual impairment has placed on people's lives so they can take walks, play sports, and see their family and friends. These glasses were recognized as one of the best inventions of 2017 (Sifferlin, 2017). For the estimated 7 million Americans who are legally blind (National Federation of the Blind, 2018), the eSight3 promises to open up a world of possibilities. At the end of 2017, over 1000 patients were using the product (Sifferlin, 2017).

Now, not all inventions are as life-changing as the eSight3. After all, another great invention of 2017 was the fidget spinner (*Time* staff, 2017). Still, it is interesting to think about the way inventions come about. Like the eSight3, inventions often make use of things that scientists and engineers had already known about for some time. Imagine editing a photo on your phone and recognizing that the technology might bring sight to the blind. Taking what we already know, adding some new ideas, and putting it all together to help others is an amazing feat of human thinking. ●

# PREVIEW

Cognitive psychology is the study of mental processes. This chapter investigates the basic cognitive processes of thinking, intelligence, and language. We first define cognition and look at the cognitive revolution that led to new understanding about the workings of the human mind. Thinking refers to the process of cognition itself. We examine types of thinking, including problem solving, reasoning, critical thinking, and creativity. We then examine the quality of mental processes, focusing on a central indicator of cognitive ability—intelligence. We next explore the way thoughts are typically expressed, focusing on the unique contribution of language to mental processes. Finally, we close by considering the role of thinking in health and wellness.

## 1. THE COGNITIVE REVOLUTION IN PSYCHOLOGY

● **cognition** The way in which information is processed and manipulated in remembering, thinking, and knowing.

**Cognition** refers to the way information is processed and manipulated in remembering, thinking, and knowing. All the things we do "in our head" and the activities you might think of as part of the mind are covered by the broad term *cognition*. Cognitive psychology is a broad field that includes the study of consciousness, memory, and cognitive neuroscience. We begin our coverage of cognition by tracing its history.

After the first decade of the twentieth century, behaviorism dominated the thinking of experimental psychologists. Behaviorists such as B. F. Skinner believed that the human mind is an abstract entity best left to philosophers, and they considered observable behavior to be psychologists' proper focus. Behaviorists had little use for the mental processes occurring in that place between your ears.

During the 1950s, psychologists' views began to change. The advent of computers provided a new way to think about the workings of the human mind (Galotti, 2017). If we could "see" what computers were doing internally, maybe we could use our observations to study human mental processes, scientists reasoned. Computer science was a key motivator in the birth of the study of human cognition.

The first modern computer, developed by mathematician John von Neumann in the late 1940s, showed that machines could perform logical operations. In the 1950s, researchers speculated that computers might offer a model to understanding how the human mind works. In many ways the advent of the computer gave psychologists an analogy or metaphor for the human mind and granted permission to study cognition in humans (Xiong & Proctor, 2018). We can think of the brain as the computer's hardware and cognition as its software.

Herbert Simon (1969) was among the pioneers in comparing the human mind to computer processing systems. In this analogy, the sensory and perceptual systems provide an "input channel," similar to the way data are entered into a computer (Figure 1). As input (information) comes into the mind, mental processes, or operations, act on it, just as the computer's software acts on the data. The processed input generates information that remains in memory in much the same way a computer stores what it has worked on. Finally, the information is retrieved from memory and "printed out" or "displayed" (so to speak) as an observable response.

By the late 1950s the cognitive revolution was in full swing, peaking in the 1980s. The term *cognitive psychology* became a label for approaches that sought to explain observable behavior by investigating mental processes and structures that cannot be observed directly.

Computers provide a logical and concrete, but oversimplified, model of human information processing. Inanimate computers and human brains function quite differently in some respects. For example, most computers receive information from a human who has already coded the information and removed much of its ambiguity. In contrast, each brain

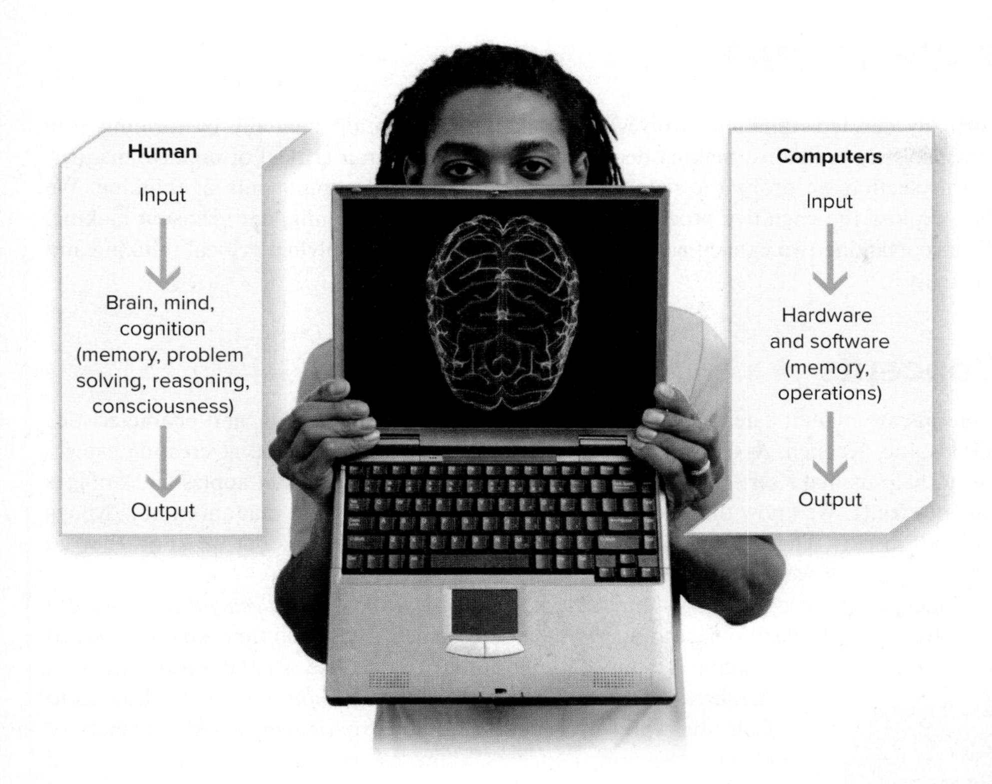


**FIGURE 1 Computers and Human Cognition** An analogy is commonly drawn between human cognition and the way computers work. The brain is analogous to a computer's hardware, and cognition is analogous to a computer's software.
©Creatas/PictureQuest Source: Simon (1969).

cell, or neuron, can respond to ambiguous information transmitted through sensory receptors such as the eyes and ears.

Computers can perform complex numerical calculations much faster and more accurately than humans. Computers can apply and follow rules more consistently and with fewer errors than humans and can represent complex mathematical patterns better than humans.

The human brain is incredibly flexible, able to learn new rules, relationships, concepts, and patterns that it can generalize to novel situations. In comparison, computers are more limited in their ability to learn, to change, and to generalize. Computers do not have the means to develop new learning goals. Furthermore, the human mind is aware of itself; the computer is not. No computer is likely to approach the richness of human consciousness. Consider the challenges involved when a computer takes over a human activity. Autonomous cars–vehicles that drive themselves–appear to be on the horizon, but devising ways to ensure that they are safe and efficient has been challenging (Mayersohn, 2018).

Computer scientists have made great strides in the area of computer perception–designing computers that process sounds (Martins & others, 2017) and recognize faces and other objects (Lopes & others, 2017). Interestingly, although the study of the mind was inspired by computers, research and innovation in computer science is inspired by the capacities of the human mind (Lu & others, 2018; Steels & Brooks, 2018).

The computer's role in cognitive psychology continues to expand. An entire scientific field called **artificial intelligence (AI)** focuses on creating machines capable of performing activities that require intelligence when people do them (Lu & others, 2018). AI is especially helpful in tasks requiring speed, persistence, and vast memory. AI systems assist in diagnosing medical illnesses and prescribing treatment, evaluating loan applicants, and advising students about which courses to take (Jarrahi, 2018). It is remarkable how far AI has permeated our lives. Recently, a painting that was created by AI sold at auction for over $400,000 (Cohn, 2018). The painting, a rather strange and distorted portrait of a man, entitled *Edmon de Belamy*, from *La Famille de Belamy*, was made by a French group called Obvious.

*Artificial intelligence (AI) created this strange portrait, Edmon de Belamy, from La Famille de Belamy.*
©Timothy A. Clary/AFP/Getty Images

● **artificial intelligence (AI)** A scientific field that focuses on creating machines capable of performing activities that require intelligence when they are done by people.

## test yourself

1. What aspect of thinking did behaviorists see as the proper focus of psychology?
2. What technological development gave psychologists a new way to look at the human mind?
3. In what ways is the human mind superior to computers?

# 2. THINKING

Formally defined, **thinking** involves manipulating information mentally by forming concepts, solving problems, making decisions, and reflecting in a critical or creative manner. In this section we probe the nature of concepts—the basic components of thinking. We then explore the cognitive processes of problem solving, reasoning, and decision making. We also examine two capacities related to enhanced problem solving: critical thinking and creativity.

● **thinking** The process of manipulating information mentally by forming concepts, solving problems, making decisions, and reflecting critically or creatively.

● **concepts** Mental categories that are used to group objects, events, and characteristics.

● **prototype model** A model emphasizing that when people evaluate whether a given item reflects a certain concept, they compare the item with the most typical item(s) in that category and look for a "family resemblance" with that item's properties.

## Concepts

**Concepts** are mental categories that are used to group objects, events, and characteristics (Goldstone, Kersten, & Carvalho, 2018). Humans are especially good at creating categories to help us make sense of information in our world. We know that apples and oranges are both fruits. We know that poodles and collies are both dogs and that ants and ladybugs are both insects. These items differ from one another in some ways but we know they go together because we have concepts for fruits, dogs, and insects.

Concepts are important for four reasons. First, they allow us to *generalize*. If we did not have concepts, each object in our world would be new to us each time we encountered it. Imagine having to think about how to use a chair every time you encountered a new member of the category *chair*. Concepts allow us to navigate the world by generalizing our experiences across members of a category. Second, concepts allow us to associate experiences and objects. Baseball, soccer, and track are sports. The concept *sport* gives us a way to compare these activities. Concepts provide the net that captures the various objects, ideas, and activities that constitute an abstract idea. Third, concepts make memory more efficient. Remember the concept of chunking in memory. Because we have a concept, many different items can be unified into a chunk, facilitating memory. Fourth, concepts provide clues about how to react to an object or experience. Maybe you have had the experience of trying an exotic new cuisine and feeling puzzled by the contents of your plate. If a friend reassures you, "That's food!" you know that given the concept *food,* it is okay to dig in. Thus, concepts tell us how to behave.

There are a variety of ways to understand how people decide that something belongs (or does not belong) in a concept. For example, the **prototype model** says that people decide whether a given item fits in a certain concept by comparing the item to the most typical item(s) in that category, looking for a "family resemblance." Birds generally fly, sing, and build nests, so we know that robins and eagles are both birds. We recognize exceptions to these properties, however, we know that a penguin is still a bird even though it does not do these things.

In the prototype model, people use characteristic properties to create a representation of the average or ideal member—the prototype—for each concept. Comparing individual cases to mental prototypes may be a good way to decide quickly whether something belongs to a particular category. As we will see later in this chapter, concepts can have negative effects when they are applied to *people* rather than to objects.

*Although it has a ducklike bill and lays eggs, the platypus is nevertheless a mammal like the tiger, as platypus females produce milk with which they feed their young. The prototypical birdlike characteristics of the platypus can lead us to think mistakenly that the platypus is a bird. Its atypical properties place the platypus on the extreme of the concept mammal.*

(first) ©John Carnemolla/Getty Images; (second) ©Ondrej Prosicky/Shutterstock

## Problem Solving

Concepts tell us *what* we think about but not *why* we think. *Why* do we engage in thinking? Consider Levi Hutchins, an ambitious young man who sought to wake up at 4 A.M. each morning. Levi had a specific goal—to beat the sun up every day. To solve this problem (and achieve his goal), he invented the alarm clock in 1787. **Problem solving** means finding an appropriate way to attain a goal when the goal is not readily available (Bassok & Novick, 2012; Fabian, 2018). Problem solving entails following several steps and overcoming mental obstacles.

● **problem solving** The mental process of finding an appropriate way to attain a goal when the goal is not readily available.

## FOLLOWING THE STEPS IN PROBLEM SOLVING

Research points to four steps in the problem-solving process.

**1. Find and Frame Problems** Recognizing that a problem exists and then considering exactly what the problem involves—that is, clearly defining it—are the first steps in solving a problem.

Many real-world problems are ill defined or vague, with no clear-cut solutions. Such problems may require a great deal of creativity. The visionaries who developed the many inventions that influence our daily lives—like the computer, phone, and light bulb—all saw problems that everyone else was content to live with. Recognizing problems involves being aware of and open to experiences (two mental habits we will examine later). It also means listening carefully to that voice in your head that occasionally sighs, "There must be a better way."

**2. Develop Good Problem-Solving Strategies** Once we find a problem and clearly define it, we need to develop strategies for solving it. Some effective strategies include creating subgoals and applying algorithms and heuristics.

**Subgoals** are intermediate goals or intermediate problems we devise to put us in a better position for reaching a final goal or solution. Imagine that you are writing a paper for a psychology class. What are some subgoaling strategies for this task? One might be locating the right books and articles on your chosen topic. At the same time that you are searching for the right publications, you will likely benefit from establishing some subgoals within your time frame for completing the project. If the paper is due in two months, you might set a subgoal of writing a first draft of the paper two weeks before it is due, another subgoal of completing your reading for the paper one month before it is due, and still another subgoal of starting your library research tomorrow. Notice that in establishing the subgoals for meeting the deadline, you worked backward. Working backward in establishing subgoals is a good strategy. You first create the subgoal that is closest to the final goal and then work backward to the subgoal that is closest to the beginning of the problem-solving effort.

● **subgoals** Intermediate goals or intermediate problems devised to put the individual in a better position for reaching the final goal or solution.

**Algorithms** are strategies that guarantee a solution to a problem. Algorithms come in different forms, such as formulas, instructions, and the testing of all possible solutions. We use algorithms in cooking (by following a recipe) and driving (by following directions to an address). These strategies have one thing in common: they lead to a single answer that is the correct solution. Algorithms are commonly used in computer science because computers can apply algorithms (formulas that might include all possible answers to a problem) very quickly (Du & others, 2018).

● **algorithms** Strategies—including formulas, instructions, and the testing of all possible solutions—that guarantee a solution to a problem.

For humans, an algorithmic strategy might take a long time. As you stare at a rack of letters during a game of Scrabble, for example, you might find yourself moving the tiles around and trying all possible combinations to make a high-scoring word. Trying all possible combinations would mean considering all possible combinations of 2, 3, 4, 5, 6, and 7 letters to see if any of these combinations make words. Fortunately, your knowledge of the English language lets you to simplify the task. Instead of using an algorithm to solve a Scrabble problem, you might rely on some rules of thumb about words and language. You know that if you have a *Q*, you are going to need a *U*. If you have an *X* and a *T*, the *T* is not going to come right before the *X*. So, rather than using an algorithm, you are using some quick rules that provide possible solutions to the problem. These shortcuts are called heuristics.

**Heuristics** are shortcut strategies or guidelines that suggest a solution to a problem but do not guarantee an answer (Bobadilla-Suarez & Love, 2018; Stanovich, 2018). In the real world, we are more likely to solve the types of problems we face with heuristics than with algorithms. Heuristics help us to narrow down the possible solutions and quickly find one that works. Heuristics are different from algorithms because they are fast, can lead to different answers to a given problem, and do not always produce the best answer.

● **heuristics** Shortcut strategies or guidelines that suggest a solution to a problem but do not guarantee an answer.

**3. Evaluate Solutions** Once we think we have solved a problem, we will not know how effective our solution is until we find out whether it works. It helps to have in mind a clear criterion, or standard against which to judge the effectiveness of the solution. For example, what will your criterion be for judging the effectiveness of your solution to the assignment of writing a psychology paper? Will you judge your solution to be effective if you simply complete the paper? If you get an *A*?

**4. Rethink and Redefine Problems and Solutions over Time** An important final step in problem solving is to rethink and redefine problems continually. Good problem solvers tend to be more motivated than the average person to improve on their past performances and to make original contributions.

## AN OBSTACLE TO PROBLEM SOLVING: BECOMING FIXATED

Good problem solvers acknowledge that they do not know everything–that strategies and conclusions are always open to revision. Optimal problem solving may require a certain amount of humility–the ability to admit that you are not perfect and that there may be better ways to solve life's problems (Haggard & others, 2018; Whitcomb & others, 2017). It is easy to fall into the trap of becoming fixated on a particular strategy for solving a problem. Sometimes solving a new problem means forgetting what we already know. One way to come up with an optimal solution to a problem is to think of at least two solutions. That way, you will not stop looking for a solution until you have considered at least two ways to accomplish your goal.

● **fixation** Using a prior strategy and failing to look at a problem from a new perspective.

● **functional fixedness** Failing to solve a problem as a result of fixation on a thing's usual functions.

**Fixation** involves using a prior strategy and failing to look at a problem from a new perspective. When we are fixated, we might feel that what worked before will always work in the present and future. **Functional fixedness** occurs when individuals fail to solve a problem because they are fixated on a thing's usual functions (Munoz-Rubke & others, 2018). Imagine having to hammer a nail but lacking a hammer. What would you do? The functionally fixed person is stuck. If you have ever used a shoe to hammer a nail, you have overcome functional fixedness to solve a problem.

One problem that requires overcoming functional fixedness is the Maier string problem, depicted in Figure 2 (Maier, 1931). The problem is to figure out how to tie two strings together when you must stand in one spot and cannot reach both strings at the same time. It seems as though you are stuck. However, there is a pair of pliers on a table. Can you solve the problem?

The solution is to use the pliers as a weight, tying them to the end of one string (Figure 3). Swing this string back and forth like a pendulum and grasp the stationary string.

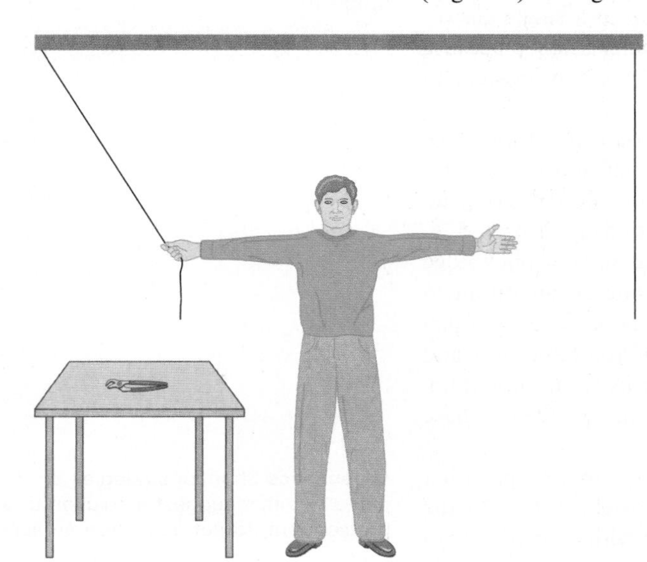

**FIGURE 2** **Maier String Problem** How can you tie the two strings together if you cannot reach them both at the same time? Source: Maier (1931).

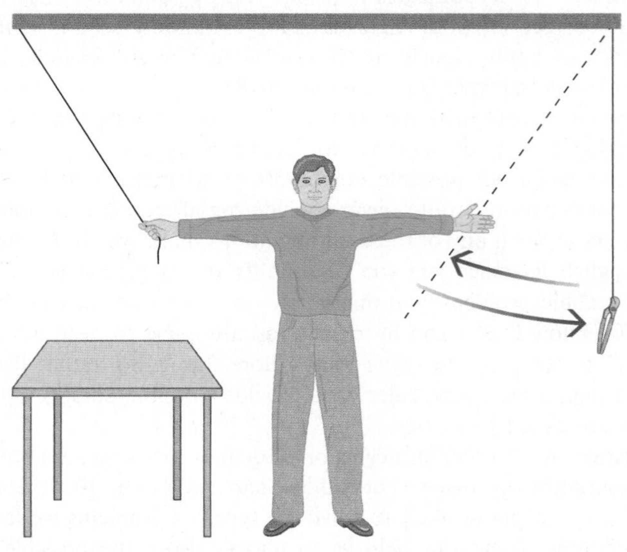

**FIGURE 3** **Solution to the Maier String Problem** Use the pliers as a weight to create a pendulum motion that brings the second string closer. Source: Maier (1931).

## psychological *inquiry*

**The Candle Problem**

How would you mount a candle on a wall so that it won't drip wax on a table or a floor while it is burning?

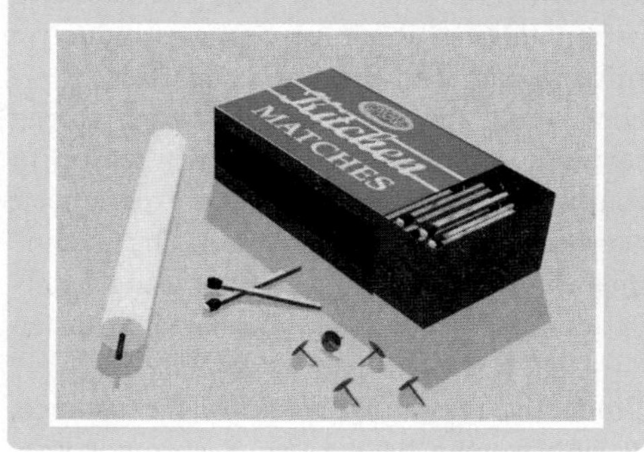


**The Nine-Dot Problem**

Take out a piece of paper and copy the arrangement of dots shown below. Without lifting your pencil, connect the dots using only four straight lines.

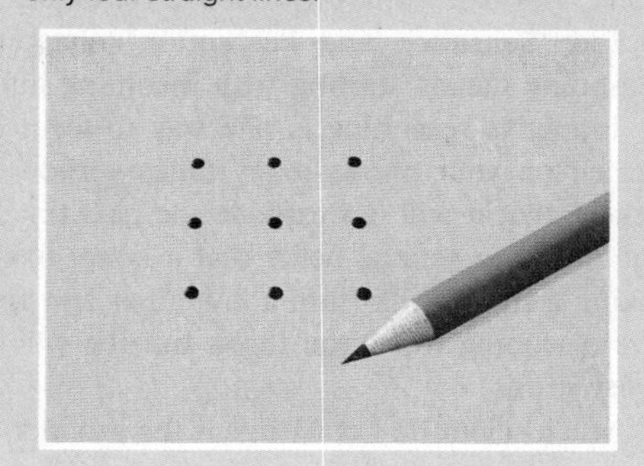

**The Six-Matchstick Problem**

Arrange six matchsticks of equal length to make four equilateral triangles, the sides of which are one matchstick long.

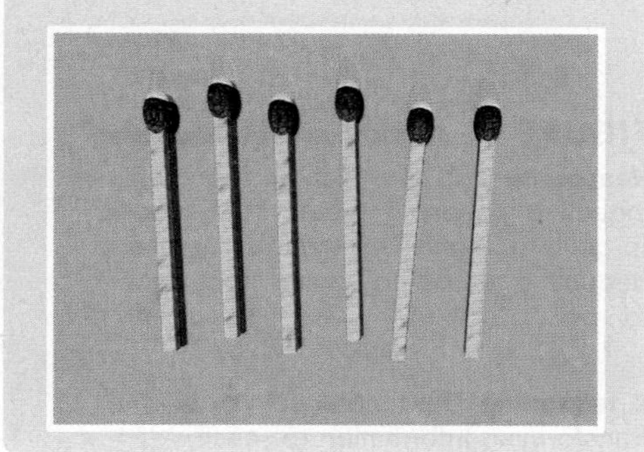

### *Thinking Outside the Box*

Above are examples of how fixation impedes problem solving. These tasks help psychologists measure creative problem solving.

Each of the problems calls for a special kind of thinking—breaking out of your usual assumptions and looking at objects in a different way. Try your hand at solving each one and then answer the questions. Solutions to the problems can be found at the end of the chapter.

1. Which of the problems was most difficult to solve? Why?
2. Do you think these problems capture an important ability, or are they more like trick questions? Why?
3. Are these problems best solved by effortful thinking or by just going with your hunches? Explain.

To solve this problem a person must disregard past experience with the usual function of pliers to find an unusual use for them–in this case, as a weight to create a pendulum.

Effective problem solving often necessitates thinking outside the box–that is, exploring novel ways of approaching tasks and challenges and finding solutions. This way of thinking can require admitting that your past strategies were not ideal or do not readily translate to a particular situation. Students who are used to succeeding in high school by cramming for tests and relying on parental pressure to get homework done may find that in college these strategies are no longer viable ways to succeed.

Sometimes successful problem solving means being *cognitively flexible*–recognizing that options are available and adapting to the situation. To explore how fixation might play a role in your own problem solving, try out the questions in the Psychological Inquiry.

## Reasoning and Decision Making

Thinking includes the higher-order mental processes of reasoning and decision making. These activities require rich connections among neurons and the ability to apply judgment. The end result of this type of thinking is an evaluation, a conclusion, or a decision.

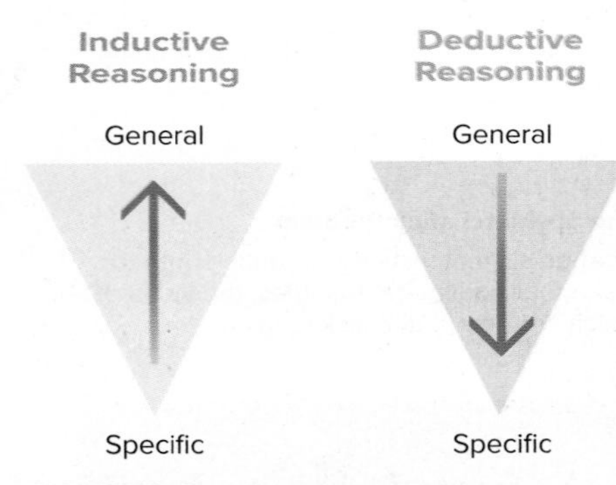


**FIGURE 4 Inductive and Deductive Reasoning** (*left*) The triangle represents inductive reasoning—going from specific to general. (*right*) The triangle represents deductive reasoning—going from general to specific.

## REASONING

**Reasoning** is the mental activity of transforming information to reach a conclusion. This type of thinking uses *reason*—weighing arguments, applying rules of logic, and coming up with sound conclusions. Reasoning is involved in problem solving and decision making. It is also a skill closely tied to critical thinking (Tversky & Liberman, 2018). Reasoning can be either inductive or deductive (Figure 4).

- **reasoning** The mental activity of transforming information to reach conclusions.

**Inductive reasoning** involves reasoning from specific observations to make generalizations. You can think of inductive reasoning as "bottom-up processing" that we discussed in the "Sensation and Perception" chapter when talking about perception. Inductive reasoning means starting with incoming information and then drawing conclusions.

- **inductive reasoning** Reasoning from specific observations to make generalizations.

Inductive reasoning is one way to form beliefs about the world. For instance, having turned on your phone many times without having it explode, you have every reason to believe that it will not explode the next time you turn it on. From your prior experiences, you form the general belief that it is not likely to become a dangerous object. Or, imagine taking a sip of milk from a container and finding that it tastes sour. You are using inductive reasoning when you throw out the whole container even though you have not tasted every drop.

Much scientific knowledge is the product of inductive reasoning. We know, for instance, that men and women are genetically different, with women having two X chromosomes and men having an X and a Y chromosome, though no one has actually tested every single human being's chromosomes to verify this generalization. Inductive reasoning is involved when we make generalizations. Psychological research is often inductive as well, studying a *sample* of participants in order to draw conclusions about the population from which the sample is drawn. In inductive reasoning, we take information and use it to draw a general conclusion.

- **deductive reasoning** Reasoning from a general case that is known to be true to a specific instance.

In contrast, **deductive reasoning** is reasoning from a general principle that we know to be true to a specific instance. Using deductive reasoning, we draw conclusions based on facts. For example, we might start with the general premise that all Texans love the Dallas Cowboys. Thus, if Jon is a Texan, we logically might surmise that Jon loves the Dallas Cowboys. Notice, however, that the logic of this deductive reasoning requires the first statement to be true: if all Texans do not love the Cowboys, Jon just might be an Eagles fan.

When psychologists develop a hypothesis from a theory, they are using a form of deductive reasoning, because the hypothesis is a specific, logical extension of the general theory. If the theory is true, then the hypothesis will be true as well. Deductive reasoning involves forming expectations of what we think is true and then applying that knowledge to incoming information.

The terms *inductive* and *deductive* are very similar, but they refer to different things. Remember that ***in***ductive means going from a specific ***in***stance to a general case. ***D***eductive means reasoning from a general principle ***d***own to a specific case.

## DECISION MAKING

Think of all the decisions that you have to make in life. Should you major in history, psychology, or business? Should you go to graduate school right after college or get a job first? Should you establish yourself in a career before settling down to have a family? Do you want fries with that? **Decision making** involves evaluating alternatives and choosing among them.

- **decision making** The mental activity of evaluating alternatives and choosing among them.

Decision making differs from reasoning. Reasoning involves following established rules to reach a sound conclusion. In decision making, such rules may not exist, some of the information might be missing, and we might not trust all of the information we have (Traczyk & others, 2018). In this sense, decision making is less certain than reasoning. Making decisions means weighing information and coming to some conclusion that we feel will maximize our outcome: Yes, we will be able to see the movie from this row in the theater; no, we will not run that red light to get to class on time.

## TWO SYSTEMS OF REASONING AND DECISION MAKING

Recall the idea of automatic and controlled processes in consciousness. Automatic processes occur without awareness or effort. Controlled processes involve deliberate reflection and conscious control of action. Psychologists often similarly divide reasoning and decision making into two levels–one that is automatic (called *system 1*) and one that is controlled or deliberate (*system 2*) (Evans & Stanovich, 2013; Pennycook & others, 2018). The automatic system involves processing that is rapid, heuristic, associative, and intuitive; it entails following one's hunches about a particular decision (Barr & others, 2015; Pennycook, Fugelsang, & Koehler, 2015). Intuitive judgment means knowing that something feels right even if the reason why is unknown (Helfrich & others, 2018; Horr, Braun, & Volz, 2014). In intuitive processing, we simply know something without being aware of why or how we know it. In contrast, the controlled system is slower, effortful, and analytical. It involves conscious reflection. This is the kind of thinking that might be required to solve a difficult math problem, for example.

Although conscious, effortful thinking is invaluable for solving many problems, research has shown that intuitive processing may also play an important role in decision making. Studies have shown that, compared with effortful reflection, intuitive decision making can sometimes be less biased and more efficient in decision making. For example, in one study participants were told that their job was to rate the popularity of particular songs (Halberstadt & Catty, 2008). Participants listened to brief snippets of the songs. Half of the participants were asked to first reflect on the reasons each song might be popular. The other half simply rendered their judgments intuitively, without much thought. Those who rendered their judgments intuitively were actually more accurate in their popularity ratings, because they based these ratings on how familiar the song was to them. Basing judgments on the feeling of familiarity was a good idea in this case: popular songs are likely to be familiar to everyone. Those who analyzed reasons were less accurate because thinking about reasons disrupted this natural association.

The popular media sometimes portray intuitive hunches as somewhat magical. However, these gut feelings do not emerge out of thin air. Rather, they are the product of learned associations such as those described in the "Learning" chapter (Kahneman & Klein, 2009; Unkelbach, 2007); of overlearned automatic processes (Halberstadt, 2010); and of implicit memory (Cheng & Huang, 2011). Gut feelings about the right answer on a test are certainly more likely to be accurate if you have put in the requisite hours of conscious, effortful study. The accuracy of intuitive judgments, then, may depend on the amount of time spent in conscious effort, even if the judgment feels like a gut feeling. So, intuitive gut feelings are not magical, and their capacity to lead to the right decision often depends on our history of effortful learning.

Both careful reflection and rapid, intuitive thought can lead to good or bad decisions. Even if we try to think a problem through carefully, our thought process can be biased and might lead us to a less than optimal decision. Similarly, intuitive processes are as rapid as they are because they often rely on heuristics. Although following these quick rules of thumb can often lead to a satisfying decision, this process can also lead to mistakes, as we now consider.

## BIASES AND HEURISTICS

In many cases, decision-making strategies are well adapted to deal with a variety of problems (Hertwig, Hoffrage, & the ABC Research Group, 2013). However, at times, reliance on heuristics can lead to biased decisions and outright errors. In addition, sometimes we are simply unaware of the influence that heuristics may have on our decisions (Nisbett & Ross, 1980; Tversky & Kahneman, 1974). Here we look at a few biases and heuristic errors, summarized in Figure 5.

One of the most powerful biases in human decision making is loss aversion. **Loss aversion** refers to the tendency to strongly prefer to avoid losses compared to acquiring gains. We dislike the prospect of losing something we already have more than we enjoy

**loss aversion** The tendency to strongly prefer to avoid losses compared to acquiring gains.

**Loss Aversion**

**Description**
Tendency to weigh potential losses more heavily than potential gains

**Example:** An investor decides not to buy stock in a new company even though the chances of financial gain outweigh the chances of financial loss.

**Confirmation Bias**

**Description**
Tendency to search for and use information that supports rather than refutes one's ideas

**Example:** A politician accepts news that supports his views and dismisses evidence that runs counter to these views.

**Base Rate Neglect**

**Description**
Tendency to ignore information about general principles in favor of very specific but vivid information

**Example:** You read a favorable expert report on a TV you are intending to buy, but you decide not to buy it when a friend tells you about a bad experience with that model.

**Hindsight Bias**

**Description**
Tendency to report falsely, after the fact, that one accurately predicted an outcome

**Example:** You read about the results of a particular psychological study and say, "I always knew that," though in fact you have little knowledge about the issues examined in the study.

**Representativeness Heuristic**

**Description**
Tendency to make judgments about group membership based on physical appearances or one's stereotype of a group rather than available base rate information

**Example:** After you are the victim of a holdup, you view police photos of possible perpetrators. All of the suspects look very similar to each other, but you choose the individual whose hair and clothing look dirtiest and most disheveled.

**Availability Heuristic**

**Description**
Prediction about the probability of an event based on the ease of recalling or imagining similar events

**Example:** A girl from an extended family in which no family member ever attended college tells her mother that she wants to be a doctor. Her mother cannot imagine her daughter in such a career and suggests that she become a home healthcare aide instead.

**FIGURE 5 Decision-Making Problems: Biases and Heuristics** Biases and heuristics (rules of thumb) affect the quality of many of the decisions we make. Source: Nisbett & Ross (1980), Tversky & Kahneman (1974); (first photo) ©Digital Vision/SuperStock; (second photo) ©stevecoleimages/Getty Images

the prospect of gaining something new, even when the prospect of a gain outweighs the loss (Kahneman & Tversky, 1984). Imagine that you have a *B*+ in a class with an optional, but likely very challenging, final exam. If you do well on the final, you could nudge your grade to an *A*–. But if you do poorly, your *B*+ could plummet to a *C*. Would you risk what you already have for the chance to get a better grade? Perhaps not.

Even when possible outcomes are mathematically the same, if information is framed as a loss people are less likely to pursue that outcome than if the same information is framed as a gain. Imagine if you were told that, out of 100 people who have a deadly virus, an experimental medicine could save 60 of them. How does the medicine sound? Now, imagine that out of those 100 people, the experimental medicine would allow 40 of them to die. The same information does not sound as favorable when framed as a loss. In decision making, losses carry about twice as much weight as gains (De Neve & others, 2018).

Loss aversion helps to explain a variety of phenomena in psychology and economics (Wang, Rieger, & Hens, 2016). For example, the *endowment effect* means that people ascribe greater value to things they already own than to objects owned by someone else. For example, in one study (Kahneman, Knetsch, & Thaler, 1990), some participants were shown a mug and were asked how much they would be willing to pay for it. Other participants were actually given the mug to keep and then were asked how much they would be willing to sell it for. In both groups the mugs were identical. However, those who owned the mug believed it was worth over three dollars more than those who just looked it over. Just by owning it made it more valuable.

Loss aversion also explains why sometimes it is so hard to cut our losses in a losing battle. The *sunk cost fallacy* refers to the fact that people are reluctant to give up on a venture because of past investment. If we were perfectly rational, we would make decisions based only on current circumstances, maximizing the benefits and minimizing the costs. However, past investment biases our judgments. Sunk cost fallacy means "throwing good money after bad."

Imagine that you have just suffered through two years of training to become an accountant. In the process, you have found that you do not enjoy accounting and you are not good at it. The courses have been a struggle and you have barely passed. Should you stick with it? If you were making a decision rationally based on current circumstances alone, you might decide to switch majors. However, doing so would also mean recognizing that the last two years have been "wasted." You have sunk a lot of resources into something you no longer even want. But sunk costs may spur you to stick it out or even try harder. Sunk costs reflect loss aversion in that we dread the thought of losing the effort, time, and money we have already put into a venture if we give up.

**Confirmation bias** is the tendency to search for and use information that supports our ideas rather than refutes them. Our decisions can become further biased because we tend to seek out and listen to people whose views confirm our own while avoiding those with dissenting views (Kruglanski & Webster, 2018; Prat-Ortega de la Rocha, 2018). Confirmation bias is sometimes called myside bias, as it involves seeking out and believing information that supports one's own beliefs. Avoiding confirmation bias means seeking out disconfirming information and applying the same rigorous analysis to both sides of an argument, even when the information seems to point in a direction we dread.

- **confirmation bias** The tendency to search for and use information that supports one's ideas rather than refutes them.

**Hindsight bias** is the tendency to report falsely, after the fact, that we accurately predicted an outcome. Sometimes called the "I knew it all along" effect, in this type of bias, people tend to view events that have happened as being more predictable than they actually were. They think of themselves as being more accurate in their predictions than they actually were (Müller & Moshagen, 2018). For instance, at the end of a long baseball season, fans might say they knew all along that which team would win the World Series.

- **hindsight bias** The tendency to report falsely, after the fact, that one has accurately predicted an outcome.

Although the hindsight bias might seem self-serving because it means remembering ourselves as having known more than we really did, this bias may be based simply on updating our knowledge about the world (Bernstein & others, 2018; Pohl & others, 2019). One reason for hindsight bias is that actual events are more vivid in our minds than all those things that did not happen, an effect called the availability heuristic.

The **availability heuristic** refers to a prediction about the probability of an event based on the ease of recalling or imagining similar events (Kudryavtsev, 2018). This heuristic means that events that are *cognitively available* are believed to be more likely to happen. Shocking events such as plane crashes stick in our minds, making it seem as if such disasters are common. But, the chance of dying in a plane crash in a given year is tiny (1 in 400,000) compared with the chance of dying in a car accident (1 in 6,500). Because car accidents are less newsworthy, they are less likely to catch our attention and remain in awareness. The availability heuristic is one reason people seem to have a difficult time believing that violent crime rates have declined. When they hear about single acts of violence, the vividness of these in memory is mistaken for their frequency.

- **availability heuristic** A prediction about the probability of an event based on the ease of recalling or imagining similar events.

The availability heuristic can reinforce generalizations about other people (Fiedler & Kutzner, 2015). Imagine, that Sofía, a Latina American girl, tells her mom that she wants to be a doctor. Her mother, who has never seen a Latina doctor, finds it hard to imagine her daughter pursuing such a career and might suggest that she try nursing instead.

Also reflective of the impact of vivid cases on decision making is **base rate neglect**, the tendency to ignore information about general principles in favor of very specific information. Imagine being told that the average exam score for a test in your psychology class was 75 percent. If you were asked to guess a random student's score, 75 percent would be a good answer–the mean tells us the central tendency of any distribution. Yet if the student provided just a little bit of information, such as how many hours he studied, you might give too much weight to that specific information, losing sight of the valuable base rate information you have–namely, the class mean.

- **base rate neglect** The tendency to ignore information about general principles in favor of very specific and vivid information.

To experience another heuristic in action, consider the following. Your psychology professor tells you she has assembled 100 men, all in their 20s, in the hallway outside your classroom. The group consists of 5 members of the U.S. National Swim Team and

95 engineers. She is going to randomly select one man and bring him into the room, and you can win $1000 if you accurately guess whether he is an Olympic-caliber swimmer or an engineer. The man stands before you. Tall and lanky, he is wearing a tight T-shirt, jeans, and flip-flops. He has sunglasses perched on his clean-shaven head. Is he an engineer or an elite swimmer? If you guessed Olympic swimmer, you have just fallen victim to the representativeness heuristic.

**representativeness heuristic** The tendency to make judgments about group membership based on physical appearance or the match between a person and one's stereotype of a group rather than on available base rate information.

The **representativeness heuristic** is the tendency to make judgments about group membership based on physical appearance or the match between a person and one's stereotype of a group rather than on available base rate information (Gualtieri & Denison, 2018). Essentially, a stereotype is the use of concepts to make generalizations about a group of people. In the example just described, the base rate information tells you that, 95 times out of 100, the man who has been randomly selected to stand in front of your class will be an engineer. The optimal approach to winning the $1000 is to shut your eyes and guess engineer, no matter what the man looks like. The representativeness heuristic, then, may lead a person to ignore base rate information and rely, instead, on individuating information that is provided about a target.

The representativeness heuristic can be damaging in the context of social judgment. Consider Lori, who has an undergraduate engineering degree and an MBA from an elite business school, applying for an executive position at an engineering firm. If there are few women in management at the firm, the company's board of directors might inaccurately view Lori as "not fitting" their prototypical manager–and miss the chance to hire an exceptional candidate.

To avoid biases produced by heuristics, a person must use the base rate information provided. Can children use base rate information in their judgments? To read about research addressing this question, see the Intersection.

Heuristics help us make decisions rapidly, but to make the best decisions, we must sometimes override these shortcuts and think more deeply, critically, and creatively. Now that you have learned about heuristics and their potential to lead to biased and inaccurate conclusions, you might be wondering whether you be less likely to be influenced by such biases in the future. Some people seem more likely to use heuristics whereas others are more likely to apply careful thought to decisions, overriding the influence of these shortcuts. Intelligence, interest in thinking through complex problems carefully, and maintaining an open mind are associated with less susceptibility to the biases promoted by heuristics (Chiesi, Primi, & Morsanyi, 2011; Toplak, West, & Stanovich, 2011). Still, such biases can influence us without our knowledge. Very bright people can recognize biases in others but miss them in their own decisions, a phenomenon called *bias blind spot* (West, Meserve, & Stanovich, 2012).

## Thinking Critically and Creatively

Problem solving and decision making are basic cognitive processes that we use multiple times each day. Certain strategies lead to better solutions and choices than others, and some people are particularly good at these cognitive exercises. In this section we examine two skills associated with superior problem solving: critical thinking and creativity.

### CRITICAL THINKING

*Critical thinking* means thinking reflectively and productively and evaluating the evidence. Recall from the chapter "What Is Psychology?" that scientists are critical thinkers. Critical thinkers grasp the deeper meaning of ideas, question assumptions, and decide for themselves what to believe. Critical thinking requires maintaining a sense of humility about what we know (and what we do not know). It means being motivated to see past the obvious.

Critical thinking is vital to effective problem solving (Sharples & others, 2018). However, it can be difficult to teach students to think critically, and schools must often balance other priorities (Chikeleze, Johnson, & Gibson, 2018; McCombs, 2013). The goal

# INTERSECTION

## Cognitive Psychology and Developmental Psychology: Can Young Children be More Rational than Adults?

When base rate information conflicts with individuating information about a specific person, adults often make mistakes (Kahneman, 2011). So, if there are 100 people in a park and only 5 of them are engineers, if adults are told that a person enjoys working with numbers and wears glasses, adults are likely to guess that that person is an engineer. Do you think children would be more or less likely than adults to make this mistake? Two recent studies addressed this question.

*Do you tend to trust the numbers or go with preexisting beliefs when making judgments about others?*

In the first study (Gualtieri & Denison, 2018), the researchers demonstrated that children can use both base rate numbers and individuating information. When kids were told there were more blue than green robots in a park, they correctly guessed that a robot wearing a white coat was likely to be blue. Also, when told that green robots are naughty and blue robots are nice, kids were able to guess that a naughty robot wearing a white coat was likely to be green.

Next, the researchers asked children (aged 4 to 6 years) to make judgments when base rate and individuating information conflicted. For example, knowing that there are more blue than green robots, would children mistakenly guess that a robot who behaves in a naughty fashion is green? The answer is that older children fell prey to the representativeness heuristic. Younger children used base-rate information and to make accurate judgments. Interestingly, the researchers tried out this task on college students. What did they find? Young adults were less likely than 4-year-olds to use base rate information when conflicting individuating information was provided (Gualtieri & Denison, 2018)! Four-year-olds rendered more rational judgments than college students.

These results challenge us to think about how, through development, people become less likely to trust the numbers and more likely to rely on social beliefs and stereotypes when rendering social judgments.

(child) ©Brian A Jackson/Shutterstock; (robot) ©Ociacia/Shutterstock

of maximizing students' scores on standardized tests can prompt teachers to concentrate on getting students to give a single correct answer in an imitative way rather than on encouraging new ideas (Zohar & Alboher Agmon, 2018). Further, many people are inclined to stay on the surface of problems rather than to stretch their minds. The cultivation of two mental habits is essential to critical thinking: mindfulness and open-mindedness.

**Mindfulness** means being alert and mentally present for one's everyday activities. The mindful person maintains an active awareness of the circumstances of his or her life. When we are mindful, we are engaged mentally in what is happening to us. According to Ellen Langer (1997, 2000, 2005), mindfulness is a key to critical thinking. Langer distinguishes *mindful* behavior from *mindless* behavior—automatic activities we perform without thought.

● **mindfulness** The state of being alert and mentally present for one's everyday activities.

In a classic study, Langer found that people (as many as 90 percent) would mindlessly give up their place in line for a copy machine when someone asked, "Can I go first? I need to make copies" as compared to when the same person simply said, "Can I go first?" (just 60 percent) (Langer, Blank, & Chanowitz, 1978). For the mindless people in the study, even a completely meaningless justification—after all, everyone in line was there to

make copies–was reason enough to step aside. A mindless person engages in automatic behavior without careful thinking. In contrast, a mindful person is engaged with the environment, responding in a thoughtful way to various experiences.

**open-mindedness** The state of being receptive to other ways of looking at things.

**Open-mindedness** means being receptive to other ways of looking at things. People often do not even know that there is another side to an issue or evidence contrary to what they believe. Simple openness to other viewpoints can help to keep individuals from jumping to conclusions. As Socrates once said, knowing what it is you do not know is the first step to true wisdom. *Actively open-minded thinking* refers to thinking that is flexible and open to questioning; it is not dogmatic or categorical (West, Toplak, & Stanovich, 2008). This thinking style means a person evaluates arguments without being biased by previous beliefs (Mellers & others, 2015). Individuals who engage in active open-minded thinking tend to be less susceptible to biases in their conclusions (Stenhouse & others, 2018; West, Meserve, & Stanovich, 2012).

Being mindful and maintaining an open mind may be more difficult than the alternative of going through life on autopilot. Critical thinking is valuable, however, because it allows us to make better predictions about the future, to evaluate situations objectively, and to effect appropriate changes. In some ways, critical thinking requires courage. When we expose ourselves to a broad range of perspectives, we risk finding out that our assumptions might be wrong. When we engage our critical minds, we may discover problems, but we are also more likely to have opportunities to make positive changes.

Understanding the role of critical thinking and being open-minded to different perspectives in controversial issues is a key interest in psychology. Sometimes the source of controversial conclusions is science itself. For scientists, objective evidence is the key to knowledge, whether that knowledge is good news or bad news. Carl Rogers, a humanistic psychologist, once famously said, "The facts are always friendly," meaning that even if the truth is uncomfortable, it is good to know it. Not everyone places faith in science. Are the actively open-minded more open to uncomfortable information when it comes from scientists? To read about this issue, see the Critical Controversy.

## CREATIVE THINKING

**creativity** The ability to think about something in novel and unusual ways and to devise unconventional solutions to problems.

**divergent thinking** Thinking that produces many solutions to the same problem.

**convergent thinking** Thinking that produces the single best solution to a problem.

Coming up with the best solution to a problem may involve thinking creatively. The word *creative* can apply to an activity or a person, and creativity as a process may be open even to people who do not think of themselves as creative. When we talk about **creativity** as a characteristic of a person, we are referring to the ability to think about something in novel and unusual ways and to devise unconventional solutions to problems (Simonton, 2016).

Creative thinking is sometimes characterized as *divergent* and *convergent*. **Divergent thinking** produces many solutions to the same problem. **Convergent thinking** produces the single best solution to a problem. Perhaps you can see how these two types of thinking might work together in creativity. Divergent thinking occurs during *brainstorming,* which happens when people openly throw out a range of possible solutions to a problem, even some that might seem crazy. Producing a lot of possible solutions, however, is ineffective unless we identify the solution that is best (An, Song, & Carr, 2016). That is where convergent thinking comes in. Convergent thinking means taking all of those possibilities and finding the right one for the job. Convergent thinking is best when a problem has only one right answer. Of course, for many problems we use both convergent and divergent thinking. Research suggests that creativity plays the biggest role in coming up with different solutions–using divergent thinking (Japardi & others, 2018).

Individuals who think creatively also show the following characteristics (Perkins, 1994):

- *Flexibility and playful thinking:* Creative thinkers are flexible and play with problems. This trait gives rise to the paradox that, although creativity takes hard work, the work goes more smoothly if it is taken lightly. In a way, humor greases the wheels of creativity (Goleman, Kaufman, & Ray, 1993). When you are joking around, you are more likely to consider any possibility and to ignore the inner censor who can condemn your ideas as off-base.

## How Does Open-Minded Thinking Relate to Views of Climate Change?

There is currently strong scientific consensus about two things. First, the Earth is getting warmer and, second, human creation of greenhouse gasses through the use of fossil fuels has contributed to that warming (NASA, 2018). The role of human activity in global climate change has been agreed upon with more than 95 percent certainty by a group of over 1000 independent scholars from all over the world (NASA, 2018). To scientists, the data speak for themselves and call for action. However, not everyone who reads about the same science draws the same conclusion. In the United States, conflicting beliefs about whether human activity causes climate change are a major political issue. People who are politically conservative tend to hold views that more pro-business and may view the science of climate change as threatening to business interests (Kahan & others, 2012). This rejection of climate science is thought to be an instance of motivated cognition where information processing is driven by political beliefs (Jost, 2017). Could actively open-minded thinking promote the acceptance of climate science?

Source: NASA

In a recent study (Stenhouse & others, 2018), a representative sample of Americans rated their political beliefs and the extent to which they believed human activity causes climate change. They also completed a measure of actively open-minded thinking, with items like, "Allowing oneself to be convinced by an opposing argument is a sign of good character" (Haran, Ritov, & Mellers, 2013). The researchers had expected to find that while conservatism would be negatively related to beliefs in climate change, conservatives who were high in actively open-minded thinking would show greater acceptance of climate science. What they found surprised them: Actively open-minded thinking predicted endorsement of human activity as a cause of climate change *regardless* of political beliefs. For all participants, whether they were conservative, liberal, or otherwise, being open to many views, looking to science for knowledge, and remaining willing to change their views was associated with greater endorsement of climate science. Thus, contrary to expectations, it was *how* people thought, not their beliefs that predicted acceptance of climate science.

Science provides important information about problems in the world, in organizations, and in one's own behavior (Baumgaertner, Carlisle, & Justwan, 2018; Kannan & Veazie, 2018). If this science is discounted, it cannot help people improve their own lives. Critical thinkers are able to encounter information that may threaten their beliefs and use that information to change their views and their behavior. Understanding how people interpret, accept, or deny scientific information is a continuing goal for cognitive psychologists.

**WHAT DO YOU THINK?**

- Are there topics about which you are skeptical of scientific findings? What are they, and why are you skeptical?
- Do you believe climate change is caused by human activity? Why or why not?
- Do you think being able to change your mind is a sign of good character?

---

- *Inner motivation:* Creative people often are motivated by the joy of creating. They tend to be less motivated by grades, money, or favorable feedback from others. Thus, creative people are inspired more by internal than by external factors (Hennessey, 2011).
- *Willingness to face risk:* Creative people make more mistakes than their less imaginative counterparts because they come up with more ideas and more possibilities. They win some; they lose some. Creative thinkers know that being wrong is not a failure–it simply means that they have discovered that one possible solution does not work.
- *Objective evaluation of work:* Most creative thinkers strive to evaluate their work objectively. They may use established criteria to make judgments or rely on the judgments of respected, trusted others. In this manner, they can determine whether further creative thinking will improve their work.

### test yourself

1. What are four reasons why concepts are important?
2. Name and explain the key steps in solving a problem.
3. Name at least two biases and two heuristics that affect the quality of our decisions and give an example of each.

# 3. INTELLIGENCE

Like *creative,* the word *intelligent* can apply to a behavior or a person. We might say that someone who decides to quit smoking has made an intelligent choice. When we apply the word to a person, however, defining *intelligent* can be trickier.

Cultures vary in the ways they define intelligence (Ortiz & others, 2018). Most European Americans think of intelligence in terms of reasoning and thinking skills, but people in Kenya consider responsible participation in family and social life an integral part of intelligence. An intelligent person in Uganda is someone who knows what to do and follows through with appropriate action. Intelligence to the Iatmul people of Papua New Guinea involves the ability to remember the names of 10,000 to 20,000 clans. The residents of the widely dispersed Caroline Islands incorporate the talent of navigating by the stars into their definition of intelligence (Figure 6).

● **intelligence** An all-purpose ability to do well on cognitive tasks, to solve problems, and to learn from experience.

In the United States, we generally define **intelligence** as an all-purpose ability to do well on cognitive tasks, to solve problems, and to learn from experience. Consider the ways we have described thinking–as problem solving, reasoning, decision making, critical analysis, and creativity. Intelligence refers to *how well* a person is able to perform these various cognitive activities.

The idea that intelligence captures a common general cognitive ability was introduced in 1904 by Charles Spearman (1904). Spearman noted that schoolchildren who did well in math also did well in reading, and he came up with the idea that intelligence is a general ability, which he called *g.* This view of intelligence suggests that general intelligence underlies performance in a variety of areas, whether it is mathematics, verbal ability, or abstract reasoning. Spearman's *g* essentially assumes that the intelligent person is a jack-of-all-cognitive trades.

## Measuring Intelligence

Psychologists measure intelligence using tests that produce a score known as the person's *intelligence quotient* (*IQ*). To understand what IQ means, let's first examine the criteria for a good intelligence test: validity, reliability, and standardization.

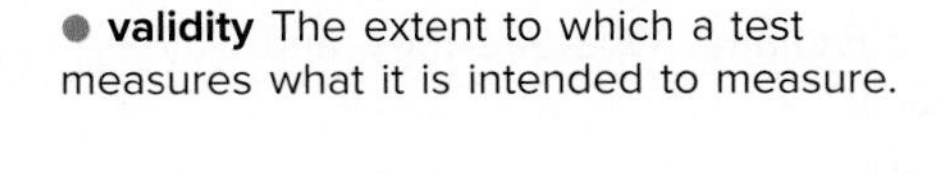
● **validity** The extent to which a test measures what it is intended to measure.

In the realm of testing, **validity** refers to the extent to which a test measures what it is intended to measure. If a test is supposed to measure intelligence, then it should measure intelligence, not some other characteristic, such as anxiety. One of the most important indicators of validity is the degree to which it predicts an individual's performance when that performance is assessed by *other measures*, or criteria, of the attribute. For example,

**FIGURE 6 Culturally Defined Intelligence** The intelligence of the Iatmul people of Papua New Guinea involves the ability to remember the names of many clans. For the residents of the 680 Caroline Islands in the Pacific Ocean east of the Philippines, intelligence includes the ability to navigate by the stars. (first) ©Images of Africa Photobank/Alamy Stock Photo; (second) ©Guido Alberto Rossi/AGE Fotostock

if an intelligence test is valid, we might expect it to predict other variables, such as grades in school or work performance. When the scores on a measure relate to important outcomes, we say the test has high *criterion validity.*

**Reliability** is the extent to which a test yields a consistent, reproducible measure of performance. That is, a reliable test is one that produces the same score over time and repeated testing.

Reliability and validity are related, but they are not the same thing. If we think that the characteristic a test measures is stable, then for a test of that characteristic to be valid, it must be reliable. However, a test can be quite reliable but not valid. A person can get the same score on a test, over and over, and yet those scores may be wrong, each and every time. Imagine that someone proposes that eye color is a good measure of intelligence. Certainly, a person's eye color is not likely to change so this measure will be very reliable. The question for validity, though, is whether eye color bears any relationship to intelligence. It does not. So, we have a reliable measure that is not valid. To keep these important terms clear, remember that *reliability* refers only to the stability of scores over time. *Validity,* in contrast, refers to the extent to which a scale measures what it purports to measure.

Good intelligence tests are not only reliable and valid but also standardized. **Standardization** involves developing uniform procedures for administering and scoring a test, as well as creating *norms,* or performance standards, for the test.

Uniform testing procedures require that the testing environment be as similar as possible for all individuals. Norms are created by giving the test to a large group of people who are representative of the population for whom the test is intended. Norms tell us which scores are considered high, low, or average. Many tests of intelligence are designed for individuals from diverse groups. So that the tests are applicable to such different groups, they may have different norms for individuals of different ages, socioeconomic statuses, and ethnic groups (Ortiz & others, 2018; Trundt & others, 2018). Figure 7 summarizes the criteria for test construction and evaluation.

**Validity**

Does the test measure what it purports to measure?

**Reliability**

Is test performance consistent?

**Standardization**

Are uniform procedures for administering and scoring the test used?

**FIGURE 7 Test Construction and Evaluation** Tests are a tool for measuring important abilities such as intelligence. Good tests show high reliability and validity and are standardized so that people's scores can be compared.
Source: Ortiz & others (2018), Trundt & others (2018).

- **reliability** The extent to which a test yields a consistent, reproducible measure of performance.
- **standardization** The development of uniform procedures for administering and scoring a test and the creation of norms (performance standards) for the test.
- **mental age (MA)** An individual's level of mental development relative to that of others.
- **intelligence quotient (IQ)** An individual's mental age divided by chronological age, multiplied by 100.

## IQ TESTS

In 1904, the French Ministry of Education asked psychologist Alfred Binet to devise a method that would determine which students did not learn effectively from regular classroom instruction. School officials wanted to reduce overcrowding by placing such students in special schools. Binet and a student (Theophile Simon) developed an intelligence test to meet this request. Test items ranged from the ability to touch one's nose or ear on command to the ability to draw designs from memory and to define abstract concepts. Binet's test is now known as the Stanford-Binet, and it is still widely used.

To measure intelligence, Binet came up with the idea of comparing a person's mental abilities to the mental abilities that are typical for a particular age group. Binet developed the concept of **mental age (MA)**, which is an individual's level of mental development relative to that of others. Binet reasoned that, because cognitive ability increases with age, we might expect a child with an intellectual disability to perform like a normally developing child *of a younger age*. To think about a person's level of intelligence, then, we might compare the person's mental age (MA) to his or her chronological age (CA), or age from birth. A very bright child has an MA considerably above CA; a less bright child has an MA considerably below CA.

The German psychologist William Stern devised the term **intelligence quotient (IQ)** in 1912. IQ consists of an individual's mental age divided by chronological age, multiplied by 100:

$$IQ = (MA/CA) \times 100$$

If mental age is the same as chronological age, then the individual's IQ is 100 (average); if mental age is above chronological age, the IQ is more than 100 (above average); if mental age is below chronological age, the IQ is less than 100 (below average). For example, a 6-year-old child with a mental age of 8 has an IQ of 133, whereas a 6-year-old child with a mental age of 5 has an IQ of 83.

**Alfred Binet (1857–1911)** Binet constructed the first intelligence test after being asked to create a measure to determine which children would benefit from instruction in France's schools.

In childhood, mental age increases as the child ages, but once the child reaches about age 16, the concept of mental age loses its meaning. That is why many experts today prefer to examine IQ scores in terms of how unusual a person's score is in comparison with the scores of other adults. For this purpose, researchers and testers use standardized norms that they have identified in the many people who have been tested.

Another measure of intelligence is the Wechsler scales, first developed by David Wechsler (1939; Wahlstrom & others, 2018). There are three versions of the scale. For those ages 16 and older, the Wechsler Adult Intelligence Scale (the WAIS) includes items such as vocabulary, working memory capacity, math problems, and the ability to complete jigsaw puzzles. For children between the ages of 6 and 16, the Wechsler Intelligence Scale for Children (the WISC) includes vocabulary and comprehension but also tasks such as putting together blocks to fit a particular pattern. Finally, a version developed for children as young as 2½ is the Wechsler Pre-School and Primary Scale of Intelligence (the WPPSI, pronounced "whipsy"). On this measure, children are asked, for instance, to point to a picture that depicts a word the examiner says, to complete a block design, and to answer basic knowledge questions (Wahlstrom & others, 2018).

If you have taken an IQ test, chances are it was one of the Wechsler scales. It is currently the most popular measure of intelligence. In addition to summary scores for general IQ, the Wechsler scales include scores for areas such as verbal comprehension, perceptual reasoning, working memory, and processing speed. These scales provide scores on various subscales rather than a single IQ score.

Both the Stanford-Binet and the Wechsler scales provide measures of Spearman's *g*. Both of these measures have a long history of research demonstrating their reliability, and they both feature standardized administration procedures and norms. Finally, they predict results that we would expect, including academic performance and life outcomes such as economic success (Damian & others, 2015; Haertel, 2018; Hafer, 2016).

Over the years, IQ tests like the Stanford-Binet and the Wechsler scales have been given to thousands upon thousands of children and adults. When the scores for many people are examined, they approximate a normal distribution. A *distribution* refers to the frequencies of scores on a scale—basically, how many people receive each of the possible scores. A **normal distribution** is a symmetrical, bell-shaped curve, with a majority of the scores falling in the middle of the possible range and few scores appearing toward the extremes of the range. To master the important idea of a normal distribution, complete the Psychological Inquiry.

● **normal distribution** A symmetrical, bell-shaped curve, with a majority of the scores falling in the middle of the possible range and few scores appearing toward the extremes of the range.

● **culture-fair tests** Intelligence tests that are intended to be culturally unbiased.

## CULTURAL BIAS IN TESTING

Many early intelligence tests were culturally biased, favoring people who were from urban rather than rural environments, of middle rather than low socioeconomic status, and of non-Latino White rather than African American ethnicity (Ortiz & others, 2018; Provenzo, 2002; Trundt & others, 2018). For example, a question on an early test asked what one should do if one finds a 3-year-old child in the street. The correct answer was "call the police." However, children from inner-city families who perceive the police as scary are unlikely to choose this answer. Similarly, children from rural areas might not choose this answer if there is no police force nearby. Such questions clearly do not measure the knowledge necessary to adapt to one's environment or to be "intelligent" in an inner-city or a rural neighborhood. In addition, members of minority groups may not speak English or may speak nonstandard English. Consequently, they may be at a disadvantage in trying to understand verbal questions that are framed in standard English, even if the content of the test is appropriate (Ortiz & others, 2018).

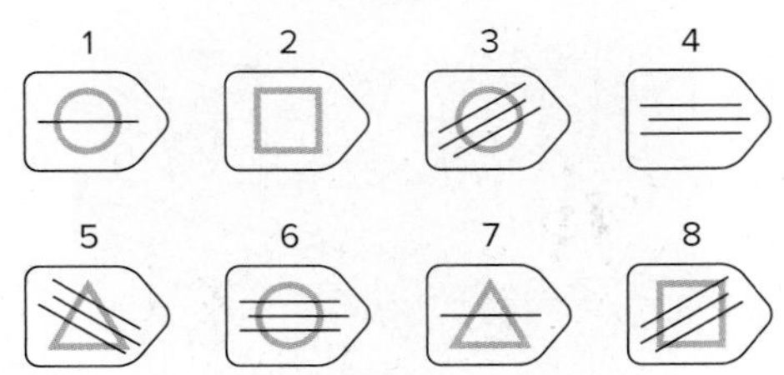


**FIGURE 8 Sample Item from the Raven Progressive Matrices Test** For this item, the respondent must choose which of the numbered figures would come next in the order. Can you explain why the right answer is number 6? Source: Adapted from *Raven's Progressive Matrices* (Advanced Progressive Matrices), 1998.

Researchers have sought to develop tests that accurately reflect a person's intelligence, regardless of cultural background (Ortiz & others, 2018; te Nijenhuis & others, 2016). **Culture-fair tests** are intelligence tests that are intended to be culturally unbiased. One type of culture-fair test includes questions that are familiar to people from all socioeconomic and ethnic backgrounds. A second type contains no verbal questions. Figure 8 shows a sample question from the Raven Progressive Matrices test. Even though tests such as the

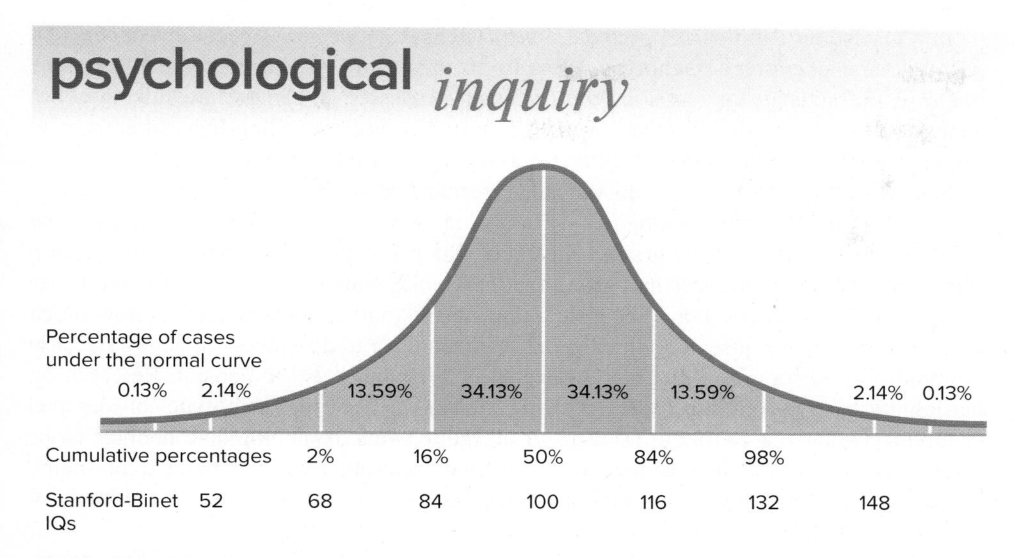


### *The Normal Curve*

This figure shows the normal curve and Stanford-Binet IQ scores. The distribution of IQ scores approximates a normal distribution. Answer the following questions, keeping in mind that the area under the curve represents the number of people who obtain a given score on the test.

1. Do most people fall in the low, medium, or high range? How do you know?
2. If someone's score was 132 on the test, how many people scored below that person's score?
3. What is the mean or average on the IQ test? Where does the mean fall on the bell-shaped curve?
4. Notice that in a normal distribution, extremely high and extremely low scores are rare. What other human characteristics might follow this pattern?

Raven are designed to be culture-fair, people with more education still score higher than do those with less education.

Why is it so hard to create culture-fair tests? Just as the definition of intelligence may vary by culture, most tests of intelligence reflect what is important to the dominant culture. If tests have time limits, the test will be biased against groups not concerned with time. If languages differ, the same words might have different meanings for different language groups. Even pictures can produce bias, because some cultures have less experience with drawings and photographs (Urbina, 2011). Because of such difficulties, some scholars suggest are no culture-fair tests, only *culture-reduced tests* (Fernández & Abe, 2018; Zhang & Sternberg, 2013).

One variable that shares a strong correlation with IQ is years of education (Plomin & von Stumm, 2018). It may seem obvious that those of higher intelligence might pursue more education. However, remember that correlation does not imply causation, so it is also possible that the causal arrow points in the other direction. That is, it may be that the correlation between IQ and education occurs because education (and other environmental factors) influence intelligence, a possibility we now consider.

## Genetic and Environmental Influences on Intelligence

Certainly, genes influence intelligence (Plomin & von Stumm, 2018) but understanding how and to what extent they do so has proved challenging.

In the chapter "Biological Foundations of Behavior" we described the concepts of genotype and phenotype. Genotype refers to an organism's genetic material. Phenotype refers to the actual characteristics the organism possesses. When we are talking about genetic influences on intelligence, we are interested in understanding how differences at the level of the genotype predict differences in the phenotype of intelligence.

Scientists long relied on a statistic called heritability to describe the extent to which the observable differences among people in a group (the phenotype) can be explained by the genetic differences of the group's members (the genotype). **Heritability** is the proportion of observable differences in a group that can be explained by differences in the genes of the group's members. For intelligence, that means that heritability tells us how much of the differences we observe in intelligence is attributable to differences in genes. Because heritability is a proportion, the highest degree of heritability is 100 percent. Research on heritability has typically involved comparing the similarity of the phenotypes of identical or monozygotic twins to that of fraternal or dizygotic twins. Assuming that identical twins share 100 percent of their genetic material, and fraternal twins 50 percent of theirs, scientists have estimated the heritability of intelligence to be about 50 percent (Plomin & von Stumm, 2018).

● **heritability** The proportion of observable differences in a group that can be explained by differences in the genes of the group's members.

Unfortunately, many controversies about the role of genetics in intelligence have arisen because of misunderstandings of the meaning of heritability. For instance, people sometimes believe that 50 percent heritability means that 50 percent of *an individual person's intelligence* is caused by genes. This is simply inaccurate. First and most important, heritability is a statistic that provides information about a group, not a single individual. This means that finding out that heritability for intelligence is 50 percent tells us nothing at all about the source of an individual person's intelligence. Heritability has no meaning when applied to a single case. Recall from the chapter "Psychology's Scientific Method" that group statistics do not apply to a specific case. That is, *statistics describe groups*, not single individuals.

Second, some have assumed, mistakenly, that if genes represent a substantial underlying cause of intelligence then a person's intelligence is "fixed" by genes. Once again, this is not true. Rather, the contribution of genes to intelligence is characterized by a dynamic relationship in which genes interact with each other and with environmental factors (Sauce & Matzel, 2018).

Third, heritability estimates can change over time and across different groups (Nisbett & others, 2012; Turkheimer & others, 2003). If a group of individuals lives in the same advantageous setting (with good nutrition, supportive parents, great schools, stable neighborhoods, and plenty of opportunities), heritability estimates for intelligence might be quite high, as this optimal environment allows genetic characteristics to flourish to their highest potential. However, if a group of individuals lives in a highly variable environment (with some individuals experiencing rich, nurturing environments full of opportunity and others experiencing less supportive contexts), genetic characteristics may be less predictive of differences in intelligence in that group, relative to environmental factors.

Fourth, it has been very difficult for scientists using molecular genetics to identify the precise genes that are involved in intelligence. Intelligence is a *polygenic trait,* meaning that a large number of genetic characteristics are involved in intelligence. Molecular genetic studies have identified some genes that work together to produce intelligence, but even these fail to explain all of the 50 percent that would account for heritability estimates (Plomin & von Stumm, 2018).

Finally, even if the heritability of a characteristic is high, the environment still matters. Take height, for example. Heritability estimates suggest that more than 90 percent of the variation in height is explained by genetic variation. Generally speaking, humans continue to get taller and taller, however, and this trend demonstrates that environmental factors such as nutrition have an impact. Similarly, in the case of intelligence, environmental interventions can change IQ scores considerably (Protzko, 2017).

Indeed, research provides strong support for the conclusion that childhood experiences can profoundly affect IQ. Recent meta-analyses have summarized research from many studies examining the effects of various childhood interventions and experiences on IQ (Protzko, 2017; Protzko, Aronson, & Blair, 2013). The results support the idea that specific experiences in childhood can influence IQ:

- *Dietary supplements:* Some supplements can promote IQ in children. If a child is deficient in some vitamins, daily supplements can improve IQ (Protzko, 2017). If a child is deficient in iodine, for example, then iodine supplements (often combined with iron) can enhance IQ (Protzko, 2017). In addition, Omega-3 fatty acids are found in breast milk, fish oil, salmon, walnuts, spinach, and avocados. When pregnant women, nursing mothers, and infants received 1,000-milligram supplements of Omega-3 fatty acids, the supplements led to an increase in children's IQs (Protzko, Aronson, & Blair, 2013).
- *Educational interventions:* Early childhood education can improve the IQs of economically disadvantaged young children, especially when the interventions involved training on complex tasks (Protzko, Aronson, & Blair, 2013). In addition, children who learn to play a musical instrument or receive other music education show higher IQs (Protzko, 2017). Learning to play a musical instrument predicts a 4-point increase in IQ.
- *Interactive reading:* Interactive reading leads to higher IQs especially when it occurs at younger ages (Protzko, Aronson, & Blair, 2013). Reading interactively means parents ask open-ended questions, encourage a child to read, and engage with the child about what they are reading.
- *Preschool:* Sending a child to preschool increases IQ by more than 4 points (Protzko, Aronson, & Blair, 2013), especially for economically disadvantaged children (those whose parents might not have been able to afford preschool except for the studies in which they were enrolled). Among these kids, attending preschool raised IQs by as much as 7 points. The effects of preschool may not be maintained if children are not continually exposed to complex cognitive challenges in their environments as they move to grade school.

One effect of education on intelligence is evident in rapidly increasing IQ test scores around the world, a phenomenon called the *Flynn effect* (Bratsberg & Rogeberg, 2018; Flynn, 1999, 2006, 2013). Scores on these tests have been rising so fast that a high percentage of people regarded as having average intelligence in 1932 would be regarded as having below-average intelligence today (Figure 9). Because the increase has taken place in a relatively short period of time, it cannot be due to heredity but rather may be due to rising levels of education attained by a much greater percentage of the world's population or to other environmental factors, such as the explosion of information to which people are now exposed (Bratsberg & Rogeberg, 2018).

Of course, environmental influences are complex. Children from wealthy families may have easy access to excellent schools, books, and tutors, but they may take such

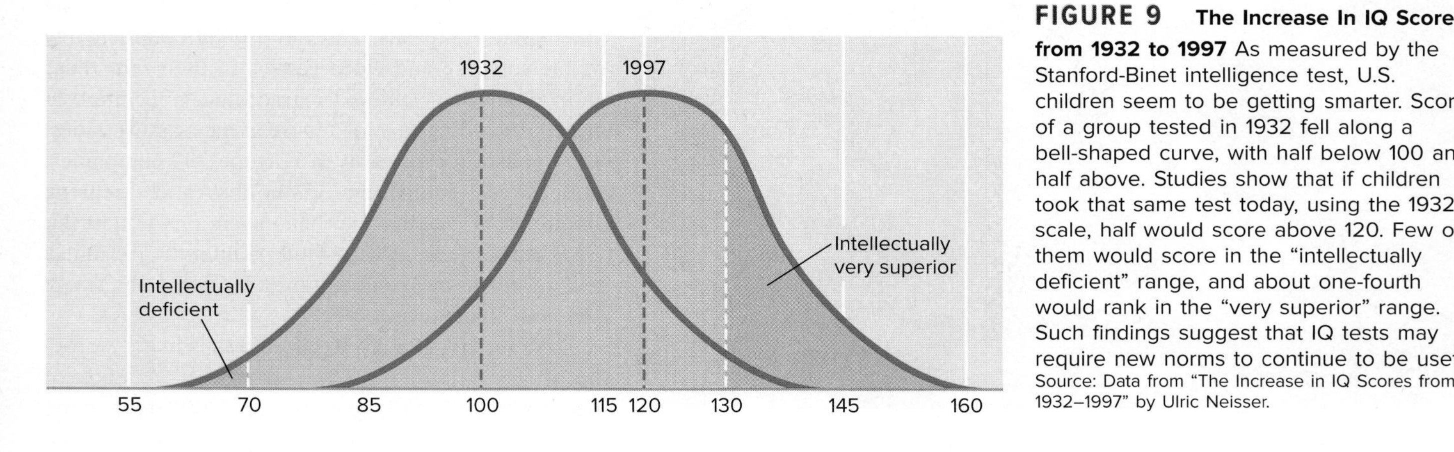


**FIGURE 9 The Increase In IQ Scores from 1932 to 1997** As measured by the Stanford-Binet intelligence test, U.S. children seem to be getting smarter. Scores of a group tested in 1932 fell along a bell-shaped curve, with half below 100 and half above. Studies show that if children took that same test today, using the 1932 scale, half would score above 120. Few of them would score in the "intellectually deficient" range, and about one-fourth would rank in the "very superior" range. Such findings suggest that IQ tests may require new norms to continue to be useful.
Source: Data from "The Increase in IQ Scores from 1932–1997" by Ulric Neisser.

opportunities for granted and not be motivated to learn and to achieve. Alternatively, poor or disadvantaged children may be highly motivated and successful. Caregivers who themselves lacked educational opportunities may instill a strong sense of the value of learning and achievement in their children.

Let's return to the idea that the word *intelligent* describes not only people but also behaviors. Mastering skills, thinking about life actively, and making decisions thoughtfully are intelligent behaviors in which people can engage regardless of the numerical intelligence quotient on their permanent record. Intelligent behavior is always an option, no matter what one's IQ score might be. As we saw in the chapter "Learning", our beliefs about cognitive ability, specifically whether it is fixed or changeable, have important implications for the goals we set for learning new skills (Dweck, 2006, 2013). We never know what we might accomplish if we try, and no one is doomed because of a number, no matter how significant that number may seem.

## Extremes of Intelligence

As we have seen, scores on IQ tests generally conform to the bell-shaped normal curve. We now examine the implications of falling on either tail of that curve.

### GIFTEDNESS

● **gifted** Possessing high intelligence (an IQ of 130 or higher) and/or superior talent in a particular area.

There are people whose abilities and accomplishments outshine those of others—the *A*+ student, the star athlete, the natural musician. People who are **gifted** have high intelligence (an IQ of 130 or higher) and/or superior talent in a particular area. Lewis Terman (1925) conducted a study of 1,500 children whose IQs averaged 150, a score that placed them in the top 1 percent. Terman's participants ("Termites") were not only academically gifted but also socially well adjusted and many went on to successful professions. Interestingly, however, the Termites did not become major creators or innovators (Winner, 2000, 2006).

Given the sweeping social and economic changes of the digital age, are today's gifted children perhaps better able than the Termites to use their gifts in innovative ways in adulthood? The results from a longitudinal study of profoundly gifted children seem to indicate just that. The Study of Mathematically Precocious Youth (SMPY), begun in the 1970s, includes 320 participants recruited before age 13 based on IQ scores. The group's average IQ estimated at 180. They are said to represent the top 1 in 10,000 IQ scores (Lubinski & others, 2001).

Tracking these individuals in their 20s, David Lubinski and colleagues (2006) found that these strikingly gifted young people were doing remarkable things. At age 23, they were pursuing doctoral degrees at a rate 50 times higher than average. They reported achievements such as receiving writing awards, creating original music and art, publishing in scholarly journals, and developing commercially viable software and video games. In their 40s, these individuals had achieved extraordinary accomplishments, including earning tenure at major universities, serving as top executives in Fortune 500 companies, collectively publishing 85 books, and securing hundreds of patents for their inventions (Lubinski, Benbow, & Kell, 2014). Thus, unlike the Termites, this group has been quite innovative (Wai, Lubinski, & Benbow, 2005).

©Rawpixel/Shutterstock

Like intelligence itself, giftedness is likely a product of both heredity and environment. A study of nearly 400,000 sibling pairs and 9,000 twin pairs that included DNA sequencing showed that the genes and environmental experiences that explain normal-range intelligence also explain exceptional intelligence (Shakeshaft & others, 2015). Certainly, individuals who enjoy world-class status in the arts, mathematics, science, and sports not only benefit from their genetic heritage but also from strong family support and years of training and practice (Bloom, 1985). Deliberate practice is an important characteristic of people who become experts in a particular domain (Ericsson & Moxley, 2012).

Of course, providing educational opportunities for youth who possess exceptionally high intelligence is just one of the many priorities faced by the educational system. For some talented students, it may be necessary to seek out opportunities outside the regular classroom. Bill Gates, Microsoft's founder, took college math classes at 13, and famed cellist Yo-Yo Ma graduated from high school at 15 and then attended the Juilliard School of Music.

To qualify for gifted education programs, children are given intelligence tests (McIntosh, Dixon, & Pierson, 2018). However, whether a child is tested may depend on factors that have nothing to do with cognitive ability. In order for a child to be tested, it is sometimes necessary for parents or teachers to nominate them as likely candidates for gifted instruction (Kornmann & others, 2015; Russell, 2018). What this means is that, for some students, qualifying for gifted instruction involves someone else's *social perception*. Being recognized as possibly gifted depends on an adult noticing that a child might be highly intelligent.

Social perception can be influenced by stereotypes. The notion that stereotypes about gifted children exist and affect who is included in gifted programs is suggested by the fact that ethnic minority groups (such as African Americans and Latino Americans), those for whom English is a second language, and people with physical and learning disabilities, are underrepresented in U.S. gifted programs (Carman, 2011; Gari, Mylonas, & Portešová, 2015).

## INTELLECTUAL DISABILITY

Just as some individuals are at the high extreme of intelligence, others are at the lower end. **Intellectual disability** (or **intellectual developmental disorder**) is a condition of limited mental ability that affects functioning in three domains:

- *Conceptual skills,* including language, reading, writing, math, reasoning, and memory
- *Social skills,* including empathy, social judgment, interpersonal communication, and the ability to make friends
- *Practical skills,* including personal care, job responsibilities, money management, recreation, and organizing school and work tasks

**intellectual disability or intellectual developmental disorder** A condition of limited mental ability that affects an individual's functioning in everyday life.

Assessment of capacities in these areas can be used to determine the amount of care the person requires for daily living–not as a function of IQ but as a gauge of the person's ability to negotiate life's challenges.

It is a relatively new idea to think about intellectual disability as involving functional impairment rather than a low IQ test score. This change represents progress in understanding the role of adaptive behaviors in determining who requires additional supports and who does not. Note that a low IQ score in the context of a person who, say, holds down a job and has warm relationships with other people, would not indicate adaptive problems. It is not unusual to find clear *functional* differences between two people who have the same low IQ. For example, looking at two individuals with a similarly low IQ, we might find that one of them is married, employed, and involved in the community while the other requires constant supervision in an institution. Such differences in social competence have led psychologists to include deficits in adaptive behavior in their definition of intellectual disability (McNicholas & others, 2017).

*Individuals with Down syndrome may excel in sensitivity toward others. The possibility that other strengths or intelligences coexist with cognitive ability (or disability) has led some psychologists to propose the need for expanding the concept of intelligence.*

©Denis Kuvaev/Shutterstock

Intellectual disability may have an organic cause, or it may be cultural and social in origin (Peters-Scheffer, Didden, & Lang, 2016). *Organic intellectual disability* is caused by a genetic disorder or brain damage; *organic* refers to the tissues or organs of the body, so there is some physical damage in organic retardation. Down syndrome, one form of organic intellectual disability, occurs when an extra chromosome is present in the individual's genetic makeup. Most people who suffer from organic retardation have an IQ between 0 and 50.

*Cultural-familial intellectual disability* is a mental deficit with no evidence of organic brain damage. Individuals with this type of disability have an IQ between 55 and 70. Psychologists suspect that such deficits result at least in part from growing up in a below-average intellectual environment. As children, individuals with this disability can be identified in school, where they often receive failing grades, need tangible rewards (candy rather than grades, for example), and are highly sensitive to what peers and adults expect of them (Vaughn, Bos, & Schumm, 2003). As adults, however, these individuals usually go unnoticed, perhaps because their environments do not tax their cognitive skills as much. It may also be that the intelligence of such individuals increases as they move toward adulthood.

A person with Down syndrome may never accomplish the amazing academic feats of gifted individuals. However, he or she may be capable of building close, warm relations with others, serving as an inspiration to loved ones, and bringing smiles into an otherwise gloomy day (Van Riper, 2007). Moreover, individuals with Down syndrome might possess different kinds of intelligence, even if they are low on general cognitive ability. The possibility that other intelligences exist alongside cognitive ability (or disability) has inspired some psychologists to suggest that we need more than one concept of intelligence.

## Theories of Multiple Intelligences

Is it more appropriate to think of an individual's intelligence as a general ability or as a number of specific abilities? Traditionally, most psychologists have viewed intelligence as a general, all-purpose problem-solving ability, termed *g* by Spearman (1904). Others have proposed that we think about different kinds of intelligence, such as *emotional intelligence*, the ability to perceive emotions in oneself and others accurately (Brackett, Rivers, & Salovey, 2011; Mayer & others, 2011). Robert Sternberg and Howard Gardner have developed influential theories presenting the viewpoint that there are *multiple intelligences.*

### STERNBERG'S TRIARCHIC THEORY AND GARDNER'S MULTIPLE INTELLIGENCES

● **triarchic theory of intelligence** Sternberg's theory that intelligence comes in three forms: analytical, creative, and practical.

Robert J. Sternberg (2018) developed the **triarchic theory of intelligence**, which says that intelligence comes in multiple (specifically, three) forms. These forms are

- *Analytical intelligence:* The ability to analyze, judge, evaluate, compare, and contrast.
- *Creative intelligence:* The ability to create, design, invent, originate, and imagine.
- *Practical intelligence:* The ability to use, apply, implement, and put ideas into practice.

Howard Gardner suggests there are nine types of intelligence, or "frames of mind" (1983, 1993, 2002). These are described here, with examples of the types of vocations in which they are reflected as strengths (Campbell, Campbell, & Dickinson, 2004):

- *Verbal:* The ability to think in words and use language to express meaning. Occupations: author, journalist, speaker.
- *Mathematical:* The ability to carry out mathematical operations. Occupations: scientist, engineer, accountant.
- *Spatial:* The ability to think three-dimensionally. Occupations: architect, artist, sailor.
- *Bodily-kinesthetic:* The ability to manipulate objects and to be physically adept. Occupations: surgeon, craftsperson, dancer, athlete.
- *Musical:* The ability to be sensitive to pitch, melody, rhythm, and tone. Occupations: composer, musician.

- *Interpersonal:* The ability to understand and interact effectively with others. Occupations: teacher, mental health professional.
- *Intrapersonal:* The ability to understand oneself. Occupations: theologian, psychologist.
- *Naturalist:* The ability to observe patterns in nature and understand natural and human-made systems. Occupations: farmer, botanist, ecologist, landscaper.
- *Existentialist:* The ability to grapple with the big questions of human existence, such as the meaning of life and death, with special sensitivity to issues of spirituality. Gardner has not identified an occupation for existential intelligence, but one career path would likely be philosopher.

According to Gardner, everyone has all of these intelligences to varying degrees. As a result, we prefer to learn and process information in different ways. People learn best when they can do so in a way that uses their stronger intelligences.

©Fuse/Getty Images

## EVALUATING THE MULTIPLE-INTELLIGENCES APPROACHES

Sternberg's and Gardner's approaches have stimulated teachers to think broadly about what makes up children's competencies. They have motivated educators to develop programs that instruct students in multiple domains. These theories have also contributed to interest in assessing intelligence and classroom learning in innovative ways, such as by evaluating student portfolios (Woolfolk, 2013).

Doubts about multiple intelligences persist, however. A number of psychologists think that the proponents of multiple intelligences have taken the concept of specific intelligences too far (Reeve & Charles, 2008). Critics argue that sufficient evidence does not exist to support the three intelligences of Sternberg or the nine intelligences of Gardner. One expert on intelligence, Nathan Brody (2007), observes that people who excel at one type of intellectual task are likely to excel at others. So, people high on one of these intelligences are likely high in them all. Other critics ask, if musical skill, for example, reflects a distinct type of intelligence, why not also label the skills of outstanding chess players, prizefighters, and poets as types of intelligence? In sum, there continues to be controversy about whether it is best to conceptualize intelligence as a general ability, specific abilities, or both (Brody, 2007; Nisbett & others, 2012).

One question that remains is whether and how we can enhance our cognitive abilities. Although there is controversy about whether these abilities can be changed (Melby-Lervåg & Hulme, 2016), there is evidence that challenging ourselves in two different ways may enhance cognition. First, you might be surprised to learn that challenging physical activity is associated with improved cognitive performance (Moreau, 2015). Second, engaging in complex cognitive tasks can improve reasoning ability over time (Au & others, 2015). Importantly, for either type of activity to pay off, we must seek out ever-more challenging activities—not rest on our laurels.

Our examination of cognitive abilities has highlighted how individuals differ in the quality of their thinking and how thoughts themselves differ. Some thoughts reflect critical thinking, creativity, or intelligence. Other thoughts are perhaps less inspired. One thing thoughts have in common is that they usually involve language. Even when we talk to ourselves, we do so with words. The central role of language in cognitive activity is the topic to which we now turn.

### *test yourself*

1. With respect to testing, what do validity, reliability, and standardization mean?
2. What two terms respectively define individuals at the high end and at the low end of intelligence?
3. How does Spearman's *g* compare with theories about multiple intelligences?

# 4. LANGUAGE

● **language** A form of communication—whether spoken, written, or signed—that is based on a system of symbols.

**Language** is a form of communication—whether spoken, written, or signed—based on a system of symbols. We need language to speak with others, listen to others, read, and write. In this section we first examine the fundamental characteristics of language and then trace the links between language and cognition.

## The Basic Properties of Language

All human languages have *infinite generativity,* the ability to produce an endless number of meaningful sentences. This superb flexibility comes from five basic rule systems:

● **phonology** A language's sound system.

● **morphology** A language's rules for word formation.

● **syntax** A language's rules for combining words to form acceptable phrases and sentences.

● **semantics** The meaning of words and sentences in a particular language.

● **pragmatics** The useful character of language and the ability of language to communicate even more meaning than is verbalized.

- **Phonology** is a language's sound system. Language is made up of basic sounds, or *phonemes.* Phonological rules ensure that certain sound sequences occur (for example, *sp, ba,* or *ar*) and others do not (for example, *zx* or *qp*) (Brentari & Lee, 2018). A good example of a phoneme in the English language is /*k*/, the sound represented by the letter *k* in the word *ski* and the letter *c* in the word *cat.* Although the /*k*/ sound is slightly different in these two words, the /*k*/ sound is described as a single phoneme in English.
- **Morphology** is a language's rules for word formation. Every word in the English language is made up of one or more morphemes. A morpheme is the smallest unit of language that carries meaning. Some words consist of a single morpheme—for example, *help.* Others are made up of more than one; for example, *helper* has two morphemes, *help* + *er.* The morpheme *-er* means "one who"—in this case, "one who helps." As you can see, not all morphemes are words; for example, *pre-, -tion,* and *-ing* are morphemes. Just as the rules that govern phonemes ensure that certain sound sequences occur, the rules that govern morphemes ensure that certain strings of sounds occur in particular sequences (White, 2018).
- **Syntax** is a language's rules for combining words to form acceptable phrases and sentences (Moody, Baker, & Blacher, 2018; White, Hacquard, & Lidz, 2018). If someone says, "John kissed Emily" or "Emily was kissed by John," you know who did the kissing and who was kissed in each case because you share that person's understanding of sentence structure. You also understand that the sentence "You didn't stay, did you?" is a grammatical sentence but that "You didn't stay, didn't you?" is unacceptable.
- **Semantics** is the meaning of words and sentences in a particular language. Every word has a unique set of semantic features (Clark, 2018; Spätgens & Schoonen, 2018). *Girl* and *woman,* for example, share many semantic features (for instance, both signify a female human being), but they differ semantically in regard to age. Words have semantic restrictions on how they can be used in sentences. The sentence "The bicycle talked the boy into buying a candy bar" is syntactically correct but semantically incorrect. The sentence violates our semantic knowledge that bicycles do not talk.
- **Pragmatics** is the useful character of language and the ability of language to communicate even more meaning than is said (Ninio & Snow, 2018). The pragmatic aspect of language allows us to use words to get the things we want. If you ever find yourself in a country in which you know only a little of the language, you will certainly take advantage of pragmatics. Wandering the streets of, say, Madrid, you might approach a stranger and ask, simply, "Autobus?" (the Spanish word for *bus*). You know that given your inflection and perhaps your desperate facial expression, the person will understand that you are looking for the bus stop.

With this basic understanding of language in place, we can examine the connections between language and cognition.

## Language and Cognition

Language is a vast system of symbols capable of expressing most thoughts; it is the vehicle for communicating most of our thoughts to one another. Although we do not always think in words, our thinking would be greatly impoverished without words.

The connection between language and thought has been of considerable interest to psychologists. Some have even argued that we cannot think without language. This proposition has produced heated controversy. Is thought dependent on language or is language dependent on thought?

*Whorf's view is that our cultural experiences with a particular concept shape a catalog of names that can be either rich or poor. Consider how rich your mental library of names for camels might be if you had extensive experience with camels in a desert world, and how poor your mental library of names for snow might be if you lived in a tropical world of palm trees and parrots. Despite its intriguing appeal, Whorf's view likely overstates the role of language in shaping thought.*

(first) ©Pegaz/Alamy Stock Photo; (second) ©White Fox/AGE Fotostock

### THE ROLE OF LANGUAGE IN COGNITION

Recall from the chapter "Memory" that memory is stored not only in the form of sounds and images but also in words. Language helps us think, make inferences, tackle difficult decisions, and solve problems. It is also a tool for representing ideas.

Today, most psychologists would accept these points. However, Benjamin Whorf (1956) went a step further: He argued that language determines the way we think, a view that has been called the *linguistic relativity hypothesis*. Whorf and fellow linguist Edward Sapir were specialists in Native American languages, and they were fascinated by the possibility that people might perceive the world differently as the result of the different languages they speak. The Inuit people in Alaska, for instance, have a dozen or more words to describe the various textures, colors, and physical states of snow. In contrast, English has relatively few words to describe snow, and thus, according to Whorf's view, English speakers *cannot see* the different kinds of snow because they have no words for them.

Whorf's bold claim appealed to many scholars. Some even tried to apply Whorf's view to gender differences in color perception. Asked to describe the colors of two sweaters, a woman might say, "One is mauve and the other is magenta," while a man might say, "They're both pink." Whorf's view of the influence of language on perceptual ability might suggest that women are able to see more colors than men simply because they have a richer color vocabulary (Hepting & Solle, 1973). It turns out that men can learn to discriminate among the various hues that women use, and this outcome suggests that Whorf's view is not accurate.

Critics of Whorf's ideas say that words merely reflect, rather than cause, the way we think. The Inuits' adaptability and livelihood in Alaska depend on their capacity to recognize various conditions of snow and ice. A skier or snowboarder who is not Inuit might also know numerous words for snow, far more than the average person, and a person who does not know the words for the different types of snow might still be able to perceive these differences.

Although the strongest form of Whorf's hypothesis—the assertion that language determines perception—seems doubtful, research has continued to demonstrate the influence of language on how we think. For instance, a set of studies showed that people were more lenient in their moral judgments when the activities were described in a foreign language (Geipel, Hadjichristidis, & Surian, 2015). Many people who are bilingual (that is, fluent in two languages) report feeling different while speaking each (Dewaele, 2016).

A set of studies demonstrated that language could influence something as fundamental as our own personalities. In those studies, researchers interviewed bilingual individuals (fluent in Spanish and English) (Ramírez-Esparza & others, 2006) who rated their own personality characteristics, once in Spanish and once in English. Across all studies, and regardless of whether the individuals lived in a Spanish-speaking or an English-speaking country, respondents reported themselves as more outgoing, nicer, and more responsible when responding to the survey in English.

## THE ROLE OF COGNITION IN LANGUAGE

Clearly, then, language can influence cognition. Researchers also study the possibility that cognition is an important foundation for language (Jackendoff, 2012).

One feature of human language that separates it from animal communication is the capacity to talk about objects that are not currently present (Hockett, 1960). A study comparing 12-month-old infants (who had not yet begun to talk) to chimpanzees suggests that this cognitive skill may underlie eventual language (Liszkowski & others, 2009). Compared to chimps, infants were more likely to communicate their desire for a toy by pointing to the place where the toy used to be. For many infants, this was the first thing they did to get their point across to another person. In contrast, chimpanzees rarely pointed to where their desired object (food) had been, except as they desperately started pointing all over the place. So, even before they can talk, humans are communicating with others about what they want and showing an appreciation of shared knowledge about objects that are no longer present.

If language is a reflection of cognition in general, we would expect to find a close link between language ability and general intellectual ability. We would anticipate, for example, that general intellectual disability is accompanied by deficits in language abilities. It is often but not always the case that individuals with intellectual disability have a reduced language proficiency. For instance, individuals with Williams syndrome—a genetic disorder that affects about 1 in 20,000 births—tend to show extraordinary verbal, social, and musical abilities while having an extremely low IQ and difficulty with motor tasks, numbers, and some reading skills (Brawn & others, 2018). Williams syndrome demonstrates that intellectual disability is not always accompanied by poor language skills.

Some research shows that people who are bilingual show greater executive function compared with those who are monolingual (those who speak only one language) (Bialystok, 2015). However, this conclusion has come under extreme scrutiny as some researchers have not found any cognitive advantage for bilingualism or have found it to be limited to very narrow tasks—not the all-purpose toolbox of executive function (Paap, Johnson, & Sawi, 2015). This controversy highlights the important role of rigorous scientific methods in research. There are a number of confounds involved in comparing bilingual to monolingual individuals. This comparison often involves comparing individuals who have immigrated at some point in their lives to those who have always lived in the same place.

Interestingly, immigrants tend to have higher IQs than nonimmigrants, so bilingual individuals might have had higher executive function to start with (Bak, 2015). The issue is even more complicated than that, however. Socioeconomic status, parental education, and a host of other issues can also affect second-language acquisition, training, and executive function. At the very least, this controversy shows that the relationship between language and cognition is complex.

In summary, although thought influences language and language influences thought, language and thought are not part of a single system. Instead, they seem to have evolved as separate but related components of the mind.

**Noam Chomsky (b. 1928)** MIT linguist Noam Chomsky was one of the early architects of the view that children's language development cannot be explained by environmental input. In Chomsky's opinion, language has strong biological underpinnings, with children biologically prewired to learn language at a certain time and in a certain way.



## Biological and Environmental Influences on Language

Everyone who uses language in some way "knows" its rules and has the ability to create an infinite number of words and sentences. Is this knowledge the product of biology, or is language acquisition and usage influenced by experiences in the environment?

### BIOLOGICAL INFLUENCES

Scientists believe that humans acquired language about 100,000 years ago. In evolutionary time, then, language is pretty new. A number of biological systems are required for language, including the brain, nervous system, and vocal apparatus. Physically equipped to do so, *Homo sapiens* went beyond grunting and shrieking to develop abstract speech. This sophisticated language ability gave humans an enormous edge over other animals and increased their chances of survival (Arbib, 2012; Fitch, 2018).

Research indicates that language evolved along with toolmaking (Morgan & others, 2015). At some point, it was no longer enough to simply watch someone do what needed to be done and then imitate that model. Early humans who could actually tell one another what to do won the evolutionary sweepstakes and survived to produce all of us. For them, language solved an enormous problem.

**Language Universals** American linguist Noam Chomsky (1975) argued that humans come into the world biologically prewired to learn language at a certain time and in a certain way. According to Chomsky and many other language experts, the strongest evidence for language's biological basis is the fact that children all over the world reach language milestones at about the same time and in about the same order, despite vast variations in the language input they receive from their environment. For example, in some cultures, such as some Samoan tribes (Schieffelin & Ochs, 1986), parents snuggle their babies but rarely talk to infants under 1 year of age, yet these infants still acquire language (Sterponi, 2010).

In Chomsky's view, children cannot possibly learn the full rules and structure of languages by only imitating what they hear. Rather, nature must provide children with a biological, prewired, universal grammar, allowing them to understand the basic rules of all languages and to apply these rules to the speech they hear. They learn language without an awareness of its underlying logic.

Think about it: The terms we used above to define the characteristics of language—*phonology, morphology, semantics,* and so forth—may be new to you, but on some level you have mastered these principles. This mastery is shown by your reading of this material, writing a paper for class, texting a friend, and talking to your parents. Like all other humans, you are engaged in the use of a rule-based language system even without knowing that you know those rules.

**Language and the Brain** There is strong evidence to back up experts who believe language has a biological foundation. Neuroscience research has shown that the brain contains particular regions that are predisposed to language use.

As we saw in the "Biological Foundations of Behavior" chapter, language processing, such as speech and grammar, mainly occurs in the brain's left hemisphere (Fuertinger & others, 2018; Tzourio-Mazoyer, Crivello, & Mazoyer, 2018). Recall the importance of two areas in the left hemisphere in terms of language: Wernicke's area (toward the middle and front) for language comprehension and Broca's area (toward the back) for speech production. Scientists used direct cortical recordings to illuminate the role of Broca's area in speech.

They found that this area is not directly involved in talking (Flinker & others, 2015). Instead, Broca's area sends and coordinates messages to sensory neurons (representing words) and motor neurons (for articulation) in preparation for speaking. Yet, during the actual act of talking, Broca's area is relatively inactive. These fascinating results point to the complex process involved in speech. Simply saying a word involves a great deal of preparatory work in the brain.

Using brain-imaging techniques such as PET scans, researchers have found that when an infant is about 9 months old, the hippocampus, the part of the brain that stores and indexes many kinds of memory, becomes fully functional (Bauer, 2009, 2013). This is also the time at which infants appear to be able to attach meaning to words—for instance, to look at a ball if someone says "ball"—suggesting links among language, cognition, and the development of the brain.

## ENVIRONMENTAL INFLUENCES

Decades ago, behaviorists opposed Chomsky's hypothesis and argued that language represents nothing more than chains of responses acquired through reinforcement (Skinner, 1957). A baby happens to babble "ma-ma," mama rewards the baby with hugs and smiles, the baby says "mama" more and more. Bit by bit, said the behaviorists, the baby's language is built up. According to behaviorists, language is a complex learned skill, much like playing the piano or dancing.

Such a view of language development is not tenable. Children learn language rapidly, and once they start talking their skills take off. In addition, there is no evidence that social environments carefully reinforce language skills (R. Brown, 1973). You probably recognize that parents often reward very young children when they mispronounce words or make up cute names for things that are not actually proper English (like calling boots "boops"). So, it is extremely unlikely that reinforcement leads to the development of language. This is not to say the environment has no role in language development. A child's experiences, the particular language to be learned, and the context in which learning takes place can strongly influence language acquisition.

Evidence for the important role of the environment in language development comes from case histories of children who have lacked exposure to language. A case of a woman who was exposed to language for the first time at age 32 provides a case in point. The woman, called "Chelsea," grew up in a rural community in a large and loving family (Curtiss, 2014). Likely due to prenatal exposure to a virus, she was born with hearing disabilities. She did not receive an accurate diagnosis of partial deafness until the age of 32 when she was fitted with her first hearing aids. With those hearing aids, Chelsea's hearing was in the normal range. Scans of Chelsea's brain reveal that it is in the normal range; her IQ falls between 77 and 89.

After 32 years in silence, Chelsea was exposed, for the first time, to the sounds of language. For three decades, Chelsea has received training both for spoken and sign language. Through the years, Chelsea has shown the ability to acquire and use a range of words. Her vocabulary and understanding of the meaning of words is remarkable, though her performance on standardized tests does not always reflect the abilities she shows in everyday life. In contrast, she has never acquired a sense of grammar. Verbal acts you likely never think about, such as putting a subject before a verb in a sentence, have escaped her. For example, in response to a picture of a boy riding a bike, Chelsea said, "Riding ride bike ride boy ride" (Curtiss, 2014, p. 124).

A remarkable aspect of this case is that in the context of these language deficits, Chelsea's math abilities are normal. She has a sense of number meanings and is able to keep a checkbook and do her own shopping. She can use her watch to tell time. Thus, this case offers two important conclusions. First, Chelsea's language deficits support the idea of a "critical period" for language development, a special time in a child's life during which language must develop or it never will. Second, the fact that Chelsea's mathematical ability appears to have been spared such deficits supports the idea (reviewed above) that, though connected, language and cognition are separable (Curtiss, 2014).

Whether the case of Chelsea confirms the idea of a critical period, her experiences and those of others who lack exposure to language in early childhood certainly support the idea that the environment is crucial to language development. Clearly, most humans do not learn language in a social vacuum. Most children are bathed in language from early infancy (Kuhl, 2012). And infants' attention to the conversations going on around them predicts language development (Vouloumanos & Curtin, 2014).

The ways adults interact with children can facilitate language learning (Golinkoff & others, 2015). For example, one study showed that when mothers immediately smiled and touched their 8-month-old infants after they had babbled, the infants subsequently made more complex speechlike sounds than when mothers responded to their infants in a random manner (Goldstein, King, & West, 2003) (Figure 10).

**FIGURE 10 The Power of Smile and Touch** Research has shown that when mothers immediately smiled and touched their 8-month-old infants after they babbled, the infants subsequently made more complex speechlike sounds than when mothers responded randomly to their infants. ©Ariel Skelley/Blend Images

Environmental influence on language development was also demonstrated in an older study examining family backgrounds, language exposure, and language acquisition. In the study, researchers observed the language environments of children from two different backgrounds: families of middle-income professionals and families living on welfare (Hart & Risley, 1995; Risley & Hart, 2006). Then they examined the children's language development. All of the children developed normally in terms of learning to talk and acquiring the basic rules of English and a fundamental vocabulary. However, the researchers found enormous differences in the sheer amount of language to which the children were exposed and in the level of the children's language development.

For example, in a typical hour, the middle-income professional parents spent almost twice as much time talking with their children as did parents of lower socioeconomic status. Each hour, the children from the middle-income families heard about 2,100 words; the children in the poorer families heard only 600 words. The researchers estimated that by age 4, the average child from the poorer family group would have *13 million* fewer words of cumulative language experience than the average child from the middle-income professional family group. These differences in exposure to words predicted grade school grades.

Before drawing strong conclusions from this famous study, it is important to note its weaknesses. First, the sample was very small. The entire "welfare" group contained just 6 families, all of them African American. The affluent group contained 13 families, only one of which was African American. Second, as you know, correlation does not imply causation. The fact that the number of words included in conversations was related to children's language development does not imply that word-exposure causes language development. Similarly, the fact that language deficits at age 3 correlated with grade school performance does not imply that these deficits caused that performance. Both of these associations might be due to the host of differences between families and especially the wide-ranging effects of poverty, including limited access to healthcare, education, and nutrition. Third, it is possible that families differed in their responses to the presence of the researcher during the visits. Poor families might have been more guarded in the presence of a stranger and might have felt less comfortable talking while being watched. This criticism suggests that the conversations drawn from the poor families might be biased.

Findings about environmental influences on language learning complicate our understanding of its foundations. In the real world of language learning, children appear to be neither exclusively biologically programmed linguists nor exclusively socially driven language experts. Children are biologically prepared to learn language but benefit enormously from being immersed in a competent language environment from an early age.

## Language Development over the Life Span

Most individuals develop a clear understanding of their language's structure, as well as a large vocabulary, during childhood. Most adults in the United States have acquired a vocabulary of nearly 50,000 words. Researchers have taken a great interest in the process by which these aspects of language develop (Parrish-Morris, Golinkoff, & Hirsh-Pasek, 2013). Their many studies have provided an understanding of the milestones of language development (Figure 11).

**FIGURE 11** **Language Milestones** All children are different and acquire language at varying rates, but these milestones provide a general sense of how language emerges in human life. (text) John W. Santrock, *Educational Psychology*. Fig. 2.14. New York, NY: McGraw-Hill Education, 2001. Copyright ©2001 by McGraw-Hill Education. All rights reserved. Used with permission. (mother and baby) ©Blend Images/SuperStock; (woman reading) ©HBSS/Corbis/Getty Images

| | |
|---|---|
| **0–6 Months** | Cooing<br>Discrimination of vowels<br>Babbling present by 6 months |
| **6–12 Months** | Babbling expands to include sounds of spoken language<br>Gestures used to communicate about objects<br>First words spoken 10–13 months |
| **12–18 Months** | Understands 50+ words on average |
| **18–24 Months** | Vocabulary increases to an average of 200 words<br>Two-word combinations |
| **2 Years** | Vocabulary rapidly increases<br>Correct use of plurals<br>Use of past tense<br>Use of some prepositions |
| **3–4 Years** | Mean length of utterances increases to 3–4 morphemes in a sentence<br>Use of yes and no questions, wh- questions<br>Use of negatives and imperatives<br>Increased awareness of pragmatics |
| **5–6 Years** | Vocabulary reaches an average of about 10,000 words<br>Coordination of simple sentences |
| **6–8 Years** | Vocabulary continues to increase rapidly<br>More skilled use of syntactical rules<br>Conversational skills improve |
| **9–11 Years** | Word definitions include synonyms<br>Conversational strategies continue to improve |
| **11–14 Years** | Vocabulary increases with addition of more abstract words<br>Understanding of complex grammar forms<br>Increased understanding of function a word plays in a sentence<br>Understands metaphor and satire |
| **15–20 Years** | Understands adult literary works |

Language researchers are fascinated by babies' speech even before the little ones say their first words. *Babbling*—endlessly repeating sounds and syllables, such as "bababa" or "dadada"—begins at the age of about 4 to 6 months and is determined by biological readiness, not by the amount of reinforcement or the ability to hear (Menn & Stoel-Gammon, 2009). Even babies who are deaf babble for a time (Lenneberg, Rebelsky, & Nichols, 1965). Babbling probably allows babies to exercise their vocal cords and helps develop the ability to articulate different sounds.

*Around the world, young children learn to speak in two-word utterances at 18 to 24 months of age.*

©Anita van Zyl/age fotostock

Patricia Kuhl's research reveals that long before they begin to learn words, infants can sort through a number of spoken sounds in search of the ones that have meaning for their culture (1993, 2000, 2011, 2012, 2015). Kuhl argues that from birth to about 6 months of age, children are "universal linguists" who are capable of distinguishing each of the sounds that make up the various different human languages. By about 6 months of age, they have started to specialize in the speech sounds (or phonology) of their native language (Figure 12).

A child's first words, uttered at the age of 10 to 13 months, name important people ("mama"), familiar animals ("kitty"), vehicles ("car"), toys ("ball"), food ("milk"), body parts ("eye"), clothes ("hat"), household items ("clock"), and greetings ("bye"). These were babies' first words a century ago, and they are babies' first words still (Bloom, 2004).

By 18 to 24 months, children usually utter two-word statements. They quickly grasp the importance of expressing concepts and the role that language plays in communicating with others (Sachs, 2009). To convey meaning in two-word statements, the child relies heavily on gesture, tone, and context. Although these two-word sentences omit many parts of speech, they are remarkably effective in conveying many messages. When a toddler demands, "Pet doggie!" parents know he means, "May I please pet the dog?" Very young children learn that language is a good way to get what they want, suggesting that they grasp another aspect of language—its pragmatics.

We continue to learn language (new words, new skills) throughout life. For many years, it was claimed that if individuals did not learn a second language prior to puberty, they would never reach native-language learners' levels in the second language (Johnson & Newport, 1991). However, research indicates a more complex conclusion: Sensitive periods likely vary across different language systems (Thomas & Johnson, 2008). For late second-language learners, such as adolescents and adults, new vocabulary is easier to learn than new sounds or new grammar (Neville, 2006). Children's ability to pronounce words with a native-like accent in a second language typically decreases with age, with an especially sharp drop occurring after about age 10 to 12.

For adults, learning a new language is a special kind of cognitive exercise. As we have seen, a great deal of language learning in infancy and childhood involves recognizing the sounds that are part of one's native tongue. This process also entails learning to ignore sounds that are *ignore* sounds that are *not* important to one's first language. For instance, in Japanese, the phonemes /*l*/ and /*r*/ are not distinguished from each other, so that, for a Japanese adult, the word *lion* is not distinguishable from the name *Ryan* (Werker & Hensch, 2015).

Mastering a new language in adulthood may involve overriding such learned habits and learning to listen to sounds that one previously ignored (Linebaugh & Roche, 2015). Indeed, adults can learn to hear and discriminate sounds that are part of a new language, and this learning can contribute to speech fluency and language skill (Evans & Iverson, 2007; Huensch & Tremblay, 2015). Research suggests that the cerebellum, located at the base of the brain, plays a role in perceiving new sounds (Guediche & others, 2015). Thus, learning a new language in adulthood involves cognitively stretching ourselves away from our assumptions and opening up to new experiences.

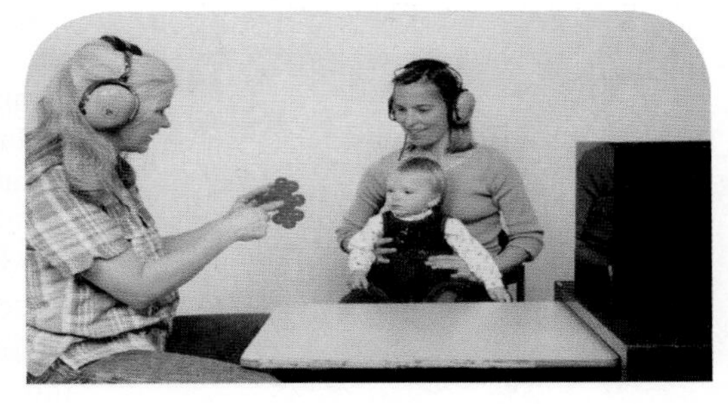

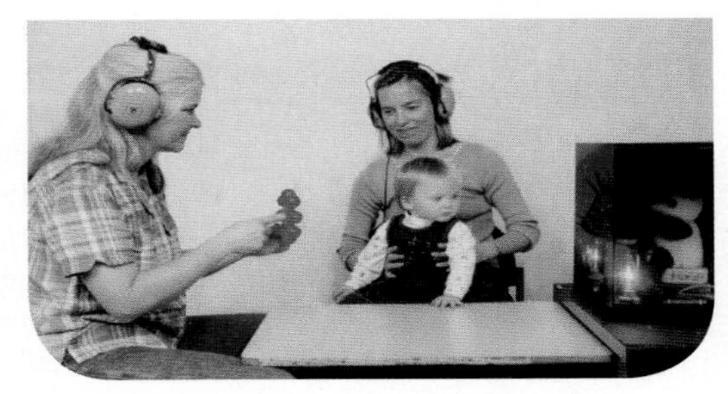

**FIGURE 12 From Universal Linguist to Language-Specific Listener** A baby is shown in Patricia Kuhl's research laboratory. In this research, babies listen to recorded voices that repeat syllables. When the sounds of the syllables change, the babies quickly learn to look at the bear. Using this technique, Kuhl has demonstrated that babies are universal linguists until about 6 months of age, but in the next 6 months they become language-specific listeners.

©2003 University of Washington, Institute for Learning and Brain Sciences (I-LABS).

# 5. THINKING, PROBLEM SOLVING, AND HEALTH AND WELLNESS

The way we think about life events can profoundly affect our experience of stress. What are your life stressors? These can be anything from losing irreplaceable notes from a class, to being yelled at by a friend, to being in a car wreck. Although everyone's body may have a similar response to stressors, not everyone perceives the same events as stressful, as we now consider.

## Cognitive Appraisal and Stress

Whether an experience "stresses us out" depends on how we think about it. You may perceive an upcoming job interview as a threatening event, whereas your roommate may perceive it as a challenging opportunity or a chance to shine. A *D* on a paper might be threatening or an incentive to work harder. To some degree, then, what is stressful depends on how we think about events–what psychologists call cognitive appraisal (Alhurani & others, 2018; Jamieson & others, 2018).

**Cognitive appraisal** refers to a person's interpretation of a situation. This appraisal includes whether the event is viewed as harmful and threatening, or challenging and a person's determination of whether he or she has the resources to cope effectively with the events. Is moving to a new apartment stressful? It depends on how you look at it and whether you have the resources you need to handle the challenge effectively.

**Coping** is essentially a kind of problem solving. It involves managing taxing circumstances, expending effort to solve life's problems, and seeking to master or reduce stress. Richard Lazarus (1993, 2000) most clearly articulated the importance of cognitive appraisal to stress and coping. In Lazarus's view, people appraise events in two steps: primary appraisal and secondary appraisal.

In *primary appraisal,* people interpret whether an event involves *harm or loss* that has already occurred, a *threat* of some future danger, or a *challenge* to be overcome. Lazarus believed that perceiving a stressor as a challenge rather than as a threat, is a good strategy for reducing stress. To understand Lazarus's concept of primary appraisal, consider two students, each of whom has a failing grade in a psychology class at midterm. Sam is almost frozen by the stress of the low grade and looks at the rest of the term as a threatening prospect. In contrast, Pam does not become overwhelmed by the harm already done and the threat of future failures. She looks at the low grade as a challenge that she can address and overcome. This initial appraisal of an event as a threat or challenge can have profound impact on health and wellness (Hase & others, 2018; Trotman & others, 2018).

Primary appraisal involves our immediate reactions to an event. What happens next? We need to figure out if we can handle whatever we are facing. Do we have what it takes to deal with the situation? *Secondary appraisal* means evaluating our resources and determining how effectively they can be used to cope with the event (Alhurani & others, 2018; Kellogg & others, 2018).

This appraisal is secondary for two reasons: It comes after primary appraisal, and it depends on the degree to which the event is appraised as harmful/threatening or challenging. For example, Sam might have some helpful resources for coping with his low midterm grade, but he views the stressful circumstance as so harmful that he does not take stock of and use his resources. Pam, in contrast, evaluates the resources she can call on to improve her grade during the second half of the term. These include asking the instructor for suggestions about how to study better for the tests in the course, setting up a time management program to include more study hours, and consulting with several high-achieving classmates about their strategies. Importantly, *rethinking* our appraisals of potential stressors can influence health and wellness.

### test yourself

1. What are the terms for a language's sound system, its rules for combining words to form acceptable sentences, and the meanings of its words and sentences?
2. State Whorf's linguistic relativity hypothesis and explain why some scholars have criticized it.
3. What evidence has neuroscience research provided for a biological foundation of language?

- **cognitive appraisal** Interpreting the events and experiences in one's life as harmful and threatening, or as challenging, and determining whether one has the resources to cope effectively.

- **coping** Managing taxing circumstances, expending effort to solve life's problems, and seeking to master or reduce stress.

## Cognitive Reappraisal

Once an event or experience has been appraised, the resulting perspective need not be set in stone. Indeed, one way of dealing with potentially stressful situations is to reappraise the event actively and come up with a new way of thinking about it.

**Cognitive reappraisal** involves regulating our feelings about an experience by reinterpreting it or thinking about it in a different way or from a different angle (Roseman & Smith, 2009). Research has shown that reappraising an event can change not only the way people feel about it, but also the brain activity linked to the experience (Holz & others, 2016).

For example, in one brain-imaging study, participants were shown images that were likely to produce negative feelings, such as a driver standing beside a car that has been in an accident (McRae & others, 2010). To examine the effects of cognitive reappraisal, the researchers told participants to look at the pictures and think about them in a way that would reduce their negative feelings. Results showed that reappraising the stimuli resulted in decreased negative feelings, decreased activation in the amygdala, and increased activation in prefrontal regions.

● **cognitive reappraisal** Regulating one's feelings about an experience by reinterpreting that experience or thinking about it in a different way or from a different angle.

Reappraising negative life events can involve a process called *benefit finding*. Benefit finding means looking at a stressful life event in a particular way, focusing on the good that has arisen in one's life as a result. Finding benefits in negative life events can be a way to make meaning out of those experiences (Mock & Boerner, 2010; C. L. Park, 2010, 2012). Finding benefits in negative life events has been related to better physical health (Bower, Moskowitz, & Epel, 2009) and better psychological functioning in the context of a variety of illnesses (Gianinazzi & others, 2016; C. L. Park, 2010, 2012; C. L. Park & others, 2009).

It may be challenging to think of negative life events as opportunities. However, the capacity to think about such events differently—to engage creatively with the notion that even objectively negative life events have helped us to become more compassionate, wiser, or better able to meet the challenges of the future—can be a powerful tool for staving off stress (King & Hicks, 2007).

### test yourself

1. What is cognitive appraisal?
2. What is cognitive reappraisal?
3. How does benefit finding relate to physical health and to body function in a variety of illnesses?

**The Candle Problem**

The solution requires a unique perception of the function of the box in which the matches came. It can become a candleholder when tacked to the wall.

**The Nine-Dot Problem**

Most people have difficulty with this problem because they try to draw the lines within the boundaries of the dots. Notice that by extending the lines beyond the dots, the problem can be solved.

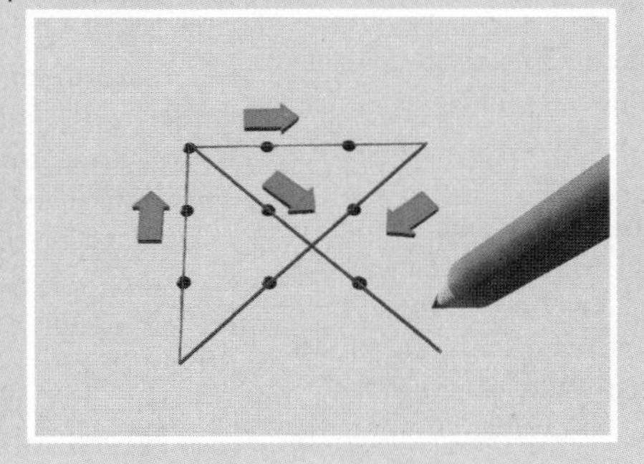

**The Six-Matchstick Problem**

Nothing in the instructions said that the solution had to be two-dimensional.

*Solutions to problems from the Psychological Inquiry feature "Thinking Outside the Box."*

SUMMARY

## 1. THE COGNITIVE REVOLUTION IN PSYCHOLOGY

Cognition is the way in which information is processed and manipulated in remembering, thinking, and knowing. The advent of the computer in the mid-twentieth century spurred a cognitive revolution in which psychologists took on the challenge of understanding human information processing. Artificial intelligence (AI), the science of creating machines capable of performing activities that require intelligence when people do them, is a byproduct of the cognitive revolution.

## 2. THINKING

Concepts are mental categories used to group objects, events, and characteristics. Concepts help us to generalize; they improve our memories; and they keep us from having to learn new things with every new instance or example of a concept. The prototype model suggests that members of a concept vary in terms of their similarity to the most typical item.

Problem solving is an attempt to find a way to attain a goal when the goal is not readily available. The four steps in problem solving are to (1) find and frame the problem, (2) develop good problem-solving strategies, (3) evaluate solutions, and (4) rethink and redefine problems and solutions over time. Among effective strategies for solving problems are setting subgoals (intermediate goals that put us in a better position to reach our goal), devising algorithms (strategies that guarantee a solution), and using heuristics (shortcuts that suggest, but do not guarantee, a solution to a problem).

Reasoning is the mental activity of transforming information to reach conclusions. Inductive reasoning is reasoning from the specific to the general. Deductive reasoning is reasoning from the general to the specific. Decision making involves evaluating alternatives and making choices among them. Biases and heuristics that may lead to problematic decision making include loss aversion, confirmation bias, hindsight bias, the availability heuristic, and the representativeness heuristic.

Critical thinking and creativity improve problem solving. Critical thinking involves thinking productively, evaluating the evidence, being mindful, and keeping an open mind. Creativity is the ability to think in novel and unusual ways and to come up with unconventional solutions. Creative thinkers are flexible and playful, self-motivated, willing to face risk, and objective in evaluating their work.

## 3. INTELLIGENCE

Intelligence consists of the ability to solve problems and to adapt to and learn from everyday experiences. Traditionally, intelligence has been measured by tests designed to compare people's performance on cognitive tasks.

A good test of intelligence meets three criteria: validity, reliability, and standardization. Validity is the extent to which a test measures what it is intended to measure. Reliability is how consistently an individual performs on a test. Standardization focuses on uniform procedures for administering and scoring a test and establishing norms.

Binet developed the first intelligence test. Individuals from age 2 through adulthood may take the current Stanford-Binet test or the age-appropriate Wechsler scale. Some intelligence tests are unfair to individuals from different cultures. Culture-fair tests are intelligence tests that are intended to be culturally unbiased.

Genes are clearly involved in intelligence. The proportion of differences in intelligence that is explained by genetic variation (or heritability) is substantial, although critics have questioned the heritability estimate. Environmental influences on intelligence have also been demonstrated. A number of interventions including interactive reading have been shown to influence children's IQs. The fact that intelligence test scores have risen considerably around the world in recent decades—called the Flynn effect—supports the role of environment in intelligence.

At the extreme ends of intelligence are giftedness and intellectual disability. People who are gifted have high intelligence (IQ of 130 or higher) and/or superior talent for a particular domain. Research has shown that individuals who are gifted are likely to make important and creative contributions. Intellectual disability (or intellectual learning disorder) is a condition of limited mental ability affecting a person's daily functioning. Intellectual disability can have an organic cause or can be cultural and social in origin.

Instead of focusing on intelligence as a single, broad cognitive ability, some psychologists view intelligence as a variety of life skills. Sternberg's triarchic theory states there are three main types of intelligence: analytical, creative, and practical. Gardner identifies nine types of intelligence, involving skills that are verbal, mathematical, spatial, bodily-kinesthetic, musical, interpersonal, intrapersonal, naturalist, and existential. The multiple-intelligences approaches have broadened the definition of intelligence and motivated educators to develop programs that instruct students in different domains.

Critics maintain that multiple-intelligences theories include factors that really are not part of intelligence, such as musical skills, and that people who are highly intelligent are likely to excel in many different areas, not just one. Skeptics also argue that there is not enough research to support the concept of multiple intelligences.

## 4. LANGUAGE

Language is a form of communication that is based on a system of symbols. All human languages have common aspects, including infinite generativity and organizational rules about structure. Also, all languages have five characteristics: phonology (the sound system of a language); morphology (the rules for combining morphemes, which are meaningful strings of sounds that contain no smaller meaningful parts); syntax (the ways words are combined to form acceptable phrases and sentences); semantics (the meaning of words and sentences); and pragmatics (the uses of language).

Although language and thought influence each other, there is increasing evidence that they evolved as separate, modular, biologically prepared components of the mind. Evolution shaped humans into linguistic creatures. Chomsky said that humans are biologically prewired to learn language at a certain time and in a certain way. In addition, there is strong evidence that particular regions in the left hemisphere of the brain are predisposed to be used for language. Experience is also crucial to language development. It is important for children to interact with language-skilled people. Children are biologically prepared to learn language but benefit enormously from being in a competent language environment from early in development.

Although we often think of language, thinking, and intelligence as fixed when we are adults, research shows that we can continue to master skills and even increase intelligence by engaging in challenging mental tasks.

## 5. THINKING, PROBLEM SOLVING, AND HEALTH AND WELLNESS

The way individuals think about life events determines whether they experience them as stressful. Cognitive appraisal is individuals' interpretation of the events in their lives as either threatening (and stressful) or challenging (and not stressful). Coping refers to people's attempts to handle situations that they perceive as stressful. Cognitive reappraisal can be a powerful tool for coping with negative life events. One type of reappraisal, benefit finding, relates to enhanced psychological and physical health.

# key *terms*

algorithms
artificial intelligence (AI)
availability heuristic
base rate neglect
cognition
cognitive appraisal
cognitive reappraisal
concepts
confirmation bias
convergent thinking
coping
creativity
culture-fair tests
decision making
deductive reasoning
divergent thinking
fixation
functional fixedness
gifted
heritability
heuristics
hindsight bias
inductive reasoning
intellectual disability or intellectual developmental disorder
intelligence
intelligence quotient (IQ)
language
loss aversion
mental age (MA)
mindfulness
morphology
normal distribution
open-mindedness
phonology
pragmatics
problem solving
prototype model
reasoning
reliability
representativeness heuristic
semantics
standardization
subgoals
syntax
thinking
triarchic theory of intelligence
validity

# apply your *knowledge*

1. To get a sense of the roles of divergent and convergent thinking in creativity, try the following exercise. First take 10 minutes and jot down all of the uses that you can think of for a cardboard box. Don't hold back–include every possibility that comes to mind. That list represents divergent thinking. Now look over the list. Which of the possible uses are most unusual or most likely to be worthwhile? That is convergent thinking.

2. Ask a few friends to define the term *intelligent.* Do they mostly describe intelligent people or intelligent behaviors? Do their definitions focus on cognitive ability or other abilities?

3. Many different intelligence tests are available online, such as www.iqtest.com/. Give this one a try and then do a web search for intelligence tests and see if you get the same results when you take a different test. Do the websites tell you how reliable the tests are? Do they provide information on standardization or validity? If your scores on the two tests are very different, what might account for this difference?

**Design elements:** Preview icon: ©Jiang Hongyan; Intersection box icon: ©D. Hurst/Alamy, ©Creative Crop/Getty Images, ©Dimitris66/Getty Images, ©Savany/Getty Images; Critical Controversy box icon: ©Ultrashock; running heads icon: ©Cre8tive Studios/Alamy; Summary icon: ©Vadarshop

# CHAPTER 9

## CHAPTER OUTLINE



©Michael H/DigitalVision/Getty Images

# Human Development

## Capes for the Tiniest Superheroes

**Based only on *Instagram* posts, a person might get the impression that 13-year-old girls are occupied by one main interest: perfecting their best "duck face."** Yet our world is full of examples of teens who defy the stereotype of adolescence as a time of obsession with the opposite sex, fashion, video games, and, yes, social media. Consider the amazing work of Rachel Maretsky, a 13-year-old from Florida. Rachel decided to transform Halloween night in 2018 for over 100 premature infants spending the night in the neonatal intensive care unit. She gathered a group of friends and family members and made super hero costumes for all of those preemies (Kekatos, 2018). One minute the ward was filled with tiny, helpless infants and their worried parents, and the next it was filled with heroes: Superman, Wonder Woman, Supergirl, Batman, Batgirl, and The Incredibles. Certainly, those children and their parents have a long road ahead. But they also have the kindness and support of a community, led by one adolescent girl. At every stage in our lives, we have a chance to defy stereotypes, to reach out and a make a difference in the lives of others, and to receive the support of others as well. Like those infants, all of us have a road ahead in which we can lay out the path for our lives. What might that path hold? How will we grow and change along the way? These fascinating questions are given scientific answers by developmental psychologists. ●

# PREVIEW

Developmental psychologists are interested in all the ways a person grows and changes throughout the time travel that is life, from its beginning to its inevitable end. We begin this chapter by examining the meaning of human development and exploring key questions in the field. We then trace the processes of physical, cognitive, and socioemotional development throughout the life span: prenatally (before birth), during childhood, and in adolescence and adulthood. We round off our tour of the human life span with a look at development and wellness.

## 1. EXPLORING HUMAN DEVELOPMENT

● **development** The pattern of continuity and change in human capabilities that occurs throughout life, involving both growth and decline.

**Development** refers to the pattern of continuity and change in human capabilities that occurs throughout the course of life. Most development involves growth, although it also is concerned with decline (such as in physical abilities). Developmental psychology studies how people change, physically and psychologically, as they age. These changes occur on three levels:

- *Physical processes* involve changes in a person's biological nature. Inherited genes; hormonal changes of puberty and menopause; and changes throughout life in the brain, height, weight, and motor skills—all of these reflect the developmental role of biological processes. Such biological growth processes are called *maturation*.
- *Cognitive processes* involve changes in an individual's thought, intelligence, and language. Observing a colorful mobile as it swings above a crib, constructing a sentence about the future, imagining oneself as a movie star, memorizing a new telephone number—these activities reflect the role of cognitive processes in development.
- *Socioemotional processes* involve changes in an individual's relationships with other people, in emotions, and in personality. An infant's smile in response to her mother's touch, a girl's development of assertiveness, an adolescent's joy at the senior prom, a young man's aggressiveness in sports, and an older couple's affection for each other all reflect the role of socioemotional processes.

*Human development is complex because it is the product of several processes. A child's growth in height and weight, a phone user's tapping out a friend's number from memory, and a young couple's joy on the occasion of their prom reflect physical, cognitive, and socioemotional processes, respectively.*

(first) ©Adam Gault/Science Source; (second) ©Studio 642/Blend Images/Getty Images; (third) ©Digital Vision/Getty Images

These physical, cognitive, and socioemotional processes are intricately interwoven. As you read this chapter, remember that you are studying the development of an integrated human being, in whom body, mind, and emotion are interdependent.

Developmental psychologists are interested in the ways that these three processes—physical, cognitive, and socioemotional—change over the human life span. Their work investigates how a person's *age* relates to different aspects of their physical, cognitive, and socioemotional characteristics. Because age is a variable that cannot be manipulated experimentally, studies on the relationship between age and other characteristics are by definition correlational in nature. This aspect of developmental research has important implications for research design, as we now consider.

## Research Methods in Developmental Psychology

Human development involves the changes that occur with age. To know what age-related differences mean, however, we must consider the kind of research presented.

In *cross-sectional studies,* people of different ages are assessed at one point in time, and differences are noted. By examining how age relates to the characteristics measured, researchers can find out whether younger individuals differ from older ones. Age differences, however, are not the same as developmental change.

A problem in cross-sectional studies is cohort effects. A cohort is a generational group consisting of people born in the same time period. *Cohort effects* are differences between individuals that stem not from their ages but from the historical and social time period in which they were born and developed (Carlson & others, 2018; Fuchs & others, 2018). For instance, people who were born in the 1940s might be less likely to have attended college than those born in the 1990s. Differences observed between these groups might be due not to their age but rather to these differing experiences.

To appreciate the limitations of a cross-sectional design, consider a study of about 28,000 people ages 18 to 88 measuring happiness and age (Yang, 2008). The study found that age was positively correlated with happiness. From this work we *might* conclude that people become happier as they age, but this conclusion is limited by its cross-sectional design. We cannot know if the happy 88-year-olds were less happy when they were in their 20s. Maybe these individuals were very happy even in their 20s. Perhaps, relatively more happy people survive into their senior years. A cross-sectional design cannot resolve these possibilities.

In contrast to a cross-sectional study, a *longitudinal study,* as described in the chapter "Psychology's Scientific Method", assesses the same participants multiple times over a lengthy period. A longitudinal study can find out not only whether age groups differ but also whether the same individuals change with respect to a particular characteristic as they age (Larzelere, Gunnoe, & Ferguson, 2018; Stanley, Petscher, & Catts, 2018).

Clearly, conclusions about developmental change in psychological characteristics require longitudinal designs (Lindenberger & others, 2011; Reiss, 2018). Using these and other methods, human development researchers have grappled with three big questions that are relevant to all of psychology, as we consider next.

- **nature** An individual's biological inheritance, especially his or her genes.
- **nurture** An individual's environmental and social experiences.

## How Do Nature and Nurture Influence Development?

Developmental psychologists seek to understand how nature and nurture influence development. **Nature** refers to an individual's biological inheritance, especially their genes; **nurture** refers to the person's environmental and social experiences.

We have previously considered the concepts of a *genotype* (the individual's genetic heritage—his or her actual genetic material) and *phenotype* (the person's observable characteristics). The phenotype shows the contributions of both nature (genetic heritage) and nurture (environment). The genotype may be expressed in various ways, depending on both the environment and characteristics of the genotype itself. Recall, for example, that a recessive gene, though part of the genotype, will not show up in the phenotype if it is paired with a dominant gene.

*Researchers often study twins to measure the influence of nature or genetics on development. Keep in mind that even among twins, the nurture, or experience, matters.*

Environmental factors can shape the developing person. Some experiences can have profoundly negative effects. For instance, persistent poverty in childhood is associated with long-term issues in emotional, cognitive, and social development (Bullock & others, 2018; Huettig & others, 2018; Pakulak, Steven, & Neville, 2018). For this reason, many scientists and policy makers view reducing poverty as a key strategy in preventing developmental problems. Bear in mind that poorer parents often hold many of the same beliefs, values, hopes, and dreams for their children that wealthier parents do; however, they simply lack the resources to provide the opportunities and material goods provided by wealthier parents (Bullock & others, 2018).

Experience can also influence the ways that genetic characteristics are expressed. An illustration of the role of environmental influences in genetic expression is a condition called *phenylketonuria (PKU)*. Caused by two recessive genes, PKU results in an inability to metabolize the amino acid phenylalanine (a major component of the artificial sweetener aspartame, used in many soft drinks and other products). Decades ago, it was thought that the genotype for PKU led to a specific phenotype: irreversible brain damage, developmental disabilities, and seizures. However, we now know that if those with the PKU genotype stick to a diet that is very low in phenylalanine, many of these phenotypic characteristics can be avoided (Bartus & others, 2018; Brown & Lichter-Konecki, 2016; De & others, 2018). Environmental precautions can change the phenotype associated with a genotype.

PKU shows that a person's measurable characteristics (phenotype) might not reflect their genetic heritage (genotype) very precisely because of experience. Instead, for each genotype, a *range* of phenotypes may be expressed, depending on environmental factors. The person we see before us emerges through the interplay of genetic and environmental experiences. Development is the product of nature, nurture, and the complex interaction of the two. One factor that must be taken into account in the development process is the developer himself or herself, as we now consider.

## What Is the Developer's Role in Development?

Because we cannot pick our genes or our parents, each of us may seem to be stuck with the genes and environment we received at birth. However, the developing human being also has a role to play in development (Turkheimer, 2011). Although you might think of nature and nurture as the raw ingredients of yourself as a person, the fact is that you take those ingredients and make them into the person you are.

Indeed, some psychologists believe that we can develop beyond what our genetic inheritance and our environment give us. They argue that a key aspect of development involves seeking optimal experiences in life (Layland, Hill, & Nelson, 2018; Ryff, 2018; Weststrate & others, 2018). They cite examples of individuals who go beyond what life has given them to achieve extraordinary things. These individuals build and shape their own lives, authoring a unique developmental path, and sometimes transforming apparent weaknesses into real strengths.

In our efforts to experience our lives in optimal ways, we develop *life themes* that involve activities, social relationships, and life goals (Bauer & others, 2018; Lieblich, 2018; Pratt & Matsuba, 2018; Weststrate & others, 2018). Some individuals are especially successful at constructing optimal life experiences. For example, Martin Luther King, Jr., Mother Teresa, Nelson Mandela, Bill and Melinda Gates, and Oprah Winfrey looked for and found meaningful life themes as they developed. Their lives were not restricted to biological survival or to settling for their particular life situations. Many of them, in fact, faced hardships early in life yet managed to contribute to the world in meaningful ways. A developmental question that naturally flows from this discussion is whether early or later life experiences are more important to a person's development over the life span.

*Microsoft founder Bill Gates and his wife Melinda have quested after—and carved out—meaningful life experiences as they have progressed through their development.*

©Rommel Demano/Getty Images

## Are Early or Later Life Experiences More Important in Development?

A key question in developmental psychology centers on the extent to which childhood experiences (nurture) determine aspects of later life. If early experiences provide the foundation for later development, does that mean that childhood experiences are likely to influence (and limit or damage) us for the rest of our lives?

Developmental psychologists debate whether early experiences or later experiences are more important. Some believe that unless infants receive warm, nurturing caregiving in their first year or so of life, they will not develop to their full potential (Glaser, 2018; Numan & Young, 2016). Other psychologists emphasize the power of later experience, arguing that important development occurs later in life as well (Chambers, 2018; Hatton & others, 2018).

*Life-span developmentalists*, who study children and adults, stress that researchers have given too little attention to adult development and aging. They argue that although early experiences contribute powerfully to development, they are not necessarily more influential than later experiences (Hershfield & others, 2013; Pauly & others, 2017). These experts say that both early and later experiences make significant contributions to development, and no one is doomed to be a prisoner of his or her childhood.

A key concept in understanding the role of negative early experiences in later development is resilience. **Resilience** is a person's ability to recover from or adapt to difficult times. Resilience means that even in the face of adversity, a person shows signs of positive functioning (Marshall, 2018; Southwick & Charney, 2018). Resilience can refer to factors that compensate for difficulties, buffering the individual from the effects of these, or to the fact that moderate difficulties may themselves help to promote development (Angelini, Bertoni, & Corazzini, 2018; McLafferty & others, 2018).

Despite undergoing hardships time and time again, resilient children grow up to be capable adults. Resilient children possess one or more advantages—such as high intelligence or a close, supportive relationship with a parent or other adult—that help them to overcome their disadvantages (Masten, 2015; 2018). Although often studied as an aspect of childhood and adolescence, resilience can also characterize development in adulthood and old age (McGinnis, 2018).

Recently, scholars have suggested that thinking about the effects of early experiences solely in terms of risk or resilience is simplistic (Ellis & others, 2017). From this perspective, we should not ask whether the effects of any experience are "good or bad" but rather how those experiences shape development. For example, accumulated evidence supports the conclusion that early adversity (that is, negative childhood experiences such as poverty, family conflict, abuse, and neglect) is related to poorer cognitive functioning, especially for self-regulation and attention (Pakulak, Stevens, & Neville, 2018). However, growing up in such circumstances might *shape* a person's cognitive development in ways that are not always negative. To read about provocative research examining this possibility, see the Critical Controversy.

*Having a supportive relationship with a parent or a competent adult outside the home can contribute to childhood resilience.*



● **resilience** A person's ability to recover from or adapt to difficult times.

### test yourself

1. What three broad processes of change do developmental psychologists study?
2. Why are longitudinal studies commonly used to investigate developmental questions? What are the limitations of cross-sectional studies with respect to studying such questions?
3. In what ways can the developing individual play a role in his or her own development?

# 2. CHILD DEVELOPMENT

In this section we focus on the three fundamental developmental processes—physical, cognitive, and socioemotional—of childhood. To understand childhood, we must begin before it even starts, with prenatal development.

## Prenatal Development

Prenatal development is a time of astonishing change, beginning with conception. *Conception* occurs when a single sperm cell from the male merges with the female's ovum (egg) to produce a *zygote,* a single cell with 23 chromosomes from the mother and 23 from the father.

# CRITICAL CONTROVERSY

## Can an Unpredictable Childhood Predict Better Cognitive Function?

Growing up in a chaotic situation can be stressful (Pakulak, Stevens, & Neville, 2018). It is easy to imagine how stressful circumstances might harm a child's developing sense of self and the world (Hill, Turiano, & Burrow, 2018; Kaiser & others, 2018). Yet, in such a situation a child might also develop the capacity to cope with difficult circumstances (Angelini, Bertoni, & Corazzini, 2018; McLafferty & others, 2018). Consider the following scale item: "When I woke up, I often didn't know what would happen to me." Might someone, endorsing this item, possess cognitive skills needed for dealing with rapidly changing circumstances? A recent set of studies tested this possibility (Young & others, 2018). Before taking a look at the research, let's briefly review the rationale behind the specific predictions tested.

First, the researchers hypothesized that experiences with an unpredictable childhood would be related to a specific cognitive skill in working memory called *updating* (Young & others, 2018). Updating refers to the ability to track information and replace old information with newer information. Successful updating gives a person the most relevant information at any given moment. This skill might be useful as one deals with a constantly changing, chaotic childhood environment. Second, the researchers predicted that those who had experienced unpredictable childhood environments would show superior updating specifically in uncertain circumstances. The idea is that people will deploy these skills only when the environment indicates they are needed.

To test their hypotheses, the researchers used an experimental manipulation to induce feelings of uncertainty in a sample of adults. Participants were randomly assigned to one of two groups. The experimental group watched a slide show conveying the sense that economic conditions are uncertain and declining (leading to high levels of uncertainty). The control group watched a slide show about the use of technology. Then, all participants completed tests of updating ability, involving tasks like being able to keep simultaneous counts of each of three different shapes presented over a number of trials. Finally, participants completed evaluations of their childhood environments, with items like the one noted above. The results showed that in the uncertain condition, those who had experienced unpredictable childhood environments performed better than those who had not (Young & others, 2018). These differences only emerged when people experienced uncertainty and did not generalize to other cognitive abilities.

©praetorianphoto/E+/Getty Images

These results show that early experiences do not simply either help or harm but rather *shape* people in ways that can be adaptive or maladaptive, depending on the circumstances. Considering the many different environments that the human species must adapt to, it makes sense that our childhood experiences shape particular cognitive skills, preparing us to solve the problems we will face in whatever situations we encounter.

**WHAT DO YOU THINK?**

- How do you think your childhood experiences have shaped your cognitive and emotional characteristics?
- What other advantages might accrue from difficult early circumstances?

### THE COURSE OF PRENATAL DEVELOPMENT

Development from zygote to fetus is divided into three periods:

- *Germinal period—weeks 1 and 2:* The germinal period begins with conception. After 1 week and many cell divisions, the zygote is made up of 100 to 150 cells. By the end of 2 weeks, the mass of cells has attached to the uterine wall.
- *Embryonic period—weeks 3 through 8:* The rate of cell differentiation intensifies, support systems for the cells develop, and the beginnings of organs appear (Figure 1a). In the third week, the neural tube, which eventually becomes the spinal cord, starts to take shape. Within the first 28 days after conception, the neural tube is formed and closes, encased inside the embryo. By the end of the embryonic period, the heart begins to beat, the arms and legs become more differentiated, the face starts to form, and the intestinal tract appears (Figure 1b).

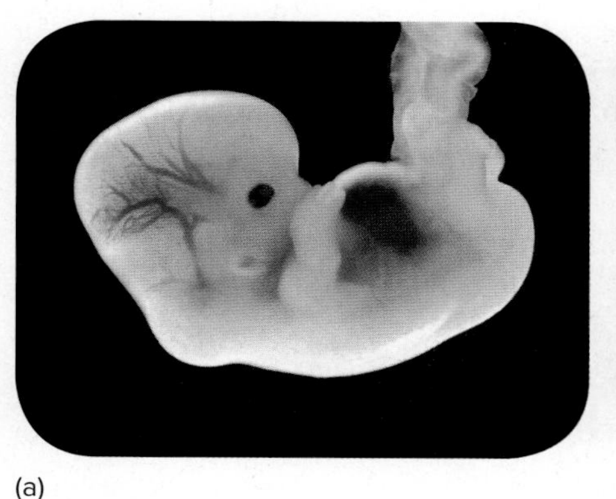

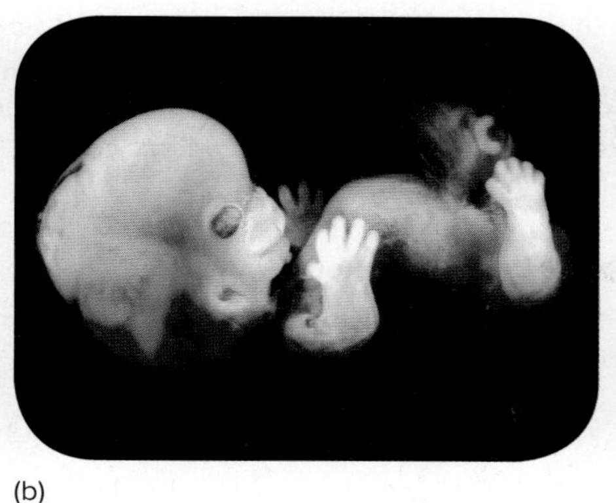

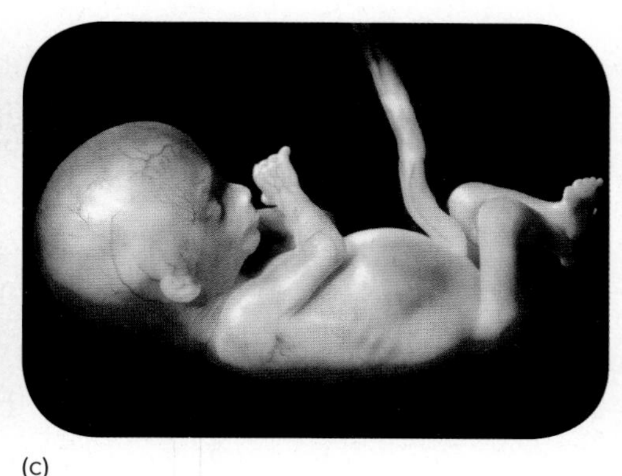

(a) (b) (c)

**FIGURE 1** **From Embryo to Fetus** (*a*) At about 4 weeks, an embryo is about 0.2 inch (less than 1 centimeter) long. The head, eyes, and ears begin to show; the head and neck are half the length of the body; the shoulders will be located where the whitish arm buds are attached. (*b*) At 8 weeks, the developing individual is about 1.6 inches (4 centimeters) long and has reached the end of its embryonic phase. It has become a fetus. Everything that will be found in the fully developed human being has now begun to form. The fetal stage is a period of growth and perfection of detail. The heart has been beating for a month, and the muscles have just begun their first exercises. (*c*) At 4½ months, the fetus is just over 7 inches (about 18 centimeters) long. When the thumb comes close to the mouth, the head may turn, and the lips and tongue begin their sucking motions—a reflex for survival. (a) ©Neil Harding/The Image Bank/Getty Images; (b) ©Joo Lee/Corbis/Getty Images; (c) ©Joo Lee/Corbis/Getty Images

- *Fetal period–months 2 through 9:* At 2 months, the fetus is the size of a kidney bean and has started to move around. At 4 months, the fetus is 5 inches long and weighs about 5 ounces (Figure 1c). At 6 months, the fetus has grown to a pound and a half. The last 3 months of pregnancy are the time when organ functioning increases and the fetus puts on considerable weight and size, adding baby fat.

Although it floats in a well-protected womb, the fetus is not immune to the larger environment surrounding the mother. Sometimes normal development is disrupted by environmental insults.

## THREATS TO THE FETUS

A *teratogen* is any agent that causes a birth defect. Teratogens include chemical substances ingested by the mother (such as nicotine if the mother smokes and alcohol if she drinks) and certain illnesses and viruses (such as rubella or the Zika virus). Substances that are ingested by the mother can lead to serious birth defects (Kinori & others, 2018; Richardson & Day, 2018).

For example, *fetal alcohol spectrum disorders (FASD)* are a cluster of abnormalities and problems that appear in the offspring of mothers who drink alcohol heavily during pregnancy (Nulman & others, 2018). These abnormalities include a small head, defects in the limbs and heart, and below-average intelligence. Heavy drinking is linked to FASD, but even moderate drinking can lead to serious problems. The best advice for a woman who is pregnant or thinking of becoming pregnant is to avoid alcohol completely.

The effects of teratogens depend on the timing of exposure. The body part or organ system that is developing when the fetus encounters the teratogen is most vulnerable (Petrelli, Weinberg, & Hicks, 2018). Genetic characteristics may buffer or worsen teratogen effects. Importantly, the environment the child encounters *after birth* influences the ultimate effects of prenatal insults.

Sexually transmitted infections (STIs) also threaten the fetus. Some STIs, such as gonorrhea, can be transferred to the baby during delivery. Others, including syphilis and the human immunodeficiency virus (HIV), can also infect the developing fetus. Besides transmission of infections to the fetus and newborns, STI exposure enhances the risk of stillbirth and a number of other problems, such as eye infections and blindness (in the case of gonorrhea). Many STIs also increase the risk of preterm birth.

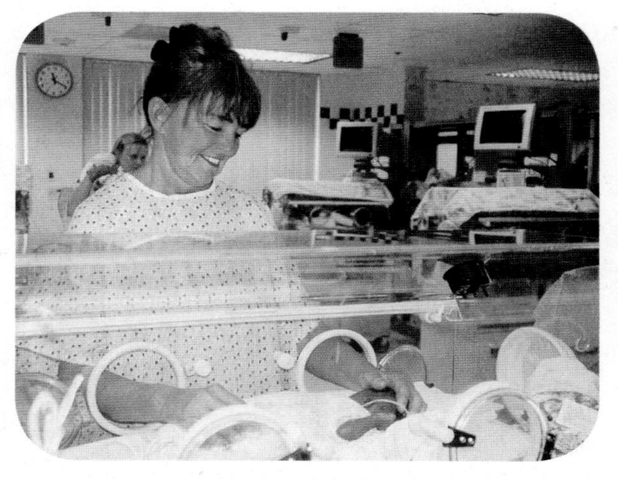

*Tiffany Field is shown massaging a newborn infant. Field's research has demonstrated the power of massage in improving the developmental outcome of at-risk infants. Under her direction, the Touch Research Institute in Miami, Florida, investigates the role of touch in a number of domains of health and well-being.*

Courtesy of Dr. Tiffany Fields/Touch Research Institutes

A *preterm infant,* one born prior to 37 weeks after conception, may also be at risk for developmental difficulties. Whether a preterm infant will have developmental problems is a complex issue, however. Preterm infants who grow up in poverty are more likely to have problems than are those who live in better socioeconomic conditions (Beauregard & others, 2018).

Postnatal experience plays a crucial role in determining the ultimate effects of preterm birth. For example, massage can improve developmental outcomes for preterm infants (Field, 2018; Wang, He, & Zhang, 2013).

## Physical Development in Infancy and Childhood

Human infants are the world's most helpless newborns. One reason for their helplessness is that they are born not quite finished. Our enormous brain sets humans apart from other animals. Getting that big brain out of the relatively small birth canal is a challenge that nature has met by sending human babies out of the womb before the brain has fully developed. The first months and years of life allow the developing human (and the environment) to put the finishing touches on that important organ.

### REFLEXES

Newborns come into the world equipped with several genetically wired reflexes that are crucial for survival. Babies are born with the ability to suck and swallow. If they are dropped in water, they will naturally hold their breath, contract their throats to keep water out, and move their arms and legs to stay afloat at least briefly. Some reflexes persist throughout life—coughing, blinking, and yawning, for example. Others, such as automatically grasping something that touches the fingers, disappear in the months following birth, as higher brain functions mature and infants develop voluntary control over many behaviors. Figure 2 shows some examples of reflexes.

### MOTOR AND PERCEPTUAL SKILLS

Relative to the rest of the body, a newborn's head is gigantic, and it flops around uncontrollably. Within 12 months, the infant becomes capable of sitting upright, standing, stooping, climbing, and often walking. During the second year, growth decelerates, but rapid

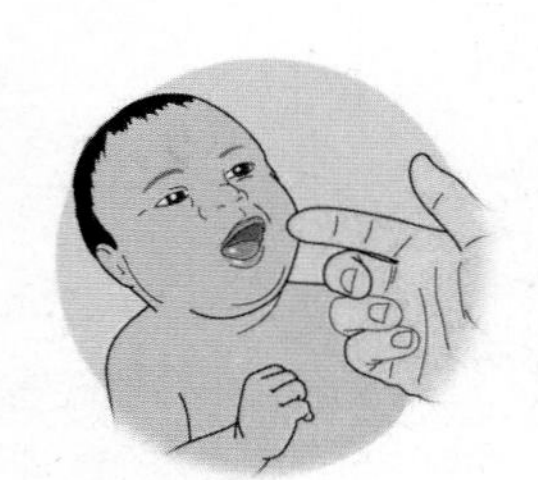

**Rooting**

*What provokes the response?* Stroking of the infant's cheek

*What the infant does* Head turns in the direction of the touch, and the infant opens his or her mouth for feeding.

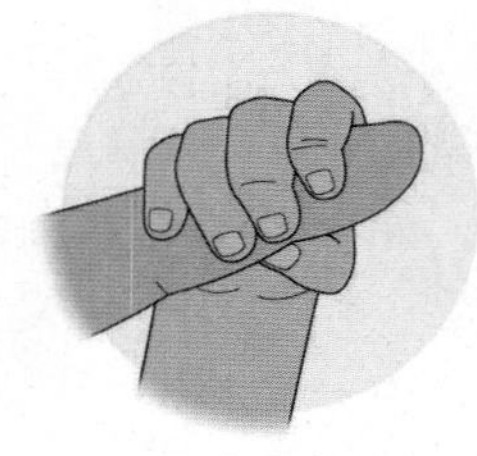

**Gripping**

*What provokes the response?* Something that is placed in the infant's hand

*What the infant does* The infant grasps the item and can hold on very well—almost enough to support his or her own weight.

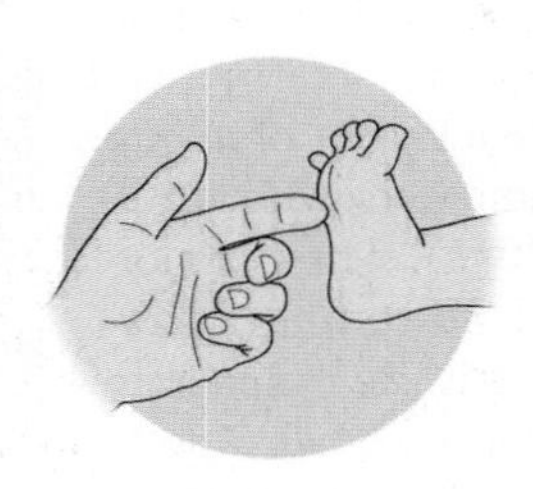

**Toe Curling**

*What provokes the response?* Stroking of the inner or outer sole of the infant's foot

*What the infant does* If the inner sole is stroked, the infant curls his or her toes. If the outer sole is stroked, the toes spread out.

**Moro or Startle**

*What provokes the response?* Sudden noise or movement

*What the infant does* The infant throws his or her head back and arms and legs out (and then cries).

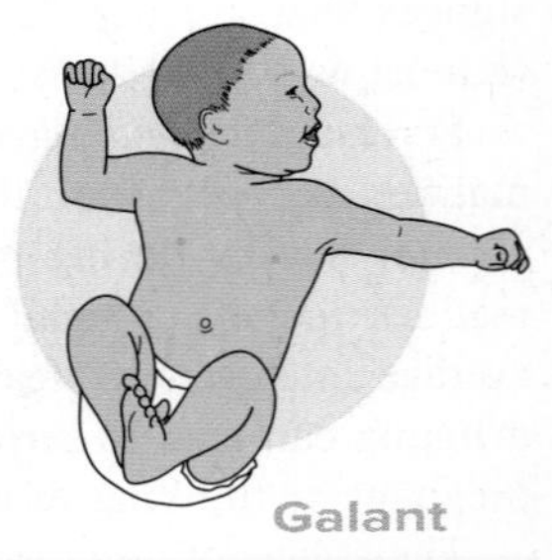

**Galant**

*What provokes the response?* Stroking of the infant's lower back, next to the spinal cord

*What the infant does* The infant curves toward the side that was stroked—and looks like a fencer when doing so.

**FIGURE 2** **Some Infant Reflexes** Infants are born with a number of reflexes to get them through life, and they are incredibly cute when they perform them. These reflexes disappear as infants mature.

gains occur in activities such as running and climbing. Researchers used to think that motor milestones—such as sitting up, crawling, and walking—unfolded as part of a genetic plan. Now, psychologists recognize that experience, not simply genetics, plays a role in motor development.

One of the most remarkable motor skills attained by infants is the ability to reach for things. Reaching may seem to be a small thing to you, but during infancy extending one's own arm to grasp an object is an enormously complex act, filled with implications (Corbetta & others, 2018). Babies who see a stuffed bunny and are able to reach for it have mastered a skill that transforms their relationship to the world: Their focus shifts from people to objects, including toys, food, Grandma's earrings, and all the things that they can now get their hands on.

Emerging between 3 and 5 months of age, the ability to reach for an object involves a wide array of processes (Corbetta & others, 2018):

- *Sensory capacities:* being able to see or hear the object
- *Motivation:* wanting to grasp the object
- *Attention:* being able to focus on a particular thing, among all the other interesting things in the baby's world
- *Bodily control:* having the ability to control posture, manage head movement, and calibrate the movement of one's arms
- *Learning:* getting positive reinforcement from the experience of attaining the object of their desire

Developmental psychologists have long studied the role of experience in the acquisition of reaching. In one study, 3-month-old infants participated in play sessions wearing "sticky mittens"—mittens with Velcro-covered palms that allow the infants to more easily "pick up" objects (toys) (Needham, Barrett, & Peterman, 2002). Being able to pick up objects with the sticky mittens led infants to look at objects longer, swat at them, and put them in their mouths (compared with infants who had not experienced the sticky mittens). However, later studies suggest that it may not have been the sticky mittens but rather being more engaged in experiences with their parents that led to these results (Williams, Corbetta, & Guan, 2015). Just getting the opportunity to play with different objects can lead babies to become more interested in all sorts of things in their environment (Corbetta, Williams, & Haynes, 2016; Williams, Corbetta, & Guan, 2015). In any case, this line of research shows how experience can affect the development of the important skill of reaching.

Infants are active developers, and their motor and perceptual skills develop together and mutually promote each other. Babies are continually coordinating their movements with information they perceive through their senses to learn how to maintain their balance, reach for objects in space, and move across various surfaces and terrains (Anderson & others, 2018). Moving from place to place in the environment teaches babies how objects and people look from different perspectives and whether surfaces will support their weight (Gibson, 2001). Actively participating in behaviors strongly influences infant development, but infants can also gain motor skills in more passive ways, by watching and modeling behavior (Gliga, 2018).

Psychologists face a daunting challenge in studying infant perception. Infants cannot talk, so how can scientists tell what they can see, hear, or feel? Researchers who study infants have no choice but to become clever methodologists, relying on what infants *can* do to understand what infants see, think, and know.

One thing infants can do is look. The **preferential looking** technique involves giving an infant a choice of what object to look at. If an infant shows a reliable preference for one stimulus (say, a picture of a face) over another (a scrambled picture of a face) when these are repeatedly presented in differing locations, we can infer that the infant can tell the two images apart. Using this technique, researchers have found that as early as *7 days old,* infants are already engaged in organized perception of faces and can put together sights and sounds. If presented with two faces with mouths moving, infants will watch the face whose mouth matches the sounds they are hearing (K. Lee & others, 2013b; Lewkowicz &

● **preferential looking** A research technique that involves giving an infant a choice of what object to look at.

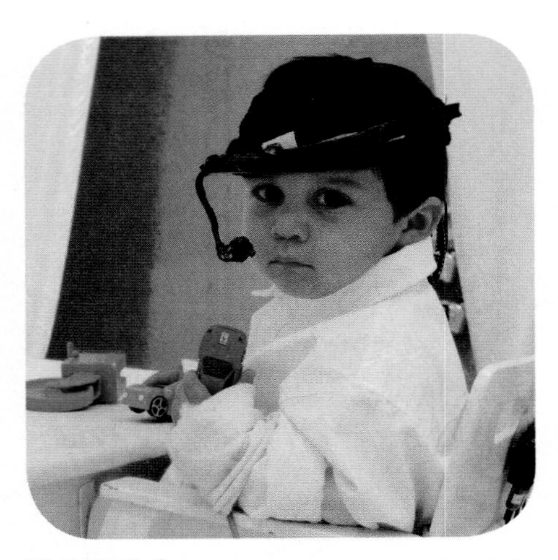

**FIGURE 3** **What Are You Looking At?** Eye-tracking technology allows infant perception researchers to identify exactly what infants are looking at. ©Chen Yu

Hansen-Tift, 2012). At 3 months, infants prefer real faces to scrambled faces and prefer their mother's face to a stranger's (Slater, Field, & Hernandez-Reif, 2007). By 6 months, babies can detect human faces more quickly than they can detect animal faces, just as adults do (Dalrymple & others, 2018).

How do researchers know where infants are looking? In some studies, researchers simply watch and record where babies are focused. An important technological advance in this domain is the use of sophisticated eye-tracking equipment (Dalyrymple & others, 2018). Figure 3 shows an infant wearing eye-tracking headgear in recent research on visually guided motor behavior and social interaction.

Eye tracking also is used to study development in many other areas, including attention, memory, and face processing (Vernetti & others, 2018; Waxman & others, 2016; Xiao & others, 2015) as well as to detect subtle differences that might reveal risks for disorders, such as autism spectrum disorders (Dalrymple & others, 2018). Such techniques have provided a great deal of information about infants' remarkable abilities, but they too are limited. Research using brain imaging suggests that infants may know more than even these clever strategies reveal (Ellis & Turk-Browne, 2018).

## THE BRAIN

As an infant plays, crawls, smiles, and frowns, his or her brain is changing dramatically. At birth and in early infancy, the brain's 100 billion neurons have only minimal connections. The infant brain literally is ready and waiting for the experiences that will create these connections (Bale, 2015; McDonald & Perdue, 2018). During the first 2 years of life, the dendrites of the neurons branch out, and the neurons become far more interconnected (Figure 4). Myelination, the process of encasing axons with fat cells (the myelin sheath described in the chapter "Biological Foundations of Behavior"), begins prenatally and continues well into adolescence and young adulthood (Gilmore, Knickmeyer, & Gao, 2018; Lebel, & Deoni, 2018; Stirrups, 2018).

During childhood, *synaptic connections* increase dramatically (Glaser, 2018). Recall from the chapter "Biological Foundations of Behavior" that a *synapse* is a gap between neurons that is bridged by chemical neurotransmitters. Nearly twice as many synapses are available as will ever be used (Huttenlocher, 1999). The connections that are made become stronger and will survive; the unused ones will be replaced by other neural pathways or disappear (Barber & others, 2018; Krogsrud & others, 2016). In the language of neuroscience, these unused connections are "pruned." Figure 5 illustrates the steep growth and later pruning of synapses during infancy in specific areas of the brain.

Brain-imaging studies show that children's brains undergo remarkable anatomical changes. Repeated brain scans of the same children up to the age of 4 years show that the amount of brain material in some areas can nearly double within as little as a year, followed by a drastic loss of tissue as unneeded cells are purged and the brain continues

**FIGURE 4** **Dendritic Spreading** Note the increase among neurons over the course of the first 15 months of life.

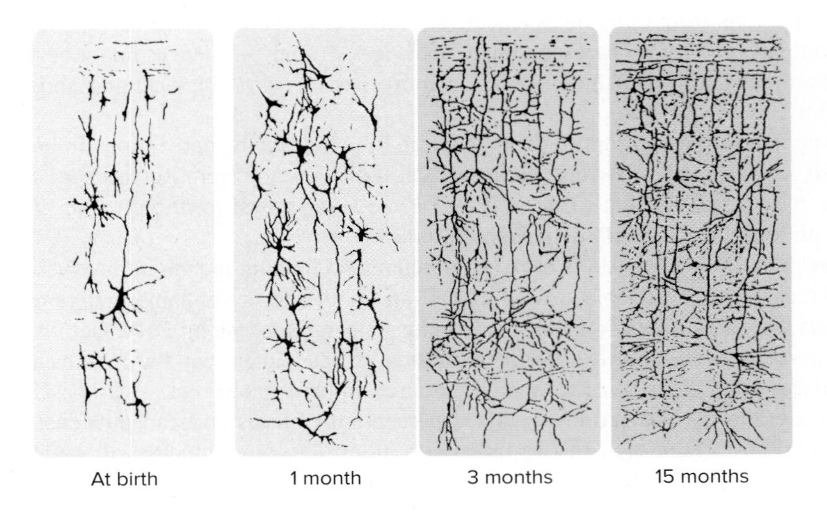

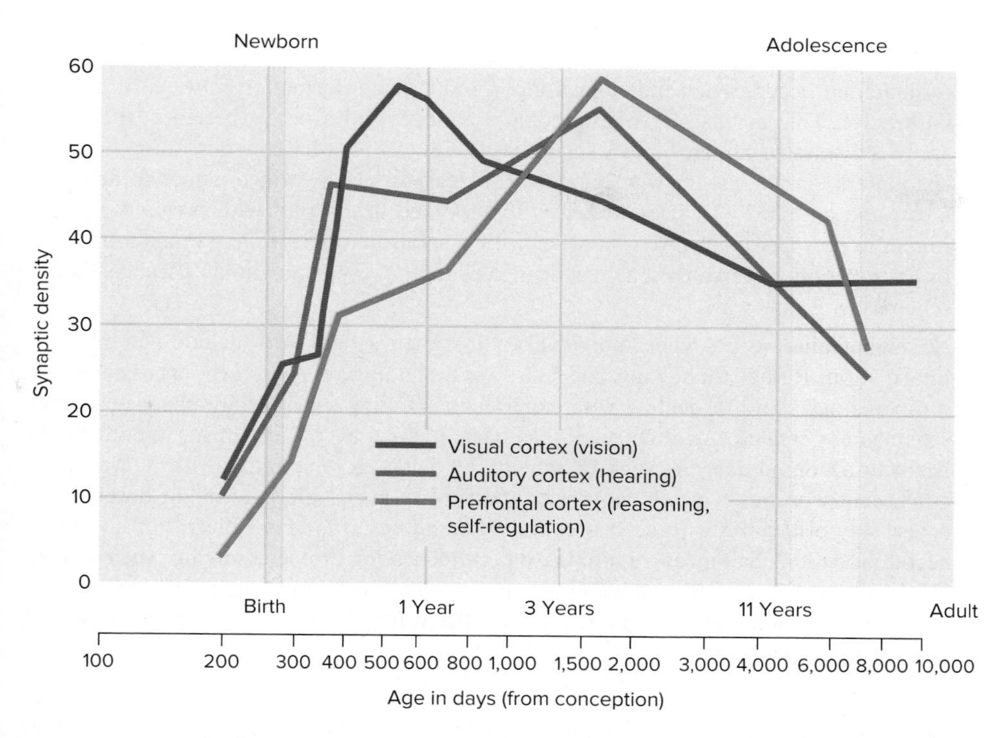


**FIGURE 5 Synaptic Density in the Human Brain from Infancy to Adulthood** The graph shows the dramatic increase and then pruning in synaptic density in three regions of the brain: visual cortex, auditory cortex, and prefrontal cortex. Synaptic density is believed to be an important indication of the extent of connectivity between neurons.

to reorganize itself. From 3 to 6 years of age, the most rapid growth takes place in the frontal lobes, which are involved in planning and organizing new actions and in maintaining attention to tasks (Gogtay & Thompson, 2010). These brain changes are not simply the result of nature; new experiences in the world also promote brain development (Cicchetti, 2016; Heuttig & others, 2018). Thus, as in other areas of development, nature and nurture operate together to promote the development of the child's brain.

To summarize, myelination begins prenatally and continues throughout childhood and into adolescence and young adulthood. In addition, the infant brain explodes with connections but these are pared away if they are not used. This process of pruning reflects the way experience shapes the brain. As the brain develops, thinking matures. That thinking, in turn, shapes the brain.

# Cognitive Development in Infancy and Childhood

*Cognitive development* refers to how thought, intelligence, and language processes change as people mature. *Cognition* refers to the way individuals think and also to their cognitive skills and abilities. In this section we review one of the most important theories in psychology–that proposed by Jean Piaget (1896–1980), the famous Swiss developmental psychologist. In addition, we consider alternatives to Piaget's view and more recent information-processing approaches to cognitive development.

**Jean Piaget (1896–1980)** Piaget, the famous Swiss developmental psychologist, changed the way we think about the development of children's minds.

©Patrick Grehan/Corbis Historical/Getty Images

## PIAGET'S THEORY OF COGNITIVE DEVELOPMENT

Piaget believed that children *actively construct* their cognitive world as they go through a series of stages. In Piaget's view, children use schemas to make sense of their experience.

Recall from the chapter "Memory" that a *schema* is a mental concept or framework that organizes and provides a structure for interpreting information. Schemas are expressed as various behaviors and skills that the child can exercise in relation to objects or situations. For example, sucking is a simple early schema. More complex schemas that occur later in childhood include licking, blowing, and crawling. In adulthood, schemas represent more complex expectations and beliefs about the world.

Piaget (1952) described two processes responsible for how schemas develop:

● **assimilation** An individual's incorporation of new information into existing knowledge.

- **Assimilation** occurs when individuals incorporate new information into existing knowledge. This means that when people are faced with a new experience, they apply old ways of doing things. An infant who sucks on whatever new thing he encounters, an adolescent who applies skills learned playing video games to driving a car, and an adult who uses strategies that worked in the past with previous romantic partners to resolve a conflict with a spouse are all using assimilation. In assimilation, a person's schemas do not change; the person simply uses existing schemas in a new way.

● **accommodation** An individual's adjustment of his or her schemas to include new information.

- **Accommodation** occurs when individuals adjust their schemas to include new information. Rather than using one's old ways of doing things, a new experience promotes new ways of dealing with experience. Existing schemas are changed or new schemas are created. An infant who has been sticking everything in her mouth might begin to accommodate the sucking schema by being more selective with it. An adolescent who has typically gone with the flow of social pressure might develop a new way of dealing with such pressure by standing up for his beliefs. For an adult, accommodation may mean rethinking old strategies for problem solving when a new challenge, such as the loss of a job, presents itself. In accommodation, schemas change. Brand-new ways of interacting with the world emerge as a function of new and different experiences.

So, whenever a person takes a new experience and incorporates it into his or her existing assumptions and ways of doing things, that is assimilation. However, if new experiences require the person to revise what they think they know about the world, that is accommodation.

According to Piaget, we go through four stages of cognitive development (Figure 6). Each stage involves a way of making sense of the world that is qualitatively different from the approach that was used in the previous stage.

**Sensorimotor Stage**

The infant constructs an understanding of the world by coordinating sensory experiences with physical actions. An infant progresses from reflexive, instinctual action at birth to the beginning of symbolic thought toward the end of the stage.

**Preoperational Stage**

The child begins to represent the world with words and images. These words and images reflect increased symbolic thinking and go beyond the connection of sensory information and physical action.

**Concrete Operational Stage**

The child can now reason logically about concrete events and classify objects into different sets.

**Formal Operational Stage**

The adolescent reasons in more abstract, idealistic, and logical ways.

11 Years of Age Through Adulthood

**FIGURE 6** **Piaget's Four Stages of Cognitive Development** Jean Piaget described how human beings, through development, become ever more sophisticated thinkers about the world. To remember the stages, try this mnemonic: "**S**mart **P**eople **C**an't **F**orget."

# psychological *inquiry*

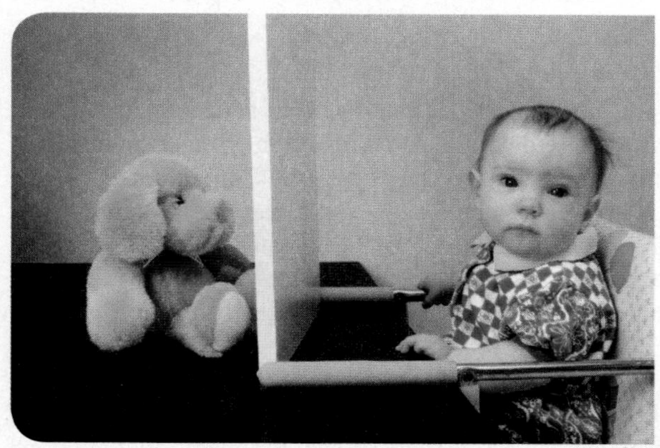

(first) ©D. Goodman/Science Source; (second) ©D. Goodman/Science Source

### *Thinking Critically About Object Permanence*

Let's revisit the classic object permanence task developed by Piaget to consider how the aspects of this task might have led Piaget to underestimate infants' abilities. Remember that from Piaget's perspective, "proving" object permanence meant that the child must search for the hidden toy, reach out, and retrieve it.

Let's assume that the child does believe that the toy exists even if he or she cannot see it. What skills must the child possess in order to enact the behaviors that Piaget thought would indicate object permanence? Answer the following questions to sharpen your understanding of this measure of object permanence.

1. Look at the two photos. Assuming that the child *does* understand that the toy still exists behind the board, what behavior must the baby exhibit to indicate that understanding?
2. What motor and perceptual skills are required for the child to enact those behaviors?
3. What motivational states (or goals) are required for the child to enact them?
4. If the baby does not reach out for the toy despite knowing that it still exists, what might the failure mean?
5. Why do you think it took over 50 years for psychologists to question the appropriateness of Piaget's methods?

**Sensorimotor Stage** Piaget's first stage, the **sensorimotor stage**, lasts from birth to about 2 years of age. You can remember this stage as the first one because as the label implies, it is based on the very limited capacities that an infant has: sensation and movement. In this stage, infants construct an understanding of the world by coordinating sensory experiences (such as seeing and hearing) with motor (physical) actions–hence the term *sensorimotor*. As newborns they have little more than reflexive patterns with which to work. By the end of this stage, 2-year-olds show complex sensorimotor patterns and are beginning to use symbols or words in their thinking.

• **sensorimotor stage** Piaget's first stage of cognitive development, lasting from birth to about 2 years of age, during which infants construct an understanding of the world by coordinating sensory experiences with motor (physical) actions.

Perhaps the biggest event of the sensorimotor stage is object permanence. **Object permanence** is Piaget's term for the accomplishment of understanding that objects and events continue to exist even when they cannot directly be seen, heard, or touched. Piaget believed that "out of sight" literally means "out of mind" for very young infants. To Piaget, object permanence is an enormous developmental milestone. Piaget studied object permanence by showing an infant an interesting toy and then covering the toy with a blanket. Piaget reasoned that if the baby knew the toy still existed, he or she would try to uncover it.

• **object permanence** Piaget's term for the crucial accomplishment of understanding that objects and events continue to exist even when they cannot directly be seen, heard, or touched.

Piaget's object permanence task has been criticized for not giving infants a chance to show their stuff. To get a sense of the limitations of Piaget's task, check out the Psychological Inquiry.

To understand Piaget's next two stages, it is vital to understand what Piaget called operations. **Operations** are mental representations of changes that are reversible. Imagine that you need to pack a very bulky sweater into a carry-on bag for an airplane flight.

• **operations** Piaget's term for mental representations of changes in objects that can be reversed.

**FIGURE 7** **Piaget's Conservation Task** The beaker test determines whether a child can think operationally—that is, can mentally reverse action and understand conservation of the substance. (*a*) Two identical beakers are presented to the child, each containing the same amount of liquid. As the child watches, the experimenter pours the liquid from B into C, which is taller and thinner than A and B. (*b*) The experimenter then asks the child whether beakers A and C have the same amount of liquid. The preoperational child says no. When asked to point to the beaker that has more liquid, the child points to the tall, thin one.
©Maya Barnes Johansen/The Image Works

You painstakingly roll the sweater into the tiniest possible cylinder and cram it into the bag. If you compare "before" and "after" photos of the sweater, you might take great pride. But what you would know, and what shows that you can perform "operations," is that when you get to your destination, that sweater, after a quick shaking out, is going to go back to its original size. The change you have made to the sweater is superficial and temporary. Nothing central has changed about that sweater because you changed its size. Not understanding that fact is what separates preoperational thought from more mature thinking.

**Preoperational Stage** Piaget's second stage of cognitive development, the **preoperational stage**, lasts from approximately 2 to 7 years of age. Preoperational children have difficulty understanding that reversing an action may restore the original conditions from which the action began—they may not, for instance, realize that your sweater is going to look the same after your trip.

● **preoperational stage** Piaget's second stage of cognitive development, lasting from about 2 to 7 years of age, during which thought is more symbolic than sensorimotor thought.

A well-known to test for operational thinking is to present a child with two identical beakers, A and B, filled with liquid to the same height (Figure 7). Next to them is a third beaker: C. Beaker C is tall and thin; beakers A and B are short and wide. The liquid is poured from B into C, and the child is asked whether the amounts in A and C are the same. The 4-year-old child invariably says that the amount of liquid in the tall, thin beaker (C) is greater than that in the short, wide beaker (A). An 8-year-old child consistently says the amounts are the same. The 4-year-old child, a preoperational thinker, cannot mentally reverse the pouring action; she cannot imagine the liquid going back from container C to container B. For Piaget, such a child has not grasped the concept of *conservation,* understanding the permanence of some attributes of objects despite superficial changes.

To sharpen your sense of preoperational thought, consider this example. While babysitting for two thirsty 4-year-olds, you give them each the same amount of apple juice poured into two different cups: one tall and thin and the other short and wide. Try as you might to explain to them that the amounts are the same, they will fight over the tall, thin cup because *it looks like more*. Now, in the same situation, older children—who are operational thinkers—would not compete for the taller cup because they understand the amounts are equal.

Preoperational thought is more symbolic than sensorimotor thought (but still limited) as children begin to represent the world with words, images, and drawings. Preoperational thought is egocentric: preoperational children cannot put themselves in someone else's shoes. Here, being egocentric does not mean being selfish. It means not realizing that, for example, another person cannot always see what they are seeing or know what they are thinking. Preoperational thinking is also intuitive, meaning that preoperational children make judgments based on gut feelings rather than logic.

**Concrete Operational Stage** Piaget's **concrete operational stage**, from 7 to 11 years of age, involves using operations and replacing intuitive reasoning with logical reasoning in concrete situations. Children in this stage can successfully complete the beaker task described above. Many of the concrete operations identified by Piaget are related to the properties of objects. For instance, when playing with Play-Doh, the child in the concrete operational stage realizes that changing its shape does not change the amount of Play-Doh.

● **concrete operational stage** Piaget's third stage of cognitive development, lasting from about 7 to 11 years of age, during which the individual uses operations and replaces intuitive reasoning with logical reasoning in concrete situations.

An important skill at this stage of reasoning is the ability to classify things into different sets or subsets and to consider their interrelations. Children in the concrete operational stage might enjoy playing games that involve sorting objects into types and identifying objects that do not fit with a group. (You might remember the childhood song that goes, "One of these things is not like the others," which aimed to coax you into performing concrete operations.)

Concrete operational thought involves logical reasoning in concrete but not hypothetical contexts. According to Piaget, this kind of abstract, logical reasoning occurs in the fourth, and final, cognitive stage.

**Formal Operational Stage** Individuals enter the **formal operational stage** of cognitive development at 11 to 15 years of age. This stage continues through the adult years. Formal operational thought is more abstract and logical than concrete operational thought. Most important, formal operational thinking includes thinking about things that are not concrete, making predictions, and using logic to come up with hypotheses about the future.

● **formal operational stage** Piaget's fourth stage of cognitive development, which begins at 11 to 15 years of age and continues through the adult years; it features thinking about things that are not concrete, making predictions, and using logic to come up with hypotheses about the future.

Unlike elementary school children, adolescents can conceive of hypothetical, purely abstract possibilities. This type of thinking is called *idealistic* because it involves comparing how things are to how they might be. Adolescents also think more logically. Unlike younger children who solve problems through trial and error, the adolescent begins to think more like a scientist. That means devising plans to solve problems and systematically testing solutions. Piaget called this type of problem solving *hypothetical-deductive reasoning*. This term denotes two qualities of adolescent thinking:

- the ability to develop *hypotheses* about ways to solve a problem such as an algebraic equation
- the ability to systematically *deduce* conclusions using logic

In summary, over the course of Piaget's four developmental stages, a person progresses from sensorimotor cognition to abstract, idealistic, and logical thought. Let's consider the current thinking about Piaget's theories of cognitive development.

## EVALUATING PIAGET'S THEORY

Piaget opened up a new way of looking at how the human mind develops (P. H. Miller, 2011). We owe him for a long list of concepts that have enduring power and fascination. We also owe Piaget for the currently accepted vision of children as active, constructive thinkers who play a role in their own development.

Nevertheless, just as other psychological theories have been criticized and amended, so have Piaget's. First, Piaget may have *overestimated* the cognitive acumen of adolescents and adults. Formal operational thought does not emerge as consistently and universally in early adolescence as Piaget envisioned (Kuhn, 2009). Many adolescents and adults do not reason as logically as Piaget proposed. Second, Piaget likely *underestimated* the cognitive capacities of very young children. As methods have improved for assessing infants and children, researchers have found that many cognitive abilities emerge earlier than Piaget envisioned (Baillargeon, Scott, & Bian, 2016; Jin & others, 2018).

## THE NATIVIST APPROACH TO INFANT COGNITION

Many scientists who study cognitive development in infancy have asserted that infants know a great deal more about the world than Piaget said. According to this *nativist* approach, infants possess primitive expectancies about events and objects that are less dependent upon experience than Piaget imagined. For instance, infants as young as 3 months of age know that objects continue to exist even when hidden, and even these very young infants have expectations about objects in the world that are more sophisticated than Piaget imagined (Baillargeon, 2014; Jin & others, 2018).

In one study, researchers presented 3-month-old infants with a puppet show featuring Minnie Mouse (Luo & Baillargeon, 2005). In the center of the stage was a flat cardboard cutout of a castle. Minnie entered stage right and proceeded toward the castle, disappearing behind it. When Minnie went behind the castle wall from one side, the infants looked for her to appear in the doorway and to come out on the other side, suggesting that even though Minnie was out of sight, she was not out of mind. Not only did these 3-month-olds realize that Minnie still existed, they also *had expectations* about where she was heading.

Such findings have led many developmental psychologists to call for an expanded appreciation for the perceptual and cognitive tools that are available to infants with very little experience (Baillargeon, Scott, & Bian, 2016; Mehr & Spelke, 2018). In a sense, babies possess a very simple sense of physics, an architecture that appears to be present as early as scientists have been able to measure it (Hespos & van Marle, 2012; Kinzler, Dupoux, & Spelke, 2013). Nativist thinkers recognize later experience as important but see it as building on this architecture (Spelke & Kinzler, 2007).

The *nativist* approach contrasts with the *empiricist* approach (Witherington, 2015). The empiricist approach emphasizes the role of experience in the world as the central driver of cognitive and perceptual development (Newcombe, 2002). The empiricist perspective points out that even if very young infants show an understanding of object permanence, that capacity might still originate in (very early) experience (Spencer & others, 2009). Still, those very young infants would have learned object permanence much earlier than Piaget asserted.

## VYGOTSKY'S SOCIOCULTURAL COGNITIVE THEORY

For Piaget, the child's active interaction with the physical world was all that was needed to go through these stages. The Russian psychologist Lev Vygotsky (1962) took a different approach, recognizing that cognitive development is an interpersonal process that happens in a cultural context (Iao & others, 2015; Wang, 2015).

Vygotsky thought of children as apprentice thinkers who develop as they interact in dialogue with more knowledgeable others, such as parents and teachers (Daniels, 2011). Vygotsky theorized that these expert thinkers spur cognitive development by interacting with a child in a way that is just above the level of sophistication the child has mastered. In effect, these interactions provide *scaffolding* that allows the child's cognitive abilities to be built higher and higher.

Furthermore, in Vygotsky's view, the goal of cognitive development is to learn the skills that will allow the individual to be competent in his or her particular culture. Expert thinkers are not simply guiding a child into a level of cognitive sophistication but also, along the way, sharing with the child important aspects of culture, such as language and customs. For Vygotsky, a child is not simply learning to think about the world–he or she is learning to think about *his or her own world.*

## INFORMATION-PROCESSING THEORY

The *information-processing theory* of development focuses on how individuals encode information, manipulate it, monitor it, and create strategies for handling it. Information-processing theory focuses on specific cognitive processes, such as memory, as we have reviewed in previous chapters.

For instance, contemporary researchers study topics such as the emergence of autobiographical memory as children come to mentally represent the events that make up their life stories (Akhtar & others, 2018; Bauer, 2015; Fivush, 2011). *Working memory*, that mental workspace that is used for problem solving (see the chapter "Memory"), is linked to many aspects of children's development (Berry & others, 2018). Children with better working memory are more advanced in reading comprehension, math skills, problem solving, and social thinking than their counterparts with less effective working memory (He & others, 2018; Kroesbergen, van't Noordende, & Kolkman, 2014). One study found that working memory in *preschool* students predicted dropout rates in high school. Students with low working memory were at higher risk of dropping out of high school, even after accounting for differences in socioeconomic status and IQ (Fitzpatrick & others, 2015).

A particularly important aspect of cognitive development in childhood is executive function. Recall that **executive function** refers to higher-order, complex cognitive processes, including thinking, planning, and problem solving. Executive function involves managing one's thoughts to engage in goal-directed behavior and to exercise self-control (Meltzer, 2018).

**executive function** Higher-order, complex cognitive processes, including thinking, planning, and problem solving.

In preschoolers, executive function involves cognitive skills such as holding back from acting on one's automatic impulses, being cognitively flexible, setting goals, and forgoing an immediate pleasure or reward for a more desirable one later (Rolan & others, 2018; Woltering & others, 2016; Zelazo & Muller, 2011). To be successful in school, one must be able to sit still, wait in line, raise one's hand before speaking, and so forth. These simple tasks require self-control and the capacity to inhibit one's automatic responses. It is not surprising that executive function during the preschool years is linked to school readiness, perhaps even more strongly than general IQ (Blair & Raver, 2015). Executive function also predicts better motor coordination and physical fitness (Oberer, Gashaj, & Roebers, 2018). Executive function predicts the development of social cognitive abilities, including theory of mind: the understanding that other people experience private knowledge and mental states (Marcovitch & others, 2015).

A large longitudinal study showed that aspects of executive function assessed in early childhood predict less risk taking, decreased dropout rates, and less drug use in adolescence, as well as better physical and psychological health, better earnings, and less criminal behavior in adulthood (some 30 years later) (Moffitt & others, 2011). Clearly, then, executive function is important. Can it be fostered by experience?

Parents and teachers play important roles in the development of executive function. Parents who model executive function and self-control can serve as scaffolds for these skills. A variety of activities increase children's executive function, such as training to improve working memory (Kirk & others, 2015) and mindfulness training (Poehlmann-Tynan & others, 2016). Sometimes very specific cognitive activities that require children to stretch the way they think, can influence executive function. For example, in one study, 5-year-olds who were instructed to complete an executive function measure as if they were someone else (for example, Batman) performed better than children who did not receive these special instructions (White & Carlson, 2016).

Of course, cognitive development is embedded in the brain. Nowhere is the intermingling of the brain and experience more apparent than when a child learns to read. For some children, this milestone is met only with great difficulty. *Developmental dyslexia* is a learning difficulty that is specific to reading (though it can include writing difficulties). Scientists define dyslexia as a deficit in the ability to map letters to sounds (Huettig & others, 2018; Stein, 2018). The precise cause of developmental dyslexia is unknown. Scientists have argued about the roles of genes, brain structures, neuronal processes, and experience in the disorder. In fact, understanding developmental dyslexia requires that we appreciate the way the developing brain and developing person are inextricably linked. To read about this conundrum, see the Intersection.

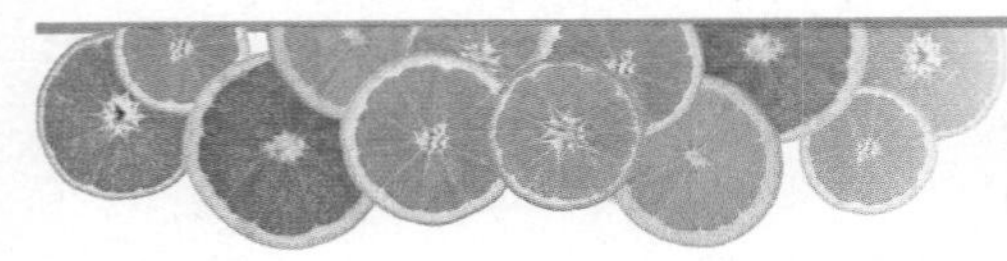

# INTERSECTION

## Developmental Psychology and Cognitive Neuroscience: Are Brain Differences the Cause or Effect of Developmental Dyslexia?

People with dyslexia have difficulty tracking the individual sounds that make up written language. This description tells us nothing about where this problem comes from. Genes play a role in developmental dyslexia and genes associated with dyslexia predict reading skill in adults (Luciano & others, 2018). But for genes to affect behavior they must do so via the brain.

*Do know someone who has dyslexia? How has it affected their life?*

Many brain imaging studies have illuminated neural mechanisms that might explain differences between people who have dyslexia and those who do not (Paz-Alonso & others, 2018; Ramus & others, 2018). For instance, typical readers show more activation on the left than the right hemisphere during reading (Banfi & others, 2018; van Setten, Maurits, & Maassen, 2018). In addition, differences in the thalamus (the brain's switchboard) and corpus callosum (the network of fibers connecting the two hemispheres) have been identified (D'Mello & Gabrieli, 2018; Ramus & others, 2018; Yu, Zuk, & Gaab, 2018).

One interesting possibility is that dyslexia involves dysfunction of *magnocellular neurons*. These very large neurons determine the *timing* of visual perception: determining what gets processed first. Because reading requires a person to look in a particular direction (for English, from left to right), these neurons may have an important role to play in directing a reader's eyes (Stein, 2018).

Considering these many findings, we might lose track of an important fact: when a person with dyslexia is compared with a typical reader, that comparison involves more than whatever genetic difference might set dyslexia into motion—it involves comparing a person who lacks a lifetime of optimal reading experiences to someone who has had them (Huettig & others, 2018). That difference in experience has enormous implications for the brain.

In typically developing children, becoming a reader changes the brain in a host of ways. In fact, the very differences observed between those who have dyslexia and those who do not are differences that appear in children before and after they learn to read (Huettig & others, 2018). Consider the magnocellular neuron explanation of dyslexia. It turns out that once children learn to read English, the "left to right" direction becomes so ingrained that readers have difficulty with tasks that involve looking from right to left (Afsari & others, 2018). So, differences in magnocellular neuron function might represent *the effects* of reading. Similarly, brain differences between adult readers and nonreaders (people who do not have a learning disability but have never been taught to read) are much like those reported for typical readers versus individuals with dyslexia (Huettig & others, 2018).

Thus, brain differences between people with dyslexia and others may reflect *experience*—not just genetics. It may be that the brain differences often considered causes of dyslexia are, instead, effects of lack of exposure to high-quality reading (Huettig & others, 2018). Given the ways that reading affects the brain, a very small difference might snowball into larger differences over the life course.

This controversy shows how experience—in this case reading—profoundly affects the brain. Individuals with dyslexia miss out on experiences that may be essential to transforming the brain into that of a reader. Many people with dyslexia are avid readers, but the way they read may not be the same process as in those without the disorder. For this reason, individuals with dyslexia warrant accommodations in educational settings so that they can maximize their achievements (Youman & others, 2018; Yu, Zuk, & Gaab, 2018).

©Steve Debenport/E+/Getty Images

# Socioemotional Development in Infancy and Childhood

When we observe newborns behind the window of a hospital nursery, one thing is clear: Humans differ from one another in terms of their emotional demeanor from the very beginning of life. Some are easygoing, some are prone to distress. Furthermore, in the earliest days of life, infants encounter a social network that will play an important role as they develop their sense of self and the world. To begin our exploration of the socioemotional aspects of development, we focus first on these raw ingredients of emotional and social characteristics that are present early in life—infant temperament and attachment.

## TEMPERAMENT

**Temperament** refers to an individual's behavioral style and characteristic ways of responding. There are a number of ways to think about infant temperament. For example, psychiatrists Alexander Chess and Stella Thomas (1977, 1996) identified three basic types of temperament in children:

- *The easy child* generally is in a positive mood, quickly establishes regular routines in infancy, and adapts easily to new experiences.
- *The difficult child* tends to react negatively and to cry frequently, engages in irregular daily routines, and is slow to accept new experiences.
- *The slow-to-warm-up child* has a low activity level, is somewhat negative, is inflexible, and is very cautious in the face of new experiences.

● **temperament** An individual's behavioral style and characteristic ways of responding.

Other researchers suggest that infant temperament also includes other dimensions, such as *effortful control* or *self-regulation* (controlling arousal and not being easily agitated), *inhibition* (being shy and showing distress in an unfamiliar situation), and *positive* and *negative affectivity* (tending to be happy and even-tempered or frustrated and sad) (Kagan, 2018; Posner & Rothbart, 2018; Rothbart & Gartstein, 2008). One study showed that mothers' memories of their children's temperament at age 4 months predicted school readiness during preschool; children with positive emotionality and high levels of self-regulation showed higher levels of school readiness (Gartstein, Putnam, & Kliewer, 2016).

The emotional characteristics that a child brings into the world are thought to serve as a foundation for later personality (Kagan, 2018). Similarly, the child's earliest social bonds might set the stage for later social relationships.

## ATTACHMENT

Just as infants require nutrition and shelter, they need warm social interaction to survive and develop. A classic study by Harry Harlow (1958) demonstrates the essential importance of warm contact. Harlow separated infant monkeys from their mothers at birth and placed them in cages with two artificial "mothers." One of the mothers was a physically cold wire mother; the other was a warm, fuzzy cloth mother (the "contact comfort" mother). Each mother could be outfitted with a feeding mechanism. Half of the infant monkeys were fed by the wire mother, half by the cloth mother. Harlow found that the infant monkeys nestled close to the cloth mother and spent little time on the wire one, even if the wire mother gave them milk (Figure 8). When afraid, the infant monkeys ran to the comfy mom.

Harlow's work shows that contact comfort, not feeding, is crucial to an infant's attachment to its caregiver. This work set the stage for our modern understanding of the vital role of warm physical contact between caregivers and infants.

**Infant attachment** is the close emotional bond between an infant and its caregiver. British psychiatrist John Bowlby (1969, 1989) theorized that the infant and the mother instinctively form an attachment. For Bowlby, the newborn comes into the world equipped to stimulate the caregiver to respond; it cries, clings, smiles, and coos. Bowlby thought that this early relationship with our primary caregiver was internalized so that it served as our schema for our sense of self and the social world. Many developmental psychologists concur that such attachment during the first year provides an important foundation for later development (Bretherton, 2012; Sroufe, Coffino, & Carlson, 2010).

● **infant attachment** The close emotional bond between an infant and its caregiver.

Mary Ainsworth devised the *strange situation test* to measure children's attachment (Ainsworth, 1979; Ainsworth & others, 2015). In this procedure, caregivers leave infants alone with a stranger and then return. Children's responses to the situation are used to classify them into one of three attachment styles. **Secure attachment** means infants use the caregiver, usually the mother, as a secure base from which to explore the environment.

● **secure attachment** The ways that infants use their caregiver, usually their mother, as a secure base from which to explore the environment.

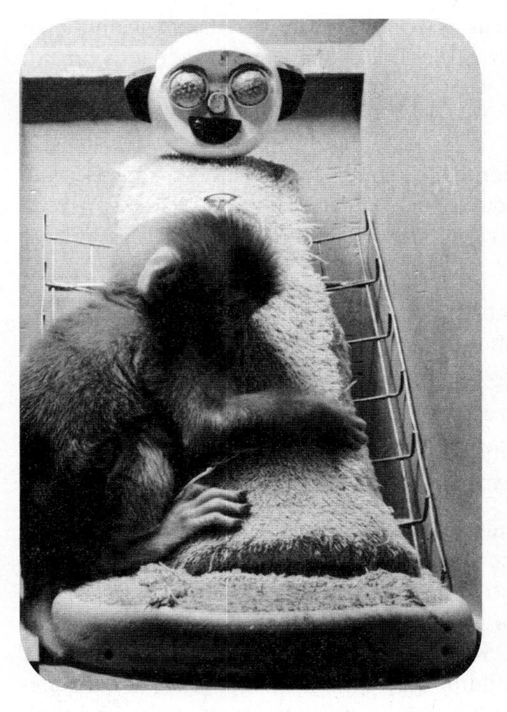
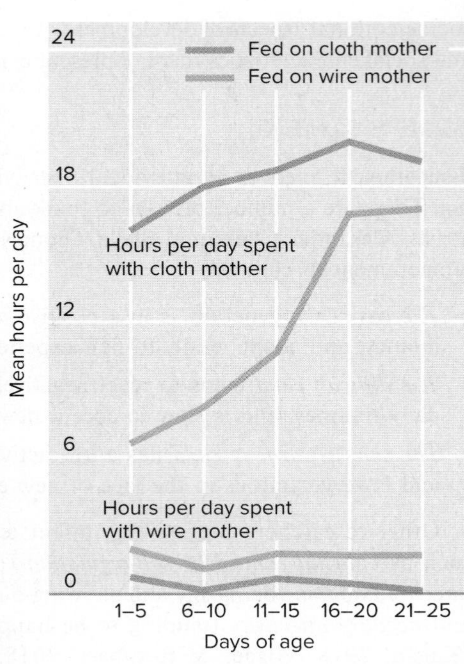


**FIGURE 8 Contact Time with Wire and Cloth Surrogate Mothers** Regardless of whether the infant monkeys were fed by a wire or a cloth mother, they overwhelmingly preferred to spend contact time with the cloth mother. ©Science Source

In the strange situation, the secure infant is upset when the mother leaves, but calms down and appears happy to see her when she returns (Behrens, Parker, & Haltigan, 2011). The securely attached infant moves freely away from the mother but also keeps tabs on her by periodically glancing at her.

● **insecure attachment** Infants do not use the caregiver as a secure base from which to explore; instead, they experience their relationship with the caregiver as unstable and unreliable. The two types of insecure attachment are avoidant and anxious/ambivalent (also called preoccupied).

In contrast, there are two types of **insecure attachment**: *avoidant* and *anxious/ambivalent*. In the strange situation, the avoidant infant might not even notice the mother has gone. The anxious/ambivalent infant (also called preoccupied) responds with intense distress, only to rage at the mother when she returns.

Although attachment theory has been very influential, it has been criticized for three main shortcomings:

- It does not adequately account for cultural variations. In some cultures infants show strong attachments to many people, not just to their primary caregiver.
- It fails to take differences in infant temperament into account. Some babies are simply more difficult than others and their personalities may color the attachment relationship.
- Finally, it fails to acknowledge that caregivers and infants likely share genetic characteristics. The attachment relationship might be a product of these shared genes.

Despite such criticisms, there is ample evidence that secure attachment is important to development (R. A. Thompson, 2013a, 2013b, 2013c). Moreover, even across cultures, maternal sensitivity to infants and mothers' willingness to serve as a secure base predict infant attachment over time (Posada & others, 2015).

From Bowlby's perspective, an infant's experiences lay the groundwork for expectations about what human relationships will be like, setting the stage for future relationships, including our romantic relationships as adults.

Given these raw ingredients of temperament and attachment, how does a human being develop in the socioemotional domain? Erik Erikson devised a theory of *psychosocial development* to address this question. Like Piaget's theory of cognitive development, Erikson's theory has guided thinking about how human beings' social and emotional capacities develop throughout the life span.

©Thomas Barwick/Getty Images

## ERIKSON'S THEORY OF SOCIOEMOTIONAL DEVELOPMENT

Erik Erikson (1902–1994) proposed eight psychosocial stages of development from infancy through old age. In Erikson's (1968) view, the first four stages take place in childhood; the last four in adolescence and adulthood (Figure 9).

Erikson's theory is important because it proposes that socioemotional development is a *lifelong* process. Each of Erikson's stages represents a developmental task that the individual must master at a particular place in the life span.

Erikson's developmental tasks are represented by two possible outcomes—one, greater strength and competence; the other, greater weakness and vulnerability. Which outcome occurs depends on whether the person's needs at each stage are well met or frustrated. Using Erikson's stages as a guide, let's consider the various ways that human beings develop in terms of their capacities for interpersonal relationships and emotional well-being in infancy and childhood.

**Erik Erikson (1902–1994)** Erikson generated one of the most important developmental theories of the twentieth century.

©Ted Streshinsky/Corbis/Getty Images

## SOCIOEMOTIONAL DEVELOPMENT IN INFANCY AND CHILDHOOD: FROM TRUST TO INDUSTRY

We examine Erikson's adolescence and adult stages later in this chapter. His four childhood stages are:

- *Trust versus mistrust:* Trust is built in infancy (birth to 18 months) when a baby's basic needs—such as comfort, food, and warmth—are met by responsive, sensitive caregivers. At this stage, the helpless infant depends on caregivers to establish a sense that the world is a predictable and friendly place.
- *Autonomy versus shame and doubt:* During toddlerhood (18 months through 3 years), children can develop either a positive sense of independence and autonomy or negative feelings of shame and doubt. In seeking autonomy, they are likely to develop a strong sense of independence. A toddler who is experiencing toilet training is learning the beginnings of self-control. The toddler's growing independence is evident in the child's insistence that no matter how difficult the task, "I can do it myself!" Similarly common is the toddler's assertion of autonomy with a simple two-letter word: "No!"
- *Initiative versus guilt:* In early childhood (3 to 5 years), preschoolers experience what it is like to forge their own interests and friendships and to take on responsibilities. If you have ever spent time with a 3-year-old, you know how often the child wants to help with whatever an adult is doing. When they experience a sense of taking on responsibility, preschoolers develop initiative. Otherwise, according to Erikson, they may feel guilty.
- *Industry versus inferiority:* Children in middle and late childhood (6 years to puberty) can achieve industry by mastering knowledge and intellectual skills. When they do not, they can feel inferior. At the end of early childhood, children are ready to turn their energy to learning academic skills. If they do not, they can develop a sense of being incompetent and unproductive. During the beginnings of elementary school, children learn the value of what Erikson called *industry,* gaining competence in academic skills and acquiring the ability to practice self-discipline and engage in hard work.

From Erikson's perspective, then, children should grow toward greater levels of autonomy and self-confidence as they progress from infancy to school age and beyond. At each stage, Erikson said, parents can facilitate the child's growth, or they can thwart it by being overly protective or neglectful.

## EVALUATING ERIKSON'S THEORY

Erikson's conclusions have had their critics (Adler, 2018; Jordan & Tseris, 2018). Erikson mainly relied on case studies, which some reject as the sole research foundation for his approach. Critics also argue that Erikson's attempt to capture each developmental stage with a single concept leaves out other important developmental tasks. For example, as we will see, Erikson said that the main task for young adults is to resolve a conflict between

**Trust Versus Mistrust**

**Developmental period:** Infancy (birth to $1\frac{1}{2}$ years)

**Characteristics:** A sense of trust requires a feeling of physical comfort and minimal amount of fear about the future. Infants' basic needs are met by responsive, sensitive caregivers.

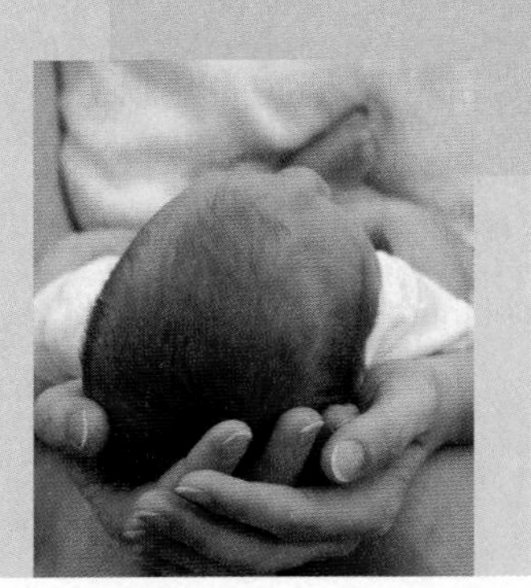

**Autonomy Versus Shame and Doubt**

**Developmental period:** Toddlerhood ($1\frac{1}{2}$ to 3 years)

**Characteristics:** After gaining trust in their caregivers, infants start to discover that they have a will of their own. They assert their sense of autonomy, or independence. They realize their will. If infants are restrained too much or punished too harshly, they are likely to develop a sense of shame and doubt.

**Initiative Versus Guilt**

**Developmental period:** Early childhood (preschool years, ages 3–5)

**Characteristics:** As preschool children encounter a widening social world, they are challenged more and need to develop more purposeful behavior to cope with these challenges. Children are now asked to assume more responsibility. Uncomfortable guilt feelings may arise, though, if the children are irresponsible and are made to feel too anxious.

**Industry Versus Inferiority**

**Developmental period:** Middle and late childhood (elementary school years, 6 years–puberty)

**Characteristics:** At no other time are children more enthusiastic than at the end of early childhood's period of expansive imagination. As children move into the elementary school years, they direct their energy toward mastering knowledge and intellectual skills. The danger at this stage involves feeling incompetent and unproductive.

**FIGURE 9 Erikson's Eight Stages of Psychosocial Development** Erikson changed the way psychologists think about development by tracing the process of growth over the entire life span. (first photo) ©Tarinoel/iStock/Getty Images; (second photo) ©Stock 4B; (third photo) ©Ariel Skelley/Getty Images; (fourth photo) ©Ariel Skelley/Getty Images; (fifth photo) ©Digital Vision; (sixth photo) ©Blue Moon Stock/Alamy Stock Photo; (seventh photo) ©McGraw-Hill Education/Ken Karp, photographer; (eighth photo) ©Ryan McVay/Getty Images

intimacy and isolation, yet another important developmental task at this life stage revolves around careers and work. Erikson's approach also fails to accommodate the struggles of those who face injustice or have disabilities (Adler, 2018; Alberts & Durrheim, 2018).

## PARENTING AND CHILDHOOD SOCIOEMOTIONAL DEVELOPMENT

Researchers have tried to identify styles of parenting associated with positive developmental outcomes. Diana Baumrind (1991, 1993, 2012) described four basic styles of interaction between parents and their children:

- **authoritarian parenting** A restrictive, punitive style in which the parent exhorts the child to follow the parent's directions.

- **Authoritarian parenting** is a strict punitive style. The authoritarian parent firmly limits and controls the child with little verbal exchange. In a difference of opinion about how to do something, for example, the authoritarian parent might say, "You must do it my way or else." Children of authoritarian parents sometimes lack social skills, show poor initiative, and compare themselves with others. Research has shown that authoritarian parenting does not deter children and adolescents of all racial/ethnic groups from engaging in delinquent behavior (Mowen & Schroeder, 2018).

- **authoritative parenting** A parenting style that encourages the child to be independent but still places limits and controls on behavior.

- **Authoritative parenting** encourages the child to be independent but still places limits and controls on behavior. This parenting style is more collaborative. Extensive verbal give-and-take is allowed, and parents are warm and nurturing toward the child. An authoritative father might put his arm around the child in a comforting way and say, "You know you should not have done that; let's talk about how you can handle the situation better next time." Children whose parents are authoritative tend to be socially competent, self-reliant, and socially responsible.

- **neglectful parenting** A parenting style characterized by a lack of parental involvement in the child's life.

- **Neglectful parenting** is distinguished by a lack of parental involvement in the child's life. Children of neglectful parents might develop a sense that other aspects of their

| Identity Versus Identity Confusion | Intimacy Versus Isolation | Generativity Versus Stagnation | Integrity Versus Despair |
|---|---|---|---|
| **Developmental period:** Adolescence (10–20 years) | **Developmental period:** Early adulthood (20s, 30s) | **Developmental period:** Middle adulthood (40s, 50s) | **Developmental period:** Late adulthood (60s– ) |
| **Characteristics:** Individuals are faced with finding out who they are, what they are all about, and where they are going in life. An important dimension is the exploration of alternative solutions to roles. Career exploration is important. | **Characteristics:** Individuals face the developmental task of forming intimate relationships with others. Erikson described intimacy as finding oneself yet losing oneself in another person. | **Characteristics:** A chief concern is to assist the younger generation in developing and leading useful lives. | **Characteristics:** Individuals look back and evaluate what they have done with their lives. The retrospective glances can be either positive (integrity) or negative (despair). |
|  |  |  |  |



parents' lives are more important than they are. Children whose parents are neglectful tend to be less competent socially, to handle independence poorly, and (especially) to show poor self-control.

- **Permissive parenting** involves placing few limits on the child's behavior. A permissive parent lets the child do what he or she wants. Some parents deliberately rear their children this way because they believe that the combination of warm involvement and few limits will produce a creative, confident child. However, children with very permissive parents typically rate poorly in social competence. They often fail to learn respect for others, expect to get their own way, and have difficulty controlling their behavior. Recall that socioemotional development involves becoming increasingly adept at controlling and regulating one's emotions and behaviors. Children may require structure from their caregivers in order to acquire these skills.

● **permissive parenting** A parenting style characterized by the placement of few limits on the child's behavior.

## Moral Development in Childhood

Another aspect of social development is how an individual becomes a person of character—someone who behaves morally. This aspect of development features yet another classic theory in developmental psychology, that of Lawrence Kohlberg (1927–1987). Moral development involves changes over time in thoughts, feelings, and behaviors regarding the principles and values that guide what people should do.

### KOHLBERG'S THEORY

Kohlberg (1958) began his study of moral thinking by creating a series of stories and asking children, adolescents, and adults questions about the stories. One story goes something like this. A man, Heinz, whose wife is dying of cancer, finds out about a drug that might save her life. He approaches the pharmacist who has the drug, but the pharmacist refuses to give it to him without being paid a very high price. Heinz is unable to scrape together the money and eventually decides to steal the drug.

**Lawrence Kohlberg (1927–1987)** Kohlberg created a provocative theory of moral development. In his view, "Moral development consists of a sequence of qualitative changes in the way an individual thinks."

©Lee Lockwood/Time & Life Pictures/Getty Images

After reading the story, each person interviewed was asked a series of questions about the moral dilemma involved. Should Heinz have stolen the drug? Kohlberg was less interested in the answer to this question than he was to how the person answered the next question: Why? Based on the reasons people gave for their answers, Kohlberg (1986) evaluated their level of moral development. Kohlberg's stages of moral development consist of three general levels:

1. *Preconventional:* The individual's moral reasoning is based on the consequences of behavior and punishments and rewards from the external world. Moral reasoning is guided by not wanting Heinz to go to jail or by feelings of concern for the druggists' profits.
2. *Conventional:* The individual abides by standards learned from parents or society's laws. At this level the person might reason that Heinz should act in accord with expectations or his role as a good husband or reason that Heinz should follow the law no matter what.
3. *Postconventional:* The individual recognizes alternative moral courses, explores the options, and then develops an increasingly personal moral code. At this level, the person might reason that saving Heinz's wife is more important than obeying a law.

Kohlberg believed that moral development is based on maturation of thought, capacity for role taking, and opportunities to discuss moral issues with a person who reasons at a stage just above one's own.

You can tell Kohlberg studied with Piaget as both placed great emphasis on a person's capacity to reason in a sophisticated way. Later approaches to moral development have focused on its social and emotional components. For Kohlberg, a sense of justice was at the heart of moral reasoning, which he believed laid the foundation for moral behavior.

## EVALUATING KOHLBERG'S THEORY

Kohlberg's ideas have stimulated considerable research about how people think about moral issues. At the same time, his theory has many critics.

One criticism is that moral *reasoning* does not necessarily mean moral *behavior.* Asked about moral reasoning, people might say things that fit into Kohlberg's advanced stages, but their actual behavior might involve cheating, lying, and stealing. Cheaters, liars, and thieves might know what is right but still choose to do what is wrong. We would not consider someone who behaves immorally to be morally developed.

**Carol Gilligan (b. 1936)** Gilligan argues that Kohlberg's approach does not give adequate attention to relationships. In Gilligan's view, "Many girls seem to fear, most of all, being alone—without friends, family, and relationships."

©Paul Hawthorne/Getty Images

Another criticism is that Kohlberg's view does not adequately reflect concern for other people and social bonds. Kohlberg's theory is called a *justice perspective* because it focuses on the rights of the individual as the key to sound moral reasoning. In contrast, the *care perspective,* which lies at the heart of Carol Gilligan's (1982) approach to moral development, views people in terms of their connectedness with others and emphasizes interpersonal communication, relationships, and concern for others. From Gilligan's perspective, this weakness in Kohlberg's approach explains why, using his measures, women generally score lower than men on moral development.

Culture can also influence whether a person approaches a moral dilemma from the perspective of justice or care (Lapsley, 2018). In Western cultures, people generally tend to have an individualistic sense of self and are therefore inclined to take a justice perspective. Such individuals might score higher in Kohlberg's scheme than their counterparts in collectivistic Asian cultures where people view the self as part of a larger group.

A final criticism of Kohlberg centers on his overestimation of the role of logical reasoning in moral judgments. Contemporary research suggests that Kohlberg overlooked the influence of emotion and intuition in moral decision making.

## CURRENT RESEARCH ON MORAL DEVELOPMENT

In addition to justice and care, contemporary research on moral reasoning includes multiple principles, or *moral foundations,* that people take into account as they reason about moral issues. From this perspective, there are at least five foundations that people consider when they are making moral judgments (Graham & others, 2012; Tatalovich & Wendell, 2018):

- *Care:* People consider kindness and compassion toward others as well as avoiding harm to others.
- *Fairness:* People think about just outcomes and seek outcomes that will be fair to all involved.
- *Loyalty*: People consider their allegiances to groups and being true to the groups to which they belong.
- *Authority:* People consider what their leaders believe and seek to obey them.
- *Purity:* People base moral judgments on whether they find a behavior to be noble or, in contrast, disgusting or animalistic.

In addition to moral reasoning, contemporary researchers have increasingly studied **prosocial behavior**, behavior that is intended to benefit other people (Carlo & others, 2016; Ferreira & others, 2016). For instance, researchers are probing how, when, and why children engage in everyday acts of kindness toward others (Carlo & others, 2011) or tell lies (Williams & others, 2016). Supportive parenting and parental monitoring relate to increased helping and comforting of others (Dodge, Coie, & Lynam, 2006). Furthermore, the capacities to empathize with others and engage in prosocial behavior are linked with the ability to engage in self-control more generally (Eisenberg, Spinrad, & Morris, 2013).

• **prosocial behavior** Behavior that is intended to benefit other people.

Other recent research has focused on determining when a child first shows signs of possessing a conscience (Carlo & others, 2016; Waller & Hyde, 2018). Having a conscience means hearing that voice in our head that tells us that something is morally good or bad. Researchers Deborah Laible and Ross Thompson (2000, 2002, 2007) examined the conversations between mothers and toddlers at times when the child did something well or got into trouble. They found that by 3 years of age, children began to show signs of early conscience development. Parent–child interactions that are clear, elaborate, and rich with emotional content and that include shared positive emotion foster this development. Childhood characteristics are important because longitudinal studies show that kind, moral children are more likely to be kind, moral adults (Dahl & Killen, 2018; Narvaez, Wang, & Cheng, 2016).

### test yourself

1. What are teratogens? Give several examples of them.
2. According to Piaget, what two processes are responsible for how people use and adapt their schemas, and what is involved in each process? What are some key aspects of Vygotsky's theory and information-processing theory?
3. What are Erikson's four childhood stages of development, and what is the central concern of each stage?

# 3. ADOLESCENCE

Adolescence is the developmental period of transition from childhood to adulthood, beginning around ages 10 to 12 and ending at 18 to 21. Adolescents are not all the same. Variations in ethnicity, culture, history, gender, socioeconomic status, and lifestyle characterize their life trajectories. In this section we examine the changes that occur in adolescence in the domains of physical, cognitive, and socioemotional development.

## Physical Development in Adolescence

Dramatic physical changes characterize adolescence, especially early adolescence. Among the major physical changes of adolescence are those involving puberty and the brain.

### PUBERTAL CHANGE

The signature physical change in adolescence is **puberty**, a period of rapid skeletal and sexual maturation that occurs mainly in early adolescence.

• **puberty** A period of rapid skeletal and sexual maturation that occurs mainly in early adolescence.

• **androgens** The class of sex hormones that predominate in males, produced by the testes in males and by the adrenal glands in both males and females.

• **estrogens** The class of sex hormones that predominate in females, produced mainly by the ovaries.

Hormonal changes lie at the core of pubertal development. The concentrations of certain hormones increase greatly during puberty (Gorday & Meyer, 2018; Quas & others, 2018). *Testosterone*—an **androgen** (the class of sex hormones that predominate in males)—is associated in boys with genital development, increased height, and voice change. *Estradiol*—an **estrogen** (the class of sex hormones that predominate in females)—is associated in girls with breast,

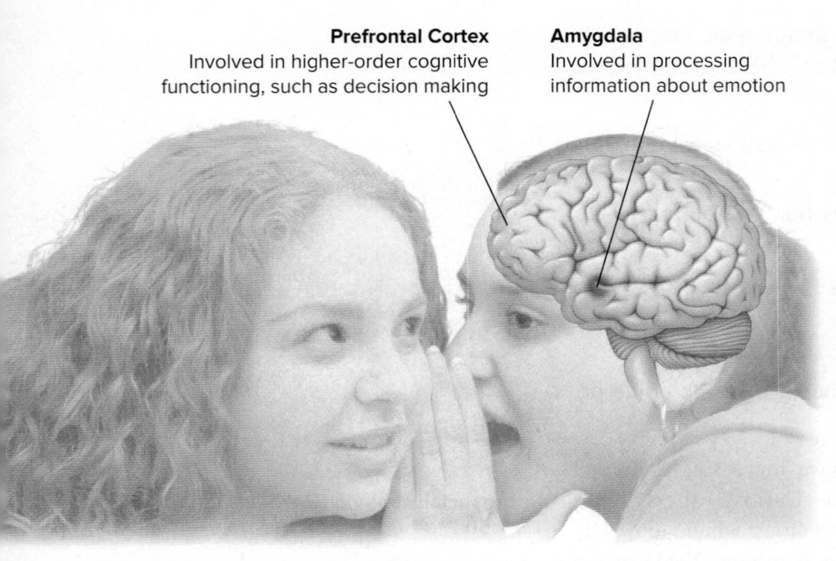
Prefrontal Cortex
Involved in higher-order cognitive functioning, such as decision making
Amygdala
Involved in processing information about emotion

**FIGURE 10 Developmental Changes in the Adolescent's Brain** The amygdala, which is responsible for processing information about emotion, matures earlier than the prefrontal cortex, which is responsible for decision making and other higher-order cognitive functions. ©BrandX Pictures/Punchstock

uterine, and skeletal development. Hormonal changes account for at least some of the emotional ups and downs of adolescence, but hormones are not solely responsible for adolescent behavior (Prendergast & Zucker, 2018; Quas & others, 2018).

Recall that physical and socioemotional development are intertwined. Nowhere is this link more apparent than in the timing of puberty. Boys and girls who mature earlier than their peers often experience different trajectories, with early-blooming boys having more positive and fewer negative outcomes than early-blooming girls. Boys who mature earlier than their peers are more popular with their peers and have higher self-esteem (Graber, Brooks-Gunn, & Warren, 2006). These boys are more successful and less likely to drink alcohol, smoke cigarettes, or engage in delinquent behaviors than late-maturing boys (Taga, Markey, & Friedman, 2006; van der Geest, Blokland, & Bijleveld, 2009).

In contrast, girls who are early bloomers are less likely to engage in academic pursuits and are less popular with their peers; they are more likely to become sexually active and to engage in unsafe sex (Blumenthal & others, 2011; Sontag-Padilla & others, 2012). Among early-blooming girls, these outcomes are at least partially due to early use of substances such as drugs and alcohol (Hendrick, Cance, & Maslowsky, 2016).

### THE ADOLESCENT BRAIN

Brain-imaging studies show important changes in the brain during adolescence (Blankenstein & others, 2018; Insel & Somerville, 2018; Morris & others, 2018; Wierenga & others, 2018). These changes focus on the earlier development of the amygdala, which involves emotion, and the later development of the prefrontal cortex, which is concerned with reasoning and decision making (Figure 10).

These brain changes may help to explain why adolescents often display very strong emotions but cannot yet control these feelings. It is as if the adolescent brain does not have the brakes to slow down emotions. Because of the relatively slow development of the prefrontal cortex, which continues to mature into early adulthood, adolescents may lack the cognitive skills to control their impulses effectively. This developmental disjunction may account for increased risk taking and other problems in adolescence (Morris & others, 2018; Steinberg, 2012, 2013).

Biological changes in the brain are linked with experiences (Dishion, 2016; Whittle & others, 2016). For instance, one study of adolescents found that resisting peer pressure was correlated with prefrontal cortex thickening and more brain connections (Paus & others, 2008). This correlational study cannot tell us if the brain changes promoted peer-pressure resistance or if this resistance promoted changes in the brain, but it does highlight the nature–nurture question that permeates the study of development.

## Cognitive Development in Adolescence

As they advance into Piaget's stage of formal operational thinking, adolescents undergo other significant cognitive changes. One characteristic of adolescent thinking, especially in early adolescence, is egocentrism. Although children are also considered egocentric, *adolescent egocentrism* has a different focus; it involves the belief that others are as preoccupied with the adolescent as he or she is. Egocentric adolescents perceive others as observing them more than actually is the case–think of the eighth-grade boy who is certain that everyone has noticed the small pimple on his face. In addition, adolescents show a belief that they are invincible (that is, incapable of being harmed). Adolescents display a particularly problematic pattern in their perception of risks; unlike adults, they underestimate risks associated with various behaviors even as they prefer riskier experiences (Modecki, 2016).

## Socioemotional Development in Adolescence

Among the key aspects of adolescent development are identity exploration and the roles that parents and peers play in adolescent development.

### IDENTITY

Recall from Figure 10 that Erikson (1968) viewed the key challenge of adolescence (his fifth stage) as *identity versus identity confusion*. Erikson's approach to the formation of identity during adolescence is one of his most important contributions. In seeking an identity, adolescents face the challenges of finding out who they are, what they are all about, and where they are going in life. Adolescents are confronted with many new roles and adult statuses—from jobs and careers to friendships and romantic relationships. If they do not adequately explore their identity during this stage, they end up confused about who they are. Erikson argued that parents should allow adolescents to explore many different roles and many paths within a particular role.

Adolescents who spend this time in their lives exploring alternatives can reach some resolution of the identity crisis and emerge with a new sense of self. Those who do not successfully resolve the crisis suffer what Erikson calls *identity confusion,* which is expressed in one of two ways: The individual either withdraws from peers and family or seeks anonymity within a crowd.

**Marcia's Theory on Identity Status** Building on Erikson's ideas, James Marcia proposed the concept of *identity status* to describe a person's progress in developing an identity (Kroger, Martinussen, & Marcia, 2010; Marcia, 1980, 2002). In Marcia's view, two dimensions of identity—exploration and commitment—are important. *Exploration* refers to investigating various options for a career and for personal values. *Commitment* involves making a decision about which identity path to follow and making a personal investment in attaining that identity. Various combinations of exploration and commitment give rise to one of four identity statuses.

Marcia's approach focuses on identity as an active construction, an outcome of a process of thinking about and trying on different identities (Klimstra & others, 2009, 2010). To understand Marcia's approach, check out the Psychological Inquiry.

**Ethnic Identity** Developing an identity in adolescence can be especially challenging for individuals from ethnic minority groups (Verkuyten, 2018). As they mature cognitively, many adolescents become acutely aware of how the majority culture views their ethnic group. In addition, an increasing number of minority adolescents face the challenge of *biculturalism* or *multiculturalism*—identifying in some ways with their ethnic minority group and in other ways with the majority culture (Romero, Piña-Watson, & Toomey, 2018).

For ethnic minority youth, feeling both a positive attachment to their minority group and an attachment to the larger culture is related to more positive academic and emotional outcomes (Serrano-Villar & Calzada, 2016). Although it might seem that being a member of an ethnic minority would make life more stressful, having a strong ethnic identity can buffer adolescents from the effects of discrimination.

In addition to ethnic identity, other aspects of one's identity can come to the fore during adolescence, including sexual orientation and gender role. We discuss these issues in depth in the chapter "Gender, Sex, and Sexuality".

*The managerial role of parenting involves effective monitoring of the adolescent's friends, social activities, and academic efforts.*

©MoMo Productions/Digital Vision/Getty Images

### PARENT AND PEER INFLUENCES

Parents and peers play important roles in adolescent development, including helping adolescents explore and answer the central questions of identity: "Who am I, and who do I hope to become?"

**Parenting** As in childhood, the preferred parenting style for most adolescents is authoritative, because this approach is associated with positive outcomes

## psychological *inquiry*

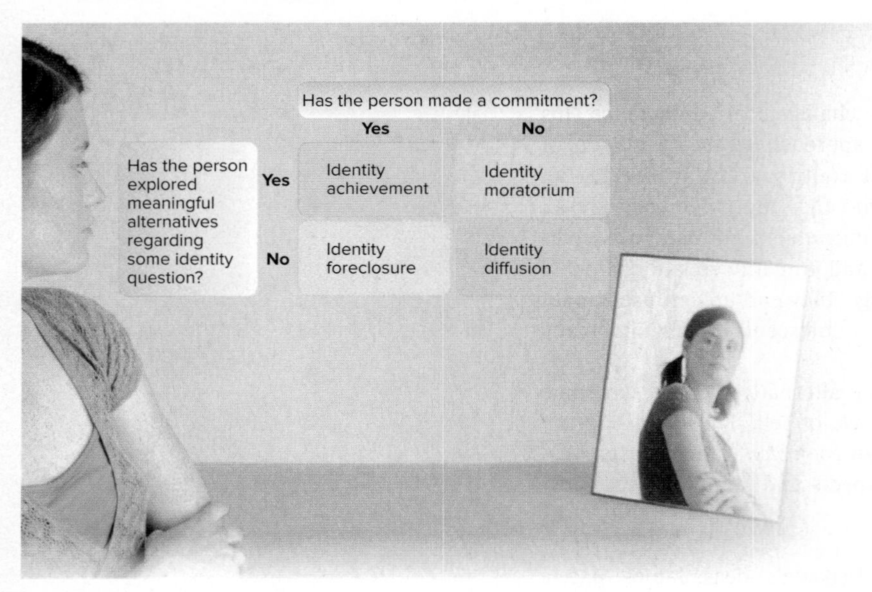

Has the person made a commitment?
Yes
No
Has the person explored meaningful alternatives regarding some identity question?
Yes
No
Identity achievement
Identity moratorium
Identity foreclosure
Identity diffusion


©PhotoAlto/PunchStock

### *Exploring Identity Exploration*

This figure summarizes Marcia's conceptualization of identity development. Notice that the different quadrants of the square represent the crossings of the two factors of commitment and exploration and that every possible combination of the two is represented. Then answer the questions that follow.

1. Imagine a young woman who comes from a family in which no one has ever attended college. What sorts of experiences might influence her journey to identity? How might her background influence her identity exploration?
2. Find your current identity status in this figure. In which quadrant is your own identity located? Do you feel that you have fully explored your potential identities? Why or why not?
3. Which path to identity do you believe is most common in young people today? Why?
4. Finding one's path in life is a common theme in popular books, TV, and film. Can you identify a book or movie that depicts the combination of exploration and resolution? Why do you think this theme is so popular?

(Baumrind, 2012). To help adolescents reach their full potential, a parent, in essence, must be an effective manager–one who locates information, makes contacts, helps to structure offsprings' choices, and provides guidance. By assuming this managerial role, parents help adolescents to avoid pitfalls and to work their way through the decisions they face.

Although adolescence is a time of establishing independence, a crucial aspect of the managerial role of parenting is effective monitoring (Romo & others, 2016). Monitoring includes supervising the adolescent's choice of social settings, activities, and friends, and his or her academic efforts. However, it is important for parents to be flexible and match their involvement with their son or daughter's life. This kind of flexible approach has been termed *vigilant care* (Omer, Satran, & Driter, 2016), an idea captures the ways that parents must allow adolescents to explore while keeping an eye out for signs of problems.

How competent the adolescent will become often depends on access to legitimate opportunities for growth, such as a quality education, community and societal support for achievement and involvement, and good jobs. Especially important in adolescence is long-term, deeply caring support from adults (Lerner & others, 2013). Successfully parenting adolescents means allowing adolescents to explore their own identity and handle increasing levels of autonomy in a positive manner, while also remaining an involved parent.

### *test yourself*

1. What characteristics of the adolescent brain help to explain why adolescents often display strong emotions that they cannot control?
2. According to Erikson, what challenges do adolescents face in trying to establish an identity, and what happens if they do not successfully resolve an identity crisis?
3. In what ways do parents and peers contribute to adolescent development?

**Peer Relations** Adolescents spend more time with peers than children do. Peer influences can be positive or negative (Dickens & others, 2018; Finan, Ohannessian, & Gordon, 2018). A significant aspect of positive peer relations is having one or more close friends. Adolescents can learn to be skilled and sensitive partners in intimate relationships by forging close friendships with selected peers (Tucker & others, 2012). However, some peers and friends can negatively impact adolescents' development. Hanging out with delinquent peers in adolescence can be a strong predictor of substance abuse, delinquent behavior, and depression (McMillan, Felmlee, & Osgood, 2018).

# 4. EMERGING ADULTHOOD, ADULT DEVELOPMENT, AND AGING

Developmental psychologists identify three approximate periods in adult development: early adulthood (20s and 30s), middle adulthood (40s and 50s), and late adulthood (60s until death). Each phase features distinctive physical, cognitive, and socioemotional changes.

Erikson believed that once issues of identity are resolved, young adults turn to the domain of intimate relationships. However, more recently, scholars have noted that after adolescence, many young people are putting off the commitments of marriage, family, and career. Jeffrey Arnett introduced the concept of *emerging adulthood* to describe this transitional period, which is partly an extended adolescence and partly a "trying on" of adult roles (Arnett, 2004, 2007, 2010, 2012). If you are a traditional-age college student, you are at this point in the life span. We begin our survey of postadolescent development by briefly examining this transitional life stage.

## Emerging Adulthood

**Emerging adulthood** is the transitional period from adolescence to adulthood (Arnett, 2004, 2006, 2007, 2012; Wood & others, 2018), from about 18 to 25 years of age. Emerging adults experiment with and explore career paths, identities, and close relationships.

● **emerging adulthood** The transitional period from adolescence to adulthood, spanning approximately 18 to 25 years of age.

Jeffrey Arnett (2006) identified five main features of emerging adulthood:

- *Identity exploration, especially in love and work:* Emerging adulthood is a time of significant changes in identity for many individuals.
- *Instability:* Residential changes peak during emerging adulthood, a time during which there also is often instability in love, work, and education.
- *Self-focus:* Emerging adults "are self-focused in the sense that they have little in the way of social obligations, [and] little in the way of duties and commitments to others, which leaves them with a great deal of autonomy in running their own lives" (Arnett, 2006, p. 10).
- *Feeling "in between":* Many emerging adults consider themselves neither adolescents nor full-fledged adults.
- *Age of possibilities, a time when individuals have an opportunity to transform their life:* Arnett (2006) described two ways in which emerging adulthood is the age of possibilities: (1) Many emerging adults are optimistic about their future; and (2) for emerging adults who have experienced difficult times while growing up, emerging adulthood presents an opportunity to guide their lives in a positive direction.

## Physical Development in Adulthood

Most of the physical changes that occur following adolescence involve declines in physical and perceptual abilities, as we now consider.

### PHYSICAL CHANGES IN EARLY ADULTHOOD

Most adults reach their peak physical development during their 20s and are the healthiest then. Unfortunately, that peak means that early adulthood is also the time when many physical skills begin to decline. Declines in strength and speed often are noticeable in the 30s. Perceptual abilities also decline. Hearing loss is very common with age. It may be hard to believe, but sensory changes occur as early as the late teens. Hearing decline begins at about 18 years old. It is so slow that most people do not notice it until much later. If you are a traditional-age college student, chances are you have already begun experiencing declines in your hearing.

## PHYSICAL CHANGES IN MIDDLE AND LATE ADULTHOOD

By the 40s or 50s, the skin has begun to wrinkle and sag because of the loss of fat and collagen in underlying tissues. Small, localized areas of pigmentation in the skin produce age spots, especially in areas exposed to sunlight such as the hands and face. Hair becomes thinner and grayer due to a lower replacement rate and a decline in melanin production. Individuals lose height in middle age, and many gain weight (Westerståhl & others, 2018). Once individuals hit their 40s, age-related vision changes usually become apparent, especially difficulty in seeing things up close and after dark.

For women, entering middle age means that menopause will soon occur. Usually in the late 40s or early 50s, a woman's menstrual periods cease completely. With menopause comes a dramatic decline in the ovaries' production of estrogen. Estrogen decline can produce uncomfortable symptoms such as *hot flashes* (sudden, brief flushing of the skin and a feeling of elevated body temperature), nausea, fatigue, and rapid heartbeat. Menopause does not produce serious psychological or physical problems for most women (Roberts & Hickey, 2016).

For both men and women, a variety of bodily systems are likely to show the effects of wear and tear as the body becomes less and less able to repair damage and regenerate itself (Parr, Coffey, & Hawley, 2013; Westerståhl & others, 2018). Physical strength declines, motor speed slows, and bones may become more brittle (especially for women). Nearly every bodily system may change with age.

Significantly, however, even as age is associated with some inevitable declines, important aspects of successful aging are within the person's control (Bertrand, Graham, & Lachman, 2013; I. C. Siegler & others, 2013a, 2013b; Moore & others, 2018). For instance, a healthy diet and regular exercise can help to slow the effects of age (Foscolou & others, 2019). Regular physical activity can have wide-ranging benefits not only for physical health but for cognitive functioning as well (Morikawa & others, 2013). Engaging in physical activity over the lifespan is associated with better cognitive functioning with age (Fondell & others, 2018).

One way older adults navigate age-related physical changes is through a process of changing their goals and developing new ways to engage in desired activities. Psychologists refer to this process as *selective optimization with compensation*, which means that older adults match their goals with their current abilities and compensate for declines by finding other ways to do the things they enjoy (Heckhausen, 2018; Venz, Pundt, & Sonnentag, 2018; Zhang & Radhakrishnan, 2018). A 75-year-old who can no longer drive might become an expert on her city's train and bus system, for example.

On the Japanese island of Okinawa, people live longer than anywhere else in the world, and Okinawa has the world's highest prevalence of *centenarians*—individuals who live to 100 years or beyond. Examination of Okinawans' lives provides insights into their longevity. Specific factors are diet (they eat nutritious foods such as grains, fish, and vegetables); lifestyle (they are easygoing and experience low stress); community (Okinawans look out for one another and do not isolate or ignore older adults); activity (they lead active lifestyles, and many older adults continue to work); and spirituality (they find a sense of purpose in spiritual matters) (Willcox & others, 2008). Just as physical changes are interwoven with socioemotional processes in childhood and adolescence, they are similarly intertwined during the later stages of life.

## BIOLOGICAL THEORIES OF AGING

Of the many proposed biological theories of aging, three especially merit attention: cellular-clock theory, free-radical theory, and hormonal stress theory.

**Cellular-Clock Theory** Leonard Hayflick's (1977) *cellular-clock theory* is that cells can divide a maximum of about 100 times and that, as we age, our cells become less capable of dividing. Hayflick found that cells extracted from adults in their 50s to 70s had divided fewer than 100 times. The total number of cell divisions was roughly related to the individual's age. Based on the way cells divide, Hayflick places the human life span's upper limit at about 120 years.

Scientists have been examining why cells lose their ability to divide (Horvath & Raj, 2018). The answer may lie at the tips of chromosomes. Each time a cell divides, the *telomeres* protecting the ends of chromosomes shorten. After about 100 replications, the telomeres are dramatically reduced, and the cell no longer can reproduce (Prescott & others, 2011).

It is not surprising then that scientists are interested in discovering ways to maintain high levels of the telomere-extending enzyme–telomerase. Some have examined how genetic manipulation of telomerase activators might influence levels of telomerase (C. Harrison, 2012). Meditation, described in the chapter "States of Consciousness", might also help to enhance telomerase activity. One study found that individuals who participated in a three-month meditation retreat showed greater telomerase activity than individuals in a control group (Jacobs & others, 2011).

**Free-Radical Theory** A second biological theory of aging is the *free-radical theory.* This theory states that people age because unstable oxygen molecules known as *free radicals* are produced inside their cells. These molecules damage DNA and other cellular structures (Mecocci & others, 2018; Redman & others, 2018). The damage done by free radicals may lead to a range of disorders, including cancer and arthritis (Valko & others, 2016).

Keep in mind, however, that although free radicals sound like enemies of a healthy body, these cells are themselves important to the body's survival. Immune cells will attack invading bacteria with free radicals to annihilate them.

**Hormonal Stress Theory** A third theory of aging, *hormonal stress theory,* argues that aging in the body's hormonal system can lower resistance to stress and increase the likelihood of disease. As individuals age, the hormones stimulated by stress stay in the bloodstream longer than is the case for younger people (Finch, 2011). These prolonged, elevated levels of stress hormones are linked to increased risks for many diseases, including cardiovascular disease, cancer, and diabetes (Gems & Partridge, 2013). Research on the hormonal stress theory has focused on the role of chronic stress in reducing immune system functioning (Naumova & others, 2013).

## AGING AND THE BRAIN

For decades, scientists believed that no new brain cells are generated past early childhood. However, researchers have discovered that adults *can* grow new brain cells throughout life (Buchman & others, 2016; Curtis, Kam, & Faull, 2011; Kazanis, 2013), although the evidence is limited to the hippocampus and the olfactory bulb (Kempermann & others, 2018). Researchers currently are studying factors that might inhibit and promote neurogenesis, including various drugs, stress, and exercise (Buchman & others, 2016). Research with rats suggests that sustained aerobic exercise (like long-distance running) leads to higher levels of neurogenesis (Nokia & others, 2016). They also are examining how grafting neural stem cells to various brain regions, such as the hippocampus, might increase neurogenesis (Doeppner & others, 2016; Srivastava & others, 2016).

Research from the Nun Study (described in the chapter "Psychology's Scientific Method") provides evidence supporting the role of experience in maintaining the brain. Recall that this study involves nearly 700 nuns in a convent in Mankato, Minnesota (Snowdon, 2003, 2007) (Figure 11). Although earlier we surveyed the aspects of the study related to happiness, this research has also investigated brain functioning. By examining the nuns' donated brains as well as those of others, neuroscientists have documented the aging brain's remarkable ability to grow and change. Even the oldest Mankato nuns lead intellectually challenging lives, and neuroscientists believe that performing stimulating mental activities increases dendritic branching. Keeping the brain actively engaged in challenging activities can help to slow the effects of age.

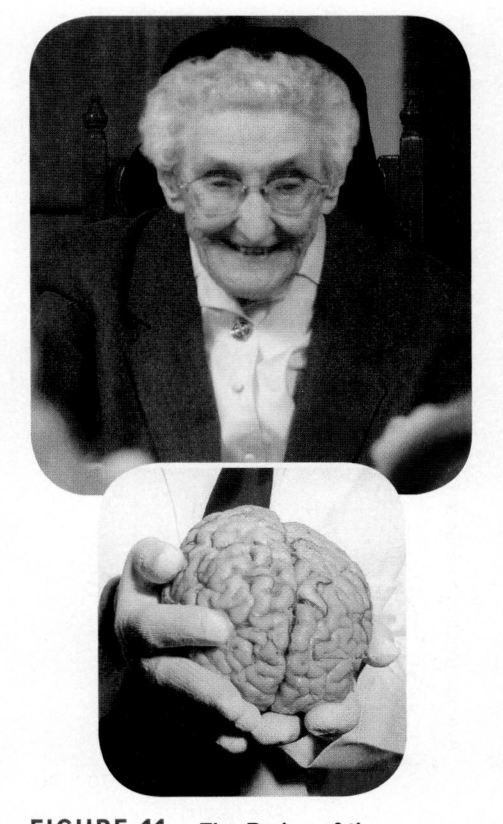

**FIGURE 11 The Brains of the Mankato Nuns** Nun Study participant Sister Nicolette Welter remained an active, contributing member of her community until her death at age 102. (*inset*) A neuroscientist holds a brain donated by a participant in the Mankato Nun Study. (Sister Nicolette Welter) ©Scott Takushi/KRT/Newscom; (brain) ©Steve Liss/Time Life Pictures/Getty Images

Even in late adulthood, the brain has the ability to repair and change itself to compensate for and adapt to age-related changes (Engeroff & others, 2018). Changes in lateralization provide one type of adaptation in aging adults. *Lateralization* is the specialization of function in one hemisphere of the brain or the other. Using neuroimaging techniques, researchers have found that brain activity in the prefrontal cortex is lateralized less in older adults than in younger adults when they are engaging in mental tasks (Brambilla & others, 2015; Raw & others, 2012). This means that for many tasks, younger adults can complete the task using just one hemisphere, while older adults will use both. Decreased lateralization in older adults might play a compensatory role in the aging brain (Brambilla & others, 2015). That is, using both hemispheres may help to maintain the mental abilities of older adults.

# Cognitive Development in Adulthood

Recall that for Piaget, each stage of cognitive development entails a way of thinking that is *qualitatively different* from that of the stage before. From Piaget's perspective, meaningful cognitive development ceases after the individual reaches the formal operational stage. Subsequent research has examined not only qualitative differences in thinking over time, but also the ebb and flow of cognitive abilities as individuals age. What kind of cognitive changes occur in adults?

## COGNITION IN EARLY ADULTHOOD

Just as physical abilities peak in early adulthood, might intellectual skills also peak during this period of life (Kitchener, King, & DeLuca, 2006)? Some experts on cognitive development argue that the typical idealism of Piaget's formal operational stage is replaced in young adulthood by more realistic, pragmatic style of thinking (Labouvie-Vief, 1986). Gisela Labouvie-Vief (2006) proposed that the increasing complexity of cultures in the past century has generated a greater need for reflective, more complex thinking that takes into account the changing nature of knowledge and the kinds of challenges contemporary thinkers face. She emphasizes that key aspects of cognitive development for young adults include deciding on a particular worldview, recognizing that the worldview is subjective, and understanding that diverse worldviews should be acknowledged. In her perspective, only some individuals attain the highest level of thinking.

## COGNITION IN MIDDLE ADULTHOOD

What happens to cognitive skills in middle adulthood? Although some cross-sectional studies indicate that middle adulthood is a time of cognitive decline, longitudinal evidence presents a different picture. K. Warner Schaie is conducting an extensive longitudinal study (started in 1956) by repeatedly measuring a host of different intellectual abilities in adults (Schaie, 1994, 2007, 2010, 2012). The highest level of functioning for four of the six intellectual abilities occurred in middle adulthood (Schaie, 2006, 2010, 2012). Only two of the six abilities declined in middle age. Based on the longitudinal data he has collected so far, Schaie concludes that *middle* (not early) adulthood is the period when many people reach their peak for a range of intellectual skills.

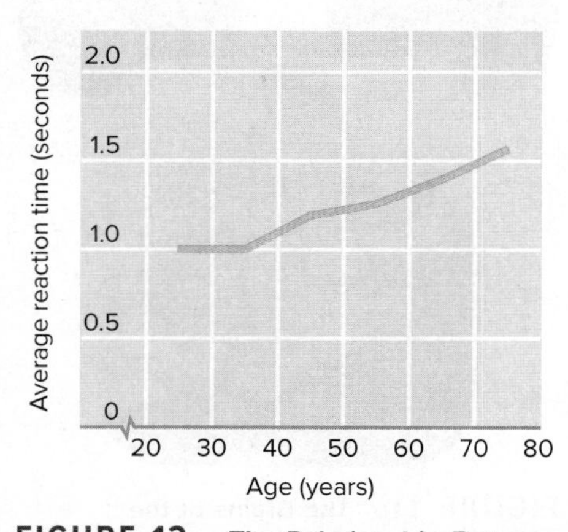


**FIGURE 12 The Relationship Between Age and Reaction Time** In one study, the average reaction time slowed for individuals in their 40s, and this decline accelerated for those in their 60s and 70s (Salthouse, 1994). The task used to assess reaction time required individuals to match numbers with symbols on a computer screen.

## COGNITION IN LATE ADULTHOOD

Many contemporary psychologists conclude that some dimensions of intelligence decline in late adulthood, whereas others are maintained or may even increase (Nyberg & Pudas, 2019). One of the most consistent findings is that when the speed of processing information is involved, older adults do not perform as well as their younger counterparts (Figure 12). This decline in speed of processing is apparent in middle-aged adults and becomes more pronounced in older adults (Aboud & others, 2018; Bopp & Verhaeghen, 2018; Weuve & others, 2018).

Older adults also tend to not do as well as younger adults in most, but not all, aspects of memory. In the area of memory involving knowledge of the world (for instance, the capital of Peru), older adults usually take longer than younger adults to remember the information, but they often are able to retrieve it (Mowrey & others, 2018). Decline occurs for working memory as well (Memel & others, 2018).

Some aspects of cognition might improve with age. One such area is **wisdom**, expert knowledge about the practical aspects of life (Nam & Cho, 2018; Staudinger & Gluck, 2011; Weststrate & others, 2018). Wisdom may increase with age because of the buildup of life experiences, but individual variations characterize people throughout their lives. Thus, not every older person has wisdom, and some young people are wise beyond their years.

**wisdom** Expert knowledge about the practical aspects of life.

Can older adults avoid declines in cognitive function? Some studies show that physical activity can be helpful in maintaining cognitive function (Fondell & others, 2018; Hamer, Terrera, & Demakakos, 2018) but the evidence is mixed (Brasure & others, 2018). It does appear that when older adults continue to increase their engagement in cognitive and physical activities, they are better able to maintain their cognitive functioning in late adulthood (C. L. Brown & others, 2012; Lindwall & others, 2012; Mitchell & others, 2012). Still, older adults tend to be less able to adapt than younger adults and thus are limited in how much they can improve their cognitive skills (Brasure & others, 2018; Finch, 2009; Salthouse, 2012).

# Socioemotional Development in Adulthood

In the physical and the cognitive domains, the developmental story is generally one of rapid growth during childhood, with continuing gains in adolescence, followed by steady decline with age. Does a similar pattern hold for socioemotional development? Let's consider the changes that characterize adult socioemotional development, first returning to Erikson's stage theory of life-span development and then looking at current research.

## SOCIOEMOTIONAL DEVELOPMENT IN EARLY ADULTHOOD

For Erikson (1968), early adulthood involves the developmental dilemma involving *intimacy versus isolation* (see Figure 10). At this stage, people either form intimate relationships with others or become socially isolated. If the young adult develops healthy friendships and an intimate relationship with a partner, intimacy will likely be achieved. A key way that a young adult achieves intimacy is through a long-term romantic relationship, often in the form of marriage.

As the idea of emerging adulthood would suggest, people are waiting longer to marry in recent decades (Schneider, Harknett, & Stimpson, 2018). In 2015, the median age for a first marriage in the United States climbed to 29.2 years for men and 27.1 years for women, higher than at any other point in history (Stritof, 2018). This trend may be good news, because divorce rates are higher for marriages in which the woman is younger than 18 compared to marriages in which she is 20 or older (Center for Family and Demographic Research, 2002).

What makes a marriage successful? John Gottman has been studying married couples since the early 1970s. He interviews couples, films their interactions, and takes measures of their heart rate and blood pressure during their interactions (Gottman, Swanson, & Swanson, 2002; Madhyastha, Hamaker, & Gottman, 2011). He follows-up on the couples every year to see how their marriages are faring. Gottman and his colleagues also study same-sex partners to try to understand what makes relationships thrive. Gottman (2006) has identified four principles at work in successful marriages:

- *Nurturing fondness and admiration:* Partners sing each other's praises. When couples put a positive spin on their talk with and about each other, marriages tend to work.
- *Turning toward each other as friends:* Partners see each other as friends and turn toward each other for support in times of stress and difficulty.
- *Giving up some power:* Bad marriages often involve one partner who is a powermonger. Healthy relationship involve each person giving up some power.
- *Solving conflicts together:* Couples work to solve problems, regulate their emotion during times of conflict, and compromise to accommodate each other.

©Rouzes/iStock/Getty Images

©Javier Pierini/Taxi/Getty Images

## SOCIOEMOTIONAL DEVELOPMENT IN MIDDLE ADULTHOOD

According to Erikson, following the resolution of the intimacy versus isolation dilemma, the adult turns to concerns about *generativity versus stagnation* (see Figure 10). *Generativity* means making a contribution to the next generation. The feeling that one has made a lasting and memorable contribution to the world is related to higher levels of psychological well-being (Ardelt, Gerlach, & Vaillant, 2018; Grossman & Gruenewald, 2018). Erikson did not think that parenting alone was a guarantee of generativity but he believed that parenting could be a way to experience this important developmental accomplishment.

## SOCIOEMOTIONAL DEVELOPMENT AND AGING

To Erikson, the later years of life are occupied by looking back—evaluating one's life and seeking meaning. Erikson called this stage *integrity versus despair* (see Figure 10). Through a process of life review and reminiscence, the older adult comes to a sense of meaning or despair. The individual is also occupied with coming to terms with his or her own death, according to Erikson. If the person has a strong sense of integrity, experiencing life as a meaningful and coherent whole, he or she faces the later years with a strong sense of meaning and low fear of death. In the absence of integrity, the older adult is filled with despair and fear.

## RESEARCH ON ADULT SOCIOEMOTIONAL DEVELOPMENT

Research on socioemotional development and aging reveals that Erikson was correct in his view that meaning is a central concern for older adults. However, he overlooked that this meaning derives not only from the past but also from the present. Let's consider recent research findings about how adults' lives change socially and emotionally over time.

In terms of social relationships, older adults often become more selective about their social networks (Carstensen, 2006, 2008, 2011; Carstensen & others, 2011). At the same time, older adults report greater happiness than their younger counterparts (Carstensen & others, 2011; Mroczek & Spiro, 2005; Ram & others, 2008; Stanley & Isaacowitz, 2012; Wrzus & others, 2012), and their satisfaction with life increases with age, even into the 80s (Stone & others, 2010).

Laura Carstensen developed *socioemotional selectivity theory* to address the narrowing of social contacts and the increase in positive emotion that occur with age (Carstensen, 2006, 2011). Her theory says that older adults are selective in their social interactions in order to maximize positive, meaningful experiences. Although younger adults may gain a sense of meaning in life from long-term goals, older adults gain a sense of meaning by focusing on satisfying relationships and activities in the *present*. Unlike younger adults, who may be preoccupied with the future, older adults embrace the present moment with increasing vitality (Giasson, Liao, & Carstensen, 2018; Hicks & others, 2012; Kotter-Grühn & Smith, 2011; Lachman & others, 2008).

Socioemotional selectivity theory posits that it is not old age itself that spurs people to maximize positive meaning in the present but, rather, limited time. Young adults who are asked to imagine having limited time (for instance, because they are about to go on a long trip) show the same pattern of maximizing time they spend with a narrow set of important friends and family members (Carstensen, 2011).

The capacity to regulate emotions, maximizing positive experiences, appears to be a central feature of aging. Across diverse samples—Norwegians, Catholic nuns, African

Americans, Chinese Americans, and non-Latino White Americans—older adults report better control of their emotions than younger adults (Charles & Carstensen, 2010).

The benefits of emotion regulation may have far-reaching consequences. In one study, adults who had expressed positive attitudes about aging some 20 years previously lived, on average, 7½ years longer than those who had expressed more negative attitudes about aging (Levy & others, 2002). An important factor in the link between attitudes and longevity was a person's belief that life was full, hopeful, and worthwhile. A recent longitudinal study found that intelligence in adolescence predicts a youthful attachment to life in old age (Stephan & others, 2018).

### test yourself

1. What are the five main features of emerging adulthood?
2. What is brain lateralization, and how might a decrease in lateralization in older adults play a role in the aging brain?
3. What do longitudinal studies indicate about intellectual abilities in middle adulthood?

# 5. HUMAN DEVELOPMENT AND HEALTH AND WELLNESS

Compared with child development, adult development is more likely to be a conscious process and therefore a kind of accomplishment (Dutt, Wahl, & Rupprecht, 2018; Recksiedler & others, 2018). In this last section we consider the active developer as the individual meets the challenges of adulthood and seek to understand how adults "grow" themselves.

## Coping and Adult Development

One way adults develop is through coping with life difficulties. Psychologist Carolyn Aldwin and her colleagues have suggested that stress and coping play a role in development (Aldwin, 2007; Aldwin, Levenson, & Kelly, 2009; Igarashi, Levenson, & Aldwin, 2018). To understand this connection, consider Piaget's ideas of assimilation and accommodation in the context of adulthood (Block, 1982). In assimilation existing cognitive structures are used to make sense out of the current environment, allowing the person to enjoy a feeling of meaning because experiences fit with preexisting schemas. However, when experience conflicts with existing schemas, it is necessary to modify current ways of thinking.

In accommodation existing schemas are modified or new structures are developed. Accommodation helps us to change so that we can make sense of life's previously incomprehensible events. When we encounter a negative life circumstance, such as an illness or a loss, we have the opportunity to change—to develop and to mature (Cárdenas & others, 2018; Roepke & others, 2018; Weststrate & others, 2018). Research shows that people who actively accommodate difficult experiences are more likely to come to a rich, complex view of themselves and the world (King & Hicks, 2007).

*Volunteering our time and talents and working with younger people can contribute to our well-being and life satisfaction as we age.*

©Ronnie Kaufman/Digital Vision/Getty Images

## Life Themes and Life-Span Development

A life theme involves a person's efforts to cultivate meaningful optimal experiences (Massimini & Delle Fave, 2000; Rathunde & Csikszentmihalyi, 2006). Consider someone who has spent much of his or her adult life pursuing wealth and career success and who turns to selfless pursuits in middle age. To contribute to the well-being of the next

### test yourself

1. How does Piaget's idea of assimilation apply to adult development?
2. How does accommodation, in Piaget's sense of the term, help adults to cope with life's difficulties?
3. What is involved when an individual pursues a life theme, such as leaving a legacy for future generations?

generation, the individual devotes more resources to helping others–for example, by volunteering or working with young people. This reorientation can ease the individual into a positive and meaningful old age.

These motivations are demonstrated by numerous individuals who use their successes for the betterment of the world. For example, former New York City Mayor Michael Bloomberg donated nearly $2 billion to cover financial aid for students applying to Johns Hopkins University. This gift means that no qualified student will be unable to attend for financial reasons.

During childhood, psychological development occurs in concert with physical development. As we become strong and skilled enough to walk, the horizons of our world open up to new discoveries. In adulthood, our developmental cues come, instead, from ourselves–where do we go, once we have managed the many tasks we faced in childhood and adolescence? Development, then, is a lifelong process that continues as we encounter opportunities to grow, to change, and to make a mark on the world in which we live.

# SUMMARY

## 1. EXPLORING HUMAN DEVELOPMENT

Development is the pattern of change in human characteristics that continues throughout the life span. Cross-sectional research on human development can show age differences. Longitudinal research shows age-related change. Strong conclusions about development require longitudinal data.

Nature (biological inheritance), nurture (environmental experience) and their interaction influence development. People are not at the mercy of either their genes or their environment when they actively construct optimal experiences. Resilience refers to the capacity of individuals to thrive during difficulties at every stage of development.

## 2. CHILD DEVELOPMENT

Prenatal development progresses through the germinal, embryonic, and fetal periods. Particular drugs and illnesses can adversely affect the fetus. These threats are called teratogens. Preterm birth is another potential problem, especially if the infant is very small or grows up in an adverse environment.

The infant's physical development is dramatic in the first year, and a number of motor milestones are reached in infancy. Extensive changes in the brain, including denser connections between synapses (followed by pruning), take place in infancy and childhood.

In Piaget's view of cognitive development, children use schemas to actively construct their world, either assimilating new information into existing schemas or adjusting schemas to accommodate that information. Piaget identified four stages of cognitive development: the sensorimotor stage, the preoperational stage, the concrete operational stage, and the formal operational stage. Two other views of children's cognitive development are Vygotsky's sociocultural cognitive theory and information-processing theory.

Understanding socioemotional development in childhood includes consideration of Erikson's psychosocial stages as well as moral development. Erikson presented a major, eight-stage psychosocial view of life-span development; its first four stages occur in childhood. In each stage, the individual seeks to resolve a particular socioemotional conflict. Kohlberg proposed a cognitive theory of moral development with three levels (preconventional, conventional, and postconventional). More recent research has focused on the development of prosocial behavior and the influence of socioemotional factors in putting moral reasoning into action.

## 3. ADOLESCENCE

Puberty is a period of rapid skeletal and sexual maturation that occurs mainly in early adolescence. Its onset occurs about two years earlier in girls than in boys. Hormonal changes trigger pubertal development.

According to Piaget, cognitive development in adolescence is characterized by the appearance of formal operational thought, the final stage in his theory. This stage involves abstract, idealistic, and logical thought.

Erikson's fifth stage of psychosocial development is identity versus identity confusion. Marcia proposed four statuses of identity based on crisis and commitment. A special concern is the development of ethnic identity. Despite great differences among adolescents, the majority develop competently.

## 4. EMERGING ADULTHOOD, ADULT DEVELOPMENT, AND AGING

Psychologists refer to the period between adolescence and adulthood as emerging adulthood, characterized by the exploration of identity through work and relationships, instability, and self-focus.

Most adults reach their peak physical performance in their 20s and are healthiest then. Physical skills begin to decline in the 30s. The cellular-clock, free-radical, and hormonal stress theories are three important biological explanations for aging. Even in late adulthood, the brain has remarkable repair capacity and plasticity.

Piaget said no new cognitive changes occur in adulthood. However, psychologists have proposed that the idealistic thinking of adolescents is replaced by the more realistic, pragmatic thinking of young adults. Longitudinal research on intelligence shows that many cognitive skills peak in middle age. Overall, older adults do not do as well on memory and other cognitive tasks and are slower to process information than younger adults.

Erikson's three stages of socioemotional development in adulthood are intimacy versus isolation (early adulthood), generativity versus stagnation (middle adulthood), and integrity versus despair (late adulthood). A special concern, beginning when individuals are in their 50s, is the challenge of understanding life's meaning. Remaining active increases the likelihood that older adults will be happy and healthy. Older adults often reduce their general social affiliations and instead are motivated to spend more time with close friends and family members. Older adults also experience more positive emotion, are happier, and are more satisfied with their lives than younger adults.

### 5. HUMAN DEVELOPMENT AND HEALTH AND WELLNESS

Though often associated with childhood, psychological development can continue throughout life. Psychologists have suggested that coping with life's difficulties is one way in which adults may develop. For adults, taking an active approach to "growing" oneself may be an important motivator in development.

Piaget's concepts of assimilation and accommodation have been applied to the process of developing through difficult times. An individual may experience meaning in life by applying his or her current understanding of the world (assimilation). In contrast, the individual may find that some experiences require a revision of that understanding (accommodation). In adulthood, people have the opportunity to pursue new goals that represent important life themes, such as leaving a legacy for the future.

## key *terms*

accommodation
androgens
assimilation
authoritarian parenting
authoritative parenting
concrete operational stage
development
emerging adulthood
estrogens
executive function
formal operational stage
infant attachment
insecure attachment
nature
neglectful parenting
nurture
object permanence
operations
permissive parenting
preferential looking
preoperational stage
prosocial behavior
puberty
resilience
secure attachment
sensorimotor stage
temperament
wisdom

## apply your *knowledge*

1. Consider the style of parenting with which you were raised. It might help to think of specific situations or moments when your parents put limits on your behavior (or did not). If you have one or more siblings, ask for their opinion, too. Do you agree with one another about your parents' style? Now give these definitions to your parents and ask which, if any, describes them. Sometimes there are as many different views of a family as there are members of that family.

2. A major part of any child's life is playing–and when kids are playing, they are often playing with toys. Using the information on perceptual and cognitive development reviewed in this chapter, design toys that you think would be a perfect fit for a child aged 2 months, 2 years, and 10 years. With respect to the child's development, what features of each toy are especially good for a child of the intended age group?

3. Go online and Google "parenting discussion boards." Click on one or two of the many sites that come up, and see what parents are talking about. What issues seem to concern them most? Do these parents appear to have a sense of the issues addressed by developmental psychologists? Does the advice that parents share with one another seem to be based on the science of psychology?

4. Set aside 15 minutes to write a brief essay as follows. Think about your life in the future, when you are 70 or 80 years old. Imagine that everything has gone as well as it possibly could, and you have achieved your life dreams. What is your life like at this stage? What things about you are the same as they are for you now as a student of psychology? What things have changed? What is your best possible older adult self? How have aspects of your life today contributed to this happily-older-after?

5. You might have heard the statement that "40 is the new 30" or "50 is the new 40." What trend do these statements reflect? What might explain this trend? What might it mean for our understanding of adult development?

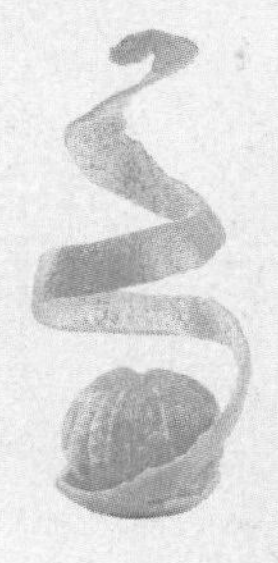

**Design elements:** Preview icon: ©Jiang Hongyan; Intersection box icon: ©D. Hurst/Alamy, ©Creative Crop/Getty Images, ©Dimitris66/Getty Images, ©Savany/Getty Images; Critical Controversy box icon: ©Ultrashock; running heads icon: ©Cre8tive Studios/Alamy; Summary icon: ©Vadarshop

# CHAPTER 10

## CHAPTER OUTLINE



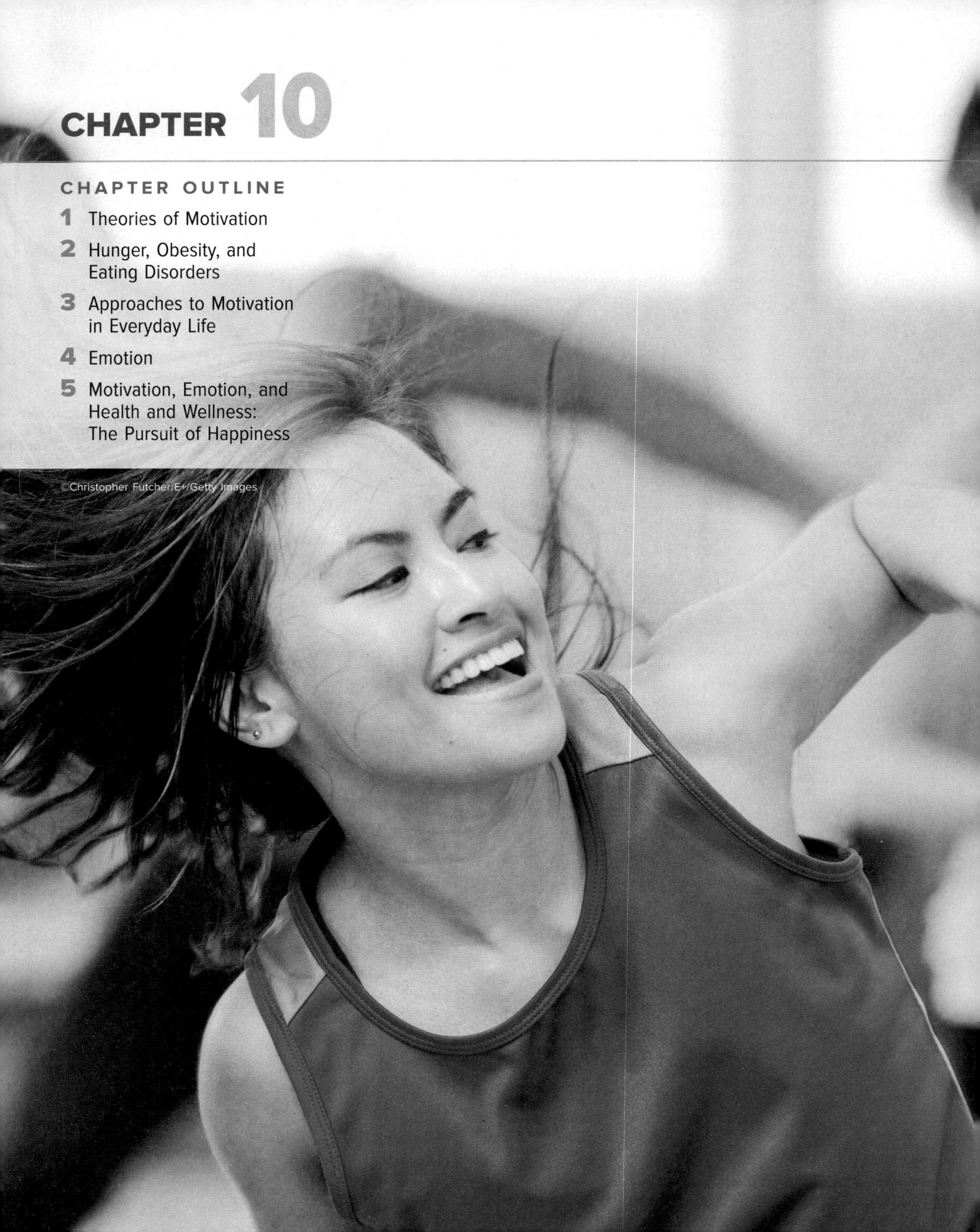

©Christopher Futcher/E+/Getty Images

# Motivation and Emotion

## A Hero on Automatic Pilot

**On September 24, 2017, shots rang out in the Burnette Chapel of Christ in Antioch, Tennessee.** As the wounded fell and people ran for cover, a church usher ran toward the gunman, placing himself between the gunmen and the worshippers (Bongioanni, 2018). The survivors of the shooting credited the man with saving their lives. Robert Engle, the usher that day, received the Civilian Medal of Honor, the highest such award given to civilians, for his heroism. The award is given by the living military service members who have received the Congressional Medal of Honor for their own heroism. But Engle did not see his actions as heroic. He acted without forethought and felt he was simply doing his job. As he put it, "I just reacted. It was like there was a hand right by me saying go, go for it" (Mojica, 2018). Of course, the typical duties of a church usher involve seating people in the pews, handing out parish bulletins, and so forth. Saving the lives of the congregation is not on the list. Yet, in a moment of terror for many, he quietly and decisively engaged the gunman. Why did he do it? How was he able to run *toward* the danger, overcoming the fearful emotion that engulfed everyone else? Whenever we ask *why* someone does something, we are looking for that person's motivation. The terms *motivation* and *emotion* come from the Latin word *movere,* which means "to move." Motivation is the *why* of what we do. When we are committed to our goals, we may achieve amazingly courageous acts. Motivation and emotion are the "go" of human life, propelling us forward. ●

# PREVIEW

This chapter examines the ways psychologists study motivation and emotion. We first review some general approaches to motivation and consider one important physiological source of motivation: hunger. We then examine motivation as it applies to everyday life. Next, we explore the rich topic of emotion. To close, we consider the ways that motivation and emotion intertwine in the pursuit of happiness.

## 1. THEORIES OF MOTIVATION

● **motivation** The force that moves people to behave, think, and feel the way they do.

**Motivation** is the force that moves people to behave, think, and feel the way they do. Motivated behavior is energized, directed, and sustained. Psychologists have proposed a variety of theories about why organisms are motivated to do what they do. In this section we explore some of the main theoretical approaches to motivation.

### The Evolutionary Approach

● **instinct** An innate (unlearned) biological pattern of behavior that is assumed to be universal throughout a species.

Early evolutionary accounts of motivation emphasized the role of instincts. An **instinct** is an innate (unlearned) biological pattern of behavior that is assumed to be universal throughout a species. Generally, an instinct is set in motion by a *sign stimulus*–something in the environment that turns on a fixed pattern of behavior. Instincts may explain a great deal of nonhuman animal behavior. In addition, some human behavior is instinctive. Recall, for example, the discussion of infant reflexes in the chapter "Human Development". Babies do not have to learn to suck; they instinctively do it when something is placed in their mouth. So, for infants, an object touching the lips is a sign stimulus. After infancy, though, it is hard to think of specific behaviors that all human beings engage in when presented with a particular stimulus.

More recently, evolutionary psychologists have emphasized how human motivation is rooted in our evolutionary past (Buss & Schmitt, 2019; Li, van Vugt, & Colarelli, 2018). Because evolutionary approaches emphasize the transmission of one's genes to future generations, these theories focus on domains of life that are especially relevant to reproduction, such as sexual behavior and behaviors relevant to competition among members of a species, such as aggression and achievement (Buss, 2018).

In general, even these behaviors are far too complex to be explained on the basis of instinct. Indeed, it would hardly seem adaptive for humans to have a fixed action pattern that is invariably set in motion by a particular signal in the environment. Adaptive human behavior is typically flexible and responsive to changes in the environment. To understand human behavior, psychologists have developed a variety of other approaches, as we now consider.

### Drive Reduction Theory

● **drive** An aroused state that occurs because of a physiological need.

● **need** A deprivation that energizes the drive to eliminate or reduce the deprivation.

Another way to think about motivation is through the constructs of drive and need. A **drive** is an aroused state of tension that occurs because of a physiological need. You can think of a drive as a psychological itch that requires scratching. Generally, we are motivated to reduce drives. A **need** is a deprivation that energizes the drive to eliminate or reduce the deprivation. Generally, psychologists think of needs as underlying our drives. You may have a need for water; the drive that accompanies that need is your feeling of being thirsty. Drive pertains to a psychological state, whereas need involves a physiological one.

Usually but not always, needs and drives are closely associated. Drives do not always follow from needs. For example, if you are deprived of oxygen because of a gas leak, you have a need for oxygen. You may feel lightheaded but never experience the drive for oxygen that might lead you to open a window. Moreover, drives sometimes seem to come out of nowhere. Having eaten a fine meal and feeling full to the point of not wanting another bite, you might nevertheless feel ready to tackle the Double Chocolate Oblivion when the waiter wheels over the dessert cart.

*Drive reduction theory* explains that as a drive becomes stronger, we are motivated to reduce it (Berridge, 2018; Hull, 1952). The goal of drive reduction is **homeostasis**, the body's tendency to maintain an equilibrium, or a steady state or balance. Hundreds of biological states in the body must be maintained within a certain range; these include temperature, blood-sugar level, potassium and sodium levels, and oxygenation. When you dive into an icy swimming pool, your body uses energy to maintain its normal temperature. When you step into the heat of a summer day, your body releases excess heat by sweating. These physiological changes occur automatically to keep your body in an optimal state of functioning. From a drive reduction perspective, then, we seek to reduce drives in order to return to a state of homeostasis.

- **homeostasis** The body's tendency to maintain an equilibrium, or a steady state or balance.

Most psychologists conclude that drive reduction theory does not provide a comprehensive framework for understanding motivation because people often behave in ways that increase rather than reduce a drive. Many things we do involve increasing (not decreasing) tensions—for example, taking a challenging course in school, raising a family, working at a difficult job, or even just watching a scary movie or going to a haunted house attraction (Kerr, Siegle, & Orsini, 2018).

## Optimum Arousal Theory

When psychologists talk about arousal, they are generally referring to a person's feelings of being alert and engaged. When we are very excited, our arousal levels are high. When we are bored, they are low. Optimal arousal theory suggests that there should be a level of arousal that is ideal for facilitating goal attainment.

You have probably noticed that motivation influences arousal levels. Sometimes you can want something (for example, to do well on a test) so much that you can become overly motivated and anxious. On the other hand, you might be so unmotivated for a task (such as doing the dishes) that you can hardly force yourself to complete it. Sometimes, to do well, you need to have an arousal level that is "just right."

Early in the twentieth century, two psychologists described how arousal can influence performance (Yerkes & Dodson, 1908). According to their formulation, known as the **Yerkes–Dodson law**, performance is best under conditions of moderate arousal rather than either low or high arousal. At the low end of arousal, you may be too lethargic to perform tasks well; at the high end, you may not be able to concentrate. To master the Yerkes-Dodson law, check out the Psychological Inquiry.

- **Yerkes–Dodson law** The psychological principle stating that performance is best under conditions of moderate arousal rather than either low or high arousal.

- **overlearning** Learning to perform a task so well that it becomes automatic.

The link between arousal and performance is one reason that individuals in many professions are trained to overlearn important procedures. **Overlearning** means learning to perform a task so well that it becomes automatic. For example, elite Navy SEALS are trained so that they can be on "automatic pilot" even during very stressful times such as the raid on Osama bin Laden's compound in Pakistan in 2011.

For individuals who must perform at their best in a crisis, success depends on knowing what to do so well that it requires little or no thought. With this extra learning, when these individuals are under conditions of high arousal, they can rely on auto pilot to do what needs to be done.

### *test yourself*

1. What is motivation?
2. What are three theoretical approaches to motivation?
3. What is overlearning, and how can it help an individual perform at his or her best?

# 2. HUNGER, OBESITY, AND EATING DISORDERS

Part of the power of motivation is tied to physiological needs. We experience strong motivational forces, for example, when we are hungry or thirsty. Furthermore, the physiological state of being hungry has often been used as a path toward understanding a variety of human motivations. We use words about hunger in contexts that are not physiological, such as when we say that someone is "craving" attention or "starving" for affection. In this section we examine the basic motivational processes underlying hunger and eating, including the related topic of eating disorders.

## psychological *inquiry*

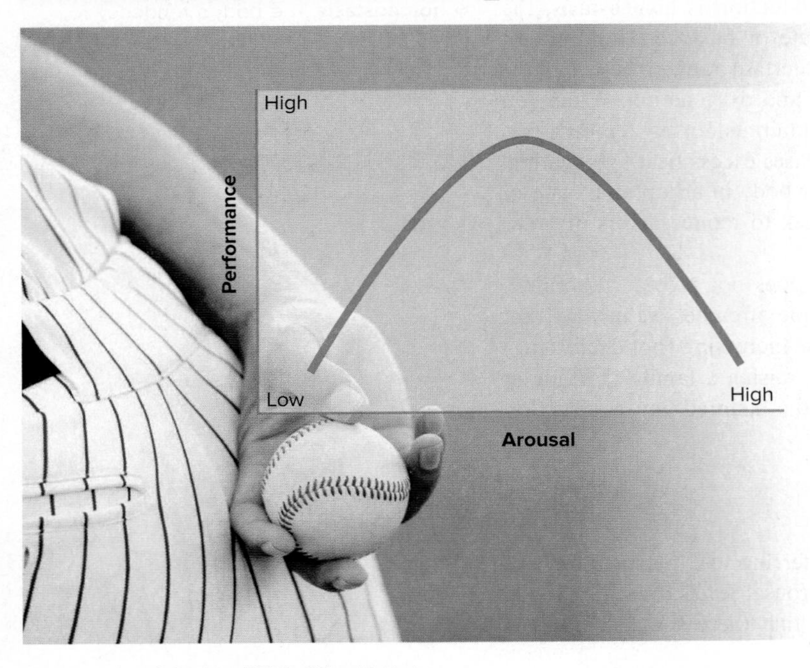


Source: Yerkes & Dodson (1908); ©Fuse/Getty Images

### *Obeying the (Yerkes–Dodson) Law*

The graph displays the relationship between arousal (shown on the X, or horizontal, axis) and performance (shown on the Y, or vertical, axis). Note that the curve resembles an inverted *V*.

Using the figure as a reference, answer the questions below.

1. What was your arousal level the last time you took an exam? If you were very nervous, your arousal level would be considered high. If you were excited and engaged but not too worried, your level would be in the medium range. If you were feeling sluggish, your arousal level would be low.
2. How did you actually do on that test? Plot your performance on the graph—find the place on the graph where your arousal level and your test performance meet up. Does it fit with the Yerkes–Dodson prediction?
3. Now think about performance in sports or the arts. Imagine your favorite athlete, musician, or actor. How might that person feel when he or she is on the spot, trying to sink a winning free throw, strike out the last batter, or impress an audience? How might arousal influence performance in those cases?
4. In many professions, individuals are forced to perform under conditions of very high arousal. These include EMTs, lifeguards, and emergency room staff. (Name some others.) How might such individuals train themselves to perform even under conditions of extreme arousal?

# The Biology of Hunger

You know you are hungry when your stomach growls and you feel hunger pangs. What role do such signals play in hunger?

## GASTRIC SIGNALS

Over a century ago, Walter Cannon and A. L. Washburn conducted an experiment that revealed a close association between stomach contractions and hunger (1912) (Figure 1). In one step of the procedure, a partially inflated balloon was passed through a tube inserted in Washburn's mouth and pushed down into his stomach. A machine that measures air pressure was connected to the balloon to monitor Washburn's stomach contractions. Every time Washburn reported hunger pangs by pushing a button, his stomach was also contracting.

Sure enough, a growling stomach needs food. The stomach tells the brain not only how full it is but also how much nutrient is present. That is why rich foods stop hunger faster than the same amount of water. The hormone cholecystokinin (CCK) helps start the digestion of food, travels to the brain through the bloodstream, and signals us to stop eating (Moss & others, 2012). Hunger involves a lot more than an empty stomach, however.

## BLOOD CHEMISTRY

Three key chemical substances play a role in hunger, eating, and *satiety* (the state of feeling full): glucose, insulin, and leptin.

*Glucose* (blood sugar) is an important factor in hunger, probably because the brain critically depends on sugar for energy. One set of sugar receptors, located in the brain, triggers hunger when sugar levels fall too low. Another set of sugar receptors is in the liver, which stores excess sugar and releases it into the blood when needed. The sugar receptors in the liver signal the brain when its sugar supply falls, and this signal also can make you hungry.

The hormone *insulin* also plays a role in glucose control. When we eat complex carbohydrates such as bread and pasta, insulin levels go up and fall off gradually. When we consume simple sugars such as candy, insulin levels rise and then fall sharply—the all-too-familiar "sugar low" (Rodin, 1984). This difference explains why we are more likely to eat again within the next several hours after eating simple sugars than after eating complex carbohydrates. Rising insulin levels lead to greater hunger.

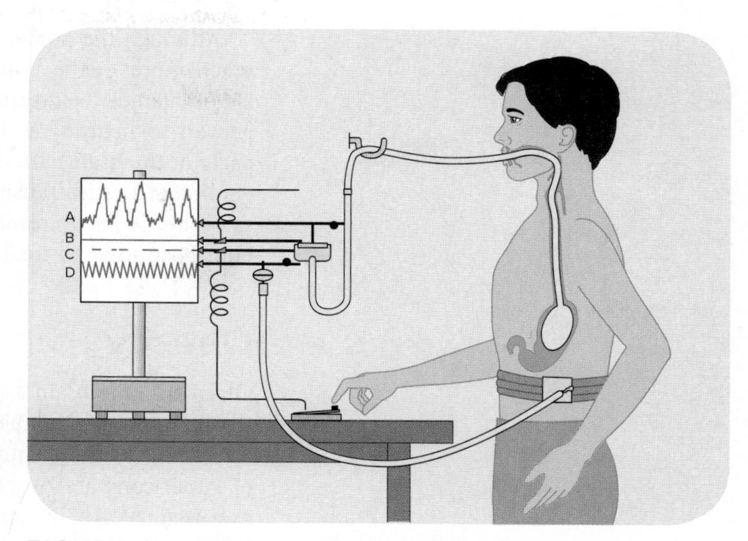


**FIGURE 1 Cannon and Washburn's Classic Experiment on Hunger** In this experiment, the researchers demonstrated that stomach contractions, which were detected by the stomach balloon, accompany a person's hunger feelings, which were indicated by pressing the key. Line A in the chart records increases and decreases in the volume of the balloon in the participant's stomach. Line B records the passage of time. Line C records the participant's manual signals of feelings of hunger. Line D records a reading from a belt placed around the participant's waist to detect movements of the abdominal wall and ensure that such movements were not the cause of changes in stomach volume. Source: Cannon & Washburn (1912).

Released by fat cells, the chemical *leptin* (from the Greek word *leptos,* meaning "thin") decreases food intake and increases energy expenditure or metabolism (Friedman, 2015). Leptin's functions were discovered in a strain of genetically obese mice, called *ob mice* (Laiglesia & others, 2018; Pelleymounter & others, 1995; Schönke & others, 2018). Because of a genetic mutation, the fat cells of ob mice cannot produce leptin. The ob mouse has a low metabolism, overeats, and gets extremely fat. Leptin appears to act as an anti-obesity hormone. If ob mice are given daily injections of leptin, their metabolic rate increases, and they become more active, eat less, and lose weight. Figure 2 shows an untreated ob mouse and an ob mouse that has received injections of leptin.

In general, leptin is associated with lower weight (Francisco & others, 2018). However, leptin is created by tissue that stores fat and, ironically, obese individuals are likely to have high levels of leptin. The problem, then, appears not to be low levels of leptin but some other issue that reduces its effectiveness (Pan & Myers, 2018). One possible explanation is that obese individuals develop resistance to leptin.

## BRAIN PROCESSES

The chapter "Biological Foundations of Behavior" described the central role of the hypothalamus in regulating important body functions, including hunger. More specifically, activity in two areas of the hypothalamus plays a role in hunger. The *lateral hypothalamus* (located on the outer portions) is involved in stimulating eating. When this area is electrically stimulated in a well-fed animal, the animal begins to eat. If this part of the hypothalamus is destroyed, even a starving animal will show no interest in food. The *ventromedial hypothalamus* (located more in the middle) is involved in reducing hunger and restricting eating. When this area of an animal's brain is stimulated, the animal stops eating. When the area is destroyed, the animal eats profusely and quickly becomes obese.

It might be confusing that these regions of the hypothalamus have very different functions but very similar names. Remember that *lateral* here refers to the outer sides (and you might *go out* to eat when hungry), whereas *ventromedial* refers to the inner portions (and you might *stay in* if you are already full).

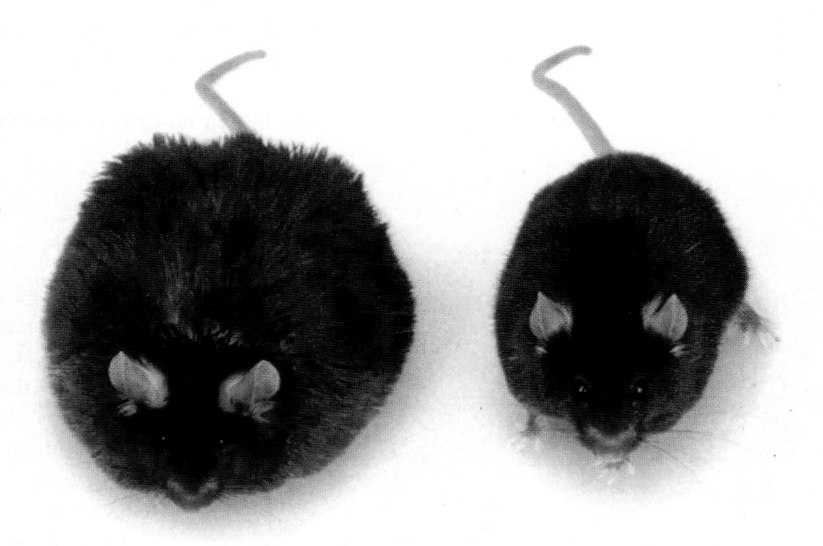

**FIGURE 2 Leptin and Obesity** The ob mouse on the left is untreated; the one on the right has been given injections of leptin.

Although the lateral and ventromedial hypothalamuses both influence hunger, there is much more to the brain's role in determining hunger than these on/off centers in the hypothalamus. Neurotransmitters (the chemical messengers that convey information from neuron to neuron) and neural circuits (clusters of neurons that often involve different parts of the brain) also function in hunger. Leptin influences eating by inhibiting the production of a neurotransmitter in the hypothalamus that induces eating. The neurotransmitter serotonin is partly responsible for the satiating effect of CCK, and serotonin antagonists have been used to treat obesity in humans.

## Obesity

Given that the brain and body are so elegantly wired to regulate eating behavior, why do so many people in the United States overeat and suffer the effects of this behavior? According to the Centers for Disease Control and Prevention (CDC, 2018), 72 percent of Americans are overweight, and nearly 40 percent are considered obese (dangerously overweight). An international comparison of 33 developed countries revealed that the United States had the highest percentage of obese adults (OECD, 2017).

Obesity is the single largest risk factor for disability, disease, and death (Pan & Myers, 2018). Obesity and overweight raise one's risk for a host of health problems, including cardiovascular disease, type II diabetes (Piché & others, 2018; Stokes & others, 2018), and cancer (Chadid & others, 2018). Overweight and obesity are global health problems.

Why so many people overeat to the point of becoming obese is a motivational puzzle, because it involves eating when one is not in need of nutrition. As is the case with much behavior, various biological, psychological, and sociocultural factors interact in diverse ways to produce eating and overeating.

### THE BIOLOGY OF OBESITY

Obesity clearly has a genetic component (Saeed, Arslan, & Froguel, 2018; Speakman & others, 2018). After the discovery of an ob gene in mice, researchers found a similar gene in humans (Nies & others, 2018). Only 10 percent of children who do not have obese parents become obese themselves, whereas 40 percent of children who have one obese parent become obese, and 70 percent of children who have two obese parents become obese.

• **set point** The weight maintained when the individual makes no effort to gain or lose weight.

Another factor in weight is **set point**, the weight maintained when the individual makes no effort to gain or lose weight. Set point is determined in part by the number of *adipose cells,* or fat cells, stored in the body (Speakman & others, 2018). When these cells are filled, the person does not get hungry. When people gain weight, they add fat cells, and even if they later lose weight, they may not be able to get rid of the extra cells. A normal-weight individual has 10 to 20 billion fat cells. An obese individual can have up to 100 billion fat cells (Hellmich, 2008). Consequently, an obese individual has to eat more to feel satisfied.

### PSYCHOLOGICAL FACTORS IN EATING AND OBESITY

©rgbdigital/iStock/Getty Images

Psychologists used to think that obesity stemmed from factors such as unhappiness and external food cues. These ideas make some sense; drowning one's sorrows in chocolate or eating some cookies just because they are there seems common enough to explain overeating. However, many psychological factors affect what, when, and how much we eat.

From an evolutionary perspective, human taste preferences developed at a time when reliable food sources were scarce. Our earliest ancestors needed a lot of calories to survive in challenging circumstances. They likely developed a preference for sweet and fatty foods. Today, many people still have a taste for such foods although modern sweet and fatty foods provide far more calories than we need, with far less nutritional value. Our early ancestors experienced a daily struggle for survival that

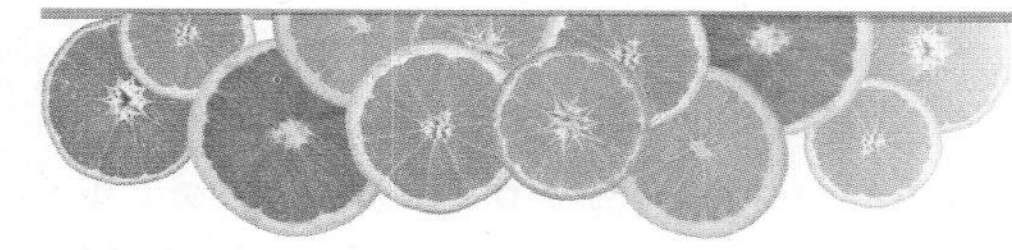
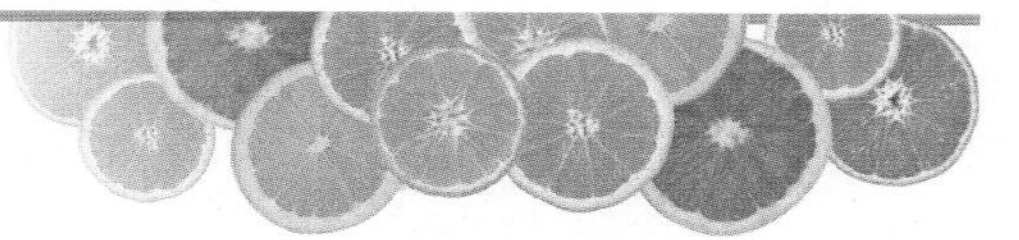

# INTERSECTION

## Perception and Eating: Can Portion Information Affect Eating?

If you have ever taken a close look at the nutritional information on the side of a snack you might notice that the information is based on how many servings are included in a pack. So, even though it seems obvious that a whole pack of cookies is a serving, the information tells you there are actually two or three servings there.

Could the presentation of serving information affect how much people eat? A recent set of studies examined whether it makes a difference if eaters, provided with the same amount of, food are given detailed or more global information about the food. Does it matter, for instance, if 11 tortilla chips are labeled as "one serving" versus "11 tortilla chips"? (Lewis & Earl, 2018). The participants in the studies all thought they were taking part in a taste test. They were presented with snack foods (in one study tortilla chips and in others gummy bears or mini rice cakes). All participants got the same amount of food in a plastic baggie. The only difference between them was the independent variable in the studies: how the food was presented. Participants were randomly assigned to be told that the baggie contained "one serving" of the snack or they were told the exact number of chips, gummy bears, or mini-rice cakes that were in the baggie. After tasting the snacks, participants rated how full they felt and how much of the snack they intended to eat in the future.

*Would you feel more full if you ate 18 gummy bears or "one serving" of gummy bears (containing 18)?*

The results? People felt more full and said they would need to eat fewer snacks in the future to feel full if they were told the actual amount of the snack they received (rather than being told it was one serving). These results are surprising—after all, everyone received the same amount of food. Yet, being given the exact count of the food presented led people to feel like it was more food. And, to the extent they thought it was more food, they actually ate less of it (Lewis & Earl, 2018).

Now imagine looking at that pack of cookies that seemed to hold one serving and being told that it actually contains 18 cookies. Perhaps small changes in the presentation of food could have cascading effects on the amount people eat and eventually contribute to healthier lifestyles.

likely burned many more calories than modern people need. In addition, learned associations of food with a particular time and place are characteristic of many organisms, including humans. If it is noon, we eat lunch; if we're in a movie theater, we eat popcorn.

Of particular concern in the battle over obesity is *how much* people eat—the size of the portions consumed (Fruhwürth & others, 2018). Indeed, growing portion sizes have been implicated in the alarming rates of obesity in the United States (Keenan & others, 2018; Kling & others, 2016). It is puzzling, though, that portion size affects eating habits. After all, a person does not have to eat all of the food on the plate. Why do people eat an entire portion of food when just a bit of it might have led to the same feeling of fullness?

Of course, parents often teach their children to "finish what's on your plate." Many people eat automatically and rely not on a feeling of fullness but rather on the sight of an empty plate or bowl as the cue to stop eating (Hetherington & Blundell-Birtill, 2018). Consider that since 1960, the average surface area of a dinner plate has increased by 36 percent (Klatell, 2012). Larger plates can change perceptions of what constitutes a meal so that cleaning one's plate means eating more and more food. People's perceptions of the amount of food it takes to make "a serving" can have consequences for their eating intentions. To read about research examining this possibility, see the Intersection.

*Uruguayan model Eliana Ramos posed for the camera in her native country. Tragically, the super-thin Eliana died at age 18 in February 2007, two years after this picture was taken, reportedly from health problems associated with anorexia nervosa.*

©Ricardo Figueredo/AP Images

Dieting is a continuing U.S. obsession. However, some people try to lose weight not because they want to improve their health but because they have an eating disorder, the topic we turn to next.

## Disordered Eating

For some people, concerns about weight and body image become a serious, debilitating disorder. For such individuals, the very act of eating is an arena where a variety of complex biological, psychological, and cultural issues are played out, often with tragic consequences.

A number of famous people have coped with eating disorders, including Paula Abdul, Mary-Kate Olsen, Kelly Clarkson, and Demi Lovato. Eating disorders are characterized by extreme disturbances in eating behavior–from eating very, very little to eating a great deal. In this section we examine three eating disorders–anorexia nervosa, bulimia nervosa, and binge eating disorder.

### ANOREXIA NERVOSA

● **anorexia nervosa** An eating disorder that involves the relentless pursuit of thinness through starvation.

**Anorexia nervosa** is an eating disorder that involves the relentless pursuit of thinness through starvation. According to the National Institute of Mental Health (NIMH), anorexia nervosa is much more common in girls and women than boys and men and affects between 0.5 and 3.7 percent of young women (NIMH, 2016a). The American Psychiatric Association (2013a) lists these main characteristics of anorexia nervosa:

- Severely restricted food intake in the pursuit of significantly low body weight compared to what is considered normal for age and height, and refusal to maintain weight at a healthy level.
- An intense fear of gaining weight that does not decrease with weight loss.
- A distorted body image. Even when individuals with anorexia nervosa are extremely thin, they never think they are thin enough.

Over time, anorexia nervosa can lead to physical changes, such as the growth of fine hair all over the body, thinning of bones and hair, severe constipation, and low blood pressure (NIMH, 2016a). Dangerous and even life-threatening complications of anorexia nervosa include damage to the heart and thyroid. Anorexia nervosa is said to have the highest mortality rate of any psychological disorder: about 5.6 percent of individuals with anorexia nervosa die within 10 years of diagnosis (Himmerich & others, 2018; NIMH, 2016a).

Anorexia nervosa typically begins in the teenage years, often following an episode of dieting and some type of life stress (Mason & others, 2018; Nagl & others, 2016). Most individuals with anorexia nervosa are non-Latino White female adolescents or young adults from well-educated middle- and upper-income families (Darcy, 2012; Dodge, 2012). They are often high-achieving perfectionists (Buzzichelli & others, 2018). In addition to perfectionism, obsessive thinking about weight and compulsive exercise are related to anorexia nervosa (Young & others, 2018). Stress is associated with disordered eating in ethnic minority college students (Kwan, Gordon, & Minnich, 2018).

### BULIMIA NERVOSA

● **bulimia nervosa** An eating disorder in which the individual (typically female) consistently follows a binge-and-purge eating pattern.

**Bulimia nervosa** is an eating disorder in which an individual (typically female) consistently follows a binge-and-purge eating pattern. The individual goes on an eating binge and then purges by self-induced vomiting or the use of laxatives. Most people with bulimia nervosa are preoccupied with food, have a strong fear of becoming overweight, and are depressed or anxious (Slade & others, 2018). Because bulimia nervosa occurs in people of normal weight, the disorder is often difficult to detect. A person with bulimia nervosa usually keeps the disorder a secret and experiences a great deal of self-disgust and shame (Blythin & others, 2018).

Bulimia nervosa can lead to complications such as a chronic sore throat, kidney problems, dehydration, gastrointestinal disorders, and dental problems, as persistent exposure to the stomach acids in vomit can wear away tooth enamel (Panico & others, 2018).

Bulimia nervosa typically begins in late adolescence or early adulthood (Uher & Rutter, 2012). The disorder affects between 1 and 4 percent of young women (NIMH, 2016a). Many young women who develop bulimia nervosa are highly perfectionistic (Kehayes & others, 2018). At the same time, they tend to have low levels of self-efficacy (Slade & others, 2018). In other words, these are young women who have very high standards but very low confidence that they can achieve their goals.

Impulsivity, negative emotion, and childhood obsessive-compulsive tendencies (see the chapter "Psychological Disorders") are also related to bulimia (Fischer & others, 2018; Hofer & others, 2018; Schaumberg & others, 2019). Bulimia nervosa is associated, too, with sexual and physical abuse in childhood (Lo Sauro & others, 2008; Nagata & others, 2018).

## ANOREXIA NERVOSA AND BULIMIA NERVOSA: CAUSES AND TREATMENTS

What is the etiology (cause) of anorexia nervosa and bulimia nervosa? For many years researchers thought that sociocultural factors, such as media images of very thin women and family pressures, were the central determinant of these disorders (Le Grange, 2016). Media images that glorify extreme thinness can influence women's body image, and emphasis on the thin ideal is related to anorexia nervosa and bulimia nervosa (Carr & Peebles, 2012). However, as powerful as these media messages might be, countless girls and women are exposed to media images of unrealistically thin women, but relatively few develop eating disorders; and many young women embark on diets, but comparatively few of them develop eating disorders.

Furthermore, eating disorders occur in cultures that do not emphasize the ideal of thinness, although the disorders may differ from Western descriptions. For instance, in Eastern cultures, individuals can show the symptoms of anorexia nervosa, but they lack the fear of getting fat that is common in North Americans with the disorder (Pike, Yamamiya, & Konishi, 2011).

Since the 1980s, researchers have moved beyond a sole focus on sociocultural factors and have increasingly probed the potential biological underpinnings of these disorders. This research has examined the interplay of social and biological factors in eating disorders. Genes play a substantial role in both anorexia nervosa and bulimia nervosa (Huckins & others, 2018; Thornton & others, 2018). In fact, genes influence many psychological characteristics (for example, perfectionism, impulsivity, obsessive-compulsive tendencies, thinness drive) and behaviors (restrained eating, binge eating, self-induced vomiting) that are associated with anorexia nervosa and bulimia nervosa (Yilmaz & others, 2018). These genes are also factors in the regulation of serotonin, and problems in regulating serotonin are related to both anorexia nervosa and bulimia nervosa (Mayhew & others, 2018).

Keep in mind that even as biological factors play a role in the emergence of eating disorders, eating disorders themselves affect the body, including the brain (Lavagnino & others, 2018; Monteleone & others, 2018; Nickel & others, 2018). Although social factors and experiences may play a role in triggering dieting, the physical effects of dieting, bingeing, and purging may change the neural networks that then sustain the disordered pattern in a kind of vicious cycle. In terms of social factors, problems in family functioning are increasingly thought to be involved in the appearance of eating disorders in adolescence (Wallis & others, 2018).

Although anorexia and bulimia nervosa are serious disorders, recovery is possible (Nickel & others, 2018). Anorexia nervosa may require hospitalization. The first target of intervention is promoting weight gain, in extreme cases through the use of a feeding tube (Kezelman & others, 2018). A common obstacle in the treatment of anorexia nervosa is that individuals with the disorder deny that anything is wrong (Dalle Grave &

*Unlike individuals with anorexia nervosa or bulimia nervosa, most people with binge eating disorder (BED) are overweight or obese.*

©Digital Vision/Getty Images

others, 2016; Wilson, Grilo, & Vitousek, 2007). Psychotherapy, family therapy, and drug treatments have been shown to be effective in treating anorexia nervosa and bulimia nervosa (Brockmeyer, Friederich, & Schmidt, 2018; Mogorovich & Caltabiano, 2018). Newer treatments for anorexia nervosa may involve noninvasive brain stimulation (Costanzo & others, 2018).

## BINGE EATING DISORDER

**Binge eating disorder (BED)** is characterized by recurrent episodes of eating more food in a short period of time than most people would eat and during which the person feels a lack of control over eating (Udo & Grilo, 2018). Individuals with BED do not try to compensate for what they have eaten by purging (APA, 2013a). Most individuals with BED are overweight or obese (McCuen-Wurst, Ruggieri, & Allison, 2018).

Individuals with BED frequently eat alone because of embarrassment or guilt, and they feel ashamed and disgusted with themselves after bingeing. The most common of all eating disorders, BED affects a broader range of ethnic groups within the United States than anorexia nervosa or bulimia nervosa (Azarbad & others, 2010). It is more common among women than men (Udo & Grilo, 2018). An estimated 2 to 5 percent of Americans will suffer from BED in their lifetime (NIMH, 2016a).

Binge eating disorder is thought to characterize approximately 8 percent of individuals who are obese. Unlike obese individuals who do not suffer from BED, binge eaters are more likely to place great value on their physical appearance, weight, and body shape (Grilo, Masheb, & White, 2010). The complications of BED are those of obesity more generally, including diabetes, hypertension, and cardiovascular disease.

● **binge eating disorder (BED)** An eating disorder characterized by recurrent episodes of eating more food in a short period of time than most people would eat and during which the person feels a lack of control over eating.

## BINGE EATING DISORDER: CAUSES AND TREATMENTS

Researchers are examining the role of biological and psychological factors in BED. Genes play a role, as does dopamine, the neurotransmitter related to reward pathways in the brain (Qasim & others, 2018; Romer & others, 2018). The fact that binge eating often occurs after stressful events suggests that binge eaters use food to regulate their emotions (Smith & others, 2018). The areas of the brain and endocrine system that respond to stress are overactive in individuals with BED (Klump & others, 2018; Mendoza, 2018). Individuals with BED may be more likely to perceive events as stressful and then seek to manage that stress by binge eating. Research using fMRI also found that the areas of the brain involved in self-regulation and impulse control, especially the prefrontal cortex, showed diminished activity in individuals with binge eating disorder (Balodis & others, 2013; Kessler & others, 2016).

Few researchers have explored the role of sociocultural factors in binge eating disorder. One study examined whether exposure to U.S. culture might increase the risk of developing BED (Swanson & others, 2012). With the research controlled for a variety of factors, the results showed that Mexican Americans and Mexicans who had immigrated to the United States were more likely to develop BED than were Mexicans who lived in Mexico (Swanson & others, 2012).

Just as treatment for anorexia nervosa first focuses on weight gain, some believe that treatment for BED should first target weight loss (Barnes & others, 2018; De Angelis, 2002). Others argue that individuals with BED must be treated for disordered eating per se, and they insist that if the underlying psychological issues are not addressed, weight loss will not be successful or permanent (de Zwaan & others, 2005; Hay & others, 2009). Research indicates that drugs targeting the functioning of the neurotransmitters serotonin and norepinephrine show some promise in treating BED (Marazziti & others, 2012; McElroy & others, 2018).

Food is unquestionably necessary for survival. Individuals struggling with disordered eating must change their relationship with this vital resource in order to survive and, eventually, thrive. Clearly, though, thriving involves more than food. We next turn to the broader implications of motivation in everyday life.

### *test yourself*

1. In Cannon and Washburn's classic study on hunger, what bodily associations were revealed?
2. What is leptin, and how does it function in the body?
3. What are some key ways that bulimia nervosa and binge eating disorder differ?

# 3. APPROACHES TO MOTIVATION IN EVERYDAY LIFE

Think about the wide range of human actions and achievements, such as Robert Engle's heroism from the opening of this chapter. Such behaviors are not easily explained by motivational approaches that focus on physiological needs. Increasingly, psychologists are recognizing the role of goals that people set for themselves in motivation. In this section, we explore the ways that psychologists have come to understand the processes that underlie everyday human behavior.

## Maslow's Hierarchy of Human Needs

Humanistic theorist Abraham Maslow (1954, 1971) proposed a **hierarchy of needs** that must be satisfied in the following sequence: physiological needs, safety, love and belongingness, esteem, and self-actualization (Figure 3). The strongest needs are at the base of the hierarchy (physiological), and the weakest are at the top (self-actualization).

● **hierarchy of needs** Maslow's theory that human needs must be satisfied in the following sequence: physiological needs, safety, love and belongingness, esteem, and self-actualization.

According to this hierarchy, people are motivated to satisfy their need for food first and to fulfill their need for safety before their need for love. If we think of our needs as calls for action, hunger and safety needs shout loudly, whereas the need for self-actualization beckons with a whisper. Maslow asserted that each lower need in the hierarchy comes from a deficiency–such as being hungry, afraid, or lonely–and that we can only see the higher-level needs in a person who has satisfied to some extent these most basic needs. Such an individual can then turn his or her attention to the fulfillment of a higher calling.

● **self-actualization** The motivation to develop one's full potential as a human being—the highest and most elusive of Maslow's proposed needs.

**Self-actualization**, the highest and most elusive of Maslow's needs, is the motivation to develop one's full potential as a human being. According to Maslow, self-actualization is possible only after the other needs in the hierarchy are met. Maslow cautions that most people stop moving up the hierarchy after they have developed a high level of esteem and do not become self-actualized.

The idea that human motives are hierarchically arranged is appealing; however, Maslow's ordering of the needs is debatable. Some people, for example, might seek greatness in a career to achieve self-esteem, while putting on hold their needs for love and belongingness. Certainly history is full of examples of individuals who, in the most difficult circumstances, were still able to engage in acts of kindness that seem to come from higher-level needs. Often, the individuals with the least financial resources are most likely to give generously to others (Manstead, 2018).

Another controversy surrounding Maslow's hierarchy of needs is the extent to which it originates with his own thinking. Specifically, Maslow's hierarchy appears to derive from a hierarchy that is part of the tradition of the Blackfoot Nation, a First Nation (or native tribe) of Canada. From the Blackfoot perspective, the triangle that you are studying was actually a *tipi*. The Blackfoot perspective on life includes the notions of self-actualization (though it provided the foundational bottom of the hierarchy). The possibility that Maslow borrowed these ideas without acknowledging their origin is supported by the fact that he spent time on a Blackfoot reservation prior to presenting his hierarchy (Lokensgard, 2014).

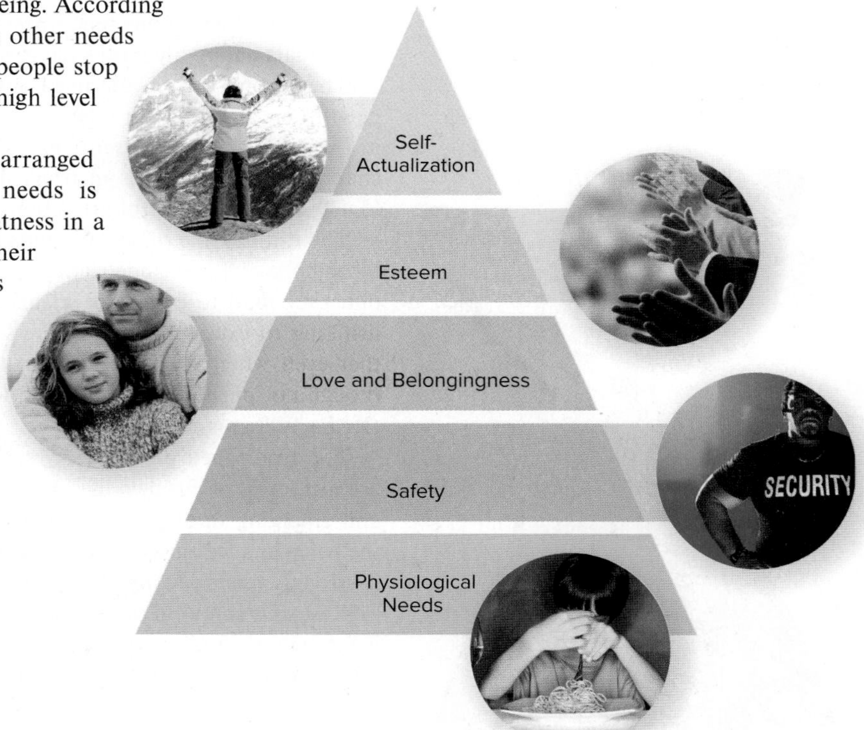


**FIGURE 3** **Maslow's Hierarchy of Needs** Abraham Maslow developed the hierarchy of human needs to show that we must satisfy basic physiological needs before we can satisfy other, higher needs. Later in his career, Maslow added self-transcendence to the top of the hierarchy. With this stage, he indicated that the very highest level of motivation involved service to others. (mountaintop photo) ©Photogl/iStock/Getty Images; (clapping photo) ©Brand X Pictures/PunchStock; (couple photo) ©Digital Vision; (security guard photo) ©Brand X Pictures; (boy with plate of food photo) ©Brooke Fasani/Corbis

Perhaps Maslow's greatest contribution to our understanding of motivation is that he asked the key question about motivation for modern people: How can we explain what humans do, once their bellies are full? That is, how do we explain the "why" of human behavior when survival is not the most pressing need? This is the kind of questioning that inspired *self-determination theory* (Ryan & Deci, 2017).

## Self-Determination Theory

● **self-determination theory** Ryan and Deci's theory asserting that all humans have three basic, innate organismic needs: competence, relatedness, and autonomy.

Psychologists Edward Deci and Richard Ryan have explored the role of motivation in optimal human functioning from a perspective that emphasizes particular kinds of needs as factors in psychological and physical well-being (Ryan & Deci, 2017). Their **self-determination theory** asserts that there are three basic organismic needs: competence, relatedness, and autonomy. The word *organismic* here means that these psychological needs are innate and exist in every person. They are basic to human growth and functioning, just as water, soil, and sunshine are necessary for plant growth. This metaphor is especially apt, because once we plant a seed, all it requires to thrive and grow is a supportive environment. Similarly, self-determination theory holds that we all have the capacity for growth and fulfillment within us, ready to emerge if given the right context.

Importantly, from the perspective of self-determination theory, these organismic needs do not arise from deficits. Self-determination theory is not a drive reduction theory. Ryan and Deci (2017) argue that these needs concern personal growth, not the filling of deficiencies. Let's examine each of these needs in depth.

The first organismic need described by self-determination theory, *competence,* is met when we feel that we are able to bring about desired outcomes. Competence motivation involves *self-efficacy* (the belief that you have the competence to accomplish a given goal or task) and *mastery* (the sense that you can gain skills and overcome obstacles). One domain in which competence needs may be met is in the realm of achievement. Some individuals are highly motivated to succeed and spend considerable effort striving to excel.

The second organismic need described by self-determination theory is *relatedness*—the need to engage in warm relations with other people. The need for relatedness is reflected in the importance of parents nurturing children's development, the intimate moments of sharing private thoughts in friendship, the uncomfortable feelings we have when we are lonely, and the powerful attraction we experience when we are in love.

The critical role of social bonds is also demonstrated in research examining the effects of being socially excluded (Bossi, Gallucci, & Ricciardelli, 2018). When people are left out, they tend to engage in a variety of self-defeating behaviors, such as overeating and drinking to excess (Jiang & others, 2018; Meisel & others, 2018). Research has shown that even when the exclusion is unintentional (for instance, when someone is ignored, though not purposely), it can lead to distress and the feeling that one's life is meaningless (K. D. Williams, 2012).

©Rubberball/Getty Images

The third need proposed by self-determination theory is *autonomy*—the sense that we are in control of our own life. Autonomy means feeling that one's behavior is self-motivated and emerging from genuine interest (Vansteenkiste & others, 2018). Of course, many of the behaviors we engage in may feel like things we are forced to do, but a sense of autonomy is strongly related to well-being (Yang, Zhang, & Sheldon, 2018).

Research supports the idea that progress on goals that serve the three organismic needs is strongly related to well-being (Werner & Milyavskaya, 2018; Zhang, Chen, & Schlegel, 2018). Further, valuing more extrinsic qualities—such as money, prestige, and physical appearance—over these organismic concerns is associated with decreased well-being, decreased self-actualization, and physical illness (Kasser & others, 2004; Steel & others, 2018b).

Self-determination theory maintains that one of the most important aspects of healthy motivation is the sense that we do the things we do because we have freely chosen to do them. When we can choose our behaviors and feel ownership over those choices, we are likely to experience heightened fulfillment (Diseth, Breidablik, & Meland, 2018; Ryan & Deci, 2017).

From the self-determination theory perspective, when our behaviors serve the needs for competence, autonomy, and relatedness, we experience intrinsic motivation (Rigby & Ryan, 2018). When our behavior, instead, serves needs for other values—such as prestige, money, or approval—our behavior is extrinsically motivated. We examine this important distinction between intrinsic and extrinsic motivation next.

## Intrinsic Versus Extrinsic Motivation

One way psychologists understand the "why" of our goals is by distinguishing between intrinsic and extrinsic motivation. **Intrinsic motivation** is based on internal factors such as organismic needs (competence, relatedness, and autonomy), as well as curiosity, challenge, and fun (Woolley & Fishbach, 2018). When we are intrinsically motivated, we engage in a behavior because we enjoy it. **Extrinsic motivation** involves external incentives such as rewards and punishments. When we are extrinsically motivated, we engage in a behavior for some external payoff or to avoid an external punishment.

- **intrinsic motivation** Motivation based on internal factors such as organismic needs (competence, relatedness, and autonomy), as well as curiosity, challenge, and fun.

- **extrinsic motivation** Motivation that involves external incentives such as rewards and punishments.

Some students study hard because they are internally motivated to put forth considerable effort and achieve high quality in their work (intrinsic motivation). Other students study hard because they want to make good grades or avoid parental disapproval (extrinsic motivation). Many psychologists believe that intrinsic motivation leads to more positive outcomes than extrinsic motivation (Rigby & Ryan, 2018). They argue that intrinsic motivation is more likely to produce competent behavior and mastery.

Many very successful individuals are both intrinsically motivated (they have high personal standards of achievement and emphasize personal effort) and extrinsically motivated (they are strongly competitive). Indeed, many of us might think of the ideal occupation as one in which we get paid (an extrinsic reward) for doing something we love to do (intrinsic motivation).

## Self-Regulation: The Successful Pursuit of Goals

Today many psychologists approach motivation in the way that you yourself might—by asking about the goals a person is trying to accomplish in everyday life.

Goal approaches to motivation include the concept of self-regulation. **Self-regulation** is the process by which an organism effortfully controls behavior in order to pursue important objectives (Carver & Scheier, 2013). A key aspect of self-regulation is getting feedback about how we are doing in our goal pursuits. Our daily mood has been proposed as a way that we may receive this feedback—that is, we feel good or bad depending on how we are doing in the areas of life we value. Note that the role of mood in self-regulation means that we cannot be happy all the time. In order to effectively pursue our goals, we have to be open to the bad news that might occasionally come our way (Tangney, Boone, & Baumeister, 2018).

- **self-regulation** The process by which an organism effortfully controls behavior in order to pursue important objectives.

Putting our personal goals into action is a potentially complex process that involves setting goals, planning for their implementation, and monitoring our progress. Individuals' success improves when they set goals that are specific and moderately challenging (Bandura, 1997; Schunk, 2012). A fuzzy, nonspecific goal is "I want to be successful." A concrete, specific goal is "I want to have a 3.5 average at the end of the semester."

Accomplishing long-term goals is facilitated by the pursuit of short-term goals. When you set long-term goals, such as "I want to be a clinical psychologist," make sure that you also create short-term goals as steps along the way, such as "I want to get an *A* on my next psychology test." Planning how to reach a goal and monitoring progress toward the goal are critical aspects of achievement. Make commitments in manageable chunks. High-achieving individuals monitor their own learning and systematically evaluate their progress toward their goals more than do low-achieving individuals (Harkin & others, 2016).

Even as we keep our nose to the grindstone in pursuing short-term goals, it is also important to have a sense of the big picture. Dedication to a long-term dream or personal

U.S. soccer star Carli Lloyd and her teammates provide role models for many American girls and boys.



mission can enhance one's sense of purpose in life. Although short-term goals can provide a feeling of accomplishment, attaching these goals to a future dream can allow individuals to experience a sense of meaning and to maintain their efforts in the face of short-term failure (Houser-Marko & Sheldon, 2008).

One way we can witness the payoff of goal pursuit is to look to individuals who have achieved the life dreams we seek. A young girl trying to become a great soccer midfielder might watch Carli Lloyd in action. A budding politician running for campus office might watch great speeches by John F. Kennedy, Ronald Reagan, or Barack Obama. Role models can be powerful sources of inspiration (Hui & Lent, 2018; McPherson, Park, & Ito, 2018; Tu & others, 2018).

A key concept in understanding how individuals successfully pursue goals is *delay of gratification*—putting off a pleasurable experience in the interest of some larger but later reward. Successful delay of gratification is evident in the student who does not go out with friends but instead stays in and studies for an upcoming test, perhaps thinking, "There will be plenty of time to party after this test is over."

Delay of gratification is challenging. Think about it—future payoffs are simply much less certain than current rewards. In a situation where rewards are few and far between, it might make sense to eat, drink, or be merry based on whatever is around right now.

Walter Mischel and his colleagues examined how children managed to delay gratification, in what have become known as the Stanford marshmallow experiments (Mischel, Shoda, & Peake, 1988; Mischel, Shoda, & Rodriguez, 1989). They placed children in a difficult situation—alone in a room with a very tempting marshmallow within reach. The children were told that if they wanted to, at any time they could ring a bell and eat the marshmallow. Otherwise, they could wait until the experimenter returned, and then they would get two marshmallows. The children were then left alone to face this self-control dilemma. In truth, the experimenter was not coming back. The researchers were interested in measuring how long the children could wait before giving in to temptation and eating the marshmallow.

There were a variety of responses to this unusual situation. Some children sat dead still, focused on the tempting marshmallow. Some stared the marshmallow down. Some smelled the marshmallow. Others turned away, sang songs, picked their nose, or did anything but pay attention to the marshmallow.

How did the children who were able to resist temptation do it? Mischel and colleagues found that the kids who were able to distract themselves from the marshmallow by focusing on "cool thoughts" (that is, non-marshmallow-related things) were better able to delay gratification. In contrast, children who remained focused on the marshmallow and all its delightful qualities—what Mischel called "hot thoughts"—ate the marshmallow sooner (Metcalfe & Mischel, 1999).

These findings have implications for self-control. Imagine that you are in a long-term romantic relationship that you wish to continue, and you meet an appealing new person to whom you are physically attracted. Should you cultivate a friendship with him or her? Maybe not, if you want to avoid temptation and preserve your current relationship. Think about all the current and potential "marshmallows" in your life—those things that have the power to distract you from achieving your long-term plans. Mischel's research with children demonstrates that avoiding these hot issues might be a good way to see a long-term plan through to its completion.

Interestingly, Mischel and his colleagues continued to study those children for many years. They found that the amount of time the children were able to delay gratification predicted their academic performance in high school and college (Mischel, 2004) and even their self-regulation skills in their 40s (Casey & others, 2011; Mischel & others, 2011). The results of these studies are striking, but recent research has called into the question the links between this single act of delay of gratification and life outcomes. To read about that work, see the Critical Controversy.

Self-regulation can be challenging. Two things that are associated with particularly poor self-regulation are impulsivity and procrastination. *Impulsivity* is the tendency to act rashly, without thinking or planning. Impulsive individuals have trouble dealing with temptation and successfully sticking to their long-term goals in a variety of domains (Bart, Abramson, & Alloy, 2018).

## Does It Matter How Long a Child Waits for That Second Marshmallow?

The famous marshmallow studies have become the stuff of psychological legend. Chances are you have seen the videos on *YouTube*. Despite their popularity and intuitive appeal, the studies have important limitations. First, compared with today's standards, the number of children in the studies falls far short. For example, the first study demonstrating this effect included only 95 children (Mischel, Shoda, & Peake, 1988). Even later investigations rarely included more than 100 children in a given study (Carlson & others, 2018). In addition, all of the children from the first study came from same preschool at Stanford University. These children were, then, likely to be the offspring of faculty, graduate students, and students associated with an elite institution of higher education. Subsequent studies have included mostly White and upper-middle-class children from large cities (New York, San Francisco, Seattle) in the United States (Carlson & others, 2018). These features of the studies are concerning, calling into question the degree to which this classic effect can be replicated and generalized. Would a larger and more diverse sample produce similar results?

©Anthony Rosenberg/iStock/Getty Images

Recently, a team of investigators set out to test whether the marshmallow study results would replicate in a diverse sample of over 900 children (Watts, Duncan, & Quan, 2018). The children were 4 years old when they participated in a delay of gratification task modeled on the original task. The treats were selected among those known to be favored by the kids. Each child was given the standard instructions: If they wanted to, at any time, they could ring a bell and eat the treat. Alternatively, they could wait for the experimenter to return and get two treats. Children were left in the room alone with the treat for 7 minutes maximum. The time children waited was recorded. Then, the researchers followed up on the children in the first grade and again at age 15. They collected information about academic achievement and behavioral problems (provided by mothers). In addition, the researchers obtained information about family social class, such as parental education and income.

The results showed that the amount of time children waited was only very weakly related to outcomes in first grade and was not related to outcomes at age 15. More importantly, the differences that emerged among the children in their capacity to delay gratification was explained almost entirely by social class. The researchers reasoned that poorer children may take what they can get when they can get it (Watts, Duncan, & Quan, 2018); after all, who knows if that second treat is really coming? Children who do not live in a world filled with ready access to treats might be more likely to jump the gun, ring the bell, and eat the treat more quickly. In addition, it may be that children from more advantaged backgrounds actually receive explicit training in waiting for rewards in an otherwise reward-rich environment.

Aside from the failure to replicate a classic finding, the study showed two additional interesting findings. First, *most kids* were able to wait the full 7 minutes, regardless of social class. The second interesting finding concerned the timing of eating the treat and outcomes at age 15. Children unable to wait for 20 seconds showed some problems at age 15. This result suggests that rather than having to struggle to delay, a child might only have to wait 20 seconds to demonstrate self-control.

Although it may be the case that failing to replicate the marshmallow study is a disappointment, for many this result has been greeted with relief. Even among those of us who would have eaten that marshmallow, the crime of doing so does not lead to a life sentence of low levels of self control.

**WHAT DO YOU THINK?**

- How long do you think you would have waited for the treat, as a child?
- What factors, other than social class, might affect a person's capacity to delay gratification?

---

Evolutionary explanations for the existence of impulsivity suggest that, in the harsh environments where they lived, early humans had to meet their survival needs quickly (Del Giudice, 2018). The modern world, however, poses different challenges, requiring people to manage multiple long-term goals. In such a context, impulsivity may lead to negative self-regulatory outcomes. But impulsivity paid off for our ancestors. This evolutionary explanation is supported by the fact that impulsivity is moderately heritable. Genetic variation explains about half of the differences we see in impulsivity (Gray & others, 2018).

## test yourself

1. What is Maslow's hierarchy of needs? Explain.
2. What is self-actualization, according to Maslow, and on what does it depend?
3. How do intrinsic motivation and extrinsic motivation differ?

*Procrastination* means intentionally putting off actions on a goal (Kaftan & Freund, 2018; van Eerde & Klingsieck, 2018). We have all experienced it: You really wanted tickets to that concert, but you waited until the last minute and it sold out. Although it is common, procrastination is a bit of a puzzle. If we really want something, why would we postpone trying to get it?

At first blush, it might seem that impulsivity and procrastination are almost opposites. After all, impulsivity means doing something quickly without thought, and procrastination means thinking about something but not doing anything. Nevertheless, these two characteristics are related, with procrastinators scoring highly on measures of impulsivity (Steel & others, 2018a; Wiklund, Yu, & Patzelt, 2018).

# 4. EMOTION

The concept of self-regulation suggests that motivation and emotion are closely linked. We feel happy or sad depending on how events influence the likelihood of our getting the things we want in life. Our emotions tell us what really matters to us. We might think, for instance, that we have lost interest in a romantic partner until that person initiates a breakup. Suddenly, we realize how much the person really means to us.

● **emotion** Feeling, or affect, that can involve physiological arousal (such as a fast heartbeat), conscious experience (thinking about being in love with someone), and behavioral expression (a smile or grimace).

Emotions are complex. The body, the mind, and the face play key roles in emotion, although psychologists debate which of these components is most significant in emotion and how they mix to produce emotional experiences. For our purposes, **emotion** is feeling, or affect, that can involve physiological arousal (such as a fast heartbeat), conscious experience (feeling joy), and behavioral expression (a smile).

## Biological Factors in Emotion

A friend whom you have been counseling about a life problem texts you, "r u home? On my way over." You get nervous. What could be going on? You feel burdened–you have a lot of work to do, and you do not have time for a talk session. When he arrives with a gift-wrapped package and a big smile, your nerves give way to relief. He announces, "Here's a present to say thanks for all your help." Your heart warms, and you feel a strong sense of your enduring bond with him. As you moved through the emotions of worry, relief, and joy, your body changed. Indeed, the body is a crucial part of our emotional experience.

©Ebtikar/Shutterstock

### THE AUTONOMIC NERVOUS SYSTEM

Recall from the chapter "Biological Foundations of Behavior" that the *autonomic nervous system (ANS)* takes messages to and from the body's internal organs, monitoring such processes as breathing, heart rate, and digestion. The ANS is divided into the sympathetic and the parasympathetic nervous systems (Figure 4). The *sympathetic nervous system (SNS)* is responsible for rapid reactions to threats. SNS arousal causes increased blood pressure, faster heart rate, more rapid breathing, and more efficient blood flow to the brain and major muscle groups. These changes prepare us for action, the "fight or flight" response. In contrast, the *parasympathetic nervous system (PNS)* calms the body, promoting processes of maintenance and healing. When the PNS is activated, blood pressure drops, heart rate and breathing slow, and food digestion increases, which is the "rest and digest" response. These two sides of the autonomic nervous system can be easy to confuse. Be sure to closely review Figure 4.

The sympathetic and parasympathetic nervous systems evolved to improve the human species' likelihood for survival. Importantly, it does not take a life-threatening situation to activate the SNS response. Just thinking about a stressful situation can activate the SNS. In addition, *emotions* are associated with SNS arousal, suggesting that such arousal plays a role in emotional experience.

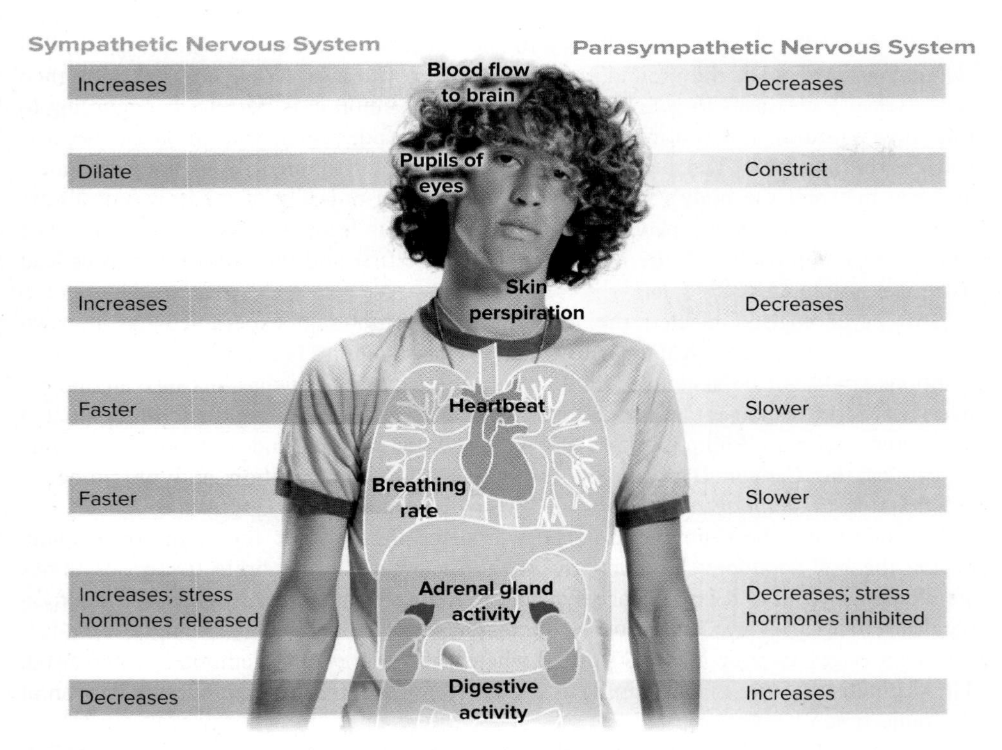


**FIGURE 4 The Autonomic Nervous System and Its Role in Arousing and Calming the Body** The two parts of the autonomic nervous system work in different ways. The sympathetic nervous system arouses the body in reaction to a stressor, evoking the "fight or flight" response. In contrast, the parasympathetic nervous system calms the body, promoting relaxation and healing. Remember, the latter system functions to "rest and digest."
©James Woodson/Getty Images

## MEASURING SNS ACTIVITY

Clearly, when the SNS is active, the body jumps into action. How might we measure these changes? One way psychologists have measured this arousal is *skin conductance level (SCL),* a rise in the skin's electrical conductivity when sweat gland activity increases. A sweaty palm conducts electricity better than a dry one. This difference provides the basis for SCL as a measure of autonomic arousal.

Another measure of arousal is the **polygraph** or lie detector, a machine examiners use to try to determine whether someone is lying. The polygraph monitors changes in the body—heart rate, breathing, and SCL—thought to be influenced by emotional states. In a typical polygraph test, the examiner asks the individual a number of neutral questions and several key, less neutral questions. If the individual's heart rate, breathing, and SCL responses increase substantially when the key questions are asked, the individual is assumed to be lying (Grubin, 2010).

• **polygraph** A machine, commonly called a lie detector, that monitors changes in the body, used to try to determine whether someone is lying.

How accurate is the lie detector? Experts argue that the polygraph errs just under 50 percent of the time (Iacono & Ben-Shakhar, 2018). The problem with the polygraph is that heart rate, breathing, and SCL can increase for reasons other than lying—for instance, because a person is *nervous* (not necessarily guilty). For this reason, the Employee Polygraph Protection Act of 1988 restricts polygraph testing outside of government agencies, and most courts do not accept the results of polygraph testing.

## THEORIES OF EMOTION

Imagine that you and your date are enjoying a picnic in the country. Suddenly, a bull runs across the field toward you. Why are you afraid? Two well-known theories of emotion that involve physiological processes provide answers to this question.

Common sense tells you that you are trembling and running away from the bull because you are afraid, but William James (1950) and Carl Lange (pronounced "Long-uh") (1922) said emotion works in the opposite way. According to the **James–Lange theory**, emotion results from physiological states triggered by stimuli in the environment: Emotion occurs *after* physiological reactions. This perspective holds that emotions are not mental events that lead to reactions; instead, physiological reactions lead to emotional states. Lange especially emphasized that each emotion—from anger to rapture—has a distinct set of physiological changes, evident in changes in heart rate, breathing patterns, sweating, and other responses.

• **James–Lange theory** The theory that emotion results from physiological states triggered by stimuli in the environment.

Let's apply the James-Lange theory to the situation with the bull. You see the bull scratching its hoof on the ground, and you begin to run away. Your aroused body then sends sensory messages to your brain, at which point emotion is perceived. According to this theory, you do not run away because you are afraid; rather, you are afraid because you are running away. You perceive a stimulus in the environment, your body responds, and you interpret the body's reaction as emotion. This ordering of events is not always easy to understand. Many people think of emotions as leading to bodily changes. The James-Lange approach says the bodily changes come first and then those responses lead us to feel an emotion.

Two psychologists rejected the idea that each emotional experience has its own particular set of physiological changes. First, Walter Cannon (1927) argued that different emotions could not be associated with specific physiological changes because autonomic nervous system responses are too diffuse and slow to account for rapid and differentiated emotional responses. Philip Bard (1934) supported this analysis, and so the theory became known as the **Cannon-Bard theory**—the proposition that emotion and physiological reactions occur *simultaneously*.

● **Cannon–Bard theory** The proposition that emotion and physiological reactions occur simultaneously.

To understand the Cannon-Bard theory, imagine the bull and the picnic once again. Seeing the bull scratching its hoof causes the thalamus of your brain to do two things simultaneously: First, it stimulates your autonomic nervous system to produce the physiological changes involved in emotion (increased heart rate, rapid breathing); second, it sends messages to your cerebral cortex, where the experience of emotion is perceived. The distinctive feature of this approach is that it proposes that these processes happen at the same time.

Unlike the James–Lange theory, which proposes that the physical reactions come first, in the Cannon–Bard theory the body plays a less important role. Figure 5 shows how the James-Lange and Cannon-Bard theories differ. Whether emotions involve discrete autonomic nervous system responses, as Lange expected, continues to be debated.

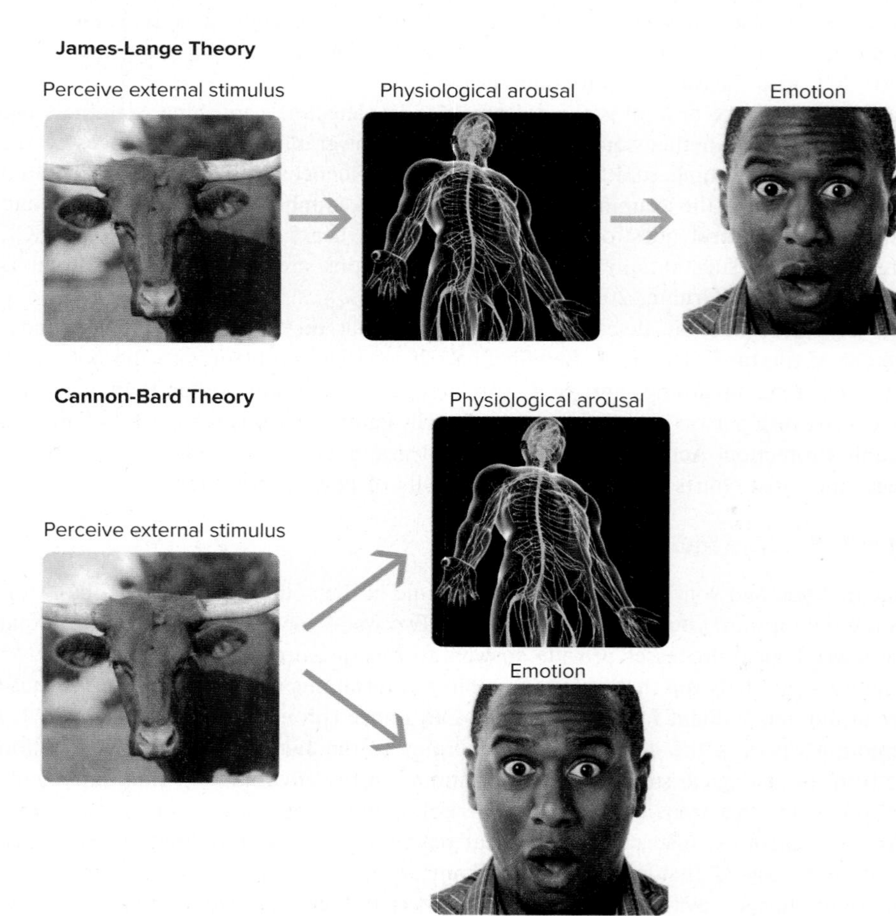


**FIGURE 5** **James–Lange and Cannon–Bard Theories** From the James–Lange perspective, the experience of fear is an outcome of physiological arousal. In the Cannon–Bard view, fear occurs at the same time as the physiological response. (longhorn) ©McGraw-Hill Education; (nervous system) ©pixologicstudio/iStock/Getty Images; (surprised face) ©drbimages/E+/Getty Images

## NEUROTRANSMITTERS AND NEURAL CIRCUITS

Contemporary researchers are keenly interested in discovering the role of neurotransmitters and charting the neural circuitry of emotions. Research suggests the involvement of neurotransmitters in emotional experience. For instance, dopamine and endorphins are linked to positive emotions such as happiness, and norepinephrine functions in regulating arousal and anxiety (Shiota & others, 2017).

With regard to the brain structures involved in emotional experience, research has focused on the limbic system and especially the amygdalae, the almond-shaped structures in the limbic system that we considered in the chapter "Biological Foundations of Behavior" (Koelsch, 2018; Pessoa, 2018). The limbic system, including the amygdalae, is involved in the experience of positive emotions (Shiota & others, 2017). However, most research has focused on the important role of the amygdalae in the experience of negative emotion, particularly fear.

Research by Joseph LeDoux and his colleagues demonstrates that the amygdalae play a central role in fear (LeDoux, 2009, 2012, 2013; LeDoux & Daw, 2018). When the amygdalae determine that danger is present, they shift into high gear, marshaling the brain's resources in an effort to protect the organism from harm. This fear system evolved to detect and respond to natural dangers that threaten survival or territory.

The brain circuitry for fear can follow two pathways: a direct pathway from the thalamus to the amygdalae or an indirect pathway from the thalamus through the sensory cortex to the amygdalae (Figure 6). The direct pathway does not convey detailed information about the stimulus, but it has the advantage of speed—and speed is a vital characteristic of information for an organism facing a threat to its survival. The indirect pathway carries nerve impulses from the sensory organs (eyes and ears, for example) to the thalamus (recall that the thalamus is a relay station for incoming sensory stimuli); from the thalamus, the nerve impulses travel to the sensory cortex, which then sends appropriate signals to the amygdalae.

The amygdalae retain fear associations for a very long time (LeDoux, 2009, 2012, 2013). This quality is useful, because once we learn that something is dangerous, we do not have to relearn it. However, we pay a penalty for this ability. Once acquired, fears may be quite difficult to unlearn.

Part of the reason fears are so difficult to change is that the amygdalae are well connected to the cerebral cortex, in which thinking and decision making primarily occur (Linnman & others, 2012). The amygdalae are in a much better position to influence the

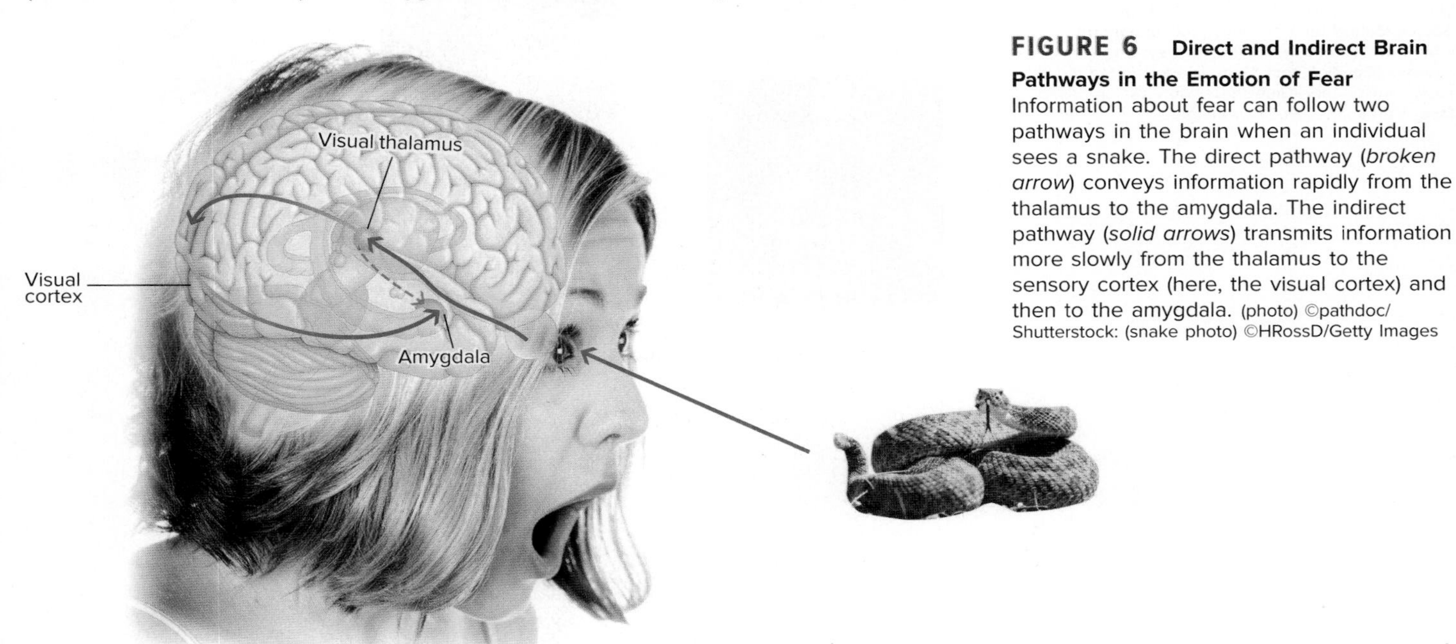


**FIGURE 6** **Direct and Indirect Brain Pathways in the Emotion of Fear** Information about fear can follow two pathways in the brain when an individual sees a snake. The direct pathway (*broken arrow*) conveys information rapidly from the thalamus to the amygdala. The indirect pathway (*solid arrows*) transmits information more slowly from the thalamus to the sensory cortex (here, the visual cortex) and then to the amygdala. (photo) ©pathdoc/Shutterstock: (snake photo) ©HRossD/Getty Images

cerebral cortex than the other way around, because they send more connections to the cerebral cortex than they get back. This may explain why it is sometimes hard to control our emotions, and why, once fear is learned, it is hard to erase.

## Cognitive Factors in Emotion

Does emotion depend on the tides of the mind? Are we happy only when we think we are happy? Cognitive theories of emotion center on the premise that emotion always has a cognitive component. Thinking is said to be responsible for feelings of love and hate, joy and sadness. Although cognitive theorists do recognize the role of the brain and body in emotion, they give cognitive processes the main credit for these responses.

### THE TWO-FACTOR THEORY OF EMOTION

● **two-factor theory of emotion** Schachter and Singer's theory that emotion is determined by two factors: physiological arousal and cognitive labeling.

In the **two-factor theory of emotion** developed by Stanley Schachter and Jerome Singer (1962), emotion is determined by two factors: physiological arousal and cognitive labeling (Figure 7). Schachter and Singer argued that we look to the external world for an explanation of *why* we are aroused. We interpret external cues and label the emotion. For example, if you feel good after someone has made a pleasant comment to you, you might label the emotion "happy." If you feel bad after you have done something wrong, you may label the feeling "guilty."

To test their theory of emotion, Schachter and Singer (1962) injected volunteer participants with epinephrine, a drug that produces high arousal. After participants received the drug, they observed someone else behave in either a euphoric way (shooting papers at a wastebasket) or an angry way (stomping out of the room). As predicted, the euphoric and angry behavior influenced the participants' cognitive interpretation of their own arousal. When they were with a happy person, they rated themselves as happy; when they were with an angry person, they said they were angry. This effect occurred, however, only when the participants were not told about the true effects of the injection. When they

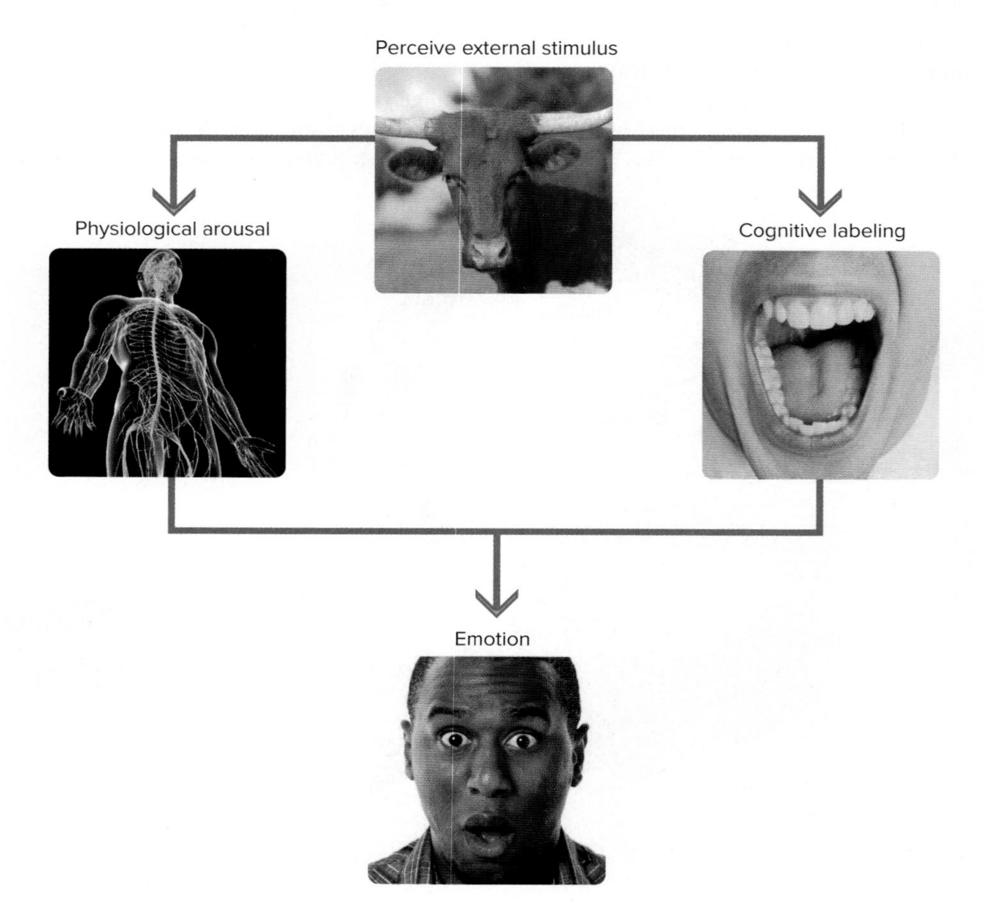


**FIGURE 7 Schachter and Singer's Two-Factor Theory of Emotion** The two-factor theory includes not only arousal but also cognitive labeling: You feel afraid of the bull because you label your physiological response "fear."
Source: Schachter & Singer (1962); (longhorn) ©McGraw-Hill Education; (nervous system) ©pixologicstudio/iStock/Getty Images; (open mouth face) ©Kristy-Anne Glubish/Design Pics; (surprised face) ©drbimages/E+/Getty Images

were told that the drug would increase their heart rate and make them jittery, they said the reason for their own arousal was the drug, not the other person's behavior. Notice, then, how external cues were only consulted if participants' feelings were ambiguous and required explanation.

The two-factor theory of emotion tells us that often our bodies send us ambiguous messages about what is going on in the world. We take those messages and look for explanations in our immediate circumstances, and that is what produces emotions. Imagine that you are late for class on an important exam day. You sprint across campus as fast as you can, arriving just in time for the test. As you look over the questions, your heart is racing, your breathing is fast, and you feel sweaty. Are you nervous about the test or just recovering from your run to the classroom? The two-factor theory suggests that you just might mistake your bodily sensations as indications that you are scared of the test.

### THE PRIMACY DEBATE: COGNITION OR EMOTION?

Which comes first, thinking or feeling? Fans of vintage episodes of TV's *Star Trek* may recognize this theme from the frequent arguments between Mr. Spock, the logical Vulcan, and Dr. McCoy, the emotional doctor on the *Enterprise*. In the 1980s and 1990s, two eminent psychologists, Richard Lazarus and Robert Zajonc, debated which was more central—cognition or emotion?

*Vintage Star Trek episodes explored the question, what comes first—thinking or feeling?*
©CBS via Getty Images

Recall from the chapter "Thinking, Intelligence, and Language" that Lazarus said that we cognitively appraise ourselves and our circumstances and that these appraisals determine how we feel about events and experiences. For Lazarus (1991), then, thinking is primary—he believed cognitive activity causes our feelings. Our appraisals—which are guided by values, goals, beliefs, and expectations—determine our emotions. Consider a student who fails a test. This event would seem to be negative to everyone. But Lazarus would say that the emotions that follow depend on appraisal. If the class is important to the student's goals, she might feel distress, but if she had been looking for a reason to change her major, she might feel relief.

Zajonc (1984) disagreed with Lazarus. Emotions are primary, he said, and our thoughts are a result of them. Zajonc famously argued that "preferences need no inferences," meaning that the way we feel about something requires no thought.

Which of the two psychologists is right? *Both* are likely correct. Lazarus talked mainly about a cluster of related events that occur over a period of time, whereas Zajonc described single events or a preference for one stimulus over another. Lazarus was concerned with love over the course of months and years, a sense of value to the community, and plans for retirement; Zajonc spoke about a car accident, an encounter with a snake, and a penchant for ice cream over spinach.

Some of our emotional reactions are virtually instantaneous and probably do not involve cognitive appraisal, such as shrieking upon detecting a snake. Other emotional circumstances, especially long-term feelings such as a depressed mood or anger toward a friend, are more likely to involve cognitive appraisal. Indeed, the direct and indirect brain pathways described earlier support the idea that some of our emotional reactions do not involve deliberate thinking, whereas others do (LeDoux, 2012).

## Behavioral Factors in Emotion

Remember that our definition of emotion includes not only physiological and cognitive components but also a behavioral component. The behavioral component can be verbal or nonverbal. Verbally, a person might show love for someone by professing it in words or might display anger by saying nasty things. Nonverbally, a person might smile, frown, show a fearful expression, or slouch.

The most interest in the behavioral dimension of emotion has focused on the nonverbal behavior of facial expressions. Emotion researchers have been intrigued by people's ability to detect emotion from a person's facial expression. In a typical research study, participants, when shown photographs like those in Figure 8, are usually able to identify six emotions: happiness, anger, sadness, surprise, disgust, and fear (Ekman & O'Sullivan, 1991).

**FIGURE 8** **Recognizing Emotions in Facial Expressions** Look at the six photographs and determine the emotion reflected in each of the six faces: (*top*) happiness, anger, sadness; (*bottom*) surprise, disgust, fear. (first) ©mheim301165/123RF; (second) ©Juanmonino/iStock/Getty Images; (third) ©Image Source; (fourth) ©gulfimages/Alamy Stock Photo; (fifth) ©Paul Burns/Digital Vision/Getty Images; (sixth) ©maurus/123RF

• **facial feedback hypothesis** The idea that facial expressions can influence emotions as well as reflect them.

Might our facial expressions not only reflect our emotions but also influence them? According to the **facial feedback hypothesis**, facial expressions can influence emotions as well as reflect them (Davis, Senghas, & Ochsner, 2009). In this view, facial muscles send signals to the brain that help us to recognize the emotion we are experiencing (Söderkvist, Ohlén, & Dimberg, 2018). For example, we feel happier when we smile and sadder when we frown. The facial feedback hypothesis provides support for the James–Lange theory of emotion discussed earlier—namely, that emotional experiences can be generated by changes in and awareness of our own bodily states.

## Sociocultural Factors in Emotion

Are the facial expressions that are associated with different emotions largely innate, or do they vary across cultures? Answering this question requires a look at research findings on sociocultural influences in emotions.

### CULTURE AND THE EXPRESSION OF EMOTION

In 1872 Charles Darwin stated in *The Expression of the Emotions in Man and Animals* that the facial expressions of human beings are innate, not learned; are the same in all cultures around the world; and have evolved from the emotions of animals (Darwin, 1965). Many psychologists still believe that emotions, and especially how they are expressed facially, have strong biological ties. For example, even if children have been blind from birth and have never observed the smile or frown on another person's face, they smile or frown the same way that children with normal vision do (Shariff & Tracy, 2011). If emotions and the facial expressions that go with them are unlearned, then they should be the same the world over. Are they?

Extensive research has examined the universality of facial expressions and the ability of people from different cultures accurately to label the emotion that lies behind facial expressions. Paul Ekman's careful observations reveal that the many faces of emotion do not differ significantly from one culture to another (Ekman, 1980, 1996, 2003).

**FIGURE 9 Disgust or Happiness?** Disgust and happiness activate specific facial muscles, no matter who is making the face. As quickly as you can, go through these diverse faces and identify which of these folks look like they just smelled sour milk (disgust) and which look like they are definitely getting the joke (happiness).
(first) ©DRB Images, LLC/E+/Getty Images; (second) ©digitalskillet/E+/Getty Images; (third) ©SIBSA Digital Pvt. Ltd./Alamy Stock Photo; (fourth) ©Vladimir Wrangel/Alamy Stock Photo; (fifth) ©themacx/iStock/Getty Images; (sixth) ©Jupiterimages/Getty Images

For example, Ekman and Wallace Friesen photographed people expressing emotions such as happiness, fear, surprise, disgust, and grief. When they showed the photographs to people from the United States, Chile, Japan, Brazil, and Borneo (an Indonesian island in the western Pacific), the participants recognized the emotions the faces were meant to show, across the various cultures (Ekman & Friesen, 1969). Similarly, in another study, members of the Fore tribe, an isolated Stone Age culture in New Guinea, were able to match descriptions of emotional situations with photographs of faces expressing fear, happiness, anger, and surprise (Ekman & Friesen, 1971). Figure 9 shows the similarity of facial expressions of emotions by many different people.

Not all psychologists believe that facial expressions of basic emotions are universal (Barrett, 2011), but all would certainly agree that cultures have different norms that govern the expression of emotion (Hampton & Varnum, 2018; Liu & others, 2018). **Display rules** are sociocultural standards that determine when, where, and how emotions should be expressed. Although feelings of happiness, fear, or sadness may be universally expressed emotions, when, where, and how people display these feelings may vary from one culture to another (Segerstrale & Molnár, 2018).

• **display rules** Sociocultural standards that determine when, where, and how emotions should be expressed.

The importance of display rules is especially evident when we evaluate the emotional expression of another. Does that grieving husband on a morning talk show seem appropriately distraught over his wife's murder? Or might he be a suspect?

Many nonverbal signals of emotion vary from one culture to another (Mesquita, 2002). For example, male-to-male kissing is commonplace in Yemen, but it is not so common in the United States. The "thumbs up" sign, which in most cultures means either that everything is okay or that one wants to hitch a ride, is an insult in Greece, similar to a raised third finger in the United States—a cultural difference to keep in mind if you find yourself backpacking through Greece.

*In the Middle Eastern country of Yemen, male-to-male kissing is commonplace, but in the United States it is less common.*
©Adam Jan/AFP/Getty Images

©Peter Griffith/Getty Images

● **negative affect** Negative emotions such as anger, guilt, and sadness.

● **positive affect** Positive emotions such as joy, happiness, and interest.

## Classifying Emotions

There are more than 200 words for emotions in the English language, indicating the complexity and variety of emotions. Not surprisingly, psychologists have created ways to classify emotions–to summarize these many emotions along various dimensions, including their valence, arousal, and motivational quality.

### VALENCE

The *valence* of an emotion refers to whether it feels pleasant or unpleasant. You probably are not surprised to know that happiness, joy, pleasure, and contentment are positively valenced emotions. In contrast, sadness, anger, and worry are negatively valenced emotions. Research has shown that emotions tend to go together based on their valence, so that if someone is sad, he or she is also likely to be angry or worried, and if a person is happy, he is or she is also likely to be feeling confident, joyful, and content (Watson, Clark, & Tellegen, 1988; Watson & Stanton, 2017).

We can classify many emotional states on the basis of valence–whether they feel pleasant or unpleasant. Using this classification, there are two broad dimensions of emotional experience: negative affect and positive affect. **Negative affect** refers to emotions such as anger, guilt, and sadness. **Positive affect** refers to emotions such as joy, happiness, and interest.

Although it seems essential to consider the valence of emotions as a way to classify them, valence does not fully capture all that we need to know about emotional states. The joy a person experiences at the birth of a child and the mild high at finding a $5 bill are both positive states, but they clearly differ. One way in which they differ is in their level of arousal.

### AROUSAL LEVEL

The *arousal level* of an emotion (sometimes called *activation level*) is the degree to which the emotion is reflected in an individual's being active, engaged, or excited versus passive, disengaged, or calm. Positive and negative emotions can be high or low in arousal. Ecstasy and excitement are examples of high-arousal positive emotions, whereas contentment and tranquility are low-arousal positive emotions. Examples of high-arousal negative emotions are rage, fury, and panic, whereas irritation and boredom represent low-arousal negative emotions.

Valence and arousal level are independent dimensions that together describe a vast number of emotional states. Using these dimensions, psychologists have created a wheel of mood states that they call a *circumplex model of emotions* (Greco, Valenza, & Scilingo, 2018; Mattek, Wolford, & Whalen, 2017). A circumplex is a graph that creates a circle from two independent dimensions. Using the dimensions of valence and arousal level, we can arrange emotional states in an organized fashion. To view the circumplex model and grasp its usefulness, see the Psychological Inquiry.

### THE MOTIVATIONAL QUALITY OF EMOTIONS

The notion that emotions can motivate action has been recognized since Darwin, who proposed that emotional expressions are themselves remnants of the actions an emotion would provoke. You can probably think of actions that are associated with emotions, even if you do not engage in those actions literally. For instance, anger might engender the behavior of striking out at another person. Joy might move us to seek out other people (in a friendlier manner). Fear might tell us to run away from whatever is making us afraid.

Psychologists have begun to classify emotions based on their relevance to motivations–as either emotions to *avoid* punishers or to *approach* rewards. Fear, for instance, is thought of as an avoidance-motivating emotion because it tells us to escape the threatening stimulus. In contrast, anger is thought to be an approach-related emotion because it directs our behavior outward. Moreover, anger is concerned with rewards: When we feel angry or frustrated, it is because something (or someone) is blocking us from what we want. Studies have shown that viewing pictures of fearful facial expressions foster behaviors that suggest avoidance, and pictures of angry faces foster approach behaviors (Wilkowski & Meier, 2010).

## psychological *inquiry*

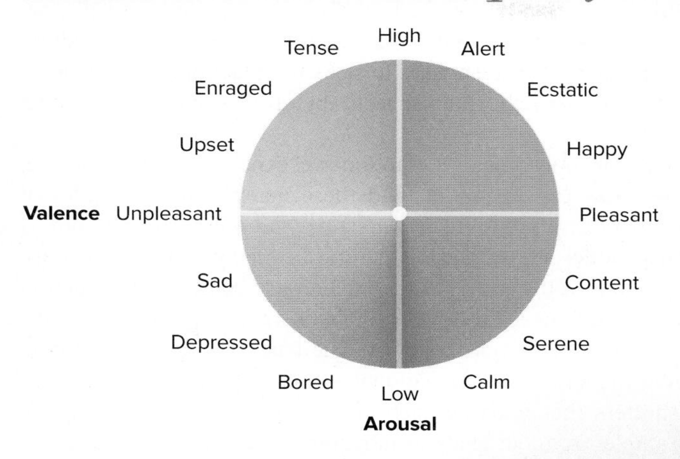


Source: Greco, Valenza, & Scilingo (2018); Mattek, Wolford, & Whalen (2017).

### *The Full Circle of Emotions*

The figure shows a commonly used representation of human emotions—the circumplex model. Note that the circle is created by two independent dimensions: valence and arousal. Emotions that are similar are closer together, and those that differ are farther apart. Using the figure as a reference, answer the following questions.

1. Locate the emotions "upset" and "sad" on the circumplex. According to the circumplex, these two feelings differ primarily in terms of their arousal. Which is higher in arousal? Do you agree with this placement of these emotions? Explain.
2. According to the model, which emotion is the exact opposite of "serene"?
3. Where would you place the following feelings on the circle: worried, proud, angry, embarrassed?

Thinking about emotions in this way can lead to unexpected predictions. For instance, consider the emotions anger and joy. Clearly, these emotions differ in their valence, but in terms of their motivational pull, both involve approach motivation and rewards. Interestingly, research suggests that positive emotions and anger share an approach motivational tendency (Pettersson & Turkheimer, 2013). When we think about emotions in a motivational context, even very different feelings can be linked together.

## The Adaptive Functions of Emotions

In considering the functions of emotions, it is fairly easy to come up with a good reason for us to have emotions such as fear and anger. Negative emotions carry direct and immediate adaptive benefits in situations that threaten survival. Negative emotions indicate clearly that something is wrong and that we must take action. Positive emotions do not signal a problem. So, what is the adaptive function of positive emotions?

- **broaden-and-build model** Fredrickson's model of positive emotion, stating that the function of positive emotions lies in their effects on an individual's attention and ability to build resources.

Confronting this question, Barbara Fredrickson proposed the **broaden-and-build model** of positive emotion (Conway & others, 2013; Fredrickson, 1998).

This model states that the function of positive emotions is to broaden the scope of attention and foster the building of resources.

The model begins with the influence of positive emotion on attention. Positive moods, such as contentment and humor, have been shown to broaden our attentional focus; they allow us to see the big picture. As a result, when in a good mood, we may be more disposed to think outside the box–to see unusual possibilities that escaped us before.

The "building" part of the model comes in as positive mood signals that there is no immediate threat in the environment, and we can explore without concern. We can take the time to make friends, to exercise to promote our health, to branch out in new ways. These activities allow us to build up strengths that we can use when we encounter life's difficulties (Papousek & others, 2010). For example, joy creates the urge to play, push the limits, and be creative.

The adaptive function of positive emotions can be seen in the quality of *resilience*. Recall from the chapter "Human Development" that resilience is the ability to bounce back from negative experiences, to be flexible and adaptable when things are not going well. Resilient individuals might be thought of as tall trees with the ability to bend but not break in response to strong winds. In contrast, people who lack resilience might be characterized as more brittle–more likely to snap or break in the face of adversity.

*According to Fredrickson's broaden-and-build model, a good mood allows us to broaden our scope of attention and explore the world, building resources for later challenges.*

One thing that allows resilient individuals to cope successfully during difficult times is their capacity to cultivate positive emotions. Michelle Tugade, Barbara Fredrickson, and Lisa Feldman Barrett (2004) found that the superior coping of resilient individuals came from their ability to use positive emotions to bounce back from negative emotional experiences. Using measures of cardiovascular activity, the researchers found that resilient individuals were better able to regulate their responses to stressful situations (for instance, being told they were about to give an important speech) by strategically experiencing positive emotion.

Of course, happiness is not the only positive emotion we experience. We also feel gratitude, awe, pride and love. How can we understand these many different shades of positive feelings? Recently, scholars have proposed a *family tree model* of positive emotions (Shiota & others, 2017). This model seeks to account for the many different positive feelings human being have. The root of the tree is the brain's reward center and the action of dopamine there. This makes sense, as all positive feelings likely have their root in this brain area that responds when something good happens. The trunk of the tree is enthusiasm, which can be considered the approach motivational aspect of positive feelings. The branches are the neurotransmitters that underlie each emotional state, which comprise the leaves of the tree. For example, oxytocin leads to nurturant love and opioids leads to pleasure and liking. The emergence of this model demonstrates the current movement of emotion science toward focusing on more differentiated emotional states and linking these to brain processes (Pressman & Cross, 2018; Shiota & others, 2017).

### *test yourself*

1. What are the key differences between the James–Lange theory and the Cannon–Bard theory of emotion?
2. What is the facial feedback hypothesis?
3. What is meant by the *valence* of an emotion and by the terms *positive affect* and *negative affect?*

# 5. MOTIVATION, EMOTION, AND HEALTH AND WELLNESS: THE PURSUIT OF HAPPINESS

Motivation is about what people want, and a quick scan of the bestseller list would seem to indicate that one thing people want very much is to be happy—or happier.

There might be good reasons to pursue happiness. The experience of negative emotions is related to disease, heart attack, and death. In contrast, the experience of positive emotions has been linked to lower levels of pain and disease (Pressman, Jenkins, & Moskowitz, 2018), as well as improved disease survival (Moskowitz, 2003) and longer lives (Petrie & others, 2018). A study examining individuals from 42 countries showed that self-reported health was strongly related to both negative and positive emotional experiences, even in developing nations (Pressman, Gallagher, & Lopez, 2013).

So, perhaps becoming happier is a worthwhile goal. Can people become happier? Let's consider the evidence.

## Biological Factors in Happiness

As we have seen, the brain is certainly at work in the experience of positive emotions. Genes also play a role. For instance, research on the heritability of well-being has tended to show that a substantial proportion of well-being differences among people can be explained by genetics. The heritability estimates for happiness range from 50 to 80 percent (Lykken, 1999). Remember from the chapter "Human Development" that heritability is a statistic that describes characteristics of a group, that heritability estimates can vary across groups and over time, and that even highly heritable characteristics can be influenced by experience. Thus, a person is not necessarily doomed to an unhappy life, even if the person has particularly miserable parents.

Recall the concept of *set point* in our discussion of weight. As it happens, there may also be a happiness set point—a person's basic level of happiness when the individual is not intentionally trying to increase his or her happiness (Sheldon & Lyubomirsky, 2007, 2012). Like weight, the happiness level may fluctuate around this set point. In investigating how to increase happiness, we must consider the role of this powerful starting spot, which is likely the result of genetic factors and personal disposition.

Other factors also complicate the pursuit of happiness. As we shall see, these include getting caught up on the hedonic treadmill and making happiness itself the direct goal.

## Obstacles in the Pursuit of Happiness

The first key challenge individuals encounter in trying to increase their happiness is the hedonic (meaning "related to pleasure") treadmill (Brickman & Campbell, 1971; Fredrick & Loewenstein, 1999). The term *hedonic treadmill* captures the idea that any aspect of life that enhances one's positive feelings is likely to do so for only a short time, because individuals generally adapt to any life change that would presumably influence their happiness. Winning the lottery, moving into a dream home, or falling in love may lead to temporary gains in the experience of joy, but eventually people go back to their baseline (Schkade & Kahneman, 1998). What a person first experiences as a life-changing improvement eventually fades to a routine (but still necessary) aspect of life, all too soon to be taken for granted. How can individuals increase their happiness if such pleasure enhancers lose their power?

A second obstacle in the goal of enhancing happiness is that pursuing happiness for its own sake is rarely a good way to get happy or happier. When happiness is the goal, the pursuit is likely to backfire (Schooler, Ariely, & Loewenstein, 2003). Indeed, those who explicitly link the pursuit of their everyday goals to happiness fare quite poorly (McIntosh, Harlow, & Martin, 1995).

In light of this difficult path, how can we enhance our happiness without having any new capacity for joy become ho-hum? How might we achieve happiness *without trying to* pursue it?

## Happiness Activities and Goal Striving

Sonja Lyubomirsky and her colleagues have suggested a promising approach to enhancing happiness (Lyubomirsky, 2011, 2013; Sheldon & Lyubomirsky, 2007, 2012). Lyubomirsky proposes beginning with intentional activities. For example, she notes that physical activity, kindness, and positive self-reflection all enhance positive affect (Lyubomirsky & others, 2011a, 2011b; Sheldon & Lyubomirsky, 2007). Engaging in altruistic behavior—habitually helping others, especially through a wide range of acts of service—is another powerful way to enhance happiness (Lyubomirsky, 2008, 2013; Mongrain & others, 2018).

One technique for engaging in positive self-reflection is to keep a gratitude journal. Studies by Robert Emmons and Michael McCullough (2004) have demonstrated the ways that being grateful can lead to enhanced happiness and psychological well-being. In one study, they asked individuals to keep a diary in which the participants counted their blessings every day. Those who counted their blessings were better off on various measures of well-being. Although some individuals seem to be naturally more grateful than others, experimental evidence indicates that even people who are not naturally grateful can benefit from taking a moment to count their blessings (Emmons & McCullough, 2003; Nezlek & others, 2018; Timmons & Ekas, 2018).

Another potentially useful approach to enhancing happiness is to commit to the pursuit of personally meaningful goals. Stop for a minute and write down the things you are typically trying to accomplish in your everyday behavior. You might identify a goal such as "to get better grades" or "to be a good friend (or partner or parent)." Such everyday goals and the pursuit of them have been shown to relate strongly to subjective well-being (Helgeson, 2018; Sheldon, 2002). Goal pursuit provides the glue that meaningfully relates a chain of life events, endowing life with beginnings, middles, and ends.

The scientific literature on goal investment offers a variety of ideas about the types of goals that are likely to enhance happiness. To optimize the happiness payoffs of goal pursuit, one ought to set goals that are important and personally valuable and that reflect the intrinsic needs of relatedness, competence, and autonomy (Sheldon, 2002). These goals also should be moderately challenging and should share an instrumental relationship with each other—so that the pursuit of one goal facilitates the accomplishment of another (Emmons & King, 1988).

©popcorner/Shutterstock

With regard to the hedonic treadmill, goal pursuit has a tremendous advantage over many other ways of trying to enhance happiness. Goals change and are changed by life experience. As a result, goal pursuit may be less susceptible to the dreaded hedonic treadmill over time. Goals accentuate the positive but do not necessarily eliminate the negative. When we fail to reach our goals, we may experience momentary increases in unhappiness (Pomerantz, Saxon, & Oishi, 2000), which can be a very good thing. Because goals can make us happy and unhappy, they keep life emotionally interesting, and their influence on happiness does not wear off over time.

Overall, goal pursuit may lead to a happier life. Goals keep the positive possible and interesting. The conclusion to be drawn from the evidence, assuming that you want to enhance your happiness, is to strive mightily for the goals that you value. You may fail now and then, but missing the mark will only make your successes all the sweeter. In a sense, devoting ourselves to goal pursuit embodies an important truth about our emotional lives. Emotions tells us how we are doing in the pursuits we value. So, an adaptive emotional life is one that is emotionally rich, including both positive and negative feelings.

### test yourself

1. Explain the term *hedonic treadmill* and give some real-world examples of it.
2. According to Lyubomirsky, how can individuals cultivate positive emotion?
3. How does committing oneself to personally meaningful goals relate to well-being?

# SUMMARY

## 1. THEORIES OF MOTIVATION

Motivated behavior is energized, directed, and sustained. Early evolutionary theorists considered motivation to be based on instinct–the innate biological pattern of behavior.

A drive is an aroused state that occurs because of a physiological need or deprivation. Drive reduction theory was proposed as an explanation of motivation, with the goal of drive reduction being homeostasis: the body's tendency to maintain equilibrium.

Optimum arousal theory focuses on the Yerkes–Dodson law, which states that performance is best under conditions of moderate rather than low or high arousal. Moderate arousal often serves us best, but there are times when low or high arousal is linked with better performance.

## 2. HUNGER, OBESITY, AND EATING DISORDERS

Stomach signals are one factor in hunger. Glucose (blood sugar) and insulin both play an important role in hunger. Glucose is needed for the brain to function, and low levels of glucose increase hunger. Insulin can cause a rise in hunger.

Leptin, a protein secreted by fat cells, decreases food intake and increases energy expenditure. The hypothalamus plays an important role in regulating hunger. The lateral hypothalamus is involved in stimulating eating; the ventromedial hypothalamus, in restricting eating.

Obesity is a serious problem in the United States. Heredity, basal metabolism, set point, and fat cells are biological factors involved in obesity. Time and place affect eating. Our early ancestors ate fruits to satisfy nutritional needs, but today we fill up on the empty calories in sweets.

Three eating disorders are anorexia nervosa, bulimia nervosa, and binge eating disorder. Anorexia nervosa is characterized by extreme underweight and starvation. Anorexia nervosa is related to perfectionism and obsessive-compulsive tendencies. Bulimia nervosa involves a pattern of binge eating followed by purging through self-induced vomiting or laxatives. Binge eating disorder involves binge eating without purging.

Anorexia nervosa and bulimia nervosa are much more common in women than men, but there is no gender difference in binge eating disorder. Although sociocultural factors were once thought to be primary in explaining eating disorders, more recent evidence points to the role of biological factors.

## 3. APPROACHES TO MOTIVATION IN EVERYDAY LIFE

According to Maslow's hierarchy of needs, our main needs are satisfied in this sequence: physiological needs, safety, love and belongingness, esteem, and self-actualization. Maslow gave the most attention to self-actualization: the motivation to develop to one's full potential.

Self-determination theory states that intrinsic motivation occurs when individuals are engaged in the pursuit of organismic needs that are innate and universal. These needs include competence, relatedness, and autonomy. Intrinsic motivation is based on internal factors. Extrinsic motivation is based on external factors, such as rewards and punishments.

Self-regulation involves setting goals, monitoring progress, and making adjustments in behavior to attain desired outcomes. Research suggests that setting intermediate goals on the path toward a long-term goal is a good strategy.

## 4. EMOTION

Emotion is feeling, or affect, that has three components: physiological arousal, conscious experience, and behavioral expression. The biology of emotion focuses on physiological arousal involving the autonomic nervous system and its two subsystems. Skin conductance level and the polygraph have been used to measure emotional arousal.

The James–Lange theory states that emotion results from physiological states triggered by environmental stimuli: Emotion follows physiological reactions. The Cannon–Bard theory states that emotion and physiological reactions occur simultaneously. Contemporary biological views of emotion increasingly highlight neural circuitry and neurotransmitters. LeDoux has charted the neural circuitry of fear, which focuses on the amygdalae and consists of two pathways, one direct and the other indirect. It is likely that positive and negative emotions use different neural circuitry and neurotransmitters.

Schachter and Singer's two-factor theory states that emotion is the result of both physiological arousal and cognitive labeling. Lazarus believed that cognition always directs emotion, but Zajonc argued that emotion directs cognition. Both probably were right.

Research on the behavioral component of emotion focuses on facial expressions. The facial feedback hypothesis states that facial expressions can influence emotions as well as reflect them.

Many psychologists believe that facial expressions of basic emotions are the same across cultures. However, display rules—nonverbal signals of body movement, posture, and gesture—vary across cultures. Differences in emoticons across cultures reinforce the idea that display rules are culture-dependent.

Emotions can be classified based on valence (pleasant or unpleasant) and arousal (high or low). Using the dimensions of valence and arousal, emotions can be arranged in a circle, or circumplex model. Emotions may also be classified in terms of whether they suggest approach or avoidance motivation.

Positive emotions may play a role in well-being by broadening our focus and allowing us to build resources. Resilience is an individual's capacity to thrive even during difficult times. Research has shown that one way resilient individuals thrive is by experiencing positive emotions. The family tree model of positive emotions suggests that all positive emotions are rooted in the brain's reward centers and that neurotransmitters in the brain give rise to the many different kinds of positive emotions we feel.

### 5. MOTIVATION, EMOTION, AND HEALTH AND WELLNESS: THE PURSUIT OF HAPPINESS

Happiness is highly heritable, and it is reasonable to believe that each person might have a happiness set point. Still, many people would like to increase their level of happiness. One obstacle to changing happiness is the hedonic treadmill: the idea that we quickly adapt to changes that might enhance happiness. Another obstacle is that pursuing happiness for its own sake often backfires.

Ways to enhance happiness include engaging in physical activity, helping others, engaging in positive self-reflection, and experiencing meaning (such as by keeping a gratitude journal). Another way to enhance happiness is to pursue personally valued goals passionately.

## key *terms*

anorexia nervosa
binge eating disorder (BED)
broaden-and-build model
bulimia nervosa
Cannon–Bard theory
display rules
drive
emotion
extrinsic motivation
facial feedback hypothesis
hierarchy of needs
homeostasis
instinct
intrinsic motivation
James–Lange theory
motivation
need
negative affect
overlearning
polygraph
positive affect
self-actualization
self-determination theory
self-regulation
set point
two-factor theory of emotion
Yerkes–Dodson law

## apply your *knowledge*

1. Ask your friends and your parents to define the word *motivation.* Compare your friends' and parents' definitions with the way psychologists define and approach motivation. What are the similarities? What are the differences? How do the definitions of your friends differ from those of your parents? Why do you think all of these variations exist?

2. To explore your own goals and sense of purpose, try the following activity. First list the top 5 or 10 goals that you are trying to accomplish in your everyday behavior. Then write your responses to the following questions that William Damon used in his interviews about life purpose (Damon, 2008):

   - Do you have any long-term goals?
   - What does it mean to have a good life?
   - What does it mean to be a good person?
   - If you were looking back on your life now, how would you like to be remembered?

   Finally, consider these questions: Are your everyday goals leading to the fulfillment of your long-term dream? How are you working in your everyday behavior to achieve your grander purposes?

3. Some psychologists believe that the ability to identify and regulate one's emotions is a kind of intelligence. Emotionally intelligent people are also thought to be better at reading the emotional expressions of others. Do a web search for "emotional intelligence tests" and take some online quizzes, or try the one at http://testyourself.psychtests.com/testid/3038. Do you think you are emotionally intelligent? Does your performance on the test seem to reflect your actual experience? What is your opinion of the test you tried? Is there information on the site showing its validity and reliability?

4. This chapter reviewed the use of autonomic nervous system activity in detecting deception. Psychologists have devised various ways to detect lying. Go online and search for information on detecting deception and lies. Is there a good way to tell if someone is being truthful? Explain.

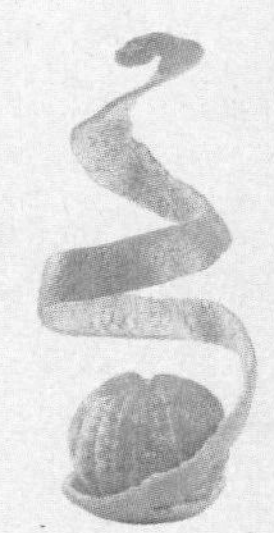

# CHAPTER 11

## CHAPTER OUTLINE



©Hero Images/Getty Images

# Gender, Sex, and Sexuality

## The International Day of the Girl

**Women make up 49 percent of the world's population.** In the United States, women have made amazing progress toward achieving equality with men (Van Bavel, Schwartz, & Esteve, 2018). They excel in business and politics and have even joined the ranks of the military elite. Yet throughout the world girls still have a long way to go before their futures will be as bright as those of their male counterparts. In much of the developing world, girls face serious obstacles even to obtaining an education. The United Nations estimates that 90 percent of adolescent girls in developing nations face either unemployment or the prospect of exploitation or abuse if they are able to find jobs (Pesce, 2018). Differences in hopes and dreams begin very early in life. By the age of 6, girls already consider boys more likely to be brilliant and better suited than girls for careers requiring a person who is really smart (Pesce, 2018). In 2012 the United Nations declared October 11 the International Day of the Girl Child. This day was set aside to draw attention to the fact that when girls and women are left out of the workforce, the world suffers. Organizations like Disney, Dove, and Facebook have joined the fight to give all children a place to dream big. There are smart and capable people with good ideas in both genders. To solve the world's many problems, we will need all the great problem solvers we can find, regardless of gender. ●

# PREVIEW

Inequality is just one of a host of contemporary issues involving gender, sex, and sexuality. In this chapter we will explore what psychology brings to these provocative topics. We begin by defining key terms related to gender, sex, and sexuality. Next, we consider the major theoretical approaches to gender development and review the psychology of gender differences. We then explore sexual orientation and examine sexual practices and behaviors. A look at several sexual variations and disorders follows, and we close the chapter by taking stock of the important place of sexuality in health and wellness.

## 1. DEFINING SEX AND GENDER

Let's start by defining the two terms we will use throughout this chapter. You have no doubt heard and used the words *sex* and *gender* frequently. Their technical definitions are key to understanding how scientists study these concepts.

### Sex and Its Biological Components

● **sex** The properties of a person that determine his or her classification as male or female.

**Sex** refers to the biological characteristics that determine a person's classification as male or female. In this section we review five physical characteristics used to classify sex: chromosomes, gonads, hormones, genitalia, and secondary sex characteristics (Hyde & others, 2018).

● **sex chromosomes** In humans, the pair of genes that differs between the sexes and determines a person's sex as male or female.

*Chromosomes* are the packages of DNA that carry our genes. Human beings have 23 pairs of chromosomes, with one of each pair being provided by each biological parent. The 23rd pair differs across the sexes. Scientists sometimes call this pair the **sex chromosomes** because it determines a person's genetic sex. In genetic females, both sex chromosomes are alike and are called X chromosomes. The pair of the chromosomes looks like an X. Genetic males have one X and one Y chromosome–the latter so named because, paired with the X chromosome, it looks like an upside-down Y (Figure 1).

● **gonads** Glands that produce sex hormones and generate ova (eggs) in females and sperm in males; collectively called gametes, the ova and sperm are the cells that eventually will be used in reproduction.

Another set of physical structures used to classify us as male or female is our gonads, a part of the endocrine system. **Gonads** are glands that produce sex hormones and generate ova (eggs) in females and sperm in males. Female gonads are the *ovaries* (located on either side of the abdomen). Male gonads are the *testes* (located in the *scrotum,* the pouch of skin that hangs below the penis).

Sex may also be classified by the hormones that these gonads produce. Hormones are chemicals produced by endocrine glands. No hormones are unique to one sex. Hormone levels vary by genetic sex. Levels of the hormones *estrogen* and *progesterone* are higher in women than in men, and levels of the hormones called *androgens* (the most common being *testosterone*) are higher in men than in women. In women, androgens are produced by the adrenal glands, and in men some of the androgens that are produced by the testes are converted into estrogens.

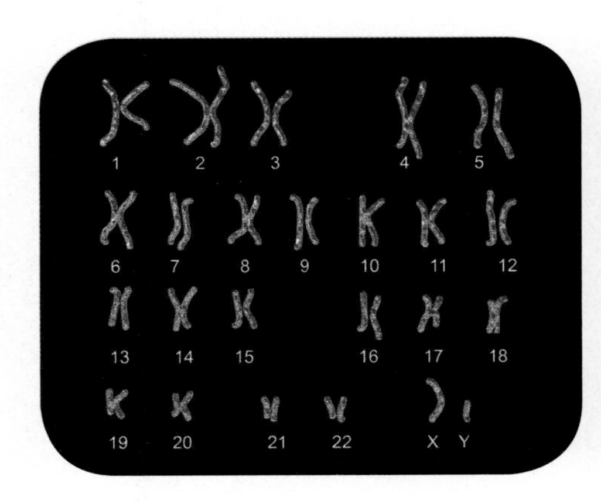


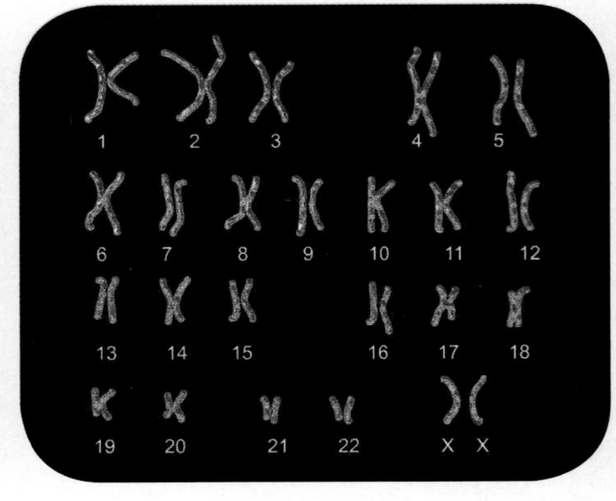


**FIGURE 1 The Difference Between Genetic Females and Genetic Males** The chromosome structures of a female (XX) and male (XY). The 23rd pair is shown at bottom right in each image. To obtain pictures of chromosomes, a cell is removed from a person's body, usually from inside the mouth, and the chromosomes are photographed under magnification.
(first) ©Kateryna Kon/Shutterstock; (second) ©Kateryna Kon/Shutterstock

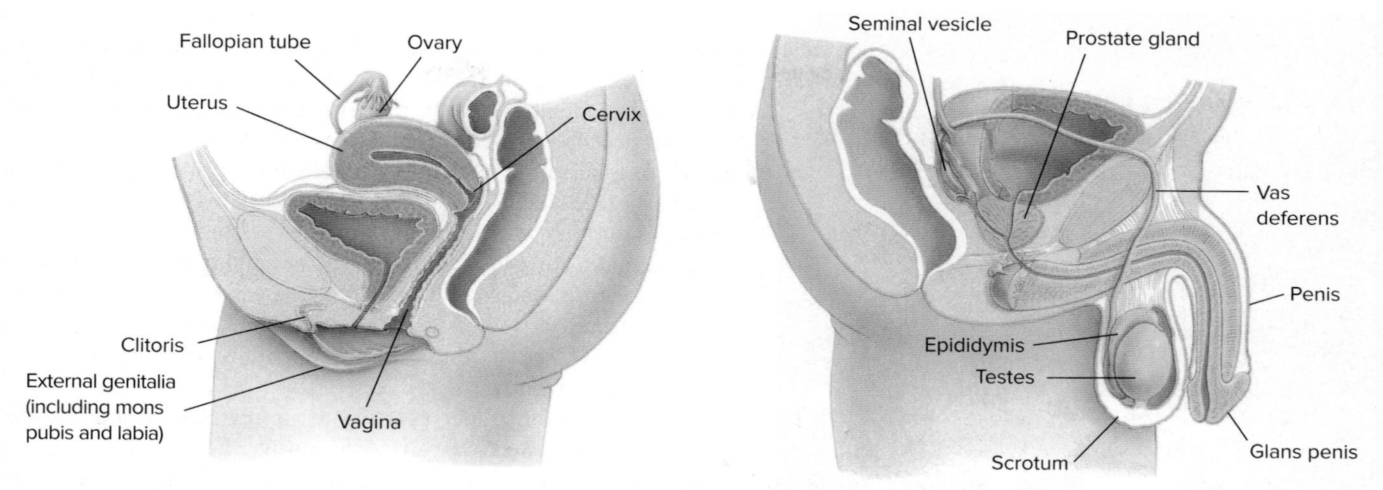


**FIGURE 2 Female and Male Internal Sex Organs and External Genitalia** These figures show the female (*left*) and male (*right*) internal sex organs and external genitalia.

Hormones secreted by the gonads spur the development of three aspects of the body that are also used in classifying us as male or female, including internal reproductive structures, external genitalia, and the secondary sex characteristics. Figure 2 shows female and male internal reproductive structures. In women, these organs allow the ovum to travel from the ovaries to the uterus. They play roles in sexual functioning, the menstrual cycle, and pregnancy. In men, the internal sex organs include the structures involved in the production and storage of sperm, and those that play a role in sexual arousal and orgasm.

The external genitalia of males and females are found between their legs (see Figure 2). The external genitalia of females, collectively called the *vulva,* include the *mons pubis* (a fleshy area just above the vagina), the *labia* (the lips surrounding the vaginal opening), and the *clitoris* (a small sensory organ at the top where the labia meet). For males, the external genitalia include the *penis* and *scrotum.*

Recall from the chapter "Human Development" that puberty is a period of rapid maturation that occurs mainly in early adolescence (Figure 3). Hormones produced during puberty drive the development of **secondary sex characteristics**, traits that differ between the two sexes but are not part of the reproductive system (Owen-Smith & others, 2018). Breasts in females and facial hair in males are secondary sex characteristics.

Physical attributes may play a role in classifying a person as male or female but physical characteristics may or may not match a person's psychological experience of himself or herself as male, female, or an alternate gender—that is, the person's gender identity.

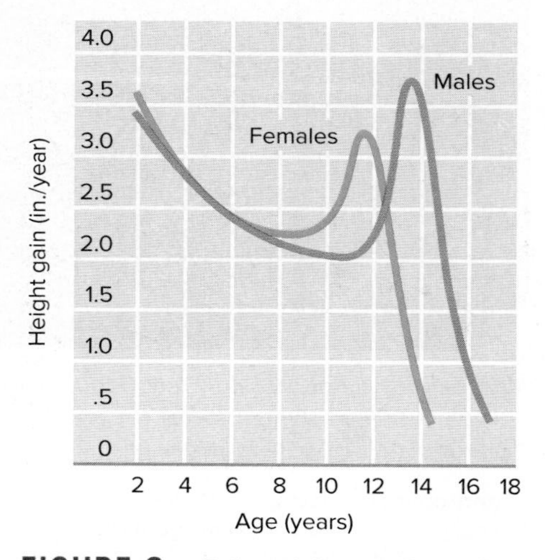


**FIGURE 3 Pubertal Growth Spurt** On average, the pubertal growth spurt begins and peaks about two years earlier for girls (starts at age 9, peaks at 11½) than for boys (starts at age 11½, peaks at 13½). Source: Data from Tanner, Whitehouse, & Takaishi (1966).

## Gender Identity

**Gender** refers to the psychological experience of being male or female that is informed by social beliefs about the characteristics thought to indicate masculinity or femininity (such as how the person looks, talks, and behaves) (Chen & others, 2018). **Gender identity** is an individual's personal sense of being male, female, or an alternate gender. Gender identity is multifaceted and goes beyond biological sex to include a person's understanding of who they are with respect to this complex issue. Gender identity is influenced by biological factors as well as socialization and experience (Eagly & Wood, 2017; Hyde & others, 2018).

Contemporary society has witnessed the emergence of many gender identities (Hyde & others, 2018; Ribeiro & others, 2018). The language of gender has changed in important ways. It may be helpful to define a few of these relatively recent gender concepts that highlight the complexity of gender.

● **secondary sex characteristics** Traits that differ between the two sexes but are not part of the reproductive system; they include breasts in females and facial hair in males.

● **gender** An individual's psychological experience of being male or female that is informed by social beliefs about the characteristics thought to indicate masculinity or femininity (such as how the person looks, talks, and behaves).

● **gender identity** An individual's personal, multifaceted sense of being male, female, or an alternate gender.

*Many successful artists, like Lady Gaga, challenge common notions of gender and sexuality*

©Kevin Mazur/WireImage/Getty Images

First, *gender expression* refers to the way a person presents themselves in terms of their subjective sense of their gender, including how a person dresses, wears their hair, and so forth. Second, *cisgender* describes a person whose gender identity fits with the sex they were assigned at birth. Most people are cisgender. Third, *non-binary* refers to the gender identity of a person who identifies as existing outside the typical "male vs. female" dichotomy (Hyde & others, 2018; Krieger, 2017). A non-binary person may identify as both male and female or as neither. It is not uncommon for those who identify as non-binary to prefer gender neutral pronouns, such as "they." Similarly, a person who identifies as *genderqueer* may view themselves as defying culturally determined gender categories (Chen & others, 2018). We will review transgender identity later in this section.

The definition of gender uses the terms *masculinity* and *femininity.* Technically, these words mean, respectively, "being like a man" and "being like a woman." What it means to be like a man or woman depends on culture and society. Psychologists study gender-related characteristics using the terms *instrumentality* and *expressiveness* to represent the broad dimensions of masculinity and femininity from a Western perspective. Instrumental attributes include being assertive, brave, independent, and dominant. Expressive traits include being nurturing, warm, gentle, and sensitive to others (Ludwikowski, Armstrong, & Lannin, 2018).

Although there are differences between men and women on these traits, with men scoring higher for instrumentality and women higher for expressiveness (Ludwikowski, Armstrong, & Lannin, 2018), these differences are not as large nor as clear-cut as you might expect (Carothers & Reis, 2013; Matud, Bethencourt, & Ibáñez, 2014). The degree of instrumentality or expressiveness a person feels may depend on the social context and the activity in which he or she is engaged (Martin, 2019). A father playing with his toddler may feel quite expressive; a WNBA guard running up the basketball court on a fast break may feel quite instrumental.

● **androgynous** Having attributes that are typically associated with both genders.

Every possible combination of instrumentality and expressiveness may be found in people of various genders. **Androgynous** means that a person is high on both instrumental and expressive qualities, having attributes that we typically associate with both genders (Bem, 1993). People who are *low* on both dimensions are referred to as undifferentiated. People who are *not* strongly gender-typed tend to have better psychological adjustment and resilience than those rated as extremely masculine or feminine (Lam & McBride-Chang, 2007). A balance between instrumentality and expressiveness is associated with a variety of positive outcomes in many cultures (Cheng, 2005; Helgeson & others, 2015; Martin, Cook, & Andrews, 2017).

It is tempting to think of *sex* as the term for biologically based differences between males and females, and *gender* or *gender identity* as terms for differences that are a product of environment or socialization. However, drawing such a simple distinction ignores the very strong relationship between the body and mind that we have emphasized throughout this text. It also seems to suggest that sex is "really" a binary distinction, more real or objectively true than gender identity. Such is not the case. To see how biological sex is less binary than you might think, see the Critical Controversy.

## Genes, Sex, and Gender Identity

Let's take a close look at the processes that connect genetic sex and gender identity. In the first few weeks after conception, genetically male and female embryos look alike. With regard to sex organs, genetically female fetuses stay the same, whereas genetically male fetuses change from this default status. The raw materials of male and female genitals and

## Isn't Gender "Really" Binary?

The term "gender binary" refers to the belief that there are two (and only two) categories of gender and that membership in one of these two categories is biologically determined (Hyde & others, 2018). *Binary* means something can take only one of two forms. The genetic contribution to sex might suggest that genes could, in conjunction with experience, give rise to two separate kinds of people. Whenever we have encountered the effects of genes on psychological characteristics, these have always affected behavior through their influence on the brain and brain development. Do the structures and functions of the brain support the conclusion that the genes that code biological sex produce male and female brains?

To probe whether there is a "male brain" vs. a "female brain," a team of neuroscientists examined MRI scans of more than 1,400 brains (Joel & others, 2015). They looked at all of the various brain regions where differences between men and women have been found. Essentially, they were looking for evidence that the differences held together, producing a measure of brain maleness or femaleness. They found that the differences did *not* hold together at all—a person might have male-typical characteristics for some brain areas but female-typical characteristics for others. So, the sex chromosomes do not lead to brains that are indelibly male or female. The brain, it seems, is a mosaic of male-like and female-like features. Regardless of whether a person is extremely masculine, feminine, or somewhere in between, their brain is likely androgynous (Joel, 2011; Joel & others, 2015).

Is there harm in taking a binary approach to gender? Janet Shibley Hyde and her colleagues (2018) enumerated the damage caused by assuming that males and females are qualitatively different kinds of people. This belief can affect the opportunities people have and the goals they seek. It can affect science, as well, if research questions are framed within this unrealistic view of gender. If this idea limits the lives of those who experience their identity outside of this binary, that is an important cost indeed (Clark & others, 2018; Nobili, Glazebrook, & Arcelus, 2018).

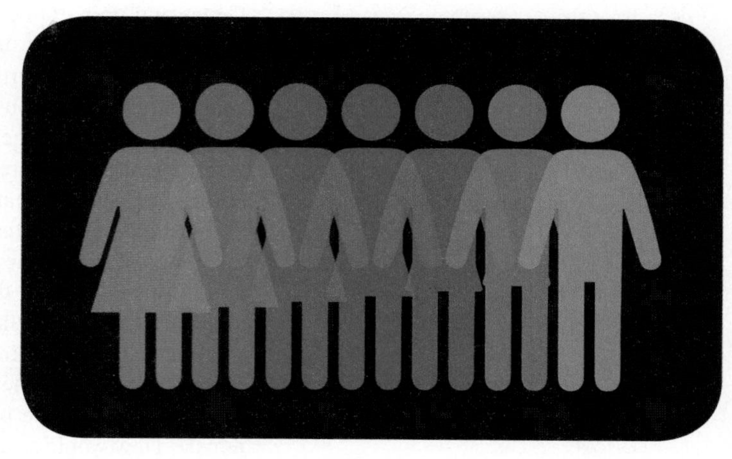
©Anne-Marie Miller/iStock/Getty Images

People whose lives challenge the gender binary have always existed across many cultures. Psychologists approach this aspect of human experience as scientists and as practitioners. As scientists, psychologists rely on the data provided by human experience that tell us gender diversity is a reality (Bragg & others, 2018; Hyde & others, 2018). As practitioners, psychologists approach people of all gender identities with compassion and respect (Chen & others, 2018; Clark & others, 2018; Krieger, 2017).

**WHAT DO YOU THINK?**

- How has the gender binary affected your life?
- How might it be adaptive for human beings to have brains that are not sex-typed?

gonads are fundamentally the same. The penis and clitoris take shape from the same embryonic structures, as do the testes (in males) and ovaries (in females), and the scrotum (in males) and the labia (in females).

What causes the development of male sexual features? A particular gene on the Y chromosome, the *SRY gene* (the sex-determining region of the Y chromosome), is activated early in the first three months of pregnancy (Cisternas, Garcia-Segura, & Cambiasso, 2018; Gonen & others, 2018). Of course, only males have a Y chromosome, so only male fetuses are exposed to the effects of the SRY gene, which causes the development of embryonic testes. The testes, then, begin to manufacture androgens that spread throughout the developing embryo, influencing the growing body and brain. Through this process, the XY embryo essentially *turns itself* into a male.

These early processes might seem to set the stage for sex and, potentially, gender identity. Prenatal hormones, for instance, play a role in brain development (Berenbaum, 2018; Cisternas, Garcia-Segura, & Cambiasso, 2018), and we might assume that these biological processes provide a foundation for our sense of ourselves as male or female.

However, the roles of nature (biological factors) and nurture (experience) in gender development are extraordinarily complex, as is illustrated by our next topics, disorders of sexual development and transgender experience.

## Disorders of Sexual Development

Genes and prenatal hormones play crucial roles in the development of the genitals, which in turn are generally used to identify a child's sex through a prenatal ultrasound or at birth. Typically determining a baby's sex is straightforward, but in rare cases the external genitalia are ambiguous. Prenatal hormone exposure, chromosomal differences, and environmental factors (such as exposure to radiation, chemicals, or some medications) can lead to genitals that are not clearly male or female, such as a very small penis, an enlarged clitoris, or genitals that appear to include both a penis and vaginal labia.

Formerly called *intersex conditions* (or *hermaphroditism*), these conditions are termed disorders of sexual development. **Disorders of sexual development (DSD)** are congenital conditions in which the development of chromosomal, gonadal, or anatomical sex is atypical (Cools & others, 2018; Meyer-Bahlburg & others, 2016). "Congenital" means present at birth. An infant with a DSD might have genitals that are not typical or that do not match with the child's genetic sex.

● **disorders of sexual development (DSD)** Congenital conditions in which the development of chromosomal, gonadal, or anatomical sex is atypical; formerly called intersex conditions or hermaphroditism.

Imagine being the parent of a child born with ambiguous genitalia, not clearly male or female. How would you feel? What would you do? Decades ago, experts thought that immediate surgery and sex assignment were crucial for parents and children (Money, Hampson, & Hampson, 1955, 1957). This plan of action rested on two (untested) assumptions (Berenbaum, 2006; Meyer-Bahlburg, 1998):

- Children cannot develop normally with ambiguous genitalia.
- Gender identity is entirely determined by socialization (nurture), not biological factors (nature).

A test of these assumptions was provided by a case in which a genetically male child was born with *typical* male genitalia. John Money, a well-known sex researcher, believed strongly that socialization was the main determinant of gender. In the 1960s, he tested his theory in the famous "John/Joan" case. The case involved one member of a pair of twin boys. A few months after birth, the penis of one of the twins was destroyed during circumcision. Money persuaded the parents to allow him to transform surgically the injured male genitals into female genitals and to agree to treat the child as a girl. Reared as a girl, according to Money, the former boy essentially became a girl (Money & Tucker, 1975). The case became famous as an example of nurture's triumph over nature.

Milton Diamond, a biologist and strong critic of Money's theory, followed up on "John/Joan" (Diamond & Sigmundson, 1997). Diamond found that over time, "Joan" became less interested in being a girl, eventually refusing to continue the process of feminization that Money had devised. We now know that "Joan" was really David Reimer, whose biography, *As Nature Made Him* (Colapinto, 2000), revealed the difficulties of his life as a boy, then a girl, then a boy, and finally a man. David struggled with traumatic gender-related experiences and depression. He died by suicide in 2004.

David's story seems to suggest that biological factors powerfully guide gender identity development and that socialization is relatively unimportant. Yet this one case may not present the full picture. Remember that it is difficult to make generalizations based on a single case study. This tragic case does not close the door on the possibility that socialization can significantly shape gender development.

Research on samples of people born with genitalia that conflict with their genetic sex points to a different conclusion—namely, that socialization is powerfully (but not perfectly) related to eventual gender identity (Berenbaum, 2006; Meyer-Bahlburg, 2005; Zucker, 1999). For example, one study showed that among genetic males born without a penis (due to a birth defect) and reared as females, 78 percent lived their adult lives as women. Of those who were reared as male, 100 percent of them were living as male (Meyer-Bahlburg, 2005).

In considering the discrepancy between those percentages, we might assume that all of these people would have experienced more stable gender identity if they had been reared in their genetic sex. However, this conclusion misses the complexity of the decision facing parents and doctors in these cases. Surgical procedures to construct a penis are difficult, costly, and not always successful (Bernabé & others, 2018; Diamond & others, 2018). The stability of sex assignment may depend on genetic and hormonal factors as well as parental reactions. And, we might ask whether stability is the most important issue for the child. Indeed, the person whose opinion matters most to this decision—the child—has not been consulted at all.

Now, experts agree that these decisions should be made based on the child's well-being, not parental distress (Chen & others, 2018; Cools & others, 2018; Hannema & de Rijke, 2018). Moreover, the "right" answer for an infant with a DSD may depend on various factors, including the type of disorder (Meyer-Bahlburg & others, 2016). Parents and medical professionals may simply have to wait until the child is mature enough to participate in important decisions that can affect sexual function and future fertility (Diamond & others, 2018; Ernst & others, 2018; Johnson & others, 2017).

## When Genetic Sex and Gender Conflict: Transgender Experience

● **transgender** Experiencing one's psychological gender as different from one's physical sex, as in the cases of biological males who identify as female and biological females who identify as male.

**Transgender** refers to experiencing one's psychological gender as different from one's biological or "natal" (meaning "at birth") sex. Transgender individuals can be biological males who identify as female or biological females who identify as male. Portrayals of transgender experience, especially among young people, have become more common on television shows like *Glee, Degrassi,* and *Grey's Anatomy.* Real-life cases of transgender people have drawn attention to this phenomenon, including *I Am Jazz,* the reality show starring Jazz Jennings, a teenager who has identified as transgender since childhood. It is estimated that over 1 million Americans identify as transgender (Peachman, 2017) and evidence exists for genetic contributions to transgender identity (Foreman & others, 2018). Previously, transgender identity was more common in genetic males ("male-to-female" or MTF) than genetic females ("female-to-male" or FTM), but recently this difference has disappeared and in some cases flipped, particularly in younger samples (Steensma, Cohen-Kettenis, & Zucker, 2018).

How do psychologists understand transgender experience? People who experience distress over their biological sex may be diagnosed with gender dysphoria (Chew & others, 2018). *Dysphoria* means discomfort or a lack of positive feelings. The American Psychiatric Association (APA) uses the term *gender dysphoria* to refer to a person's discomfort with his or her natal gender (APA, 2013b; Steensma & Wensing-Kruger, 2018).

However, there is considerable debate over whether such individuals should be considered as having a disorder at all. They might, instead, be viewed as experiencing distress because they feel they are living in the wrong body and because they face discrimination and misunderstanding (Chew & others, 2018). The issue of whether transgender individuals are suffering from a disorder is complex, as a diagnosis is often required in order to gain insurance coverage for (costly) treatment. Increasingly, mental health professionals are called upon not to treat these individuals but to provide evaluations of their suitability for various treatments.

Generally, transitioning as a transgender person involves gradual stages that move from reversible gender-affirming treatments to permanent ones (Nobili, Glazebrook, & Arcelus, 2018; Owen-Smith & others, 2018).

*Caitlyn Jenner (formerly Olympic star Bruce Jenner) was lauded for her courage in coming out as transgender.*

The first stage may involve coming out to family, friends, and coworkers and dressing and living as their preferred gender identity. Then the person might receive *gender-affirming hormones* that support that identity, followed by surgery to remove secondary sex characteristics (such as breasts) (Agarwal & others, 2018), and potentially culminating in *gender-affirming surgery,* formerly known as *sex reassignment surgery*. Surgery involves the surgical reconstruction of the genitals (Falcone & others, 2018; Hsiao & others, 2018). The majority of transgender individuals undergo hormone treatment only, while about a third also receive gender-affirming surgery (Grant & others, 2011). Importantly, these differences in treatment may not reflect preferences but financial realities, as people often must pay for treatment out of pocket (Heyes & Latham, 2018; Puckett & others, 2018).

Among youth who identify as transgender, many will ultimately adopt the gender identity of their genetic sex; however, some will continue to identify as transgender (Steensma & Cohen-Kettenis, 2018; Temple Newhook & others, 2018). Because it is difficult to distinguish between these two groups during childhood, some experts advocate offering medications to delay puberty so that youth can have a "time-out" from sexual development. This time-out prevents the permanent bodily changes spurred by puberty, giving the person and their parents the opportunity to fully contemplate the path ahead (Chew & others, 2018).

### test yourself

1. Explain the difference between sex and gender.
2. Discuss the causes of the differentiation of the sexes.
3. What is transgender?

Not all trans people desire treatment to change their bodies. Some trans individuals embrace their identity as a quality that challenges the gender binary. For them, being transgender means living according to the belief that a person can be a man who happens to have a vagina or a woman who has a penis (Lev, 2007)—as an individual who occupies a different but valid gender territory (Meyer-Bahlburg, 2010; Pfafflin, 2010). In many ways, transgender experience reflects and informs a growing recognition that gender identity is enormously complex.

*Research on infants from 3 to 8 months of age found that males spent more time looking at boy toys, such as trucks and machines, than other toys.*



# 2. THEORIES OF GENDER DEVELOPMENT

For most people, genetic sex and gender identity are experienced as a reasonably good fit. Nevertheless, we might wonder how a person who is XX or XY comes to think of him- or herself as female or male. Various theories of gender development have addressed this question. In this section we examine the major theoretical approaches to gender development. These theories focus on cisgender men and women. As you read about them, you might consider how each might seek to understand alternate gender identities.

## Biological Approaches

A number of biological factors—including genes, gonads, and hormones—identify a person as male or female. Biological approaches to gender draw links between these aspects of the person's biological sex and his or her eventual psychological feelings of gender. Scientists who study biological factors in gender development focus on variables such as genes, prenatal hormones, and brain structures and functions, as these differ between males and females and potentially account for the experiences of ourselves in those sexes. Importantly, research on the biological bases of gender does not simply focus on how biological factors (genes, hormones, and so on) *determine* gender development but also on how such factors contribute to gender development in interaction with experience (Berenbaum, 2018; Berenbaum & Beltz, 2016).

Biologically based research has looked at differences between the sexes in infancy, searching for clues to gender-related characteristics in the earliest days of life. In infancy, boys are larger and more active than girls (Fausto-Sterling, 2016). In one study, 1-day-old infants were shown two stimuli: a human face and a mobile made out of a picture of that face (Connellan & others, 2000). Baby girls spent more time looking at the human face, while the baby boys were more interested in the mobile.

Similarly, research on infants from 3 to 8 months of age found that males spent more time looking at typical boy toys, including trucks and machines, and females spent more time looking at typical girl toys, such as dolls (Alexander, Wilcox, & Woods, 2009). Nonhuman primates exhibit similar differences (Alexander & Hines, 2002; Hassett, Siebert, & Wallen, 2008). In humans, such differences are thought to be biologically, not socially, based because very young infants have not yet had social experiences that might influence gender development.

## Evolutionary Psychology

The evolutionary psychology approach to gender views the differences between the sexes through the lens of natural selection and adaptation. From this perspective, the factors that produce gender are the product of millions of years of natural selection.

Recall from the chapter "What Is Psychology?" that, according to Charles Darwin's theory of evolution, a species' characteristics reflect natural selection, the process by which the environment determines the adaptiveness of particular genetic characteristics. Organisms with the fittest genes are most likely to survive and reproduce. This slow process is responsible for creating the typical characteristics of any species.

Applying these ideas to gender, evolutionary psychologists assert that the differences we see between contemporary men and women can be explained by the *selection pressures,* or environmental challenges, that confronted our distant human ancestors (Buss, 2016; Cosmides & Tooby, 2013; Lewis & others, 2017). To understand the potential role of selection pressures on gender, evolutionary psychologists focus on sexual selection and the differing reproductive challenges faced by men and women.

### SEXUAL SELECTION

Differences between male and female members of the same species abound in nature. For instance, the beautiful peacock with the colorful tail and the cardinal with brilliant red feathers are both males, while the female members of those species are duller in appearance. What accounts for these sex differences within species?

Darwin (1871) proposed that many sex differences that occur within species have evolved through sexual selection. **Sexual selection** means that the male and female members of a species differ from each other because of differences in competition and choice. *Competition* occurs among members of the same sex as they vie for the opportunity to mate with members of the opposite sex. Members of that opposite sex in turn exercise *choice,* selecting the lucky one (or ones) with whom they will mate. In peacocks, males use their amazing plumage to compete with one another for females, and females select the prettiest male with whom to reproduce.

• **sexual selection** According to Darwin's theory of evolution, differentiation between the male and female members of a species that can be traced to differences in competition and choice.

Who chooses and who competes? Generally, the sex that invests the most in producing offspring is the one that chooses, and the other sex is the one that competes (Bateman, 1948; Clutton-Brock, 2007, 2010; Puts, 2016). Applying these ideas to humans, evolutionary psychologists believe that differences between women and men are evidence that sexual selection has occurred in our species. Women are the sex that gives birth, and as such they ought to do the choosing. Men, on the other hand, show characteristics that are thought to be well suited for competing. Evolutionary psychologists explain human males' physical size as an adaptation that helps men compete with one another for female mates (Puts, 2016).

*This male peacock uses his beautiful plumage to attract female mates.*

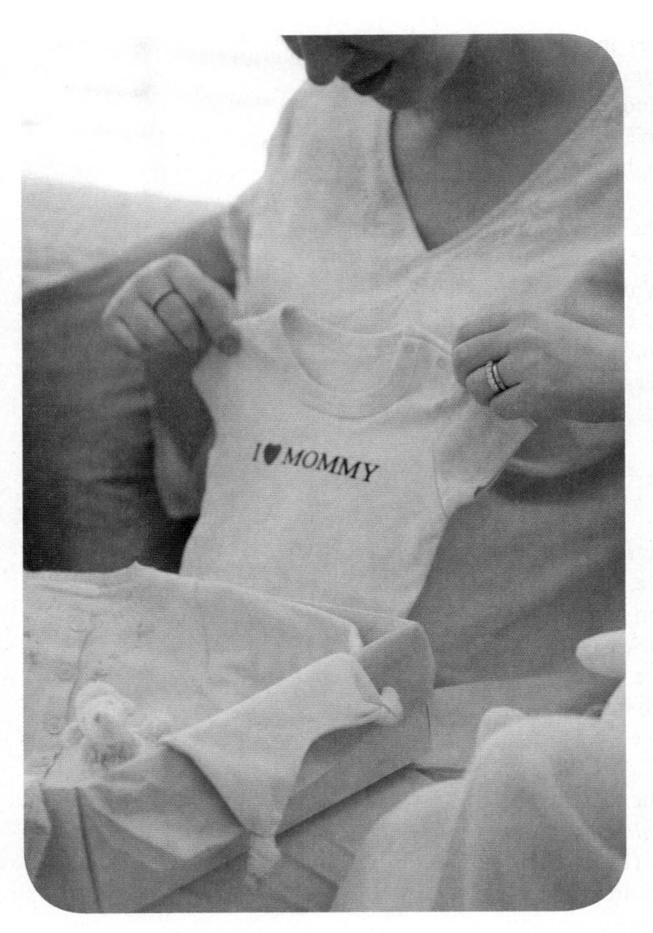


©Barry Austin/Photodisc/Getty Images

Sexual selection is more complicated in human beings than in other species. Human infants are so helpless that it makes sense from a survival standpoint for men to invest in their offspring. This means that sometimes men are the choosers and women are the competitors vying for the men who are most likely to invest in their children. This aspect of sexual selection is of particular interest in humans because of the different challenges men and women face in reproducing.

### REPRODUCTIVE CHALLENGES FOR MEN AND WOMEN

Men and women share the same evolutionary goal—to reproduce—but accomplishing that objective presents different challenges to each sex. Women experience pregnancy and childbirth. They can reproduce only about once per year and have a limited time of fertility. Thus, evolutionary psychologists believe that women must be choosy in selecting sexual partners, putting a premium on high *quality*—seeking sexual partners who have adequate resources to invest in a family.

Men do not bear the obligation of childbearing, and they are generally fertile from puberty onward. Therefore, say evolutionary theorists, they can focus on *quantity,* reproducing as often as possible. Evolutionary psychologists suggest that men should be less selective than women about sexual behavior (Buss, 2016; Geary, 2010; Lewis & others, 2017). A sticking point for this strategy, though, is that, as noted above, babies are so helpless that it is adaptive for men to invest in their offspring.

Further, men have an additional problem. Because the moment when the egg is fertilized by the sperm is a mystery for the parties involved, a man cannot be certain whether the child in whom he is investing his resources is genetically *his* child. Evolutionarily speaking, for a man, the worst-case scenario is to invest his resources to ensure the survival of someone else's offspring.

How might men avoid this dreaded outcome? Evolutionary psychologists point out that across cultures, men are likely to prefer women who are younger than they are (Buss, 2016). This preference for younger women may be a way for a man to minimize the chances that his betrothed is already pregnant with someone else's offspring.

Sex differences that emerge shortly after birth, as well as cross-cultural similarities in mate preferences, would seem to support biological and evolutionary theories of gender development. But, let's stop and think about the potential role of the social environment in the emergence of gender. Family and friends begin to buy pink and blue baby clothes before a child is even born. That child is introduced to a social network with strong expectations about gender-appropriate behavior. If a little boy shows even a slight preference for playing with a truck, we might smile and conclude, "He's *all boy*." If the same child expresses interest in trying on a dress or playing with a doll, we might respond differently. Might these different social responses influence the child's developing sense of self?

Consider too that the male preference for younger sexual partners may reflect social expectations or the power differences that exist between men and women in many cultures. These considerations reflect concerns that are represented in two additional views of gender development: social cognitive approaches and social role theory.

## Social Cognitive Approaches

Social cognitive theories of gender development focus on how children *learn* about gender and how they come to occupy a particular gender identity. These approaches emphasize both the way that children internalize information about gender (Bem, 1983, 1993) and the way the environment reinforces gender-related behavior (Bussey & Bandura, 2004).

From this perspective, gender behavior is learned through reward and punishment, observational learning, and modeling (Bandura & Bussey, 2004; Bussey & Bandura, 2004), processes we examined in the chapter "Learning". From this perspective, modeling is an especially potent mechanism for transmitting values (Bandura, 1986; Bussey & Bandura, 2004). Children gain information about gender from models of each sex. Who leaves for work every day? Who does the housekeeping? When children see their parents and other adults engaging in behavior (and as they observe whether and how these behaviors are reinforced), they learn about how *men* and *women* behave.

In subtle ways, children may be rewarded for engaging in gender-conforming behavior and punished for engaging in *gender-nonconforming behavior* (Becerra-Culqui & others, 2018)–activities and preferences that do not fit the expectations for their sex. Examples of gender-conforming behavior include girls playing with dolls and boys playing with trucks. Examples of gender-nonconforming behavior include girls playing with a model railroad set and boys playing dress-up or house.

The social environment responds to behaviors in various ways, coloring the child's perception of their appropriateness. A girl might learn that pretending to be a professional football player does not please her parents. A boy might pick up on his mother's subtle frown when he announces that he wants to try on her high-heeled shoes (Mesman & Groeneveld, 2018). Although clearly times have changed, controversies that erupt over mothers' allowing their sons to wear nail polish or long hair tell us that society can still respond harshly when behavior crosses the lines of gender expectations.

Peers play a role in gender development. Especially after age 6, peer groups often segregate into boy groups and girl groups (Maccoby, 2002) (Figure 4). Peers are stricter than most parents in rewarding gender-conforming behavior and punishing gender-nonconforming behavior, especially for boys (Pasterski, Golombok, & Hines, 2011).

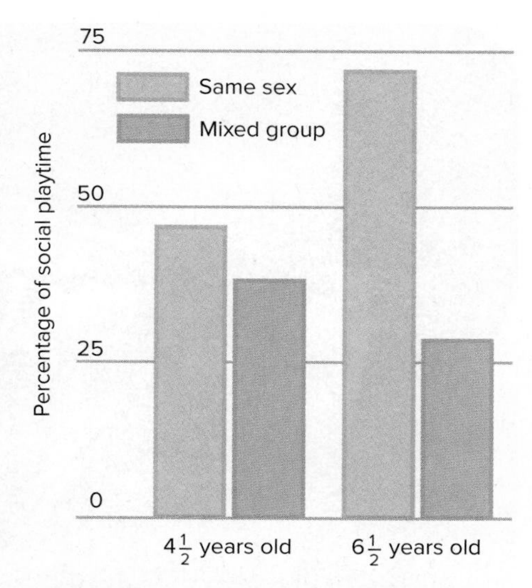


**FIGURE 4 Developmental Changes in Percentage of Time Spent in Same-Sex and Mixed-Group Settings** Observations of children show that they are more likely to play in same-sex groups than mixed groups. This tendency increases between 4 and 6 years of age. Source: Maccoby (2002).

Through these varied experiences, children learn that gender is an important organizing principle in social life, and they come to recognize that boys and girls, and men and women, are different in ways that matter (Leaper, 2013). Children develop a *gender schema*–a mental framework for understanding what is considered appropriate behavior for females and males in their culture (Martin & Ruble, 2010). Recall that schemas are mental frameworks we use to understand the world. The gender schema is a product of learning and serves as a cognitive framework by which children interpret further experiences related to gender.

While acknowledging biological differences between males and females, social cognitive psychologists believe that social and cultural factors have a much stronger influence on eventual gender identity (Bandura & Bussey, 2004; Mesman & Groeneveld, 2018). From this perspective, differences in men's and women's career and life choices can be explained by differences in the availability of role models and beliefs about self-efficacy and personal control.

## Social Role Theory

Alice Eagly proposed that to understand gender, we must recognize the larger social and cultural institutions surrounding gender identity (Eagly, 1987, 2009, Eagly & Wood, 2010, 2013, 2017). **Social role theory**, introduced by Eagly, is a theory of gender development that acknowledges the physical differences between the sexes that, historically, led men and women to perform different tasks; but it also points out the ways that these differences color social expectations and create and support social structures that limit opportunities for both sexes. Like evolutionary theory, social role theory begins by acknowledging that women are more innately and directly involved in reproduction than men, and men are larger and stronger than women. Eagly proposed that these differences resulted in a *division of labor* between the sexes, with women being more involved in the home and with childrearing and men being more likely to work outside the home.

● **social role theory** Eagly's theory of gender development that, while acknowledging the physical differences between the sexes, argues that these differences color social expectations and create social structures that limit opportunities for both sexes.

Social role theory asserts that this division of labor can lead to important beliefs about what it means to be a woman or a man. The activities and occupations we see men and women performing give rise to expectations and beliefs about what it means to be a male

*Traditional gender roles and gender stereotypes often (but not always, as the photo shows) shape individuals' life goals and career choices.*

©Peter Cade/Iconica/Getty Images

or female person, what a male or female person *ought* to do, and what we believe that person *can* do. In this way, the division of labor spawns the social construct of **gender roles**, expectations for how a female person and how a male person should think, act, and feel (Eagly, 2009, Eagly & Wood, 2017).

Gender roles are related to **gender stereotypes**–overly general beliefs and expectations about what women and men are like (Ellemers, 2018). Gender stereotypes might suggest that women are warm, caring, and emotional and that men are strong, dominant, and rational. Social role theory asserts that each of us internalizes these roles and stereotypes and comes to evaluate our own behavior and choices according to their gender typicality (Buckley, 2018; Yang & others, 2018).

For example, gender roles and gender stereotypes might influence our life goals (Ellemers, 2018). If a particular occupation (say, an engineer or a nurse) conflicts with our perceived gender role, we may view it as less desirable and less likely to bring us success. Notably, when men and women make choices that are guided by gender roles and gender stereotypes, they tend to become more and more different from each other in their behaviors, attitudes, and aspirations, with each sex engaging in more stereotypical pursuits. In turn, these sex-based differences, driven by gender roles and stereotypes, maintain the social structure (Eagly & Wood, 2010).

Social role theory recognizes the institutional structures and patterns of opportunity that perpetuate gender differences (Eagly & Wood, 2010; Eagly & Wood, 2017). Differences between men and women in access to education and in the treatment they receive from teachers, for instance, helps to explain differences in career choices (Makarova, Aeschlimann, & Herzog, 2016; Saw, Chang, & Chan, 2018).

Gender roles can be especially important to outcomes when the content of these roles conflicts with success. For example, in 2017, the median income for women in the United States was about 80 percent of men's median income (Institute for Women's Policy Research, 2018). Why do women make less than men? The answer to that question is complex, but one possible factor is the conflict between gender role expectations for women and the negotiation context. According to the female gender role, women are expected to be gentle and supportive, not demanding and difficult. Thus, gender role expectations might contribute to an unfair playing field for women in negotiating for things like pay (Mazei & others, 2015).

● **gender roles** Roles that reflect the individual's expectation for how a female person and how a male person should think, act, and feel.

● **gender stereotypes** Overly general beliefs and expectations about what women and men are like.

Social role theory predicts that as social structures change, gender differences should decline–and this prediction has been borne out (Carothers & Reis, 2013; Eagly & Diekman, 2003). For example, in countries where there is little gender difference in education and women earn comparable salaries to men, women are less likely to prefer men with resources (Van Bavel, Schwartz, & Esteve, 2018). Such results challenge the evolutionary perspective on gender differences. Still, gender roles continue to dictate many aspects of modern life. Mothers who work outside the home may find that they are still expected to do the majority of the housework and childcare (Shockley & Allen, 2018).

## Evaluating the Theoretical Approaches to Gender

In summary, scholars think about gender development in a number of ways, including biological, evolutionary, social cognitive, and social role perspectives. These theories are not mutually exclusive, and a comprehensive understanding of gender might well take all of them into account.

Biology alone would not seem to offer a sufficient explanation for gender. Indeed, wide variations occur within each sex, for there are certainly girls and women who are assertive and dominant, as well as boys and men who are submissive and subordinate (Hyde, 2014).

| Theoretical Approach | Summary | Research Questions |
|---|---|---|
| **Biological** | Focuses on the various biological processes that underlie differences between men and women. Researchers from this perspective examine variables such as genes, hormones, and brain structures and functions to identify the biological underpinnings of gender. | • How does prenatal hormone exposure relate to later sex-typed behavior?<br>• How do genetic factors influence the development of gender identity? |
| **Evolutionary** | Focuses on the ways that differences between men and women can be understood as serving adaptive functions for our distant ancestors. Sexual selection is used to explain gender differences in behavior, and sex differences in reproductive challenges are thought to underlie differences in sexual behavior. | • How do men and women differ in terms of engaging in casual sex?<br>• Do sex differences in nonhuman primates show the same patterns as those found in humans? |
| **Social Cognitive** | Focuses on how processes such as learning (including modeling and rewards and punishers) and the development of cognitive schemas associated with sex lead to conceptions of male and female behavior. | • When do children learn that a person's sex makes a difference in how he or she is treated by others?<br>• How do peer groups react to children who behave in gender-atypical ways? |
| **Social Role** | Focuses on the ways that the division of labor between the sexes leads to expectations about what is appropriate behavior for members of each sex. The division of labor leads to the construction of gender roles and stereotypes that influence the opportunities and aspirations of men and women. | • Do women seek out different opportunities in cultures that have more egalitarian attitudes toward the sexes?<br>• Do gender differences we see in one culture translate to another? |

**FIGURE 5** **Summary of Major Theoretical Approaches to Gender and Gender Development** Note how each approach focuses on a different aspect of human life, ranging from genetic and hormonal influences to relationships, psychological processes, and social structures.

Yet biological differences between the sexes are likely more significant than the social cognitive approach acknowledges: Just ask the parents whose daughter insists on playing with dolls instead of trucks or those who witness their son turning a stuffed bunny into a weapon.

Similarities in patterns of gender differences across different cultures support evolutionary psychology approaches. However, the application of sexual selection to human behavior has been strongly criticized. Some suggest that gender differences can be better explained by social factors, such as group cooperation, than by natural selection (Hyde & Else-Quest, 2013; Roughgarden, Oishi, & Akçay, 2006).

Certainly, having role models is a factor in the attitudes that men and women form about their choices of life goals, as the social cognitive view suggests. Further, there is no question that social roles are also important. Indeed, it is shocking to consider that although we live in a world where in some nations a woman can serve as national leader, in other countries a girl is not permitted even to go to school, and a woman cannot leave home unless a male family member accompanies her.

Biological, evolutionary, social cognitive, and social role theorists approach gender development from different levels of analysis, and each approach poses different questions for researchers to investigate (Figure 5). Throughout the rest of this chapter, we often will refer to these broad perspectives to see how each one applies in regard to the specific topics and issues addressed. Each of these theories, for example, has something to say about whether and how the sexes should differ from each other on various attributes, our next topic.

### *test yourself*

1. What are four major theoretical approaches to gender development? What is the main idea behind each?
2. Explain sexual selection, a key concept of the evolutionary psychology approach.
3. What are gender roles and gender stereotypes? What does social role theory say about them?

## 3. THE PSYCHOLOGY OF GENDER DIFFERENCES

To think about gender differences, let's start with a game we will call "Who are more ______?" For each adjective below, answer as quickly as you can with either "Men" or "Women."

| Who are more . . . | Assertive | Rational |
|---|---|---|
| | Emotional | Aggressive |
| | Strong | Sexually adventurous |
| | Creative | Reserved |
| | Verbal | Active |

Now, for each of those descriptors, think of someone you know who is of the opposite sex to your answer and who is very high on the quality described. What does this game tell you about gender stereotypes? Even though you might be aware of cultural stereotypes for gender differences, in fact individual men and women vary widely with respect to a number of qualities.

In this section we will review the research on gender differences in four main areas:

- Emotion, empathy, and helping
- Cognitive ability
- Aggression
- Sexuality

Because gender cannot be manipulated, research comparing men and women is by definition correlational–so causal claims are not justified. Correlation does not imply causation. Also, as we review these topics, ask yourself how the four approaches to gender development–biological, evolutionary, social cognitive, and social role theory–might explain each.

## Emotion, Empathy, and Helping

You probably know the stereotype about gender and emotion: Women are emotional and men are not. This stereotype is powerful and pervasive across cultures (Ellemers, 2018; LaFrance & Vial, 2016). However, men and women are often more alike in the way they experience emotion than the stereotype would lead us to believe (Carothers & Reis, 2013).

For many emotional experiences, researchers do not find gender differences (Hyde, 2014). Where differences do emerge, women report more feelings of sadness and anxiety than men do, and men report more anger and irritability than women do (Schirmer, 2013). Women also consistently report higher levels of disgust than men do (Al-Shawaf, Lewis, & Buss, 2018; Timmers, Bossio, & Chivers, 2018). Neuroimaging studies suggest that the responsiveness of the amygdalae to emotion-arousing stimuli varies according to gender, with women being more responsive to negative stimuli and men being more responsive to positive stimuli (Stevens & Hamann, 2012).

Understanding these differences requires consideration of gender-related beliefs about emotion and the contexts in which emotions are experienced (Brannon, 1999; Brody, 1999). Men and women are aware of the gender-specific expectations for emotional behavior (Schirmer, 2013). For example, women may be judged harshly for expressions of anger, while men may be evaluated as weak if they express worry or sadness.

● **empathy** A feeling of oneness with the emotional state of another person.

**Empathy** is a person's feeling of oneness with the emotional state of another person. When we feel empathy for someone, we feel what that person is feeling. Women do report themselves as more empathetic than men (Carothers & Reis, 2013). Empathy requires an appreciation of another person's mental state, suggesting the important role of theory of mind in this capacity. Theory of mind, as noted in the chapter "States of Consciousness", is the ability to understand the inner life of another person. When the sexes are compared on measures of theory of mind and differences are found, women tend to show an advantage (Baron-Cohen & others, 2001; Hall & Matsumoto, 2004; Ibanez & others, 2013; Khorashad & others, 2018).

Empathy is a strong predictor of an individual's willingness to help another in need. If women are more empathetic than men, are they also more helpful? The answer to this question is "It depends" (Van der Graaff & others, 2018). Women are more likely than men to help when doing so does not involve risks to personal safety. For instance, women donate more money to charitable causes than men do (Leslie, Snyder, & Glomb, 2013). In contrast, men are more likely than women to help in situations in which a perceived danger is present (for instance, picking up a hitchhiker) and in which they feel competent to help (as in assisting someone with a flat tire) (Eagly & Crowley, 1986).

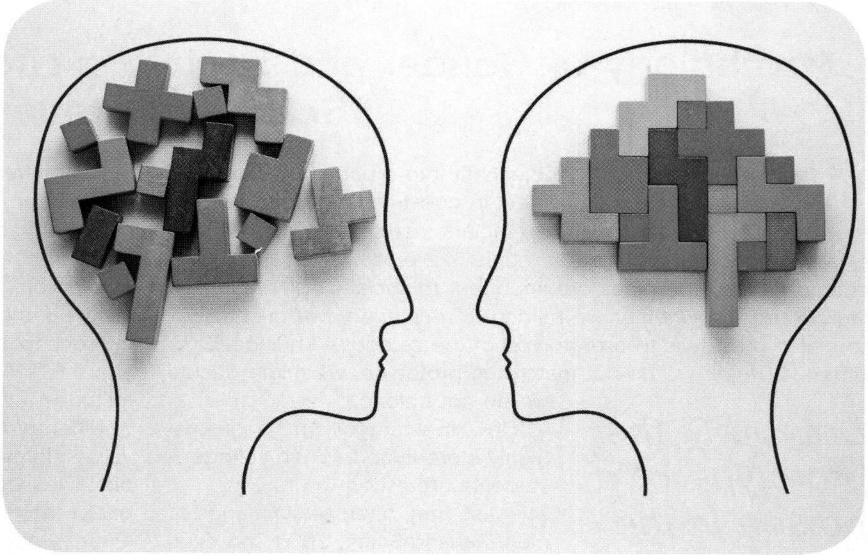

## Cognitive Ability

Are there gender differences in cognitive ability? Summarizing a large body of research in this area, Janet Shibley Hyde (2005) found that where differences did emerge, they were quite small, with girls scoring higher on some measures of verbal ability and boys scoring higher on spatial tasks (Hyde, 2005).

©Radachynskyi/iStock/Getty Images

As an example of girls' superior performance on verbal tasks, one study examined the verbal performance of fourth-graders in 33 different countries (Mullis & others, 2003; Ogle & others, 2003). In every country, the average performance of girls on verbal tasks was higher than the average performance of boys.

In turn, research has revealed that, at least by preschool age, boys show greater accuracy in performing tasks requiring mental rotation of objects in space (Levine & others, 1999; Loring-Meier & Halpern, 1999). The gender difference in mental rotation persists in adulthood (Hegarty, 2018; Heil & others, 2018). Interestingly, the difference is smaller when the rotating objects are human figures rather than abstract forms (Doyle & Voyer, 2018).

A gender difference that is a source of interest for many researchers, as well as for the general public, is the under-representation of women in math and science careers (often called STEM for science, technology, engineering, and math). Considering that women constitute half of the world's population, the percentage of women in STEM fields is quite low. In 2014, women made up about 20 percent of computer scientists and physicists (National Science Foundation, 2017). Is it possible that the lack of women in STEM is due to the small differences in cognitive abilities described above? Based on the most recent evidence, the answer to that question is no.

First, the remarkable dearth of women in STEM does not apply to all science fields. Women are well represented in social and life sciences (like psychology and biology) (Cheryan & others, 2017). The gender difference in STEM appears to be specific to computer science, engineering, and physics. A recent analysis of a worldwide database of over 400,000 adolescents showed that in nearly all countries, girls and boys were equally capable of undertaking challenging science coursework (Stoet & Geary, 2018). Looking at the data carefully, the researchers found that people were likely to pursue careers that used their personal strengths. However, the percentage of girls for whom science and math were personal academic strengths was always far lower than the percentage of women pursuing STEM majors in college (Stoet & Geary, 2018).

Apparently girls who are talented in math and science choose not to pursue careers in these fields. What might explain the choices made by women who are capable of entering science careers but choose not to pursue them? That choice is likely to be a product of many interrelated factors, including what activities a woman feels she is especially good at and likes to do, the role models she encounters, the social support she receives from family and friends, and the likelihood that a particular career path will ultimately lead to the life she envisions for herself in the future. An important factor in a woman's decision making might be whether or not she feels like she fits into the scientist category. To read about research probing this issue, see the Intersection.

## INTERSECTION

### Psychology of Gender and Social Psychology: Do You "Match" the Scientist Category?

When we judge whether objects fit into a particular category, we often compare the object in question to *a prototype* of that category. Prototypes are exemplars that capture the essence of a category. For example, an apple is a prototype of the category *fruit*. Prototypes are important to social judgments as well. To decide whether we belong to a category, we might try to match ourselves to a prototype of the category (Ehrlinger & others, 2018). If we do not match the prototype, we might decide we do not belong.

*Do you fit the prototype of a person in the career you would like to pursue?*

Now, the category of scientist is highly stereotyped. When college students are asked to draw a scientist, they often draw images of men (Farland-Smith, 2017) and even the word *scientist* conjures images of a bearded man in a lab coat wearing glasses (McCoy & others, 2018). Women are rarely featured as scientists in movies and when they are, they are typically childless (Steinke & Tavarez, 2018). Could the idea of the "protoypical scientist" affect whether women pursue STEM?

In a series of studies, researchers asked college students to rate the traits of a typical student in a calculus-based physics class required for STEM majors (McPherson, Park, & Ito, 2018) and then to rate themselves on those same traits. The traits were science-relevant (intelligent, logical), expressive (caring, warm), and instrumental (powerful, self-confident) characteristics. Results showed students thought that STEM majors would be less expressive and less instrumental than themselves (McPherson, Park, & Ito, 2018). Importantly, students whose self-ratings were very different from their image of a typical STEM student reported less interest in STEM majors.

With these results in mind, the researchers took their question to the next level. They obtained self-ratings on the same traits from an actual sample of nearly 800 students in a calculus-based physics class. Were these STEM students really so different from everyone else? They were not: STEM majors did not differ from other students on these dimensions (McPherson, Park, & Ito, 2018).

The choices we make as we pursue our life dreams are affected not only by our abilities but by the opportunities we see as possible. When we think of what we want to be when we grow up, the image in our mind's eye may be informed by misconceptions and stereotypes. When young women think about STEM careers, they may have inaccurate and negative attitudes toward women scientists, viewing them as unrelatable or different from themselves in terms of their life goals and values. Interestingly, when young women are reminded of the obstacles women scientists likely faced as they pursued their goals, they come to see these woman as more relatable (Pietri & others, 2018).

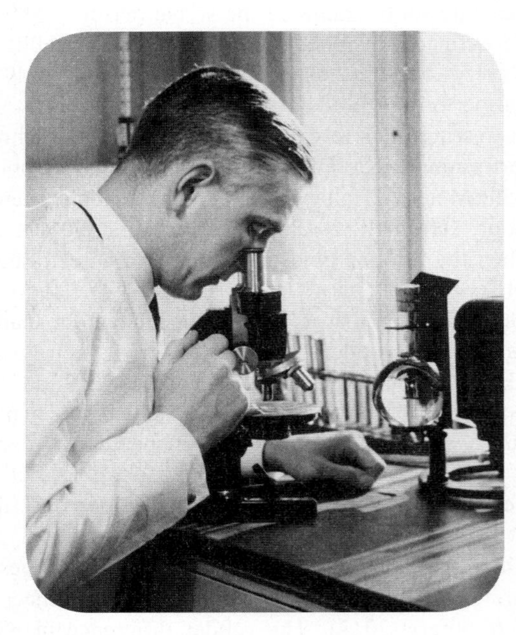

©George Marks/Retrofile RF/Getty Images

## Aggression

**Aggression** is behavior that is intended to harm another person. A consistent finding in the research literature is that men are far more likely than women to engage in physical aggression (Björkqvist, 2018; Provençal, Booij, & Tremblay, 2015). Yet, the relationship between gender and aggression is more nuanced than this simple conclusion suggests.

**Overt aggression** refers to physically or verbally harming another person directly. Boys and men are higher on overt aggression than girls and women throughout life (Björkqvist, 2018; Widom & others, 2018). Men are more likely than women to be chronically hostile and to commit violent crimes (Hachtel & others, 2018).

Women's smaller physical size may be one reason they are less likely to engage in overt aggression. To understand aggressive tendencies in girls and women, researchers have focused instead on **relational aggression**, behavior that is meant to harm the social standing

- **aggression** Behavior that is intended to harm another person.
- **overt aggression** Physically or verbally harming another person directly.
- **relational aggression** Behavior that is meant to harm the social standing of another person.

of another person through activities such as gossiping and spreading rumors (Coyne & Ostrov, 2018).

Relational aggression differs from overt aggression in that it requires some social and cognitive skill. To be relationally aggressive, a person must understand how to plant rumors and the likelihood that a piece of information will be damaging to the intended party (Loflin & Barry, 2016). Relationally aggressive individual may not seem to be aggressive to outsiders, as the aggressive acts typically are committed secretly. Girls are not necessarily more relationally aggressive than boys. Rather, relational aggression comprises a greater percentage of girls' overall aggression than it does for boys (Björkqvist, 2018).

Although relational aggression does not lead to the physical injury that might result from overt aggression, it can be extremely painful nevertheless. For example, a victim of relational aggression, Tyler Clementi, was a talented, creative college student who also happened to be gay. In 2010, he committed suicide after being cyberbullied by classmates at Rutgers University (Parker, 2012). The main perpetrator was convicted of multiple crimes, including invasion of privacy.

*Tyler Clementi's mother commemorates her son, who was just 18 years old at his death.*



## Sexuality

Broadly speaking, **sexuality** refers to the ways people experience and express themselves as sexual beings. Sexuality involves activity that is associated with sexual pleasure. Although stereotypes might point to large gender differences in sexuality, with men being more preoccupied with sex than women, research has shown that differences are smaller and less consistent than those stereotypes suggest. In some cases, it is clear that social expectations influence people's responses to questions about their sexual behavior. For instance, men often report having more sex partners than women do. In a study using a fake lie detector test (called the *bogus pipeline*), however, this difference disappeared when men and women thought that the researchers could tell if they were lying (Alexander & Fisher, 2003).

● **sexuality** The ways people experience and express themselves as sexual beings.

Do men at least *think about* having sex more often than women do? In one study, undergraduate participants kept tallies of how many times they thought about sex, food, and sleep for a week (Fisher, Moore, & Pittenger, 2012). Men did report thinking about sex more than women did; however, men also thought about food and sleep more than women did. The researchers concluded that men may be more focused than women on their own physical needs.

The evolutionary perspective on gender strongly predicts gender differences in sexual behavior–specifically, that women should be more selective and men less so when it comes to casual sex (Buss, 2016). To test this prediction, Russell Clark and Elaine Hatfield (1989) sent five male and five female experimenters (judged to be slightly unattractive to moderately attractive) to a college campus with a mission. They were to approach members of the opposite sex whom they found quite attractive and say, "I have been noticing you around campus. I find you very attractive." Then they were to ask one of three questions:

- "Would you like to go out with me?"
- "Would you like to go to my apartment with me?"
- "Would you like to go to bed with me?"

The independent variables in this study were the sex of the person approached and the type of question asked. The dependent variable was whether that person said yes or no to the question. The results showed no differences between men and women in their answers to the "going out" question–about half of each sex said yes. However, dramatic sex differences emerged for the other two questions: The large majority of men said yes to the "apartment" question (most women said no) and to the "bed" question (all of the women said no). The Psychological Inquiry shows the results.

## psychological *inquiry*

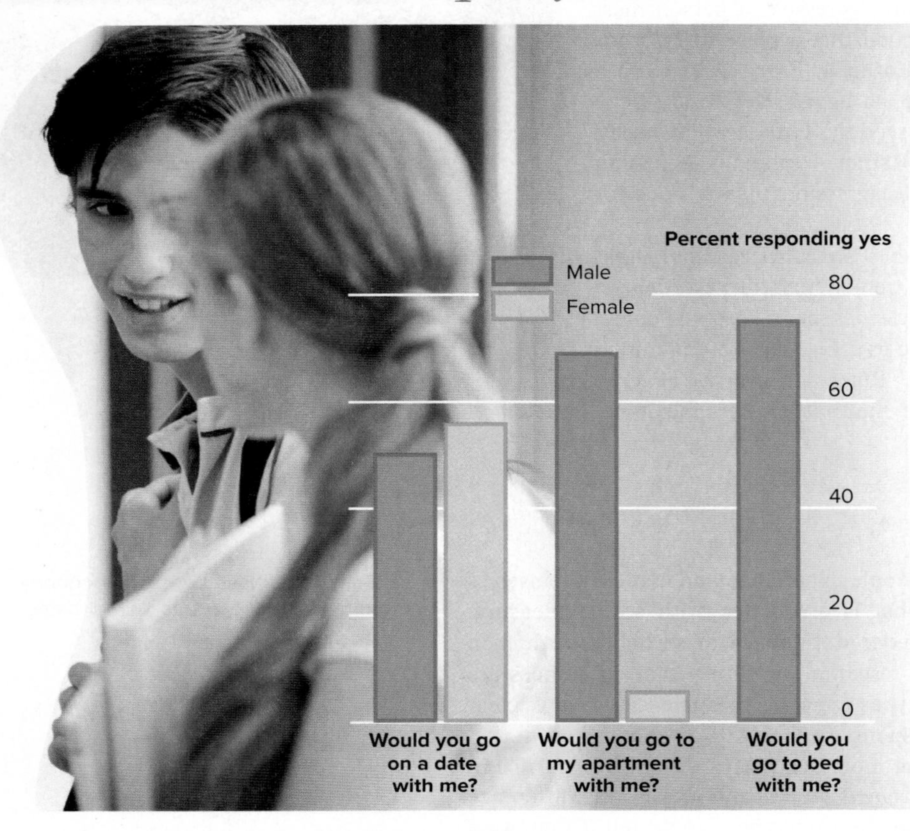


Source: Clark & Hatfield (1989); (photo) ©PhotoAlto/Sigrid Olsson/Getty Images

### *Sex and Casual Sex*

The figure shows the results of the Clark and Hatfield study (1989). Recall that the experimenters approached men and women on a college campus and asked one of three questions. Review the details of the study and answer the following questions.

1. This study was an experiment. What are the independent and dependent variables?
2. Why do you think that men were more likely to say yes to the "bed" question than they were to the "date" question?
3. Recall that in this study, the experimenters were judged to range from slightly unattractive to moderately attractive and were told to approach people whom they found to be quite attractive. How might these circumstances have influenced the results?
4. Perhaps the most striking aspect of this experiment's results is the big gender difference on the "bed" question. Most men said yes and not a single woman did. What is another question that might have produced a similarly stunning gender difference?
5. Imagine that you strongly favor the social role theory of gender development. How would you explain these results from that perspective?

©Ariel Skelley/Getty Images

Interestingly, men who said no to the "bed" question felt the need to explain themselves with statements like "I have a girlfriend" or "I'm married." In contrast, women who were asked if they would like to go to bed with a male experimenter were more likely to give responses such as "You've got to be kidding" and "What is wrong with you? Leave me alone" (Clark & Hatfield, 1989, p. 52). For many years, this study was recognized as supporting the predictions that men are more interested in casual sex than women are and that women are choosier than men.

If you think about this study long enough, you might see that there is a *confound* in the study design. As described in the chapter "Psychology's Scientific Method", a confound in an experiment is a variable, other than the independent variable, that systematically differs across the groups and that might explain the results. Terri Conley noted that although men and women in the study differed in their willingness to say yes to a proposal for casual sex, they were responding to proposers who systematically differed in terms of their sex as well: Women were always approached *by men,* and men were always approached *by women* (Conley, 2011). Isn't it possible, Conley asked, that the sex of the person doing the asking might have influenced whether those who were approached said yes to the proposal?

In a series of studies, Conley showed that the proposer's characteristics influence whether the approached person accepts or rejects a proposal for casual sex (Conley, 2011). For instance, she found that both men and women rated a male stranger as potentially more dangerous than a female stranger. Would women be so choosy if a familiar person rather than a stranger approached them? Conley discovered that women were more likely to report that they would say yes to casual sex if it was offered by a familiar person, such as an attractive friend, or by a celebrity, such as Johnny Depp. She also found that bisexual women were more likely to say they would engage in casual sex with a female, but not a male, who approached them.

So gender differences in sexuality are less dramatic than stereotypes would tell us. A meta-analysis of research examining gender differences in sexuality found differences on the following: Men engaged in more masturbation, viewed more pornography, engaged in more casual sex, and had more permissive attitudes about casual sex than did women (Petersen & Hyde, 2010).

Men and women differ sexually in other ways. Compared with men, women tend to show more changes in their sexual patterns and sexual desires over their lifetime (Luoto, Krams, & Rantala, 2018; Morales Knight & Hope, 2012; Ponseti & others, 2018b). Women are more likely than men, for instance, to have had sexual experiences with same- and opposite-sex partners, even if they identify strongly as heterosexual or lesbian. Women are more likely than men to identify as bisexual (Fahs & Koerth, 2018).

In contrast, male sexuality may be more limited to specific targets of attraction. One study compared the sexual arousal of heterosexual women, lesbian women, heterosexual men, and gay men while they watched erotic films of various sexual acts featuring male and female actors or bonobo apes (Chivers, Bouchard, & Timmers, 2015; Dawson & Chivers, 2018; Chivers, Seto, & Blanchard, 2007). Physiological measures of sexual arousal showed that both heterosexual women and lesbian women were aroused by films showing sexual activity. However, gay men were aroused only by such films that included men, and heterosexual men were aroused only by such films that included women.

## Evaluating the Evidence for Gender Differences

With regard to emotion, empathy, and helping, women show some advantage in reading the emotions of others, but gender differences in these domains require us to consider the social context. Gender differences appear to be strongest in the area of physical aggression. Differences are weaker in the domains of cognitive ability and sexuality. Janet Shibley Hyde (2005) conducted a meta-analysis of meta-analyses. Recall that a meta-analysis is a statistical summary of all the available data about a particular research question. In her analysis, Hyde pulled together the very best and most definitive data available to address the question of gender differences across a host of domains. Hyde found strong support for what she called the **gender similarities hypothesis**–the idea that men and women (and boys and girls) are much more similar than they are different (Hyde, 2005, 2006, 2007, 2014). Evidence for gender differences must be understood in this context of a great deal of similarity and overlap between men and women on most characteristics.

One way in which men and women clearly differ is that men generally are sexually attracted to women, whereas women typically are sexually attracted to men. Of course, these patterns of attraction are not always the case, as human beings differ from one another in their sexual orientation, our next topic.

● **gender similarities hypothesis** Hyde's proposition that men and women (and boys and girls) are much more similar than they are different.

### *test yourself*

1. What is the gender similarities hypothesis? How might even small gender differences lead to larger differences later in life?
2. How do overt aggression and relational aggression differ? How does gender relate to types of aggression?
3. Identify at least four ways in which men and women differ in their patterns of sexual behavior, thoughts, and/or feelings.

# 4. SEXUAL ORIENTATION

A person's **sexual orientation** is the direction of their erotic interests. Sexual orientation is not just sexual behavior. A man may have sex with other men while in prison but may never think of himself as homosexual. A woman might always feel sexually attracted to

● **sexual orientation** The direction of an individual's erotic interests.

other women but never act on those feelings. When we talk about sexual orientation, we mean a *whole range* of human experiences that interest psychologists, including behaviors, desires, feelings, fantasies, and a person's sense of identity.

## Defining Sexual Orientation

- **heterosexual** Referring to a sexual orientation in which the individual is generally sexually attracted to members of the opposite sex.
- **homosexual** Referring to a sexual orientation in which the individual is generally sexually attracted to members of the same sex.
- **bisexual** Referring to a sexual orientation in which the individual is sexually attracted to people of both sexes.
- **pansexual** A person whose sexual attractions do not depend on the biological sex, gender, or gender identity of others.
- **asexual** A person who experiences a lack of sexual attraction to others or has no sexual orientation.

A person who identifies as **heterosexual** is generally sexually attracted to members of the opposite sex. A person who identifies as **homosexual** is generally sexually attracted to members of the same sex. Women who are primarily attracted to women may identify as *lesbian.* Some people identify as **bisexual**, meaning that they are sexually attracted to people of both sexes. Some people identify as pansexual (Sprott & Benoit Hadcock, 2018). **Pansexual** orientation means that the person's sexual attractions do not depend on the biological sex, gender, or gender identity of others. Finally, some people identify as **asexual**. Asexuality means the person experiences a lack of sexual attraction to others and may feel they have no sexual orientation (Bogaert, Ashton, & Lee, 2018).

Despite the widespread use of labels for sexual orientation, some scholars argue that they are misleading. Instead, erotic attractions may be fluid, and these categories ignore the potential flexibility of human sexual attraction and behavior (L. M. Diamond, 2008b; Diamond, Dickenson, & Blair, 2017). In some cultures, engaging in same-sex sexual activity is not viewed as an indication of the person's identity (Nanda, 2008), but in Western societies, there is a strong belief that sexual orientation is a stable attribute. Longitudinal studies have shown very high stability for heterosexuality over time (Kinnish, Strassberg, & Turner, 2005; Mock & Eibach, 2011). Non-heterosexual individuals may be more likely to shift their erotic interests, especially in adolescence (Berona & others, 2018; Katz-Wise & Hyde, 2015).

Related to this issue is the very definition of bisexuality. Some people (mistakenly) think that bisexuality is simply a steppingstone to homosexuality (Matsick & Rubin, 2018). Evidence supports the notion that bisexuality is a stable orientation that involves attraction to both sexes (Israel, 2018; Lippa, 2013; Mock & Eibach, 2011). Indeed, even when a bisexual person is in a committed relationship, their sexual orientation does not change to match that relationship (Hayfield, Campbell, & Reed, 2018).

## Occurrence of the Different Sexual Orientations

*Roy and Silo, same-sex partners who raised their adopted daughter Tango, are chinstrap penguins like this parent and offspring.*



Homosexual behavior is relatively common in nature, having been observed in 1,500 different species, including rats, nonhuman primates, giraffes, ostriches, guppies, cats, bison, dolphins, and fruit flies (Sommer & Vasey, 2006). Long-term same-sex partnerships occur in nonhuman species. In 2004, the *New York Times* reported the story of Roy and Silo, two male penguins who appeared to share a long-term monogamous sexual relationship at the Central Park Zoo, even raising their adopted daughter Tango (they have since broken up) (D. Smith, 2004). In humans, homosexuality is present in all cultures, regardless of whether a culture is tolerant or not. Obviously, the majority of people, regardless of culture, are heterosexual.

It is difficult to know precisely how many gays, lesbians, bisexuals (and others) there are in the world, partly because fears of discrimination may prevent people from answering honestly on surveys. Estimates of the frequency of non-heterosexual sexual orientations range from 2 percent to 15 percent of the population (Berona & others, 2018; Zietsch & others, 2008). Demographer Gary Gates (2011) summarized the available U.S. data and concluded that approximately 3.8 percent or 9 million Americans are gay, lesbian, or bisexual, which is essentially the population of New Jersey. Interestingly, the largest sexual minority group appears to be those who identify as bisexual (Brown, 2017).

## Origins of Sexual Orientation: A Scientific Puzzle

©Betsie Van Der Meer/Taxi/Getty Images

What is the source of sexual orientation? Scientists have speculated extensively about this question. Charles Darwin (1862) himself commented, "We do not even in the least know the final cause of sexuality. The whole subject is hidden in darkness."

Since Darwin's time, scientists have learned something about factors that *do not* predict sexual orientation. First, being reared by a gay parent *does not* increase the chances of being gay (Golombok & Tasker, 1996; Patterson & Farr, 2016; Patterson & Wainright, 2010). In fact, the vast majority of gay people have heterosexual parents, so it does not seem that observational learning or modeling play a role in the development of sexual orientation. Nor does a particular parenting style relate to the emergence of sexual orientation (Bell, Weinberg, & Hammersmith, 1981). Given the many different ways parents interact with their children and the fact that the vast majority of people are heterosexual, it is highly unlikely that heterosexuality is explained by particular parenting strategies. Finally, same-sex sexual experience or experimentation in childhood does not predict eventual adult homosexuality (Bailey, 2003; Bogaert, 2000).

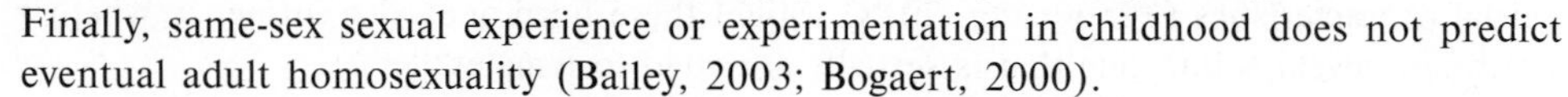

So, what factors might account for sexual orientation? Before we probe this question, let's pause to consider some key issues in the science behind sexual orientation.

### THINKING CRITICALLY ABOUT SEXUAL ORIENTATION

Scientists approach the puzzle of sexual orientation with an openness to the different potential answers empirical data might suggest. Before exploring the current evidence for various explanations of sexual orientation, it may be helpful to review five important issues for critical thinkers.

- *Unlikelihood of a single cause:* For any psychological characteristic, it is unlikely that a single cause can be identified, and sexual orientation is no exception. Keep in mind that it is very probable that many factors work together to foster sexual orientation and that factors that have not even been considered will likely emerge in the future.
- *Within-group variation:* There is a great deal of variation within any group of people who share the same sexual orientation. Heterosexual men are sexually attracted to women, but that attraction may be the only thing that any two heterosexual men have in common. Similarly, gay men share a sexual attraction to men, but any two gay men may have little else in common.
- *Research challenges:* Comparing people with different sexual orientations presents challenges. One such challenge is representativeness. Heterosexual and homosexual participants are often recruited in different ways. Gay, lesbian and bisexual participants are sometimes recruited only from Gay Pride events, for example, and so they may not be representative of all homosexual and bisexual people. Small sample sizes can also be an issue due to the difficulty of recruiting gay participants. In one study in 2000, just 6 gay men were compared to 256 "non-gay" men (Lippa, 2000). Recall that studies using larger samples are more likely to yield generalizable results.
- *Explaining sexual orientation does not mean explaining only homosexuality:* Finally, any good theory of sexual orientation should explain how *any of us* (straight, gay, or otherwise) becomes sexually oriented toward people of a particular sex. As scientists, we want to explain the sexual orientations of people who are attracted to men or women or both.

With these cautions in mind, let's look at the evidence concerning sexual orientation.

## GENETIC INFLUENCES

Twin studies have sought to estimate the heritability of sexual orientation. Recall from the chapter "Thinking, Intelligence, and Language" that heritability is a statistic that tells us the extent to which we can explain observed differences in a given characteristic based on differences in genes. A study of nearly 4,000 twins in Sweden demonstrated that the heritability of same-sex sexual behavior was about 35 percent in men and 19 percent in women (Långström & others, 2010). These estimates suggest that genes are associated with sexual orientation but not as strongly as they are for other characteristics, such as intelligence.

Of course, genes do not affect psychological characteristics as directly as they do a physical characteristic like eye color. We therefore need to consider other factors that might provide the bridge between genes and the psychological experience of sexual orientation.

## PRENATAL HORMONES AND BRAIN DIFFERENCES

One way in which genes might influence sexual orientation is through their effect on brain development. Recall that prenatal androgens play a crucial role in the development of sexual characteristics (Berenbaum, 2018). Might these hormones also influence whether the brain develops into one that is sexually attracted to females?

One strategy for examining the link between prenatal hormones and sexual orientation is to identify physical features that are associated with prenatal testosterone. The idea is that once we identify the effects of prenatal testosterone on various physical features of the body, we can look at those features and see whether they differ in adults who are either gay or straight.

The best known of these features is the ratio between the second and fourth digits on the hand (the pointer and the ring finger), called the *2D:4D ratio*. This ratio is influenced by prenatal testosterone and men tend to have a ring finger that is longer than their pointer; for women the two fingers are nearly the same length (Fink & Manning, 2018; Salmon & Hehman, 2018). Thus, women tend to have larger 2D:4D ratios than men. If prenatal testosterone exposure is related to developing a brain that is attracted to females, we might expect lesbian women to show a pattern more similar to heterosexual men (a smaller 2D:4D ratio). Evidence for such a difference was reported in a recent study comparing identical twin sisters, only one of whom was lesbian or bisexual (Watts & others, 2018). However, other studies have failed to support this prediction in non-twin samples (Rahman & Wilson, 2003; Vásquez-Amézquita & others, 2018; Voracek & others, 2011).

Researchers have also examined whether sexual orientation is associated with brain differences. A recent brain imaging study examined patterns of brain structures that characterize gender differences in the brains of four groups: gay men, lesbian women, heterosexual men, and heterosexual women (Manzouri & Savic, 2018). Results showed differences across the male groups but not the female groups. Brain structural differences for gay men were more similar to women than heterosexual men. These brain differences likely emerge from an interaction of genetics, prenatal hormones, and possibly experiences (Gavrilets, Friberg, & Rice, 2018; Manzouri & Savic, 2018; Roselli, 2018). Indeed, in trying to interpret these brain characteristics, we must keep in mind that habitual patterns of *behavior* can also influence brain structure and function. Behavioral similarities between heterosexual women and gay men may contribute to similarities in brain structure.

## SOCIAL FACTORS

What about social experience? We have seen that there is no evidence that specific parenting styles "cause" sexual orientation. Still, some scientists have attempted to explain sexual orientation as a function of early childhood experience. Gender-nonconforming behaviors—activities that run counter to gender stereotypes—have received particular focus (Bem, 1996; Rieger, Linsenmeier, & Bailey, 2009; Rieger & others, 2008).

Homosexual adults are more likely than heterosexual adults to remember themselves as having engaged in gender-nonconforming behaviors (Bailey & Zucker, 1995; Lippa, 2008). Moreover, some evidence suggests that in videos of their childhood activities, gay and lesbian adults pursued more gender-atypical activities as children (Rieger & others, 2008).

For boys, gender-nonconforming behavior may be related to eventual sexual development, but the picture is not clear-cut. For example, one study compared 66 extremely gender-nonconforming boys to 56 gender-conforming boys (Green, 1987). Among the nonconforming boys, 75 percent were either bisexual or homosexual at a follow-up during adolescence or young adulthood. Among the gender-conforming boys, 96 percent were heterosexual at follow-up.

Although this study is sometimes used as evidence of the role of gender-nonconforming behavior in the development of sexual orientation (Bem, 1996), take a good look at those percentages. Although gender-nonconforming boys were more likely to be homosexual or bisexual, note that the percentage of boys in the gender-conforming group who eventually emerged as gay or bisexual falls within the typical percentages found in the general population. Thus, boys who are quite gender typical in their behavior can certainly turn out to be gay (or bisexual or straight).

©T.M.O. Pictures/Alamy Stock Photo

Studies of childhood behavior and sexual orientation are correlational. One challenge of correlational research is the potential for a third variable to explain the relationship between the variables of interest. In thinking about an individual's gender-nonconforming behavior in childhood and his or her eventual sexual orientation, you might note that factors such as genes and prenatal hormone exposure might explain both of these variables (Berenbaum, 2018; Cohen-Bendahan, van de Beek, & Berenbaum, 2005).

Consider, too, that gender-nonconforming boys may experience a very different social response than gender-nonconforming girls. In fact, many women report having been tomboys (Peplau & others, 1999). Girls who engage in boyish activities are frequently popular among their peers, and the vast majority of tomboys turn out to be heterosexual (Peplau & others, 1999). Social responses to gender-nonconforming boys may be more negative (Van Beusekom & others, 2018). Parents and peers may label a gender-nonconforming boy as homosexual, and that labeling may influence the boy's sense of self and his emerging identity (Hegarty, 2009).

### AN UNSOLVED PUZZLE

Clearly, scientists have devised a number of ways to identify factors associated with sexual orientation. However, as we have seen, many questions remain. Although we may not still be in the "darkness" described by Darwin, it is fair to say that the room remains dimly lit.

Similar to many other psychological characteristics, an individual's sexual orientation most likely depends on a combination of genetic, hormonal, cognitive, and environmental factors (Gavrilets, Friberg, & Rice, 2018). Most experts on sexual orientation believe that no one factor alone causes sexual orientation and that the relative weight of each factor can vary within people of the same orientation (Jeffery & others, 2018).

We know that no matter what a person's sexual orientation might be, they cannot be talked out it. Indeed, Qazi Rahman, a researcher who studies the neurobiology of sexual orientation, asserted that "there is no argument anymore–if you are gay, you are born gay" (quoted in Nicholson, 2008). Whether one is homosexual, heterosexual, bisexual, or some alternative orientation, sexual orientation is not a choice but an integral part of the functioning human being and his or her sense of self (Worthington & others, 2008).

## Gay and Lesbian Functioning

We may not know definitively why people are gay or lesbian, but research has uncovered some interesting things about gay people. Here we briefly review selected findings as they relate to individual adjustment and well-being, gay and lesbian relationships, and gay and lesbian families.

## INDIVIDUAL ADJUSTMENT AND WELL-BEING

Researchers typically find no differences among lesbians, gays, bisexuals, and heterosexuals in a wide range of attitudes and behaviors, as well as in psychological adjustment. Gay men and lesbian women are likely to differ from heterosexuals in terms of the gender typicality of their hobbies, activities, and occupations (Lippa, 2000). Note, however, that if gay men and women live in households that are headed by two men or two women, they will inevitably engage in gender-atypical behavior (for instance, women doing the yard work or men cooking and cleaning) simply because someone has to do those tasks.

One factor in the well-being of gays and lesbians is coping with prejudice and discrimination (Garrison, Doane, & Elliott, 2018). Among gay men and lesbians polled in one survey, 90 percent reported that discrimination against homosexuals remains a serious problem (Page, 2012). In addition, it is important to note that some sexual minority individuals are also members of ethnic minorities as well. These people exemplify *intersectionality*, the idea that a person may occupy many different identities at once (Ghavami & Peplau, 2018) and the combination of identities may affect the person's life in a unique way. For example, an African American women who identifies as lesbian may face different challenges because of the convergence of her unique experience as a woman, an ethnic minority member, and a sexual minority person (Warner, Settles, & Shields, 2018).

Attitudes toward gays and lesbians have become increasingly more positive in U.S. society. For example, in 2016, 63 percent of Americans reported believing that homosexuality should be accepted, compared with just 51 percent in 2006 (Brown, 2017). Younger Americans are particularly likely to support gay rights. In a 2015 poll, among those ages 18 to 29, 70 percent supported marriage equality (Pew Research Center, 2015).

This increased acceptance likely stems in part from the greater openness of gay people about their lives. Individuals who know someone who is gay are less likely to report prejudicial attitudes toward gay people (Smith, Axelton, & Saucier, 2009). Polls have shown a steady increase in the number of Americans who know a gay person. In a 2013 poll, 79 percent of respondents reporting knowing someone who is gay (Murray, 2013)–a large increase from a 1984 survey in which only 24 percent reported knowing a gay or bisexual person (Harris Interactive, 2006).

For gays, lesbians, and bisexuals, being open about their sexual orientation is a strong predictor of psychological and physical health (Biegel, 2018; Cohen & others, 2016; Hammack & others, 2018), although the benefits of coming out may depend on the social reaction (Legate, Ryan, & Weinstein, 2012). Living in accord with one's sexual orientation is a matter of living authentically, and being "out" to other people is part of being true to oneself (Ryan & Ryan, 2018).

*Lesbian women and gay men are similar to heterosexual women and heterosexual men in many respects.*

©David Jakle/Image Source/Getty Images

## GAY AND LESBIAN RELATIONSHIPS

Research consistently shows that gay men and lesbian women report greater satisfaction in their relationships than do heterosexual couples (Balsam & others, 2008; Kurdek, 2004; MacIntosh, Reissing, & Andruff, 2010). What might explain this higher relationship satisfaction? One possibility is that heterosexual people feel more pressure to get married and stay married, regardless of their personal choices, and they may be supported to stay in unsatisfying relationships (Green, Bettinger, & Zacks, 1996).

John Gottman and his colleagues (2003) conducted a longitudinal study of gay, lesbian, and heterosexual couples that included video-recorded interactions over 12 years. Gottman's team found that compared with heterosexual couples, gay and lesbian partners were better able to manage conflicts. They were more likely to use humor and affection in dealing with conflicts, took a more positive attitude toward negative feedback from their partners, and let conflicts go once they had been resolved (Gottman & others, 2003).

Despite the fact that gay couples report higher satisfaction with their relationships, for many years, research showed that gay couples were more likely to end their relationships than heterosexual married couples were (Kurdek, 2004; Lau, 2012). A possible reason for this difference is that the legal status of marriage, previously unavailable to gay couples, promotes relationship stability (Shulman, Gotta, & Green, 2012), and divorce makes dissolving relationships more difficult. In keeping with this idea, research shows that the legal tie of marriage is associated with relationship stability among same-sex couples (Balsam & others, 2008).

### GAY AND LESBIAN FAMILIES

Increasingly gay families include kids. Available evidence suggests that approximately 37 percent of gay, lesbian, bisexual, or transgender households include children (Gates, 2013). Children reared by gay parents tend to be as well-adjusted as those from heterosexual households and are just as likely to be accepted by their peers (Chan, Raboy, & Patterson, 1998; Farr & Patterson, 2013; Goldberg, 2010; Golombok & others, 2003; Patterson & Farr, 2016; Patterson & Wainright, 2010). Research examining the well-being of children who have same-sex and opposite-sex parents consistently shows that what matters is a warm relationship with their parents, not the parents' gender or sexual orientation (Golombok & others, 2018; Wainright & Patterson, 2008).

***test yourself***

1. Name various factors that might influence sexual orientation.
2. What is gender-nonconforming behavior? What is the evidence for the role of gender-nonconforming behavior in the development of sexual orientation?
3. What are some factors associated with gay and lesbian well-being?

# 5. SEXUAL BEHAVIORS AND PRACTICES

Talking about sexual behaviors can sometimes be uncomfortable and embarrassing but also interesting, enlightening, and exciting. In this section, we take up this hot topic and explore the ways that research has addressed it.

## Sexual Behaviors

What constitutes sexual behavior—what we commonly refer to as "sex"? In 1998, when President Bill Clinton was asked whether he had engaged in sex with White House intern Monica Lewinsky, he was widely ridiculed for replying that "it depends" on what sex is. Yet Clinton may have been representing a more general confusion. What counts as sex? Most people might answer that question with "vaginal intercourse," but what about other sexual behaviors, such as anal sex and oral sex? If someone has engaged in these practices, is he or she still a "virgin"? If your significant other reported to you that he or she had recently engaged in oral sex with another person, would you consider that sexual infidelity? What if he or she had spent an hour sexting an attractive friend? These are the kinds of questions that come up in trying to define sexual behavior.

One possibility is to define sex as activities involved in reproduction. By this definition. many gay men and women are virgins, as are adolescents who engage exclusively in, say, oral sex. Further, masturbation would not qualify as a sexual behavior at all.

Another approach is to define sexual behavior by the arousal and sexual response that occur when the behavior is performed. Though broader, this definition still might leave out people who could say that they are engaged in sexual behavior. For instance, if a person is unable to experience sexual arousal but performs oral sex on a partner, has that person "had sex"? Alternatively, we might broaden the definition a great deal and define sexual behaviors to include behaviors that are specific to each individual and that are pleasurable in a particular way—one that is unusually intimate and personal.

Confusion over what counts as sex can lead to potentially risky behavior. For example, for many adolescents, oral sex appears to be a recreational activity and a safe alternative to intercourse (Goldstein & Halpern-Felsher, 2018). Engaging in oral sex, of course, does not increase the risk of pregnancy, and one study showed that among adolescents girls, those who reported having engaged in oral sex prior to vaginal sex were nearly four times less likely to experience teen pregnancy (Reese & others, 2013). As we will consider later in this chapter, however, oral sex exposes individuals to the risk of contracting sexually transmitted infections.

## Sexual Practices

When people in the United States engage in sexual behavior, what do they do, and how often? Alfred Kinsey and his colleagues conducted the earliest research on this topic in 1948. Kinsey is widely recognized as the father of sexology, a pioneer who brought scientific attention to sexual behavior. Kinsey collected data wherever he could find it, interviewing anyone who was willing to discuss the intimate details of his or her sex life.

*The Kinsey Reports,* published in two volumes, presented his findings for men (Kinsey, Pomeroy, & Martin, 1948) and women (Kinsey, Martin, & Pomeroy, 1953). Among the findings that shocked his readers were Kinsey's estimates of the frequency of bisexuality in men (nearly 12 percent) and women (7 percent) and his estimate that at least 50 percent of married men had been sexually unfaithful. Although acknowledged for initiating the scientific study of sexual behavior, Kinsey's work was limited by the lack of representative samples.

More recent data provide more representative answers to the question "What, exactly, are people doing when they say they are having sex?" In 2002, the Centers for Disease Control conducted a study of sexual behaviors in the United States (Mosher, Chandra, & Jones, 2005). The researchers found that among people 15 to 44 years old, 10 percent of men and 8 percent of women had never had sex, including vaginal intercourse, oral sex, and anal sex. Among adults 25 to 44 years old, 97 percent had engaged in vaginal intercourse and 90 percent in oral sex. Forty percent of men had engaged in anal sex, and 35 percent of women had done so.

What do gay men and lesbian women do when they "have sex"? Research is limited but suggests that among gay men, mutual masturbation, oral sex, and anal sex are common, although as many as a third of gay men report never having engaged in anal sex (Reisner & others, 2009; Rice & others, 2016). Among lesbian women, practices include genital-to-genital contact (body rubbing), mutual fondling and masturbation, penetration with the hands or other objects, and oral sex (Marrazzo, Coffey, & Bingham, 2005; Mercer & others, 2007; Ybarra & others, 2016).

How often do people have sex? Answers to this question come from a survey given to large samples of adults in the United States. Starting in 1989, the survey asked participants how many times they had had sex in the past year. Results spanning the years from 1989 until 2014, including over 26,000 people, showed that sexual frequency declined over time (Twenge, Sherman, & Wells, 2017). Between 1989 and 1994, respondents estimated having sex approximately 60 times in the past year. In comparison, from 2010 to 2014, that number had dropped to about 54 times. Interestingly, this drop appears to exist because younger generations are having less sex. Another interesting trend from these data is a difference that has emerged in the link between marriage and sexual frequency. Prior to 2003, married (or partnered) adults reported having more sex than unmarried (or unpartnered) adults. However, that difference disappeared in 2003 and by 2014, unmarried (or unpartnered) individuals reported having more sex than married (or partnered) people (Twenge, Sherman, & Wells, 2017). We will address the implications of sexual frequency for relationship satisfaction and personal well-being at the end of this chapter.

## The Human Sexual Response Pattern

Regardless of the specific behavior, similar physical processes are involved in sexual responses. To examine the physiological processes involved in sexual activity, William Masters and Virginia Johnson (1966) carefully observed and measured the physiological responses of 382 female and 312 male volunteers as they masturbated or had vaginal intercourse. Masters and Johnson identified a **human sexual response pattern** consisting of four phases—excitement, plateau, orgasm, and resolution.

• **human sexual response pattern** Masters and Johnson's model of human sexual response, consisting of four phases—excitement, plateau, orgasm, and resolution.

The *excitement phase* begins the process of erotic responsiveness; it lasts from several minutes to several hours, depending on the nature of the sex play involved. Engorgement of blood vessels and increased blood flow in genital areas, along with muscle tension, characterize the excitement phase. The most obvious signs of response in this phase are lubrication of the vagina and partial erection of the penis.

The second phase of the human sexual response, the *plateau phase,* is a continuation and heightening of the arousal begun in the excitement phase. The increases in breathing, pulse rate, and blood pressure that occurred during the excitement phase become more intense, penile erection and vaginal lubrication are more complete, and orgasm is closer.

The third phase of the human sexual response cycle is *orgasm.* How long does orgasm last? Typically about 3 to 15 seconds. Orgasm involves an explosive discharge of neuromuscular tension and an intensely pleasurable feeling. With orgasm comes the release of the neurotransmitter oxytocin, which, as we saw in the chapter "Biological Foundations of Behavior", plays a role in social bonding.

Following orgasm, the individual enters the *resolution phase,* in which blood vessels return to their normal state. A sex difference in this phase is that females may be stimulated to orgasm again without delay, whereas males enter a *refractory period* during which they cannot have another orgasm.

Working around the same time as Masters and Johnson was sex therapist Helen Singer Kaplan (1974). Kaplan studied sexual response through the lens of her clinical practice, during which she talked with people about their sexual experiences. Kaplan's view of the sexual response differed from Masters and Johnson's in that she added a key initial stage: *desire*. Kaplan discovered that for many of her clients, sexual desire was sometimes lacking. Kaplan's work highlighted the very important role of motivation in sexual activity. Clearly, she argued, without the desire to have sex, the stages described by Masters and Johnson might never get started. We will return to the human sexual response and sexual desire later in this chapter when we survey sexual disorders.

## Cognition and Other Factors in Sexual Behavior

Sexual behavior is influenced by a variety of factors—sensation, perception, cognition, and emotion (Crooks & Baur, 2014). Finding someone sexually attractive may involve seeing the person, getting to know him or her, and feeling emotionally attached. Certainly, our thoughts play an important role in our sexuality. We might be sexually attracted to someone but understand that we must inhibit our sexual urges until the relationship has had time to develop. We have the cognitive capacity to respect our partners and not take sexual advantage of them. We also have the cognitive resources to generate sexual images—to become sexually aroused just by thinking about something erotic.

Recall from the chapter "Memory" that scripts are mental schemas for events. Sexuality is influenced by *sexual scripts,* patterns of expectancies for how people should behave sexually (Stulhofer, Busko, & Landripet, 2010). We carry these scripts with us in our memories, and men and women may have different sexual scripts (McCabe, Tanner, & Heiman, 2010). Not surprisingly, sexual scripts can be influenced by what we see on television or in films (Seabrook & others, 2016). They can also be infused with religious and moral beliefs (Hernandez-Kane & Mahoney, 2018). Sexual scripts can be problematic

Donald Marshall's work focused on the sexual practices of the people of the South Pacific island of Mangaia.



when they contain beliefs about coercion or talking someone into engaging in sexual behavior (Landgraf & von Treskow, 2017). These scripts may be missing crucial information about the important role of consent in sexuality, as we address later.

## THE INFLUENCE OF CULTURE

The influence of culture on sexuality was demonstrated dramatically in a classic analysis by John Messenger (1971) of the people living on the small island of Inis Beag off the coast of Ireland. They knew nothing about tongue kissing or hand stimulation of the penis, and they detested nudity. For both females and males, premarital sex was out of the question. Men avoided most sexual experiences because they believed that sexual intercourse reduced their energy level and was bad for their health. In this group, sexual intercourse occurred only at night, taking place as quickly as possible. As you might suspect, female orgasm was rare in this culture (Messenger, 1971).

In contrast, around the same time that Messenger was studying the people of Inis Beag, Donald Marshall (1971) studied the Mangaian culture in the South Pacific. In Mangaia, young boys were taught about masturbation and were encouraged to engage in it as much as they liked. At age 13, the boys underwent a ritual initiating them into sexual manhood. First, their elders instructed them about sexual strategies, including how to aid their female partner in having orgasms. Two weeks later, the boy had intercourse with an experienced woman who helped him hold back from ejaculation until she experienced orgasm with him. By the end of adolescence, Mangaians had sex pretty much every day. Mangaian women reported a high frequency of orgasm.

Few cultures are as isolated and homogeneous as those of Inis Beag and Mangaia. In the United States, sexual behaviors and attitudes reflect the country's diverse multicultural population, falling somewhere in the middle of a continuum going from repressive to open.

## SEX EDUCATION

One way that societies teach youth about sex and sexuality is through formal education. The role of sex education in the socialization of young people is especially important because many parents feel uncomfortable talking openly with their children about sexual practices (Holman & Koenig Kellas, 2018). Increasingly the vacuum of education about sex and sexuality has been filled by friends (Pariera, 2018) and, unfortunately, online pornography (Vogels & O'Sullivan, 2018). Most people concerned with sex education share two simple and uncontroversial goals: to encourage the very young to delay sexual activity (what is called the "sexual debut") and to reduce teen pregnancy and sexually transmitted infections. However, there are many different opinions on *how* to achieve these goals.

Youth who learn about the fact that latex condoms protect against many sexually transmitted infections are not more likely to engage in sex and are more likely to use protection.



*Comprehensive* sex education involves providing students with comprehensive knowledge about sexual behavior, birth control, and the use of condoms in protecting against sexually transmitted infections, while encouraging them to delay sexual activity and practice abstinence.

Another form of sex education is the *abstinence-only* approach. Abstinence-only educational programs emphasize that sexual behavior outside of marriage is harmful at any age (Family and Youth Services Bureau, 2014). Instructors can present contraceptives and condoms only in terms of their failure rates.

Which approach to sex education most effectively delays sexual activity and prevents teen pregnancy? Comprehensive sex education is far superior to abstinence-only programs in achieving these goals. Adolescents who experienced comprehensive sex education are less likely to report adolescent pregnancies than those who received abstinence-only sex education or no sex education (Kohler, Manhart, & Lafferty, 2008). Importantly, sex education programs that emphasize contraceptive knowledge *do not* increase the incidence of sexual intercourse and are more likely to reduce the risk of adolescent pregnancy and sexually transmitted infections than abstinence-only programs (Constantine, 2008; M. E. Eisenberg & others, 2008; Hampton, 2008). In comparison, abstinence-only programs do not delay the initiation of sexual intercourse and do not reduce HIV-risk behaviors (Butler, Sorace, & Beach, 2018; Jaramillo & others, 2017; Kirby, 2008; Underhill, Montgomery, & Operario, 2007).

A study of more than 350 middle and high school sex educators found that many felt they were limited in the breadth of information they could share with students concerning topics such as communicating about sex, teen parenting, abortion, and sexual orientation (M. E. Eisenberg & others, 2013). Perhaps in part due to such issues, the United States has a higher rate of adolescent pregnancy and childbearing than other developed countries. Importantly, the teen pregnancy and birth rate has declined almost continuously over the last 20 years. In 2010 the rate was over 57 per 1,000 females, and by 2015 it had fallen to 22.3 per 1,000 females, the lowest rate ever recorded in the United States (CDC, 2017).

Preventing unplanned pregnancy and delaying sexual debut are not the only things that are important about a person's developing sexuality. Education might also be aimed at helping young people feel a sense of control of their own bodies and choices (Cense, 2018; Palmer & others, 2017). Scientists introduced the idea of *sexual competence* as a way to ascertain whether a person is ready for their first experience of sexual intercourse (Wellings & others, 2013; van der Doef & Reinders, 2018). Instead of focusing on the person's age, sexual competence means that a person's sexual experiences will involve a reliable form of contraception and two equally willing participants who feel a sense of personal autonomy.

The importance of personal autonomy and lack of coercion in sexual experiences is reflected in the movement toward *affirmative consent* at many universities (Silver & Hovick, 2018). Affirmative consent means that, rather than simply assuming both partners are comfortable with sexual activity, each partner provides, by words or actions, a knowing and voluntary indication that they are willing to engage in sexual activity. Affirmative consent means that both partners have provided unambiguous permission with regard to their willingness to engage in the sexual activity.

### test yourself

1. What are some different ways that people define sexual behavior, or "sex"?
2. What do studies indicate about the frequency of sexual behavior in contemporary society?
3. What are two kinds of sex education, and how effective is each?

# 6. SEXUAL VARIATIONS AND DISORDERS

If we think of sexual behavior as any behavior that involves sexual pleasure, then we can say that there are many different kinds of sexual behavior. When it comes to sexual pleasure, in fact, variation is the norm. In this section we consider some variant sexual behaviors and draw a contrast between behavior that is pleasurable but not harmful versus behavior that is harmful. We also consider some common disorders of sexual desire and response.

## Fetishes

People are sexually aroused by different activities. A man might be sexually stimulated by wearing women's clothing. A woman might be turned on by wearing a necktie. A **fetish** is an object or activity that arouses sexual interest and desire. Fetishes include erotic materials (such as pornographic images and films), clothing, and other physical objects (Joyal, 2018; Rees & Garcia, 2017). A person with a *transvestic fetish* (who may be heterosexual or homosexual) gets sexual pleasure from wearing clothing of the opposite sex. In *sadomasochism,* one person (the sadistic partner) gains sexual

• **fetish** An object or activity that arouses sexual interest and desire.

pleasure from dominating another person (the masochist), who in turn enjoys being dominated.

These behaviors may be unusual, but they are not considered abnormal. Indeed, unusual sexual practices are typically considered harmless variations as long as three principles are not violated (Beech, Miner, & Thornton, 2016; Wright, 2018):

- The individuals are consenting adults.
- They do not experience personal distress.
- They are not putting themselves in danger of physical harm or death as a result of their activities.

When a variation in sexual behavior violates one or more of these principles (Di Lorenzo & others, 2018; Sorrentino & others, 2018), however, it may qualify as a *paraphilic disorder*, considered next.

## Paraphilic Disorders

● **paraphilic disorders** Sexual disorders that feature recurrent sexually arousing fantasies, urges, or behaviors involving nonhuman objects; the suffering or humiliation of oneself or one's partner; or children or other nonconsenting individuals.

The American Psychiatric Association (2013a) defines **paraphilic disorders** as psychological disorders that involve

- Sexual interests that cause personal distress (beyond that simply resulting from societal disapproval)
- Sexual desires or behaviors that involve another person's psychological distress, injury, or death
- Desire for sexual behavior involving unwilling persons or those who cannot give legal consent

Figure 6 lists the various paraphilic disorders that the American Psychiatric Association recognizes.

| Paraphilic Disorder | Focus |
| --- | --- |
| **Exhibitionistic Disorder** | Exposing one's genitals to a stranger |
| **Fetishistic Disorder** | Using nonliving objects for sexual pleasure |
| **Frotteuristic Disorder** | Touching and rubbing against a person who has not given consent—for instance, in a crowded subway car |
| **Pedophilic Disorder** | Sexual activity with a prepubescent child |
| **Sexual Masochism Disorder** | Acts in which the individual derives sexual excitement from being humiliated, beaten, bound, or otherwise made to suffer |
| **Sexual Sadism Disorder** | Acts in which the individual derives sexual excitement from the psychological or physical suffering of the victim |
| **Transvestic Disorder** | Cross-dressing by a man or woman that causes distress or interferes with daily functioning |
| **Voyeuristic Disorder** | Observing unsuspecting individuals, usually strangers, who are naked or in the process of disrobing or engaging in sexual activity |

**FIGURE 6 Types of Paraphilic Disorders** Recall that sexual variations are considered harmless if (1) the individuals are consenting adults; (2) they do not experience personal distress; and (3) they are not putting themselves in danger of physical harm as a result of their activities. For some of the paraphilic disorders listed here, the issue is one of consent; for others the variations may only qualify as a disorder if they cause the person distress or interfere with daily living. Can you identify which of these principles apply to each?
Source: American Psychiatric Association (APA) (2013a).

What causes paraphilic disorders? There is no one answer to this question. Each disorder may have its own origin. Some experts have suggested that principles of classical conditioning can explain the emergence of some paraphilic disorders (DeFeo, 2015; Woods & others, 2018). Recall that in classical conditioning, a conditioned stimulus (CS) is paired with another stimulus, the unconditioned stimulus (US), which provokes an unconditioned response (UR). After frequent pairings, the CS comes to evoke the response even in the absence of the US. Using this framework, we might speculate that a man with a shoe fetish may have been around shoes when he masturbated as a boy and that these experiences led to the fetish. For other paraphilic disorders, however, it is likely that more than associative learning is involved.

## Pedophilic Disorder

**Pedophilic disorder** is a psychological disorder in which an adult or an older adolescent sexually fantasizes about or engages in sexual behavior with children who have not reached puberty.

**pedophilic disorder** A paraphilic disorder in which an adult or an older adolescent sexually fantasizes about or engages in sexual behavior with individuals who have not reached puberty.

The causes of pedophilic disorder are not well understood. It is not the case that those who sexually abuse children were themselves sexually abused as children. Adults who sexually abuse children are more likely than other sex offenders to report that they experienced sexual abuse in childhood (Fazio, 2018), but the vast majority of individuals who have been sexually molested as children do *not* themselves go on to molest others.

People who are sexually attracted to children show an array of features that suggest the disorder might have neurodevelopmental origins. People with pedophilic disorder tend to be short in stature and have especially short legs (Fazio & others, 2017). They are more likely to be left-handed and show mild physical anomalies of the face and head (such as non-detached ear lobes) (Babchishin & others, 2018). These associations suggest *prenatal* factors may play a role in the development of pedophilic disorder.

In addition, pedophilic disorder is associated with a history of head injuries (causing unconsciousness) in childhood (Fazio, 2018; Seto, 2017, 2018). The disorder is related to a pattern of cognitive distortions, including minimizing the harm of pedophilic activities, believing that sexual impulses are uncontrollable, and thinking that sexual relationships with children are consensual (Hall & Hall, 2007). Neuroscientific studies suggest that individuals who are sexually attracted to children show a pervasive pattern of brain dysfunction, related to connections between brain regions (Cantor & Blanchard, 2012; Cazala & others, 2018; Holoyda & Kellaher, 2016; Ponseti, Bruhn & others, 2018a) and low levels of GABA (Ristow & others, 2018). Individuals with pedophilic disorder also have low self-esteem, poor social skills, and low IQ (Hall & Hall, 2007). Pedophilic disorder is more common in men than women (Seto, 2017; 2018).

Given the potential damage that pedophilic behavior can inflict on its victims, identifying strategies for treatment and prevention is paramount. Therapies target the learned associations between children and sexual arousal or have focused on training offenders in skills needed to recognize and avoid risky situations, such as being around children. Unfortunately, these treatments have been relatively ineffective (Cantor, 2018; Seto, 2018).

Biological treatments for pedophilia seek to reduce sexual desire in these individuals. Castration (either surgically, through removal of the testes, or chemically, with drugs that reduce testosterone) has been used to treat sex offenders who victimize children (Turner & Briken, 2018). Hundreds of surgical castrations of sex offenders have been performed throughout Europe, and nine U.S. states have laws that *require* chemical or surgical castration for sex offenders who commit crimes against children as a condition of parole (Seto, 2018; Zhao, 2018).

©chrisstockphoto/Alamy Stock Photo

It is difficult to evaluate the effectiveness of castration because individuals are not randomly assigned to the treatment, and those who undergo the procedure may be particularly motivated to change their behavior (Seto, 2018). Furthermore, some critics have suggested that castration is used primarily to punish, not to treat, and as such is unethical (Malón, 2012; R. G. Wright, 2008).

Acknowledging the difficulties in treating pedophilic disorder, it may be that preventing the disorder and implementing interventions aimed at child-victims are the best goals (Seto, 2017, 2018). With respect to preventing pedophilic disorder, given the evidence for a neurodevelopmental basis for the disorder, enhanced prenatal care and early parenting interventions might be helpful in reducing the occurrence of the disorder. With respect to preventing abuse and protecting children, educating children to distinguish appropriate and inappropriate touch and empowering them to share their feelings with a trusted adult if someone is making them uncomfortable are important goals.

## Disorders of Sexual Desire and Sexual Response

Paraphilic disorders are unusual. More common disorders of sexuality involve problems either in sexual desire or in the physical sexual response described by Masters and Johnson.

With regard to sexual desire disorders, up to a quarter of men and nearly half of women report sometimes being troubled with a general lack of interest in sex (Clayton & others, 2018; O'Loughlin, Basson, & Brotto, 2018). Lack of sexual desire in both men and women can stem from a variety sources, including low levels of androgen, stress, anxiety and depression, physical illnesses, and various medications. Treatments for lack of sexual desire include drug therapies, psychological therapies, and relationship counseling.

In men, two common disorders of sexual response are *erectile dysfunction,* the failure of the penis to become erect, and *premature ejaculation,* the experience of orgasm before the person wishes it. As we have seen, the male genitalia are complex, and the male sexual response involves a number of physiological reactions, from erection to ejaculation. It is not surprising that, at times, this elegant machinery does not function optimally.

In most cases, erectile dysfunction involves a combination of psychological and physical factors (Wessells, 2018). Erectile dysfunction may be a symptom of an underlying physical illness, such as diabetes, and is more likely to occur with age. Treatment typically involves medications, such as Viagra, that allow the individual to experience erection (Fahmy & Aljaeid, 2018).

Premature ejaculation is the most common sexual complaint among men under the age of 40 (Kim & others, 2018). Psychological, physical, and relationship factors can play a role in premature ejaculation. The problem may be treated with drugs or therapy and may also involve working together with one's sexual partner to develop greater mastery over the sexual response.

For women, disorders of sexual response include problems in sexual arousal and in the experience of orgasm. For some women, dysfunction in arousal is explained by problems in the autonomic nervous system that disrupt the engorgement of the labia and lubrication of the vagina; for other women, the subjective feeling of arousal is absent even when these physical changes occur (O'Loughlin, Basson, & Brotto, 2018). Disorders of sexual orgasm in women involve delayed or absent orgasm during sexual activity. Both of these types of disorders can be related to the experience of childhood sexual abuse, as well as to strict religious beliefs and negative sexual attitudes (Alexander & others, 2018). These disorders of sexual response may be treated with androgens or through psychotherapy. Addressing underlying physical causes can also sometimes improve sexual function.

The occasional occurrence of erectile dysfunction or premature ejaculation in males, and problems with arousal and orgasm in females, are common and normal. It is when these problems cause distress for the individual or difficulties in important relationships that they are considered disorders in need of treatment.

## Variations, Disorders, and the Meaning of Normality

A theme throughout this discussion has been whether variations in sexual behavior are problems that require professional help or whether they represent harmless differences that simply reflect human diversity. The difficulties people have in talking about sexuality only perpetuate anxiety, shame, and concern about sex. People are not ashamed to admit that they like certain foods and dislike others. Imagine if we treated sexual tastes in a similarly open way.

### test yourself

1. What three principles must not be violated for a variation in sexual behavior to be considered harmless?
2. Why is it difficult to determine the effectiveness of surgical or chemical castration as a treatment for pedophilia?
3. Give examples of sexual response disorders experienced by men, as well as examples of such disorders experienced by women.

# 7. SEXUALITY AND HEALTH AND WELLNESS

Many people view healthy sexual activity is an important component of the good life. In this section, we consider the implications of sexuality first for physical health and second, for relationship functioning and psychological well-being.

## Sexual Behavior and Physical Health

A key consideration in sexual health is sexually transmitted infections. A **sexually transmitted infection (STI)** is contracted primarily through sexual activity—vaginal, oral, or anal sex. STIs are can have implications for a person's future fertility, risk of cancer, and life expectancy.

**sexually transmitted infection (STI)** An infection that is contracted primarily through sexual activity—vaginal intercourse as well as oral and anal sex.

### TYPES AND CAUSES OF SEXUALLY TRANSMITTED INFECTIONS

Some STIs are *bacterial* in origin, such as gonorrhea, syphilis, and chlamydia. These infections can be treated effectively with antibiotics, especially if caught early (CDC, 2018a). Early detection means recognizing the symptoms and seeking medical attention. Figure 7 shows the symptoms of these infections as well as their long-term consequences.

Other STIs are caused by *viruses*, as in the case of genital herpes, human papilloma virus (HPV), and human immunodeficiency virus (HIV). Figure 7 describes the symptoms of these viral STIs. There is no cure for genital herpes, but medications can treat symptoms and reduce recurrences. The HPV vaccine (called *Gardasil*) can prevent HPV infection (CDC, 2018b). Vaccination is important because some strains of HPV can lead to cancer.

HIV is not curable, but early treatment prevent the development of AIDS. HIV causes **acquired immune deficiency syndrome (AIDS)**. Without treatment, most people with HIV are vulnerable to germs that a healthy immune system can destroy. People whose behavior puts them at high risk for HIV infection may be eligible for medications called "Pre-Exposure Prophylaxis," or PrEP (CDC, 2018c; Raifman & Sherman, 2018). PrEP involves taking medication daily and is effective in reducing the risk of HIV infection if used consistently (CDC, 2018c).

**acquired immune deficiency syndrome (AIDS)** A sexually transmitted infection, caused by the human immunodeficiency virus (HIV), which destroys the body's immune system.

A final common STI is trichomoniasis, caused by a parasite (CDC, 2018a). Symptoms include vaginal or penile discharge, itching, and irritation. This infection can be cured with antibiotic treatment. The inflammation caused by the trichomoniasis can increase a person's risk of contracting another STI so treatment is important.

Although rates of HIV infections have dropped, the numbers of diagnoses of other STIs have continued to rise, reaching record highs in 2017 (Howard, 2018).

| | Symptoms | Long-Term Consequences |
|---|---|---|
| **Bacterial Infections** | | |
| Gonorrhea | Burning when urinating and, in men, white, yellow, or green discharge from the penis. Gonorrhea can also infect the throat when passed via oral sex. | In women, untreated gonorrhea can lead to pelvic inflammatory disease, increasing the risk of pregnancy complications and infertility. In men, it can cause an inflammation in the genital tract, which can lead to scarring, blocked sperm ducts, and infertility issues. |
| Syphilis | The first sign of syphilis is a small painless sore, called a chancre. Within a few weeks of the chancre healing, the person may develop a rash that begins on the trunk, eventually covering the body. | Complications of late-stage syphilis include damage to the brain, nerves, eyes, heart, blood vessels, liver, bones and joints. Babies born to women who have syphilis can become infected and may suffer a number of complications as a result. |
| Chlamydia | Most people who have chlamydia have no symptoms. In women, symptoms may include abnormal vaginal discharge and/or a burning sensation when urinating. Men may experience discharge from the penis, a burning sensation when urinating, and pain/swelling in the testicles. | If left untreated, chlamydia can cause serious, permanent damage to a woman's reproductive system. |
| **Viral Infections** | | |
| Genital herpes | Symptoms can be extremely mild and include pain/itching in the genitals, small red bumps or tiny white blisters that become scabs. | Herpes sores increase the risk of transmitting other STDs and may lead to bladder problems in some cases. Babies born to infected mothers can experience serious problems, including brain damage, blindness, and death. |
| Human papilloma virus (HPV) | HPV infections appear as warts on or around the genital area. Other varieties of HPV can cause warts on hands, fingers, elbows and feet. | Certain strains of HPV can cause cervical cancer and may also contribute to cancers of the genitals, anus, mouth, and upper respiratory tract. |
| Human immunodeficiency virus (HIV) | A person can carry HIV for a long time without experiencing symptoms. However, some people may develop a set of flu-like symptoms. | Left untreated, HIV infection may develop into AIDS. |

**Note.** All sexually transmitted diseases are preventable. Practicing safe sex can greatly reduce your chances of being infected. Regular STD testing is important for individuals who are sexually active. Some of these infections can be spread by means other than sexual contact, such as by needle sharing among those who use injectable drugs of abuse. Information is from the CDC (2018a).

**FIGURE 7** **Sexually Transmitted Infections** Source: CDC (2018a).

## PRACTICING SAFE SEX

Many sensual activities such as kissing, French kissing, cuddling, massage, and mutual masturbation (that does not involve the exchange of bodily fluids) involve no risk of an STI. Sexual activities that involve penetration, including vaginal, anal, and oral sex are riskier behaviors that can be made less risky with the use of proper protection.

Latex condoms are key in the prevention of STIs. In your own sexual experience, the wisest course of action is always to protect yourself by using a latex condom. When correctly used, latex condoms help to prevent or significantly reduce the risk of transmission of many STIs (Hodges & Holland, 2018; Johnson, O'Leary, & Flores, 2018).

Programs to promote safe sex are especially effective if they include the eroticization of condom use—that is, making condoms a part of the sensual experience of foreplay (Hood, Shook, & Belgrave, 2017; Scott-Sheldon & Johnson, 2006). Fear tactics are relatively less effective and programs emphasizing active skill building (for example, role-playing the use of condoms), self-efficacy, and positive attitudes about condom use are effective with most groups (Albarracín & others, 2016; Albarracin, Durantini, & Earl, 2006; Durantini & others, 2006). Making safe sex sexy is a great way to practice safe sex (Ellis, Rajagopal, & Kiviniemi, 2018).

## Sexual Behavior and Psychological Well-Being

*This couple probably had no trouble talking openly about their preferences and safety concerns before embarking on this bike ride. Shouldn't sex be like that too?*

©H. Mark Weidman Photography/Alamy Stock Photo

The relationship of sexual behavior to well-being can depend on why the person is engaging in that behavior. Having sex in order to be close to another person is related to enhanced well-being, but engaging in sex to avoid bad feelings is linked to decreases in well-being (Impett, Peplau, & Gable, 2005). In a study of newlyweds, frequency of sexual behavior was associated with higher relationship satisfaction to the extent that the individual members of the couple perceived the partner as responsive to their needs (Gadassi & others, 2016). When partners are mutually engaged in meeting each other's sexual needs, they both experience higher levels of sexual and relationship satisfaction (Impett, Muise, & Harasymchuk, 2018).

Does sexual frequency matter to couples? For couples in a relationship, it is important to keep in mind that sexual intimacy exists in the context of a larger relationship, but sexual satisfaction does matter to relationship satisfaction throughout a relationship (Hernandez & Mahoney, 2018; Maas & others, 2018; Schoenfeld & others, 2017). Sexual intimacy can create a deep bond between partners (McNulty, Wenner, & Fisher, 2016). A study of "sexual afterglow" in newlywed couples showed that having sex led to enhanced sexual satisfaction for 48 hours afterward (Meltzer & others, 2017). The stronger the couples' sexual afterglow, the more satisfied they were in their marriages over time.

Frequency of sexual behavior is positively related to psychological well-being, but only up to a point. Essentially, once a week appears to be the frequency at which this relationship levels off so that having sex more than once a week fails to increase well-being (Muise, Schimmack, & Impett, 2016). In this sense, sexual activity is similar to financial resources. For both sexual frequency and income, these variables are positively related to well-being but that relationship levels off once a particular level is met.

Throughout the life span, sexual activities remain a source of pleasure and the experience of intimacy with another (Mroczek & others, 2013). Older couples tend to focus more on the quality rather than quantity of sex with their partners (Forbes, Eaton, & Krueger, 2017; Macleod, Busija, & McCabe, 2018). Importantly, partnered sexual activity is a strong predictor of satisfaction in relationships among older individuals even when those activities do not include vaginal intercourse (Træen & others, 2018). Sexuality is also an important part of life in the context of disability (Rohleder & others, 2018). Like everyone else, people with disabilities can benefit from open conversations about sexuality with their partners (Valvano & others, 2018).

### test yourself

1. What is a sexually transmitted infection (STI)?
2. What contraceptive device is key in efforts to protect individuals from contracting STIs? Against what infections does it offer the most protection?
3. How does sexual behavior relate to personal well-being?

SUMMARY

## 1. DEFINING SEX AND GENDER

*Sex* refers to biological aspects that are used to classify a person as male or female. Biological features that serve in this capacity include genes, gonads, hormones, genitals, and secondary sexual characteristics. Gender identity refers to the person's psychological sense of himself or herself as male or female. Gender is sometimes described in terms of a person's level of instrumentality or expressiveness.

Disorders of sexual development are conditions in which a person's genetic, genital, or gonadal sex is atypical. In these cases, the sex in which the child was raised is the most consistent predictor of eventual gender identity.

Individuals who feel trapped in the wrong biological sex are referred to as *transgender.* Transgender individuals are sometimes considered to be suffering from gender dysphoria, which involves intense distress over one's birth sex. Treatment for transgender individuals generally involves steps ranging from reversible interventions to irreversible changes such as gender-affirming surgery.

## 2. THEORIES OF GENDER DEVELOPMENT

Perspectives on gender development include biological, evolutionary psychology, social cognitive, and social role theories. Biological approaches focus on the ways that genes, hormones, and brain structures relate to gender differences. Evolutionary psychology views gender through the lens of Darwinian natural selection and asserts that human beings have evolved through a process of sexual selection in which men compete for mates and women choose their male partners. Social cognitive approaches to gender emphasize how learning, modeling, and cognitive schemas influence the development of gender. Social role theory states that a division of labor between the sexes that is based on male or female physical differences can lead to the social construction of gender roles and gender stereotypes. Social role theory predicts that as social structures change, gender differences should decline.

## 3. THE PSYCHOLOGY OF GENDER DIFFERENCES

Stereotypes tells us that women are more emotional than men, but research suggests this difference may be due to social expectations. Women tend to perform better than men in tasks requiring theory of mind ability. In addition, women are more likely than men to help another person if it is safe to offer assistance, while men are more likely than women to help if helping involves risk. In regard to cognition, girls are better at verbal tasks and boys are better at spatial tasks, although these differences are relatively small. In terms of aggression, males tend to be more overtly aggressive than females. Females are more relationally aggressive than overtly aggressive.

Sexuality refers to the ways people experience and express themselves as sexual beings. Many stereotypes about gender differences in sexuality have not been supported by research. Men do report more frequent sexual arousal and are more likely than women to masturbate. They have more permissive attitudes about casual premarital sex as well. Women are more likely than men to show fluidity in their sexual attractions.

## 4. SEXUAL ORIENTATION

*Sexual orientation* refers to the direction of a person's erotic interest and includes heterosexuality, homosexuality, bisexuality, pansexuality, and asexuality. Sexual orientation is generally measured using questionnaires. The vast majority of people are heterosexual; the number of homosexual or bisexual individuals is between 2 and 15 percent of the population.

Possible explanations for sexual orientation include genetic factors, prenatal hormone exposure, and brain differences. Genes explain a relatively small amount of the variation we see in sexual orientation. Social factors do not seem to play a large role in sexual orientation.

Gay men and lesbian women are similar to their heterosexual counterparts in many ways, but they do show higher levels of relationship satisfaction and are more likely to break up than heterosexual married couples. Gay men and lesbian women who are legally married are less likely to break up than those without such unions. Children with gay parents tend to be as well-adjusted as children with heterosexual parents.

## 5. SEXUAL BEHAVIORS AND PRACTICES

Vaginal intercourse is the most common sexual practice for men and women. Both men and women report engaging in oral sex more than anal sex. Contemporary people appear to be having less sex than previous generations. Regardless of the particular sexual activity, the human sexual response pattern is characterized by four stages—excitement, plateau, orgasm, and resolution.

Sexual desire is a key element in sexual behavior. Sensation, perception, and cognition are all important components of sexual activity. Culture plays a role in sexuality as well.

Some people worry that providing adolescents with comprehensive sex education will lead to premature sexual activity. However, research strongly suggests that comprehensive sex education does not encourage sexual behavior and is crucial to preventing unwanted pregnancy.

## 6. SEXUAL VARIATIONS AND DISORDERS

In regard to sexual tastes and activities, variation is the norm. A fetish is an object that a person finds sexually arousing.

Paraphilic disorders are sexual disorders featuring recurrent sexually arousing fantasies, urges, or behaviors involving nonhuman objects; the suffering or humiliation of oneself or one's partner; or children or other nonconsenting individuals. Pedophilic disorder is a particularly harmful paraphilic disorder involving sexual attraction to prepubescent children. It is very difficult to treat.

Disorders of sexual desire and sexual response are relatively common. Two common disorders of sexual response in men are erectile dysfunction and premature ejaculation. In women, common sexual response disorders include problems in arousal and inability to experience orgasm.

## 7. SEXUALITY AND HEALTH AND WELLNESS

Sexually transmitted infections (STIs) are infections that can be spread through sexual contact, including vaginal, anal, and oral sex. Bacterial infections include gonorrhea, syphilis, and chlamydia. Viral infections include genital herpes, human papilloma virus, and HIV. When used properly and consistently, latex condoms offer excellent protection against many STIs, including HIV.

Sexual behavior is positively related to relationship functioning and psychological wellness. Sexuality is an important aspect of psychological well-being throughout the life span and in the context of disability.

# key *terms*

acquired immune deficiency syndrome (AIDS)
aggression
androgynous
asexual
bisexual
disorders of sexual development (DSD)
empathy
fetish
gender
gender identity
gender roles
gender similarities hypothesis
gender stereotypes
gonads
heterosexual
homosexual
human sexual response pattern
overt aggression
pansexual
paraphilic disorders
pedophilic disorder
relational aggression
secondary sex characteristics
sex
sex chromosomes
sexuality
sexually transmitted infection (STI)
sexual orientation
sexual selection
social role theory
transgender

# apply your *knowledge*

1. Ask your parents about your gender-related behavior as a child and about their views on how their parenting influenced your gender development. Do their recollections ring true with your memories? What factors do you think played a role in your gender development?
2. Set aside a day and keep a gender-awareness diary. Try to notice every time you have an experience in which your gender matters to your life. From the moment you get up in the morning until you go to bed at night, if you are man, ask yourself, "Would I be doing this if I were a woman?" If you are a woman, ask yourself, "Would I be doing this if I were a man?" When you see a woman performing an activity, ask yourself, "Would this seem appropriate to me if a man were doing it?" Write down your thoughts and feelings about these activities, and reflect on the role of gender in your daily life.
3. The evolutionary psychology approach to gender suggests that men are more likely to seek women who are younger than they are and that women are more likely to seek older men with resources. Check out personal ads, either from the local newspaper or online, and examine those placed by men and women. Do the ads reflect evolutionary psychology's predictions about what men and women look for in a partner?
4. States differ in terms of their laws regarding gay and lesbian marriage, adoption rights, and employment protections. Research your own state's legal policies toward the rights of gay men and women. Summarize those rights. Does your state also have laws about the protection of transgender rights?
5. Conduct web searches for "transgender experience" and "gender identity disorder." How do the sites you find differ in their discussions of a person who feels trapped in the wrong sex?

**Design elements:** Preview icon: ©Jiang Hongyan; Intersection box icon: ©D. Hurst/Alamy, ©Creative Crop/Getty Images, ©Dimitris66/Getty Images, ©Savany/Getty Images; Critical Controversy box icon: ©Ultrashock; running heads icon: ©Cre8tive Studios/Alamy; Summary icon: ©Vadarshop

# CHAPTER 12

CHAPTER OUTLINE

# Personality

## Symbols of Who We Really Are

### Looking in the mirror each day, you have seen yourself.

Throughout your life, you have seen your reflected image change from the face of a small child to the way you look now. You will see it change further as you grow older. Our faces are a symbol of ourselves, a basis for personal identity. Yet, faces can change—sometimes drastically. Adults who experience facial disfigurement often experience distress about the fact that people can no longer see who they "really are" (Rifkin & others, 2018). In fact, it was the sense that the face is a vital symbol of personal identity that led to reluctance to attempt face transplants. However, such transplants have transformed the lives of people who receive them. In 2006, Andy Sandness was 21 years old when he attempted to die by suicide, sending a bullet through his chin and destroying most of his face (Bever, 2017). A decade later, another 21-year-old, Rudy Ross, died by suicide. His 19-year-old widow, Lily, was 8 months pregnant and she donated Rudy's face, along with other organs. Andy received Rudy's face in a 60-hour surgery. A year later, Andy was able to meet Lily and her son. It was an intense experience for Lily—seeing her husband's face on another man. For Andy it was an opportunity to express his undying gratitude and to assure Lily that her gift would not be wasted (Bever, 2017).

Andy's appearance has changed forever. He now has Rudy's mole and rosy cheeks, and bears a resemblance to Rudy's young son. But behind that face—that mix of Rudy and Andy—the person is still, and always will be, Andy. As much as faces may define us superficially, there is something else about us that continues to provide a sense of identity. Age and life experiences can change us, but something about us endures throughout life. That "something" is personality, the focus of this chapter.

# PREVIEW

Personality psychology explores the psychological attributes that underlie who we really are—the unified and enduring core characteristics that account for our existence as a unique individual throughout the life span. In this chapter, we survey the field of personality from a variety of perspectives. We begin with classic theories from psychodynamic and humanistic thinkers and then examine more contemporary approaches, including the trait, life story, social cognitive, and biological perspectives. We then look at personality assessment. Finally, we consider the role of personality in health and wellness.

## 1. PSYCHODYNAMIC PERSPECTIVES

● **personality** A pattern of enduring, distinctive thoughts, emotions, and behaviors that characterize the way an individual adapts to the world.

● **psychodynamic perspectives** Theoretical views emphasizing that personality is primarily unconscious (beyond awareness).

**Personality** is a pattern of enduring, distinctive thoughts, emotions, and behaviors that characterize the way an individual adapts to the world. Psychologists have approached these enduring characteristics in a variety of ways, focusing on different aspects of the person.

**Psychodynamic perspectives** on personality emphasize that personality is primarily unconscious. According to this viewpoint, the enduring patterns that make up personality are largely unavailable to our conscious awareness, and they powerfully shape our behaviors in ways that we cannot readily comprehend (Marmor, 2018; Tangolo, 2018). Psychodynamic theorists use the word *unconscious* differently from how other psychologists do. From the psychodynamic perspective, aspects of our personality are unconscious because they *must* be: These mysterious, unconscious forces are simply too frightening to be part of our awareness (Northoff, 2018).

Psychodynamic theorists believe that behavior is only a surface characteristic and that to truly understand someone's personality, we have to explore the symbolic meanings of that behavior and the deep inner workings of the mind (Newirth, 2018). Psychodynamic theorists also stress that early childhood experience shapes adult personality. The psychodynamic view of personality was introduced by Sigmund Freud.

### Freud's Psychoanalytic Theory

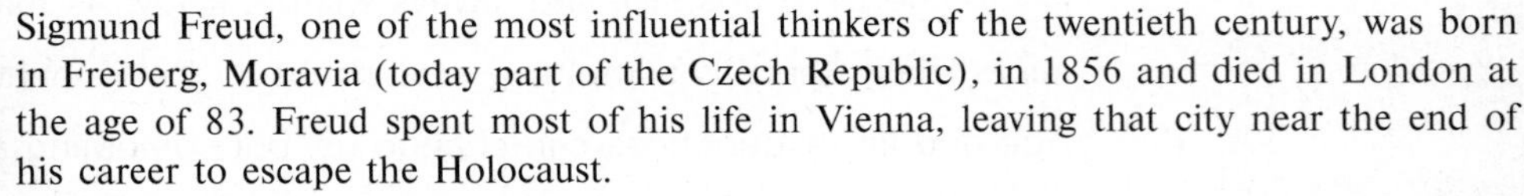

Sigmund Freud, one of the most influential thinkers of the twentieth century, was born in Freiberg, Moravia (today part of the Czech Republic), in 1856 and died in London at the age of 83. Freud spent most of his life in Vienna, leaving that city near the end of his career to escape the Holocaust.

**Sigmund Freud (1856–1939)** Freud's theories have strongly influenced how people in Western cultures view themselves and the world.

©Ingram Publishing

Freud has had such a phenomenal impact that just about everyone has an opinion about him, even those who have never studied his work. If you ask others what they think of Freud, you will likely get a variety of interesting answers. Some might comment that Freud was a cocaine addict. Freud did use cocaine early in his career, but he stopped using the drug when he learned of its harmful effects. Others might claim that Freud hated women. As we will see, Freud's theory of development did include the notion that women are morally inferior to men. However, Freud was never satisfied with his approach to the psychology of women. He welcomed women interested in pursuing careers in psychoanalysis, and many of his earliest followers were women. Finally, people might declare that Freud thought everything was about sex. That claim, it turns out, is true, except that by *sex* Freud did not mean sexual activity in the usual sense. Freud defined sex as organ pleasure. *Anything* that is pleasurable is sex, according to Freud.

For Freud, the sexual drive was the most important motivator in human life. Freud thought that the human sex drive was the main determinant of personality development, and he felt that psychological disorders, dreams, and all human behavior represent the conflict between unconscious sexual drive and the demands of civilized human society.

Freud developed *psychoanalysis,* his approach to personality, through his work with patients suffering from hysteria. *Hysteria* refers to physical symptoms that have no physical cause. For instance, a person might be unable to see, even with perfectly healthy eyes, or unable to walk, despite having no physical injury.

In Freud's day (the Victorian era, a time marked by strict rules regarding sex), many young women suffered from hysterical symptoms, physical problems that could not be explained by actual physical illness. In his practice, Freud spent long hours listening to these women talk about their symptoms. Freud came to understand that the hysterical symptoms stemmed from unconscious conflicts, centered on experiences in which the person's drive for pleasure was thwarted by the social pressures of Victorian society. Moreover, the particular symptoms were related symbolically to these underlying conflicts.

For instance, one of Freud's patients, Fraulein Elisabeth Von R., suffered from leg pains that prevented her from standing or walking. Through analysis, Freud discovered that Fraulein Elisabeth had had a number of experiences in which she wanted nothing more than to take a walk but had been prevented from doing so by her duty to her ill father. Fraulein Elisabeth's symptoms were not due to a single experience, but rather to *many repeated* experiences, all related to walking.

Based on such observations, Freud concluded that hysterical symptoms were *overdetermined*, meaning that those symptoms had *many* causes in the unconscious. Eventually, Freud came to use hysterical symptoms as his metaphor for understanding dreams, slips of the tongue, and all human behavior. Everything we do, he said, has a multitude of unconscious causes.

Drawing from his analyses of patients (as well as himself), Freud developed a model of human personality. He saw personality as like an iceberg, existing mostly below the level of awareness, just as the massive part of an iceberg lies beneath the surface of the water. Figure 1 illustrates this analogy and depicts the extensiveness of the unconscious part of our mind, in Freud's view. Notice how only the tiniest bit of the personality is the conscious mind. Most of who we are is cloaked in the unconscious.

- **id** The Freudian structure of personality consisting of unconscious drives; the individual's reservoir of sexual energy.
- **ego** The Freudian structure of personality that deals with the demands of reality.
- **superego** The Freudian structure of personality that serves as the harsh internal judge of our behavior; what we often call conscience.

## STRUCTURES OF PERSONALITY

The three structures of personality described by Freud are shown in Figure 1. Freud (1924) called these structures the id, the ego, and the superego. You can get a better feel for these Latin labels by considering their English translations: The id is literally the "it," the ego is the "I," and the superego is the "above-I."

The **id** consists of unconscious drives and is the individual's reservoir of sexual energy. This "it" is a pool of amoral and often vile urges pressing for expression. In Freud's view, the id has no contact with reality. The id works according to the *pleasure principle:* the Freudian concept that the id seeks immediate gratification.

The world would be pretty scary if personalities were all id. As young children mature, they learn that they cannot act on every impulse. They cannot snatch every candy or slug other children. They must negotiate with others to get the things they want. As children experience the constraints of reality, a new element of personality is formed–the **ego**, the Freudian structure of personality that deals with the demands of reality. According to Freud, the ego abides by the *reality principle.* It tries to get the id what it wants within the norms of society. Whereas the id is completely unconscious, the ego is partly conscious. It houses our higher mental functions–reasoning, problem solving, and decision making, for example.

The id and ego do not consider whether something is right or wrong. Rather, the **superego** is the harsh internal judge of our behavior. The superego is reflected in what we often call conscience and evaluates the morality of our behavior.

The ego acts as a mediator between the conflicting demands of the id and the superego, as well as the real world. Your ego might say, for example, "I will have sex only in a committed relationship and always practice safe sex." Your id, however, screams, "Sex! Now!" and your superego commands, "Sex? Don't even think about it."

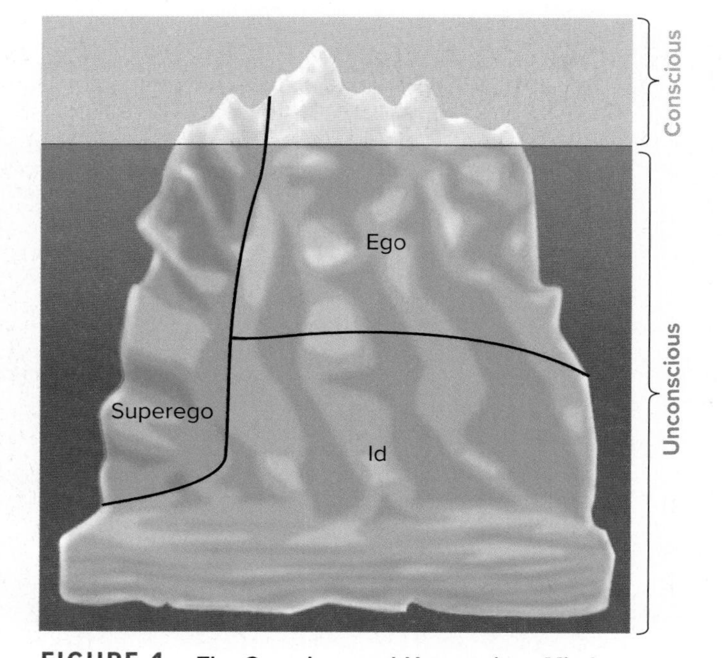


**FIGURE 1 The Conscious and Unconscious Mind**
The iceberg can be used as an analogy to illustrate how much of the mind is unconscious in Freud's theory. The conscious mind is the part of the iceberg above water; the unconscious mind is the part below water. Notice that the id is totally unconscious, whereas the ego and the superego can operate at either the conscious or the unconscious level.
Source: Freud (1924).

## DEFENSE MECHANISMS

**defense mechanisms** The Freudian term for tactics the ego uses to reduce anxiety by unconsciously distorting reality.

The conflicts that erupt among the demands of the id, the superego, and reality create a great deal of anxiety for the ego. The ego has strategies for dealing with this anxiety, called defense mechanisms. **Defense mechanisms** are tactics the ego uses to *reduce* anxiety by unconsciously *distorting* reality. For example, imagine that Jason's id is pressing to express an unconscious desire to have sex with his mother. Clearly, acting on this impulse would not please the superego or society at large. If he became aware of this impulse, Jason might recoil in horror. Instead, Jason's ego might use a defense mechanism of *displacement.* Displacement means directing unacceptable impulses at a less threatening target. So, Jason might develop a relationship with a girlfriend who looks and acts like his mother. Through displacement, the ego allows Jason to express his id impulse in a way that will not land him in trouble. Of course, Jason's friends might chuckle at the resemblance between his mother and his girlfriend, but you can bet that Jason will never notice.

Figure 2 describes several defense mechanisms, many of which were introduced and developed by Freud's daughter Anna, who followed in her father's career footsteps. All defense mechanisms reduce anxiety by distorting reality. Defense mechanisms are unconscious; we are not aware that we are calling on them.

*Repression* is the most powerful and pervasive defense mechanism. To reduce the anxiety caused by unacceptable id impulses, repression pushes these impulses back into the unconscious. Freud said, for example, that our early childhood experiences, many of which he believed were sexually laden, are too threatening for us to deal with consciously, so we reduce the anxiety of childhood conflict through repression.

Defense mechanisms have been used to explain prejudice–that is, holding negative attitudes toward a group of people because of their race, ethnicity, or other characteristics.

| Defense Mechanism | How It Works | Example |
|---|---|---|
| Repression | The master defense mechanism; the ego pushes unacceptable impulses out of awareness, back into the unconscious mind. | A young girl was sexually abused by her uncle. As an adult, she can't remember anything about the traumatic experience. |
| Rationalization | The ego replaces a less acceptable motive with a more acceptable one. | A college student does not get into the fraternity of his choice. He tells himself that the fraternity is very exclusive and that a lot of students could not get in. |
| Displacement | The ego shifts feelings toward an unacceptable object to another, more acceptable object. | A woman can't take her anger out on her boss, so she goes home and takes it out on her husband. |
| Sublimation | The ego replaces an unacceptable impulse with a socially acceptable one. | A man with strong sexual urges becomes an artist who paints nudes. |
| Projection | The ego attributes personal shortcomings, problems, and faults to others. | A man who has a strong desire to have an extramarital affair accuses his wife of flirting with other men. |
| Reaction Formation | The ego transforms an unacceptable motive into its opposite. | A woman who fears her sexual urges becomes a religious zealot. |
| Denial | The ego refuses to acknowledge anxiety-producing realities. | A man won't acknowledge that he has cancer even though a team of doctors has diagnosed his cancer. |
| Regression | The ego seeks the security of an earlier developmental period in the face of stress. | A woman returns home to mother every time she and her husband have a big argument. |

**FIGURE 2** **Defense Mechanisms** Defense mechanisms reduce anxiety in various ways, in all instances by distorting reality.

The defense mechanism of *projection* involves seeing the impulses a person fears in him- or herself in others. We might say that prejudicial attitudes involve projecting one's own impulses onto others. The defense mechanism of *reaction formation*–feeling consciously the exact opposite of one's true unconscious feeling–has also been used to understand anti-gay bigotry. Research shows that high levels of homophobia are associated with high levels of unconscious same-sex attraction (Weinstein & others, 2012).

## PSYCHOSEXUAL STAGES OF PERSONALITY DEVELOPMENT

Freud believed that human beings go through universal stages of personality development and that at each developmental stage we experience sexual pleasure in one part of the body more than in others. Each stage is named for the location of sexual pleasure at that stage. *Erogenous zones* are parts of the body that have especially strong pleasure-giving qualities at particular stages of development.

- *Oral stage (first 18 months):* The infant's pleasure centers on the mouth. Sucking, chewing, and biting are the chief sources of pleasure that reduce tension in the infant.
- *Anal stage (18 to 36 months):* During a time when most children are experiencing toilet training, the child's greatest pleasure involves the anus and urethra and their functions. Freud recognized that there is pleasure in "going" and "holding it" as well as in the experience of control over one's parents in deciding when to do either.
- *Phallic stage (3 to 6 years):* The name of Freud's third stage comes from the Latin word *phallus,* which means "penis." Pleasure focuses on the genitals as the child discovers that self-stimulation is enjoyable.

In Freud's view, the phallic stage has a special importance in personality development because it triggers the Oedipus complex. This name comes from the Greek tragedy in which Oedipus unknowingly kills his father and marries his mother. The **Oedipus complex** is the boy's intense desire to replace his father and enjoy the affections of his mother. Eventually, the boy recognizes that his father might punish him for these incestuous wishes, specifically by cutting off the boy's penis. *Castration anxiety* refers to the boy's intense fear of being mutilated by his father. To reduce this conflict, the boy identifies with his father, adopting the male gender role. The intense castration anxiety is repressed into the unconscious and serves as the foundation for the development of the superego.

● **Oedipus complex** According to Freud, a boy's intense desire to replace his father and enjoy the affections of his mother.

Freud recognized differences between boys and girls in the phallic stage. Because a girl does not have a penis, she cannot experience castration anxiety, Freud reasoned. Instead, she compares herself to boys and realizes that she is missing something–a penis–and thus experiences not castration anxiety but "castration completed," resulting in *penis envy*–the intense desire to obtain a penis by eventually marrying and bearing a son. Without castration anxiety, a girl cannot develop a superego in the same sense that boys do. In this way, for Freud, anatomy is destiny: The physical fact that girls lack a penis means they cannot develop a superego. Thus, Freud concluded, women are morally inferior to men.

Although noting that his views ran counter to the feminist thinkers of his time, Freud stood firm that the sexes are not equal in every way. He considered women to be somewhat childlike in their development and thought it was good that fathers, and eventually husbands, should guide them through life. He asserted that the only hope for women's moral development is education.

- *Latency period (6 years to puberty):* This phase is not a developmental stage but rather a kind of psychic time-out. After the drama of the phallic stage, the child sets aside all interest in sexuality.
- *Genital stage (adolescence and adulthood):* The genital stage is the time of sexual reawakening, a point when the source of sexual pleasure shifts to someone outside the family. Freud believed that in adulthood, individuals become capable of the two hallmarks of maturity: love and work. However, Freud felt that human beings are inevitably subject to intense conflict, reasoning that everyone, no matter how well adjusted, still has an id pressing for expression. Adulthood, even in the best of circumstances, still involves reliving the unconscious conflicts of childhood.

| Stage | Adult Extensions (Fixations) | Sublimations | Reaction Formations |
|---|---|---|---|
| Oral | Smoking, eating, kissing, oral hygiene, drinking, chewing gum | Seeking knowledge, humor, wit, sarcasm, being a food or wine expert | Speech purist, food faddist, prohibitionist, dislike of milk |
| Anal | Notable interest in one's bowel movements, love of bathroom humor, extreme messiness; or, alternatively, extreme cleanliness, stubbornness, and a strong desire for simplicity and structure | Interest in painting or sculpture, being overly giving, great interest in statistics | Extreme disgust with feces, fear of dirt, prudishness, irritability |
| Phallic | Heavy reliance on masturbation, flirtatiousness, expressions of virility | Interest in poetry, love of love, interest in acting, striving for success | Puritanical attitude toward sex, excessive modesty |

**FIGURE 3** **Defense Mechanisms and Freudian Stages** If a person is fixated at a psychosexual stage, the fixation can color his or her personality in many ways, including the defense mechanisms the person might use to cope with anxiety.

Freud argued that the individual may become stuck in any of these developmental stages if he or she is overdisciplined or overindulged at a given stage. For example, a parent might wean a child too early (or not early enough) or be too strict (or too lax) in toilet training. *Fixation* occurs when a particular psychosexual stage colors an individual's adult personality. For instance, an *anal retentive* person (someone who is obsessively neat and organized) is fixated at the anal stage. The construct of fixation thus explains how, according to Freud, childhood experiences can have an enormous impact on adult personality. Figure 3 illustrates possible links between adult personality characteristics and fixation at the oral, anal, and phallic stages.

## Psychodynamic Critics and Revisionists

Because Freud was among the first theorists to explore personality, some of his ideas have needed updating and revision over time, while others have been tossed out altogether. In particular, Freud's critics have said that his ideas about sexuality, early experience, social factors, and the unconscious mind were misguided (Adler, 1927; Erikson, 1968; Friedman, Alfonso, & Downey, 2015; Fromm, 1947; Horney, 1945; Jung, 1917; Kohut, 1977; Rapaport, 1967; Sullivan, 1953). They stress the following points:

- Sexuality is not the pervasive force that Freud believed it to be. Furthermore, the Oedipus complex is not as universal as Freud maintained. Freud's concepts were heavily influenced by the setting in which he lived—turn-of-the-century Vienna, a society that, compared with contemporary society, was sexually repressed and male-dominated.
- The first five years of life are not as powerful in shaping adult personality as Freud thought. Later experiences warrant attention.
- The ego and conscious thought processes play a larger role in personality than Freud believed. Achievement, thinking, and reasoning are not always tied to sexual impulses.
- Sociocultural factors are much more important than Freud believed. In stressing the id's dominance, Freud placed more emphasis on the biological basis of personality. More contemporary psychodynamic scholars have especially emphasized the interpersonal setting of the family and the role of early social relationships in personality development (Stern & others, 2018).

A number of dissenters and revisionists to Freud's theory have been influential in the development of psychodynamic theories. Erik Erikson, whose psychosocial stages we examined in the chapter "Human Development", is among these. Here we briefly consider three other thinkers—Karen Horney, Carl Jung, and Alfred Adler—who made notable revisions to Freud's approach.

## HORNEY'S SOCIOCULTURAL APPROACH

Karen Horney (1885–1952) rejected the notion that anatomy is destiny. She argued that sociocultural influences on personality development should be investigated as well (Horney, 1937). Consider Freud's concept of penis envy. Horney pointed out that women might envy the penis not because of unconscious issues but because of the status that society bestows on those who have one. Further, she suggested that both sexes envy the attributes of the other, with men coveting women's reproductive capacities (Horney, 1967).

Horney believed that the need for security, not sex, is the prime motive in human existence. She reasoned that an individual whose needs for security are met should be able to develop his or her capacities to the fullest extent. She viewed psychological health as allowing the person to express talents and abilities freely and spontaneously.

**Karen Horney (1885–1952)** Horney developed the first feminist criticism of Freud's theory. Horney's view emphasizes women's positive qualities and self-evaluation.



## JUNG'S ANALYTICAL THEORY

Freud's contemporary Carl Jung (1875–1961) shared Freud's interest in the unconscious, but he believed that Freud underplayed the role of the unconscious mind in personality. In fact, Jung believed that the roots of personality go back to the dawn of humanity.

The **collective unconscious** is Jung's term for the impersonal, deepest layer of the unconscious mind, shared by all human beings because of their common ancestral past. Describing the collective unconscious as "impersonal" emphasizes that it is the same across all humanity. In Jung's theory, the experiences of a common past have made a deep, permanent impression on the human mind (Hunt, 2012).

Jung posited that the collective unconscious contains **archetypes**, emotionally laden ideas and images that have symbolic meaning for all people. Jung concluded that these archetypes emerge in art, literature, religion, and dreams (Faber & Mayer, 2009; Morgan, 2012; Neumann, 2015). Archetypes are essentially predispositions to respond to the environment in particular ways.

Jung used the terms *anima* and *animus* to identify two common archetypes. He believed each of us has a passive feminine side—the anima—and an assertive masculine side—the animus. The *persona* is another archetype. Jung thought that the persona represents the public mask that we all wear during social interactions; he believed that it is an essential archetype because the persona allows us always to keep some secret part of ourselves hidden from others.

**Carl Jung (1875–1961)** Swiss psychoanalytic theorist Jung developed the concepts of the collective unconscious and archetypes.



## ADLER'S INDIVIDUAL PSYCHOLOGY

Alfred Adler (1870–1937) was one of Freud's earliest followers, although his relationship with Freud was quite brief and his approach to personality was drastically different. In Adler's **individual psychology**, people are motivated by purposes and goals—thus, perfection, not pleasure, is the key motivator in human life. Adler argued that people have the ability to take their genetic inheritance and their environmental experiences and act upon them creatively to become the person they want to be.

Adler thought that everyone strives for superiority by seeking to adapt, improve, and master the environment (Kern & Curlette, 2015). Striving for superiority is our response to the uncomfortable feelings of inferiority that we experience as infants and young children when we interact with bigger, more powerful people. *Compensation* is Adler's term for the individual's attempt to overcome imagined or real inferiorities or weaknesses by developing one's own abilities. Adler believed that compensation is normal, and he said that we often make up for a weakness in one ability by excelling in a different one. For example, a person of small stature and limited physical abilities (like Adler himself) might compensate by excelling in academics (Abramson, 2015).

Adler (1928) believed that birth order could have a profound influence on personality. He viewed firstborn children as being particularly vulnerable because they begin life at the center of their parents' attention but then are knocked off their pedestal by their siblings. Adler believed that firstborn children are more likely to suffer from

- **collective unconscious** Jung's term for the impersonal, deepest layer of the unconscious mind, shared by all human beings because of their common ancestral past.
- **archetypes** Jung's term for emotionally laden ideas and images in the collective unconscious that have rich and symbolic meaning for all people.
- **individual psychology** Adler's view that people are motivated by purposes and goals and that perfection, not pleasure, is thus the key motivator in human life.

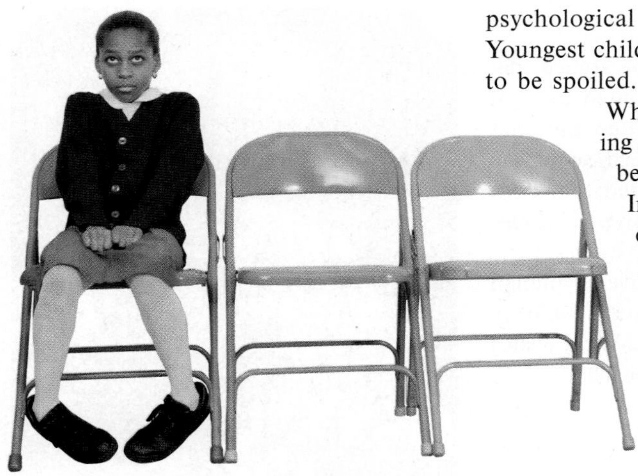

©Big Cheese Photo/Getty Images

psychological disorders throughout their lives and to engage in criminal behavior. Youngest children, however, also are potentially in trouble because they are most likely to be spoiled.

What is the healthiest birth order position? According to Adler, those (including Adler) who are middle children are in a particularly advantageous situation because they have older siblings as built-in inspiration for superiority striving. Importantly, though, Adler did not believe that anyone is doomed by birth order. Rather, sensitive parents could help children in any position in the family to negotiate their needs for superiority.

Many students (but especially middle children) find Adler's approach to the effects of birth order on personality to be fascinating. Adler only *theorized* about birth order; he did not conduct empirical research to investigate whether birth order affects personality–either as he proposed or in any other way. The current science of birth order has shown that despite its intuitive appeal, birth order does not relate in a systematic way to personality (Damian & Roberts, 2015a; Damian & Roberts, 2015b; Rohrer, Egloff, & Schmukle, 2015).

## Evaluating the Psychodynamic Perspectives

Although psychodynamic theories have diverged from Freud's original psychoanalytic version, they share some core principles:

- Personality is determined both by current experiences *and* by early life experiences.
- Personality can be better understood by examining it developmentally–as a series of stages that unfold with the individual's physical, cognitive, and socioemotional development.
- We mentally transform our experiences, giving them meaning that shapes our personality.
- The mind is not all conscious; unconscious motives lie behind some of our puzzling behavior.
- The individual's inner world often conflicts with the outer demands of reality, creating anxiety that is not easy to resolve.
- Personality and adjustment are important topics of psychological inquiry.

Psychodynamic perspectives have come under fire for a variety of reasons. Some critics say that psychodynamic theorists overemphasize the influence of early family experiences on personality and do not acknowledge that people retain the capacity for change and adaptation throughout life. Moreover, some psychologists believe that Freud and Jung put too much faith in the unconscious mind's ability to control behavior. Others complain that Freud placed too much importance on sexuality in explaining personality.

Some have argued, too, that psychoanalysis is not a theory that researchers can test through empirical studies. However, numerous empirical studies on concepts such as defense mechanisms and the unconscious have proved this criticism to be unfounded (Cramer, 2008a, 2008b, 2009a, 2009b; Porcerelli & others, 2017; Weinstein & others, 2012). At the same time, we could look at this argument about empirical testing of psychoanalysis in a different way: Although it is certainly possible to test hypotheses derived from psychoanalytic theory through research, the question remains whether psychoanalytically oriented individuals who believe strongly in Freud's ideas would be open to research results that called for serious changes in the theory.

In light of these criticisms, it may be hard to appreciate why Freud continues to have an impact on psychology. It is useful to keep in mind that Freud made a number of important contributions, including being the first to propose that childhood is crucial to later functioning, that development might be understood in terms of stages, and that unconscious processes might play a significant role in human life (Benet-Martínez & others, 2015).

### test yourself

1. What three structures of personality did Freud describe, and how did he define each?
2. What are Freud's psychosexual stages of personality development?
3. What criticisms have been leveled at psychodynamic theories of personality?

# 2. HUMANISTIC PERSPECTIVES

**Humanistic perspectives** stress a person's capacity for personal growth and positive human qualities. Humanistic psychologists believe that we all have the ability to control our lives and to achieve what we desire.

● **humanistic perspectives** Theoretical views of personality that stress a person's capacity for personal growth and positive human qualities.

Such perspectives contrast with both psychodynamic perspectives and behaviorism, discussed in the chapter "Learning". Humanistic theorists sought to move beyond Freudian psychoanalysis and behaviorism to a theory that might capture the rich and potentially positive aspects of human nature.

## Maslow's Approach

A leading architect of the humanistic movement was Abraham Maslow (1908–1970), whose hierarchy of needs we considered in the chapter "Motivation and Emotion". Maslow believed that we can learn the most about human personality by focusing on the very best examples of human beings—self-actualizers.

Recall that at the top of Maslow's (1954, 1971) hierarchy was the need for self-actualization. Self-actualization is the motivation to develop to one's full potential as a human being. Maslow described self-actualizers as spontaneous, creative, and possessing a childlike capacity for awe. According to Maslow, a person at this optimal level of existence would be tolerant of others, have a gentle sense of humor, and be likely to pursue the greater good. Self-actualizers also maintain a capacity for "peak experiences," or breathtaking moments of spiritual insight. As examples of self-actualized individuals, Maslow included Pablo Casals (cellist), Albert Einstein (physicist), Ralph Waldo Emerson (writer), William James (psychologist), Thomas Jefferson (politician), Eleanor Roosevelt (humanitarian, diplomat), and Albert Schweitzer (humanitarian).

Created more than 40 years ago, Maslow's list of self-actualizers is limited. Because he concentrated on people who were successful in a particular historical context, Maslow's self-actualizers include only those who had opportunities for success in that setting. Maslow listed considerably more men than women, and mostly individuals from Western cultures and of European ancestry. Today, we might add to Maslow's list individuals such as the Dalai Lama (Tenzin Gyatso), Tibetan spiritual and political leader, and Malala Yousafzai, the Pakistani girl who defied the Taliban and, even after being shot in the head, became an activist for education for girls. Both of them are winners of the Nobel Peace Prize, with Yousafzai being the youngest winner of the prize to date, at just 17 years old.

## Rogers's Approach

The other key figure in the development of humanistic psychology, Carl Rogers (1902–1987), began his career as a psychotherapist struggling to understand the unhappiness of the individuals he encountered in therapy. Rogers's work established the foundations for more contemporary studies of personal growth and self-determination.

Like Freud, Rogers began his inquiry into human nature with troubled people. Based on his clinical observations, Rogers (1961) devised his own approach to personality. He believed that we are all born with the raw ingredients of a fulfilling life. We simply need the right conditions to thrive. Just as a sunflower seed, once planted in rich soil and given water and sunshine, will grow into a strong and healthy flower, all humans will flourish in the appropriate environment.

**Carl Rogers (1902–1987)** Rogers was a pioneer in the development of the humanistic perspective.



This analogy is particularly apt and reveals the differences between Rogers's view of human nature and Freud's. A sunflower seed does not have to be directed away from its dark natural tendencies by social constraints, nor does it have to reach a difficult compromise between its vile true impulses and reality. Instead, given the appropriate environment, it will grow into a beautiful flower. Rogers believed that, similarly, each person is born with natural capacities for growth and fulfillment. We are also endowed with an

©Thorsten Indra/Alamy Stock Photo

innate sense–a gut feeling–that allows us to evaluate whether an experience is good or bad for us. Finally, we are all born with a need for positive regard from others. We need to be loved, liked, or accepted by people around us. As children interacting with our parents, we learn early on to value the feeling that they value us, and we gain a sense of self-worth.

## EXPLAINING UNHAPPINESS

If we have innate tendencies toward growth and fulfillment, why are so many people so unhappy? The problem arises when our need for positive regard from others is not met *unconditionally*. **Unconditional positive regard** means being accepted, valued, and treated positively regardless of one's behavior. Rogers noted that often others value us only when we behave in particular ways that meet particular standards. **Conditions of worth** are the standards we must live up to in order to receive positive regard from others. For instance, parents might give their son positive regard only when he achieves in school or chooses a profession that they themselves value. According to Rogers, as we grow up, people who are central to our lives condition us to move away from our genuine feelings and to earn their love by pursuing those goals that they value, even if those goals do not reflect our deepest wishes.

Rogers's theory includes the idea that we develop a *self-concept,* our conscious representation of who we are and who we wish to become, during childhood. This idea is quite different from Freud's ego. For Rogers, the self-concept is the hub of human functioning. Optimally, this self-concept reflects our genuine, innate desires. However, conditions of worth can become part of the self-concept. As a result, we can become alienated from our real feelings and strive to actualize a self that does not represent our authentic desires. A person who dedicates himself or herself to such goals might be very successful by outward appearances but might feel utterly unfilled. Such an individual might be able to check off all the important boxes in life's to-do lists, and complete all that he or she is "supposed to do," but never feel truly happy.

● **unconditional positive regard** Rogers's construct referring to the individual's need to be accepted, valued, and treated positively regardless of the person's behavior.

● **conditions of worth** The standards that the individual must live up to in order to receive positive regard from others.

## PROMOTING OPTIMAL FUNCTIONING

To remedy this situation, Rogers believed that the person must reconnect with his or her true feelings and desires. He proposed that to achieve this reconnection, the individual must experience a relationship that includes three essential qualities: unconditional positive regard, empathy, and genuineness. We will consider each of these qualities in turn.

First, Rogers said that regardless of what they do, people need to receive unconditional positive regard. Although an individual might lack unconditional positive regard in childhood, he or she can experience this unconditional acceptance from others later, in friendships and/or romantic relationships or during sessions with a therapist. Even when a person's behavior is inappropriate, obnoxious, or unacceptable, he or she still needs the respect, comfort, and love of others. Research supports the notion that an enduring, stable sense of self-esteem is more likely to emerge if we feel good about ourselves, without having to live up to external standards (Barry & others, 2018; Crocker & Park, 2012; Geukes & others, 2017).

Second, Rogers said that individuals can become more fulfilled by interacting with people who are empathetic toward them. Empathy involves being a sensitive listener and understanding another's true feelings.

Genuineness is a third requirement in the individual's path to becoming a fully functioning human being. Being genuine means being open with one's feelings and dropping all pretenses and facades. The importance that Rogers placed on the therapist's acting genuinely in the therapeutic relationship demonstrates his strong belief in the positive character of human nature. Rogers believed that we can help others simply by being present for them as the authentic individuals we really are. Research on being genuine or authentic supports Rogers's assertion that being true to ourselves is associated with stable self-esteem (Davis & others, 2015; Kernis, 2003; Showers, Ditzfeld, & Zeigler-Hill, 2015) and well-being more generally (Baker & others, 2017; Peets & Hodges, 2018; Wickham & others, 2016).

Thus, according to Rogers, unconditional positive regard, empathy, and genuineness are three essential ingredients of healthy human relations. Anyone—a manager, teacher, counselor, member of the clergy—who is interested in promoting optimal human functioning can apply these principles.

## Evaluating the Humanistic Perspectives

The humanistic perspectives emphasize that the way we perceive ourselves and the world around us is an essential element of personality. Humanistic psychologists also stress that we need to consider the whole person and the positive side of human nature. Their emphasis on conscious experience has given us the view that personality contains a well of potential that can be developed to its fullest.

Some critics believe that humanistic psychologists are too optimistic about human nature. Others argue that humanistic approaches do not hold individuals accountable for their behaviors if all negative human behavior is seen as emerging out of negative situations.

Self-determination theory, which we considered in the chapter "Motivation and Emotion", demonstrates the way that psychologists have studied humanistic ideas (Ryan & Deci, 2017). Their work bears witness to the enduring impact of humanistic perspectives on contemporary personality psychology.

### test yourself

1. What do the humanistic perspectives on personality emphasize?
2. What name did Maslow give to the motivation to develop to one's full human potential?
3. According to Rogers, what three qualities do individuals need to receive in a relationship in order to connect with their feelings and desires? How did Rogers define each quality?

# 3. TRAIT PERSPECTIVES

If you are setting up a friend on a blind date, you are likely to describe the person in terms of his or her *traits,* or lasting personality characteristics. For decades, trait perspectives have been the dominant approach to understanding personality differences.

## Trait Theories

According to **trait theories**, personality consists of broad, enduring dispositions that tend to lead to characteristic responses. These enduring dispositions are called *traits*. In other words, we can describe people in terms of the ways they behave, such as whether they are outgoing, friendly, private, or hostile. People who have a strong tendency to behave in certain ways are referred to as "high" on the traits; those with a weak tendency to behave in these ways are "low" on the traits. Although trait theorists hold different views about which traits make up personality, they agree that traits are the fundamental building blocks of personality (Ashton & Lee, 2018; Costa & McCrae, 2017; Schermer & Goffin, 2018).

● **trait theories** Theoretical views stressing that personality consists of broad, enduring dispositions (traits) that tend to lead to characteristic responses.

Gordon Allport (1897–1967), sometimes referred to as the father of American personality psychology, was particularly bothered by the negative view of humanity that psychoanalysis portrayed. He rejected the notion that the unconscious was central to an understanding of personality and believed that to understand healthy people, we must focus on their lives *in the present*, not on their childhood experiences. In defining personality, Allport (1961) stressed each person's uniqueness and capacity to adapt to the environment. He was dedicated to the idea that psychology should have relevance to issues facing modern society, and his scholarship has influenced not only personality psychology but also the psychology of religion and prejudice (Allport, 1954).

Allport (1961) believed that personality psychology should focus on understanding healthy, well-adjusted individuals. He described healthy, mature people as having the following characteristics:

- A positive but objective sense of self and others
- Interest in issues beyond their own experience
- A sense of humor

- Common sense
- A unifying philosophy of life—typically but not always provided by religious faith

Allport asserted that traits were the optimal way to understand personality. He defined traits as mental structures that make different situations the same for the person. For instance, if Carly is sociable, she is likely to behave in an outgoing fashion whether she is at a party or in a group study session. Allport's definition implies that behavior should be consistent across different situations.

We get a sense of the down-to-earth quality of Allport's approach to personality by looking at his study of traits. In the late 1930s, Allport and his colleague H. S. Odbert (1936) sat down with two big unabridged dictionaries and pulled out all the words that could be used to describe a person—a method called the *lexical approach*. This approach reflects the idea that if a trait is important to people in real life, it ought to be represented in the natural language people use to talk about one another. Allport and Odbert started with 18,000 words and gradually pared down that list to 4,500.

Clearly, 4,500 traits would make for a very long questionnaire. Do we really need them all? Imagine that you are asked to rate a person, Ignacio, on some traits. You use a scale from 1 to 5, with 1 meaning "not at all" and 5 meaning "very much." If you give Ignacio a 5 on "outgoing," what do you think you might give him on "shy"? So, we may not need 4,500 traits to summarize the way we describe personality. Still, how might we whittle down these descriptors further without losing something important?

With advances in statistical methods and the advent of computers, the lexical approach became considerably less cumbersome. Researchers began to analyze trait words to look for underlying structures that might explain their overlap. Specifically, a statistical procedure called *factor analysis* allowed researchers to identify the traits that go together. Factor analysis essentially tells us what items on a scale people are responding to as if they mean the same thing. For example, if Ignacio got a 5 on "outgoing," he probably would get a 5 on "talkative" and a 1 or 2 on "shy." Factor analysis involves taking the various ratings and reducing them to a few underlying factors that explain their overlap.

One important characteristic of factor analysis is that it relies on the scientist to interpret the meaning of the factors, and the researcher must make some decisions about how many factors are sufficient to explain the data (Goldberg & Digman, 1994). In 1963, W. T. Norman reanalyzed the Allport and Odbert traits and concluded that only five factors were needed to summarize these traits. Norman's research set the stage for the dominant approach in personality psychology today: the five-factor model (Digman, 1990).

## The Five-Factor Model of Personality

Pick a friend and jot down 10 of that friend's most notable personality traits. Did you perhaps list "reserved" or "a good leader"? "Responsible" or "unreliable"? "Sweet," "kind," or "friendly"? Maybe "creative"? Researchers in personality psychology have found that there are essentially five broad personality dimensions that are represented in the natural language; these dimensions also summarize the various ways psychologists have studied traits (Costa & McCrae, 2017).

- **big five factors of personality** The five broad traits that are thought to describe the main dimensions of personality: neuroticism (emotional instability), extraversion, openness to experience, agreeableness, and conscientiousness.

The **big five factors of personality**—the broad traits that are thought to describe the main dimensions of personality—are neuroticism (the tendency to worry and experience negative emotions, sometimes identified by its opposite, emotional stability), extraversion, openness to experience, agreeableness, and conscientiousness. Openness to experience is often the most difficult to understand. This trait refers to a tendency to enjoy intellectual pursuits, to be interested in art and culture, and to engage in creative pursuits. Today it is most commonly labeled "openness to experience," but it was previously termed "intellect" and "culture." Personality psychologists typically refer to the traits as N, E, O, A, and C. If you scramble the first letters of the trait names, you can create an anagram and get the word *OCEAN*. Figure 4 more fully defines the big five traits.

| Openness | Conscientiousness | Extraversion | Agreeableness | Neuroticism (emotional instability) |
|---|---|---|---|---|
| • Imaginative or practical | • Organized or disorganized | • Sociable or retiring | • Softhearted or ruthless | • Calm or anxious |
| • Interested in variety or routine | • Careful or careless | • Fun-loving or somber | • Trusting or suspicious | • Secure or insecure |
| • Independent or conforming | • Disciplined or impulsive | • Energetic or reserved | • Helpful or uncooperative | • Self-satisfied or self-pitying |

**FIGURE 4** **The Big Five Factors of Personality** Each of the broad traits encompasses more narrow traits and characteristics. Use the acronym *OCEAN* to remember the big five personality factors: openness, conscientiousness, extraversion, agreeableness, and neuroticism. Source: Costa & McCrae (2017); King & Trent (2013); Ozer & Benet-Martínez (2006).

To find out where you stand on these traits, see the Psychological Inquiry.

Each of the big five traits has been the topic of extensive research (Costa & McCrae, 2017; King & Trent, 2013; Ozer & Benet-Martínez, 2006). The following is a just a sampling of the interesting work that the five-factor model has inspired:

- *Neuroticism* is related to feeling negative emotion more often than positive emotion in one's daily life. Neuroticism predicts health complaints (Carver & Connor-Smith, 2010) and coronary heart disease risk (Dermody & others, 2016; Koelsch, Enge, & Jentschke, 2012). In a longitudinal study tracking older individuals for nearly seven years, neuroticism predicted dying during the study (Fry & Debats, 2009). In older adults, neuroticism is linked to higher levels of mortality following bereavement (Bratt, Stenström, & Rennemark, 2016). Neuroticism is associated with lower levels of psychological well-being (Sobol-Kwapinska, 2016) and higher risk of a number of psychological disorders (Paulus & others, 2016). However, among individuals who had been diagnosed with serious disease, neuroticism predicted lower levels of smoking (Weston & Jackson, 2015). Neuroticism is also negatively related to risky stock portfolios (Oehler & others, 2018).
- Individuals high in *extraversion* are more likely than others to engage in social activities (Emmons & Diener, 1986). People rate extraverts as smiling, standing energetically, and dressing stylishly (Durante & Griskevicius, 2016; Naumann & others, 2009). Extraversion is a very strong correlate of psychological well-being (Womick & King, 2016) and is negatively related to symptoms of psychological disorders, especially depression (Watson & others, 2015). Extraverts post more selfies online (Guo & others, 2018) and catch more Pokemon when playing Pokemon Go (Khalis & Mikami, 2018). Extraversion positively predicts impulse buying at restaurants (Su & Lu, 2018), greater frequency of sexual activity (Allen & Walter, 2018), as well as higher lifetime earnings (Gensowski, 2018).
- *Openness to experience* is related to liberal values, open-mindedness, tolerance (McCrae & Sutin, 2009), and creativity (Gocłowska & others, 2018). Openness is also associated with superior cognitive functioning and IQ across the life span (Sharp & others, 2010) as well as greater functional connectivity in the brain (Beaty & others, 2018). Openness to experience is related to producing innovative ideas in the workplace, especially when a person has held a job for a long time (Woods & others, 2018). Individuals who rate themselves as open to experience are more likely to pursue entrepreneurial goals (for instance, starting their own business) and to experience success in those pursuits (Zhao, Seibert, & Lumpkin, 2010). One meta-analysis found that openness to experience was linked to living longer (Ferguson & Bibby, 2012).
- *Agreeableness* is related to generosity, altruism (Caprara & others, 2010), religious faith (Ward & King, 2018), and more satisfying social relationships (Tov, Nai, & Lee, 2016). In online dating profiles, agreeableness is negatively related to lying about oneself (J. A. Hall & others, 2010; Stanton, Ellickson-Larew, & Watson, 2016). Agreeableness is negatively related to lifetime earnings (Gensowski, 2018) but positively related to sexual fidelity and lower levels of aggression (Allen & Walter, 2018).

# psychological *inquiry*

### *Your Personality Traits: Who Are You?*

Use the following scale to rate yourself on the trait items listed below. Next to each item, write the number from the scale that best corresponds to how you rate yourself with respect to that trait.

| Disagree strongly | Disagree moderately | Disagree a little | Neither agree nor disagree | Agree a little | Agree moderately | Agree strongly |
|---|---|---|---|---|---|---|
| **1** | **2** | **3** | **4** | **5** | **6** | **7** |

### *I See Myself As:*

**1.** ______ extraverted, enthusiastic.
**2.** ______ critical, quarrelsome.
**3.** ______ dependable, self-disciplined.
**4.** ______ anxious, easily upset.
**5.** ______ open to new experiences, complex.
**6.** ______ reserved, quiet.
**7.** ______ sympathetic, warm.
**8.** ______ disorganized, careless.
**9.** ______ calm, emotionally stable.
**10.** ______ conventional, uncreative.

You have just completed the Ten-Item Personality Inventory, or TIPI (Gosling, Rentfrow, & Swann, 2003), a measure of the big five traits. All of the even-numbered items are *reverse-scored,* meaning your ratings should be reversed for these. (Reverse items are included in scales to fully identify a characteristic and to make sure that respondents are reading items carefully.) So, if you gave item number 2 a rating of 7, it should be a 1; a rating of 6 should be a 2, and so on. The first step in calculating your scores is to reverse your scores on these even-numbered items. Then average together your ratings for the following items for each trait, using the steps in the table below.

| Trait | Items | Sum of Your Ratings | Your Score (divide the sum by 2) | Low Score | Medium Score | High Score |
|---|---|---|---|---|---|---|
| **Emotional Stability (the opposite of neuroticism)** | 4, 9 | _____ | _____ | 3.41 | 4.83 | 6.25 |
| **Extraversion** | 1, 6 | _____ | _____ | 2.99 | 4.44 | 5.89 |
| **Openness to Experience** | 5, 10 | _____ | _____ | 4.13 | 5.38 | 6.45 |
| **Agreeableness** | 2, 7 | _____ | _____ | 4.12 | 5.23 | 6.34 |
| **Conscientiousness** | 3, 8 | _____ | _____ | 4.08 | 5.40 | 6.72 |

The last three columns provide information about what those scores mean. The "medium scores" reflect the mean score found in a sample of more than 1,800 participants. The "low scores" are the mean minus 1 standard deviation. The "high scores" are the mean plus 1 standard deviation. Now answer the following questions.

**1.** Do your scores reflect your sense of who you really are? Explain.

**2.** Why do you think the researchers included one reverse-scored item for each trait?

**3.** The guides for low, medium, and high scores were provided by data from a sample of college students at the University of Texas. Do you think these norms might differ at your school? Why or why not?

**4.** Although this is a very short assessment, scores on this scale are highly correlated with scores on longer scales measuring the same traits (Ehrhart & others, 2009). What does it mean to say that the scores are highly correlated?

- *Conscientiousness* is a key factor in a variety of life domains. Conscientiousness predicts a higher college grade-point average (McAbee & Oswald, 2013), better work performance (S. D. Brown & others, 2011), and higher lifetime earnings (Gensowski, 2018). These links to life success clash with another finding: conscientiousness shares a weak negative relationship with intelligence (Reuter & others, 2018). It appears that conscientiousness serves as an excellent compensation for less-than-outstanding intelligence, leading to higher levels of goal direction and education (Gensowski, 2018; Reuter & others, 2018), Low levels of conscientiousness are linked with higher rates of criminal behavior and substance abuse (Vize, Miller & Lynam, 2018). Conscientiousness is the most consistent personality predictor of health and longevity (Gallagher & others, 2018; Jokela & others, 2013).

Keep in mind that because the five factors are theoretically independent of one another, a person can be any combination of them. Do you know a neurotic extravert or an agreeable introvert, for example? Reading about the correlates of personality traits can sometimes be dissatisfying. If you are low in conscientiousness, are you doomed to be unsuccessful in your career? In many ways, the role of personality traits in our life depends on the situations in which we find ourselves. Traits can be strengths or weaknesses, depending on the types of situations we encounter and the kinds of situations we seek out for ourselves (King & Trent, 2013). Even a trait like agreeableness may be a liability when the situation calls for confrontational behavior. For instance, a woman whose marriage is breaking up might wish for a divorce lawyer who treats her kindly but might prefer one who is less than agreeable at the bargaining table. Eminent psychologist Lee Cronbach (1957, p. 679) once said, "If for each environment there is a best organism, for every organism there must be a best environment." If our personalities are not particularly well suited to a situation, we can change that situation or create one that fits better.

A great context for thinking about the fit between a person and a situation is time of day. Are you the kind of person who tries to schedule your day so none of your classes meet before 10 a.m.? Or do you try to have all your classes finish by 10 a.m.? To read about the psychology of morningness and eveningness, see the Intersection.

## TRAITS AND PERSONALITY DEVELOPMENT

Although it is an assumption of the trait approach that these aspects of personality are relatively stable, numerous studies show that personality traits can change throughout life (Costa, McCrae, & Löckenhoff, 2019). Increasingly, personality psychologists have come to think of these changes in traits as representing personality development because they very often indicate a change from less to greater psychological maturity (Ferschmann & others, 2018; Roberts, 2018).

For example, in an important meta-analysis, Brent Roberts and his colleagues analyzed 92 different longitudinal studies that included thousands of participants from age 12 to over 80 and measured aspects of the big five across the life course (Roberts, Walton, & Viechtbauer, 2006). They found consistent evidence for trait changes throughout life, even into adulthood. Social dominance (a facet of extraversion), conscientiousness, and emotional stability (the opposite of neuroticism) were found to increase—especially between the ages of 20 and 40. Social vitality, another facet of extraversion, and openness to experience increased most during adolescence but then declined in old age. Agreeableness showed a steady rise over the life course. Especially between ages 17 and 24, individuals were likely to become more responsible and less distressed (Blonigen & others, 2008; Klimstra & others, 2009). In general, changes in personality traits across adulthood occur in a direction suggesting that people become more socially mature with time (Roberts & Mroczek, 2008).

## THE BIG FIVE ACROSS CULTURES

If the traits identified in the big five truly capture human personality, they should do so in different cultures and in different languages. Do the big five show up in the assessment of personality in cultures around the world? Many studies suggest that they do. A version of the five factors appears in people in countries as diverse as Canada, Finland, Poland,

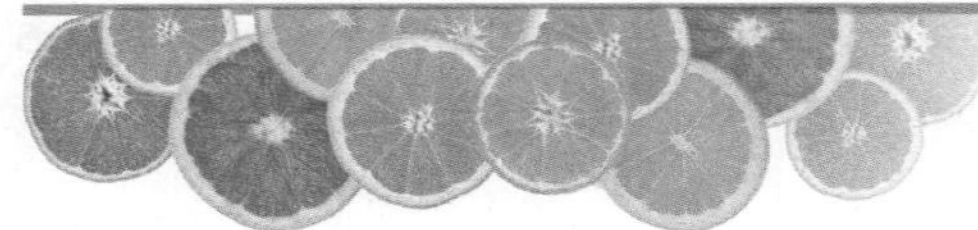

# INTERSECTION

## Personality and Sleep Science: Are You a Morning Person or an Evening Person—and Does It Matter?

©Aila Images/Shutterstock

©leungchopan/Shutterstock

Consider the following questions:

- In order to feel at your very best, what time would you get up in the morning, if you had complete control over your plans for the day?
- Imagine you have to take an important test that is likely to be mentally exhausting. You must be at your very best. You can start the test at any time during a day. It is completely up to you. What time would you choose to start the exam?

Items like these are used to measure *circadian preference*, the time of day when a person is most likely to wake up easily and to feel most alert (Horne & Norbury, 2018). Simply, circadian preference tells us the extent to which someone is a morning person (sometimes called a lark) or an evening person (sometimes called an owl). A recent meta-analysis showed that circadian preferences are related to the big five traits. Conscientiousness is associated with morningness, and openness to experience and extraversion are linked to eveningness (Gorgol, Stolarski, & Matthews, 2018; Lipnevich & others, 2017). But circadian preferences are not simply the same thing as the big five personality factors.

*How might night owls create better situations for themselves?*

Does the degree to which one is a morning or evening person matter? Morning and evening people do differ from each other in terms of their behavioral patterns (Kroese & others, 2018). Although the associations are not large, fortune favors the larks of the world (Taylor & Hasler, 2018). Not only is morningness associated with higher life satisfaction and lower distress, but switching to a lark-like schedule leads to higher levels of happiness (Hasler, Buysse, & Germain, 2016). Morning people are likely to be more active during the day and less likely to be depressed, to smoke, and to be bothered by daytime sleepiness (Taylor & Hasler, 2018). Interestingly, eveningness shares a small positive correlation with intelligence, yet morningness (which is unrelated to cognitive ability) is associated with better academic outcomes (Diaz-Morales & Escribano, 2013), perhaps due to its link with conscientiousness (Gorgol, Stolarski, & Matthews, 2018).

What explains the lark advantage in life outcomes? It turns out that much of it is explained by sleep quality. Quite simply, larks get better sleep and are more well-rested (Demirhan & others, 2018). It is easy to see how this sleep advantage would translate into many benefits in well-being, health, and occupational outcomes.

Consider the fit that exists between larks and the social world. School and work start times are often in the morning. Imagine a lark and an owl showing up to take an exam for an early-morning class: One is bright-eyed and ready. The other is feeling jet-lagged. Now imagine how a lark might feel starting the day at noon or doing their most important work at 10 p.m.

China, and Japan (Paunonen & others, 1992; X. Zhou & others, 2009). Among the big five, the factors most likely to emerge across cultures and languages are extraversion, agreeableness, and conscientiousness (De Raad & others, 2010). Personality traits like the big five have also been used to address another way of thinking about people—as types. For a variety of reasons, many personality psychologists are not enthusiastic about thinking about people in this way. To read about the most recent evidence from research on personality types, see the Critical Controversy.

### ANIMAL STUDIES ON THE BIG FIVE

Researchers have found evidence for at least some of the big five personality traits in animals (Weiss, 2018), including domestic dogs (Gosling, 2008; Gosling, Kwan, & John, 2003) and hyenas (Gosling & John, 1999). In addition, studies have turned up evidence

## *Are There Personality* Types?

If you have ever completed a personality test online you have probably received feedback about the *type* of person you are—Gryffindor, Slitherin, Bart Simpson, or Spongebob Squarepants, for example. As the popularity of the big five personality traits suggests, personality psychologists do not commonly think about personality in terms of types (Haslam, Holland, & Kuppens, 2012; Ofrat, Krueger, & Clark, 2018; Rosenström & Jokela, 2017). Classifying people using types can be misleading because it ignores how much of a trait a person has. Still, some scholars do think that types are useful (Alessandri & Vecchione, 2017; Sârbescu & Boncu, 2018).

When we put people into types, we must have some boundary that separates one type from another and there is great concern about those boundary lines. You may have heard of the Myers Briggs Type Indicator (MBTI) (Briggs & Myers, 1998), developed in the 1940s by a mother–daughter team with no training in assessment. Based on a book by Carl Jung, the MBTI provides feedback on personality types based on four dimensions: extraversion vs. introversion, sensing vs. intuiting, thinking vs. feeling, and judgment vs. perception.

These MBTI dimensions create categories that are labeled with letters; for example, an extraverted person who relies on sensation, thinking, and judgment would be called an ESTJ. Importantly, the MBTI is neither reliable (people get different scores with repeated testing) nor valid (it does not predict what it should) (Grant, 2013). How is it possible that people get different "type" feedback on repeated testing? When a cutoff score is used to classify people, a change of even 1 point can change the person's "type." Personality psychologists do not typically put much faith in the MBTI.

More recently, researchers have tried to identify personality types in samples of over 1.5 million people in the United States and Great Britain who had completed measures of the big five (Gerlach & others, 2018). Four types were identified by profiles of trait scores:

- ***Role Models*** were high on extraversion, openness to experience, conscientiousness, and agreeableness and low in neuroticism. So, role models had "good personalities."
- ***Self-Centered*** types were low on agreeableness, conscientiousness, and openness to experience.
- ***Reserved*** types were low on both neuroticism and openness to experience.
- ***Average*** types were essentially about average on everything. This was the largest group.

What do you think of these types? Certainly, finding out that you are "average"—although it makes perfect statistical sense—does not give the same satisfaction as being told you belong in Ravenclaw.

Of course, the true test of any typology of personality will lie in its ability to predict behavior and to do so better than continuous traits (Loehlin & Martin, 2018). The idea that there are types of personalities has fascinated human beings for centuries. Perhaps the most interesting question might be why we are so attracted to the idea of classifying people as types.

**WHAT DO YOU THINK?**

- What makes the type approach appealing?
- Based on your scores on the big five, which type are you?

©Craig Russell/Shutterstock

©Craig Russell/Shutterstock

for general personality traits (such as overall outgoingness) in orangutans, geese, lizards (Weinstein, Capitanio, & Gosling, 2008), and fish (Wilson & Godin, 2010), among others. Studies showing the existence of traits in nonhuman primates are especially important in exploring the likely evolutionary roots of human personality (Latzman, Boysen, & Schapiro, 2018; Weiss, 2018).

## Evaluating the Trait Perspectives

As already noted, the trait approach is the dominant perspective on personality psychology today. The emergence of the five-factor model has provided personality psychologists with a common language and a set of tools for understanding a host of important topics, including the prediction of behavior, psychological well-being, psychological disorders, and health and illness.

Despite strong evidence for the big five, some personality researchers say that these traits might not end up being the ultimate list of broad traits; they argue that more specific traits are better predictors of behavior. One alternative, the HEXACO model, incorporates a sixth dimension, honesty/humility, to capture the moral dimensions of personality (Ashton & Lee, 2018). Using this model, personality is explained by the following traits: ***h***onesty/***h***umility, ***e***motional stability, e***x***traversion, ***a***greeableness, ***c***onscientiousness, and ***o***penness to experience.

The trait approach has been faulted for missing the importance of *situational* factors in personality and behavior (Kammrath & Scholer, 2013). For example, a person might rate herself as introverted among new people but very outgoing with family and friends. Further, some have criticized the trait perspective for painting an individual's personality with very broad strokes (Uher, 2015). A great deal of contemporary personality science focuses on lower-level facets of the five factors in an effort to get a more fine-grained view of the person (Helle & others, 2018; Lucchetti & others, 2018; Vize, Miller, & Lynam, 2018).

### *test yourself*

1. How do trait theorists define personality?
2. What kind of work did the lexical approach of Allport and Odbert involve, and what key idea about personality traits did it reflect?
3. What traits are included in the big five factors of personality? Define them.

# 4. PERSONOLOGICAL AND LIFE STORY PERSPECTIVES

If two people have the same levels of the big five traits, do they essentially have the same personality? Researchers who approach personality from the personological and life story perspectives do not think so (Adler & others, 2018; McAdams, 2018). One of the goals of personality psychology is to understand how each of us is unique. **Personological and life story perspectives** stress that the way to understand the uniqueness of each person is to focus on his or her life history and life story.

**personological and life story perspectives** Theoretical views of personality stressing that the way to understand the person is to focus on the person's life history and life story.

## Murray's Personological Approach

Henry Murray (1893–1988) was a young biochemistry graduate student when he became interested in the psychology of personality after meeting Carl Jung and reading his work. Murray went on to become the director of the Psychological Clinic at Harvard at the same time that Gordon Allport was a member of that faculty. Murray and Allport saw personality very differently. Whereas Allport was most comfortable focusing on conscious experience and traits, Murray embraced the psychodynamic notion of unconscious motivation.

Murray coined the word *personology* to refer to the study of the whole person. He believed that to understand a person, we have to know that person's history, including the physical, psychological, and sociological aspects of the person's life.

Murray applied his insights into personality during World War II, when he was called upon by the Office of Strategic Services (a precursor to the CIA) to develop a psychological profile of Adolf Hitler. That document, produced in 1943, accurately predicted that Hitler would commit suicide rather than be taken alive. Murray's analysis of Hitler was the first "offender profile," and it has served as a model for modern criminal profiling.

Henry Murray's psychological profile of Adolf Hitler, developed in 1943 during World War II, serves as a model for criminal profiling today.



The aspect of Murray's research that has had the most impact on contemporary personality psychology is his approach to motivation. Murray believed that our motives are largely unknown to us. This circumstance complicates the study of motivation, because it means that researchers cannot simply ask people to say what it is they want. To address the issue, Murray, along with Christiana Morgan, developed the Thematic Apperception Test (TAT), to which we will return later in this chapter (Morgan & Murray, 1935).

For the TAT, a person looks at an ambiguous picture and writes or tells a story about what is going on in the scene. A variety of scoring procedures have been devised for analyzing the unconscious motives that are revealed in imaginative stories (C. P. Smith, 1992). These scoring procedures involve *content analysis,* a procedure in which a psychologist takes the person's story and codes it for different images, words, and so forth. Although Murray posited 22 different unconscious needs, three have been the focus of most current research:

- *Need for achievement:* an enduring concern for attaining excellence and overcoming obstacles
- *Need for affiliation:* an enduring concern for establishing and maintaining interpersonal connections
- *Need for power:* an enduring concern for having an impact on the social world

David Winter (2005) analyzed the motives revealed in inaugural addresses of U.S. presidents. He found that certain needs revealed in these speeches corresponded to later events during the person's presidency. For instance, presidents who scored high on need for achievement (such as Jimmy Carter) were less successful during their terms. Note that the need for achievement is about striving for personal excellence and may have little to do with playing politics, negotiating interpersonal relationships, or delegating responsibility. Presidents who scored high on need for power tended to be judged as more successful (John F. Kennedy, Ronald Reagan), and presidents whose addresses suggested a high need for affiliation tended to experience scandal during their presidencies (Richard M. Nixon). A recent analysis of President Donald J. Trump's inaugural address suggested high levels of power motivation as well as achievement motivation (Winter, 2018).

## The Life Story Approach to Identity

Following in the Murray tradition, Dan McAdams (2018) developed the *life story approach* to identity. His work centers on the idea that each of us has a unique life story, representing our memories of what makes us who we are. This life story is a constantly changing narrative that provides us with a sense of coherence. For McAdams, our life story is our very identity.

McAdams (1989) also introduced the concept of intimacy motivation. The *intimacy motive* is an enduring concern for warm interpersonal encounters for their own sake. Intimacy motivation is revealed in the warm, positive interpersonal imagery in the stories people tell. Intimacy motive has been shown to relate to positive outcomes. For instance, college men who were high on intimacy motivation showed heightened levels of happiness and reduced levels of work strain some 30 years later (McAdams & Bryant, 1987). A study of the coming-out stories of gay men and lesbians demonstrated that intimacy-related imagery (for example, experiencing falling in love or warm acceptance from others) was associated with well-being and personality development (King & Smith, 2005).

Research by David Winter (2005) has analyzed presidential motives in inaugural addresses such as those delivered by Richard M. Nixon (first) and John F. Kennedy (second). Winter found that certain needs revealed in these speeches corresponded to later events during these individuals' terms in office.

Other personality psychologists have relied on narrative accounts of experiences as a means of understanding how individuals create meaning in life events. In one study, parents of children with Down syndrome wrote the story of how they found out about their child's diagnosis. Parents whose stories ended happily scored higher on measures of happiness, life meaning, and personal growth than others. Parents who told stories about struggling to make sense of the experience tended to mature psychologically over time (King & others, 2000). By using narratives, personal documents (such as diaries), and even letters and speeches, personality psychologists search for the deeper meaning that cannot be revealed through tests that ask people directly about whether specific items capture their personality traits.

Finally, some personality psychologists use the life story approach to understand individual lives. *Psychobiography* is a type of inquiry in which personality psychologists attempt to apply personality theory to one person's life (Kasser, 2017; Schultz & Lawrence, 2017). Erik Erikson's study of Gandhi's life, described in the chapter "Psychology's Scientific Method", is an example of a psychobiography. Psychobiographies have been written about a diverse array of figures, including Sigmund Freud, Gordon Allport, John F. Kennedy, George W. Bush, Osama bin Laden, and Elvis Presley.

## Evaluating the Personological and Life Story Perspectives

Studying individuals through narratives and personal interviews provides an extraordinarily rich opportunity for the researcher. Imagine having the choice of reading someone's diary versus seeing that person's scores on a questionnaire measuring traits. Not many would pass up the chance to read the diary.

However, such studies are difficult and time-consuming. Personologist Robert W. White (1992) referred to the study of narratives as exploring personality "the long way." Collecting interviews and narratives is often just the first step. Turning these personal stories into scientific data means transforming them into numbers, and that process involves extensive coding and content analysis. Further, for narrative studies to be worthwhile, they must tell us something we could not have found out in a much easier way (King, 2003). Moreover, psychobiographical inquiries tend to reflect the biases of the scholars who conduct them, may violate the privacy of the subjects of inquiry, and may not serve the scientific goal of generalizability (Young & Collins, 2018).

### test yourself

1. What did Murray mean by personology, and what did he believe was essential to understanding who a person really is?
2. On what does McAdams say our identities depend?
3. What is the intimacy motive? What has research revealed about it?

# 5. SOCIAL COGNITIVE PERSPECTIVES

● **social cognitive perspectives** Theoretical views of personality emphasizing the influence of conscious awareness, beliefs, expectations, and goals.

**Social cognitive perspectives** on personality emphasize the influence of conscious awareness, beliefs, expectations, and goals. While incorporating principles from behaviorism (see the chapter "Learning"), social cognitive psychologists explore the person's ability to reason; to think about the past, present, and future; and to reflect on the self. They emphasize the person's individual interpretation of situations and thus focus on the uniqueness of each person by examining how behavior is tailored to the diversity of situations in which people find themselves.

Social cognitive theorists are not interested in broad traits such as the big five. Rather, they investigate how more specific factors, such as beliefs, relate to behavior and performance. In this section we consider the two major social cognitive approaches, developed respectively by Albert Bandura and Walter Mischel.

## Bandura's Social Cognitive Theory

In his social cognitive approach to learning, Albert Bandura took the basic tenets of behaviorism (see the chapter "Learning") and added a recognition of the role of mental processes in determining behavior (Bandura, 1986, 2011a). Applying these principles to personality, Bandura's social cognitive theory states that behavior, environment, and person/cognitive factors are *all* important in understanding personality.

Bandura coined the term *reciprocal determinism* to describe the way behavior, environment, and person/cognitive factors interact to create personality (Figure 5). Reciprocal determinism means that the relationships among the person, his or her behavior, and the environment are all two-way streets. The environment can determine a person's behavior, but the person can act to change the environment. Similarly, person/cognitive factors can both influence behavior and be influenced by behavior. Our behavior—for instance, doing well on a test—can influence our beliefs about ourselves and in turn influence future behaviors.

From Bandura's perspective, then, behavior is a product of a variety of forces—some of which come from the situation and some of which the person brings to the situation. We now review the important processes and variables Bandura uses to understand personality.

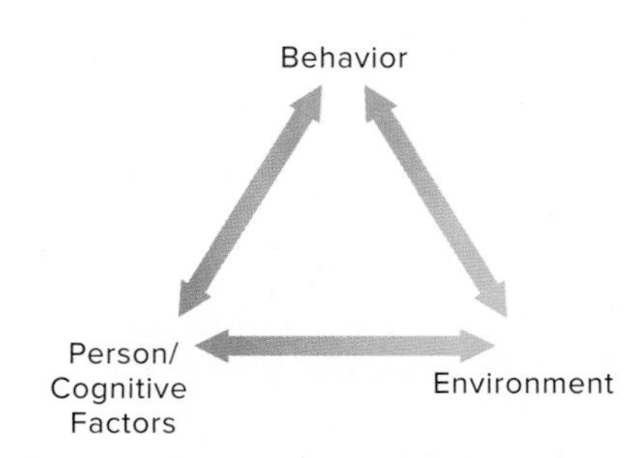


**FIGURE 5 Bandura's Social Cognitive Theory** Bandura's social cognitive theory emphasizes reciprocal influences of behavior, environment, and person/cognitive factors. Notice that from Bandura's perspective, all of those arrows are double-headed, meaning that causation goes in both directions.

## OBSERVATIONAL LEARNING

Recall from the chapter "Learning" Bandura's belief that observational learning is a key aspect of how we learn. By observing how others behave and noticing the consequences of their actions, we might come to adopt the behavior ourselves. For example, a boy might observe that his mother's hostile exchanges with other people are an effective way to get what she wants. Later, when the boy is with his peers, he might adopt the same strategy. Social cognitive theorists believe that we acquire a wide range of behaviors, thoughts, and feelings by watching others' behavior and that our observations strongly shape our personality (Bandura, 2009, 2011a).

**Albert Bandura (b. 1925)** Bandura's practical, problem-solving social cognitive approach has made a lasting mark on personality theory and therapy.



## PERSONAL CONTROL

Social cognitive theorists emphasize that we can regulate and control our own behavior despite our changing environment (Bandura, 2011a; Damen & others, 2015; Mischel, 2004). For example, a young executive who observes her boss behave in an overbearing and sarcastic manner toward his subordinates may find the behavior distasteful and go out of her way to encourage and support her own staff. Psychologists commonly describe a sense of behavioral control as coming from inside the person (an *internal locus of control*) or outside the person (an *external locus of control*). When we feel that we ourselves are controlling our choices and behaviors, the locus of control is internal, but when other influences are controlling them, the locus of control is external.

Consider the question of whether you will perform well on your next test. With an internal locus of control, you believe that you are in command of your choices and behaviors, and your answer will depend on what you can realistically do (for example, study hard or attend a special review session). With an external locus of control, however, you might say that you cannot predict how things will go because so many outside factors influence performance, such as whether the test is difficult, how the curve is set in the course, and whether the instructor is fair. Feeling a strong sense of personal control is vital to many aspects of performance, behavior, and well-being (Cheng & others, 2018; Gooding, Callan, & Hughes, 2018; Zigarmi, Galloway, & Roberts, 2018).

## SELF-EFFICACY

**Self-efficacy** is the belief that one has the competence to accomplish a given goal or task and produce positive change. Bandura and others have shown that self-efficacy is related to a number of positive developments in people's lives, including solving problems and becoming more sociable (Bandura, 2011a).

• **self-efficacy** The belief that one can accomplish a given goal or task and produce positive change.

Self-efficacy influences whether people even try to develop healthy habits, as well as how much effort they expend in coping with stress, how long they persist in the face of obstacles, and how much stress and pain they experience (Becker, Kang, & Stuifbergen, 2012; Schutte & Malouff, 2016; Zahodne & others, 2015). We will return to the topics of personal control and self-efficacy at the end of this chapter.

## Mischel's Contributions

Like Bandura, Walter Mischel was a social cognitive psychologist who explored how personality influences behavior. Mischel left his mark on the field of personality in two notable ways. First, his critique of the idea of consistency in behavior ignited a flurry of controversy. Second, he proposed the CAPS model, a new way of thinking about personality.

### MISCHEL'S CRITIQUE OF CONSISTENCY

Whether we are talking about unconscious sexual conflicts, traits, or motives, all of the approaches we have considered so far maintain that these various personality characteristics are enduring influences on behavior. In 1968 Walter Mischel's book *Personality and Assessment* shattered this assumption and nearly ended the psychological study of personality.

To understand Mischel's argument, recall Gordon Allport's definition of a trait as a characteristic that ought to make different situations equivalent for a given person. This quality of traits suggests that a person should behave consistently in different situations–in other words, the individual should exhibit *cross-situational consistency.* For example, an outgoing person should act in a highly sociable way, no matter whether she is at a party or in the library. However, Mischel looked at the research compiled on trait prediction of behavior and found it to be lacking. He concluded that there was no evidence for cross-situational consistency in behavior–and thus no evidence for the existence of personality as it had been previously conceptualized.

Rather than understanding personality as consisting of broad, internal traits that produce consistent behavior across situations, Mischel said that personality often changes according to a given situation. Mischel asserted that behavior is discriminative; that is, a person looks at each situation and responds accordingly. Mischel's view is called *situationism,* the idea that personality and behavior often vary considerably from one context to another.

Personality psychologists responded to Mischel's situationist attack in various ways (Donnellan, Lucas, & Fleeson, 2009; Funder, 2009; Hogan, 2009). Researchers showed that it is not a matter of *whether* personality predicts behavior but *when and how* it does so, often in combination with situational factors (Sherman, Nave, & Funder, 2010). The research findings can be summarized as follows:

- The narrower and more limited a trait is, the more likely it will predict behavior.
- Some people are consistent on some traits, and other people are consistent on other traits.
- Personality traits exert a stronger influence on an individual's behavior when situational influences are less powerful. A very powerful situation is one that contains many clear cues about how a person is supposed to behave. For example, even a highly talkative person typically sits quietly during a class lecture. In weaker situations, however, such as during leisure time, the person may spend most of the time talking.

Importantly, individuals select the situations they are in (Webb & others, 2018). Consequently, even if situations determine behavior, traits play a role by influencing which situations people choose–such as going to a party or staying home to study (Emmons & Diener, 1986).

Let's pause and reflect on what it means to be consistent. You might believe that being consistent is part of being a genuine, honest person and that tailoring behavior to different situations means being fake. On the other hand, consider that a person who never changes his or her behavior to fit a situation might be unpleasant to have around. For example, think about someone who cannot put aside his competitive drive even when playing checkers with a 4-year-old. Clearly, adaptive behavior might involve sometimes being consistent and sometimes tailoring behavior to fit the situation.

Mischel (2004, 2009) developed an approach to personality that he felt captured the nuances of the relationship between the individual and situations in producing behavior. Imagine trying to study personality without using traits or broad motives. What would you focus on? Mischel's answer to this dilemma was his CAPS theory.

### CAPS THEORY

Recall Mischel's work on delay of gratification from the chapter "Motivation and Emotion" (Carlson & others, 2018). Early studies showed that the longer children waited for a treat, the better they fared later in life in a variety of ways. Mischel's approach to personality is concerned with just such stability (or coherence) in the pattern of behavior *over time,* not with consistency across differing situations. That is, Mischel and his colleagues have studied how behaviors in very different situations have a coherent pattern, such as a child's waiting to eat the marshmallow and that same individual's (as a grown college student) deciding to stay home and study instead of going out to party.

In keeping with the social cognitive emphasis on the person's cognitive abilities and mental states, Mischel conceptualized personality as a set of interconnected **cognitive affective processing systems (CAPS)** (Kell, 2018; Meehan & others, 2018; Mischel, 2009; Shoda & others, 2013). This label captures how the CAPS approach understands personality: It involves information processing (cognitive) and emotional experience (affective) interacting to systematically determine behavior, as the person encounters different situations. According to this approach, our thoughts and emotions about ourselves and the world affect our behavior and become linked in ways that matter to behavior (Kammrath & Scholer, 2013).

Personal control and self-efficacy are psychological connections that a person has made among situations, beliefs, and behaviors. For example, Raoul may be excited by the challenge of a new assignment from his boss and think about all the possible strategies to complete the project and get down to work immediately. Yet this go-getter may respond differently to other challenges, depending on who gives the assignment, what it is, or whether he feels he can do a good job.

From the CAPS perspective, it makes no sense to ask a person "How extraverted are you?" because the answer is always, "It depends." A person may be outgoing in one situation (on the first day of class) and not so in another (right before an exam), and that unique pattern of flexibility is what personality is all about.

©Image Source/Getty Images

● **cognitive affective processing systems (CAPS)** Mischel's theoretical model for describing how individuals' thoughts and emotions about themselves and the world affect their behavior and become linked in ways that matter to that behavior.

## Evaluating the Social Cognitive Perspectives

Social cognitive theory focuses on the interactions of individuals with their environments. The social cognitive approach has fostered a scientific climate for understanding personality that highlights the observation of behavior. Social cognitive theory emphasizes the influence of cognitive processes in explaining personality and suggests that people have the ability to control their environment.

Critics of the social cognitive perspective on personality take issue with one or more aspects of the theory. For example, they charge that

- The social cognitive approach is too concerned with situational influences on personality. It ignores the role played by traits and other enduring qualities of personality.
- Social cognitive theory overlooks the role biology plays in personality.
- In its attempt to incorporate both the situation and the person into its view of personality, social cognitive psychology tends to lead to very specific predictions for each person in any given situation, making generalizations impossible.

### *test yourself*

1. In what ways did Bandura react to and modify Skinner's approach to understanding human functioning?
2. What is self-efficacy, and what kinds of positive life developments have been linked to it?
3. With what is Mischel's cognitive affective processing systems (CAPS) approach centrally concerned?

# 6. BIOLOGICAL PERSPECTIVES

The notion that physiological processes influence personality has been around since ancient times. Around 400 B.C.E., Hippocrates, the father of medicine, described human beings as having one of four basic personalities based on levels of particular bodily fluids (called *humours*). For Hippocrates, a "sanguine" personality was a happy, optimistic individual who happened to have an abundance of blood. A "choleric" person was quick-tempered, with too much yellow bile. A "phlegmatic" personality referred to a placid, sluggish individual with too much phlegm (mucus produced by the respiratory system), and a "melancholic" pessimist had too much black bile.

Hippocrates' ideas about bodily fluids have fallen by the wayside, but personality psychologists have long acknowledged that personality involves the brain and biological processes. Psychologists' beliefs about these interacting processes in personality, though, were based on assumptions, not direct study. For instance, Freud's psychosexual stages demonstrate his strong belief in the connection between the mind (personality) and the body; Allport defined traits as "*neuro*psychic" structures and personality as a "psycho*physical*" system; and Murray once declared, "No brain, no personality." More recently, with advances in method and theory, biological perspectives on personality have become more prominent (Markett, Montag, & Reuter, 2018; McNaughton & Smillie, 2018; Toschi & others, 2018). The biological approach to personality seeks to link personality processes with physical aspects of the person, including the brain and genes.

## Personality and the Brain

The brain is clearly important in personality as in other psychological phenomena. Recall the case of Phineas Gage, described in the chapter "Biological Foundations of Behavior". A key effect of Gage's horrific accident was that it changed his personality. He went from being gentle, kind, and reliable to being angry, hostile, and untrustworthy.

A great deal of research is currently addressing the ways in which brain activity is associated with various personality traits. For example, research has shown that conscientiousness is related to cortical thickness (Lewis & others, 2018) and a network of brain areas involved in goal pursuit (Reuter & others, 2018). Extraversion predicts responses to humor in the amygdala (Berger & others, 2018). More recently, researchers have begun to explore the ways that traits influence the meaning of brain structure or activity differences (Kong & others, 2015). Hans Eysenck and Jeffrey Gray have proposed two theoretical approaches to the biology of personality.

### EYSENCK'S RETICULAR ACTIVATION SYSTEM THEORY

British psychologist Hans Eysenck (1967) was among the first to describe the role of a particular brain system in personality. He developed an approach to extraversion/introversion based on the role of arousal in personality and behavior. In the chapter "States of Consciousness", we discussed the meaning of arousal as a state of engagement with the environment. In the chapter "Biological Foundations of Behavior", we noted that the reticular formation is located in the brain stem and plays a role in wakefulness or arousal. Eysenck focused on the *reticular activation system (RAS),* which is the name given to the reticular formation and its connections.

Eysenck posited that all of us share an optimal arousal level, a level at which we feel comfortably engaged with the world. However, Eysenck proposed, the RAS of extraverts and introverts differs with respect to the baseline level of arousal. You know that an extravert tends to be outgoing, sociable, and dominant and that an introvert is quieter and more reserved and passive. According to Eysenck, these behavioral differences reflect different arousal regulation strategies (Figure 6). Extraverts wake up in the morning under-aroused, *below* the optimal level, whereas introverts start out *above* the optimal level.

If *you* were feeling under-engaged with life, what might you do? You might listen to loud music or hang out with friends—in other words, behave like an extravert. If, on the other hand, you were feeling over-aroused or too stimulated, what would you do? You might spend time alone, keep distractions to a minimum, maybe sit quietly and read a book—in other words, you might act like an introvert. Thus, from Eysenck's perspective, we can understand the continuum of extraversion/introversion as demonstrating patterns of behavior aimed at regulating arousal around our baseline. According to Eysenck, extraverts experience a baseline that is below the optimal; introverts experience a baseline that is above the optimal.

Research has not shown that extraverts and introverts differ in terms of baseline arousal. Instead, researchers have found that a process similar to what Eysenck proposes for arousal—not involving the activation of RAS, but rather blood flow in the striatum, a part of the basal ganglia—plays a role in dopamine levels (Hermes & others, 2011;

**FIGURE 6 Eysenck's Reticular Activation System Theory** Eysenck viewed introversion and extraversion as characteristic behavioral patterns that aim to regulate arousal around the individual's baseline level. (first photo) ©drbimages/E+/Getty Images; (second photo) ©Stockbyte/Getty Images

Wacker, 2018; Wacker & Smillie, 2015). Recall that dopamine is the neurotransmitter linked with the experience of reward. From this approach, introverts have higher baseline blood flow, and extraverts have lower baseline blood flow to this region of the brain. Because extraverts are motivated to bring their dopamine levels up, they are more likely to seek out arousing and rewarding experiences and thus behave in extraverted ways.

## GRAY'S REINFORCEMENT SENSITIVITY THEORY

Jeffrey Gray proposed a neuropsychology of personality, called *reinforcement sensitivity theory,* that has been the subject of much research (Corr, 2016; Gray, 1987; Kaye, White, & Lewis, 2018). On the basis of animal learning principles, Gray posited that two neurological systems—the *behavioral activation system (BAS)* and the *behavioral inhibition system (BIS)*—could be viewed as underlying personality, as Figure 7 shows.

According to Gray, these systems explain differences in an organism's attention to rewards and punishers in the environment. An organism sensitive to rewards is more likely to learn associations between behaviors and rewards and therefore to show a characteristic pattern of seeking out rewarding opportunities. In contrast, an organism with a heightened sensitivity to punishers in the environment is more likely to learn associations between behaviors and negative consequences. Such an organism shows a characteristic pattern of avoiding such consequences.

In Gray's theory, the BAS is sensitive to rewards in the environment, predisposes one to feelings of positive emotion, and underlies the trait of extraversion (Wacker, 2018). In contrast, the BIS is sensitive to punishments and is involved in avoidance learning; it predisposes the individual to feelings of fear and underlies the trait of neuroticism (McNaughton & Smillie, 2018).

Gray's conceptual model of reinforcement sensitivity proposed interacting brain systems as primarily responsible for the behavioral manifestations of the BAS and BIS. Research has provided some evidence for the biological underpinnings of these systems. The amygdalae, the prefrontal cortex, and the anterior cingulated cortex appear to serve together as a system for affective style (Davidson, 2005; McNaughton & Corr, 2008) and are particularly implicated in the BAS or extraversion (McNaughton & Smillie, 2018).

BAS
Behavioral Activation System
Sensitive to
Environmental reward
Behavior
Seek positive consequences/rewards
Character of emotion
Positive
Personality trait
Extraversion
BIS
Behavioral Inhibition System
Sensitive to
Environmental punishment
Behavior
Avoid negative consequences/punishments
Character of emotion
Negative
Personality trait
Neuroticism


**FIGURE 7 Gray's Reinforcement Sensitivity Theory** Gray theorized that two neurological systems, the BAS and the BIS, explain differences in an organism's attention to environmental rewards and punishments and in this way shape personality. Source: Corr (2016); Gray (1987); (top photo) ©McGraw-Hill Education/Ken Karp, photographer; (bottom photo) ©xubingruo/Getty Images

## THE ROLE OF NEUROTRANSMITTERS

Neurotransmitters have also been implicated in personality in ways that fit Gray's model (De Pascalis, Sommer, & Scacchia, 2018; Fischer, Lee, & Verzijden, 2018). As noted above, the neurotransmitter dopamine functions in the experience of reward. Dopamine is vital to learning that certain behaviors are rewarding, sending the message, "Do it again!" Research has shown that dopamine is a factor in BAS or extraversion (Wacker & Smillie, 2015) suggesting that the dopaminergic system in extraverts is well prepared to learn associations between environmental cues and rewards.

Even stronger than the link between dopamine and extraversion is the relationship between the neurotransmitter serotonin and neuroticism (Aluja & others, 2018;

Delvecchio & others, 2016). In this case, neuroticism is associated with low levels of circulating serotonin. As well, neuroticism may be related to a certain serotonin transporter gene and to the binding of serotonin in the thalamus (Cao & others, 2018; Kruschwitz & others, 2015; Wannemüller & others, 2018). Interestingly, the influence of this gene on personality may depend on experience. Whether individuals who have this genetic characteristic actually develop into worriers depends on their social experiences (Laceulle & others, 2015; Pluess & others, 2010).

Keep in mind that finding associations between neurotransmitters and personality does not tell us about the potential causal pathways between these variables. Extraversion is linked to dopamine, neuroticism to serotonin. Yet, behavior can influence brain processes, and patterns of behavior can determine brain activity and neurotransmitter levels. One thing that behavior cannot influence, at least not yet, is genes, another important biological factor in personality.

## Personality and Behavioral Genetics

● **behavioral genetics** The study of the inherited underpinnings of behavioral characteristics.

**Behavioral genetics** is the study of the inherited underpinnings of behavioral characteristics. A great deal of research in behavioral genetics has involved twin studies, and the hub of this work is, appropriately, the University of Minnesota, located in the Twin Cities (Minneapolis and St. Paul).

Twin studies show that genetic factors explain a substantial amount of the observed differences in each of the big five traits. Remember that to conduct these studies, researchers compare identical twins, who share 100 percent of their genes, with fraternal twins, who share just 50 percent. All of the participants complete questionnaires measuring their traits. Then the researchers see if the identical twins are more similar to each other than the fraternal twins.

Heritability estimates for the five factors are about 50 percent (Bouchard & Loehlin, 2001; Jang, Livesley, & Vernon, 1996; Keyes & others, 2015). As noted in the chapter "Biological Foundations of Behavior", heritability statistics have come into question and as such these estimates are likely higher than reality. Still, they suggest a substantial role of genes in explaining differences between people on personality traits.

Even aspects of personality that are not traits reveal genetic influence. For example, autobiographical memories about one's childhood and early family experiences (the kind of data that the personologist might find interesting) are influenced by genetics. Robert Krueger and his colleagues examined retrospective reports on the quality of family environments in a sample of twins who were reared apart (Krueger, Markon, & Bouchard, 2003). Participants rated their adoptive families on a variety of characteristics such as parental warmth, feelings of being wanted, and the strictness of their parents. These twins, though obviously sharing genetics, were reared by different families, so they were describing different experiences. Yet their recollections of their early family experiences were similar, and the heritability estimate for family cohesion ranged from 40 to 60 percent.

©Greatstock Photographic Library/Alamy Stock Photo

Understanding the role of genetic factors in personality is enormously complex. Research on non-twin samples often suggests much lower heritability, for reasons that are not well understood (South & Krueger, 2008). Furthermore, because genes and environment are often intertwined, it is very difficult to tease apart whether, and how, genes or experience explains enduring patterns of behavior. For instance, a little girl who is genetically predisposed to engage in disruptive behavior may often find herself in a time-out or involved in arguments with parents or teachers. When that child emerges as an adult with a "fighting spirit" or lots of "spunk," are those adult traits the product of genes, experiences, or both? Finally, most traits are probably influenced by multiple genes (Abdellaoui & others, 2018; Davis & others, 2019), making the task of identifying specific molecular links very challenging.

## Evaluating the Biological Perspectives

Exploring the biological aspects of personality is a vital, continuing goal in personality psychology. This work ties the field of personality to animal learning models, advances in brain imaging, and evolutionary theory. However, a few cautions are necessary in thinking about biological variables and their place in personality.

As we considered above, biology can be the effect, not the cause, of personality. To be sure that you grasp this idea, first recall that personality is the individual's characteristic pattern of behavior, thoughts, and feelings. Then recall from previous chapters that behavior, thoughts, and feelings are physical events in the body and brain. If traits predispose individuals to particular and consistent behaviors, thoughts, and emotional responses, traits may play a role in forging particular habitually used pathways in the brain. Recall, too, from the chapter "Memory" that memory may be thought of as patterns of activation among neurons. The autobiographical memories that interest personologists, then, might be viewed as well-worn patterns of activation. To the extent that personality represents a person's characteristic pattern of thought or the accumulation of memories over the life span, personality may not only be influenced by the brain–it may also play a role in the brain's very structure and functions.

### *test yourself*

1. According to Eysenck, what part of the brain influences whether a person is an introvert or an extravert?
2. How does Gray's reinforcement sensitivity theory of personality explain extraversion and neuroticism?
3. What is behavioral genetics, and what kind of study is commonly used in research in this area?

# 7. PERSONALITY ASSESSMENT

One of the great contributions of personality psychology is its development of rigorous methods for measuring mental processes. Psychologists use a number of scientifically developed methods to evaluate personality. They assess personality for different reasons–from career counseling and job selection to clinical evaluation and criminal risk.

## Self-Report Tests

The most commonly used method of measuring personality characteristics is the **self-report test** (also called an *objective test* or an *inventory*), which directly asks people whether specific items describe their personality traits. Self-report personality tests include items such as

- I am easily embarrassed.
- I love to go to parties.
- I like to watch cartoons on TV.

Respondents choose from a limited number of answers (yes or no, true or false, agree or disagree).

**self-report test** A method of measuring personality characteristics that directly asks people whether specific items describe their personality traits; also called an objective test or an inventory.

One problem with self-report tests is *social desirability.* To grasp the idea of social desirability, imagine answering the item "I am lazy at times." This statement is probably true for everyone, but would you feel comfortable admitting it? When motivated by social desirability, individuals say what they think will make them look better. One way to measure the influence of social desirability is to give individuals a questionnaire that is designed to tap into this tendency. Such scales typically contain universally true but threatening items ("I like to gossip at times," "I have never said anything intentionally to hurt someone's feelings"). If scores on a trait item correlate with this measure of social desirability, we know that the test takers were probably not being straightforward on their trait ratings.

Another way to get around social desirability issues is to design scales so that it is virtually impossible for the respondent to know what the researcher is trying to measure. One means of accomplishing this goal is to use an **empirically keyed test**, a type of self-report test that is created by first identifying two groups that are known to be different. The researcher would give these two groups a large number of questionnaire items and

**empirically keyed test** A type of self-report test that presents many questionnaire items to two groups that are known to be different in some central way.

then see which items show the biggest differences between the groups. Those items would become part of the scale to measure the group difference. For instance, a researcher might want to develop a test that distinguishes between individuals with a history of substance abuse and those with no such history. The researcher might generate a long list of true/false items asking about a variety of topics but not mentioning substance abuse. These questions would be presented to the members of the two groups, and on the basis of the responses, the researcher can then select the items that best discriminate between the members of the differing groups. Empirically keyed tests require that we have two groups we know in advance differ on an important variable.

Note that an empirically keyed test avoids the issue of social desirability because the items that distinguish between the two groups are not related in any obvious way to the actual purpose of the test. For instance, those without a substance abuse history might typically respond "true" to the item "I enjoy taking long walks," whereas those with a history of substance abuse might respond "false"; but this item does not mention substance use, and there is no clear reason why it should distinguish between these groups.

Indeed, an important consideration with respect to empirically keyed tests is that researchers often do *not* know why a given test item distinguishes between two groups. Imagine, for example, that an empirically keyed test of achievement motivation includes an item such as "On TV, I prefer to watch sports, not romantic movies." A researcher might find that this item does a good job of distinguishing between higher-paid versus lower-paid managers in a work setting. However, does this item measure achievement motivation or, instead, simply the respondents' gender? Because empirically keyed tests depend on knowing in advance that two groups differ, there may be reasons other than the one the researcher is focusing on that might lead to differences on items.

## MMPI

● **Minnesota Multiphasic Personality Inventory (MMPI)** The most widely used and researched empirically keyed self-report personality test.

The **Minnesota Multiphasic Personality Inventory (MMPI)** is the most widely used and researched empirically keyed self-report personality test. The MMPI was initially constructed in the 1940s to assess "abnormal" personality tendencies. The most recent version of the inventory, the MMPI-2 RF, is still widely used around the world to assess personality and predict outcomes (Butcher & others, 2011; Tarescavage, Scheman, & Ben-Porath, 2018). The scale features 567 items and provides information on a variety of personality characteristics. The MMPI also includes items meant to assess whether the respondent is lying or trying to make a good impression (social desirability). The MMPI is used to assess mental health (Lee, Graham, & Arbisi, 2018; Stanley & others, 2018), as a tool in hiring decisions (Roberts & others, 2018), to help people make career choices (Caillouet & others, 2010; Moyle & Hackston, 2018), and in forensic settings, assessing criminal risk (Olver, Coupland, & Kurtenbach, 2018; Sellbom & Wygant, 2018).

## ASSESSMENT OF THE BIG FIVE FACTORS

Paul Costa and Robert McCrae (1992) constructed the Neuroticism Extraversion Openness Personality Inventory–Revised (or NEO-PI-R, for short), a self-report test assessing the five-factor model: neuroticism, extraversion, openness, agreeableness, and conscientiousness. Other measures of the big five traits have relied on the lexical approach and offer the advantage of being available without a fee.

Unlike empirically keyed tests, measures of the big five generally contain straightforward items; for instance, the trait "talkative" might show up on an extraversion scale. These items have what psychologists call **face validity**, which means that the items seem on the surface to be testing the characteristic in question. Measures of the big five typically involve items that are obvious in terms of what they measure, but not all self-report assessments have this quality.

● **face validity** The extent to which a test item appears to fit the particular trait it is measuring.

It is likely that you could give a reasonably good assessment of your own levels of traits such as neuroticism and extraversion. What about the more mysterious aspects of yourself and others? If you are like most people, you think of psychological assessments as tools to find out things you do not already know about yourself. For that objective, psychologists might turn to projective tests.

## Projective Tests

A **projective test** presents individuals with an ambiguous stimulus and asks them to describe it or tell a story about it–in other words, to *project* their own meaning onto the stimulus. Projective tests are based on the assumption that the ambiguity of the stimulus allows individuals to interpret it based on their feelings, desires, needs, and attitudes. Based on the defense mechanism of projection, projective tests are especially designed to elicit the individual's unconscious feelings and conflicts, providing an assessment that goes deeper than the surface of personality (Sahly & others, 2011).

Projective tests attempt to get inside the mind to discover how the test taker really feels and thinks; that is, they aim to go beyond the way the individual overtly presents himself or herself. These tests are theoretically aligned with psychodynamic perspectives on personality, which give more weight to the unconscious than do other perspectives. Projective techniques require content analysis; the examiner must code the responses for the underlying motivations revealed in the story.

Perhaps the most famous projective test is the **Rorschach inkblot test**, developed in 1921 by Swiss psychiatrist Hermann Rorschach. The test consists of 10 cards, half in black-and-white and half in color, which the individual views one at a time (Figure 8). The test taker is asked to describe what he or she sees in each of the inkblots. The individual may say, for example, "I see two fairies having a tea party" or "This is a picture of the female reproductive organs." These responses are scored based on indications of various underlying psychological characteristics (Mihura & others, 2018).

The Rorschach's usefulness in research is controversial. The test's reliability and its validity have been questioned (Garb & others, 2001; Hunsley & Bailey, 2001; Weiner, 2004). If the Rorschach were reliable, two different scorers would agree on the personality characteristics of the individual being tested. If the Rorschach were valid, it would predict behavior outside of the testing situation; that is, it would predict, for example, whether an individual will attempt suicide, become severely depressed, cope successfully with stress, or get along well with others. Research shows that the Rorschach does not meet these criteria of reliability and validity (Lilienfeld, Wood, & Garb, 2000).

Although sometimes administered in clinical (Huprich, 2013) and applied settings (Piotrowski, 2015), the Rorschach is not commonly used in personality research. However, the projective method itself remains a tool for studying personality, especially in the form of the Thematic Apperception Test (TAT).

The **Thematic Apperception Test (TAT)**, developed by Henry Murray and Christiana Morgan in the 1930s, is designed to elicit stories that reveal something about an individual's personality. The TAT consists of a series of pictures like the one in Figure 9, each on an individual card or slide. The TAT test taker is asked to tell a story about each of the pictures, including events leading up to the situation described, the characters' thoughts and feelings, and the way the situation turns out. The TAT is now more commonly referred to as a *Picture Story Exercise (PSE).*

PSE methods are used in clinical practice and in research. The stories can be coded for motivational content, including need for achievement, affiliation, power, intimacy, and a variety of other needs (Schultheiss & Brunstein, 2005) as well as unconscious defense mechanisms (Cramer, 2015). In contrast with the Rorschach, TAT measures have shown reliability and validity (Aydinli & others, 2015; Schüler & others, 2015). The coding schemes used for PSEs can also be applied to any number of texts, including social media posts (Dufner, Arslan, & Denissen, 2018).

## Other Assessment Methods

Self-report questionnaires and projective techniques are just two of the multitude of assessment methods developed and used by personality psychologists. Many personality psychologists incorporate interviews (Alea, 2018) as well as friend or peer ratings of individuals' traits or other characteristics (Malesza & Kaczmarek, 2018). Personality

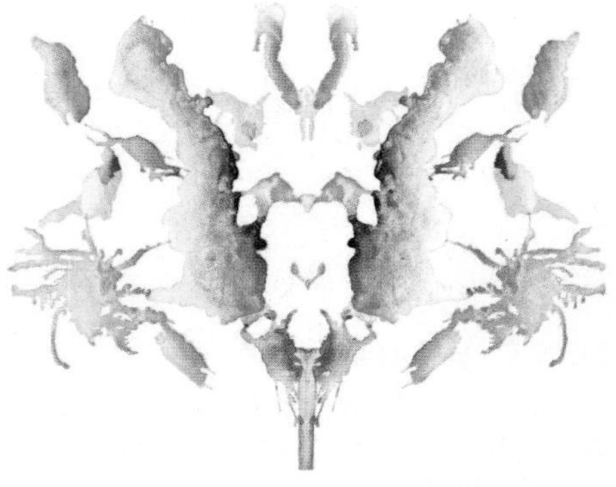

**FIGURE 8 Type of Stimulus Used in the Rorschach Inkblot Test** What do you see in this figure? Do you see two green seahorses? Or a pair of blue spiders? A psychologist who relies on the Rorschach test would examine your responses to find out who you are. ©zmeel/E+/Getty Images

- **projective test** A personality assessment test that presents individuals with an ambiguous stimulus and asks them to describe it or tell a story about it—to project their own meaning onto the stimulus.

- **Rorschach inkblot test** A famous projective test that uses an individual's perception of inkblots to determine his or her personality.

- **Thematic Apperception Test (TAT)** A projective test that is designed to elicit stories that reveal something about an individual's personality.

**FIGURE 9 Picture from the Thematic Apperception Test (TAT)** What are this man and woman thinking and feeling? How did they come to this situation, and what will happen next? A psychologist who uses the TAT would analyze your story to find out your unconscious motives. ©Science History Images/Alamy Stock Photo

psychologists also measure behavior directly by observing a person either live or in a video (Hall & others, 2018). In addition, cognitive assessments have become more common in personality psychology, as researchers investigate topics such as the relationships between personality and processes of attention and memory. Personality psychologists also use a host of psychophysiological measures, such as heart rate and skin conductance. Increasingly, personality psychologists are incorporating brain imaging as well (McNaughton & Smillie, 2018).

Whether personality assessments are being used by clinical psychologists, psychological researchers, or other practitioners, the choice of assessment instrument depends greatly on the researcher's theoretical perspective. Figure 10 summarizes which methods are associated with each of the theoretical perspectives. The figure also summarizes each approach, including its major assumptions, and gives a sample research question addressed by each. Personality psychology is a diverse field, unified by a shared interest in understanding those aspects of the person that make the individual who he or she really is.

## test yourself

1. What is an empirically keyed test?
2. What is a common problem with self-report tests?
3. What technique does the TAT (or PSE) involve?

| Approach | Summary | Assumptions | Typical Methods | Sample Research Question |
|---|---|---|---|---|
| **Psychodynamic** | Personality is characterized by unconscious processes. Childhood experiences are of great importance to adult personality. | The most important aspects of personality are unconscious. | Case studies, projective techniques. | How do unconscious conflicts lead to dysfunctional behavior? |
| **Humanistic** | Personality evolves out of the person's innate, organismic motives to grow and actualize the self. These healthy tendencies can be undermined by social pressure. | Human nature is basically good. By getting in touch with who we are and what we really want, we can lead happier, healthier lives. | Questionnaires, interviews, observation. | Can situations be changed to support individuals' organismic values and enhance their well-being? |
| **Trait** | Personality is characterized by five general traits that are represented in the natural language that people use to describe themselves and others. | Traits are relatively stable over time. Traits predict behavior. | Questionnaires, observer reports. | Are the five factors universal across cultures? |
| **Personological and Life Story** | To understand personality, we must understand the whole person. We all have unique life experiences, and the stories we tell about those experiences make up our identities. | The life story provides a unique opportunity to examine the personality processes associated with behavior, development, and well-being. | Written narratives, TAT stories or PSE, autobiographical memories, interviews, and psychobiography. | How do narrative accounts of life experiences relate to happiness? |
| **Social Cognitive** | Personality is the pattern of coherence that characterizes a person's interactions with the situations he or she encounters in life. The individual's beliefs and expectations, rather than global traits, are the central variables of interest. | Behavior is best understood as changing across situations. To understand personality, we must understand what each situation means for a given person. | Multiple observations over different situations; video-recorded behaviors rated by coders; questionnaires. | When and why do individuals respond to challenging tasks with fear versus excitement? |
| **Biological** | Personality characteristics reflect underlying biological processes such as those carried out by the brain, neurotransmitters, and genes. Differences in behaviors, thoughts, and feelings depend on these processes. | Biological differences among individuals can explain differences in their personalities. | Brain imaging, twin studies, molecular genetic studies. | Do genes explain individual differences in extraversion? |

**FIGURE 10** **Approaches to Personality Psychology** This figure summarizes the broad approaches to personality described in this chapter. Many researchers in personality do not stick with just one approach but apply the various theories and methods that are most relevant to their research questions.

# 8. PERSONALITY AND HEALTH AND WELLNESS

Personality comprises a set of enduring characteristics that influence behavior. As such, personality affects many behaviors that impact physical health and psychological wellness, as we consider in this final section.

## Personality and Physical Health

We first survey personality characteristics that are linked, respectively, to health and to illness.

### CONSCIENTIOUSNESS

Conscientiousness is not the sexiest personality trait, but it might well be the most important of the big five when it comes to longevity and healthy living (Turiano & others, 2015). A variety of studies show that conscientious people tend to do all the things that they are told are good for their health, such as getting regular exercise, avoiding drinking and smoking, wearing seatbelts, and checking smoke detectors (Hakulinen & others, 2015; O'Connor & others, 2009; Turiano & others, 2012). Conscientiousness is correlated with better health and lower stress (Jokela, 2018; Sutin, Stephan, & Terracciano, 2018). Conscientious individuals have a lower mortality risk than their counterparts who are less conscientious (Turiano & others, 2015). A fascinating study found that teachers' ratings of the responsibility and studiousness of elementary schools students predicted a lower risk of death at age 52 (Spengler & others, 2016). In addition, a recent study showed that it is impossible to be *too* conscientious. Across a variety of important life outcomes, conscientiousness was never a negative influence (Nickel, Roberts, & Chernyshenko, 2018).

### PERSONAL CONTROL

Another personality characteristic associated with taking the right steps toward a long, healthy life is personal control. Feeling in control can reduce stress during difficult times and can lead to the development of problem-solving strategies to deal with hardship. Personal control has been linked to lower risk of cancer and cardiovascular disease because of its link to healthy behavior (Stürmer, Hasselbach, & Amelang, 2006; Williams & others, 2016). Personal control has been related to emotional well-being, successful coping with a stressful event, healthy behavior change, and good health (Mercer & others, 2018; Nuccitelli & others, 2018; Shukla & Rishi, 2018; Wilson & others, 2018).

### SELF-EFFICACY

Self-efficacy is related to success in a wide variety of positive life changes, including achieving weight loss (Varkevisser & others, 2018), exercising regularly (Siow & others, 2018), quitting smoking (Warner & others, 2018), reducing substance abuse (Gause & others, 2018), and practicing safe sex (Safren & others, 2018). Evidence shows a link between self-efficacy and cardiovascular functioning following heart failure (Ha & others, 2018). Individuals high in self-efficacy are not only less likely to suffer a second hospitalization due to heart failure but also more likely to live longer (Bachmann & others, 2015; Maeda & others, 2012; Sarkar, Ali, & Whooley, 2009).

If there is a problem to be fixed, self-efficacy—having a can-do attitude—is related to finding a solution. In one study, smokers were randomly assigned to one of three conditions. In the *self-efficacy condition,* individuals were told they had been chosen for the study because they had great potential to quit smoking (Warnecke & others, 2001). Then they participated in a 14-week program on smoking cessation. In the *treatment-alone condition,* individuals participated in the 14-week smoking cessation program but were told that they had been randomly selected for it. In the *no-treatment control condition,* individuals did not participate in the smoking cessation program. At the end of the 14 weeks, individuals in the self-efficacy condition were more likely to have quit smoking than their counterparts in the other two conditions. The Psychological Inquiry shows the results.

## psychological *inquiry*

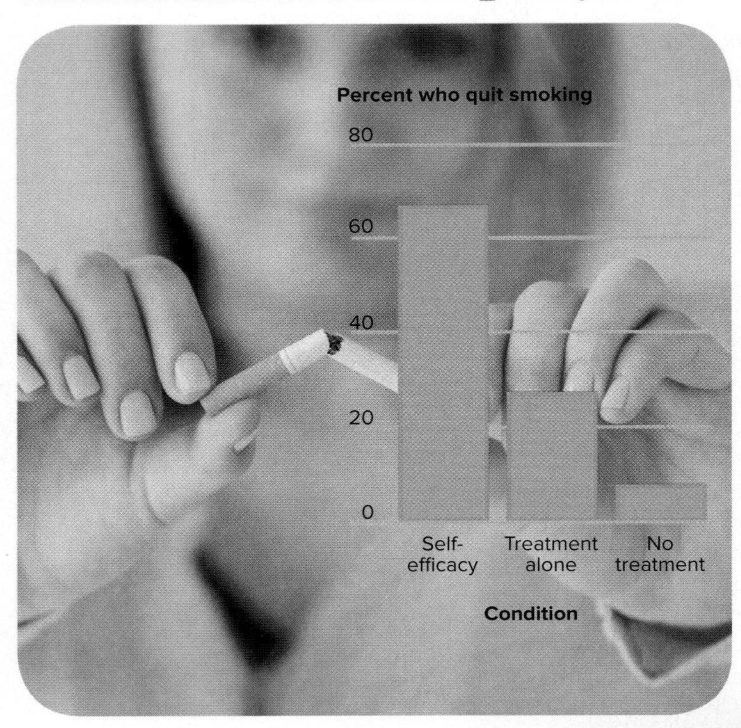


©Tetra Images/Getty Images Source: Warnecke, Morera, Turner, Mermelstein, Johnson, Parsons, Crittenden, Freels, & Flay, (2001).

### *A Can-Do Attitude Means You Can Quit Smoking*

The figure shows the results of the study on self-efficacy and smoking cessation (Warnecke & others, 2001). Smokers were randomly assigned to one of three conditions—self-efficacy, treatment alone, and no treatment. Notice that the Y, or vertical, axis shows the dependent variable, the percentage of participants who quit smoking. The X, or horizontal, axis shows the independent variable, the groups to which participants were assigned. Try your hand at answering the following questions.

1. Why were participants randomly assigned to groups?
2. If the researchers concluded that the self-efficacy manipulation caused these differences, would their conclusion be justified? Explain.
3. How might the results of this study be generalized to groups who wish to change other behaviors?
4. How would you design a correlational study that would examine the relationship between self-efficacy and smoking cessation?

## OPTIMISM

A factor that is often linked to positive functioning and adjustment is optimism.

Optimism is having the general expectation that good things are more likely than bad things to occur in the future (Carver & Scheier, 2018). Numerous studies reveal that those who hold these positive expectancies for the future are physically and mentally healthier than pessimists (Kubzansky & others, 2018). Optimism is related to effective immune system functioning (Dantzer & others, 2018; Segerstrom & Sephton, 2010). Optimism also is associated with better cardiovascular health (Hernandez & others, 2015) and better outcomes among individuals with coronary heart disease (Carver & Scheier, 2018).

As you think about the traits we have examined—conscientiousness, personal control, self-efficacy, and optimism—and their relationship to good health, keep in mind that you can *cultivate* these qualities. Studies show that even conscientiousness, the most stable of these characteristics, can increase, especially in young adulthood. Although these characteristics are generally associated with wellness, other aspects of personality are linked to health problems, as we now consider.

## PERSONALITY TYPES: THE TYPE A/TYPE B AND TYPE D BEHAVIOR PATTERNS

In the late 1950s, a secretary for two cardiologists, Meyer Friedman and Ray Rosenman, observed that the chairs in their waiting rooms were tattered and worn, but only on the front edges. The cardiologists themselves had noticed the impatience of their cardiac patients, who often arrived exactly on time and were in a great hurry to leave. Intrigued by this consistency, they conducted an eight-year study of 3,000 healthy men between the ages of 35 and 59 to find out whether people with certain behavioral characteristics might be prone to heart problems (Friedman & Rosenman, 1974). During the eight years, one group of men had twice as many heart attacks or other forms of heart disease as the other men.

Friedman and Rosenman described the common personality characteristics of the men who developed coronary disease as the **Type A behavior pattern**, a cluster of characteristics—being excessively competitive, hard-driven, impatient, and hostile. Rosenman and Friedman labeled the behavior of the healthier group, who were more relaxed and easygoing, the **Type B behavior pattern**.

- **Type A behavior pattern** A cluster of characteristics—including being excessively competitive, hard-driven, impatient, and hostile—related to a higher incidence of heart disease.

- **Type B behavior pattern** A cluster of characteristics—including being relaxed and easygoing—related to a lower incidence of heart disease.

Subsequent research showed that the link between Type A behavior and coronary disease is not as strong as Friedman and Rosenman believed (Suls & Swain, 1998; R. B. Williams, 2001, 2002). However, certain components of Type A are linked with coronary risk (Spielberger, 2004), especially hostility (Mwendwa & others, 2013). People who are hostile are more likely to develop heart disease than their less angry counterparts (Eng & others, 2003; K. A. Matthews & others, 2004). People with hostile feelings tend to have strong physiological reactions to stress: Their heart races, their breathing quickens, and their muscles tense up (Vella & others, 2012).

The **Type D behavior pattern** describes individuals who are generally distressed, frequently experience negative emotions, and are socially inhibited (Allen & others, 2018). Even after adjustment for depression, Type D individuals face a threefold increased risk of adverse cardiovascular events (Denollet & Conraads, 2011; Lin & others, 2018). A meta-analysis found that Type D individuals with cardiovascular disease are at a higher risk for major adverse cardiac events and have a lower health-related quality of life (O'Dell & others, 2011). The Type D behavior pattern is related to lower quality of life, higher levels of depression, poor health behaviors, and poor coping with illness (Gramer, Haar, & Mitteregger, 2018; Kupper & others, 2018; Mizutani, & others, 2018).

- **Type D behavior pattern** A cluster of characteristics—including being generally distressed, having negative emotions, and being socially inhibited—related to adverse cardiovascular outcomes.

## Personality and Psychological Well-Being

Among the most consistent findings in personality research is the strong association between personality traits and psychological well-being. Specifically, neuroticism is strongly related to lower levels of well-being, while extraversion is related to higher levels (Womick & King, 2018). The links between these two traits and well-being have even been found in orangutans (Weiss, King, & Perkins, 2006). What explains these connections?

As defined by psychologists, **subjective well-being** is a person's assessment of his or her level of positive affect and negative affect and an evaluation of his or her life in general (Diener, 2012a). This definition provides a clue as to why the traits of neuroticism and extraversion are so strongly related to well-being. Neurotic individuals experience more negative affect than others, and their moods are more changeable. David Watson, a personality and clinical psychologist who specializes in the study of mood, has suggested that negative emotion is at the very core of the trait of neuroticism (Miller, Vachon, & Lynam, 2009; Watson & Clark, 1997).

- **subjective well-being** A person's assessment of his or her own level of positive affect relative to negative affect and an evaluation of his or her life in general.

Interestingly, however, research has shown that neurotics can be happy—especially if they are also extraverted (Hotard & others, 1989). Indeed, Watson suggests that positive emotion is the core of the trait of extraversion (Watson & Naragon, 2009). Research has shown that extraverts are happier than introverts even when they are alone (Lucas, 2008). In fact, research has supported the conclusion that extraverts are happier regardless of what they are doing or with whom they are doing it (Lucas, 2007; McNiel, Lowman, & Fleeson, 2010).

If you are not very conscientious, or you are a pessimist with an external locus of control, or you are hostile, or neurotic, or an introvert—or a hostile, neurotic introvert—you may be feeling your mood deflating. If personality is stable, what good is it to find out that your personality—who you really are—might put you at risk for illness and make you miserable?

A positive way to think about these issues is to focus on the difference between traits and states (Magee & Biesanz, 2018; Tamir & Thornton, 2018). Recall that traits are enduring characteristics—the way you generally are. In contrast, states (such as positive or negative moods) are briefer experiences. Having a trait, such as neuroticism, that

### test yourself

1. What are four personality characteristics that are associated with positive functioning and positive life changes?
2. How have various researchers defined optimism?
3. What is the Type A behavior pattern, and what specific aspect of it is most often linked to coronary disease?

predisposes you to feelings of worry (a state) does not mean that your overall well-being must suffer. Instead, recognizing that you tend to be neurotic may be an important step in noting when your negative moods are potentially being fed by this trait and are not necessarily the result of objective events. Finding out that you have a personality style associated with higher levels of stress or lower levels of happiness does not mean that you are doomed. Rather, you can use this information to cultivate good habits and to make the most of your unique qualities.

Remember, too, that personality characteristics influence health through their relationships to behaviors and the experience of stress. Even a person who is very low in conscientiousness can engage in healthy behaviors. Consider that characteristics such as locus of control and self-efficacy involve your beliefs about the world, and these aspects of personality are changeable. Recall that in the Psychological Inquiry in this section self-efficacy was manipulated by simply telling people they had high potential to change. Believing in *your own* potential may be the first step to enhancing your health and wellness.

# SUMMARY

## 1. PSYCHODYNAMIC PERSPECTIVES

Freud developed psychoanalysis through his work with patients suffering from hysterical symptoms (physical symptoms with no physical cause). Freud viewed these symptoms as representing conflicts between sexual drive and duty. Freud believed that most personality—which, in his theory, includes the id, ego, and superego—is unconscious. The ego uses various defense mechanisms, Freud said, to reduce anxiety.

A number of theorists criticized and revised Freud's approach. Horney said that the need for security, not sex or aggression, is our most important need. Jung developed the concept of the collective unconscious, a storehouse of archetypes. Adler's individual psychology stresses that people are striving toward perfection.

Weaknesses of the psychodynamic perspectives include overreliance on reports from the past and overemphasis on the unconscious mind. Strengths of psychodynamic approaches include recognizing the importance of childhood, conceptualizing development through stages, and calling attention to the role of unconscious processes in behavior.

## 2. HUMANISTIC PERSPECTIVES

Humanistic perspectives stress a person's capacity for personal growth and positive human qualities. Maslow developed the concept of a hierarchy of needs, with self-actualization being the highest human need. In Rogers's approach, each of us is born with a tendency toward growth, a sense of what is good and bad for us, and a need for unconditional positive regard. Because we are often denied unconditional positive regard, we may become alienated from our innate growth tendencies. In order to reconnect with these innate tendencies, Rogers felt, a person requires a relationship that includes unconditional positive regard, empathy, and genuineness.

The humanistic perspectives recognize positive human capacities, but critics suggest the approach is too optimistic and may downplay personal responsibility.

## 3. TRAIT PERSPECTIVES

Trait theories emphasize that personality consists of traits—broad, enduring dispositions that lead to characteristic responses. Allport stated that traits should produce consistent behavior in different situations, and he used the lexical approach to personality traits, which involves using all the words in the natural language that could describe a person as a basis for understanding the traits of personality.

The current dominant perspective in personality psychology is the five-factor model. The big five traits include openness to experience, conscientiousness, extraversion, agreeableness, and neuroticism. Studying people in terms of their traits has value, but trait approaches are criticized for focusing on broad dimensions and not attending to each person's uniqueness.

## 4. PERSONOLOGICAL AND LIFE STORY PERSPECTIVES

Murray described personology as the study of the whole person. Contemporary followers of Murray study personality through narrative accounts and interviews. McAdams introduced the life story approach to identity, which views identity as a constantly changing story with a beginning, a middle, and an end. Psychobiography is a form of personological investigation that applies personality theory to one person's life. Life story approaches to personality reveal the richness of each person's unique life story, but it is difficult to carry out and is time-consuming.

## 5. SOCIAL COGNITIVE PERSPECTIVES

Social cognitive theory states that behavior, environment, and person/cognitive factors are important in understanding personality. In Bandura's view, these factors reciprocally interact.

Two important concepts in social cognitive theory are self-efficacy and personal control. Self-efficacy is the belief that one can master a situation and produce positive outcomes. Personal control refers to individuals' beliefs about whether the outcomes of their actions depend on their own acts (internal) or on events outside of their control (external).

Mischel's controversial book *Personality and Assessment* stressed that people do not behave consistently across different situations but rather tailor their behavior to suit particular situations. Personality psychologists countered that personality does predict behavior for some people some of the time. Mischel developed a revised approach to personality centered on cognitive affective processing systems (CAPS). According to CAPS, personality is best understood as a person's habitual emotional and cognitive reaction to specific situations.

A particular strength of social cognitive theory is its focus on cognitive processes. However, social cognitive approaches have not given adequate attention to enduring individual differences, to biological factors, and to personality as a whole.

## 6. BIOLOGICAL PERSPECTIVES

Eysenck suggested that introversion/extraversion can be understood as reflecting differences in arousal regulation. Gray developed a reinforcement sensitivity theory of personality, suggesting that extraversion and neuroticism can be understood as two neurological systems that respond to rewards (the behavioral activation system, or BAS) and punishments (the behavioral inhibition system, or BIS) in the environment.

Research has found that dopamine is associated with behavioral approach (extraversion) and serotonin with behavioral avoidance (neuroticism). Behavioral genetic studies have shown that the heritability of personality traits is approximately 50 percent. Studies of biological processes in personality are valuable but can overestimate the causal role of biological factors.

## 7. PERSONALITY ASSESSMENT

Self-report tests assess personality by asking participants about their preferences and behaviors. One problem in self-report research is the tendency for individuals to respond in socially desirable ways. Empirically keyed tests avoid social desirability problems by using items that distinguish between groups even if we do not know precisely why the items do so.

The Minnesota Multiphasic Personality Inventory (MMPI) is the most widely used empirically keyed personality test. The most popular test for assessing the big five traits is the NEO-PI-R, which uses self-report items to measure each of the traits.

Projective tests, designed to assess unconscious aspects of personality, present individuals with an ambiguous stimulus, such as an inkblot or a picture, and ask them to tell a story about it. Projective tests are based on the assumption that individuals will project their personalities onto these stimuli. The Thematic Apperception Test (TAT) is a projective test that has been used in personality research. Today, the TAT is more commonly termed the Picture Story Exercise (PSE). Other assessment methods include behavioral observation, reports from peers, and psychophysiological and neuropsychological measures.

## 8. PERSONALITY AND HEALTH AND WELLNESS

Conscientiousness and personal control relate to health and longevity through their association with healthy lifestyle choices. Self-efficacy is also related to the ability to make positive changes in lifestyle. Optimism is another personality characteristic that is related to better health.

The Type A behavior pattern is a set of characteristics including hostility, time urgency, and competitiveness. Type B behavior, in contrast, refers to a more easygoing style. With regard to predicting cardiovascular disease, the crucial aspect of Type A appears to be hostility. The Type D personality is prone to distress, and this type has been linked to poorer health outcomes.

Personality traits that are related to health and wellness can also be thought of as states. Thus, even if you are low on these wellness traits, you can still benefit by seeking out states that foster positive attributes.

# key *terms*

archetypes
behavioral genetics
big five factors of personality
cognitive affective processing systems (CAPS)
collective unconscious
conditions of worth
defense mechanisms
ego
empirically keyed test
face validity
humanistic perspectives
id
individual psychology
Minnesota Multiphasic Personality Inventory (MMPI)
Oedipus complex
personality
personological and life story perspectives
projective test
psychodynamic perspectives
Rorschach inkblot test
self-efficacy
self-report test
social cognitive perspectives
subjective well-being
superego
Thematic Apperception Test (TAT)
trait theories
Type A behavior pattern
Type B behavior pattern
Type D behavior pattern
unconditional positive regard

# apply your *knowledge*

1. Consider a facet of your personality that you might want to change. From the perspective of Freud's psychoanalytic theory and Rogers's humanistic theory, could you change this aspect of your personality? If so, how?
2. How important has your childhood been in the development of your adult personality? Choose an experience or series of experiences in childhood and describe how they are represented in your current personality.
3. If you are a fan of reality television, try your hand at identifying the personality characteristics of the individuals involved. Are any of the folks from *Real Housewives* or *Survivor* particularly neurotic or conscientious? If you prefer fictional shows, consider your favorite characters: What are the traits these individuals express?
4. Look at your own social networking profile. Do you think you are expressing the "real you"? If so, how?

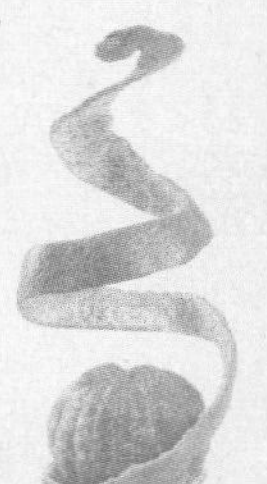

**Design elements:** Preview icon: ©Jiang Hongyan; Intersection box icon: ©D. Hurst/Alamy, ©Creative Crop/Getty Images, ©Dimitris66/Getty Images, ©Savany/Getty Images; Critical Controversy box icon: ©Ultrashock; running heads icon: ©Cre8tive Studios/Alamy; Summary icon: ©Vadarshop

# CHAPTER 13

## CHAPTER OUTLINE





127

128

# Social Psychology

## Reaching Out to Other Tribes

**In February of 2017, Jewish cemeteries in Philadelphia and near St. Louis were attacked by vandals who overturned headstones and spray-painted Nazi symbols in those hallowed grounds.** Some of the graves in the cemeteries were of individuals who had come to the United States in search of religious freedom. Now, their final resting place was marred by bigotry. A woman whose great-grandfather was buried in one of the cemeteries said, "To come to the U.S. and create this amazing life where everyone felt safe and secure and able to be who they were, that was an incredible thing... For this to have happened where my family has been laid to rest was just heartbreaking. These are unconscionable acts" (Victor, 2017). The Jewish community was rocked by the violation that hearkened back to the horrors of the Holocaust during World War II. Almost immediately, help was offered by a group of Muslims who set up an online crowdfunding site to raise money to repair the damage. The group set a goal of $20,000 which was reached in a mere 3 hours. In all, they raised over $130,000. Although most donors were Muslims, some were not, including J.K. Rowling and Ellen DeGeneres.

Jews, Muslims, Christians, Hindus, people of other faiths, and nonbelievers do not agree on everything. They may disagree on many things. But reaching out a hand of friendship and support, even to those who differ from us, is possible for everyone. We all differ from each other in ways big and small. Understanding how we negotiate our differences and come to share the world in peace and mutual respect is at the core of social psychology.

# PREVIEW

We begin our study of social psychology by examining social cognition and then exploring social behavior, including altruism and aggression. We next look at conformity, obedience, and social influence before considering how the groups to which we belong shape our interactions with other groups. We probe the world of close relationships, including attraction and love. Finally, we consider the vital role of social connections in health and wellness.

## 1. DEFINING SOCIAL PSYCHOLOGY

We need other people to survive. Our thoughts and emotions are often about the people we care about. Our goals and motives often include interpersonal relationships. Our behavior is often directed toward (or in response to) another person. It is hard to think of an aspect of our lives that is not in some way connected to other people. This fundamental property of human existence, its social nature, is the focus of social psychology. **Social psychology** is the study of how people think about, influence, and relate to other people.

● **social psychology** The study of how people think about, influence, and relate to other people.

*Social psychology* is sometimes confused with *sociology*. Sociology is the study of human societies, organizations, and institutions. Although both sociology and social psychology are interested in human social behavior, sociology focuses on the group level. Social psychology, in contrast, is interested in how individuals influence groups and how groups influence individuals. Unlike sociologists, social psychologists often focus on the immediate social situation to understand what causes people to behave as they do. Social psychologists are interested in studying how a person's thoughts, feelings, and behaviors are influenced by the actual (or imagined) presence of others.

Within psychology, social psychology is most closely aligned with personality psychology. Social psychologists and personality psychologists are both interested in understanding and predicting behavior. What distinguishes them from each other is where they look for the causes of behavior. Typically, personality psychologists look within the person and his or her traits, motives, and so forth. Social psychologists typically focus on the situational factors that lead to behavior (Pettigrew, 2019).

### Features of Social Psychology

Social psychology shares many characteristics with other areas of psychology, but it is distinctive in at least two ways. These include its connection to real-life events and its reliance on experimental methods. Let's review each of these features.

#### SOCIAL PSYCHOLOGY IS CONNECTED TO REAL LIFE

There are few issues reported in the news today that social psychologists have not studied or will not study in the near future. Whether it is the latest political campaign or social media obsession, social psychologists have likely weighed in with scientific evidence. In fact, since its earliest days, social psychology has been inspired by real-life events.

The emergence of social psychology as a field can be traced back to the years after the U.S. Civil War in the late 1800s (Morawski & Bayer, 2013). Imagine what the country was like at that time. The nation was recovering from an incredibly bloody battle that almost ended the union. Former slaves and former slave owners had to find a way to live together in peace. There were many problems to be solved, to say the least. It was at this time that people began to consider whether the new science of psychology might be useful in solving these problems. To this day, racism, prejudice, and attitudes in general are central topics of inquiry in social psychology (Tropp & Molina, 2019).

Similarly, after World War II, social psychology saw enormous growth as scientists dedicated themselves to understanding the events that led to the war, the rise of the Nazis, and the Holocaust. Later, during the civil rights movement in the United States, social psychologists were interested in studying all of the ways that changing situational factors might change a person's life for the better.

Not only do social psychologists take inspiration from real-life events, but their research has important implications for many aspects of everyday life. Social psychological research includes topics like leadership, organizational behavior, marketing, and persuasion. Social psychology places many topics from other areas of psychology–including neuroscience, perception, cognition, learning, motivation, and emotion–into a social context. From a social psychological perspective, because human beings are innately social creatures, it makes sense to always consider the social context of any psychological process.

### SOCIAL PSYCHOLOGICAL RESEARCH IS (OFTEN) EXPERIMENTAL

Although some social psychological research is correlational in nature, more often than not social psychologists use experimental methods (Stroebe, 2018). That means that social psychologists are likely to manipulate an independent variable–for example, an aspect of the social context–to draw causal conclusions about its effects on some outcome (the dependent variable). These experiments are often inspired by observations of the phenomena in the social world.

## An Example: The Bystander Effect

To give you a sense of the flavor of social psychology, let's review a classic study, which is drawn from real life and which uses experimental methods–the two distinctive features of social psychology. In 1964, a young woman named Kitty Genovese was brutally murdered in New York City. She was attacked at about 3 A.M. in a courtyard surrounded by apartment buildings. It took the slayer approximately 30 minutes to kill Genovese. Thirty-eight neighbors watched the gory scene from their windows and heard Genovese's screams. Media reports declared that no one helped or called the police. Those reports turned out to be erroneous (Nadler, 2019). Nevertheless, inspired by this case, social psychologists John Darley and Bibb Latané (1968) devised a number of studies to examine when the presence of others would lead individuals to be less likely to help a person in distress.

©Chris Schmidt/E+/Getty Images

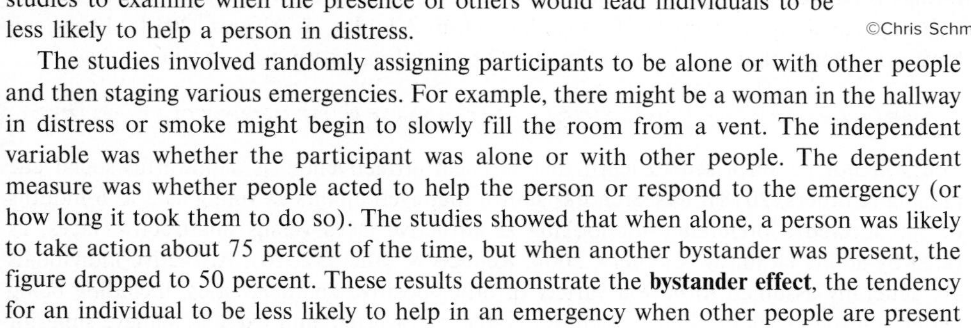

The studies involved randomly assigning participants to be alone or with other people and then staging various emergencies. For example, there might be a woman in the hallway in distress or smoke might begin to slowly fill the room from a vent. The independent variable was whether the participant was alone or with other people. The dependent measure was whether people acted to help the person or respond to the emergency (or how long it took them to do so). The studies showed that when alone, a person was likely to take action about 75 percent of the time, but when another bystander was present, the figure dropped to 50 percent. These results demonstrate the **bystander effect**, the tendency for an individual to be less likely to help in an emergency when other people are present (Hortensius & de Gelder, 2018).

- **bystander effect** The tendency of an individual who observes an emergency to help less when other people are present than when the observer is alone.

Why does the bystander effect occur? According to Darley and Latané (1970), there are five steps to helping in an emergency. The actor (that is, the person observing the event) must

- Notice the event
- Understand that it is an emergency
- Take responsibility for aiding the victim
- Know how to help
- Help

The presence of other people appears to short-circuit the process at some point, but where? Evidence suggests two factors may be at work. First, actors may use other people as a guide for behavior. If no one else is helping, maybe one ought not to help either. Perhaps, then, the presence of others who are not helping indicates that it is not an emergency or sends the message that people are not supposed to help. Second, diffusion of responsibility is a strong factor. The presence of others may have the effect of draining responsibility from each person present.

### test yourself

1. Give three examples of the strong tie between social psychology and historical events.
2. Identify the five steps of helping in an emergency.
3. What is the bystander effect?

# 2. SOCIAL COGNITION

● **social cognition** The area of social psychology that explores how people select, interpret, remember, and use social information.

● **social neuroscience** The study of social thoughts, feelings, and behavior that incorporates a range of measures of brain and body functioning

**Social cognition** is the area of social psychology that explores how people select, interpret, remember, and use social information. Essentially, it is the way in which individuals think in social situations. **Social neuroscience** refers to the study of social thoughts, feelings, and behavior that incorporates a range of measures of brain and body functioning. You can think of social neuroscience as uniting the fields of social psychology and neuroscience (Amodio, Harmon-Jones, & Berkman, 2019). Many aspects of social cognition have been studied in the context of social neuroscience, as we will review below.

## Person Perception

*Person perception* refers to the processes by which we use social stimuli to form impressions of others (Uleman & Sarribay, 2019). One important social cue is the face. Seeing only a face, we automatically process information about how trustworthy and dominant a person is likely to be (Feldman Hall & others, 2018; Verosky & others, 2018). As we have seen in the chapter "Biological Foundations of Behavior", the right hemisphere and occipital lobe of the human brain are especially wired to respond to this very important social cue (Kamps, Morris, & Dilks, 2019; Powell, Kosakowski, & Saxe, 2018).

Alexander Todorov and his colleagues (2005; Olivola, Tingley, & Todorov, 2018) have examined how perception of faces can influence political elections. They asked people to rate the competence of individuals from photographs of their faces. The faces were of candidates in the 2000, 2002, and 2004 U.S. House and Senate elections. Respondents' ratings accurately predicted the outcome for about *70 percent* of the elections. Faces reveal information about the candidates, particularly how competent and trustworthy the perceivers felt each office-seeker would be (Franklin & Zebrowitz, 2016).

The trustworthiness of a face can have profound implications (Zebrowitz, 2018). In a recent series of studies, participants were shown pictures of unfamiliar individuals who held political office and asked to rate how corruptible the person seemed to be. The ratings predicted whether the politicians actually had been convicted of political corruption and violation of campaign finance laws (Lin, Adolphs, & Alvarez, 2018). Faces can have other important implications for social perception, as we now consider.

● **stereotype** A generalization about a group's characteristics that does not consider any variations from one individual to another.

### PHYSICAL ATTRACTIVENESS AND OTHER PERCEPTUAL CUES

You will not be surprised to learn that physical attractiveness is a powerful social cue (Zhang & others, 2018). Research has shown that even infants as young as 3 to 6 months of age showed a preference for looking at attractive faces versus unattractive faces, as rated by adults (Ramsey & others, 2004; Rennels & others, 2016). Attractive individuals are generally assumed to have a variety of other positive characteristics, including being better adjusted, socially skilled, friendly, likable, extraverted, and likely to achieve superior job performance (Mello & Garcia-Marques, 2018; Putz, Kocsor, & Bereczkei, 2018). These positive expectations for physically attractive individuals have been referred to as the "beautiful is good" stereotype.

A **stereotype** is a generalization about a group's characteristics that does not consider any variations from one individual to another. Stereotypes are a natural extension of the limits on human cognitive processing and our reliance on concepts in cognitive processing (Fiske & Tablante, 2015). We simplify the task of understanding people by classifying them as members of groups or categories with which we are familiar. It takes more mental effort to consider a person's individual characteristics than it does to label him or her as a member of a particular group or category. In this sense, stereotypes are *heuristics*, the mental shortcuts we reviewed in the chapter "Thinking, Intelligence, and Language". Recall that heuristics serve as quick rules of thumb for judgments. Stereotypes often influence the way we think about other people (Johnson, Kopp, & Petty, 2018).

Is there any truth to the "beautiful is good" stereotype? Attractive people may indeed possess a number of positive characteristics (O'Connor & Gladstone, 2018; Wolbring & Riordan, 2016). Does that mean that attractiveness is naturally related to, for example, better social skills? Not necessarily.

*What makes a face attractive? Research has found that "averageness" is an essential component.*

One way that stereotypes can influence individuals is through **self-fulfilling prophecy**. In a self-fulfilling prophecy, expectations cause individuals to act in ways that serve to make the expectations come true. Robert Rosenthal and Lenore Jacobson conducted a classic self-fulfilling prophecy study (1968). The researchers told grade-school teachers that five students were likely to be "late bloomers"–that these students had high levels of ability that would likely shine forth over time. In reality, however, the researchers had randomly selected the students. Nonetheless, a year later, the researchers found that teachers' expectations for the "late bloomers" were reflected in student performance: The academic performance of these five was beyond that of other students. Self-fulfilling prophecy shows the potential power of stereotypes and other sources of expectations on human behavior.

● **self-fulfilling prophecy** Social expectations that cause an individual to act in such a way that expectations are realized.

Let's apply self-fulfilling prophecy to physically attractive individuals. Attractive people may receive differential treatment from others throughout their lives. This special treatment increases the likelihood that the attractive individuals might well develop enhanced social skills and be more self-confident than others.

Another relevant question is "What makes a face attractive?" *People* magazine's "50 Most Beautiful People" issue might lead you to conclude that attractiveness is about being exceptional in some physical way. Consider Beyoncé's radiant smile or Ryan Gosling's icy blue eyes. It turns out, though, that very attractive faces are actually *average*.

Using computer technology that allowed them to digitally "average" the faces of a large group of individuals of varying attractiveness, Langlois and her colleagues (1994) created composite faces. A large sample of college students then rated the individual faces and the composites. The results showed that individual faces were less attractive than faces that were created by averaging 8, 16, or 32 other faces. These researchers concluded that attractive faces are "just average." Although "averageness" is not the only predictor of attractiveness, Langlois and her colleagues suggest that being average is an essential component (along with variables such as symmetry and youthfulness) of facial attractiveness.

Recent research has added another fascinating contributor to what makes a face attractive: attention. The more we attend to a face, the more attractive it becomes, as compared to faces that have not captured our attention (Störmer & Alvarez, 2016).

### FIRST IMPRESSIONS

When we first meet someone, typically the new acquaintance quickly makes an impression. That first impression can have lasting effects (Hall, Horgan, & Murphy, 2019; Uleman & Sarribay, 2019). Why are first impressions so powerful? One possibility is the primacy effect (see the chapter "Memory"): the tendency to attend to and remember what they learned first (N. H. Anderson, 1965). How quickly do we make these initial impressions of others? In one study, individuals needed just a 100-millisecond exposure time to unfamiliar faces to form an impression (Willis & Todorov, 2006).

Are first impressions correct? A number of studies have shown that they can be. Based on photographs or very brief interactions or videos, people are able to accurately discern a person's self-esteem (Hirschmüller & others, 2018), romantic interest in them (Campbell & others, 2018), propensity for violence (Fowler, Lilienfeld, & Patrick, 2009; Rogers & others, 2018), and personality (Hall, Horgan, & Murphy, 2019; Murphy & others, 2018). Indeed, after watching a video for just *5 seconds*, judgments of extraversion, conscientiousness, and intelligence match very well with targets' self-reports of those traits, and after 1 minute, a reasonably accurate impression across traits was formed (Hall, Horgan, & Murphy, 2019).

Of course, once you become acquainted with someone, you have a lot more information to use to form an opinion of the person. The process by which we come to understand the causes of others' behavior and form an impression of them as individuals is called *attribution.*

## Attribution

Attributions are explanations of the causes of behavior (Scherer, 2018; Weiner, 2018). We can observe someone's actions, such as a friend giving money to a homeless person. To determine the underlying cause of that behavior, what it means about that friend, we often have to make inferences. Making inferences means taking the information we have and coming up with a good guess about who someone is and what the person is likely to do in the future. The results of those inferences are our attributions. What factors play a role in the attributions we make about behaviors? This question is addressed by attribution theory.

**Attribution theory** views people as motivated to discover the underlying causes of behavior as part of their effort to make sense of the behavior (Heider, 1958; Kelley, 1973; Weiner, 2018). Attributions vary along three dimensions:

- *Internal/external causes:* Internal attributions are causes inside and specific to the person, such as his or her traits and abilities. External attributions are causes outside the person, such as social pressure, aspects of the social situation, the weather, and luck. Did Beth get a *D* on the test because she didn't study or because the test was too hard?
- *Stable/unstable causes:* Whether the cause of behavior is relatively enduring and permanent or temporary influences attributions. Did Taylor honk her car horn because she is a hostile person or because she happened to be in a big hurry that day?
- *Controllable/uncontrollable causes:* We perceive that people have power over some causes (for instance, by preparing delicious food for a picnic) but not others (rain on picnic day). So, if a rainstorm spoils Henry's picnic, we would not hold that against him.

- **attribution theory** The view that people are motivated to discover the underlying causes of behavior as part of their effort to make sense of the behavior.
- **fundamental attribution error** Observers' overestimation of the importance of internal traits and underestimation of the importance of external situations when they seek explanations of an actor's behavior.
- **representativeness heuristic** The tendency to make judgments about group membership based on physical appearance or the match between a person and one's stereotype of a group rather than on available base rate information.
- **false consensus effect** A person's overestimation of the degree to which everybody else thinks or acts the way he or she does.

## ATTRIBUTIONAL ERRORS

In attribution theory, the person who produces the behavior to be explained is called the *actor.* The person who offers a causal explanation of the actor's behavior is called the *observer.* Actors often explain their own behavior in terms of external causes. That means that Beth might say she did poorly on the test because it was, in fact, too hard. In contrast, observers frequently explain the actor's behavior in terms of internal causes. Taylor might explain that she honked at a car that was slow to move when the light turned green because she was in a hurry to get to the hospital to see her ill father, but the other driver might think she was rude.

The **fundamental attribution error** refers to the tendency of observers to overestimate the importance of internal traits and underestimate the importance of external factors when they explain an actor's behavior (Gollwitzer & Bargh, 2018; Jones & Harris, 1967; Repacholi & others, 2016) (Figure 1). To consider how important this error might be, think of it in the context of coerced criminal confessions (Kassin & others, 2018). Jurors are likely to miss the role of situational factors when they learn an accused person has confessed. When we make the fundamental attribution error, we explain a person's behavior using their traits or character, neglecting situational factors.

Although it is called the *fundamental* attribution error, this error is not universal. Cross-cultural studies show that Westerners tend to attribute causes of behavior to the person. In contrast, those from collectivistic cultures are more likely to look to the situation to explain the behavior of others (Triandis, 2018).

**Observer** Tends to give internal, trait explanations of actor's behavior

"She's late with her report because she can't concentrate on her own responsibilities."


**Actor** Tends to give external, situational explanations of own behavior

"I'm late with my report because other people keep asking me to help them with their projects."


**FIGURE 1 The Fundamental Attribution Error** In this situation, the supervisor is the observer, and the employee is the actor. Source: Gollwitzer & Bargh, (2018); Jones & Harris (1967); Repacholi, Meltzoff, Toub, & Ruba, (2016); (top photo) ©Kris Timken/Blend Images; (bottom photo) ©langstrup/123RF

## HEURISTICS IN SOCIAL INFORMATION PROCESSING

When we make attributions, we are engaging in social information processing. Just as heuristics are useful in general information processing, they can play a role in *social* information processing. Heuristics can be helpful tools for navigating the complex social landscape, but they can lead to mistakes. Because these mistakes occur in the social context, their consequences can be serious. As an example, recall the **representativeness heuristic.** When we use this heuristic, we ignore unbiased information in favor of the resemblance between a person and our image of a typical member of a group. If a woman does not look like any of the other engineers we know, we may not view her as capable of the job.

One common heuristic is the false consensus effect. The **false consensus effect** means overestimating the degree to which everybody else thinks or acts the way we do.

Ask yourself: "How many students at my school support the death penalty?" The false consensus effect tells us that your answer is likely to depend on whether *you* support the death penalty.

The fundamental attribution error and the false consensus effect are both related to the special significance of our own thoughts and circumstances. Both of these effects reflect the vast amount of information we have about ourselves relative to the more limited information we have about other people, and they suggest the special place of the self in social information processing.

## The Self as a Social Object

Each of us carries around mental representations of ourselves. We can think of the self as our schema, as described in the chapter "Memory", for who we are, what we are like (and not like), and how we feel about these perceptions. The self is different from other social objects because we know so much more about ourselves than we do about others (Crocker & Brummelman, 2019).

The self is special as well because we value ourselves. One of the most important self-related variables is *self-esteem,* the degree to which we have positive or negative feelings about ourselves (Orth, Erol, & Luciano, 2018). In general, research has shown that it is good to feel good about oneself, especially if those feelings are stable and not overly inflated (Crocker & Brummelman, 2019; Harris & others, 2018).

Individuals with high self-esteem often possess a variety of **positive illusions**–rosy views of themselves that are not necessarily rooted in reality. Indeed, research shows that many of us think of ourselves as "above average" on valued characteristics, including how trustworthy, objective, and capable we are. A recent meta-analysis showed that these overly positive views of the self are generally associated with better adjustment (Dufner & others, 2018).

● **positive illusions** Favorable views of the self that are not necessarily rooted in reality.

**Self-serving bias** refers to the tendency to take credit for our successes and to deny responsibility for our failures when we make attributions about our own behavior. Think about taking an exam. If you do well, you are likely to take credit for that success ("I'm smart"); you tend to make internal attributions. If you do poorly, however, you are more likely to blame situational factors ("The test was too hard"); you tend to make external attributions. You might note that self-serving bias suggests a twist on the fundamental attribution error. We look to situational factors to explain our failures (as in the fundamental attribution error). However, we are happy to take credit for our successes, making personal attributions for these.

● **self-serving bias** The tendency to take credit for one's successes and to deny responsibility for one's failures.

### SELF-OBJECTIFICATION

**Self-objectification** refers to the tendency to see oneself as an object in others' eyes. Researchers have focused on how women have been socialized to think of themselves and their bodies as objects in the social world (Roberts, Calogero, & Gervais, 2018). Making women aware of their status as sexual objects can induce body image concerns, shame, and restricted eating (Moradi & Huang, 2008). Chronic feelings of objectification are associated with lower self-esteem and higher levels of depression (Carrotte & Anderson, 2018; Miner-Rubino, Twenge, & Fredrickson, 2002). Women who feel objectified are less likely to reject sexism and less likely to engage in social activism (Calogero, 2013). Self-objectification can interfere with task performance. For example, a recent study showed that getting a compliment on one's appearance (although it lifted mood) was negatively related to math performance, not only for women but for men as well (Kahalon, Shnabel, & Becker, 2018).

● **self-objectification** The tendency to see oneself primarily as an object in the eyes of others.

Self-objectification research suggests that reminding women of the fact that they are often judged based on their appearance has important implications for their feelings and behavior. A similar process has been found for members of stereotyped groups.

### STEREOTYPE THREAT

● **stereotype threat** An individual's fast-acting, self-fulfilling fear of being judged based on a negative stereotype about his or her group.

**Stereotype threat** is an individual's fast-acting, self-fulfilling fear of being judged based on a negative stereotype about his or her group. A person who experiences stereotype threat is well aware of stereotypical expectations for him or her as a member of a group. In stereotype-relevant situations, the individual experiences anxiety about living "down" to expectations and consequently underperforms. Research has shown that when a test is presented to African American and European American students who have first simply checked a box indicating their ethnicity, the African Americans perform more poorly (Steele & Aronson, 1995, 2004). When attention is not drawn to ethnicity, no differences in performance emerged.

Stereotype threat undermines performance on math tests by women compared with that of men, even when both groups have equally strong math training (Spencer, Steele, & Quinn, 1999). Women can experience stereotype in leadership positions as well (Hoyt & Murphy, 2016). European American men, too, can fall prey to stereotype threat; in a study of golf ability, European American men performed more poorly than African American men when they were told the test measured "natural athletic ability" (Stone, 2002). Studies have also shown that boys are more likely than girls to be affected by stereotype threat in academic endeavors, especially reading, that are more stereotypically associated with girls (Pansu & others, 2016).

How exactly does stereotype threat interfere with performance? There are likely many processes at work, including anxiety, distraction, loss of motivation and effort (Davies & others, 2016; Spencer, Logel, & Davies, 2016). What factors might help prevent the consequences of stereotype threat? In one study, African American schoolchildren who were asked their race prior to a math test did not perform as well unless the test was presented to them as a challenge, not as a threat (Alter & others, 2010).

### SOCIAL COMPARISON

● **social comparison** The process by which individuals evaluate their thoughts, feelings, behaviors, and abilities in relation to those of others.

Have you ever felt great about getting a *B* on a test, only to feel deflated after finding out a friend got an *A*? Comparing ourselves to other people is one way we come to understand our own behavior. **Social comparison** is the process by which we evaluate our thoughts, feelings, behaviors, and abilities in relation to those of others. Social comparison tells us what our distinctive characteristics are and aids us in building an identity.

Over 60 years ago, Leon Festinger (1954) proposed a theory of social comparison. The theory states that when no objective means are available to evaluate our opinions and abilities, we compare ourselves with others. Extended and modified over the years, Festinger's theory continues to provide an important rationale for how individuals come to know themselves. *Upward* social comparisons—comparing ourselves to those who are better off than we are—can foster feelings of envy and inadequacy. Social media can lead to these feelings, as most people post only very positive portrayals of their lives on Instagram or Facebook (Appel, Gerlach, & Crusius, 2016). *Downward* social comparisons—that is, comparing ourselves with others who are less fortunate—can make us feel better about our own lives (Huang, 2016).

## Attitudes

● **attitudes** An individual's opinions and beliefs about people, objects, and ideas—how the person feels about the world.

**Attitudes** are our opinions and beliefs about people, objects, and ideas—how we feel about the world. Social psychologists are interested in how attitudes affect behavior (and vice versa) and in whether and how attitudes can change (Albarracín, Chan, & Jang, 2019).

### CAN ATTITUDES PREDICT BEHAVIOR?

People sometimes say one thing but do another. On a survey, you might report positive attitudes about recycling but still pitch an aluminum soda can in the trash. Studies over the past half-century indicate some of the conditions under which attitudes guide actions (Briñol & Petty, 2012):

- *When the person's attitudes are strong:* If you are very passionate about recycling, you are less likely to pitch that soda can in the trash than someone who has only a weak attitude (Ajzen, 2001).
- *When the person shows a strong awareness of an attitude and rehearses and practices it:* For example, a person who has been asked to give a speech about the benefits of recycling is more likely to recycle than is an individual with the same attitude about recycling who has not done so (Fazio & Olsen, 2007; Fazio & others, 1982).
- *When the person has a vested interest:* People are more likely to act on attitudes when the issue at stake is something that will affect them personally. A classic study examined whether students would show up for a rally protesting a change that would raise the legal drinking age from 18 to 21 (Sivacek & Crano, 1982). Although generally students were against the change, only those in the critical age group (from 18 to 20) were likely to show up to protest.

In sum, if an attitude is strong, if it is one a person has thought about and rehearsed a great deal, and if it is about an issue that has direct implications for a person's life, that attitude is likely to predict behavior.

Attitudes are an important topic for the field of social psychology. Social psychologists are interested in just about every question you can imagine asking about attitudes, including where they come from, what they predict, and whether they can be changed.

## CAN BEHAVIOR PREDICT ATTITUDES?

Does the link between attitudes and behaviors run in both directions? Social psychologists offer two main explanations for how behavior influences attitudes: cognitive dissonance theory and self-perception theory.

**Cognitive Dissonance Theory** **Cognitive dissonance**, another concept introduced by Festinger (1957), is the psychological discomfort (*dissonance*) caused by having two inconsistent thoughts. According to the theory, we feel uneasy when we notice an inconsistency between what we believe and what we do.

● **cognitive dissonance** An individual's psychological discomfort (dissonance) caused by having two inconsistent thoughts.

In a classic study, Festinger and J. Merrill Carlsmith (1959) asked college students to engage in a series of very boring tasks, such as sorting spools into trays and turning wooden pegs. These participants were later asked to persuade another student (who was in fact a confederate) to participate in the study by telling him that the task was actually interesting and enjoyable. Half of the participants were randomly assigned to be paid $1 for telling this white lie, and the other half received $20. Afterward, all of the participants rated how interesting and enjoyable the task really was.

Those who were paid only $1 to tell the lie rated the task as significantly more enjoyable than those who were paid $20. Festinger and Carlsmith reasoned that those paid $20 to tell the lie could attribute their behavior to the high value of the money they received ($20 in 1959 had the buying power of $170 today). On the other hand, those who were paid $1 experienced cognitive dissonance: "How could I *lie* for just $1? If I said I liked the task, I must have really liked it." The inconsistency between what they *did* (tell a lie) and what they *were paid for doing it* (just $1) moved these individuals to change their attitudes about the task.

When attitudes and behavior conflict, we can reduce cognitive dissonance in one of two ways: change our behavior to fit our attitudes or change our attitudes to fit our behavior. In the classic study above, participants changed their attitudes about the task to match their behavior. If you pitched that soda can in the trash, for example, you might feel dissonance ("Wait, I believe in recycling, yet I just pitched that can") and relieve that dissonance by telling yourself, "Recycling is not really *that* important." Through cognitive dissonance, your behavior changed your attitude.

*Working hard to get into a group inspires loyalty through cognitive dissonance.*

©Lorado/E+/Getty Images

One type of dissonance reduction is called effort justification. *Effort justification* means coming up with a rationale for the amount of work we put into getting something, typically by increasing the value associated with things that are difficult to attain.

Effort justification explains the strong group loyalty that emerges after enduring difficult experiences to get into groups, such as initiation rites for sororities or fraternities, boot camp in the Marines, and the rigors of medical school en route to becoming a physician. From a cognitive dissonance perspective, individuals in these situations are likely to think, "If it's this tough to get into, it must be worth it." Working hard to get into a group can change our attitudes about that group. In some U.S. presidential elections, many voters have to wait in line for hours to cast their votes. You can imagine that many of them feel that the right to vote is extraordinarily important to them, after the long wait. Working hard for something increases its value to us.

**Self-Perception Theory** **Self-perception theory** is Daryl Bem's (1967) take on how behavior influences attitudes. According to self-perception theory, individuals make inferences about their attitudes by observing their behavior. That is, behaviors can cause attitudes, because when we are questioned about our attitudes, we think back on our behaviors for information. If you stood in line for five hours to vote and someone asked about your attitude toward voting, for example, you might think, "Well, I have waited all this time; it must be very important to me." Your behavior has led you to recognize something about yourself that you had not noticed before. According to Bem, we are especially likely to look to our behavior to determine our attitudes when those attitudes are unclear.

• **self-perception theory** Bem's theory on how behaviors influence attitudes, stating that individuals make inferences about their attitudes by perceiving their behavior.

Figure 2 compares cognitive dissonance theory and self-perception theory. Both theories have merit in explaining the connection between attitudes and behavior, and these opposing views bring to light the complexity that may exist in this connection. Both theories suggest that behavior can change attitudes. Another route to attitude change is persuasion.

Festinger's Cognitive Dissonance Theory
We are motivated toward consistency between attitudes and behavior and away from inconsistency.
Example: "I hate my job. I need to develop a better attitude toward it or else quit."
Bem's Self-Perception Theory
We make inferences about our attitudes by perceiving and examining our behavior and the context in which it occurs, which might involve inducements to behave in certain ways.
Example: "I am spending all of my time thinking about how much I hate my job. I really must not like it."


**FIGURE 2** **Two Theories of the Connections Between Attitudes and Behavior** Although we often think of attitudes as causing behavior, *behavior* can change *attitudes*, through either dissonance reduction or self-perception.
(photo) ©Photodisc/Getty Images

## PERSUASION

Persuasion involves trying to change someone's attitude–and often his or her behavior as well (Petty, 2018). Teachers, lawyers, and sales representatives study techniques that will help them sway their audiences (children, juries, and buyers). Presidential candidates have arsenals of speechwriters and image consultants to help ensure that their words are persuasive. Advertisers are skilled persuaders who draw upon a full array of techniques to sell everything from cornflakes to carpets to cars.

Carl Hovland and his colleagues originally identified the various elements of persuasion (Hovland, Janis, & Kelley, 1953; Janis & Hovland, 1959):

*Apple CEO Tim Cook calls on his powers of persuasion whenever Apple introduces a new product.*

©Monica Davey/Epa/REX/Shutterstock

- *The communicator (source):* A key factor in persuasion is the person doing the persuading. Is the person delivering the message (or the source of the message) viewed as credible (or believable)? Trustworthiness, expertise, power, attractiveness, likability, and similarity are all credibility characteristics that help a communicator change people's attitudes or convince them to act.
- *The medium:* Another persuasion factor is the medium or technology used to get the message across. Is the message presented in print, on TV, on Twitter, or on YouTube? Because it presents live images, video is generally a more powerful medium than print sources for changing attitudes. Social media have become a key way that persuaders get their message out (Ordenes & others, 2018). Of course, the effects of the medium of a message may depend on who is receiving it.
- *The target (audience):* The audience or target of a message can play a role in message persuasiveness. Younger people are more likely to change their attitudes than older ones. And individuals with weak attitudes are more easily persuaded than those with strong ones.
- *The message:* The final aspect of persuasion is the message itself. What kind of message is persuasive? Some messages involve strong logical arguments, and others focus on inducing emotions such as fear and anger in the audience. Which is more likely to work and when? The elaboration likelihood model addresses this question.

The **elaboration likelihood model** identifies two pathways of persuasion: a central route and a peripheral route (Petty, 2018; Petty & Cacioppo, 1986). The *central route* works by engaging the audience thoughtfully with a sound, logical argument. The *peripheral route* involves factors that are not relevant to the logic or quality of the argument. Peripheral factors include things like the source's attractiveness (rather than credibility) and the emotional power of an appeal. The peripheral route is most effective when people are not paying close attention or lack the time or energy to think about the message. As you might guess, television advertisers often use the peripheral route to persuasion on the assumption that during the commercials you are probably not paying full attention to the screen. The central route is more persuasive when people have the ability and the motivation to pay attention.

● **elaboration likelihood model** Theory identifying two ways to persuade: a central route and a peripheral route.

### Successful Persuasion

Sooner or later, nearly everyone will be in a position of selling something to someone. Social psychologists have studied ways in which social psychological principles influence whether a salesperson makes that sale (Cialdini, 1993; Falk & Scholz, 2018).

One strategy is called the *foot-in-the-door* technique (Freedman & Fraser, 1966). The foot-in-the-door strategy involves making a smaller request ("Would you be interested in a three-month trial subscription to a magazine?") at the beginning, saving the biggest demand ("How about a full year?") for last. The foot-in-the-door strategy relies on the notion that in agreeing to the smaller offer, the customer has created a relationship with the seller, expressing a level of trust.

A different strategy is called the *door-in-the-face* technique (Cialdini & others, 1975). The door-in-the-face technique involves making the biggest pitch first ("Would you be interested in a full-year subscription?"), which the customer probably will reject, and then making a smaller, "concessionary" demand ("Okay, then, how about a three-month trial?").

This technique relies on the fact that the customer feels a sense of obligation: You let him off the hook with that big request; maybe he should be nice and take the smaller offer.

**Resisting Persuasion** Advertisers and salespeople work their hardest to persuade us to buy their products. How do we resist their appeals? One way to resist persuasion is through *inoculation* (McGuire, 2003; McGuire & Papageorgis, 1961). This means that just as administering a vaccine inoculates individuals from a virus by introducing a weakened or dead version of that virus to the immune system, giving people a weak version of a persuasive message and allowing them time to argue against it can help individuals avoid persuasion.

Such "inoculation" helps college students resist plagiarism (Compton & Pfau, 2008) as well as credit card marketing appeals (Compton & Pfau, 2004). When individuals are warned that they are going to be hit with persuasive appeals and are given arguments to help them resist these pitches, they are better able to do so (Petty, 2018).

### test yourself

1. What do psychologists mean by a stereotype, and how do they define a stereotype threat?
2. What is involved in making a fundamental attribution error? Give an example of such an error.
3. Identify and briefly explain the four elements of persuasion.

# 3. SOCIAL BEHAVIOR

We do not just think socially; we also behave in social ways. Two particular types of behavior that have interested psychologists represent the extremes of human social activity: altruism and aggression.

## Altruism

Jake Tobin had less than 300 meters left to finish a boys' junior varsity cross country race when he was passed by Luke Fortner, a senior from another school. Luke is legally blind and was running with an aide. Jake saw Luke fall on a particularly precarious stretch of the race. At that moment, Jake, a sophomore at Cazenovia High School in Auburn, New York, forgot all about competing. He put his arms around his competitor and helped him up (Associated Press, 2018). Jake's display of sportsmanship and kindness was rightly praised. Sometimes human beings are capable of unexpected kindness even in the midst of fierce competition.

Indeed, people engage in a surprising range of extreme acts of kindness. Some give away nearly every cent they own to charities. In everyday life, we witness and perform "random acts of kindness"—maybe adding a quarter to someone's expired parking meter or giving up our seat on a bus to someone in need. All of these acts are *prosocial behaviors*—they all involve helping another person (Marsh, 2019). Such acts of kindness bear the markings of altruism. **Altruism** means giving to another person with the ultimate goal of benefiting that person, even if it incurs a cost to oneself. Are acts of kindness truly altruistic?

● **altruism** Unselfish interest in helping another person.

● **egoism** Giving to another person to ensure reciprocity; to gain self-esteem; to present oneself as powerful, competent, or caring; or to avoid censure from oneself and others for failing to live up to society's expectations.

Psychologists debate whether human behavior is ever truly altruistic. Altruistic motives contrast with selfish or egoistic motives (Cialdini, 1991). **Egoism** means helping another person for personal gain, such as to feel good or avoid guilt. Kindness might also serve selfish purposes by ensuring *reciprocity*, meaning that we help another person to increase the chances that the person will return the favor. When a person behaves kindly toward another and expects something in return (reciprocity), that is not altruism. Rather, altruism means doing something good for another even if it poses a cost to oneself and even if the act can never be repaid (Ferguson & others, 2018).

Altruism has presented a puzzle for evolutionary psychologists (Cornwallis, 2018). How can behavior that rewards others, and not oneself, be adaptive? One way to explain this puzzle is to note that prosocial behavior is often extended among family members, because helping a relative also means promoting the survival of the family's genes. Evolutionary theorists believe that reciprocity in relationships with nonfamily members is essentially the mistaken application of a heuristic that made sense in human evolutionary history—to engage in selfless acts of kindness to one's own family (Piccinini & Schulz, 2018).

Acts of kindness seem to have one powerful payoff for those who do them: Helping others strongly and consistently leads to increased positive mood (Aknin & others, 2015;

Snippe & others, 2018). Prosocial spending, or spending money on others rather than oneself, is linked to greater well-being, potentially universally (Aknin & others, 2013). Does the fact that prosocial behavior leads to feelings of pleasure mean that such behavior is always selfish?

Feelings of pleasure are linked with adaptive behaviors, those things we need to do to survive and reproduce. We enjoy eating. We enjoy sex. Is it possible that the strong link between pleasure and kindness demonstrates that prosocial behavior is an important adaptation for humans who depend on one another for survival? Interestingly, kindness is not exclusive to humans. Ethology—the study of animal behavior—has examined whether acts of kindness occur in nonhuman animals. Ethologists have found that nonhuman primates demonstrate altruistic acts of kindness (Burkart, Bruegger, & van Schaik, 2018; Engelmann & Hermann, 2016).

Setting aside the question of whether such acts are altruistic, in this section we review biological, psychological, and sociocultural factors that predict prosocial behavior. As you read, consider whether you think altruism is a problem to be solved or a natural aspect of human life.

©Mel Curtis/Getty Images

## BIOLOGICAL FACTORS IN PROSOCIAL BEHAVIOR

Research has shown that genetics play a role in prosocial behavior. Genetic factors explain between 30 and 69 percent of the differences we see in the tendency to engage in kind acts (Knafo-Noam, Vertsberger, & Israel, 2018). Prosociality is linked as well to the oxytocin receptor gene (Marsh, 2019). Such a link makes sense as oxytocin is associated with social bonding. High levels of serotonin are associated with prosocial behavior (Gärtner & others, 2018). In addition, dopamine receptors in the brain are associated with prosocial behavior (Knafo-Noam,Vertsberger, & Israel, 2018).

In terms of brain structures, research suggests that when we feel compassion for another person, areas of the midbrain associated with the perception of pain and self-awareness are likely to be active (Becker & others, 2018; Shamay-Tsoory & Lamm, 2018). These same areas are associated with nurturing parental behaviors, suggesting that neural factors associated with the parent-child relationship are involved in kindness toward others.

## PSYCHOLOGICAL FACTORS IN PROSOCIAL BEHAVIOR

Among the psychological factors thought to play a role in prosocial behavior are empathy, personality, and mood.

**Empathy** As we discussed in the chapter "Gender, Sex, and Sexuality", *empathy* is a person's feeling of oneness with the emotional state of another. When we feel empathy for someone, we feel what that person is feeling. Empathy allows us to put ourselves in another person's shoes. We can feel empathy even for those we do not particularly like, as demonstrated by the playing of "Sweet Caroline" (a tradition of the Boston Red Sox) at Yankee Stadium during the game with their archrivals following the Boston Marathon bombing in 2013.

For many scientists, empathy is the foundation for prosocial behavior (Batson, 2002, 2006, 2012; Davis, 2018). When we are feeling empathy for someone else's plight, we are moved to action—not to make ourselves feel better but out of genuine concern for the other person. However, recently, the limits of empathy in prosocial behavior have been highlighted. Empathy may make us more likely to behave prosocially only to those with whom we feel similar, such members of our own groups, rather than deserving strangers (Bloom, 2017).

Understanding the relationship of empathy to prosocial behavior is complicated by the fact that empathy is a highly desirable characteristic and even those who are not especially altruistic are likely to rate themselves as high on this valued trait (Ward & King, 2018). Who would not want to be thought of as an empathetic person? A recent study sought to avoid this problem by using brain imaging to provide an objective measure of empathy and examine its relationship to extreme altruism (Brethel-Haurwitz & others, 2018). To read about the study, see the Intersection.

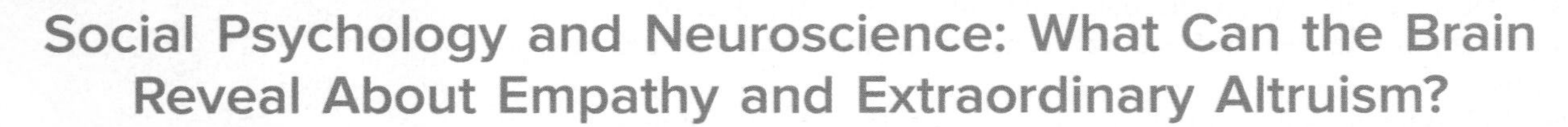

INTERSECTION

## Social Psychology and Neuroscience: What Can the Brain Reveal About Empathy and Extraordinary Altruism?

Many of us engage in small acts of kindness every day—putting money in an expired parking meter or paying for the order behind us in a drive-through. These prosocial behaviors pale in comparison with the actions taken by *extraordinary altruists*. Extraordinary altruists are those who have taken action that poses risk to themselves and that benefits a complete stranger. One act of extraordinary altruism involves donating a kidney to an unknown stranger. Of course, a person can live with only one kidney, but the donation procedures carry some risk and the donor's body is forever changed. Are extraordinary altruists especially high in empathy?

*Would you consider performing an extraordinary act of altruism?*

A recent study (Brethel-Haurwitz & others, 2018) focused on an area of the brain called the *anterior insula*. This area of the brain is activated by two experiences: feeling pain oneself and observing another person experiencing pain (Becker & others, 2018; Shamay-Tsoory & Lamm, 2018). Thus, the extent to which the anterior insula responds similarly to one's own and another's pain is neural indication of empathy.

The study involved two groups of participants: 25 altruistic kidney donors (people who had donated a kidney to an unknown stranger) and 27 others matched on various characteristics (age, gender, ethnicity, income, education and so forth). These individuals had also reported that they would *not* consider donating a kidney to a stranger (Brethel-Haurwitz & others, 2018). Both groups had two kinds of experiences while their brains were scanned. First, they watched a monitor that showed another person's hand experiencing painful pressure to the right thumbnail. Second, they watched as their own hand was subjected to the same experience.

Comparing brain activation across the groups showed that the anterior insula responded more similarly across the two experiences among the extraordinary altruists than among the control group. This means that compared with the control group, the extraordinary altruists processed another person's pain in the same way they processed their own. Interestingly, the two groups did not differ in their self-reports of empathy (Brethel-Haurwitz & others, 2018). These results highlight how brain imaging can provide an objective assessment of the important capacity for empathy.

©Hinterhaus Productions/DigitalVision/Getty Images

**Personality** Agreeableness (see the chapter "Personality") is the big five personality trait most strongly associated with prosocial behaviors (Graziano & Habashi, 2015). Similarly, the trait of honesty/humility in the HEXACO model predicts prosocial behavior (Thielmann & Hilbig, 2018). Interestingly, there are also strong *negative* relationships between prosocial behaviors and a set of "dark" traits (Wertag & Bratko, 2018). These traits include being narcissistic, manipulative, and callous and cold toward others. It may be that low levels of these traits are more closely tied to being kind than are high levels of niceness (Turner, Foster, & Webster, 2019). An interesting recent study showed that even among people who are low on agreeableness, engaging in kind acts lowered depression (Mongrain & others, 2018).

**Mood** Our mood can determine whether or not we engage in kind behaviors. The research literature strongly concludes that happy people are more likely than unhappy people to help others (Ferguson & others, 2018; Snyder & Lopez, 2007). Does it then follow that being in a bad mood makes people less helpful? Not necessarily, because adults (especially) generally understand that doing good for another person can be a mood booster. When people are in a bad mood, they might be likely to help if they think that doing so will improve their mood.

### SOCIOCULTURAL FACTORS IN PROSOCIAL BEHAVIOR

Two sociocultural factors that influence prosocial behavior are socioeconomic status and the media.

**Socioeconomic Status** Socioeconomic status is a sociocultural factor in prosocial behavior. Although they have less, those of lower socioeconomic status tend to be more likely to help others than those who have more (Piff, Kraus, & Keltner, 2018). Even children from lower socioeconomic backgrounds are more generous (Miller, Kahle, & Hastings, 2015). Compared with wealthier individuals, those from poorer backgrounds tend be more attuned to the suffering of others (Manstead, 2018). It may be that relative wealth promotes a focus on maintaining one's standing in the world, to the detriment of reaching out to help those in need (Piff, Kraus, & Keltner, 2018).

**Media Influences** Media—including music, TV, film, and video games—can influence prosocial behavior. Whether it is on YouTube or TV, seeing someone perform an act of kindness can move us to behave kindly as well (Ellithorpe, Ewoldsen, & Oliver, 2015). Listening to music with prosocial lyrics, watching television shows with positive content, and playing prosocial video games enhances prosocial thoughts, empathy, and acts of kindness and reduces aggressive behavior (Coyne & others, 2018). The effects of prosocial media are especially strong for acts of kindness toward strangers.

The human ability to engage in kindness sits alongside the capacity to cause others harm. Some evolutionary scientists have suggested that altruism, especially when it is directed at the members of one's own group, may coexist with hostile actions toward other groups (Arrow, 2007). A soldier may perform selfless acts of altruism for his or her country, but for a person on the other side of the combat, that behavior is harmful. Many scholars have begun to recognize that altruism or prosociality exists at one end of the spectrum of human behavior, with aggression on the other (Davis, 2018; Marsh, 2019; Sonne & Gash, 2018).

## Aggression

**Aggression** refers to social behavior with the objective of harming someone either physically or verbally. Ethologists note aggression in nonhuman animals (Lorenz, 1965; Tinbergen, 1969). However, in the animal kingdom, most hostile encounters do not escalate to killing or even severe harm. Much of the fighting is ritualistic and involves threat displays—for example, a bear's laid-back ears, lowered head, and bellowing.

● **aggression** Behavior that is intended to harm another person.

Evolutionary theorists believe that human beings are not much different from other animals. A basic theme of their theory is the survival of the fittest. Thus, they conclude that early in human evolution the survivors were probably aggressive individuals (Wrangham, 2018). In this section we will review biological, psychological, and sociocultural influences on aggression.

*In the animal world, aggression often is ritualistic and typically involves threat displays, such as a bear's laid-back ears, lowered head, and bellowing.*

©Don Hammond/Design Pics

### BIOLOGICAL INFLUENCES IN AGGRESSION

Researchers who approach aggression from a biological viewpoint examine the influence of genetics and neurobiological factors.

**Genes** The importance of genes to aggression is clear in selective breeding of animals. After a number of breedings among only aggressive animals and among only docile animals, vicious and timid strains of animals emerge. The vicious strains attack nearly anything in sight; the timid strains rarely fight, even when attacked.

The genetic basis for aggression is more difficult to demonstrate in humans than nonhuman animals and may depend on the type of aggression studied (Tremblay, Vitaro, & Côté, 2018; Wrangham, 2018; Zhang-James &

others, 2018). Specifically, twin studies have shown that physical aggression that is proactive in nature (that is, unprovoked aggression) may be more influenced by genes, but reactive aggression may be more susceptible to environmental effects (Wrangham, 2018).

**Neurobiological Factors** Although humans do not have a specific aggression center in the brain, aggressive behavior often results when areas such as the limbic system are stimulated by electric currents (Aaronson & Lloyd, 2015; Herbert, 1988; Wood & Liossi, 2006). Brain imaging research has compared the brains of individuals who have committed violent crimes to those of nonviolent criminals. This research shows that the brains of violent individuals (some of whom have committed murder) have deficits in areas that are associated with empathy and compassion (including the insula) as well as areas of the limbic system, including the amygdala (Bogerts, Schöne, & Breitschuh, 2018, Haller, 2018). In addition, violent individuals show dysfunction in areas of the brain associated with control of aggressive impulses, including the brain's frontal lobes (Bogerts, Schöne, & Breitschuh, 2018; Nordstrom & others, 2011).

Neurotransmitters–particularly, lower levels of serotonin–have been linked to aggressive behavior (Bedrosian & Nelson, 2018; da Cunha-Bang & others, 2018). However, the link between serotonin and aggression is small (Duke & others, 2013).

Hormones are another biological factor that may play a role in aggression, as noted in the chapter "Gender, Sex, and Sexuality". The hormone that is typically implicated in aggressive behavior is testosterone. Animal research has shown that testosterone is related to aggression (Cunningham & McGinnis, 2007), but the link between testosterone and aggression in humans is likely more complex. For instance, one study showed that high testosterone only predicted aggression in boys when those children had also experienced harsh discipline in the home (Chen, Raine, & Granger, 2018).

## PSYCHOLOGICAL INFLUENCES IN AGGRESSION

Psychological influences on aggression include personality characteristics, frustrating and aversive circumstances, cognitive determinants, and observational learning factors.

**Personality Characteristics** Some people are more likely to behave aggressively than others. Not surprisingly, low levels of agreeableness are associated with more aggressive behavior (Wang & others, 2017). In addition, a constellation of traits–including low levels of agreeableness, low levels of conscientiousness, and high levels of neuroticism–is associated with aggression (Settles & others, 2012). A meta-analysis showed that individuals who are high on hostility and irritability are more likely to behave aggressively, whether provoked or not (Bettencourt & others, 2006). Individuals high on traits of narcissism, manipulativeness, and callousness toward others are also more likely to behave aggressively (Paulhus, Curtis, & Jones, 2018; Tetreault, Bates, & Bolam, 2018).

**Frustrating and Aversive Circumstances** Many years ago, John Dollard and his colleagues (1939) proposed that *frustration,* the blocking of an individual's attempts to reach a goal, triggers aggression. The *frustration-aggression hypothesis* states that frustration always leads to aggression. When people are frustrated in their desires, they will lash out.

Psychologists later recognized that frustration is just one of many aversive experiences that can lead to aggression (Groves & Anderson, 2018). You might notice that you are more grumpy and short-tempered when you have a headache or a toothache, for example. Circumstances like physical pain, personal insults, crowding, and unpleasant events can all lead to aggression. Aversive circumstances also include factors in the physical environment, such as the weather. Murder, rape, and assault increase when temperatures are the highest, as well as in the hottest years and the hottest cities (Groves & Anderson, 2018). Long-term changes in temperatures are associated with increased aggression in adolescents (Younan & others, 2018). Other aversive circumstances, such as poverty or being treated unfairly, can also predict aggression. Even as research reviewed above showed that lower socioeconomic status was associated with greater kindness, it is also positive associated with aggression (Greitemeyer & Sagioglou, 2018).

*Aversive circumstances that might stimulate aggression include factors in the physical environment such as noise and crowding.*

©Sandy Huffaker/Getty Images

**Cognitive Determinants** Aggressive behavior often starts with aggressive thoughts. Aspects of the environment can put aggressive thoughts in our heads through priming. Recall from the chapter "Memory" that priming can involve making something salient to a person, even subliminally or without the person's awareness. Research by Leonard Berkowitz showed that the mere presence of a weapon (such as a gun) may prime hostile thoughts and produce aggression (Berkowitz, 1990; Berkowitz & LePage, 1996). The tendency for the presence of firearms to enhance aggression is known as the *weapons effect*. A recent meta-analysis suggested that the effect of the presence of a weapon on aggressive thoughts, feelings, and behavior is much weaker than Berkowitz thought (Benjamin, Kepes, & Bushman, 2018).

**Observational Learning Factors** Social cognitive theorists believe that individuals learn aggression through observation and reinforcement. Watching others engage in aggressive actions can evoke aggression, as you might recall from the classic Bobo doll study described in the chapter "Learning" (Bandura, Ross, & Ross, 1961). One of the strongest predictors of aggression is witnessing aggression in one's own family (Ferguson & others, 2008). Watching television provides a ready opportunity to observe aggression in our culture, which we consider further in the discussion below on media violence.

## SOCIOCULTURAL INFLUENCES IN AGGRESSION

Aggression and violence are more common in some cultures than others. In this section, we review sociocultural influences on aggression, including the culture of honor and media influences.

**The Culture of Honor** Dov Cohen has examined how cultural norms about masculine pride and family honor may foster aggressive behavior (Cohen, 2001; Nisbett & Cohen, 2018; Vandello & others, 2009). In *cultures of honor*, a man's reputation is thought to be an essential aspect of his economic survival. Such cultures see insults to a man's honor as diminishing his reputation and view violence as a way to compensate for that loss. In these cultures, family pride might lead to so-called honor killings in which, for example, a female rape victim is slain by her male family members so that they, in turn, are not "contaminated" by the rape.

Cohen has examined how, in the United States, southerners are more likely than northerners to be aggressive when honor is at stake. In one study, Cohen and his colleagues (1996) had men who were from either the North or the South take part in an experiment

*Social psychologists sometimes ask participants in a study to assign the amount of hot sauce a person must drink as a measure of aggression. Do you think that is a good operational definition of aggression?*

©flashgun/iStock/Getty Images

that required them to walk down a hallway. A member of the study passed all the men, bumping against them and quietly calling them a derogatory name. The southerners were more likely than the northerners to think their masculine reputation was threatened, to become physiologically aroused by the insult, and to engage in actual aggressive or dominant acts. In contrast, the northerners were less likely to perceive a random insult as "fightin' words."

**Media** Images of violence pervade U.S. popular media: newscasts, television shows, sports broadcasts, movies, video games, Internet videos, and song lyrics. Do portrayals of violence lead to aggression? This question sparks intense controversy among social psychologists.

Some critics reject the conclusion that TV violence causes aggression (Savage & Yancey, 2008). Other scholars insist that TV violence can prompt aggressive or antisocial behavior in children (Brown & Tierney, 2011; Bushman & Huesmann, 2012; Comstock, 2012). Of course, television violence is not the only cause of aggression in children or adults. Like all social behaviors, aggression has multiple determinants (Matos, Ferreira, & Haase, 2012). Certainly, the link between TV violence and aggression in children is influenced by children's personality traits and attitudes toward violence.

Another type of media that has interested psychologists is violent pornography. Violent pornography includes films, videos, websites, and magazines portraying the degradation of women in a sexual context. Do such media foster violence toward women? Based on several meta-analyses and on research of their own, Neil Malamuth and his colleagues concluded that pornography consumption does have a small effect on male sexual aggression and is related to increased tolerance of violence toward women (Hald, Malamuth, & Yuen, 2010; Malamuth, Addison, & Koss, 2000). Yet Malamuth and his colleagues caution that pornography is only one of a number of factors that may lead to sexual violence against women (Hald, Malamuth, & Yuen, 2010; Vega & Malamuth, 2007). The most problematic materials are those that depict women enjoying being the victims of male sexual violence (Hald, Malamuth, & Yuen, 2010). Such violent pornography reinforces the *rape myth*—the false belief that women desire coercive sex.

As we discussed earlier, research shows that prosocial video games foster prosocial behavior. Do violent video games foster aggression? Correlational studies have linked violent video game exposure to aggression and low levels of empathy in children and adolescents (Calvert & others, 2017). Some experimental evidence shows that playing a violent video game can lead to more aggressive thoughts and behaviors in children and adults (Anderson & Bushman, 2018).

However, it is important to recognize that psychological research on video gaming has often been flawed by not accounting for factors such as the difficulty of game play. In fact, studies have shown that the effects of video games on aggressive behavior may be more a function of how difficult and frustrating the games are than whether they have violent content (Engelhardt, Hilgard, & Bartholow, 2015). A recent meta-analysis suggested that the link between violent video game exposure and aggression is likely much weaker than previously estimated (Hilgard & others, 2017).

Conducting laboratory studies of aggression involves coming up with an operational definition of aggression. Often these behaviors are not very similar to real-world acts of aggression. Researchers might provide participants the opportunity to "aggress" against another, for instance, by subjecting the individual to a blast of loud noise, dispensing a mild electrical shock, or administering a large dose of Tabasco to swallow. Whether these operational definitions of aggression are applicable to real-life violence is a matter of much debate (Savage & Yancey, 2008).

Perhaps more importantly, critics of research on the link between violent video games and aggression argue that this research often employs small samples and does not equalize gaming experiences across both violent and nonviolent games (Hilgard & others, 2017; Markey, Markey, & French, 2015). In addition, many studies have not consistently assessed the influence of important third variables, such as family violence, in predicting both video-game use and aggression (Ferguson, 2015; Ferguson & Kilburn, 2010; Ferguson & others, 2008).

## test yourself

1. What is the difference between altruism and egoism?
2. What are the various psychological influences contributing to aggression?
3. What have researchers found about the influence of prosocially oriented video games? What have they learned about the effects of violent video games?

# 4. SOCIAL INFLUENCE

Another topic of interest to social psychologists is how our behavior is influenced by that of other individuals and groups. This section explores key aspects of social influence: conformity, obedience, and group influence.

## Conformity and Obedience

After World War II, psychologists sought answers to the disturbing question of how ordinary people could be influenced to commit the atrocities inflicted on Jews, Gypsies, and other minorities during the Holocaust. Many people engaged in terrible actions because everyone else was doing it or because they were told to do it by an authority figure. Researchers wanted to understand the processes by which people allowed themselves to be controlled by the social situation in this way. This interest gave rise to research on conformity and obedience as well as to three classic studies in social psychology that we will encounter along the way.

### CONFORMITY

**Conformity** is a change in a person's behavior to coincide more closely with a group standard. When we conform, we do something we might not have done otherwise because everyone else is doing it. Conformity takes many forms and affects many aspects of people's lives in positive and negative ways. Conformity is at work when we obey the rules and regulations that allow society to run smoothly. Consider how chaotic it would be if people did not conform to social norms such as stopping at a red light, driving on the correct side of the road, and not punching others in the face.

• **conformity** A change in a person's behavior to coincide more closely with a group standard.

Conformity can also be a powerful way to increase group cohesion. Even something as simple as marching in step together or singing a song along with a group can lead to enhanced cooperation among group members (Mogan, Fischer, & Bulbulia, 2017). Some of the most important rituals in which humans participate involve conforming to particular actions: We march, stand, kneel, dance–in unison. Such behaviors increase our sense of belonging (Jackson & others, 2018).

Conformity can also be destructive. Conformity is at work, for example, when a person comes to college and starts drinking heavily at parties, even though he or she might have never consumed alcohol before. Conformity is a powerful social force. You can feel the pressure of conformity for yourself if, the next time you get on an elevator with other people, you do not turn around to face the door. We begin our exploration of conformity by considering a classic study by Solomon Asch.

**Asch's Experiment** Put yourself in this situation: You are taken into a room where you see five other people seated at a table. A person in a white lab coat enters the room and announces that you are about to participate in an experiment on perceptual accuracy. The group is shown two cards–the first having only a single vertical line on it and the second having three vertical lines of varying length. You are told that the task is to determine which of the three lines on the second card is the same length as the line on the first card. You look at the cards and think, "What a snap. It's so obvious which is the same."

What you do not know is that the other people in the room are confederates who are working with the experimenter. On the first several trials, everyone agrees about which line matches the standard. Then on the fourth trial, each of the others picks the same *incorrect* line. As the last person to make a choice, you have the dilemma of responding as your eyes tell you or conforming to what the others before you said. How would you answer?

Solomon Asch conducted this classic experiment on conformity in 1951. Asch instructed the confederates to give incorrect responses on 12 of 18 trials. To his surprise, Asch (1951) found that participants conformed to the incorrect answers 35 percent of the time.

Why would people go along with a group even when they have clear-cut information disputing the others, such as the lines in the Asch experiment? We will review biological, psychological, cultural answers to this question.

**Biological Factors in Conformity** A number of biological factors are involved in conformity. First, there is evidence that genes play a role in a person's tendency to conform (Chen & others, 2018). In addition, brain imaging studies suggest the brain views not conforming as a mistake and conforming as a good thing. For example, finding out that one's views *do not* fit with those of a group is associated with activation of the brain area associated with monitoring for errors, suggesting that moments of not conforming are viewed as wrong (Klucharev & others, 2009; Wasylyshyn & others, 2018). In addition, conforming is associated with activation in the brain's reward centers (Izuma, 2017; Wu, Luo, & Feng, 2016). Conformity can be an important aspect of cooperation. Research shows that when people engage in a cooperative task (even if they are doing different aspects of the task), their brains conform with each other's, showing synchronous patterns of brain activity (Hu & others, 2018).

Another biological factor in conformity is oxytocin, the neurotransmitter and hormone associated with social bonding. A number of double-blind experiments have shown that participants randomly assigned to receive oxytocin (rather than a placebo) are more likely to show conformity (Hertz & others, 2016; Pfundmair & others, 2018; Stallen & others, 2012).

**Psychological Factors in Conformity** Imagine walking into the first meeting of a group you have just joined. You do not know the members very well and are unfamiliar with how they run things. You are very likely to use the behavior of others to direct your own: When in Rome, do as the Romans do. But why, precisely, would you do that? For one thing, you lack knowledge of the group's customs. For another, you are new and want them to like you. These two reasons are the main psychological factors identified as contributing to conformity: informational social influence and normative social influence.

● **informational social influence** The influence other people have on us because we want to be right.

**Informational social influence** refers to the influence other people have on us because we want to be right (Shi & others, 2018). The social group can provide us with information that we do not have or may help us see things in ways that had not occurred to us. As a result, we may conform because we have come to agree with the group. The tendency to conform based on informational social influence depends especially on two factors: how confident we are in our own judgment and how well informed we perceive the group to be. For example, if you know little about computers and three of your acquaintances who are IT geeks tell you not to buy a particular brand of computer, you are likely to conform to their recommendation. They have knowledge you lack, and you want to make the right choice. So, informational social influence is driven by the desire to be correct.

● **normative social influence** The influence others have on us because we want them to like us.

In contrast, **normative social influence** is the influence others have on us because we want them to like us (Schultz & others, 2018). Whether the group is an inner-city gang or members of a profession such as medicine or law, if a particular group is important to us, we might adopt the clothing style of the group, use the same slang words, and assume the attitudes that characterize the group's members (Barreto & Hogg, 2018). On your first day of work at a new job, you might think about what you saw others wearing at your interview and follow suit because you want to fit in. That's normative social influence. Normative social influence is driven by the desire to gain approval from others.

In sum, we have two reasons for conformity: Informational social influence means we conform to be right; normative social influence means we conform to be liked.

**Cultural Factors in Conformity** Individualistic cultures value independence and individual accomplishments and emphasize differences and uniqueness. Collectivistic cultures value the group, emphasize group harmony, and believe that accomplishments depend on individuals' carrying out their roles in the larger social network. It is not surprising, then, that collectivism has been associated with greater levels of conformity. One research review, summarizing 133 experiments following Asch's design, found that individualism within cultures was negatively correlated with conformity (Bond & Smith, 1996).

## OBEDIENCE

● **obedience** Behavior that complies with the explicit demands of the individual in authority.

**Obedience** is behavior that complies with the explicit demands of the individual in authority. We are obedient when an authority figure demands that we do something, and we do it. Note that in conformity, people change their thinking or behavior so that it will be more like that of others, while in obedience, there is an explicit demand made on the person.

Obedient behavior sometimes can be distressingly cruel. One of the most infamous examples of the destructive nature of obedience is the Nazi crimes against Jews and others during World War II. More recent examples include the obedience of radical Muslims instructed to participate in suicide attacks against Israelis and westerners and that of U.S. military personnel at Abu Ghraib prison in Iraq, who justified their horrendous abuse of detainees by asserting that they were "just following orders" (A. G. Miller, 2004). Millions of people throughout history have obeyed commands to commit terrible acts. A classic and controversial experiment in social psychology provides insight into obedience.

**Milgram's Experiment** Stanley Milgram (1965, 1974) was a social psychologist interested in how susceptible people can be to following orders. Initially, Milgram was interested in finding out if Americans would be as likely as Germans were to obey commands to harm another person. The studies he conducted demonstrated the profound effect of obedience.

To get a sense for his studies, imagine that, as part of a psychology experiment on the effects of punishment on memory, you are asked to deliver a series of electric shocks to another person. Your role is to be the "teacher" and to punish the mistakes made by the "learner." Each time the learner makes a mistake, you are to increase the intensity of the shock.

You are introduced to the learner, a nice 50-year-old man who mumbles something about having a heart condition. Strapped to a chair in the next room, he communicates with you through an intercom. The apparatus in front of you has 30 switches, ranging from 15 volts (slight) to 450 volts (marked as beyond dangerous: "XXX").

As the trials proceed, the learner quickly runs into trouble and is unable to give the correct answers. As you increase the intensity of the shock, the learner says that he is in pain. At 150 volts, he demands to have the experiment stopped. At 180 volts, he cries out that he cannot stand it anymore. At 300 volts, he yells about his heart condition and pleads to be released. If you hesitate in shocking the learner, however, the experimenter tells you, "You must go on. The experiment requires that you continue."

Eventually the learner stops responding altogether, and the experimenter tells you that not responding is the same as a wrong answer. The learner is unresponsive. He might be injured or even dead. Would you keep going? Do you think most people would? As shown in Figure 3, when Milgram conducted this study, the majority of the teachers obeyed the experimenter: Almost two-thirds delivered the full 450 volts. By the way, the 50-year-old man was a confederate and was not being shocked at all. Of course, the teachers were unaware that the learner was only pretending to be shocked.

"You must go on. The experiment requires that you continue." Imagine that with those simple statements the experimenter was able to calmly command people (as far as they knew) to shock a man to unconsciousness and possibly death. Such is the power of obedience to authority.

The ethics of Milgram's studies are controversial. Under today's ethical guidelines, it is unlikely that these experiments would have been approved. Milgram noted that participants were generally favorable about the importance of his work; however, the influence of cognitive dissonance in these responses

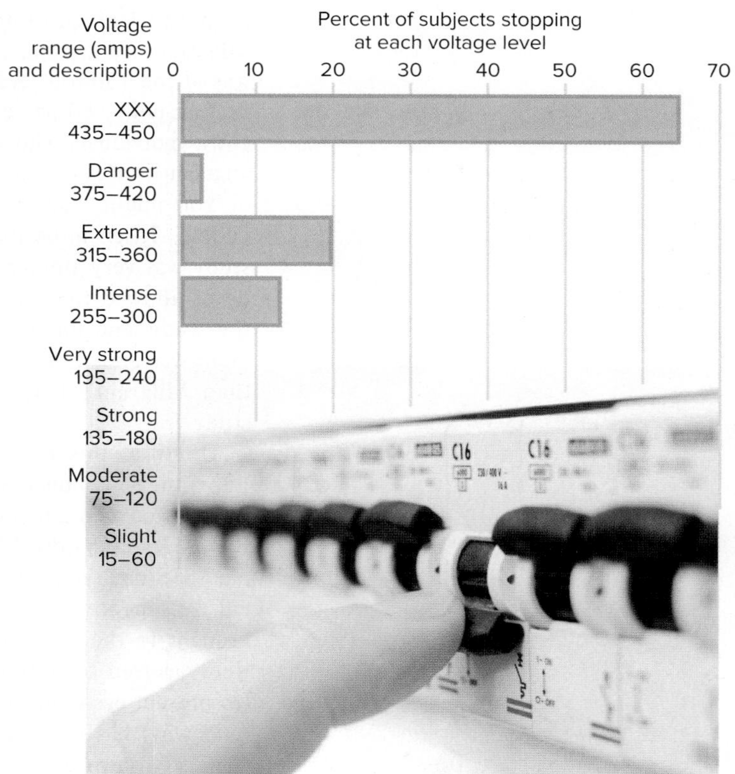


**FIGURE 3** **Milgram Obedience Study** A 50-year-old man, the "learner," is strapped into a chair. The experimenter makes it look as if a shock generator is being connected to his body through several electrodes. The chart shows the percentage of "teachers" who stopped shocking the learner at each voltage level.
©BernardaSv/iStock/Getty Images

## psychological *inquiry*

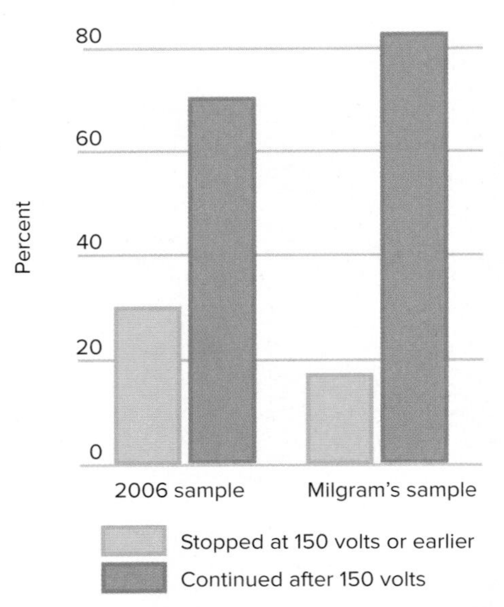


Source: Data from Burger (2009).

### *Obedience Then and Now*

The figure shows the results of Burger's obedience study, conducted in 2006 and published in 2009, and the results of one of Milgram's studies. The vertical, or Y axis, shows the percent of participants who stopped or continued shocking the learner after that individual first expressed a desire to end the study. Try answering the questions below the figure.

1. Does this comparison surprise you? Why or why not?
2. Burger did not allow participants who knew of Milgram's study to take part in his study. How might the results have differed if these individuals had been permitted to participate?
3. If you had been a "teacher" in this study, what do you think you would have done?

cannot be ignored (Turowetz & Hollander, 2018). Nonetheless, we are still learning from Milgram's data. A meta-analysis of his experiments suggested that the critical decision was at the 150-volt level, when the learner first requested that the experiment be halted. At that point, 80 percent of those who were going to stop did so (Packer, 2008). Apparently, individuals who were going to disobey were those who responded not to the later anguished cries of pain but to the learner's first request to be set free.

You might wonder whether Milgram's results would apply to more contemporary people. To examine this question, Jerry Burger (2009) recreated Milgram's study. His study was very similar to Milgram's with one key exception: Burger's participants were never allowed to go higher than 150 volts. At 150 volts, the confederate asked to end the study, and immediately after participants decided whether to continue, the experiment was ended. Surprisingly, Burger's participants were only slightly less likely to obey than Milgram's had been. The Psychological Inquiry probes the results of Burger's study.

Often, at this point, students of psychology are introduced to the Stanford Prison Experiment, conducted by Philip Zimbardo in 1971 (Resnick, 2018). Zimbardo and his students created a mock prison in the basement of a Stanford University building (Haney, Banks, & Zimbardo, 1973; Zimbardo, 1972, 1973). Twenty-four healthy young men were paid $15/day (equivalent to about $94 in 2018) to play either prisoners or guards in the jail. Prisoners were "arrested," booked and fingerprinted at the local police station, and brought to the "prison." They were placed in cells, wore uncomfortable uniforms, and were referred to only by numbers. The guards wore uniforms and mirrored sunglasses (to prevent eye contact with prisoners) and wielded wooden batons. What happened next (and why) has become a point of contention in social psychology. Read about it in the Critical Controversy.

### EXERTING PERSONAL CONTROL

After reading about the landmark studies by Asch and Milgram, you may be questioning the value of conformity and obedience and wondering what it might take for people to stand up to group pressure or to resist the demands of an authority figure. It can be

## *What Happened in the Stanford Prison Experiment?*

The Stanford Prison Experiment is a landmark in social psychology and popular culture. It has even been made into a movie (with Billy Crudup playing Zimbardo). But what really happened during the few days those young men were assigned to play guards and prisoners in a mock jail? According to Zimbardo's account, their roles strongly dictated participant behavior. Guards behaved sadistically toward the prisoners, and prisoners became docile and lost their sense of self. One prisoner, said Zimbardo, experienced a psychological breakdown. So horrific were the events that unfolded that the experiment, planned to last for 2 weeks, was stopped after just 6 days. Zimbardo claimed the study showed the strong power of roles in determining behavior. He said the prisoners did not ask to leave the study because they had so internalized their roles. Further, he suggested that the guards' actions revealed an important truth about the human capacity for evil: given the opportunity, human beings will engage in vile behavior toward others (Zimbardo, 2007).

Recently, a French journalist uncovered audiotapes that had been made during the study and interviewed some of the men who had participated all those years ago (Blum, 2018; Le Texier, 2018). What he found was quite different from the story typically shared in psychology courses. Perhaps most importantly, Zimbardo failed to emphasize that prior to the start of the experiment, he and his assistants had strongly encouraged the guards to play a "tough guard" and use fear to control the prisoners (Blum, 2018). If guards were too mild, a research assistant pressed them to be more aggressive. One notoriously mean guard said in a recent interview that he was just trying to please the experimenters and had modeled his behavior after a character in the classic film *Cool Hand Luke* (Blum, 2018).

The typical interpretation of the Stanford Prison Experiment rests on Zimbardo's assertion that guards and prisoners behaved as they did naturally, with no interference from him or the students helping with the study. We now know that this is not true. In fact, an attempt to replicate the study showed that without the encouragement given to guards to be tough, it is unlikely any would have behaved aggressively (Haslam & Reicher, 2003).

A serious ethical issue with the study was that numerous prisoners *did* ask to leave the study but were told they could not. In fact, the prisoner who had the mental breakdown said he had faked his distress to get out of the study. He had assumed that he would be able to study while making money in the mock jail (Blum, 2018).

*Philip Zimbardo*



The enduring impact of the Stanford Prison Experiment in psychology is a bit of a puzzle. It was not, after all, much of an experiment and the results were not published in a peer-reviewed journal. Leon Festinger himself called it not science but rather "a happening" (Blum, 2018). A study purporting to show the strong effect of roles on social behavior has transformed into a difficult happening indeed, the meaning of which is now entwined in complex issues of memory, truth, and notoriety.

**WHAT DO YOU THINK?**

- Why do you think people placed so much stock in the report of the Stanford Prison Experiment?
- Zimbardo and the former participants disagree strongly about what took place during the study. Who do you believe and why?

---

difficult to go against the crowd and risk being wrong or rejected. When people believe that they have control over their own actions, they are less likely to conform (Feldman & Chandrashekar, 2018).

*Reactance* refers to the motivation to reject attempts to control us (Brehm, 2000; Hall & others, 2018). Reactance occurs when a person feels that someone or something is taking

Individuals forced to wait in long lines to vote may show reactance and become even more determined to exercise their rights.

©Rob Crandall/Shutterstock

away his or her choices. Sometimes when authority figures overreach, reactance propels people to defy those authorities. Reactance might explain high levels of voter turnout in elections in places where authorities attempt to limit voting.

Daily life requires some amount of conformity and obedience, but there are times when all of us must exert personal control over our actions. Although it may not be easy to resist the group or authority, living with the knowledge that you compromised your own moral integrity may be more difficult in the long run.

## Group Influence

Scenes of mobs rioting are all too common in the media. A team wins a championship, and fans who would never otherwise break the law can be seen setting fire to cars and looting businesses. People at a political rally who might otherwise never even raise their voices to someone else are captured on video punching individuals who favor a different candidate. Teammates, fraternity and sorority members, bandmates, and members of various clubs harm and even kill new members during hazing rituals. Make no mistake, the perpetrators in these instances are often people with no history of violence who genuinely have no hostility toward the person harmed. None of them, acting alone, would have performed destructive, even murderous, acts. Why does being in a group lead to such behavior? This central question has driven research in the social psychology of group influence.

### DEINDIVIDUATION

● **deindividuation** The reduction in personal identity and erosion of the sense of personal responsibility when one is part of a group.

One process that sheds light on the behavior of individuals in groups is **deindividuation**, which occurs when being part of a group reduces personal identity and erodes the sense of personal responsibility (Ritchey & Ruback, 2018). An example of the effects of deindividuation is the wild street celebrations that erupt after a team's victory in the World Series or Super Bowl.

One explanation for the effects of deindividuation is that groups give us anonymity. When we are part of a group, we may act in an uninhibited way because we believe that no one will be able to identify us. The Ku Klux Klan demonstrates a variety of ways that human beings can deindividuate: acting in groups, often under cover of darkness, and wearing white hoods to conceal identity (Ritchey & Ruback, 2018).

Nowhere is the deindividuating cloak of anonymity more apparent than in anonymous online communication (Chung, 2018; Perfumi & others, 2018). Indeed, cyberbullying is highest when people feel they are completely anonymous online (Kowalski, Limber, & McCord, 2018).

*Why do individuals who would never perform destructive acts when alone perpetrate them when in a group?*

©Patrick Fallon/Cal Sport Media/Newscom

### SOCIAL CONTAGION

Have you ever noticed that a movie you watched in a crowded theater seemed funnier than it did when you watched it alone at home? People laugh more when others are laughing. Babies cry when other babies are crying. The effects of others on our behavior can take the form of **social contagion**, imitative behavior involving the spread of actions, emotions, and ideas. Social contagion effects have been observed in varied phenomena, including shopping online or in stores (Bilgicer & others, 2015), gun shot injuries (Papachristos, Wildeman, & Roberto, 2015), the popularity of dog breeds (Herzog, 2006), ethnic hostility (Bauer & others, 2018), the spread of childhood obesity (Datar & Nicosia, 2018), and the way members of sports teams seem to all have bad performances during the same game (Boss & Kleinart, 2015).

● **social contagion** Imitative behavior involving the spread of actions, emotions, and ideas.

One way to observe social contagion is to sit in a quiet but crowded library and start coughing. You will soon notice others doing the same thing. Similarly, imagine that you are walking down the sidewalk and come upon a group of people who are all looking up. How likely is it that you can avoid the temptation of looking up to see what is so interesting?

## GROUP PERFORMANCE

Are two or three heads better than one? Some studies reveal that we accomplish more in groups; others show that we are more productive when we work alone (Meyer, Schermuly, & Kauffeld, 2016; Wolf & others, 2015). Social psychologists use the terms *social facilitation* and *social loafing* to describe the varying ways the presence of others can influence performance.

**Social Facilitation** If you have ever given a presentation in a class, you might have noticed that you did a much better job when you were standing in front of your classmates than during any of your practice runs. **Social facilitation** occurs when an individual's performance improves because of the presence of others. Robert Zajonc (1965) argued that the presence of other individuals arouses us. The arousal produces energy and facilitates our performance in groups. If our arousal is too high, however, we are unable to learn new or difficult tasks efficiently. Social facilitation, then, improves our performance on well-learned tasks. For new or difficult tasks, we might be best advised to work things out on our own before trying them in a group.

● **social facilitation** Improvement in an individual's performance because of the presence of others.

**Social Loafing** Another factor in group performance is the degree to which one's behavior is monitored. **Social loafing** refers to each person's tendency to exert less effort in a group because of reduced accountability for individual effort. The effect of social loafing is lowered group performance. The larger the group, the more likely it is that an individual can loaf without detection. Social loafing can be reduced by making individuals' contributions more identifiable and unique, simplifying the evaluation of these contributions, and making the group's task more attractive (Chen & Cheng, 2018).

● **social loafing** Each person's tendency to exert less effort in a group because of reduced accountability for individual effort.

## GROUP DECISION MAKING

Many of the decisions we make take place in groups–juries, teams, families, clubs, school boards, and the U.S. Senate, for example. What happens when people put their minds to the task of making a group decision? How do they decide whether a criminal is guilty, whether a country should attack another, where a family should go on vacation, or whether sex education should be part of a school curriculum? Three aspects of group decision making bear special mention: risky shift and group polarization; groupthink; and majority and minority influence.

**Risky Shift and Group Polarization** Imagine that you have a friend, Ann, who works as an accountant. All her life Ann has longed to be a writer. In fact, she believes that she has the next great American novel in her head; she just needs time and energy to devote to writing it. Would you advise Ann to quit her job and go for it? What if you knew beforehand that her chances of success were 50–50? How about 60–40? How much risk would you advise Ann to take?

In one investigation, participants were presented with fictitious dilemmas like this one and were asked how much risk the characters in the scenarios should take (Stoner, 1961).

When the individuals discussed the dilemmas as a group, they endorsed riskier decisions than when they were queried alone. The so-called **risky shift** is the tendency for a group decision to be riskier than the average decision made by the individual group members (Westfall, Judd, & Kenny, 2015). Essentially, risky shift means that after group discussion, people start to move toward a riskier choice than their first decision.

● **risky shift** The tendency for a group decision to be riskier than the average decision made by the individual group members.

However, people do not always make riskier decisions in a group than when alone. Instead, a group discussion can move individuals more strongly in the direction of the position they initially held (Moscovici, 1985). The **group polarization effect** is the solidification and further strengthening of an individual's position as a consequence of a group discussion or interaction. For example, in 2013, a YouTube clip surfaced of (now former) Rutgers men's basketball coach Mike Rice abusing players during a practice. Administrators had seen the video months earlier and had decided that a fine, suspension, and anger management courses would be appropriate consequences. However, after the wider public saw and discussed the clip, it became clear that a more extreme punishment was required, and Rice was fired.

● **group polarization effect** The solidification and further strengthening of an individual's position as a consequence of a group discussion or interaction.

Why would conversation lead to more extreme opinions? First, during the discussion, new, more persuasive arguments can strengthen an original position. Second, social comparison can have influence. The administrators at Rutgers certainly wanted to see themselves as standing up for what was right. Comparing their response to the public outcry revealed they needed to do more to achieve that goal.

**Groupthink: Getting Along but Being Very Wrong** **Groupthink** refers to the impaired group decision making that occurs when making the right decision is less important than maintaining group harmony. Instead of engaging in an open discussion of all the available information, in groupthink, members of a group place the highest value on conformity and unanimity. Members are encouraged to "get with the program." Those who dissent are met with very strong disapproval. Groupthink can occur in different types of groups, ranging from government (Barr & Mintz, 2018) to medical decision-making teams (Ryan & others, 2018) to street gangs (Gebo, 2018). Symptoms of groupthink include overestimating the power and morality of one's group, closed-mindedness and unwillingness to hear all sides of an argument, and pressure for uniformity. Groupthink can occur whenever groups value conformity over accuracy.

● **groupthink** The impaired group decision making that occurs when making the right decision is less important than maintaining group harmony.

Groupthink can result in disastrous decisions. Irving Janis (1972) introduced the concept of groupthink to explain a number of enormous decision-making errors throughout history. Such errors include the lack of U.S. preparation for the Japanese bombing of Pearl Harbor during World War II, the escalation of the Vietnam War in the 1960s, the Watergate coverup in 1974, and the *Challenger* space shuttle disaster in 1986.

Groupthink has also been suggested as being involved in the failure to heed warnings of the 9/11 terrorist attacks, the abuse of prisoners at Abu Ghraib, the lack of action to circumvent activities leading to the recession of 2008, and the unresponsiveness of officials to allegations that former team physician Larry Nassar was sexually assaulting student athletes at Michigan State University. If you look at your favorite news source today, you will likely find some evidence of groupthink lurking behind negative events.

©Scott Olson/Getty Images

Groupthink can be prevented if groups avoid isolation, allow the airing of all sides of an argument, have an impartial leader, include outside experts in the debate, and encourage members who are strongly identified with the group to speak out in dissent (Packer, 2009). The decision in 2011 for the Navy SEALS to conduct an assassination raid on Osama bin Laden's compound involved an open discussion. Although most of President Obama's advisors hedged their bets, Vice President Biden specifically advised against the raid, whereas then–CIA Director Leon Panetta explicitly recommended going in (Landler, 2012).

**Majority and Minority Influence** Most groups make decisions by voting, and even in the absence of groupthink, the majority usually wins. The majority exerts influence on group decision making through both informational influence (they have greater opportunity to share their views) and normative influence (they set group norms). Those who do not go along may be ignored or even given the boot.

Prospects might seem dim for minority opinion holders, but they *can* make a difference. Because the minority is outnumbered, it cannot win through normative pressure. Instead, it must do its work through informational pressure. If the minority presents its views consistently and confidently, then the majority is more likely to listen to the minority's perspectives. A powerful way that minority opinion holders can have influence is by winning over former majority members to their points of view (Perez & others, 2018).

### test yourself

1. Compare and contrast informational social influence and normative social influence.
2. What is the difference between conformity and obedience?
3. What do the concepts of risky shift and group polarization reveal about decision making in a group context?

# 5. INTERGROUP RELATIONS

Conflicts between groups, especially ethnic and cultural groups, are rampant around the world. The terrorist organization ISIS attacks Paris and Brussels; the wronged nations retaliate. Israelis and Palestinians fight over territory in the Middle East, each claiming religious and historical rights to the disputed land. In countries across Africa, tribal chiefs try to craft a new social order favorable to their own rule. A variety of concepts introduced by social psychologists can help us understand the intensity of conflicts between groups and can provide insight into how to reduce them.

## Group Identity

Think about the groups of which you are a member—your religious and social organizations, your ethnic group, your nationality. When someone asks you to identify yourself, how often do you respond by mentioning these group memberships? And how much does it matter whether the people you associate with are members of the same groups as you?

### SOCIAL IDENTITY

**Social identity** refers to the way we define ourselves in terms of our group membership. In contrast to personal identity, which can be highly individualized, social identity assumes some commonalities with others (Crocetti, Prati, & Rubini, 2018; Verkuyten, 2018). A person's social identity might include identifying with a religious group, a country, a social organization, a political party, and many other groups. These diverse forms of social identity reflect the numerous ways people connect to groups and social categories. Social psychologist Kay Deaux (2001) identified five distinct types of social identity: ethnicity and religion, personal relationships, vocations and avocations, political affiliations, and stigmatized groups (Figure 4).

● **social identity** The way individuals define themselves in terms of their group membership.

**FIGURE 4** **Types of Identity** When we identify ourselves, we draw on a host of different characteristics associated with the various social groups to which we belong. Source: Deaux (2001); (first photo) ©Radius Images/Getty Images; (second photo) ©R.M. Nunes/Shutterstock; (third photo) ©Jacob Lund/Shutterstock; (fourth photo) ©moodboard/Mike Watson Images/Getty Images; (fifth photo) ©RichLegg/Getty Images

For many people, ethnic identity and religious identity are central to their social identity (Margolis, 2018; Verkuyten, 2018). Ethnic identity can be a source of pride. In the United States, special events celebrate the rich cultural contributions of many different groups to the society. Such experiences may provide individuals with an important resource in coping with biases they encounter (Yip, 2018). Feeling connected to one's ethnic group may buffer individuals from the stressful effects of injustice (Hakim, Molina, & Branscombe, 2018; Wang & others, 2018).

Social psychologist Henry Tajfel (1978), a Holocaust survivor, wanted to explain the extreme violence and prejudice that his religious group (Jews) experienced. Tajfel developed **social identity theory**, which states that our social identities are a crucial part of our self-image and a valuable source of positive feelings about ourselves. To feel good about ourselves, we need to feel good about the groups to which we belong. For this reason, individuals invariably think of the group to which they belong as an *ingroup,* a group that has special value in comparison with other groups. Those other groups are called *outgroups*. To improve our self-image, we continually compare our ingroups with outgroups. In the process, we often focus more on the differences between the two groups than on their similarities. Moreover, we begin to see outgroups as more similar to each other: "They" are all the same (Shilo & others, 2018).

● **social identity theory** Tajfel's theory that social identity, based on group membership, is a crucial part of self-image and a valuable source of positive feelings about oneself.

Research by Tajfel (and many others who have used his theory) shows how easy it is to lead people to think in terms of "us" and "them" (Tajfel, 1978). In one experiment, Tajfel had participants look at a screen featuring a huge number of dots and estimate how many dots were displayed. He then assigned the participants to groups based on an arbitrary situation—whether they overestimated or underestimated the number of dots. Once assigned to one of the two groups, the participants were asked to award money to other participants. Tajfel found that individuals awarded money to members of their ingroup, not to participants in the outgroup, even though the group assignment had been essentially arbitrary. If we favor the members of a group that was formed on such a trivial basis, it is no wonder that we show intense ingroup favoritism when differences are not so trivial.

## ETHNOCENTRISM

● **ethnocentrism** The tendency to favor one's own ethnic group over other groups.

**Ethnocentrism** is the tendency to favor one's own ethnic group over other groups. Ethnocentrism is not simply taking pride in one's group; it involves asserting the group's superiority over other groups. As such, ethnocentrism encourages ingroup/outgroup or we/they thinking (Bizumic, 2018). Consequently, ethnocentrism implies that ethnic outgroups are not just different: they are worse than one's group. Hence, ethnocentrism may underlie prejudice.

## PREJUDICE

● **prejudice** An unjustified negative attitude toward an individual based on the individual's membership in a group.

**Prejudice** is an unjustified negative attitude toward an individual based on the individual's membership in a particular group. The group can be made up of people of a specific ethnicity, sex, age, religion—essentially, people who are different in some way from a prejudiced person (Craig, Rucker, & Richeson, 2018).

Prejudice is a worldwide phenomenon that can be seen in eruptions of hatred throughout human history. In the Balkan Peninsula of eastern Europe, the Serbs' prejudice against Bosnians prompted the Serb policy of "ethnic cleansing." The prejudice of the Hutus against the Tutsis in Rwanda led them to go on a murderous rampage, attacking the Tutsis with machetes.

A powerful example of destructive prejudice within U.S. society is racial prejudice against African Americans. When African people were brought to colonial America as slaves, they were considered property and treated inhumanely. In the first half of the twentieth century, most African Americans still lived in the South and remained largely segregated based on skin color, with restaurants, movie theaters, and buses maintaining separate areas for Whites and Blacks.

It is useful at this point to note that talking openly about race and ethnicity can be awkward. Even coming up with labels to use to describe different groups of people can be difficult. In the United States, typical labels have changed from "Black" and "White"

*Ethnic identity evokes ethnic pride. Here, Chinese American children touch the "lion" in the streets of New York City's Chinatown on the day of Chinese New Year, in hopes of receiving good luck and prosperity.*

©Roberto Soncin Gerometta/Getty Images

to "African American" and "European American." But even these labels are not without problems. Many times labels are based not on information about the person's origins, but solely on the color of the person's skin. Nelson Mandela, for instance, was not African American. He was African. How do we distinguish between Mandela and F. W. de Klerk, the former (White) South African president who shared the Nobel Peace Prize with Mandela in 1993 for abolishing apartheid? In our discussion here, we will use the terms *Black* and *White* when in a particular study the actual ethnic background of targets of social judgment is not specified. In these instances, the only cue to the person's background, or anything else about that person, is skin color. Unfortunately, skin color can have a remarkably negative effect on how people are treated.

Despite progress over the years, there remain notable racial disparities among Americans, in terms of poverty, wealth, employment, education, and access to healthcare. Research continues to demonstrate the influence of race in U.S. life. In one study, researchers sent out 5,000 résumés in response to 1,200 job ads placed in newspapers in Chicago and Boston. The résumés were identical in qualifications. They differed only in whether the candidates' names were stereotypically White or Black. "White" names included Meredith, Emily, Brad, and Greg. "Black" names included Tamika, Lakisha, Darnell, and Kareem.

The researchers found that even with identical qualifications, the applicants with White-sounding names were 50 percent more likely to be called for an interview (Bertrand & Mullainathan, 2004; Patacchini, Ragusa, & Zenou, 2015). Results like these have prompted some to consider banning names of applicants on résumés. Such effects are not limited to employment. Churches are most likely to respond to e-mails from individuals with White-sounding names, compared to those with Black- or Latino-sounding names and especially compared to those with Asian-sounding names (Wright & others, 2015).

©David Maung/Bloomberg via Getty Images

Race not only influences employment but also broader economic decisions. For example, one study reported that Black and Latinx home buyers were much more likely to be given less financially advantageous mortgages (Bayer, Ferreira, & Ross, 2016). Another study examined the way race influenced the advice that bankruptcy attorneys gave to clients. Declaring bankruptcy means that a person is admitting that he or she is unable to repay debts. This legal claim can allow people to start the arduous process of regaining financial solvency. The two ways of declaring bankruptcy are Chapter 7 and Chapter 13. Chapter 7 bankruptcy is less expensive and often less burdensome than Chapter 13. An analysis of bankruptcy cases across the United States showed that African Americans were more likely than Whites to file for Chapter 13 rather than Chapter 7 bankruptcy (Braucher, Cohen, & Lawless, 2012).

Why would a group of individuals choose the more difficult and expensive form of bankruptcy? Could attorneys be steering African Americans toward this more burdensome path? To address these questions, the researchers conducted an experiment involving a random sample of bankruptcy lawyers. Participants read scenarios in which potential clients were identified as either "Reggie and Latisha" or "Todd and Alison." Even when all other aspects of the cases were identical, lawyers were more likely to recommend that Todd and Alison declare Chapter 7 and that Reggie and Latisha pursue Chapter 13 (Braucher, Cohen, & Lawless, 2012).

Such results are troubling. It is important to keep in mind that these responses to Black-sounding names might reflect subtle and potentially unconscious racial biases. Because racial prejudice is socially unacceptable, few people today would readily admit to holding racist or prejudicial views. Today, prejudiced individuals are more likely than before to appear unprejudiced on the surface while nevertheless holding racist views at a deeper, potentially unconscious, level.

To confront this problem, social psychologists examine prejudicial attitudes on two levels—explicit racism and implicit racism. *Explicit racism* is a person's conscious and openly shared attitude, which might be measured using a questionnaire. *Implicit racism* refers to attitudes that exist on a deeper, hidden level. Implicit attitudes must be measured with a method that does not require awareness. For example, implicit racism is sometimes measured using the Implicit Associations Test (IAT), a computerized survey that assesses the ease with which a person can associate a Black or White person with good things (for example, flowers) or bad things (for example, misery) (Greenwald & others, 2009; Sriram & Greenwald, 2009). This test is based on the idea that preexisting biases may make it easier to associate some social stimuli with positive rather than negative items. Although the IAT is widely used, scholars have raised concerns about its validity (Blanton, Jaccard, & Burrows, 2015; Blanton & others, 2009).

One study showed that while explicit prejudice predicted the things that White students said while interacting with a Black partner, implicit prejudice predicted nonverbal aspects of the interaction, such as White students' facial expressions and how close they sat to their interaction partner (Dovidio, Kawakami, & Gaertner, 2002).

Certainly both explicit and implicit prejudice can affect the well-being of individuals who are the target of prejudice (Allen & others, 2019; Russell & others, 2018; Yip, 2018). For example, a study examined the vital statistics for over 31 million infants born in the United States between 2002 and 2012 (Orchard & Price, 2017). Those data showed that Black mothers were 60 percent more likely than White mothers to give birth to low birth weight or preterm infants. The researchers combined the birth data with data collected as part of Project Implicit, which involves collecting implicit and explicit measures of racism from nearly 2 million adults across the United States. Those data were used to identify counties as high or low in racism. When they combined the birth data with the racism scores, the researchers found that the racial gap in infant birth weight was 14 percent higher in counties characterized by high levels of implicit racism and 22 percent higher in counties characterized by high levels of explicit racism (Orchard & Price, 2017).

Why do people develop prejudice? Social psychologists have explored a number of possible reasons. One contributor is realistic conflict between groups, especially when resources are scarce. For example, immigrants often compete with established low-income members of a society for jobs—a situation that can lead to persistent conflict between the two groups. Cultural learning is also clearly involved. Children can adopt the prejudicial attitudes of their families and friends before they even meet a person from an outgroup. In addition, when people feel bad about themselves, they might bolster their self-esteem by demeaning outgroup members.

A final factor that might underlie prejudice comes from the limits on our information-processing abilities. As already noted, individuals have a limited capacity for effortful thought, but we face a complex social environment. To simplify the challenge of understanding others' behavior, people use categories or stereotypes. Stereotypes can be a powerful force in developing and maintaining prejudicial attitudes. Recall that stereotypes are generalizations about a group that deny variations within the group. At the root of prejudice is a particular kind of stereotype: a negative generalization about a group that is applied to all members of that group (Craig, Rucker, & Richeson, 2018).

### DISCRIMINATION

**Discrimination** is an unjustified negative or harmful action toward a member of a group simply because the person belongs to that group. Discrimination occurs when negative emotional reactions combine with prejudicial beliefs and are translated into behavior. Since the passage of the Civil Rights Act of 1964 (revised in 1991), it has been unlawful to deny someone employment on the basis of gender or ethnicity, as we will review in the chapter "Industrial and Organizational Psychology".

● **discrimination** An unjustified negative or harmful action toward a member of a group simply because the person belongs to that group.

## Ways to Improve Intergroup Relations

People show bias against others based on innumerable characteristics: race, gender, gender identification, sexuality, disability status, weight, and socioeconomic status, to name just a few. Considering the evidence described so far, one might feel a bit hopeless. Why can't we all just get along? Social psychologists have not simply documented the existence of prejudice and discrimination; they have also tried to devise ways to improve relations among different groups. Here we consider two of these—optimal group contact and changing the prejudice habit.

### OPTIMAL GROUP CONTACT

One way to improve intergroup relations might be for people to come to know one another better. However, in daily life many people interact with individuals from other ethnic groups, and this contact does not necessarily lead to tolerance or warm relations. Indeed, researchers have consistently found that contact by itself—attending the same school or working in the same company—does not necessarily improve relations among people of different ethnic backgrounds. So, rather than focusing on contact per se, researchers have examined how *various features* of a contact situation may be optimal for reducing prejudice and promoting intergroup harmony (Craig, Rucker, & Richeson, 2018; Durrheim & Dixon, 2018).

Gordon Allport (1954), whose contributions to personality psychology we examined in the chapter "Personality", theorized that particular aspects of the contact between groups could help to reduce prejudice. According to Allport, intergroup contact is likely to reduce prejudice when group members

- Think that they are of equal status
- Feel that an authority figure sanctions their positive relationships
- Believe that friendship might emerge from the interaction
- Engage in cooperative tasks in which everyone has something to contribute

Research supports many of Allport's ideas (Pettigrew & Tropp, 2006). In particular, studies have examined the role of *task-oriented cooperation*—working together toward a shared goal—in reducing tensions between groups. Two examples of the power of task-oriented cooperation are Sherif's Robbers Cave Study and Aronson's jigsaw classroom.

It may be hard to imagine in our post-*Survivor* era, but even before Jeff Probst started handing out color-coded "buffs" on the TV show *Survivor*, Muzafer Sherif and his colleagues (1961) had the idea of exploring group processes by assigning 11-year-old boys to two competitive groups (the "Rattlers" and the "Eagles") in a summer camp called Robbers Cave (see the Psychological Inquiry). Sherif, disguised as a janitor so that he could observe

## psychological *inquiry*

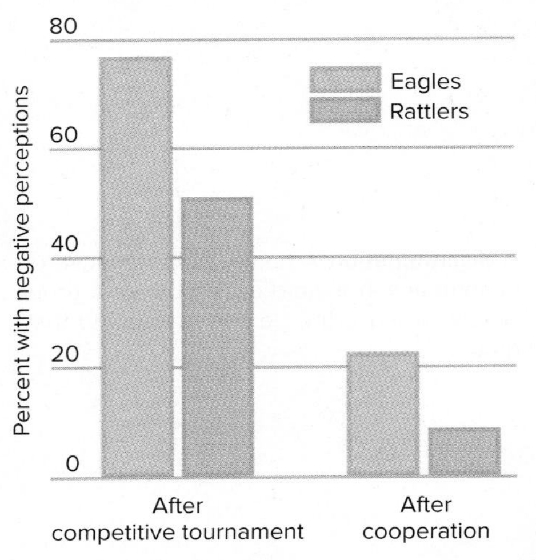


Source: Data from Sherif, Harvey, White, Hood, & Sherif, (1961).

### *Improving Group Relations Through Cooperative Activities*

The figure illustrates the results of Sherif's (1961) Robbers Cave Study. The graph shows the negative feelings expressed by members of the Eagles and Rattlers toward the other group (the outgroup) after a competitive tournament and after cooperative activity. Try your hand at answering these questions.

1. When did hostility between the groups peak? When did it drop?
2. What is up with the Eagles? What are some reasons why they might be more negative about the Rattlers?
3. In your own life, are there examples of holding particular attitudes toward a group different from your own? How have your attitudes changed, and what events preceded these changes?

the boys, arranged for the two groups to compete in baseball, touch football, and tug-of-war. If you have watched reality television, you have some idea how this experiment went. In short order, relations between the groups deteriorated. Members of each group expressed negative opinions of members of the other group, and the Rattlers and Eagles became battling factions.

What could bring these clashing groups together? Sherif created tasks that required the joint efforts of both groups, such as working together to repair the camp's only water supply. When the groups were required to work cooperatively to solve problems, the Rattlers and Eagles developed more positive relationships.

Sherif's idea was later tested in the real world in Austin, Texas, when ethnic tensions and violence erupted among African Americans, Mexican Americans, and European Americans in desegregated schools. Social psychologist Eliot Aronson was asked to help address the problem, and he devised the *jigsaw classroom* (1986), where all of the students had to pull together to get the "big picture."

Let's say there is an ethnically diverse class of 30 students. The academic goal for all students is to learn about the life of Rosa Parks. The class might be broken up into five study groups of six students each, with the groups being as equal as possible in ethnic composition and academic achievement level. Learning about Parks's life becomes a class project divided into six parts, with one part given to each member of the six-person group. The components might be various books about Parks or information about different aspects of her life. The parts are like the pieces of a jigsaw puzzle: They have to be put together to form the complete puzzle.

U.S. teachers have used the jigsaw approach in their classrooms, and it has been associated with increased self-esteem, better academic performance, friendships among classmates, and improved interethnic perceptions (Nolan & others, 2018; Slavin, 2006). Indeed, one meta-analysis found that real-life contact interventions, such as jigsaw classrooms, do tend to reduce prejudice and that such changes are long-lasting (Lemmer & Wagner, 2015).

### BREAKING THE PREJUDICE HABIT

Given that much of prejudice in contemporary life is likely to be implicit—meaning that it happens automatically and can occur unconsciously—it is important to ask whether we can change not only explicit attitudes but implicit ones as well. Implicit prejudice rests on automatic associations: You see a person from a different ethnic, racial, or religious group, and stereotypical thoughts pop into your head. In this sense, prejudice is a habitual way of thinking.

Can we short-circuit these automatic connections and reduce implicit prejudice? A study by Patricia Devine and her colleagues (2012) suggests that we can. Non-African American participants were randomly assigned to an experimental group that received an intervention to reduce implicit prejudice or a control group that simply completed the dependent measures. Based on the idea that to change racial attitudes people must be aware of them, the first step was to measure implicit racial prejudice using the IAT and give the participants their scores. These scores can be surprising to many people who feel they are not prejudiced against people of color.

Next, participants in the experimental group were trained in various ways to break the prejudice habit. This training to introduce new habits of the mind included noticing stereotypic thoughts about African Americans and replacing them with more individualized information about the person. Participants were also trained to think about individuals who do not fit the stereotype of various outgroups, and they were encouraged to put themselves in the other's position and consider things from that person's perspective. Finally, participants were urged to seek out contact with members of the outgroup. The results showed that, six weeks later, participants who had experienced this intervention did show reductions in implicit bias against African Americans. In addition, these individuals were more likely to express concerns about the problems of discrimination in U.S. society. Subsequent research has shown that making a conscious effort to stop automatic prejudicial thoughts can reduce prejudice (Johnson, Kopp, & Petty, 2018).

These results, and those of contact interventions, suggest that even though the problem of racial tension in the United States and across the world may seem insurmountable, it is possible to improve relations among groups.

### test yourself

1. What does social identity theory say about groups?
2. What is prejudice? Give two real-world examples, either historical or contemporary.
3. According to Allport, what particular aspects of the contact between groups could help to reduce prejudice?

# 6. CLOSE RELATIONSHIPS

Along with good health and happiness, close relationships figure prominently in people's notions of a good life. Because close romantic relationships are so crucial for most of us, it is no wonder that social psychologists are interested in studying this vital part of human existence. A vast literature has accumulated in social psychology that focuses on attraction, love, and intimacy.

## Attraction

At the beginning of this chapter, we discussed one key factor in interpersonal attraction: namely, physical attractiveness. Research on interpersonal attraction has illuminated a variety of other factors that play a role in the dynamic of attraction.

### PROXIMITY AND SIMILARITY

Even in the age of Internet dating, it is very unlikely that you are going to become attracted to someone without meeting the person. *Proximity,* or physical closeness, is a strong predictor of attraction. You are more likely to become attracted to someone you pass in the hall every day than to a person you rarely see. One potential mechanism for the role of proximity in attraction is the mere exposure effect (Zajonc, 1968, 2001). The **mere exposure effect** is the phenomenon that the more we encounter someone or something (a person, a word, an image), the more probable it is that we will start liking the person or thing even if we do not realize we have seen it before.

• **mere exposure effect** The phenomenon that the more individuals encounter someone or something, the more probable it is that they will start liking the person or thing even if they do not realize they have seen it before.

In addition to proximity, similarity plays an important role in attraction (Hampton, Fisher Boyd, & Sprecher, 2018). We have all heard that opposites attract, but what is true of magnets is not usually true of human beings. We like to associate with people who are similar to us (Singh & others, 2017). Our friends and lovers are much more like us than unlike us. We share similar attitudes, behavior patterns, taste in clothes, intelligence, personality, other friends, values, lifestyle, and physical attractiveness.

The concept of *consensual validation* explains why people are attracted to others who are similar to them. Our own attitudes and behavior are supported when someone else's attitudes and behavior are familiar—their attitudes and behavior validate ours.

*As love matures, passionate love tends to give way to affectionate love.*

©Blend Images/Image Source

Another reason that similarity matters is that we tend to shy away from the unknown. Similarity implies that we will enjoy doing things with another person who has comparable tastes and attitudes.

## Love

Some relationships never progress much beyond the attraction stage. Others deepen to friendship and perhaps even to love. Social psychologists have long puzzled over exactly what love is (Berscheid, 2006, 2010; Shiota & others, 2017). One way to think about love is to consider the types of love that characterize different human relationships—for instance, friendships versus romantic relationships (Hendrick & Hendrick, 2009; Sternberg & Sternberg, 2018). Here we consider two types of love: romantic love and affectionate love.

Poets, playwrights, and musicians through the ages have celebrated the fiery passion of romantic love—and lamented the searing pain when it fails. Think about songs and books that hit the top of the charts. Chances are, they are about romantic love. **Romantic love**, also called **passionate love**, is love with strong components of sexuality and infatuation, and it often predominates in the early part of a love relationship (Hendrick & Hendrick, 2006). This is the kind of sexually charged feeling we usually mean when we talk about being "in love."

● **romantic love or passionate love** Love with strong components of sexuality and infatuation, often dominant in the early part of a love relationship.

Love is more than just passion, however (Gable, 2018). **Affectionate love**, also called **companionate love**, is the type of love that occurs when individuals desire to have the other person near and have a deep, caring affection for the person. There is a growing belief that the early stages of love have more romantic ingredients and that as love matures, passion tends to give way to affection (Berscheid & Regan, 2005).

● **affectionate love or companionate love** Love that occurs when individuals desire to have another person near and have a deep, caring affection for the person.

## Models of Close Relationships

What makes long-term romantic relationships last? Two theoretical approaches to this sometimes bewildering question include social exchange theory and the investment model.

### SOCIAL EXCHANGE THEORY

The social exchange approach to close relationships focuses on the costs and benefits of one's romantic partner. **Social exchange theory** is based on the notion of social relationships as involving an exchange of goods, the objective of which is to minimize costs and maximize benefits. This theory looks at human relations as an exchange of rewards between actors.

● **social exchange theory** The view of social relationships as involving an exchange of goods, the objective of which is to minimize costs and maximize benefits.

From the social exchange perspective, the most important predictor of a relationship's success is *equity*—a feeling on the part of the individuals in the relationship that each is doing his or her "fair share." Essentially, social exchange theory asserts that the partners keep a mental balance sheet, tallying the pluses and minuses associated with each other—what they put in ("I paid for our last date") and what they get out ("He brought me flowers").

As relationships progress, equity may no longer apply. In fact, research shows that over time, this kind of accounting not only is less likely to explain what happens in a relationship but also becomes distasteful to the partners. Happily married couples are less likely to keep track of "what I get versus what I give," and they avoid thinking about the costs and benefits of their relationships (Gable, 2018; Kashdan & others, 2018). Surely we can all think of long-term relationships in which one partner remains committed even when the benefits are hard for the outsider to see—as in the case where the person's romantic partner is gravely ill for a long time.

### THE INVESTMENT MODEL

Another way to think about long-term romantic relationships is to focus on the underlying factors that characterize stable, happy relationships compared with others. The **investment model** examines the ways that commitment, investment, and the availability of attractive

● **investment model** A model of long-term relationships that examines the ways that commitment, investment, and the availability of attractive alternative partners predict satisfaction and stability in relationships.

alternative partners predict satisfaction and stability in relationships (Day & Impett, 2018; Hadden & others, 2018; Rusbult, Agnew, & Arriaga, 2012).

From the investment model perspective, long-term relationships are likely to continue when both partners are committed to the relationship and both have invested a great deal; in addition, relationships are more enduring when there are few tempting alternatives for the partners. For example, college students who are committed to their romantic partners are less likely to cheat on them sexually during spring break (Drigotas, Safstrom, & Gentilia, 1999).

Commitment to a relationship also predicts a willingness to sacrifice for a romantic partner. In one study, individuals were given a chance to climb up and down a short staircase, over and over, to spare their partner from having to do so. Those who were more committed to their partner worked harder climbing up and down to spare their loved one the burden (Van Lange & others, 1997). When two partners are deeply invested in a relationship, they can also bring out the best aspects of each other, mutually helping themselves grow into their best possible selves (Day & Impett, 2018; Rusbult, Finkel, & Kumashiro, 2009).

### test yourself

1. Explain the concept of consensual validation.
2. What is the difference between romantic love and affectionate love, and what is another name for each?
3. What does social exchange theory say about happy romantic relationships?

## 7. SOCIAL PSYCHOLOGY AND HEALTH AND WELLNESS

The principles of social psychology have provided a strong foundation for ongoing research in the areas of health and wellness. In this concluding section, we glimpse some of the significant connections that researchers have uncovered among social contacts, physical health, and psychological wellness.

A long list of studies has shown that social ties are an important, if not the *most* important, variable in predicting health. For example, in a landmark study, social isolation had six times the effect on mortality rates that cigarette smoking had (House, Landis, & Umberson, 1988). A longitudinal study involving over 5,000 adults over the age of 50 found that loneliness was associated with increased risk for cardiovascular disease (Valtorta & others, 2018). Loneliness is linked with impaired physical health and psychological distress (Kobayashi & Steptoe, 2018; Segrin, McNelis, & Pavlich, 2018). A study of nearly half a million adults in the United Kingdom found that social isolation predicted higher risk of a heart attack or stroke and increased mortality associated with these events (Hakulinen & others, 2018). Without a doubt, being connected to others is crucial to human survival (Cacioppo & Cacioppo, 2018).

Social isolation and loneliness are not the same thing. Social isolation means having few social ties and being objectively alone. Loneliness is the feeling of distress associated with feeling socially isolated. A person can feel lonely even when they are surrounded by other people (Pinel, 2018). These two variables can combine to create a particularly bad combination in predicting mortality. In combination they are stronger predictors of death than either alone (Beller & Wagner, 2018).

Having many different social ties may be especially important during difficult times (Deckx & others, 2018). Individuals who participate in more diverse social networks–for example, having a close relationship with a partner; interacting with family members, friends, neighbors, and fellow workers; and belonging to social and religious groups–live longer than those with a narrower range of social relationships (Valente, 2017; Vogt & others, 1992).

One study investigated the effects of diverse social ties on susceptibility to getting a common cold (S. Cohen & others, 1998). Individuals reported the extent of their participation in 12 types of social ties. Then they were given nasal drops containing a cold virus and monitored for the appearance of a cold. Individuals with more diverse social ties were less likely to get a cold than their counterparts with less diverse social networks.

Each of us has times in our life when we feel lonely, particularly when we are going through major life transitions. For example, when individuals leave the familiar world of their hometown and family to begin college, they can feel especially lonely. Indeed, experiencing loneliness at the beginning of one's college career is quite common and normal.

### test yourself

1. What are some physical illnesses in which social isolation plays a significant role, according to researchers?
2. What kinds of social networks are especially important in times of trouble?
3. If a friend were struggling with loneliness, what strategy would you recommend for coping with it?

If you are lonely, there are strategies you can use to become better connected with others. You might consider joining activities, such as volunteering your time for a cause in which you believe. When interacting with others, you will improve your chances of developing enduring relationships if you are considerate, honest, trustworthy, and cooperative. If you cannot get rid of your loneliness on your own, you might want to contact the counseling services at your college.

Having completed this chapter's survey of social psychology, you may be surprised to learn that we have barely scratched the surface of this broad and deep field: The branch of psychology that focuses on the ways human beings relate to one another is a rich, intriguing area of study. In the next few days, think about the stories that are making the headlines and that you are talking about with your friends. Reflecting back on this chapter, you might notice that social psychology would have something to say about most of these topics.

## 1. DEFINING SOCIAL PSYCHOLOGY

Social psychology is the scientific study of how people think about, influence, and relate to other people. This broad subfield of psychology is relevant to everyday life and typically relies on experimental methods. An example of social psychology in action is provided by classic research on the bystander effect. The bystander effect means that individuals who observe an emergency are less likely to help when someone else is present than when they are alone.

## 2. SOCIAL COGNITION

The face conveys information to social perceivers, including attractiveness. Self-fulfilling prophecy means that our expectations of others can have a powerful impact on their behavior.

Attributions are our thoughts about why people behave as they do and about who or what is responsible for the outcome of events. Attribution theory views people as motivated to discover the causes of behavior as part of their effort to make sense of it. The dimensions used to make sense of the causes of human behavior include internal/external, stable/unstable, and controllable/uncontrollable.

The fundamental attribution error is observers' tendency to overestimate traits and to underestimate situations when they explain an actor's behavior. Self-serving bias means attributing our successes to internal causes and blaming our failures on external causes. Heuristics are used as shortcuts in social information processing. One such heuristic is a stereotype—a generalization about a group's characteristics that does not consider any variations among individuals in the group.

The self is our mental representation of our own characteristics. Self-esteem refers to the attitude we take toward ourselves. Stereotype threat is an individual's fast-acting, self-fulfilling fear of being judged based on a negative stereotype about his or her group. In order to understand ourselves better, we might engage in social comparison, evaluating ourselves through comparison with others.

Attitudes are our feelings—about people, objects, and ideas. Attitudes predict behavior when an individual's attitudes are strong, when the person is aware of his or her attitudes and expresses them often, and when the person has a vested interest in the attitude. Sometimes changes in behavior precede changes in attitude.

According to cognitive dissonance theory, our strong need for cognitive consistency causes us to change our behavior to fit our attitudes or to change our attitudes to fit our behavior. Self-perception theory stresses the importance of making inferences about attitudes by observing our own behavior, especially when our attitudes are not clear.

## 3. SOCIAL BEHAVIOR

Altruism is an unselfish interest in helping someone else. Reciprocity often is involved in altruism. Genes play a role in prosocial behavior, along with the neurotransmitters serotonin, dopamine, and oxytocin. The experience of empathy is linked to helping, as is the personality trait of agreeableness. Individuals who are in a good mood are more helpful.

Aggression is behavior meant to harm another person. Evidence for genetic and neurobiological factors is mixed and generally less clear-cut than that suggested by research with animals. Psychological factors in aggression include frustrating and aversive circumstances. Sociocultural factors include cross-cultural variation, the culture of honor, and violence in the media.

## 4. SOCIAL INFLUENCE

Conformity involves a change in behavior to coincide with that of a group. Factors that influence conformity include informational social influence (going along to be right) and normative social influence (going along to be liked). Asch conducted a classic experiment on conformity in 1951.

Obedience is behavior that complies with the explicit demands of an authority. Milgram's experiments demonstrated the power of obedience.

People often change their behavior when they are in a group. Deindividuation refers to the lack of inhibition and diffusion of responsibility that can occur in groups. Social contagion refers to imitative behaviors involving the spread of behavior, emotions, and ideas. Our performance in groups can be improved through social facilitation and impaired by social loafing.

Risky shift refers to the tendency for a group decision to be riskier than the average decision made by the individual group members. The group polarization effect is the solidification and further strengthening of a position as a consequence of group discussion or interaction. Groupthink involves impaired decision making resulting from valuing group harmony over accuracy.

## 5. INTERGROUP RELATIONS

Social identity is our definition of ourselves in terms of our group memberships. Social identity theory states that when individuals are assigned to a group, they invariably think of it as the ingroup. Identifying with the group allows the person to have a positive self-image. Ethnocentrism is the tendency to favor one's own ethnic group over others.

Prejudice is an unjustified negative attitude toward an individual based on membership in a group. The underlying reasons for prejudice include competition between groups over scarce resources, a person's motivation to enhance his or her self-esteem, cognitive processes that tend to categorize and stereotype others, and cultural learning. Prejudice is also based on stereotypes. The cognitive process of stereotyping can lead to discrimination, an unjustified negative or harmful action toward a member of a group simply because he or she belongs to that group. Discrimination results when negative emotional reactions combine with prejudicial beliefs and are translated into behavior.

An effective strategy for enhancing the effects of intergroup contact is to set up task-oriented cooperation among individuals from different groups.

## 6. CLOSE RELATIONSHIPS

We tend to be attracted to people whom we see often and who are similar to us. Romantic love (passionate love) includes feelings of infatuation and sexual attraction. Affectionate love (companionate love) is more akin to friendship and includes deep, caring feelings for another.

Social exchange theory states that a relationship is likely to be successful if individuals feel that they get as much out of the relationship as they put into it. The investment model focuses on commitment, investment, and the availability of attractive alternatives in predicting relationship success.

## 7. SOCIAL PSYCHOLOGY AND HEALTH AND WELLNESS

Social isolation is a strong risk factor for a range of physical illnesses. Loneliness relates to a number of negative health outcomes, including impaired physical health and early death. Individuals who participate in more diverse social networks live longer than those with a narrower range of social relationships. Loneliness often emerges when people make life transitions, so it is not surprising that loneliness is common among college freshmen. Strategies that can help to reduce loneliness include participating in activities with others and taking the initiative to meet new people.

# key *terms*

affectionate love or companionate love
aggression
altruism
attitudes
attribution theory
bystander effect
cognitive dissonance
conformity
deindividuation
discrimination
egoism
elaboration likelihood model
ethnocentrism
false consensus effect
fundamental attribution error
group polarization effect
groupthink
informational social influence
investment model
mere exposure effect
normative social influence
obedience
positive illusions
prejudice
representativeness heuristic
risky shift
romantic love or passionate love
self-fulfilling prophecy
self-objectification
self-perception theory
self-serving bias
social cognition
social comparison
social contagion
social exchange theory
social facilitation
social identity
social identity theory
social loafing
social neuroscience
social psychology
stereotype
stereotype threat

# apply your *knowledge*

1. Check out this website to see how the averaging of faces works: www.faceresearch.org/demos/average. Pick some faces you consider unattractive. What happens when you average them together? If you have a digital photograph of yourself and some friends, see what happens when you average those faces. Do you agree that average faces are more attractive than any single face?

2. Many people are surprised by the results of the IAT when they take this implicit measure. Try it yourself at https://implicit.harvard.edu/implicit. Do you think your results are valid? Explain.

3. We are often unaware of how many attributions we make about the behavior of others. To demonstrate this point to yourself, spend some time in a crowded area observing the interactions of others (alternatively, watch some scenes in television shows or movies). Take careful notes about the social behaviors that occur and then document your impressions of why the individuals behaved as they did. What cues did you use in making your attributions about their behavior? Did your knowledge of the fundamental attribution error influence your attributions? Why or why not?

4. Choose a day when you will engage in altruistic behavior. Act as kindly toward others as you can without telling anyone what you are up to. Keep track of your thoughts and feelings as you experience this day of kindness. How does it influence your feelings about altruism?

5. Interview the happiest couple you know. Ask the partners individually about the things that they think help make their relationship work. Then examine your notes. How do the characteristics of your "ideal" couple's relationship compare with the findings of research on close relationships?

# CHAPTER 14

## CHAPTER OUTLINE

# Industrial and Organizational Psychology

## Would You Work Even if You Didn't Have To?

**For many people a job is a means to an end.** We work to make money. Looking at how some of the world's wealthiest people spend their time, though, it is clear that these individuals work hard and work a lot—even though they have more than enough money to never work again. Tycoons in business and technology—such as Bill Gates (worth $76 billion), and Mark Zuckerberg—maintain long workdays, as do enormously successful writers, musicians, actors, and athletes. At 34 years old, Zuckerberg had an estimated personal worth of $61.4 billion. Even spending $100,000 a day, he would need to live over *1600 years* to spend it all. Just finding ways to spend all that money might become stressful. Why do people with sufficient wealth to never work at all still devote long hours and great effort to work?

Work is more than a way to earn money. It is an opportunity to use our skills and abilities and to feel successful and effective. It offers a context for meaningful relationships with others. In addition, work provides us with a sense of identity and purpose.

# PREVIEW

In this chapter we first examine the origins of industrial-organizational (I-O) psychology. We then investigate each of the two major domains of this approach—the "I" or industrial psychology side, concerned with personnel selection, and the "O" or organizational psychology side, including the topics of management style, workers' attitudes and behavior, and leadership. We pay special attention to one aspect of the "O" side, organizational culture. Finally, we complete our survey of the I-O field by exploring the crucial role of work in health and well-being.

## 1. ORIGINS OF INDUSTRIAL AND ORGANIZATIONAL PSYCHOLOGY

● **industrial and organizational (I-O) psychology** The field of psychology that applies the science of human behavior to work and the workplace.

**Industrial and organizational (I-O) psychology** applies the science of human behavior to work and the workplace (Grand & others, 2018). I-O psychologists are interested in many topics related to work, including how to select the right person for a job, how attitudes influence job performance, and the ways people work together in groups. Many of these topics are also studied in other areas, such as cognition, personality, and motivation. I-O psychology is unique, however, in that it examines these topics in the important real-world context of work. We will examine each side of industrial and organizational psychology in separate sections but the two areas overlap a great deal, and some topics, such as motivation, are a focal point in both areas. Industrial, the "I" side, is more concerned with maximizing efficiency, safety, cost effectiveness, and personnel selection. Organizational, the "O" side, targets the human relations processes that contribute to feelings of fulfillment, including job satisfaction, leadership, and organizational climate.

The idea that the principles of science should be applied to work settings has been around for only about 100 years. Contemporary I-O psychology has roots in the history of industry and the two world wars. Here we review three important influences on the development of I-O psychology: scientific management, ergonomics, and the human relations approach to management.

### Scientific Management

● **scientific management** The managerial philosophy that emphasizes the worker as a well-oiled machine and the determination of the most efficient methods for performing any work-related task.

The pioneers in applying scientific methods to the workplace were not psychologists but engineers. They focused on **scientific management**—the managerial philosophy that emphasizes the worker as a well-oiled machine and finding the most efficient methods for performing any work-related task. Yet these engineers sounded like psychologists at times. One of them, Frederick Winslow Taylor, was the mastermind of scientific management (Litterer, 2018; Schachter, 2018). Taylor (1911) suggested these guidelines, which have continuing influence today:

- Jobs should be carefully analyzed to identify the best way to perform them.
- Employees should be hired according to the characteristics associated with success at a task. Identify such characteristics by examining people who are already successful at a job.
- Employees should be trained at the job they will perform.
- Employees should be rewarded for productivity, to encourage high levels of performance.

The assembly line demonstrates the spirit of scientific management. Before the twentieth century, individuals or teams created an entire single product, assembling it from beginning to end—whether the product was a car or a dress. In 1901, Ransom E. Olds invented the *assembly line,* which revolutionized the automobile industry: Each individual laborer assembled only one part of a car. Henry Ford, founder of Ford Motor Company, added a motorized conveyor belt so that the car being assembled automatically moved along while workers stayed in the same spot. Ford had Frederick Taylor conduct *time and motion studies* to identify the precise movements needed to complete a task and eliminate unnecessary movements. Completed in 1913, the first moving assembly line was a boon to productivity and efficiency. By 1916, Ford Motor Company was producing twice as many cars as all of its competitors combined.

With the start of World War I in 1914, psychologists played a growing role in the application of science to the workplace, especially the military, addressing recruitment, selection, and morale. Between the two world wars, the field that would become known as I-O psychology expanded beyond the military into a variety of settings, including private industry, as it became ever more apparent that applying scientific research to the work environment would help employers improve efficiency (Bryan & Vinchur, 2013).

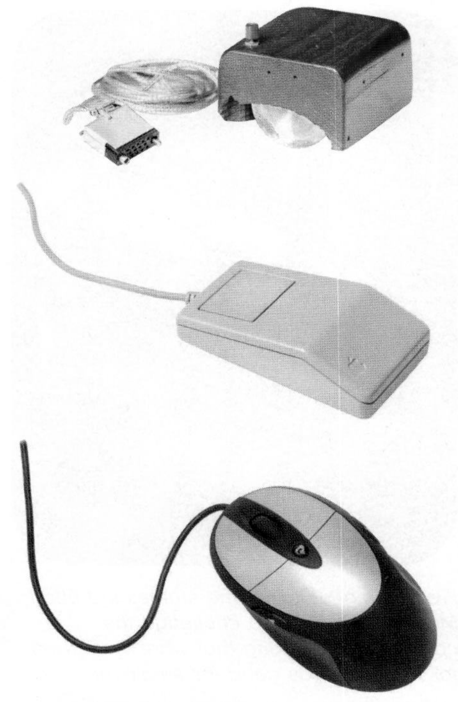

**FIGURE 1 Building a Better Mouse** The figure shows the evolution of the computer mouse from its wooden-box beginnings (*first*) to its later, sleeker forms (*second, third*). The evolution has continued with the development of the touchpad or trackpad (*fourth*)—a built-in mouse substitute in laptop computers. The mouse and the touchpad are tools that many of us take for granted, but they are the product of design decisions that have improved their utility and efficiency.
(first) ©Apic/Getty Images; (second) ©Nor Gal/Shutterstock; (third) ©Brand X Pictures/Getty Images; (fourth) ©goldy/Getty Images

## Ergonomics: Where Psychology Meets Engineering

Many occupations involve the interaction of humans with tools. Whether the tools are computers or hand-press drills, many people earn a living by working with the help of machines. Understanding and enhancing the safety and efficiency of the human-machine interaction is the central focus of **ergonomics**, also called **human factors**, a field that combines engineering and psychology to improve the fit between tools and the human body (Thatcher & others, 2018; Visser & others, 2018). Desks, chairs, switches, buttons—all of the objects people use every day—are the product of design decisions aimed at promoting efficiency and safety on the job.

Ergonomic specialists represent a range of expertise, from perception, attention, and cognition experts (people who have good ideas about the placement of buttons on a control panel), to learning psychologists (people who design training programs for the use of machines), to social and environmental researchers (people who address issues such as living in a constrained environment like that of the space shuttle). To appreciate the role of ergonomics in daily life, see Figure 1, which shows how the design of something as common as the computer mouse reflects expert attention to the human-machine relationship.

Scientific management and ergonomics focus on efficiency and safety. However, from the late 1920s to the present day, a third, different approach has shaped thinking about the workplace. This third influence on I-O psychology—the historic Hawthorne studies—drew attention to the larger context of the workplace as a social environment, and to the worker as a person with feelings, motivations, and attitudes.

## The Hawthorne Studies and the Human Relations Approach

A defining moment in I-O history occurred after the end of World War I. A series of studies was conducted at the Western Electric Hawthorne Works, a plant outside Chicago, from 1927 to 1932 under the leadership of psychologist and sociologist Elton Mayo. In what are known as the Hawthorne studies, Mayo and his colleagues were initially interested in testing how various work conditions (such as room lighting, humidity, or work hours) would affect productivity. What they found surprised them: *Any change* at all increased productivity. Just being studied led workers to work harder and harder. These results led to the coining of the term **Hawthorne effect**, which refers to the tendency of people to perform better simply due to being singled out and made to feel important.

- **ergonomics or human factors** A field that combines engineering and psychology to focus on understanding and enhancing the safety and efficiency of the human–machine interaction.

- **Hawthorne effect** The tendency of individuals to perform better simply because of being singled out and made to feel important.

*His landmark Hawthorne studies led Elton Mayo (1880–1949) to challenge the conventional thinking that what was good for business was good for employees.*



Later analyses suggested that the Hawthorne results might have resulted from a variety of factors, including the beginning of the Great Depression (Franke & Kaul, 1978) or the fact that workers received feedback about their performance (Chiesa & Hobbs, 2008; Parsons, 1974) but the Hawthorne studies are landmark for persuasively showing that the workplace is a social system populated by people. When workers felt that what they did mattered to someone, they performed better.

Mayo was critical of management's obsession with efficiency and its effect on the human side of business. Emphasizing the time-and-motion aspects of a job, Mayo said, detracts from the experience of craftsmanship and the capacity of workers to identify with the products they are creating. He believed that traditional approaches to the science of work erroneously assumed that what was good for business was good for the employee. Mayo's Hawthorne studies moved researchers away from scientific management toward a *human relations approach to management.*

The **human relations approach** emphasizes the psychological characteristics of workers and managers and stresses the significance of factors such as morale, attitudes, values, and humane treatment of workers (Collings, Wood, & Szamosi, 2018). The human relations view sees the workplace as a vital social system, emphasizing positive interpersonal relations among coworkers, teamwork, leadership, job attitudes, and the social skills of managers. For this view, fulfilling work meets important human needs beyond purely economic ones.

● **human relations approach** A management approach emphasizing the psychological characteristics of workers and managers, stressing the importance of factors such as morale, attitudes, values, and humane treatment of workers.

Great places to work are sometimes highlighted in the media. It seems like everyone knows that Google (now Google/Alphabet) is an amazing organization. What makes it so great? Some of the benefits include an on-site roller hockey rink, a 7-acre sports complex, 25 different cafés, and free massages. Google also covers all health expenses and provides on-site mammograms to the 33 percent of employees who are women. Not everyone can work at Google, of course. In the following sections, as we survey the topics of interest to I-O psychologists, let's see if we can determine what makes a workplace great, including how these qualities apply to Google and other successful companies.

### *test yourself*

1. What does the managerial philosophy known as scientific management emphasize?
2. What is ergonomics, and with what aspects of the workplace is it concerned?
3. Why are the Hawthorne studies important?

## 2. INDUSTRIAL PSYCHOLOGY

Industrial psychology focuses on enhancing efficiency and productivity through the appropriate use of a firm's employees—its *human resources.* The field of industrial psychology has a four-pronged emphasis:

- *Job analysis:* Organizing and describing the tasks involved in a job
- *Employee selection:* Matching the best person to each job
- *Training:* Bringing new employees up to speed on the details of a position
- *Performance appraisal:* Evaluating whether an employee is doing a good job

Let's explore each of these aspects of industrial psychology.

### Job Analysis

**Job analysis** is the process of generating a description of what a job involves, including the knowledge and skills that are necessary to carry out the job's functions.

● **job analysis** The process of generating a description of what a job involves, including the knowledge and skills that are necessary to carry out the job's functions.

An effective job analysis includes three elements (Brannick, Cadle, & Levine, 2012; Landau & Rohmert, 2017). First, the analysis must follow a systematic procedure that is set up in advance. Second, it must break down the job into small units so that each aspect can be easily understood. Third, the analysis should lead to an employee manual that accurately characterizes the job.

A job analysis can focus on the job itself or on the attributes of a person who is suited for the job (Robinson-Morral & others, 2018; Sackett & others, 2016). A job-oriented analysis outlines what the job entails (say, analyzing scientific data) and what it requires (like, expertise with statistics software). A person-oriented job analysis gives what are often called **KSAOs** (or **KSAs**). The acronym stands for *k*nowledge, *s*kills, *a*bilities, and *o*ther characteristics. Knowledge refers to what the person needs to know to do the job. Skills are what the individual must be able to do. Abilities include the person's capacity to learn the job and to gain new skills. Other characteristics may also be important. For a child-care worker, for instance, the ability to chase energetic toddlers may be required.

*Enthusiasm can be an important job qualification. Patagonia seeks to hire people who are passionate climbers and hikers.*



Increasingly, employers focus on the *competencies* that are central to a job. Competencies refer to a person's capacity to put the KSAOs into action and apply them effectively in the workplace. Competencies refer not only to what a person *can do,* but to what he or she *will do* on the job (Nixon & Braithwaite, 2018; van Vianen, 2018).

Creating a job analysis typically involves collecting information from a variety of informants, including job analysts, people who already have the job, supervisors, and trained observers. These people may be asked to complete a questionnaire about the importance of various skills to a job, or they might be directed to describe the essential elements of the job in an interview.

● **KSAOs or KSAs** Common elements in a person-oriented job analysis; an acronym for **k**nowledge, **s**kills, **a**bilities, and **o**ther characteristics.

Job analyses establish a foundation for other aspects of personnel decision making. A thorough job analysis can provide information that directs hiring decisions and performance evaluations. Quite simply, a manager cannot select the right person for the job or evaluate job performance without knowing what the job formally requires. In addition, job analyses can guide training and provide information to I-O researchers who are interested in examining how aspects of jobs relate to outcomes, such as productivity, absenteeism, and work stress.

A job analysis is also important in the legal realm. The KSAOs mentioned in a job analysis must be clearly relevant to the specific job. Some job attributes have caused controversy–for example, should height and physical fitness be considered job-relevant characteristics for police officers? The requirement of such attributes historically has excluded some women and others of shorter stature from police duty, and the courts have struck down many such requirements.

A thorough job analysis should accurately describe the essential and nonessential functions of a job. *Essential functions* are the fundamental, necessary duties of a job as defined by the employer, usually in writing. For example, a child-care worker must be capable of being physically active, and a data analyst must be able to use advanced statistical techniques. *Nonessential functions* are aspects of the job that are desirable but not necessary. For example, a pizza delivery person must have a valid driver's license, but driving is not essential for a kitchen worker at the pizza shop. The difference between essential and nonessential job functions is important in the context of workers with disabilities.

The Americans with Disabilities Act (ADA) of 1990 (see Figure 2) determines what qualifies as fair treatment for a person with a disability. The ADA made it illegal to refuse employment or promotion to a person with a disability based on *nonessential* job functions (Chi & others, 2018). According to the ADA, a person with a disability is qualified for a position if he or she is able to perform the *essential* job functions, with or without reasonable accommodations. Accommodations may include changes in

**FIGURE 2 Excerpts from the Americans with Disabilities Act of 1990, Title I** Passed in 1990, the Americans with Disabilities Act forbids discrimination in the workplace based on disability or illness.
Source: The Americans with Disabilities Act (ADA) of 1990.

*No (employer) shall discriminate against a qualified individual with a disability because of the disability of such individual in regard to job application procedures, the hiring, advancement, or discharge of employees, employee compensation, job training, and other terms, conditions, and privileges of employment.*

. . . [T]he term "discriminate" includes

1. limiting, segregating, or classifying a job applicant or employee in a way that adversely affects the opportunities or status of such applicant or employee because of (his or her) disability . . . ;

2. utilizing standards, criteria, or methods of administration that have the effect of discrimination on the basis of disability; or that perpetuate the discrimination of others . . . ;

3. excluding or otherwise denying equal jobs or benefits to a qualified individual because of the known disability of an individual with whom the qualified individual is known to have a relationship or association;

4. not making reasonable accommodations to the known physical or mental limitations of an otherwise qualified individual with a disability who is an applicant or employee, unless such (employer) can demonstrate that the accommodation would impose an undue hardship . . . ;

5. using qualification standards, employment tests or other selection criteria that screen out or tend to screen out an individual with a disability . . . unless the standard, test or other selection criteria, as used by the covered entity, is shown to be job-related for the position in question and is consistent with business necessity; and

6. failing to select and administer tests concerning employment in the most effective manner to ensure that, when such test is administered to a job applicant or employee who has a disability that impairs sensory, manual, or speaking skills, such test results accurately reflect the skills, aptitude, or whatever other factor of such applicant or employee that such test purports to measure, rather than reflecting the impaired sensory, manual, or speaking skills of (the individual). . . .

The term "qualified individual with a disability" means an individual with a disability who, with or without reasonable accommodation, can perform the essential functions of the employment position that such individual holds or desires. . . . [I]f an employer has prepared a written description before advertising or interviewing applicants for the job, this description shall be considered evidence of the essential functions of the job.

facilities, equipment, or policies that permit an otherwise qualified individual with disabilities to perform the essential functions of a job. An accommodation is considered reasonable–and is required–if it effectively allows the person to perform the essential job tasks while not placing undue burden on the employer. Most importantly, *nonessential* functions cannot be used as grounds for not hiring a person with a disability. Such regulations promote fairness and help to diversify the workforce, bringing many unique perspectives to bear on an organization's goals (Burke & Welbes, 2018; Follmer & Jones, 2018).

An accurate job analysis increases the likelihood that people will feel they have been treated fairly in hiring and promotion decisions (Chun, Brockner, & De Cremer, 2018; Reynolds & Helfers, 2018). For example, an employee who is very shy may understand being turned down for a promotion if the job analysis for the position clearly indicates that it requires an active leadership style.

A job analysis is more formal and exact than a job description, which is generally of interest to job seekers. Job descriptions allow people to evaluate their interest in a particular occupation. The U.S. Department of Labor has produced a huge online database called O*NET (www.onetonline.org/) that compiles job descriptions for thousands of occupations. The descriptions are based on authoritative ratings and interviews with experts in the various occupations, and new occupations are added frequently. The site can be searched for jobs by various categories and requirements, such as whether they are "green" occupations and what their growth rate is expected to be in the coming years. Figure 3 presents the descriptions from the U.S. Department of Labor for the jobs of

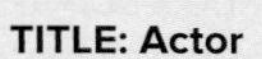

**TITLE: Actor**
Portrays role in dramatic production to interpret character or present characterization to audience: Rehearses part to learn lines and cues as directed. Interprets serious or comic role by speech, gesture, and body movement to entertain or inform audience for stage, motion picture, television, radio, or other media production. May write or adapt own material. May dance and sing. May direct self and others in production. May read from script or book, utilizing minimum number of stage properties and relying mainly on changes of voice and inflection to hold audience's attention and be designated Dramatic Reader.

**TITLE: Predatory-Animal Hunter**
Hunts, traps, and kills predatory animals to collect bounty: Hunts quarry using dogs, and shoots animals. Traps or poisons animals depending on environs and habits of animals sought. Removes designated parts, such as ears or tail from slain animals, using knife, to present as evidence of kill for bounty. May skin animals and treat pelts for marketing. May train dogs for hunting. May be designated according to animal hunted as Cougar Hunter; Coyote Hunter; Wolf Hunter.

**TITLE: Personal Shopper**
Selects and purchases merchandise for department store customers, according to mail or telephone requests. Visits wholesale establishments or other department stores to purchase merchandise which is out-of-stock or which store does not carry. Records and processes mail orders and merchandise returned for exchange. May escort customer through store.

**FIGURE 3** **Sample Job Descriptions** Do you aspire to a career as an actor, a predatory-animal hunter, or a personal shopper? If so, the description reproduced here from the U.S. Department of Labor's *Dictionary of Occupational Titles* will give you a distinct flavor of the job and its day-to-day responsibilities. Source: U.S. Department of Labor's Dictionary of Occupational Titles; (first photo) ©Pictorial Press Ltd/Alamy Stock Photo; (second photo) ©PressLab/Shutterstock; (third photo) ©Mike Watson Images/Alamy Stock Photo

actor, predatory-animal hunter, and personal shopper. Unlike job analysis, a job description often has information about expected pay range.

Are you good at memorization? Does "removing designated parts" of an animal sound interesting to you? How about "escorting a customer through a store"? Job descriptions may be a first step for job seekers interested in finding a good match to their interests and skills.

According to O*NET, the occupations in the United States that are expected to grow fastest through 2026 are solar photovoltaic installer (individual who assembles and installs solar panels on roofs), wind turbine technician, and home health aide. The Psychological Inquiry shows the relevant data and the percentage increase in other fast-growing jobs.

## Employee Selection

Managers must select the best candidates from among the pool of recruits. That pool can be huge. Google/Alphabet gets over 2 million job applicants a year, from all over the world.

## psychological *inquiry*

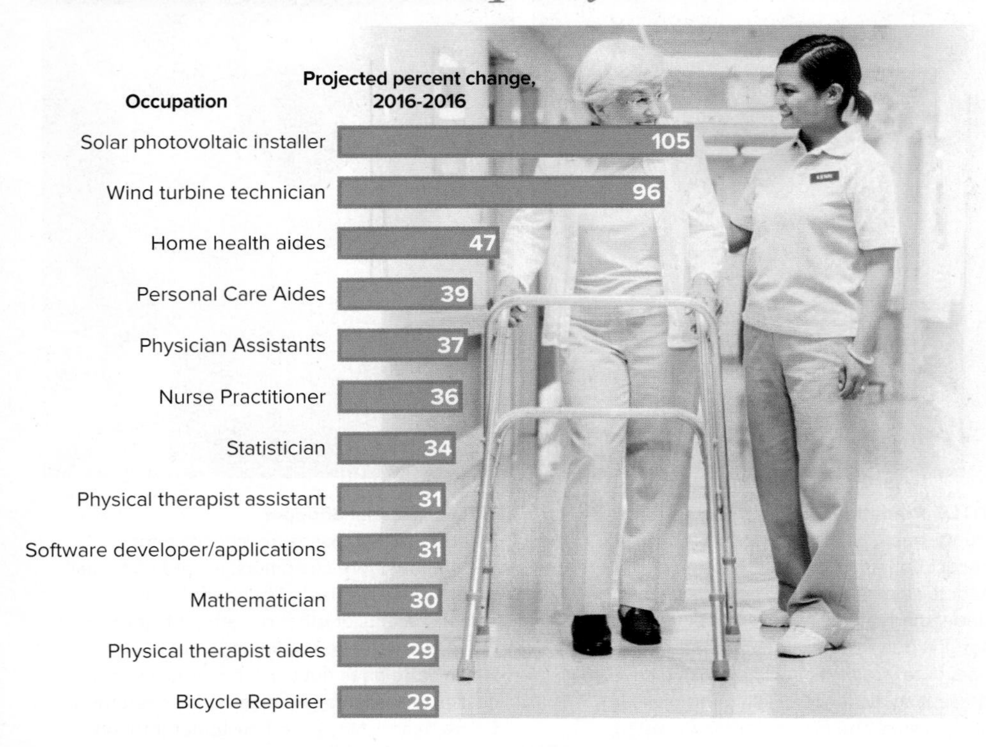


Source: Bureau of Labor Statistics (April 13, 2018); (photo) ©Andersen Ross/Getty Images

### *The Fastest-Growing Jobs in the United States*

This figure presents the projected percentage change in demand for the fastest-growing jobs in the United States from 2016 to 2026 (Bureau of Labor Statistics, 2018). The jobs listed had differing 2017 wages. For solar photovoltaic installers, the median income is $39,490, while for physician's assistants and nurse practitioners the median is just over $100,000. The median income for statisticians is $84,900. Notice how many of these jobs represent health and environmental interests. Try your hand at answering the questions below.

1. Which of the listed occupations in the figure has the lowest projected growth?
2. Consider the pay that is described above (photovoltaic installers, physician assistants, nurse practitioners, and statisticians) for each of these occupations. What does the median mean? What percentage of statisticians make more than $84,900? Do you think the wages are appropriate for each occupation? Why or why not?
3. Imagine how this list might differ from similar lists compiled 20 years ago. Which careers do you think are the newest arrivals? Why?
4. Many of the fastest-growing jobs relate to a Green Economy and sustainability. What do these data tell you about U.S. society today and in the coming years?

Where do qualified applicants come from? An analysis of 50 different companies who filled more than 500,000 positions in 2013 identified how those companies found new hires. Figure 4 shows some of the results. Clearly, the most common way for companies to fill new positions was to hire from within. For new outsiders, *referrals* were the most popular way that candidates ended up landing jobs (Crispin & Mehler, 2014). A referral means that a potential candidate was identified through current or former employees' social networks. If the candidate is ultimately hired, the referring employee may receive a bonus (Burks & others, 2015; Derfler-Rozin, Baker, & Gino, 2018).

How powerful are referrals in leading to hires? Referred candidates had a one in five chance of being hired—pretty good odds in a tough job market. Many employers rely on referrals. For example, Wegmans Food Markets appear regularly on lists of best places to work. At Wegmans, one in five employees have family members who also are employed by the company.

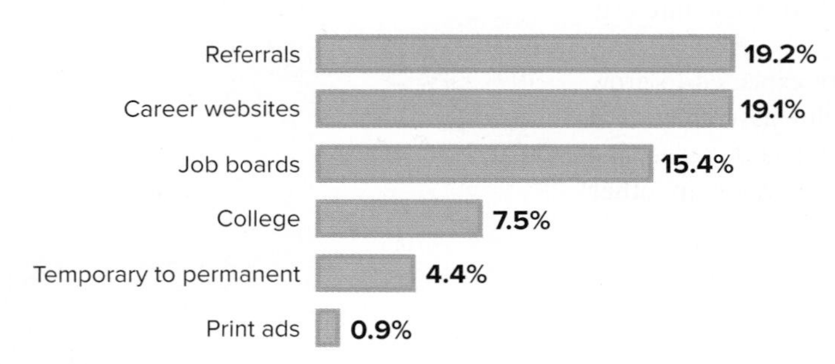


**FIGURE 4** **How Did New Hires Get Their Foot in the Door?** This figure shows the results of a 2013 survey of 50 companies reporting where their new hires came from. How might these figures influence your next job search? Source: Adapted from Crispin & Mehler (2014).

Employers also use online sites like Monster.com and Indeed.com (Darnold & Rynes, 2013). Another online resource for employers are *job boards,* websites that employers develop and use to advertise openings (Ajunwa & Greene, 2018; Hellester, Kuhn, & Shen, 2018). Social media increasingly play a role in recruiting and hiring (Waite & Morote, 2018). It is important for job seekers to show maturity and good sense in their online presence. College students may also encounter prospective employers at job fairs held on campus (Minifie, Bell, & Zhang, 2018). Preparing for these meetings can help job applicants make the best possible impression on interviewers (Hamilton & Davison, 2018).

Industrial psychologists have played a significant role in developing techniques for selecting people and placing them in positions that match their strengths. Based on a job analysis, the KSAOs necessary for a particular job should be clear. The next step is to measure the KSAOs of the recruits in order to evaluate their appropriateness for a position. These measures include testing and interviews, as well as work samples and exercises.

## TESTING

Managers or human resource personnel may administer tests to applicants to find out if they are good matches for a position (Evers, Anderson, & Voskuijl, 2017). Organizations use psychological tests that assess factors such as personality traits and motivation. An **integrity test** is designed to assess whether the candidate is likely to be honest on the job (Billings & Dages, 2018; Minifie, Bell, & Zhang, 2018). An *overt integrity test* contains items that ask the individual to give his or her attitude about lying. A sample item might be "It's okay to lie if you know you won't get caught."

● **integrity test** A type of job-screening examination that is designed to assess whether a candidate will be honest on the job.

Not surprisingly, most employers hope to hire conscientious employees who will treat others with respect and be highly motivated to excel at work. Employers also want workers who will be honest, not steal from the workplace, or engage in cheating. However, a key drawback with the use of tests to screen individuals for these characteristics is that people can provide fake answers to make a good impression. A number of strategies have been devised to overcome this problem (Meade & others, 2018; Pelt, van der Linden, & Born, 2018).

Many employers are increasingly interested in a person's adaptability (Kim & Ployhart, 2018; Oprins, Bosch, & Venrooij, 2018). Adaptable people are effective, creative problem solvers even when unanticipated obstacles arise. Employers want to hire people who are flexible and able to handle change. Adaptable workers are able to work with people who are different from them, to work effectively in changing contexts, and to deal calmly with emergencies and crises (Sony & Mekoth, 2016).

How do employers assess a candidate's adaptability? They might use a situational judgment test. A **situational judgment test** presents a job candidate with realistic, hypothetical scenarios and asks the individual to identify the most appropriate response (Caponecchia, Zheng, & Regan, 2018; Lievens & others, 2018; Weng & others, 2018). As the name implies, these tests ask people to describe how they would handle different circumstances. These tests assess not just knowledge and skill but competencies–how the applicant uses their knowledge and skills effectively. Situational judgment tests are less obvious than some other methods of testing and therefore may be less susceptible to faking.

● **situational judgment test** A type of job-screening examination that presents job candidates with realistic, hypothetical scenarios and asks them to identify the most appropriate response.

Perhaps the strongest predictor of success at a job is general intelligence (Ones, Viswesvaran, & Dilchert, 2017; Van Iddekinge & others, 2018). As described in the chapter "Thinking, Intelligence, and Language", **intelligence** represents an all-purpose ability to learn new skills and perform well on many cognitive tasks. Employers of all kinds are interested in finding out whether applicants have the cognitive ability to succeed in a position. An IQ (called the Wonderlic test) is even given to professional football players.

● **intelligence** An all-purpose ability to do well on cognitive tasks, to solve problems, and to learn from experience.

A problem for employers is that intelligence tests may be biased against individuals from different sociocultural backgrounds (te Nijenhuis & others, 2016). These biases leave employers open to legal action if the tests they use exclude people who are well qualified for a job but do not perform well on the test.

## INTERVIEWS

Perhaps the most common way that job candidates are evaluated is through an interview (Buehl & others, 2018). An interview is, of course, a conversation between two (or more) people. Interviewers and interviewees have different goals. The interviewer wants to find the best person for a position. The interviewee wants to get the job. Balancing these two goals is one of the reasons effective interviewing can be a challenge.

Imagine interviewing for your dream job–to be a high school English teacher. During the interview, the school principal asks if you might also be able to teach history or coach the volleyball team. If you really want the job, it might not seem like a stretch to say, "Yes, I might be able to do those things" (if only you had taken even a single college history class or paid better attention to last summer's Olympic Games). Certainly, job candidates try to put their best foot forward and refrain from revealing their failings (Buehl & others, 2018; Swider, Barrick, & Harris, 2016). *Interviewer illusion* refers to interviewers' mistaken belief in their own ability to tell if a job applicant is being truthful (Nisbett, 1987).

Interviewers must also separate irrelevant factors from those that matter to the job. During an interview, a person may display a lot of different qualities, not all of which are relevant to the position in question. Interviews reveal not only whether a person is qualified for a job but also aspects of their personality, interview skills, and general cognitive ability (Caldwell, Beverage, & Converse, 2018). Interviewers can be affected by factors such as whether the person has a firm handshake (Stewart & others, 2008) and the ease with which the candidate establishes rapport with the interviewer (Barrick, Swider, & Stewart, 2010). Although social skills are important in life in general, they are not necessarily important for every job. Certainly, for interviews to serve their purpose, they must be about more than simply whether the interviewer likes the candidate. The interviewer must focus on qualities that directly relate to the job.

As we saw in the chapter "Social Psychology", first impressions are made very rapidly. This first impression may have nothing to do with a person's ability, for example, to program a computer or to develop a new drug. First impressions can also be subject to gender and ethnic biases, and since the Civil Rights Act of 1964 (revised in 1991), it has been illegal in the United States to deny someone employment on the basis of gender or ethnicity. Although first impressions can influence even highly structured interviews, their influence fades as the interview progresses (Barrick, Swider, & Stewart, 2016). This means that all candidates should be given the same amount of time for an interview and the same opportunity to demonstrate their relevant skills. Figure 5 lists the provisions of the Civil Rights Act that set the standards for fair personnel decisions in the United States.

Interviewers can improve the quality of the information they obtain by asking the same questions of all candidates. In a **structured interview**, candidates are asked specific questions that methodically seek to obtain truly useful information for the interviewer. Rather than posing the question, "Do you get along with others?" the interviewer might ask the candidate, "Can you tell me about a time when you had a conflict with someone at work and how you resolved it?" During a structured interview, interviewers take notes or record the interviews in order to avoid memory biases.

● **structured interview** A kind of interview in which candidates are asked specific questions that methodically seek to obtain truly useful information for the interviewer.

**FIGURE 5 Excerpts from the Civil Rights Act of 1964, Title VII (Revised, 1991)** The Civil Rights Act forbids discrimination based on race, national origin, sex, or religious affiliation.
Source: Civil Rights Act of 1964, Title VII (Revised, 1991)

It shall be an unlawful employment practice for an employer:

1. to fail or refuse to hire or to discharge any individual, or otherwise to discriminate against any individual with respect to his compensation, terms, conditions, or privileges of employment, because of such individual's race, color, religion, sex, or national origin;

or

2. to limit, segregate, or classify his employees or applicants for employment in any way which would deprive or tend to deprive any individual of employment opportunities or otherwise adversely affect his status as an employee, because of such individual's race, color, religion, sex, or national origin.

It shall be an unlawful employment practice for an employment agency to fail or refuse to refer for employment, or otherwise to discriminate against, any individual because of his race, color, religion, sex, or national origin, or to classify or refer for employment any individual on the basis of his race, color, religion, sex, or national origin.

It shall be an unlawful employment practice for any employer, labor organization, or joint labor-management committee controlling apprenticeship or other training or retraining, including on-the-job training programs, to discriminate against any individual because of his race, color, religion, sex, or national origin in admission to, or employment in, any program established to provide apprenticeship or other training.

Unlike unstructured interviews, structured interviews put all of the candidates on equal footing and give them all the same chance to show their stuff (Alonso, Moscoso, & Salgado, 2017). Interestingly, compared to unstructured interviews, job candidates perform better in structured interviews (Culbertson, Weyhrauch, & Huffcutt, 2017) and these interviews are also more likely to predict actual job performance (Scherbaum & others, 2018).

Recently, some organizations have moved to conducting initial interviews online, using interfaces such as *Skype*. This practice allows companies to save money on travel and to interview people from a broader geographic area. Online interview performance may differ from face-to-face interactions, however, and job seekers might wish to practice online (Bondarouk, Ruël, & Ter Harmsel, 2018).

### WORK SAMPLES AND EXERCISES

Businesses may also require applicants to submit work samples. For a job such as photographer, copywriter, or graphic designer, for instance, the candidate typically must present samples. Work samples let prospective employers see what a candidate has been able to accomplish in ways words cannot capture.

Another evaluation method requires candidates to complete mock job-related tasks that allow the direct assessment of their skills. These activities might include an "in-basket" exercise in which candidates organize and prioritize a pile of potential assignments and a "leaderless group" exercise in which prospective employees are observed in a group problem-solving task without anyone being in charge.

Clearly, the process of evaluating and selecting people for a job can be complex. For this reason, rather than relying on an internal human resources department, some organizations outsource testing to firms dedicated to evaluating the abilities of prospective employees (Kleinmann & Ingold, 2019).

*Applying for a job in fields such as graphic design and photography often requires showing a portfolio of work samples.*



## Training

You got the job! Now, what was that job again? Once a new employee is hired, the challenge facing the organization (and the new recruit) is to learn all that is necessary to carry out the job effectively. Three aspects of training are orientation, formal training, and mentoring.

### ORIENTATION

Learning the ropes of a new workplace can be difficult for new hires. To help them overcome the hurdles, most firms have a program of **orientation**, which generally involves introducing newly hired employees to the organization's goals, familiarizing them with its rules and regulations, and letting them know how to get things done. Studies show that orientation programs are effective, especially for instilling an understanding of organizational values and philosophies and socializing new employees (Sitzmann & Weinhardt, 2018).

- **orientation** A program by which an organization introduces newly hired employees to the organization's goals, familiarizes them with its rules and regulations, and lets them know how to get things done.

Some organizations use computer-based orientation programs (Jaworski & others, 2018). One study examined the implications of using computer-based versus in-person orientation programs (Wesson & Gogus, 2005). Although both methods provided new employees with information, the computer-based orientation fell short on social factors. Employees who received a computer-based orientation might have learned how to work the copy machine or get a computer repaired, but they probably did not come away with a list of their acquaintances from their orientation or a sense of the social culture of their new workplace.

### FORMAL TRAINING

**Training** involves teaching a new employee the essential requirements to do a job well. Training needs vary by occupation. The position of home health aide requires only basic on-the-job training; other positions, such as airline pilot, require extensive training.

- **training** Teaching a new employee the essential requirements to do the job well.

The foundation of any training program is to establish the goals of the training and a sense for how the trainer will know that the person is ready. An assumption of training is that whatever the employee learns in training will generalize to the real world when they start working. Training is an important function that is directly related to eventual job performance (Caloghirou & others, 2018). Research shows that sound training has a positive impact on the company's bottom line (Riley, Michael, & Mahoney, 2017).

Certainly, organizations vary with respect to the value they place on training. This difference is shown, for example, by the degree of training provided in different companies for similar jobs. Consider that trainees at the Container Store get 241 hours of training, in contrast with the 7 hours of training that is the retail-industry average.

Although we have considered training primarily in relation to beginning a new job, employee learning and the expansion of employee skills (what is called *employee development* or *management training*) are important throughout a career, for employees and firms alike. Even experts can benefit from development programs (Nerstad & others, 2018). I-O psychologists, in consultation with organizations, often develop these programs.

### MENTORING

• **mentoring** A relationship between an experienced employee—a mentor—and a novice, in which the more experienced employee serves as an advisor, a sounding board, and a source of support for the newer employee.

**Mentoring** is a relationship between an experienced employee and a novice in which the more experienced employee–the *mentor*–serves as an advisor, a sounding board, and a source of support for the newer employee. Mentoring may benefit both the employee and the organization, as mentors guide new employees through the beginning of their career and help them achieve their goals within the organization, as well as provide a strong interpersonal bond.

Some organizations assign individuals to mentors. Assigned mentors may not be as effective as those that emerge naturally–and having an incompetent mentor may be worse than having no mentor at all (Menges, 2016; Ragins, Cotton, & Miller, 2000). "Natural" mentoring relationships, however, may be based on common interests and other similarities and as such may be less likely to develop for women and for members of ethnic minorities in fields that are dominated by European American men. In such situations, assigned mentors who are sensitive and open and who have time to devote to new protégés are especially important. At a minimum, coworkers who differ in every other way share one common bond: the organization (Illies & Reiter-Palmon, 2018).

## Performance Appraisal

• **performance appraisal** The evaluation of a person's success at meeting his or her organization's goals.

Industrial psychologists are also interested in **performance appraisal**, the evaluation of a person's success at meeting their organization's goals.

Performance appraisal is important. It allows employees to get feedback and make appropriate changes in their work habits. It also guides decisions about promotions and raises, as well as terminations (firings). Regular performance appraisals provide a paper trail, justifying promotion and termination decisions. Within the U.S. government, for example, firing must be performance based. This requirement means that before a government employer can terminate someone, there must be documented evidence of poor performance. In Canada, this regulation applies to private businesses as well.

In some occupations, objective measures can be used to gauge performance. These might include the number of products a factory worker makes per hour, the dollar amount of sales by a sales representative, the number of days late to work, the number of legal cases won, and the number of surgeries performed. Of course, not all jobs provide such measurable output. Also, it may not be clear what a "high number" is: How high would the number have to be in order to be "good"? Simple counts, taken out of context, may not be informative. For example, consider a sales agent with a very challenging territory who sets a selling record for that territory even though her sales fall below the average of other representatives who are assigned to less difficult areas.

Finally, focusing on objective counts may miss the quality of a person's work. For these reasons, many performance evaluations, while including an assessment of objective numbers, also entail subjective ratings made by a supervisor or panel of experts. These ratings typically involve multiple items that are meant to assess different aspects of performance, such as work quality and efficiency.

## FACTORS PREDICTING PERFORMANCE APPRAISALS

Much research in I-O psychology examines predictors of performance appraisals. Work performance is related to deep knowledge and experience at a job, but the strongest predictor of work performance among the many different qualities studied is general cognitive ability (De Kock & others, 2018; Schmidt, Beck, & Gillespie, 2013). One meta-analysis summarizing 22,000 studies showed that general cognitive ability predicted job performance across a variety of jobs, situations, and organizations (Ones, Viswesvaran, & Dilchert, 2017).

Other characteristics that have been examined as predictors of job performance are called *psychological capital*. Psychological capital includes positive qualities such as self-efficacy, optimism, hope, and resilience, which serve as important resources in the workplace. These attributes predict increased employee performance (Allessandri & others, 2018) and decreased work absences (Ozturk & Karatepe, 2018). The psychological capital approach has been applied in various organizational settings including manufacturing, education, and the military.

Recall from the chapter "Personality" that self-efficacy is the belief that one has the ability to take on a particular task or goal and see it through. A great deal of research supports the relationship between self-efficacy and success in a variety of settings (de Haan & others, 2013; Fu & others, 2010; Laguna, 2013; Tay, Ang, Van Dyne, 2006). Self-efficacy is thought to enhance effort and activity that are needed to achieve difficult goals in the workplace (De Clercq, Haq, & Azeem, 2018; Schmidt, Beck, & Gillespie, 2013).

## SOURCES OF BIAS IN PERFORMANCE APPRAISALS

Factors other than work quality can influence a performance evaluation. Supervisors are human, and in evaluating the work of others, they are engaged in a social process. They have expectations and look for confirming information. As subjective judgments, performance appraisals can be prone to biases and errors.

A common error in performance appraisals is the **halo effect**. This effect occurs when a rater gives an employee the same rating on all of the items being evaluated, even though the individual varies across the dimensions being assessed. In making halo effect errors, the rater allows his or her general impression of the person to guide the ratings (Tziner & Rabenu, 2018). So, for example, the supervisor might give someone a 9 on a 1-to-10 scale for all assessment items, even though the employee's work quality was a 9 but his efficiency was closer to a 5.

● **halo effect** A bias, common in performance appraisals, that occurs when a rater gives an employee the same rating on all of the items being evaluated, even though the individual varies across the dimensions being assessed.

● **360-degree feedback** A method of performance appraisal whereby an employee's performance is rated by a variety of individuals, including himself or herself, a peer, a supervisor, a subordinate, and perhaps a customer or client.

## 360-DEGREE FEEDBACK

A way to improve the validity of performance evaluations is to collect feedback from a variety of sources. To this end, appraisers use a method called 360-degree feedback. In **360-degree feedback** an employee's performance is rated by a variety of people, including himself or herself, a peer, a supervisor, a subordinate, and perhaps a customer or client. Although there is some agreement among the different raters using the 360-degree feedback process, there is also more likely to be variability, suggesting that ratings are indeed about the person's performance and not a general impression (Cormack & others, 2018; Karkoulian, Assaker, & Hallak, 2016).

Web-based evaluation systems have simplified the logistics of the 360-degree feedback approach, illustrated in Figure 6. Recently, in response to a variety of scandals in its highest ranks, the U.S. military adopted the 360-degree feedback approach, incorporating lower-level officers in evaluations of high-ranking individuals.

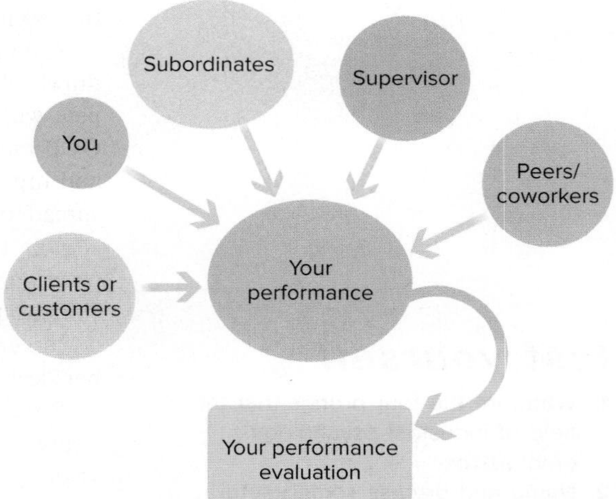


**FIGURE 6** **360-Degree Feedback** 360-degree feedback means that everyone who is affected by your work has some input in evaluating your performance.
Source: Cormack & others (2018); Karkoulian, Assaker, & Hallak (2016).

## THE IMPORTANCE OF FAIRNESS

A performance appraisal can be stressful for both the evaluator(s) and the evaluated employee. Few people relish telling someone that her work has been rated poorly, and the temptation might be to send off the evaluation by e-mail. Talking about evaluations face-to-face is vital to perceptions of fair treatment. Sitting down with a supervisor and openly discussing the evaluation enhances feelings of fairness in the process, even when the ratings are poor (Harrington & Lee, 2015; Tziner & Rabenu, 2018). A person who has received a negative performance review should be given a chance to do better in the future (Dahlin, Chuang, & Roulet, 2018). Organizations might offer counseling or developmental opportunities to poorly performing employees.

Performance evaluation systems must not discriminate based on gender or ethnicity. In order to enhance the legal defensibility of a termination decision, a job analysis should define the dimensions that will be used in the performance appraisal; the raters should be trained; employees should have a chance to appeal the ratings; and the organization should meticulously document performance (Barrett & Kernan, 1987).

The experience of being fired from a job can be economically and emotionally devastating (Anusic, Yap, & Lucas, 2014; Denissen & others, 2018). People who feel they have been treated unfairly may take legal action. The use of multiple raters in performance evaluations is associated with greater success in defending firing decisions in court (Werner & Bolino, 1997).

## ORGANIZATIONAL CITIZENSHIP BEHAVIOR

● **organizational citizenship behavior (OCB)** Discretionary actions on the part of an employee that promote organizational effectiveness but are not included in the person's formal responsibilities.

One type of behavior that may not find its way into a performance evaluation is **organizational citizenship behavior (OCB)**—discretionary actions on an employee's part that promote organizational effectiveness but are not included in the person's formal responsibilities (Organ, 2018; Podsakoff, MacKenzie, & Podsakoff, 2018). OCB includes behaviors such as coming in early, staying late, and helping a colleague with an assignment. Conscientiousness is associated with higher levels of OCB, yet even those low on conscientiousness engage in OCB when they are especially happy at their jobs (Klotz & others, 2018).

OCB is thought to influence organizations in two ways. First, it may directly impact productivity and economic success (Meynhardt, Brieger, & Hermann, 2018). Second, OCB may have a more general influence on the social system of the workplace, making fellow employees feel more positive about their jobs (Marinova, Cao, & Park, 2018; Organ, 2018). As such, OCB occupies the middle ground in I-O psychology, influencing both the efficiency and profitability of business (the "I" side) and the wider social climate of the organization (the "O" side).

Although OCB is certainly associated with many positive outcomes, it may have its drawbacks. OCB may appear to be altruistic but it might be engaged in as a way to compete with others or to get ahead in an organization (Lemmon & Wayne, 2015). Also, if OCB interferes with completing one's actual job duties, it can take a toll on performance and organizational success. Finally, individuals who engage in OCB may find themselves spread too thin and exhausted (Gabriel & others, 2018; Klotz & others, 2018; Organ, 2018).

One thing that influences the effects of OCB is the wider social context of the organization. Is showing up for work early every day an example of OCB, or is it simply "kissing up" (Eastman, 1994) or playing office politics (Snell & Wong, 2007)? Did your coworker text you that reminder at 5 A.M. to be helpful or to point out that she was at her desk working while you were still asleep?

Research shows that responses to OCB can depend on the quality of a supervisor in a given organization (Schyns & Schilling, 2013; Tepper & others, 2004). When a supervisor is prone to hostile behaviors, emotional outbursts, public criticism, or sarcastic comments, even apparently kind behavior can have a negative effect on the job satisfaction of coworkers. With a hostile supervisor, OCB might raise suspicions among coworkers. As such, the meaning of a behavior may differ depending on its organizational context. That context is the domain of organizational psychology.

### test yourself

1. What are the four prongs that the field of industrial psychology emphasizes?
2. Name and discuss some useful functions of job analyses.
3. Identify and define the three key aspects of job training.

# 3. ORGANIZATIONAL PSYCHOLOGY

As we have seen, industrial psychology, the "I" in I-O, introduced the idea of human resources. Now, let's turn to its "O" counterpart, organizational psychology, which focuses on research and practice involving human relations (Kozlowski, Mak, & Chao, 2016; Latham, 2019; Pulakos, Mueller-Hanson, & Arad, 2019).

Organizational psychology emphasizes the psychological experiences of work. It examines how the relationships among people at work influence their job satisfaction and commitment, as well as their efficiency and productivity. Although it may seem reasonable to expect companies to concentrate on "the bottom line," focusing exclusively on the economic results of work may not always be the best way to do business. As the following discussion reveals, other factors also matter, including management approaches, job satisfaction, employee commitment, the meaning of work, and leadership styles.

## Approaches to Management

Managers are in a position of power in an organization. They make decisions about personnel, direct activities, and ensure that the staff does the work correctly and on time. A manager's approach to this role can have widespread impact on organizational success as well as on employees' lives (Fallatah & Laschinger, 2016; Trus & others, 2018). To appreciate the importance of management styles to business, we first consider the historic contrast between American and Japanese automakers.

● **Theory X managers** Managers who assume that work is innately unpleasant and that people have a strong desire to avoid it; such managers believe that employees need direction, dislike responsibility, and must be kept in line.

### THE "JAPANESE" MANAGEMENT STYLE

In the 1980s, as the U.S. car industry noted of the rising dominance of Japanese cars in the U.S. market, Japanese management principles became popular. U.S. automakers adopted the so-called Japanese principles of quality control and worker participation in organizational decision making. Interestingly, an American engineer and statistician, W. Edwards Deming, originally suggested these principles that became famous as the Japanese style.

In the 1940s, Deming developed ideas about management that focused on quality; indeed, he has been called the father of the quality revolution. His philosophy of management was not well received in the United States, however, as American industry was wedded to scientific management with its emphases on efficiency and the bottom line. After World War II, Deming played a large role in the successful rebuilding of the Japanese economy, particularly the car industry.

Deming had a lot to say about management. One of his key points was that industry must embrace innovation and plan for the future, not remain narrowly focused on economic results. He compared the results-oriented management of the typical U.S. factory to driving a car with our eyes fixed on the rearview mirror (Deming, 1986). Results, he stressed, tell us about past performance–how we did. What concerned Deming, however, was what we are going to do *next.* Deming called upon industry to make a long-term commitment to having an eye always trained on the future. He emphasized innovation and a managerial style that takes risks, makes decisions based on quality, and fosters strong relationships with suppliers, employees, and customers.

The contrast between Frederick Taylor's approach to scientific management and Deming's innovation-oriented thinking can also be seen in other psychological approaches to management styles, as we now consider.

*So great were the contributions of American statistician W. Edwards Deming (1900–1993) in the recovery of the Japanese economy after World War II that the prime minister of Japan, on behalf of Emperor Hirohito, honored him with the Order of the Sacred Treasures, second class, in 1960.*



### THEORY X AND THEORY Y

In his book *The Human Side of Enterprise,* Douglas McGregor (1960) identified two general approaches to management, which he termed Theory X and Theory Y. **Theory X managers** assume that work is innately unpleasant and that people have a strong desire to avoid it. Such managers believe that employees need direction, dislike responsibility, and must be kept in line. Theory X managers motivate workers by exerting control and threatening punishment.

**Theory Y managers** Managers who assume that engaging in effortful behavior is natural to human beings; they recognize that people seek out responsibility and that motivation can come from allowing employees to suggest creative and meaningful solutions.

In contrast, **Theory Y managers**, those with the outlook that McGregor advocated, assume that engaging in effortful behavior is natural to human beings–that even at play, people often work hard. Theory Y managers recognize that people seek out responsibility and that motivation can come from allowing employees to suggest creative and meaningful solutions to problems. These managers assume that people have untapped creative and intellectual potential that can benefit the organization.

Though nearly 60 years have passed since his book was published, McGregor's distinction between the two managerial styles remain a source of inspiration, particularly for practitioners in I-O psychology who consult with organizations to enhance managerial effectiveness.

## STRENGTHS-BASED MANAGEMENT

**strengths-based management** A management style emphasizing that maximizing an employee's existing strengths is much easier than trying to build such attributes from the ground up.

Donald Clifton, a former CEO of the Gallup polling organization, emphasized the vast potential of employees. Similar to Theory Y managers, Clifton stressed that managers need to identify and make use of their employees' strengths. Clifton's **strengths-based management** emphasized that maximizing an employee's existing strengths is a much easier proposition than trying to build such attributes from the ground up. By "strength" Clifton meant the consistent ability to attain a near-perfect performance on a given task (Clifton & Nelson, 1995; Hodges & Clifton, 2004). To develop worker strengths, a manager must recognize that each person has unique talents and that discovering these and putting them to use is crucial not only to an effective organization but also to the worker's sense of fulfillment (Kong & Ho, 2016).

Focusing on employee strengths can have a powerful influence on profits. A study of 65 organizations found that only 4 were taking a strengths-based approach (Clifton & Harter, 2003). Unlike the other 61, those 4 showed an increase in productivity equal to $1,000 per employee. In real-money terms, that translates into about $5.4 million for the average company. The various management styles are summarized in Figure 7.

Managers are important because they strongly influence how people feel at work. A dream job can be ruined by a lousy manager. Or a great manager might make a boring job seem important and worthwhile. How people feel about their occupations is another topic that interests I-O psychologists.

| Approach | Theorist | Manager's Mission | Manager's Problem-Solving Strategy | Manager's Focus When Things Are Going Well |
|---|---|---|---|---|
| "Japanese" style | Deming | Focus on the future, always seeking innovation and high quality. Forge strong relationships with people in every aspect of the organization. | Take risks, think about the future, and try something new. | Keep looking to the future, to potential innovation, and to risks. |
| Theory X | McGregor | Control employees, enforce rules, and make sure everyone is working hard. Keep the ship afloat. | Punish employees who fail. | Reward employees who succeed, and don't rock the boat. |
| Theory Y | McGregor | Challenge employees with responsibility; let them apply their talents, insights, and abilities. | Look to employees for input; harness their wisdom and insight to solve the problem. | Talk to employees about their insights into success and what to do next. |
| Strengths-based | Clifton | Identify employee strengths and match employees with jobs that will maximize these. | Reexamine the fit between employee strengths and assigned tasks. | Continue to build on employee strengths. |

**FIGURE 7** **Approaches to Management** Different approaches to management can have different consequences for employees and companies. Managers vary not only in general philosophy but also in problem-solving strategies and responses to success.
Source: Clifton & Harter (2003).

## Job Satisfaction

I-O psychologists are keenly interested in people's attitudes about their jobs. **Job satisfaction** is the extent to which an individual is content in his or her job. Job satisfaction is a relatively recent idea. In the past, many people simply did whatever their parents did to earn a living. However, economic conditions and social change have allowed more individuals access to education and employment, so the question has become not only whether a job puts money in the bank and food on the table but whether an individual feels fulfilled by his or her occupation.

**job satisfaction** The extent to which a person is content in his or her job.

Job satisfaction matters to organizations. It is related to lower job turnover and absenteeism (Chen & others, 2015; Lu & others, 2016), higher organizational citizenship (Organ, 2018; Pan, 2015), and performance (Eggerth, 2015; Judge & others, 2001). The most common way to measure job satisfaction is with employee rating scales. Job satisfaction can be assessed globally, as with an item such as "How happy are you with your job, overall?" or in terms of more specific factors such as pay, work responsibilities, variety of tasks, promotional opportunities, and coworkers.

One factor that is not as strongly related to job satisfaction as you might expect is pay (Block & others, 2015; Judge & others, 2010; Yao, Locke, & Jamal, 2018). Among those who are making the minimum wage, some people are quite satisfied with their jobs. And among those who are earning a six-figure salary, some are dissatisfied. One study found that job satisfaction did not depend on the amount of money per se but rather on the person's perception that his or her pay was fair (Cohen-Charash & Spector, 2001; Paoline & others, 2018).

The amount a job pays is only modestly related to a person's level of job satisfaction. Still, job seekers might be excused for assuming that higher pay will lead to positive things in life, including the ability to buy desired items, to support one's family, to save for the future, and to experience freedom from economic worries. Given these benefits of higher income, we might wonder if a higher-paying job will lead to higher levels of well-being.

To read about the complex relationship between income and happiness, see the Critical Controversy.

Possibly it is the person, rather than the job, that matters most for job satisfaction. A 50-year longitudinal study revealed that a worker's emotional disposition was linked to job satisfaction 50 years later (Staw, Bell, & Clausen, 1986). Some individuals may simply be predisposed to be more satisfied than others. There may not be one perfect job but rather a very good but different job for each of us. Research demonstrates that the fit between the person and the job is the most important aspect of job satisfaction (Judge & Zapata, 2015; Liu, Tang, & Yang, 2015; Mateos-Romero & del Mar Salinas-Jiménez, 2018).

Job satisfaction is just one of the attitudes that I-O psychologists have probed. Another fertile area of research focuses on worker commitment, as we now consider.

Employees may be committed to their organizations based on their strong bonds with coworkers.



## Employee Commitment

By the time an employee has completed training, the organization has already dedicated a great deal of resources to the person. Clearly, it is in the organization's interest to keep the employee around. Especially during times of organizational change, understanding employee commitment is important to industry and psychologists.

I-O psychologists have examined work commitment as a key determinant of work-related outcomes (Ennis, Gong, & Okpozo, 2018; Jiang & Johnson, 2018; Seifert & others, 2016). A highly

# CRITICAL CONTROVERSY

## Are the Extremely Rich Happier than Those Who Are Very Rich?

How does money relate to happiness? The answer to this question, like so many in psychology, is "it depends." First, research shows that income does share a small positive correlation with well-being (Aknin, Wiwad, & Hanniball, 2018; Ng & Diener, 2018). In addition, people's happiness shows a small but positive increase as their income grows (Diener, Tay, & Oishi, 2013). Finally, until recently research has pointed to the conclusion that the association between income and well-being is characterized by diminishing returns. So, the positive relationship between income and happiness primarily applies to low and medium levels of income, with the relationship leveling off at about $75,000/year. Once a person makes $75,000 per year, more money no longer predicts greater happiness (Diener & Biswas-Diener, 2002; Kahneman & Deaton, 2010; Ward & King, 2019).

Importantly, however, most studies have included very few people who might be considered extremely wealthy. So, the typical study of the association between money and happiness levels may be missing action at the very, very high end on the income scale. Two recent studies (Donnelly & others, 2018) included over 4,000 millionaires to see if the very wealthy (those with net worth over $8 million) might differ from the extremely wealthy (those with net worth over $10 million). In this research, the extremely wealthy were a bit happier than their very wealthy counterparts. Interestingly, this difference depended on the source of the money. Among the extremely wealthy, those who became that way via inheritance were not happier than the very wealthy. In contrast, those who *earned* the money were happier than the very wealthy (Donnelly & others, 2018).

Of course, money does not contribute directly to well-being. Rather, how that money is spent matters most. For example, spending money on experiences (like travel or concerts) rather than on things leads to higher boosts in well-being (Gilovich, Kumar, & Jampol, 2015). However, and importantly, research shows that experiences typically cost more than objects (Lee, Hall, & Wood, 2018) and those who spend money on experiences often have more money to begin with. In addition, spending money on others (or donating to charity) instead of spending on oneself is associated with higher well-being (Aknin, Wiwad, & Hanniball, 2018).

©fokke baarssen/Shutterstock

A key source of the money we have is the work we do. Research in this area reveals one of the ways work influences well-being: by providing financial resources. Where these resources come from and how we use them may affect our happiness, profoundly.

**WHAT DO YOU THINK?**

- Why do you think inherited wealth did not predict higher happiness, compared with earned wealth?
- Do you believe that money can buy happiness? Why or why not?

---

influential framework emphasizes three types of commitment—affective, continuance, and normative—that are essential to understanding an employee's level of dedication to the workplace (Meyer, Becker, & Vandenberghe, 2004):

- **affective commitment** A kind of job commitment deriving from the employee's emotional attachment to the workplace.

- **Affective commitment** refers to the person's emotional attachment to the workplace. A person with a strong affective commitment identifies closely with the goals of the organization and wants to be a part of it. Affective commitment is associated with feelings of "we-ness," of identifying with the group that is one's workplace (Morin & others, 2016). People with strong affective commitment are loyal to an organization because they want to be. Affective commitment is thought to result in better job performance because it predicts working harder (Riketta, 2002).

- **continuance commitment** A kind of job commitment deriving from the employee's perception that leaving the organization would be too costly, both economically and socially.

- **Continuance commitment** derives from the employee's perception that leaving the organization would be too costly, both economically and socially. The person may dread the hassle of relocation or the effort that a new job search would entail. Such people might remain with an organization because of the feeling that they "have to." Continuance commitment has been shown to be either unrelated or negatively related to job performance and citizenship behaviors (Vandenberghe & Panaccio, 2015).

- **Normative commitment** is the sense of obligation an employee feels toward the organization because of the investment the organization has made in the person's personal and professional development. If an organization has subsidized a person's education, for example, the employee might feel that she owes it to her boss to stick around. Normative commitment means being committed because one feels one "ought to."

**normative commitment** A kind of job commitment deriving from the employee's sense of obligation to the organization for the investment it has made in the individual's personal and professional development.

## The Meaning of Work

Occupations define people in fundamental ways (Frieder, Wang, & Oh, 2018). People identify with their work, and the work shapes many aspects of their lives. Work is an important influence on their financial standing, leisure activities, home location, friendships, and health. One of the strongest predictors of job satisfaction is feeling that one is engaged in something meaningful or significant. In one study, individuals who were asked about the meaning associated with their work reported that contributing to the economic maintenance of one's family, having a job that allowed them to have a positive impact on the organization, and work as self-expression were important ways their work had meaning for them (Wrzesniewski, Dutton, & Debebe, 2003).

A trend in the U.S. workforce that is detrimental to job satisfaction and the meaningfulness of work is the disappearance of long-term careers for an increasing number of adults, especially men in private-sector jobs (Greenhaus & Callanan, 2013). Among the reasons for the disappearance of many long-term jobs is the dramatic rise in technology and companies' use of cheaper labor in other countries. More and more workers, both young and older adults, are working at a series of jobs, and many work in short-term jobs as part of a "gig economy" (Pfeffer, 2016). Early careers are especially unstable because some young workers move from "survival jobs" to "career jobs" as they seek one that matches their personal interests and goals (Greenhaus & Callanan, 2013).

Individuals' perspectives on their work and its place in their lives can have an impact on their job performance, their workplace, and their lives in general (Jones & George, 2007). I-O psychologist Amy Wrzesniewski and her colleagues (1997) studied 300 workers and found that their perceptions of their occupation had a substantial impact on important aspects of their work and well-being. Some described their occupation as a "job," one that involved no training and allowed no personal control and little freedom. These people tended to focus on the material benefits of work. Another group of participants identified their occupation as a "career." They saw their occupation as a steppingstone to greater advancement and accordingly focused on the attainment of better pay, promotions, and moving up the organizational ladder. A final group viewed their occupation as a "calling." They perceived the occupation as requiring a great deal of training and as involving personal control and freedom. For these individuals, work was not a means to financial ends but rather a valuable endeavor in and of itself. Indeed, some saw their occupation as their "mission in life." Importantly, all of these people were describing the same job–that of hospital maintenance worker. Other research has uncovered similar results for administrative assistants, with about equal numbers having each work orientation (Wrzesniewski, 2003).

People who view their occupation as a calling are more likely to experience work as meaningful and fulfilling. They show higher levels of life satisfaction and job satisfaction. These individuals are more likely to engage in organizational citizenship behaviors, to devote more time to work, and to miss work less often (Bartel, Wrzesniewski, & Wiesenfeld, 2007; Wrzesniewski, 2003). Those with a calling orientation also derive more satisfaction from the work domain than from hobbies or leisure activities.

You might think that those who view their work as a calling must have just gotten lucky and found the right job for themselves. Wrzesniewski (2003) argues, however, that the ability to view one's occupation as a calling is a "portable" resource that a person can take from one context to another. She uses the term **job crafting** to refer to the physical and cognitive changes individuals can make within the constraints of a task to make the work "their own." Job crafting is associated with heightened work evaluations but especially when the crafting involves extending one's responsibilities to do a bit more (rather than less) (Weseler & Niessen, 2016).

**job crafting** The physical and cognitive changes individuals can make within the constraints of a task to make the work "their own."

*I-O psychologists study the qualities of effective leaders such as Glenn "Doc" Rivers, here during one of his seasons with the Boston Celtics.*



For example, one hospital maintenance worker took it upon himself to start rotating the artwork on the walls of the hospital rooms as he cleaned them. Doing so was not part of his written job description–it was his idea for improving the quality of life for patients facing long hospital stays. Job crafting means taking advantage of the freedom one has to bring fulfillment to an occupation (Berg, Grant, & Johnson, 2010; Kim, Im, & Qu, 2018; Rai, 2018).

## Leadership

Nearly every organization has a leader. In a business it may be a CEO, on a jury it is the foreperson, and on a team it is the captain or coach. I-O psychologists are especially interested in understanding what makes an effective leader and what effect leadership characteristics have on organizations.

Leaders are not necessarily the same as managers. Even in informal groups at work, someone may be perceived as a leader regardless of his or her formal title. Furthermore, not all managers are effective leaders. A leader is a person who influences others, motivates them, and enables them to succeed. In terms of personality, a meta-analysis summarizing 94 studies of effective leadership showed that conscientiousness, extraversion, and openness to experience were the strongest personality predictors of effective leadership (Judge & others, 2002).

What leaders do, for better or worse, matters a great deal to organizational outcomes (Chen, Zhou, & Klyver, 2018; Lee, 2018; Randel & others, 2018). Leadership may be especially crucial during an internal crisis, such as when two organizations merge or when the organization reduces its workforce (Uhl-Bien & Arena, 2018). Two major types of leadership are transactional leadership and transformational leadership.

### TRANSACTIONAL LEADERSHIP

Sometimes a leader is simply "the person in charge." That is, as a leader she sees herself as responsible for running operations but not changing things. A **transactional leader** is an individual who emphasizes the exchange relationship between the worker and the leader (Northouse, 2018), applying the principle "You do a good job and I will reward you."

● **transactional leader** An individual in a leadership capacity who emphasizes the exchange relationship between the worker and the leader and who applies the principle that a good job should be rewarded.

Like a Theory X manager, a transactional leader believes that people are motivated by the rewards (or punishers) they receive for their work, and such a leader gives clear and structured directions to followers. The transactional leader works within the goals of the existing organizational system ("that's how we do it around here") and may exhibit management by exception–stepping in only when a problem arises. With regard to personality traits, transactional leaders tend to be characterized by low conscientiousness and low agreeableness (Zopiatis & Constanti, 2012).

### TRANSFORMATIONAL LEADERSHIP

While a transactional leader primarily concentrates on keeping the ship sailing, a different type of leader focuses on defining the direction of the ship. An individual with this leadership style dedicates thought to the meaning of leadership itself and to the impact she might have in improving an organization. A **transformational leader** is a dynamic individual who brings charisma, passion, and vision to the position (Northouse, 2018; Tepper & others, 2018). A transformational leader is concerned not with enforcing the rules but with changing them.

● **transformational leader** An individual in a leadership capacity who is dynamic and who brings charisma, passion, and vision to the position.

What are transformational leaders like? Research shows that transformational leaders tend to rate themselves high on conscientiousness, extraversion, and openness to experience (Zopiatis & Constanti, 2012). Transformational leaders are more likely to be happy as well (Jin, Seo, & Shapiro, 2016).

Four elements of transformational leadership have been described (Harms & Crede, 2010; Simola, Barling, & Turner, 2010):

- Transformational leaders exert idealized influence. They do what they believe is right and serve as a role model for employees.
- Transformational leaders motivate by inspiring others to do their very best.
- Transformational leaders are devoted to intellectually stimulating their employees. They make it clear that they need input from employees because they themselves do not have all the answers.
- Transformational leaders provide individualized consideration to their employees, showing a sincere concern for each person's well-being.

Transformational leaders can help people do more than they believed possible. In one study, elite UK Royal Marine recruits were more likely to make it through the challenges of boot camp if they had a transformational leader (Hardy & others, 2010). Transformational leaders can be especially inspiring for workers whose jobs do not involve a great deal of personal autonomy and freedom (Den Hartog & Belschak, 2012). One reason transformational leaders improve worker satisfaction and job attitudes is that they create opportunities for workers to fulfill the central human needs of relatedness, autonomy, and competence (Kovjanic & others, 2012).

Transformational leadership is associated with positive organizational outcomes in a wide variety of settings, from sports teams (Charbonneau, Barling, & Kelloway, 2001) to profit-oriented businesses (Barling, Weber, & Kelloway, 1996; Tikhomirov & Spangler, 2010) to the military (Hardy & others, 2010). Transformational leaders strive to foster trust in the organization, to persuade employees about the meaningfulness of their work, and finally to strengthen employees' **organizational identity**–their feelings of oneness with the organization and its goals (Böhm & others, 2015).

● **organizational identity** Employees' feelings of oneness with the organization and its goals.

Clearly, employees' lives can be affected by the qualities of their leaders. To read about the ways the mental lives of leaders relate to employee well-being, see the Intersection.

Transformational leadership is one way psychologists understand positive leadership but it may not represent all of the facets of being a positive leader. For example, Ken Lay was thought to be a transformational leader. He was an American businessman and founder and CEO of the Enron Corporation. Under his leadership, Enron engaged in illegal behaviors that led to the largest bankruptcy in history at the time (McLean & Elkind, 2004). Public scandals like Enron led psychologists to look for alternative approaches to positive leadership (Hoch & others, 2018; Weiss & others, 2018). One of the most important is called servant leadership. **Servant leadership** means putting the needs of employees, customers, and communities first (Greenleaf, 1997). The servant leader emphasizes serving others over other priorities and views him or herself as servant first, leader second. Although servant leaders share some attributes to transformational leaders, there are differences between these types of leaders (Hoch & others, 2018). Servant leaders put the needs of employees above organizational goals; transformational leaders are more likely to prioritize the organization (Gregory Stone, Russell, & Patterson 2004). Servant leaders model a service orientation. Employees are more likely to adopt a similar style in their work when they see a servant leader in action (Wang, Xu, & Liu, 2018). Importantly, when people feel that the work they do is helping others they tend to experience work as more meaningful (Allan, Duffy, & Collisson, 2018).

● **servant leadership** Leading by putting the needs of employees, customers, and communities first. The servant leader is a servant first, leader second.

One notable difference between transactional and transformational leaders lies in their approach to the workplace culture. Transactional leaders *work within* the context of that culture, whereas transformational leaders seek to *define and redefine* it (Northouse, 2018). Industry analysts widely consider the dynamic culture of organizations such as Google to be their biggest asset. What does it mean to talk about organizational culture? In the next section we probe this fascinating topic.

### test yourself

1. With what is the field of organizational psychology primarily concerned?
2. How do Theory X and Theory Y managers differ?
3. Define transactional and transformational leadership. How do these styles differ?

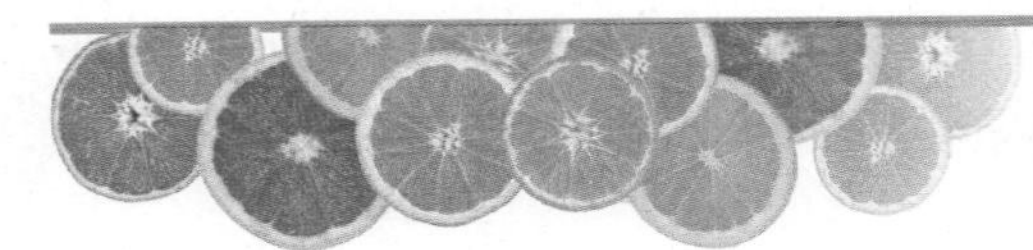

# INTERSECTION

## Psychology of Consciousness and I/O Psychology: How Does Leader Mindfulness Affect Employee Well-Being?

Mindfulness is a conscious state of being non-judgmentally aware of one's own thoughts and experiences. A mindful person is aware of his or her bodily sensations, feelings, and surroundings without becoming preoccupied by any given sensation, thought, or feeling. The mindful person is able to maintain non-judgmental awareness of experience. Research has linked mindfulness to many aspects of psychological well-being (Pratscher & others, 2018). So, it is not surprising that being mindful in the workplace is related to higher well-being for employees and leaders alike (Reb & Choi, 2014; Roche, Haar, & Luthans, 2014).

*Have you ever had a mindful boss? Would you be a mindful boss?*

Recent research has examined how a *leader's* mindfulness might relate to employee outcomes. For example, a set of studies showed that employees who had highly mindful leaders felt more respected and were more productive than those who did not (Reb & others, 2018).

Could having a mindful leader have benefits for employee well-being? A recent study examined this question by collecting data from 65 leaders and 153 employees (Pinck & Sonnentag, 2018). All of the participants completed measures of mindfulness (with items like "Even when I make a big mistake, I treat myself with understanding") and well-being, including positive mood and job satisfaction. In addition, leaders completed measures of transformational leadership (with items like "I challenge my employees to think about old problems in new ways"). The results of the study showed, first, that, indeed, leader mindfulness was associated with better mood and job satisfaction among employees. The analyses pointed as well to the important conclusion that being mindful predicted leaders adopting a transformational leadership style, which itself predicted more positive outcomes for employees. When leaders were aware of their own thoughts and feelings they were also more likely to embrace a vision for their organization and see that vision to fruition. Mindful, transformational leaders, then, had happier employees. We might think of mindfulness as something that happens "inside a person's head," benefiting primarily that individual (Pratscher & others, 2018). But this research shows how a mindful stance can affect the way people engage with their work roles with benefits far beyond the individual.

©FatCamera/E+/Getty Images

# 4. ORGANIZATIONAL CULTURE

● **organizational culture** An organization's shared values, beliefs, norms, and customs.

**Organizational culture** refers to an organization's shared values, beliefs, norms, and customs. How do people dress? Do they socialize? Is it okay to decorate cubicles with personal items? Can the employees talk to the CEO? These are the kinds of questions a new employee might ask, and the answers reveal the formality, warmth, and status consciousness of the workplace culture. Organizational culture describes the "flavor" of an organization—the "way we get things done around here" (Deal & Kennedy, 1982).

Even unspoken aspects of organizational culture can influence the everyday behavior of people in an organization. Recall groupthink from the chapter "Social Psychology". Groupthink occurs when people in a group squelch dissent and seek consensus above all else. An open climate may produce greater conflict, but conflict over important matters may be a good thing. An open climate characterizes the Harley-Davidson Motor Company. Because many Harley-Davidson employees are themselves motorcycle enthusiasts, their ideas are welcome at any time. In Harley's open-door policy, everyone can talk to everyone else. This free exchange is valued because the company's success relies on its passion for motorcycles. Such openness reveals a strong level of respect for the contributions of people across the organization.

## Positive Organizational Culture

©monkeybusinessimages/Getty Images

Positive organizational culture stems from a variety of factors, including active leadership, explicit policies, and less tangible aspects like the "feel" of an organization. Creating positive organizational culture can be as simple as giving employees reinforcement for doing good work. Leaders who reward outstanding performance and acknowledge the contributions that employees make to an organization may foster achievement motivation and promote success. A positive climate can be nurtured by leaders who incorporate fairness and safety into the cultural climate as part of a well-functioning workplace, rather than treating these concerns as hassles to be endured (Glavas, 2016).

Positive organizational culture involves compassion and leadership characterized by integrity and moral virtue. Compassion can be expressed in creative, humane corporate policies. For example, the Boston Consulting Group values work-life balance and issues a "red zone report" when individuals are working too many long weeks. Workers can also receive $10,000 for volunteering at a nonprofit. At another "best place" to work—NetApp, a data storage company in Sunnyvale, California—a top executive asks managers to notify him if they catch someone doing something right. He then calls 10 to 20 employees *every day* to thank them.

Sometimes, business may seem to require a lack of compassion. For example, downsizing is an increasingly popular corporate strategy to enhance profitability. **Downsizing** refers to dramatically cutting the workforce, especially during difficult economic times. By downsizing, companies often intend to send the message to stockholders that they are taking profit seriously. Certainly downsizing has human costs for those who are laid off (Cameron, 2003, 2005). Does sacrificing staff members pay off economically? Perhaps not. An analysis of numerous studies did not identify a clear economic benefit to downsizing (Datta & Basuil, 2015).

● **downsizing** A dramatic cutting of the workforce that has become a popular business strategy to enhance profitability.

Related to compassion is moral virtue. Employees who believe their organization is committed to doing the right thing may be better able to cope with difficult circumstances (Nikandrou & Tsachouridi, 2015). Organizations with top leaders perceived as fostering a culture of virtuousness showed higher productivity and higher-quality output after downsizing (Cameron, 2003).

## Toxic Factors in the Workplace

Not all work settings are positive. *Workplace incivility* refers to rude or disrespectful behaviors that reveal a lack of regard for others, such as spreading rumors, sending inflammatory e-mails, and sabotaging the work of fellow employees. Such incivility can spiral into a variety of other negative behaviors. Here we focus on two extreme cases of such incivility: sexual harassment and workplace aggression and violence.

### SEXUAL HARASSMENT

**Sexual harassment** is unwelcome behavior of a sexual nature that offends, humiliates, or intimidates another person. In the workplace, sexual harassment includes unwanted sexual advances, requests for sexual favors, and other verbal or physical conduct of a sexual nature (Holland & Cortina, 2016).

● **sexual harassment** Unwelcome behavior or conduct of a sexual nature that offends, humiliates, or intimidates another person.

In the United States, sexual harassment is an illegal form of sexual discrimination that violates Title VII of the Civil Rights Act of 1964. The victim of sexual harassment can be a man or woman and need not be the opposite sex of the perpetrator. The victim need not be the person harassed; it can be anyone affected by the offensive conduct. For example, a man who works in a setting in which women are routinely demeaned may find his workplace toxic. A woman who is offended by sexual comments made to other women

**What to Do If You Think You Are Being Sexually Harassed**

1. Keep careful records. Write down times, dates, places, and names of individuals who have witnessed the behavior.
2. Build a paper trail related to the harassment. If someone has sent you offensive or troubling e-mails, letters, or phone messages, keep them. Information that is documented may be helpful in pursuing a complaint.
3. Talk to a trusted friend, counselor, or therapist who will keep the information confidential. An objective third party may have suggestions for resolving the problem. If the harassment is occurring at work, consult with the human resources department. If it is taking place at school, talk to someone at your college's counseling center.
4. Write a letter to the individual you believe is harassing you. If you feel uncomfortable talking to the harasser in person, a letter may be a good alternative. The letter should include not only a description of specific examples of the behavior and your feelings about it, but also a statement of what you would like to happen next. Keep a copy of the letter for yourself.
5. If you have concerns about your safety or have been assaulted, immediately call the police. Most students do not report sexual harassment but wish they could. Reporting sexual harassment can be a challenge, but it is important. Sexual harassment is likely to be repeated if the perpetrator does not get feedback about the problem behavior.

**FIGURE 8** **Coping with Sexual Harassment** A serious problem on college campuses, sexual harassment can crop up in relations between students, students and their professors, and members of the university staff. If you feel that you are being sexually harassed, first consider that someone can sexually harass you without meaning to and that the solution can be as simple as informing the person that their behavior makes you uncomfortable. If talking to the person alone is uncomfortable, take someone with you for support. If you feel that confronting the person might be dangerous, there are other steps you can take, as described in the figure. ©Tomwang112/Getty Images

or among men at her workplace may also be the victim of sexual harassment. The harasser can be a coworker, supervisor, or even someone who is not an employee.

Many people meet their romantic partners at work, of course. Sexual conduct is unlawful only when it is unwelcome. According to the U.S. Equal Employment Opportunity Commission (EEOC), over 7,000 cases of sexual harassment were reported in 2017 (EEOC, 2018). Women filed approximately 83 percent of the complaints. For cases resolved in favor of the plaintiff, the amount of benefits totaled $46.3 million. Estimates of the frequency of sexual harassment in the workplace vary from 40 to 75 percent for women and 13 to 31 percent for men (McDonald, 2012). Sexual harassment is more likely in organizations with poor social ties among workers and poor relationships between employees and management (Rubino & others, 2018; Snyder, Scherer, & Fisher, 2012).

Sexual harassment is related to reduced well-being and job satisfaction and heightened distress and intentions to quit a job (Bell & others, 2018; Holland & Cortina, 2016). Being harassed is linked to depression, anxiety, and feelings of hopelessness, humiliation, and helplessness (McDonald, 2012). Sexual harassment is costly to organizations–predicting lower productivity, poor time management, and high levels of worker turnover (Jiang & others, 2015)

Sexual harassment has two forms: quid pro quo and hostile work environment. *Quid pro quo sexual harassment* refers to unwelcome sexual advances, requests for sexual favors, and verbal or physical conduct of a sexual nature in which submission is made either explicitly or implicitly a condition of the victim's employment. That is, the harassed individual is expected to tolerate the behavior or submit to sexual demands to be hired or to keep a job. Quid pro quo sexual harassment can also occur if rejection of the inappropriate conduct becomes the basis for employment decisions affecting the victim. For example, a woman who rejects her boss's advances may be denied a promotion or may get a negative performance evaluation.

*Hostile work environment sexual harassment* refers to unwelcome sexual behavior when this conduct has the purpose or effect of interfering with a person's work performance or creating an intimidating or offensive work environment. Behaviors contributing to a hostile environment include sexually graphic humor, suggestive remarks, ridiculing someone's body, and inappropriate touching.

Victim distress can be compounded when organizations fail to respond effectively to sexual harassment claims. Research examining over 6,000 sexual harassment victims in the U.S. military demonstrated that an organization's tendency to minimize the negative effects of harassment, to retaliate against the victim, and to seek to remedy the situation in unsatisfactory ways are strong predictors of victim distress (Bergman & others, 2002).

No one has to tolerate inappropriate sexual conduct at work or school. For information on how to cope with sexual harassment, see Figure 8.

## WORKPLACE AGGRESSION AND VIOLENCE

Aggression is behavior meant to harm another person. Aggression in the workplace includes verbal abusiveness, intimidating behavior, and bullying. Such behavior can have negative effects on workers. Nonsexual aggression is strongly related to lower job satisfaction (Jaradat & others, 2018; Valentine & Fleischman, 2018). Bullying, aggressive behavior that includes repeatedly threatening, mean-spirited teasing, or physically hurting another person (Kuehn, Wagner, & Velloza, 2018), can also be a serious problem in the workplace (Glambeck, Skogstad, & Einarsen, 2018).

At the extreme end of aggression is workplace violence, which includes physical assault and homicide (Barclay & Aquino, 2010; Dillon, 2012). Workplace violence falls within the realm of workplace safety. According to the Occupational Safety and Health Administration (OSHA) Act of 1970, an employer is required to "furnish each of his employees... a place of employment which... free from recognized hazards that are causing or are likely to cause death or serious physical harm to his employees" (OSHA, 2002).

High-profile cases of workplace violence often grab the headlines. For example, on Christmas night in 2000, Michael McDermott, a software tester for Edgewater Technology in Wakefield, Massachusetts, went to his workplace and stashed 24 boxes of ammunition, two rifles, a shotgun, a pistol, and a bayonet. On the day after Christmas, after a morning spent at work and chatting with coworkers, he strode into the human resources department and, within a few minutes, killed seven people. He was convicted of seven counts of murder in 2002 (Blades, 2006).

Nearly 2 million Americans report being the victim of workplace violence each year (OSHA, 2015). Many more cases likely go unreported. Unfortunately, many U.S. workplaces have no formal policy for workplace violence. Understanding and preventing workplace violence is a concern for both employers and I-O psychologists (Yang & Caughlin, 2017).

Workplace violence may occur between coworkers, but it also includes violence perpetrated by outsiders such as customers, clients, or patients (Beattie & others, 2018). Consider a store clerk confronted by a robber, a teacher faced with a hostile high school student in the classroom, or a nurse dealing with a physically abusive patient—all are in a position to become victims of violence. Employers are expected to anticipate and take action to prevent victimization in such circumstances.

No organization can identify every potential problem but they can take steps to prevent workplace violence (Shier & others, 2018; Siegel, 2018). Examples of strategies include:

- Create a humane environment in which employees feel they are being treated fairly. Individuals who perceive that they have been treated unfairly are more likely to aggress, verbally and physically.
- Strive for an open approach to resolving conflicts. Commitment to solving problems head-on can defuse difficult situations before they escalate to violence.
- Establish zero-tolerance policies toward violent behavior, and ensure that the policy covers employees, clients, customers, patients, visitors, and anyone else who may come into the organization.

### *test yourself*

1. What is meant by organizational culture?
2. Name some key factors in a positive organizational culture.
3. What is sexual harassment? Discuss its two forms.

# 5. I-O PSYCHOLOGY AND HEALTH AND WELLNESS

It is no surprise that work affects health and wellness. In this last section we review the link between unemployment and well-being, the experience of job stress, and ways to cope with it.

## Unemployment

The importance of work is never more apparent than when people lose their jobs. Unemployment is related to physical problems (such as heart attack, stroke, obesity), psychological disorders (such as anxiety and depression), marital and family troubles, and homicide and other crimes (Aguilar-Palacio & others, 2018; Diette & others, 2018; Egan, Daly, & Delaney, 2016; González-Val & Marcén, 2018; Kaspersen & others, 2015; Müller & others, 2015).

Compared to the unemployed, people who are employed full-time have lower stress and depression and report better health behaviors, including healthier eating and physical activity (Rosenthal & others, 2012). A 15-year longitudinal study of 24,000 people living in Germany found that unemployment was devastating to well-being (Lucas &

others, 2004; Luhmann & others, 2012). People recovered much of the happiness they had enjoyed prior to becoming unemployed but many failed to return fully to those levels. A research review concluded that unemployment was associated with an increased mortality risk, especially for people in the early and middle stages of their careers (Roelfs & others, 2011). Physical exercise can buffer the effects of unemployment on health (Colombo, Rotondi, & Stanca, 2018).

In difficult economic times, people may experience repeated spells of unemployment. One study found that among those who had experienced repeated unemployment, being employed even temporarily between bouts of unemployment predicted better coping (Booker & Sacker, 2012). So, the experience of work itself can serve as a buffer against the effects of unemployment. Yet work can also be a source of stress.

## Stress at Work

**job stress** The experience of stress on the job and in the workplace setting.

**role conflict** The kind of stress that arises when a person tries to meet the demands of more than one important life role, such as worker and mother.

**Job stress** refers to the experience of stress at work. A key source of job stress is role conflict. **Role conflict** may occur when a person tries to meet the demands of more than one important life role, such as employee and mother. Because work may compete with other valued activities for our time and energy, it can be difficult to resolve the demands of our various valued roles: Should I stay at work and finish this project, or head home for dinner with my family?

Some jobs are more stressful than others. Coworker support and clear job requirements are related to lower levels of stress (French & others, 2018; Leiter, Day, & Price, 2015; Matthews, Bulger, & Barnes-Farrell, 2010). Four characteristics of work settings are linked with employee stress and health problems:

- High job demands, such as having a heavy workload and time pressure
- Inadequate opportunities to participate in decision making
- A high level of supervisor control
- Lack of clarity about the criteria for competent performance

**burnout** A distressed psychological state in which a person experiences emotional exhaustion and little motivation for work.

When work stress becomes chronic, individuals may fall victim to **burnout**, a distressed psychological state in which a person experiences emotional exhaustion and little work motivation. Burnout may include feelings of being overworked and underappreciated and can feature depersonalization, confusion, worry, and resentment (Woodhead, Northrop, & Edelstein, 2016). Symptoms can be physical (exhaustion, headaches, gastrointestinal problems, suppressed immune function, sleep disturbance), behavioral (increased use of alcohol, drugs, caffeine; absenteeism; and social withdrawal), and emotional (increased cynicism and negativity, hopelessness, irritability, emotional distancing, depression, and anxiety).

## Managing Job Stress

Stress at work does not always lead to burnout, especially if people develop enjoyable leisure activities. Indeed, an important aspect of life, beyond work, is relaxation and leisure. **Leisure** refers to the pleasant times before or after work when individuals are free to pursue activities and interests of their own choosing, like hobbies, sports, and reading. Using leisure time to help others can be a particularly engaging way to recover from work-related stress.

**leisure** The pleasant times before or after work when individuals are free to pursue activities and interests of their own choosing, such as hobbies, sports, and reading.

Might taking regular vacations also help people combat job stress? Vacations increase well-being for most people (Blank & others, 2018; Syrek & others, 2018). One study found that in the days and weeks at work just after a vacation, people were less exhausted, had fewer health complaints, and were putting forth more efficient effort than in the week at work prior to the vacation (Fritz & Sonnentag, 2006). Check out the Psychological Inquiry for the results of that study.

## psychological *inquiry*

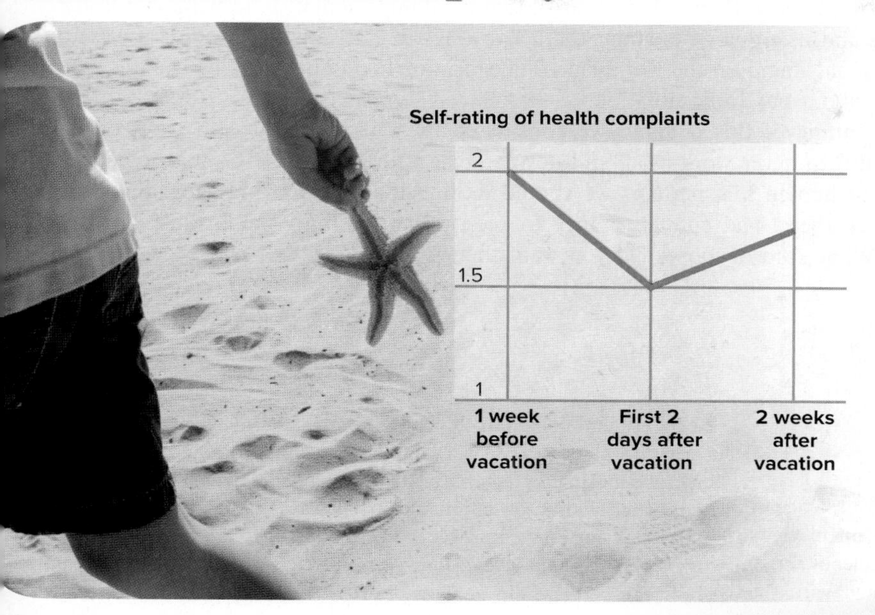


urce: Fritz, & Sonnentag (2006); (photo) ©Cultura Motion/Shutterstock

### *You Need a Vacation!*

This graph shows the results of a study examining employees' health complaints before and after they took a vacation (Fritz & Sonnentag, 2006). The Y axis (vertical) is the self-rated score on health complaints, and the X axis (horizontal) represents time. Employees rated their health complaints on 12 items (for example, "Have you slept less because of worries?"). The 4-point scale ranged from 1 (not at all) to 4 (much more than normal). Consider these questions:

1. When were health complaints at their lowest and highest?
2. If the researchers had measured the employees' level of satisfaction with life, do you think the pattern would look the same? Explain.
3. Was this a correlational study or an experiment? What does your answer mean for the conclusions that can be drawn from this study?
4. In this study, participants completed self-report measures of their health. Was that a wise research decision or not? Explain.

Taking vacations can also be associated with living longer. In a longitudinal study, 12,338 men 35 to 57 years of age were assessed each year for five years on the question of whether they took vacations (Gump & Matthews, 2000). Compared with those who never took vacations, men who went on annual vacations were 21 percent less likely to die over a nine year period and 32 percent less likely to die of coronary heart disease. The same concerns that lead men to skip a vacation—such as not trusting anyone to fill in for them and fearing that they will get behind in their work and someone will replace them—tend to promote heart disease. Such apprehensions are characteristic of the Type A behavioral pattern we examined in the chapter "Personality".

The benefits of time away from work are often short-lived (de Bloom, Geurts, & Kompier, 2012). Why do they wear off so quickly? One contributing factor is that often a person's workload right after vacation is very heavy (Kühnel & Sonnentag, 2011; Sonnentag & Fritz, 2015). Vacations that allow people to fully detach from work and enjoy themselves are more likely to continue to influence well-being down the line (de Bloom, Geurts, & Kompier, 2012; Sonnentag & Fritz, 2015). A key source of stress in today's world is the ever-present smartphone that places work emails at the touch of a button, distracting from relaxation (Ayeh, 2018).

In addition to developing enjoyable leisure activities and taking regular vacations, what else can you do to cope with work stress? Dealing with job stress in a healthy way involves taking care of your body as well as your mind (Fahey, Insel, & Roth, 2016). Meet your physical needs by eating right, exercising, and getting enough sleep.

Because work stress, like all stress, is about our perception of experience, it makes sense to hone your coping skills and periodically to monitor your patterns of behavior and well-being (Donatelle, 2015). Are your work goals realistic? Are you taking work-related issues too personally? What are your strengths, and how can you use them to do what you do best?

At times, we might view working hard as just that—hard. However, work can be a vital part of living a fulfilling life. Indeed, Mihaly Csikszentmihalyi (1990) found that while we are working, we are 10 times more likely to experience **flow**—the optimal experience of a

● **flow** The optimal experience of a match between one's skills and the challenge of a task.

match between our skills and the challenge of a task–even though, ironically, we are also 6 times more likely to wish we were somewhere else when on the job.

When we think of work as a calling, we might find ourselves listening for that call with an open mind and heart. Remember, though, that a calling orientation to work is not just about waiting and listening. It is about the active way we craft any job, finding a way to place our personal stamp on the workplace. Transforming a job into a calling is a decision that we make about our work situation.

At the beginning of this chapter, we considered the question "Why do people with sufficient wealth to never work at all still devote great effort to work?" Given the central role of work in human life, perhaps we should rethink that question. Imagine that you, like Mark Zuckerberg, had enough money to keep you more than comfortable for over 1,600 years. What kind of job would you want then?

### test yourself

1. What role conflicts do you—or someone you know well—experience?
2. Define burnout and name some physical, behavioral, and emotional symptoms of burnout.
3. What have researchers discovered about the benefits of taking a vacation?

# SUMMARY

## 1. ORIGINS OF INDUSTRIAL AND ORGANIZATIONAL PSYCHOLOGY

Industrial and organizational (I-O) psychology applies the science of psychology to work and the workplace. Scientific management views workers as well-oiled machines and seeks to maximize efficiency. Ergonomics, or human factors, is a field of study concerned with the relationship between human beings and the tools or machines they use in their work. Ergonomics is focused on promoting safety and efficiency. The Hawthorne studies, conducted by Mayo and his colleagues, showed that just being made to feel special increased productivity. This work gave rise to the human relations approach to management.

## 2. INDUSTRIAL PSYCHOLOGY

Job analysis is the systematic description of the knowledge and skills necessary to carry out a job. Procedures involved in personnel selection include testing, interviews, work samples, and other exercises. Job training is a key goal for industrial psychologists. Dimensions of training include orientation, formal training, and mentoring, and ongoing employee development.

Performance appraisal gives feedback to employees and guides decisions about promotions, raises, and termination. One strategy to avoid errors in performance appraisal is 360-degree feedback, which involves rating a worker through the input of a range of individuals, including coworkers, managers, and customers. Organizational citizenship behavior refers to discretionary behaviors that a person engages in that are not part of the specific job description.

## 3. ORGANIZATIONAL PSYCHOLOGY

The way managers approach their jobs is an important focus of research in organizational psychology. Deming, an American, developed the "Japanese" management style, stressing innovation, future orientation, and quality. McGregor introduced Theory X and Theory Y management styles. Strengths-based management, developed by Clifton, asserts that the best approach to management is one that matches individuals' strengths with their jobs.

Job satisfaction is a person's attitude toward his or her occupation. Job satisfaction is not strongly associated with wages and may relate in important ways to the personality characteristics of the worker and the fit between the person and the job.

Employee commitment is an individual's feeling of loyalty to his or her workplace. Three types of commitment are affective commitment (a person's emotional attachment to a job), continuance commitment (a person's perception that leaving a job would be too costly or difficult), and normative commitment (a person's feeling that he or she should stick with a job because of obligation).

Because our jobs define us in many ways, the way we think about work influences our lives more generally. Research has shown that people can perceive the same position as a job, a career, or a calling. Those who perceive their work as a calling show numerous positive benefits.

A transactional leader is one who emphasizes the exchange relationship between the boss and employees. This leader is likely to take action only in reaction to events. In contrast, a transformational leader is a dynamic individual who brings charisma and vision to the position.

## 4. ORGANIZATIONAL CULTURE

Organizational culture refers to an organization's shared beliefs, values, customs, and norms. Positive organizational culture can be nurtured through positive reinforcement, as well as genuine concern for the well-being of workers. Compassion and virtue also promote positive organizational culture.

Factors such as sexual harassment and workplace violence represent the negative side of organizational culture. Sexual harassment is illegal and may take the form of either quid pro quo (the demand for sexual favors in return for employment or continued employment) or hostile workplace environment. Workplace violence is a growing concern for employers and I-O psychologists. Employers must create a safe environment for workers, including doing all that they can to foresee and prevent possible violence.

## 5. I-O PSYCHOLOGY AND HEALTH AND WELLNESS

Unemployment can take a toll on psychological and physical health. Job stress is stress experienced at the workplace. Role conflict, a key source of such stress, results from trying to meet multiple demands in a limited amount of time. Sources of job stress include high demands, inadequate opportunity to participate in decision making, high levels of supervisor control, and unclear criteria for performance. At the extreme, work stress can lead to burnout.

One way to manage job stress is to enrich one's life while not at work. Engaging in satisfying leisure activities can promote workplace wellness. Enjoying time off can have benefits for individuals when they are back on the job.

# key *terms*

affective commitment
burnout
continuance commitment
downsizing
ergonomics or human factors
flow
halo effect
Hawthorne effect
human relations approach
industrial and organizational (I-O) psychology
integrity test
intelligence
job analysis
job crafting
job satisfaction
job stress
KSAOs or KSAs
leisure
mentoring
normative commitment
organizational citizenship behavior (OCB)
organizational culture
organizational identity
orientation
performance appraisal
role conflict
scientific management
servant leadership
sexual harassment
situational judgment test
strengths-based management
structured interview
Theory X managers
Theory Y managers
360-degree feedback
training
transactional leader
transformational leader

# apply your *knowledge*

1. You might be interested in discovering your personal strengths so that you can identify the occupations that might be best for you. A variety of measures assess vocational abilities, and you can visit your campus career center to check these out. In addition, positive psychologists have developed an assessment tool that measures strengths of character such as achievement motivation, loyalty, sense of humor, capacity to love and be loved, and integrity. To determine your character strengths, visit the Values in Action website at https://www.viacharacter.org/www/.

2. Browse the *Wall Street Journal* and read the latest news about the corporate world. Can you detect principles of scientific management or human relations approaches in the corporations documented in the stories? What types of corporate leadership do the articles describe?

3. Ask some friends and family members to describe their jobs to you. Where do the descriptions fall with respect to the distinctions between job, career, and calling discussed in this chapter? In light of what you know about your respondents, how much do you think this distinction reflects the job itself and how much reflects the person?

4. Pick someone you know who shows the qualities of a good leader. Interview the individual about times he or she has been in a leadership role. How did the individual manage challenges? How did the person view the people he or she led? What perspective did the person bring to the position of leader? Do you think your candidate fits the Theory X or Theory Y management profile? Is the individual a transactional or transformational leader? Explain your conclusions.

5. If you are interested in exploring possible careers, check out the *Occupational Outlook Handbook* at http://www.bls.gov/ooh/. You might be surprised at some of the jobs that are out there.

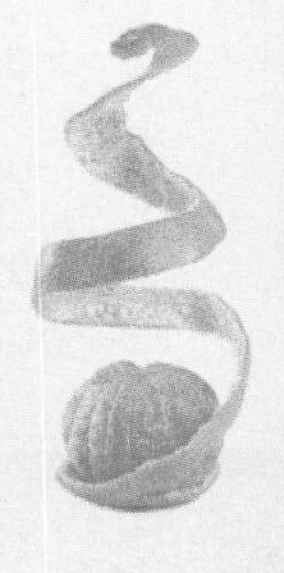

**Design elements:** Preview icon: ©Jiang Hongyan; Intersection box icon: ©D. Hurst/Alamy, ©Creative Crop/Getty Images, ©Dimitris66/Getty Images, ©Savany/Getty Images; Critical Controversy box icon: ©Ultrashock; running heads icon: ©Cre8tive Studios/Alamy; Summary icon: ©Vadarshop

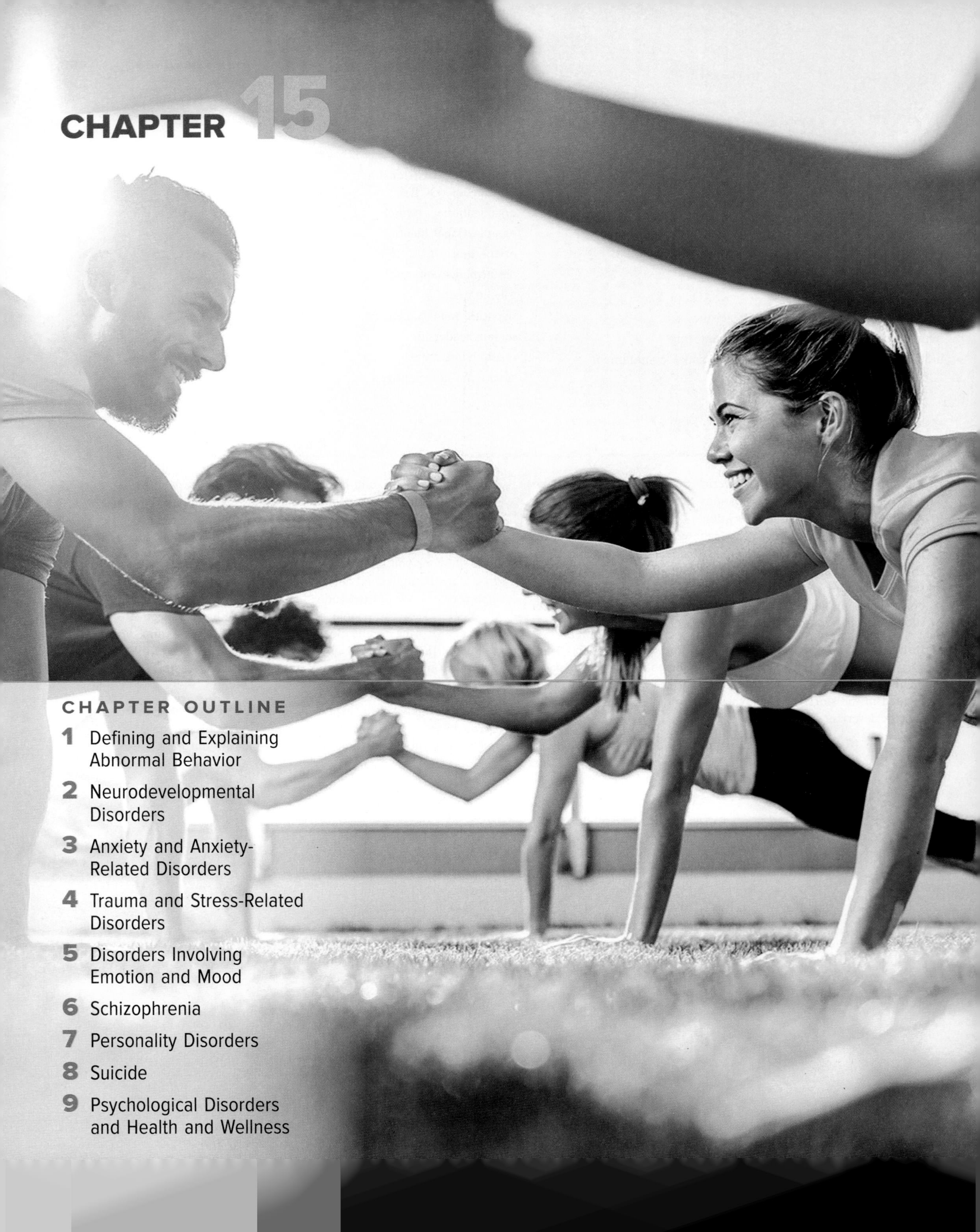

# CHAPTER 15

CHAPTER OUTLINE

# Psychological Disorders

## Making Castles from Life's Stones

**Sitting in her office, Erica Crompton, a writer living and working in London, could not help but notice the bars on the windows of the building.** The bars were there for security reasons, as is common. However, Erica could not escape the idea that they were part of a conspiracy: She was convinced that she had committed some heinous act she could not remember and the police were spying on her to collect evidence. Someone somewhere was sending her a message that she would soon be behind bars. Walking down the street, every passing police officer was a threat, someone waiting to arrest her. What those working in the office with Erica did not know was that she had schizophrenia, a severe psychological disorder. Erica long hid her diagnosis from others, fearful of being judged negatively. She struggled to keep up appearances from 9 to 5, every day. Now working as a freelance writer and mental health advocate, Erica's message to the world is this: We can take the stones life throws at us and build castles (Crompton, 2017). She views herself, as all of us must, as a work in progress. She has created a life that allows her the flexibility to get regular therapy and maintain her medications.

Individuals with psychological disorders are not so different from the rest of us. They are brothers, sisters, grandparents, uncles, aunts, and parents, classmates, and coworkers—people with life stories to share (Crompton, 2018). Psychological disorders may make their lives more difficult and our relationships with them more challenging, but they cannot take away the humanity that binds them to us. ●

# PREVIEW

This chapter surveys psychological disorders. We first explore the meaning of the word *abnormal* and examine approaches to understanding abnormal behavior. We then survey a number of disorders. In the concluding section, we consider the influence of the stigma associated with psychological disorders on the health and wellness of those who experience them.

## 1. DEFINING AND EXPLAINING ABNORMAL BEHAVIOR

● **abnormal behavior** Behavior that is deviant, maladaptive, or personally distressful over a relatively long period of time.

What makes behavior abnormal? Abnormal behavior is certainly statistically unusual or atypical. Alicia Keyes, Cam Newton, and Mark Zuckerberg are atypical—but we do not categorize them as abnormal. Three criteria help identify abnormal behavior. **Abnormal behavior** is behavior that is deviant, maladaptive, or personally distressful over a relatively long period of time. Let's examine the three criteria more closely:

- Abnormal behavior is *deviant*. Deviant means that a behavior does not conform to accepted social standards. When atypical behavior deviates from what is acceptable in a culture, it often is considered abnormal. A woman who washes her hands four times an hour and takes seven showers a day is abnormal because her behavior deviates from what we consider acceptable. The *context* of behavior may determine whether it is deviant. If the woman who repeatedly washes her hands and takes showers works in a sterile lab with live viruses or radioactive material, her behavior might be acceptable.
- Abnormal behavior is *maladaptive*. Maladaptive behavior interferes with a person's ability to function effectively in the world. A man who believes he can harm other people through his breathing may go to great lengths to avoid people for what he believes is their own good. His belief separates him from society and prevents his everyday functioning; thus, his behavior is maladaptive. Behavior that presents a danger to the person or other people is maladaptive (and abnormal).
- Abnormal behavior involves *personal distress* over a long period of time, meaning the person finds it troubling. A woman who secretly makes herself vomit after every meal may never be seen by others as deviant (because they do not know about it), but this pattern of behavior may cause her to feel intense shame and guilt.

Only one of the three criteria described above needs to be present for behavior to be labeled "abnormal," but typically two or all three may be present. When abnormal behavior persists, it may lead to the diagnosis of a psychological disorder.

*Accomplished people—such as singer-songwriter Alicia Keys, NFL superstar Cam Newton, and Facebook CEO Mark Zuckerberg—are atypical but not abnormal. However, when atypical behavior deviates from cultural norms, it often is considered abnormal.*

(first) ©Allstar Picture Library/Alamy Stock Photo; (second) ©Maddie Meyer/Getty Images; (third) ©Simon Dawson/Bloomberg/Getty Images

# Theoretical Approaches to Psychological Disorders

What causes people to develop a psychological disorder–that is, to behave in deviant, maladaptive, and personally distressful ways? Theorists have suggested various approaches for answering this question.

## THE BIOLOGICAL APPROACH

The biological approach attributes psychological disorders to organic, internal causes. This approach primarily focuses on the brain, genetic factors, and neurotransmitter functioning as the sources of abnormality. This is the approach taken by the American Psychiatric Association (2001, 2006, 2013a). This organization creates the diagnostic categories for mental health professionals. It defines abnormal behavior in medical terms–as an illness that affects or is manifested in a person's brain and can affect the way the individual thinks, behaves, and interacts with others. This approach reflects the **medical model**. The medical model describes psychological disorders as medical diseases with a biological origin.

● **medical model** The view that psychological disorders are medical diseases with a biological origin.

## THE PSYCHOLOGICAL APPROACH

The psychological approach emphasizes the contributions of experiences, thoughts, emotions, and personality characteristics to psychological disorders. Psychologists might focus on the influence of childhood experiences or personality traits in the development and course of psychological disorders. Behavioral psychologists probe the rewards and punishers in the environment that determine abnormal behavior. Social cognitive psychologists focus on observational learning, cognitions, and beliefs as factors that foster or maintain abnormal behavior.

## THE SOCIOCULTURAL APPROACH

The sociocultural approach looks to social contexts and variables, like culture or gender. The criterion of deviance suggests the important role of sociocultural factors in psychological disorders. Cultures establish the norms by which people evaluate behavior, telling us whether it is socially acceptable (Causadias, Korous, & Cahill, 2018; De Vaus & others, 2018). In evaluating behavior as deviant, culture matters in complex ways (Sue & others, 2014).

Importantly, cultural norms can be mistaken, limiting, and prejudicial (Kent, 2016; Potter, 2012). People who fight to change the established social order are sometimes labeled deviant. In the late nineteenth and early twentieth centuries, women in Britain who protested for women's right to vote were labeled mentally ill. When someone's behavior challenges social expectations, we must be open to the possibility that such actions are an adaptive response to injustice. By challenging what everyone thinks is true and expressing ideas that seem strange, they may make others feel uncomfortable. But, justifiable demands for social change are not abnormal. Further, definitions of what is normal change as societal norms change. Consider that cigarette smoking was not only acceptable in the 1960s, it was promoted as a healthy way to relax.

Cultural variation in what it means to be normal or abnormal makes it difficult to compare psychological disorders across different cultures. Many of the diagnostic categories we trace in this chapter primarily reflect Western (and often U.S.) notions of normality, and applying these to other cultures can be inappropriate (Kawasaka, 2018; Rubington & Weinberg, 2015). As people move from one culture to another, evaluations of their behavior must take into account the norms in their culture of origin (Hassan & others, 2016; Lee, Choi, & Matejkowski, 2013). Historically, people entering the United States from other countries were examined at Ellis Island, and many were judged to be mentally impaired simply because of differences in language and customs.

| Disorder | Culture | Description/Characteristics |
| --- | --- | --- |
| Amok | Malaysia, Philippines, Africa | This disorder involves sudden, uncontrolled outbursts of anger in which the person may injure or kill someone. Amok is often found in males who are emotionally withdrawn before the onset of the disorder. After the attack on someone, the individual feels exhausted and depressed and does not remember the rage and attack. |
| Anorexia Nervosa | Western cultures, especially the United States | This eating disorder involves a relentless pursuit of thinness through starvation and can eventually lead to death. |
| Koro | China and Southeast Asia | This disorder in China and Southeast Asia involves the terrifying belief that one's genitalia are retracting into one's abdomen. |

**FIGURE 1** **Some Culture-Related Disorders** Although many psychological disorders are universal, some are associated with specific cultures, as this figure illustrates. Sources: Collado, Lim, & MacPherson (2016); Hunt (2018); Polanczyk, Salum, Sugaya, Caye, & Rohde (2015).

The sociocultural perspective stresses the ways that cultures influence the understanding and treatment of psychological disorders. The frequency and intensity of psychological disorders vary and depend on social, economic, technological, and religious aspects of cultures (Collado, Lim, & MacPherson, 2016; Hunt, 2018; Polanczyk & others, 2015). Some disorders are culture-related, as indicated in Figure 1.

Sociocultural researchers also stress the role of social factors—such as gender, ethnicity, socioeconomic status, and family relationships—on psychological disorders. For instance, poverty creates stressful circumstances that can contribute to the development of a psychological disorder (Chen & Miller, 2013; Lund, 2015).

### THE BIOPSYCHOSOCIAL MODEL

Biological, psychological, and sociocultural factors often act in combination with one another to produce a psychological disorder. From the *biopsychosocial perspective,* none of these factors is necessarily viewed as more important than another; rather, biological, psychological, and social factors are *all* significant ingredients in producing both normal and abnormal behavior. Further, these factors may combine in unique ways, so that one depressed person might differ from another in terms of the key factors associated with the development of the disorder.

Why do we need to consider these many factors? As you will see throughout this chapter, generally speaking, there is no one gene or experience that leads inevitably to the development of a disorder. Two people can share the same gene—one develops a disorder, but another does not. Similarly, two people might have the same experience, such as childhood neglect, and one might develop a disorder while the other does not. Thus, to understand the development of psychological disorders, we must consider a variety of *interacting* factors from each of the domains of experience.

An important idea representing the ways different factors influence the development of psychological disorders is the **vulnerability-stress hypothesis** (also called the **diathesis-stress model**). The vulnerability-stress hypothesis suggests that preexisting conditions (such as genetic characteristics, personality dispositions, or experiences) may put a person at risk of developing a psychological disorder. A vulnerability can lead to a psychological disorder, when combined with stressful experience.

● **vulnerability-stress hypothesis or diathesis-stress model** Theory suggesting that preexisting conditions—such as genetic characteristics, personality dispositions, or experiences—may put a person at risk of developing a psychological disorder.

Psychologists study these processes is by examining the interactions between genes and environmental circumstances, or gene × environment (G × E) interactions (Maglione & others, 2018; Pérez-Pérez & others, 2018).

# Classifying Abnormal Behavior

To understand, prevent, and treat abnormal behavior, psychiatrists and psychologists have devised systems classifying those behaviors into specific psychological disorders. Classifying disorders provides a common basis for communicating. If one psychologist says that her client is experiencing depression, another psychologist understands that a particular pattern of abnormal behavior has led to this diagnosis. A classification system can also help clinicians make predictions about the likelihood of a particular disorder's occurrence, who might be most susceptible to it, and what the best treatment might be. A classification system may also benefit the person suffering from psychological symptoms. Finding out a disorder has a name can be a comforting signal that they may reasonably expect relief.

However, labeling a problem can have serious negative implications because of the potential for creating *stigma,* a mark of shame that may cause others to avoid or to act negatively toward a person (Eno Louden & others, 2018; M. L. Smith & others, 2018).

Indeed, being diagnosed with a psychological disorder can influence a person's life profoundly because of what the diagnosis means to the person, his or her family, and the larger social world. We return to the issue of stigma at the end of this chapter.

## THE *DSM* CLASSIFICATION SYSTEM

In 1952, the American Psychiatric Association (APA) published the first major classification of psychological disorders in the United States, the *Diagnostic and Statistical Manual of Mental Disorders*. Its current version, ***DSM-5***, was approved in 2013. Throughout the history of the *DSM,* the number of diagnoses has increased dramatically. *DSM-5* includes new diagnoses such as binge eating disorder and gambling addiction.

The *DSM* is not the only diagnostic system. The World Health Organization devised the *International Classification of Diseases and Related Health Problems (ICD-10),* which includes a chapter on mental and behavioral disorders. One of the goals of *DSM-5* was to bring diagnoses closer to the *ICD-10* but the two manuals remain different in important ways.

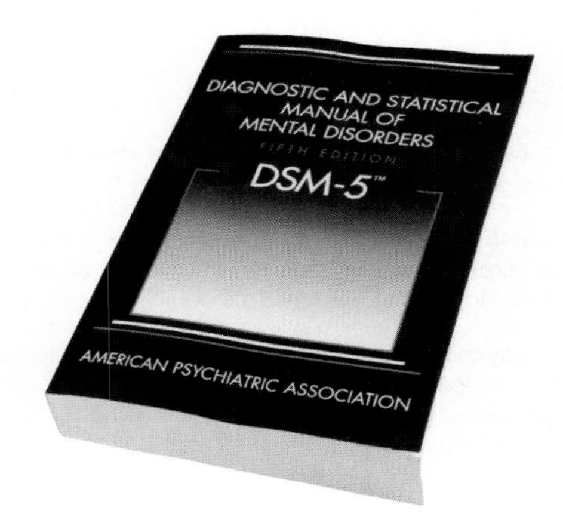


©Studio 101/Alamy Stock Photo

● **DSM-5** The fifth edition of the *Diagnostic and Statistical Manual of Mental Disorders;* the major classification of psychological disorders in the United States.

## CRITIQUES OF THE *DSM*

A central criticism of the *DSM* is that it is rooted in the medical model–treating psychological disorders as if they are medical illnesses and taking an overly biological view of conditions that may be rooted in social experience (Cooke & Kinderman, 2018). Even as research has shed light on the complex interaction of genetic, neurobiological, cognitive, social, and environmental factors in psychological disorders, *DSM-5* continues to reflect only the medical model, neglecting factors such as poverty, unemployment, and trauma (Borsboom, Cramer, & Kalis, 2018; Surís, Holliday, & North, 2016).

Another criticism of the *DSM* is that it focuses only on problems. Critics argue that emphasizing *strengths* as well as weaknesses might help to destigmatize psychological disorders (Roten, 2007). Other criticisms of *DSM-5* include:

- It relies too much on social norms and subjective judgments.
- Too many new categories of disorders have been added, some of which do not have consistent research support.
- Loosening the standards for some existing diagnoses will add to the already very high rates of these.

Considering critiques of the *DSM*, you might be wondering what all the fuss is about. One reason for concern is that generally U.S. insurance companies will only reimburse for treatments of diagnoses that appear in *DSM-5.* Another key concern is that part of the medical model is the assumption that, optimally, disorders would be treated through medical means. Generally, that means prescribing medications. If diagnostic criteria are loosened, many more people might be given powerful psychoactive drugs, perhaps unnecessarily. It is imperative that the *DSM* get it right.

Let's consider one distinctive change in *DSM-5.* Previous editions of the manual included a disorder called *somatoform disorder*. Somatoform disorder referred to a person's experience of having a physical symptom without any indication of a physical cause for the symptom. The disorder is now called *somatic symptom disorder*. In **somatic symptom disorder** a person experiences one or more bodily (somatic) symptoms and experiences excessive thoughts and feelings about these symptoms (APA, 2013a). Note that the idea of having no physical cause for the symptoms is no longer a defining feature (Erkic & others, 2018; Heimann & others, 2018).

● **somatic symptom disorder** A psychological disorder in which a person experiences one or more bodily (somatic) symptoms and experiences excessive thoughts and feelings about these symptoms that interfere with everyday functioning.

Previously, the person must have demonstrated efforts to find a medical explanation for the symptom, and the focus was on the fact that these symptoms are not physically "real." As you can imagine, patients often found this aspect of the diagnosis insulting, as if doctors were saying, "It's all in your head." Now the focus is on the experience of distressing thoughts and feelings related to the symptoms. People diagnosed with somatic symptom disorder have often endured many medical procedures (including surgeries and medications) in an effort to treat their physical symptoms. These experiences can, understandably, lead to a lack of trust (Luyten & Fonagy, 2016). By focusing on psychological symptoms (rather than the absence of physical causes associated with the bodily symptoms experienced), it is hoped that psychologists and psychiatrists might regain that trust.

● **comorbidity** When two or more disorders are experienced at the same time.

● **risk factors** Characteristics, experiences, or exposures that increase the likelihood of a person developing a disorder.

● **psychotherapy** A nonmedical process that helps individuals with psychological disorders recognize and overcome their problems.

### FINAL TERMS AND CAUTIONS

Before reviewing psychological diagnoses, let's clarify common terms and issues. First, many people with psychological disorders have more than one diagnosis simultaneously. An adult may have both depression and an anxiety disorder. The term **comorbidity** means that a person has two or more disorders at the same time.

Throughout our review, we will consider the etiology of disorders. *Etiology* refers to the causes of disorders. For most disorders there is not a single known cause. Instead, researchers have identified risk factors. **Risk factors** are characteristics, experiences, or exposures that increase the likelihood of a person developing a disorder. Risk factors are correlated with the development of a disorder. Of course, correlation does not imply causation. Many people with a particular risk factor may never develop a disorder.

In our review, we will briefly touch on common treatments. These treatments, our focus in the chapter "Therapies", are often divided into two types, psychotherapy and medication. **Psychotherapy** is a nonmedical process that helps people with psychological disorders recognize and overcome their problems. Medications are drugs that are used to treat the symptoms of psychological disorders. These often address dysregulation of neurotransmitters in the brain.

Finally, a caution: People who are learning about psychological disorders often begin to recognize symptoms of disorders in themselves or others. Only trained professionals can diagnose a psychological disorder.

### *test yourself*

1. What three criteria distinguish abnormal behavior from normal behavior?
2. Why is it important to have formal systems for classifying abnormal behavior into specific psychological disorders?
3. What are some criticisms of *DSM-5*?

## 2. NEURODEVELOPMENTAL DISORDERS

● **neurodevelopmental disorders** A class of psychological disorders that typically appear in childhood and are traced to genetic differences, atypical brain development, or prenatal exposure to substances that adversely affect development.

**Neurodevelopmental disorders** typically appear in childhood (APA, 2013a) and are traced to genetic differences, atypical brain development, or prenatal exposure to substances that adversely affect development. Next, we review two neurodevelopmental disorders–autism spectrum disorder and attention-deficit/hyperactivity disorder.

### Autism Spectrum Disorder

● **autism spectrum disorder** A neurodevelopmental disorder involving persistent deficits in social communication and social interaction across a variety of settings as well as restrictive repetitive behaviors, interests, and activities.

**Autism spectrum disorder** (ASD) is characterized by two key features:

1. Persistent deficits in social communication and social interaction across a variety of settings.
2. Restrictive repetitive behaviors, interests, and activities.

Symptoms of ASD are likely to color behavior throughout life (Ke, Whalon, & Yun, 2018; Pallathra & others, 2018). Infants may prefer not to be cuddled. Children may not develop the ability to speak. Adults may have problems communicating. Repetitive behaviors in childhood may include hand flapping, head banging, or being preoccupied by activities, like opening and closing a door. Later in life, restrictive interests might involve an enthusiastic or obsessive interest in a topic, like trains (Berry, Russell, & Frost, 2018).

©UrsaHoogle/E+/Getty Images

It was once thought that about 5 children in 1000 had ASD. More recent estimates are that ASD affects 1 in 69 8-year-olds (Christensen & others, 2018). There are likely many reasons for the increase, such as greater awareness of ASD (Muhle & others, 2018). ASD, which occurs in all ethnic groups and SES levels, is 2 to 5 times more common in boys than in girls (Christensen & others, 2018).

ASD is called a *spectrum* because the impairment it causes is extremely variable (Cohen & others, 2018; Golya & McIntyre, 2018;

Zimmerman & others, 2018). At one end of the spectrum, people cannot speak and have profound difficulties in self-care and independent living. At the other end, people may succeed in school, careers, and relationships with others (Zimmerman & others, 2018). Temple Grandin (2006), an accomplished scientist with ASD, described how she has had to memorize that non-autistic people think in words, not images, and their facial expressions reveal their feelings. High-functioning people with ASD were once diagnosed with *Asperger's Syndrome.* Now that the diagnosis acknowledges the spectrum of function, this label is not used. Some people with ASD are effective self-advocates, asserting that ASD should be viewed as a type of valuable *neurodiversity* (Dean, 2018).

Theories of ASD try to explain its symptoms as responses to central problems in cognition, motivation, and sensation. For example, one explanation of ASD focuses on theory of mind (Jones & others, 2018). *Theory of mind* refers to understanding that other people have subjective experiences that differ from our own. From this perspective, children with ASD navigate the social world without this understanding (Baron-Cohen, 1995; 2011). Another theory holds that people with ASD have profoundly lower social motivation than typically developing people. This difference affects what infants attend to and what they learn from experience (Chevallier & others, 2012; Clements & others, 2018), potentially affecting brain development. A final approach to ASD notes that people with ASD are often very sensitive to sights, sounds, and tactile sensations and have problems integrating sensory experiences (Little & others, 2018; Reiersen, 2018; Robertson & Baron-Cohen, 2017). For a person with ASD the world can be an overwhelming cacophony of stimulation (Bogdashina, 2016; Tavassoli & others, 2018).

A diagnosis of ASD often begins when parents and pediatricians notice potential signs, such as language delays (CDC, 2018a). Despite widespread awareness of ASD, most children are diagnosed after age 3; many are diagnosed after age 6 (May & Williams, 2018; Ozonoff & others, 2018; Zwaigenbaum & Penner, 2018). A concern is that children of diverse ethnic, racial, and socioeconomic backgrounds may not receive the evaluations they need to access treatments (Durkin & others, 2017).

Because early intervention strongly predicts better outcomes (Noyes-Grosser & others, 2018; Vinen & others, 2018), scientists have searched for ways to identify children with ASD before age 3. In a landmark study, Julie Osterling and Geraldine Dawson (1994) found evidence of early signs of ASD in home videos. They had a team of coders rate videos of children's first birthday parties. For half of the videos, the birthday child would later be diagnosed with ASD; the others would develop typically. Coders were unaware of whether a child would eventually be diagnosed with ASD.

The results? Even at just one year, children who would be diagnosed with ASD were less likely than typically developing kids to look when someone called their name; to point at or show an object to another person; and to look at a person's face when interacting with them (Osterling & Dawson, 1994). Subsequent research has shown that, compared with typically developing children, very young children who will develop ASD show low levels of joint attention (looking at objects with another person) and low levels of attention to other children (Clifford & Dissanayake, 2008; Wilson & others, 2017). Currently, many infants in the United States are screened for ASD at 18 and 24 months of age (Broder-Fingert, Feinberg, & Silverstein, 2018; Salisbury & others, 2018). Screenings monitor the child's communication and social abilities (CDC, 2018a).

To identify ASD risk as early as possible, scientists have tried to identify *biomarkers,* measurable physical qualities that signal the presence of a disorder. Researchers have identified markers in blood (Howsmon & others, 2018) and saliva (Hicks & others, 2018) that appear to distinguish children with ASD from the typically developing and those with other developmental disorders. Biomarkers for ASD may someday allow interventions to begin even before symptoms appear (Jaffee, 2018).

## THE ETIOLOGY OF AUTISM SPECTRUM DISORDER

Currently, there is strong scientific consensus about two things that *do not* cause ASD. First, specific parenting styles do not produce ASD (Muhle & others, 2018). Second, vaccines do not cause ASD (Dudley & others, 2018; Hotez, 2018).

● **illusory correlation** A cognitive bias that occurs when two vivid events happen close in time and they are mistakenly perceived as linked, meaningfully.

The mistaken perception that vaccines cause ASD is an example of *illusory correlation*. **Illusory correlation** means that when two vivid events occur at the same time, they are mistakenly perceived as linked. Because vaccines are given at the same time that communication and social skill delays are noticed, adults are more likely to think the delays are caused by vaccines. They are not.

Risk factors for ASD include older parental age (Muhle & others, 2018), maternal obesity, diabetes, and hypertension, and prenatal exposure to some chemicals (Hisle-Gorman & others, 2018). Maternal infections, such as rubella, during pregnancy are also risk factors (Spann & others, 2017). Preterm birth, birth complications, and infant seizures shortly after birth predict ASD (Gross, 2018; Hisle-Gorman & others, 2018). The two most important factors in ASD are genes and the brain.

**Genetic and Brain Differences** Genes play a large role in the development of ASD (J. Wang & others, 2018). Children whose siblings have ASD are at higher risk and the heritability estimate for ASD is over 80 percent (Yip & others, 2018). Molecular genetic studies link ASD to genes involved in cell regulation and communication (Brandler & others, 2018; J. Wang & others, 2018).

Problems at the molecular level can affect how the brain develops prenatally and beyond. At-risk infants show an atypical pattern of brain development (Muhle & others, 2018). In one study, among at-risk infants at age 6 months, networks in the brain (including temporal, parietal, and occipital lobes, and Broca's area) were less able to communicate efficiently, and this inefficiency predicted severity of ASD symptoms at one year (Lewis & others, 2017).

Brain imaging studies show differences that reflect the social symptoms of ASD. A study of adults with ASD found deficits in the brain's reward pathways in response to social stimuli (Supekar & others, 2018). Other studies suggest deficits in mirror neuron functioning (Fründt & others, 2018) and emotional face processing (Leung & others, 2018).

**Etiological Diversity** There is no one cause of ASD. It appears to be *etiologically diverse*, meaning underlying causes vary from person to person (Betancur, 2011; Müller & Fishman, 2018). Recall the term phenotype–the actual characteristics of an organism. Etiological diversity means that people with ASD may share similar phenotypes but the underlying causes differ across persons. One way to understand this complexity is to note that there are only so many ways to be human. A child, no matter their genes, will not sprout wings and fly. They will be, always, human. People with ASD may share symptoms, like hand flapping or restricted interests, for different underlying reasons. These many reasons produce similar symptoms because those symptoms are within the realm of what human beings do.

You may know someone who has some level of traits associated with ASD. Parents and siblings of kids with ASD often show subclinical levels of ASD traits, like being less socially engaged (Rubenstein & others, 2018; Ruzich & others, 2017). Thinking of ASD in this way highlights that those with ASD are not qualitatively different from others; they are not only on the autism spectrum but also on the *human* spectrum.

● **applied behavior analysis or behavior modification** The use of operant conditioning principles to change human behavior.

## TREATMENT

There is no cure for ASD, but treatments can greatly improve the lives of many people with ASD. Behavioral treatment, called **applied behavior analysis**, as reviewed in the "Learning" chapter, is used to treat ASD (Thompson, 2013). This intense treatment uses reinforcement, shaping, and discrimination (Thompson, 2013; Strand & Eldevik, 2018). A meta-analysis showed that applied behavior analysis interventions improved IQ scores, communication, and language skills among children with ASD (Makrygianni & others, 2018). Medications may also be used to treat especially troubling symptoms (tantrums or self-harm) (Nylander & others, 2018).

It is common for children with ASD to receive a dual diagnosis of ASD and attention-deficit/hyperactivity disorder (Ghirardi & others, 2018), our next topic.

## Attention-Deficit/Hyperactivity Disorder

**Attention-deficit/hyperactivity disorder** (or ADHD) involves persistent problems in sustaining attention and difficulty engaging in quiet activities for a prolonged period. ADHD has three main symptoms (APA, 2013):

**attention-deficit/hyperactivity disorder (ADHD)** A common psychological disorder in which the individual exhibits one or more of the following: inattention, hyperactivity, and impulsivity.

1. *Inattention*: A tendency to wander off tasks, lack of persistence, and difficulty sustaining focus.
2. *Hyperactivity*: Excessive activity when it is inappropriate.
3. *Impulsivity*: Taking actions without planning or thinking.

Symptoms must occur before age 12 and appear across a variety of settings. A fifth-grader who is fidgety at school but can sit for hours constructing a complex Lego set at home is unlikely to have ADHD.

ADHD occurs in most cultures in about 5 percent of children (APA, 2013), but there are big differences across countries in ADHD rates (Sayal & others, 2018). Boys are more likely than girls to be diagnosed with ADHD (Mowlem & others, 2018). Experts once thought children "grow out" of ADHD, but about 70 percent of those diagnosed as children continue to experience symptoms in later in life (Uchida & others, 2018; Zhu & others, 2018).

In the United States, ADHD is one of the most common psychological disorders of childhood. In 2016, over 9 percent of American children aged 4 to 17 were diagnosed with ADHD at some point (CDC, 2018b). Rates are higher for White/European American children than for children in other ethnic/racial groups (Fairman, Peckham, & Sclar, 2017).

High rates of ADHD have prompted concern that psychiatrists, parents, and teachers are treating normal childhood behavior as a disorder (Armstrong 2017; Koutsoklenis & Gaitanidis, 2017; Timimi, 2017; Wakefield, 2016). Some argue that without a specific genetic or brain-related explanation, the ADHD diagnosis should be dropped. However, most psychological disorders lack such explanations. Moreover, left untreated, ADHD predicts serious negative outcomes.

ADHD predicts lower academic performance (Gray & others, 2017; Khalis, Mikami, & Hudec, 2018; Liu & others, 2017; Sjöwall & others, 2017) and poorer peer relations (Thorell & others, 2017). Compared with their typically developing peers, youth with ADHD are more likely to engage in delinquency (Philipp-Wiegmann & others, 2018). Adults diagnosed in childhood show poorer educational outcomes, higher rates of relationship difficulties, increased likelihood of incarceration, and lower SES (Faraone & others, 2015; Owens & others, 2017). These negative outcomes can be prevented by effective treatments (Thapar & Cooper, 2016).

An ADHD diagnosis involves interviews with the child and parents, and standard assessments completed by parents and teachers. ADHD symptoms can occur in other disorders (Caplan, 2017; Holland & Sayal, 2018), so it is important for children to be carefully assessed. Some groups, such as children from disadvantaged backgrounds, may have less access to evaluation and high-quality treatment (Rowland & others, 2018).

### THE ETIOLOGY OF ADHD

Very premature birth (Scott & others, 2017), low birth weight (Hanć & others, 2018), and prenatal exposure to alcohol and smoking (Frey & others, 2018; He & others, 2017) are risk factors for ADHD. Childhood lead exposure (Kim & others, 2018) in combination with factors such as poverty (Perera & others, 2018) is also associated with ADHD. Exposure to some pesticides can, together with genetic risk, heighten the risk of ADHD (Chang & others, 2018). Longitudinal studies show that children who experience more adverse events (physical, sexual, or verbal abuse and neglect) are more likely to be diagnosed with ADHD (Brown & others, 2017; Jimenez & others, 2017).

Twin studies show that up to 70 percent of the variance in ADHD symptoms is accounted for by genetic variability (Eilertsen & others, 2018). ADHD is *polygenic*, meaning that it is related to the interaction of two or more genes (Faraone & Larsson, 2018). Molecular genetic studies have identified specific genetic locations associated with ADHD (Bidwell & others, 2017), including the genes responsible for transporting dopamine and serotonin (Faraone & Larsson, 2018; Klein & others, 2017). Genes associated with ADHD are not specific to the disorder but may represent general risk for psychological disorders (Guo & others, 2017; van Hulzen & others, 2017).

Genetic differences are thought to affect brain development in ways that contribute to ADHD. For example, one approach to ADHD is the *delayed maturation hypothesis* (Klein & others, 2017; Rubia, 2018). This hypothesis says that in children with ADHD, the brain (especially the prefrontal cortex) develops more slowly compared to typically developing people (Beare & others, 2017; Bouziane & others, 2018). ADHD is associated with reduced cortical thickness (Cherkasova & others, 2017; Newman & others, 2016; Shaw & others, 2007) and fewer connections between the prefrontal cortex and other brain regions (Beare & others, 2017; Bouziane & others, 2018).

This research fits with cognitive approaches that emphasize problems in executive function as the root cause of problems in ADHD (Barkley, 1997; Carey & Bogdan, 2018; Graham, 2017). Preschoolers with poorer working memory function and difficulty regulating extreme positive emotions are more likely to show ADHD symptoms in adolescence (Sjöwall & others, 2017). Differences in working memory (rather than ADHD) may explain the lower academic performance among children with ADHD (Orban & others, 2018; Simone & others, 2017).

Another neurobiological focus is the reward centers of the brain, where people with ADHD have less brain volume (Hoogman & others, 2017; Hulst & others, 2017; Stevens & others, 2018). ADHD is associated with dysregulation in the neurotransmitter dopamine and pathways that carry this important neurotransmitter (Fernández-Jaén & others, 2018; Volkow & others, 2017). In addition to dopamine, dysregulation of acetylcholine and melatonin in infancy predict the development of ADHD (Hellmer & Nyström, 2017). Such findings fit with symptoms related to regulating reward motivation.

Diagnosis of ADHD requires that someone (often a child's teacher) notice symptoms. To read about a study that found a surprising variable that might bring a child to a teacher's attention, see the Critical Controversy.

©Vgstockstudio/Shutterstock

### TREATMENT

Stimulant medication (Ritalin or Adderall) is often the first line of treatment for ADHD (Pelham & others, 2017). It may be surprising that people who are too active would be treated with stimulants. These medications increase the amount of circulating dopamine (Schrantee & others, 2016). This increase in dopamine means the child does not have to engage in activity to experience the pleasure that dopamine evokes.

Children and adults with ADHD can also benefit from nonmedical interventions (Levelink & others, 2018). Often combined with medication, these interventions include physical exercise (Den Heijer & others, 2017; LaCount & Hartung, 2018), sports training (Altszuler & others, 2017), meditation (Chimiklis & others, 2018), academic tutoring and training (Tamm & others, 2017), and driving safety (Bruce & others, 2017).

Psychotherapy can be effective in treating ADHD in children whose symptoms do not respond to medication or who are very young (Daley & Dupaul, 2016; Sprich & others, 2016). Psychotherapy is also effective in treating ADHD in adults (Knouse, Teller, & Brooks, 2017) and parents of children with ADHD (Sprich & others, 2016).

## *test yourself*

1. What are four different theoretical perspectives on the origins of autism spectrum disorder?
2. Define etiological diversity.
3. Name five risk factors for ADHD.

## *Could Birth Month Predict an ADHD Diagnosis?*

Recently researchers identified one fact about a child that predicts ADHD diagnosis: being born in August (Jena, Barnett, & Layton, 2018). Why August? Many states in the United States have rules for when a child can start kindergarten. Typically, a child who turns 5 before September 1 may enroll in public school. This means that August-born children start school almost immediately after their 5th birthday. Compare those children to kids born in September. Entering kindergarten, they are almost 6 years old. So, even though all of the children are in the same grade, kids born in August are up to a year younger than everyone else.

Compared with their (older) classmates, August-born children might show signs of immaturity. A teacher may wonder whether a child's inability to sit still or pay attention indicates ADHD. Might immaturity be mistaken for a disorder?

To find out, researchers (Layton & others, 2018) used the medical records of over 400,000 children born in the United States from 2007 to 2009. In 2015, they collected data about ADHD diagnosis and treatment and compared children born in August with those born in September. The results? In states with a September 1 cutoff for kindergarten, the rate of ADHD in August-born children was up to 34 percent greater than the rate for those born in September. No other two months differed in this way. And, in states without a September 1 cutoff no difference in between August- and September-born children was found. Clearly, teachers and physicians must be mindful of children's age (not just their grade in school) when evaluating their behaviors.

**WHAT DO YOU THINK?**

- Why do you think parents decide to send children born in August to kindergarten?
- If a teacher suggested your child might have ADHD, what would you do?

# 3. ANXIETY AND ANXIETY-RELATED DISORDERS

Think about how you felt as you noticed police lights flashing behind your speeding car. Did you feel jittery and nervous and experience tightness in your stomach? These are symptoms of anxiety, an unpleasant feeling of fear and dread.

People with high levels of anxiety worry a lot, but their anxiety does not necessarily impair their ability to function. In contrast, people who have **anxiety disorders** experience fears that are uncontrollable, disproportionate to the actual danger the person might be in, and disruptive of life. They feature motor tension (jumpiness, trembling), hyperactivity (dizziness, a racing heart), and apprehensive expectations and thoughts.

- **anxiety disorders** Disabling (uncontrollable and disruptive) psychological disorders that feature motor tension, hyperactivity, and apprehensive expectations and thoughts.

*DSM-5* recognizes 12 types of anxiety disorders. In this section, we survey four of the most common anxiety disorders:

- Generalized anxiety disorder
- Panic disorder
- Specific phobia
- Social anxiety disorder

We also consider a disorder that is not classified by *DSM-5* as an anxiety disorder but that is related to the experience of anxiety, obsessive-compulsive disorder (categorized under obsessive-compulsive and related disorders).

## Generalized Anxiety Disorder

● **generalized anxiety disorder** An anxiety disorder marked by persistent anxiety for at least six months, and in which the individual is unable to specify the reasons for the anxiety.

When you are worried about getting a speeding ticket, you know why you are anxious; there is a specific cause. **Generalized anxiety disorder** is different from such everyday feelings of anxiety in that sufferers experience persistent anxiety for at least six months and are unable to specify the reasons for their anxiety (APA, 2013). People with generalized anxiety disorder are nervous most of the time and worry a great deal. That worry can take a physical toll, so that people with generalized anxiety disorder may suffer from fatigue, muscle tension, stomach problems, and difficulty sleeping.

What biopsychosocial factors play a role in generalized anxiety disorder? Among the biological factors are genetic predisposition, deficiency in the neurotransmitter GABA (the brain's brake pedal), respiratory system abnormalities, and problems in regulating the sympathetic nervous system (Strawn & others, 2018; Strobbe & Campanella, 2018; Taillieu & others, 2018; W. Wang & others, 2018). Psychological and sociocultural factors include having harsh (or even impossible) self-standards; overly strict, critical, or cold parents; difficulty dealing with uncertainty; automatic negative thoughts when feeling stressed; and a history of uncontrollable traumas or stressors (such as an abusive parent) (Fergusson, McLeod, & Horwood, 2013; Gillett & others, 2018; Goodwin, Yiend, & Hirsch, 2017; Long & others, 2015).

● **panic disorder** An anxiety disorder in which the individual experiences recurrent, sudden onsets of intense terror, often without warning and with no specific cause.

*Many experts interpret Edvard Munch's painting* The Scream *as an expression of the terror brought on by a panic attack.*



## Panic Disorder

Much like everyone else, you might have a specific experience that sends you into a panic. You are just about to dash across a street when you see a big truck coming right at you. Your heart races, your hands shake, and you might break into a sweat. In this situation, you know why you are experiencing panic.

In **panic disorder**, however, a person experiences recurrent, sudden onsets of intense terror, often without warning and with no specific cause. Panic attacks can produce extreme shortness of breath, chest pains, trembling, sweating, dizziness, and a feeling of helplessness (Tully, Sardinha, & Nardi, 2017). People with panic disorder may feel as if they are having a heart attack.

Charles Darwin, who proposed the theory of evolution, suffered from intense panic disorder (Barloon & Noyes, 1997), as has former NFL running back Earl Campbell.

What factors underlie panic disorder? In terms of biology, people may have a genetic predisposition to the disorder. Of particular interest to researchers are genes that direct neurotransmitters such as norepinephrine, GABA, and serotonin (Watanabe & others, 2017). Another brain chemical, lactate, which plays a role in brain metabolism, is elevated in those with panic disorder (Riske & others, 2017; Strawn & others, 2018). Interestingly, experimental research shows that increasing lactate levels can produce panic attacks (Bernik & others, 2017; Leibold & others, 2015).

Other research points to the involvement of genes involved in hormone regulation and responses to stress (Wichmann & others, 2018). Panic disorder appears to share biological features with physical illnesses, such as asthma (Meuret & others, 2018), hypertension (Abreu & others, 2018), and cardiovascular disease (Tural & Iosifescu, 2018).

With regard to psychological influences, learning processes, as described in the chapter "Learning", have been considered in panic disorder. Classical conditioning research has shown that learned associations between bodily cues of respiration and fear can play a role in panic attacks (Kellner & others, 2018). Interestingly, in humans carbon dioxide ($CO_2$) is a very strong conditioned stimulus for fear (Feinstein & others, 2013), suggesting that we may be biologically prepared to learn an association between high concentrations of $CO_2$ and fear. Thus, some learning researchers suggest that at the heart of panic attacks are such learned associations (Cooper, Grillon, & Lissek, 2018).

Also, the learning concept of *generalization* may apply to panic attack. Recall that in classical conditioning generalization means showing a conditioned response (in this case, fear) to stimuli other than the particular one used in learning. People who suffer from panic attacks are more likely to display overgeneralization of fear learning (Duits & others, 2015; Spalding, 2018). It may be that genetic characteristics predispose people to develop such associations when they encounter particularly stressful life events, especially involving separation (Morimoto & others, 2018). This is a vulnerability-stress explanation.

In terms of sociocultural factors, women are nearly twice as likely as men to have panic attacks (Boyd & others, 2015). Possible reasons for this difference include differences in hormones and neurotransmitters (Fodor & Epstein, 2002), as well as the different ways men and women cope with anxiety-provoking situations (Schmidt & Koselka, 2000; Sun, Lu, & Qu, 2018).

## Specific Phobia

Many people are afraid of spiders and snakes; thinking about letting a tarantula crawl over one's face is likely to give anyone the willies. It is not uncommon to be afraid of particular objects or situations such as extreme heights. For most of us, these fears do not interfere with daily life. A fear becomes a phobia when a situation is dreaded so intensely that a person goes to almost any length to avoid it. A fear of snakes that keeps a city-dweller from leaving his apartment is clearly disproportionate to the actual chance of encountering a snake. **Specific phobia** is an anxiety disorder in which an individual has an irrational, overwhelming, persistent fear of a particular object or situation.

● **specific phobia** An anxiety disorder in which the individual experiences an irrational, overwhelming, persistent fear of a particular object or situation.

Specific phobias come in many forms, as shown in Figure 2.

Where do specific phobias come from? Answering this question involves first acknowledging that fear plays an important role in adaptive behavior. Fear tells us when we are in danger and need to take to action. The importance of this function suggests that fears should be relatively quickly learned, because learning to fear things that will hurt us keeps us out of harm's way. Specific phobias might be viewed, then, as an unfortunate variant of this adaptive process (Coelho & Purkis, 2009; Muris & Merckelbach, 2012). Women are more likely than men to experience specific phobias (Steinhausen & others, 2016).

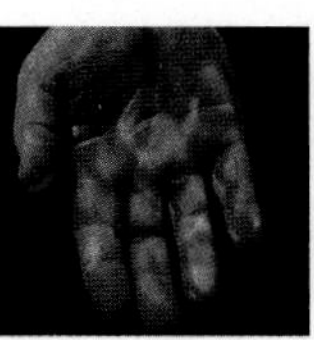

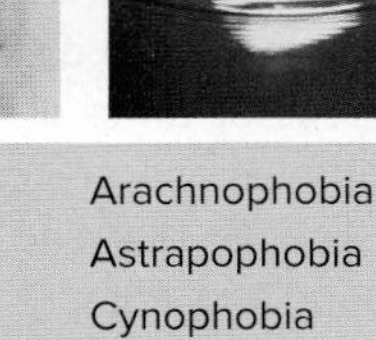

| | | | | | |
|---|---|---|---|---|---|
| Acrophobia | Fear of high places | Arachnophobia | Fear of spiders | Mysophobia | Fear of dirt |
| Aerophobia | Fear of flying | Astrapophobia | Fear of lightning | Nyctophobia | Fear of darkness |
| Ailurophobia | Fear of cats | Cynophobia | Fear of dogs | Ophidiophobia | Fear of nonpoisonous snakes |
| Algophobia | Fear of pain | Gamophobia | Fear of marriage | Thanatophobia | Fear of death |
| Amaxophobia | Fear of vehicles, driving | Hydrophobia | Fear of water | Xenophobia | Fear of strangers |
| | | Melissophobia | Fear of bees | | |

**FIGURE 2** **Specific Phobias** This figure features examples of specific phobias—psychological disorders characterized by irrational, overwhelming, and persistent fear of a particular object or situation. photos (first) ©Fuse/Getty Images; (second) ©Flying Colors Ltd./Getty Images; (third) ©Digital Archive Japan/Alamy Stock Photo; (fourth) ©Comstock Images/Alamy Stock Photo; (fifth) ©believeinme33/123RF; (sixth) ©Peter Dazeley/Photographer's Choice/Getty Images; (seventh) ©Creatas/PunchStock/Getty Images; (eighth) ©Tom Mareschal/Alamy Stock Photo; (spider) ©pets in frames/Shutterstock

Many explanations of specific phobias view them as based on experiences, memories, and learned associations (Meir Drexler & Wolf, 2018; Pittig & others, 2018). Perhaps, for example, the individual with a fear of heights experienced a fall from a high place earlier in life and therefore associates heights with pain (a classical conditioning explanation). Alternatively, he or she may have heard about or watched others who demonstrated terror of high places (an observational learning explanation), as when a little girl develops a fear of heights after sitting next to her terrified mother and observing her clutch the handrails, white-knuckled, as the roller coaster creeps steeply uphill.

Not all people who have a specific phobia can easily identify experiences that explain them, so other factors may also be at play (Coelho & Purkis, 2009). Each specific phobia may have its own neural correlates (Lueken & others, 2011), and some people may be especially prone to phobias (van der Merwe & others, 2019). Women are more likely than men to experience specific phobias and another risk factor having a parent who has a psychological disorder, even if that disorder is not a specific phobia (Steinhausen & others, 2016).

## Social Anxiety Disorder

Imagine how you might feel just before you first meet the parents of the person you hope to marry. You might dread making some awful gaffe, ruining their first impression of you. **Social anxiety disorder (SAD)** (also called **social phobia**) is an intense fear of being humiliated or embarrassed in social situations (Oliveira & others, 2018; Morrison & Heimberg, 2013).

**social anxiety disorder (SAD) or social phobia** An anxiety disorder in which the individual has an intense fear of being humiliated or embarrassed in social situations.

Where does SAD come from? Genes appear to play a role (Torvik & others, 2016), along with neural circuitry involving the thalamus, amygdalae, and cerebral cortex (Jacob & others, 2018; Weidt & others, 2016). A number of neurotransmitters may be involved, including oxytocin (Ma & others, 2016; Olofsdotter & others, 2018). SAD may involve vulnerabilities, such as genetic characteristics, that lay a foundation of risk, combined with learning experiences in a social context (Pejic & others, 2013; Sharma & others, 2016).

In *DSM-5*, the disorders we have covered so far are classified as anxiety disorders (APA, 2016; Gallo & others, 2013; Kupfer, 2015). Our next topic–obsessive-compulsive disorder (or OCD)–is not included under the umbrella of anxiety disorders. Instead, OCD has its own separate category. Nonetheless, as we will see, anxiety is relevant to this disorder.

## Obsessive-Compulsive Disorder

Just before leaving on a long road trip, you find yourself checking to be sure you locked the front door. Going to bed the night before an early flight, you check your alarm clock a few times to be sure it will wake you for your 8 A.M. plane. This kind of checking behavior is a normal part of worry.

In contrast, **obsessive-compulsive disorder (OCD)** involves anxiety-provoking thoughts that will not go away and/or urges to perform repetitive, ritualistic behaviors to prevent or produce some future situation. *Obsessions* are recurrent thoughts, and *compulsions* are recurrent behaviors. People with OCD dwell on normal doubts and repeat their behavioral routines, sometimes hundreds of times a day.

**obsessive-compulsive disorder (OCD)** Psychological disorder in which the individual has anxiety-provoking thoughts that will not go away and/or urges to perform repetitive, ritualistic behaviors to prevent or produce some future situation.

The most common compulsions are excessive checking, cleansing, and counting. A person with OCD might believe that she has to touch the doorway with her left hand whenever she enters a room and count her steps as she walks across the room. If she does not complete this ritual, she may be overcome with fear that something terrible will happen. Indeed, most people feel extraordinarily anxious if they do not act out their compulsions (Dougherty & others, 2018; Laposa & others, 2015). Actor and game show host Howie Mandel has coped with OCD.

### FACTORS CONTRIBUTING TO OCD

There seems to be a genetic component to OCD (Fernandez, Leckman, & Pittenger, 2018). Research also points to low levels of the neurotransmitters serotonin and dopamine

(D. L. Murphy & others, 2013; Winter & others, 2018) and high levels of glutamate (Naaijen & others, 2018) in the brain pathways linked with OCD.

Brain-imaging, EEG, and animal studies suggest neurological links for OCD. The brain seems to engage in a hyperactive monitoring of behavior in those with OCD (Endrass & others, 2013), and brain activation during learning may predispose people with OCD to a chronic feeling that something is not quite right (Gehring, Himle, & Nisenson, 2000).

One interpretation of these data is that the frontal cortex or basal ganglia are so active or so strongly connected to other areas of the brain in people with OCD that numerous impulses reach the thalamus, generating obsessive thoughts or compulsive actions (Apergis-Schoute & others, 2018; Rotge & others, 2009). Essentially, the brain fails to get the "finished" message (Montiero & Feng, 2016).

Learning processes are also implicated in OCD (Endrass & others, 2013; Ramos & others, 2018). A person who engages in compulsive behaviors often feels like they must do it to fend off some dreaded outcome. For instance, consider a woman who feels compelled to check the locks on her apartment door 10 times so that she knows she has not put herself in danger by leaving the door unlocked. Having locked the door once, she is, of course, safe from this feared result. But she checks nine more times just to be sure.

Can you see the vicious cycle of her compulsion? Over and over again, she performs the ritual and nothing bad happens. As long as she performs this ritual, she will never discover that the terrible outcome would not have happened anyway. This example suggests that *avoidance learning* might be an important contributor to the maintenance of compulsive symptoms. Recall that avoidance learning is a powerful form of negative reinforcement that occurs when the organism learns that by making a particular response, an unpleasant or aversive stimulus can be avoided completely. That response is maintained even in the absence of any aversive stimulus. The unpleasant stimulus is no longer around, but the avoiding organism will never discover that fact (Pittig & others, 2018).

The notion that those with OCD may get "stuck" in the vicious cycle of avoidance learning is supported by studies showing that OCD is associated with reduced flexibility in picking up on changes in the rules of learning tasks (Bradbury, Cassin, & Rector, 2011; Pushkarskaya & others, 2018).

Not surprisingly, people with OCD show a cognitive bias associated with overestimating personally relevant threats (Rouel, Stevenson, & Smith, 2018). As noted above, from a cognitive perspective, people with OCD show an inability to turn off negative, intrusive thoughts by ignoring or effectively dismissing them.

Thus, the science of OCD suggests that these people are preoccupied with avoiding a dreaded outcome, are prone to see that outcome as worse and more likely than it actually is, and are likely to be bothered by lingering doubts about whether they have avoided it. Once they find a way to fend off the feared result, they are likely to have difficulty unlearning that strategy. Some psychologists propose that, fundamentally, OCD symptoms reflect intolerance of uncertainty (Giele & others, 2016; Gillett & others, 2018).

## OCD-RELATED DISORDERS

*DSM-5* expanded the disorders that are thought to be related to OCD. All of these disorders involve repetitive behavior, and like OCD, issues with uncertainty and anxiety. Some of the new additions are listed here:

- *Hoarding disorder* involves compulsive collecting, poor organizational skills, and difficulty discarding, as well as cognitive deficits in information-processing speed, decision making, and procrastination (Kress & others, 2016; Pushkarskaya & others, 2018). People with this disorder find it difficult to throw things away; they are troubled by the feeling of uncertainty—the sense that they might need, for instance, old newspapers, at a later time (Castriotta & others, 2018).
- *Excoriation disorder* (or skin picking) refers to a particular compulsion, picking at one's skin, sometimes to the point of injury (Sampaio & Grant, 2018). Skin picking is more common among women than men and is seen as a symptom of autism spectrum disorder. Infections and complications with healing are issues with this disorder.

- *Trichotillomania* (hair pulling) is a disorder in which the person compulsively pulls at his or her hair, from the scalp, eyebrows, and other body areas (Chamberlain & others, 2018). Hair pulling from the scalp can lead to patches of baldness that the person may go to great lengths to disguise.
- *Body dysmorphic disorder* involves a distressing preoccupation with imagined or slight flaws in one's physical appearance (Hong & others, 2018). People with the disorder cannot stop thinking about their appearance, comparing their appearance to others, checking themselves in the mirror, and so forth. Occurring about equally in men and women, this disorder can involve maladaptive behaviors such as compulsive exercise and bodybuilding and repeated cosmetic surgery.

### test yourself

1. Define four anxiety disorders.
2. What are the central features of obsessive-compulsive disorder?
3. How is anxiety related to OCD?

## 4. TRAUMA AND STRESS-RELATED DISORDERS

Many psychological disorders involve a combination of factors, including genetic characteristics and experiences. Some psychological disorders, though, are more clearly linked to extremely negative experiences. In this section, we review two types of disorders that involve trauma: post-traumatic stress disorder and dissociative disorders. Traumatic experiences may involve the threat of death or serious injury or sexual violence, in which a person feels intense fear and helplessness (Chopko, Palmieri, & Adams, 2018). Traumas can involve a single horrific incident or a pattern of negative experiences.

### Post-Traumatic Stress Disorder

If you are ever in a car accident, you may have a nightmare or two about it. You might even find yourself reliving the experience for some time. This normal recovery process takes on a devastating character in **post-traumatic stress disorder (PTSD)**, a disorder that develops through exposure to a traumatic event that overwhelms the person's abilities to cope. *DSM-5* has expanded the kinds of experiences that might foster PTSD, recognizing that the disorder can occur not only in people who directly experience a trauma but also in those who witness it and those who only *hear* about it (APA, 2013). The symptoms of PTSD vary but may include the following:

**post-traumatic stress disorder (PTSD)** Psychological disorder that develops through exposure to a traumatic event, a severely oppressive situation, physical or emotional abuse, or a natural or an unnatural disaster.

- Flashbacks in which the individual relives the event. A flashback can make the person lose touch with reality and reenact the event for seconds, hours, or, very rarely, days. A person having a flashback—which can come in the form of images, sounds, smells, and/or feelings—usually believes that the traumatic event is happening all over again.
- Avoiding emotional experiences and avoiding talking about emotions with others.
- Emotional numbness and a reduced ability to feel emotions.
- Excessive arousal, resulting in an exaggerated startle response or an inability to sleep.
- Difficulties with memory and concentration.
- Impulsive behavior.

Source: U.S. Navy photo by Lance Cpl. Brian L. Wickliffe

PTSD can occur after a variety of extremely disturbing events. Such events can include natural disasters (such as hurricanes or earthquakes), combat and war-related trauma, unnatural disasters (such as car accidents, plane crashes, terrorist attacks, or mass shootings), childhood abuse and victimization, and sexual violence. Health crises are also linked to the development of PTSD (S. K. Smith & others, 2018). As many as 1 in 5 adults diagnosed with cancer developed PTSD symptoms within 4 years (Chan & others, 2018).

Different traumas can have different consequences for symptoms, such as survivor guilt, lingering feelings of betrayal and powerlessness, or enduring worries about safety (Badour, Resnick, & Kilpatrick, 2017).

©tommaso79/Shutterstock

What traumatic experiences share is their capacity to shatter the basic assumptions of life, including beliefs about the fairness of existence and one's place in the world. Traumatic life experiences challenge a person's capacity to cope. PTSD symptoms can follow a trauma immediately or after months or even years have passed (Dikmen-Yildiz, Ayers, & Phillips, 2018). Most people who are exposed to a traumatic event experience some of the symptoms in the days and weeks following exposure (National Center for PTSD, 2018).

One type of traumatic event linked to PTSD that is unfortunately common for American college students is sexual victimization (Dworkin & others, 2017; Rosellini & others, 2017). Such traumas can include rape, sexual assault, or sexual harassment. Rape refers to forced sexual intercourse, including both verbal and physical force. Sexual assault may or may not include force and includes actions such as grabbing or fondling. Sexual harassment is unwelcome conduct of a sexual nature that offends, humiliates, or intimidates another. In comparison with women who have not been victims of a violent crime, women who have experienced sexual victimization are approximately six times more likely to develop PTSD (Gilmore & others, 2017; Kilpatrick, 2000).

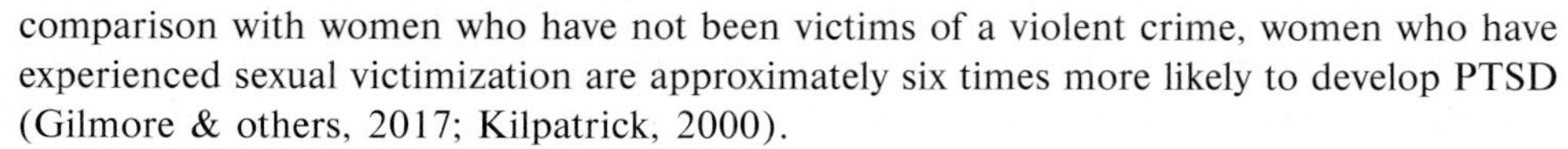

How can survivors of sexual victimization be helped? In addition to treatment for psychological disorders, sexual assault survivors benefit from strong social support (Dworkin, Ullman, & others, 2018). People who have access to information and medical and legal help are better able to cope with this trauma. Unfortunately, too often, victims of sexual assault are unaware of the resources available to them (Holland, Rabelo, & Cortina, 2017). For this reason, many colleges and universities have taken steps to better educate their communities about such services, about the laws surrounding sexual assault and harassment, and their expectations for appropriate behavior. An important way to prevent PTSD is to prevent sexual victimization.

What causes PTSD? Clearly, one factor is the traumatic event. However, not everyone exposed to the same event develops PTSD (Chopko, Palmieri, & Adams, 2018). Therefore, other factors must influence a person's vulnerability to the disorder. These include a history of previous traumatic events and conditions, such as abuse and psychological disorders (John, Cisler, & Sigel, 2017), personality characteristics (Meyer & others, 2018), cultural background (Alford, 2016), and genetic predisposition (Bharadwaj & others, 2018; Mehta & others, 2018). These preexisting conditions make people more vulnerable to PTSD when they encounter stressful events. Thus, PTSD may be best explained by a vulnerability-stress model.

Trauma can profoundly affect the way a person copes with other life events (John, Cisler, & Sigel, 2017; Kim & others, 2018). Traumas can alter the delicate balance of neurotransmitters, hormones, and other biological systems, such that PTSD can influence how the body and brain react to stress (Mehta & others, 2018; Young & others, 2018). PTSD is associated with decreased volume in the hippocampus, the brain structure most associated with integrating memories (Logue & others, 2018; Quidé, Andersson, & El-Hage, 2018).

Treatments for PTSD include psychotherapies using classical conditioning paradigms to break the links between current experiences and deep feelings of trauma (Downs, 2018; Foa & others, 2018) as well as therapies aimed at changing beliefs and behavior (Brown & others, 2018). In addition, group therapy with other survivors of similar trauma can be helpful (Levi & others, 2017). Among survivors of sexual assault, self-defense training can help restore a sense of personal control and efficacy (Pinciotti & Orcutt, 2018). Finally, medications may help people with PTSD (Downs, 2018), often in conjunction with intensive psychotherapy.

## Dissociative Disorders

Have you ever been on a long car ride and completely lost track of time, so that you could not even remember a stretch of miles along the road? Have you been so caught up in a daydream that you were unaware of the passage of time? These are examples of normal dissociation. *Dissociation* refers to psychological states in which the person feels disconnected from immediate experience.

At the extreme of dissociation are those who persistently feel a sense of disconnection. **Dissociative disorders** involve a sudden loss of memory or change in identity. Under extreme stress or shock, a person's conscious awareness becomes separated or split (dissociated) from previous memories and thoughts. People with dissociative disorders may have problems putting together different aspects of consciousness, so that experiences at different levels of awareness might be perceived as though they are happening to someone else. In *DSM-5,* dissociative disorders are not included as a trauma-related disorder but are placed in close proximity to these to reflect the level of overlap between PTSD and dissociative disorders (APA, 2013). Indeed, some people with PTSD also experience dissociation (Ford & others, 2018; Melara & others, 2018). Both dissociative disorders and PTSD are thought to be rooted, in part, in extremely traumatic life events (Elklit, Hyland, & Shevlin, 2014).

● **dissociative disorders** Psychological disorders that involve a sudden loss of memory or change in identity due to the dissociation (separation) of the individual's conscious awareness from previous memories and thoughts.

Psychologists believe that dissociation is a way of dealing with extreme stress (Krause-Utz & Elzinga, 2018; Zamir & others, 2018). The idea that dissociative disorders are related to problems in pulling together emotional memories is supported by findings showing lower volume in the hippocampus and amygdalae in people with dissociative disorders (McDonald & White, 2013; D. Scott & others, 2018). The hippocampus is especially involved in consolidating memory and organizing life experience into a coherent whole.

Dissociative disorders may be the most controversial of all diagnostic categories, with some psychologists believing that they are often mistakenly diagnosed and others arguing that they are underdiagnosed (Freeland & others, 1993; Rydberg, 2017; Sar, Akyuz, & Dogan, 2007). Two kinds of dissociative disorders are dissociative amnesia and dissociative identity disorder.

## DISSOCIATIVE AMNESIA

Amnesia is the inability to recall important events. Amnesia can result from a blow to the head that produces trauma in the brain. **Dissociative amnesia** is a type of amnesia characterized by extreme memory loss that stems from extensive psychological stress (Radulovic, Lee, & Ortony, 2018). People experiencing dissociative amnesia remember everyday tasks like how to hail a cab or use a phone. They forget only aspects of their own identity and autobiographical experiences.

● **dissociative amnesia** Dissociative disorder characterized by extreme memory loss that is caused by extensive psychological stress.

Sometimes those suffering from dissociative amnesia will also unexpectedly travel away from home, occasionally assuming a new identity (Mamarde & others, 2013). For instance, on August 28, 2008, Hannah Upp, a 23-year-old middle school teacher in New York City, disappeared while out for a run (Marx & Didziulis, 2009). She had no wallet, no identification, no phone, and no money. Her family and friends posted flyers around the city and messages on the Internet. As days went by, they became increasingly concerned that something terrible had happened. Finally, Hannah was found floating face down in the New York harbor on September 16, sunburned and dehydrated but alive. She remembered nothing of her experiences. To her, it felt like she had gone out for a run and 10 minutes later was being pulled from the harbor. After recovering from her first experience, Hannah disappeared again years later and has not been found (Aviv, 2018).

Dissociative amnesia is believed to be caused by extremely stressful events. Treatment for this disorder is likely to involve psychotherapy that provides the person an opportunity to process their traumatic memories in a safe context.

## DISSOCIATIVE IDENTITY DISORDER

**Dissociative identity disorder (DID)**, formerly called *multiple personality disorder,* is the most dramatic, least common, and most controversial dissociative disorder. People with this disorder have two or more distinct personalities or identities (Costabile & others, 2018; Parry, Lloyd, & Simpson, 2018). Each identity has its own memories, behaviors, and relationships. One identity dominates at one time, another takes over at another time. People sometimes report that a wall of amnesia separates their different identities (Morton, 2017) however, research suggests that memory does transfer across these identities, even if the person believes it does not (Huntjens & others, 2014; Kong, Allen, & Glisky, 2008).

● **dissociative identity disorder (DID)** Dissociative disorder in which the individual has two or more distinct personalities or selves, each with its own memories, behaviors, and relationships; formerly called multiple personality disorder.

The shift between identities usually occurs under stress (Sar, Akyuz, & Dogan, 2007) but sometimes can also be controlled by the person (Kong, Allen, & Glisky, 2008).

A famous real-life example of dissociative identity disorder is the "three faces of Eve" case, based on the life of a woman named Chris Sizemore (Thigpen & Cleckley, 1957) (Figure 3). Eve White was the original dominant personality. She had no knowledge of her second personality, Eve Black, although Eve Black had been alternating with Eve White for a number of years. Eve White was quiet and serious. Eve Black was mischievous and uninhibited. Eve Black would emerge at inappropriate times, leaving Eve White with hangovers, bills, and a reputation in local bars that she could not explain. During treatment, a third personality emerged: Jane. More mature than the other two, Jane seems to have developed as a result of therapy.

**FIGURE 3** **The Three Faces of Eve** Chris Sizemore, the subject of the 1950s book and film *The Three Faces of Eve,* is shown here with a work she painted, titled *Three Faces in One.*

©Gerald Martineau/The Washington Post/Getty Images

The factors that contribute to DID remain something of a mystery. Extraordinarily severe sexual or physical abuse during early childhood has been linked to the condition (J. G. Scott & others, 2018). Some psychologists believe that a child can cope with intense trauma by dissociating from the experience and developing other alternate selves as protectors. Sexual abuse has occurred in as many as 70 percent or more of DID cases (Foote & others, 2006); however, the majority of people who have been sexually abused do not develop DID. The vast majority of people with DID are women. A genetic predisposition might also exist, as the disorder tends to run in families (Dell & Eisenhower, 1990). Finally, a recent brain imaging study showed that those with DID had lower cortical thickness and cortical surface area than matched healthy controls (Reinders & others, 2018). These findings are particularly interesting because the brain differences are traced to genetic and prenatal factors. Thus, these differences might represent a vulnerability to DID.

Until the 1980s, only about 300 cases of DID had ever been reported (Suinn, 1984). In the past 30 years, hundreds more cases have been diagnosed (Dorahy & van der Hart, 2014). Social cognitive scholars note that diagnoses have increased whenever the popular media present a case, as in the miniseries *Sybil* or the film *Split*. From this perspective, people develop multiple identities through social contagion. After exposure to these examples, people may be more likely to view multiple identities as a real condition. Some experts believe that DID is a *social construction*—that it represents a category some people adopt to make sense of their experiences (Spanos, 1996). Rather than being a single person with many conflicting feelings, wishes, and potentially awful experiences, the person compartmentalizes different aspects of the self into independent identities. In some cases, therapists have been accused of creating alternate personalities. Encountering a person who appears to have a fragmented sense of self, the therapist may begin to treat each fragment as its own "personality" (Spiegel, 2006).

Cross-cultural comparisons shed light on whether DID is primarily a response to traumatic events or the result of a social contagion. If dissociation is a response to trauma, people with similar levels of traumatic experience should show similar degrees of dissociation, regardless of their exposure to cultural messages about dissociation. In China, the popular media *do not* commonly portray cases of DID and professional knowledge of the disorder is rare. A study comparing people from China and Canada (where DID is widely publicized) found reports of traumatic experience to be similar across groups and to relate to dissociative experiences similarly as well (Ross & others, 2008), casting some doubt on the idea that dissociative experiences are entirely a product of social contagion.

Because DID is rare, research on treatments is limited. One study showed that long-term, in-depth, intensive psychotherapy led to improvement in functioning (Myrick & others, 2017). A key concern is that therapists remain objective in treatment and avoid evoking multiple identities in the patient.

## test yourself

1. What are three symptoms of PTSD?
2. Use the vulnerability-stress approach to understand dissociative identity disorder.
3. Describe two types of treatment for PTSD.

*This painting by Vincent Van Gogh,* Portrait of Dr. Gachet, *reflects the extreme melancholy that characterizes the depressive disorders.*



● **depressive disorders** Psychological disorders in which the individual suffers from depression—an unrelenting lack of pleasure in life.

● **major depressive disorder (MDD)** Psychological disorder involving a significant depressive episode and depressed characteristics, such as lethargy and hopelessness, for at least two weeks.

# 5. DISORDERS INVOLVING EMOTION AND MOOD

Usually, our emotions tell us how we are doing in life. We feel good or bad depending on our progress toward achieving important goals. For some people, the link between experience and emotions is off-kilter. They may feel sad for no reason or feel elated in the absence of any great accomplishment. Many psychological disorders involve this kind of dysregulation in a person's emotional life. In this section we examine two such disorders: depressive disorders and bipolar disorders.

## Depressive Disorders

Everyone feels blue sometimes. A romantic breakup, the death of a loved one, or a personal failure can cast a dark cloud over life. Sometimes, however, a person might feel unhappy and not know why. **Depressive disorders** are disorders in which the individual suffers from *depression*–an unrelenting lack of pleasure in life.

Depression is common. A recent study found that over 20 percent of Americans reported at least one major depressive episode in their lifetime (Hasin & others, 2018)–about twice the population of the state of Texas.

A number of successful people have been diagnosed with depression, including musicians Sheryl Crow, Eric Clapton, and Peter Gabriel; actors Drew Barrymore and Jim Carrey; artist Pablo Picasso; photographer Diane Arbus; famed architect Frank Lloyd Wright; and J. K. Rowling, the author of the *Harry Potter* series.

**Major depressive disorder (MDD)** involves a significant depressive episode and depressed characteristics, such as lethargy and hopelessness, for at least two weeks. MDD has been called the leading cause of disability in the United States (NIMH, 2018). The symptoms of MDD may include the following:

- Depressed mood for most of the day
- Reduced interest or pleasure in activities that were once enjoyable
- Significant weight loss or gain, or significant decrease or increase in appetite
- Trouble sleeping, or sleeping too much
- Fatigue or loss of energy
- Feeling worthless or guilty in an excessive or inappropriate manner
- Problems in thinking, concentrating, or making decisions
- Recurrent thoughts of death and suicide
- No history of manic episodes (periods of euphoric mood)

People who experience less extreme depressive mood for over two months may be diagnosed with *persistent depressive disorder*. This disorder includes symptoms such as hopelessness, lack of energy, poor concentration, and sleep problems. A variety of biological, psychological, and sociocultural factors have been implicated in the development of depressive disorders.

### BIOLOGICAL FACTORS

The biological factors implicated in depressive disorders include brain structure and function, neurotransmitters, and genes. Depression is associated with lower levels of brain activity in a section of the prefrontal cortex that is involved in generating actions (Duman & others, 2012) and with problems in processing in the brain's reward center (Antonesei, Murayama, & McCabe, 2018; Howland, 2012; Zahavi & others, 2016). A depressed person's brain may not recognize opportunities for pleasurable experiences.

Depression also likely involves problems in regulating neurotransmitters, such as serotonin, norepinephrine, and others (Moran & others, 2018). Medical treatments for depression seek to increase the amount of circulating serotonin in the brain (Taciak, Lysenko, &

Mazurek, 2018). Some evidence indicates that people with depressive disorder appear to have too few receptors for the neurotransmitters serotonin and norepinephrine (Healy, 2015). The relationship of neurotransmitters to depression is likely complex and involves many of these chemicals in concert.

Genes explain about 40 percent of the variance we see in depression (Shadrina, Bondarenko, & Slominsky, 2018; Sullivan, Neale, & Kendler, 2000). Research seeking to identify precise genetic locations associated with depression has produced mixed results (Yu & others, 2018). For instance, depression has been linked to features of the serotonin transporter gene called 5-HTTLPR (Schneck & others, 2016; Schneider & others, 2018). A classic and controversial study showed that this genetic characteristic predicted depression but only in concert with a stressful social environment, suggesting a stress × gene interaction (Caspi & others, 2003). Recently over 70 scientists collaborated on a very large meta-analysis combining data from nearly 40,000 people seeking to replicate this pattern (Culverhouse & others, 2018). The results of the analysis showed no evidence for a stress × gene interaction. The only two predictors of depression were experiencing life stress and being a woman (Culverhouse & others, 2018). Whether the serotonin transporter gene plays a role in depression, with or without stressful events, remains a controversial topic of research.

Keep in mind that depression, sometimes called the "common cold" of psychological disorders, is so commonplace that any biological characteristics associated with the disorder cannot be rare. Indeed, it is estimated that all humans carry some level of genetic risk for depression (Wray & others, 2018).

## PSYCHOLOGICAL FACTORS

A key factor in the development of depression is stressful or negative life events (Bergamini & others, 2018; Culverhouse & others, 2018). Many people report experiencing depression after the loss of a loved one (Hasin & others, 2018). Thus, it makes sense that psychological explanations of depression often draw on the ways people learn from and cope with negative life events.

One behavioral view of depression focuses on learned helplessness (see the chapter "Learning"). Recall that learned helplessness refers to an individual's feelings of powerlessness following exposure to aversive circumstances, such as prolonged stress, over which the individual has no control. When people cannot control negative circumstances, they may feel helpless and stop trying to change their situation (Smallheer, Vollman, & Dietrich, 2018). This helplessness spirals into a feeling of hopelessness (Ribeiro & others, 2018). An advantage of the learned helplessness approach is that, because scientists can induce learned helplessness in animals, animal models can be used to examine how such experiences affect the brain and body (Shirayama & others, 2015).

Cognitive explanations of depression focus on thoughts and beliefs that can contribute to and prolong this sense of hopelessness. Cognitive approaches recognize that thoughts can be overly negative, exaggerated, self-defeating, and too general. From this perspective, automatic negative thoughts reflect illogical self-defeating beliefs that shape the experiences of people who are depressed (Beck, 1967; Beck & Haigh, 2014). Habitual negative thoughts magnify negative experiences (Shim & others, 2018). A person who is depressed might overgeneralize about a minor occurrence—say, turning in a work assignment late—and believe that he or she is worthless. The accumulation of cognitive distortions can lead to depression.

*The incidence of depression is high among people living in poverty, as well as single women who are the heads of households.*

(first) ©DebbiSmirnoff/Getty Images; (second) ©Africa Studio/Shutterstock

The course of depression can be influenced not only by what people think but also by *how* they think. Depressed individuals may ruminate on negative experiences and feelings, replaying them over and over again in their mind (Constantin, English, & Mazmanian, 2018). This tendency to ruminate is associated with the development of depression (Connolly & Alloy, 2018).

Another cognitive view of depression focuses on the *attributions* people make—their attempts to explain the cause of what happens. Research from this perspective examines how particular styles of attributions relate to depression (O'Sullivan & others, 2018; Rodriguez, Pu, & Foiles, 2018).

*Pessimistic* attributional style means blaming oneself for negative events and expecting the negative events to recur in the future (Abramson, Seligman, & Teasdale, 1978). The pessimist explains negative events as having internal causes ("It is my fault I failed the exam"), stable causes ("I'm going to fail again and again"), and global causes ("Failing this exam shows that I don't have the ability to do well in any of my courses").

This pessimistic attributional style contrasts with an optimistic attributional style. Optimists make external attributions for bad things that happen ("I did badly on the test because it's hard to know what a professor wants on the first exam"). They also recognize that these causes can change ("I'll do better on the next one") and that they are specific ("It was only one test"). Optimistic attributional style relates to better outcomes, ranging from lower rates of depression, less distress, and decreased suicide risk in a variety of samples (Hirsch & Rabon, 2015; Stein & others, 2016; Tindle & others, 2012).

### SOCIOCULTURAL FACTORS

Individuals with a low socioeconomic status (SES), especially people living in poverty, are more likely to develop depression than those with higher SES (Evans & Erickson, 2019; Han & others, 2018; Williams, Priest, & Anderson, 2016). Depression increases as standards of living and employment circumstances worsen (Lorant & others, 2007). Studies have found very high rates of depression in Native American groups, among whom poverty, hopelessness, and alcoholism are widespread (Evans & Erickson, 2019; Hishinuma & others, 2018). Recall the concept of intersectionality from the chapter "Gender, Sex, and Sexuality". Individuals who belong to a minority group or groups, including LGBT, African American, Latinx, Asian, and so forth, are at higher risk for depression than those who do not belong to these groups (Ching & others, 2018; Evans & Erickson, 2019).

Women are nearly twice as likely as men to be diagnosed with depression (Culverhouse & others, 2018; Wilson & others, 2018), a gender difference that is consistent across many cultures. The Psychological Inquiry provides a closer look at gender differences in depression.

## Bipolar Disorder

Just as we all have down times, there are times when things seem to be going phenomenally well. For people with bipolar disorder, the ups and downs of life take on an extreme, often harmful tone. **Bipolar disorder** is characterized by extreme mood swings that include one or more episodes of *mania*—an overexcited, unrealistically optimistic state. During a manic episode, the person feels euphoric and energetic and might sleep very little. A manic state also features impulsivity that can lead to trouble, such as spending one's life savings on a foolish business venture.

• **bipolar disorder** Psychological disorder characterized by extreme mood swings that include one or more episodes of mania—an overexcited, unrealistically optimistic state.

The severity of manic episodes is used to distinguish between two types of bipolar disorder. *Bipolar I disorder* involves extreme manic episodes during which a person may hallucinate—that is, see or hear things that are not there. *Bipolar II disorder* refers to the milder version in which the person may experience less extreme euphoria.

Most people with bipolar disorder experience multiple cycles of depression interspersed with mania. These people can have manic and depressive episodes four or more times a year, but cycles usually are separated by six months to a year. Bipolar disorder is equally common in women and men. Academy Award–winning actor Catherine Zeta-Jones, famed

# psychological *inquiry*

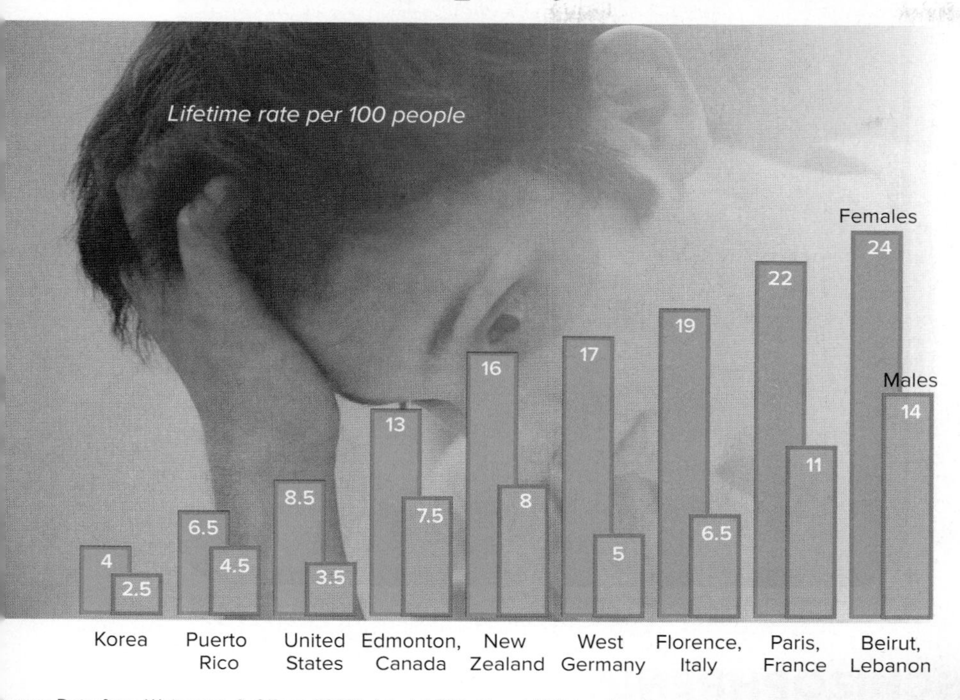


Source: Data from Weissman & Olfson (1995); (photo) ©McGraw-Hill Education/Gary He, photographer

### *Depression Among Women and Men Across Cultures*

The graph shows the rates of depression for women and men in nine different cultures (Weissman & Olfson, 1995). The rates represent the number of diagnosed cases per 100 people.

1. Which cultures have the highest and lowest levels of depression overall? What might account for these differences?
2. Which places have the biggest gender difference in depression? What might account for these differences?
3. In order to be diagnosed with depression, a person has to seek treatment for the disorder. How might gender influence a person's willingness to seek treatment?
4. How does your answer to question 3 influence the conclusions you would draw from the data illustrated in the graph?

dancer and choreographer Alvin Ailey, and the late actor Carrie Fisher (Princess Leia in *Star Wars*) were diagnosed with bipolar disorder.

What factors play a role in the development of bipolar disorder? Genetic influences are stronger predictors of bipolar disorder than of depression (Ament & others, 2015; Fabbri & Serretti, 2016; Serdarevic & others, 2018). An individual with an identical twin who has bipolar disorder has about a 70 percent probability of also having the disorder, and a fraternal twin has a more than 10 percent probability (Figure 4).

Bipolar disorder is also associated with differences in brain activity. Figure 5 shows the metabolic activity in the cerebral cortex of an individual cycling through depressive and manic phases. Notice the decrease in metabolic activity in the brain during depression and the increase in metabolic activity during mania (Baxter & others, 1995). In addition to high levels of norepinephrine and low levels of serotonin, studies link dysregulated glutamate to bipolar disorder (Howes & others, 2018; Rutherford & others, 2018).

In addition to these biological factors, experience can influence bipolar disorder. For instance, childhood experiences with physical, sexual, and verbal abuse are associated with earlier onset of bipolar disorder and with greater difficulty in treatment (Agnew-Blais & Danese, 2016; Stevelink & others, 2018).

Can children develop bipolar disorder? Practitioners and researchers have recognized symptoms in children that fit with the diagnosis (Birmaher & others, 2018; MacPherson, Weinstein, & West, 2018). A key dilemma is that treating bipolar disorder in adults involves medications that have not been approved for use in children. The potential side effects of these drugs could put children's health and development at risk. To address this issue, *DSM-5* included a new diagnosis, *disruptive mood dysregulation disorder*, which is considered a depressive disorder in children who show persistent irritability and recurrent episodes of out-of-control behavior (APA, 2013). This decision is not without controversy. As we saw with ADHD, it is not clear that children who are prone to wild mood swings are not simply being children.

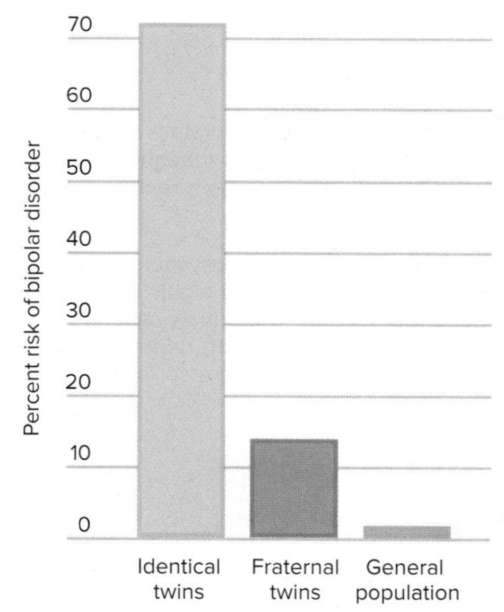


**FIGURE 4 Risk of Bipolar Disorder in Identical and Fraternal Twins If One Twin Has the Disorder, and in the General Population** Notice how much stronger the similarity of bipolar disorder is in identical twins, compared with fraternal twins and the general population. These statistics suggest a strong genetic role in the disorder.

Source: Data from *Annual Review of Neuroscience*, vol. 20, 1997. Annual Reviews. www.annualreviews.org

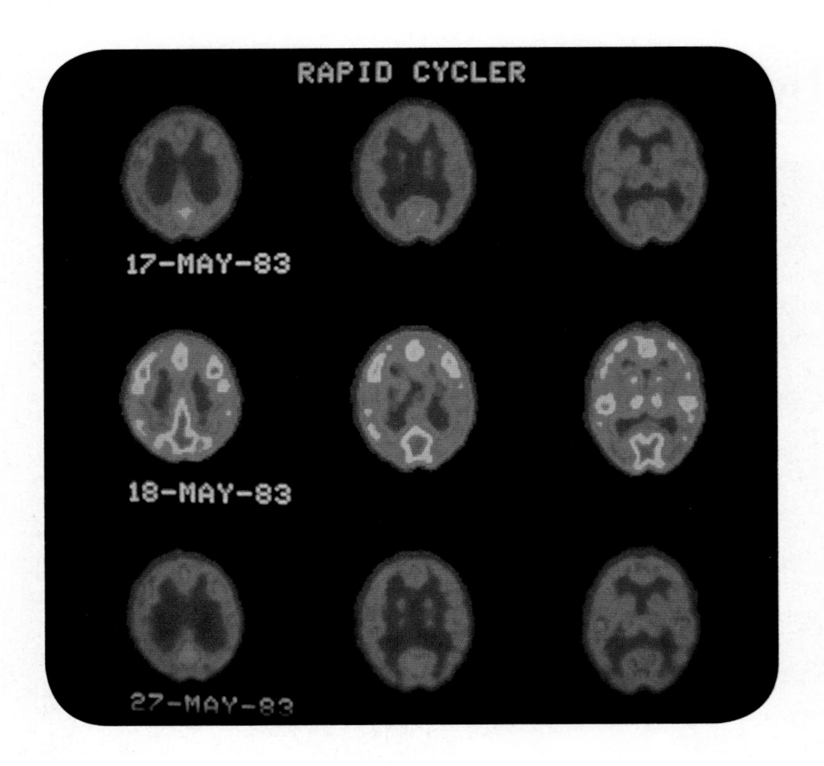


**FIGURE 5 Brain Metabolism in Mania and Depression** These images are of PET scans for an individual with bipolar disorder, who is described as a rapid cycler because of how quickly severe mood changes occur. The scans in the top and bottom rows show the person's brain in a depressed state. The scans in the middle row show the person in a manic state. The PET scans reveal how the brain's energy consumption falls in depression and rises in mania. The red areas in the middle row reflect rapid consumption of glucose. Courtesy of Dr. Michael Phelps, UCLA School of Medicine

### *test yourself*

1. What are the features of major depressive disorder?
2. Identify at least two biological, two psychological, and two sociocultural factors in depression.
3. What are the essential characteristics of bipolar disorder, and how are they different in bipolar I versus bipolar II?

# 6. SCHIZOPHRENIA

Have you ever listened to a radio talk show and realized that the host was saying exactly what you were just thinking? Have you ever been thinking about a friend and the person called you at that very moment? Do these moments mean something special about you or are they coincidences? For people with severe psychological disorders, such random experiences take on special and personal meaning.

**Psychosis** refers to a state in which a person's perceptions and thoughts are fundamentally removed from reality. *DSM-5* recognizes a class of disorders called "schizophrenia spectrum and other psychotic disorders." Within this group is one of the most debilitating psychological disorders, schizophrenia.

- **psychosis** Psychological state in which a person's perceptions and thoughts are fundamentally removed from reality.

- **schizophrenia** Severe psychological disorder characterized by highly disordered thought processes; individuals suffering from schizophrenia may be referred to as psychotic because they are so far removed from reality.

**Schizophrenia** is a severe psychological disorder that is characterized by highly disordered thought processes. People with schizophrenia may see things that are not there, hear voices inside their heads, and live in a terrifying world of twisted logic. They may say odd things, show inappropriate emotion, and move their bodies in strange ways. Often, they are socially withdrawn and isolated.

Schizophrenia is usually diagnosed in early adulthood, around age 18 for men and 25 for women. The suicide risk for people with schizophrenia is eight times that for the general population (Depp & others, 2016; McGinty, Haque, & Upthegrove, 2018; Pompili & others, 2007).

## Symptoms of Schizophrenia

Psychologists classify the symptoms of schizophrenia into positive symptoms, negative symptoms, and cognitive deficits (NIMH, 2016c).

### POSITIVE SYMPTOMS

*Positive symptoms* involve a distortion or an excess of normal function. They are "positive" because they reflect something added above and beyond normal behavior. Positive symptoms of schizophrenia include hallucinations, delusions, thought disorders, and movement disorders.

**Hallucinations** are sensory experiences that occur in the absence of real stimuli. Hallucinations are usually auditory–the person might complain of hearing voices–or visual. Much less commonly, they take the form of smells or tastes (Winton-Brown & others, 2015). Visual hallucinations involve seeing things that are not there. For example, at the age of 21, while serving in Vietnam as a medical corpsman for the Marines, Moe Armstrong experienced a psychotic break. Dead Vietcong soldiers appeared to talk to him, beg him for help, and did not seem to realize that they were dead. Armstrong, now a successful businessman and a sought-after public speaker who holds two master's degrees, relies on medication to keep such experiences at bay (Bonfatti, 2005).

● **hallucinations** Sensory experiences that occur in the absence of real stimuli.

**Delusions** are false, unusual, and sometimes magical beliefs that are not part of an individual's culture. A delusional person might think that he is Jesus Christ or Muhammad; another might imagine that her thoughts are being broadcast over the radio. Delusions can be difficult to change.

● **delusions** False, unusual, and sometimes magical beliefs that are not part of an individual's culture.

For people with schizophrenia, delusional beliefs that might seem completely illogical to the outsider are experienced as all too real. At one point in his life, Bill Garrett, a college student with schizophrenia, was convinced that a blister on his hand was a sign of gangrene. So strong was his belief that he tried to cut off his hand with a knife, before being stopped by his family (M. Park, 2009).

**Thought disorder** refers to unusual, sometimes bizarre thought processes. The thoughts of people with schizophrenia can be disorganized and confused. Often those with schizophrenia do not make sense when they talk or write. For example, someone with schizophrenia might say, "Well, Rocky, babe, happening, but where, when, up, top, side, over, you know, out of the way, that's it. Sign off." Such speech has no meaning for the listener. The person might also make up new words (*neologisms*) (Etlouba & others, 2018).

● **thought disorder** The unusual, sometimes bizarre thought processes that are characteristic positive symptoms of schizophrenia.

A person with schizophrenia can also show **referential thinking**, which means ascribing personal meaning to completely random events. The individual might believe that a dead bird on the sidewalk is a sign from God or that a person walking nearby is an agent from the government. Molly Watson was diagnosed with schizophrenia in her 30s. She described how, during her first psychotic episode, she was convinced that car license plate numbers were important messages to be followed or avoided (Watson, 2015).

● **referential thinking** Ascribing personal meaning to completely random events.

**Movement disorders** involve unusual mannerisms, body movements, and facial expressions (Haralanov & others, 2018). The individual may repeat certain motions over and over or, in extreme cases, may become catatonic. **Catatonia** is a state of immobility and unresponsiveness that lasts for long periods of time.

● **movement disorders** The unusual mannerisms, body movements, and facial expressions that are characteristic positive symptoms of schizophrenia.

● **catatonia** State of immobility and unresponsiveness lasting for long periods of time.

### NEGATIVE SYMPTOMS

In contrast to positive symptoms, schizophrenia's *negative symptoms* reflect social withdrawal, behavioral deficits, and the loss or decrease of normal functions. One negative symptom is **flat affect**, which is displaying little or no emotion (Compton & others, 2018). People with schizophrenia also may be unable to read the emotions of others (Frajo-Apor & others, 2016). They may show a deficient ability to plan, initiate, and engage in goal-directed behavior.

● **flat affect** The display of little or no emotion—a common negative symptom of schizophrenia.

### COGNITIVE SYMPTOMS

Cognitive symptoms of schizophrenia include deficits in executive functioning (Giraldo-Chica & others, 2018), including difficulty sustaining attention, problems holding information in memory, and inability to interpret information and make decisions (Fernandes & others, 2018).

## Causes of Schizophrenia

Much research has investigated biological, psychological, and sociocultural factors in schizophrenia.

## psychological *inquiry*

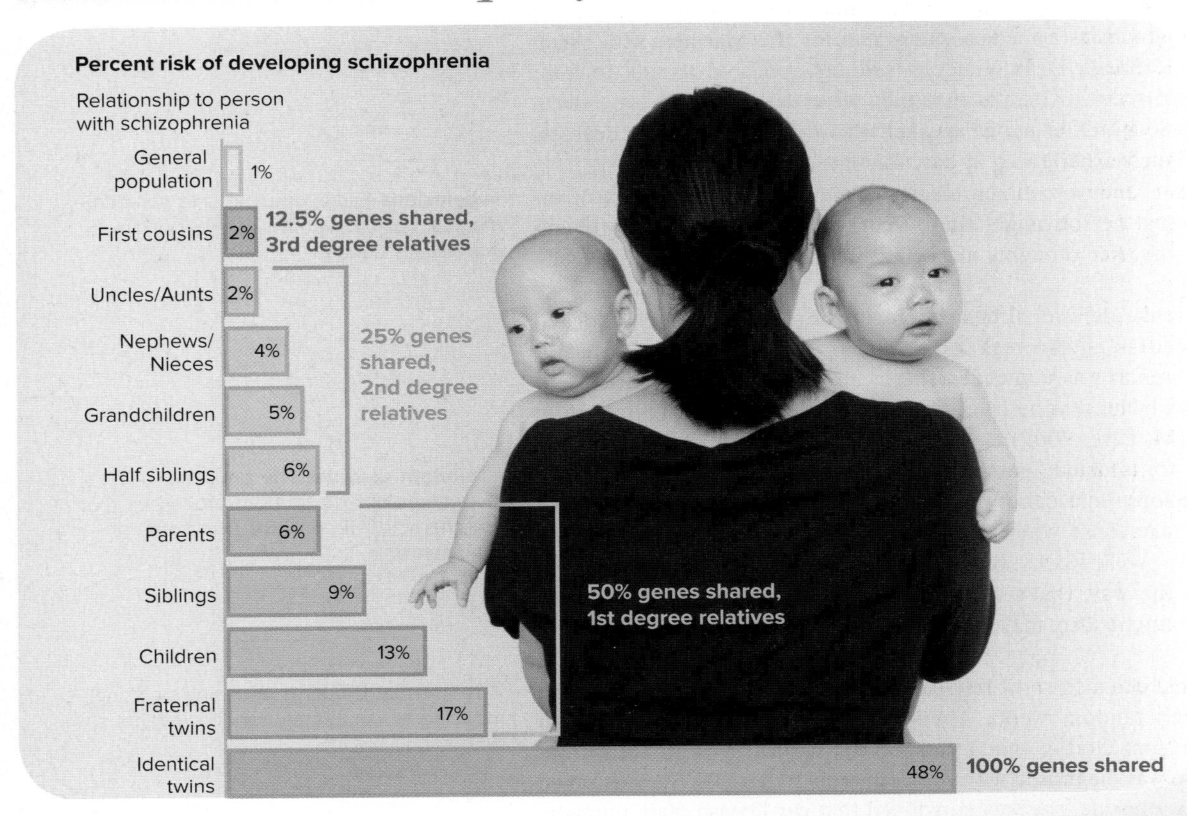


Source: Greenwood & others (2018); McCarthy (2018); (photo) ©Big Cheese Photo/Getty Images

### *The Association of Genes with Schizophrenia*

This figure shows that as genetic relatedness to an individual with schizophrenia increases, so does the lifetime risk of developing schizophrenia. Using the grap answer these questions:

1. Which familial relations hav the lowest and highest lev of genetic overlap (shared genes)?
2. What is the difference in genetic overlap between identical twins and non-twi siblings?
3. What is the difference in ri of schizophrenia between identical twins and non-twi siblings of individuals with schizophrenia?
4. What do you think accounts for the differences in your answers to questions 2 and 3?

## BIOLOGICAL FACTORS

Research strongly supports biological explanations of schizophrenia, including genetics differences, brain differences, and problems in regulating neurotransmitters.

**Genes** Schizophrenia is at least partially explained by genetic factors (Greenwood & others, 2018; McCarthy, 2018). The Psychological Inquiry shows the results of research examining the role of genetics in schizophrenia.

**Structural Brain Abnormalities** Studies have found structural brain abnormalities in people with schizophrenia, specifically enlarged ventricles (Kubota & others, 2015; Zhao & others, 2018). Ventricles are fluid-filled spaces, and enlargement of the ventricles indicates deterioration in other brain tissue. These changes can occur over time, suggesting that as schizophrenia progresses, the brain deteriorates.

People with schizophrenia also have a smaller prefrontal cortex and lower activity in this area of the brain than healthy individuals (Pillai & others, 2016). The prefrontal cortex is the region where thinking, planning, and decision making take place. Recall from the chapter "Human Development" that the prefrontal cortex continues to develop into early adulthood. It may be telling that the emergence of symptoms of schizophrenia (typically in young adulthood), happens during the time when the prefrontal cortex becomes fully connected.

Still, differences between the brains of healthy people and those with schizophrenia are small. Microscopic studies of brain tissue after death reveal small changes in the distribution or characteristics of brain cells in persons with schizophrenia. At least some of these changes seem to have occurred prenatally because they are not accompanied by glial cells, which are always present when a brain injury occurs after birth (Vuillermot &

others, 2010). Problems in prenatal development may predispose a brain to develop schizophrenic symptoms later in life (Fatemi & Folsom, 2009; McCarthy, 2018). In addition, recent research shows some of these brain differences are present *prior to* the emergence of symptoms (Zhao & others, 2018).

**Neurotransmitter Regulation** Whether it is differences in amount of dopamine, its production, or its uptake, there is good evidence that problems regulating the neurotransmitter dopamine play a role in schizophrenia (Vyas & others, 2018).

A link between dopamine and psychotic symptoms was first noticed when the drug L-dopa (which increases dopamine levels) was given to people as a treatment for Parkinson disease. In addition to relieving Parkinson symptoms, L-dopa led some people to experience psychosis (Janowsky, Addario, & Risch, 1987; Madras, 2013). Further, drugs that reduce psychotic symptoms often block dopamine (Kesby & others, 2018).

Previously we have encountered dopamine as the "feel good" neurotransmitter that helps us recognize rewarding stimuli in the environment and is related to being outgoing and sociable. How can a neurotransmitter that is associated with good things play a crucial role in schizophrenia?

One way to think about this puzzle is to view dopamine as a neurochemical messenger that shouts out, "Hey! This is important!" whenever we encounter opportunities for reward. Imagine what it might be like to be bombarded with such messages about even the smallest details of life (Roiser & others, 2010). Private thoughts might take on such dramatic proportions that they sound like someone else's voice talking inside the person's head. Fleeting ideas, such as "The traffic lights are turning red *because* I am in a hurry," suddenly seem not silly but true. Hallucinations, delusions, and referential thinking may be expressions of the person's attempts to make sense of such extraordinary feelings (Kapur, 2003).

Another neurotransmitter that is thought to play a role in schizophrenia is glutamate, a neurotransmitter that sends the message for other neurons to fire. In the brain, the majority of excitatory messages are sent by glutamate. Although initially it was hypothesized that low levels of glutamate led to schizophrenia, it appears that schizophrenia is associated with abnormalities in specific types of glutamate receptors (Howes, McCutcheon, & Stone, 2015; Wijtenburg & others, 2018). Some of the drugs used to treat schizophrenia have the effect of increasing glutamate.

## PSYCHOLOGICAL FACTORS

Psychologists used to explain schizophrenia as rooted in childhood experiences with unresponsive parents. Such explanations have fallen by the wayside. Contemporary theorists do recognize that stress may contribute to the development of this disorder. Experiences are now viewed through the lens of the vulnerability-stress hypothesis, suggesting that individual with schizophrenia may have biological risk factors that interact with experience to produce the disorder.

## SOCIOCULTURAL FACTORS

Sociocultural background is not considered to be a *cause* of schizophrenia, but sociocultural factors do appear to affect the *course* of the disorder. Across cultures, people with schizophrenia in developing, nonindustrialized nations tend to have better outcomes than those in developed, industrialized nations (Jablensky, 2000; Myers, 2010). This difference may be due to the fact that in developing nations, family and friends are more accepting and supportive of people with schizophrenia. In Western samples, marriage, warm and supportive friends (Jablensky & others, 1992; Wiersma & others, 1998), and employment are related to better outcomes for people with schizophrenia (Rosen & Garety, 2005).

Some experts call for a focus on preventing schizophrenia by identifying those at risk and intervening early to reduce the level of disability they experience (Murru & Carpiniello, 2018; Walder & others, 2012). Early intervention can be important because a strong predictor of relapse (that is, having symptoms again after treatment) is the amount of time a person spends in a psychotic state without treatment (Allott & others, 2018; Karson & others, 2016). Intervening after a person's first psychotic break and preventing further such experiences is an important goal. The contemporary thinking is that a psychotic episode should be thought of as similar to a seizure—as a potentially damaging event (Wannan & others, 2018). The quicker the person is treated and the psychoses ended, the better the prognosis (Allott & others, 2018).

Is there a way to know who might be at risk for schizophrenia? Research suggests that among those with a family history of schizophrenia, lower levels of social functioning distinguished those who went on to develop schizophrenia from others (Cornblatt & others, 2012). Indeed, an especially brutal aspect of psychosis is that it takes people out of a shared reality, putting them in a terrifying and lonely place (Lim & others, 2018).

### test yourself

1. What is schizophrenia?
2. What is meant by positive and negative symptoms of schizophrenia?
3. How is dopamine thought to be involved in schizophrenia?

## 7. PERSONALITY DISORDERS

Imagine that your very personality—who you really are—is the core of your life difficulties. **Personality disorders** are chronic, maladaptive cognitive-behavioral patterns that are thoroughly integrated into a person's personality. Personality disorders affect a person's sense of self and capacity for relationships with others (Livesly & Larstone, 2018; Trull, Carpenter, & Widiger, 2013). Such disorders are relatively common. In a representative U.S. sample, researchers found that 15 percent had a personality disorder (Grant & others, 2004).

● **personality disorders** Chronic, maladaptive cognitive-behavioral patterns that are thoroughly integrated into an individual's personality.

*DSM-5* lists 10 personality disorders (Figure 6). Below, we survey the two personality disorders that have been studied most extensively: antisocial personality disorder and borderline personality disorder. As we review below, both of these disorders are associated with dire consequences.

| Personality Disorder | Description |
|---|---|
| Paranoid Personality Disorder | Paranoia, suspiciousness, and deep distrust of others. People with this disorder are always on the lookout for danger and the slightest social mistreatment. They may be socially isolated. |
| Schizoid Personality Disorder | Extreme lack of interest in interpersonal relationships. People with this disorder are emotionally cold and apathetic, and they are generally detached from interpersonal life. |
| Schizotypal Personality Disorder | Socially isolated and prone to odd thinking. People with this disorder often have elaborate and strange belief systems and attribute unusual meanings to life events and experiences. |
| Antisocial Personality Disorder | Manipulative, deceitful, and amoral. People with this disorder lack empathy for others, are egocentric, and are willing to use others for their own personal gain. |
| Borderline Personality Disorder | Emotionally volatile and unstable sense of self. These individuals are prone to mood swings, excessive self-criticism, extreme judgments of others, and are preoccupied with being abandoned. |
| Histrionic Personality Disorder | Attention-seeking, dramatic, lively, and flirtatious. These individuals are inappropriately seductive in their interactions with others. |
| Narcissistic Personality Disorder | Self-aggrandizing yet overly dependent on the evaluations of others. People with this disorder view themselves as entitled and better than others. They show deficits in empathy and in understanding the feelings of others. |
| Avoidant Personality Disorder | Socially inhibited and prone to feelings of inadequacy, anxiety, and shame. These individuals feel inadequate and hold back in social situations. They have unrealistic standards for their own behavior and avoid setting goals, taking personal risks, or pursuing new activities. |
| Dependent Personality Disorder | Dependent on others for emotional and physical needs. People with this disorder perceive others as powerful and competent and themselves as childlike and helpless. |
| Obsessive-Compulsive Personality Disorder | Conforming rigidly to rules. These individuals show an excessive attachment to moral codes and are excessively orderly in daily life. |

**FIGURE 6 The 10 Personality Disorders Included in *DSM-5*** Diagnoses of these disorders require that the person be over the age of 18, and all involve pervasive aspects of the person that color their cognition, emotion, and behavior. Note that some of the labels are potentially confusing. Schizoid and schizotypal personality disorders are not the same thing as schizophrenia (though schizotypal personality disorder may proceed to schizophrenia). Further, obsessive-compulsive personality disorder is not the same thing as obsessive-compulsive disorder.

## Antisocial Personality Disorder

**Antisocial personality disorder (ASPD)** is characterized by guiltlessness, law-breaking, exploitation of others, irresponsibility, and deceit. People with ASPD are bold, cold and callous, mean, and impulsive (McKinley, Patrick, & Verona, 2018). Those with this disorder are aggressive and potentially violent (Raine, 2018a). ASPD is far more common in men than in women (McKinley, Patrick, & Verona, 2018; Olson-Ayala & Patrick, 2018).

**antisocial personality disorder (ASPD)** Psychological disorder characterized by guiltlessness, law-breaking, exploitation of others, irresponsibility, and deceit.

ASPD is characterized by

- Failure to conform to social norms or obey the law
- Deceitfulness, lying, or conning others for personal profit or pleasure
- Impulsivity
- Irritability and aggressiveness, getting into physical fights or perpetrating assaults
- Reckless disregard for the safety of self or others
- Consistent irresponsibility, inconsistent work behavior, not paying bills
- Lack of remorse, showing indifference to the pain of others, or rationalizing behavior that hurts or mistreats others

ASPD is related to criminal behavior, but not all people with ASPD engage in crime, and not all criminals suffer from ASPD. Those with ASPD can be successful. There are antisocial physicians, clergy, journalists, law enforcement officers, and just about any other occupation. Still, these people tend to exploit others, lack empathy, and break the rules.

A number of factors seem to intertwine to produce ASPD. Genes play a role in the disorder (Patrick & Brislin, 2018). Brain differences between those with ASPD and others are apparent especially in areas of the brain thought to undergird empathy and moral decision-making (Raine, 2018b). Childhood abuse is related to ASPD, but there is evidence that genetic differences may distinguish abused children who go on to commit violent acts from those who do not (Caspi & others, 2002; Lynam & others, 2007).

People with ASPD show lower levels of autonomic nervous system arousal and are less stressed than others by aversive circumstances, including punishment (Portnoy & Farrington, 2015). They have the ability to keep their cool while engaging in deception (Verschuere & others, 2005), suggesting they might be able to fool a polygraph. The underaroused autonomic nervous system may be a key difference between adolescents who become antisocial adults and those whose behavior improves during adulthood (DeLisi & others, 2018; Raine, Venables, & Williams, 1990).

There is continuity in antisocial behavior and nervous system differences from childhood into adolescence and beyond (Ascione & others, 2018; DeLisi & others, 2018; Trentham, Hensley, & Policastro, 2018; Wagner, Hastings, & Rubin, 2018; Whipp & others, 2018). This continuity and the genetic contribution to the disorder has led Adrian Raine (2018a), an expert on ASPD, to suggest it should be regarded as a neurodevelopmental disorder.

*Psychopaths* are a subgroup of those with ASPD (Raine, 2018b). They are remorseless predators who engage in violence to get what they want. Examples are serial killers John Wayne Gacy (who murdered 33 boys and young men) and Ted Bundy (who murdered at least 30 young women).

Research on prison inmates with ASPD (all of whom committed violent offenses) shows that those who are classified as psychopaths have less gray matter in areas of the brain associated with empathy than those who are not (Decety, Skelly, & Kiehl, 2013; Gregory & others, 2012).

A challenge in treating people with ASPD, including psychopaths, is their ability to con even mental health professionals. Those with ASPD may resist engaging in a therapeutic relationship because it involves giving up a sense of power (Black, 2017). Many never seek therapy, and others end up in prison, where treatment is rarely an option.

*John Wayne Gacy* (top) *and Ted Bundy* (bottom) *exemplify the subgroup of people with ASPD who are also psychopathic.*

*Impulsivity (and risk-taking) can be a symptom of borderline personality disorder.*

©Martinan/iStock/Getty Images

## Borderline Personality Disorder

**Borderline personality disorder (BPD)** is a pervasive pattern of instability in interpersonal relationships, self-image, and emotions. People with BPD are impulsive, insecure, and emotional. BPD is related to self-harming behaviors such as cutting and suicide (Paris, 2018).

At the very core of borderline personality disorder is profound instability–in mood, in sense of self, in relationships. Four essential features characterize BPD (Trull & Brown, 2013):

- Unstable affect
- Unstable sense of self and identity, including self-destructive impulsive behavior and chronic feelings of emptiness
- Negative interpersonal relationships that are unstable, intense, and characterized by extreme shifts between idealization and devaluation
- Self-harm, including recurrent suicidal behavior, gestures, or threats or self-mutilating behavior

● **borderline personality disorder (BPD)** Psychological disorder characterized by a pervasive pattern of instability in interpersonal relationships, self-image, and emotions and by marked impulsivity beginning by early adulthood and present in a variety of contexts.

To cope with their unstable emotional lives, those with BPD may engage in a variety of maladaptive behaviors, among them drinking alcohol and using illicit substances (Barker & others, 2015). BPD is more common in women than men, among those with lower SES, and among those younger than 30 (Tomko & others, 2013). A renowned expert on BPD, Marsha Linehan, revealed that she herself has struggled with the disorder (Carey, 2011a).

Potential causes of BPD likely include biological factors and childhood experiences. The role of genes in BPD has been demonstrated in a variety of studies and across cultures (Jang & Vernon, 2018; Mulder, 2012; Reichborn-Kjennerud & others, 2015). Many people with BPD report experiences of childhood sexual abuse, physical abuse, and neglect (Linehan, 2018; Paris, 2018). It is not clear, however, that abuse is a primary cause of the disorder (Trull, Carpenter, & Widiger, 2013). Rather, childhood abuse experiences may combine with genetic factors in promoting BPD (Jang & Vernon, 2018).

Cognitive factors associated with BPD include a tendency to hold the irrational beliefs that one is powerless and innately unacceptable and that other people are dangerous and hostile (Linehan, 2018). People with BPD also display *hypervigilance:* the tendency to be constantly on the alert, looking for threatening information in the environment (Izurieta Hidalgo & others, 2016).

People with BPD are very sensitive to how others treat them. They tend to see the world in either-or terms, a thinking style called *splitting* (Fertuck, Fischer, & Beeney, 2018). For example, they typically view other people as either hated enemies with no positive qualities or as beloved, idealized friends who can do no wrong.

For some time, experts thought BPD was untreatable, but as many as 50 percent of individuals with BPD improve within two years. Once improved they are unlikely to relapse (Gunderson, 2008). A key part of improvement appears to be reducing social stress, such as leaving an abusive romantic partner or establishing a sense of trust in a therapist (Gunderson & others, 2018). In the chapter "Therapies", we will review dialectical behavior therapy as a treatment for BPD (Linehan, 2018).

### test yourself

1. How are personality disorders defined?
2. To what sorts of behaviors is antisocial personality disorder related?
3. How is borderline personality disorder defined, and what are four features that characterize it?

# 8. SUICIDE

Thinking about suicide is not necessarily abnormal, but attempting or completing the act of suicide is. Sadly, many people who might seem to be successful have died by suicide, such as grunge icon Kurt Cobain and actor Robin Williams.

In the United States in 2016, 45,000 people died by suicide and suicide was the 10th leading cause of death (NIMH, 2018). For Americans aged 10 to 24, suicide is the second leading cause of death. In the United States there are twice as many suicides as homicides (NIMH, 2018).

Given these grim statistics, psychologists work to reduce the frequency and intensity of suicidal impulses. You can do your part. Figure 7 provides good advice on what to do and what not to do if you encounter someone who is threatening suicide.

What might prompt a person to end their life? Biological, psychological, and sociocultural circumstances can be contributing factors.

**What to Do**

1. Ask direct, straightforward questions in a calm manner. For example, "Are you thinking about hurting yourself?"
2. Be a good listener and be supportive. Emphasize that unbearable pain can be survived.
3. Take the suicide threat very seriously. Ask questions about the person's feelings, relationships, and thoughts about the type of method to be used. If a gun, pills, rope, or other means is mentioned and a specific plan has been developed, the situation is dangerous. Stay with the person until help arrives.
4. Encourage the person to get professional help and assist him or her in getting help. If the person is willing, take the person to a mental health facility or hospital.

**What Not to Do**

1. Don't ignore the warning signs.
2. Don't refuse to talk about suicide if the person wants to talk about it.
3. Don't react with horror, disapproval, or repulsion.
4. Don't offer false reassurances ("Everything will be all right") or make judgments ("You should be thankful for . . .").
5. Don't abandon the person after the crisis seems to have passed or after professional counseling has begun.

**FIGURE 7** **When Someone Is Threatening Suicide** Do not ignore the warning signs if you think someone you know is considering suicide. Talk to a counselor if you are reluctant to say anything to the person yourself. (photo) ©Nathan Lau/Design Pics/Corbis

## Biological Factors

Genes appear to play a role in suicide (Erlangsen & others, 2018; Sokolowski, Wasserman, & Wasserman, 2018). Genetic characteristics related to suicide may also predispose people to depression (Consoloni & others, 2018; Youssef & others, 2018). Neurotransmitters are also linked to suicide (Malhi & others, 2018). A number of studies link suicide with low levels of serotonin and serotonin-linked genes (Consoloni & others, 2018; Mann & others, 2018).

There are families that appear to be plagued by suicide, such as the Hemingways. Five members of that family, spread across generations, died by suicide, including the writer Ernest Hemingway and his granddaughter Margaux, a model and actor. In 2009, Nicholas Hughes—a successful marine biologist and the son of Sylvia Plath, a poet who died by suicide—tragically died by suicide. In considering these examples, you might note that, yes, these individuals shared genes with family members who died by suicide, but they had also experienced the suicide of a family member—an experience that might have put them at risk.

Poor physical health, especially when it is chronic, is a risk factor for suicide (Large & others, 2018; Prince, 2018). A recent study showed that people with a cancer diagnosis had a 20 percent higher risk of suicide than others (Henson & others, 2018). Another study showed that the highest risk for suicide was within one year of diagnosis (S. M. Wang & others, 2018).

## Psychological Factors

Psychological factors that can contribute to suicide include psychological disorders and traumatic experiences (Gilmore & others, 2017; Prince, 2018). Approximately 90 percent of people who die by suicide are thought to have a psychological disorder (American Foundation for Suicide Prevention, 2018; Fan & others, 2018; NIMH, 2018), most commonly depression and anxiety (Bentley & others, 2016; Zalpuri & Rothschild, 2016). Depression and PTSD predict suicide risk among combat veterans (Bullman, Schneiderman, & Gradus, 2018). Substance abuse is also a risk factor for suicide (Kaplan & others, 2018). An immediate, highly stressful event—such as the loss of a loved one, losing one's job, or an unwanted pregnancy—can lead people to threaten and/or to complete suicide (Gvion & Levi-Belz, 2018). In a recent study of adolescents, being the victim of relational aggression predicted suicide attempts (Massing-Schaffer & others, 2018).

A recent study sought to distinguish between those who are thinking about suicide and those who would actually attempt to die by suicide (Nock & others, 2018). Suicide attempts were predicted by risk taking or engaging in reckless behavior and, interestingly, failing to answer questions about one's thoughts of suicide (Nock & others, 2018). It might be that those who are especially likely to attempt suicide are also those least likely to admit to those thoughts and feelings.

*Suicide tends to run in families. Five suicides occurred in different generations of the Hemingway family, including author Ernest and his granddaughter Margaux.*

(first) ©Bettmann/Getty Images; (second) ©Pierre Vauthey/Sygma/Sygma via Getty Images

An expert on suicide, Thomas Joiner (2005) has proposed a comprehensive theory of the phenomenon. His *interpersonal theory of suicide* states that suicide involves two factors (Hagan & others, 2015; Hames, Hagan, & Joiner, 2013):

- A desire to die
- The acquired capability for suicide

The desire to die, from this perspective, emerges when a person's social needs are not met. People who feel they do not belong, are chronically lonely, and who perceive themselves to be a burden on others are more likely to experience a desire to die (Barzilay & others, 2015; Hames, Hagan, & Joiner, 2013; King & others, 2018).

Even among those with a desire to die, however, a key variable is the person's acquired capability to complete a suicide attempt. A fear of death and a strong desire to avoid pain prevent most people from attempting suicide. Research suggests that one way people might overcome these natural motivations is to develop a tolerance for pain through previous experiences of injury (Joiner, Ribeiro, & Silva, 2012; Martin & others, 2018). Past experience can extinguish the fear response, allowing people to complete the act of suicide (Heffer & Willoughby, 2018).

The interpersonal theory continues to be tested. Research supports the idea that feeling burdensome and not belonging predict suicidal intentions in adolescents (Barzilay & others, 2015) and middle-aged adults (Van Orden & others, 2016). In addition, recent research suggests that these factors can be especially potent predictors when the person feels hopeless (Martin & others, 2018).

## Sociocultural Factors

Suicide rates vary worldwide; the lowest rates occur in countries with cultural and religious norms against suicide. Nations with the highest suicide rates in 2018 were Lithuania, Russia, Guyana, and South Korea (World Population Review, 2018). Among the nations with the lowest rates are the Bahamas, Jamaica, Grenada, and Barbados. Of 176 nations, the United States ranks 25th (World Population Review, 2018).

Research has linked suicide to the culture of honor. Recall that in honor cultures, individuals are more likely to defend their personal honor with aggression. A set of studies examined suicide and depression in the United States, comparing states in the South (a region with a culture of honor) with other areas. Even accounting for a host of other factors, suicide rates were higher in southern states (Osterman & Brown, 2011). Honor-related suicides are more likely to occur in the context of public, reputation-damaging events (Roberts, Miller, & Azrael, 2018). Compared with other suicide deaths, people who die by honor-related suicides are more likely to be suffering from depression but not seeking treatment (Roberts, Miller, & Azrael, 2018).

There are gender differences in suicide. Men are more likely to complete suicide than women and are more likely to use a firearm (NIMH, 2018). For women, suicide rates are highest (about 10 per 100,000 people) for those aged 45 to 54. For men suicide rates are highest (32 per 100,000) for those 65 and older.

### test yourself

1. What are the two requirements for suicide as described by the interpersonal theory of suicide?
2. Give at least two biological, two psychological, and two sociocultural factors in suicide.
3. From the perspective of the three criteria for abnormal behavior, how does *thinking* about suicide compare with *attempting* suicide?

# 9. PSYCHOLOGICAL DISORDERS AND HEALTH AND WELLNESS

Labeling psychological disorders can make it seem like they happen only to other people. But psychological disorders are not just about *other* people; they are about people, period. Between 18 and 32 percent of Americans ages 18 and older suffer from a psychological disorder in a given year—at least 43.6 million U.S. adults (Center for Behavioral Health Statistics and Quality, 2015).

Chances are you or someone you know will experience a psychological disorder. Figure 8 shows how common many psychological disorders are in the United States.

Psychological disorders present a challenge to living a healthy, fulfilling life. For those who are diagnosed with one or more disorders, significant obstacles in the pursuit of a fulfilling life are stigma, stereotypes, prejudice, and discrimination.

The power of the label of mental illness was shown dramatically in a classic and controversial study by David Rosenhan (1973). He recruited eight adults (including a stay-at-home mother, a psychology graduate student, a pediatrician, and some psychiatrists), none with a psychological disorder, to see a psychiatrist at various hospitals. These "pseudo-patients" were instructed to act in a normal way except to complain about hearing voices that said things like "empty" and "thud." All of them were admitted to the hospital and diagnosed with schizophrenia. After admission to the hospital, the pseudo patients behaved normally and stopped complaining of symptoms: They no longer heard voices. All eight expressed an interest in leaving the hospital and behaved cooperatively. Yet, all eight were kept in the hospital from 3 to 52 days. None of the mental health professionals they encountered ever questioned the diagnosis that had been given to these people, and all were discharged with the label "schizophrenia in remission." The label "schizophrenia" had stuck to the pseudo-patients, leading the professionals around them to interpret their very normal behavior as abnormal. This label can color how others perceive everything a person does.

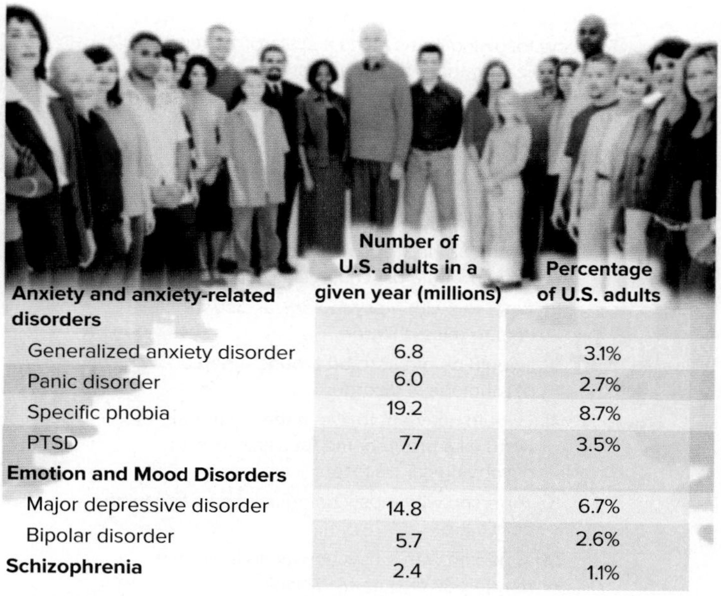

| | Number of U.S. adults in a given year (millions) | Percentage of U.S. adults |
|---|---|---|
| **Anxiety and anxiety-related disorders** | | |
| Generalized anxiety disorder | 6.8 | 3.1% |
| Panic disorder | 6.0 | 2.7% |
| Specific phobia | 19.2 | 8.7% |
| PTSD | 7.7 | 3.5% |
| **Emotion and Mood Disorders** | | |
| Major depressive disorder | 14.8 | 6.7% |
| Bipolar disorder | 5.7 | 2.6% |
| **Schizophrenia** | 2.4 | 1.1% |

**FIGURE 8** **The 12-Month Prevalence of the Most Common Psychological Disorders** Psychological disorders are more common than you might expect. (photo) ©Ryan McVay/Getty Images

If a person has a psychological disorder, can they still be a good friend? A good parent? A competent worker? A significant concern for people with psychological disorders is the negative attitudes that others might have about people with mental illness (Ezell & others, 2018). Stigma can be a significant barrier for people coping with a psychological disorder and for their families and loved ones (Hinshaw, 2018; Oexle & Corrigan, 2018). Fear of stigma can prevent individuals from talking about their problems and seeking treatment (Schomerus & others, 2018; Stanley, Hom, & Joiner, 2018). Bias against those with psychological disorders can be far-reaching (Batastini, Lester, & Thompson, 2018; Eno Louden & others, 2018; Rai & others, 2018), and is experienced by family members (Ergetie & others, 2018) and practitioners who treat those with serious psychological disorders (Vayshenker & others, 2018). To test your own attitudes about people with psychological disorders, complete the exercise in Figure 9.

## Consequences of Stigma

People with psychological disorders can face stigma, prejudice, and discrimination, complicating an already difficult situation. Stigma can also negatively affect physical health.

### PREJUDICE AND DISCRIMINATION

Labels of psychological disorders can be damaging because they may lead to negative stereotypes, which, as reviewed in the chapter "Social Psychology", play a role in prejudice. For example, the label "schizophrenic" often has negative connotations such as "frightening" and "dangerous."

Vivid cases of extremely harmful behavior by people with psychological disorders can perpetuate the stereotype that people with such disorders are violent. You have likely heard of such cases. In 2007, Cho Seung-Hui, a college student, murdered 32 students and faculty at Virginia Tech University. James Eagan Holmes committed a mass shooting in an Aurora, Colorado, movie theater in July 2012, leaving 12 dead and 70 injured. The following December, Adam Lanza killed his mother and then 20 children and 6 adults at Sandy Hook Elementary School in Newtown, Connecticut. In 2018, Nikolas Cruz allegedly murdered 17 people in a Florida high school.

Rate the following items using a scale of 1–5, with 1 indicating that you completely *disagree* with the statement and 5 indicating that you completely *agree* with the statement.

*1 = completely disagree 2 = slightly agree*
*3 = moderately agree 4 = strongly agree*
*5 = completely agree*

_____ 1. I would rather not live next door to a person with a psychological disorder.
_____ 2. A person with a psychological disorder is unfit to raise children.
_____ 3. I would be afraid to be around a person with a psychological disorder.
_____ 4. I would not want to live in the same neighborhood as a group home for persons with psychological disorders.
_____ 5. A person with a psychological disorder cannot hold a job.
_____ 6. A person with a psychological disorder is dangerous or potentially violent.

**Total** _____

Add up your score and divide by 6. If your score is 3 or higher, you may want to rethink your attitudes about individuals with psychological disorders.

It may be revealing to ask yourself how you would respond to these statements if the words "person with a psychological disorder" were replaced with "woman," "African American," or "gay man or lesbian." Sometimes even individuals who would not think of themselves as being prejudiced against other groups find themselves biased against the mentally ill.

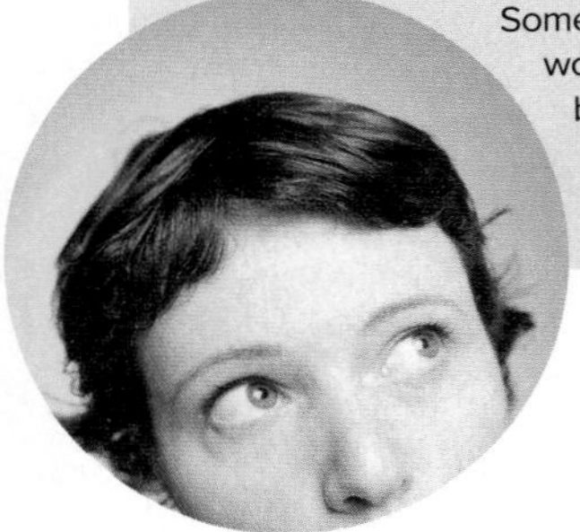

**FIGURE 9 Test Your Attitudes About People with Psychological Disorders**
Take the survey to discover and evaluate your own attitudes. (first) ©Ingram Publishing/AGE Fotostock; (second) ©Ingram Publishing/AGE Fotostock

Aside from committing these horrific acts, these four people have something else in common—they were all described as having a history of psychological disorders. For Cho, it was depression and anxiety; for Lanza, it was a type of autism spectrum disorder, anxiety, depression, and anorexia. Holmes was reported to suffer from schizophrenia or a personality disorder. Although a specific diagnosis has not been identified, Cruz had a history of mental illness and treatments.

Such vivid cases may give the erroneous impression that people who suffer from psychological disorders are prone to violence. Once again, we encounter an *illusory correlation.* The impression that people with psychological disorders are dangerous is an illusion. Consider that these young men share other qualities, too. For instance, they were all young men. They are no more representative of people with psychological disorders than they are representative of young men.

Consider, too, that after the Sandy Hook killings, many commentators noted that to do such a thing, one *must* have a psychological disorder, by definition (Estes, 2012; Solomon, 2012). Whether or not one believes that statement is true, it leads to at least two unfortunate potential inferences. First, it suggests that people who commit horrific acts cannot be held responsible for those acts, because their behaviors are symptoms of a disorder. Second, it suggests that such acts are something that people with psychological disorders do. This conclusion is untrue. People with psychological disorders (especially those in treatment) are no more likely to be violent than the general population. People with psychological disorders are more likely to be the *victims* of violence than the perpetrators (Corrigan & others, 2002; Hiroeh & others, 2001).

People with psychological disorders are often aware of the stigma attached to these conditions (Brohan & others, 2010; Corrigan, 2015; Corrigan & Al-Khouja, 2018). They themselves may have previously held such negative attitudes. People with psychological disorders need help, but seeking that assistance may involve sacrificing their status as mentally healthy for a new, stigmatized identity (Thornicroft & others, 2009; Yen & others, 2009).

Among the most feared aspects of stigma is discrimination. As we saw in the chapter "Social Psychology", discrimination means acting prejudicially toward a person who is a member of a stigmatized group. In the workplace, discrimination against a person with a psychological disorder is illegal. The Americans with Disabilities Act (ADA) of 1990 forbids employers from refusing employment or a promotion to someone with a psychological disorder when the person's condition does not prevent performance of the job's essential functions (Cleveland, Barnes-Farrell, & Ratz, 1997). A person's appearance or behavior may be unusual or irritating, but as long as that individual is able to complete the duties required of a position, he or she cannot be denied employment or promotion (Follmer & Jones, 2018; Yanos, 2018).

If you doubt the power of the stigma of mental illness, check out the Intersection.

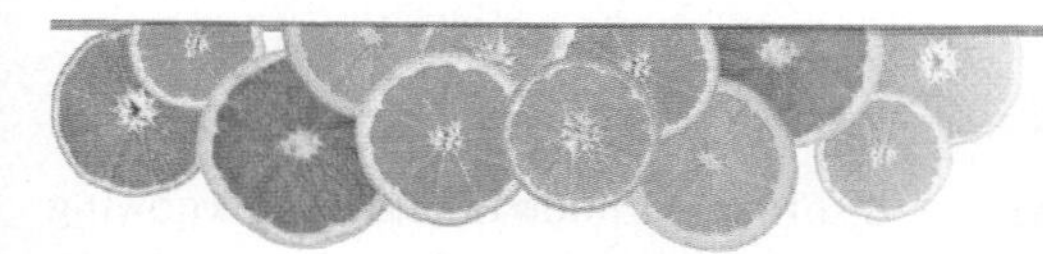

# INTERSECTION

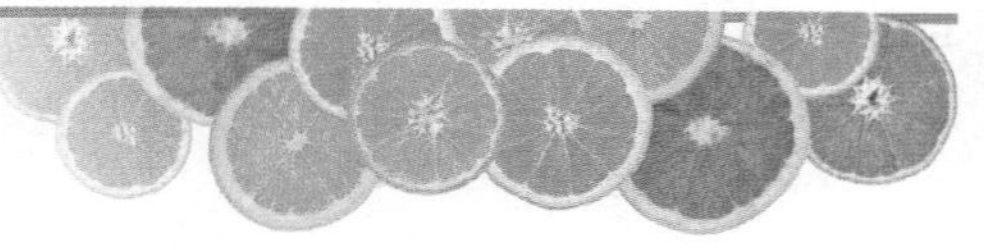

## Clinical Psychology and Social Psychology: How Does the Stigma of Mental Illness Affect Social Interactions?

Imagine participating in the following study. You must fill out a form that asks some basic questions and whether you have been hospitalized in the last 12 months. You are told that, as part of the study, you will be interacting with a partner a week later. To help you get to know the person (who is in the next room), you are provided with their information form. On the form, the person has indicated that they were hospitalized in the last year because they have a diagnosis of schizophrenia. Then the experimenter tells you that you can sign up for one of three topics for next week. On the list, the person in the next room has already indicated their preferred topic. You can avoid meeting the person if you pick a different topic. Would you?

*How is having a psychological disorder different from other stigmatized identities?*

College students in a recent study faced this situation (Lucas & Phelan, 2018). The partner (who did not actually exist) was identified either as not having been hospitalized (the control condition) or as having one of three disorders: panic disorder, depression, or schizophrenia (the experimental conditions). In the control and panic disorder conditions, 90 percent of the participants selected the same topic as the partner. However, when the partner mentioned having depression only 60 percent signed up for that interaction. When the partner mentioned having schizophrenia, less than half of the participants selected that topic.

A small entry on a form mentioning a psychological disorder was all that it took to move people to avoid contact with a person. This powerful stigma can have profound implications. Certainly, throughout our review of psychological disorders we have not encountered evidence that being socially isolated from others is optimal for anyone. A great deal of research is aimed at understanding the stigma attached to psychological disorders and reducing prejudice against those who are already suffering (Koike & others, 2018). In addition to education, contact with a person who has a disorder can improve attitudes (Morgan & others, 2018). If your first response to someone with a disorder is to avoid contact, much is lost, including the opportunity to reduce your own prejudices and potentially to make a new friend.

©sturti/E+/Getty Images

### PHYSICAL HEALTH

Compared with their psychologically healthy counterparts, people with psychological disorders are more likely to be physically ill (Gittelman, 2008), to be obese, to smoke, to drink excessively, and to lead sedentary lives (Beard, Weisberg, & Keller, 2010; Chou & others, 2013; H.-Y. Lin & others, 2013).

You might think, these physical health issues are the least of their worries. If people with schizophrenia want to smoke, why not let them? This type of thinking reveals the subtle way that prejudice toward those with psychological disorders can affect their lives. It sells short the capacity of treatments to help those with disorders, and more importantly, it fails to acknowledge that these people can lead healthy, meaningful lives.

Health-promotion programs can work for people with a psychological disorder (Bonfioli & others, 2018; Farholm & Sørensen, 2016; Rosenbaum & others, 2014; Sharma & others, 2018). When we disregard the potential of physical health interventions for people with psychological disorders to make positive life changes, we reveal our own biases.

## Overcoming Stigma

How can we effectively combat the stigma of psychological disorders? An obstacle to changing people's attitudes toward individuals with psychological disorders is that mental illness is often invisible. A person can have a disorder without others ever knowing about it. Indeed, we may be unaware of *many* courageous lives around us that are being lived within the challenging context of psychological disorders, because worries about being stigmatized keep the affected individuals from "coming out" (Corrigan & others, 2015). Thus, stigma leads to a catch-22: Positive examples of people coping with psychological disorders are often missing from our experience because those who are doing well (understandably) shun public disclosure of their disorders.

A critical step toward eliminating stigma is to create a positive environment for people with disorders. Without fear of stigma, they can become empowering positive role models for others. We must recognize that those with psychological disorders have strengths to offer (Yanos, 2018).

After reading this chapter, you know that many admired people have dealt with psychological disorders. Their diagnoses do not detract from their accomplishments. To the contrary, their accomplishments are all the more remarkable in the context of the challenges they have faced.

### test yourself

1. What did the classic study by Rosenhan reveal about the power of labels that are applied to individuals?
2. What social and physical effects can result from the stigma with which some people view psychological disorders?
3. What are some critical considerations in efforts to eliminate stigma toward individuals with psychological disorders?

## SUMMARY

### 1. DEFINING AND EXPLAINING ABNORMAL BEHAVIOR

Abnormal behavior is deviant, maladaptive, or personally distressful. Theoretical perspectives on the causes of psychological disorders include biological, psychological, sociocultural, and biopsychosocial approaches.

Biological approaches view psychological disorders as diseases with origins in neurological, biochemical, and genetic factors. Psychological approaches include behavioral, social cognitive, and trait perspectives. Sociocultural approaches emphasize the larger social and cultural context and factors such as marriage, socioeconomic status, ethnicity, gender, and culture. Biopsychosocial approaches view the interactions among biological, psychological, and social factors as significant forces in producing both normal and abnormal behavior. The vulnerability-stress hypothesis (or the diathesis-stress model) suggests that some factors may predispose a person to develop a psychological disorder in response to stressful experiences.

The *Diagnostic and Statistical Manual of Mental Disorders (DSM)* is the classification system clinicians use to diagnose psychological disorders. Some psychologists contend that *DSM-5* perpetuates the medical model of psychological disorders, that it labels everyday problems as psychological disorders, and that it fails to address strengths.

### 2. NEURODEVELOPMENTAL DISORDERS

Neurodevelopmental disorders are diagnosed in childhood and often traced to atypical brain development, genetic differences, or prenatal exposure to substances that adversely affect development. Autism spectrum disorder (ASD) is typically diagnosed in early childhood and involves deficits in communication and social relationships. The level of impairment associated with ASD varies. ASD is linked to genetics and brain development, but no single cause has been identified. Typical treatment is intense behavioral-oriented therapies. Attention-deficit/hyperactivity disorder (ADHD) is characterized by problems maintaining attention, excessive, inappropriate activity, and high levels of impulsivity. ADHD is typically diagnosed in childhood and, left untreated, can have numerous negative consequences. Genetic and brain differences, especially in the prefrontal cortex and reward centers, are linked to ADHD. Treatment typically involves stimulant medications. Nonmedical treatments such as psychotherapy can also be effective.

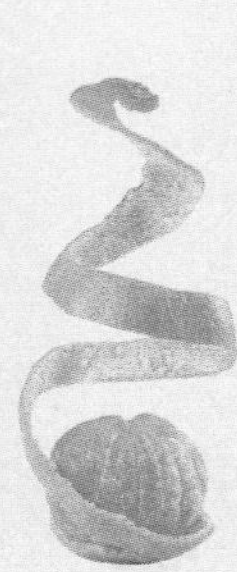

### 3. ANXIETY AND ANXIETY-RELATED DISORDERS

Anxiety disorders involve unrealistic and debilitating high levels of anxiety. Generalized anxiety disorder involves a high level of anxiety with no specific reason for the anxiety. Panic disorder involves attacks marked by the sudden onset of intense terror. Specific phobia is irrational, overwhelming fear of a specific object, like snakes, or a situation, like flying. Social anxiety disorder is the intense fear that one will do something embarrassing or humiliating in public. Obsessive-compulsive disorder involves anxiety-provoking thoughts that will not go away (obsession) and/or urges to perform repetitive behaviors (compulsion).

### 4. TRAUMA AND STRESS-RELATED DISORDERS

Some psychological disorders are tied to traumatic events. One such disorder, post-traumatic stress disorder (PTSD), includes flashbacks, emotional numbing, and excessive arousal. Dissociative disorders are also linked to traumatic experience. Dissociative amnesia involves memory loss caused by extensive psychological stress. In dissociative identity disorder, formerly called multiple personality disorder, two or more distinct personalities are present in the same person.

### 5. DISORDERS INVOLVING EMOTION AND MOOD

In depressive disorder, the individual experiences a serious depressive episode and depressed characteristics such as lethargy and hopelessness. Biological explanations focus on heredity, brain features, and neurotransmitter regulation. Psychological explanations include behavioral and cognitive perspectives. Sociocultural explanations emphasize socioeconomic and ethnic factors and gender.

Bipolar disorder is characterized by extreme mood swings that include one or more episodes of mania (an overexcited, unrealistic, optimistic state). Individuals with bipolar I disorder have more extreme manic episodes than those with bipolar II.

### 6. SCHIZOPHRENIA

Schizophrenia spectrum disorder is a severe psychological disorder characterized by highly disordered thought processes. Positive symptoms of schizophrenia are behaviors and experiences that are present in individuals with schizophrenia but absent in healthy people, such as hallucinations, delusions, thought disorder, and movement disorders. Negative symptoms are behaviors and experiences that are part of healthy human life that are absent for those with this disorder; they include flat affect and an inability to plan or engage in goal-directed behavior.

Biological factors in schizophrenia include genes and the neurotransmitter dopamine. Psychological and sociocultural factors are not viewed as stand-alone causes of schizophrenia, but they are related to the course of the disorder.

## 7. PERSONALITY DISORDERS

Personality disorders are chronic, maladaptive cognitive-behavioral patterns that are thoroughly integrated into an individual's personality. Antisocial personality disorder (ASPD) is characterized by guiltlessness, law-breaking, exploitation of others, irresponsibility, and deceit. Individuals with this disorder often lead a life of crime and violence. Psychopaths–remorseless predators who engage in violence to get what they want–are a subgroup of individuals with ASPD. Biological factors for ASPD include genetic, brain, and autonomic nervous system differences.

Borderline personality disorder is a pervasive pattern of instability in interpersonal relationships, self-image, and emotions. This disorder is related to self-harming behaviors such as cutting and suicide. The potential causes of BPD are complex and include biological and cognitive factors and childhood experiences.

## 8. SUICIDE

Theorists have proposed biological, psychological, and sociocultural explanations of how people die by suicide. The interpersonal theory of suicide suggests that it requires the desire to die and the acquired capability to kill oneself.

## 9. PSYCHOLOGICAL DISORDERS AND HEALTH AND WELLNESS

Stigma can create a significant barrier for people coping with a psychological disorder and for their loved ones. Fear of being labeled can prevent individuals from getting treatment and from talking about their problems with family and friends. In addition, the stigma attached to psychological disorders can lead to prejudice and discrimination toward individuals who are struggling with these problems.

We can combat stigma by acknowledging the strengths and the achievements of individuals coping with psychological disorders. By creating a positive environment for people with disorders, we encourage them to be open about their struggles and to thrive, with the result that they can become positive role models for others.

# key *terms*

abnormal behavior
antisocial personality disorder (ASPD)
anxiety disorders
applied behavior analysis or behavior modification
attention-deficit/hyperactivity disorder (ADHD)
autism spectrum disorder
bipolar disorder
borderline personality disorder (BPD)
catatonia
comorbidity
delusions
depressive disorders
dissociative amnesia
dissociative disorders
dissociative identity disorder (DID)
*DSM-5*
flat affect
generalized anxiety disorder
hallucinations
illusory correlation
major depressive disorder (MDD)
medical model
movement disorders
neurodevelopmental disorders
obsessive-compulsive disorder (OCD)
panic disorder
personality disorders
post-traumatic stress disorder (PTSD)
psychosis
psychotherapy
referential thinking
risk factors
schizophrenia
social anxiety disorder (SAD) or social phobia
somatic symptom disorder
specific phobia
thought disorder
vulnerability-stress hypothesis or diathesis-stress model

# apply your *knowledge*

1. Spend 15 to 20 minutes observing an area with a large number of people, such as a mall, a cafeteria, or a stadium during a game. Identify and make a list of behaviors you would classify as abnormal. How does your list of behaviors compare with the definition of *abnormal* provided in the chapter? What would change in the list if you were in a different setting, such as a church, a bar, or a library? What does this exercise tell you about the meaning of *abnormal?*
2. If you have never encountered anyone with schizophrenia, meet Moe Armstrong by checking out this YouTube video: www.youtube.com/watch?v=p-_j1ZNKzsg
3. Although we might think of people who contend with psychological disorders as troubled and downtrodden, they (like all people) have the capacity to be astonishingly creative. Check out the website maintained by the National Art Exhibitions of the Mentally Ill (NAEMI) to experience some amazing creations of artists who suffer from mental illness. Go to www.naemi.org and click on "Enter" to view each artist's work. How does your exploration of this artwork influence your feelings about mental illness?
4. Go online and search for message boards where individuals with different psychological disorders share with one another. How do the discussion boards reflect what you have learned about these disorders?

**Design elements:** Preview icon: ©Jiang Hongyan; Intersection box icon: ©D. Hurst/Alamy, ©Creative Crop/Getty Images, ©Dimitris66/Getty Images, ©Savany/Getty Images; Critical Controversy box icon: ©Ultrashock; running heads icon: ©Cre8tive Studios/Alamy; Summary icon: ©Vadarshop

# PREVIEW

The science of psychology has led to the development of various treatments to help relieve psychological suffering. These different forms of therapy are the focus of this chapter. We first consider psychological and biological approaches to treating disorders. Then we turn to a consideration of psychotherapy, including evaluations of its effectiveness and descriptions of the numerous approaches to psychotherapy devised by psychologists. Next, we examine biological and sociocultural approaches to therapy. Finally, we consider the broad array of benefits that therapy offers for physical health and psychological wellness.

## 1. APPROACHES TO TREATING PSYCHOLOGICAL DISORDERS

● **clinical psychology** The area of psychology that integrates science and theory to prevent and treat psychological disorders.

● **psychotherapy** A nonmedical process that helps individuals with psychological disorders recognize and overcome their problems.

● **biological therapies or biomedical therapies** Treatments that reduce or eliminate the symptoms of psychological disorders by altering aspects of bodily functioning.

**Clinical psychology** is the area of psychology that integrates science and theory to prevent and treat psychological disorders. To treat psychological disorders, clinical psychologists use psychotherapy. **Psychotherapy** is a nonmedical process that helps individuals with psychological disorders recognize and overcome their problems. Psychotherapists employ a number of strategies including talking, interpreting, listening, rewarding, and modeling (Prochaska & Norcross, 2018). As we saw in the chapter "Psychological Disorders", the medical model views psychological disorders as akin to diseases requiring specific treatments, typically medications. Such **biological therapies**, also called **biomedical therapies**, are treatments that reduce or eliminate the symptoms of psychological disorders by altering aspects of bodily functioning.

Both psychotherapy and biological therapies share the goal of relieving the suffering of individuals with psychological disorders, but they differ in their focus and in the types of professionals who are able to deliver them, as we now consider.

### The Psychological Approach to Therapy

Psychotherapy is practiced by a variety of mental health professionals, including clinical psychologists, counselors, and social workers. Figure 1 lists the main types of mental health professionals, their degrees, the years of education required, and the nature of their training.

Sometimes referred to as "talk therapy," psychotherapy is provided by professionals who receive training to develop expertise in diagnosing disorders, administering psychological assessments, as well as performing therapy to help those with psychological disorders. Licensing and certification are two ways in which society retains control over psychotherapy practitioners. Laws at the state level are used to license or certify such professionals. These laws specify the training individuals must have and provide for some assessment of an applicant's skill through formal examination.

During graduate school, those seeking a PhD in clinical psychology begin to see clients under the supervision of a licensed clinical psychologist. In addition to completing their graduate work, these individuals complete a clinical internship–one year spent providing supervised therapy in an accredited site–to hone their therapeutic skills. In practice, psychotherapy may be given alone or in conjunction with medication which (as we review below) is typically administered by psychiatrists and other medical doctors.

### The Biological Approach to Therapy

Generally speaking, those who administer biological therapies are required to have completed the training to become a medical doctor (that is, an MD). *Psychiatrists* are medical doctors who specialize in treating psychological disorders. In the United States, psychiatrists complete medical school and then spend an additional four years in a psychiatric residency program. During their residency, these individuals continue training in diagnosing disorders, understanding the effects of drug therapies on disorders, and practicing psychotherapy.

| Professional Type | Degree; Education Beyond Bachelor's Degree | Nature of Training |
|---|---|---|
| Clinical Psychologist | PhD or PsyD<br>5–7 years | Requires both clinical and research training. Includes a 1-year internship in a psychiatric hospital or mental health facility. Some universities have developed PsyD programs, which have a stronger clinical than research emphasis. The PsyD training program takes as long as the clinical psychology PhD program and also requires the equivalent of a 1-year internship. |
| Psychiatrist | MD<br>7–9 years | Four years of medical school, plus an internship and residency in psychiatry, is required. A psychiatry residency involves supervision in therapies, including psychotherapy and biomedical therapy. |
| Counseling Psychologist | MA, PhD, PsyD, or EdD<br>3–7 years | Similar to clinical psychologist but with emphasis on counseling and therapy. Some counseling psychologists specialize in vocational counseling. Some counselors complete master's degree training, others PhD or EdD training, in graduate schools of psychology or education. |
| School Psychologist | MA, PhD, PsyD, or EdD<br>3–7 years | Training in graduate programs of education or psychology. Emphasis on psychological assessment and counseling practices involving students' school-related problems. Training is at the master's or doctoral level. |
| Social Worker | MS W/DSW or PhD<br>2–5 years | Graduate work in a school of social work that includes specialized clinical training in mental health facilities. |
| Psychiatric Nurse | RN, MA, or PhD<br>0–5 years | Graduate work in a school of nursing with special emphasis on care of mentally disturbed individuals in hospital settings and mental health facilities. |
| Occupational Therapist | BS, MA, or PhD<br>0–5 years | Emphasis on occupational training with focus on physically or psychologically handicapped individuals. Stresses getting individuals back into the mainstream of work. |
| Pastoral Counselor | None to PhD or DD (Doctor of Divinity)<br>0–5 years | Requires ministerial background and training in psychology. An internship in a mental health facility as a chaplain is recommended. |
| Counselor | MA or MEd<br>2 years | Graduate work in a department of psychology or department of education with specialized training in counseling techniques. |

**FIGURE 1** **Main Types of Mental Health Professionals** Professionals with varying levels of training have taken on the challenge of helping people with psychological disorders.

For licensing in the United States, psychiatrists are required to demonstrate proficiency in different approaches to psychotherapy that we will review later in this chapter.

Although psychologists and psychiatrists can both administer psychotherapy, for the most part only psychiatrists can prescribe medications. When a psychotherapist believes that a client would benefit from medication, he or she might refer that client to a trusted psychiatrist to obtain a prescription.

For a number of years, psychologists have sought to obtain the right to prescribe drug treatments to their clients. The motivation for this movement is often a shortage of psychiatrists in some areas. Currently, the states that permit psychologists to prescribe drugs are Idaho, Illinois, Iowa, Louisiana, and New Mexico. In these states, clinical psychologists complete additional training in medicine to qualify for prescription privileges. Other states have also considered granting psychologists these privileges, often in response to a lack of psychiatrists to treat those with psychological disorders in many areas.

Those who support the idea that psychologists ought to have prescription privileges argue that this change in regulations would make treatment more efficient for those with psychological disorders. In addition, they note that a psychologist's likely first impulse is to treat with psychotherapy, rather than medication, reducing the potential overuse of strong drugs when they are not needed. Those who oppose such a change note that psychoactive drugs are powerful and affect many bodily systems. They feel that additional training simply cannot provide the level of expertise required to prescribe and monitor these medicines. Further, those with psychological disorders may also have physical illnesses that psychologists would not be trained to diagnose or treat.

### test yourself

1. Define psychotherapy and biological therapy.
2. What are the differences between a clinical psychologist and a psychiatrist in training and the types of treatment provided?
3. Describe two arguments from both sides regarding whether psychologists should be allowed to prescribe drug treatment.

# 2. PSYCHOTHERAPY

Although there are different types of psychotherapies, they all involve a trained professional engaging in an interpersonal relationship with someone who is suffering. Later in this section, we will review the specific types of psychotherapies that have been developed from broad theoretical approaches in psychology. Before we do so, let's consider some general issues that are common to all forms of psychotherapy.

## Central Issues in Psychotherapy

Psychotherapy can be a very desirable type of treatment. One study showed that 90 percent of those surveyed said that they would rather talk to someone than take medicines for their problems (Duncan & others, 2010). Still, a person seeking psychotherapy might wonder whether it works, whether some therapies work better than others, what factors influence a therapy's effectiveness, and how various forms of therapy differ. In this section, we address these questions.

### DOES PSYCHOTHERAPY WORK?

There are many debates in psychology, but the effectiveness of psychotherapy in treating psychological disorders is *not* one of them. Many studies have been conducted to answer the question "Does psychotherapy work?" and the answer is a resounding yes (American Psychological Association, 2012). A vast body of research and multiple meta-analyses support this conclusion (Carpenter & others, 2018; Hopkinson & others, 2018; Kline & others, 2018; McAleavey & others, 2017; Munder & others, 2018; Weitz & others, 2018). Individuals who experience 12 to 14 sessions of psychotherapy are more likely to improve than those who receive a placebo treatment or no treatment at all, and they are likely to maintain these improvements for two to three years, provided that the treatment they receive is based on sound psychological theory (Lambert, 2013). The Psychological Inquiry shows the results of an analysis of treatment outcomes.

### DOES ONE THERAPY WORK BETTER THAN OTHERS?

People who are contemplating seeing a psychotherapist do not just want to know *whether* psychotherapy in general works, but also *which form* of psychotherapy is most effective. In some ways, this question pits the different brands of psychotherapy against one another in a kind of competition. It is important to bear in mind that it is human nature for psychologists to have allegiances or loyalties to the brand of psychotherapy they use and in which they were trained. The results of many studies addressing the "which therapy is the best" question show that, although there is strong research supporting the notion that therapy is effective, no one therapy has been shown to be significantly more effective than the others, overall (Duncan & Reese, 2013; Gelo, Pritz, & Rieken, 2014; Lambert, 2001; Lemmens & others, 2015; Luborsky & others, 2002; Wampold, 2001; Werbart & others, 2013).

Indeed, the answer to the question "Which therapy works the best?" may be "It depends on the person's diagnosis." That is, some therapies might be more effective than others for particular psychological disorders (Nasser, 2013; Reid & others, 2018; Strosahl & Robinson, 2018). Some psychologists believe that, for patients to improve, therapies must be tailored to particular disorders and therapists should rely on proven treatments for those disorders (Chambless, 2002; David, Cristea, & Hofmann, 2018). This perspective, called **empirically supported treatment**, means that for any given psychological disorder, treatment decisions should be based on the body of research that has been conducted showing which type of therapy works best. Proponents of empirically supported treatment say that, ideally, each disorder would be treated using the particular type of therapy that has been shown by research to work best for that disorder (David, Cristea, & Hofmann, 2018; Mulkens & others, 2018; Strauss & others, 2018).

● **empirically supported treatment** An approach to treating psychological disorders that advocates making treatment decisions based on the body of research that has shown which type of therapy works best.

Other psychologists argue that targeting particular disorders with specific treatments amounts to taking an overly medical approach (Horvath, 2013; S. D. Miller & others, 2013).

## psychological *inquiry*

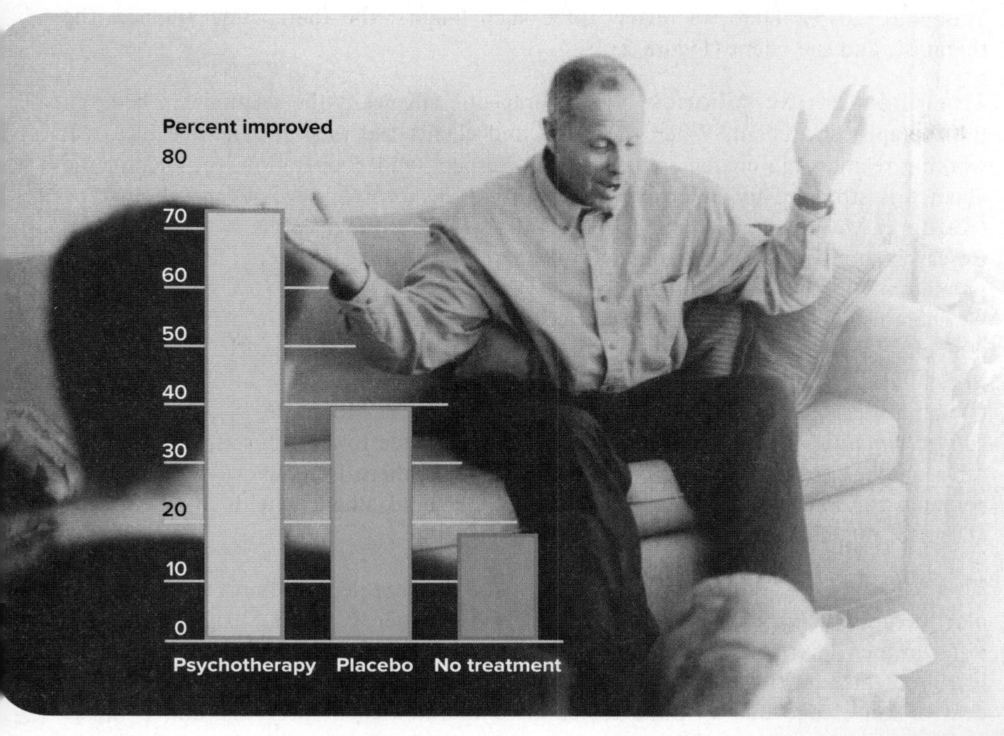


### *Does Therapy Work?*

This figure provides a summary of numerous studies and reviews of research in which clients were randomly assigned to a no-treatment control group, a placebo control group, or a psychotherapy treatment (Lambert, 2001). Note that the group to which individuals were assigned is indicated on the X (horizontal) axis, and the percent of individuals who improved is shown on the Y (vertical) axis. Use the graph to answer the following questions.

1. Which group improved most, and which improved least?
2. Why might those in the no-treatment group have improved?
3. What does the difference between the psychotherapy group and the placebo group indicate?
4. Do these results allow us to infer causal relationships between therapy and improvement? Explain.

ɔurce: Data from Lambert (2001); (photo) ©Geoff Manasse/Photodisc/Getty Images

In medicine, drugs (like antibiotics) are specifically prescribed to treat particular illnesses (like strep throat). Critics of empirically supported treatment note that psychotherapies are not like drugs or medicines that target a particular disease. These psychologists are concerned that closely dictating what therapists should do takes away the flexibility that potentially might be vital for improvement (Shedler, 2018).

Relying on empirical research in making treatment decisions is challenging because the evidence is not always clear-cut: For instance, research is not always conducted on appropriate samples (that is, people who are actually diagnosed with particular disorders), or the samples may not be representative of the people clinicians see in practice (Wampold, 2013). A key challenge in relying on empirical evidence to guide treatment decisions is that such evidence is limited or nonexistent for many disorders. Moreover, relying on research to direct decisions leaves the clinician in the dark when research-recommended treatments do not work for a particular client.

A special task force appointed by the president of the American Psychological Association reached a compromise between these two positions (APA Presidential Task Force on Evidence-Based Practice, 2006). The task force endorsed evidence-based practice. **Evidence-based practice** means that decisions about treatment are made based on three criteria:

- the best available research
- the therapist's clinical judgment
- client characteristics, culture, and preferences.

● **evidence-based practice** Integration of the best available research with clinical expertise in the context of client characteristics, culture, and preferences.

Although evidence-based practice recognizes the importance of scientific evidence, it also permits flexibility for clinicians to consider a broad range of factors in deciding on a course of therapy. A key concern with evidence-based practice is that all three criteria be given equal weighting (Mulkens & others, 2018; Stewart, Chambless, & Stirman, 2018).

• Participates actively
• Draws on personal strengths, abilities, skills, and motivation
• Develops confidence and trust in therapist
• Becomes more hopeful and less alienated
• Participates actively
• Provides genuine support
• Monitors quality of relationship with client


**FIGURE 2 Factors in Effective Psychotherapy** This figure emphasizes the qualities and behaviors of therapists and clients that are essential to a successful therapeutic alliance and effective psychotherapy.
Sources: Cuijpers, Reijnders, & Huibers, (2019); Laska, Gurman, & Wampold (2014); (photo) ©Andrea Morini/Getty Images

● **therapeutic alliance** The relationship between the therapist and client; an important element of successful psychotherapy.

## FACTORS IN EFFECTIVE PSYCHOTHERAPY

Research has also addressed the factors that play an important role in determining the effectiveness of psychotherapy (Cuijpers, Reijnders, & Huibers, 2019; Laska, Gurman, & Wampold, 2014). Here we review three such factors: the therapeutic alliance, the therapist, and the client (Figure 2).

**The Therapeutic Alliance** The **therapeutic alliance** is the relationship between the therapist and client. When therapists and clients feel they are engaged in a real working relationship characterized by trust, respect, and cooperation, the therapeutic alliance is strong. This alliance is an important element of successful psychotherapy (Kazdin & McWhinney, 2018; Nienhuis & others, 2018; Prochaska & Norcross, 2018). Research shows that a poor alliance can be a key predictor of clients leaving therapy prematurely (Anderson, Bautista, & Hope, 2018).

Therapists may treat clients who are different from themselves in many ways, from ethnicity, to gender, to religious faith, to sexuality and gender identity. Knowing how to establish rapport and convey acceptance to diverse individuals is an important skill (Benuto, Casas, & O'Donohue, 2018; Pepping, Lyons, & Morris, 2018). A mindset of *cultural humility*–taking a humble and respectful attitude toward those from other cultures and acknowledging that one cannot know all there is to know about another person's cultural experience–allows therapists to build alliances with diverse clients (Davis & others, 2018).

**The Therapist** Whether psychotherapy works or not depends more on the particular therapist than on the type of therapy used (Beutler & others, 2012). Therapists differ in their level of expertise and experience, their deep knowledge about psychological problems and treatments. Therapists with high expertise not only possess a great deal of knowledge but continue to learn, to monitor client progress, and to make changes when necessary. Therapists who are viewed as genuine and empathetic are more likely to be able to establish a strong therapeutic alliance with clients (Nienhuis & others, 2018).

Research has also shown that the match between a therapist's style and a client's personality can influence whether therapy is effective (Swift & others, 2018). For example, if a client has a strong resistance to changing, a therapist who is more laid back and less directive may have greater success than one who engages directly with the client (Beutler & others, 2012).

**The Client** Another major factor in therapeutic outcomes is the person seeking treatment. Indeed, meta-analyses suggest that the quality of the client's participation is the most important determinant of whether therapy is successful (Bohart & Tallman, 2010; Coyne & others, 2017; McKay, Imel, & Wampold, 2006; Wampold, 2001). Even though individuals often seek therapy due to difficulties and problems in their lives, it is their strengths, abilities, skills, and motivation that account for therapeutic success (Hubble & Miller, 2004; Wampold & Brown, 2005). A review of the extensive evidence on therapeutic efficacy concluded: "The data make abundantly clear that therapy does not make clients work, but rather clients make therapy work" (Hubble & Miller, 2004, p. 347).

## HOW DO PSYCHOTHERAPIES DIFFER?

All psychotherapies involve therapists and clients interacting together in a relationship, but each type of psychotherapy provides a different approach that guides the type of interaction that occurs during treatment. There are two ways to differentiate the types of therapy: (1) the extent to which they focus on insight versus immediate symptoms and skills; and (2) whether they are directive or not (Laska, Gurman, & Wampold, 2014):

- *Insight versus symptoms and skill development:* Some treatments focus on gaining insight into the deeper causes of a problem; others focus on identifying the person's immediate symptoms and helping the person develop specific skills to manage those symptoms. Behavioral therapies do not emphasize insight.

- *Directive versus nondirective:* Some treatments call upon the therapist to be quite outspoken in giving advice to the client; these treatments also tend to encourage the therapist to play an active role in the client's life. In contrast, other treatments prompt the client to drive the interaction, with the therapist taking a less active role in treatment.

The remainder of this section focuses on four main approaches to psychotherapy: psychodynamic, humanistic, behavioral, and cognitive therapy, as well as eclectic approaches to therapy that combine many different techniques.

## Psychodynamic Therapies

The **psychodynamic therapies** stress the importance of the unconscious mind, extensive interpretation by the therapist, and the role of early childhood experiences in the development of an individual's problems. The goal of psychodynamic therapies is to help individuals gain insight into the unconscious conflicts that underlie their problems (Haliburn, Stevenson, & Halovic, 2018; Mullin & others, 2018). Many psychodynamic approaches grew out of Freud's psychoanalytic theory of personality.

- **psychodynamic therapies** Treatments that stress the importance of the unconscious mind, extensive interpretation by the therapist, and the role of early childhood experiences in the development of an individual's problems.

**Psychoanalysis** is Freud's therapeutic technique for analyzing an individual's unconscious thoughts. Freud believed that a person's current problems could be traced to childhood experiences, many of which involved unconscious sexual conflicts. To free the person from these unconscious conflicts, the psychoanalyst interprets aspects of what the person shares about his or her life. A psychoanalyst may ask a person to simply say aloud whatever comes to mind in response to, for instance, the symptoms that have brought him or her to treatment. This process is called *free association*.

- **psychoanalysis** Freud's therapeutic technique for analyzing an individual's unconscious thoughts.

The analyst might also ask the person to share his or her dreams. **Dream analysis** is a psychoanalytic technique for interpreting a person's dreams. Psychoanalysts believe that dreams contain information about unconscious thoughts, wishes, and conflicts (Freud, 1911). From this perspective, dreams give us an outlet to express symbolically our unconscious wishes, a mental theater in which our deepest and most secret desires can be played out. According to Freud, every dream, even our worst nightmare, contains a hidden, disguised wish. The sheer horror we feel during a nightmare might itself disguise that unconscious wish.

- **dream analysis** A psychoanalytic technique for interpreting a person's dreams.

The key aspect of the therapeutic alliance from a psychodynamic perspective is transference. **Transference** is the psychoanalytic term for the client's relating to the analyst in ways that reproduce or relive important relationships in the individual's life. A person might interact with an analyst as if the analyst were a parent or lover, for example. Freud believed that transference is a necessary part of the psychoanalytic relationship, as it models the way that individuals relate to important people in their lives.

- **transference** A client's relating to the psychoanalyst in ways that reproduce or relive important relationships in the individual's life.

Contemporary psychodynamic therapies differ from Freudian psychoanalysis in many ways. However, practitioners of these approaches still probe unconscious thoughts about early childhood experiences to gain insight into their clients' current problems (Haliburn, Stevenson, & Halovic, 2018; Mullin & others, 2018). Contemporary psychoanalysts accord more power to the conscious mind and to a person's current relationships, and they generally place less emphasis on sex (Calderon & others, 2018). The focus of such treatment may involve helping the individual develop the story of his or her experience—putting words on experiences that lack labels (Rosenbaum & others, 2012). Newer approaches to psychodynamic therapies are likely to incorporate emotional expression and warm support as well (Haliburn, Stevenson, & Halovic, 2018).

Like other forms of psychotherapy, psychodynamic therapies can be effective in alleviating symptoms (Driessen & others, 2015; Knekt & others, 2016; Lambert, 2013). One study showed that short-term and long-term psychodynamic therapy continued to predict positive outcomes for clients 10 years later, though long-term therapy performed somewhat better (Knekt & others, 2016).

## Humanistic Therapies

The underlying philosophy of humanistic therapies is captured by the metaphor of how an acorn, if provided with appropriate conditions, will grow, pushing naturally toward its

©Perfect Picture Parts/Alamy Stock Photo

actualization as an oak tree. In **humanistic therapies**, people are encouraged toward self-understanding and personal growth. The humanistic therapies are unique in their emphasis on the person's self-healing capacities. In contrast with psychodynamic therapies, humanistic therapies emphasize conscious rather than unconscious thoughts, the present rather than the past, and self-fulfillment rather than illness (Palacios, 2018; Timulak, 2018).

**Client-centered therapy** (also called *Rogerian therapy* or *nondirective therapy*) is a form of humanistic therapy, developed by Carl Rogers, in which the therapist provides a warm, supportive atmosphere to improve the client's self-concept and to encourage the person to gain insight into problems (Rogers, 1961, 1980). The goal of client-centered therapy is to help clients identify and understand their own genuine feelings and become more *congruent,* bringing their actual self closer to their ideal self.

One way to achieve this goal is through active listening and **reflective speech**, a technique in which the therapist mirrors the client's own feelings back to the client. For example, as a woman is describing her grief over the traumatic loss of her husband in a drunk-driving accident, the therapist might suggest "You sound angry" to help her identify her feelings.

As noted in the chapter "Personality", Rogers believed that humans require three essential elements to grow: unconditional positive regard, empathy, and genuineness. These three elements are reflected in his approach to therapy:

- *Unconditional positive regard:* The therapist constantly recognizes the inherent value of the client, providing a context for personal growth and self-acceptance.
- *Empathy:* The therapist strives to put himself or herself in the client's shoes–to feel the emotions the client is feeling.
- *Genuineness:* The therapist is a real person in his or her relationship with the client, sharing feelings and not hiding behind a facade.

For genuineness to coexist with unconditional positive regard, that regard must be a sincere expression of the therapist's true feelings. The therapist may distinguish between the person's behavior and the person himself or herself. Although the person is acknowledged as a valuable human being, the client's behavior can be evaluated negatively: "You are a good person but your actions are not." Rogers's positive view of humanity extended to his view of therapists. He believed that by being genuine with the client, the therapist could help the client improve.

● **humanistic therapies** Treatments, unique in their emphasis on clients' self-healing capacities, that encourage clients to understand themselves and to grow personally.

● **client-centered therapy** A form of humanistic therapy, developed by Carl Rogers, in which the therapist provides a warm, supportive atmosphere to improve the client's self-concept and to encourage the client to gain insight into problems; also called Rogerian therapy or nondirective therapy.

● **reflective speech** A technique in which the therapist mirrors the client's own feelings back to the client.

## Behavior Therapies

The two approaches we have reviewed thus far, psychodynamic and humanistic, differ in important ways. However, both of these approaches are called *insight therapies* because they encourage self-awareness as the key to psychological health. Both of these approaches assume that once people have insight into the causes of their problems, they will improve. We now turn to therapies that take a different approach. In behavior therapies, insight is irrelevant to the goal of treatment. Instead, behavior therapies offer action-oriented strategies to help people change their *behavior*, not their underlying thoughts or emotions.

**Behavior therapies** use principles of learning to reduce or eliminate maladaptive behavior. Behavior therapies are based on the behavioral and social cognitive theories of learning. Behavior therapists assume that overt symptoms are the central problem and that even if clients discover why they are depressed, that does not mean the depression will cease. To alleviate anxiety or depression, then, behavior therapists focus on eliminating the problematic symptoms or behaviors rather than on helping individuals understand why they are depressed (Foa & McLean, 2016; Reid & others, 2018).

● **behavior therapies** Treatments, based on the behavioral and social cognitive theories of learning, that use principles of learning to reduce or eliminate maladaptive behavior.

Although initially based almost exclusively on the learning principles of classical and operant conditioning, behavior therapies have diversified in recent years. As social cognitive theory grew in popularity, behavior therapists increasingly included observational learning, cognitive factors, and self-instruction (encouraging people to change what they say to themselves) in their treatments.

## CLASSICAL CONDITIONING TECHNIQUES

Classical conditioning has been used in treating phobias. Recall that phobias are irrational fears that interfere with an individual's life, such as fear of heights, dogs, flying, or public speaking. **Systematic desensitization** is a method of behavior therapy that treats anxiety by teaching the client to associate deep relaxation with increasingly intense anxiety-producing situations Lehrer, 2018; Miller-Matero & Eshelman, 2018).

Desensitization involves exposing someone to a feared situation in a real or an imagined way, or using virtual reality (Carl & others, 2018). A therapist might first ask the client which aspects of the feared situation are the most and least frightening. The therapist then arranges these circumstances in order from most to least frightening. The next step is to teach the individual to relax. The client learns to recognize the presence of muscular contractions or tension in various parts of the body and then to tighten and relax different muscles. Once the individual is relaxed, the therapist asks the person to imagine the least feared stimulus in the hierarchy. Subsequently, the therapist moves up the list of items, from least to most feared, while the client remains relaxed. Eventually, the client can imagine the scariest circumstance without fear.

In systematic desensitization, if you are afraid of, say, spiders, the therapist might initially have you watch someone handle a spider and then ask you to engage in increasingly more feared behaviors. You might first go into the same room with a spider, next approach the spider, and then touch the spider. Eventually, you might play with the spider. Figure 3 shows an example of a desensitization hierarchy.

Recall from the chapter "Learning" that aversive conditioning consists of repeated pairings of an undesirable behavior with aversive stimuli to decrease the behavior's positive associations. Through aversive conditioning, people can learn to avoid behaviors such as smoking, overeating, and drinking alcohol. Electric shocks, nausea-inducing substances, bad smells, and verbal insults are some of the noxious stimuli used in aversive conditioning (Kang & others, 2018; Mantsch & Twining, 2018). The Psychological Inquiry illustrates conditioning principles in practice.

1. A month before an examination
2. Two weeks before an examination
3. A week before an examination
4. Five days before an examination
5. Four days before an examination
6. Three days before an examination
7. Two days before an examination
8. One day before an examination
9. The night before an examination
10. On the way to the university on the day of an examination
11. Before the unopened doors of the examination room
12. Awaiting distribution of examination papers
13. The examination paper lies facedown before her
14. In the process of answering an examination paper

**FIGURE 3 A Desensitization Hierarchy Involving Test Anxiety** In this hierarchy, the individual begins with her least feared circumstance (a month before the exam) and moves through each of the circumstances until reaching her most feared circumstance (being in the process of answering the exam questions). At each step of the way, the person replaces fear with deep relaxation and successful visualization. (photo) ©FatCamera/Getty Images

## OPERANT CONDITIONING TECHNIQUES

The idea behind using operant conditioning as a therapy approach is that just as maladaptive behavior patterns are learned, they can be unlearned. Using operant conditioning, unhealthy behaviors are replaced with healthy ones. Therapy involves conducting a careful analysis of the person's environment to determine which factors need modification. Especially important is changing the consequences of the person's behavior to ensure that healthy, adaptive replacement behaviors are followed by positive reinforcement.

Applied behavior analysis, described in the chapter "Psychological Disorders", involves establishing positive reinforcement connections between behaviors and rewards so that individuals engage in appropriate behavior and extinguish inappropriate behavior. This type of therapy is often used with individuals on the autism spectrum. It may strike you as unusual that behavioral approaches do not emphasize gaining insight and self-awareness. However, for the very reason that they do not stress these goals, such treatments may be particularly useful with individuals whose cognitive abilities are limited, such as adults with developmental disabilities or children.

# Cognitive Therapies

**Cognitive therapies** emphasize that cognitions, or thoughts, are the main source of psychological problems; these therapies attempt to change the individual's feelings and behaviors by changing cognitions.

Cognitive therapies differ from psychoanalytic therapies by focusing on symptoms and skill development rather than insight into the past or to root causes of the client's problems. Clients in cognitive therapy may gain insight, but that insight is about the automatic thoughts that underlie their problems. Just knowing this, however, will not change the thoughts: They must be replaced with healthy cognitions. Compared with humanistic

- **systematic desensitization** A method of behavior therapy that treats anxiety by teaching the client to associate deep relaxation with increasingly intense anxiety-producing situations.

- **cognitive therapies** Treatments emphasizing that cognitions (thoughts) are the main source of psychological problems and that attempt to change the individual's feelings and behaviors by changing cognitions.

## Psychological *inquiry*

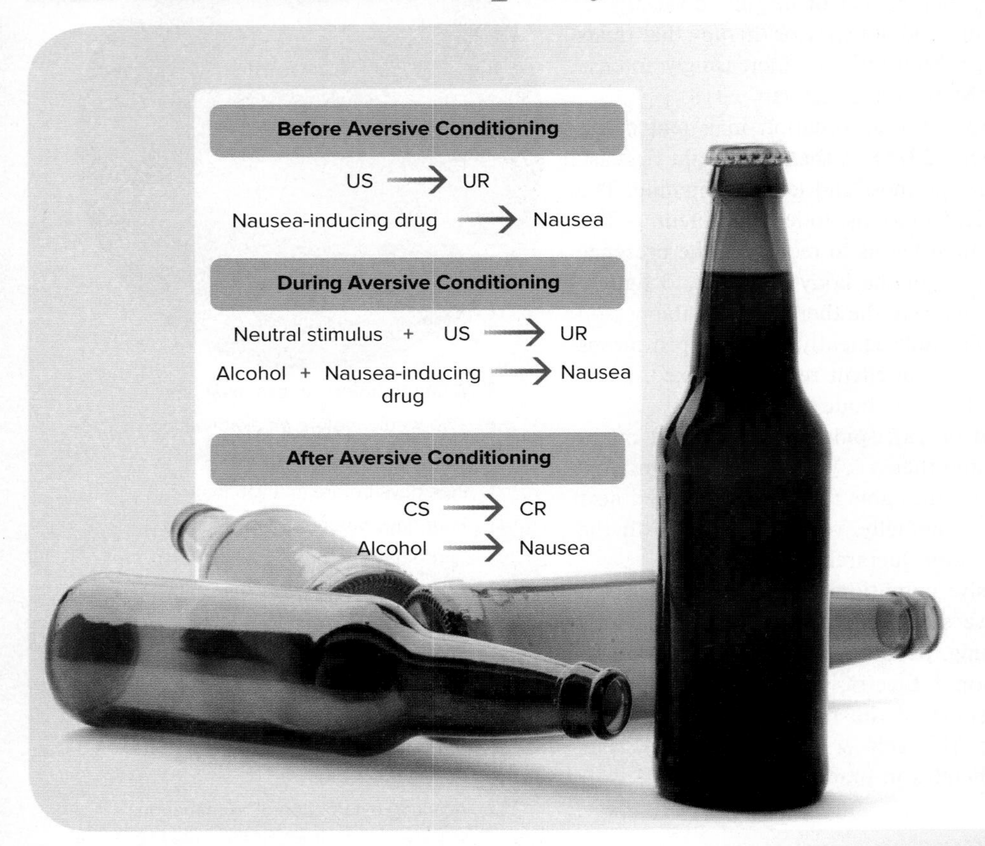


### *Classical Conditioning: The Backbone of Aversive Conditioning*

This figure demonstrates how classical conditioning principles underlie the process of aversive conditioning. It specifically shows how classical conditioning can provide a conditional aversion to alcohol. In studying the figure, recall the abbreviations US (unconditioned stimulus), UR (unconditioned response), CS (conditioned stimulus), and CR (conditioned response). Try your hand at answering the questions below.

1. In the example illustrated in the figure, what is the conditioned stimulus?
2. What is the likely effect of alcohol *prior to* aversion therapy? Is this effect learned (that is, a conditioned response) or not (an unconditioned response)?
3. What role, if any, does the person's motivation play in the process of conditioning?
4. Looking over the steps in aversive conditioning, how do you think classical conditioning might be applied to prevent psychological problems?

(photo) ©TokenPhoto/iStock/Getty Images

therapies, cognitive therapies are more directive. Cognitive therapists guide individuals in identifying their irrational and self-defeating thoughts. Then they use various techniques to get clients to challenge these thoughts and to consider different, more positive ways of thinking (Beck & others, 2018; Medalia, Beck, & Grant, 2018).

### FOUNDATIONS OF COGNITIVE THERAPIES

All cognitive therapies involve these basic assumptions: Human beings have control over their feelings, and how individuals feel about something depends on how they think about it (Beck, 2006; Ellis, 2005). Cognitive therapy involves getting people to recognize these connections and helping them use thinking to change their feelings. *Cognitive restructuring,* a general concept for changing a pattern of thought that is presumed to be causing maladaptive behavior or emotion, is central to cognitive therapies.

Unfortunately, thoughts that lead to emotions can happen so rapidly that we are not even aware of them. Thus, the first goal of therapy is to bring these automatic thoughts into awareness so that they can be changed. The therapist helps clients to identify their own automatic thoughts and to keep records of their thought content and emotional reactions.

With the therapist's assistance, clients learn to recognize logical errors in their thinking and to challenge the accuracy of these automatic thoughts. Logical errors in thinking can lead individuals to the following erroneous beliefs (Carson, Butcher, & Mineka, 1996):

- Perceiving the world as harmful while ignoring evidence to the contrary—for example, when a young woman still feels worthless after a friend has just told her how much other people genuinely like her.

- Overgeneralizing on the basis of limited examples—such as a man's seeing himself as worthless because one person stopped dating him.
- Magnifying the importance of undesirable events—for example, viewing a single failure as the end of the world.
- Engaging in absolutist thinking—such as exaggerating the importance of someone's mildly critical comment and perceiving it as proof of total inadequacy.

Cognitive therapy has been used successfully in treating a wide array of disorders, including depression, anxiety disorders, personality disorders, and schizophrenia (Beck & others, 2018). It has also been effective with children and adolescents (Racey & others, 2018; Shearer & others, 2018).

Figure 4 describes some of the most widely used cognitive therapy techniques.

| Cognitive Therapy Technique | Description | Example |
|---|---|---|
| Challenge Idiosyncratic Meanings | Explore personal meaning attached to the client's words and ask the client to consider alternatives. | When a client says he will be "devastated" by his spouse leaving, ask just how he would be devastated and ways he could avoid being devastated. |
| Question the Evidence | Systematically examine the evidence for the client's beliefs or assertions. | When a client says she can't live without her spouse, explore how she lived without the spouse before she was married. |
| Reattribution | Help the client distribute responsibility for events appropriately. | When a client says that his son's failure in school must be his fault, explore other possibilities, such as the quality of the school. |
| Examine Options and Alternatives | Help the client generate alternative actions to maladaptive ones. | If a client considers leaving school, explore whether tutoring or going part-time to school are good alternatives. |
| Decatastrophize | Help the client evaluate whether he is overestimating the nature of a situation. | If a client states that failure in a course means he must give up the dream of medical school, question whether this is a necessary conclusion. |
| Fantasize Consequences | Explore fantasies of a feared situation: if unrealistic, the client may recognize this; if realistic, work on effective coping strategies. | Help a client who fantasizes "falling apart" when asking the boss for a raise to role play the situation and develop effective skills for making the request. |
| Examine Advantages and Disadvantages | Examine advantages and disadvantages of an issue, to instill a broader perspective. | If a client says he "was just born depressed and will always be that way," explore the advantages and disadvantages of holding that perspective versus other perspectives. |
| Turn Adversity to Advantage | Explore ways that difficult situations can be transformed into opportunities. | If a client has just been laid off, explore whether this is an opportunity for her to return to school. |
| Guided Association | Help the client see connections between different thoughts or ideas. | Draw the connections between a client's anger at his wife for going on a business trip and his fear of being alone. |
| Scaling | Ask the client to rate her emotions or thoughts on scales to help gain perspective. | If a client says she was overwhelmed by an emotion, ask her to rate it on a scale from 0 (not at all present) to 100 ("I fell down in a faint"). |
| Thought Stopping | Provide the client with ways of stopping a cascade of negative thoughts. | Teach an anxious client to picture a stop sign or hear a bell when anxious thoughts begin to snowball. |
| Distraction | Help the client find benign or positive distractions to take attention away from negative thoughts or emotions temporarily. | Have a client count to 200 by 13s when he feels himself becoming anxious. |
| Labeling of Distortions | Provide labels for specific types of distorted thinking to help the client gain more distance and perspective. | Have a client keep a record of the number of times a day she engages in all-or-nothing thinking—seeing things as all bad or all good. |

**FIGURE 4** **Cognitive Therapy Techniques** Cognitive therapists develop strategies to help change the way people think.
Sources: Racey & others (2018); Shearer & others (2018).

## COGNITIVE-BEHAVIOR THERAPY

**cognitive-behavior therapy** A therapy that combines cognitive therapy and behavior therapy with the goal of developing self-efficacy.

**Cognitive-behavior therapy (CBT)** is a combination of cognitive therapy, with its emphasis on reducing self-defeating thoughts, and behavior therapy, with its emphasis on changing behavior (Linehan, 2018). In CBT, the therapist takes a directive role, engaging in a dialogue to help the client identify automatic thoughts and the feelings they produce and then working with the client to change those thoughts while also focusing on changing behavior. In CBT, the client may be given homework assignments directed at these behavioral changes.

*Self-instructional methods* are cognitive-behavior techniques aimed at teaching individuals to modify their own behavior (Lee & DiGiuseppe, 2018). Using self-instructional techniques, cognitive-behavior therapists prompt clients to change what they say to themselves. The therapist gives the client examples of constructive statements, known as *reinforcing self-statements,* which the client can repeat in order to take positive steps to cope with stress or meet a goal. The therapist also encourages the client to practice the statements through role playing and strengthens the client's newly acquired skills through reinforcement.

An important aspect of cognitive-behavior therapy is *self-efficacy,* the belief that one can master a situation and produce positive outcomes (Bandura, 2001, 2010, 2011b, 2012). At each step of the therapy process, clients need to bolster their confidence by telling themselves things such as "I'm going to master my problem," "I can do it," "I'm improving," and "I'm getting better." As they gain confidence and engage in adaptive behavior, the successes become intrinsically motivating. Before long, individuals persist (with considerable effort) in their attempts to solve personal problems because of the positive outcomes that were set in motion by self-efficacy.

CBT is the most common form of therapy used today, and it has proved effective in treating a host of disorders in adults and in children (March & others, 2018; Ruocco, Gordon, & McLean, 2016; van Steensel & Bögels, 2015).

The four psychotherapies—psychodynamic, humanistic, behavior, and cognitive—are compared in Figure 5.

# Therapy Integrations

**integrative therapy** Use of a combination of techniques from different therapies based on the therapist's judgment of which particular methods will provide the greatest benefit for the client.

Many psychotherapists identify themselves as not adhering to one particular method. Rather, they refer to themselves as "eclectic" or "integrative." **Integrative therapy** is a combination of techniques from different therapies based on the therapist's judgment of which particular methods will provide the greatest benefit for the client (Prochaska & Norcross, 2018). For example, a therapist might use a behavioral approach to treat an individual with panic disorder and a cognitive approach to treat a client with depressive disorder.

Because clients present a wide range of problems, it makes sense for therapists to use the best tools in each case rather than to adopt a "one size fits all" program. Sometimes a given psychological disorder is so difficult to treat that it requires the therapist to bring all possible tools to bear (Vohs & others, 2018). For example, borderline personality disorder (see the

| | Cause of Problem | Therapy Emphasis | Nature of Therapy and Techniques |
|---|---|---|---|
| **Psychodynamic Therapies** | Client's problems are symptoms of deep-seated, unresolved unconscious conflicts. | Discover underlying unconscious conflicts and work with client to develop insight. | Psychoanalysis, including free association and dream analysis: therapist interprets heavily. |
| **Humanistic Therapies** | Client is not functioning at an optimal level of development. | Develop awareness of inherent potential for growth. | Person-centered therapy, including unconditional positive regard, genuineness, accurate empathy, and active listening; self-appreciation emphasized. |
| **Behavior Therapies** | Client has learned maladaptive behavior patterns. | Learn adaptive behavior patterns through changes in the environment and rewards and punishers. | Observation of behavior and its controlling conditions; therapies based on classical conditioning, operant conditioning. |
| **Cognitive Therapies** | Client has developed inappropriate thoughts. | Change feelings and behaviors by changing cognitions. | Conversation with client designed to get him or her to change irrational and self-defeating beliefs. |

**FIGURE 5** **Therapy Comparisons** Different therapies address the same problems in very different ways. Many therapists use the tools that seem right for any given client and his or her problems. Sources: March & others (2018); Ruocco, Gordon, & McLean (2016); van Steensel & Bögels (2015).

chapter "Psychological Disorders") involves emotional instability, impulsivity, and self-harming behaviors, and this disorder responds to a therapy called *dialectical behavior therapy,* or *DBT* (Coyle, Shaver, & Linehan, 2018; Lois & Miller, 2018). A recent meta-analysis showed DBT to be effective in treating suicidal impulses (DeCou, Comtois, & Landes, 2018).

Like psychodynamic approaches, DBT assumes that early childhood experiences are important to the development of borderline personality disorder. However, DBT employs a variety of techniques, including homework assignments, cognitive interventions, intensive individual therapy, and group sessions involving others with the disorder. Group sessions focus on mindfulness training as well as emotional and interpersonal skills training.

Recall from the chapter "Psychological Disorders" that borderline personality disorder was once thought to be an incurable condition—one that would persist despite great effort to help people overcome the disorder. The effects of DBT on this severe personality disorder are striking (McCauley & others, 2018). We have seen that changes in thinking and behavior can affect the brain. Research has demonstrated that therapy can affect brain structure and function (Aguilar & others, 2018). How does DBT affect the brain? To read about research answering this question, see the Intersection.

## INTERSECTION

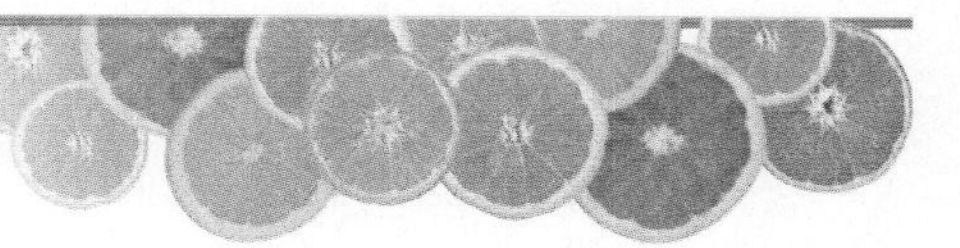

### Clinical Psychology and Neuroscience: How Does Dialectical Behavior Therapy Affect the Brain?

Borderline personality disorder is a common but severe disorder that affects a person's capacity to regulate emotion. Those who have the disorder may feel that they are on an emotional roller coaster and their very sense of self may be affected by that roller coaster. In addition, those who love individuals with the disorder may feel that they have to "walk on eggshells" because they do not know what might send the person into an emotional spiral. Brain imaging comparisons of those with borderline personality disorder and healthy controls reveal that borderline personality disorder is linked with a lack of connections between prefrontal areas of the brain responsible for planning and self-control with those areas associated with emotional reactions, such as the amygdalae (Schulze, Schmahl, & Niedtfeld, 2016).

*How do the ways you think, feel, and act affect your brain?*

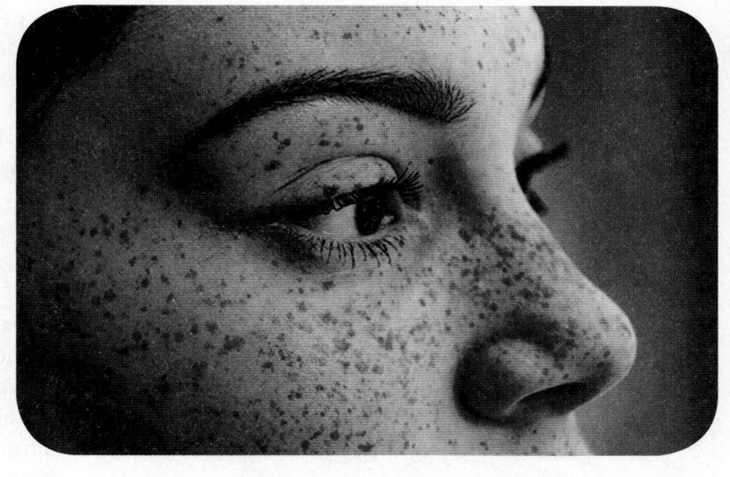

©Talia Ali/EyeEmGetty Images

A recent study sought to examine the ways that DBT, the intensive therapy described in the main text, might affect the brains of women with borderline personality disorder (Mancke & others, 2018). This study compared women receiving DBT (the experimental group) to a control group of women with borderline personality disorder who continued to receive whatever treatment they were receiving at the beginning of the study (including psychotherapy or medication). Participants in the experimental group received DBT for 12 weeks as part of a residential program. Participants underwent brain imaging before beginning therapy and again after 12 weeks of treatment.

The study had two important results. First, measurements before and after therapy showed that in comparison with the control group, women who received DBT had increased volume of grey matter in areas of the brain associated with emotion regulation. Second, those changes in grey matter were correlated with symptom changes—in other words, changes observed in the brain translated to actual improvements in emotion regulation (Mancke & others 2018).

This particular study cannot tell us what specific aspects of DBT led to these brain changes. Still, it is an important first step in understanding the processes that underlie improvement in people with borderline personality disorder.

Personality disorders affect all aspects of a person's psychological experience—the way they typically think, feel, and act. These disorders are part of "who a person is." Thus, it makes sense that an intense psychotherapy that reaches the person in a comprehensive way should affect the very organ that is the origin of these experiences. These results are not only relevant to DBT and borderline personality disorder. They demonstrate, once again, the remarkable plasticity of the brain as it learns new skills.

## test yourself

1. Describe what psychotherapy is, and identify four psychotherapeutic approaches.
2. What specific behavior therapy technique is used to treat phobias? How does it work?
3. What is cognitive-behavior therapy?
4. What is integrative therapy?

At their best, integrative therapies are effective, systematic uses of a variety of therapeutic approaches (Prochaska & Norcross, 2018). However, one worry about integrative therapies is that their increased use might result in an unsystematic, haphazard application of therapeutic techniques that some therapists say would be no better than a narrow, dogmatic approach (Lazarus, Beutler, & Norcross, 1992). In addition, relying on integrative approaches requires practitioners to master the skills and knowledge needed for each type of therapy we have reviewed (Byrne, Salmon, & Fisher, 2018).

Another integrative method is to combine psychotherapy with drug therapy. A mental health team that includes a psychiatrist and a clinical psychologist might conduct this integrative therapy. The use of medication to treat psychological disorders is a type of biological approach to therapy, our next topic.

# 3. BIOLOGICAL THERAPIES

Biological therapies, typically administered by psychiatrists or other medical doctors, involve altering aspects of bodily functioning to treat psychological disorders. Drug therapy is the most common form of biological therapy. Electroconvulsive therapy and psychosurgery are much less widely used biological therapies.

## Drug Therapy

Although people have long used medicine and herbs to alleviate symptoms of emotional distress, it was not until the twentieth century that drug treatments revolutionized mental health care. Psychotherapeutic drugs are used to treat many disorders. In this section we explore the effectiveness of drugs in treating various disorders—including anxiety disorders, depressive disorders, bipolar disorder, and schizophrenia. As you read about these various treatments, you will note that the reasons why a particular drug works for a particular problem are not always understood. Rather, these drugs are used because they work—and research continues to explore the reasons for their effectiveness.

● **antianxiety drugs** Drugs that reduce anxiety by making the individual calmer and less excitable; commonly known as tranquilizers.

### ANTIANXIETY DRUGS

**Antianxiety drugs**, commonly known as tranquilizers, make individuals calmer and less excitable. Benzodiazepines are the antianxiety drugs that generally offer the greatest relief for anxiety symptoms. They work by binding to the receptor sites of neurotransmitters that become overactive during anxiety. The most frequently prescribed benzodiazepines include Xanax, Valium, and Librium (Bernard & others, 2018).

Benzodiazepines are relatively fast-acting, taking effect within hours. Side effects of benzodiazepines include drowsiness, loss of coordination, fatigue, and mental slowing. These effects can be hazardous when a person is driving or operating machinery, especially when the individual starts taking the medication. Benzodiazepines also have been linked to abnormalities in babies born to mothers who took them during pregnancy (Freeman & others, 2018). Further, combining benzodiazepines with alcohol and with other medications can lead to problems such as depression (Dell'Osso & Lader, 2012).

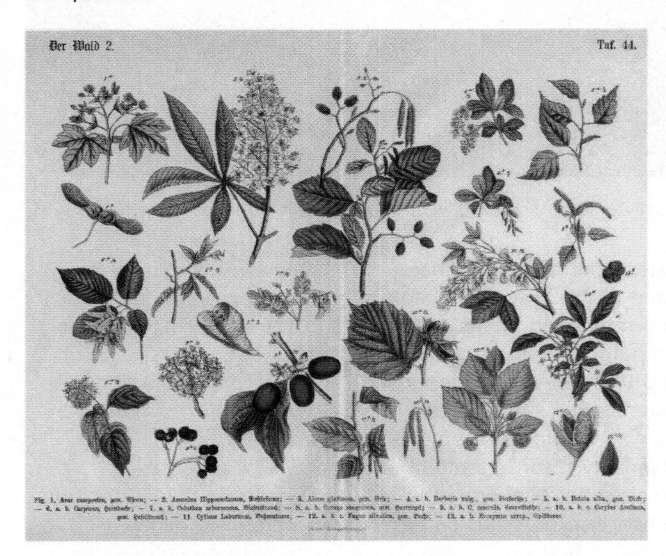


*People have used medicinal herbs to treat emotional distress since ancient times.*



A key concern with benzodiazepines is that they are addictive. "Beta blockers" pose a lower risk of addiction. These drugs, such as propranolol, were originally developed as treatments for cardiovascular issues, including irregular heart rhythm and high blood pressure. They block the activation of receptors that control heart rate and have been used effectively for anxiety issues, including stage fright, but research support for the use of these drugs in treating anxiety disorders is still preliminary (Rosenberg & others, 2018; Steenen & others, 2016).

## ANTIDEPRESSANT DRUGS

**Antidepressant drugs** regulate mood. The four main classes of antidepressant drugs are tricyclics, such as Elavil; tetracyclics, such as Avanza; monoamine oxidase (MAO) inhibitors, such as Nardil; and selective serotonin reuptake inhibitors, such as Prozac, Paxil, and Zoloft. These antidepressants are all thought to help alleviate depressed mood through their effects on neurotransmitters in the brain. In different ways, they all allow the person's brain to increase or maintain its level of important neurotransmitters. Let's take a close look at each of these types of antidepressants.

● **antidepressant drugs** Drugs that regulate mood.

*Tricyclics,* so-called because of their three-ringed molecular structure, are believed to work by increasing the level of certain neurotransmitters in the bloodstream, especially norepinephrine and serotonin (Duric & Duman, 2013; X. Zhou & others, 2015). You might recall the role of low serotonin levels in negative mood (the chapter "Personality") and aggression (the chapter "Social Psychology"). Tricyclics reduce the symptoms of depression in approximately 60 to 70 percent of cases, usually taking two to four weeks to improve mood. Adverse side effects may include restlessness, faintness, trembling, sleepiness, and memory difficulties. A meta-analysis of 30 years of studies concluded that the older antidepressant drugs, such as the tricyclics, reduced depression more effectively than the newer antidepressant drugs (Undurraga & Baldessarini, 2012).

Related to the tricyclics are *tetracyclic* antidepressants (named for their four-ringed structure). Tetracyclics are also called *noradrenergic and specific serotonergic antidepressants,* or NaSSAs. These drugs increase the levels of both norepinephrine and serotonin in the brain.

*MAO inhibitors* are thought to work because they block monoamine oxidase, an enzyme that breaks down serotonin and norepinephrine in the brain (Youdim, 2018). Scientists believe that the blocking action of MAO inhibitors allows these neurotransmitters to remain in the brain's synapses and help regulate mood. MAO inhibitors are not as widely used as the tricyclics because they are more potentially harmful to the body. However, some individuals who do not respond to the tricyclics do respond to MAO inhibitors (Nishida & others, 2009). MAO inhibitors may be especially risky because of their potential interactions with certain fermented foods (such as cheese) and other drugs, leading to high blood pressure and risk of stroke.

Psychiatrists and general practitioners increasingly prescribe a type of antidepressant called *selective serotonin reuptake inhibitors* (SSRIs). SSRIs target serotonin and work mainly by interfering only with the reabsorption of serotonin in the brain. Figure 6 shows how this process is thought to work.

SSRIs are the most commonly prescribed antidepressants because they are thought to be effective with the fewest side effects. Still, they can have negative effects, including insomnia, anxiety, headache, diarrhea, and impaired sexual function (Jern & others, 2015; Nguyen & Sin, 2015). SSRIs can also produce withdrawal symptoms if individuals stop taking them (Canady, 2018).

In addition to depressive disorder, antidepressant drugs are often prescribed for anxiety disorders as well as obsessive-compulsive disorder, post-traumatic stress disorder, and some eating and sleep disorders (Amitai & others, 2016; Sestan-Pesa & Horvath, 2016). In fact, in 2005, less than half of the individuals in the United States who had taken prescribed antidepressants were doing so for depression (Olfson & Marcus, 2009).

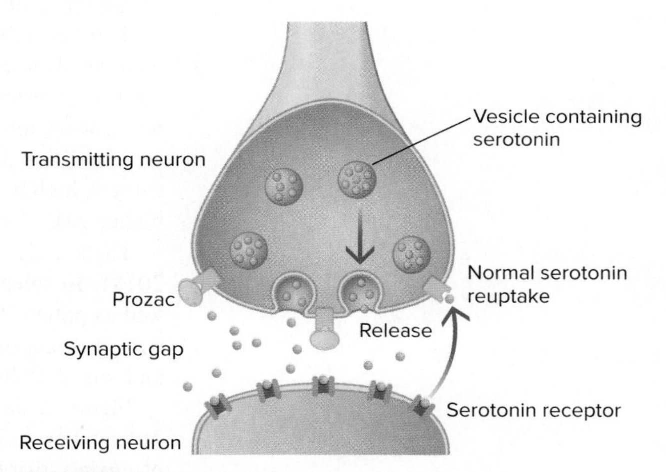


**FIGURE 6 How the Antidepressant Prozac Is Hypothesized to Work** Secreted by a transmitting neuron, serotonin moves across the synaptic gap and binds to receptors in a receiving neuron. Excess serotonin in the synaptic gap is normally reabsorbed by the transmitting neuron. The antidepressant Prozac blocks this reuptake of serotonin by the transmitting neuron, however, leaving excess serotonin in the synaptic gap. The excess serotonin is transmitted to the receiving neuron and circulated through the brain. The result is a reduction of the serotonin deficit found in individuals with depression.

## MEDICATION FOR BIPOLAR DISORDER

● **lithium** The lightest of the solid elements in the periodic table of elements, widely used to treat bipolar disorder.

**Lithium** is widely used to treat bipolar disorder. Lithium is the lightest of the solid elements in the periodic table of elements. Lithium is thought to stabilize mood by influencing levels of norepinephrine and serotonin, but the exact mechanism of its effect is unknown (McCarthy & others, 2018; Papiol, Schulze, & Alda, 2018). Sometimes people are diagnosed with bipolar disorder because their disorder responds to lithium (Song & others, 2015). The amount of lithium that circulates in the bloodstream must be carefully monitored because the effective dosage is precariously close to toxic levels. Kidney and thyroid gland complications as well as weight gain can arise as a consequence of lithium therapy (Post, 2018). Lithium may be combined with antidepressant drugs during depressive episodes.

## ANTIPSYCHOTIC DRUGS

● **antipsychotic drugs** Powerful drugs that diminish agitated behavior, reduce tension, decrease hallucinations, improve social behavior, and produce better sleep patterns in individuals with a severe psychological disorder, especially schizophrenia.

**Antipsychotic drugs** are powerful drugs that diminish agitated behavior, reduce tension, decrease hallucinations, improve social behavior, and produce better sleep patterns in individuals who have a severe psychological disorder, especially schizophrenia. Antipsychotic drugs do not cure schizophrenia. They treat only the symptoms of the disorder, not its causes. If an individual with schizophrenia stops taking the medication, the symptoms return. Because schizophrenia is a chronic disorder, many individuals take these medicines for decades.

Two types of antipsychotic drugs used to treat schizophrenia are neuroleptics and atypical antipsychotic medication. *Neuroleptics* (also called *first-generation antipsychotics*), including Haldol (haloperidol), Loxitane (loxapine), and Thorazine (chlorpromazine), are thought to block dopamine's action in the brain (Bogers & others, 2018). *Atypical antipsychotic medications* (also called *second-generation antipsychotics*), including Clozaril (clozapine) and Risperdal (risperidone), appear to influence dopamine as well as serotonin (Delcourte & others, 2018).

Both neuroleptics and atypical antipsychotic medications have shown some effectiveness in reducing schizophrenia's symptoms (Lee & others, 2018; Pyne & others, 2018). These types of medications differ, however, in their side effects.

Two serious side effects of antipsychotic medication are tardive dyskinesia and metabolic syndrome. *Tardive dyskinesia* is a neurological disorder characterized by involuntary random movements of the facial muscles, tongue, and mouth, as well as twitching of the neck, arms, and legs (Carbon & others, 2018; Solmi & others, 2018). *Metabolic syndrome* is a condition associated with obesity and risk for diabetes and heart disease. Neuroleptics carry a higher risk of tardive dyskinesia, and atypical antipsychotic medications carry a higher risk of metabolic syndrome (Scaini & others, 2018).

These side effects can influence patient compliance with treatment (Pyne & others, 2018). In selecting treatments for patients, then, psychiatrists must weigh these risks as well as patient factors that might make them vulnerable to these side effects. Finally, along with medication, individuals with schizophrenia may need training in vocational, family, and social skills.

Figure 7 summarizes the drugs used to treat various psychological disorders, the disorders they target, their effectiveness, and their side effects. Notice that for some types of anxiety disorders, such as agoraphobia, MAO inhibitors (antidepressant drugs) might be used rather than antianxiety drugs.

# Electroconvulsive Therapy

● **electroconvulsive therapy (ECT)** A treatment, sometimes used for depression, that sets off a seizure in the brain; also called shock therapy.

The goal of **electroconvulsive therapy (ECT)**, sometimes called *shock therapy,* is to set off a seizure in the brain. It may seem strange that causing someone to have a seizure might help cure a psychological disorder, but this idea has been around for quite some time. Hippocrates, the ancient Greek father of medicine, first noticed that malaria-induced convulsions would sometimes cure individuals who were thought to be insane (Endler, 1988). Following Hippocrates, many other medical doctors noted that head traumas,

| Psychological Disorder | Drug | Effectiveness | Side Effects |
|---|---|---|---|
| **Everyday anxiety** | Antianxiety drugs; antidepressant drugs | Substantial improvement short term | Antianxiety drugs: less powerful the longer people take them; may be addictive<br>Antidepressant drugs: see below under depressive disorders |
| **Generalized anxiety disorder** | Antianxiety drugs | Not very effective | Less powerful the longer people take them; may be addictive |
| **Panic disorder** | Antianxiety drugs | About half show improvement | Less powerful the longer people take them; may be addictive |
| **Agoraphobia** | Tricyclic drugs and MAO inhibitors | Majority show improvement | Tricyclics: restlessness, fainting, and trembling<br>MAO inhibitors: toxicity |
| **Specific phobias** | Antianxiety drugs | Not very effective | Less powerful the longer people take them; may be addictive |
| **Depressive disorders** | Tricyclic drugs, MAO inhibitors, SSRI drugs, and tetracyclic drugs | Majority show moderate improvement | Tricyclics: cardiac problems, mania, confusion, memory loss, fatigue<br>MAO inhibitors: toxicity<br>SSRI drugs: nausea, nervousness, insomnia, and in a few cases, suicidal thoughts<br>Tetracyclics: drowsiness, increased appetite, weight gain |
| **Bipolar disorder** | Lithium | Large majority show substantial improvement | Toxicity |
| **Schizophrenia** | Neuroleptics; atypical antipsychotic medications | Majority show partial improvement | Neuroleptics: irregular heartbeat, low blood pressure, uncontrolled fidgeting, tardive dyskinesia, and immobility of face<br>Atypical antipsychotic medications: metabolic syndrome; less extensive side effects than with neuroleptics, but can have a toxic effect on white blood cells |

**FIGURE 7** **Drug Therapy for Psychological Disorders** This figure summarizes the types of drugs used to treat various psychological disorders.

seizures, and convulsions brought on by fever would sometimes lead to the apparent cure of psychological problems.

In the early twentieth century, doctors induced seizures by insulin overdose and other means and used this procedure primarily to treat schizophrenia. In 1937, Ugo Cerletti, an Italian neurologist specializing in epilepsy, developed an efficient procedure to induce seizures using electrical shock, and ECT gained wide use in mental institutions (Faedda & others, 2010). Unfortunately, in earlier years, ECT was used indiscriminately, sometimes even to punish patients, as illustrated in the classic film *One Flew Over the Cuckoo's Nest*, starring Jack Nicholson.

Today, doctors use ECT primarily to treat severe depression, bipolar disorder, and post-traumatic stress disorder (Agarkar, Hurt, & Young, 2018; Ahmadi & others, 2018; Rivas-Grajales & others, 2018), and it has also been used in treating OCD (Agrawal, Das, & Thirthalli, 2018). ECT is given mainly to individuals who have not responded to drug therapy or psychotherapy, and its administration involves little discomfort. The patient receives anesthesia and muscle relaxants before the current is applied; this medication allows the individual to sleep through the procedure, minimizes convulsions, and reduces the risk of physical injury (Stripp, Jorgensen, & Olsen, 2018). Although in the past electrical current was passed through the person's entire brain, increasingly ECT is applied only to the right hemisphere to prevent damage to verbal abilities (Oltedal & others, 2018).

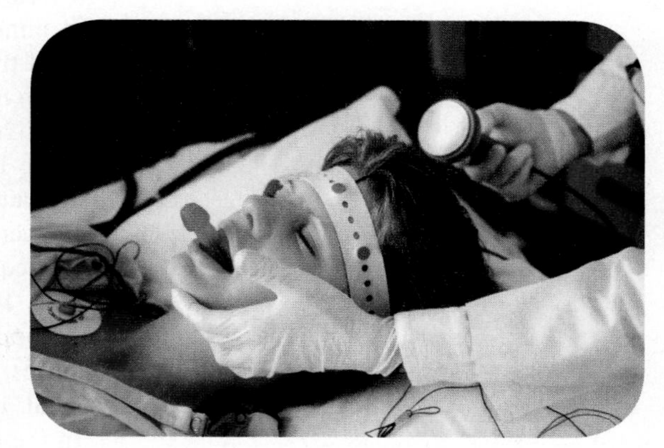

*Electroconvulsive therapy (ECT), commonly called shock therapy, causes a seizure in the brain. ECT is still administered to as many as 100,000 people a year, mainly to treat major depressive disorder.*



How effective is ECT? One analysis of the use of ECT compared its effectiveness in treating depression with that of cognitive therapy and antidepressant drugs (Seligman, 1994). ECT was as effective as cognitive therapy or drug therapy, with about four out of five individuals showing marked improvement from all three therapies.

What sets electroconvulsive therapy apart from other treatments is the rapid relief it can produce in a person's mood (Agarkar, Hurt, & Young, 2018). ECT may be especially effective as a treatment for acute depression in individuals who are at great risk of suicide (Liang & others, 2018). A recent study compared fMRI brain scans before and after ECT and found that the procedure weakened the brain's responses to negative stimuli (Miskowiak & others, 2018). Studies have also shown that hippocampus volume increases after ECT, but this enlargement may not relate to outcomes post-treatment (Oltedal & others, 2018).

ECT is controversial. Its potential side effects remain a source of debate and contradictory findings (Verwijk & others, 2012). These possible effects include memory loss and other cognitive impairments (Jones & McCollum, 2018). Some individuals treated with ECT have reported prolonged and profound memory loss (Koitabashi, Oyaizu, & Ouchi, 2009). Despite these potential problems, some psychiatrists argue that for certain individuals, this invasive treatment can have life-enhancing—and even life-saving—benefits (Huuhka & others, 2012; Martínez-Amorós & others, 2012).

**deep brain stimulation** A procedure for treatment-resistant depression that involves the implantation of electrodes in the brain that emit signals to alter the brain's electrical circuitry.

More recently, practitioners have been treating psychological disorders by applying electrical stimulation in very precise locations in the brain. In **deep brain stimulation**, doctors surgically implant electrodes in the brain that emit signals to alter the brain's electrical circuitry. For instance, deep brain stimulation of the nucleus accumbens (part of the brain's reward pathways) has been effective in treating severe depression (Kisely & others, 2018; Riva-Posse & others, 2018). Deep brain stimulation has also been used to treat bipolar disorder (Gippert & others, 2017) and OCD (Karas & others, 2018).

## Psychosurgery

**psychosurgery** A biological therapy, with irreversible effects, that involves removal or destruction of brain tissue to improve the individual's adjustment.

**Psychosurgery** is a biological intervention that involves the removal or destruction of brain tissue to improve the individual's adjustment. The effects of psychosurgery cannot be reversed.

In the 1930s, Portuguese physician Antonio Egas Moniz developed a surgical procedure in which an instrument was inserted into the brain and rotated, severing fibers connecting the frontal lobe and the thalamus. Moniz theorized that by severing the connections between these structures, the surgeon could alleviate the symptoms of severe mental disorders (Soares & others, 2013). In 1949, Moniz received the Nobel Prize for developing the procedure, which he felt should be used with extreme caution and only as a last resort.

After hearing about Moniz's procedure, American neurologist Walter Freeman became the champion of *prefrontal lobotomies* (a term Freeman coined). Freeman developed his own technique, performed using a device similar to an ice pick, in surgeries that lasted mere minutes. A dynamic and charismatic advocate, in the 1950s and 1960s Freeman traveled the country in a van he called the "lobotomobile," demonstrating the surgery in state-run mental institutions. During his career, Freeman performed over 3,000 lobotomies (El-Hai, 2005). Prefrontal lobotomies were conducted on tens of thousands of patients from the 1930s through the 1960s. These numbers speak not only to Freeman's persuasive charm but also to the desperation many physicians felt in treating institutionalized patients with severe psychological disorders (Lerner, 2005).

Subsequent research questioned the lobotomy procedure (Landis & Erlick, 1950; Mettler, 1952). Many individuals who received lobotomies suffered permanent and profound brain damage (Soares & others, 2013). Ethical concerns arose because, in many instances, giving consent for the lobotomy was a requirement for release from a mental hospital. Like ECT, lobotomies were being used as a form of punishment and control.

In the late 1970s new regulations classified the procedure as experimental and established safeguards for patients. Fortunately, crude lobotomies are no longer performed, and Freeman's technique is certainly not typical of contemporary psychosurgery. Modern psychosurgery is quite precise. For the most part, deep brain stimulation (which may involve surgery to implant electrodes) has replaced conventional surgical removal of brain tissue.

Today, only several hundred patients who have severely debilitating conditions undergo psychosurgery each year. Psychosurgery may be performed for OCD, major depression, or bipolar disorder rather than for schizophrenia (Shelton & others, 2010; van Vliet & others, 2013). Just as Moniz originally suggested, the procedure is now used only as a last resort—and with the utmost caution.

Considering interventions like ECT, deep brain stimulation, or psychosurgery, you might wonder how people feel as they decide whether to pursue these treatments that might be recommended by a mental health professional. To read about some of the issues involved in mental health decision making, see the Critical Controversy.

### *test yourself*

1. How do antianxiety drugs work, and why do so many people take them?
2. What are SSRIs, and through what process do they have their effect?
3. Describe the procedure used in electroconvulsive therapy (ECT).

## *Who Should Decide What Treatment is Best for a Person?*

When someone has a physical illness, that person has a great deal of autonomy in deciding on a course of action. Should the same be true for a person with a psychological disorder? Consider that sometimes a person with a disorder may not have insight into their own illness (Powers, 2017). A young woman with anorexia nervosa may not recognize that she is putting herself in danger by continuing to diet. A man experiencing psychosis may not recognize that his perceptions are not real. People with a substance abuse disorder may not realize their risk of overdose. At times like these, professionals or family members may believe that it is in the person's best interest to take action. Additionally, when people engage in behaviors that break the law, they may be forced to undergo treatment as part of a court order. If individuals present an imminent danger to themselves, their health, or to other people, they may be forced into treatment. This type of treatment can range from assisted outpatient treatment to forced hospitalization. Requiring a person to undergo treatment poses legal and ethical challenges and potentially violates the person's autonomy (Hem & others, 2018; Tochkov & Williams, 2018). Forced hospitalization can be extremely stressful, and people might feel as if they have been imprisoned. We know that when people have a say in their treatment, better outcomes are likely (Swift & others, 2018). Does treatment work if it is forced on a person? Unfortunately, very little research has addressed this question (Burns, Kisely, & Rugkåsa, 2017; Jain, Christopher, & Appelbaum, 2018).

Recently, individuals with psychological disorders have begun to create *psychiatric advance directives* (Belluck, 2018). These directives are similar to those that many people have for medical treatments. Medical advance directives involve specifying who should make decisions if one is unable to do so and whether or not a person wishes to receive extreme life-supportive measures if they lose consciousness. Psychiatric advance directives or PADs are legal documents that a person with a serious psychological disorder can create to specify the types of treatment they prefer and those they do not wish to receive (Maylea & others, 2018). They also allow the person to provide names of people who should participate in their treatment decisions. PADs allow people to make decisions about psychiatric treatment before they are too ill to play an active role in decision making.

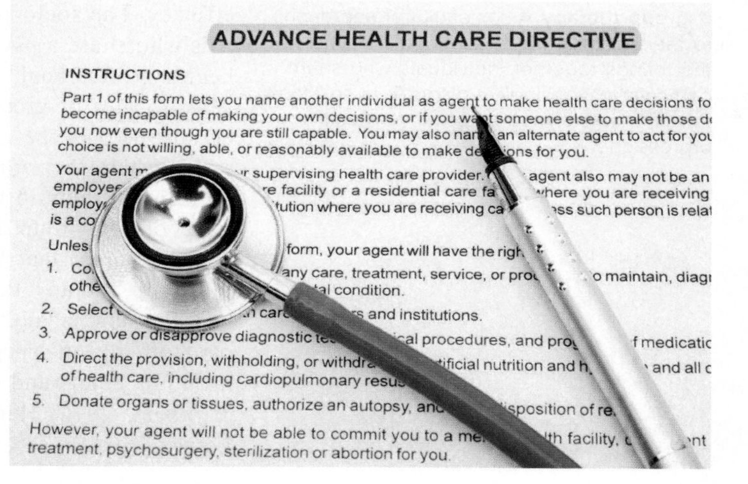


©rallef/Shutterstock

Although not all states in the United States treat PADs as legally binding, these documents can be an important source for information for medical professionals from the persons who know the most about their illnesses—the patients themselves. Patients can specify what treatments have worked in the past and what side effects they have experienced. For instance, one man with bipolar disorder and borderline personality disorder suggested that rather than being restrained, isolated, or medicated, it would be very helpful to hear someone say, "Everything is going to be okay" (Belluck, 2018). Although PADs are controversial, many psychiatrists have positive attitudes toward them (Gieselmann & others, 2018). It remains unclear how a psychiatrist should resolve conflicts that might erupt between his or her own opinion on optimal treatment and patient preferences.

**WHAT DO YOU THINK?**

- Would a doctor be justified in ignoring a psychiatric advance directive if she felt it was not the right course of action?
- How does a psychiatric advance directive differ from a medical advance directive?

# 4. SOCIOCULTURAL APPROACHES AND ISSUES IN TREATMENT

In the treatment of psychological disorders, behavior therapies modify the person's behavior, cognitive therapies alter the person's thinking, and biological therapies change the person's body. This section focuses on sociocultural approaches to the treatment of psychological disorders. These methods view the individual as part of a system of relationships that are influenced by various social and cultural factors (Mihelicova, Brown, & Shuman, 2018; Stuart, Schultz, & Ashen, 2018).

We first review some common sociocultural approaches, including group therapy, family and couples therapy, self-help support groups, and community mental health programs. We then examine various cultural perspectives on therapy.

## Group Therapy

There is good reason to believe that individuals who share a psychological problem may benefit from observing others who are coping with a similar problem and that helping others cope can in turn improve individuals' feelings of competence and efficacy. The sociocultural approach known as **group therapy** brings together individuals who share a psychological disorder in sessions that are typically led by a mental health professional.

● **group therapy** A sociocultural approach to the treatment of psychological disorders that brings together individuals who share a particular psychological disorder in sessions that are typically led by a mental health professional.

Advocates of group therapy stress that individual therapy has limited effectiveness because it puts the client outside the normal context of relationships. It is these very relationships, they argue, that may hold the key to successful therapy. Many psychological problems develop in the context of interpersonal relationships—within one's family, marriage, or peer group, for example. By taking into account the context of these important groups, therapy may be more successful.

Group therapy takes many diverse forms—including psychodynamic, humanistic, behavior, and cognitive therapy—in addition to approaches that do not reflect the major psychotherapeutic perspectives. In addition, it can be used with a range of populations, including adults and children with shared psychological issues or experiences (Castillo & others, 2016; Hansen, 2016). Six features characterize group therapy (Yalom & Leszcz, 2006):

- *Information:* Individuals receive information about their problems from either the group leader or other group members.
- *Universality:* Individuals are able to see that they are not alone. Others share their experiences.
- *Altruism:* Group members support one another with advice and sympathy and learn that they have something to offer others.
- *Experience of a positive family group:* A therapy group often resembles a family, with the leaders representing parents and the other members of the group representing siblings. In this new family, old wounds may be healed and new, more positive family ties made.
- *Development of social skills:* Corrective feedback from peers may identify flaws in the individual's interpersonal skills. For example, an individual may come to see that he or she is self-centered if five other group members comment on the person's self-centeredness; in individual therapy, the individual might not believe the therapist.
- *Interpersonal learning:* The group can serve as a training ground for practicing new behaviors and relationships. A hostile person may learn that he or she can get along better with others by behaving less aggressively, for example.

## Family and Couples Therapy

Our relationships with family members and significant others are certainly an important part of human life. Sometimes these vital relationships can benefit from the intervention of a helpful outsider. **Family therapy** is group therapy among family members (Lebow, 2016; Wagenaar & Baars, 2012). **Couples therapy** is group therapy with married or unmarried couples whose major problem lies within their relationship. These approaches stress that although one person may have some abnormal symptoms, those symptoms are a function of the family or couple relationships (Burgess Moser & others, 2018). Psychodynamic, humanistic, and behavior therapies may be used in family and couples therapy.

- **family therapy** Group therapy with family members.

- **couples therapy** Group therapy with married or unmarried couples whose major problem lies within their relationship.

Four of the most widely used family therapy techniques are described below:

- *Validation:* The therapist expresses an understanding and acceptance of each family member's feelings and beliefs and thus validates the person. When the therapist talks with each family member, he or she finds something positive to say.
- *Reframing:* The therapist helps families reframe problems as family problems, not an individual's problems. A delinquent adolescent girl's problems are reframed in terms of how each family member contributed to the situation. The parents' lack of attention to the girl or their own marital conflict may be involved, for example.
- *Structural change:* The family therapist tries to restructure the coalitions in a family. In a mother–son coalition, the therapist might suggest that the father take a stronger disciplinarian role to relieve the mother of some of the burden. Restructuring might be as simple as suggesting that the parents explore satisfying ways of being together, such as going out once a week for a quiet dinner.
- *Detriangulation:* In some families, one member is the scapegoat for two other members who are in conflict but pretend not to be. For example, parents of a girl with anorexia nervosa might insist that their marriage is fine but find themselves in subtle conflict over how to handle the child. The therapist tries to disentangle, or detriangulate, this situation by shifting attention away from the child to the conflict between the parents.

Couples therapy proceeds in much the same way as family therapy. Couples therapy addresses diverse problems and challenges such as alcohol abuse, jealousy, sexual issues, infidelity, gender roles, two-career families, divorce, remarriage, and the special concerns

*In family therapy, the assumption is that particular patterns of interaction among the family members cause the observed abnormal symptoms.*

©Alvis Upitis/Media Bakery

of stepfamilies (Hirschfeld & Wittenborn, 2016; Sandberg & Knestel, 2011). Conflict in close relationships frequently involves poor communication, so the therapist tries to improve the communication between the partners (Weeks, Fife, & Peterson, 2016; Williamson & others, 2016).

## Self-Help Support Groups

Self-help support groups are voluntary organizations of individuals who get together on a regular basis to discuss topics of common interest. A professional does not conduct the group; rather, a paraprofessional or a member of the common-interest group takes the lead. *Paraprofessionals* are individuals who have been taught by a professional to provide some mental health services but who do not have formal mental health training. Some paraprofessionals may themselves have had a disorder; for example, a chemical dependency counselor may also be a recovering addict. The group leader and members provide support to help individuals with their problems.

Self-help support groups play a valuable role in Americans' mental health care (Brown, 2018; Norcross & others, 2013), and there are many thousands of support groups in the United States. In addition to reaching so many people in need of help, these groups are important because they are relatively inexpensive. They also serve people who are otherwise unlikely to receive help, such as those with less education and fewer resources than patients who receive other types of mental health care.

Self-help support groups provide members with a sympathetic audience for social sharing and emotional release. The social support, role modeling, and sharing of concrete strategies for solving problems that unfold in self-help groups add to their effectiveness. A woman who has been raped might not believe a therapist who tells her that, with time, she will put the pieces of her shattered life back together. The same message from another rape survivor—someone who has had to work through the same feelings of rage, fear, and violation—might be more believable.

Alcoholics Anonymous (AA), founded in 1935 by a reformed alcoholic and a physician, is one of the best-known self-help groups (Kelly, 2013). Some studies show a positive effect for AA (Karriker-Jaffe & others, 2018; Pagano & others, 2013), but others do not (Kaskutas, 2009). Researchers continue to explore whether AA is beneficial.

For individuals who tend to cope by seeking information and affiliation with similar peers, self-help support groups can reduce stress and promote adjustment. However, as reviewed in the chapter "Social Psychology", groups can be positive or negative influences on individuals, and group leaders may need to monitor these processes.

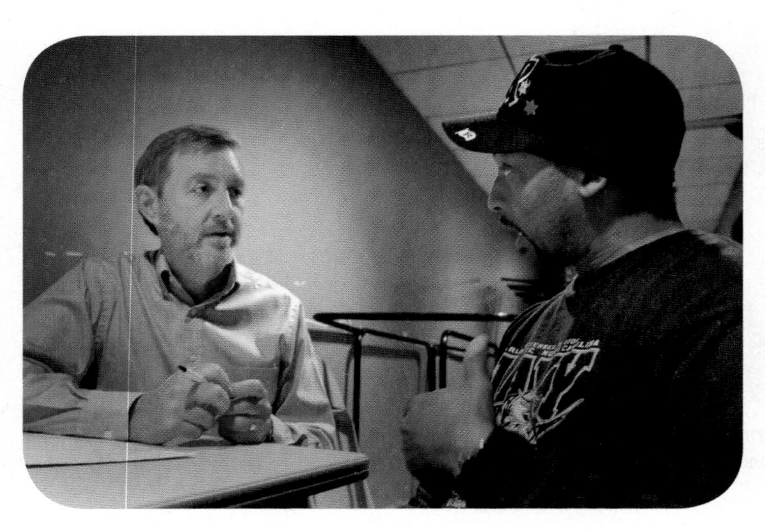

*Community mental health counselors can serve as a lifeline to many local citizens.*

©Gerald Martineau/The Washington Post/Getty Images

## Community Mental Health

The community mental health movement was born in the 1960s as society's attitude toward people with psychological disorders began to change. The deplorable conditions of some psychiatric facilities at the time were one catalyst for the movement. Advocates of community mental health maintained that individuals with psychological disorders ought to remain within society with their families rather than being locked away in institutions and that they should receive treatment in community mental health centers. This movement also reflected economic concerns, as it was thought that institutionalizing people was considerably more expensive than treating them in the community.

With the passage of the Community Mental Health Act of 1963, large numbers of individuals with psychological disorders were transferred from mental institutions to community-based facilities in a process called *deinstitutionalization.* Although at least partially motivated by a desire to treat individuals with psychological disorders more effectively and humanely, deinstitutionalization has been linked to rising rates of homelessness.

Community mental health programs train teachers, ministers, family physicians, nurses, and others who interact with community members to offer lay counseling and workshops. Clients receive help in areas ranging from coping with stress to reducing their drug use to developing assertiveness (Jones & others, 2018). Advocates and providers of community mental health care believe that the best way to treat a psychological disorder is through prevention (Markström & others, 2018).

An explicit goal of community mental health programs is to help people who are disenfranchised from society, such as those living in poverty, to lead happier, more productive lives (Leamy & others, 2016). A key concept involved in this effort is *empowerment*–assisting individuals to develop the skills they need to control their own lives. Community mental health involves reaching people where they are and in whatever type of community they occupy to help them optimize their lives (Rowe & Guerin, 2018). Importantly, most community mental health programs rely on financial support from local, state, and federal governments. The success of community mental health services depends on the resources and commitment of the communities they serve.

## Cultural Perspectives

The psychotherapies discussed earlier in this chapter–psychodynamic, humanistic, behavior, and cognitive–center on the individual. This focus is compatible with the needs of people in Western cultures such as the United States, where the emphasis is on the individual rather than the group (family, community, or ethnic group). However, these psychotherapies may not be as effective with people who live in collectivistic cultures that place more importance on the group (Hays, 2016). Some psychologists argue that family therapy is likely to be more effective with people in cultures that place a high value on the family, such as Latino and Asian cultures (Y. Guo, 2005).

Considering how to provide psychotherapy effectively within a specific cultural framework is enormously complex. Cultures may differ, for instance, in how they view the appropriateness of talking with an elder about personal problems or in talking about one's feelings at all. Cultural issues in therapy include factors such as socioeconomic status, ethnicity, gender, country of origin, current culture, and religious beliefs and traditions (Davis & others, 2018).

**Cross-cultural competence** refers both to how skilled a therapist feels about being able to manage cultural issues that might arise in therapy and to how the client perceives the therapist's ability (Ang & Van Dyne, 2015; Asnaani & Hofmann, 2012). Dominant features of cross-cultural competence are demonstrating respect for cultural beliefs and practices and balancing the goals of a particular therapeutic approach with the goals and values of a culture. Keep in mind that cultural humility involves the realization that even if a person is well-versed in another culture he or she cannot know precisely what it is like to belong to that culture (Davis & others, 2018).

• **cross-cultural competence** A therapist's assessment of his or her ability to manage cultural issues in therapy and the client's perception of those abilities.

### ETHNICITY

Many ethnic minority individuals prefer discussing problems with parents, friends, and relatives rather than mental health professionals (Boyd-Franklin & others, 2013; Hays, 2016). Might therapy be most successful when the therapist and the client are from the same ethnic background?

Researchers have found that when there is an ethnic match between the therapist and the client and when ethnic-specific services are provided, clients are less likely to drop out of therapy early and in many cases have better treatment outcomes (Jackson & Greene, 2000; Swift & others, 2018). Ethnic-specific services include culturally appropriate greetings and arrangements (for example, serving tea rather than coffee to Chinese American clients), providing flexible hours for treatment, and employing a bicultural/bilingual staff.

©FilippoBacci/Getty Images

### GENDER

One byproduct of changing gender roles for women and men is reevaluation of the goal of psychotherapy. Traditionally, the goal has been autonomy or self-determination for the client. However, those goals may reveal an older view of psychological health as involving an unrealistic level of independence from others. Human beings need each other. Interpersonal relationships may be especially important to women's lives. Incorporating relational connections in therapy is an important goal, particularly in therapy with women. Therapy, for everyone, should involve a balance of emphasis on autonomy/self-determination and relatedness/connection to others (Enns, 2018).

Feminist therapists believe that traditional psychotherapy continues to carry considerable gender bias and has not adequately addressed the specific concerns of women. Thus, several alternative nontraditional therapies have arisen that aim to help clients break free from traditional gender roles and stereotypes. In terms of improving clients' lives, the goals of feminist therapists are no different from those of other therapists. However, feminist therapists seek to challenge the power dynamic that is implied in the traditional therapist–client relationship and maintain a sense of equality across these roles.

Feminist therapists believe that improvement depends in part on understanding how bias and discrimination in women's lives can contribute to the development of psychological disorders (Enns, 2018; Huft & Jonathan, 2018). Essentially, feminist psychotherapy involves acknowledging and exploring the ways that an unfair society shapes women's lives and provides a context for their struggles. These therapists work to facilitate client empowerment and to identify and harness client strengths, rather than to focus exclusively on addressing weaknesses.

Finally, of course, many people simultaneously occupy multiple cultural, gender, sexuality identities and the experience of intersectionality is an important focus of psychotherapy and training (Gutierrez, 2018).

### *test yourself*

1. Why might group therapy be more successful than individual therapy?
2. What are four common family therapy techniques? Briefly describe each.
3. What social and economic forces drove the community mental health movement?

## 5. THERAPIES AND HEALTH AND WELLNESS

Therapy is generally aimed at relieving psychological symptoms. A therapy is considered effective if it frees a person from the negative effects of psychological disorders. Does therapy have larger implications related to a person's psychological wellness and even physical health? Researchers have examined this interesting question in a variety of ways.

For example, people who learn that they have cancer are undoubtedly under stress. Might psychotherapeutic help aimed at reducing this stress improve patients' ability to cope with the disease? Research indicates that therapy does have positive effects. One study revealed that group-based cognitive therapy that focused on improving prostate cancer patients' stress management skills was effective in improving their quality of life (Penedo & others, 2006). Another study found that individual cognitive-behavior therapy reduced symptom severity in cancer patients undergoing chemotherapy (Sikorskii & others, 2006).

As well, psychotherapy directed at relieving psychological disorders such as depression can have important benefits for physical health (Purdy, 2013). Depression is associated with coronary heart disease, for example (Linke & others, 2009). Psychotherapy that reduces depression is likely, then, to reduce the risk of heart disease (Mavrides & Nemeroff, 2013). A research review also showed evidence of positive effects of psychotherapy on health behavior and physical illness, including habits and ailments such as smoking, chronic pain, chronic fatigue syndrome, and asthma (Eells, 2000).

Psychotherapy might also be a way to *prevent* psychological and physical problems. One study demonstrated the benefits of incorporating therapy into physical health care (Smit & others, 2006). Individuals waiting to see their primary health care provider received either physical health treatment as usual or that same treatment plus brief psychotherapy (a simple version of cognitive-behavior therapy). The brief psychotherapy included a self-help manual, instructions in mood management, and six short telephone conversations with a prevention worker. The overall rate of depression was significantly lower in the psychotherapy group, and this difference was cost-effective. That is, the use of brief psychotherapy as part of regular physical checkups was both psychologically and economically advantageous.

Finally, although typically targeted at relieving distressing symptoms, might psychotherapy enhance psychological well-being? This question is important because the absence of psychological symptoms (the goal of most psychotherapy) is not the same thing as the presence of psychological wellness. Just as an individual who is without serious physical illness is not necessarily at the height of physical health, a person who is relatively free of psychological symptoms still might not show the qualities we associate with psychological thriving. Studies have found that a lack of psychological wellness may predispose individuals to relapse or make them vulnerable to problems (Fava & Bech, 2015; Ryff, Singer, & Love, 2004). Research has demonstrated that individuals who show not only a decrease in symptoms but also an increase in well-being are less prone to relapse (Gu & others, 2015).

*Psychotherapy can improve cancer patients' ability to cope with the disease.*



Therapists have developed a treatment approach aimed at enhancing well-being. **Well-being therapy (WBT)** is a short-term, problem-focused, directive therapy that encourages clients to accentuate the positive (Fava, 2016; Guidi, Rafanelli, & Fava, 2018). The first step in WBT is recognizing the good things in one's life when they happen. The initial WBT homework assignment asks clients to monitor their own happiness levels and keep track of moments of well-being. Clients are encouraged to note even small pleasures in their lives—a beautiful spring day, a relaxing chat with a friend, the great taste of morning coffee. Clients then identify thoughts and feelings that are related to the premature ending of these moments.

**well-being therapy (WBT)** A short-term, problem-focused, directive therapy that encourages clients to accentuate the positive.

WBT is about learning to notice and savor positive experiences and coming up with ways to promote and celebrate life's good moments. WBT is effective in enhancing well-being, and it may also allow individuals to enjoy sustained recovery from mental disorders (Fava, 2016; Guidi, Rafanelli, & Fava, 2018).

Life is complicated and filled with potential pitfalls. We all need help from time to time, and therapy is one way to get that help. Through therapy we can improve ourselves—physically and psychologically—to become the best person we can be. Like all human relationships, a therapeutic relationship is complex and challenging but potentially rewarding, making positive change possible for an individual through a meaningful association with another.

## test yourself

1. How might psychotherapy prevent physical illnesses?
2. How might psychotherapy affect coping with physical disease?
3. What is well-being therapy, and what steps does it involve on the client's part?

SUMMARY

## 1. APPROACHES TO TREATING PSYCHOLOGICAL DISORDERS

Two approaches to treating psychological disorders are psychotherapy and biological therapies. Psychotherapy, administered by a range of different professionals, is the process that mental health professionals use to help individuals recognize, define, and overcome their disorders and improve their adjustment. Biological treatments involve drugs and other procedures that change the functioning of the body. In most states, only medical doctors can prescribe drugs to treat psychological disorders. Psychologists have endeavored to obtain prescription privileges, arguing that doing so would make treatment more efficient for clients.

## 2. PSYCHOTHERAPY

Research strongly shows that psychotherapies are successful in treating psychological disorders, though no therapy is conclusively more effective than any other. Psychologists debate whether treatment decisions should be based on empirical research or clinical judgment. Evidence-based practice means taking research into account, combined with the clinician's judgment and client characteristics.

Three factors that influence the effectiveness of therapy are the therapeutic alliance, the therapist, and the client. Types of psychotherapy differ in terms of how much they focus on gaining insight versus treating specific symptoms and gaining skills. They also differ in how directive or nondirective the therapist is.

Psychodynamic approaches to therapy focus on the unconscious and the need for the psychotherapist to interpret the client's thoughts, dreams, and childhood experiences. This form of therapy is based on the notion that gaining insight into unconscious conflicts is the key to treating psychological disorders.

Humanistic therapies encourage clients to understand themselves and to grow personally. Client-centered therapy, developed by Carl Rogers, is a type of humanistic therapy that includes active listening, reflective speech, unconditional positive regard, empathy, and genuineness.

Behavior therapies use principles of learning to reduce or eliminate maladaptive behavior. They are based on the behavioral and social cognitive theories of personality. Behavior therapies seek to eliminate symptoms or behaviors rather than to help individuals to gain insight into their problems.

Two behavior therapy techniques based on classical conditioning are systematic desensitization and aversive conditioning. In systematic desensitization, anxiety is treated by getting the individual to associate deep relaxation with increasingly intense anxiety-producing situations. In aversive conditioning, pairings of the undesirable behavior with aversive stimuli are repeated to decrease the behavior's pleasant associations.

In operant conditioning approaches to behavior therapy, a careful analysis of the person's environment is conducted to determine which factors need modification. Applied behavior analysis is the application of operant conditioning to change human behavior. Its main goal is to replace maladaptive behaviors with adaptive ones.

Cognitive therapies emphasize that the individual's cognitions (thoughts) are the main source of abnormal behavior. Cognitive therapies attempt to change the person's feelings and behaviors by changing cognitions. Cognitive-behavior therapy combines cognitive therapy and behavior therapy techniques. Self-efficacy and self-instructional methods are used in this approach.

Up to half of all practicing therapists refer to themselves as "integrative" or "eclectic." Integrative therapy uses a combination of techniques from different therapies based on the therapist's judgment of which specific techniques will provide the greatest benefit for the client.

## 3. BIOLOGICAL THERAPIES

Biological approaches to therapy include drugs, electroconvulsive therapy (ECT), and psychosurgery. Psychotherapeutic drugs that treat psychological disorders fall into four main categories: antianxiety drugs, antidepressant drugs, medication for bipolar disorder, and antipsychotic drugs.

Benzodiazepines are the most commonly used antianxiety drugs. Antidepressant drugs regulate mood; the three main classes are tricyclics, MAO inhibitors, and SSRI drugs. Lithium is used to treat bipolar disorder. Antipsychotic drugs are administered to treat severe psychological disorders, especially schizophrenia.

Practitioners use electroconvulsive therapy to alleviate severe depression when other interventions have failed. Psychosurgery is an irreversible procedure in which brain tissue is destroyed. Though rarely used today, psychosurgery is more precise than it was in the days of prefrontal lobotomies.

## 4. SOCIOCULTURAL APPROACHES AND ISSUES IN TREATMENT

Group therapies emphasize that relationships can hold the key to successful therapy. Family therapy is group therapy with family members. Four widely used family therapy techniques are validation, reframing, structural change, and detriangulation. Couples therapy is group therapy with married or unmarried couples whose major problem is within their relationship.

Self-help support groups are voluntary organizations of individuals who get together on a regular basis to discuss topics of common interest. They are conducted without a professional therapist.

The community mental health movement was born out of the belief that individuals suffering from psychological disorders should not be locked away from their families and communities. The deinstitutionalization that resulted from the movement caused the homeless population to rise, however. Empowerment is often a goal of community mental health.

Psychotherapy's traditional focus on the individual may be successful in individualistic Western cultures. However, individual-centered psychotherapies may not work as well in collectivistic cultures. Therapy is often more effective when there is an ethnic match between the therapist and the client, although culturally sensitive therapy can be provided by a therapist with a different background from the client's.

Psychotherapy's emphasis on independence and self-reliance may be problematic for the many women who place a strong emphasis on connectedness in relationships. Feminist therapies have emerged to address that problem.

## 5. THERAPIES AND HEALTH AND WELLNESS

Psychotherapy has been shown to help individuals cope with serious physical diseases. Psychotherapy can also aid individuals by alleviating physical symptoms directly or by reducing psychological problems, such as depression, that are related to physical illness. Research has shown moreover that brief psychotherapy may be a cost-effective way to *prevent* serious psychological disorders.

Psychotherapy aims not only at reducing the presence of psychological illness but also at enhancing psychological wellness and personal growth. Individuals who gain in wellness are less likely to fall prey to recurrent psychological distress. Interventions such as well-being therapy have been designed to promote wellness itself.

# key *terms*

antianxiety drugs
antidepressant drugs
antipsychotic drugs
behavior therapies
biological therapies or biomedical therapies
client-centered therapy
clinical psychology
cognitive-behavior therapy
cognitive therapies
couples therapy
cross-cultural competence
deep brain stimulation
dream analysis
electroconvulsive therapy (ECT)
empirically supported treatment
evidence-based practice
family therapy
group therapy
humanistic therapies
integrative therapy
lithium
psychoanalysis
psychodynamic therapies
psychosurgery
psychotherapy
reflective speech
systematic desensitization
therapeutic alliance
transference
well-being therapy (WBT)

# apply your *knowledge*

1. To experience Rogerian therapy firsthand, watch a video of Carl Rogers describing his approach and participating in a session with a client at https://www.youtube.com/watch?v=ZBkUqcqRChg
2. To get a good sense of how cognitive-behavior therapy works, see this clip at www.youtube.com/watch?v=ds3wHkwiuCo
3. Behavioral and cognitive approaches may be helpful in modifying a behavior that would not be considered abnormal but that an individual might still want to change (for example, procrastinating, eating unhealthy food, or watching too much TV). Think about a behavior that you would like to do more or less frequently; then imagine that you are a behavior therapist or a cognitive therapist and describe some recommendations you might make during a therapy session.
4. For which kinds of problems would you be most likely to choose one of the sociocultural approaches to therapy? Which method would you choose? Do some research and see whether you can find a local group or therapist who would be helpful to someone with these kinds of problems. Where would you turn if an appropriate resource were not available in your area?

# CHAPTER 17

CHAPTER OUTLINE

# Health Psychology

## The Healthiest Sport?

**Whether it is an extramural kickball team or a formal tennis match, sports are fun and can be a great way to connect with friends.** Engaging in sports is more than just a good time, though. Sports give people a way to be physically active. Scientists have long known that people who regularly take part in sports and other active leisure activities live longer (Paffenbarger & others, 1986). Of course, all types of sports come with some risk—ranging from tennis elbow to some nasty bruises from dodge-ball. Swimming can be especially easy on joints. Is one sport better than the others for longevity? A recent study addressed this question, following over 8500 people for over 25 years (Schnohr & others, 2018). The researchers tracked fitness habits and how long people lived. The study compared those who were inactive to people who engaged in various physical activities. Overall, engaging in physical exercise led to longer lives than being inactive. But the types of activities mattered to a surprising degree. For example, those who primarily worked out in a fitness club enjoyed only an extra 1.5 years compared with inactive people. In contrast, tennis was associated with nearly an extra decade of life! Similarly, badminton and soccer players gained over 5 years. Although the reasons for these differences are not entirely clear, the researchers noted that the healthiest activities involved interaction with other people (Schnohr & others, 2018). When we are active our bodies benefit, but when we are active with other people the benefits are even greater. ●

# PREVIEW

In this chapter, we focus on health psychology: the field devoted to promoting healthy practices and understanding the psychological processes that underlie health and illness. We begin by defining the field. Then we examine the various ways that psychologists explain the process of making healthy life changes and the resources on which individuals can draw to effect positive change. Next we survey what psychologists know about stress and coping, and we consider psychological perspectives on making wise choices in three vital areas: physical activity, diet, and the decision to smoke or not to smoke. We end with a look at psychology's role in shaping a good life.

## 1. HEALTH PSYCHOLOGY AND BEHAVIORAL MEDICINE

● **health psychology** A subfield of psychology that emphasizes psychology's role in establishing and maintaining health and preventing and treating illness.

● **behavioral medicine** An interdisciplinary field that focuses on developing and integrating behavioral and biomedical knowledge to promote health and reduce illness; overlaps with health psychology.

**Health psychology** emphasizes psychology's role in establishing and maintaining health and preventing and treating illness. Health psychologists emphasize that lifestyle choices, behaviors, and psychological characteristics can play important roles in health (Podina & Fodor, 2018; Van Cappellen & others, 2018; Weston & others, 2018). A related discipline, **behavioral medicine**, is an interdisciplinary field that focuses on developing and integrating behavioral and biomedical knowledge to promote health and reduce illness (Behrman & others, 2018; Larson & others, 2018). The concerns of health psychology and behavioral medicine overlap, but they are distinct. Health psychology primarily focuses on behavioral, social, and cognitive influences, whereas behavioral medicine is more concerned with direct policy implications of biomedical, behavioral, and social factors. Although clearly related, health psychology differs from behavioral medicine in that it focuses more on the individual and his or her thoughts, feelings, and behavior as these relate to health.

Health psychology and behavioral medicine both inform two related fields: health promotion and public health. *Health promotion* involves helping people change their lifestyle to optimize health and assisting them in achieving balance in physical, emotional, social, spiritual, and intellectual health and wellness. *Public health* is concerned with studying health and disease in large populations to guide policymakers. Public health experts identify public health concerns, set priorities, and design interventions for health promotion. An important goal of public health is to ensure that all populations have access to cost-effective healthcare, health promotion services, and health-promoting behaviors and resources.

*The "Click It or Ticket" program, promoting seatbelt use, reflects the efforts of individuals working in the related fields of health promotion and health psychology.*

©Andre Jenny/Alamy Stock Photo

### The Biopsychosocial Model

The interests of health psychologists and behavioral medicine researchers are broad—ranging from increasing specific health behaviors, like dental flossing (Hamilton & others, 2018), to preventing disease (Kippax, 2018), to identifying ways to cope with stress (Cohen, Murphy, & Prather, 2019), and to exploring psychological responses to illness (Roberts & others, 2018). The biopsychosocial model we examined in the chapter "Psychological Disorders" applies to health psychology as well, because health psychology integrates biological, psychological, and social factors in health (Bennett & others, 2018; Wiechman, Hoyt, & Patterson, 2018).

For example, stress is a focal point of study across the broad field of psychology. Study of the brain and behavior (the chapter "Biological Foundations of Behavior"), for instance, acknowledges the impact of stress on the autonomic nervous system. Furthermore, an individual's state of consciousness (in the chapter "States of Consciousness"), as well as the particular ways in which that person thinks about events (in the chapter "Thinking, Intelligence, and Language"), can influence the experience of stress. Stressful events also affect our emotions (in the chapter "Motivation and Emotion"), which are themselves

**TABLE 1 All the things you already know about Health Psychology.** We have already reviewed many important topics in Health Psychology. Here are just a few.

| Chapter | Implications for Health and Wellness |
| --- | --- |
| **3 Biological Foundations** | Acute stress is often adaptive but chronic stress can take a toll on our bodies, especially our immune system. |
| **4 Sensation and Perception** | Healthy behaviors can help to protect our precious senses. |
| **5 States of Consciousness** | Engaging in meditation can be a great way to relieve stress and allow our bodies to recover from stressful circumstances. |
| **6 Learning** | The experience of stress can be decreased by optimal levels of predictability, personal control, and having outlets for frustration. |
| **7 Memory** | Incorporating cognitive challenges in our everyday behavior can help to keep memory sharp with age. |
| **8 Thinking, Intelligence, and Language** | Cognitive appraisal (that is, how we think about potentially stressful events) can have a large impact on the amount of stress we experience. We can make events less stressful by changing the way we think about them. |
| **9 Human Development** | Actively coping with difficult life circumstances is associated with higher levels of wisdom and maturity. |
| **10 Motivation and Emotion** | The human pursuit of happiness is affected by biological factors, and actively pursuing life goals can help to enhance happiness. |
| **11 Gender, Sex, and Sexuality** | Practicing safe sex allows people to prevent sexually transmitted infections. |
| **12 Personality** | Conscientiousness, personal control, optimism, and self-efficacy are personality characteristics associated with better health and longevity. |
| **13 Social Psychology** | Social relationships are among the most important predictors of physical health. |
| **14 Industrial and Organizational Psychology** | Unemployment can be extremely stressful and is associated with negative physical and psychological changes. |
| **15 Psychological Disorders** | Stigma is a key stressor for those who have psychological disorders. In addition, stigma may prevent health professionals from realizing that these individuals can benefit from health behavior interventions. |
| **16 Therapies** | Therapy can be an excellent way to learn to better manage stress and enhance psychological well-being. |

psychological and physical events. Aspects of our personalities, too, may be associated with stress (in the chapter "Personality") and can influence our health. Finally, social contexts, relationships (in the chapter "Social Psychology"), and work experiences (in the chapter "Industrial and Organizational Psychology") can shape both an individual's experience of stress and his or her ability to cope with it. Throughout the Science of Psychology, you have learned a great deal about health psychology in each chapter's Health and Wellness section. Table 1 highlights the many ways we have already seen that psychology is implicated in health and wellness.

## The Relationship Between Mind and Body

From the biopsychosocial perspective, the many diverse aspects of the person are strongly intertwined. Our bodies and minds are closely connected, a link introduced in the chapter "What Is Psychology?". After suffering a heart attack, one health psychologist ruefully noted that none of his colleagues in the field had thought to ask him whether heart disease was part of his family history, ignoring the obvious question that a medical doctor would ask first.

Although the mind is responsible for much of what happens in the body, it is not the only factor. Even as we consider the many ways that psychological processes contribute to health and disease, we must understand that sometimes illness happens for other reasons–affecting even those who have led healthy lives.

Although it might be more exciting to think about ways the mind may influence health, it is important to appreciate that the body may influence the mind as well. That is, how we feel physically may have implications for how we think. Health psychology and behavioral medicine are concerned not only with how psychological states influence health, but also with how health and illness may influence the person's psychological experience, including cognitive abilities, stress, and coping. A person who is feeling psychologically run-down may not realize that the level of fatigue is in fact the beginning stage of an illness. In turn, physical health can be a source of good feelings. The mind and body are never truly separate.

### test yourself

1. What factors does the field of health psychology emphasize as keys to good health?
2. With what is the field of health promotion concerned?
3. Name three societal issues with which you might be concerned if you worked in the field of public health.

# 2. MAKING POSITIVE LIFE CHANGES

One of health psychology's missions is to help individuals identify and implement ways they can effectively change their behaviors for the better. **Health behaviors**—practices that have an impact on physical well-being—include adopting a healthy approach to stress, exercising, eating right, brushing one's teeth, performing breast and testicular exams, not smoking, drinking in moderation (or not at all), and practicing safe sex. Before exploring what health psychologists have learned about the best ways to make healthy behavioral changes, we focus on the process of change itself.

● **health behaviors** Practices that have an impact on physical well-being, such as adopting a healthy approach to stress, exercising, eating right, brushing one's teeth, performing breast and testicular exams, not smoking, drinking in moderation (or not at all), and practicing safe sex.

## Theoretical Models of Change

In many instances, changing behaviors begins by changing attitudes. Psychologists have sought to understand specifically how changing attitudes can lead to behavioral changes. Social cognitive theories emphasize the crucial role of beliefs about one's ability to make healthy changes, as well as the individual's knowledge and skills.

What factors play a role in healthy behavior changes? One way this question has been answered is in the **theory of reasoned action** (Ajzen & Albarracín, 2007; Ajzen & Fishbein, 2005; Hagger, Polet, & Lintunen, 2018). The theory suggests that effective change requires that individuals

- Have specific intentions about their behaviors
- Hold positive attitudes about a new behavior
- Perceive that their social group looks favorably on the new behavior as well

● **theory of reasoned action** Theoretical model stating that effective change requires individuals to have specific intentions about their behaviors, as well as positive attitudes about a new behavior, and to perceive that their social group looks favorably on the new behavior as well.

The **theory of planned behavior** includes all of these three components but adds a fourth: the person's perceptions of *control* over the outcome (Ajzen, 2012a, 2012b). If you smoke and want to quit smoking, these theories tell us you will be more successful if you devise an explicit intention of quitting, feel good about it, believe that your friends support you, and believe that you have control over your smoking. Emphasis on control is what makes the theory of planned behavior different from the theory of reasoned action.

● **theory of planned behavior** Theoretical model that includes the basic ideas of the theory of reasoned action but adds the person's perceptions of control over the outcome.

The theory of reasoned action and its extension, the theory of planned behavior, have accurately predicted whether individuals successfully develop intentions to engage in healthy behaviors, including cancer screening and decision making (Saab & others, 2018), HIV prevention and safer sex practices (Montanaro, Kershaw, & Bryan, 2018), prevention of smoking (Record & others, 2018) and binge drinking (Barratt & Cooke, 2018), exercise (Doherty & others, 2018), healthy eating (Close & others, 2018), and substance abuse (Pinedo, Zemore, & Rogers, 2018).

One potential limitation of these approaches is that they consider health decision making to be a rational process. Sometimes our health decisions are based on strong, automatic emotional reactions rather than information or even social norms (Klaassen & others, 2018). In particular, the experience of *anticipated regret*—the feeling that we will look back on our decision with negative emotion—can powerfully influence health decision making (Lacombe-Duncan, Newman, & Baiden, 2018; Mertes, 2017).

Regardless of their primary focus on thoughts or feelings or both, all theoretical models of health-related behavioral changes make predictions about the type of intervention that should be most successful in producing durable change.

| Stage | Description | Example |
|---|---|---|
| 1 **Precontemplation** | Individuals are not yet ready to think about changing and may not be aware that they have a problem that needs to be changed. | Overweight individuals are not aware that they have a weight problem. |
| 2 **Contemplation** | Individuals acknowledge that they have a problem but may not yet be ready to change. | Overweight individuals know they have a weight problem but aren't yet sure they want to commit to losing weight. |
| 3 **Preparation/ Determination** | Individuals are preparing to take action. | Overweight individuals explore options they can pursue in losing weight. |
| 4 **Action/Willpower** | Individuals commit to making a behavioral change and enact a plan. | Overweight individuals begin a diet and start an exercise program. |
| 5 **Maintenance** | Individuals are successful in continuing their behavior change over time. | Overweight individuals are able to stick with their diet and exercise regimens for 6 months. |

**FIGURE 1 Stages of Change Model Applied to Losing Weight** The stages of change model has been applied to many different health behaviors, including losing weight. Sources: DiClemente (2018); Norcross, Loberg, & Norcross (2012); Prochaska, Redding, & Evers (2015).

## The Stages of Change Model

The **stages of change model** describes the process by which individuals give up bad habits and adopt healthier lifestyles. The model breaks down behavioral changes into five steps, recognizing that real change does not occur overnight with one monumental decision (DiClemente, 2018; Norcross, Loberg, & Norcross, 2012; Prochaska, Redding, & Evers, 2015) (Figure 1). Rather, change occurs in progressive stages, each characterized by particular issues and challenges. Those stages are:

- Precontemplation
- Contemplation
- Preparation/Determination
- Action/Willpower
- Maintenance

● **stages of change model** Theoretical model describing a five-step process by which individuals give up bad habits and adopt healthier lifestyles.

### PRECONTEMPLATION

The *precontemplation stage* occurs when individuals are not yet genuinely thinking about changing. They may not even be aware that they have a problem behavior. Individuals who drink to excess but are not aware that their drinking is affecting their work may be in this precontemplation phase. At this stage, raising one's consciousness about the problem is crucial.

A woman who smokes may find her consciousness raised by the experience of becoming pregnant. A man who is stopped for drunk driving may be forced to take a good look at his drinking. Similarly, overweight individuals may not recognize their problem until they see photos of themselves taken at a family reunion—or until they learn that a meal consisting of a McDonald's Big Mac, large fries, and large chocolate shake amounts to over 2,000 calories, the recommended caloric intake for an adult woman for an entire day.

It is common for people in the precontemplation phase to deny that their current pattern of behavior is a problem. The individual might defend such behaviors, claiming that "I don't drink/smoke/eat that much." Those who are overweight may discover that they do eat "that much" when they start keeping track of calories.

©Andrey Armyagov/Shutterstock

## CONTEMPLATION

In the *contemplation stage*, people acknowledge the problem but may not be ready to commit to change. As the name of the stage suggests, at this point individuals are actively thinking about change. They might reevaluate the place of this behavior in their life, and they may have mixed feelings about giving up an unhealthy habit. For example, how will they deal with missing their friends on a smoke break? Or turning down an invitation to go out drinking? Or packing a healthy lunch instead of heading to the drive-thru? They may weigh the short-term gains of the harmful behavior against the long-term benefits of changing.

As we considered in the chapter "Learning", future rewards can be difficult to pursue when immediate pleasures beckon. Sure, it would be nice to be thinner, but losing weight is going to take time, and that hot fudge sundae is right there, looking very delicious. Nevertheless, in the contemplation phase, individuals may begin to separate themselves, mentally, from the typical overeater or smoker and start to define themselves as someone who is ready to change.

## PREPARATION/DETERMINATION

At the *preparation/determination stage,* people are getting ready to take action. At this point, self-belief and especially beliefs about one's ability to "see it through" are very important. A key consideration in this stage is whether individuals truly feel they are ready to change. Events such as the diagnosis of an illness can lead a person to feel ready to change (Kumar & others, 2018).

During this stage, individuals start thinking concretely about how they might take on their new challenge. For example, they explore options for the best ways to quit smoking or drinking or investigate different exercise programs. Individuals who want to lose weight might think about joining a gym to get regular exercise or setting the alarm clock for a 6 A.M. run.

## ACTION/WILLPOWER

At the *action/willpower stage*, individuals commit to making a real behavioral change and enact an effective plan. An important challenge at this stage is finding ways to support the new, healthy behavior pattern. One approach is to find reinforcements or rewards for the new behavior. Individuals who have quit smoking might focus on how much better food tastes after they have given up cigarettes. Successful dieters might treat themselves to a shopping trip to buy new, smaller-size clothes. Acknowledging, enjoying, and celebrating accomplishments can motivate consistent behavior.

Another source of support for new behaviors is the individual's social network. Friends, family, and members of a support group can help by providing encouragement and reinforcement for positive change. Members of a family might all quit smoking at the same time or join the individual in physical activities or healthier eating.

Finally, people may focus on alternative behaviors that replace the unhealthy ones. Instead of bar hopping, they might join a group dedicated to activities not associated with drinking alcohol, such as a dance club or community theater group. In other words, effective change also means avoiding tempting situations.

©svetikd/E+/Getty Images

## MAINTENANCE

In the *maintenance stage*, individuals successfully avoid temptation and consistently pursue healthy behaviors. They may anticipate tempting situations and avoid them or actively prepare for them. If smokers seeking to kick the habit know that they always enjoy a cigarette after a big meal out with friends, they might mentally prepare themselves for that temptation before going out. Successful dieters might post a consciousness-raising photograph on the refrigerator.

At some point, people in the maintenance stage may find that actively fighting the urge to indulge in unhealthy behaviors is no longer necessary. *Transcendence* means that they are no longer consciously engaged in maintaining their healthy lifestyle; rather, the lifestyle has become a part of who they are. They are now nonsmokers, healthy eaters, or committed runners.

### RELAPSE

One challenge during the maintenance stage is to avoid **relapse**, a return to the former unhealthy patterns. Contrary to popular belief, relapse is a common aspect of change. That is, for most people, real change takes many attempts. Relapse can be discouraging and can lead a person to feel like a failure. However, the *majority* of people who eventually do change do not succeed on the first try. Rather, they try and fail and try again, cycling through the five stages several times before achieving a stable, healthy lifestyle. Consequently, individuals who are experts in changing health behavior consider relapse to be normal (DiClemente, 2018).

● **relapse** A return to former unhealthy patterns.

If you have ever tried to adopt a healthier lifestyle by dieting, starting an exercise program, or quitting smoking, you might know how regretful you feel when you experience relapse. One slip, however, does not mean you will never reach your goal. Rather, when a slip-up occurs, you have an opportunity to learn, to think about what led to the relapse, and to devise a strategy for preventing it in the future. Successful dieters, for example, do not let one lapse ruin the week. Individuals who successfully keep weight off are those who do not get too down on themselves when they relapse (Pedersen & others, 2018; Phelan & others, 2003).

### EVALUATION OF THE STAGES OF CHANGE MODEL

The stages of change model has been applied successfully to a broad range of healthy behaviors, including exercise, smoking cessation, diet, and so forth (Edwards-Stewart & others, 2017; Romain, Horwath, & Bernard, 2018). Although it has proven to be relevant to a variety of behaviors, the model has its critics (Brug & others, 2004; DuPont & others, 2017; Joseph, Breslin, & Skinner, 1999). Some have questioned whether the stages are mutually exclusive, discrete categories and whether individuals move from one stage to another sequentially as has been proposed (Littell & Girvin, 2002). For example, some individuals might feel themselves to be in both action/willpower and maintenance at the same time or may move from contemplation back to precontemplation.

Critics of the model also point out that it refers more to changing attitudes than to modifying behavior (West, 2005). Recall from the chapter "Social Psychology" that the relationship between attitudes and behavior can be complex. Furthermore, all of the stages might be understood as promoting a sense of self-efficacy, rather than producing change itself (West, 2005).

No theoretical model is perfect. One advantage of the stages of change model is that it can serve as a powerful tool for therapists who are trying to help clients institute healthy behavior patterns. Sometimes, sharing the model with individuals who are trying to change provides them with a useful language to use in understanding the change process, helps to reduce their uncertainty, and encourages them to develop realistic expectations for the difficult journey ahead.

***test yourself***

1. How does the theory of planned behavior expand upon, or extend, the theory of reasoned action?
2. Name and briefly describe the five stages of the stages of change model.
3. What positive advice would you give to someone who experiences relapse when dieting or trying to quit smoking?

# 3. RESOURCES FOR EFFECTIVE LIFE CHANGE

Making positive changes to promote health can be challenging. Fortunately, there are various psychological, social, and cultural resources and tools at our disposal to help us in the journey to a healthier lifestyle. In this section we consider some of the tools that can help us achieve effective change and, ultimately, lead a healthier life.

## Motivation

Recall from the chapter "Motivation and Emotion" that motivation refers to the "why" of behavior. Motivational tools for self-change involve changing for the right reasons. Change is most effective when you are doing it for yourself, rather than because others want you to change. One study found that individuals who were pressured to lose weight were less

Religious faith may also be an important factor in good health because it provides a sense of purpose and meaning in life and acts as a buffer for stressful events (Krok, 2015; Negru-Subtirica & others, 2017). Belief in the enduring meaningfulness of one's life can help one keep perspective and see life's hassles in the context of a bigger picture. The Psychological Inquiry breaks down the various factors that might play a role in the association between religious faith and health.

Given these associations, it is not surprising that accumulated evidence suggests religious faith is associated with longer survival (Chong & others, 2018; Shor & Roelfs, 2013; Wallace & others, 2018). Importantly, it appears that the strong link between religiosity and longevity may be a peculiarly American finding (VanderWeele, 2017). Examining this association across 59 nations showed that religious faith was associated with self-reported health and longevity only in highly religious nations (Stavrova, 2015). These results suggest that the fit that exists between a person and the larger social context may determine whether religious faith predicts better health and longer life.

### *test yourself*

1. Name three tools or resources on which we can draw in trying to make positive life changes.
2. Discuss the importance of motivation in efforts at self-change.
3. Identify and describe three types of benefits provided by social support.

# 4. TOWARD A HEALTHIER MIND (AND BODY): CONTROLLING STRESS

Complete the following sentence: "I wish I could stop ______." If you could change one thing about your behavior, what would you choose? Would the change perhaps have to do with feeling stressed out much of the time? Maybe you wish you could quit worrying so much or stop facing every daily challenge with tension. Let's look at the problems that can arise when you feel chronically stressed and the ways you can better manage your stress.

## Stress and Its Stages

As described in the chapter "Biological Foundations of Behavior", *stress* is an individual's response to environmental *stressors,* the circumstances and events that threaten well-being, disrupt goal achievement, and tax coping abilities (Cohen, Murphy, & Prather, 2019). We often think of negative life events as stressful, but positive occasions–such as graduating from college, getting married, and starting a new job–can also produce stress if these events present significant changes. Hans Selye (1974, 1983), the founder of stress research, focused on the physical response to stressors, especially the wear and tear on the body due to the demands placed on it. After observing patients with different problems–the death of someone close, loss of income, arrest for embezzlement–Selye concluded that any number of environmental events or stimuli would produce the same stress symptoms: loss of appetite, muscular weakness, and decreased interest in the world.

**general adaptation syndrome (GAS)** Selye's term for the common effects of stressful demands on the body, consisting of three stages: alarm, resistance, and exhaustion.

**General adaptation syndrome (GAS)** is Selye's term for the common effects on the body when stressful demands are placed on it (Figure 2). The GAS consists of three stages: alarm, resistance, and exhaustion. Selye's model is especially useful in helping us understand the link between stress and health.

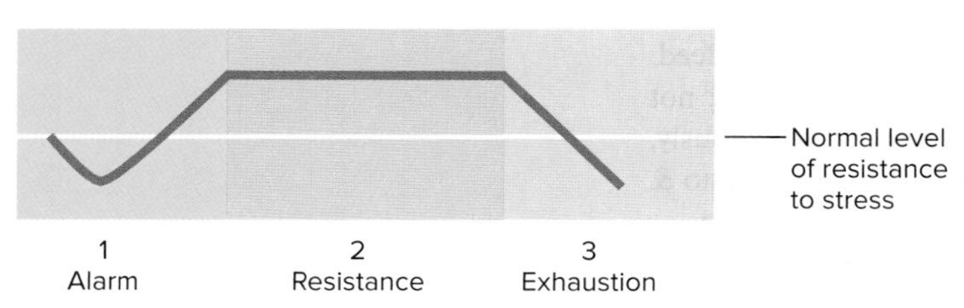


**FIGURE 2** **Selye's General Adaptation Syndrome** The general adaptation syndrome (GAS) describes an individual's response to stress in terms of three stages: (1) alarm, in which the body mobilizes its resources; (2) resistance, in which the body strives mightily to endure the stressor; and (3) exhaustion, in which resistance becomes depleted.

The body's first reaction to a stressor, in the *alarm stage,* is a temporary state of shock during which resistance to illness and stress falls below normal limits. In trying to cope with the initial effects of stress, the body quickly releases hormones that, in a short time, adversely affect the functioning of the immune system—our body's network of natural defenses. During this time the individual is prone to infections from illness and injury.

In the *resistance stage* of Selye's general adaptation syndrome, a number of glands throughout the body manufacture different hormones that protect the individual in many ways. Endocrine and sympathetic nervous system activity are not as high as in the alarm stage, although they still are elevated. During the resistance stage, the body's immune system can fight off infection with remarkable efficiency. Similarly, hormones that reduce the inflammation normally associated with injury circulate at high levels.

If the body's all-out effort to combat stress fails and the stress persists, the individual moves into the *exhaustion stage.* At this point, the wear and tear on the body takes its toll; the person might collapse from fatigue or succumb to illness. Serious, possibly irreversible damage to the body, such as a heart attack or even death, may occur.

The body system that plays the greatest role in Selye's GAS is called the **hypothalamic-pituitary-adrenal axis (HPA axis)**. The HPA axis is a complex set of interactions among the hypothalamus (part of the brain's limbic system), the pituitary gland (the master gland of the endocrine system), and the adrenal glands (endocrine system glands that are located on top of each kidney). The HPA axis regulates various body processes, including digestion, immune system responses, emotion, and energy expenditure. The axis also controls reactions to stressful events, and these responses will be our focus here.

● **hypothalamic-pituitary-adrenal axis (HPA axis)** The complex set of interactions among the hypothalamus, the pituitary gland, and the adrenal glands that regulates various body processes and controls reactions to stressful events.

When the brain detects a threat in the environment, it signals the hypothalamus to produce corticotropin-releasing hormone (CRH). In turn, CRH stimulates the pituitary gland to produce another hormone that causes the adrenal glands to release cortisol. Cortisol is itself the "stress hormone" that directs cells to make sugar, fat, and protein available so the body can take quick action. Cortisol also suppresses the immune system.

In the chapter "Biological Foundations of Behavior" we distinguished between acute stress and chronic stress. Acute stress can sometimes be adaptive, and in acute stress cortisol plays an important role in helping us to take the necessary action to avoid dire consequences. Typically, once the body has dealt with a given stressor, our cortisol level returns to normal. However, under chronic stress, the HPA axis can remain activated over the long haul.

The activity of the HPA axis varies from one person to the next. These differences may be explained by genes as well as by particular stressful experiences (Cohen, Murphy, & Prather, 2018; Young & others, 2018). Research has shown that prenatal stress can influence the development of the HPA axis (Biggio & others, 2018; W. Zhang & others, 2018). When the HPA is chronically active, various systems in the body suffer, as we now consider.

## Stress and the Immune System

Chronic stress can have serious implications for the body, particularly for the immune system. Interest in links between the immune system and stress spawned the field of **psychoneuroimmunology**, which explores connections among psychological factors (such as attitudes and emotions), the nervous system, and the immune system (Halaris & others, 2019).

● **psychoneuroimmunology** A new field of scientific inquiry that explores connections among psychological factors (such as attitudes and emotions), the nervous system, and the immune system.

The immune system and the central nervous system are similar in their modes of receiving, recognizing, and integrating signals from the external environment. The central nervous system and the immune system both possess "sensory" elements, which receive information from the environment and other parts of the body, and "motor" elements, which carry out an appropriate response. Both systems also rely on chemical mediators for communication. CRH, the hormone discussed above, is shared by the central nervous system and the immune system, uniting the stress and immune responses.

A variety of research supports the idea that stress can profoundly influence the immune system (Castellazzi & others, 2018; Edwards & others, 2018; Grinberg, O'Hara, & Sbarra, 2018). Acute stressors (sudden, stressful, one-time life events or stimuli) can produce immunological changes. For example, in relatively healthy HIV-infected individuals, as well as in individuals with cancer, acute stressors are associated with poorer immune system functioning (Boland & Pockley, 2018; Flentje & others, 2018).

In addition to acute stressors, chronic stressors (long-lasting agents of stress) are associated with an increasing downturn in immune system responsiveness (H. Zhang & others, 2018). This effect has been documented in a number of circumstances, including worries about living next to a nuclear reactor, failures in close relationships (divorce, separation, and marital distress), negative relationships with family and friends, and burdensome caregiving for a family member with a progressive illness (Grinberg, O'Hara, & Sbarra, 2018; Prather & others, 2018).

A goal of psychoneuroimmunology is to determine the precise links among psychological factors, the brain, and the immune system (Cohen, Murphy, & Prather, 2019; Halaris & others, 2019; Hutchinson, 2018). Hypotheses about the interaction that causes vulnerability to disease include the following:

- Stressful experiences lower the efficiency of immune systems, making individuals more susceptible to disease.
- Stress directly promotes disease-producing processes.
- Stressful experiences may cause the activation of dormant viruses that diminish the individual's ability to cope with disease.

These hypotheses may lead to better treatments for some of the most challenging diseases, including cancer and AIDS.

Sheldon Cohen and his colleagues have conducted a number of studies on the effects of stress, emotion, and social support on immunity and susceptibility to infectious disease (Cohen, 2016). Cohen and his colleagues (1998) found that adults who faced interpersonal or work-related stress for at least a month were more likely than their less-stressed counterparts to catch a cold after exposure to viruses. In the study, 276 adults were exposed to viruses and then quarantined for five days. The longer people had experienced major stress, the more likely they were to catch a cold. Individuals who reported high stress for the preceding two years tripled their risk of catching a cold (Figure 3). Those who experienced work-related stress for a month or longer were nearly five times more likely to develop colds than individuals without chronic stress. Those who experienced interpersonal stress for a month or more were twice as likely to catch a cold.

Cohen concluded that stress-triggered changes in the immune system and hormones might create greater vulnerability to infection. These findings suggest that when we know we are under stress, we need to take better care of ourselves than usual, although often we do just the opposite (Cohen & others, 2009, 2012, 2013). Research has probed the ways that many events can affect immune system functioning. See the Intersection to discover how economic factors can influence health and immunity.

## Stress and Cardiovascular Disease

There is also reason to believe that stress can increase an individual's risk for cardiovascular disease (Ochoa, Wu, & Terada, 2018). Chronic emotional stress is associated with high blood pressure, heart disease, and early death (Ogilvie & others, 2016; Roy, Riley, & Sinha, 2018). Apparently, the surge in adrenaline caused by severe emotional stress causes the blood to clot more rapidly, and blood clotting is a major factor in heart attacks (Kivimäki & others, 2018; Strike & others, 2006).

Emotional stress also can contribute to cardiovascular disease in other ways. Individuals who have had major life changes (such as the loss of a loved one) have a higher incidence of cardiovascular disease and early death (Mostofsky & others, 2012; Vitaliano & others, 2018). Job loss can also play a role. A longitudinal study of involuntary unemployment among workers 50 years and older over a 10-year period revealed that displaced workers have a twofold increase in the risk of stroke (Gallo & others, 2006).

The body's internal reactions to stress are not the only risk. People in a chronically stressed condition are more likely to take up smoking, start overeating, and avoid exercising (Dalton & Hammen, 2018; van den Berk-Clark & others, 2018). All of these stress-related behaviors are linked with the development of cardiovascular disease.

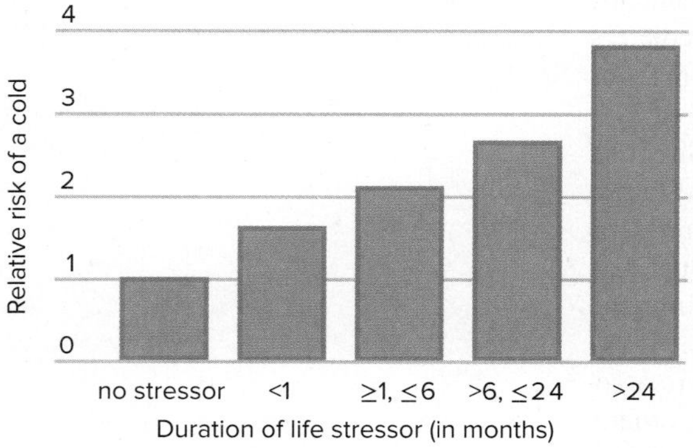

**FIGURE 3 Stress and the Risk of Developing a Cold** In a study by Cohen and others (1998), the longer individuals had a life stressor, the more likely they were to develop a cold. The four-point scale is based on the odds (0 = lower; 4 = higher) of getting a cold. Source: Cohen, Frank, Doyle, Skoner, Rabin, & Gwaltney (1998).

## Stress and Cancer

Given the association of stress with poor health behaviors such as smoking, it is not surprising that stress has also been related to cancer risk (Fischer, Ziogas, & Anton-Culver, 2018; Haldar & Ben-Eliyahu, 2018; Nezu & others, 2013).

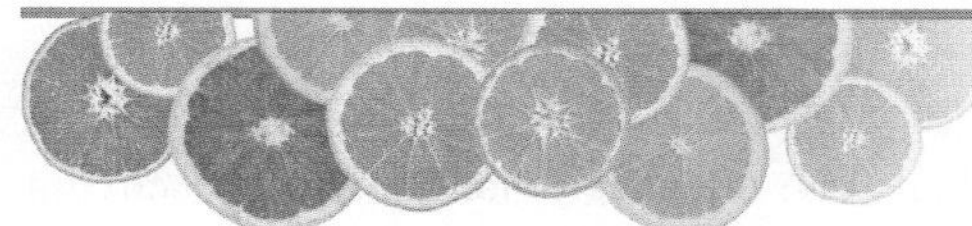

# INTERSECTION

## Health Psychology and Social Psychology: Can Economic Stress Age the Immune System?

In 2007, the United States experienced a massive economic downturn known as the Great Recession. The Great Recession involved a host of potentially stressful economic events, including increases in job losses, declines in house values, and increased home foreclosures (Flanagan & Wilson, 2013). Some people were left jobless and homeless. Not surprisingly, this time period also saw an uptick in health problems, including increases in symptom complaints, depression, and substance use and abuse (Cagney & others, 2014; Tsai, 2015). Stressful events can influence health through their impact on the immune system. Did the Great Recession influence immune functioning?

*Have any national events stressed you out lately? Do you think they have taken a toll on your health?*

One way to answer this question involves a particular organ, the thymus gland. This gland is located in the chest, between the lungs and just behind the sternum (or breastbone). The thymus gland is important to immune function because it is responsible for producing new killer T-cells, the immune system's weapon for fighting disease. An interesting aspect of the thymus gland is that it begins to shrink after puberty. As we age, the thymus gland becomes smaller and smaller. The thymus gland is also sensitive to stress. During severe stress, thymus functioning decreases, leaving the person vulnerable to disease.

To examine the relationships among aspects of the Great Recession and immune function, researchers involved in the Detroit Neighborhood Health Study measured various aspects of neighborhoods throughout the Detroit, MI area (McClure & others, 2018). Within each neighborhood, the researchers measured the number of abandoned homes, foreclosure rate, number of empty lots, and rate of unemployment. Next, they took blood samples from 277 people living in those neighborhoods to get a measure of thymus gland function. The results showed that these economic indicators were negatively related to thymus gland functioning. In effect, the Great Recession aged the thymus glands of those living in neighborhoods most affected.

Importantly, the researchers did not stop there. They were interested in finding out whether there were any variables that might help to explain the link between neighborhood factors and immune function. Seeing empty lots and foreclosure signs in one's neighborhood might be stressful, but could that alone explain the associations uncovered? The researchers found that the key to this link was social cohesion—the extent to which people felt their neighborhood was a close-knit group of friends. Essentially, this means it was not so much the physical changes to the neighborhood but the social meaning of these changes that was associated with impaired immune system function. The loss of home value is painful, but losing friends and no longer feeling like part of a group helped explain the association between economic factors and immune function. Among those who maintained a sense of cohesion, immune function was less severely affected. These results show how real-world events can influence health and illustrates the kinds of psychological experiences that boost or weaken our bodies' natural defense against disease.

©Andy Dean Photography/Alamy Stock Photo

Stress sets in motion biological changes involving the autonomic, endocrine, and immune systems. If the immune system is not compromised, it appears to help provide resistance to cancer and slow its progress. Researchers have found, however, that the physiological effects of stress inhibit a number of cellular immune responses (Edwards & others, 2018; Hayakawa, 2012; Prather & others, 2018). Cancer patients show diminished natural killer (NK)-cell activity in the blood (Cacalano, 2016; David & Massagué, 2018) (Figure 4). Low NK-cell activity is linked with the development of further malignancies, and the length of survival for the cancer patient is related to NK-cell activity (Kaur & others, 2018; Parham & Guethlein, 2018).

Thus, stress is clearly a factor not only in immune system functioning and cardiovascular health but also in the risk for cancer. Once a person has cancer, stress is especially problematic in terms of tumor growth and recovery (Gu & others, 2018; Le & others, 2016; Nagaraja & others, 2013). In light of these links, understanding the psychological

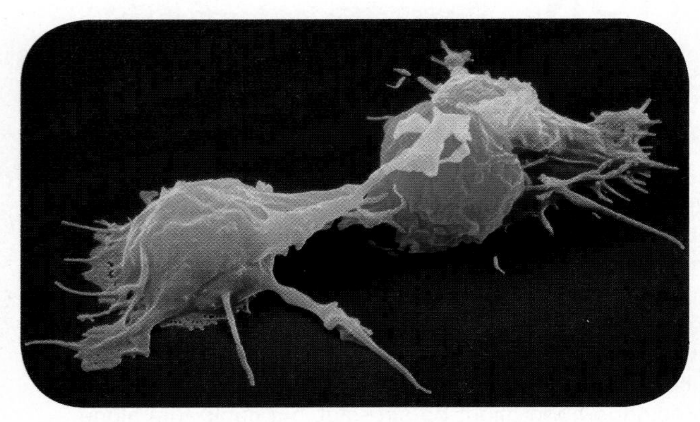

**FIGURE 4** **NK Cells and Cancer** Two natural-killer (NK) cells (*yellow*) are shown attacking a leukemia cell (*red*). Notice the blisters that the leukemia cell has developed to defend itself. Nonetheless, the NK cells are surrounding the leukemia cell and are about to destroy it. ©Eye of Science/Science Source

processes by which individuals can effectively handle stressful circumstances is a crucial topic in health psychology.

# Coping with Stress

What stresses you out? Stressors can be anything from losing irreplaceable notes from a class, to being yelled at by a friend, to failing a test, to being in a car wreck.

Although everyone's body may have a similar response to stressors, not everyone perceives the same events as stressful. Indeed, whether or not an experience stresses us out depends on how we think about that experience. As reviewed in the chapter "Thinking, Intelligence, and Language", *cognitive appraisal* refers to an individual's interpretation of an experience as either threatening or challenging and the person's determination of whether he or she has the resources to cope effectively with the event. Coping means managing taxing circumstances, expending effort to solve life's problems, and seeking to master or reduce stress.

## TYPES OF COPING

Research has identified two types of coping. **Problem-focused coping** is the cognitive strategy of squarely facing one's troubles and trying to solve them. For example, if you are having trouble with a class, you might go to the campus study skills center and sign up for a program to learn how to study more effectively. In taking this step, you have faced your problem and attempted to do something about it. Problem-focused coping might involve coming up with goals and implementation intentions, the problem-solving steps we examined earlier in this chapter. A meta-analysis revealed that problem-focused coping was linked to a lower level of psychopathology in areas such as anxiety, depression, eating disorders, and substance use disorders (Aldao, Nolen-Hoeksema, & Schweizer, 2010).

● **problem-focused coping** The coping strategy of squarely facing one's troubles and trying to solve them.

● **emotion-focused coping** The coping strategy that involves responding to the stress that one is feeling—trying to manage one's emotional reaction—rather than focusing on the problem itself.

**Emotion-focused coping** involves responding to the stress that you are feeling–trying to manage your emotional reaction–rather than confronting the problem itself. In emotion-focused coping, you might avoid the source of your stress, rationalize what has happened to you, deny the problem is occurring, laugh it off, or call on your religious faith for support. If you use emotion-focused coping, you might avoid going to a class that is a problem for you. You might say the class does not matter, deny that you are having difficulty with it, joke about it with your friends, or pray that you will do better.

Although problem-focused coping is generally associated with better outcomes, in some circumstances emotion-focused coping can be helpful. Denial is one of the main protective psychological mechanisms for navigating the flood of feelings that occurs when the reality of death or dying becomes too great.

For example, one study found that following the death of a loved one, bereaved individuals who directed their attention away from their negative feelings had fewer health problems and were rated as better adjusted by their friends, compared with bereaved individuals who did not use this coping strategy (Coifman & others, 2007; Galatzer-Levy, Huang, & Bonanno, 2018). Denial can be used to avoid the destructive impact of shock by postponing the time when a person has to deal with stress. In other circumstances, however, emotion-focused coping can be problematic. Denying that your ex does not love you anymore keeps you from getting on with life. Yet emotion-focused coping may be useful in situations in which there is no solution to a problem, such as long-term grieving over the loss of a loved one. In such cases, the emotion itself might be the stressor.

©dolgachov/Getty Images

Many individuals successfully use both problem-focused and emotion-focused coping when adjusting to a stressful circumstance. For example, in one study individuals said they used both problem-focused and emotion-focused coping strategies in 98 percent of the stressful encounters they face (Folkman & Lazarus, 1980). Over the long term, though, problem-focused coping usually works best (Lovell & Gaszka, 2018).

## Strategies for Successful Coping

Successful coping can improve even the most stressful situations. Several specific factors are associated with effective coping, including a sense of personal control, a healthy immune system, personal resources, and positive emotions.

When one is experiencing stressful life events, multiple coping strategies often work better than a single strategy, as is true with any problem-solving challenge (Folkman & Moskowitz, 2004). People who have experienced a stressful life event or a cluster of difficulties (such as a parent's death, a divorce, and a significant loss of income) might actively embrace problem solving and consistently take advantage of opportunities for positive experiences, even in the context of the bad times they are going through. Positive emotion can give them a sense of the big picture, help them devise a variety of possible solutions, and allow them to make creative connections.

Optimism can play a strong role in effective coping. Recall from the chapter "Personality" that optimism is the expectancy that good things are likely to occur in the future (Bouchard & others, 2018; Carver & Scheier, 2009). Having an optimistic view of what lies ahead tends to help people engage constructively with potentially threatening information (Aspinwall & Pengchit, 2013; Aspinwall & Tedeschi, 2010a, 2010b).

Optimists face life's challenges from a position of strength. For instance, when an optimist finds out that tanning, a favorite pastime, is related to an elevated risk of skin cancer, the information is important but not overwhelming. In contrast, pessimists are already living in a bleak world and prefer not to hear more bad news.

Another personal quality that appears to promote thriving during difficult times is hardiness. **Hardiness** is characterized by a sense of commitment rather than alienation and of control rather than powerlessness; a hardy individual sees problems as challenges rather than as threats (Krauss & others, 2018; Maddi & others, 2017). Hardiness is exemplified by the basketball player whose team is down by two points with seconds remaining on the clock when he shouts, "Coach! Give me the ball!"

● **hardiness** A personality trait characterized by a sense of commitment rather than alienation and of control rather than powerlessness; a perception of problems as challenges rather than threats.

The links among hardiness, stress, and illness were the focus of the Chicago Stress Project, which studied male business managers 32 to 65 years of age over a five-year period (Kobasa, Maddi, & Kahn, 1982; Maddi, 1998). During the five years, most of the managers experienced stressful events such as divorce, job transfers, the death of a close friend, unfavorable performance evaluations at work, and reporting to an unpleasant boss. In one aspect of the study, managers who developed an illness, ranging from the flu to a heart attack, were compared with those who did not (Kobasa, Maddi, & Kahn, 1982). Those who did not were more likely to have hardy personalities. Another aspect of the study investigated whether hardiness, along with exercise and social support, provided a buffer against stress and reduced illness in executives' lives (Kobasa & others, 1986). When all three factors were present in an executive's life, the level of illness dropped dramatically (Figure 5).

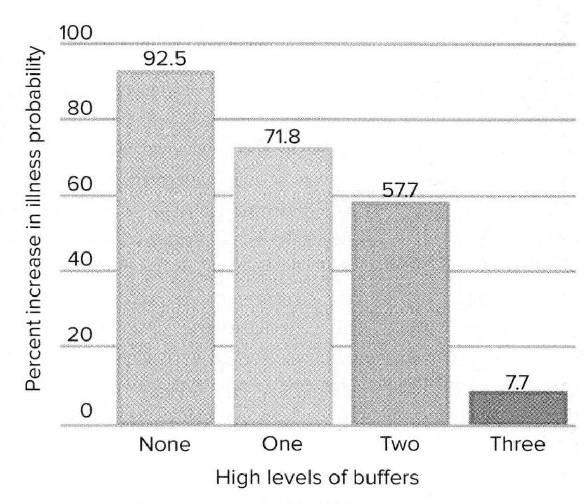


**FIGURE 5 Illness in High-Stress Business Executives** In one study of high-stress business executives (all of whom were selected for this analysis because they were above the stress mean for the entire year of the study), a low level of all three buffers (hardiness, exercise, and social support) involved a high probability of at least one serious illness in that year. High levels of one, two, and all three buffers decreased the likelihood of at least one serious illness occurring in the year of the study.

Source of data: *Journal of Psychosomatic Research*, vol. 29, no. 5, S. C. Kobasa, S. R. Maddi, M. C. Puccette, and M. A. Zola, "Relative effectiveness of hardiness, exercise and social support as resources against illness," pp. 525–533.

Other researchers also have found support for the role of hardiness in illness and health (Bartone & others, 2012; Sandvik & others, 2013). The results of this research on hardiness suggest the power of multiple factors, rather than any single factor, in cushioning individuals against stress and maintaining their health (Krauss & others, 2018; Maddi & others, 2017).

We have seen in this discussion that certain psychological capacities, such as optimism and hardiness, can help us avoid the effects of stress; we can thrive even during potentially threatening circumstances by changing the way we think. One significant stressor in life is illness itself. Can the way we think influence the likelihood of being diagnosed with a serious illness? Can it affect the eventual outcome of that illness? Research pointing to the links between psychological characteristics and better health outcomes can sometimes create a burden on individuals who are struggling with illness. To read about this issue, see the Critical Controversy.

## How Powerful Is the Power of Positive Thinking?

Research demonstrating the role of psychological variables in health, disease, and mortality is extremely appealing because it gives us a sense we have some control over our physical health. Yet, as assuring as such findings might be, these factors are not a psychological recipe for immortality.

When scientists find a link between some psychological factor and an important health outcome, the popular media often latch onto the results as if they mean that such factors play a causal role in disease. Such research can sometimes lead to victim blaming: thinking that a person is ill or has died because of a deficit of hardiness or optimism. Even the most optimistic, hardy nonsmoker who eats well and exercises can develop cancer. Indeed, based on a large-scale analysis of various tissues, scientists have estimated that as much as 80 percent of risk for cancer is random (Tomasetti & Vogelstein, 2015). As much as we wish to feel we have control over all of the factors that might affect someone's health, some health outcomes are a matter of bad luck.

A compelling case in point is provided by research on "fighting spirit" in battling breast cancer. In a study published 35 years ago, 69 women were interviewed three months after undergoing surgery for breast cancer (Greer, Morris, & Pettingale, 1979). Based on the interviews, the researchers categorized the women's responses to breast cancer as "denial," "fighting spirit," "quiet resignation," or "helplessness." The researchers then contacted the women five years later to see whether they had experienced a recurrence. The results showed that women whose responses were characterized by either denial or fighting spirit were less likely to have had a recurrence of cancer. This study led to the conclusion that women with breast cancer should be encouraged to adopt a fighting attitude toward their cancer. The idea that a fighting spirit is important to breast cancer survival continues to hold sway in interventions for women coping with the disease (Coyne & Tennen, 2010).

Crucially, this finding—based on a single study with a relatively small sample—has not withstood the test of time. Subsequent research studies, especially those employing much larger samples, have failed to show any link between adopting a fighting spirit and breast cancer outcomes (Petticrew, Bell, & Hunter, 2002; Phillips & others, 2008; M. Watson & others, 2005).

Although the reality that a fighting spirit does not improve a woman's chances of beating cancer might seem disappointing, many have welcomed this news. As one expert commented, such findings "may help to remove any continuing feelings of guilt or sense of blame for breast cancer relapse from those women who worry because they cannot always maintain a

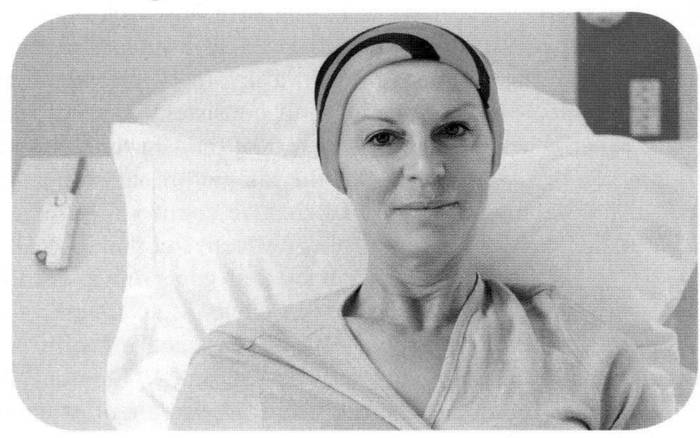

©Eric Audras/Getty Images

fighting spirit or a positive attitude" (Dobson, 2005, p. 865). The widespread belief that adopting a fighting spirit is key to cancer survival imposes a burden on individuals already dealing with a difficult life experience.

Does this conclusion mean that psychosocial variables have no role to play in disease? Certainly not. Psychological factors, like motivation, optimism, and social support can play a large role in how people cope with disease, tolerate difficult treatments, and whether and how they are able to engage in life even during challenging times (Brockway & Shapiro, 2018; Dumontier & others, 2018; Humphries & others, 2018). Knowing about a person's psychosocial characteristics may prompt professionals to provide much-needed information about treatment and the potential for long-term recovery. Indeed, among the factors that (happily) complicate this type of research are that many cancers have effective treatments and that, especially with early detection, relatively few individuals die or experience a recurrence (Coyne & Tennen, 2010). For many individuals, hearing the "C word" can be a very stressful experience. Coming to understand that cancer, if it is detected early, is often treatable and even curable can be a psychological challenge (Aldaz & others, 2018).

**WHAT DO YOU THINK?**

- In the 1979 study, fighting and denial both were associated with better outcomes. Why do you think people latched onto fighting spirit rather than denial as a key intervention?
- If someone you love were diagnosed with cancer, how would the research reported here influence the support you provide to that person?

## Stress Management Programs

Nearly every day we are reminded that stress is bad for our health. "Avoid stress" may be a good prescription, but life is full of potentially stressful experiences. Sometimes just checking e-mail or answering a cell phone can be an invitation for stress. Sometimes, too, trying to manage stress on our own can be overwhelming. Thus, it makes sense to explore options for breaking the stress habit.

Because many people have difficulty in regulating stress, psychologists have developed various techniques that people can learn to apply themselves (Dyrbye & others, 2017; Yusufov & others, 2018). **Stress management programs** teach individuals how to appraise stressful events, develop coping skills, and put these skills into use in everyday life. Effective stress management programs are generally based on the principles of cognitive-behavior therapy (Dear & others, 2018), as described in the chapter "Therapies". Some stress management programs are broad in scope, teaching a range of techniques to handle stress; others teach a specific technique, such as relaxation or assertiveness training.

● **stress management program** A regimen that teaches individuals how to appraise stressful events, how to develop skills for coping with stress, and how to put these skills into use in everyday life.

Stress management programs are often taught through workshops, which are becoming more common in the workplace. Aware of the costs in lost productivity due to stress-related disorders, many organizations have become increasingly motivated to help their workers identify and cope with the stressful circumstances in their lives (Dyrbye & others, 2017). Colleges and universities similarly run stress management programs for students (Yusufov & others, 2018). If you are finding the experience of college extremely stressful and having difficulty coping with the pressures, you might consider enrolling in a stress management program at your school or in your community.

Do stress management programs work? In one study, researchers randomly assigned men and women with hypertension (blood pressure greater than 140/90) to one of three groups (Linden, Lenz, & Con, 2001). One group received 10 hours of individual stress management training; a second group was placed in a waitlist control group and eventually received stress management training; and a third group (a control group) received no such training. The two groups that received the stress management training showed significantly reduced blood pressure. The control group experienced no reduction in blood pressure. Also, the reduced blood pressure in the first two groups was linked to a reported decrease in psychological stress and improved ability to cope with anger.

Coping effectively with stress is essential for physical and mental health. Still, there is a lot more we can do to promote our health. Healthful living—establishing healthy habits and evaluating and changing behaviors that interfere with good health—helps us avoid the damaging effects of stress.

Just as the biopsychosocial perspective predicts, healthy changes in one area of life can have benefits that overflow to others. In the next section, we take a close look at habits and behaviors that directly influence our physical (and psychological) health and wellness.

### *test yourself*

1. What is Selye's term for the pattern of common effects on the body when demands are placed on it?
2. How does the HPA axis function in regulating stress? How is the body affected when the HPA axis is chronically active?
3. What personality characteristic applies to an individual who faces difficulties with a sense of commitment and control and who perceives problems as challenges rather than threats?

# 5. TOWARD A HEALTHIER BODY (AND MIND): BEHAVING AS IF YOUR LIFE DEPENDS UPON IT

There's no escaping it: Getting stress under control is crucial for a healthy mind and body. Where health and wellness are concerned, it is also important to make wise behavioral choices when it comes to physical activity, diet and nutrition, and smoking.

## Becoming Physically Active

Imagine that there was a time when, to change a TV channel, people had to get up and walk a few feet to turn a knob. Consider the time when people physically had to go to the library and hunt through card catalogs and shelves to find information rather than going online and Googling. As our daily tasks have become increasingly easy, we have become less active, and inactivity is a serious health problem (Cooper & Morton, 2018).

Any activity that expends physical energy can be part of a healthy lifestyle. It can be as simple as taking the stairs instead of an elevator, walking or biking to class instead of driving, going ice skating instead of to a movie, or getting up and dancing instead of sitting at the bar. Older people are among the most inactive, and physical activity can

**FIGURE 6** **The Jogging Hog**
**Experiment** Jogging hogs reveal the dramatic effects of exercise on health. In one investigation, a group of hogs was trained to run approximately 100 miles per week (Bloor & White, 1983). Then the researchers narrowed the arteries that supplied blood to the heart. The hearts of the jogging hogs developed extensive alternate pathways for blood supply, and 42 percent of the threatened heart tissue was salvaged, compared with only 17 percent in a control group of non-jogging hogs. ©UCSD School of Medicine

● **exercise** Structured activities whose goal is to improve health.

especially benefit older adults (Koster, Stenholm, & Schrack, 2018). One study of older adults revealed that the more energy they expended in daily activities, the longer they were likely to live (Manini & others, 2006). A recent study showed that older adults who were randomly assigned to a physical activity intervention showed healthier blood pressure six months later compared with control participants who were given information about healthy aging (Kerr & others, 2018). The experimental group was also more likely to remain physically active.

In addition to being related to life expectancy, physical activity correlates with a host of other positive outcomes, including a lower probability of developing cardiovascular and metabolic diseases including diabetes, declining cognitive functioning, and dementia (Shih & others, 2018), weight loss in overweight individuals (Hall, 2013), positive coping with stress (Head, Singh, & Bugg, 2012), and improvements in self-esteem and body image (Ginis, Bassett, & Conlin, 2012). Even in the absence of weight loss, physical activity has positive effects on diabetes (Camps, Verhoef, & Westerterp, 2016) and survival among those with cardiovascular disease (Moholdt, Lavie, & Nauman, 2018). Physical exercise has also been shown to reduce levels of anxiety (Zheng & others, 2018) and depression (McDowell & others, 2018).

Even a real pig can benefit from exercise; Figure 6 shows a hog getting a workout. In this study, a group of hogs was trained to run approximately 100 miles a week (Bloor & White, 1983). After training, the researchers narrowed the arteries that supplied blood to the hogs' hearts. Compared to a control group of untrained hogs, the jogging hogs developed extensive alternative pathways that provided a blood supply to their hearts. These results suggest that being physically active is like investing energy in a wellness bank account: Activity enhances physical well-being and gives us the ability to face life's potential stressors energetically.

Exercise is one special type of physical activity. **Exercise** formally refers to structured activities whose goal is to improve health. Although exercise designed to strengthen muscles and bones or to improve flexibility is important to fitness, many health experts emphasize the benefits of **aerobic exercise**, which is sustained activity–jogging, swimming, or cycling, for example–that stimulates heart and lung functioning.

In one study, exercise literally meant the difference between life and death for middle-aged and older adults (Blair & others, 1989). More than 10,000 men and women were divided into categories of low fitness, medium fitness, and high fitness. Then they

## psychological *inquiry*

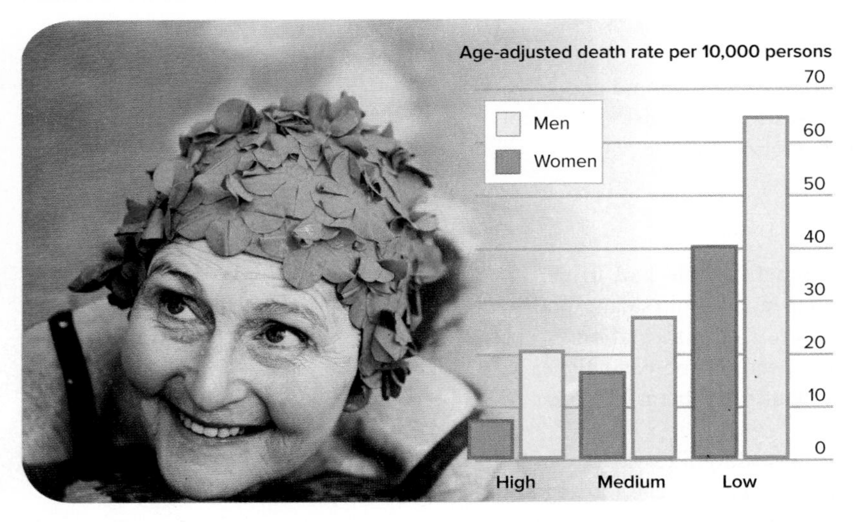


Source of data: Blair, Kohl, Paffenbarger, Clark, Cooper, & Gibbons (1989); (photo): ©Stockbyte/PunchStock

### *Physical Activity: A Matter of Life and Death*

This graph shows the results of an eight-year longitudinal study of over 10,000 men and women (Blair & others, 1989). The X (horizontal) axis shows the fitness level of participants, and the Y (vertical) axis shows the death rates within those groups. Note that results are separated for men and women. Using the figure, answer the following questions.

1. Which groups had the highest and lowest death rates?
2. Comparing the results for men and women separately, what role does gender play in mortality? What might explain this difference?
3. Because this is a correlational study, the results cannot be assumed to show that a low fitness level causes mortality. What third variables might explain the relationship between activity level and mortality?

were studied over eight years. Sedentary participants (low fitness) were more than twice as likely to die during the study's eight-year time span than those who were moderately fit and more than three times as likely to die as those who were highly fit. The positive effects of physical fitness occurred for both men and women. The Psychological Inquiry examines the study's results.

• **aerobic exercise** Sustained activity—jogging, swimming, or cycling, for example—that stimulates heart and lung functioning.

One reason that exercise plays a role in how long people live may involve telomeres. Recall from the chapter "Human Development" that telomeres protect the tips of chromosomes and become significantly shorter as individuals get older; that shortening is theorized to be a main reason for aging (Broer & others, 2013; Shay, 2018). A recent study focused on family members who were serving as caregivers of loved ones with dementia. Caregivers were randomly assigned to an aerobic exercise group or to a control group (who received no treatment). The results? Along with lowering BMI and stress and increasing fitness, aerobic exercise led to longer telomeres in the experimental group, compared with controls (Puterman & others, 2018).

Health experts recommend that adults engage in at least 30 minutes of moderate physical activity on most, or preferably all, days of the week and that children exercise for 60 minutes. Most advise that you should try to raise your heart rate to at least 60 percent of your maximum rate. However, only about one-fifth of adults attain these recommended levels of physical activity. Figure 7 lists examples of the physical activities that qualify as moderate (and, for comparison, vigorous) activities. Both moderate and intense activities may produce important physical and psychological gains, but intense activity has more widespread benefits. Take a look at Figure 7 and see how a person might transform moderate activity (such as walking briskly) into a vigorous activity (such as walking briskly uphill or while carrying a load).

A major obstacle to promoting exercise in the United States is that many U.S. cities are not designed in ways that promote walking or cycling. Advocates for change say that by making life too easy and far too accommodating to cars and drivers, urban designers have created an *obesogenic* (obesity-promoting) environment—a context where it is challenging for people to engage in healthy activities. Countries such as the Netherlands and Denmark have adopted urban planning strategies that promote walking and biking and discourage car use. In the Netherlands, 60 percent of all journeys taken by people over age 60 are by bicycle (Henderson, 2008).

| Moderate | Vigorous |
| --- | --- |
| Walking briskly (3–4 mph) | Walking briskly uphill or with a load |
| Swimming, moderate effort | Swimming, fast treading crawl |
| Cycling for pleasure or transportation (≤10 mph) | Cycling, fast or racing (>10 mph) |
| Racket sports, table tennis | Racket sports, singles tennis, racquetball |
| Conditioning exercise, general calisthenics | Conditioning exercise, stair ergometer, ski machine |
| Golf, pulling cart or carrying clubs | Golf, practice at driving range |
| Canoeing, leisurely (2.0–3.9 mph) | Canoeing, rapidly (≥4 mph) |
| Home care, general cleaning | Moving furniture |
| Mowing lawn, power mower | Mowing lawn, hand mower |
| Home repair, painting | Fix-up projects |

**FIGURE 7 Moderate and Vigorous Physical Activities** At a minimum, adults should strive for 30 minutes of moderate activity each day. That activity can become even more beneficial if we "pump it up" to vigorous. (first photo) ©Reed Kaestner/Corbis/Getty Images; (second photo) ©LWA/Sharie Kennedy/Blend Images

Environmental contexts that invite physical activity increase activity levels. For example, one quasi-experimental study examined the effects on activity of changes to the physical environment. The study focused on an urban neighborhood in which a greenway (a biking and walking trail) was retrofitted to connect with pedestrian sidewalks. Researchers counted the number of people outside engaging in physical activity in that neighborhood for a two-hour period at various times over two years. Compared to two other similar neighborhoods, the neighborhood with the trail featured more people being active, walking, and biking (Fitzhugh, Bassett, & Evans, 2010). Environmental features that encourage physical activity are also associated with health and wellness. In one study, elderly people who lived near parks, tree-lined streets, and areas for taking walks showed higher longevity over a five-year study period (Takano, Nakamura, & Watanabe, 2002).

One hint for becoming more physically active is not to limit yourself to only a few options. There are many activities that require physical exertion. Choose one that you genuinely like. Important factors in sticking to an exercise plan include self-efficacy, making active choices, and experiencing positive reinforcement and social support (Newsom & others, 2018). Finding a buddy who is interested in working out with you might be a powerful motivator.

## Eating Right

As described in "Motivation and Emotion", obesity and overweight are serious public health concerns not only in the United States but throughout the world. In recent years, the percentage of individuals who are overweight or obese has been increasing at an alarming rate. As Figure 8 indicates, the prevalence of being overweight or obese in the United States changed little from 1960 to 1980; after 1980 the rate began a gradual rise. However, from 2009 onward the percentage of U.S. adults who were overweight or obese soared. In 2016, over 70 percent of U.S. adults qualified as overweight and nearly 40 percent as obese (CDC, 2018a).

Exercising regularly is one great way to lose weight, and making healthy dietary choices is another. Eating right means eating sensible, nutritious foods. Despite the growing variety of choices Americans can make in the grocery store, many of us are unhealthy eaters. We take in too much sugar and not enough foods high in vitamins, minerals, and fiber, such as fruits, vegetables, and grains. We eat too much fast food and too few well-balanced meals—choices that increase our fat and cholesterol intake, both of which are implicated in long-term health problems.

Healthy eating does not mean trying out every fad diet that comes along but rather incorporating tasty, healthful foods into meals and snacks. Healthy eating is not something that people should do just to lose weight: It is about establishing and maintaining lifelong healthy food habits. Several health goals can be accomplished through a sound nutritional

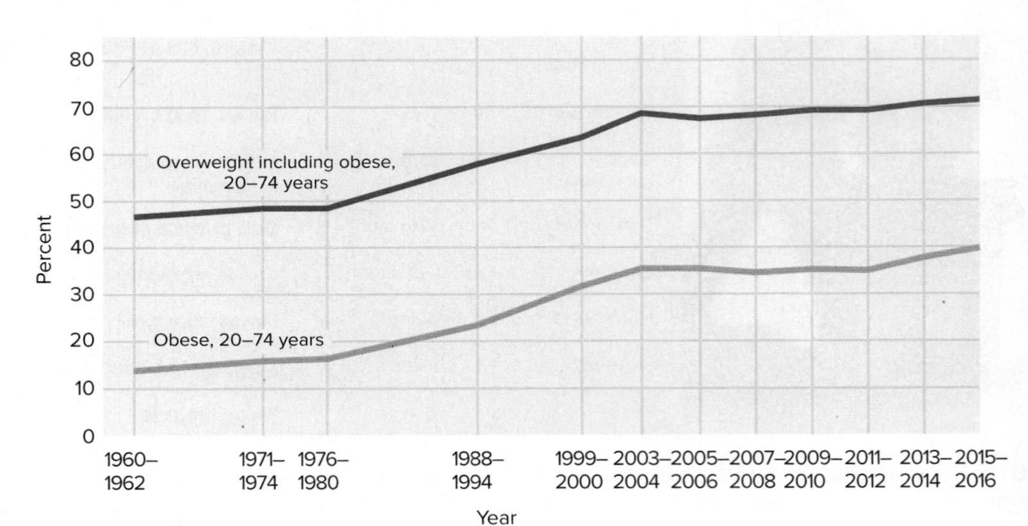


**FIGURE 8 Changes in the Percentage of U.S. Adults 20 to 74 Years of Age Classified as Overweight or Obese, 1960–2012** Being overweight or obese poses the greatest overall health risk for Americans today. In this graph, the vertical axis (or Y axis) shows the percentage of people considered overweight or obese, and the horizontal axis (or X axis) shows the years for these values. Source: Centers for Disease Control and Prevention (CDC) (2018a).

plan. Not only does a well-balanced diet provide more energy, but it also can lower blood pressure and lessen the risk for cancer and tooth decay (Fahey, Insel, & Roth, 2016).

Losing weight and opting for healthier foods can be difficult, especially when one is just starting out. Many weight-loss fads promise weight loss with no effort, no hunger, and no real change in one's food consumption. These promises are unrealistic. Making genuine, enduring changes in eating behavior is hard work. This reality does not mean adopting a pessimistic attitude. Rather, positive expectations and self-efficacy are essential because the task at hand is challenging.

The National Weight Control Registry is an ongoing study of people who have lost at least 40 pounds and kept it off for at least two years. Research on these successful dieters gives us important tips on how people who keep the weight off achieve this goal (L. G. Ogden & others, 2012). Another study of approximately 2,000 U.S. adults found that exercising 30 minutes a day, planning meals, and weighing themselves daily were the main strategies of successful dieters (Kruger, Blanck, & Gillespie, 2006) (Figure 9).

The truth is that keeping weight off is an ongoing process. The goal is difficult, but accomplishing it is a testament to the power of belief in oneself.

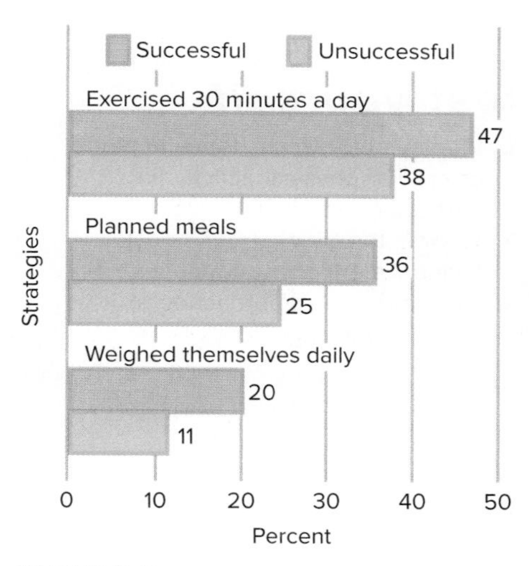


**FIGURE 9 Comparison of Strategies in Successful and Unsuccessful Dieters** Losing weight—and keeping it off—can be challenging, but reaching these goals is not impossible. Success in dieting depends on engaging in physical activity, planning meals, and monitoring progress. Source: Kruger, Blanck, & Gillespie (2006).

## Quitting Smoking

Another health-related goal is giving up smoking. Smoking harms nearly every bodily organ and system, and it is the leading preventable cause of death in the United States (CDC, 2018b). Smoking is associated with all causes of mortality for both men and women. Fewer people smoke today than in the past, and almost half of the living adults who ever smoked have quit. Still, in 2016, nearly 16 percent of American adults still smoked (CDC, 2018b). Children of smokers are at higher risk for respiratory and middle-ear diseases (CDC, 2017).

Quitting smoking has enormous health benefits. Figure 10 shows that when individuals quit smoking, their risk of fatal lung cancer declines over time.

It is difficult to imagine that there is a person living today who is not aware that smoking causes cancer, and there is little doubt that most smokers would like to quit. However, their addiction to nicotine makes quitting a challenge. Nicotine, the active drug in cigarettes, is a stimulant that increases the smoker's energy and alertness, a pleasurable and reinforcing experience. In addition, nicotine stimulates neurotransmitters that have a calming or pain-reducing effect (Johnstone & others, 2006; Plaza-Zabala & others, 2010).

Research confirms that giving up smoking can be difficult, especially in the early days of quitting. There are various ways to quit smoking. Common methods include:

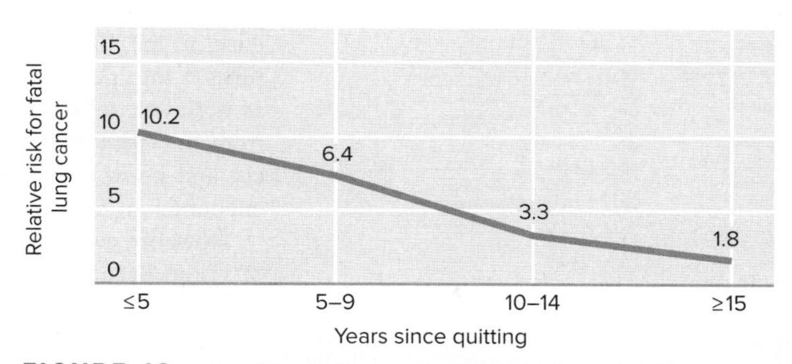


**FIGURE 10 Fatal Lung Cancer and Years Since Quitting Smoking** One study compared more than 43,000 former male smokers with almost 60,000 men who had never smoked (Enstrom, 1999). For comparison purposes, a zero (0) level was assigned as the risk for fatal lung cancer for men who had never smoked. Over time, the relative risk for smokers who had quit declined, but even after 15 years it was still above that of nonsmokers. Source: Enstrom (1999).

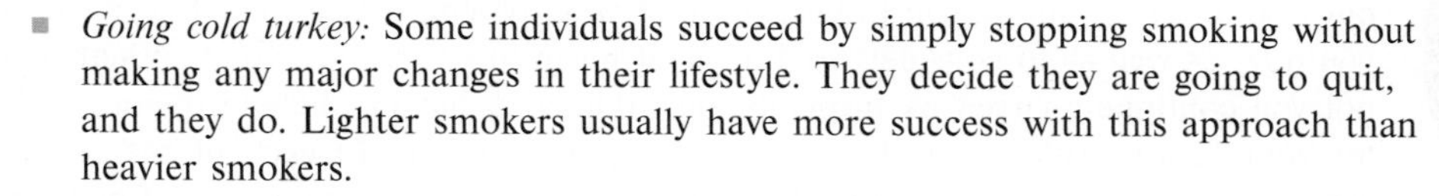

- *Going cold turkey:* Some individuals succeed by simply stopping smoking without making any major changes in their lifestyle. They decide they are going to quit, and they do. Lighter smokers usually have more success with this approach than heavier smokers.
- *Using a substitute source of nicotine:* Nicotine gum, the nicotine patch, the nicotine inhaler, and nicotine spray work on the principle of supplying small amounts of nicotine to diminish the intensity of withdrawal.
- *Seeking therapeutic help:* Some smokers get professional help to kick the habit. Interventions may include psychotherapy and medications, often in combination with each other.

No single method is foolproof for quitting smoking. Often a combination of these approaches is the best strategy. Furthermore, quitting for good typically requires more than one try, as the stages of change model would suggest.

©Image Source/Getty Images

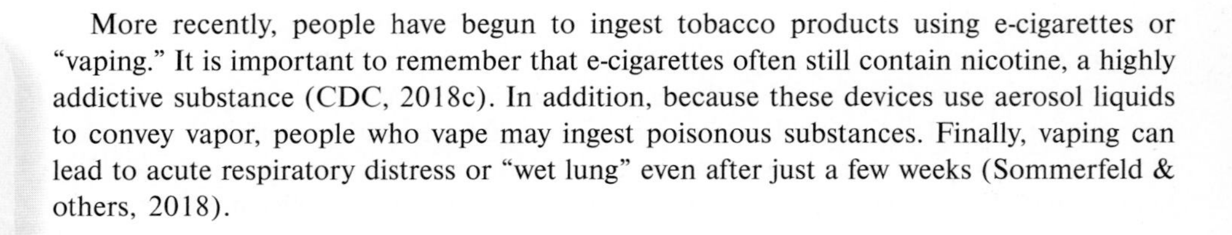

More recently, people have begun to ingest tobacco products using e-cigarettes or "vaping." It is important to remember that e-cigarettes often still contain nicotine, a highly addictive substance (CDC, 2018c). In addition, because these devices use aerosol liquids to convey vapor, people who vape may ingest poisonous substances. Finally, vaping can lead to acute respiratory distress or "wet lung" even after just a few weeks (Sommerfeld & others, 2018).

### test yourself

1. Identify and discuss three benefits of regular physical activity (in particular, exercise).
2. What is the biggest health risk facing Americans today?
3. Describe three approaches to quitting smoking.

# 6. PSYCHOLOGY AND YOUR GOOD LIFE

In this chapter, we have examined how the mental and physical aspects of your existence intertwine and influence each other in dynamic ways. The field of health psychology serves to illustrate how all of the various areas of psychology converge to reveal that interplay.

As a human being, you are both a physical entity and a system of mental processes that are themselves reflected in that most complex physical organ: the human brain. At every moment, both body and mind are present and affecting each other. Caring for your brain and mind—the resources that make it possible for you to read this book, study for tests, listen to lectures, fall in love, share with friends, help others, and make a difference in the world—is worthy of being a life mission.

Many pages ago, we defined psychology as the scientific study of behavior and mental processes, broadly meaning the things we do, think, and feel. Reflect for a moment on the psychological dimensions of vision. In the chapter "Sensation and Perception" we examined the processes by which those amazing sense organs, our eyes, detect color, light, dark, shape, and depth. We probed the ways that the brain takes that information and turns it into perception—how a pattern of colors, shapes, and light comes to be perceived as a flower, a fall day, a sunset. Visual systems, we discovered, are generally the same from one person to the next. Thus, you can memorize the different parts of the human eye and know that your understanding is true for just about all the human eyes you will encounter in life.

However, even something as deceptively simple as perceiving a sunset through the sense of vision becomes amazingly complex when we put it in the context of a human life. Is that sunset the first you see while on your honeymoon, or right after a painful romantic breakup, or on the eve of the first day of your life as a new parent? Placing even the most ordinary moment in the framework of a human life renders it remarkably complex and undeniably fascinating.

*An experience as deceptively simple as perceiving a sunset becomes stunningly complex in the context of a human life.*

©Aleksander Rubtsov/Cultura/Getty Images

This fascination is one of the primary motivations for the science of psychology itself. Individuals have always pondered the mysteries of human behavior, thought, and emotion. Why do we do the things we do? How do we think and feel? In this book, we have explored the broad range of topics that have interested psychologists throughout the history of this young science.

Coming to the close of this introduction to psychology allows you to look back but also ahead. It allows you to take stock of what psychology has come to mean to you now, as well as to consider what it might mean to you in the future. Whether or not you continue coursework in psychology, this book has highlighted opportunities for your future exploration about yourself and your world. In each of the real-life examples of human experience we have considered in the text—moments of heroism, weakness, joy, pain, and more—psychology has had a lesson to share with respect to the person that is *you*. Making the most of what you have learned about psychology means making the most of yourself and your life.

SUMMARY

## 1. HEALTH PSYCHOLOGY AND BEHAVIORAL MEDICINE

Health psychology is a multidimensional field that emphasizes biological, psychological, and social factors in human health. Closely aligned with health psychology is behavioral medicine, which combines medical and behavioral knowledge to reduce illness and promote health. Related fields are health promotion, which is concerned with identifying ways to foster healthy behaviors, and public health, which focuses on understanding disease at the population level and directing public policy.

Health psychology and behavioral medicine demonstrate the biopsychosocial model by examining the interaction of biological, psychological, and social variables as they relate to health and illness. Stress is an example of a biological, psychological, and social construct.

Health psychology and behavioral medicine bring the relationship of the mind and body to the forefront. These approaches examine the reciprocal relationships between the mind and body: how the body is influenced by psychological states and how mental life is influenced by physical health.

## 2. MAKING POSITIVE LIFE CHANGES

The theory of reasoned action suggests that we can make changes by devising specific intentions for behavioral change. We are more likely to follow through on our intentions if we feel good about the change and if we feel that others around us also support the change. The theory of planned behavior incorporates these factors as well as our perceptions of control over the behavior.

The stages of change model posits that personal change occurs in a series of five steps: precontemplation, contemplation, preparation/determination, action/willpower, and maintenance. Each stage has its own challenges. Relapse is a natural part of the journey toward change.

## 3. RESOURCES FOR EFFECTIVE LIFE CHANGE

Motivation is an important part of sustaining behavioral change. Change is more effective when the person does it for intrinsic reasons (because he or she really wants to) rather than extrinsic reasons (to gain rewards). Implementation intentions are the specific ways individuals plan to institute changes successfully.

Social relationships are strongly related to health and survival. Social support refers to the aid provided by others to a person in need. Support can take the form of tangible assistance, information, or emotional support. Social support has been found to have strong relations to functioning and coping with stress.

Religious faith is associated with enhanced health. One reason for this association is that religions often frown on excess and promote healthy behavior. Religious participation also allows individuals to benefit from a social group. Finally, religion provides a meaning system on which to rely in times of difficulty.

## 4. TOWARD A HEALTHIER MIND (AND BODY): CONTROLLING STRESS

Stress is the response of individuals when life circumstances threaten them and tax their ability to cope. Selye characterized the stress response with his concept of a general adaptation syndrome (GAS), which has three stages: alarm, resistance, and exhaustion.

The hypothalamic-pituitary-adrenal axis (HPA axis) comprises the interactions among the hypothalamus, pituitary gland, and adrenal glands. This axis plays an important role in human responses to stress. Chronic stress takes a toll on the body's natural disease-fighting abilities. Stress is also related to cardiovascular disease and cancer.

Kicking the stress habit means remembering that stress is a product of how we think about life events. Coping may be divided into the categories of problem-focused coping and emotion-focused coping. Overall, problem-focused coping is more adaptive than emotion-focused coping. Hardiness and optimism are associated with thriving during stressful times.

## 5. TOWARD A HEALTHIER BODY (AND MIND): BEHAVING AS IF YOUR LIFE DEPENDS UPON IT

Exercise has many positive psychological and physical benefits. Tips for increasing one's activity level include starting small by making changes in one's routine to incorporate physical activity (such as walking instead of driving to school); trying a variety of activities to find something one likes; finding an exercise partner; and swapping exercise for sedentary activities such as TV viewing. Keeping track of progress helps the individual to monitor his or her goal progress.

Overweight and obesity pose the greatest health risks to Americans today. They can be largely avoided by eating right, which means selecting nutritious foods and maintaining healthy eating habits for a lifetime, not just while on a diet. A combination of healthy eating and exercise is the best way to achieve weight loss.

Despite widespread knowledge that smoking causes cancer, some people still smoke. Methods of quitting include going cold turkey, using a substitute source of nicotine, and seeking therapy. Although difficult at first, quitting smoking can be achieved, though quitting for good usually takes more than one try. Usually a combination of methods is the best strategy for quitting.

## 6. PSYCHOLOGY AND YOUR GOOD LIFE

More than any other science, psychology is about you—understanding how you work. This book has aimed to show the relevance of psychology to your health and wellness and to help you appreciate the many, and deep, connections between this comparatively new science and your everyday life.

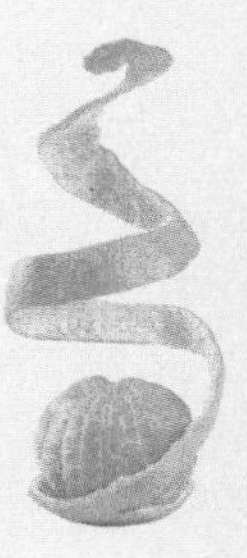

## key *terms*

aerobic exercise
behavioral medicine
emotion-focused coping
exercise
general adaptation syndrome (GAS)
hardiness
health behaviors
health psychology
hypothalamic-pituitary-adrenal axis (HPA axis)
implementation intentions
problem-focused coping
psychoneuroimmunology
relapse
social support
stages of change model
stress management program
theory of planned behavior
theory of reasoned action

## apply your *knowledge*

1. Take one day and become a stress detective. Every time a friend mentions how stressed out he or she is feeling, ask your friend to describe the source of the stress. What is the stressful event? How is the person appraising the event? How might he or she appraise the situation in ways that would help decrease stress?
2. Interview someone you know who has successfully lost weight, quit smoking, or started an exercise program. Ask the person about his or her experience of each of the stages of change. Does the theory fit your friend's experience? Why or why not?
3. Select one bad habit you would like to break for one week—for example, smoking, eating sugary foods, or putting off getting aerobic exercise. Keep a journal of your progress each day in avoiding the bad habit. How easy or difficult did you find this little test in healthy life change?
4. Search the web on the topic of stress management or coping with stress. Visit three or four sites and critically evaluate the suggestions made on the sites. How are they similar to the suggestions given in the text? How much information is available to evaluate the claims on the sites? Based on your critical evaluation, is the advice something you would follow or not? Explain.
5. One method that has helped to decrease unhealthy behaviors, such as smoking, is to make them more expensive. Some local governments have suggested imposing taxes on unhealthy foods, such as sugary soft drinks. Would such a tax be useful? Would you be in favor of such a tax, or opposed? Why?
6. Turn to the Table of Contents of this book. Consider which chapters or topics you found most interesting as you explored psychology. Go to your school's library and locate the journals that are devoted to that area (you can ask a librarian for help). Browse a recent issue of one of the journals. What kinds of topics are scientists studying? If a particular study described in this book sounded interesting, you can probably obtain it online. Search for the authors and take a look at the original article. What did the authors conclude? What did you learn?

**Design elements:** Preview icon: ©Jiang Hongyan; Intersection box icon: ©D. Hurst/Alamy, ©Creative Crop/Getty Images, ©Dimitris66/Getty Images, ©Savany/Getty Images; Critical Controversy box icon: ©Ultrashock; running heads icon: ©Cre8tive Studios/Alamy; Summary icon: ©Vadarshop

# GLOSSARY

**360-degree feedback** A method of performance appraisal whereby an employee's performance is rated by a variety of individuals, including himself or herself, a peer, a supervisor, a subordinate, and perhaps a customer or client.

## A

**abnormal behavior** Behavior that is deviant, maladaptive, or personally distressful over a relatively long period of time.

**absolute threshold** The minimum amount of stimulus energy that a person can detect.

**accommodation** An individual's adjustment of his or her schemas to include new information.

**acquired immune deficiency syndrome (AIDS)** A sexually transmitted infection, caused by the human immunodeficiency virus (HIV), which destroys the body's immune system.

**acquisition** The initial learning of the connection between the unconditioned stimulus and the conditioned stimulus when these two stimuli are paired.

**action potential** The brief wave of positive electrical charge that sweeps down the axon.

**activation-synthesis theory of dreaming** Theory that dreaming occurs when the cerebral cortex synthesizes neural signals generated from activity in the lower part of the brain and that dreams result from the brain's attempts to find logic in random brain activity that occurs during sleep.

**addiction** Either a physical or a psychological dependence, or both, on a drug.

**adrenal glands** Glands at the top of each kidney that are responsible for regulating mood, energy level, and the ability to cope with stress.

**aerobic exercise** Sustained activity–jogging, swimming, or cycling, for example–that stimulates heart and lung functioning.

**affectionate love or companionate love** Love that occurs when individuals desire to have another person near and have a deep, caring affection for the person.

**affective commitment** A kind of job commitment deriving from the employee's emotional attachment to the workplace.

**afferent nerves or sensory nerves** Nerves that carry information about the external environment *to* the brain and spinal cord via sensory receptors.

**aggression** Behavior that is intended to harm another person.

**alcoholism** A disorder that involves long-term, repeated, uncontrolled, compulsive, and excessive use of alcoholic beverages and is associated with impairment of the drinker's health and social relationships.

**algorithms** Strategies–including formulas, instructions, and the testing of all possible solutions–that guarantee a solution to a problem.

**all-or-nothing principle** The principle that once the electrical impulse reaches a certain level of intensity (its threshold), it fires and moves all the way down the axon without losing any intensity.

**altruism** Unselfish interest in helping another person.

**amnesia** The loss of memory.

**amygdala** An almond-shaped structure within the base of the temporal lobe that is involved in the discrimination of objects that are necessary for the organism's survival, such as appropriate food, mates, and social rivals. There is one amygdala in each hemisphere of the brain.

**androgens** The class of sex hormones that predominate in males, produced by the testes in males and by the adrenal glands in both males and females.

**androgynous** Having attributes that are typically associated with both genders.

**anorexia nervosa** An eating disorder that involves the relentless pursuit of thinness through starvation.

**anterograde amnesia** A memory disorder that affects the retention of new information and events.

**antianxiety drugs** Drugs that reduce anxiety by making the individual calmer and less excitable; commonly known as tranquilizers.

**antidepressant drugs** Drugs that regulate mood.

**antipsychotic drugs** Powerful drugs that diminish agitated behavior, reduce tension, decrease hallucinations, improve social behavior, and produce better sleep patterns in individuals with a severe psychological disorder, especially schizophrenia.

**antisocial personality disorder (ASPD)** Psychological disorder characterized by guiltlessness, law-breaking, exploitation of others, irresponsibility, and deceit.

**anxiety disorders** Disabling (uncontrollable and disruptive) psychological disorders that feature motor tension, hyperactivity, and apprehensive expectations and thoughts.

**apparent movement** The perception that a stationary object is moving.

**applied behavior analysis or behavior modification** The use of operant conditioning principles to change human behavior.

**archetypes** Jung's term for emotionally laden ideas and images in the collective unconscious that have rich and symbolic meaning for all people.

**artificial intelligence (AI)** A scientific field that focuses on creating machines capable of performing activities that require intelligence when they are done by people.

**asexual** A person who experiences a lack of sexual attraction to others or has no sexual orientation.

**assimilation** An individual's incorporation of new information into existing knowledge.

**association cortex or association area** The region of the cerebral cortex that is the site of the highest intellectual functions, such as thinking and problem solving.

**associative learning** Learning that occurs when an organism makes a connection, or an association, between two events.

**Atkinson–Shiffrin theory** Theory stating that memory storage involves three separate systems: sensory memory, short-term memory, and long-term memory.

**attention-deficit/hyperactivity disorder (ADHD)** A common psychological disorder in which the individual exhibits one or more of the following: inattention, hyperactivity, and impulsivity.

**attention** The process of focusing awareness on a narrow aspect of the environment.

**attitudes** An individual's opinions and beliefs about people, objects, and ideas–how the person feels about the world.

**attribution theory** The view that people are motivated to discover the underlying causes of behavior as part of their effort to make sense of the behavior.

**auditory nerve** The nerve structure that receives information about sound from the hair cells of the inner ear and carries these neural impulses to the brain's auditory areas.

**authoritarian parenting** A restrictive, punitive style in which the parent exhorts the child to follow the parent's directions.

**authoritative parenting** A parenting style that encourages the child to be independent but still places limits and controls on behavior.

**autism spectrum disorder** A neurodevelopmental disorder involving persistent deficits in social communication and social interaction across a variety of settings as well as restrictive repetitive behaviors, interests, and activities.

**autobiographical memory** A special form of episodic memory, consisting of a person's recollections of his or her life experiences.

**automatic processes** States of consciousness that require little attention and do not interfere with other ongoing activities.

**autonomic nervous system** The body system that takes messages to and from the body's internal organs, monitoring such processes as breathing, heart rate, and digestion.

**availability heuristic** A prediction about the probability of an event based on the ease of recalling or imagining similar events.

**aversive conditioning** A form of treatment that consists of repeated pairings of a stimulus with a very unpleasant stimulus.

**avoidance learning** An organism's learning that it can altogether avoid a negative stimulus by making a particular response.

**axon** The part of the neuron that carries information away from the cell body toward other cells.

## B

**barbiturates** Depressant drugs, such as Nembutal and Seconal, that decrease central nervous system activity.

**basal ganglia** Large neuron clusters located above the thalamus and under the cerebral cortex that work with the cerebellum and the cerebral cortex to control and coordinate voluntary movements.

**base rate neglect** The tendency to ignore information about general principles in favor of very specific and vivid information.

**behavioral approach** An approach to psychology focusing on the scientific study of observable behavioral responses and their environmental determinants.

**behavioral genetics** The study of the inherited underpinnings of behavioral characteristics.

**behavioral medicine** An interdisciplinary field that focuses on developing and integrating behavioral and biomedical knowledge to promote health and reduce illness; overlaps with health psychology.

**behavior** Everything we do that can be directly observed.

**behaviorism** A theory of learning that focuses solely on observable behaviors, discounting the importance of mental activity such as thinking, wishing, and hoping.

**behavior therapies** Treatments, based on the behavioral and social cognitive theories of learning, that use principles of learning to reduce or eliminate maladaptive behavior.

**big five factors of personality** The five broad traits that are thought to describe the main dimensions of personality: neuroticism (emotional instability), extraversion, openness to experience, agreeableness, and conscientiousness.

**binding** In the sense of vision, the bringing together and integration of what is processed by different neural pathways or cells.

**binge eating disorder (BED)** An eating disorder characterized by recurrent episodes of eating more food in a short period of time than most people would eat and during which the person feels a lack of control over eating.

**binocular cues** Depth cues that depend on the combination of the images in the left and right eye and on the way the two eyes work together.

**biological approach** An approach to psychology focusing on the body, especially the brain and nervous system.

**biological rhythms** Periodic physiological fluctuations in the body, such as the rise and fall of hormones and accelerated and decelerated cycles of brain activity, that can influence behavior.

**biological therapies or biomedical therapies** Treatments that reduce or eliminate the symptoms of psychological disorders by altering aspects of bodily functioning.

**bipolar disorder** Psychological disorder characterized by extreme mood swings that include one or more episodes of mania—an overexcited, unrealistically optimistic state.

**bisexual** Referring to a sexual orientation in which the individual is sexually attracted to people of both sexes.

**borderline personality disorder (BPD)** Psychological disorder characterized by a pervasive pattern of instability in interpersonal relationships, self-image, and emotions and by marked impulsivity beginning by early adulthood and present in a variety of contexts.

**bottom-up processing** The operation in sensation and perception in which sensory receptors register information about the external environment and send it up to the brain for interpretation.

**brain stem** The stemlike brain area that includes much of the hindbrain (excluding the cerebellum) and the midbrain; it connects with the spinal cord at its lower end and then extends upward to encase the reticular formation in the midbrain.

**broaden-and-build model** Fredrickson's model of positive emotion, stating that the function of positive emotions lies in their effects on an individual's attention and ability to build resources.

**bulimia nervosa** An eating disorder in which the individual (typically female) consistently follows a binge-and-purge eating pattern.

**burnout** A distressed psychological state in which a person experiences emotional exhaustion and little motivation for work.

**bystander effect** The tendency of an individual who observes an emergency to help less when other people are present than when the observer is alone.

## C

**Cannon–Bard theory** The proposition that emotion and physiological reactions occur simultaneously.

**case study or case history** An in-depth look at a single individual.

**catatonia** State of immobility and unresponsiveness lasting for long periods of time.

**cell body** The part of the neuron that contains the nucleus, which directs the manufacture of substances that the neuron needs for growth and maintenance.

**central nervous system (CNS)** The brain and spinal cord.

**cerebral cortex** Part of the forebrain, the outer layer of the brain, responsible for the most complex mental functions, such as thinking and planning.

**chromosomes** In the human cell, threadlike structures that come in 23 pairs, one member of each pair originating from each parent, and that contain the remarkable substance DNA.

**circadian rhythms** Daily behavioral or physiological cycles that involve the sleep/wake cycle, body temperature, blood pressure, and blood sugar level.

**classical conditioning** Learning process in which a neutral stimulus becomes associated with an innately meaningful stimulus and acquires the capacity to elicit a similar response.

**client-centered therapy** A form of humanistic therapy, developed by Carl Rogers, in which the therapist provides a warm, supportive atmosphere to improve the client's self-concept and to encourage the client to gain insight into problems; also called Rogerian therapy or nondirective therapy.

**clinical psychology** The area of psychology that integrates science and theory to prevent and treat psychological disorders.

**cognition** The way in which information is processed and manipulated in remembering, thinking, and knowing.

**cognitive-behavior therapy** A therapy that combines cognitive therapy and behavior therapy with the goal of developing self-efficacy.

**cognitive affective processing systems (CAPS)** Mischel's theoretical model for describing how individuals' thoughts and emotions about themselves and the world affect their behavior and become linked in ways that matter to that behavior.

**cognitive appraisal** Interpreting the events and experiences in one's life as harmful and threatening, or as challenging, and determining whether one has the resources to cope effectively.

**cognitive approach** An approach to psychology focusing on the mental processes involved in knowing: how we direct our attention, perceive, remember, think, and solve problems.

**cognitive dissonance** An individual's psychological discomfort (dissonance) caused by having two inconsistent thoughts.

**cognitive reappraisal** Regulating one's feelings about an experience by reinterpreting that experience or thinking about it in a different way or from a different angle.

**cognitive theory of dreaming** Theory proposing that dreaming can be understood by applying the same cognitive concepts used to study the waking mind.

**cognitive therapies** Treatments emphasizing that cognitions (thoughts) are the main source of psychological problems and that attempt to change the individual's feelings and behaviors by changing cognitions.

**collective unconscious** Jung's term for the impersonal, deepest layer of the unconscious mind, shared by all human beings because of their common ancestral past.

**comorbidity** When two or more disorders are experienced at the same time.

**concepts** Mental categories that are used to group objects, events, and characteristics.

**concrete operational stage** Piaget's third stage of cognitive development, lasting from about 7 to 11 years of age, during which the individual uses operations and replaces intuitive reasoning with logical reasoning in concrete situations.

**conditioned response (CR)** The learned response to the conditioned stimulus that occurs after conditioned stimulus–unconditioned stimulus pairing.

**conditioned stimulus (CS)** A previously neutral stimulus that eventually elicits a conditioned response after being paired with the unconditioned stimulus.

**conditions of worth** The standards that the individual must live up to in order to receive positive regard from others.

**cones** The receptor cells in the retina that allow for color perception.

**confederate** A person who is given a role to play in an experiment so that the social context can be manipulated.

**confirmation bias** The tendency to search for and use information that supports one's ideas rather than refutes them.

**conformity** A change in a person's behavior to coincide more closely with a group standard.

**connectionism or parallel distributed processing (PDP)** The theory that memory is stored throughout the brain in connections among neurons, several of which may work together to process a single memory.

**consciousness** An individual's awareness of external events and internal sensations under a condition of arousal, including awareness of the self and thoughts about one's experiences.

**continuance commitment** A kind of job commitment deriving from the employee's perception that leaving the organization would be too costly, both economically and socially.

**control group** The participants in an experiment who are as much like the experimental group as possible and who are treated in every way like the experimental group except for a manipulated factor, the independent variable.

**controlled processes** The most alert states of human consciousness, during which individuals actively focus their efforts toward a goal.

**convergence** A binocular cue to depth and distance in which the muscle movements in an individual's two eyes provide information about how deep and/or far away something is.

**convergent thinking** Thinking that produces the single best solution to a problem.

**coping** Managing taxing circumstances, expending effort to solve life's problems, and seeking to master or reduce stress.

**corpus callosum** The large bundle of axons that connects the brain's two hemispheres, responsible for relaying information between the two sides.

**correlational research** Research that examines the relationship between variables in order to find out whether and how two variables change together.

**counterconditioning** A classical conditioning procedure for changing the relationship between a conditioned stimulus and its conditioned response.

**couples therapy** Group therapy with married or unmarried couples whose major problem lies within their relationship.

**creativity** The ability to think about something in novel and unusual ways and to devise unconventional solutions to problems.

**critical thinking** The process of reflecting deeply and actively, asking questions, and evaluating the evidence.

**cross-cultural competence** A therapist's assessment of his or her ability to manage cultural issues in therapy and the client's perception of those abilities.

**cross-sectional design** A type of correlational study in which variables are measured at a single point in time.

**culture-fair tests** Intelligence tests that are intended to be culturally unbiased.

# D

**decay theory** Theory stating that when an individual learns something new, a neurochemical memory trace forms but then disintegrates over time, suggesting that the passage of time always increases forgetting.

**decision making** The mental activity of evaluating alternatives and choosing among them.

**deductive reasoning** Reasoning from a general case that is known to be true to a specific instance.

**deep brain stimulation** A procedure for treatment-resistant depression that involves the implantation of electrodes in the brain that emit signals to alter the brain's electrical circuitry.

**defense mechanisms** The Freudian term for tactics the ego uses to reduce anxiety by unconsciously distorting reality.

**deindividuation** The reduction in personal identity and erosion of the sense of personal responsibility when one is part of a group.

**delusions** False, unusual, and sometimes magical beliefs that are not part of an individual's culture.

**demand characteristic** Any aspect of a study that communicates to the participants how the experimenter wants them to behave.

**dendrites** Treelike fibers projecting from a neuron, which receive information and orient it toward the neuron's cell body.

**deoxyribonucleic acid (DNA)** A complex molecule in the cell's chromosomes that carries genetic information.

**dependent variable** The outcome; the variable that may change in an experiment in response to changes in the independent variable.

**depressants** Psychoactive drugs that slow down mental and physical activity.

**depressive disorders** Psychological disorders in which the individual suffers from depression—an unrelenting lack of pleasure in life.

**depth perception** The ability to perceive objects three-dimensionally.

**descriptive research** Research that determines the basic dimensions of a phenomenon—defining what it is, how often it occurs, and so on.

**descriptive statistics** Mathematical procedures that are used to describe and summarize sets of data in a meaningful way.

**development** The pattern of continuity and change in human capabilities that occurs throughout life, involving both growth and decline.

**difference threshold** The degree of difference that must exist between two stimuli before the difference is detected.

**discrimination (in classical conditioning)** The process of learning to respond to certain stimuli and not others.

**discrimination (in operant conditioning)** Responding appropriately to stimuli that signal that a behavior will or will not be reinforced.

**discrimination** An unjustified negative or harmful action toward a member of a group simply because the person belongs to that group.

**disorders of sexual development (DSD)** Congenital conditions in which the development of chromosomal, gonadal, or anatomical sex is atypical; formerly called intersex conditions or hermaphroditism.

**display rules** Sociocultural standards that determine when, where, and how emotions should be expressed.

**dissociative amnesia** Dissociative disorder characterized by extreme memory loss that is caused by extensive psychological stress.

**dissociative disorders** Psychological disorders that involve a sudden loss of memory or change in identity due to the dissociation (separation) of the individual's conscious awareness from previous memories and thoughts.

**dissociative identity disorder (DID)** Dissociative disorder in which the individual has two or more distinct personalities or selves, each with its own memories, behaviors, and relationships; formerly called multiple personality disorder.

**divergent thinking** Thinking that produces many solutions to the same problem.

**divided attention** Concentrating on more than one activity at the same time.

**divided consciousness view of hypnosis** Hilgard's view that hypnosis involves a splitting of consciousness into two separate components: one that follows the hypnotist's commands and the other that acts as a "hidden observer."

**dominant-recessive genes principle** The principle that, if one gene of a pair is dominant and one is recessive, the dominant gene overrides the recessive gene. A recessive gene exerts its influence only if both genes of a pair are recessive.

**double-blind experiment** An experimental design in which neither the experimenter nor the participants are aware of which participants are in the experimental group and which are in the control group until the results are calculated.

**downsizing** A dramatic cutting of the workforce that has become a popular business strategy to enhance profitability.

**dream analysis** A psychoanalytic technique for interpreting a person's dreams.

**drive** An aroused state that occurs because of a physiological need.

***DSM-5*** The fifth edition of the *Diagnostic and Statistical Manual of Mental Disorders;* the major classification of psychological disorders in the United States.

## E

**efferent nerves or motor nerves** Nerves that carry information *out of* the brain and spinal cord to other areas of the body.

**egoism** Giving to another person to ensure reciprocity; to gain self-esteem; to present oneself as powerful, competent, or caring; or to avoid censure from oneself and others for failing to live up to society's expectations.

**ego** The Freudian structure of personality that deals with the demands of reality.

**elaboration likelihood model** Theory identifying two ways to persuade: a central route and a peripheral route.

**elaboration** The formation of a number of different connections around a stimulus at any given level of memory encoding.

**electroconvulsive therapy (ECT)** A treatment, sometimes used for depression, that sets off a seizure in the brain; also called shock therapy.

**emerging adulthood** The transitional period from adolescence to adulthood, spanning approximately 18 to 25 years of age.

**emotion-focused coping** The coping strategy that involves responding to the stress that one is feeling—trying to manage one's emotional reaction—rather than focusing on the problem itself.

**emotion** Feeling, or affect, that can involve physiological arousal (such as a fast heartbeat), conscious experience (thinking about being in love with someone), and behavioral expression (a smile or grimace).

**empathy** A feeling of oneness with the emotional state of another person.

**empirically keyed test** A type of self-report test that presents many questionnaire items to two groups that are known to be different in some central way.

**empirically supported treatment** An approach to treating psychological disorders that advocates making treatment decisions based on the body of research that has shown which type of therapy works best.

**empirical method** Gaining knowledge through the observation of events, the collection of data, and logical reasoning.

**encoding** The first step in memory; the process by which information gets into memory storage.

**endocrine system** The body system consisting of a set of glands that regulate the activities of certain organs by releasing their chemical products into the bloodstream.

**episodic memory** The retention of information about the where, when, and what of life's happenings—that is, how individuals remember life's episodes.

**ergonomics or human factors** A field that combines engineering and psychology to focus on understanding and enhancing the safety and efficiency of the human-machine interaction.

**estrogens** The class of sex hormones that predominate in females, produced mainly by the ovaries.

**ethnocentrism** The tendency to favor one's own ethnic group over other groups.

**evidence-based practice** Integration of the best available research with clinical expertise in the context of client characteristics, culture, and preferences.

**evolutionary approach** An approach to psychology focusing on evolutionary ideas such as adaptation, reproduction, and natural selection as the basis for explaining specific human behaviors.

**executive function** Higher-order, complex cognitive processes, including thinking, planning, and problem solving.

**exercise** Structured activities whose goal is to improve health.

**experiment** A carefully regulated procedure in which the researcher manipulates one or more variables believed to influence some other variable.

**experimental group** The participants in an experiment who receive the drug or other treatment under study; those who are exposed to the change that the independent variable represents.

**experimenter bias** The influence of the experimenter's expectations on the outcome of the research.

**explicit memory or declarative memory** The conscious recollection of information, such as specific facts or events and, at least in humans, information that can be verbally communicated.

**external validity** The degree to which an experimental design actually reflects the real-world issues it is supposed to address.

**extinction (in classical conditioning)** The weakening of the conditioned response when the unconditioned stimulus is absent.

**extinction (in operant conditioning)** Decreases in the frequency of a behavior when the behavior is no longer reinforced.

**extrinsic motivation** Motivation that involves external incentives such as rewards and punishments.

## F

**face validity** The extent to which a test item appears to fit the particular trait it is measuring.

**facial feedback hypothesis** The idea that facial expressions can influence emotions as well as reflect them.

**false consensus effect** A person's overestimation of the degree to which everybody else thinks or acts the way he or she does.

**family therapy** Group therapy with family members.

**feature detectors** Neurons in the brain's visual system that respond to particular features of a stimulus.

**fetish** An object or activity that arouses sexual interest and desire.

**figure-ground relationship** The principle by which we organize the perceptual field into stimuli that stand out (figure) and those that are left over (ground).

**fixation** Using a prior strategy and failing to look at a problem from a new perspective.

**flashbulb memory** The memory of emotionally significant events that people often recall with more accuracy and vivid imagery than everyday events.

**flat affect** The display of little or no emotion—a common negative symptom of schizophrenia.

**flow** The optimal experience of a match between one's skills and the challenge of a task.

**forebrain** The brain's largest division and its most forward part.

**formal operational stage** Piaget's fourth stage of cognitive development, which begins at 11 to 15 years of age and continues through the adult years; it features thinking about things that are not concrete, making predictions, and using logic to come up with hypotheses about the future.

**frequency theory** Theory regarding how the inner ear registers the frequency of sound, stating that the perception of a sound's frequency depends on how often the auditory nerve fires.

**frontal lobes** The portions of the cerebral cortex behind the forehead that are involved in personality, intelligence, and the control of voluntary muscles.

**functional fixedness** Failing to solve a problem as a result of fixation on a thing's usual functions.

**functionalism** James's approach to mental processes, emphasizing the functions and purposes of the mind and behavior in the individual's adaptation to the environment.

**fundamental attribution error** Observers' overestimation of the importance of internal traits and underestimation of the importance of external situations when they seek explanations of an actor's behavior.

## G

**gender** An individual's psychological experience of being male or female that is informed by social beliefs about the characteristics thought to indicate masculinity or femininity (such as how the person looks, talks, and behaves).

**gender identity** An individual's personal, multifaceted sense of being male, female, or an alternate gender.

**gender roles** Roles that reflect the individual's expectation for how a female person and how a male person should think, act, and feel.

**gender similarities hypothesis** Hyde's proposition that men and women (and boys and girls) are much more similar than they are different.

**gender stereotypes** Overly general beliefs and expectations about what women and men are like.

**general adaptation syndrome (GAS)** Selye's term for the common effects of stressful demands on the body, consisting of three stages: alarm, resistance, and exhaustion.

**generalization (in classical conditioning)** The tendency of a new stimulus that is similar to the original conditioned stimulus to elicit a response that is similar to the conditioned response.

**generalization (in operant conditioning)** Performing a reinforced behavior in a different situation.

**generalized anxiety disorder** An anxiety disorder marked by persistent anxiety for at least six months, and in which the individual is unable to specify the reasons for the anxiety.

**genes** The units of hereditary information, consisting of short segments of chromosomes composed of DNA.

**genotype** An individual's genetic heritage; one's actual genetic material.

**gestalt psychology** A school of thought interested in how people naturally organize their perceptions according to certain patterns.

**gifted** Possessing high intelligence (an IQ of 130 or higher) and/or superior talent in a particular area.

**glands** Organs or tissues in the body that create chemicals that control many bodily functions.

**glial cells or glia** The second of two types of cells in the nervous system; glial cells provide support, nutritional benefits, and other functions and keep neurons running smoothly.

**gonads** Glands that produce sex hormones and generate ova (eggs) in females and sperm in males; collectively called gametes, the ova and sperm are the cells that eventually will be used in reproduction.

**group polarization effect** The solidification and further strengthening of an individual's position as a consequence of a group discussion or interaction.

**group therapy** A sociocultural approach to the treatment of psychological disorders that brings together individuals who share a particular psychological disorder in sessions that are typically led by a mental health professional.

**groupthink** The impaired group decision making that occurs when making the right decision is less important than maintaining group harmony.

## H

**habituation** Decreased responsiveness to a stimulus after repeated presentations.

**hallucinations** Sensory experiences that occur in the absence of real stimuli.

**hallucinogens** Psychoactive drugs that modify a person's perceptual experiences and produce visual images that are not real.

**halo effect** A bias, common in performance appraisals, that occurs when a rater gives an employee the same rating on all of the items being evaluated, even though the individual varies across the dimensions being assessed.

**hardiness** A personality trait characterized by a sense of commitment rather than alienation and of control rather than powerlessness; a perception of problems as challenges rather than threats.

**Hawthorne effect** The tendency of individuals to perform better simply because of being singled out and made to feel important.

**health behaviors** Practices that have an impact on physical well-being, such as adopting a healthy approach to stress, exercising, eating right, brushing one's teeth, performing breast and testicular exams, not smoking, drinking in moderation (or not at all), and practicing safe sex.

**health psychology** A subfield of psychology that emphasizes psychology's role in establishing and maintaining health and preventing and treating illness.

**heritability** The proportion of observable differences in a group that can be explained by differences in the genes of the group's members.

**heterosexual** Referring to a sexual orientation in which the individual is generally sexually attracted to members of the opposite sex.

**heuristics** Shortcut strategies or guidelines that suggest a solution to a problem but do not guarantee an answer.

**hierarchy of needs** Maslow's theory that human needs must be satisfied in the following sequence: physiological needs, safety, love and belongingness, esteem, and self-actualization.

**hindbrain** Located at the skull's rear, the lowest portion of the brain, consisting of the medulla, cerebellum, and pons.

**hindsight bias** The tendency to report falsely, after the fact, that one has accurately predicted an outcome.

**hippocampus** The structure in the limbic system that has a special role in the storage of memories.

**homeostasis** The body's tendency to maintain an equilibrium, or a steady state or balance.

**homosexual** Referring to a sexual orientation in which the individual is generally sexually attracted to members of the same sex.

**hormones** Chemical messengers that are produced by the endocrine glands and carried by the bloodstream to all parts of the body.

**humanistic approach** An approach to psychology focusing on a person's positive qualities, the capacity for positive growth, and the freedom to choose one's destiny.

**humanistic perspectives** Theoretical views of personality that stress a person's capacity for personal growth and positive human qualities.

**humanistic therapies** Treatments, unique in their emphasis on clients' self-healing capacities, that encourage clients to understand themselves and to grow personally.

**human relations approach** A management approach emphasizing the psychological characteristics of workers and managers, stressing the importance of factors such as morale, attitudes, values, and humane treatment of workers.

**human sexual response pattern** Masters and Johnson's model of human sexual response, consisting of four phases—excitement, plateau, orgasm, and resolution.

**hypnosis** An altered state of consciousness or a psychological state of altered attention and expectation in which the individual is unusually receptive to suggestions.

**hypothalamic-pituitary-adrenal axis (HPA axis)** The complex set of interactions among the hypothalamus, the pituitary gland, and the adrenal glands that regulates various body processes and controls reactions to stressful events.

**hypothalamus** A small forebrain structure, located just below the thalamus, that monitors three pleasurable activities—eating, drinking, and sex—as well as emotion, stress, and reward.

**hypothesis** An educated guess that derives logically from a theory; a prediction that can be tested.

# I

**id** The Freudian structure of personality consisting of unconscious drives; the individual's reservoir of sexual energy.

**illusory correlation** A cognitive bias that occurs when two vivid events happen close in time and they are mistakenly perceived as linked, meaningfully.

**implementation intentions** Specific strategies for dealing with the challenges of making a life change.

**implicit memory or nondeclarative memory** Memory in which behavior is affected by prior experience without a conscious recollection of that experience.

**independent variable** A manipulated experimental factor; the variable that the experimenter changes to see what its effects are.

**individual psychology** Adler's view that people are motivated by purposes and goals and that perfection, not pleasure, is thus the key motivator in human life.

**inductive reasoning** Reasoning from specific observations to make generalizations.

**industrial and organizational (I-O) psychology** The field of psychology that applies the science of human behavior to work and the workplace.

**infant attachment** The close emotional bond between an infant and its caregiver.

**inferential statistics** Mathematical methods that are used to indicate whether the data sufficiently support a research hypothesis.

**informational social influence** The influence other people have on us because we want to be right.

**inner ear** The part of the ear that includes the oval window, cochlea, and basilar membrane and whose function is to convert sound waves into neural impulses and send them to the brain.

**insecure attachment** Infants do not use the caregiver as a secure base from which to explore; instead, they experience their relationship with the caregiver as unstable and unreliable. The two types of insecure attachment are avoidant and anxious/ambivalent (also called preoccupied).

**insight learning** A form of problem solving in which the organism develops a sudden insight into or understanding of a problem's solution.

**instinct** An innate (unlearned) biological pattern of behavior that is assumed to be universal throughout a species.

**instinctive drift** The tendency of animals to revert to instinctive behavior that interferes with learning.

**integrative therapy** Use of a combination of techniques from different therapies based on the therapist's judgment of which particular methods will provide the greatest benefit for the client.

**integrity test** A type of job-screening examination that is designed to assess whether a candidate will be honest on the job.

**intellectual disability or intellectual developmental disorder** A condition of limited mental ability that affects an individual's functioning in everyday life.

**intelligence** An all-purpose ability to do well on cognitive tasks, to solve problems, and to learn from experience.

**intelligence quotient (IQ)** An individual's mental age divided by chronological age, multiplied by 100.

**interference theory** The theory that people forget not because memories are lost from storage but because other information gets in the way of what they want to remember.

**internal validity** The degree to which changes in the dependent variable are due to the manipulation of the independent variable.

**intrinsic motivation** Motivation based on internal factors such as organismic needs (competence, relatedness, and autonomy), as well as curiosity, challenge, and fun.

**investment model** A model of long-term relationships that examines the ways that commitment, investment, and the availability of attractive alternative partners predict satisfaction and stability in relationships.

## J

**James–Lange theory** The theory that emotion results from physiological states triggered by stimuli in the environment.

**job analysis** The process of generating a description of what a job involves, including the knowledge and skills that are necessary to carry out the job's functions.

**job crafting** The physical and cognitive changes individuals can make within the constraints of a task to make the work "their own."

**job satisfaction** The extent to which a person is content in his or her job.

**job stress** The experience of stress on the job and in the workplace setting.

## K

**kinesthetic senses** Senses that provide information about movement, posture, and orientation.

**KSAOs or KSAs** Common elements in a person-oriented job analysis; an acronym for *k*nowledge, *s*kills, *a*bilities, and *o*ther characteristics.

## L

**language** A form of communication—whether spoken, written, or signed—that is based on a system of symbols.

**latent content** According to Freud, a dream's hidden content; its unconscious and true meaning.

**latent learning or implicit learning** Unreinforced learning that is not immediately reflected in behavior.

**law of effect** Thorndike's law stating that behaviors followed by positive outcomes are strengthened and that behaviors followed by negative outcomes are weakened.

**learned helplessness** An organism's learning through experience with negative stimuli that it has no control over negative outcomes.

**learning** A systematic, relatively permanent change in behavior that occurs through experience.

**leisure** The pleasant times before or after work when individuals are free to pursue activities and interests of their own choosing, such as hobbies, sports, and reading.

**levels of processing** A continuum of memory processing from shallow to intermediate to deep, with deeper processing producing better memory.

**limbic system** A loosely connected network of structures under the cerebral cortex, important in both memory and emotion. Its two principal structures are the amygdala and the hippocampus.

**lithium** The lightest of the solid elements in the periodic table of elements, widely used to treat bipolar disorder.

**long-term memory** A relatively permanent type of memory that stores huge amounts of information for a long time.

**longitudinal design** A special kind of systematic observation, used by correlational researchers, that involves obtaining measures of the variables of interest in multiple waves over time.

**loss aversion** The tendency to strongly prefer to avoid losses compared to acquiring gains.

## M

**major depressive disorder (MDD)** Psychological disorder involving a significant depressive episode and depressed characteristics, such as lethargy and hopelessness, for at least two weeks.

**manifest content** According to Freud, the surface content of a dream, containing dream symbols that disguise the dream's true meaning.

**mean** A measure of central tendency that is the average for a sample.

**median** A measure of central tendency that is the middle score in a sample.

**medical model** The view that psychological disorders are medical diseases with a biological origin.

**meditation** The attainment of a peaceful state of mind in which thoughts are not occupied by worry; the meditator is mindfully present to his or her thoughts and feelings but is not consumed by them.

**memory** The retention of information or experience over time as the result of three key processes: encoding, storage, and retrieval.

**mental age (MA)** An individual's level of mental development relative to that of others.

**mental processes** The thoughts, feelings, and motives that each of us experiences privately but that cannot be observed directly.

**mentoring** A relationship between an experienced employee—a mentor—and a novice, in which the more experienced employee serves as an advisor, a sounding board, and a source of support for the newer employee.

**mere exposure effect** The phenomenon that the more individuals encounter someone or something, the more probable it is that they will start liking the person or thing even if they do not realize they have seen it before.

**meta-analysis** A statistical procedure that summarizes a large body of evidence from the research literature on a particular topic, allowing the researcher to assess the strength of the relationship between the variables.

**midbrain** Located between the hindbrain and forebrain, an area in which many nerve-fiber systems ascend and descend to connect the higher and lower portions of the brain; in particular, the midbrain relays information between the brain and the eyes and ears.

**middle ear** The part of the ear that channels sound through the eardrum, hammer, anvil, and stirrup to the inner ear.

**mindfulness** The state of being alert and mentally present for one's everyday activities.

**Minnesota Multiphasic Personality Inventory (MMPI)** The most widely used and researched empirically keyed self-report personality test.

**mirror neurons** Nerve cells in the brain that are activated (in human and nonhuman primates) both when an action is performed and when the organism observes the action being performed by another.

**mode** A measure of central tendency that is the most common score in a sample.

**monocular cues** Powerful depth cues available from the image in one eye, either the right or the left.

**morphology** A language's rules for word formation.

**motivated forgetting** Forgetting that occurs when something is so painful or anxiety-laden that remembering it is intolerable.

**motivation** The force that moves people to behave, think, and feel the way they do.

**motor cortex** A region in the cerebral cortex that processes information about voluntary movement, located just behind the frontal lobes.

**movement disorders** The unusual mannerisms, body movements, and facial expressions that are characteristic positive symptoms of schizophrenia.

**myelin sheath** A layer of fat cells that encases and insulates most axons.

## N

**naturalistic observation** The observation of behavior in a real-world setting.

**natural selection** Darwin's principle of an evolutionary process in which organisms that are better adapted to their environment will survive and produce more offspring.

**nature** An individual's biological inheritance, especially his or her genes.

**need** A deprivation that energizes the drive to eliminate or reduce the deprivation.

**negative affect** Negative emotions such as anger, guilt, and sadness.

**negative punishment** The removal of a stimulus following a given behavior in order to decrease the frequency of that behavior.

**negative reinforcement** The removal of a stimulus following a given behavior in order to increase the frequency of that behavior.

**neglectful parenting** A parenting style characterized by a lack of parental involvement in the child's life.

**neocortex** The outermost part of the cerebral cortex, making up 80 percent of the cortex in the human brain.

**nervous system** The body's electrochemical communication circuitry.

**neural networks** Networks of nerve cells that integrate sensory input and motor output.

**neurodevelopmental disorders** A class of psychological disorders that typically appear in childhood and are traced to genetic differences, atypical brain development, or prenatal exposure to substances that adversely affect development.

**neurons** One of two types of cells in the nervous system; neurons are the type of nerve cell that handles the information-processing function.

**neuroscience** The scientific study of the structure, function, development, genetics, and biochemistry of the nervous system, emphasizing that the brain and nervous system are central to understanding behavior, thought, and emotion.

**neurotransmitters** Chemical substances that are stored in very tiny sacs within the terminal buttons and involved in transmitting information across a synaptic gap to the next neuron.

**noise** Irrelevant and competing stimuli—not only sounds but also any distracting stimuli for the senses.

**normal distribution** A symmetrical, bell-shaped curve, with a majority of the scores falling in the middle of the possible range and few scores appearing toward the extremes of the range.

**normative commitment** A kind of job commitment deriving from the employee's sense of obligation to the organization for the investment it has made in the individual's personal and professional development.

**normative social influence** The influence others have on us because we want them to like us.

**nurture** An individual's environmental and social experiences.

# O

**obedience** Behavior that complies with the explicit demands of the individual in authority.

**object permanence** Piaget's term for the crucial accomplishment of understanding that objects and events continue to exist even when they cannot directly be seen, heard, or touched.

**observational learning** Learning that involves observing and imitating another's behavior.

**obsessive-compulsive disorder (OCD)** Psychological disorder in which the individual has anxiety-provoking thoughts that will not go away and/or urges to perform repetitive, ritualistic behaviors to prevent or produce some future situation.

**occipital lobes** Structures located at the back of the head that respond to visual stimuli.

**Oedipus complex** According to Freud, a boy's intense desire to replace his father and enjoy the affections of his mother.

**olfactory epithelium** The lining of the roof of the nasal cavity, containing a sheet of receptor cells for smell.

**open-mindedness** The state of being receptive to other ways of looking at things.

**operant conditioning or instrumental conditioning** A form of associative learning in which the consequences of a behavior change the probability of the behavior's recurrence.

**operational definition** A definition that provides an objective description of how a variable is going to be measured and observed in a particular study.

**operations** Piaget's term for mental representations of changes in objects that can be reversed.

**opioids** A class of drugs that act on the brain's endorphin receptors. These include opium and its natural derivatives (sometimes called opiates) as well as chemicals that do not occur naturally but that have been created to mimic the activity of opium. These drugs (also called narcotics) depress activity in the central nervous system and eliminate pain.

**opponent-process theory** Theory stating that cells in the visual system respond to complementary pairs of red-green and blue-yellow colors; a given cell might be excited by red and inhibited by green, whereas another cell might be excited by yellow and inhibited by blue.

**optic nerve** The structure at the back of the eye, made up of axons of the ganglion cells, that carries visual information to the brain for further processing.

**organizational citizenship behavior (OCB)** Discretionary actions on the part of an employee that promote organizational effectiveness but are not included in the person's formal responsibilities.

**organizational culture** An organization's shared values, beliefs, norms, and customs.

**organizational identity** Employees' feelings of oneness with the organization and its goals.

**orientation** A program by which an organization introduces newly hired employees to the organization's goals, familiarizes them with its rules and regulations, and lets them know how to get things done.

**outer ear** The outermost part of the ear, consisting of the pinna and the external auditory canal.

**ovaries** Sex-related endocrine glands that produce hormones involved in female sexual development and reproduction.

**overlearning** Learning to perform a task so well that it becomes automatic.

**overt aggression** Physically or verbally harming another person directly.

# P

**pain** The sensation that warns an individual of damage to the body.

**pancreas** A dual-purpose gland under the stomach that performs both digestive and endocrine functions.

**panic disorder** An anxiety disorder in which the individual experiences recurrent, sudden onsets of intense terror, often without warning and with no specific cause.

**pansexual** A person whose sexual attractions do not depend on the biological sex, gender, or gender identity of others.

**papillae** Rounded bumps above the tongue's surface that contain the taste buds, the receptors for taste.

**parallel processing** The simultaneous distribution of information across different neural pathways.

**paraphilic disorders** Sexual disorders that feature recurrent sexually arousing fantasies, urges, or behaviors involving nonhuman objects; the suffering or humiliation of oneself or one's partner; or children or other nonconsenting individuals.

**parasympathetic nervous system** The part of the autonomic nervous system that calms the body.

**parietal lobes** Structures at the top and toward the rear of the head that are involved in registering spatial location, attention, and motor control.

**pedophilic disorder** A paraphilic disorder in which an adult or an older adolescent sexually fantasizes about or engages in sexual behavior with individuals who have not reached puberty.

**perception** The process of organizing and interpreting sensory information so that it makes sense.

**perceptual constancy** The recognition that objects are constant and unchanging even though sensory input about them is changing.

**perceptual set** A predisposition or readiness to perceive something in a particular way.

**performance appraisal** The evaluation of a person's success at meeting his or her organization's goals.

**peripheral nervous system (PNS)** The network of nerves that connects the brain and spinal cord to other parts of the body.

**permissive parenting** A parenting style characterized by the placement of few limits on the child's behavior.

**personality** A pattern of enduring, distinctive thoughts, emotions, and behaviors that characterize the way an individual adapts to the world.

**personality disorders** Chronic, maladaptive cognitive-behavioral patterns that are thoroughly integrated into an individual's personality.

**personological and life story perspectives** Theoretical views of personality stressing that the way to understand the person is to focus on the person's life history and life story.

**phenotype** An individual's observable characteristics.

**phonology** A language's sound system.

**physical dependence** The physiological need for a drug that causes unpleasant withdrawal symptoms such as physical pain and a craving for the drug when it is discontinued.

**pituitary gland** A pea-sized gland just beneath the hypothalamus that controls growth and regulates other glands.

**placebo effect** A phenomenon in which the expectation of the participants, rather than actual treatment, produces an outcome.

**placebo** In a drug study, a harmless substance that has no physiological effect, given to participants in a control group so that they are treated identically to the experimental group except for the active agent.

**place theory** Theory regarding how the inner ear registers the frequency of sound, stating that each frequency produces vibrations at a particular spot on the basilar membrane.

**plasticity** The brain's special physical capacity for change.

**polygraph** A machine, commonly called a lie detector, that monitors changes in the body, used to try to determine whether someone is lying.

**population** The entire group about which the investigator wants to draw conclusions.

**positive affect** Positive emotions such as joy, happiness, and interest.

**positive illusions** Favorable views of the self that are not necessarily rooted in reality.

**positive psychology** A branch of psychology that emphasizes human strengths.

**positive punishment** The presentation of a stimulus following a given behavior in order to decrease the frequency of that behavior.

**positive reinforcement** The presentation of a stimulus following a given behavior in order to increase the frequency of that behavior.

**post-traumatic stress disorder (PTSD)** Psychological disorder that develops through exposure to a traumatic event, a severely oppressive situation, physical or emotional abuse, or a natural or an unnatural disaster.

**pragmatics** The useful character of language and the ability of language to communicate even more meaning than is verbalized.

**prediction** A statement about the specific expectation for the outcome of a study.

**preferential looking** A research technique that involves giving an infant a choice of what object to look at.

**prejudice** An unjustified negative attitude toward an individual based on the individual's membership in a group.

**preoperational stage** Piaget's second stage of cognitive development, lasting from about 2 to 7 years of age, during which thought is more symbolic than sensorimotor thought.

**preparedness** The species-specific biological predisposition to learn in certain ways but not others.

**primary reinforcer** A reinforcer that is innately satisfying; a primary reinforcer does not require any learning on the organism's part to make it pleasurable.

**priming** The activation of information that people already have in storage to help them remember new information better and faster.

**proactive interference** Situation in which material that was learned earlier disrupts the recall of material that was learned later.

**problem-focused coping** The coping strategy of squarely facing one's troubles and trying to solve them.

**problem solving** The mental process of finding an appropriate way to attain a goal when the goal is not readily available.

**procedural memory** Memory for skills.

**projective test** A personality assessment test that presents individuals with an ambiguous stimulus and asks them to describe it or tell a story about it—to project their own meaning onto the stimulus.

**prosocial behavior** Behavior that is intended to benefit other people.

**prospective memory** Remembering information about doing something in the future; includes memory for intentions.

**prototype model** A model emphasizing that when people evaluate whether a given item reflects a certain concept, they compare the item with the most typical item(s) in that category and look for a "family resemblance" with that item's properties.

**psychoactive drugs** Drugs that act on the nervous system to alter consciousness, modify perception, and change mood.

**psychoanalysis** Freud's therapeutic technique for analyzing an individual's unconscious thoughts.

**psychodynamic approach** An approach to psychology focusing on unconscious thought, the conflict between biological drives (such as the drive for sex) and society's demands, and early childhood family experiences.

**psychodynamic perspectives** Theoretical views emphasizing that personality is primarily unconscious (beyond awareness).

**psychodynamic therapies** Treatments that stress the importance of the unconscious mind, extensive interpretation by the therapist, and the role of early childhood experiences in the development of an individual's problems.

**psychological dependence** The strong desire to repeat the use of a drug for emotional reasons, such as a feeling of well-being and reduction of stress.

**psychology** The scientific study of behavior and mental processes.

**psychoneuroimmunology** A new field of scientific inquiry that explores connections among psychological factors (such as attitudes and emotions), the nervous system, and the immune system.

**psychopathology** The scientific study of psychological disorders and the development of diagnostic categories and treatments for those disorders.

**psychosis** Psychological state in which a person's perceptions and thoughts are fundamentally removed from reality.

**psychosurgery** A biological therapy, with irreversible effects, that involves removal or destruction of brain tissue to improve the individual's adjustment.

**psychotherapy** A nonmedical process that helps individuals with psychological disorders recognize and overcome their problems.

**puberty** A period of rapid skeletal and sexual maturation that occurs mainly in early adolescence.

**punishment** A consequence that decreases the likelihood that a behavior will occur.

## R

**random assignment** The assignment of participants to experimental groups by chance, to reduce the likelihood that a study's results will be due to preexisting differences between groups.

**random sample** A sample that gives every member of the population an equal chance of being selected.

**range** A measure of dispersion that is the difference between the highest and lowest scores.

**reasoning** The mental activity of transforming information to reach conclusions.

**referential thinking** Ascribing personal meaning to completely random events.

**reflective speech** A technique in which the therapist mirrors the client's own feelings back to the client.

**reinforcement** The process by which a stimulus or event (a reinforcer) following a particular behavior increases the probability that the behavior will happen again.

**relapse** A return to former unhealthy patterns.

**relational aggression** Behavior that is meant to harm the social standing of another person.

**reliability** The extent to which a test yields a consistent, reproducible measure of performance.

**REM sleep** An active stage of sleep during which dreaming occurs.

**renewal** The recovery of the conditioned response when the organism is placed in a novel context.

**replication** Repeating a study in a new sample to see if results are the same as in previous work. A direct replication employs the very same methods as the original study. A conceptual replication employs different methods to test the same prediction.

**representativeness heuristic** The tendency to make judgments about group membership based on physical appearance or the match between a person and one's stereotype of a group rather than on available base rate information.

**research participant bias** In an experiment, the influence of participants' expectations, and of their thoughts on how they should behave, on their behavior.

**resilience** A person's ability to recover from or adapt to difficult times.

**resting potential** The stable, negative charge of an inactive neuron.

**reticular activating system** A network of structures including the brain stem, medulla, and thalamus that are involved in the experience of arousal and engagement with the environment.

**reticular formation** A system in the midbrain comprising a diffuse collection of neurons involved in stereotyped patterns of behavior such as walking, sleeping, and turning to attend to a sudden noise.

**retina** The multilayered, light-sensitive surface in the eye that records electromagnetic energy and converts it to neural impulses for processing in the brain.

**retrieval** The memory process that occurs when information that was retained in memory comes out of storage.

**retroactive interference** Situation in which material that was learned later disrupts the retrieval of information that was learned earlier.

**retrograde amnesia** Memory loss for a segment of the past but not for new events.

**retrospective memory** Remembering information from the past.

**risk factors** Characteristics, experiences, or exposures that increase the likelihood of a person developing a disorder.

**risky shift** The tendency for a group decision to be riskier than the average decision made by the individual group members.

**rods** The receptor cells in the retina that are sensitive to light but not very useful for color vision.

**role conflict** The kind of stress that arises when a person tries to meet the demands of more than one important life role, such as worker and mother.

**romantic love or passionate love** Love with strong components of sexuality and infatuation, often dominant in the early part of a love relationship.

**Rorschach inkblot test** A famous projective test that uses an individual's perception of inkblots to determine his or her personality.

## S

**sample** The subset of the population chosen by the investigator for study.

**schedules of reinforcement** Specific patterns that determine when a behavior will be reinforced.

**schema** A preexisting mental concept or framework that helps people to organize and interpret information. Schemas from prior encounters with the environment influence the way individuals encode, make inferences about, and retrieve information.

**schizophrenia** Severe psychological disorder characterized by highly disordered thought processes; individuals suffering from schizophrenia may be referred to as psychotic because they are so far removed from reality.

**science** The use of systematic methods to observe the natural world and to draw conclusions.

**scientific management** The managerial philosophy that emphasizes the worker as a well-oiled machine and the determination of the most efficient methods for performing any work-related task.

**script** A schema for an event, often containing information about physical features, people, and typical occurrences.

**secondary reinforcer** A reinforcer that acquires its positive value through an organism's experience; a secondary reinforcer is a learned or conditioned reinforcer.

**secondary sex characteristics** Traits that differ between the two sexes but are not part of the reproductive system; they include breasts in females and facial hair in males.

**secure attachment** The ways that infants use their caregiver, usually their mother, as a secure base from which to explore the environment.

**selective attention** The act of focusing on a specific aspect of experience while ignoring others.

**self-actualization** The motivation to develop one's full potential as a human being–the highest and most elusive of Maslow's proposed needs.

**self-determination theory** Deci and Ryan's theory asserting that all humans have three basic, innate organismic needs: competence, relatedness, and autonomy.

**self-efficacy** The belief that one can accomplish a given goal or task and produce positive change.

**self-fulfilling prophecy** Social expectations that cause an individual to act in such a way that expectations are realized.

**self-objectification** The tendency to see oneself primarily as an object in the eyes of others.

**self-perception theory** Bem's theory on how behaviors influence attitudes, stating that individuals make inferences about their attitudes by perceiving their behavior.

**self-regulation** The process by which an organism effortfully controls behavior in order to pursue important objectives.

**self-report test** A method of measuring personality characteristics that directly asks people whether specific items describe their personality traits; also called an objective test or an inventory.

**self-serving bias** The tendency to take credit for one's successes and to deny responsibility for one's failures.

**semantic memory** A person's knowledge about the world, including his or her areas of expertise; general knowledge, such as of things learned in school, and everyday knowledge.

**semantics** The meaning of words and sentences in a particular language.

**semicircular canals** Three fluid-filled circular tubes in the inner ear containing the sensory receptors that detect head motion caused when an individual tilts or moves the head and/or the body.

**sensation** The process of receiving stimulus energies from the external environment and transforming those energies into neural energy.

**sensorimotor stage** Piaget's first stage of cognitive development, lasting from birth to about 2 years of age, during which infants construct an understanding of the world by coordinating sensory experiences with motor (physical) actions.

**sensory adaptation** A change in the responsiveness of the sensory system based on the average level of surrounding stimulation.

**sensory memory** Memory system that involves holding information from the world in its original sensory form for only an instant, not much longer than the brief time it is exposed to the visual, auditory, and other senses.

**sensory receptors** Specialized cells that detect stimulus information and transmit it to sensory (afferent) nerves and the brain.

**serial position effect** The tendency to recall the items at the beginning and end of a list more readily than those in the middle.

**servant leadership** Leading by putting the needs of employees, customers, and communities first. The servant leader is a servant first, leader second.

**set point** The weight maintained when the individual makes no effort to gain or lose weight.

**sex chromosomes** In humans, the pair of genes that differs between the sexes and determines a person's sex as male or female.

**sex** The properties of a person that determine his or her classification as male or female.

**sexual harassment** Unwelcome behavior or conduct of a sexual nature that offends, humiliates, or intimidates another person.

**sexuality** The ways people experience and express themselves as sexual beings.

**sexually transmitted infection (STI)** An infection that is contracted primarily through sexual activity—vaginal intercourse as well as oral and anal sex.

**sexual orientation** The direction of an individual's erotic interests.

**sexual selection** According to Darwin's theory of evolution, differentiation between the male and female members of a species that can be traced to differences in competition and choice.

**shaping** Rewarding successive approximations of a desired behavior.

**short-term memory** Limited-capacity memory system in which information is usually retained for only as long as 30 seconds unless the individual uses strategies to retain it longer.

**signal detection theory** An approach to perception that focuses on decision making about stimuli under conditions of uncertainty.

**situational judgment test** A type of job-screening examination that presents job candidates with realistic, hypothetical scenarios and asks them to identify the most appropriate response.

**sleep** A natural state of rest for the body and mind that involves the reversible loss of consciousness.

**social anxiety disorder (SAD) or social phobia** An anxiety disorder in which the individual has an intense fear of being humiliated or embarrassed in social situations.

**social cognition** The area of social psychology that explores how people select, interpret, remember, and use social information.

**social cognitive behavior view of hypnosis** The perspective that hypnosis is a normal state in which the hypnotized person behaves the way the individual believes that a hypnotized person should behave.

**social cognitive perspectives** Theoretical views of personality emphasizing the influence of conscious awareness, beliefs, expectations, and goals.

**social comparison** The process by which individuals evaluate their thoughts, feelings, behaviors, and abilities in relation to those of others.

**social contagion** Imitative behavior involving the spread of actions, emotions, and ideas.

**social exchange theory** The view of social relationships as involving an exchange of goods, the objective of which is to minimize costs and maximize benefits.

**social facilitation** Improvement in an individual's performance because of the presence of others.

**social identity theory** Tajfel's theory that social identity, based on group membership, is a crucial part of self-image and a valuable source of positive feelings about oneself.

**social identity** The way individuals define themselves in terms of their group membership.

**social loafing** Each person's tendency to exert less effort in a group because of reduced accountability for individual effort.

**social neuroscience** The study of social thoughts, feelings, and behavior that incorporates a range of measures of brain and body functioning

**social psychology** The study of how people think about, influence, and relate to other people.

**social role theory** Eagly's theory of gender development that, while acknowledging the physical differences between the sexes, argues that these differences color social expectations and create social structures that limit opportunities for both sexes.

**social support** Information and feedback from others indicating that one is loved and cared for, esteemed and valued, and included in a network of communication and mutual obligation.

**sociocultural approach** An approach to psychology focusing on the ways in which social and cultural environments influence behavior.

**somatic nervous system** The body system consisting of the sensory nerves, whose function is to convey information from the skin and muscles to the CNS about conditions such as pain and temperature, and the motor nerves, whose function is to tell muscles what to do.

**somatic symptom disorder** A psychological disorder in which a person experiences one or more bodily (somatic) symptoms and experiences excessive thoughts and feelings about these symptoms that interfere with everyday functioning.

**somatosensory cortex** A region in the cerebral cortex that processes information about body sensations, located at the front of the parietal lobes.

**specific phobia** An anxiety disorder in which the individual experiences an irrational, overwhelming, persistent fear of a particular object or situation.

**spontaneous recovery** The process in classical conditioning by which a conditioned response can recur after a time delay, without further conditioning.

**stages of change model** Theoretical model describing a five-step process by which individuals give up bad habits and adopt healthier lifestyles.

**standard deviation** A measure of dispersion that indicates how much the scores in a sample differ from the mean in the sample.

**standardization** The development of uniform procedures for administering and scoring a test and the creation of norms (performance standards) for the test.

**stem cells** Unique primitive cells that have the capacity to develop into most types of human cells.

**stereotype** A generalization about a group's characteristics that does not consider any variations from one individual to another.

**stereotype threat** An individual's fast-acting, self-fulfilling fear of being judged based on a negative stereotype about his or her group.

**stimulants** Psychoactive drugs–including caffeine, nicotine, amphetamines, and cocaine–that increase the central nervous system's activity.

**storage** The retention of information over time and how this information is represented in memory.

**stream of consciousness** Term used by William James to describe the mind as a continuous flow of changing sensations, images, thoughts, and feelings.

**strengths-based management** A management style emphasizing that maximizing an employee's existing strengths is much easier than trying to build such attributes from the ground up.

**stress management program** A regimen that teaches individuals how to appraise stressful events, how to develop skills for coping with stress, and how to put these skills into use in everyday life.

**stressors** Circumstances and events that threaten individuals and tax their coping abilities and that cause physiological changes to ready the body to handle the assault of stress.

**stress** The responses of individuals to environmental stressors.

**structuralism** Wundt's approach to discovering the basic elements, or structures, of mental processes; so called because of its focus on identifying the structures of the human mind.

**structured interview** A kind of interview in which candidates are asked specific questions that methodically seek to obtain truly useful information for the interviewer.

**subgoals** Intermediate goals or intermediate problems devised to put the individual in a better position for reaching the final goal or solution.

**subjective well-being** A person's assessment of his or her own level of positive affect relative to negative affect and an evaluation of his or her life in general.

**subliminal perception** The detection of information below the level of conscious awareness.

**superego** The Freudian structure of personality that serves as the harsh internal judge of our behavior; what we often call conscience.

**suprachiasmatic nucleus (SCN)** A small brain structure that uses input from the retina to synchronize its own rhythm with the daily cycle of light and dark; the body's way of monitoring the change from day to night.

**sustained attention or vigilance** The ability to maintain attention to a selected stimulus for a prolonged period of time.

**sympathetic nervous system** The part of the autonomic nervous system that arouses the body to mobilize it for action and thus is involved in the experience of stress.

**synapses** Tiny spaces between neurons; the gaps between neurons are referred to as synaptic gaps.

**syntax** A language's rules for combining words to form acceptable phrases and sentences.

**systematic desensitization** A method of behavior therapy that treats anxiety by teaching the client to associate deep relaxation with increasingly intense anxiety-producing situations.

# T

**temperament** An individual's behavioral style and characteristic ways of responding.

**temporal lobes** Structures in the cerebral cortex that are located just above the ears and are involved in hearing, language processing, and memory.

**testes** Sex-related endocrine glands in the scrotum that produce hormones involved in male sexual development and reproduction.

**thalamus** The forebrain structure that sits at the top of the brain stem in the brain's central core and serves as an important relay station.

**Thematic Apperception Test (TAT)** A projective test that is designed to elicit stories that reveal something about an individual's personality.

**theory** A broad idea or set of closely related ideas that attempts to explain observations and to make predictions about future observations.

**theory of mind** Individuals' understanding that they and others think, feel, perceive, and have private experiences.

**theory of planned behavior** Theoretical model that includes the basic ideas of the theory of reasoned action but adds the person's perceptions of control over the outcome.

**theory of reasoned action** Theoretical model stating that effective change requires individuals to have specific intentions about their behaviors, as well as positive attitudes about a new behavior, and to perceive that their social group looks favorably on the new behavior as well.

**Theory X managers** Managers who assume that work is innately unpleasant and that people have a strong desire to avoid it; such managers believe that employees need direction, dislike responsibility, and must be kept in line.

**Theory Y managers** Managers who assume that engaging in effortful behavior is natural to human beings; they recognize that people seek out responsibility and that motivation can come from allowing employees to suggest creative and meaningful solutions.

**therapeutic alliance** The relationship between the therapist and client; an important element of successful psychotherapy.

**thermoreceptors** Sensory nerve endings under the skin that respond to changes in temperature at or near the skin's surface and provide input to keep the body's temperature at 98.6 degrees Fahrenheit.

**thinking** The process of manipulating information mentally by forming concepts, solving problems, making decisions, and reflecting critically or creatively.

**third variable problem** The circumstance in which a variable that has not been measured accounts for the relationship between two other variables. Third variables are also known as confounds.

**thought disorder** The unusual, sometimes bizarre thought processes that are characteristic positive symptoms of schizophrenia.

**tip-of-the-tongue (TOT) phenomenon** A type of effortful retrieval associated with a person's feeling that he or she knows something (say, a word or a name) but cannot quite pull it out of memory.

**tolerance** The need to take increasing amounts of a drug to get the same effect.

**top-down processing** The operation in sensation and perception, launched by cognitive processing at the brain's higher levels, that allows the organism to sense what is happening and to apply that framework to information from the world.

**training** Teaching a new employee the essential requirements to do the job well.

**trait theories** Theoretical views stressing that personality consists of broad, enduring dispositions (traits) that tend to lead to characteristic responses.

**tranquilizers** Depressant drugs, such as Valium and Xanax, that reduce anxiety and induce relaxation.

**transactional leader** An individual in a leadership capacity who emphasizes the exchange relationship between the worker and the leader and who applies the principle that a good job should be rewarded.

**transference** A client's relating to the psychoanalyst in ways that reproduce or relive important relationships in the individual's life.

**transformational leader** An individual in a leadership capacity who is dynamic and who brings charisma, passion, and vision to the position.

**transgender** Experiencing one's psychological gender as different from one's physical sex, as in the cases of biological males who identify as female and biological females who identify as male.

**triarchic theory of intelligence** Sternberg's theory that intelligence comes in three forms: analytical, creative, and practical.

**trichromatic theory** Theory stating that color perception is produced by three types of cone receptors in the retina that are particularly sensitive to different, but overlapping, ranges of wavelengths.

**two-factor theory of emotion** Schachter and Singer's theory that emotion is determined by two factors: physiological arousal and cognitive labeling.

**Type A behavior pattern** A cluster of characteristics—including being excessively competitive, hard-driven, impatient, and hostile—related to a higher incidence of heart disease.

**Type B behavior pattern** A cluster of characteristics—including being relaxed and easygoing—related to a lower incidence of heart disease.

**Type D behavior pattern** A cluster of characteristics—including being generally distressed, having negative emotions, and being socially inhibited—related to adverse cardiovascular outcomes.

## U

**unconditional positive regard** Rogers's construct referring to the individual's need to be accepted, valued, and treated positively regardless of the person's behavior.

**unconditioned response (UR)** An unlearned reaction that is automatically elicited by the unconditioned stimulus.

**unconditioned stimulus (US)** A stimulus that produces a response without prior learning.

**unconscious thought** According to Freud, a reservoir of unacceptable wishes, feelings, and thoughts that are beyond conscious awareness.

## V

**validity** The extent to which a test measures what it is intended to measure.

**variable** Anything that can change.

**vestibular sense** Sense that provides information about balance and movement.

**volley principle** Modification of frequency theory stating that a cluster of nerve cells can fire neural impulses in rapid succession, producing a volley of impulses.

**vulnerability-stress hypothesis or diathesis-stress model** Theory suggesting that preexisting conditions—such as genetic characteristics, personality dispositions, or experiences—may put a person at risk of developing a psychological disorder.

## W

**Weber's law** The principle that two stimuli must differ by a constant minimum percentage (rather than a constant amount) to be perceived as different.

**well-being therapy (WBT)** A short-term, problem-focused, directive therapy that encourages clients to accentuate the positive.

**wisdom** Expert knowledge about the practical aspects of life.

**working memory** A combination of components, including short-term memory and attention, that allow individuals to hold information temporarily as they perform cognitive tasks; a kind of mental workbench on which the brain manipulates and assembles information to guide understanding, decision making, and problem solving.

## Y

**Yerkes–Dodson law** The psychological principle stating that performance is best under conditions of moderate arousal rather than either low or high arousal.

# REFERENCES

## A

**Aaronson, A., & Lloyd, R. B.** (2015). Aggression after traumatic brain injury: A review of the current literature. *Psychiatric Annals, 45* (8), 422–426.

**Abbott, B. B., Schoen, L. S, & Badia, P.** (1984). Predictable and unpredictable shock: Behavioral measures of aversion and physiological measures of stress. *Psychological Bulletin, 96* (1), 45–71.

**Abdellaoui, A., Nivard, M. G., Hottenga, J. J., Fedko, I., Verweij, K. J., Baselmans, B. M., ... & Cacioppo, J. T.** (2018). Predicting loneliness with polygenic scores of social, psychological and psychiatric traits. *Genes, Brain and Behavior*, e12472.

**Abidi, M., Bruce, J., Le Blanche, A., Bruce, A., Jarmolowicz, D. P., Csillik, A., ... & de Marco, G.** (2018). Neural mechanisms associated with treatment decision making: An fMRI study. *Behavioural Brain Research, 349*, 54–62.

**Aboud, K. S., Huo, Y., Kang, H., Ealey, A., Resnick, S. M., Landman, B. A., & Cutting, L. E.** (2018). Structural covariance across the lifespan: Brain development and aging through the lens of internetwork relationships. *Human Brain Mapping, 40* (1), 125–136.

**Abraham, A., Barnett, C., Katzberg, H. D., Lovblom, L. E., Perkins, B. A., & Bril, V.** (2018). Sex differences in neuropathic pain intensity in diabetes. *Journal of the Neurological Sciences, 388*, 103–106.

**Abrams, L., & Rodriguez, E. L.** (2005). Syntactic class influences phonological priming of tip-of-the-tongue resolution. *Psychonomic Bulletin and Review, 12* (6), 1018–1023.

**Abramson, C. I.** (2009). A study in inspiration: Charles Henry Turner (1867–1923) and the investigation of insect behavior. *Annual Review of Entomology, 54*, 343–359.

**Abramson, L. Y., Seligman, M. E. P., & Teasdale, J.** (1978). Learned helplessness in humans: Critique and reformulation. *Journal of Abnormal Psychology, 87* (1), 49–74.

**Abramson, Z.** (2015). The meaning of neurosis according to Adler. *Journal of Individual Psychology, 71* (4), 426–439.

**Abreu, A. R., Molosh, A. I., Johnson, P. L., & Shekhar, A.** (2018). Role of medial hypothalamic orexin system in panic, phobia and hypertension. *Brain Research*. doi: 10.1016/j.brainres.2018.09.010 (in press)

**Adams, E. J., Nguyen, A. T., & Cowan, N.** (2018). Theories of working memory: Differences in definition, degree of modularity, role of attention, and purpose. *Language, speech, and hearing services in schools, 49*(3), 340–355.

**Adamsky, A., Kol, A., Kreisel, T., Doron, A., Ozeri-Engelhard, N., Melcer, T., ... & London, M.** (2018). Astrocytic activation generates de novo neuronal potentiation and memory enhancement. *Cell*, 174, 59–71.

**Adelman, R. M., Herrmann, S. D., Bodford, J. E., Barbour, J. E., Graudejus, O., Okun, M. A., & Kwan, V. Y.** (2017). Feeling closer to the future self and doing better: Temporal psychological mechanisms underlying academic performance. *Journal of Personality, 85* (3), 398–408. doi:10.1111/jopy.12248

**Ader, R.** (1974). Letter to the editor: Behaviorally conditioned immunosuppression. *Psychosomatic Medicine, 36*, 183–184.

**Adler, A.** (1927). *The theory and practice of individual psychology.* Fort Worth: Harcourt Brace.

**Adler, A.** (1928). Characteristics of the first, second, and third child. *Children, 3* (5), *14–52.*

**Adler, J. M.** (2018). Bringing the (disabled) body to personality psychology: A case study of Samantha. *Journal of personality, 86* (5), 803–824.

**Adler, J. M., Waters, T. E., Poh, J., & Seitz, S.** (2018). The nature of narrative coherence: An empirical approach. *Journal of Research in Personality, 74*, 30–34.

**Adler, N. J., & Aycan, Z.** (2018). Cross-cultural interaction: What we know and what we need to know. *Annual Review of Organizational Psychology and Organizational Behavior, 5*, 307–333.

**Adolphs, R.** (2009). The social brain: Neural basis of social knowledge. *Annual Review of Psychology* (vol. 60, pp. 693–716). Palo Alto, CA: Annual Reviews.

**Afsari, Z., Keshava, A., Ossandón, J. P., & König, P.** (2018). Interindividual differences among native right-to-left readers and native left-to-right readers during free viewing task. *Visual Cognition, 26*, 1–12.

**Agarkar, S., Hurt, S. W., & Young, R. C.** (2018). Speed of antidepressant response to electroconvulsive therapy in bipolar disorder vs. major depressive disorder. *Psychiatry Research, 265*, 355–359.

**Agarwal, C. A., Scheefer, M. F., Wright, L. N., Walzer, N. K., & Rivera, A.** (2018). Quality of life improvement after chest wall masculinization in female-to-male transgender patients: A prospective study using the BREAST-Q and Body Uneasiness Test. *Journal of Plastic, Reconstructive & Aesthetic Surgery, 71* (5), 651–657.

**Agnew-Blais, J., & Danese, A.** (2016). Childhood maltreatment and unfavourable clinical outcomes in bipolar disorder: A systematic review and meta-analysis. *The Lancet Psychiatry, 3* (4), 342–349.

**Agrawal, A., Das, S., & Thirthalli, J.** (2018). When obsessive compulsive disorder responds only to electroconvulsive therapy: A rare case for maintenance electroconvulsive therapy? *Journal of Neurosciences in Rural Practice, 9* (3), 450.

**Agresz, P.** (2017). Mysterious cases in the neuroscientific field: The girl who has never felt pain. *Patrick's Cases.* https://patrickscasestudies.wordpress.com/2017/10/31/the-girl-who-lives-without-pain/

**Aguilar, E. J., Corripio, I., García-Martí, G., Grasa, E., Martí-Bonmatí, L., Gómez-Ansón, B., ... & Brabban, A.** (2018). Emotional fMR auditory paradigm demonstrates normalization of limbic hyperactivity after cognitive behavior therapy for auditory hallucinations. *Schizophrenia Research, 193*, 304–312.

**Aguilar-Palacio, I., Carrera-Lasfuentes, P., Sánchez-Recio, R., Alonso, J. P., & Rabanaque, M. J.** (2018). Recession, employment and self-rated health: A study on the gender gap. *Public Health, 154*, 44–50.

**Ahmadi, N., Moss, L., Hauser, P., Nemeroff, C., & Atre-Vaidya, N.** (2018). Clinical outcome of maintenance electroconvulsive therapy in comorbid posttraumatic stress disorder and major depressive disorder. *Journal of Psychiatric Research, 105*, 132–136.

**Åhs, F., Rosén, J., Kastrati, G., Fredrikson, M., Agren, T., & Lundström, J. N.** (2018). Biological preparedness and resistance to extinction of skin conductance responses conditioned to fear relevant animal pictures: A systematic review. *Neuroscience & Biobehavioral Reviews, 95*, 430–437.

**Aiken, A., Clare, P. J., Wadolowski, M., Hutchinson, D., Najman, J. M., Slade, T., ... & Mattick, R. P.** (2018). Age of alcohol initiation and progression to binge drinking in adolescence: A prospective cohort study. *Alcoholism: Clinical and Experimental Research, 42* (1), 100–110.

**Ainsworth, M. D. S.** (1979). Infant–mother attachment. *American Psychologist, 34* (10), 932–937.

**Ainsworth, M. D. S., Blehar, M. C., Waters, E., & Wall, S. N.** (2015). *Patterns of attachment: A psychological study of the strange situation.* New York: Psychology Press.

**Ajunwa, I., & Greene, D.** (2018). Platforms at work: Automated hiring platforms and other new intermediaries in the organization of work. *Research in the Sociology of Work, 33*. (in press)

**Ajzen, I.** (2001). Nature and operation of attitudes. *Annual Review of Psychology* (vol. 52, pp. 27–58). Palo Alto, CA: Annual Reviews.

**Ajzen, I.** (2012a). Attitudes and persuasion. In K. Deaux & M. Snyder (Eds.), *The Oxford handbook of personality and social psychology* (pp. 367–394). New York: Oxford University Press.

**Ajzen, I.** (2012b). The theory of planned behavior. In P. A. M. Van Lange, A. W. Kruglanski, & E. T. Higgins (Eds.), *Handbook of theories of social psychology.* Thousand Oaks, CA: Sage.

**Ajzen, I., & Albarracín, D.** (2007). Predicting and changing behavior: A reasoned action approach. In I. Ajzen, D. Albarracín, & R. Hornik (Eds.), *Prediction and change in health behavior* (pp. 1–22). Mahwah, NJ: Erlbaum.

**Ajzen, I., & Fishbein, M.** (2005). The influence of attitudes on behavior. In D. Albarracín, B. T. Johnson, & M. P. Zanna (Eds.), *The handbook of attitudes* (pp. 173–221). Mahwah, NJ: Erlbaum.

**Akhtar, S., & Barlow, J.** (2018). Forgiveness therapy for the promotion of mental well-being: A systematic review and meta-analysis. *Trauma, Violence, & Abuse, 19* (1), 107–122. doi:10.1177/1524838016637079

**Akhtar, S., Justice, L. V., Morrison, C. M., & Conway, M. A.** (2018). Fictional first memories. *Psychological science, 29*(10), 1612–1619.

**Aknin, L. B., Barrington-Leigh, C. P., Dunn, E. W., Helliwell, J. F., Burns, J., Biswas-Diener, R., ... & Norton, M. I.** (2013). Prosocial spending and well-being: Cross-cultural evidence for a psychological universal. *Journal of Personality and Social Psychology, 104* (4), 635–652.

**Aknin, L. B., Broesch, T., Hamlin, J. K., & Van de Vondervoort, J. W.** (2015). Prosocial behavior leads to happiness in a small-scale rural society. *Journal of Experimental Psychology: General, 144* (4), 788–795.

**Aknin, L. B., Wiwad, D., & Hanniball, K. B.** (2018). Buying well-being: Spending behavior and happiness. *Social and Personality Psychology Compass, 12* (5), e12386.

**Aktar, T., Chen, J., Ettelaie, R., Holmes, M., & Henson, B.** (2017). Human roughness perception and possible factors effecting roughness sensation. *Journal of Texture Studies, 48* (3), 181–192.

**Al'bertin, S. V.** (2018). Effects of conditioned reflex retraining regime on search behavior in a radial maze in rats. *Neuroscience and Behavioral Physiology, 48* (2), 207–212.

**Albarracín, D., Chan, M. S., & Jang, D.** (2019). Attitudes and attitude change: Social and personality considerations about specific and general patterns of behavior. In K. Deaux & M. Snyder (Eds.), *The Oxford handbook of personality and social psychology* (2nd ed., pp. 439–464). New York: Oxford University Press.

**Albarracin, D., Durantini, M. R., & Earl, A.** (2006). Empirical and theoretical conclusions of an analysis of outcomes of HIV-prevention interventions. *Current Directions in Psychological Science, 15* (2), 73–78.

**Albarracín, D., Wilson, K., Durantini, M. R., Sunderrajan, A., & Livingood, W.** (2016). A meta-intervention to increase completion of an HIV-prevention intervention: Results from a randomized controlled trial in the state of Florida. *Journal of Consulting and Clinical Psychology, 84* (12), 1052–1065.

**Alberts, C., & Durrheim, K.** (2018). Future direction of identity research in a context of political struggle: A critical appraisal of Erikson. *Identity, 18* (4), 295–305.

**Aldao, A., Nolen-Hoeksema, S., & Schweizer, S.** (2010). Emotion-regulation strategies across psychopathology: A meta-analytic review. *Clinical Psychology Review, 30* (2), 217–237.

**Aldaz, B. E., Treharne, G. J., Knight, R. G., Conner, T. S., & Perez, D.** (2018). 'It gets into your head as well as your body': The experiences of patients with cancer during oncology treatment with curative intent. *Journal of Health Psychology, 23* (1), 3–16.

**Aldwin, C. M.** (2007). *Stress, coping, and development* (2nd ed.). New York: Guilford.

**Aldwin, C. M., Levenson, M. R., & Kelly, L. L.** (2009). Lifespan developmental perspectives on stress-related growth. In C. L. Park, S. Lechner, A. Stanton, & M. Antoni (Eds.), *Positive life changes in the context of medical illness.* Washington, DC: American Psychological Association.

**Alea, N.** (2018). Does the life story interview make us make sense? Spontaneous and cued redemption and contamination in life story scenes. *Imagination, Cognition and Personality, 37* (3), 271–292.

**Alessandri, G., Consiglio, C., Luthans, F., & Borgogni, L.** (2018). Testing a dynamic model of the impact of psychological capital on work engagement and job performance. *Career Development International, 23* (1), 33–47.

**Alessandri, G., & Vecchione, M.** (2017). Resilient, undercontrolled, and overcontrolled personality types across cultures. In A. T. Church (Ed.), *The Praeger handbook of personality across cultures: Culture and characteristic adaptations* (vol. 2, pp. 211–246). Santa Barbara, CA: Praeger/ABC-CLIO.

**Alexander, G. M., & Hines, M.** (2002). Sex differences in response to children's toys in nonhuman primates (*Cercopithecus aethiops sabaeus*). *Evolution and Human Behavior, 23* (6), 467–479.

**Alexander, G. M., Wilcox, T., & Woods, R.** (2009). Sex differences in infants' visual interest in toys. *Archives of Sexual Behavior, 38* (3), 427–433.

**Alexander, M., Bashir, K., Alexander, C., Marson, L., & Rosen, R.** (2018). Randomized trial of clitoral vacuum suction versus vibratory stimulation in neurogenic female orgasmic dysfunction. *Archives of Physical Medicine and Rehabilitation, 99* (2), 299–305.

**Alexander, M. G., & Fisher, T. D.** (2003). Truth and consequences: Using the bogus pipeline to examine sex differences in self-reported sexuality. *Journal of Sex Research, 40* (1), 27–35.

**Alexander, P. A.** (2018). Looking down the road: Future directions for research on depth and regulation of strategic processing. *British Journal of Educational Psychology, 88*(1), 152–166.

**Alexandrou, A. M., Saarinen, T., Mäkelä, S., Kujala, J., & Salmelin, R.** (2017). The right hemisphere is highlighted in connected natural speech production and perception. *NeuroImage, 152,* 628–638.

**Alford, C. F.** (2016). *Trauma, culture, and PTSD.* New York: Springer.

**Alhurani, A. S., Dekker, R., Ahmad, M., Miller, J., Yousef, K. M., Abdulqader, B., ... & Moser, D. K.** (2018). Stress, cognitive appraisal, coping, and event free survival in patients with heart failure. *Heart & Lung, 47*(3), 205–210.

**Allan, B. A., Duffy, R. D., & Collisson, B.** (2018). Helping others increases meaningful work: Evidence from three experiments. *Journal of Counseling Psychology, 65* (2), 155.

**Allen, A. M., Thomas, M. D., Michaels, E. K., Reeves, A. N., Okoye, U., Price, M. M., ... & Chae, D. H.** (2019). Racial discrimination, educational attainment, and biological dysregulation among midlife African American women. *Psychoneuroendocrinology, 99,* 225–235.

**Allen, M. S., & Walter, E. E.** (2018). Linking big five personality traits to sexuality and sexual health: A meta-analytic review. *Psychological Bulletin, 144* (10), 1081.

**Allen, M. T., Handy, J. D., Blankenship, M. R., & Servatius, R. J.** (2018). The distressed (Type D) personality factor of social inhibition, but not negative affectivity, enhances eyeblink conditioning. *Behavioural Brain Research, 345,* 93–103.

**Allott, K., Fraguas, D., Bartholomeusz, C. F., Díaz-Caneja, C. M., Wannan, C., Parrish, E. M., ... & Rapado-Castro, M.** (2018). Duration of untreated psychosis and neurocognitive functioning in first-episode psychosis: A systematic review and meta-analysis. *Psychological Medicine, 48* (10), 1592–1607.

**Allport, G. W.** (1954). *The nature of prejudice.* Cambridge, MA: Perseus.

**Allport, G. W.** (1961). *Pattern and growth in personality.* New York: Holt, Rinehart & Winston.

**Allport, G. W., & Odbert, H. S.** (1936). Trait-names: *A psycho-lexical study* (no. 211). Princeton, NJ: Psychological Review Monographs.

**Almeida, J., Pajtas, P. E., Mahon, B. Z., Nakayama, K., & Caramazza, A.**(2013). Affect of the unconscious: Visually suppressed angry faces modulate our decisions. *Cognitive, Affective, and Behavioral Neuroscience, 13* (1), 94–101.

**Alonso, P., Moscoso, S., & Salgado, J. F.** (2017). Structured behavioral interview as a legal guarantee for ensuring equal employment opportunities for women: A meta-analysis. *The European Journal of Psychology Applied to Legal Context, 9* (1), 15–23.

**Al-Shawaf, L., Lewis, D. M., & Buss, D. M.** (2018). Sex differences in disgust: Why are women more easily disgusted than men? *Emotion Review, 10* (2), 149–160.

**Altenor, A., Volpicelli, J. R., & Seligman, M. E. P.** (1979). Debilitated shock escape is produced by both short- and long-duration inescapable shock: Learned helplessness vs. learned inactivity. *Bulletin of the Psychonomic Society, 14* (5), 337–339.

**Alter, A. L., Aronson, J., Darley, J. M., Rodriguez, C., & Ruble, D. N.** (2010). Rising to the threat: Reducing stereotype threat by reframing the threat as a challenge. *Journal of Experimental Social Psychology, 46,* 166–171.

**Altszuler, A. R., Morrow, A. S., Merrill, B. M., Bressler, S., Macphee, F. L., Gnagy, E. M., ... & Pelham, W. E., Jr.** (2017). The effects of stimulant medication and training on sports competence among children with ADHD. *Journal of Clinical Child & Adolescent Psychology, 48* (supl), S155–S167. doi: 10.1080/15374416.2016.1270829

**Aluja, A., Balada, F., Blanco, E., Fibla, J., & Blanch, A.** (2018). Twenty candidate genes predicting neuroticism and sensation seeking personality traits: A multivariate analysis association approach. *Personality and Individual Differences.* doi: 10.1016/j.paid.2018.03.041

**Alvarez-Bolado, G., Grinevich, V., & Puelles, L.** (2015). Editorial: Development of the hypothalamus. *Frontiers in Neuroanatomy, 9,* 83.

**Ambron, E., Miller, A., Kuchenbecker, K. J., Buxbaum, L. J., & Coslett, H.** (2018). Immersive low-cost virtual reality treatment for phantom limb pain: Evidence from two cases. *Frontiers in Neurology, 9,* 67.

**Ament, S. A., Szelinger, S., Glusman, G., Ashworth, J., Hou, L., Akula, N., ... & Roach, J. C.** (2015). Rare variants in neuronal excitability genes influence risk for bipolar disorder. *Proceedings of the National Academy of Sciences USA, 112* (11), 3576–3581.

**American Foundation for Suicide Prevention.** (2018). *About suicide.* http://afsp.org/about-suicide/ (accessed December 19, 2018)

**American Psychiatric Association (APA).** (2001). *Mental illness.* Washington, DC: Author.

**American Psychiatric Association (APA).** (2006). *American Psychiatric Association practice guidelines for the treatment of psychiatric disorders.* Washington, DC: Author.

**American Psychiatric Association (APA).** (2013a). *Diagnostic and statistical manual of mental disorders (DSM-5).* Washington, DC: Author.

**American Psychiatric Association (APA).** (2013b). *Gender dysphoria.* Arlington, VA: Author.

**American Psychiatric Association (APA).** (2016). *Anxiety disorders: DSM-5 selections.* Arlington, VA: Author.

**American Psychological Association.** (2012). Research shows psychotherapy effective but underutilized. *APA.org.* http://www.apa.?org/news/?press/?releases/?2012/08/?psychotherapy-?effective.aspx (accessed April 10, 2016)

**Amitai, M., Taler, M., Carmel, M., Michaelovsky, E., Eilat, T., Yablonski, M., ... & Fennig, S.** (2016). The relationship between plasma cytokine levels and response to selective serotonin reuptake inhibitor treatment in children and adolescents with depression and/or anxiety disorders. *Journal of Child and Adolescent Psychopharmacology, 26* (8), 727–732.

**Amodio, D. M., Harmon-Jones, E., & Berkman, E. T.** (2019). Neuroscience approaches to social and personality psychology. In K. Deaux & M. Snyder (Eds.), *The Oxford handbook of personality and social psychology,* (2nd ed., pp. 97–132). New York: Oxford University Press.

**Amunts, K., Schlaug, G., Jancke, L., Steinmetz, H., Schleicher, A., Dabringhaus, A., & Zilles, K.** (1997). Motor cortex and hand motor skills: Structural compliance in the human brain. *Human Brain Mapping, 5* (3), 206–215.

**An, D., Song, Y., & Carr, M.** (2016). A comparison of two models of creativity: Divergent thinking and creative expert performance. *Personality and Individual Differences, 90,* 78–84.

**Anacker, C., Denny, C. A., & Hen, R.** (2015). Regulation of hippocampal memory traces by neurogenesis. *Neurogenesis, 2* (1), e1025180.

**Andel, R., Crowe, M., Pedersen, N. L., Mortimer, J., Crimmins, E., Johansson, B., & Gatz, M.** (2005). Complexity of work and risk of Alzheimer's disease: A population-based study of Swedish twins. *Journals of Gerontology: B: Psychological Sciences and Social Sciences, 60* (5), P251–P258.

**Anderson, C. A., & Bushman, B. J.** (2018). Media violence and the general aggression model. *Journal of Social Issues, 74* (2), 386–413.

**Anderson, D. I., Dahl, A., Campos, J. J., Chand, K., He, M., & Uchiyama, I.** (2018). Availability of peripheral optic flow influences whether infants cross a visual cliff. *Journal of Motor Learning and Development, 6* (s1), S76–S88.

**Anderson, K. N., Bautista, C. L., & Hope, D. A.** (2018). Therapeutic alliance, cultural competence and minority status in premature termination of psychotherapy. *The American Journal of Orthopsychiatry.* doi: 10.1037/ort0000342

**Anderson, L. C., & Petrovich, G. D.** (2018). Distinct recruitment of the hippocampal, thalamic, and amygdalar neurons projecting to the prelimbic cortex in male and female rats during context-mediated renewal of responding to food cues. *Neurobiology of Learning and Memory, 150,* 25–35.

**Anderson, N. H.** (1965). Primacy effects in personality impression formation using a generalized order effect paradigm. *Journal of Personality and Social Psychology, 2* (1), 1–9.

**Anderson, R.** (2018). Toward a sacred science–Reflecting forward. *The Humanistic Psychologist, 46* (1), 1.

**Andoh, J., Milde, C., Tsao, J. W., & Flor, H.** (2018). Cortical plasticity as a basis of phantom limb pain: Fact or fiction? *Neuroscience, 387,* 85–91.

**Ang, S., & Van Dyne, L.** (2015). *Handbook of cultural intelligence.* New York: Routledge.

**Angelini, V., Bertoni, M., & Corazzini, L.** (2018). Does paternal unemployment affect young adult offspring's personality? *Journal of Human Capital, 12,* 542–567.

**Anobile, G., Turi, M., Cicchini, G. M., & Burr, D. C.** (2015). Mechanisms for perception of numerosity or texture-density are governed by crowding-like effects. *Journal of Vision, 15* (5), 4.

**Antico, L., Guyon, A., Mohamed, Z. K., & Corradi-Dell'Acqua, C.** (2018). Beyond unpleasantness: Social exclusion affects the experience of pain, but not of equally-unpleasant disgust. *Cognition, 181,* 1–11.

**Antonesei, A., Murayama, K., & McCabe, C.** (2018). T88. Reduced neural response to reward in major depression disorder using a fMRI reinforcement learning task. *Biological Psychiatry, 83* (9), S162–S163.

**Antón-Méndez, I., Schütze, C. T., Champion, M. K., Gollan, & Tamar, H.** (2012). What the tip-of-the-tongue (TOT) says about homophone frequency inheritance. *Memory and Cognition, 40* (5), 802–811.

**Antony, J. W., Schönauer, M., Staresina, B. P., & Cairney, S. A.** (2018). Sleep spindles and memory reprocessing. *Trends in Neurosciences, 42* (1), 1–3.

**Anusic, I., Yap, S. C. Y., & Lucas, R. E.** (2014). Testing set-point theory in a Swiss national sample: Reaction and adaptation to major life events. *Social Indicators Research, 19* (3), 1265–1288.

**APA.** (2018). Mary Whiton Calkins, 1905 APA President. http://www.apa.org/about/governance/president/bio-mary-whiton-calkins.aspx

**APA Presidential Task Force on Evidence-Based Practice.** (2006). Evidence-based practice in psychology. *American Psychologist, 61* (4), 271–285.

**Apergis-Schoute, A. M., Bijleveld, B., Gillan, C. M., Fineberg, N. A., Sahakian, B. J., & Robbins, T. W.** (2018). Hyperconnectivity of the ventromedial prefrontal cortex in obsessive-compulsive disorder. *Brain and Neuroscience Advances, 2.* doi: 10.1177/2398212818808710

**Appel, H., Gerlach, A. L., & Crusius, J.** (2016). The interplay between Facebook use, social comparison, envy, and depression. *Current Opinion in Psychology, 9,* 44–49.

**Arbib, M. A.** (2012). *How the brain got language: The mirror system hypothesis.* New York: Oxford University Press.

**Arcaro, M. J., Thaler, L., Quinlan, D. J., Monaco, S., Khan, S., Valyear, K. F., Goebel, R., Dutton, G. N., Goodale, M. A., Kastner, S., & Culham, J. C.** (2018). Psychophysical and neuroimaging responses to moving stimuli in a patient with the Riddoch phenomenon due to bilateral visual cortex lesions. *Neuropsychologia.* doi: 10.1016/j.neuropsychologia.2018.05.008

**Ardelt, M., Gerlach, K. R., & Vaillant, G. E.** (2018). Early and midlife predictors of wisdom and subjective well-being in old age. *The Journals of Gerontology: Series B, 73* (8), 1514–1525.

**Arendt, J.** (2018). Approaches to the pharmacological management of jet lag. *Drugs, 78,* 1419–1431.

**Armstrong, T.** (2017). *The myth of the ADHD child, revised edition: 101 ways to improve your child's behavior and attention span without drugs, labels, or coercion.* New York: Penguin.

**Arnett, J. J.** (2004). *Emerging adulthood.* New York: Oxford University Press.

**Arnett, J. J.** (2006). Emerging adulthood: Understanding the new way of coming of age. In J. J. Arnett & J. L. Tanner (Eds.), *Emerging adults in America.* Washington, DC: American Psychological Association.

**Arnett, J. J.** (2007). Socialization in emerging adulthood. In J. E. Grusec & P. D. Hastings (Eds.), *Handbook of socialization.* New York: Oxford University Press.

**Arnett, J. J.** (2010). Oh, grow up! Generational grumbling and the new life stage of emerging adulthood. *Perspectives on Psychological Science. 5* (1), 89–92.

**Arnett, J. J.** (Ed.). (2012). *Adolescent psychology around the world.* New York: Psychology Press.

**Aronson, E.** (1986, August). *Teaching students things they think they already know all about: The case of prejudice and desegregation.* Paper presented at the meeting of the American Psychological Association, Washington, DC.

**Arrow, H.** (2007). The sharp end of altruism. *Science, 318* (5850), 581–582.

**Asarnow, L. D., McGlinchey, E., & Harvey, A. G.** (2014). The effects of bedtime and sleep duration on academic and emotional outcomes in a nationally representative sample of adolescents. *Journal of Adolescent Health, 54* (3), 350–356.

**Asch, S. E.** (1951). Effects of group pressure on the modification and distortion of judgments. In H. S. Guetzkow (Ed.), *Groups, leadership, and men.* Pittsburgh: Carnegie University Press.

**Ascione, F. R., McDonald, S. E., Tedeschi, P., & Williams, J. H.** (2018). The relations among animal abuse, psychological disorders, and crime: Implications for forensic assessment. *Behavioral Sciences & The Law, 36* (6), 717–729. doi: 10.1002/bsl.2370

**Ashton, J. C., Dowie, M. J., & Glass, M.** (2017). The endocannabinoid system and human brain functions: Insight from memory, motor, and mood pathologies. In E. Murillo-Rodriguez (Ed). *The endocannabinoid system* (pp. 115–186). New York: Academic Press.

**Ashton, M. C., & Lee, K.** (2018). How well do big five measures capture HEXACO scale variance? *Journal of Personality Assessment.* doi: 10.1080/00223891.2018.1448986 (in press)

**Ashworth, D. K., Sletten, T. L., Junge, M., Simpson, K., Clarke, D., Cunnington, D., & Rajaratnam, S. M.** (2015). A randomized controlled trial of cognitive behavioral therapy for insomnia: An effective treatment for comorbid insomnia and depression. *Journal of Counseling Psychology, 62* (2), 115–123.

**Asnaani, A., & Hofmann, S. G.** (2012). Collaboration in multicultural therapy: Establishing a strong therapeutic alliance across cultural lines. *Journal of Clinical Psychology, 68* (2), 187–197.

**Aspinwall, L. G., & Pengchit, W.** (2013). Positive psychology. In M. D. Gellman & J. R. Turner (Eds.), *Encyclopedia of behavioral medicine.* New York: Springer.

**Aspinwall, L. G., & Tedeschi, R. G.** (2010a). The value of positive psychology for health psychology: Progress and pitfalls in examining the relation of positive phenomena to health. *Annals of Behavioral Medicine, 39* (1), 4–15.

**Aspinwall, L. G., & Tedeschi, R. G.** (2010b). Of babies and bathwater: A reply to Coyne and Tennen's views on positive psychology and health. *Annals of Behavioral Medicine, 39* (1), 27–34.

**Associated Press.** (2018, October 19). Youngster shows sportsmanship, kindness in race. *Business Mirror.* https://businessmirror.com.ph/youngster-shows-sportsmanship-kindness-in-race/

**Atkinson, R. C., & Shiffrin, R. M.** (1968). Human memory: A proposed system and its control processes. In K. W. Spence & J. T. Spence (Eds.), *The psychology of learning and motivation: II* (pp. 89–195). Oxford, UK: Academic Press.

**Au, J., Sheehan, E., Tsai, N., Duncan, G. J., Buschkuehl, M., & Jaeggi, S. M.** (2015). Improving fluid intelligence with training on working memory: A meta-analysis. *Psychonomic Bulletin and Review, 22* (2), 366–377.

**Aubin, S., Jennum, P., Nielsen, T., Kupers, R., & Ptito, M.** (2018). Sleep structure in blindness is influenced by circadian desynchrony. *Journal of Sleep Research, 27* (1), 120–128.

**Avena-Koenigsberger, A., Misic, B., & Sporns, O.** (2018). Communication dynamics in complex brain networks. *Nature Reviews Neuroscience, 19* (1), 17–33.

**Aviv, R.** (2018, April 2). How a young woman lost her identity. *The New Yorker.* https://www.newyorker.com/magazine/2018/04/02/how-a-young-woman-lost-her-identity

**Aydinli, A., Bender, M., Chasiotis, A., van de Vijver, F. J., & Cemalcilar, Z.** (2015). Implicit and explicit prosocial motivation as antecedents of volunteering: The moderating role of parenthood. *Personality and Individual Differences, 74,* 127–132.

**Ayeh, J. K.** (2018). Distracted gaze: Problematic use of mobile technologies in vacation contexts. *Tourism Management Perspectives, 26,* 31–38.

**Azarbad, L., Corsica, J., Hall, B., & Hood, M.** (2010). Psychosocial correlates of binge eating in Hispanic, African American, and Caucasian women presenting for bariatric surgery. *Eating Behaviors, 11* (2), 79–84.

## B

**Babchishin, K. M., Seto, M. C., Fazel, S., & Långström, N.** (2018). Are there early risk markers for pedophilia? A nationwide case-control study of child sexual exploitation material offenders. *The Journal of Sex Research.* doi: 10.1080/00224499.2018.1492694

**Babiloni, C., Marzano, N., Soricelli, A., Cordone, S., Millán-Calenti, J. C., Del Percio, C., & Buján, A.** (2016). Cortical neural synchronization underlies primary visual consciousness of qualia: Evidence from event-related potentials. F*rontiers in Human Neuroscience, 10.*

**Babiloni, C., Vecchio, F., Cappa, S., Pasqualetti, P., Rossi, S., Miniussi, C., & Rossini, P. M.** (2006). Functional frontoparietal connectivity during encoding and retrieval processes follows HERA model: A high resolution study. *Brain Research Bulletin, 68* (4), 203–212.

**Bach, M., & Hoffmann, M. B.** (2000). Visual motion detection in man is governed by non-retinal mechanisms. *Vision Research, 40* (18), 2379–2385.

**Bachhuber, M. A., Saloner, B., Cunningham, C. O., & Barry, C. L.** (2014). Medical cannabis laws and opioid analgesic overdose mortality in the United States, 1999–2010. *JAMA Internal Medicine, 174* (10), 1668–1673.

**Bachmann, J. M., Wallston, K. A., Roumie, C. L., Munoz, D., Patel, N., & Kripalani, S.** (2015). Health self-efficacy is associated with increased physical activity in patients with coronary heart disease. *Circulation, 132* (Suppl. 3), A11771.

**Baddeley, A. D.** (2010a). Long-term and working memory: How do they interact? In L. Backman & L. Nyberg (Eds.), *Memory, aging, and the brain.* New York: Psychology Press.

**Baddeley, A. D.** (2010b). Working memory. *Current Biology, 20* (4), R136–R140.

**Baddeley, A. D.** (2012). Working memory: Theories, models, and controversies. *Annual Review of Psychology* (vol. 63, pp. 1–29). Palo Alto, CA: Annual Reviews.

**Baddeley, A. D.** (2017). *Exploring working memory.* London: Routledge.

**Baddeley, J. L., & Singer, J. A.** (2010). A loss in the family: Silence, memory, and narrative identity after bereavement. *Memory, 18* (2), 198–207.

**Badour, C. L., Resnick, H. S., & Kilpatrick, D. G.** (2017). Associations between specific negative emotions and DSM-5 PTSD among a national sample of interpersonal trauma survivors. *Journal of Interpersonal Violence, 32* (11), 1620–1641.

**Bagga, P., Pickup, S., Crescenzi, R., Martinez, D., Borthakur, A., D'Aquilla, K., ... & Hariharan, H.** (2018). In vivo GluCEST MRI: Reproducibility, background contribution and source of glutamate changes in the MPTP model of Parkinson's disease. *Scientific Reports, 8* (1), 2883.

**Bahrick, H. P.** (1984). Semantic memory content in permastore: Fifty years of memory for Spanish learned in school. *Journal of Experimental Psychology: General, 113* (1), 1–29.

**Bahrick, H. P.** (2000). Long-term maintenance of knowledge. In E. Tulving & F. I. M. Craik (Eds.), *The Oxford handbook of memory* (pp. 347–362). New York: Oxford University Press.

**Bahrick, H. P.** (2005). The long-term neglect of long-term memory: Reasons and remedies. In A. F. Healey (Ed.), *Experimental cognitive psychology and its applications* (pp. 89–100). Washington, DC: American Psychological Association.

**Bahrick, H. P., Bahrick, P. O., & Wittlinger, R. P.** (1974). Long-term memory: Those unforgettable high-school days. *Psychology Today, 8,* 50–56.

**Bahrick, H. P., Hall, L. K., & Da Costa, L. A.** (2008). Fifty years of memory of college grades: Accuracy and distortions. *Emotion, 8* (1), 13–22.

**Bailey, J. M.** (2003). Biological perspectives on sexual orientation. In L. D. Garnets & D. C. Kimmel (Eds.), *Psychological perspectives on lesbian, gay, and bisexual experiences* (2nd ed., pp. 50–85). New York: Columbia University Press.

**Bailey, J. M.** (2018). The fraternal birth order effect is robust and important. *Archives of Sexual Behavior, 47* (1), 17–19.

**Bailey, J. M., & Zucker, K. J.** (1995). Childhood sex-typed behavior and sexual orientation: A conceptual and quantitative review. *Developmental Psychology, 31* (1), 43–55.

**Baillargeon, R.** (2014). Cognitive development in infancy. *Annual Review of Psychology* (vol. 65, pp. 172–176). Palo Alto, CA: Annual Reviews.

**Baillargeon, R., Scott, R. M., & Bian, L.** (2016). Psychological reasoning in infancy. *Annual Review of Psychology* (vol. 67, pp. 159–186). Palo Alto, CA: Annual Reviews.

**Bak, T. H.** (2015). Beyond a simple "yes" and "no." *Cortex, 73,* 332–333.

**Baker, Z. G., Tou, R. Y., Bryan, J. L., & Knee, C. R.** (2017). Authenticity and well-being: Exploring positivity and negativity in interactions as a mediator. *Personality and Individual Differences, 113,* 235–239.

**Bale, T. L.** (2015). Epigenetic and transgenerational reprogramming of brain development. *Nature Reviews: Neuroscience, 16* (6), 332–344.

**Balodis, I. M., Molina, N. D., Kober, H., Worhunsky, P. D., White, M. A., Rajita, S., ... & Potenza, M. N.** (2013). Divergent neural substrates of inhibitory control in binge eating disorder relative to other manifestations of obesity. *Obesity, 21* (2), 367–377.

**Balsam, K. F., Beauchaine, T. P., Rothblum, E. D., & Solomon, S. E.** (2008). Three-year follow-up of same-sex couples who had civil unions in Vermont, same-sex couples not in civil unions, and heterosexual married couples. *Developmental Psychology, 44* (1), 102–116.

**Balter, M.** (2010). Did working memory spark creative culture? *Science, 328* (5975), 160–163.

**Bandura, A.** (1986). *Social foundations of thought and action.* Englewood Cliffs, NJ: Prentice-Hall.

**Bandura, A.** (1997). Self-efficacy. New York: Freeman.

**Bandura, A.** (2001). Social cognitive theory: An agentic perspective. *Annual Review of Psychology* (vol. 52, pp. 1–26). Palo Alto, CA: Annual Reviews.

**Bandura, A.** (2009). Vicarious learning. In D. Matsumoto (Ed.), *Cambridge dictionary of psychology.* New York: Cambridge University Press.

**Bandura, A.** (2010). Self-efficacy. In D. Matsumoto (Ed.), *Cambridge dictionary of psychology.* New York: Cambridge University Press.

**Bandura, A.** (2011a). Social cognitive theory. In P. A. M. van Lange, A. W. Kruglanski, & E. T. Higgins (Eds.), *Handbook of social psychological theories.* (pp. 349–373). Thousand Oaks, CA: Sage.

**Bandura, A.** (2011b). The social and policy impact of social cognitive theory. In M. Mark, S. Donaldson, & B. Campbell (Eds.), *Social psychology and evaluation* (pp. 33–70). New York: Guilford.

**Bandura, A.** (2012). On the functional properties of perceived self-efficacy revisited. *Journal of Management, 38* (1), 9–44.

**Bandura, A., & Bussey, K.** (2004). On broadening the cognitive, motivational, and sociostructural scope of theorizing about gender development and functioning: Comment on Martin, Ruble, and Szkrybalo (2002). *Psychological Bulletin, 130* (5), 691–701.

**Bandura, A., Ross, D., & Ross, S. A.** (1961). Transmission of aggression through imitation of aggressive models. *Journal of Abnormal and Social Psychology, 63* (3), 575–582.

**Banfi, C., Koschutnig, K., Moll, K., Schulte-Körne, G., Fink, A., & Landerl, K.** (2018). White matter alterations and tract lateralization in children with dyslexia and isolated spelling deficits. *Human Brain Mapping.* doi: 10.1002/hbm.24410

**Banyard, V. L., & Williams, L. M.** (2007). Women's voices on recovery: A multi-method study of the complexity of recovery from child sexual abuse. *Child Abuse and Neglect, 31* (3), 275–290.

**Baraban, M., Koudelka, S., & Lyons, D. A.** (2018). Ca 2+ activity signatures of myelin sheath formation and growth in vivo. *Nature Neuroscience, 21* (1), 19.

**Barber, J. P., & Sharpless, B. A.** (2015). On the future of psychodynamic therapy research. *Psychotherapy Research, 25* (3), 309–320.

**Barber, T. W., Veysey, D., Billah, B., & Francis, P.** (2018). Normal brain metabolism on FDG PET/MRI during childhood and adolescence. *Nuclear Medicine Communications, 39* (11), 1022–1032.

**Barclay, L. J., & Aquino, K.** (2010). Workplace aggression and violence. In S. Zedeck (Ed.), *APA handbook of industrial and organizational psychology.* Washington, DC: American Psychological Association.

**Bard, P.** (1934). Emotion. In C. Murchison (Ed.), *Handbook of general psychology.* Worcester, MA: Clark University Press.

**Bargh, J. A., Lee-Chai, A., Barndollar, K., Gollwitzer, P. M., & Trötschel, R.** (2001). The automated will: Nonconscious activation and pursuit of behavioral goals. *Journal of Personality and Social Psychology, 81* (6), 1014–1027.

**Barker, A. T., Jalinous, R., & Freeston, I. L.** (1985). Non-invasive magnetic stimulation of human motor cortex. *Lancet, 1* (8437), 1106–1107.

**Barker, V., Romaniuk, L., Cardinal, R. N., Pope, M., Nicol, K., & Hall, J.** (2015). Impulsivity in borderline personality disorder. *Psychological Medicine, 45* (9), 1955–1964.

**Barkley, R. A.** (1997). Behavioral inhibition, sustained attention, and executive functions: Constructing a unifying theory of ADHD. *Psychological Bulletin, 121* (1), 65–95.

**Barling, J., Weber, T., & Kelloway E. K.** (1996). Effects of transformational leadership training on attitudinal and financial outcomes: A field experiment. *Journal of Applied Psychology, 81* (6), 827–832.

**Barloon, T., & Noyes, Jr., R.** (1997). Charles Darwin and panic disorder. *Journal of the American Medical Association, 277* (2), 138–141.

**Barnacle, G. E., Tsivilis, D., Schaefer, A., & Talmi, D.** (2018). Local context influences memory for emotional stimuli but not electrophysiological markers of emotion-dependent attention. *Psychophysiology, 55*(4), e13014.

**Barnes, R. D., Ivezaj, V., Pittman, B. P., & Grilo, C. M.** (2018). Early weight loss predicts weight loss treatment response regardless of binge-eating disorder status and pretreatment weight change. *International Journal of Eating Disorders.* doi: 10.1002/eat.22860

**Baron-Cohen, S.** (1995). *Mindblindness: An essay on autism and theory of mind.* Cambridge, MA: MIT Press.

**Baron-Cohen, S.** (2008). Autism, hypersystematizing, and the truth. *Quarterly Journal of Experimental Psychology, 61* (1), 64–75.

**Baron-Cohen, S.** (2011). The empathizing-systematizing (E-S) theory of autism: A cognitive developmental account. In U. Goswami (Ed.), Wiley-Blackwell *handbook of childhood cognitive development* (2nd ed.). New York: Wiley-Blackwell.

**Baron-Cohen, S., Wheelwright, S., Hill, J., Raste, Y., & Plumb, I.** (2001). The "reading of mind in the eyes" test revised version: A study with normal adults, and adults with Asperger syndrome or high-functioning autism. *Journal of Child Psychology and Psychiatry, 42* (2), 241–251.

**Barr, K., & Mintz, A.** (2018). Public policy perspective on group decision-making dynamics in foreign policy. *Policy Studies Journal, 46,* S69–S90.

**Barr, N., Pennycook, G., Stolz, J. A., & Fugelsang, J. A.** (2015). Reasoned connections: A dual-process perspective on creative thought. *Thinking and Reasoning, 21* (1), 61–75.

**Barrash, J., Stuss, D. T., Aksan, N., Anderson, S. W., Jones, R. D., Manzel, K., & Tranel, D.** (2018). "Frontal lobe syndrome"? Subtypes of acquired personality disturbances in patients with focal brain damage. *Cortex, 106,* 65–80.

**Barratt, J. M., & Cooke, R.** (2018). Do gender and year of study affect the ability of the theory of planned behaviour to predict binge-drinking intentions and episodes? *Drugs: Education, Prevention and Policy, 25* (2), 181–188.

**Barreto, N. B., & Hogg, M. A.** (2018). Influence and leadership in small groups: Impact of group prototypicality, social status, and task competence. *Journal of Theoretical Social Psychology, 2* (1), 26–33.

**Barrett, G. V., & Kernan, M. G.** (1987). Performance appraisal and terminations: A review of court decisions since *Brito v. Zia* with implications for personnel practices. *Personnel Psychology, 40* (3), 489–503.

**Barrett, L. F.** (2011). Was Darwin wrong about emotional expressions? *Current Directions in Psychological Science, 20* (6), 400–406.

**Barrick, M. R., Swider, B., & Stewart, G. L.** (2010). Initial evaluations in the interview: Relationships with subsequent interviewer evaluations and employment offers. *Journal of Applied Psychology, 95* (6), 1037–1046.

**Barrouillet, P., De Paepe, A., & Langerock, N.** (2012). Time causes forgetting from working memory. *Psychonomic Bulletin and Review, 19* (1), 87–92.

**Barry, C. T., McDougall, K. H., Anderson, A. C., & Bindon, A. L.** (2018). Global and contingent self-esteem as moderators in the relations between adolescent narcissism, callous-unemotional traits, and aggression. *Personality and Individual Differences, 123,* 1–5.

**Barry, T. J., Lenaert, B., Hermans, D., Raes, F., & Griffith, J. W.** (2018). Meta-Analysis of the Association Between Autobiographical Memory Specificity and Exposure to Trauma. *Journal of Traumatic Stress, 31*(1), 35–46.

**Bart, C. P., Abramson, L. Y., & Alloy, L. B.** (2018). Impulsivity and behavior-dependent life events mediate the relationship of reward sensitivity and depression, but not hypomania, among at-risk adolescents. *Behavior Therapy*. doi: 10.1016/j.beth.2018.09.001

**Bartel, C. A., Wrzesniewski, A., & Wiesenfeld, B.** (2007). The struggle to establish organizational membership: Newcomer socialization in remote work contexts. In C. A. Bartel., S. Blader, & A. Wrzesniewski (Eds.), *Identity and the modern organization.* Mahwah, NJ: Erlbaum.

**Bartlett, N. T., & Hurd, P. L.** (2018). Fraternal birth order effects on personality: Will reasonable claims require extraordinary evidence? *Archives of Sexual Behavior, 47* (1), 21–25.

**Bartone, P. T., Hystad, S. W., Eid, J., & Brevik, J. L.** (2012). Psychological hardiness and coping style as risk/resilience factors for alcohol abuse. *Military Medicine, 177* (5), 517–524.

**Bartoshuk, L. M.** (2018). Taste. *Stevens' Handbook of Experimental Psychology and Cognitive Neuroscience, 2,* 1–33.

**Bartsch, L. M., Singmann, H., & Oberauer, K.** (2018). The effects of refreshing and elaboration on working memory performance, and their contributions to long-term memory formation. *Memory & Cognition,* 1–13.

**Barttfeld, P., Uhrig, L., Sitt, J. D., Sigman, M., Jarraya, B., & Dehaene, S.** (2015). Signature of consciousness in the dynamics of resting-state brain activity. *Proceedings of the National Academy of Sciences USA, 112* (3), 887–892.

**Bartus, A., Palasti, F., Juhasz, E., Kiss, E., Simonova, E., Sumanszki, C., & Reismann, P.** (2018). The influence of blood phenylalanine levels on neurocognitive function in adult PKU patients. *Metabolic Brain Disease, 33,* 1609–1615.

**Barušs, I., & Rabier, V.** (2014). Failure to replicate retrocausal recall. *Psychology of Consciousness: Theory, Research, and Practice, 1*(1), 82–91.

**Barzilay, S., Feldman, D., Snir, A., Apter, A., Carli, V., Hoven, C. W., Wasserman, C., Sarchiapone, M., & Wasserman, D.** (2015). The interpersonal theory of suicide and adolescent suicidal behavior. *Journal of Affective Disorders, 183,* 68–74.

**Bassok, M., & Novick, L. R.** (2012). Problem solving. In K. J. Holyoak & R. G. Morrison (Eds.), *The Oxford handbook of thinking and reasoning.* New York: Oxford University Press.

**Batastini, A. B., Lester, M. E., & Thompson, R. A.** (2018). Mental illness in the eyes of the law: Examining perceptions of stigma among judges and attorneys. *Psychology, Crime & Law, 24* (7), 673–686.

**Bateman, A. J.** (1948). Intra-sexual selection in *Drosophila. Heredity, 2,* 349–368.

**Batson, C. D.** (2002). Addressing the altruism question experimentally. In S. G. Post, L. G. Underwood, J. P. Schloss, & W. B. Hurlbut (Eds.), *Altruism and altruistic love.* New York: Oxford University Press.

**Batson, C. D.** (2006). "Not all self-interest after all": Economics of empathy-induced altruism. In D. DeCremer, M. Zeelenberg, & J. K. Murnigham (Eds.), *Social psychology and economics* (pp. 281–299). Mahwah, NJ: Erlbaum.

**Batson, C. D.** (2012). History of prosocial behavior research. In A. W. Kruglanski & W. Stroebe (Eds.), *Handbook of the history of social psychology.* New York: Psychology Press.

**Bauer, J. J., Graham, L. E., Lauber, E. A., & Lynch, B. P.** (2019). What growth sounds like: Redemption, self-improvement, and eudaimonic growth across different life narratives in relation to well-being. *Journal of Personality, 87,* 546–565.

**Bauer, M., Cahlíková, J., Chytilová, J., & Želinský, T.** (2018). Social contagion of ethnic hostility. *Proceedings of the National Academy of Sciences, 115* (19) 4881–4886.

**Bauer, P. J.** (2009). Learning and memory: Like a horse and carriage. In A. Needham & A. Woodward (Eds.), *Learning and the infant mind.* New York: Oxford University Press.

**Bauer, P. J.** (2013). Memory. In P. D. Zelazo (Ed.), *The Oxford handbook of developmental psychology* (vol. 1, pp. 505–564). New York: Oxford University Press.

**Bauer, P. J.** (2015). Development of episodic and autobiographical memory: The importance of remembering forgetting. *Developmental Review, 38,* 146–166.

**Baum, W. M.** (2017). *Understanding behaviorism: Behavior, culture, and evolution.* New York: John Wiley & Sons.

**Baumeister, R. F., & Leary, M. R.** (2000). The need to belong: Desire for interpersonal attachments as a fundamental human motivation. In E. T. Higgins & A. W. Kruglanski (Eds.), *Motivational science: Social and personality perspectives* (pp. 24–49). New York: Psychology Press.

**Baumgaertner, B., Carlisle, J. E., & Justwan, F.** (2018). The influence of political ideology and trust on willingness to vaccinate. *PloS One, 13* (1), e0191728.

**Baumrind, D.** (1991). Parenting styles and adolescent development. In J. Brooks-Gunn, R. Lerner, & A. C. Petersen (Eds.), *The encyclopedia of adolescence* (vol. 2). New York: Garland.

**Baumrind, D.** (1993). The average expectable environment is not good enough: A response to Scarr. *Child Development, 64* (5), 1299–1307.

**Baumrind, D.** (2012). Authoritative parenting revisited: History and current status. In R. Larzelere, A. S. Morris, & A. W. Harist (Eds.), *Authoritative parenting.* Washington, DC: American Psychological Association.

**Baxter, Jr., L. R., Phelps, M. E., Mazziotta, J. C., Schwartz, J. M., Gerner, R. H., Selin, C. E., & Sumida, R. M.** (1995). Cerebral metabolic rates for glucose in mood disorders: Studies with positron emission tomography and fluorodeoxyglucose F 18. *Archives of General Psychiatry, 42* (5), 441–447.

**Bayer, P., Ferreira, F., & Ross, S. L.** (2016). What drives racial and ethnic differences in high-cost mortgages? The role of high-risk lenders. *NBER Working Paper No. 22004.* Cambridge, MA: National Bureau of Economic Research.

**Bazov, I., Sarkisyan, D., Kononenko, O., Watanabe, H., Yakovleva, T., Hansson, A. C., ... & Bakalkin, G.** (2018). Dynorphin and κ-opioid receptor dysregulation in the dopaminergic reward system of human alcoholics. *Molecular Neurobiology, 55,* 7049–7061.

**Beard, C., Weisberg, R. B., & Keller, M. B.** (2010). Health-related quality of life across the anxiety disorders: Findings from a sample of primary care patients. *Journal of Anxiety Disorders, 24* (6), 559–564.

**Beare, R., Adamson, C., Bellgrove, M. A., Vilgis, V., Vance, A., Seal, M. L., & Silk, T. J.** (2017). Altered structural connectivity in ADHD: A network based analysis. *Brain Imaging and Behavior, 11* (3), 846–858.

**Beattie, J., Griffiths, D., Innes, K., & Morphet, J.** (2018). Workplace violence perpetrated by clients of healthcare: A need for safety and trauma-informed care. *Journal of Clinical Nursing.* doi: 10.1111/jocn.14683

**Beaty, R. E., Chen, Q., Christensen, A. P., Qiu, J., Silvia, P. J., & Schacter, D. L.** (2018). Brain networks of the imaginative mind: Dynamic functional connectivity of default and cognitive control networks relates to openness to experience. *Human Brain Mapping, 39* (2), 811–821.

**Beauregard, J. L., Drews-Botsch, C., Sales, J. M., Flanders, W. D., & Kramer, M. R.** (2018). Does socioeconomic status modify the association between preterm birth and children's early cognitive ability and kindergarten academic achievement in the United States? *American Journal of Epidemiology,* kwy068.

**Becerra-Culqui, T. A., Liu, Y., Nash, R., Cromwell, L., Flanders, W. D., Getahun, D., ... & Quinn, V. P.** (2018). Mental health of transgender and gender nonconforming youth compared with their peers. *Pediatrics,* e20173845.

**Becher, E. H., McGuire, J. K., McCann, E. M., Powell, S., Cronin, S. E., & Deenanath, V.** (2018). Extension-based divorce education: A quasi-experimental design study of the Parents Forever program. *Journal of Divorce & Remarriage.* doi: 10.1080/10502556.2018.1466256

**Beck, A.** (1967). *Depression.* New York: Harper & Row.

**Beck, A. T.** (2006). How an anomalous finding led to a new system of psychotherapy. *Nature Medicine, 12* (10), 1139–1141.

**Beck, A. T., & Haigh, E.** (2014). The generic cognitive model. *Annual Review of Clinical Psychology* (vol. 10, pp. 1–24). Palo Alto, CA: Annual Reviews.

**Beck, A. T., Himelstein, R., Bredemeier, K., Silverstein, S. M., & Grant, P.** (2018). What accounts for poor functioning in people with schizophrenia: A re-evaluation of the contributions of neurocognitive v. attitudinal and motivational factors. *Psychological Medicine,* 1–10.

**Becker, B., Geng, Y., Zhao, W., Zhou, F., Ma, X., Yao, S., & Kendrick, K. M.** (2018). Oxytocin facilitates empathic and self-embarrassment ratings by attenuating amygdala and anterior insula responses. *Frontiers in Endocrinology, 9,* 572.

**Becker, H., Kang, S. J., & Stuifbergen, A.** (2012). Predictors of quality of life for long-term cancer survivors with preexisting disabling conditions. *Oncology Nursing Society, 39* (2), E122–E131.

**Bedrosian, T. A., & Nelson, R. J.** (2018). The biology of human aggression. In J. L. Ireland, P. Birch, & C. A. Ireland (Eds.), *The Routledge international handbook of human aggression: Current issues and perspectives.* New York: Routledge.

**Beech, A. R., Miner, M. H., & Thornton, D.** (2016). Paraphilias in the DSM-5. *Annual Review of Clinical Psychology* (vol. 12). Palo Alto, CA: Annual Reviews.

**Beeli, G., Esslen, M., & Jäncke, L.** (2005). Synaesthesia: When coloured sounds taste sweet. *Nature, 434* (7029), 38.

**Behrens, K. Y., Parker, A. C., & Haltigan, J. D.** (2011). Maternal sensitivity assessed during the strange situation procedure predicts child's attachment quality and reunion behaviors. *Infant Behavior and Development, 34* (2), 378–381.

**Behrman, P., Redding, C. A., Raja, S., Newton, T., Beharie, N., & Printz, D.** (2018). Society of Behavioral Medicine (SBM) position statement: Restore CDC funding for firearms and gun violence prevention research. *Translational Behavioral Medicine,* ibx040. doi: 10.1093/tbm/ibx040

**Beier, K. T., Steinberg, E. E., DeLoach, K. E., Xie, S., Miyamichi, K., Schwarz, L., Gao, X. J., Kremer, E. J., Malenka, R. C., & Luo, L.** (2015). Circuit architecture of VTA dopamine neurons revealed by systematic input-output mapping. *Cell, 162* (3), 622–634.

**Bell, A. P., Weinberg, M. S., & Hammersmith, S. K.** (1981). *Sexual preference: Its development in men and women.* Bloomington: Indiana University Press.

**Bell, M. E., Dardis, C. M., Vento, S. A., & Street, A. E.** (2018). Victims of sexual harassment and assault in the military: Understanding risks and promoting recovery. *Military Psychology,* 1–10.

**Beller, J., & Wagner, A.** (2018). Loneliness, social isolation, their synergistic interaction, and mortality. *Health Psychology, 37* (9), 808–813.

**Belluck, P.** (December 3, 2018). Specifying mental health care before they're too ill to choose. *New York Times,* A1.

**Bem, D.** (1967). Self-perception: An alternative explanation of cognitive dissonance phenomena. *Psychological Review, 74* (3), 183–200.

**Bem, D. J.** (1996). Exotic becomes erotic: A developmental theory of sexual orientation. *Psychological Review, 103* (2), 320–335.

**Bem, S. L.** (1983). Gender schema theory and its implications for child development: Raising gender-aschematic children in a gender-schematic society. *Signs, 8* (4), 598–616.

**Bem, S. L.** (1993). *The lenses of gender: Transforming the debate on sexual inequality.* New Haven, CT: Yale University Press.

**Benet-Martínez, V., Donnellan, M. B., Fleeson, W., Fraley, R. C., Gosling, S. D., King, L. A., Robins, R. W., & Funder, D. C.** (2015). Six visions for the future of personality psychology. In R. J. Larsen & M. L. Cooper (Eds.), *APA handbook of personality and social psychology* (vol. 4, pp. 665–689). Washington, DC: American Psychological Association.

**Benjamin, A. J., Jr., Kepes, S., & Bushman, B. J.** (2018). Effects of weapons on aggressive thoughts, angry feelings, hostile appraisals, and aggressive behavior: A meta-analytic review of the weapons effect literature. *Personality and Social Psychology Review.* doi: 10.1177/1088868317725419

**Benjamin, D. J., Berger, J. O., Johannesson, M., Nosek, B. A., Wagenmakers, E. J., Berk, R., ... Johnson, V. E.** (2018). Redefine statistical significance. *Nature Human Behaviour, 2*(1), 6–10. doi: 10.1038/s41562-017-0189-z

**Benjamin, S., MacGillivray, L., Schildkrout, B., Cohen-Oram, A., Lauterbach, M. D., & Levin, L. L.** (2018). Six Landmark Case Reports Essential for Neuropsychiatric Literacy. *The Journal of Neuropsychiatry and Clinical Neurosciences, 30*(4), 279–290.

**Bennett, J. B., Lucas, G. M., Linde, B. D., Neeper, M. A., Hudson, M., & Gatchel, R. J.** (2018). A process model of health consciousness: Its application to the prevention of workplace prescription drug misuse. *Journal of Applied Biobehavioral Research,* e12130.

**Bentley, K. H., Franklin, J. C., Ribeiro, J. D., Kleiman, E. M., Fox, K. R., & Nock, M. K.** (2016). Anxiety and its disorders as risk factors for suicidal thoughts and behaviors: A meta-analytic review. *Clinical Psychology Review, 43,* 30–46.

**Benuto, L. T., Casas, J., & O'Donohue, W. T.** (2018). Training culturally competent psychologists: A systematic review of the training outcome literature. *Training and Education in Professional Psychology, 12* (3), 125–134.

**Berenbaum, S. A.** (2006). Psychological outcome in children with disorders of sex development: Implications for treatment and understanding typical development. *Annual Review of Sex Research, 17* (1), 1–38.

**Berenbaum, S. A.** (2018). Beyond pink and blue: The complexity of early androgen effects on gender development. *Child Development Perspectives, 12* (1), 58–64.

**Berenbaum, S. A., & Beltz, A. M.** (2016). How early hormones shape gender development. *Current Opinion in Behavioral Sciences, 7,* 53–60.

**Berg, J., Grant, A., & Johnson, V.** (2010). When callings are calling: Crafting work and leisure in pursuit of unanswered occupational callings, *Organization Science, 21* (5), 973–994.

**Bergamini, G., Mechtersheimer, J., Azzinnari, D., Sigrist, H., Buerge, M., Dallmann, R., ... & Ferger, B.** (2018). Chronic social stress induces peripheral and central immune activation, blunted mesolimbic dopamine function, and reduced reward-directed behaviour in mice. *Neurobiology of Stress, 8,* 42–56.

**Berger, P., Bitsch, F., Nagels, A., Straube, B., & Falkenberg, I.** (2018). Personality modulates amygdala and insula connectivity during humor appreciation: An event-related fMRI study. *Social Neuroscience, 13* (6), 756–768.

**Bergman, M. E., Langhout, R. D., Palmieri, P. A., Cortina, L. M., & Fitzgerald, L. F.** (2002). The (un) reasonableness of reporting: Antecedents and consequences of reporting sexual harassment. *Journal of Applied Psychology, 87* (2), 230–242.

**Berke, D. S., Reidy, D. E., Miller, J. D., & Zeichner, A.** (2017). Take it like a man: Gender-threatened men's experience of gender role discrepancy, emotion activation, and pain tolerance. *Psychology of Men & Masculinity, 18* (1), 62–69.

**Berkowitz, L.** (1990). On the formation and regulation of anger and aggression: A cognitive-neoassociationistic analysis. *American Psychologist, 45* (4), 494–503.

**Berkowitz, L., & LePage, A.** (1996). Weapons as aggression-eliciting stimuli. In S. Fein & S. Spencer (Eds.), *Readings in social psychology: The art and science of research* (pp. 67–73). Boston: Houghton Mifflin.

**Bernabé, K. J., Nokoff, N. J., Galan, D., Felsen, D., Aston, C. E., Austin, P., ... & Ellens, R.** (2018). Preliminary report: Surgical outcomes following genitoplasty in children with moderate to severe genital atypia. *Journal of Pediatric Urology, 14* (2), 157–e1.

**Bernard, M. M. T., Luc, M., Carrier, J. D., Fournier, L., Duhoux, A., Cote, E., ... & Roberge, P.** (2018). Patterns of benzodiazepines use in primary care adults with anxiety disorders. *Heliyon, 4* (7), e00688.

**Bernik, M., Ramos, R. T., Hetem, L. A. B., & Graeff, F.** (2017). Effect of single doses of pindolol and d-fenfluramine on flumazenil-induced anxiety in panic disorder patients. *Behavioural Brain Research, 357–358,* 82–87.

**Bernstein, D. M., Kumar, R., Masson, M. E., & Levitin, D. J.** (2018). Fluency misattribution and auditory hindsight bias. *Memory & Cognition,* 1–13.

**Berntsen, D., & Rubin, D. C.** (2002). Emotionally charged autobiographical memories across the life span: The recall of happy, sad, traumatic, and involuntary memories. *Psychology and Aging, 17* (4), 636–652.

**Berona, J., Stepp, S. D., Hipwell, A. E., & Keenan, K. E.** (2018). Trajectories of sexual orientation from adolescence to young adulthood: Results from a community-based urban sample of girls. *Journal of Adolescent Health, 63* (1), 57–61.

**Berridge, K. C.** (2018). Evolving concepts of emotion and motivation. *Frontiers in Psychology, 9.*

**Berron, D., Neumann, K., Maass, A., Schütze, H., Fliessbach, K., Kiven, V., ... & Düzel, E.** (2018). Age-related functional changes in domain-specific medial temporal lobe pathways. *Neurobiology of Aging, 65,* 86–97.

**Berry, E. D., Waterman, A. H., Baddeley, A. D., Hitch, G. J., & Allen, R. J.** (2018). The limits of visual working memory in children: Exploring prioritization and recency effects with sequential presentation. *Developmental Psychology, 54* (2), 240–253.

**Berry, K., Russell, K., & Frost, K.** (2018). Restricted and repetitive behaviors in autism spectrum disorder: A review of associated features and presentation across clinical populations. *Current Developmental Disorders Reports, 5* (2), 108–115.

**Berscheid, E.** (2006). Searching for the meaning of "love." In R. J. Sternberg & K. Weis (Eds.), *The new psychology of love* (pp. 171–183). New Haven, CT: Yale University Press.

**Berscheid, E.** (2010). Love in the fourth dimension. *Annual Review of Psychology* (vol. 61, pp. 1–25). Palo Alto, CA: Annual Reviews.

**Berscheid, E., & Regan, P. C.** (2005). *The psychology of interpersonal relationships.* New York: Prentice-Hall.

**Bertels, J., Bayard, C., Floccia, C., & Destrebecqz, A.** (2018). Rapid detection of snakes modulates spatial orienting in infancy. *International Journal of Behavioral Development, 42* (4), 381–387.

**Bertisch, S. M., Pollock, B. D., Mittleman, M. A., Buysse, D. J., Bazzano, L. A., Gottlieb, D. J., & Redline, S.** (2018). Insomnia with objective short sleep duration and risk of incident cardiovascular disease and all-cause mortality: Sleep Heart Health Study. *Sleep, 41* (6), zsy047.

**Bertrand, M., & Mullainathan, S.** (2004). Are Emily and Greg more employable than Lakisha and Jamal? A field experiment on labor market discrimination. *American Economic Review, 94* (4), 991–1013.

**Bertrand, R. M., Graham, E. K., & Lachman, M. E.** (2013). Personality development in adulthood and old age. In R. M. Lerner, M. A. Easterbrooks, J. Mistry, & I. B. Weiner (Eds.), *Handbook of psychology* (2nd ed., vol. 6, pp. 475–494). Hoboken, NJ: Wiley.

**Besedovsky, L., Lange, T., & Born, J.** (2012). Sleep and immune function. *Pflugers Archives, 463* (1), 121–137.

**Beshears, J., Choi, J. J., Laibson, D., Madrian, B. C., & Milkman, K. L.** (2015). The effect of providing peer information on retirement savings decisions. *Journal of Finance, 70* (3), 1161–1201.

**Besnard, P., Passilly-Degrace, P., & Khan, N. A.** (2016). Taste of fat: A sixth taste modality? *Physiological Reviews, 96,* 151–176. doi: 10.1152/physrev.00002.2015

**Betancur, C.** (2011). Etiological heterogeneity in autism spectrum disorders: More than 100 genetic and genomic disorders and still counting. *Brain Research, 1380,* 42–77.

**Bettencourt, B. A., Talley, A., Benjamin, A. J., & Valentine, J.** (2006). Personality and aggressive behavior under provoking and neutral conditions: A meta-analytic review. *Psychological Bulletin, 132* (5), 751–777.

**Beutler, L. E., Forrester, B., Gallagher-Thompson, D., Thompson, L., & Tomlins, J. B.** (2012). Common, specific, and treatment fit variables in psychotherapy outcome. *Journal of Psychotherapy Integration, 22* (3), 255–281.

**Bever, L.** (November 10, 2017). The unforgettable moment a widow touched the face that once belonged to her husband. *Washington Post.* https://www.washingtonpost.com/news/to-your-health/wp/2017/11/10/the-unforgettable-moment-a-widow-touched-the-face-that-once-belonged-to-her-husband/?noredirect=on&utm_term=.0d2f23e260cf (accessed December 21, 2018)

**Bharadwaj, R. A., Jaffe, A. E., Chen, Q., Deep-Soboslay, A., Goldman, A. L., Mighdoll, M. I., ... & Mattay, V. S.** (2018). Genetic risk mechanisms of posttraumatic stress disorder in the human brain. *Journal of Neuroscience Research, 96* (1), 21–30.

**Bialystok, E.** (2015). Bilingualism and the development of executive function: The role of attention. *Child Development Perspectives, 9* (2), 117–121.

**Bidwell, L., Gray, J. C., Weafer, J., Palmer, A. A., de Wit, H., & MacKillop, J.** (2017). Genetic influences on ADHD symptom dimensions: Examination of a priori candidates, gene-based tests, genome-wide variation, and SNP heritability. *American Journal of Medical Genetics Part B: Neuropsychiatric Genetics, 174* (4), 458–466.

**Biegel, S.** (2018). *The right to be out: Sexual orientation and gender identity in America's public schools* (2nd ed.). Minneapolis: University of Minnesota Press.

**Biggio, F., Talani, G., Locci, V., Pisu, M. G., Boero, G., Ciarlo, B., ... & Serra, M.** (2018). Low doses of prenatal ethanol exposure and maternal separation alter HPA axis function and ethanol consumption in adult male rats. *Neuropharmacology, 131,* 271–281.

**Bilefsky, D.** (2018). Gleefully or warily, Canadians usher in era of legalized marijuana. *New York Times* (Oct. 17, 2018), A4.

**Bilgicer, T., Jedidi, K., Lehmann, D. R., & Neslin, S. A.** (2015). Social contagion and customer adoption of new sales channels. *Journal of Retailing, 91* (2), 254–271.

**Billings, S. W., & Dages, K. D.** (2018). Cross-cultural validity of integrity assessments for lower-level and higher-level jobs. *International Journal of Selection and Assessment, 26* (1), 66–74.

**Birmaher, B., Merranko, J. A., Goldstein, T. R., Gill, M. K., Goldstein, B. I., Hower, H., ... & Axelson, D.** (2018). A risk calculator to predict the individual risk of conversion from subthreshold bipolar symptoms to Bipolar Disorder I or II in youth. *Journal of the American Academy of Child & Adolescent Psychiatry, 57* (10), 755–763.

**Biscocho, D., Cook, J. G., Long, J., Shah, N., & Leise, E. M.** (2018). GABA is an inhibitory neurotransmitter in the neural circuit regulating metamorphosis in a marine snail. *Developmental Neurobiology*. doi: 10.1002/dneu.22597

**Biswas-Diener, R., Vittersø, J., & Diener, E.** (2005). Most people are pretty happy, but there is cultural variation: The Inughuit, the Amish, and the Maasai. *Journal of Happiness Studies, 6,* 205–226.

**Bizumic, B.** (2018). *Ethnocentrism: Integrated perspectives*. New York: Routledge.

**Björkqvist, K.** (2018). Gender differences in aggression. *Current Opinion in Psychology, 19,* 39–42.

**Black, D. W.** (2017). The treatment of antisocial personality disorder. *Current Treatment Options in Psychiatry, 4* (4), 295–302.

**Black, S. E., Grönqvist, E., & Öckert, B.** (2018). Born to lead? The effect of birth order on noncognitive abilities. *Review of Economics and Statistics, 100* (2), 274–286.

**Blackhart, G. C., Brown, K. E., Clark, T., Pierce, D. L. & Shell, K.** (2012). Assessing the adequacy of post-experimental inquiries in deception research and the factors that promote participant honesty. *Behavioral Research Methods, 44,* 24–40.

**Blackwell, L. S., Trzesniewski, K. H., & Dweck, C. S.** (2007). Implicit theories of intelligence predict achievement across an adolescent transition: A longitudinal study and an intervention. *Child Development, 78* (1), 246–263.

**Blades, H. B.** (2006). Killer coworker: The case of Michael McDermott, the Christmas killer. *Forensic Examiner, 15* (3), 48–52.

**Blagrove, M., & Akehurst, L.** (2000). Personality and dream recall frequency: Further negative findings. *Dreaming, 10* (3), 139–148.

**Blagrove, M. T., Edwards, C., van Rijn, E., Reid, A., Malinowski, J. E., Bennett, P., ... & Ruby, P.** (2018). Insight from the consideration of REM dreams, non-REM dreams and daydreams. *Psychology of Consciousness: Theory, Research, and Practice*. (in press)

**Blair, C., & Raver, C. C.** (2015). School readiness and self-regulation: A developmental psychobiological approach. *Annual Review of Psychology* (vol. 66, pp. 711–731). Palo Alto, CA: Annual Reviews.

**Blair, S. N., Kohl, H. W., Paffenbarger, Jr., R. S., Clark, D. G., Cooper, K. H., & Gibbons, L. W.** (1989). Physical fitness and all-cause mortality: A prospective study of healthy men and women. *Journal of the American Medical Association, 262* (17), 2395–2401.

**Blanco, M., Hickman, J. S., Olson, R. L., Bocanegra, J. L., Hanowski, R. J., Nakata, A., ... & Bowman, D.** (2009). *Investigating critical incidents, driver restart period, sleep quantity, and crash countermeasures in commercial vehicle operations using naturalistic data collection: A final report* (Contract No. DTFH61-01-00049, Task Order #23). Washington, DC: Federal Motor Carrier Safety Administration.

**Blank, C., Gatterer, K., Leichtfried, V., Pollhammer, D., Mair-Raggautz, M., Duschek, S., ... & Schobersberger, W.** (2018). Short vacation improves stress-level and well-being in German-speaking middle-managers—A randomized controlled trial. *International Journal of Environmental Research and Public Health, 15* (1), 130. doi: 10.3390/ijerph15010130

**Blankenstein, N. E., Schreuders, E., Peper, J. S., Crone, E. A., & van Duijvenvoorde, A. C.** (2018). Individual differences in risk-taking tendencies modulate the neural processing of risky and ambiguous decision-making in adolescence. *NeuroImage, 172,* 663–673.

**Blanton, H., Jaccard, J., & Burrows, C. N.** (2015). Implications of the Implicit Association Test D–Transformation for psychological assessment. *Assessment, 22* (4), 429–440.

**Blanton, H., Jaccard, J., Klick, J., Mellers, B., Mitchell, G., & Tetlock, P. E.** (2009). Strong claims and weak evidence: Reassessing the predictive validity of the IAT. *Journal of Applied Psychology, 94* (3), 567–582.

**Block, J.** (1982). Assimilation, accommodation, and the dynamics of personality development. *Child Development, 53* (2), 281–295.

**Block, J. H., Millán, J. M., Román, C., & Zhou, H.** (2015). Job satisfaction and wages of family employees. *Entrepreneurship Theory and Practice, 39* (2), 183–207.

**Block, S. D., Shestowsky, D., Segovia, D. A., Goodman, G. S., Schaaf, J. M., & Alexander, K. W.** (2012). "That never happened": Adults' discernment of children's true and false memory reports. *Law and Human Behavior, 36* (5), 365–374.

**Blonigen, D. M., Carlson, M. D., Hicks, B. M., Krueger, R. F., & Iacono, W. G.** (2008). Stability and change in personality traits from late adolescence to early adulthood: A longitudinal twin study. *Journal of Personality, 76* (2), 229–266.

**Bloom, B.** (1985). *Developing talent in young people*. New York: Ballantine.

**Bloom, P.** (2004). Myths of word learning. In D. G. Hall & S. R. Waxman (Eds.), *Weaving a lexicon* (pp. 205–224). Cambridge, MA: MIT Press.

**Bloom, P.** (2017). *Against empathy: The case for rational compassion*. New York: Random House.

**Bloor, C., & White, F.** (1983). Unpublished manuscript. La Jolla: University of California, San Diego.

**Blum, B.** (June 7, 2018). The lifespan of a lie. *The Medium*. https://medium.com/s/trustissues/the-lifespan-of-a-lie-d869212b1f62

**Blumenthal, H., Leen-Feldner, E. W., Babson, K. A., Gahr, J. L., Trainor, C. D., & Frala, J. L.** (2011). Elevated social anxiety among early maturing girls. *Developmental Psychology, 47* (4), 1133–1140.

**Blythin, S. P., Nicholson, H. L., Macintyre, V. G., Dickson, J. M., Fox, J. R., & Taylor, P. J.** (2018). Experiences of shame and guilt in anorexia and bulimia nervosa: A systematic review. *Psychology and Psychotherapy: Theory, Research and Practice*. doi: 10.1111/papt.12198

**Bobadilla-Suarez, S., & Love, B. C.** (2018). Fast or frugal, but not both: Decision heuristics under time pressure. *Journal of Experimental Psychology: Learning, Memory, and Cognition, 44* (1), 24–33.

**Boerner, K. E., Birnie, K. A., Caes, L., Schinkel, M., & Chambers, C. T.** (2014). Sex differences in experimental pain among healthy children: A systematic review and meta-analysis. *PAIN, 155* (5), 983–993.

**Bogaert, A. F.** (2000). Birth order and sexual orientation in a national probability sample. *Journal of Sex Research, 37* (4), 361–368.

**Bogaert, A. F., Ashton, M. C., & Lee, K.** (2018). Personality and sexual orientation: Extension to asexuality and the HEXACO model. *The Journal of Sex Research, 55* (8), 951–961.

**Bogdashina, O.** (2016). *Sensory perceptual issues in autism and Asperger syndrome: Different sensory experiences—different perceptual worlds*. Philadelphia: Jessica Kingsley Publishers.

**Bogers, J. P., Schulte, P. F., Broekman, T. G., Moleman, P., & de Haan, L.** (2018). Dose reduction of high-dose first-generation antipsychotics or switch to ziprasidone in long-stay patients with schizophrenia: A 1-year double-blind randomized clinical trial. *European Neuropsychopharmacology, 28* (9), 1024–1034.

**Bogerts, B., Schöne, M., & Breitschuh, S.** (2018). Brain alterations potentially associated with aggression and terrorism. *CNS Spectrums, 23* (2), 129–140.

**Bohart, A. C., & Tallman, K.** (2010). Clients: The neglected common factor in psychotherapy. In B. L. Duncan, S. D. Miller, B. E. Wampold, & M. A. Hubble (Eds.), *The heart and soul of change: Delivering what works in therapy* (2nd ed., pp. 83–111). Washington, DC: American Psychological Association.

**Böhm, S. A., Dwertmann, D. J., Bruch, H., & Shamir, B.** (2015). The missing link? Investigating organizational identity strength and transformational leadership climate as mechanisms that connect CEO charisma with firm performance. *Leadership Quarterly, 26* (2), 156–171.

**Bohn, A., & Berntsen, D.** (2011). The reminiscence bump reconsidered: Children's prospective life stories show a bump in young adulthood. *Psychological Science, 22* (2), 197–202.

**Boland, J. W., & Pockley, A. G.** (2018). Influence of opioids on immune function in patients with cancer pain: from bench to bedside. *British Journal of Pharmacology, 175* (14), 2726–2736.

**Bond, R., & Smith, P. B.** (1996). Culture and conformity: A meta-analysis of studies using Asch's (1952, 1956) line judgment task. *Psychological Bulletin, 119* (1), 111–137.

**Bondarouk, T., Ruël, H., & Ter Harmsel, B.** (2018). 'Video killed the F2F-interview star': A mixed-method study into the effect of pre-recorded video interviews as a selection tool. In P. Novo Melo & C. Machado (Eds.), *Management and Technological Challenges in the Digital Age* (pp. 65–98). Cham: CRC Press.

**Bonfatti, J. F.** (2005). Hope holds the key: Finding inspiration. *Schizophrenia Digest* (Summer), 31–34.

**Bonfioli, E., Mazzi, M. A., Berti, L., & Burti, L.** (2018). Physical health promotion in patients with functional psychoses receiving community psychiatric services: Results of the PHYSICO-DSM-VR study. *Schizophrenia Research, 193,* 406–411.

**Bongioanni, C.** (March 24, 2018). One stopped a church shooter, another tended to others during a mass shooting: Annual MOH tribute honors citizen heroes. *Stars and Stripes*. https://www.stripes.com/news/us/one-stopped-a-church-shooter-another-tended-to-others-during-a-mass-shooting-annual-moh-tribute-honors-citizen-heroes-1.518499

**Booker, C. L., & Sacker, A.** (2012). Psychological well-being and reactions to multiple unemployment events: Adaptation or sensitization? *Journal of Epidemiology and Community Health, 66* (9), 832–838.

**Boomsma, D. I., Helmer, Q., Nieuwboer, H. A., Hottenga, J. J., de Moor, M. H., van Den Berg, S. M., ... & Willemsen, G.** (2018). An extended twin-pedigree study of neuroticism in the Netherlands Twin Register. *Behavior Genetics, 48* (1), 1–11.

**Bopp, K. L., & Verhaeghen, P.** (2018). Aging and n-back performance: A meta-analysis. *The Journals of Gerontology: Series B*. (in press)

**Bornstein, D.** (October 2, 2018). The power of student peer leaders. *New York Times,* online opinion. https://www.nytimes.com/2018/10/02/opinion/college-student-aid-education.html?rref=collection%2Fsectioncollection%2Fopinion&action=click&contentCollection=opinion®ion=stream&module=stream_unit&version=search&contentPlacement=1&pgtype=sectionfront

**Borsboom, D., Cramer, A., & Kalis, A.** (2018). Brain disorders? Not really... Why network structures block reductionism in psychopathology research. *Behavioral and Brain Sciences*. doi: 10.1017/S0140525X17002266 1-54.

**Borsook, D., Youssef, A. M., Barakat, N., Sieberg, C. B., & Elman, I.** (2018). Subliminal (latent) processing of pain and its evolution to conscious awareness. *Neuroscience & Biobehavioral Reviews, 88,* 1–15.

**Bosak, J., Eagly, A., Diekman, A., & Sczesny, S.** (2018). Women and men of the past, present, and future: Evidence of dynamic gender stereotypes in Ghana. *Journal of Cross-Cultural Psychology, 49* (1), 115–129.

**Boss, M., & Kleinert, J.** (2015). Explaining social contagion in sport applying Heider's balance theory: First experimental results. *Psychology of Sport and Exercise, 16* (Pt. 3), 160–169.

**Bossi, F., Gallucci, M., & Ricciardelli, P.** (2018). How social exclusion modulates social information processing: A behavioural dissociation between facial expressions and gaze direction. *PloS one, 13* (4), e0195100.

**Bostan, A. C., & Strick, P. L.** (2018). The basal ganglia and the cerebellum: Nodes in an integrated network. *Nature Reviews Neuroscience, 19,* 338–350.

**Bouchard, L. C., Carver, C. S., Mens, M. C., & Scheier, M. F.** (2018). Optimism, health, and well-being. In D. S. Dunn (Ed.), *Positive psychology: Established and emerging issues.* (pp. 112–130). New York, NY: Routledge/Taylor & Francis Group. http://proxy.mul.missouri.edu/login?url=http://search.ebscohost.com/login.aspx?direct=true&AuthType=ip,cookie,url,uid&db=psyh&AN=2017-45272-008&site=ehost-live&scope=site

**Bouchard, Jr., T. J., & Loehlin, J. C.** (2001). Genes, evolution, and personality. *Behavior Genetics, 31* (3), 243–273.

**Bouchard, T. J., Lykken, D. T., Tellegen, A., & McGue, M.** (1996). Genes, drives, environment, and experience: EPD theory–revised. In C. P. Benbow & D. Lubinski (Eds.), *Psychometrics and social issues concerning intellectual talent.* Baltimore: Johns Hopkins University Press.

**Bouton, M. E., & Schepers, S. T.** (2015). Renewal after the punishment of free operant behavior. *Journal of Experimental Psychology: Animal Learning and Cognition, 41* (1), 81–90.

**Bouziane, C., Caan, M. W., Tamminga, H. G., Schrantee, A., Bottelier, M. A., de Ruiter, M. B., ... & Reneman, L.** (2018). ADHD and maturation of brain white matter: A DTI study in medication naive children and adults. *NeuroImage: Clinical, 17,* 53–59.

**Bower, J. E., Moskowitz, J. T., & Epel, E.** (2009). Is benefit finding good for your health? Pathways linking positive life changes after stress and physical health outcomes. *Current Directions in Psychological Science, 18* (6), 337–341.

**Bowlby, J.** (1969). *Attachment and loss* (vol. 1). London: Hogarth.

**Bowlby, J.** (1989). *Secure and insecure attachment.* New York: Basic.

**Bowman, N. A.** (2010). College diversity experiences and cognitive development: A meta-analysis. *Review of Educational Research, 80* (1), 4–33.

**Boyd, A., Van de Velde, S., Vilagut, G., de Graaf, R., O'Neill, S., Florescu, S., Alonso, J., & Kovess-Masfety, V.** (2015). Gender differences in mental disorders and suicidality in Europe: Results from a large cross-sectional population-based study. *Journal of Affective Disorders, 173,* 245–254.

**Boyd-Franklin, N., Cleek, E. N., Wofsky, M., & Mundy, B.** (Eds.). (2013). *Therapy in the real world.* New York: Guilford.

**Boyle, P. A., Yu, L., Wilson, R. S., Leurgans, S. E., Schneider, J. A., & Bennett, D. A.** (2018). Person-specific contribution of neuropathologies to cognitive loss in old age. *Annals of Neurology, 83* (1), 74–83.

**Boywitt, C. D., & Meiser, T.** (2012). The role of attention for context-context binding of intrinsic and extrinsic features. *Journal of Experimental Psychology: Learning, Memory, and Cognition, 38* (4), 1099–1107.

**Brackett, M. A., Rivers, S. E., & Salovey, P.** (2011). Emotional intelligence: Implications for personal, social, academic, and workplace success. *Social and Personality Psychology Compass, 5,* 88–103.

**Bradbury, C., Cassin, S. E., & Rector, N. A.** (2011). Motor inhibition and cognitive flexibility in obsessive-compulsive disorder. *Psychiatry Research, 187* (1-2), 160–165.

**Bradford, A. C., Bradford, W. D., Abraham, A., & Adams, G. B.** (2018). Association between US state medical cannabis laws and opioid prescribing in the Medicare Part D population. *JAMA Internal Medicine, 178* (5), 667–672.

**Bragg, S., Renold, E., Ringrose, J., & Jackson, C.** (2018). "More than boy, girl, male, female": Exploring young people's views on gender diversity within and beyond school contexts. *Sex Education, 18* (4), 420–434.

**Brambilla, M., Manenti, R., Ferrari, C., & Cotelli, M.** (2015). Better together: Left and right hemisphere engagement to reduce age-related memory loss. *Behavioural Brain Research, 293,* 125–133.

**Brandler, W. M., Antaki, D., Gujral, M., Kleiber, M. L., Whitney, J., Maile, M. S., ... & Pang, T.** (2018). Paternally inherited cis-regulatory structural variants are associated with autism. *Science, 360* (6386), 327–331.

**Brannick, M., Cadle, A., & Levine, E. L.** (2012). Job analysis for knowledge, skills, abilities, and other characteristics, predictor measures, and performance outcomes. In N. Schmitt (Ed.), *The Oxford handbook of personnel assessment and selection* (pp. 119–146). Oxford, UK: Oxford University Press.

**Brannon, L.** (1999). *Gender: Psychological perspectives* (2nd ed.). Boston: Allyn & Bacon.

**Brascamp, J., Sterzer, P. Blake, R., & Knapen, T.** (2018). Multistable perception and the role of the frontoparietal cortex in perceptual inference. *Annual Review of Psychology, 69,* 77–103.

**Brasure, M., Desai, P., Davila, H., Nelson, V. A., Calvert, C., Jutkowitz, E., ... & McCarten, J. R.** (2018). Physical activity interventions in preventing cognitive decline and Alzheimer-type dementia: A systematic review. *Annals of Internal Medicine, 168* (1), 30–38.

**Bratsberg, B., & Rogeberg, O.** (2018). Flynn effect and its reversal are both environmentally caused. *Proceedings of the National Academy of Sciences,* 201718793.

**Bratt, A. S., Stenström, U., & Rennemark, M.** (2016). The role of neuroticism and conscientiousness on mortality risk in older adults after child and spouse bereavement. *Aging and Mental Health, 20* (6), 559–566.

**Braucher, J., Cohen, D., & Lawless, R. M.** (2012). Race, attorney influence, and bankruptcy chapter choice. *Journal of Empirical Legal Studies.* http://ssrn.com/abstract=1989039 (accessed April 5, 2016)

**Brauchli, C., Elmer, S., Rogenmoser, L., Burkhard, A., & Jäncke, L.** (2018). Top-down signal transmission and global hyperconnectivity in auditory-visual synesthesia: Evidence from a functional EEG resting-state study. *Human Brain Mapping, 39* (1), 522–531.

**Braun, B., Weinland, C., Kornhuber, J., & Lenz, B.** (2018). Religiosity, guilt, altruism and forgiveness in alcohol dependence: Results of a cross-sectional and prospective cohort study. *Alcohol and Alcoholism, 53* (4), 426–434. doi:10.1093/alcalc/agy026

**Braun, M. H., Lukowiak, K., Karnik, V., & Lukowiak, K.** (2012). Differences in neuronal activity explain differences in memory forming abilities of different populations of *Lymnaea stagnalis. Neurobiology of Learning and Memory, 97* (1), 173–182.

**Brawn, G., Kohnen, S., Tassabehji, M., & Porter, M.** (2018). Functional basic reading skills in Williams syndrome. *Developmental Neuropsychology, 43,* 454–477.

**Brawn, T. P., Nusbaum, H. C., & Margoliash, D.** (2018). Differential development of retroactive and proactive interference during post-learning wakefulness. *Learning & Memory, 25*(7), 325–329.

**Brazeau, H., & Davis, C. G.** (2018). Hope and psychological health and well-being following spinal cord injury. *Rehabilitation Psychology, 63* (2), 258–266. doi:10.1037/rep0000209

**Brehm, J. W.** (2000). Reactance. In A. E. Kazdin (Ed.), *Encyclopedia of psychology* (vol. 7, pp. 10–12). Washington, DC: American Psychological Association.

**Breland, K., & Breland, M.** (1961). The misbehavior of animals. *American Psychologist, 16* (11), 681–684.

**Brentari, D., & Lee, J. L.** (Eds.). (2018). *Shaping phonology.* Chicago: University of Chicago Press.

**Brethel-Haurwitz, K. M., Cardinale, E. M., Vekaria, K. M., Robertson, E. L., Walitt, B., VanMeter, J. W., & Marsh, A. A.** (2018). Extraordinary altruists exhibit enhanced self–other overlap in neural responses to distress. *Psychological Science, 29* (10), 1631–1641.

**Bretherton, I.** (2012). Afterword. In K. H. Brisch, *Treating attachment disorders* (2nd ed.). New York: Guilford.

**Brewer, N., & Wells, G. L.** (2011). Eyewitness identification. *Current Directions in Psychological Science, 20* (1), 24–27.

**Brickman, P., & Campbell, D. T.** (1971). Hedonic relativism and planning the good society. In M. H. Appley (Ed.), Adaptation-level *theory* (pp. 287–302). New York: Academic.

**Bridge, D. J., Chiao, J. Y., & Paller, K. A.** (2010). Emotional context at learning systematically biases memory for facial information. *Memory and Cognition, 38* (2), 125–133.

**Briggs, K. C., & Myers, I. B.** (1998). Myers-Briggs *Type Indicator.* Palo Alto, CA: Consulting Psychologists Press.

**Bringmann, A., Syrbe, S., Görner, K., Kacza, J., Francke, M., Wiedemann, P., & Reichenbach, A.** (2018). The primate fovea: Structure, function and development. *Progress in Retinal and Eye Research, 66,* 49–84.

**Briñol, P., & Petty, R. E.** (2012). History of attitudes and persuasion research. In A. W. Kruglanski & W. Stroebe (Eds.), *Handbook of the history of social psychology.* New York: Psychology Press.

**Broberg, D. J., & Bernstein, I. L.** (1987). Candy as a scapegoat in the prevention of food aversions in children receiving chemotherapy. *Cancer, 60* (9), 2344–2347.

**Brockmeyer, T., Friederich, H. C., & Schmidt, U.** (2018). Advances in the treatment of anorexia nervosa: A review of established and emerging interventions. *Psychological Medicine, 48* (8), 1228–1256.

**Brockway, J. P., & Shapiro, C. L.** (2018). Improving adherence to endocrine therapy in women with HR-positive breast cancer. *Breast Cancer, 32,* 235–249.

**Broder-Fingert, S., Feinberg, E., & Silverstein, M.** (2018). Improving screening for autism spectrum disorder: Is it time for something new? *Pediatrics,* e20180965.

**Brody, L. R.** (1999). *Gender, emotion, and the family.* Cambridge, MA: Harvard University Press.

**Brody, N.** (2007). Does education influence intelligence? In P. C. Kyllonen, R. D. Roberts, & L. Stankov (Eds.), *Extending intelligence.* Mahwah, NJ: Erlbaum.

**Broer, L., Codd, V., Nyholt, D. R., Deelen, J., Mangino, M., Willemsen, G., ... & Boomsma, D. I.** (2013). Meta-analysis of telomere length in 19,713 subjects reveals high heritability, stronger maternal inheritance, and a paternal age effect. *European Journal of Human Genetics, 21* (10), 1163–1168.

**Brohan, E., Elgie, R., Sartorius, N., & Thornicroft, G.** (2010). Self-stigma, empowerment, and perceived discrimination among people with schizophrenia in 14 European countries: The GAMIAN-Europe study. *Schizophrenia Research, 122* (1–3), 232–238.

**Brown, A.** (2017, June 13). *Five key findings about LGBT Americans.* Pew Research. http://www.pewresearch.org/fact-tank/2017/06/13/5-key-findings-about-lgbt-americans/

**Brown, A. S.** (2004). *The déjà vu experience.* New York: Psychology Press.

**Brown, A. S.** (2012). *The tip of the tongue state.* New York: Taylor & Francis.

**Brown, A. S., & Marsh, E. J.** (2010). Digging into déjà vu: Recent research findings on the possible mechanisms. In B. H. Ross (Ed.,) *The psychology of learning and motivation* (vol. 53, pp. 33–62). Burlington, VT: Academic Press.

**Brown, C. L., Gibbons, L. E., Kennison, R. F., Robitaille, A., Lindwall, M., Mitchell, M. B., ... & Piccinin, A. M.** (2012). Social activity and cognitive functioning over time: A coordinated analysis of four longitudinal studies. *Journal of Aging Research.* doi: 10.1155.2012/287438

**Brown, C. S., & Lichter-Konecki, U.** (2016). Phenylketonuria (PKU): A problem solved? *Molecular Genetics and Metabolism Reports, 6,* 8–12.

**Brown, D.** (2007). Evidence-based hypnotherapy for asthma: A critical review. *International Journal of Clinical and Experimental Hypnosis, 55* (2), 220–249.

**Brown, N. M., Brown, S. N., Briggs, R. D., Germán, M., Belamarich, P. F., & Oyeku, S. O.** (2017). Associations between adverse childhood experiences and ADHD diagnosis and severity. *Academic Pediatrics, 17* (4), 349–355.

**Brown, N. W.** (2018). *Psychoeducational groups: Process and practice* (4th ed.). New York: Routledge.

**Brown, P., & Tierney, C.** (2011). Media role in violence and the dynamics of bullying. *Pediatric Reviews, 32,* 453–454.

**Brown, R.** (1973). *A first language: The early stages.* Cambridge, MA: Harvard University Press.

**Brown, S. D., Lent, R. W., Telander, K., & Tramayne, S.** (2011). Social cognitive career theory, conscientiousness, and work performance: A meta-analytic path analysis. *Journal of Vocational Behavior, 79* (1), 81–90.

**Brown, S. L., Nesse, R. N., Vinokur, A. D., & Smith, D. M.** (2003). Providing social support may be more beneficial than receiving it: Results from a prospective study of mortality. *Psychological Science, 14* (4), 320–327.

**Brown, W. J., Dewey, D., Bunnell, B. E., Boyd, S. J., Wilkerson, A. K., Mitchell, M. A., & Bruce, S. E.** (2018). A critical review of negative affect and the application of CBT for PTSD. *Trauma, Violence, & Abuse, 19* (2), 176–194.

**Bruce, C. R., Unsworth, C. A., Dillon, M. P., Tay, R., Falkmer, T., Bird, P., & Carey, L. M.** (2017). Hazard perception skills of young drivers with attention deficit hyperactivity disorder (ADHD) can be improved with computer based driver training: An exploratory randomised controlled trial. *Accident Analysis & Prevention, 109,* 70–77.

**Bruck, M., & Ceci, S. J.** (2012). Forensic developmental psychology in the courtroom. In D. Faust & M. Ziskin (Eds.), *Coping with psychiatric and psychological testimony.* New York: Cambridge University Press.

**Brug, J., Conner, M., Harré, N., Kremers, S., McKellar, S., & Whitelaw, S.** (2004). The transtheoretical model and stages of change: A critique. Observations by five commentators on the paper by J. Adams and M. White (2004) Why don't stage-based activity promotion interventions work? *Health Education Research, 20* (2), 244–258.

**Bryan, L. K., & Vinchur, A. J.** (2013). Industrial-organizational psychology. In D. K. Freedheim & I. B. Weiner (Eds.), *Handbook of psychology* (2nd ed., vol. 1, pp. 407–428). Hoboken, NJ: Wiley.

**Bryant, J. B.** (2012). Pragmatic development. In E. L. Bavin (Ed.), *The Cambridge handbook of child language.* New York: Cambridge University Press.

**Bryner, J.** (October 2, 2018). Nobel Prize in physics shared by woman for 1st time in 55 years. *Live Science.* https://www.livescience.com/63727-nobel-prize-in-physics-2018.html

**Bucherelli, C., Baldi, E., Mariottini, C., Passani, M. B., & Blandina, P.** (2006). Aversive memory reactivation engages in the amygdala only some neurotransmitters involved in consolidation. *Learning and Memory, 13,* 426–430.

**Buchman, A. S., Yu, L., Boyle, P. A., Schneider, J. A., De Jager, P. L., & Bennett, D. A.** (2016). Higher brain BDNF gene expression is associated with slower cognitive decline in older adults. *Neurology, 86* (8), 735–741.

**Buchmeier, A. L., Baker, J. C., Reuter-Yuill, L. M., & MacNeill, B. R.** (2018). Considerations for preference and reinforcer assessments with older adults with developmental disabilities. *Behavior Analysis: Research and Practice, 18* (1), 103–116.

**Buckley, T. R.** (2018). Black adolescent males: Intersections among their gender role identity and racial identity and associations with self-concept (global and school). *Child Development, 89* (4), e311–e322.

**Buehl, A. K., Melchers, K. G., Macan, T., & Kühnel, J.** (2018). Tell me sweet little lies: How does faking in interviews affect interview scores and interview validity? *Journal of Business and Psychology.* doi: 10.1007/s10869-018-9531-3

**Buján, A., Galdo-Álvarez, S., Lindín, M., & Díaz, F.** (2012). An event-related potentials study of face naming: Evidence of phonological retrieval deficit in the tip-of-the-tongue state. *Psychophysiology, 49* (7), 980–990.

**Bullman, T., Schneiderman, A., & Gradus, J. L.** (2018). Relative importance of posttraumatic stress disorder and depression in predicting risk of suicide among a cohort of Vietnam veterans. *Suicide and Life-Threatening Behavior.* doi: 10.1111/sltb.12482

**Bullock, H. E., Griffin, K. M., Kent, A. H., & Toolis, E. E.** (2018). Translating psychological research on social class and socioeconomic status. *Translational Issues in Psychological Science, 4* (2), 119–121. doi: 10.1037/tps0000160

**Bureau of Labor Statistics.** (April 13, 2018). Fastest growing occupations 2016–2026. https://www.bls.gov/ooh/fastest-growing.htm

**Burger, J. M.** (2009). Replicating Milgram: Would people still obey today? *American Psychologist, 64* (1), 1–11.

**Burgess Moser, M., Johnson, S. M., Dalgleish, T. L., Wiebe, S. A., & Tasca, G. A.** (2018). The impact of blamer-softening on romantic attachment in emotionally focused couples therapy. *Journal of Marital and Family Therapy, 44* (4), 640–654.

**Burgos, J. E.** (2018). Is a nervous system necessary for learning? *Perspectives on Behavior Science,* 1–26.

**Burkart, J. M., Bruegger, R. K., & van Schaik, C. P.** (2018). Evolutionary origins of morality: Insights from nonhuman primates. *Frontiers in Sociology, 3,* 17.

**Burke, P., & Welbes, J.** (2018). Minneapolis–St. Paul International Airport: Instilling a culture of accessibility for people with disabilities that goes above and beyond requirements. *Journal of Airport Management, 12* (2), 198–206.

**Burks, S. V., Cowgill, B., Hoffman, M., & Housman, M.** (2015). The value of hiring through employee referrals. *Quarterly Journal of Economics, 130* (2), 805–839.

**Burns, S. A., Elsner, A. E., Sapoznik, K. A., Warner, R. L., & Gast, T. J.** (2019). Adaptive optics imaging of the human retina. *Progress in Retinal and Eye Research, 68,* 1–30.

**Burns, T., Kisely, S., & Rugkåsa, J.** (2017). Randomised controlled trials and outpatient commitment. *The Lancet Psychiatry, 4* (12), e31.

**Burr, J. A., Han, S., Lee, H. J., Tavares, J. L., & Mutchler, J. E.** (2017). Health benefits associated with three helping behaviors: Evidence for incident cardiovascular disease. *The Journals of Gerontology: Series B, 73* (3), 492–500.

**Burton, C. M., & King, L. A.** (2004). The health benefits of writing about peak experiences. *Journal of Research in Personality, 38,* 150–163.

**Burton, C. M., & King, L. A.** (2008). The effects of (very) brief writing on health: The 2-minute miracle. *British Journal of Health Psychology, 13,* 9–14.

**Burton, C. M., & King, L. A.** (2009). The benefits of writing about positive experiences: Applying the broaden and build model. *Psychology and Health, 24,* 867–879.

**Bushman, L., & Huesmann, L. R.** (2012). Effects of media violence on aggression. In D. G. Singer & J. L. Singer (Eds.), *Handbook of children and the media* (2nd ed.). Thousand Oaks, CA: Sage.

**Buss, D. M.** (2015). *Evolutionary psychology: The new science of the mind* (5th ed.). New York: Psychology Press.

**Buss, D. M.** (2018). Sexual and emotional infidelity: Evolved gender differences in jealousy prove robust and replicable. *Perspectives on Psychological Science, 13* (2), 155–160.

**Buss, D. M., & Schmitt, D. P.** (2019). Mate preferences and their behavioral manifestations. *Annual Review of Psychology.* (in press)

**Bussey, K., & Bandura, A.** (2004). Social cognitive theory of gender development and functioning. In A. H. Eagly, A. Beall, & R. Sternberg (Eds.), *The psychology of gender* (2nd ed., pp. 92–119). New York: Guilford.

**Bussy, G., Charrin, E., Brun, A., Curi, A., & des Portes, V.** (2011). Implicit procedural learning in fragile X and Down syndrome. *Journal of Intellectual Disabilities Research, 55* (5), 521–528.

**Butcher, J. N., Beutler, L. E., Harwood, T. M., & Blau, K.** (2011). The MMPI-2. In T. M. Harwood, L. E. Beutler, & G. Groth-Marnat (Eds.), *Integrative assessment of adult personality* (3rd ed.). New York: Guilford.

**Butler, R. S., Sorace, D., & Beach, K. H.** (2018). Institutionalizing sex education in diverse US school districts. *Journal of Adolescent Health, 62* (2), 149–156.

**Buxton, O. M., Chang, A. M., Spilsbury, J. C., Bos, T., Emsellem, H., & Knutson, K. L.** (2015). Sleep in the modern family: Protective family routines for child and adolescent sleep. *Sleep Health, 1* (1), 15–27.

**Buzzichelli, S., Marzola, E., Amianto, F., Fassino, S., & Abbate-Daga, G.** (2018). Perfectionism and cognitive rigidity in anorexia nervosa: Is there an association? *European Eating Disorders Review.* doi: 10.1002/erv.2591

**Byrd, W. C.** (2015). College diversity is (but doesn't have to be) for whites. *Contexts, 14* (3), 74–75.

**Byrne, A., Salmon, P., & Fisher, P.** (2018). A case study of the challenges for an integrative practitioner learning a new psychological therapy. *Counselling and Psychotherapy Research, 18* (4), 369–376.

**Byrne, R. W., Hobaiter, C., & Klailova, M.** (2011). Local traditions in gorilla manual skill: Evidence for observational learning of behavioral organization. *Animal Cognition, 14* (5), 683–693.

## C


**Cacalano, N.** (2016). Regulation of natural killer cell function by STAT3. *Frontiers in Immunology, 7.* 128.

**Cacioppo, J. T., & Cacioppo, S.** (2018). Loneliness in the modern age: An evolutionary theory of loneliness (ETL). *Advances in Experimental Social Psychology, 58,* 127–197.

**Cacioppo, J. T., Cacioppo, S., & Petty, R. E.** (2018). The neuroscience of persuasion: A review with an emphasis on issues and opportunities. *Social Neuroscience, 13* (2), 129–172.

**Cagney, K. A., Browning, C. R., Iveniuk, J., & English, N.** (2014). The onset of depression during the Great Recession: Foreclosure and older adult mental health. *American Journal of Public Health, 10,* 498–505.

**Caillouet, B. A., Boccaccini, M. T., Varela, J. G., Davis, R. D., & Rostow, C. D.** (2010). Predictive validity of the MMPI-2 PSY-5 scales and facets for law enforcement officer employment outcomes. *Criminal Justice and Behavior, 37,* 217–238.

**Calderon, A., Schneider, C., Target, M., Midgley, N., & IMPACT Consortium.** (2018). 'Interaction structures' between depressed adolescents and their therapists in short-term psychoanalytic psychotherapy and cognitive behavioural therapy. *Clinical Child Psychology and Psychiatry.* doi: 10.1177/1359104518807734

**Caldwell, C., Beverage, M. S., & Converse, P. D.** (2018). Selecting for flair factors: Improving the selection process. *Business and Management Research, 7*(1). doi: 10.5430/bmr.v7n1p1

**Calogero, R. M.** (2013). Objects don't object: Evidence that self-objectification disrupts women's social activism. *Psychological Science, 24* (3), 312–318.

**Caloghirou, Y., Giotopoulos, I., Korra, E., & Tsakanikas, A.** (2018). How do employee training and knowledge stocks affect product innovation? *Economics of Innovation and New Technology, 27* (4), 343–360.

**Calvert, S. L., Appelbaum, M., Dodge, K. A., Graham, S., Nagayama Hall, G. C., Hamby, S., ... & Hedges, L. V.** (2017). The American Psychological Association Task Force assessment of violent video games: Science in the service of public interest. *American Psychologist, 72* (2), 126–143.

**Cameron, K. S.** (2003). Organizational virtuousness and performance. In K. S. Cameron, J. E. Dutton, & R. E. Quinn (Eds.), *Positive organizational scholarship: Foundations of a new discipline* (pp. 48–65). San Francisco: Berrett-Koehler.

**Cameron, K. S.** (2005). Organizational downsizing. In N. Nicholson, P. G. Audia, & M. M. Pilluta (Eds.), *The Blackwell encyclopedia of management.* Malden, MA: Blackwell.

**Campbell, I. G., Grimm, K. J., de Bie, E., & Feinberg, I.** (2012). Sex, puberty, and the timing of sleep EEG measured adolescent brain maturation. *Proceedings of the National Academy of Sciences USA, 109* (15), 5740–5743.

**Campbell, K., Nelson, J., Parker, M. L., & Johnston, S.** (2018). Interpersonal chemistry in friendships and romantic relationships. *Interpersona: An International Journal on Personal Relationships, 12* (1), 34–50.

**Campbell, L., Campbell, B., & Dickinson, D.** (2004). *Teaching and learning through multiple intelligences.* Boston: Allyn & Bacon.

**Camps, S. G., Verhoef, S. P., & Westerterp, K. R.** (2016). Physical activity and weight loss are independent predictors of improved insulin sensitivity following energy restriction. *Obesity, 24* (2), 291–296.

**Canady, V. A.** (2018). Mental health experts weigh in on NYT analysis of SSRI withdrawal concerns. *Mental Health Weekly, 28* (15), 1–3.

**Cannon, W. B.** (1927). The James–Lange theory of emotions: A critical examination and an alternative theory. *American Journal of Psychology, 39,* 106–124.

**Cannon, W. B., & Washburn, A. L.** (1912). An explanation of hunger.*American Journal of Physiology, 29,* 441–454.

**Cantor, J. M.** (2018). Can pedophiles change? *Current Sexual Health Reports, 10* (4), 203–206.

**Cantor, J. M., & Blanchard, T.** (2012). White matter volumes in pedophiles, hebephiles, and teleiophiles. *Archives of Sexual Behavior, 41,* 749–752.

**Cao, H., Harneit, A., Walter, H., Erk, S., Braun, U., Moessnang, C., ... & Romanczuk-Seiferth, N.** (2018). The 5-HTTLPR polymorphism affects network-based functional connectivity in the visual-limbic system in healthy adults. *Neuropsychopharmacology, 43* (2), 406–414.

**Capitanio, J.** (2017). Animal studies in psychology. https://www.apa.org/ed/precollege/psn/2017/01/animal-studies.aspx

**Caplan, R.** (2017). ADHD in pediatric epilepsy: Fact or fiction? *Epilepsy Currents, 17* (2), 93–95.

**Capogrosso, M., Wagner, F. B., Gandar, J., Moraud, E. M., Wenger, N., Milekovic, T., ... & Bloch, J.** (2018). Configuration of electrical spinal cord stimulation through real-time processing of gait kinematics. *Nature Protocols, 13* (9), 2031.

**Caponecchia, C., Zheng, W. Y., & Regan, M. A.** (2018). Selecting trainee pilots: Predictive validity of the WOMBAT situational awareness pilot selection test. *Applied Ergonomics, 73,* 100–107.

**Caprara, G. V., Alessandri, G., Di Giunta, L., Panerai, L., & Eisenberg, N.** (2010). The contribution of agreeableness and self-efficacy beliefs to prosociality. *European Journal of Personality, 24* (1), 36–55.

**Caprara, G. V., Fagnani, C., Alessandri, G., Steca, P., Gigantesco, A., Sforza, L. L. C., & Stazi, M. A.** (2009). Human optimal functioning: The genetics of positive orientation towards self, life, and the future. *Behavior Genetics, 39* (3), 277–284.

**Carbon, M., Kane, J. M., Leucht, S., & Correll, C. U.** (2018). Tardive dyskinesia risk with first- and second-generation antipsychotics in comparative randomized controlled trials: A meta-analysis. *World Psychiatry, 17* (3), 330–340.

**Cárdenas, M., Barrientos, J., Meyer, I., Gómez, F., Guzmán, M., & Bahamondes, J.** (2018). Direct and indirect effects of perceived stigma on posttraumatic growth in gay men and lesbian women in Chile. *Journal of Traumatic Stress, 31* (1), 5–13.

**Carey, B.** (2011a, November 25). Finding purpose after living with delusion. *New York Times.* http://www.nytimes.com/2011/11/26/health/man-uses-his-schizophrenia-to-gather-clues-for-daily-living.html (accessed April 9, 2016)

**Carey, C. E., & Bogdan, R.** (2018). Executive function and genomic risk for attention-deficit/hyperactivity disorder: Testing intermediate phenotypes in the context of polygenic risk, *Journal of the American Academy of Child & Adolescent Psychiatry 57,* 146–148.

**Carl, E., Stein, A. T., Levihn-Coon, A., Pogue, J. R., Rothbaum, B., Emmelkamp, P., ... & Powers, M. B.** (2018). Virtual reality exposure therapy for anxiety and related disorders: A meta-analysis of randomized controlled trials. *Journal of Anxiety Disorders.* doi: 10.1016/j.janxdis.2018.08.003

**Carlo, G., Christ, C., Laible, D., & Gulseven, Z.** (2016). An evolving and developing field of study: Prosocial morality from a biological, cultural, and developmental perspective. In T. K. Shackelford & R. D. Hansan (Eds.), *The evolution of morality* (pp. 53–76). Switzerland: Springer International Publishing.

**Carlo, G., Knight, G. P., McGinley, M., & Hayes, R.** (2011). The roles of parental inductions, moral emotions, and moral cognitions in prosocial tendencies among Mexican American and European American early adolescents. *Journal of Early Adolescence, 31,* 757–781.

**Carlson, S. M., Shoda, Y., Ayduk, O., Aber, L., Schaefer, C., Sethi, A., ... & Mischel, W.** (2018). Cohort effects in children's delay of gratification. *Developmental Psychology, 54* (8), 1395–1407.

**Carman, C. A.** (2011). Stereotypes of giftedness in current and future educators. *Journal for the Education of the Gifted, 34* (5), 790–812.

**Carmona, J. E., Holland, A. K., & Harrison, D. W.** (2009). Extending the functional cerebral systems theory of emotion to the vestibular modality: A systematic and integrative approach. *Psychological Bulletin, 135* (2), 286–302.

**Carothers, B. J., & Reis, H. T.** (2013). Men and women are from Earth: Examining the latent structure of gender. *Journal of Personality and Social Psychology, 104* (2), 385–407.

**Carpenter, J. K., Andrews, L. A., Witcraft, S. M., Powers, M. B., Smits, J. A., & Hofmann, S. G.** (2018). Cognitive behavioral therapy for anxiety and related disorders: A meta-analysis of randomized placebo-controlled trials. *Depression and Anxiety.* doi: 10.1002/da.22728

**Carr, A., Slade, L., Yuill, N., Sullivan, S., & Ruffman, T.** (2018). Minding the children: A longitudinal study of mental state talk, theory of mind, and behavioural adjustment from the age of 3 to 10. *Social Development.* doi: 10.1111/sode.12315

**Carr, R., & Peebles, R.** (2012). Developmental considerations of media exposure risk for eating disorders. In J. Lock (Ed.), *The Oxford handbook of child and adolescent eating disorders: Developmental perspectives.* New York: Oxford University Press.

**Carrier, L. M., Rosen, L. D., Cheever, N. A., & Lim, A. F.** (2015). Causes, effects, and practicalities of everyday multitasking. *Developmental Review, 35,* 64–78.

**Carrotte, E., & Anderson, J. R.** (2018). A systematic review of the relationship between trait self-objectification and personality traits. *Personality and Individual Differences, 132,* 20–31.

**Carrozza, A.** (2018, November 12). Program pairs Air Force veteran and rescue dog. *Veterinarian's Money Digest.* https://www.vmdtoday.com/news/zoetis-program-pairs-air-force-veteran-and-rescue-dog

**Carson, R. C., Butcher, J. N., & Mineka, S.** (1996). *Abnormal psychology and life* (10th ed.). New York: HarperCollins.

**Carstensen, L. L.** (2006). The influence of a sense of time on human development. *Science, 312* (5782), 1913–1915.

**Carstensen, L. L.** (2008, May). *Long life in the twenty-first century.* Paper presented at the meeting of the Association of Psychological Science, Chicago.

**Carstensen, L. L.** (2011). *A long bright future: Happiness, health, and financial security in an age of increased longevity.* New York: Broadway Books.

**Carstensen, L. L., Turan, B., Scheibe, S., Ram, N., Ersner-Hershfield, H., Samanez-Larkin, G. R., Brooks, K. P., & Nesselroade, J. R.** (2011). Emotional experience improves with age: Evidence based on over 10 years of sampling. *Psychology and Aging, 26* (1), 21–33.

**Carvalho, F. M., & Spence, C.** (2018). The shape of the cup influences aroma, taste, and hedonic judgements of specialty coffee. *Food Quality and Preference, 68,* 315–321.

**Carver, C. S., & Connor-Smith, J.** (2010). Personality and coping. *Annual Review of Psychology* (vol. 61, pp. 679–704). Palo Alto, CA: Annual Reviews.

**Carver, C. S., & Scheier, M. F.** (2009). Optimism. In M. R. Levy & R. H. Hoyle (Eds.), *Handbook of individual differences in social behavior* (pp. 330–342). New York: Guilford.

**Carver, C. S., & Scheier, M. F.** (2013). Self-regulatory perspectives on personality. In H. A. Tennen, J. M. Suls, & I. B. Weiner (Eds.), *Handbook of psychology* (2nd ed., vol. 5, pp. 119–140). Hoboken, NJ: Wiley.

**Clifton, D. O., & Harter, J. K.** (2003). Strengths investment. In K. S. Cameron, J. E. Dutton, & R. E. Quinn (Eds.), *Positive organizational scholarship* (pp. 111–121). San Francisco: Berrett & Koehler.

**Clifton, D. O., & Nelson, P.** (1995). *Soar with your strengths.* New York: Random House.

**Close, M. A., Lytle, L. A., Chen, D. G., & Viera, A. J.** (2018). Using the theory of planned behavior to explain intention to eat a healthful diet among Southeastern United States office workers. *Nutrition & Food Science, 48* (2), 365–374.

**Clutton-Brock, T. H.** (2007). Sexual selection in males and females. *Science, 318* (5858), 1882–1885.

**Clutton-Brock, T. H.** (2010). We do not need a sexual selection 2.0–nor a theory of genial selection. *Animal Behaviour, 79* (3), e7–e10.

**Coa, K. I., Epstein, J. B., Ettinger, D., Jatoi, A., McManus, K., Platek, M. E., Price, W., Stewart, M., Teknos, T. N., & Moskowitz, B.** (2015). The impact of cancer treatment on the diets and food preferences of patients receiving outpatient treatment. *Nutrition and Cancer, 67* (2), 339–353.

**Coddington, L. T., & Dudman, J. T.** (2018). The timing of action determines reward prediction signals in identified midbrain dopamine neurons. *Nature Neuroscience, 21,* 1563–1573.

**Codoñer-Franch, P., & Gombert, M.** (2018). Circadian rhythms in the pathogenesis of gastrointestinal diseases. *World Journal of Gastroenterology, 24* (38), 4297.

**Coelho, C. M., & Purkis, H.** (2009). The origins of specific phobias: Influential theories and current perspectives. *Review of General Psychology, 13* (4), 335–348.

**Cohen, D.** (2001). Cultural variation: Considerations and implications. *Psychological Bulletin, 127* (4), 451–471.

**Cohen, D., Nisbett, R. E., Bowdle, B. F., & Schwarz, N.** (1996). Insult, aggression, and the southern culture of honor: An "experimental ethnography." *Journal of Personality and Social Psychology, 70* (5), 945–960.

**Cohen, G., & de Chazal, P.** (2015). Automated detection of sleep apnea in infants: A multi-modal approach. *Computers in Biology and Medicine, 63,* 118–123.

**Cohen, J. M., Blasey, C., Taylor, C. B., Weiss, B. J., & Newman, M. G.** (2016). Anxiety and related disorders and concealment in sexual minority young adults. *Behavior Therapy, 47* (1), 91–101.

**Cohen, S.** (2016). Psychological stress, immunity, and physical disease. In R. Sternberg, F. Fiske, & D. Foss (Eds.), *Scientists making a difference: The greatest living behavioral and brain scientists talk about their most important contributions* (pp. 419–423). Cambridge UK: Cambridge University Press.

**Cohen, S., Doyle, W. J., Alper, C. M., Janicki-Deverts, D., & Turner, R. B.** (2009). Sleep habits and susceptibility to the common cold. *Archives of Internal Medicine, 169* (1), 62–67.

**Cohen, S., Frank, E., Doyle, W., Skoner, D. P., Rabin, B. S., & Gwaltney, J. M.** (1998). Types of stressors that increase susceptibility to the common cold in healthy adults. *Health Psychology, 17* (3), 214–223.

**Cohen, S., Fulcher, B. D., Rajaratnam, S. M., Conduit, R., Sullivan, J. P., St. Hilaire, M. A., ... & Braga-Kenyon, P.** (2018). Sleep patterns predictive of daytime challenging behavior in individuals with low-functioning autism. *Autism Research, 11* (2), 391–403.

**Cohen, S., Janicki-Deverts, D., Crittenden, C. N., & Sneed, R. S.** (2012). Personality and human immunity. In S. C. Segerstrom (Ed.), *The Oxford handbook of psychoneuroimmunology.* New York: Oxford University Press.

**Cohen, S., Janicki-Deverts, D., Turner, R. B., Casselbrant, M. L., Li-Korotky, H. S., Epel, E. S., & Doyle, W. J.** (2013). Association between telomere length and experimentally induced upper viral infection in healthy adults. *Journal of the American Medical Association, 309* (7), 699–705.

**Cohen, S., Murphy, M. L. M., & Prather, A. A.** (2019). Ten surprising facts about stressful life events and disease risk. *Annual Review of Psychology, 70,* 7.1–7.21. doi: 10.1146/annurev-psych-010418-102857

**Cohen-Bendahan, C. C., van de Beek, C., & Berenbaum, S. A.** (2005). Prenatal sex hormone effects on child and adult sex-typed behavior: Methods and findings. *Neuroscience and Biobehavioral Reviews, 29* (2), 353–384.

**Cohen-Charash, Y., & Spector, P. E.** (2001). The role of justice in organizations: A meta-analysis. *Organizational Behavior and Human Decision Processes, 86* (2), 278–321.

**Cohn, G.** (October 21, 2018). Up for bid, AI art signed 'Algorithm'. *New York Times,* C1.

**Coifman, K. G., Bonanno, G. A., Ray, R. D., & Gross, J. J.** (2007). Does repressing coping promote resilience? Affective-autonomic response discrepancy during bereavement. *Journal of Personality and Social Psychology, 92* (4), 745–758.

**Colapinto, J.** (2000). *As nature made him.* New York: HarperAcademic.

**Collado, A., Lim, A. C., & MacPherson, L.** (2016). A systematic review of depression psychotherapies among Latinos. *Clinical Psychology Review, 45,* 193–209.

**Collibee, C., & Furman, W.** (2018). A moderator model of alcohol use and dating aggression among young adults. *Journal of Youth and Adolescence, 47* (3), 534–546.

**Collings, D. G., Wood, G. T., & Szamosi, L. T.** (2018). Human resource management: A critical approach. In D.G. Collings, G. T. Wood, & L. T. Szamosi (Eds.), *Human Resource Management,* 2nd ed. (pp. 1–23). London: Routledge.

**Collins, K. L., Russell, H. G., Schumacher, P. J., Robinson-Freeman, K. E., O'Conor, E. C., Gibney, K. D., ... & Tsao, J. W.** (2018). A review of current theories and treatments for phantom limb pain. *The Journal of Clinical Investigation, 128* (6), 2168–2176.

**Colloca, L.** (2019). The placebo effect in pain therapies. *Annual Review of Pharmacology and Toxicology, 59,* 191–211.

**Colombo, E., Rotondi, V., & Stanca, L.** (2018). Macroeconomic conditions and health: Inspecting the transmission mechanism. *Economics & Human Biology, 28,* 29–37.

**Coltheart, M., Cox, R., Sowman, P., Morgan, H., Barnier, A., Langdon, R., ... & Polito, V.** (2018). Belief, delusion, hypnosis, and the right dorsolateral prefrontal cortex: A transcranial magnetic stimulation study. *Cortex, 101,* 234–248.

**Compton, J. A., & Pfau, M.** (2004). Use of inoculation to foster resistance to credit card marketing targeting college students. *Journal of Applied Communication Research, 32* (4), 343–364.

**Compton, J. A., & Pfau, M.** (2008). Inoculating against pro-plagiarism justifications: Rational and affective strategies. *Journal of Applied Communication Research, 36* (1), 98–119.

**Compton, M. T., Lunden, A., Cleary, S. D., Pauselli, L., Alolayan, Y., Halpern, B., ... & Bernardini, F.** (2018). The aprosody of schizophrenia: Computationally derived acoustic phonetic underpinnings of monotone speech. *Schizophrenia Research, 197,* 392–399.

**Comstock, G.** (2012). The use of television and other film-related media. In D. G. Singer & J. L. Singer (Eds.), *Handbook of children and the media* (2nd ed.). Thousand Oaks, CA: Sage.

**Conley, T. D.** (2011). Perceived proposer personality characteristics and gender differences in acceptance of casual sex offers. *Journal of Personality and Social Psychology, 100* (2), 309–329.

**Connellan, J., Baron-Cohen, S., Wheelwright, S., Batki, A., & Ahluwalia, J.** (2000). Sex differences in human neonatal social perception. *Infant Behavior & Development, 23* (1), 113–118.

**Connolly, S. L., & Alloy, L. B.** (2018). Negative event recall as a vulnerability for depression: Relationship between momentary stress-reactive rumination and memory for daily life stress. *Clinical Psychological Science, 6* (1), 32–47.

**Consoloni, J. L., Lefebvre, M. N., Zendjidjian, X., Olié, E., Mazzola-Pomietto, P., Desmidt, T., ... & Haffen, E.** (2018). Serotonin transporter gene expression predicts the worsening of suicidal ideation and suicide attempts along a long-term follow-up of a major depressive episode. *European Neuropsychopharmacology, 28* (3), 401–414.

**Constantin, K., English, M. M., & Mazmanian, D.** (2018). Anxiety, depression, and procrastination among students: Rumination plays a larger mediating role than worry. *Journal of Rational-Emotive & Cognitive-Behavior Therapy, 36* (1), 15–27.

**Constantine, N. A.** (2008). Converging evidence leaves policy behind: Sex education in the United States. *Journal of Adolescent Health, 42* (4), 324–326.

**Conway, A. M., Tugade, M. M., Catalino, L. I., & Fredrickson, B. L.** (2013). The broaden-and-build theory of positive emotions: Form, function, and mechanisms. In S. A. David, I. Boniwell, & A. Conley Ayers (Eds.), *The Oxford handbook of happiness.* (pp. 17–34). New York: Oxford University Press.

**Conway, M., & Rubin, D.** (1993). The structure of autobiographical memory. In A. F. Collins, S. E. Gathercole, M. A. Conway, & P. E. Morris (Eds.), *Theories of memory.* Hillsdale, NJ: Erlbaum.

**Cook, S. L., Woods, S., Methven, L., Parker, J. K., & Khutoryanskiy, V. V.** (2018). Mucoadhesive polysaccharides modulate sodium retention, release and taste perception. *Food Chemistry, 240,* 482–489.

**Cooke, A., & Kinderman, P.** (2018). But what about real mental illnesses? Alternatives to the disease model approach to schizophrenia. *Journal of Humanistic Psychology, 58* (1), 47–71.

**Cools, M., Nordenström, A., Robeva, R., Hall, J., Westerveld, P., Flück, C., ... & Pasterski, V.** (2018). Caring for individuals with a difference of sex development (DSD): A consensus statement. *Nature Reviews Endocrinology,* 1.

**Cooper, J. M., Abrahamsson, K. E., & Prosser, R. A.** (2018). Circadian rhythm and sleep-wake systems share the dynamic extracellular synaptic milieu. *Neurobiology of Sleep and Circadian Rhythms, 5,* 15–36.

**Cooper, M., & Morton, J.** (2018). Digital health and obesity: How technology could be the culprit and solution for obesity. In H. Rivas & K.Wac (Eds.), *Digital health: Scaling healthcare to the world* (pp. 169–178). Cham, Switzerland: Springer.

**Cooper, R. M., & Zubek, J. P.** (1958). Effects of enriched and restricted early environments on the learning ability of bright and dull rats. *Canadian Journal of Psychology, 12* (3), 159–164.

**Cooper, S. E., Grillon, C., & Lissek, S.** (2018). Impaired discriminative fear conditioning during later training trials differentiates generalized anxiety disorder, but not panic disorder, from healthy control participants. *Comprehensive Psychiatry, 85,* 84–93.

**Corbetta, D., Wiener, R. F., Thurman, S. L., & McMahon, E.** (2018). The embodied origins of infant reaching: Implications for the emergence of eye-hand coordination. *Kinesiology Review, 7* (1), 10–17.

**Corbetta, D., Williams, J. L., & Haynes, J. M.** (2016). Bare fingers, but no obvious influence of "prickly" Velcro! In the absence of parents' encouragement, it is not clear that "sticky mittens" provide an advantage to the process of learning to reach. *Infant Behavior and Development, 42,* 168–178.

**Corder, G., Castro, D. C., Bruchas, M. R., & Scherrer, G.** (2018). Endogenous and exogenous opioids in pain. *Annual Review of Neuroscience, 41,* 453–473.

**Cordon, I. M., Melinder, A. M., Goodman, G. S., & Edelstein, R. S.** (2013). Children's and adults' memory for emotional pictures: Examining age-related patterns using the developmental affective photo system. *Journal of Experimental Child Psychology, 114* (2), 339–356.

**Cormack, C. L., Jensen, E., Durham, C. O., Smith, G., & Dumas, B.** (2018). The 360-degree evaluation model: A method for assessing competency in graduate nursing students. A pilot research study. *Nurse Education Today, 64,* 132–137.

**Cornblatt, B. A., Carrion, R. E., Addington, J., Seidman, L., Walker, E. F., Cannon, T. D., … & Lencz, T.** (2012). Risk factors for psychosis: Impaired social and role functioning. *Schizophrenia Bulletin, 38* (6), 1247–1257.

**Cornelius, T., Gettens, K., Lenz, E., Wojtanowski, A. C., Foster, G. D., & Gorin, A. A.** (2018). How prescriptive support affects weight loss in weight-loss intervention participants and their untreated spouses. *Health Psychology, 37* (8), 775.

**Cornish, M. A., Woodyatt, L., Morris, G., Conroy, A., & Townsdin, J.** (2018). Self-forgiveness, self-exoneration, and self-condemnation: Individual differences associated with three patterns of responding to interpersonal offenses. *Personality and Individual Differences, 129,* 43–53. doi: 10.1016/j.paid.2018.03.003

**Cornwallis, C. K.** (2018). Cooperative breeding and the evolutionary coexistence of helper and nonhelper strategies. *Proceedings of the National Academy of Sciences, 115,* 1684–1686.

**Corr, P. J.** (2016). Reinforcement sensitivity theory of personality questionnaires: Structural survey with recommendations. *Personality and Individual Differences, 89,* 60–64.

**Corrigan, P. W.** (2015). Challenging the stigma of mental illness: Different agendas, different goals. *Psychiatric Services, 66* (12), 1347–1349.

**Corrigan, P. W., & Al-Khouja, M. A.** (2018). Three agendas for changing the public stigma of mental illness. *Psychiatric Rehabilitation Journal, 41* (1), 1.

**Corrigan, P. W., Larson, J. E., Michaels, P. J., Buchholz, B. A., Rossi, R. D., Fontecchio, M. J., Castro, D., Gause, M., Krzyżanowski, R., & Rüsch, N.** (2015). Diminishing the self-stigma of mental illness by coming out proud. *Psychiatry Research, 229* (1–2), 148–154.

**Corrigan, P. W., Rowan, D., Green, A., Lundin, R., River, P., Uphoff-Wasowski, K., White, K., & Kubiak, M. A.** (2002). Challenging two mental illness stigmas: Personal responsibility and dangerousness. *Schizophrenia Bulletin, 28* (2), 293–309.

**Cosmides, L., & Tooby, J.** (2013). Evolutionary psychology: New perspectives on cognition and motivation. *Annual Review of Psychology* (vol. 64, pp. 201–229). Palo Alto, CA: Annual Reviews.

**Costa, P. T., & McCrae, R. R.** (1992). *Revised NEO personality inventory.* Odessa, FL: Psychological Assessment Resources.

**Costa, P. T., Jr., & McCrae, R. R.** (2017). The NEO Inventories as instruments of psychological theory. In T. A. Widiger (Ed.), *The Oxford handbook of the five factor model.* (pp. 11–37). New York: Oxford University Press.

**Costa, P. T., Jr., McCrae, R. R., & Löckenhoff, C. E.** (2019). Personality across the life span. *Annual Review of Psychology, 70,* 423–448.

**Costabile, T., Bilo, L., De Rosa, A., Pane, C., & Saccà, F.** (2018). Dissociative identity disorder: Restoration of executive functions after switch from alter to host personality. *Psychiatry and Clinical Neurosciences, 72* (3), 189–189.

**Costanzo, F., Menghini, D., Maritato, A., Castiglioni, M. C., Mereu, A., Varuzza, C., … & Vicari, S.** (2018). New treatment perspectives in adolescents with anorexia nervosa: The efficacy of non-invasive brain-directed treatment. *Frontiers in Behavioral Neuroscience, 12,* 133.

**Cowan, N.** (2008). What are the differences between long-term, short-term, and working memory? In W. S. Sossin, L. C. Lacaille, V. F. Castellucci, & S. Belleville (Eds.), *Essence of memory: Progress in brain research* (vol. 169, pp. 323–338). New York: Elsevier.

**Cowan, N.** (2010). The magical mystery four: How is working memory capacity limited, and why? *Current Directions in Psychological Science, 19* (1), 51–57.

**Cowan, N.** (2015). George Miller's magical number of immediate memory in retrospect: Observations on the faltering progression of science. *Psychological Review, 122* (3), 536–541.

**Cox, C. R., Seidenberg, M. S., & Rogers, T. T.** (2015). Connecting functional brain imaging and parallel distributed processing. *Language, Cognition, and Neuroscience, 30* (4), 380–394.

**Cox, K., & McAdams, D. P.** (2012). The transforming self: Service narratives and identity change in emerging adulthood. *Journal of Adolescent Research, 27* (1), 18–43.

**Cox, M. J., Janssen, T., Lopez-Vergara, H., Barnett, N. P., & Jackson, K. M.** (2018). Parental drinking as context for parental socialization of adolescent alcohol use. *Journal of Adolescence, 69,* 22–32.

**Cox, R. E., & Bryant, R. A.** (2008). Advances in hypnosis research: Methods, designs, and contributions of intrinsic and instrumental hypnosis. In M. R. Nash & A. J. Barnier (Eds.), *The Oxford handbook of hypnosis: Research theory and practice* (pp. 311–336). New York: Oxford University Press.

**Coyle, T. N., Shaver, J. A., & Linehan, M. M.** (2018). On the potential for iatrogenic effects of psychiatric crisis services: The example of dialectical behavior therapy for adult women with borderline personality disorder. *Journal of Consulting and Clinical Psychology, 86* (2), 116–124.

**Coyne, A. E., Constantino, M. J., Ravitz, P., & McBride, C.** (2018). The interactive effect of patient attachment and social support on early alliance quality in interpersonal psychotherapy. *Journal of Psychotherapy Integration, 28*(1), 46–59. doi: 10.1037/int0000074

**Coyne, J. C., & Tennen, H.** (2010). Positive psychology in cancer care: Bad science, exaggerated claims, and unproven medicine. *Annals of Behavioral Medicine, 39* (1), 16–26.

**Coyne, S. M., & Ostrov, J. M.** (Eds.). (2018). *The development of relational aggression.* New York: Oxford University Press.

**Coyne, S. M., Padilla-Walker, L. M., Holmgren, H. G., Davis, E. J., Collier, K. M., Memmott-Elison, M. K., & Hawkins, A. J.** (2018). A meta-analysis of prosocial media on prosocial behavior, aggression, and empathic concern: A multidimensional approach. *Developmental Psychology, 54* (2), 331–347.

**Cracco, L., Appleby, B. S., & Gambetti, P.** (2018). Fatal familial insomnia and sporadic fatal insomnia. *Handbook of Clinical Neurology, 153,* 271–299.

**Craig, M. A., Rucker, J. M., & Richeson, J. A.** (2018). The pitfalls and promise of increasing racial diversity: Threat, contact, and race relations in the 21st century. *Current Directions in Psychological Science, 27* (3), 188–193.

**Craik, F. I. M., & Lockhart, R. S.** (1972). Levels of processing: A framework for memory research. *Journal of Verbal Learning and Verbal Behavior, 11* (6), 671–684.

**Craik, F. I. M., & Tulving, E.** (1975). Depth of processing and retention of words in episodic memory. *Journal of Experimental Psychology: General, 104* (3), 268–294.

**Cramer, P.** (2008a). Longitudinal study of defense mechanisms: Late childhood to late adolescence. *Journal of Personality, 75* (1), 1–23.

**Cramer, P.** (2008b). Seven pillars of defense mechanism theory. *Social and Personality Psychology Compass, 2* (5), 1963–1981.

**Cramer, P.** (2009a). The development of defense mechanisms from pre-adolescence to early adulthood: Do IQ and social class matter? A longitudinal study. *Journal of Research in Personality, 43* (3), 464–471.

**Cramer, P.** (2009b). An increase in early adolescent undercontrol is associated with the use of denial. *Journal of Personality Assessment, 91* (4), 331–339.

**Cramer, P.** (2015). Defense mechanisms: 40 years of empirical research. *Journal of Personality Assessment, 97* (2), 114–122.

**Crispin, G., & Mehler, M.** (2014). A CareerXroads "lab" report: Filling the gaps. *Source of Hire Report 2014.* http://www.careerxroads.com/news/2014_SourceOfHire.pdf (accessed April 6, 2016)

**Crocetti, E., Prati, F., & Rubini, M.** (2018). The interplay of personal and social identity. *European Psychologist, 23* (4), 300–310.

**Crocker, J., & Brummelman, E.** (2019). The self: Dynamics of persons and their situations. In K. Deaux & M. Snyder (Eds.), *The Oxford handbook of personality and social psychology, 2nd edition.* (pp. 265–288). New York: Oxford University Press.

**Crocker, J., & Park, L. E.** (2012). Contingencies of self-worth. In M. R. Leary & J. P. Tangney (Eds.), *Handbook of self and identity* (2nd ed., pp. 309–326). New York: Guilford.

**Crompton, E.** (2018, June 30). Experiencing trauma in childhood doesn't mean we're doomed to fail. https://metro.co.uk/2018/06/30/experiencing-trauma-childhood-doesnt-mean-doomed-fail-7658475/

**Crompton, E.** (2017, September 26). Under pressure from 9 to 5. *The New York Times,* D4.

**Cronbach, L. J.** (1957). The two disciplines of scientific psychology. *American Psychologist, 12* (1), 671–684.

**Cronin, D. A., & Irwin, D. E.** (2018). Visual working memory supports perceptual stability across saccadic eye movements. *Journal of Experimental Psychology: Human Perception and Performance, 44* (11), 1739–1759.

**Crooks, R. L., & Baur, K.** (2014). *Our sexuality* (12th ed.). Boston: Cengage.

**Cross, Z. R., Kohler, M. J., Schlesewsky, M., Gaskell, M. G., & Bornkessel-Schlesewsky, I.** (2018). Sleep-dependent memory consolidation and incremental sentence comprehension: Computational dependencies during language learning as revealed by neuronal oscillations. *Frontiers in Human Neuroscience, 12,* 18.

**Crowley, S. J., & Carskadon, M. A.** (2010). Modifications to weekend recovery sleep delay circadian phase in older adolescents. *Chronobiology International, 27* (7), 1469–1492.

**Csikszentmihalyi, M.** (1990). *Flow: The psychology of optimal experience.* New York: HarperPerennial.

**Cuevas, J., & Dawson, B. L.** (2018). A test of two alternative cognitive processing models: Learning styles and dual coding. *Theory and Research in Education, 16*(1), 40–64.

**Cuijpers, P., Reijnders, M., & Huibers, M. J.** (2019). The role of common factors in psychotherapy outcomes. *Annual Review of Clinical Psychology, 15.* (in press)

**Culbertson, S. S., Weyhrauch, W. S., & Huffcutt, A. I.** (2017). A tale of two formats: Direct comparison of matching situational and behavior description interview questions. *Human Resource Management Review, 27* (1), 167–177.

**Culverhouse, R. C., Saccone, N. L., Horton, A. C., Ma, Y., Anstey, K. J., Banaschewski, T., … & Goldman, N.** (2018). Collaborative meta-analysis finds no evidence of a strong interaction between stress and 5-HTTLPR genotype contributing to the development of depression. *Molecular Psychiatry, 23* (1), 133–142.

**Cunningham, C. A., & Egeth, H. E.** (2018). The capture of attention by entirely irrelevant pictures of calorie-dense foods. *Psychonomic Bulletin & Review, 25* (2), 586–595.

**Cunningham, R. L., & McGinnis, M. Y.** (2007). Factors influencing aggression toward females by male rats exposed to anabolic androgenic steroids during puberty. *Hormones and Behavior, 51* (1), 135–141.

**Curry, O. S., Rowland, L. A., Van Lissa, C. J., Zlotowitz, S., McAlaney, J., & Whitehouse, H.** (2018). Happy to help? A systematic review and meta-analysis of the effects of performing acts of kindness on the well-being of the actor. *Journal of Experimental Social Psychology, 76,* 320–329.

**Curtis, M. A., Kam, M., & Faull, R. L.** (2011). Neurogenesis in humans. *European Journal of Neuroscience, 33,* 1170–1174.

**Curtiss, S.** (2014). The case of Chelsea: The effects of late age at exposure to language on language performance and evidence for the modularity of language and mind. In C. T. Schutze & L. Stockall (Eds.), Connections: Papers by and for Sarah Van Wagenen. *UCLA Working Papers in Linguistics, 18,* 115–146.

**Curwen, C.** (2018). Music-colour synaesthesia: Concept, context and qualia. *Consciousness and Cognition, 61,* 94–106.

# D

**D'Angelo, M. C., & Humphreys, K. R.** (2015). Tip-of-the-tongue states reoccur because of implicit learning, but resolving them helps. *Cognition, 142,* 166–190.

**D'Esposito, M., & Postle, B. R.** (2015). The cognitive neuroscience of working memory. *Annual Review of Psychology* (vol. 66, pp. 115–142). Palo Alto, CA: Annual Reviews.

**da Cunha-Bang, S., Fisher, P. M., Hjordt, L. V., Perfalk, E., Beliveau, V., Holst, K., & Knudsen, G. M.** (2018). Men with high serotonin 1B receptor binding respond to provocations with heightened amygdala reactivity. *Neuroimage, 166,* 79–85.

**Da Paz, N. S., Wallander, J. L., & Tiemensma, J.** (2018). Effects of written disclosure on psychophysiological stress among parents of children with autism: A randomized controlled pilot study. *Research in Autism Spectrum Disorders, 53,* 7–17.

**Dadwal, P., Mahmud, N., Sinai, L., Azimi, A., Fatt, M., Wondisford, F. E., Miller, F. D., & Morshead, C. M.** (2015). Activating endogenous neural precursor cells using metformin leads to neural repair and functional recovery in a model of childhood brain injury. *Stem Cell Reports, 5* (2), 166–173.

**Dahl, A., & Killen, M.** (2018). A developmental perspective on the origins of morality in infancy and early childhood. *Frontiers in Psychology, 9.*

**Dahlin, K. B., Chuang, Y. T., & Roulet, T. J.** (2018). Opportunity, motivation, and ability to learn from failures and errors: Review, synthesis, and ways to move forward. *Academy of Management Annals, 12* (1), 252–277.

**Dai, J., Pleskac, T. J., & Pachur, T.** (2018). Dynamic cognitive models of intertemporal choice. *Cognitive Psychology, 104,* 29–56.

**Daley, D., & DuPaul, G.** (2016). Nonpharmacological interventions for preschool children with attention-deficit/hyperactivity disorder. *Journal of the American Academy of Child & Adolescent Psychiatry, 55* (10), S329–S330.

**Dalle Grave, R., El Ghoch, M., Sartirana, M., & Calugi, S.** (2016). Cognitive behavioral therapy for anorexia nervosa: An update. *Current Psychiatry Reports, 18* (1), 1–8.

**Dalrymple, K. A., Wall, N., Spezio, M., Hazlett, H. C., Piven, J., & Elison, J. T.** (2018). Rapid face orienting in infants and school-age children with and without autism: Exploring measurement invariance in eye-tracking. *PloS one, 13* (8), e0202875.

**Dalton, E. D., & Hammen, C. L.** (2018). Independent and relative effects of stress, depressive symptoms, and affect on college students' daily health behaviors. *Journal of Behavioral Medicine,* 1–12. doi: 10.1007/s10865-018-9945-4

**Damen, T. G., van Baaren, R. B., Brass, M., Aarts, H., & Dijksterhuis, A.** (2015). Put your plan into action: The influence of action plans on agency and responsibility. *Journal of Personality and Social Psychology, 108* (6), 850–866.

**Damian, R. I., & Roberts, B. W.** (2015a). The associations of birth order with personality and intelligence in a representative sample of U.S. high school students. *Journal of Research in Personality, 58,* 96–105.

**Damian, R. I., & Roberts, B. W.** (2015b). Settling the debate on birth order and personality. *Proceedings of the National Academy of Sciences USA, 112* (46), 14119–14120.

**Damian, R. I., Su, R., Shanahan, M., Trautwein, U., & Roberts, B. W.** (2015). Can personality traits and intelligence compensate for background disadvantage? Predicting status attainment in adulthood. *Journal of Personality and Social Psychology, 109* (3), 473–489.

**Damon, W.** (2008). *The path to purpose: Helping our children find their calling in life.* New York: Free Press.

**Danckert, J., & Merrifield, C.** (2018). Boredom, sustained attention and the default mode network. *Experimental Brain Research, 236* (9), 2507–2518.

**Dang, L. C., Samanez-Larkin, G. R., Castrellon, J. J., Perkins, S. F., Cowan, R. L., & Zald, D. H.** (2018). Individual differences in dopamine D 2 receptor availability correlate with reward valuation. *Cognitive, Affective, & Behavioral Neuroscience.* (in press)

**Daniels, H.** (2011). Vygotsky and psychology. In U. Goswami (Ed.), Wiley-Blackwell *handbook of childhood cognitive development* (2nd ed.). New York: Wiley-Blackwell.

**Danner, D. D., Snowdon, D. A., & Friesen, W. V.** (2001). Positive emotions in early life and longevity: Findings from the Nun Study. *Journal of Personality and Social Psychology, 80,* 804–813.

**Dantzer, R., Cohen, S., Russo, S., & Dinan, T.** (2018). Resilience and immunity. *Brain, Behavior, and Immunity.* doi: 10.1016/j.bbi.2018.08.010 (in press)

**Danvers, A. F., & Shiota, M. N.** (2018). Dynamically engaged smiling predicts cooperation above and beyond average smiling levels. *Evolution and Human Behavior, 39* (1), 112–119.

**Darcy, E.** (2012). Gender issues in child and adolescent eating disorders. In J. Lock (Ed.), *The Oxford handbook of child and adolescent eating disorders: Developmental perspectives.* New York: Oxford University Press.

**Darley, J. M., & Latané, B.** (1968). Bystander intervention in emergencies: Diffusion of responsibility. *Journal of Personality and Social Psychology, 8* (4, Pt. 1), 377–383.

**Darley, J. M., & Latané, B.** (1970). *The unresponsive bystander: Why doesn't he help?* New York: Appleton-Century-Crofts.

**Darnold, T. C., & Rynes, S. L.** (2013). Recruitment and job choice research: Same as it ever was? In N. W. Schmitt, S. Highhouse, & I. B. Weiner (Eds.), *Handbook of psychology* (2nd ed., vol. 12, pp. 104–142). Hoboken, NJ: Wiley.

**Darwin, C.** (1862). *On the various contrivances by which British and foreign orchids are fertilised by insects, and on the good effects of intercrossing.* London: John Murray.

**Darwin, C.** (1871). *The descent of man and selection in relation to sex.* London: John Murray.

**Darwin, C.** (1965). *The expression of the emotions in man and animals.* Chicago: University of Chicago Press. (original work published 1872)

**Darwin, C.** (1979). *On the origin of species.* New York: Avenal Books. (original work published 1859)

**Datar, A., & Nicosia, N.** (2018). Assessing social contagion in body mass index, overweight, and obesity using a natural experiment. *JAMA Pediatrics, 172* (3), 239–246.

**Datta, D. K., & Basuil, D. A.** (2015). Does employee downsizing really work? In M. Andresen & C. Nowak (Eds.), *Human resource management practices* (pp. 197–221). Switzerland: Springer International Publishing.

**Dauvilliers, Y., Schenck, C. H., Postuma, R. B., Iranzo, A., Luppi, P. H., Plazzi, G., … & Boeve, B.** (2018). REM sleep behaviour disorder. *Nature Reviews Disease Primers, 4* (1), 19.

**David, C. J., & Massagué, J.** (2018). Contextual determinants of TGFβ action in development, immunity and cancer. *Nature Reviews Molecular Cell Biology, 19,* 419–435.

**David, D., Cristea, I., & Hofmann, S. G.** (2018). Why cognitive behavioral therapy is the current gold standard of psychotherapy. *Frontiers in Psychiatry, 9,* 4.

**Davidson, P. S., Cook, S. P., & Glisky, E. L.** (2006). Flashbulb memories for September 11th can be preserved in older adults. *Neuropsychology, Development, and Cognition, B: Aging and Neuropsychological Cognition, 13* (2), 196–206.

**Davidson, R. J.** (2005). Neural substrates of affective style and value. In Y. Christen (Series Ed.) & J.-P. Changeux, A. R. Damasio, W. Singer, & Y. Christen (Vol. Eds.), *Research and perspectives in neurosciences: Neurobiology of human values* (pp. 67–90). Germany: Springer-Verlag.

**Davidson, R. J., Kabat-Zinn, J., Schumacher, J., Rosenkranz, M. M., Daniel, S., Saki, F., … & Sheridan, J. F.** (2003). Alterations in brain and immune function produced by mindfulness meditation. *Psychosomatic Medicine, 65* (4), 564–570.

**Davidson, T. L., & Riley, A. L.** (2015). Taste, sickness, and learning. *American Scientist, 103* (3), 204–211.

**Davies, G., Greenhough, B., Hobson-West, P., & Kirk, R. G.** (2018). Science, culture, and care in laboratory animal research: Interdisciplinary perspectives on the history and future of the 3Rs. *Science, Technology and Human Values, 43,* 603–621.

**Davies, L. C., Conner, M., Sedikides, C., & Hutter, R. R. C.** (2016). Math question type and stereotype threat: Evidence from educational settings. *Social Cognition, 34,* 192–216.

**Davis, A. K., & Maney, D. L.** (2018). The use of glucocorticoid hormones or leucocyte profiles to measure stress in vertebrates: What's the difference? *Methods in Ecology and Evolution, 9* (6), 1556–1568.

**Davis, C., Zai, C. C., Adams, N., Bonder, R., & Kennedy, J. L.** (2019). Oxytocin and its association with reward-based personality traits: A multilocus genetic profile (MLGP) approach. *Personality and Individual Differences, 138,* 231–236.

**Davis, D. E., Choe, E., Meyers, J., Wade, N., Varjas, K., Gifford, A., … & Worthington, Jr., E. L.** (2016). Thankful for the little things: A meta-analysis of gratitude interventions. *Journal of Counseling Psychology, 63* (1), 20.

**Davis, D. E., DeBlaere, C., Owen, J., Hook, J. N., Rivera, D. P., Choe, E., … & Placeres, V.** (2018). The multicultural orientation framework: A narrative review. *Psychotherapy, 55* (1), 89–100.

**Davis, D., & Loftus, E. F.** (2018). Eyewitness Science in the 21st Century: What Do We Know and Where Do We Go from Here? *Stevens' Handbook of Experimental Psychology and Cognitive Neuroscience, 1,* 1–38.

**Davis, J. I., Senghas, A., & Ochsner, K. N.** (2009). How does facial feedback modulate emotional experience? *Journal of Research in Personality, 43* (5), 822–829.

**Davis, M. H.** (2018). *Empathy: A social psychological approach*. London: Routledge.

**Davis, W. E., Hicks, J. A., Schlegel, R. J., Smith, C. M., & Vess, M.** (2015). Authenticity and self-esteem across temporal horizons. *Journal of Positive Psychology, 10* (2), 116–126.

**Dawson, S. J., & Chivers, M. L.** (2018). The effect of static versus dynamic stimuli on visual processing of sexual cues in androphilic women and gynephilic men. *Royal Society Open Science, 5* (6), 172286.

**Day, L. C., & Impett, E. A.** (2018). Giving when it costs: How interdependent self-construal shapes willingness to sacrifice and satisfaction with sacrifice in romantic relationships. *Journal of Social and Personal Relationships, 35* (5), 722–742.

**De, S. F., Romani, C., Geberhiwot, T., MacDonald, A., & Palermo, L.** (2018). Language processing and executive functions in early treated adults with phenylketonuria (PKU). *Cognitive Neuropsychology, 35,* 148–170.

**De Angelis, T.** (2002). Binge-eating disorder: What's the best treatment? *Monitor on Psychology, 33* (3), 30.

**de Bloom, J., Geurts, S. A., & Kompier, M. A.** (2012). Effects of short vacations, vacation activities and experiences on employee health and well-being. *Stress and Health, 28* (4), 305–318.

**De Clercq, D., Haq, I. U., & Azeem, M. U.** (2018). Self-efficacy to spur job performance: Roles of job-related anxiety and perceived workplace incivility. *Management Decision, 56* (4), 891–907.

**de Haan, E., Duckworth, A., Birch, D., & Jones, C.** (2013). Executive coaching outcome research: The contribution of common factors such as relationship, personality match, and self-efficacy. *Consulting Psychology, 65* (1), 40–57.

**De Kock, F. S., Lievens, F., & Born, M. P.** (2018). The profile of the 'Good Judge' in HRM: A systematic review and agenda for future research. *Human Resource Management Review.* (in press)

**de Lange, F. P., Heilbron, M., & Kok, P.** (2018). How do expectations shape perception? *Trends in Cognitive Sciences, 22,* 764–779.

**De Neve, J. E., Ward, G., De Keulenaer, F., Van Landeghem, B., Kavetsos, G., & Norton, M. I.** (2018). The asymmetric experience of positive and negative economic growth: Global evidence using subjective well-being data. *Review of Economics and Statistics, 100* (2), 362–375.

**De Nunzio, A. M., Farina, D., & Falla, D.** (2017). A novel training approach to reducing phantom limb pain. *Physiotherapy, 103,* e131.

**De Pascalis, V., Sommer, K., & Scacchia, P.** (2018). Extraversion and behavioural approach system in stimulus analysis and motor response initiation. *Biological Psychology, 137,* 91–106.

**De Raad, B., Barelds, D. P., Levert, E., Ostendorf, F., Mlačić, B., Di Blas, L., ... & Katigbak, M. S.** (2010). Only three factors of personality description are fully replicable across languages: A comparison of 14 trait taxonomies. *Journal of Personality and Social Psychology, 98* (1), 160–173.

**De Vaus, J., Hornsey, M. J., Kuppens, P., & Bastian, B.** (2018). Exploring the east-west divide in prevalence of affective disorder: A case for cultural differences in coping with negative emotion. *Personality and Social Psychology Review, 22* (3), 285–304.

**de Zwaan, M., Mitchell, J. E., Crosby, R. D., Mussell, M. P., Raymond, N. C., Specker, S. M., & Seim, H. C.** (2005). Short-term cognitive behavioral treatment does not improve outcome of a comprehensive very-low-calorie diet program in obese women with binge eating disorder. *Behavior Therapy, 36* (1), 89–99.

**Deal, T. E., & Kennedy, A. A.** (1982). *Corporate cultures: The rites and rituals of corporate life.* New York: Penguin.

**Dean, R.** (2018). Neurodiversity and the rejection of cures. In A. Cureton & T. E. Hill (Eds.), *Disability in practice: Attitudes, policies, and relationships* (pp. 115–133). New York: Oxford University Press.

**Dear, B. F., Fogliati, V. J., Fogliati, R., Gandy, M., McDonald, S., Talley, N., ... & Jones, M.** (2018). Transdiagnostic internet-delivered cognitive-behaviour therapy (CBT) for adults with functional gastrointestinal disorders (FGID): A feasibility open trial. *Journal of Psychosomatic Research, 108,* 61–69.

**Deaux, K.** (2001). Social identity. In J. Worell (Ed.), *Encyclopedia of gender and women.* San Diego: Academic.

**Decety, J., Skelly, L. R., & Kiehl, K. A.** (2013). Brain response to empathy-eliciting scenarios involving pain in incarcerated individuals with psychopathy. *JAMA Psychiatry, 70* (6), 638–645.

**Decimo, I., Bifari, F., Krampera, M., & Fumagalli, G.** (2012). Neural stem cell niches in health and diseases. *Current Pharmaceutical Design, 18* (13), 1755–1783.

**Deckx, L., van den Akker, M., Buntinx, F., & van Driel, M.** (2018). A systematic literature review on the association between loneliness and coping strategies. *Psychology, Health & Medicine, 23,* 899–916.

**DeCou, C. R., Comtois, K. A., & Landes, S. J.** (2018). Dialectical behavior therapy is effective for the treatment of suicidal behavior: A meta-analysis. *Behavior Therapy.* doi: 10.1016/j.beth.2018.03.009

**Dedania, V. S., Ozgonul, C., Zacks, D. N., & Besirli, C. G.** (2018). Novel classification system for combined hamartoma of the retina and retinal pigment epithelium. *Retina, 38* (1), 12–19.

**DeFeo, J.** (2015). Understanding sexual, paraphilic, and gender dysphoria disorders in DSM-5. *Journal of Child Sexual Abuse, 24* (2), 210–215.

**Dehaene, S.** (2018). The error-related negativity, self-monitoring, and consciousness. *Perspectives on Psychological Science, 13* (2), 161–165.

**Dehaene, S., & Changeux, J. P.** (2011). Experimental and theoretical approaches to conscious processing. *Neuron, 70,* 200–207.

**Dehaene, S., Lau, H., & Kouider, S.** (2017). What is consciousness, and could machines have it? *Science, 358,* 486–492.

**Del Casale, A., Ferraculi, S., Rapinesi, C., Serata, D., Caltagirone, S. S., Savoja, V., ... & Girardi, P.** (2015). Pain perception and hypnosis: Findings from recent functional neuroimaging studies. *International Journal of Clinical and Experimental Hypnosis, 63* (2), 144–170.

**Del Giudice, M.** (2018). *Evolutionary psychopathology: A unified approach.* New York: Oxford University Press.

**Delcourte, S., Ashby Jr, C. R., Rovera, R., Kiss, B., Adham, N., Farkas, B., & Haddjeri, N.** (2018). The novel atypical antipsychotic cariprazine demonstrates dopamine D2 receptor-dependent partial agonist actions on rat mesencephalic dopamine neuronal activity. *CNS Neuroscience & Therapeutics.* doi: 10.1111/cns.12867

**DeLisi, M., Drury, A. J., Caropreso, D., Heinrichs, T., Tahja, K. N., & Elbert, M. J.** (2018). Antisocial personality disorder with or without antecedent conduct disorder: The differences are psychiatric and paraphilic. *Criminal Justice and Behavior, 45* (6), 902–917.

**D'Mello, A. M., & Gabrieli, J. D.** (2018). Cognitive neuroscience of dyslexia. *Language, Speech, and Hearing Services in Schools, 49* (4), 798–809.

**Dell, P. F., & Eisenhower, J. W.** (1990). Adolescent multiple personality disorder: A preliminary study of eleven cases. *Journal of the American Academy of Child & Adolescent Psychiatry, 29* (3), 359–366.

**Dell'Osso, B., & Lader, M.** (2012). Do benzodiazepines still deserve a major role in the treatment of psychiatric disorders? A critical reappraisal. *European Psychiatry, 28* (1), 7–20.

**della Monica, C., Johnsen, S., Atzori, G., Groeger, J. A., & Dijk, D. J.** (2018). Rapid eye movement sleep, sleep continuity and slow wave sleep as predictors of cognition, mood, and subjective sleep quality in healthy men and women, aged 20–84 years. *Frontiers in Psychiatry, 9.*

**Delvecchio, G., Bellani, M., Altamura, A. C., & Brambilla, P.** (2016). The association between the serotonin and dopamine neurotransmitters and personality traits. *Epidemiology and Psychiatric Sciences, 25* (2), 109–112.

**Deming, W. E.** (1986). *Out of the crisis.* Cambridge, MA: MIT Press.

**Demirhan, E., Randler, C., Beşoluk, Ş., & Horzum, M. B.** (2018). Gifted and non-gifted students' diurnal preference and the relationship between personality, sleep, and sleep quality. *Biological Rhythm Research, 49* (1), 103–117.

**Den Hartog, D. N., & Belschak, F. D.** (2012). When does transformational leadership enhance employee proactive behavior? The role of autonomy and role breadth self-efficacy. *Journal of Applied Psychology, 97* (1), 194–202.

**Den Heijer, A. E., Groen, Y., Tucha, L., Fuermaier, A. B., Koerts, J., Lange, K. W., Thome, J., & Tucha, O.** (2017). Sweat it out? The effects of physical exercise on cognition and behavior in children and adults with ADHD: A systematic literature review. *Journal of Neural Transmission, 124* (1), 3–26.

**Deng, Y., Xiang, R., Zhu, Y., Li, Y., Yu, S., & Liu, X.** (2019). Counting blessings and sharing gratitude in a Chinese prisoner sample: Effects of gratitude-based interventions on subjective well-being and aggression. *The Journal of Positive Psychology, 14* (3), 303–311. doi: 10.1080/17439760.2018.1460687.

**Denissen, J. J., Luhmann, M., Chung, J. M., & Bleidorn, W.** (2018). Transactions between life events and personality traits across the adult lifespan. *Journal of Personality and Social Psychology.* doi: 10.1037/pspp0000196 (in press)

**Dennis, A. A., Astell, A., & Dritschel, B.** (2012). The effects of imagery on problem-solving ability and autobiographical memory. *Journal of Behavior Therapy and Experimental Psychiatry, 43* (Suppl. 1), S4–S11.

**Denollet, J., & Conraads, V. M.** (2011). Type D personality and vulnerability to adverse outcomes of heart disease. *Cleveland Clinic Journal of Medicine, 78* (Suppl. 1), S13–S19.

**Denson, T. F., Blundell, K. A., Schofield, T. P., Schira, M. M., & Krämer, U. M.** (2018). The neural correlates of alcohol-related aggression. *Cognitive, Affective, & Behavioral Neuroscience, 18* (2), 203–215.

**Depp, C. A., Moore, R. C., Perivoliotis, D., Holden, J. L., Swendsen, J., & Granholm, E. L.** (2016). Social behavior, interaction appraisals, and suicidal ideation in schizophrenia: The dangers of being alone. *Schizophrenia Research, 172* (1–3), 195–200.

**Derfler-Rozin, R., Baker, B., & Gino, F.** (2018). Compromised ethics in hiring processes? How referrers' power affects employees' reactions to referral practices. *Academy of Management Journal, 61* (2), 615–636.

**Dermody, S. S., Wright, A. G., Cheong, J., Miller, K. G., Muldoon, M. F., Flory, J. D., ... & Manuck, S. B.** (2016). Personality correlates of midlife cardiometabolic risk: The explanatory role of higher-order factors of the five-factor model. *Journal of Personality, 84* (6), 765–776.

**Destin, M.** (2018). Socioeconomic mobility, identity, and health: Experiences that influence immunology and implications for intervention. *American Psychologist,* doi: 10.1037/amp0000297 (in press)

**Destin, M., Rheinschmidt-Same, & Richeson, J. A.** (2017). Status-based identity: A conceptual approach integrating the social psychological study of socioeconomic status and identity. *Personality and Social Psychology Review, 12,* 270–289.

**Devine, E. G., Peebles, K. R., & Martini, V.** (2017). Strategies to exclude subjects who conceal and fabricate information when enrolling in clinical trials. *Contemporary Clinical Trials Communications, 5,* 67–71.

**Devine, P. G., Forscher, P. S., Austin, A. J., & Cox, W. T.** (2012). Long-term reduction in implicit race bias: A prejudice habit-breaking intervention. *Journal of Experimental Social Psychology, 48* (6), 1267–1278.

**Dewaele, J. M.** (2016). Why do so many bi- and multilinguals feel different when switching languages? *International Journal of Multilingualism, 13* (1), 92–105.

**Di Lorenzo, G., Gorea, F., Longo, L., & Ribolsi, M.** (2018). Paraphilia and paraphilic disorders. In E. A. Jannini & A. Siracusano (Eds.), *Sexual dysfunctions in mentally ill patients* (pp. 193–213). Cham: Springer.

**di Volo, M., Morozova, E. O., Lapish, C. C., Kuznetsov, A., & Gutkin, B.** (2018). Dynamical ventral tegmental area circuit mechanisms of alcohol-dependent dopamine release. *European Journal of Neuroscience.* doi: 10.1111/ejn.14147

**Diamond, D. A., Swartz, J., Tishelman, A., Johnson, J., & Chan, Y. M.** (2018). Management of pediatric patients with DSD and ambiguous genitalia: Balancing the child's moral claims to self-determination with parental values and preferences. *Journal of Pediatric Urology,* 14, 416.e1–416.e5

**Diamond, L. M.** (2008b). Female bisexuality from adolescence to adulthood: Results from a 10-year longitudinal study. *Developmental Psychology, 44* (1), 5–14.

**Diamond, L. M., Dickenson, J. A., & Blair, K. L.** (2017). Stability of sexual attractions across different timescales: The roles of bisexuality and gender. *Archives of Sexual Behavior, 46* (1), 193–204.

**Diamond, L. M., & Savin-Williams, R. C.** (2013). Same-sex activity in adolescence: Multiple meanings and implications. In R. F. Fassinger & S. L. Morrow (Eds.), *Sex in the margins.* Washington, DC: American Psychological Association.

**Diamond, M., & Sigmundson, H. K.** (1997). Sex reassignment at birth: A long term review and clinical implications. *Archives of Pediatrics and Adolescent Medicine, 151* (3), 298–304.

**Diaz-Morales, J. F., & Escribano, C.** (2013). Circadian preference and thinking styles: Implications for school achievement. *Chronobiology International, 30,* 1231–1239.

**Díaz-Morales, J. F., & Escribano, C.** (2015). Social jetlag, academic achievement, and cognitive performance: Understanding gender/sex differences. *Chronobiology International, 32* (6), 822–831.

**Dickens, D. D., Jackman, D. M., Stanley, L. R., Swaim, R. C., & Chavez, E. L.** (2018). Alcohol consumption among rural African American and White adolescents: The role of religion, parents, and peers. *Journal of Ethnicity in Substance Abuse, 17* (3), 273–290.

**DiClemente, C. C.** (2018). *Addiction and change: How addictions develop and addicted people recover.* New York: Guilford.

**Dien, J.** (2009). A tale of two recognition systems: Implications of the fusiform face area and the visual word form area for lateralized object recognition models. *Neuropsychologia, 47* (1), 1–16.

**Diener, E.** (1999). Introduction to the special section on the structure of emotion. *Journal of Personality and Social Psychology, 76,* 803–804.

**Diener, E.** (2012a). New findings and future directions for subjective well-being research. *American Psychologist, 67* (8), 590–597.

**Diener, E.** (2012b). Positive psychology: Past, present, and future. In S. J. Lopez & C. R. Snyder (Eds.), *The Oxford handbook of positive psychology* (2nd ed.). New York: Oxford University Press.

**Diener, E., & Biswas-Diener, R.** (2002). Will money increase subjective well-being? *Social Indicators Research, 57* (2), 119–169. doi: 0.1023/A:1014411319119

**Diener, E., & Diener, C.** (1996). Most people are happy. *Psychological Science, 7,* 181–185.

**Diener, E., Emmons, R. A., Larsen, R. J., & Griffin, S.** (1985). The Satisfaction with Life Scale. *Journal of Personality Assessment, 49,* 71–75.

**Diener, E., Tay, L., & Oishi, S.** (2013). Rising income and the subjective well-being of nations. *Journal of Personality and Social Psychology, 104,* 267–276.

**Dieterich, M., & Brandt, T.** (2018). The parietal lobe and the vestibular system. *Handbook of Clinical Neurology, 151,* 119–140.

**Diette, T. M., Goldsmith, A. H., Hamilton, D., & Darity, W.** (2018). Race, unemployment, and mental health in the USA: What can we infer about the psychological cost of the Great Recession across racial groups? *Journal of Economics, Race, and Policy, 1* (2–3), 75–91.

**DiFrancesco, M. W., Shamsuzzaman, A., McConnell, K. B., Ishman, S. L., Zhang, N., Huang, G., ... & Amin, R. S.** (2018). Age-related changes in baroreflex sensitivity and cardiac autonomic tone in children mirrored by regional brain gray matter volume trajectories. *Pediatric Research, 83* (2), 498–505.

**Digman, J. M.** (1990). Personality structure: Emergence of the five-factor model. *Annual Review of Psychology* (vol. 41, pp. 417–440). Palo Alto, CA: Annual Reviews.

**Dikmen-Yildiz, P., Ayers, S., & Phillips, L.** (2018). Longitudinal trajectories of post-traumatic stress disorder (PTSD) after birth and associated risk factors. *Journal of Affective Disorders, 229,* 377–385.

**Dillon, B. L.** (2012). Workplace violence: Impact, causes, prevention. *Work, 42* (1), 15–20.

**Ding, L., Li, L., Chen, S., & Jia, J.** (2018). Speech paired sensory feedbacks enhancing the perception of embodiment of the reflection of face. *Annals of Physical and Rehabilitation Medicine, 61,* e344–e345.

**Diseth, Å., Breidablik, H. J., & Meland, E.** (2018). Longitudinal relations between perceived autonomy support and basic need satisfaction in two student cohorts. *Educational Psychology, 38* (1), 99–115.

**Dishion, T. J.** (2016). Social influences on executive functions development in children and adolescents: Steps toward a social neuroscience of predictive adaptive responses. *Journal of Abnormal Child Psychology, 44* (1), 57–61.

**Dittmar, H., Bond, R., Hurst, M., & Kasser, T.** (2014). The relationship between materialism and personal well-being: A meta-analysis. *Journal of Personality and Social Psychology, 107* (5), 879–924.

**Dobson, D., & Dobson, K. S.** (2018). Evidence-based *practice of cognitive-behavioral therapy.* New York: Guilford Publications.

**Dobson, R.** (2005). "Fighting spirit" after cancer diagnosis does not improve outcome. *British Medical Journal, 330* (7496), 865.

**Dodge, E.** (2012). Family evolution and process during the child and adolescent years in eating disorders. In J. Lock (Ed.), *The Oxford handbook of child and adolescent eating disorders: Developmental perspectives.* New York: Oxford University Press.

**Dodge, K. A., Coie, J. D., & Lynam, D.** (2006). Aggression and antisocial behavior in youth. In W. Damon & R. Lerner (Eds.), *Handbook of child psychology* (6th ed.). New York: Wiley.

**Doeppner, T. R., Traut, V., Heidenreich, A., Kaltwasser, B., Bosche, B., Bähr, M., & Hermann, D. M.** (2017). Conditioned medium derived from neural progenitor cells induces long-term post-ischemic neuroprotection, sustained neurological recovery, neurogenesis, and angiogenesis. *Molecular Neurobiology, 54,* 1531–1540.

**Doherty, J., Giles, M., Gallagher, A. M., & Simpson, E. E. A.** (2018). Understanding pre-, peri-and post-menopausal women's intentions to perform muscle-strengthening activities using the Theory of Planned Behaviour. *Maturitas, 109,* 89–96.

**Dollard, J., Doob, L. W., Miller, N. E., Mowrer, O. H., & Sears, R. R.** (1939). *Frustration and aggression.* New Haven, CT: Yale University Press.

**Domenech, P., & Koechlin, E.** (2015). Executive control and decision-making in the prefrontal cortex. *Current Opinion in Behavioral Sciences, 1,* 101–106.

**Domhoff, G. W.** (2018). Dreaming is an intensified form of mind-wandering, based in an augmented portion of the default network. In K.C.R. Fox & K. Christoff, (Eds.), *The Oxford handbook of spontaneous thought: Mind-wandering, creativity, and dreaming* (pp. 355–370). New York: Oxford University Press.

**Domhoff, G. W., & Fox, K. C. R.** (2015). Dreaming and the default network: A review, synthesis, and counterintuitive research proposal. *Consciousness and Cognition, 33,* 342–353.

**Domjan, M.** (2005). Pavlovian conditioning: A functional perspective. *Annual Review of Psychology* (vol. 56, pp. 179–206). Palo Alto, CA: Annual Reviews.

**Domjan, M.** (2015). The Garcia-Koelling selective association effect: A historical and personal perspective. *International Journal of Comparative Psychology, 28.* http://escholarship.org/uc/item/5sx993rm (accessed March 1, 2016)

**Donatelle, R. J.** (2015). *Health: The basics* (11th ed.). Upper Saddle River, NJ: Pearson.

**Donnellan, M. B., Lucas, R. E., & Fleeson, W.** (2009). Introduction to personality and assessment at age 40: Reflections on the legacy of the person-situation debate and the future of person-situation integration. *Journal of Research in Personality, 43* (2), 117–119.

**Donnelly, G. E., Zheng, T., Haisley, E., & Norton, M. I.** (2018). The amount and source of millionaires' wealth (moderately) predict their happiness. *Personality and Social Psychology Bulletin, 44* (5), 684–699.

**Dorahy, M. J., & van der Hart, O.** (2014). DSM-5's "PTSD with dissociative symptoms": Challenges and future directions. *Journal of Trauma and Dissociation.* PMID: 24983300

**Dougherty, D. D., Brennan, B. P., Stewart, S. E., Wilhelm, S., Widge, A. S., & Rauch, S. L.** (2018). Neuroscientifically informed formulation and treatment planning for patients with obsessive-compulsive disorder: A review. *JAMA Psychiatry, 75* (10), 1081–1087.

**Dovidio, J. F., Kawakami, K., & Gaertner, S. L.** (2002). Implicit and explicit prejudice and interracial interaction. *Journal of Personality and Social Psychology, 82* (1), 62–68.

**Downs, D. L.** (2018). PTSD: A systematic approach to diagnosis and treatment. *Current Psychiatry, 17* (4), 35–42.

**Doyen, S., Klein, O., Pichon, C. L., & Cleeremans, A.** (2012). Behavioral priming: It's all in the mind, but whose mind? *PloS One, 7* (1), e29081.

**Doyle, R. A., & Voyer, D.** (2018). Photographs of real human figures: Item types and persistent sex differences in mental rotation. *Quarterly Journal of Experimental Psychology.* doi: 10.1177/1747021817742079.

**Driessen, E., Hegelmaier, L. M., Abbass, A. A., Barber, J. P., Dekker, J. J., Van, H. L., Jansma, E. P., & Cuijpers, P.** (2015). The efficacy of short-term psychodynamic psychotherapy for depression: A meta-analysis update. *Clinical Psychology Review, 42,* 1–15.

**Drigotas, S. M., Safstrom, C. A., & Gentilia, T.** (1999). An investment model prediction of dating infidelity. *Journal of Personality and Social Psychology, 77* (3), 509–524.

**Du, D. C., Vinh, H. H., Trung, V. D., Hong Quyen, N. T., & Trung, N. T.** (2018). Efficiency of Jaya algorithm for solving the optimization-based structural damage identification problem based on a hybrid objective function. *Engineering Optimization, 50* (8), 1233–1251.

**Dudley, M. Z., Salmon, D. A., Halsey, N. A., Orenstein, W. A., Limaye, R. J., O'Leary, S. T., & Omer, S. B.** (2018). *The clinician's vaccine safety resource guide.* Cham: Springer.

**Dufner, M., Arslan, R. C., & Denissen, J. J.** (2018). The unconscious side of Facebook: Do online social network profiles leak cues to users' implicit motive dispositions? *Motivation and Emotion, 42* (1), 79–89.

**Dufner, M., Gebauer, J. E., Sedikides, C., & Denissen, J. J.** (2018). Self-enhancement and psychological adjustment: A meta-analytic review. *Personality and Social Psychology Review.* doi: 10.1177/1088868318756467

**Duits, P., Cath, D. C., Lissek, S., Hox, J. J., Hamm, A. O., Engelhard, I. M., van den Hout, M. A., & Baas, J. M.** (2015). Updated meta-analysis of analysis of classical fear conditioning in the anxiety disorders. *Depression and Anxiety, 32* (4), 239–253.

**Duke, A. A., Bègue, L., Bell, R., & Eisenlohr-Moul, T.** (2013). Revisiting the serotonin–aggression relationship in humans: A meta-analysis. *Psychological Bulletin, 139* (5), 1148–1172.

**Duman, R. S., Li, N., Liu, R. J., Duric, V., & Aghajanian, G.** (2012). Signaling pathways underlying the rapid antidepressant actions of ketamine. *Neuropharmacology, 62* (1), 35–41.

**Dumontheil, I., & Klingberg, T.** (2012). Brain activity during a visuospatial memory task predicts arithmetical performance 2 years later. *Cerebral Cortex, 22* (5), 1078–1085.

**DuMontier, C., Clough-Gorr, K. M., Silliman, R. A., Stuck, A. E., & Moser, A.** (2018). Health-related quality of life in a predictive model for mortality in older breast cancer survivors. *Journal of the American Geriatrics Society*, 66, 1115–1122.

**Dunbar, R. M.** (2014). The social brain: Psychological underpinnings and implications for the structure of organizations. *Current Directions in Psychological Science, 23* (2), 109–114.

**Duncan, A. E., Scherrer, J., Fu, Q., Bucholz, K. K., Heath, A. C., True, W. R., Haber, J. R., Howell, D., & Jacob, T.** (2006). Exposure to paternal alcoholism does not predict development of alcohol-use disorders in offspring: Evidence from an offspring-of-twins study. *Journal of Studies on Alcohol, 67* (5), 649–656.

**Duncan, B. L., Miller, S. D., Wampold, B. E., & Hubble, M. A.** (Eds.). (2010). *The heart and soul of change: Delivering what works in therapy* (2nd ed.). Washington, DC: American Psychological Association.

**Duncan, B. L., & Reese, R. J.** (2013). Empirically supported treatments, evidence-based treatments, and evidence-based practice. In G. Stricker, T. A. Widiger, & I. B. Weiner (Eds.), *Handbook of psychology* (2nd ed., vol. 8, pp. 489–514). Hoboken, NJ: Wiley.

**Duncan, L. E., Ratanatharathorn, A., Aiello, A. E., Almli, L. M., Amstadter, A. B., Ashley-Koch, A. E., ... & Bradley, B.** (2018). Largest GWAS of PTSD (N = 20 070) yields genetic overlap with schizophrenia and sex differences in heritability. *Molecular Psychiatry, 23* (3), 666–673.

**Dunlop, W., & Tracy, J. L.** (2013). Sobering stories: Narratives of self-redemption predict behavioral change and improved health among recovering alcoholics. *Journal of Personality and Social Psychology, 104* (3), 576–590.

**Dunn, D. S.** (Ed.) (2018). *Positive psychology: Established and emerging issues.* New York: Routledge/Taylor & Francis Group.

**Dunn, E. W., Aknin, L. B., & Norton, M. I.** (2008). Spending money on others promotes happiness. *Science, 319,* 1687–1688.

**Dunne, F. J., Getachew, H., Cullenbrooke, F., & Dunne, C.** (2018). Pain and pain syndromes. *British Journal of Hospital Medicine, 79* (8), 449–453.

**Dunsmoor, J. E., & Kroes, M. C.** (2019). Episodic memory and Pavlovian conditioning: ships passing in the night. *Current Opinion in Behavioral Sciences, 26,* 32–39.

**Dupont, H. B., Candel, M. J., Lemmens, P., Kaplan, C. D., van de Mheen, D., & De Vries, N. K.** (2017). Stages of change model has limited value in explaining the change in use of cannabis among adolescent participants in an efficacious motivational interviewing intervention. *Journal of Psychoactive Drugs, 49* (5), 363–372.

**Durante, K. M., & Griskevicius, V.** (2016). Evolution and consumer behavior. *Current Opinion in Psychology, 10,* 27–32.

**Durantini, M. R., Albarracin, D., Mitchell, A. L., Earl, A. N., & Gillette, J. C.** (2006). Conceptualizing the influence of social agents of behavior change: A meta-analysis of the effectiveness of HIV-prevention interventionists for different groups. *Psychological Bulletin, 132,* 212–248.

**Duric, V., & Duman, R. S.** (2013). Depression and treatment response: Dynamic interplay of signaling pathways and altered neural responses. *Cellular and Molecular Life Sciences, 70* (1), 39–53.

**Durkin, M. S., Maenner, M. J., Baio, J., Christensen, D., Daniels, J., Fitzgerald, R. ... & Yeargin-Allsopp, M.** (2017). Autism spectrum disorder among US children (2002–2010): Socioeconomic, racial, and ethnic disparities. *American Journal of Public Health, 107,* 1818–1826.

**Durrheim, K., & Dixon, J.** (2018). Intergroup contact and the struggle for social justice. In P. L. Hammack (Ed.), *The Oxford handbook of social psychology and social justice* (pp. 367–378). New York: Oxford University Press.

**Dutt, A. J., Wahl, H. W., & Rupprecht, F. S.** (2018). Mindful vs. mind full: Processing strategies moderate the association between subjective aging experiences and depressive symptoms. *Psychology and Aging, 33* (4), 630–642.

**Dweck, C. S.** (2006). *Mindset.* New York: Random House.

**Dweck, C. S.** (2013). Social development. In P. D. Zelazo (Ed.), *The Oxford handbook of developmental psychology* (vol. 2, pp. 167–190). New York: Oxford University Press.

**Dweck, C.** (2006). *Mindset.* New York: Random House.

**Dworkin, E. R., Menon, S. V., Bystrynski, J., & Allen, N. E.** (2017). Sexual assault victimization and psychopathology: A review and meta-analysis. *Clinical Psychology Review, 56,* 65–81.

**Dworkin, E. R., Ullman, S. E., Stappenbeck, C., Brill, C. D., & Kaysen, D.** (2018). Proximal relationships between social support and PTSD symptom severity: A daily diary study of sexual assault survivors. *Depression and Anxiety, 35* (1), 43–49.

**Dyrbye, L. N., Shanafelt, T. D., Werner, L., Sood, A., Satele, D., & Wolanskyj, A. P.** (2017). The impact of a required longitudinal stress management and resilience training course for first-year medical students. *Journal of General Internal Medicine, 32* (12), 1309–1314.

**Dyshniku, F., Murray, M. E., Fazio, R. L., Lykins, A. D., & Cantor, J. M.** (2015). Minor physical anomalies as a window into the prenatal origins of pedophilia. *Archives of Sexual Behavior, 44* (8), 2151–2159. doi: 10.1007/s10508-015-0564-7


# E


**Eagly, A. H.** (1987). *Sex differences in social behavior: A social-role interpretation.* Hillsdale, NJ: Erlbaum.

**Eagly, A. H.** (2009). The his and hers of prosocial behavior: An examination of the social psychology of gender. *American Psychologist, 64* (8), 644–658.

**Eagly, A. H., & Crowley, M.** (1986). Gender and helping behavior: A meta-analytic review of the social psychological literature. *Psychological Bulletin, 100* (3), 283–308.

**Eagly, A. H., & Diekman, A. B.** (2003). The malleability of sex differences in response to changing social roles. In L. G. Aspinwall & U. M. Staudinger (Eds.), *A psychology of human strengths: Fundamental questions and future directions for a positive psychology* (pp. 103–115). Washington, DC: American Psychological Association.

**Eagly, A. H., & Wood, W.** (2010). Gender roles in a biosocial world. In P. van Lange, A. Kruglanski, & E. T. Higgins (Eds.), *Handbook of theories in social psychology.* Thousand Oaks, CA: Sage.

**Eagly, A. H., & Wood, W.** (2013). The nature–nurture debates: 25 years of challenges in understanding the psychology of gender. *Perspectives on Psychological Science, 8*(3), 340–357.

**Eagly, A., & Wood, W.** (2017). Gender identity: Nature and nurture working together. *Evolutionary Studies in Imaginative Culture, 1* (1), 59–62.

**Eastman, K. K.** (1994). In the eyes of the beholder: An attributional approach to ingratiation and organizational citizenship behavior. *Academy of Management Journal, 37* (5), 1379–1391.

**Eckerberg, B., Lowden, A., Nagai, R., & Akerstedt, T.** (2012). Melatonin treatment effects on adolescent students' sleep timing and sleepiness in a placebo-controlled crossover study. *Chronobiology International, 29* (9), 1239–1248.

**Eder, A. B., Krishna, A., & Van Dessel, P.** (2019). Operant evaluative conditioning. *Journal of Experimental Psychology: Animal Learning and Cognition, 45,* 102–110.

**Edwards, J. P., Walsh, N. P., Diment, P. C., & Roberts, R.** (2018). Anxiety and perceived psychological stress play an important role in the immune response after exercise. *Exercise Immunology Review, 24,* 26–34.

**Edwards-Stewart, A., Prochaska, J. O., Smolenski, D. J., Saul, S. F., & Reger, G. M.** (2017). Self-identified problem behaviors and stages of change among soldiers. *Military Behavioral Health, 5*(3), 203–207.

**Eells, T. D.** (2000). Can therapy affect physical health? *Journal of Psychotherapy Practice and Research, 9* (2), 100–104.

**Eftekhar, A., Norton, J. J., McDonough, C. M., & Wolpaw, J. R.** (2018). Retraining reflexes: Clinical translation of spinal reflex operant conditioning. *Neurotherapeutics, 15,* 669–683.

**Egan, M., Daly, M., & Delaney, L.** (2016). Adolescent psychological distress, unemployment, and the Great Recession: Evidence from the National Longitudinal Study of Youth 1997. *Social Science and Medicine, 156,* 98–105.

**Eggerth, D. E.** (2015). Job satisfaction, job performance, and success. In P. J. Hartung, M. L. Savickas, & W. B. Walsh (Eds.), *APA handbook of career intervention* (vol. 2, pp. 453–463). Washington, DC: American Psychological Association.

**Ehrhart, M. G., Ehrhart, K. H., Roesch, S. C., Chung-Herrera, B. G., Nadler, K., & Bradshaw, K.** (2009). Testing the latent factor structure and construct validity of the Ten-Item Personality Inventory. *Personality and Individual Differences, 47* (8), 900–905.

**Ehrlinger, J., Plant, E. A., Hartwig, M. K., Vossen, J. J., Columb, C. J., & Brewer, L. E.** (2018). Do gender differences in perceived prototypical computer scientists and engineers contribute to gender gaps in computer science and engineering? *Sex Roles, 78* (1-2), 40-51.

**Eichenlaub, J. B., van Rijn, E., Gareth Gaskell, M., Lewis, P. A., Maby, E., Malinowski, J., ... & Blagrove, M.** (2018). Incorporation of recent waking-life experiences in dreams correlates with frontal theta activity in REM sleep. *Social Cognitive and Affective Neuroscience, 13,* 637-647.

**Eilertsen, E. M., Gjerde, L. C., Kendler, K. S., Røysamb, E., Aggen, S. H., Gustavson, K., ... & Ystrom, E.** (2018). Development of ADHD symptoms in preschool children: Genetic and environmental contributions. *Development and Psychopathology.* doi: 10.1017/S095457941800073

**Eisenberg, M. E., Bernat, D. H., Bearinger, L. H., & Resnick, M. D.** (2008). Support for comprehensive sexuality education: Perspectives from parents of school-age youth. *Journal of Adolescent Health, 42* (4), 352-359.

**Eisenberg, M. E., Madsen, N., Oliphant, J. A., & Sieving, R. E.** (2013). Barriers to providing sexuality education that teachers believe students need. *Journal of School Health, 83* (5), 335-342.

**Eisenberg, N., Spinrad, T. L., & Morris, A. S.** (2013). Prosocial development. In P. D. Zelazo (Ed.), *The Oxford handbook of developmental psychology.* New York: Oxford University Press.

**Ekman, P. & Friesen, W. V.** (1969). The repertoire of nonverbal behavior: Categories, origins, usage, and coding. *Semiotica, 1* (1), 49-98.

**Ekman, P.** (1980). *The face of man.* New York: Garland.

**Ekman, P.** (1996). Lying and deception. In N. L. Stein, C. Brainerd, P. A. Ornstein, & B. Tversky (Eds.), *Memory for everyday emotional events.* Mahwah, NJ: Erlbaum.

**Ekman, P.** (2003). *Emotions inside out: 130 years after Darwin's* The Expression of Emotions in Man and Animal (pp. 1-6). New York: Annals of the New York Academy of Science.

**Ekman, P., Davidson, R. J., & Friesen, W. V.** (1990). The Duchenne smile: Emotional expression and brain physiology: II. *Journal of Personality and Social Psychology, 58* (2), 342-353.

**Ekman, P., & Friesen, W. V.** (1971). Constants across cultures in the face and emotion. *Journal of Personality and Social Psychology, 17* (2), 124-129.

**Ekman, P., & O'Sullivan, M.** (1991). Facial expressions: Methods, means, and moues. In R. S. Feldman & B. Rime (Eds.), *Fundamentals of nonverbal behavior.* Cambridge, UK: Cambridge University Press.

**Elba, I., & Ivy, J. W.** (2018). Increasing the post-use cleaning of gym equipment using prompts and increased access to cleaning materials. *Behavior Analysis in Practice, 11* (4), 390-394.

**El-Hai, J.** (2005). *The lobotomist: A maverick medical genius and his tragic quest to rid the world of mental illness.* Hoboken, NJ: Wiley.

**Elkins, G. R., Barabasz, A. F., Council, J. R., & Spiegel, D.** (2015). Advancing research and practice: The revised APA Division 30 definition of hypnosis. *American Journal of Clinical Hypnosis, 57* (4), 378-385.

**Elkins, G., Johnson, A., & Fisher, W.** (2012). Cognitive hypnotherapy for pain management. *American Journal of Clinical Hypnosis, 54* (4), 294-310.

**Elklit, A., Hyland, P., & Shevlin, M.** (2014). Evidence of symptom profiles consistent with posttraumatic stress disorder and complex posttraumatic stress disorder in different trauma samples. *European Journal of Psychotraumatology.* doi: 10.3402/ejpt.v5.24221

**Ellemers, N.** (2018). Gender stereotypes. *Annual Review of Psychology, 69,* 275-298.

**Ellis, A.** (2005). Why I (really) became a therapist. *Journal of Clinical Psychology, 61* (8), 945-1031.

**Ellis, B. J., Bianchi, J., Griskevicius, V., & Frankenhuis, W. E.** (2017). Beyond risk and protective factors: An adaptation-based approach to resilience. *Perspectives on Psychological Science, 12,* 561-587.

**Ellis, C. T., & Turk-Browne, N. B.** (2018). Infant fMRI: A model system for cognitive neuroscience. *Trends in Cognitive Sciences, 22,* 375-387.

**Ellis, E. M., Rajagopal, R., & Kiviniemi, M. T.** (2018). The interplay between feelings and beliefs about condoms as predictors of their use. *Psychology & Health, 33* (2), 176-192.

**Ellithorpe, M. E., Ewoldsen, D. R., & Oliver, M. B.** (2015). Elevation (sometimes) increases altruism: Choice and number of outcomes in elevating media effects. *Psychology of Popular Media Culture, 4* (3), 236-250.

**Elsey, J. W., Van Ast, V. A., & Kindt, M.** (2018). Human memory reconsolidation: A guiding framework and critical review of the evidence. *Psychological Bulletin,* 144, 797-848.

**Emmons, R. A., & Diener, E.** (1986). Situation selection as a moderator of response consistency and stability. *Journal of Personality and Social Psychology, 51* (5), 1013-1019.

**Emmons, R. A., & King, L. A.** (1988). Conflict among personal strivings: Immediate and long-term implications for psychological and physical well-being. *Journal of Personality and Social Psychology, 54* (6), 1040-1048.

**Emmons, R. A., & McCullough, M. E.** (2003). Counting blessings versus burdens: An experimental investigation of gratitude and subjective well-being in daily life. *Journal of Personality and Social Psychology, 84* (2), 377-389.

**Emmons, R. A., & McCullough, M. E.** (Eds.). (2004). *The psychology of gratitude.* New York: Oxford University Press.

**Endler, N. S.** (1988). The origins of electroconvulsive therapy (ECT). *Convulsive Therapy, 4* (1), 5-23.

**Endrass, T., Koehne, S., Riesel, A., & Kathmann, N.** (2013). Neural correlates of feedback processing in obsessive-compulsive disorder. *Journal of Abnormal Psychology, 122* (2), 387-396.

**Eng, P. M., Fitzmaurice, G., Kubzansky, L. D., Rimm, E. B., & Kawachi, I.** (2003). Anger expression and risk of stroke and coronary heart disease among male health professionals. *Psychosomatic Medicine, 65* (1), 100-110.

**Engel, A. K., & Singer, W.** (2001). Temporal binding and the neural correlates of sensory awareness. *Trends in Cognitive Science, 5* (1), 16-25.

**Engelhardt, C. R., Hilgard, J., & Bartholow, B. D.** (2015). Acute exposure to difficult (but not violent) video games dysregulates cognitive control. *Computers in Human Behavior, 45,* 85-92.

**Engelmann, J. M., & Herrmann, E.** (2016). Chimpanzees trust their friends. *Current Biology, 26,* 1-5.

**Engen, H. G., & Singer, T.** (2015). Compassion-based emotion regulation up-regulates experienced positive affect and associated neural networks. *Social, Cognitive, and Affective Neuroscience, 10* (9), 1291-1301.

**Engeroff, T., Vogt, L., Fleckenstein, J., Füzéki, E., Matura, S., Pilatus, U., ... & Banzer, W.** (2018). Lifespan leisure physical activity profile, brain plasticity and cognitive function in old age. *Aging & Mental Health,* doi: 10.1080/13607863.2017.1421615

**Engle, R. W.** (2018). Working memory and executive attention: A revisit. *Perspectives on Psychological Science, 13* (2), 190-193.

**Ennis, M. C., Gong, T., & Okpozo, A. Z.** (2018). Examining the mediating roles of affective and normative commitment in the relationship between transformational leadership practices and turnover intention of government employees. *International Journal of Public Administration, 41* (3), 203-215.

**Enns, C. Z.** (2018). Feminist therapy and empowerment. In C. B Travis, J. W. White, A. Rutherford, W. S. Williams, S. L. Cook, & K. F. Wyche (Eds.), *APA handbooks in psychology series. APA handbook of the psychology of women: Perspectives on women's private and public lives* (pp. 3-19). Washington, DC, US: American Psychological Association.

**Eno Louden, J., Manchak, S. M., Ricks, E. P., & Kennealy, P. J.** (2018). The role of stigma toward mental illness in probation officers' perceptions of risk and case management decisions. *Criminal Justice and Behavior, 45* (5), 573-588.

**Enstrom, J. E.** (1999). Smoking cessation and mortality trends among two United States populations. *Journal of Clinical Epidemiology, 52* (9), 813-825.

**Equal Employment Opportunity Commission (EEOC).** (2018). Charges alleging sexual harassment FY 2010-FY 2017. *EEOC.* https://www.eeoc.gov/eeoc/statistics/enforcement/sexual_harassment_new.cfm

**Ergetie, T., Yohanes, Z., Asrat, B., Demeke, W., Abate, A., & Tareke, M.** (2018). Perceived stigma among non-professional caregivers of people with severe mental illness, Bahir Dar, northwest Ethiopia. *Annals of General Psychiatry, 17* (1), 42.

**Erickson, C. K.** (2018). *The science of addiction: From neurobiology to treatment.* New York: Norton.

**Ericsson, K. A., & Moxley, J. H.** (2012). A critique of Howard's argument for innate limits in chess performance or why we need an account based on acquired skill and deliberate practice. *Applied Cognitive Psychology, 26* (4), 649-653.

**Erikson, E. H.** (1968). *Identity: Youth and crisis.* New York: Norton.

**Erikson, E. H.** (1969). *Gandhi's truth.* New York: Norton.

**Erkic, M., Bailer, J., Fenske, S. C., Schmidt, S. N., Trojan, J., Schröder, A., ... & Mier, D.** (2018). Impaired emotion processing and a reduction in trust in patients with somatic symptom disorder. *Clinical Psychology & Psychotherapy, 25* (1), 163-172.

**Erlangsen, A., Appadurai, V., Wang, Y., Turecki, G., Mors, O., Werge, T., ... & Nudel, R.** (2018). Genetics of suicide attempts in individuals with and without mental disorders: A population-based genome-wide association study. *Molecular Psychiatry,* 1.

**Ernst, M. M., Liao, L. M., Baratz, A. B., & Sandberg, D. E.** (2018). Disorders of sex development/intersex: Gaps in psychosocial care for children. *Pediatrics, 142* (2), e20174045.

**Estes, A. C.** (2012, December 17). Newtown, mental health and the dangers of oversimplifying gun control. *Vice.* http://www.vice.com/read/newtown-mental-health-and-the-dangers-of-oversimplifying-gun-control (accessed April 10, 2016)

**Etlouba, Y., Laher, A., Motara, F., Moolla, M., & Ariefdien, N.** (2018). First presentation with psychotic symptoms to the emergency department. *The Journal of Emergency Medicine, 55,* 78-86.

**Ettenberg, A., Fomenko, V., Kaganovsky, K., Shelton, K., & Wenzel, J. M.** (2015). On the positive and negative affective responses to cocaine and their relation to drug self-administration in rats. *Psychopharmacology, 232* (13), 2636-2375.

**Evans, B. G., & Iverson, P.** (2007). Plasticity in vowel perception and production: A study of accent change in young adults. *Journal of the Acoustical Society of America, 121* (6), 3814-3826.

**Evans, C. R., & Erickson, N.** (2019). Intersectionality and depression in adolescence and early adulthood: A MAIHDA analysis of the national longitudinal study of adolescent to adult health, 1995-2008. *Social Science & Medicine, 220,* 1-11.

**Evans, J. St. B. T., & Stanovich, K. E.** (2013). Dual-process theories of higher cognition: Advancing the debate. *Perspectives on Psychological Science, 8* (3), 223-241.

**Evers, A., Anderson, N., & Voskuijl, O.** (Eds.) (2017). *The Blackwell handbook of personnel selection.* New York: Wiley-Blackwell.

**Eysenck, H. J.** (1967). *The biological basis of personality.* Springfield, IL: Thomas.

**Ezell, J. M., Choi, C. W. J., Wall, M. M., & Link, B. G.** (2018). Measuring recurring stigma in the lives of individuals with mental illness. *Community Mental Health Journal, 54* (1), 27–32.

## F

**Fabbri, C., & Serretti, A.** (2016). Genetics of long-term treatment outcome in bipolar disorder. *Progress in Neuropsychopharmacology and Biological Psychiatry, 65,* 17–24.

**Faber, M. A., & Mayer, J. D.** (2009). Resonance to archetypes in media: There's some accounting for taste. *Journal of Research in Personality, 43* (3), 307–322.

**Fabian, J.** (2018). *Creative thinking and problem solving.* New York: CRC Press.

**Fader, L., Whitaker, J., Lopez, M., Vivace, B., Parra, M., Carlson, J., & Zamora, R.** (2018). Tibia fractures and NSAIDs. Does it make a difference? A multicenter retrospective study. *Injury.* doi: 10.1016/j.injury.2018.09.024

**Faedda, G. L., Becker, I., Baroni, A., Tondo, L., Aspland, E., & Koukopoulos, A.** (2010). The origins of electroconvulsive therapy: Prof. Bini's first report on ECT. *Journal of Affective Disorders, 120* (1–3), 12–15.

**Fahey, T. D., Insel, P. M., & Roth, W. T.** (2016). *Fit and well* (12th ed.). New York: McGraw-Hill.

**Fahmy, U. A., & Aljaeid, B. M.** (2018). Tadalafil transdermal delivery with alpha-lipoic acid self nanoemulsion for treatment of erectile dysfunction by diabetes mellitus. *International Journal of Pharmacology, 14* (7), 945–951.

**Fahs, B., & Koerth, K. M.** (2018). Female bisexuality: Identity, fluidity, and cultural expectations. In D. J. Swan & S. Habibi (Eds.), *Bisexuality* (pp. 113–126). Cham: Springer.

**Fairman, K. A., Peckham, A. M., & Sclar, D. A.** (2017). Diagnosis and treatment of ADHD in the United States: Update by gender and race. *Journal of Attention Disorders.* doi: 10.1177/1087054716688534

**Falcone, M., Garaffa, G., Gillo, A., Dente, D., Christopher, A. N., & Ralph, D. J.** (2018). Outcomes of inflatable penile prosthesis insertion in 247 patients completing female to male gender reassignment surgery. *BJU International, 121* (1), 139–144.

**Falk, E., & Scholz, C.** (2018). Persuasion, influence, and value: Perspectives from communication and social neuroscience. *Annual Review of Psychology, 69,* 329–356.

**Fallatah, F., & Laschinger, H. K.** (2016). The influence of authentic leadership and supportive professional practice environments on new graduate nurses' job satisfaction. *Journal of Research in Nursing, 21* (2), 125–136.

**Family and Youth Services Bureau.** (2014). State abstinence education grant program. *Family and Youth Services Bureau.* http://www.acf.hhs.gov/programs/fysb/resource/aegp-fact-sheet (accessed March 22, 2016)

**Fan, S. S., Cox, B., Wallace, A., Spencer, L., Oquendo, M., & Blumberg, H. P.** (2018). Commonalities and distinctions in white matter integrity associated with suicide behavior between adolescents and young adults with bipolar disorder and major depressive disorder. *Biological Psychiatry, 83* (9), S293.

**Fantoni, E. R., Chalkidou, A., O'Brien, J. T., Farrar, G., & Hammers, A.** (2018). A systematic review and aggregated analysis on the impact of amyloid PET brain imaging on the diagnosis, diagnostic confidence, and management of patients being evaluated for Alzheimer's disease. *Journal of Alzheimer's Disease, 63,* 783–796.

**Faraone, S. V., Asherson, P. A., Banaschewski, T., Biederman, J., Buitelaar, J. K., Ramos-Quiroga, J. A., ... & Franke, B.** (2015). Attention-deficit hyperactivity disorder. *Nature Reviews Disease Primers, 1,* 15020. doi: 10.1038/nrdp.2015.20

**Faraone, S. V., & Larsson, H.** (2018). Genetics of attention deficit hyperactivity disorder. *Molecular Psychiatry,* 1.

**Farholm, A., & Sørensen, M.** (2016). Motivation for physical activity and exercise in severe mental illness: A systematic review of intervention studies. *International Journal of Mental Health Nursing, 25* (3), 194–205.

**Farland-Smith, D.** (2017). The evolution of the analysis of the draw-a-scientist test. In P. Katz (Ed.), *Drawing for science education* (pp. 171–178). Rotterdam: SensePublishers.

**Farmer, R. F., Seeley, J. R., Gau, J. M., Klein, D. N., Merikangas, K. R., Kosty, D. B., ... & Lewinsohn, P. M.** (2018). Clinical features associated with an increased risk for alcohol use disorders among family members. *Psychology of Addictive Behaviors, 32* (6), 628–638.

**Farr, R. H., & Patterson, C. J.** (2013). Lesbian and gay adoptive parents and their children. In A. E. Goldberg & K. R. Allen (Eds.), LGBT-parent *families: Innovations in research and implications for practice* (pp. 39–55). New York: Springer.

**Fatemi, S. H., & Folsom, T. D.** (2009). The neurodevelopmental hypothesis of schizophrenia, revisited. *Schizophrenia Bulletin, 35* (3), 528–548.

**Fausto-Sterling, A.** (2016). How else can we study sex differences in early infancy? *Developmental Psychobiology, 58* (1), 5–16.

**Fava, G. A.** (2016). Well-being *therapy: Treatment manual and clinical application.* Basel: Karger Medical and Scientific Publishers.

**Fava, G. A., & Bech, P.** (2015). The concept of euthymia. *Psychotherapy and Psychosomatics, 85* (1), 1–5.

**Faymonville, M. E., Boly, M., & Laureys, S.** (2006). Functional neuroanatomy of the hypnotic state. *Journal of Physiology, Paris, 99,* 463–469.

**Fazio, R. H., Chen, J.-M., McDonel, E. C., & Sherman, S. J** (1982). Attitude accessibility, attitude-behavior consistency, and the strength of the object-evaluation association. *Journal of Experimental Social Psychology, 18* (4), 339–357.

**Fazio, R. H., & Olsen, A.** (2007). Attitudes. In M. A. Hogg & J. Cooper (Eds.), *The Sage handbook of social psychology* (concise 2nd ed.). Thousand Oaks, CA: Sage.

**Fazio, R. L.** (2018). Toward a neurodevelopmental understanding of pedophilia. *The Journal of Sexual Medicine, 15,* 1205–1207.

**Fazio, R. L., Dyshniku, F., Lykins, A. D., & Cantor, J. M.** (2017). Leg length versus torso length in pedophilia: Further evidence of atypical physical development early in life. *Sexual Abuse: Journal of Research and Treatment, 29* (5), 500–514. doi: 10.1177/1079063215609936

**Feijó, L. M., Tarman, G. Z., Fontaine, C., Harrison, R., Johnstone, T., & Salomons, T.**. (2018). Sex-specific effects of gender identification on pain study recruitment. *Journal of Pain, 19* (2), 178–185.

**Feinstein, J. S., Buzza, C., Hurlemann, R., Follmer, R. L., Dahdaleh, N. S., Coryell, W. H., Welsh, M. J., Tranel, D., & Wemmie, J. A.** (2013). Fear and panic in humans with bilateral amygdala damage. *Nature Neuroscience, 16* (3), 270–272.

**Feldman, G., & Chandrashekar, S. P.** (2018). Laypersons' beliefs and intuitions about free will and determinism: New insights linking the social psychology and experimental philosophy paradigms. *Social Psychological and Personality Science, 9* (5), 539–549.

**Feldman Hall, O., Dunsmoor, J. E., Tompary, A., Hunter, L. E., Todorov, A., & Phelps, E. A.** (2018). Stimulus generalization as a mechanism for learning to trust. *Proceedings of the National Academy of Sciences, 115* (7), E1690–E1697.

**Ferguson, C. J.** (2015). Do Angry Birds make for angry children? A meta-analysis of video game influences on children's and adolescents' aggression, mental health, prosocial behavior, and academic performance. *Perspectives on Psychological Science, 10* (5), 646–666.

**Ferguson, C. J., & Kilburn, J.** (2010). Much ado about nothing: The misestimation and overinterpretation of violent video game effects in Eastern and Western nations: Comment on Anderson et al. (2010). *Psychological Bulletin, 136,* 174–178.

**Ferguson, C. J., Rueda, S. M., Cruz, A. M., Ferguson, D. E., Fritz, S., & Smith, S. M.** (2008). Violent video games and aggression: Causal relationship or byproduct of family violence and intrinsic violence motivation? *Criminal Justice and Behavior, 35* (3), 311–332.

**Ferguson, E., & Bibby, P. A.** (2012). Openness to experience and all-cause mortality: A meta-analysis and r (equivalent) from risk ratios and odds ratios. *British Journal of Health Psychology, 17* (1), 85–102.

**Ferguson, E., Zhao, K., O'Carroll, R. E., & Smillie, L. D.** (2018). Costless and costly prosociality: Correspondence among personality traits, economic preferences, and real-world prosociality. *Social Psychological and Personality Science.* doi: 10.1177/1948550618765071

**Fergusson, D. M., McLeod, G. F., & Horwood, L. J.** (2013). Childhood sexual abuse and adult developmental outcomes: Findings from a 30-year longitudinal study in New Zealand. *Child Abuse and Neglect, 37* (9), 664–674.

**Fernandes, T., Martins, T., Mustafé, G., Mendes, D., Pegoraro, L. F., & Dantas, C. D. R.** (2018). Executive function of chronic schizophrenia patients in a seven-year follow-up. *Schizophrenia Bulletin, 44* (Suppl. 1), S349.

**Fernández, A. L., & Abe, J.** (2018). Bias in cross-cultural neuropsychological testing: Problems and possible solutions. *Culture and Brain, 6,* 1–35.

**Fernandez, T. V., Leckman, J. F., & Pittenger, C.** (2018). Genetic susceptibility in obsessive-compulsive disorder. *Handbook of Clinical Neurology, 148,* 767–781.

**Fernández-Jaén, A., Albert, J., Fernández-Mayoralas, D. M., López-Martín, S., Fernández-Perrone, A. L., Jimenez de la Peña, M., ... & López Arribas, S.** (2018). Cingulate cortical thickness and dopamine transporter (DAT1) Genotype in children and adolescents with ADHD. *Journal of Attention Disorders, 22* (7), 651–660.

**Ferreira, T., Cadima, J., Matias, M., Vieira, J. M., Leal, T., & Matos, P. M.** (2016). Preschool children's prosocial behavior: The role of mother–child, father–child, and teacher–child relationships. *Journal of Child and Family Studies.* doi: 10.1007/s10826-016-0369-x

**Ferrie, J. E., Shipley, M. J., Akbaraly, T. N., Marmot, M. G., Kivimaki, M., & Singh-Manoux, A.** (2011). Change in sleep duration and cognitive function: Findings from the Whitehall II Study. *Sleep, 34* (5), 565–573.

**Ferschmann, L., Fjell, A. M., Vollrath, M. E., Grydeland, H., Walhovd, K. B., & Tamnes, C. K.** (2018). Personality traits are associated with cortical development across adolescence: A longitudinal structural MRI study. *Child Development, 89* (3), 811–822.

**Fertuck, E. A., Fischer, S., & Beeney, J.** (2018). Social cognition and borderline personality disorder:

Splitting and trust impairment findings. *Psychiatric Clinics, 41* (4), 613–632.

**Festinger, L.** (1954). A theory of social comparison processes. *Human Relations, 7,* 117–140.

**Festinger, L.** (1957). *A theory of cognitive dissonance.* Evanston, IL: Row Peterson.

**Festinger, L., & Carlsmith, J. M.** (1959). Cognitive consequences of forced compliance. *Journal of Abnormal and Social Psychology, 58,* 203–210.

**Fiedler, K., & Krueger, J. I.** (2013). Afterthoughts on precognition: No cogent evidence for anomalous influences of consequent events on preceding cognition. *Theory & Psychology, 23* (3), 323–333.

**Fiedler, K., & Kutzner, F.** (2015). Reasoning biases: Implications for research in judgment and decision making. In G. Keren & G. Wu (Eds.), *The Wiley Blackwell handbook of judgment and decision making* (pp. 380–403). New York: Wiley.

**Field, T.** (2018). Postnatal anxiety prevalence, predictors and effects on development: A narrative review. *Infant Behavior and Development, 51,* 24–32.

**Fields, R. D., Woo, D. H., & Basser, P. J.** (2015). Glial regulation of the neuronal connectome through local and long-distant communication. *Neuron, 86* (2), 374–386.

**Finan, L. J., Ohannessian, C. M., & Gordon, M. S.** (2018). Trajectories of depressive symptoms from adolescence to emerging adulthood: The influence of parents, peers, and siblings. *Developmental Psychology, 54* (8), 1555.

**Finch, C. E.** (2009). The neurobiology of middle-age has arrived. *Neurobiology and Aging, 30* (4), 515–520.

**Finch, C. E.** (2011). Inflammation and aging. In E. Masoro & S. Austad (Eds.), *Handbook of the biology of aging* (7th ed.). New York: Elsevier.

**Fink, B., & Manning, J. T.** (2018). Direct versus indirect measurement of digit ratio: New data from Austria and a critical consideration of clarity of report in 2D:4D studies. *Early Human Development, 127,* 28–32.

**Finn, A. S., Kalra, P. B., Goetz, C., Leonard, J. A., Sheridan, M. A., & Gabrieli, J. D.** (2016). Developmental dissociation between the maturation of procedural memory and declarative memory. *Journal of Experimental Child Psychology, 142,* 212–220.

**Fischer, A., Ziogas, A., & Anton-Culver, H.** (2018). Perception matters: Stressful life events increase breast cancer risk. *Journal of Psychosomatic Research, 110,* 46–53.

**Fischer, R., Lee, A., & Verzijden, M. N.** (2018). Dopamine genes are linked to Extraversion and Neuroticism personality traits, but only in demanding climates. *Scientific Reports, 8* (1), 1733.

**Fischer, S., Wonderlich, J., Breithaupt, L., Byrne, C., & Engel, S.** (2018). Negative urgency and expectancies increase vulnerability to binge eating in bulimia nervosa. *Eating Disorders, 26* (1), 39–51.

**Fisher, O., O'Donnell, S. C., & Oyserman, D.** (2017). Social class and identity-based motivation. *Current Opinion in Psychology, 18,* 61–66.

**Fisher, T. D., Moore, Z. T., & Pittenger, M. J.** (2012). Sex on the brain? An examination of frequency of sexual cognitions as a function of gender, erotophilia, and social desirability. *Journal of Sex Research, 49* (1), 69–77.

**Fiske, S. T., & Tablante, C. B.** (2015). Stereotyping: Processes and content. In M. Mikulincer, P. R. Shaver, E. Borgida, & J. A. Bargh (Eds.), *APA handbook of personality and social psychology* (vol. 1, pp. 457–507). Washington, DC: American Psychological Association.

**Fitch, W. T.** (2018). What animals can teach us about human language: The phonological continuity hypothesis. *Current Opinion in Behavioral Sciences, 21,* 68–75.

**Fitzhugh, E. C., Bassett, Jr., D. R., & Evans, M. F.** (2010). Urban trails and physical activity: A natural experiment. *American Journal of Preventive Medicine, 39* (3), 259–262.

**Fitzpatrick, C., Archambault, I., Janosz, M., & Pagani, L. S.** (2015). Early childhood working memory forecasts high school dropout risk. *Intelligence, 53,* 160–165.

**Fivush, R.** (2011). The development of autobiographical memory. *Annual Review of Psychology* (vol. 62, pp. 559–582). Palo Alto, CA: Annual Reviews.

**Flanagan, C., & Wilson, E.** (2013). Home value and homeownership rates: Recession and post-recession comparisons from 2007–2009 to 2010–2012. *American Community Survey Brief* (pp. 12–20). Washington, DC: U.S. Census Bureau.

**Flentje, A., Kober, K. M., Carrico, A. W., Neilands, T. B., Flowers, E., Heck, N. C., & Aouizerat, B. E.** (2018). Minority stress and leukocyte gene expression in sexual minority men living with treated HIV infection. *Brain, Behavior, and Immunity, 70,* 335–345.

**Flinker, A., Korzeniewska, A., Shestyuk, A. Y., Franaszczuk, P. J., Dronkers, N. F., Knight, R. T., & Crone, N. E.** (2015). Redefining the role of Broca's area in speech. *Proceedings of the National Academy of Sciences USA, 112* (9), 2871–2875.

**Flynn, J. R.** (1999). Searching for justice: The discovery of IQ gains over time. *American Psychologist, 54* (1), 5–20.

**Flynn, J. R.** (2006). The history of the American mind in the 20th century: A scenario to explain gains over time and a case for the irrelevance of *g.* In P. C. Kyllonen, R. D. Roberts, & L. Stankov (Eds.), *Extending intelligence.* Mahwah, NJ: Erlbaum.

**Flynn, J. R.** (2013). *Are we getting smarter?* New York: Cambridge University Press.

**Foa, E., & McLean, C. P.** (2016). The efficacy of exposure therapy for anxiety-related disorders and its underlying mechanisms: The case of OCD and PTSD. *Annual Review of Clinical Psychology* (vol. 12, pp. 1–28). Palo Alto, CA: Annual Reviews.

**Foa, E. B., McLean, C. P., Zang, Y., Rosenfield, D., Yadin, E., Yarvis, J. S., ... & Fina, B. A.** (2018). Effect of prolonged exposure therapy delivered over 2 weeks vs 8 weeks vs present-centered therapy on PTSD symptom severity in military personnel: A randomized clinical trial. *JAMA, 319* (4), 354–364.

**Fodor, I., & Epstein, J.** (2002). Agoraphobia, panic disorder, and gender. In J. Worell (Ed.), *Encyclopedia of women and gender.* San Diego: Academic.

**Folkman, S., & Lazarus, R. S.** (1980). An analysis of coping in a middle-aged community sample. *Journal of Health and Social Behavior, 21* (3), 219–239.

**Folkman, S., & Moskowitz, J. T.** (2004). Coping: Pitfalls and promises. *Annual Review of Psychology* (vol. 54, pp. 745–744). Palo Alto, CA: Annual Reviews.

**Follmer, K. B., & Jones, K. S.** (2018). Mental illness in the workplace: An interdisciplinary review and organizational research agenda. *Journal of Management, 44* (1), 325–351.

**Fondberg, R., Lundström, J. N., Blöchl, M., Olsson, M. J., & Seubert, J.** (2018). Multisensory flavor perception: The relationship between congruency, pleasantness, and odor referral to the mouth. *Appetite, 125,* 244–252.

**Fondell, E., Townsend, M. K., Unger, L. D., Okereke, O. I., Grodstein, F., Ascherio, A., & Willett, W. C.** (2018). Physical activity across adulthood and subjective cognitive function in older men. *European Journal of Epidemiology, 33* (1), 79–87.

**Foote, B., Smolin, Y., Kaplan, M., Legatt, M. E., & Lipschitz, D.** (2006). Prevalence of dissociative disorders in psychiatric outpatients. *American Journal of Psychiatry, 163* (4), 566–568.

**Forbes, M. K., Eaton, N. R., & Krueger, R. F.** (2017). Sexual quality of life and aging: A prospective study of a nationally representative sample. *The Journal of Sex Research, 54* (2), 137–148.

**Ford, E. S., Cunningham, T. J., Giles, W. H., & Croft, J. B.** (2015). Trends in insomnia and excessive daytime sleepiness among U.S. adults from 2002 to 2012. *Sleep Medicine, 16* (3), 372–378.

**Ford, J. D., Charak, R., Modrowski, C. A., & Kerig, P. K.** (2018). PTSD and dissociation symptoms as mediators of the relationship between polyvictimization and psychosocial and behavioral problems among justice-involved adolescents. *Journal of Trauma & Dissociation, 19* (3), 325–346.

**Foreman, M., Hare, L., York, K., Balakrishnan, K., Sánchez, F. J., Harte, F., ... & Harley, V. R.** (2018). A genetic link between gender dysphoria and sex hormone signalling. *The Journal of Clinical Endocrinology & Metabolism,* jc.2018-01105. doi: 10.1210/jc.2018-01105.

**Forgas, J. P., Dunn, E., & Granland, S.** (2008). Are you being served... ? An unobtrusive experiment of affective influences on helping in a department store. *European Journal of Social Psychology, 38,* 333–342.

**Foscolou, A., Magriplis, E., Tyrovolas, S., Chrysohoou, C., Sidossis, L., Matalas, A. L., ... & Panagiotakos, D.** (2019). The association of protein and carbohydrate intake with successful aging: A combined analysis of two epidemiological studies. *European Journal of Nutrition, 58* (2), 807–817.

**Fowler, K. A., Lilienfeld, S. O., & Patrick, C. J.** (2009). Detecting psychopathy from thin slices of behavior. *Psychological Assessment, 21* (1), 68–78.

**Fox, K. C., & Christoff, K.** (Eds.). (2018). *The Oxford handbook of spontaneous thought: Mind-wandering, creativity, and dreaming.* Oxford University Press.

**Frajo-Apor, B., Pardeller, S., Kemmler, G., Welte, A. S., & Hofer, A.** (2016). Emotional intelligence deficits in schizophrenia: The impact of non-social cognition. *Schizophrenia Research, 172* (1–3), 131–136.

**Francisco, V., Pino, J., Campos-Cabaleiro, V., Ruiz-Fernández, C., Mera, A., Gonzalez-Gay, M. A., ... & Gualillo, O.** (2018). Obesity, fat mass and immune system: Role for leptin. *Frontiers in Physiology, 9,* 640.

**Franke, R. H., & Kaul, J. D.** (1978). The Hawthorne experiments: First statistical interpretation. *American Sociological Review, 43* (5), 623–643.

**Frankenhuis, W. E., & Tiokhin, L.** (2018). Bridging evolutionary biology and developmental psychology: Toward an enduring theoretical infrastructure. *Child Development, 89* (6), 2303–2306. doi: 10.1111/cdev.13019.

**Frankl, V. E.** (2006). *Man's search for meaning* (3rd ed., reprint; I. Lasch, trans.). Boston: Beacon. (original work published 1946)

**Franklin, Jr., R. G., & Zebrowitz, L. A.** (2016). The influence of political candidates' facial appearance on older and younger adults' voting choices and actual electoral success. *Cogent Psychology, 3* (1), 1151602.

**Franklin, M. S., Smallwood, J., Zedelius, C. M., Broadway, J. M., & Schooler, J. W.** (2016). Unaware yet reliant on attention: Experience sampling reveals that mind-wandering impedes implicit learning. *Psychonomic Bulletin & Review, 23* (1), 223–229.

**Frattaroli, J.** (2006). Experimental disclosure and its moderators: A meta-analysis. *Psychological Bulletin, 132,* 823–865.

**Fredrick, S., & Loewenstein, G.** (1999). Hedonic adaptation. In D. Kahneman, E. Diener, & N. Schwarz (Eds.), Well-being: *The foundations of hedonic psychology* (pp. 302–329). New York: Russell Sage Foundation.

**Fredrickson, B. L.** (1998). What good are positive emotions? *Review of General Psychology, 2* (3), 300–319.

**Freedman, J. L., & Fraser, S. C.** (1966). Compliance without pressure: The foot-in-the-door technique. *Journal of Personality and Social Psychology, 4* (2), 195–202.

**Freeland, A., Manchanda, R., Chiu, S., Sharma, V., & Merskey, H.** (1993). Four cases of supposed multiple personality disorder: Evidence of unjustified diagnoses. *Canadian Journal of Psychiatry, 38* (4), 245–247.

**Freeman, M. P., Góez-Mogollón, L., McInerney, K. A., Davies, A. C., Church, T. R., Sosinsky, A. Z., ... & Cohen, L. S.** (2018). Obstetrical and neonatal outcomes after benzodiazepine exposure during pregnancy: Results from a prospective registry of women with psychiatric disorders. *General Hospital Psychiatry, 53,* 73–79.

**French, K. A., Dumani, S., Allen, T. D., & Shockley, K. M.** (2018). A meta-analysis of work–family conflict and social support. *Psychological Bulletin, 144* (3), 284–314.

**Freud, S.** (1911). *The interpretation of dreams* (3rd ed.; A. A. Brill, trans.). New York: Macmillan. (original work published 1899)

**Freud, S.** (1924). *A general introduction to psychoanalysis.* New York: Washington Square Press.

**Freud, S.** (1963). Letter to Oskar Pfister. In H. Meng & E. L. Freud (Eds.) & E. Mosbacher (Trans.), *Psychoanalysis and faith: The letters of Sigmund Freud and Oskar Pfister.* New York: Basic Books. (original work published 1918)

**Frey, S., Eichler, A., Stonawski, V., Kriebel, J., Wahl, S., Gallati, S., ... & Moll, G. H.** (2018). Prenatal alcohol exposure is associated with adverse cognitive effects and distinct whole-genome DNA methylation patterns in primary school children. *Frontiers in Behavioral Neuroscience, 12,* 125.

**Frieder, R. E., Wang, G., & Oh, I. S.** (2018). Linking job-relevant personality traits, transformational leadership, and job performance via perceived meaningfulness at work: A moderated mediation model. *Journal of Applied Psychology, 103* (3), 324–333.

**Friedman, J.** (2015). Leptin and the regulation of food intake and body weight. *Journal of Nutritional Science and Vitaminology, 61* (Suppl.), S202.

**Friedman, J. P., & Jack, A. I.** (2018). Mapping cognitive structure onto the landscape of philosophical debate: An empirical framework with relevance to problems of consciousness, free will and ethics. *Review of Philosophy and Psychology, 9* (1), 73–113.

**Friedman, M., & Rosenman, R.** (1974). *Type A behavior and your heart.* New York: Knopf.

**Friedman, R. C., Alfonso, C. A., & Downey, J. I.** (2015). Editorial: Psychodynamic psychiatry and psychoanalysis: Two different models. *Psychodynamic Psychiatry, 43* (4), 513–521.

**Friedman, R., Myers, P., & Benson, H.** (1998). Meditation and the relaxation response. In H. S. Friedman (Ed.), *Encyclopedia of mental health* (vol. 2). San Diego: Academic.

**Frischholz, E. J., Braun, B. G., Sachs, R. G., Schwartz, D. R., Lewis, J., Shaeffer, D., Westergaard, C., & Pasquotto, J.** (2015a). Construct validity of the Dissociative Experiences Scale: II. Its relationship to hypnotizability. *American Journal of Clinical Hypnosis, 57* (2), 102–109.

**Frischholz, E. J., Spiegel, D., Trentalange, M. J., & Spiegel, H.** (2015b). The Hypnotic Induction Profile and absorption. *American Journal of Clinical Hypnosis, 57* (2), 122–128.

**Fritz, C., & Sonnentag, S.** (2006). Recovery, well-being, and performance-related outcomes: The role of work overload and vacation experiences. *Journal of Applied Psychology, 91* (4), 936–945.

**Fromm, E.** (1947). *Man for himself.* New York: Holt, Rinehart & Winston.

**Fruhwürth, S., Vogel, H., Schürmann, A., & Williams, K. J.** (2018). Novel insights into how overnutrition disrupts the hypothalamic actions of leptin. *Frontiers in Endocrinology, 9,* 89.

**Fründt, O., Schulz, R., Schöttle, D., Cheng, B., Thomalla, G., Braaß, H., ... & Bäumer, T.** (2018). White matter microstructure of the human mirror neuron system is related to symptom severity in adults with autism. *Journal of Autism and Developmental Disorders, 48* (2), 417–429.

**Fry, P. S., & Debats, D. L.** (2009). Perfectionism and the five-factor personality traits as predictors of mortality in older adults. *Journal of Health Psychology, 14* (4), 513–524.

**Fu, F. Q., Richards, K. A., Hughes, D. E., & Jones, E.** (2010). Motivating salespeople to sell new products: The relative influence of attitudes, subjective norms, and self-efficacy. *Journal of Marketing, 74* (6), 61–76.

**Fu, Q., Liu, Y. J., Dienes, Z., Wu, J., Chen, W., & Fu, X.** (2017). Neural correlates of subjective awareness for natural scene categorization of color photographs and line-drawings. *Frontiers in Psychology, 8.*

**Fuchs, F., Monet, B., Ducruet, T., Chaillet, N., & Audibert, F.** (2018). Effect of maternal age on the risk of preterm birth: A large cohort study. *PloS one, 13* (1), e0191002.

**Fuchs, X., Flor, H., & Bekrater-Bodmann, R.** (2018). Psychological factors associated with phantom limb pain: A review of recent findings. *Pain Research and Management,* 5080123. doi: 10.1155/2018/5080123

**Fuertinger, S., Zinn, J. C., Sharan, A. D., Hamzei-Sichani, F., & Simonyan, K.** (2018). Dopamine drives left-hemispheric lateralization of neural networks during human speech. *Journal of Comparative Neurology, 526* (5), 920–931.

**Fujiwara, E., Levine, B., & Anderson, A. K.** (2008). Intact implicit and reduced explicit memory for negative self-related information in repressive coping. *Cognitive, Affective, and Behavioral Neuroscience, 8* (3), 254–263.

**Funder, D. C.** (2009). Persons, behaviors, and situations: An agenda for personality psychology in the postwar era. *Journal of Research in Personality, 43* (2), 120–126.

**Furman, A. J., Meeker, T. J., Rietschel, J. C., Yoo, S., Muthulingam, J., Prokhorenko, M., ... & Seminowicz, D. A.** (2018). Cerebral peak alpha frequency predicts individual differences in pain sensitivity. *Neuroimage, 167,* 203–210.

## G

**Gable, S. L.** (2018). Satisfying and meaningful close relationships. In J. P. Forgas & R. F. Baumeister, (Eds.), *The social psychology of living well.* London: Routledge.

**Gabriel, A. S., Koopman, J., Rosen, C. C., & Johnson, R. E.** (2018). Helping others or helping oneself? An episodic examination of the behavioral consequences of helping at work. *Personnel Psychology, 71* (1), 85–107.

**Gadassi, R., Bar-Nahum, L. E., Newhouse, S., Anderson, R., Heiman, J. R., Rafaeli, E., & Janssen, E.** (2016). Perceived partner responsiveness mediates the association between sexual and marital satisfaction: A daily diary study in newlywed couples. *Archives of Sexual Behavior, 45* (1), 109–120.

**Galatzer-Levy, I. R., Huang, S. H., & Bonanno, G. A.** (2018). Trajectories of resilience and dysfunction following potential trauma: A review and statistical evaluation. *Clinical Psychology Review,* 63, 41–55.

**Gallagher, S., O' Riordan, A., McMahon, G., & Creaven, A. M.** (2018). Evaluating personality as a moderator of the association between life events stress and cardiovascular reactivity to acute stress. *International Journal of Psychophysiology, 126,* 52–59.

**Gallo, K. P., Thompson-Hollands, J., Pincus, D. B., & Barlow, D. H.** (2013). Anxiety disorders. In G. Stricker, T. A. Widiger, & I. B. Weiner (Eds.), *Handbook of psychology* (2nd ed., vol. 8, pp. 147–170). Hoboken, NJ: Wiley.

**Gallo, W. T., Bradley, E. H., Dubin, J. A., Jones, R. N., Falba, T. A., Teng, H. M., & Kasi, S. V.** (2006). The persistence of depressive symptoms in older workers who experience involuntary job loss: Results from the health and retirement survey. *Journals of Gerontology: B: Psychological Sciences and Social Sciences, 61* (4), S221–S228.

**Galotti, K. M.** (2017). *Cognitive psychology in and out of the laboratory* (6th ed.). Thousand Oaks, CA: Sage.

**Gannon, B. M., Baumann, M. H., Walther, D., Jimenez-Morigosa, C., Sulima, A., Rice, K. C., & Collins, G. T.** (2018). The abuse-related effects of pyrrolidine-containing cathinones are related to their potency and selectivity to inhibit the dopamine transporter. *Neuropsychopharmacology, 43* (12), 2399–2407.

**Garamszegi, L. Z., Zagalska-Neubauer, M., Canal, D., Blázi, G., Laczi, M., Nagy, G., ... & Zsebők, S.** (2018). MHC-mediated sexual selection on birdsong: Generic polymorphism, particular alleles and acoustic signals. *Molecular Ecology, 27* (11), 2620–2633.

**Garb, H. N., Wood, J. M., Nezworski, M. T., Grove, W. M., & Stejskal, W. J.** (2001). Toward a resolution of the Rorschach controversy. *Psychological Assessment, 13* (4), 433–448.

**Garcia, J.** (1989). Food for Tolman: Cognition and cathexis in concert. In T. Archer & L. Nilsson (Eds.), *Aversion, avoidance, and anxiety.* Mahwah, NJ: Erlbaum.

**Garcia, J., Ervin, F. R., & Koelling, R. A.** (1966). Learning with prolonged delay of reinforcement. *Psychonomic Science, 5* (3), 121–122.

**Garcia, J., & Koelling, R. A.** (1966). Relation of cue to consequence in avoidance learning. *Psychonomic Science, 4*(3), 123–124.

**Garcia, J., & Koelling, R. A.** (2009). Specific hungers and poison avoidance as adaptive specializations of learning. In D. Shanks (Ed.), *Psychology of learning.* Thousand Oaks, CA: Sage.

**Gardner, H.** (1983). *Frames of mind.* New York: Basic.

**Gardner, H.** (1993). *Multiple intelligences.* New York: Basic.

**Gardner, H.** (2002). The pursuit of excellence through education. In M. Ferrari (Ed.), *Learning from extraordinary minds.* Mahwah, NJ: Erlbaum.

**Gari, A., Mylonas, K., & Portešová, S.** (2015). An analysis of attitudes towards the gifted students with learning difficulties using two samples of Greek and Czech primary school teachers. *Gifted Education International, 31* (3), 271–286.

**Garnett, C. V., Crane, D., Brown, J., Kaner, E. F. S., Bever, F. R., Muirhead, C. R., ... & Michie, S.** (2018). Behavior change techniques used in digital behavior change interventions to reduce excessive alcohol consumption: A meta-regression. *Annals of Behavioral Medicine, 52* (6), 530–543.

**Garrett, B. L.** (2011). *Convicting the innocent: Where criminal prosecutions go wrong.* Cambridge, MA: Harvard University Press.

**Garrison, S. M., Doane, M. J., & Elliott, M.** (2018). Gay and lesbian experiences of discrimination, health, and well-being surrounding the presidential election. *Social Psychological and Personality Science, 9* (2), 131–142.

**Gärtner, A., Strobel, A., Reif, A., Lesch, K. P., & Enge, S.** (2018). Genetic variation in serotonin function impacts on altruistic punishment in the ultimatum game: A longitudinal approach. *Brain and Cognition, 125,* 37–44.

**Gärtner, H., Minnerop, M., Pieperhoff, P., Schleicher, A., Zilles, K., Altenmüller, E., & Amunts, K.** (2013). Brain morphometry shows effects of long-term musical practice in middle-aged keyboard players. *Frontiers in Psychology, 4,* 636. doi: 10.3389/fpsyg.2013.00636

**Gartstein, M. A., Putnam, S. P., & Kliewer, R.** (2016). Do infant temperament characteristics predict core academic abilities in preschool-aged children? *Learning and Individual Differences, 45,* 299–306.

**Gates, G. J.** (2011, April). *How many people are lesbian, gay, bisexual, and transgender? Williams Institute.*

ideomotor responding: A real-simulator comparison. *Contemporary Hypnosis, 22* (3), 123–137.

**Green, R.** (1987). *The "sissy boy syndrome" and the development of homosexuality.* New Haven, CT: Yale University Press.

**Green, R. J., Bettinger, M., & Zacks, E.** (1996). Are lesbian couples fused and gay male couples disengaged? Questioning gender straitjackets. In J. Laird & R. J. Green (Eds.), *Lesbian and gays in couples and families: A handbook for therapists* (pp. 185–230). New York: Jossey-Bass.

**Greenhaus, J. H., & Callanan, G. A.** (2013). Career dynamics. In N. W. Schmitt, S. Highhouse, & I. B. Weiner (Eds.), *Handbook of psychology* (2nd ed., vol. 12, pp. 593–614). Hoboken, NJ: Wiley.

**Greenleaf, R. K.** (1997). The servant as leader. In R. P. Vecchio (Ed.), *Leadership: Understanding the dynamics of power and influence in organizations* (pp. 429–438). Notre Dame, IN: University of Notre Dame Press.

**Greenwald, A. G., Poehlman, T. A., Uhlmann, E., & Banaji, M. R.** (2009). Understanding and using the Implicit Association Test: III. Meta-analysis of predictive validity. *Journal of Personality and Social Psychology, 97* (1), 17–41.

**Greenwood, J. D.** (2015). *A conceptual history of psychology: Exploring the tangled web* (2nd ed.). Cambridge, UK: Cambridge University Press.

**Greenwood, T., Lazzeroni, L., Calkins, M., Freedman, R., Green, M., Gur, R., ... & Radant, A.** (2018). Genome-wide association of endophenotypes for schizophrenia from the Consortium On the Genetics of Schizophrenia (COGS) study. *Biological Psychiatry, 83* (9), S428–S429.

**Greer, S., Morris, T., & Pettingale, K. W.** (1979). Psychological response to breast cancer: Effect on outcome. *The Lancet, 2* (8146), 785–787.

**Gregory Stone, A., Russell, R. F., & Patterson, K.** (2004). Transformational versus servant leadership: A difference in leader focus. *Leadership & Organization Development Journal, 25* (4), 349–361.

**Gregory, R. L.** (2015). *Eye and brain: The psychology of seeing.* Princeton, NJ: Princeton University Press.

**Gregory, S., Ffytche, D., Simmons, A., Kumari, V., Howard, M., Hodgins, S., & Blackwood, N.** (2012). The antisocial brain: Psychopathy matters. *Archives of General Psychiatry, 69* (9), 962–972.

**Greitemeyer, T., & Sagioglou, C.** (2018). Does low (vs. high) subjective socioeconomic status increase both prosociality and aggression? *Social Psychology, 49,* 76–87.

**Griffin, S. C., Curran, S., Chan, A. W., Finn, S. B., Baker, C. I., Pasquina, P. F., & Tsao, J. W.** (2017). Trajectory of phantom limb pain relief using mirror therapy: Retrospective analysis of two studies. *Scandinavian Journal of Pain, 15,* 98–103.

**Grigoryan, G., Korkotian, E., & Segal, M.** (2012). Selective facilitation of LPTP in the ventral hippocampus by calcium stores. *Hippocampus, 22* (7), 1635–1644.

**Grilo, C. M., Masheb, R. M., & White, M. A.** (2010). Significance of overvaluation of shape/weight in binge-eating disorder: Comparative study with overweight and bulimia nervosa. *Obesity, 18* (3), 499–504.

**Grinberg, A. M., O'Hara, K. L., & Sbarra, D. A.** (2018). Preliminary evidence of attenuated blood pressure reactivity to acute stress in adults following a recent marital separation. *Psychology & Health, 33* (3), 430–444.

**Gross, R.** (2018). Pre- and perinatal risk factors for autism spectrum disorder: An update. *Biological Psychiatry, 83* (9), S149.

**Grossi, E., Buscema, M. P., Snowdon, D., & Antuono, P.** (2007). Neuropathological findings processed by artificial neural networks (ANNs) can perfectly distinguish Alzheimer's patients from controls in the Nun Study. *BMC Neurology, 7,* 15.

**Grossi, G., Jeding, K., Söderström, M., Osika, W., Levander, M., & Perski, A.** (2015). Self-reported sleep lengths ≥ 9 hours among Swedish patients with stress-related exhaustion: Associations with depression, quality of sleep, and levels of fatigue. *Nordic Journal of Psychiatry, 69* (4), 292–299.

**Grossman, M. R., & Gruenewald, T. L.** (2018). Failure to meet generative self-expectations is linked to poorer cognitive-affective well-being. *The Journals of Gerontology: Series B.* gby069

**Groves, C. L., & Anderson, C. A.** (2018). Aversive events and aggression. *Current Opinion in Psychology, 19,* 144–148.

**Grubin, D.** (2010). The polygraph and forensic psychiatry. *Journal of the American Academy of Psychiatry and the Law Online, 38* (4), 446–451.

**Grünblatt, E., Ruder, J., Monoranu, C. M., Riederer, P., Youdim, M. B., & Mandel, S. A.** (2018). Differential alterations in metabolism and proteolysis-related proteins in human Parkinson's disease substantia nigra. *Neurotoxicity Research, 33* (3), 560–568.

**Gu, C., Ramos, J., Begley, U., Dedon, P. C., Fu, D., & Begley, T. J.** (2018). Phosphorylation of human TRM9L integrates multiple stress-signaling pathways for tumor growth suppression. *Science Advances, 4* (7), eaas9184.

**Gualtieri, S., & Denison, S.** (2018). The development of the representativeness heuristic in young children. *Journal of Experimental Child Psychology, 174,* 60–76.

**Guediche, S., Holt, L. L., Laurent, P., Lim, S. J., & Fiez, J. A.** (2015). Evidence for cerebellar contributions to adaptive plasticity in speech perception. *Cerebral Cortex, 25* (7), 1867–1877.

**Guell, X., Gabrieli, J. D., & Schmahmann, J. D.** (2018). Triple representation of language, working memory, social and emotion processing in the cerebellum: convergent evidence from task and seed-based resting-state fMRI analyses in a single large cohort. *NeuroImage, 172,* 437–449.

**Guidi, J., Rafanelli, C., & Fava, G. A.** (2018). The clinical role of well-being therapy. *Nordic Journal of Psychiatry.* doi: 10.1080/08039488.2018.1492013

**Gump, B., & Matthews, K.** (2000, March). Are vacations good for your health? The 9-year mortality experience after the multiple risk factor intervention trial. *Psychosomatic Medicine, 62,* 608–612.

**Gunderson, E. A., Sorhagen, N. S., Gripshover, S. J., Dweck, C. S., Goldin-Meadow, S., & Levine, S. C.** (2018). Parent praise to toddlers predicts fourth-grade academic achievement via children's incremental mindsets. *Developmental Psychology, 54,* 397–409.

**Gunderson, J.** (2008). Borderline personality disorder: An overview. *Social Work in Mental Health, 6* (1–2), 5–12.

**Gunderson, J. G., Herpertz, S. C., Skodol, A. E., Torgersen, S., & Zanarini, M. C.** (2018). Borderline personality disorder. *Nature Reviews Disease Primers, 4,* 18029.

**Guntrip, H.** (2018). *Psychoanalytic theory, therapy and the self.* First published 1971. London: Routledge.

**Guo, M., Liu, R. D., Ding, Y., Hu, B., Zhen, R., Liu, Y., & Jiang, R.** (2018). How are extraversion, exhibitionism, and gender associated with posting selfies on WeChat friends' circle in Chinese teenagers? *Personality and Individual Differences, 127,* 114–116.

**Guo, W., Samuels, J. F., Wang, Y., Cao, H., Ritter, M., Nestadt, P. S., ... & Geller, D. A.** (2017). Polygenic risk score and heritability estimates reveals a genetic relationship between ASD and OCD. *European Neuropsychopharmacology, 27* (7), 657–666.

**Guo, Y.** (2005). Filial therapy for children's behavioral and emotional problems in mainland China. *Journal of Child and Adolescent Psychiatric Nursing, 18* (4), 171–180.

**Gurevitch, J., Koricheva, J., Nakagawa, S., & Stewart, G.** (2018). Meta-analyses and the science of research synthesis. *Nature, 555,* 175–182.

**Gurin, P., Dey, E. L., Hurtado, S., & Gurin, G.** (2002). Diversity and higher education: Theory and impact on educational outcomes. *Harvard Educational Review, 72* (3), 330–366.

**Gutchess, A., & Kensinger, E. A.** (2018). Shared mechanisms may support mnemonic benefits from self-referencing and emotion. *Trends in Cognitive Sciences.*

**Gutierrez, D.** (2018). The role of intersectionality in marriage and family therapy multicultural supervision. *The American Journal of Family Therapy, 46* (1), 14–26.

**Guttman, N., & Kalish, H. I.** (1956). Discriminability and stimulus generalization. *Journal of Experimental Psychology, 51* (1), 79–88.

**Gvion, Y., & Levi-Belz, Y.** (2018). Serious suicide attempts: Systematic review of psychological risk factors. *Frontiers in Psychiatry, 9,* 56.

**Gwernan-Jones, R., & Burden, R. L.** (2010). Are they just lazy? Student teachers' attitudes about dyslexia. *Dyslexia: An International Journal of Research and Practice, 16* (1), 66–86.

## H

**Ha, F. J., Hare, D. L., Cameron, J. D., & Toukhsati, S. R.** (2018). Heart failure and exercise: A narrative review of the role of self-efficacy. *Heart, Lung and Circulation, 27* (1), 22–27.

**Hachisuka, J., Chiang, M. C., & Ross, S. E.** (2018). Itch and neuropathic itch. *Pain, 159* (3), 603–609.

**Hachtel, H., Nixon, M., Bennett, D., Mullen, P., & Ogloff, J.** (2018). Motives, offending behavior, and gender differences in murder perpetrators with or without psychosis. *Journal of Interpersonal Violence.* doi: 10.1177/0886260518774304

**Hadamitzky, M., Sondermann, W., Benson, S., & Schedlowski, M.** (2018). Placebo effects in the immune system. *International Review of Neurobiology, 138,* 39–59.

**Hadden, B. W., Harvey, S. M., Settersten Jr, R. A., & Agnew, C. R.** (2018). What do I call us? The investment model of commitment processes and changes in relationship categorization. *Social Psychological and Personality Science.* doi: 10.1177/1948550617745115

**Haeger, A., Pouzat, C., Luecken, V., N'Diaye, K., Elger, C. E., Kennerknecht, I., ... & Dinkelacker, V.** (2018). P34. Working memory for faces in congenital prosopagnosia: Altered neural representations in the fusiform face area. *Clinical Neurophysiology, 129* (8), e80–e81.

**Haertel, E. H.** (2018). Tests, test scores, and constructs. *Educational Psychologist, 53* (3), 203–216.

**Hafer, R. W.** (2016). Cross-country evidence on the link between IQ and financial development. *Intelligence, 55,* 7–13.

**Hagadorn, J. A., & Seilacher. A.** (2009). Hermit arthropods 500 million years ago? *Geology, 37* (4), 295–298.

**Hagan, C. R., Podlogar, M. C., Chu, C., & Joiner, T. E.** (2015). Testing the interpersonal theory of suicide: The moderating role of hopelessness. *International Journal of Cognitive Therapy, 8* (2), 99–113.

**Haggard, M., Rowatt, W. C., Leman, J. C., Meagher, B., Moore, C., Fergus, T., ... & Howard-Snyder, D.** (2018). Finding middle ground between intellectual arrogance and intellectual servility: Development and assessment of the limitations-owning intellectual humility scale. *Personality and Individual Differences, 124,* 184–193.

**Hagger, M. S., Luszczynska, A., de Wit, J., Benyamini, Y., Burkert, S., Chamberland, P. E., ... & Gollwitzer, P. M.,** (2016). Implementation intention and planning interventions in health psychology:

**Freeland, A., Manchanda, R., Chiu, S., Sharma, V., & Merskey, H.** (1993). Four cases of supposed multiple personality disorder: Evidence of unjustified diagnoses. *Canadian Journal of Psychiatry, 38* (4), 245–247.

**Freeman, M. P., Góez-Mogollón, L., McInerney, K. A., Davies, A. C., Church, T. R., Sosinsky, A. Z., ... & Cohen, L. S.** (2018). Obstetrical and neonatal outcomes after benzodiazepine exposure during pregnancy: Results from a prospective registry of women with psychiatric disorders. *General Hospital Psychiatry, 53,* 73–79.

**French, K. A., Dumani, S., Allen, T. D., & Shockley, K. M.** (2018). A meta-analysis of work-family conflict and social support. *Psychological Bulletin, 144* (3), 284–314.

**Freud, S.** (1911). *The interpretation of dreams* (3rd ed.; A. A. Brill, trans.). New York: Macmillan. (original work published 1899)

**Freud, S.** (1924). *A general introduction to psychoanalysis.* New York: Washington Square Press.

**Freud, S.** (1963). Letter to Oskar Pfister. In H. Meng & E. L. Freud (Eds.) & E. Mosbacher (Trans.), *Psychoanalysis and faith: The letters of Sigmund Freud and Oskar Pfister.* New York: Basic Books. (original work published 1918)

**Frey, S., Eichler, A., Stonawski, V., Kriebel, J., Wahl, S., Gallati, S., ... & Moll, G. H.** (2018). Prenatal alcohol exposure is associated with adverse cognitive effects and distinct whole-genome DNA methylation patterns in primary school children. *Frontiers in Behavioral Neuroscience, 12,* 125.

**Frieder, R. E., Wang, G., & Oh, I. S.** (2018). Linking job-relevant personality traits, transformational leadership, and job performance via perceived meaningfulness at work: A moderated mediation model. *Journal of Applied Psychology, 103* (3), 324–333.

**Friedman, J.** (2015). Leptin and the regulation of food intake and body weight. *Journal of Nutritional Science and Vitaminology, 61* (Suppl.), S202.

**Friedman, J. P., & Jack, A. I.** (2018). Mapping cognitive structure onto the landscape of philosophical debate: An empirical framework with relevance to problems of consciousness, free will and ethics. *Review of Philosophy and Psychology, 9* (1), 73–113.

**Friedman, M., & Rosenman, R.** (1974). *Type A behavior and your heart.* New York: Knopf.

**Friedman, R. C., Alfonso, C. A., & Downey, J. I.** (2015). Editorial: Psychodynamic psychiatry and psychoanalysis: Two different models. *Psychodynamic Psychiatry, 43* (4), 513–521.

**Friedman, R., Myers, P., & Benson, H.** (1998). Meditation and the relaxation response. In H. S. Friedman (Ed.), *Encyclopedia of mental health* (vol. 2). San Diego: Academic.

**Frischholz, E. J., Braun, B. G., Sachs, R. G., Schwartz, D. R., Lewis, J., Shaeffer, D., Westergaard, C., & Pasquotto, J.** (2015a). Construct validity of the Dissociative Experiences Scale: II. Its relationship to hypnotizability. *American Journal of Clinical Hypnosis, 57* (2), 102–109.

**Frischholz, E. J., Spiegel, D., Trentalange, M. J., & Spiegel, H.** (2015b). The Hypnotic Induction Profile and absorption. *American Journal of Clinical Hypnosis, 57* (2), 122–128.

**Fritz, C., & Sonnentag, S.** (2006). Recovery, well-being, and performance-related outcomes: The role of work overload and vacation experiences. *Journal of Applied Psychology, 91* (4), 936–945.

**Fromm, E.** (1947). *Man for himself.* New York: Holt, Rinehart & Winston.

**Fruhwürth, S., Vogel, H., Schürmann, A., & Williams, K. J.** (2018). Novel insights into how overnutrition disrupts the hypothalamic actions of leptin. *Frontiers in Endocrinology, 9,* 89.

**Fründt, O., Schulz, R., Schöttle, D., Cheng, B., Thomalla, G., Braaß, H., ... & Bäumer, T.** (2018). White matter microstructure of the human mirror neuron system is related to symptom severity in adults with autism. *Journal of Autism and Developmental Disorders, 48* (2), 417–429.

**Fry, P. S., & Debats, D. L.** (2009). Perfectionism and the five-factor personality traits as predictors of mortality in older adults. *Journal of Health Psychology, 14* (4), 513–524.

**Fu, F. Q., Richards, K. A., Hughes, D. E., & Jones, E.** (2010). Motivating salespeople to sell new products: The relative influence of attitudes, subjective norms, and self-efficacy. *Journal of Marketing, 74* (6), 61–76.

**Fu, Q., Liu, Y. J., Dienes, Z., Wu, J., Chen, W., & Fu, X.** (2017). Neural correlates of subjective awareness for natural scene categorization of color photographs and line-drawings. *Frontiers in Psychology, 8.*

**Fuchs, F., Monet, B., Ducruet, T., Chaillet, N., & Audibert, F.** (2018). Effect of maternal age on the risk of preterm birth: A large cohort study. *PloS one, 13* (1), e0191002.

**Fuchs, X., Flor, H., & Bekrater-Bodmann, R.** (2018). Psychological factors associated with phantom limb pain: A review of recent findings. *Pain Research and Management,* 5080123. doi: 10.1155/2018/5080123

**Fuertinger, S., Zinn, J. C., Sharan, A. D., Hamzei-Sichani, F., & Simonyan, K.** (2018). Dopamine drives left-hemispheric lateralization of neural networks during human speech. *Journal of Comparative Neurology, 526* (5), 920–931.

**Fujiwara, E., Levine, B., & Anderson, A. K.** (2008). Intact implicit and reduced explicit memory for negative self-related information in repressive coping. *Cognitive, Affective, and Behavioral Neuroscience, 8* (3), 254–263.

**Funder, D. C.** (2009). Persons, behaviors, and situations: An agenda for personality psychology in the postwar era. *Journal of Research in Personality, 43* (2), 120–126.

**Furman, A. J., Meeker, T. J., Rietschel, J. C., Yoo, S., Muthulingam, J., Prokhorenko, M., ... & Seminowicz, D. A.** (2018). Cerebral peak alpha frequency predicts individual differences in pain sensitivity. *Neuroimage, 167,* 203–210.

## G

**Gable, S. L.** (2018). Satisfying and meaningful close relationships. In J. P. Forgas & R. F. Baumeister, (Eds.), *The social psychology of living well.* London: Routledge.

**Gabriel, A. S., Koopman, J., Rosen, C. C., & Johnson, R. E.** (2018). Helping others or helping oneself? An episodic examination of the behavioral consequences of helping at work. *Personnel Psychology, 71* (1), 85–107.

**Gadassi, R., Bar-Nahum, L. E., Newhouse, S., Anderson, R., Heiman, J. R., Rafaeli, E., & Janssen, E.** (2016). Perceived partner responsiveness mediates the association between sexual and marital satisfaction: A daily diary study in newlywed couples. *Archives of Sexual Behavior, 45* (1), 109–120.

**Galatzer-Levy, I. R., Huang, S. H., & Bonanno, G. A.** (2018). Trajectories of resilience and dysfunction following potential trauma: A review and statistical evaluation. *Clinical Psychology Review,* 63, 41–55.

**Gallagher, S., O' Riordan, A., McMahon, G., & Creaven, A. M.** (2018). Evaluating personality as a moderator of the association between life events stress and cardiovascular reactivity to acute stress. *International Journal of Psychophysiology, 126,* 52–59.

**Gallo, K. P., Thompson-Hollands, J., Pincus, D. B., & Barlow, D. H.** (2013). Anxiety disorders. In G. Stricker, T. A. Widiger, & I. B. Weiner (Eds.), *Handbook of psychology* (2nd ed., vol. 8, pp. 147–170). Hoboken, NJ: Wiley.

**Gallo, W. T., Bradley, E. H., Dubin, J. A., Jones, R. N., Falba, T. A., Teng, H. M., & Kasi, S. V.** (2006). The persistence of depressive symptoms in older workers who experience involuntary job loss: Results from the health and retirement survey. *Journals of Gerontology: B: Psychological Sciences and Social Sciences, 61* (4), S221–S228.

**Galotti, K. M.** (2017). *Cognitive psychology in and out of the laboratory* (6th ed.). Thousand Oaks, CA: Sage.

**Gannon, B. M., Baumann, M. H., Walther, D., Jimenez-Morigosa, C., Sulima, A., Rice, K. C., & Collins, G. T.** (2018). The abuse-related effects of pyrrolidine-containing cathinones are related to their potency and selectivity to inhibit the dopamine transporter. *Neuropsychopharmacology, 43* (12), 2399–2407.

**Garamszegi, L. Z., Zagalska-Neubauer, M., Canal, D., Blázi, G., Laczi, M., Nagy, G., ... & Zsebők, S.** (2018). MHC-mediated sexual selection on birdsong: Generic polymorphism, particular alleles and acoustic signals. *Molecular Ecology, 27* (11), 2620–2633.

**Garb, H. N., Wood, J. M., Nezworski, M. T., Grove, W. M., & Stejskal, W. J.** (2001). Toward a resolution of the Rorschach controversy. *Psychological Assessment, 13* (4), 433–448.

**Garcia, J.** (1989). Food for Tolman: Cognition and cathexis in concert. In T. Archer & L. Nilsson (Eds.), *Aversion, avoidance, and anxiety.* Mahwah, NJ: Erlbaum.

**Garcia, J., Ervin, F. R., & Koelling, R. A.** (1966). Learning with prolonged delay of reinforcement. *Psychonomic Science, 5* (3), 121–122.

**Garcia, J., & Koelling, R. A.** (1966). Relation of cue to consequence in avoidance learning. *Psychonomic Science, 4*(3), 123–124.

**Garcia, J., & Koelling, R. A.** (2009). Specific hungers and poison avoidance as adaptive specializations of learning. In D. Shanks (Ed.), *Psychology of learning.* Thousand Oaks, CA: Sage.

**Gardner, H.** (1983). *Frames of mind.* New York: Basic.

**Gardner, H.** (1993). *Multiple intelligences.* New York: Basic.

**Gardner, H.** (2002). The pursuit of excellence through education. In M. Ferrari (Ed.), *Learning from extraordinary minds.* Mahwah, NJ: Erlbaum.

**Gari, A., Mylonas, K., & Portešová, S.** (2015). An analysis of attitudes towards the gifted students with learning difficulties using two samples of Greek and Czech primary school teachers. *Gifted Education International, 31* (3), 271–286.

**Garnett, C. V., Crane, D., Brown, J., Kaner, E. F. S., Bever, F. R., Muirhead, C. R., ... & Michie, S.** (2018). Behavior change techniques used in digital behavior change interventions to reduce excessive alcohol consumption: A meta-regression. *Annals of Behavioral Medicine, 52* (6), 530–543.

**Garrett, B. L.** (2011). *Convicting the innocent: Where criminal prosecutions go wrong.* Cambridge, MA: Harvard University Press.

**Garrison, S. M., Doane, M. J., & Elliott, M.** (2018). Gay and lesbian experiences of discrimination, health, and well-being surrounding the presidential election. *Social Psychological and Personality Science, 9* (2), 131–142.

**Gärtner, A., Strobel, A., Reif, A., Lesch, K. P., & Enge, S.** (2018). Genetic variation in serotonin function impacts on altruistic punishment in the ultimatum game: A longitudinal approach. *Brain and Cognition, 125,* 37–44.

**Gärtner, H., Minnerop, M., Pieperhoff, P., Schleicher, A., Zilles, K., Altenmüller, E., & Amunts, K.** (2013). Brain morphometry shows effects of long-term musical practice in middle-aged keyboard players. *Frontiers in Psychology, 4,* 636. doi: 10.3389/fpsyg.2013.00636

**Gartstein, M. A., Putnam, S. P., & Kliewer, R.** (2016). Do infant temperament characteristics predict core academic abilities in preschool-aged children? *Learning and Individual Differences, 45,* 299–306.

**Gates, G. J.** (2011, April). *How many people are lesbian, gay, bisexual, and transgender? Williams Institute.*

http://williamsinstitute.law.ucla.edu/research/census-lgbt-demographics-studies/how-many-people-are-lesbian-gay-bisexual-and-transgender/ (accessed March 22, 2016)

**Gates, G.** (2013, February). LGBT parenting in the United States. *Williams Institute.* http://williamsinstitute.law.ucla.edu/research/census-lgbt-demographics-studies/lgbt-parenting-in-the-united-states/ (accessed March 22, 2016)

**Gathercole, S. E., & Alloway, T. P.** (2008). *Working memory and learning: A practical guide.* Thousand Oaks, CA: Sage.

**Gause, N. K., Elliott, J. C., Delker, E., Stohl, M., Hasin, D., & Aharonovich, E.** (2018). Association between change in self-efficacy to resist drinking and drinking behaviors among an HIV-infected sample: Results from a large randomized controlled trial. *Journal of Health Psychology, 23* (6), 829–839.

**Gavrilets, S., Friberg, U., & Rice, W. R.** (2018). Understanding homosexuality: Moving on from patterns to mechanisms. *Archives of Sexual Behavior, 47* (1), 27–31.

**Gayet, S., Paffen, C. L., & Van der Stigchel, S.** (2018). Visual working memory storage recruits sensory processing areas. *Trends in Cognitive Sciences, 22* (3), 189–190.

**Geary, D. C.** (2010). *Male, female: The evolution of human sex differences* (2nd ed.). Washington, DC: American Psychological Association.

**Gebo, E.** (2018). Gangs and gang violence. In A. J. Trevino, (Ed.), *The Cambridge handbook of social problems* (vol. 2, pp. 363–380). New York: Cambridge University Press.

**Gehring, W. J., Himle, J., & Nisenson, L. G.** (2000). Action monitoring dysfunction in obsessive-compulsive disorder. *Psychological Science, 11* (1), 1–6.

**Geiker, N. R. W., Astrup, A., Hjorth, M. F., Sjödin, A., Pijls, L., & Markus, C. R.** (2018). Does stress influence sleep patterns, food intake, weight gain, abdominal obesity and weight loss interventions and vice versa? *Obesity Reviews, 19* (1), 81–97.

**Geipel, J., Hadjichristidis, C., & Surian, L.** (2015). How foreign language shapes moral judgment. *Journal of Experimental Social Psychology, 59,* 8–17.

**Gelo, O., Pritz, A., & Rieken, B.** (Eds.). (2014). *Psychotherapy research.* New York: Springer.

**Gems, D., & Partridge, L.** (2013). Genetics of longevity in model organisms: Debates and paradigm shifts. *Annual Review of Physiology* (vol. 75, pp. 621–644). Palo Alto, CA: Annual Reviews.

**Gensowski, M.** (2018). Personality, IQ, and lifetime earnings. *Labour Economics, 51,* 170–183.

**Geraerts, E., Lindsay, D. S., Merckelbach, H., Jelicic, M., Raymaekers, L., Arnold, M. M., & Schooler, J. W.** (2009). Cognitive mechanisms underlying recovered-memory experiences of childhood sexual abuse. *Psychological Science, 20* (1), 92–98.

**Gerlach, M., Farb, B., Revelle, W., & Nunes Amaral, L. A.** (2018). A robust data-driven approach identifies four personality types across four large data sets. *Nature Human Behaviour, 2,* 735–742.

**Germain, A.** (2012). Parasomnias I: Nightmares. In C. M. Morin & C. A. Espie (Eds.), *The Oxford handbook of sleep and sleep disorders* (pp. 555–576). New York: Oxford University Press.

**Gerson, S. A., Simpson, E. A., & Paukner, A.** (2016). Drivers of social cognitive development in human and non-human primate infants. In J.A. Sommerville & J. Decety, (Eds.), *Social cognition: Development across the lifespan.* (pp. 116–146). New York: Routledge.

**Geukes, K., Nestler, S., Hutteman, R., Dufner, M., Küfner, A. C., Egloff, B., ... & Back, M. D.** (2017). Puffed-up but shaky selves: State self-esteem level and variability in narcissists. *Journal of Personality and Social Psychology, 112* (5), 769–786.

**Geurten, M., Lloyd, M., & Willems, S.** (2017). Hearing "quack" and remembering a duck: Evidence for fluency attribution in young children. *Child Development, 88* (2), 514–522.

**Ghavami, N., & Peplau, L. A.** (2018). Urban middle school students' stereotypes at the intersection of sexual orientation, ethnicity, and gender. *Child Development, 89* (3), 881–896.

**Ghirardi, L., Brikell, I., Kuja-Halkola, R., Freitag, C. M., Franke, B., Asherson, P., ... & Larsson, H.** (2018). The familial co-aggregation of ASD and ADHD: a register-based cohort study. *Molecular Psychiatry, 23* (2), 257–262.

**Gianinazzi, M. E., Rueegg, C. S., Vetsch, J., Lüer, S., Kuehni, C. E., Michel, G., & Swiss Pediatric Oncology Group (SPOG).** (2016). Cancer's positive flip side: Posttraumatic growth after childhood cancer. *Supportive Care in Cancer, 24* (1), 195–203.

**Giasson, H. L., Liao, H. W., & Carstensen, L. L.** (2018). Counting down while time flies: Implications of age-related time acceleration for goal pursuit across adulthood. *Current Opinion in Psychology.* (in press)

**Gibson, E. J.** (2001). *Perceiving the affordances.* Mahwah, NJ: Erlbaum.

**Giele, C. L., van den Hout, M. A., Engelhard, I. M., Dek, E. C., Toffolo, M. B., & Cath, D. C.** (2016). Perseveration induces dissociative uncertainty in obsessive-compulsive disorder. *Journal of Behavior Therapy and Experimental Psychiatry, 52,* 1–10.

**Gieselmann, A., Simon, A., Vollmann, J., & Schöne-Seifert, B.** (2018). Psychiatrists' views on different types of advance statements in mental health care in Germany. *International Journal of Social Psychiatry, 64* (8), 737–744.

**Gilbert, E., Foulk, T., & Bono, J.** (2018). Building personal resources through interventions: An integrative review. *Journal of Organizational Behavior, 39* (2), 214–228.

**Gill, M., Chan-Golston, A. M., Rice, L. N., Roth, S. E., Crespi, C. M., Cole, B. L., ... & Prelip, M. L.** (2018). Correlates of social support and its association with physical activity among young adolescents. *Health Education & Behavior, 45* (2), 207–216.

**Gillett, C. B., Bilek, E. L., Hanna, G. L., & Fitzgerald, K. D.** (2018). Intolerance of uncertainty in youth with obsessive-compulsive disorder and generalized anxiety disorder: A transdiagnostic construct with implications for phenomenology and treatment. *Clinical Psychology Review, 60,* 100–108.

**Gilligan, C.** (1982). *In a different voice.* Cambridge, MA: Harvard University Press.

**Gillihan, S. J., & Farah, M. J.** (2005). Is self special? A critical review of evidence from experimental psychology and cognitive neuroscience. *Psychological Bulletin, 131* (1), 76–97.

**Gil-Mohapel, J., Simpson, J. M., Ghilan, M., & Christie, B. R.** (2011). Neurogenesis in Huntington's disease: Can studying adult neurogenesis lead to the development of new therapeutic strategies? *Brain Research, 1406,* 84–105.

**Gilmore, A. K., Walsh, K., Badour, C. L., Ruggiero, K. J., Kilpatrick, D. G., & Resnick, H. S.** (2017). Suicidal ideation, posttraumatic stress, and substance abuse based on forcible and drug- or alcohol-facilitated/incapacitated rape histories in a national sample of women. *Suicide and Life-Threatening Behavior, 48* (2), 183–192.

**Gilmore, J. H., Knickmeyer, R. C., & Gao, W.** (2018). Imaging structural and functional brain development in early childhood. *Nature Reviews Neuroscience, 19* (3), 123–137.

**Gilovich, T., Kumar, A., & Jampol, L.** (2015). A wonderful life: Experiential consumption and the pursuit of happiness. *Journal of Consumer Psychology, 25,* 152–165.

**Ginis, K. A., M., Bassett, R. L., & Conlin, C.** (2012). Body image and exercise. In E. O. Acevedo (Ed.), *The Oxford handbook of exercise psychology.* New York: Oxford University Press.

**Gippert, S. M., Switala, C., Bewernick, B. H., Kayser, S., Bräuer, A., Coenen, V. A., & Schlaepfer, T. E.** (2017). Deep brain stimulation for bipolar disorder–review and outlook. *CNS Spectrums, 22* (3), 254–257.

**Giraldo-Chica, M., Rogers, B. P., Damon, S. M., Landman, B. A., & Woodward, N. D.** (2018). Prefrontal-thalamic anatomical connectivity and executive cognitive function in schizophrenia. *Biological Psychiatry, 83* (6), 509–517.

**Gittelman, M.** (2008). Editor's introduction: Why are the mentally ill dying? *International Journal of Mental Health, 37* (1), 3–12.

**Glambek, M., Skogstad, A., & Einarsen, S.** (2018). Workplace bullying, the development of job insecurity and the role of laissez-faire leadership: A two-wave moderated mediation study. *Work & Stress.* doi: 10.1080/02678373.2018.1427815

**Glaser, D.** (2018). Early experience, attachment and the brain. In J. Corrigall & H. Wilkinson (Eds.), *Revolutionary connections* (pp. 117–133). London: Routledge.

**Glavas, A.** (2016). Corporate social responsibility and organizational psychology: An integrative review. *Frontiers in Psychology, 7* (144), 1–13.

**Glaw, X. M., Garrick, T. M., Terwee, P. J., Patching, J. R., Blake, H., & Harper, C.** (2009). Brain donation: Who and why? *Cell and Tissue Banking, 10* (3), 241–246.

**Gliga, T.** (2018). Telling apart motor noise from exploratory behaviour, in early development. *Frontiers in Psychology, 9,* 1939.

**Glynn, R. W., Byrne, N., O'Dea, S., Shanley, A., Codd, M., Keenan, E., ... & Clarke, S.** (2018). Chemsex, risk behaviours and sexually transmitted infections among men who have sex with men in Dublin, Ireland. *International Journal of Drug Policy, 52,* 9–15.

**Gocłowska, M. A., Ritter, S. M., Elliot, A. J., & Baas, M.** (2018). Novelty seeking is linked to openness and extraversion, and can lead to greater creative performance. *Journal of Personality.* doi: 10.1111/jopy.12387

**Godden, D. R., & Baddeley, A. D.** (1975). Context-dependent memory in two natural environments: On land and under water. *British Journal of Psychology, 66* (3), 325–331.

**Gogtay, N., & Thompson, P. M.** (2010). Mapping gray matter development: Implications for typical development and vulnerability to psychopathology. *Brain and Cognition, 72* (1), 6–15.

**Goldberg, A. E.** (2010). Introduction: Lesbian and gay parents and their children–Research and contemporary issues. In *Lesbian and gay parents and their children: Research on the family life cycle* (pp. 3–14). Washington, DC: American Psychological Association.

**Goldberg, L. R., & Digman, J. M.** (1994). Revealing structure in the data: Principles of exploratory factor analysis. In S. Strack & M. Lorr (Eds.), *Differentiating normal and abnormal personality* (pp. 216–242). New York: Springer.

**Goldstein, M. H., King, A. P., & West, M. J.** (2003). Social interaction shapes babbling: Testing parallels between birdsong and speech. *Proceedings of the National Academy of Sciences USA, 100* (13), 8030–8035.

**Goldstein, R., & Halpern-Felsher, B.** (2018). Adolescent oral sex and condom use: How much should we worry and what can we do? *Journal of Adolescent Health 62,* 363–364.

**Goldstone, R. L., Kersten, A., & Carvalho, P. F.** (2018). Categorization and concepts. In S. L.

Thompson-Schill (Ed.), *Stevens' handbook of experimental psychology and cognitive neuroscience, language and thought* (4th ed., vol. 3, pp. 275–318). New York: Wiley.

**Goleman, D., Kaufman, P., & Ray, M.** (1993). *The creative mind.* New York: Plume.

**Golinkoff, R. M., Can, D. D., Soderstrom, M., & Hirsh-Pasek, K.** (2015). (Baby) talk to me: The social context of infant-directed speech and its effects on early language acquisition. *Current Directions in Psychological Science, 24* (5), 339–344.

**Göllner, L. M., Ballhausen, N., Kliegel, M., & Forstmeier, S.** (2018). Delay of gratification, delay discounting and their associations with age, episodic future thinking, and future time perspective. *Frontiers in Psychology, 8,* 2304.

**Gollwitzer, A., & Bargh, J. A.** (2018). Social psychological skill and its correlates. *Social Psychology, 49,* 88–102.

**Golombok, S., Blake, L., Slutsky, J., Raffanello, E., Roman, G. D., & Ehrhardt, A.** (2018). Parenting and the adjustment of children born to gay fathers through surrogacy. *Child Development, 89* (4), 1223–1233.

**Golombok, S., Perry, B., Burston, A., Murray, C., Mooney-Somers, J., Stevens, M., & Golding, J.** (2003). Children with lesbian parents: A community study. *Developmental Psychology, 39* (1), 20–33.

**Golombok, S., & Tasker, F.** (1996). Do parents influence the sexual orientation of their children? Findings from a longitudinal study of lesbian families. *Developmental Psychology, 32* (1), 3–11.

**Golya, N., & McIntyre, L. L.** (2018). Variability in adaptive behaviour in young children with autism spectrum disorder. *Journal of Intellectual & Developmental Disability, 43* (1), 102–111.

**Gonen, N., Futtner, C. R., Wood, S., Garcia-Moreno, S. A., Salamone, I. M., Samson, S. C., ... & Lovell-Badge, R.** (2018). Sex reversal following deletion of a single distal enhancer of Sox9. *Science,* eaas9408. doi: 10.1126/science.aas9408

**González-Cutre, D., Megías, Á., Beltrán-Carrillo, V. J., Cervelló, E., & Spray, C. M.** (2018). Effects of a physical activity program on post-bariatric patients: A qualitative study from a self-determination theory perspective. *Journal of Health Psychology.* doi: 10.1177/1359105318770729

**González-Maeso, J., & Sealfon, S. C.** (2009). Psychedelics and schizophrenia. *Trends in Neuroscience, 32* (4), 225–232.

**González-Val, R., & Marcén, M.** (2018). Unemployment, marriage and divorce. *Applied Economics, 50* (13), 1495–1508.

**Gooding, P. L., Callan, M. J., & Hughes, G.** (2018). The association between believing in free will and subjective well-being is confounded by a sense of personal control. *Frontiers in Psychology, 9.*

**Goodman, G. S.** (1991). Stress and children's testimony: Commentary on Peters. In J. Doris (Ed.), *The suggestibility of children's recollections* (pp. 77–82). Washington, DC: American Psychological Association.

**Goodman, G. S.** (2005). Wailing babies in her wake. *American Psychologist, 60* (8), 872–881.

**Goodman, G. S.** (2006). Children's eyewitness memory: A modern history and contemporary commentary. *Journal of Social Issues, 62* (4), 811–832.

**Goodman, G. S., Quas, J. A., Batterman-Faunce, J. M., Riddlesberger, M., & Kuhn, J.** (1997). Children's reactions to and memory for a stressful experience: Influences of age, knowledge, anatomical dolls, and parental attachment. *Applied Developmental Sciences, 1* (2), 54–75.

**Goodwin, H., Yiend, J., & Hirsch, C. R.** (2017). Generalized anxiety disorder, worry and attention to threat: A systematic review. *Clinical Psychology Review, 54,* 107–122.

**Goosens, K. A.** (2011). Hippocampal regulation of aversive memories. *Current Opinion in Neurobiology, 21* (3), 460–466.

**Gorday, J. Y., & Meyer, A.** (2018). Linking puberty and error-monitoring: Relationships between self-reported pubertal stages, pubertal hormones, and the error-related negativity in a large sample of children and adolescents. *Developmental Psychobiology.* doi: 10.1002/dev.21625

**Gordon, P. C., Zrenner, C., Desideri, D., Belardinelli, P., Zrenner, B., Brunoni, A. R., & Ziemann, U.** (2018). Modulation of cortical responses by transcranial direct current stimulation of dorsolateral prefrontal cortex: A resting-state EEG and TMS-EEG study. *Brain Stimulation. 11,* 1024–1032.

**Gorgol, J., Stolarski, M., & Matthews, G.** (2018). On the moderating role of chronotype on the association between IQ and conscientiousness: The compensation effect occurs only in Evening-types. *Biological Rhythm Research.* doi: 10.1080/09291016.2018.1526483

**Göritz, C., & Frisén, J.** (2012). Neural stem cells and neurogenesis in the adult. *Cell: Stem Cell, 10* (6), 657–659.

**Gorman, D. M., Ponicki, W. R., Zheng, Q., Han, D., Gruenewald, P. J., & Gaidus, A. J.** (2018). Violent crime redistribution in a city following a substantial increase in the number of off-sale alcohol outlets: A Bayesian analysis. *Drug and Alcohol Review, 37* (3), 348–355.

**Gosling, S. D.** (2008). Personality in non-human animals. *Social and Personality Psychology Compass, 2* (2), 985–1001.

**Gosling, S. D., & John, O. P.** (1999). Personality dimensions in nonhuman animals: A cross-species review. *Current Directions in Psychological Science, 8* (3), 69–75.

**Gosling, S. D., Kwan, V. S. Y., & John, O.** (2003). A dog's got personality: A cross-species comparison of personality judgments in dogs and humans. *Journal of Personality and Social Psychology, 85* (6), 1161–1169.

**Gosling, S. D., Rentfrow, P. J., & Swann, Jr., W. B.** (2003). A very brief measure of the Big-Five personality domains. *Journal of Research in Personality, 37,* 504–528.

**Gosling, S. D., Sandy, C. J., John, O. P., & Potter, J.** (2010). Wired but not WEIRD: The promise of the Internet in reaching more diverse samples. *Behavioral and Brain Sciences, 33* (2–3), 94–95.

**Gosseries, O., Yu, Q., LaRocque, J. J., Starrett, M. J., Rose, N. S., Cowan, N., & Postle, B. R.** (2018). Parietal-occipital interactions underlying control-and representation-related processes in working memory for nonspatial visual features. *Journal of Neuroscience,* 2747–17. doi: 10.1523/JNEUROSCI.2747-17.2018

**Gottlieb, G.** (2007). Probabilistic epigenesis. *Developmental Science, 10* (1), 1–11.

**Gottman, J. M.** (2006, April 26). Love special: Secrets of long-term love. *New Scientist.* https://www.newscientist.com/article/mg19025491-400-love-special-secrets-of-long-term-love/ (accessed March 15, 2016)

**Gottman, J. M., Levenson, R. W., Swanson, C., Swanson, K., Tyson, R., & Yoshimoto, D.** (2003). Observing gay, lesbian and heterosexual couples' relationships: Mathematical modeling of conflict interaction. *Journal of Homosexuality, 45* (1), 65–91.

**Gottman, J. M., Swanson, C., & Swanson, K.** (2002). A general systems theory of marriage: Nonlinear difference equation modeling of marital interaction. *Personality and Social Psychology Review, 6* (4), 326–340.

**Graber, J. A., Brooks-Gunn, J., & Warren, M. P.** (2006). Pubertal effects on adjustment in girls: Moving from demonstrating effects to identifying pathways. *Journal of Youth and Adolescence, 35* (3), 391–401.

**Graham, J., Haidt, J., Koleva, S., Motyl, M., Iyer, R., Wojcik, S., & Ditto, P. H.** (2012). Moral foundations theory: The pragmatic validity of moral pluralism. *Advances in Experimental Social Psychology, 47,* 55–130.

**Graham, S.** (2017). Attention-deficit hyperactivity disorder (ADHD), learning disabilities (LD), and executive functioning: Recommendations for future research. *Contemporary Educational Psychology, 50,* 97–101. doi:10.1016/j.cedpsych.2017.01.001

**Grainger, J., Dufau, S., & Ziegler, J. C.** (2016). A vision of reading. *Trends in Cognitive Sciences, 20,* 171–179.

**Gramer, M., Haar, J., & Mitteregger, M.** (2018). Type D personality and cardiovascular reactivity in active performance situations: Gender and task-specific influences. *Personality and Individual Differences, 132,* 74–78.

**Grand, J. A., Rogelberg, S. G., Allen, T. D., Landis, R. S., Reynolds, D. H., Scott, J. C., ... & Truxillo, D. M.** (2018). A systems-based approach to fostering robust science in industrial-organizational psychology. *Industrial and Organizational Psychology, 11* (1), 4–42.

**Grandin, T.** (2006). *Thinking in pictures: My life with autism.* New York: Random House.

**Grant, A.** (2013). Goodbye to MBTI, the fad that won't die. *Psychology Today.* https://www.psychologytoday.com/us/blog/give-and-take/201309/goodbye-mbti-the-fad-won-t-die

**Grant, B. F., Stinson, F. S., Dawson, D. A., Chou, P., Dufour, M. C., Compton, W., Pickering, R. P., & Kaplan, K.** (2004). Prevalence and co-occurrence of substance use disorders and independent mood and anxiety disorders: Results from the national epidemiologic survey on alcohol and related conditions. *Archives of General Psychiatry, 61* (8), 807–816.

**Grant, J. M., Mottet, L. A. Tanis, J., Harrison, J., Herman, J. L., & Keisling, M.** (2011). *Injustice at every turn: A report of the national transgender discrimination survey.* Washington: National Center for Transgender Equality and National Gay and Lesbian Task Force.

**Gravina, N. E., King, A., & Austin, J.** (2019). Training leaders to apply behavioral concepts to improve safety. *Safety Science, 112,* 66–70.

**Gray, J. A.** (1987). *The psychology of fear and stress.* Cambridge, UK: Cambridge University Press.

**Gray, J. C., MacKillop, J., Weafer, J., Hernandez, K. M., Gao, J., Palmer, A. A., & de Wit, H.** (2018). Genetic analysis of impulsive personality traits: Examination of a priori candidates and genome-wide variation. *Psychiatry Research, 259,* 398–404.

**Gray, S. A., Dueck, K., Rogers, M., & Tannock, R.** (2017). Qualitative review synthesis: The relationship between inattention and academic achievement. *Educational Research, 59* (1), 17–35.

**Graziano, W. G., & Habashi, M. M.** (2015). Searching for the prosocial personality. In D. A. Schroeder & W. A. Graziano (Eds.), *The Oxford handbook of prosocial behavior* (pp. 231–255). New York: Oxford University Press.

**Greco, A., Valenza, G., & Scilingo, E. P.** (2018). Brain dynamics during arousal-dependent pleasant/unpleasant visual elicitation: An electroencephalographic study on the circumplex model of affect. *IEEE Transactions on Affective Computing.* doi: 10.1109/TAFFC.2018.2879343

**Green, E., Chase, R. M., Zayzay, J., Finnegan, A., & Puffer, E. S.** (2018). The impact of the 2014 Ebola virus disease outbreak in Liberia on parent preferences for harsh discipline practices: A quasi-experimental, pre-post design. *Global Mental Health, 5.* doi: 10.1017/gmh.2017.24

**Green, J. P., Page, R. A., Handley, G. W., & Rasekhy, R.** (2005). The "hidden observer" and ideomotor responding: A real-simulator comparison. *Contemporary Hypnosis, 22* (3), 123–137.

**Green, R.** (1987). *The "sissy boy syndrome" and the development of homosexuality.* New Haven, CT: Yale University Press.

**Green, R. J., Bettinger, M., & Zacks, E.** (1996). Are lesbian couples fused and gay male couples disengaged? Questioning gender straitjackets. In J. Laird & R. J. Green (Eds.), *Lesbian and gays in couples and families: A handbook for therapists* (pp. 185–230). New York: Jossey-Bass.

**Greenhaus, J. H., & Callanan, G. A.** (2013). Career dynamics. In N. W. Schmitt, S. Highhouse, & I. B. Weiner (Eds.), *Handbook of psychology* (2nd ed., vol. 12, pp. 593–614). Hoboken, NJ: Wiley.

**Greenleaf, R. K.** (1997). The servant as leader. In R. P. Vecchio (Ed.), *Leadership: Understanding the dynamics of power and influence in organizations* (pp. 429–438). Notre Dame, IN: University of Notre Dame Press.

**Greenwald, A. G., Poehlman, T. A., Uhlmann, E., & Banaji, M. R.** (2009). Understanding and using the Implicit Association Test: III. Meta-analysis of predictive validity. *Journal of Personality and Social Psychology, 97* (1), 17–41.

**Greenwood, J. D.** (2015). *A conceptual history of psychology: Exploring the tangled web* (2nd ed.). Cambridge, UK: Cambridge University Press.

**Greenwood, T., Lazzeroni, L., Calkins, M., Freedman, R., Green, M., Gur, R., ... & Radant, A.** (2018). Genome-wide association of endophenotypes for schizophrenia from the Consortium On the Genetics of Schizophrenia (COGS) study. *Biological Psychiatry, 83* (9), S428–S429.

**Greer, S., Morris, T., & Pettingale, K. W.** (1979). Psychological response to breast cancer: Effect on outcome. *The Lancet, 2* (8146), 785–787.

**Gregory Stone, A., Russell, R. F., & Patterson, K.** (2004). Transformational versus servant leadership: A difference in leader focus. *Leadership & Organization Development Journal, 25* (4), 349–361.

**Gregory, R. L.** (2015). *Eye and brain: The psychology of seeing.* Princeton, NJ: Princeton University Press.

**Gregory, S., Ffytche, D., Simmons, A., Kumari, V., Howard, M., Hodgins, S., & Blackwood, N.** (2012). The antisocial brain: Psychopathy matters. *Archives of General Psychiatry, 69* (9), 962–972.

**Greitemeyer, T., & Sagioglou, C.** (2018). Does low (vs. high) subjective socioeconomic status increase both prosociality and aggression? *Social Psychology, 49,* 76–87.

**Griffin, S. C., Curran, S., Chan, A. W., Finn, S. B., Baker, C. I., Pasquina, P. F., & Tsao, J. W.** (2017). Trajectory of phantom limb pain relief using mirror therapy: Retrospective analysis of two studies. *Scandinavian Journal of Pain, 15,* 98–103.

**Grigoryan, G., Korkotian, E., & Segal, M.** (2012). Selective facilitation of LPTP in the ventral hippocampus by calcium stores. *Hippocampus, 22* (7), 1635–1644.

**Grilo, C. M., Masheb, R. M., & White, M. A.** (2010). Significance of overvaluation of shape/weight in binge-eating disorder: Comparative study with overweight and bulimia nervosa. *Obesity, 18* (3), 499–504.

**Grinberg, A. M., O'Hara, K. L., & Sbarra, D. A.** (2018). Preliminary evidence of attenuated blood pressure reactivity to acute stress in adults following a recent marital separation. *Psychology & Health, 33* (3), 430–444.

**Gross, R.** (2018). Pre- and perinatal risk factors for autism spectrum disorder: An update. *Biological Psychiatry, 83* (9), S149.

**Grossi, E., Buscema, M. P., Snowdon, D., & Antuono, P.** (2007). Neuropathological findings processed by artificial neural networks (ANNs) can perfectly distinguish Alzheimer's patients from controls in the Nun Study. *BMC Neurology, 7,* 15.

**Grossi, G., Jeding, K., Söderström, M., Osika, W., Levander, M., & Perski, A.** (2015). Self-reported sleep lengths ≥ 9 hours among Swedish patients with stress-related exhaustion: Associations with depression, quality of sleep, and levels of fatigue. *Nordic Journal of Psychiatry, 69* (4), 292–299.

**Grossman, M. R., & Gruenewald, T. L.** (2018). Failure to meet generative self-expectations is linked to poorer cognitive-affective well-being. *The Journals of Gerontology: Series B.* gby069

**Groves, C. L., & Anderson, C. A.** (2018). Aversive events and aggression. *Current Opinion in Psychology, 19,* 144–148.

**Grubin, D.** (2010). The polygraph and forensic psychiatry. *Journal of the American Academy of Psychiatry and the Law Online, 38* (4), 446–451.

**Grünblatt, E., Ruder, J., Monoranu, C. M., Riederer, P., Youdim, M. B., & Mandel, S. A.** (2018). Differential alterations in metabolism and proteolysis-related proteins in human Parkinson's disease substantia nigra. *Neurotoxicity Research, 33* (3), 560–568.

**Gu, C., Ramos, J., Begley, U., Dedon, P. C., Fu, D., & Begley, T. J.** (2018). Phosphorylation of human TRM9L integrates multiple stress-signaling pathways for tumor growth suppression. *Science Advances, 4* (7), eaas9184.

**Gualtieri, S., & Denison, S.** (2018). The development of the representativeness heuristic in young children. *Journal of Experimental Child Psychology, 174,* 60–76.

**Guediche, S., Holt, L. L., Laurent, P., Lim, S. J., & Fiez, J. A.** (2015). Evidence for cerebellar contributions to adaptive plasticity in speech perception. *Cerebral Cortex, 25* (7), 1867–1877.

**Guell, X., Gabrieli, J. D., & Schmahmann, J. D.** (2018). Triple representation of language, working memory, social and emotion processing in the cerebellum: convergent evidence from task and seed-based resting-state fMRI analyses in a single large cohort. *NeuroImage, 172,* 437–449.

**Guidi, J., Rafanelli, C., & Fava, G. A.** (2018). The clinical role of well-being therapy. *Nordic Journal of Psychiatry.* doi: 10.1080/08039488.2018.1492013

**Gump, B., & Matthews, K.** (2000, March). Are vacations good for your health? The 9-year mortality experience after the multiple risk factor intervention trial. *Psychosomatic Medicine, 62,* 608–612.

**Gunderson, E. A., Sorhagen, N. S., Gripshover, S. J., Dweck, C. S., Goldin-Meadow, S., & Levine, S. C.** (2018). Parent praise to toddlers predicts fourth-grade academic achievement via children's incremental mindsets. *Developmental Psychology, 54,* 397–409.

**Gunderson, J.** (2008). Borderline personality disorder: An overview. *Social Work in Mental Health, 6* (1–2), 5–12.

**Gunderson, J. G., Herpertz, S. C., Skodol, A. E., Torgersen, S., & Zanarini, M. C.** (2018). Borderline personality disorder. *Nature Reviews Disease Primers, 4,* 18029.

**Guntrip, H.** (2018). *Psychoanalytic theory, therapy and the self.* First published 1971. London: Routledge.

**Guo, M., Liu, R. D., Ding, Y., Hu, B., Zhen, R., Liu, Y., & Jiang, R.** (2018). How are extraversion, exhibitionism, and gender associated with posting selfies on WeChat friends' circle in Chinese teenagers? *Personality and Individual Differences, 127,* 114–116.

**Guo, W., Samuels, J. F., Wang, Y., Cao, H., Ritter, M., Nestadt, P. S., ... & Geller, D. A.** (2017). Polygenic risk score and heritability estimates reveals a genetic relationship between ASD and OCD. *European Neuropsychopharmacology, 27* (7), 657–666.

**Guo, Y.** (2005). Filial therapy for children's behavioral and emotional problems in mainland China. *Journal of Child and Adolescent Psychiatric Nursing, 18* (4), 171–180.

**Gurevitch, J., Koricheva, J., Nakagawa, S., & Stewart, G.** (2018). Meta-analyses and the science of research synthesis. *Nature, 555,* 175–182.

**Gurin, P., Dey, E. L., Hurtado, S., & Gurin, G.** (2002). Diversity and higher education: Theory and impact on educational outcomes. *Harvard Educational Review, 72* (3), 330–366.

**Gutchess, A., & Kensinger, E. A.** (2018). Shared mechanisms may support mnemonic benefits from self-referencing and emotion. *Trends in Cognitive Sciences.*

**Gutierrez, D.** (2018). The role of intersectionality in marriage and family therapy multicultural supervision. *The American Journal of Family Therapy, 46* (1), 14–26.

**Guttman, N., & Kalish, H. I.** (1956). Discriminability and stimulus generalization. *Journal of Experimental Psychology, 51* (1), 79–88.

**Gvion, Y., & Levi-Belz, Y.** (2018). Serious suicide attempts: Systematic review of psychological risk factors. *Frontiers in Psychiatry, 9,* 56.

**Gwernan-Jones, R., & Burden, R. L.** (2010). Are they just lazy? Student teachers' attitudes about dyslexia. *Dyslexia: An International Journal of Research and Practice, 16* (1), 66–86.

## H

**Ha, F. J., Hare, D. L., Cameron, J. D., & Toukhsati, S. R.** (2018). Heart failure and exercise: A narrative review of the role of self-efficacy. *Heart, Lung and Circulation, 27* (1), 22–27.

**Hachisuka, J., Chiang, M. C., & Ross, S. E.** (2018). Itch and neuropathic itch. *Pain, 159* (3), 603–609.

**Hachtel, H., Nixon, M., Bennett, D., Mullen, P., & Ogloff, J.** (2018). Motives, offending behavior, and gender differences in murder perpetrators with or without psychosis. *Journal of Interpersonal Violence.* doi: 10.1177/0886260518774304

**Hadamitzky, M., Sondermann, W., Benson, S., & Schedlowski, M.** (2018). Placebo effects in the immune system. *International Review of Neurobiology, 138,* 39–59.

**Hadden, B. W., Harvey, S. M., Settersten Jr, R. A., & Agnew, C. R.** (2018). What do I call us? The investment model of commitment processes and changes in relationship categorization. *Social Psychological and Personality Science.* doi: 10.1177/1948550617745115

**Haeger, A., Pouzat, C., Luecken, V., N'Diaye, K., Elger, C. E., Kennerknecht, I., ... & Dinkelacker, V.** (2018). P34. Working memory for faces in congenital prosopagnosia: Altered neural representations in the fusiform face area. *Clinical Neurophysiology, 129* (8), e80–e81.

**Haertel, E. H.** (2018). Tests, test scores, and constructs. *Educational Psychologist, 53* (3), 203–216.

**Hafer, R. W.** (2016). Cross-country evidence on the link between IQ and financial development. *Intelligence, 55,* 7–13.

**Hagadorn, J. A., & Seilacher. A.** (2009). Hermit arthropods 500 million years ago? *Geology, 37* (4), 295–298.

**Hagan, C. R., Podlogar, M. C., Chu, C., & Joiner, T. E.** (2015). Testing the interpersonal theory of suicide: The moderating role of hopelessness. *International Journal of Cognitive Therapy, 8* (2), 99–113.

**Haggard, M., Rowatt, W. C., Leman, J. C., Meagher, B., Moore, C., Fergus, T., ... & Howard-Snyder, D.** (2018). Finding middle ground between intellectual arrogance and intellectual servility: Development and assessment of the limitations-owning intellectual humility scale. *Personality and Individual Differences, 124,* 184–193.

**Hagger, M. S., Luszczynska, A., de Wit, J., Benyamini, Y., Burkert, S., Chamberland, P. E., ... & Gollwitzer, P. M.,** (2016). Implementation intention and planning interventions in health psychology:

Recommendations from the Synergy Expert Group for research and practice. *Psychology and Health, 31* (7), 814–839.

**Hagger, M. S., Polet, J., & Lintunen, T.** (2018). The reasoned action approach applied to health behavior: Role of past behavior and tests of some key moderators using meta-analytic structural equation modeling. *Social Science & Medicine, 213,* 85–94.

**Hahn, J., Günter, M., & Autenrieth, S.** (2015). Impact of sleep on innate immune cells. *Brain, Behavior, and Immunity, 49* (Suppl.), e43.

**Haidle, M. N.** (2010). Working memory capacity and the evolution of modern cognitive capacities—Implications from animal and early human tool use. *Current Anthropology, 51/S1, Working memory: Beyond language and symbolism,* Wenner-Gren Symposium (Suppl. 1), S149–S166.

**Hakim, N. H., Molina, L. E., & Branscombe, N. R.** (2018). How discrimination shapes social identification processes and well-being among Arab Americans. *Social Psychological and Personality Science, 9* (3), 328–337.

**Hakulinen, C., Elovainio, M., Batty, G. D., Virtanen, M., Kivimäki, M., & Jokela, M.** (2015). Personality and alcohol consumption: Pooled analysis of 72,949 adults from eight cohort studies. *Drug and Alcohol Dependence, 151,* 110–114.

**Hakulinen, C., Pulkki-Råback, L., Virtanen, M., Jokela, M., Kivimäki, M., & Elovainio, M.** (2018). Social isolation and loneliness as risk factors for myocardial infarction, stroke and mortality: UK Biobank cohort study of 479,054 men and women. *Heart.* heartjnl-2017

**Halaris, A., Bechter, K., Haroon, E., Leonard, B. E., Miller, A., Pariante, C., & Zunszain, P.** (2019). The future of psychoneuroimmunology: Promises and challenges. In A. Javed & K.N. Fountoulakis (Eds.), *Advances in Psychiatry* (pp. 235–266). Cham: Springer.

**Halberstadt, J.** (2010). Dumb but lucky: Fortuitous affect cues and their disruption by analytic thought. *Social and Personality Psychology Compass, 4* (1), 64–76.

**Halberstadt, J., & Catty, S.** (2008). Analytic thought disrupts familiarity-based decision making. *Social Cognition, 26* (6), 755–765.

**Hald, G. M., Malamuth, N. M., & Yuen, C.** (2010). Pornography and attitudes supporting violence against women: Revisiting the relationship in nonexperimental studies. *Aggressive Behavior, 36* (1), 14–20.

**Haldar, R., & Ben-Eliyahu, S.** (2018). Reducing the risk of post-surgical cancer recurrence: a perioperative anti-inflammatory anti-stress approach. *Future Oncology, 14*(11), 1017–1021.

**Haliburn, J., Stevenson, J., & Halovic, S.** (2018). Integration in the psychodynamic psychotherapy of severe personality disorders: The conversational model. *Journal of Personality Disorders, 32* (1), 70–86.

**Hall, J. A., Back, M. D., Nestler, S., Frauendorfer, D., Schmid Mast, M., & Ruben, M. A.** (2018). How do different ways of measuring individual differences in zero-acquaintance personality judgment accuracy correlate with each other? *Journal of Personality, 86* (2), 220–232.

**Hall, J. A., Horgan, T. G., & Murphy, N. A.** (2019). Nonverbal communication. *Annual Review of Psychology, 70,* 271–294.

**Hall, J. A., & Matsumoto, D.** (2004). Gender differences in judgments of multiple emotions from facial expressions. *Emotion, 4* (2), 201–206.

**Hall, J. A., Park, N., Song, H., & Cody, M. J.** (2010). Strategic misrepresentation in online dating: The effects of gender, self-monitoring, and personality traits. *Journal of Social and Personal Relationships, 27* (1), 117–135.

**Hall, K. D.** (2013). Diet versus exercise in "the biggest loser" weight loss competition. *Obesity, 21* (5), 957–959.

**Hall, M. G., Sheeran, P., Noar, S. M., Boynton, M. H., Ribisl, K. M., Parada, H., Jr., ... & Brewer, N. T.** (2018). Negative affect, message reactance and perceived risk: how do pictorial cigarette pack warnings change quit intentions? *Tobacco Control, 27* (e2), e136–e142.

**Hall, R. C. W., & Hall, R. C. W.** (2007). A profile of pedophilia: Definition, characteristics of offenders, recidivism, treatment outcomes, and forensic issues. *Mayo Clinic Proceedings, 82* (4), 457–471.

**Hall, W., West, R., Marsden, J., Humphreys, K., Neale, J., & Petry, N.** (2018). It is premature to expand access to medicinal cannabis in hopes of solving the US opioid crisis. *Addiction, 113* (6), 987–988.

**Haller, J.** (2018). The role of central and medial amygdala in normal and abnormal aggression: A review of classical approaches. *Neuroscience & Biobehavioral Reviews, 85,* 34–43.

**Halliwell, B.** (2019). Making sense of neurodegeneration: A unifying hypothesis. In J. A. S. Kelso (Ed.), *Learning to live together: Promoting social harmony* (pp. 115–120). Cham: Springer.

**Hamer, M., Terrera, G. M., & Demakakos, P.** (2018). Physical activity and trajectories in cognitive function: English Longitudinal Study of Ageing. *Journal of Epidemiology and Community Health, 72* (6), 477–483.

**Hames, J. L., Hagan, C. R., & Joiner, T. E.** (2013). Interpersonal processes in depression. *Annual Review of Clinical Psychology* (vol. 9, pp. 355–377). Palo Alto, CA: Annual Reviews.

**Hamilton, K., Orbell, S., Bonham, M., Kroon, J., & Schwarzer, R.** (2018). Dental flossing and automaticity: A longitudinal moderated mediation analysis. *Psychology, Health & Medicine, 23* (5), 619–627.

**Hamilton, R. H., & Davison, H. K.** (2018). The search for skills: Knowledge stars and innovation in the hiring process. *Business Horizons, 61* (3), 409–419.

**Hammack, P. L., Frost, D. M., Meyer, I. H., & Pletta, D. R.** (2018). Gay men's health and identity: Social change and the life course. *Archives of Sexual Behavior, 47*(1), 59–74.

**Hammoud, M. Z., & Milad, M. R.** (2018). Symptom changes in posttraumatic stress disorder and major depressive disorder after transcranial magnetic stimulation: Mechanisms of where and how in the brain. *Biological Psychiatry, 83* (3), 200–202.

**Hampton, A. J., Fisher Boyd, A. N., & Sprecher, S.** (2018). You're like me and I like you: Mediators of the similarity-liking link assessed before and after a getting-acquainted social interaction. *Journal of Social and Personal Relationships.* doi: 10.1177/0265407518790411

**Hampton, J.** (2008). Abstinence-only programs under fire. *Journal of the American Medical Association, 299* (17), 2013–2015.

**Hampton, R. S., & Varnum, M. E.** (2018). The cultural neuroscience of emotion regulation. *Culture and Brain, 6* (2), 130–150.

**Han, K. M., Han, C., Shin, C., Jee, H. J., An, H., Yoon, H. K., ... & Kim, S. H.** (2018). Social capital, socioeconomic status, and depression in community-living elderly. *Journal of Psychiatric Research, 98,* 133–140.

**Han, P., Mohebbi, M., Unrath, M., Hummel, C., & Hummel, T.** (2018). Different neural processing of umami and salty taste determined by umami identification ability independent of repeated umami exposure. *Neuroscience, 383,* 74–83.

**Hanć, T., Szwed, A., Słopień, A., Wolańczyk, T., Dmitrzak-Węglarz, M., & Ratajczak, J.** (2018). Perinatal risk factors and ADHD in children and adolescents: A hierarchical structure of disorder predictors. *Journal of Attention Disorders, 22* (9), 855–863.

**Hancox, J. E., Quested, E., Ntoumanis, N., & Thøgersen-Ntoumani, C.** (2018). Putting self-determination theory into practice: Application of adaptive motivational principles in the exercise domain. *Qualitative Research in Sport, Exercise and Health, 10* (1), 75–91.

**Haney, C., Banks, C., & Zimbardo, P.** (1973). Interpersonal dynamics in a simulated prison. *International Journal of Criminology and Penology, 1,* 69–97.

**Hanley, A., Garland, E. L., & Black, D. S.** (2014). Use of mindful reappraisal coping among meditation practitioners. *Journal of Clinical Psychology, 70* (3), 294–301.

**Hannema, S. E., & de Rijke, Y. B.** (2018). Improving laboratory assessment in disorders of sex development through a multidisciplinary network. *Sexual Development, 12* (1–3), 135–139.

**Hannum, R. D., Rosellini, R. A., & Seligman, M. E. P.** (1976). Learned helplessness in the rat: Retention and immunization. *Developmental Psychology, 12* (5), 449–454.

**Hanowski, R. J., Olson, R. L., Hickman, J. S., & Bocanegra, J.** (2009, September). *Driver distraction in commercial vehicle operations.* Paper presented at the First International Conference on Driver Distraction and Inattention, Gothenburg, Sweden.

**Hansen, S.** (2016). Kids together: A group therapy program for children using cognitive-behavioral play therapy interventions. In A. A. Drewes & C. E. Schaefer (Eds.), *Play therapy in middle childhood* (pp. 153–169). Washington, DC: American Psychological Association.

**Hao, N., Liu, M., Ku, Y., Hu, Y., & Runco, M. A.** (2015). Verbal divergent thinking facilitated by a pleasurable incubation interval. *Psychology of Aesthetics, Creativity, and the Arts, 9* (3), 286–295.

**Harackiewicz, J. M., & Priniski, S. J.** (2018). Improving student outcomes in higher education: The science of targeted intervention. *Annual Review of Psychology, 69,* 409–435.

**Haralanov, S., Haralanova, E., Milushev, E., Shkodrova, D., & Claussen, C. F.** (2018). Objective and quantitative equilibriometric evaluation of individual locomotor behaviour in schizophrenia: Translational and clinical implications. *Journal of Evaluation in Clinical Practice.* doi: 10.1111/jep.12917

**Haran, U., Ritov, I., & Mellers, B. A.** (2013). The role of actively open-minded thinking in information acquisition, accuracy, and calibration. *Judgment and Decision Making, 8,* 188–201.

**Hardy, L., Arthur, C. A., Jones, G., Shariff, A., Munnoch, K., Isaacs, I., & Allsopp, A. J.** (2010). The relationship between transformational leadership behaviors, psychological, and training outcomes in elite military recruits. *Leadership Quarterly, 21* (1), 20–32.

**Harker, L. A., & Keltner, D.** (2001). Expressions of positive emotion in women's college yearbook pictures and their relationship to personality and life outcomes across adulthood. *Journal of Personality and Social Psychology, 80,* 112–124.

**Harkin, B., Webb, T. L., Chang, B. P., Prestwich, A., Conner, M., Kellar, I., Benn, Y., & Sheeran, P.** (2016). Does monitoring goal progress promote goal attainment? A meta-analysis of the experimental evidence. *Psychological Bulletin, 142* (2), 198–229.

**Harlow, H. F.** (1958). The nature of love. *American Psychologist, 13,* 673–685.

**Harms, P. D., & Crede, M.** (2010). Emotional intelligence and transformational and transactional leadership: A meta-analysis. *Journal of Leadership and Organizational Studies, 17* (1), 5–17.

**Harrington, J. R., & Lee, J. H.** (2015). What drives perceived fairness of performance appraisal? Exploring the effects of psychological contract fulfillment on employees' perceived fairness of performance appraisal in U.S. federal agencies. *Public Personnel Management, 44* (2), 214–238.

**Harris Interactive.** (2006, October 10). Seven out of ten heterosexuals today know someone gay. *PR Newswire.* http://www.prnewswire.com/news-releases/seven-out-of-ten-heterosexuals-today-know-someone-gay-56396747.html (accessed March 22, 2016)

**Harris, C. B., Sutton, J., & Barnier, A. J.** (2010). Autobiographical forgetting. In S. D. Sala (Ed.), *Forgetting.* New York: Psychology Press.

**Harris, M. A., Wetzel, E., Robins, R. W., Donnellan, M. B., & Trzesniewski, K. H.** (2018). The development of global and domain self-esteem from ages 10 to 16 for Mexican-origin youth. *International Journal of Behavioral Development, 42* (1), 4–16.

**Harrison, C.** (2012). Ageing: Telomerase gene therapy increases longevity. *Nature Reviews: Drug Discovery, 11,* 518.

**Hart, B., & Risley, T. R.** (1995). *Meaningful differences in the everyday experience of young Americans.* Baltimore: Paul H. Brookes.

**Hart, S. J., Green, S. R., Casp, M., & Belger, A.** (2010). Emotional priming effects during Stroop task performance. *NeuroImage, 49,* 2662–2670.

**Hase, A., O'Brien, J., Moore, L. J., & Freeman, P.** (2018). The relationship between challenge and threat states and performance: A systematic review. *Sport, Exercise, and Performance Psychology.* (in press)

**Hasin, D. S., Sarvet, A. L., Meyers, J. L., Saha, T. D., Ruan, W. J., Stohl, M., & Grant, B. F.** (2018). Epidemiology of adult DSM-5 major depressive disorder and its specifiers in the United States *JAMA Psychiatry, 75* (4), 336–346. doi: 10.1001/jamapsychiatry.2017.4602

**Haslam, N., Holland, E., & Kuppens, P.** (2012). Categories versus dimensions in personality and psychopathology: A quantitative review of taxometric research. *Psychological Medicine, 42* (5), 903–920.

**Haslam, S. A., & Reicher, S.** (2003). Beyond Stanford: Questioning a role-based explanation of tyranny. *SPSP Dialogue, 18,* 22–25.

**Hasler, B. P., Buysse, D. J., & Germain, A.** (2016). Shifts toward morningness during behavioral sleep interventions are associated with improvements in depression, positive affect, and sleep quality. *Behavioral Sleep Medicine, 14* (6), 624–635. doi:10.1080/15402002.2015.1048452

**Hassabis, D., Kumaran, D., Summerfield, C., & Botvinick, M.** (2017). Neuroscience-inspired artificial intelligence. *Neuron, 95*(2), 245–258.

**Hassan, G., Ventevogel, P., Jefee-Bahloul, H., Barkil-Oteo, A., & Kirmayer, L. J.** (2016). Mental health and psychosocial well-being of Syrians affected by armed conflict. *Epidemiology and Psychiatric Sciences, 25* (2), 129–141.

**Hassett, J. M., Siebert, E. R., & Wallen, K.** (2008). Sex differences in rhesus monkey toy preferences parallel those of children. *Hormones and Behavior, 54* (3), 359–364.

**Hasson, U., Chen, J., & Honey, C. J.** (2015). Hierarchical process memory: Memory as an integral component of information processing. *Trends in Cognitive Sciences, 19* (6), 304–313.

**Hastings, M. H., Maywood, E. S., & Brancaccio, M.** (2018). Generation of circadian rhythms in the suprachiasmatic nucleus. *Nature Reviews Neuroscience, 19,* 453–469.

**Hatton, S. N., Franz, C. E., Elman, J. A., Panizzon, M. S., Hagler Jr, D. J., Fennema-Notestine, C., ... & Kremen, W. S.** (2018). Negative fateful life events in midlife and advanced predicted brain aging. *Neurobiology of Aging, 67,* 1–9.

**Hauser, K. F., & Knapp, P. E.** (2018). Opiate drugs with abuse liability hijack the endogenous opioid system to disrupt neuronal and glial maturation in the central nervous system. *Frontiers in Pediatrics, 5,* 294.

**Haviland-Jones, J., Rosario, H. H., Wilson, P., & McGuire, T. R.** (2005). An environmental approach to positive emotion: Flowers. *Evolutionary Psychology, 3* (1), 104–132.

**Hay, P. P., Bacaltchuk, J., Stefano, S., & Kashyap, P.** (2009). Psychological treatments for bulimia nervosa and binging. *Cochrane Database of Systematic Reviews, 4,* CD000562.

**Hayakawa, Y.** (2012). Targeting NKG2D in tumor surveillance. *Expert Opinion on Therapeutic Targets, 16* (6), 587–599.

**Hayfield, N., Campbell, C., & Reed, E.** (2018). Misrecognition and managing marginalisation: Bisexual people's experiences of bisexuality and relationships. *Psychology & Sexuality, 9,* 221–236.

**Hayflick, L.** (1977). The cellular basis for biological aging. In C. E. Finch & L. Hayflick (Eds.), *Handbook of the biology of aging.* New York: Van Nostrand.

**Haynes, E. E., Strauss, C. V., Stuart, G. L., & Shorey, R. C.** (2018). Drinking motives as a moderator of the relationship between dating violence victimization and alcohol problems. *Violence Against Women, 24*(4), 401–420.

**Hays, P. A.** (2016). *Addressing cultural complexities in practice: Assessment, diagnosis, and therapy* (3rd ed.). Washington, DC: American Psychological Association.

**Hayworth, K. J.** (2012). Dynamically partitionable autoassociative networks as a solution to the neural binding problem. *Frontiers in Computational Neuroscience, 6,* 73.

**Hazelden Betty Ford Foundation.** (June 10, 2015). *Survey finds risky opioid use among college-age youth, with limited knowledge of the danger or where to get help.* http://www.hazeldenbettyford.org/about-us/news-media/press-release/2015-opioid-use-among-college-youth

**He, J., Guo, D., Zhai, S., Shen, M., & Gao, Z.** (2018). Development of social working memory in preschoolers and its relation to theory of mind. *Child Development.* doi: 10.1111/cdev.13025

**He, Y., Chen, J., Zhu, L. H., Hua, L. L., & Ke, F. F.** (2017). Maternal smoking during pregnancy and ADHD: Results from a systematic review and meta-analysis of prospective cohort studies. *Journal of Attention Disorders.* doi: 10.1177/1087054717696766 (in press)

**Head, D., Singh, T., & Bugg, J. M.** (2012). The moderating role of exercise on stress-related effects on the hippocampus and memory. *Neuropsychology, 26* (2), 133–143.

**Healy, D.** (2015). Serotonin and depression. *British Medical Journal, 350,* h1771.

**Hebb, D. O.** (1949). *The organization of behavior: A neuropsychological theory.* New York: Wiley.

**Hebb, D. O.** (1980). *Essay on mind.* Mahwah, NJ: Erlbaum.

**Heckhausen, J.** (2018). The motivation of developmental regulation. In J. Heckhausen & H. Heckhausen *Motivation and Action* (3rd ed., pp. 745–782). Cham: Springer.

**Heffer, T., & Willoughby, T.** (2018). The role of emotion dysregulation: A longitudinal investigation of the interpersonal theory of suicide. *Psychiatry Research, 260,* 379–383.

**Hegarty, M.** (2018). Ability and sex differences in spatial thinking: What does the mental rotation test really measure? *Psychonomic Bulletin & Review, 25* (3), 1212–1219.

**Hegarty, P.** (2009). Toward an LGBT-informed paradigm for children who break gender norms: A comment on Drummond et al. (2008) and Rieger et al. (2008). *Developmental Psychology, 45* (4), 895–900.

**Heide, M., Huttner, W. B., & Mora-Bermúdez, F.** (2018). Brain organoids as models to study human neocortex development and evolution. *Current Opinion in Cell Biology, 55,* 8–16.

**Heider, F.** (1958). *The psychology of interpersonal relations.* Hillsdale, NJ: Erlbaum.

**Heil, M., Krüger, M., Krist, H., Johnson, S. P., & Moore, D. S.** (2018). Adults' sex difference in a dynamic mental rotation task. *Journal of Individual Differences, 39,* 48–52.

**Heimann, P., Herpertz-Dahlmann, B., Buning, J., Wagner, N., Stollbrink-Peschgens, C., Dempfle, A., & von Polier, G. G.** (2018). Somatic symptom and related disorders in children and adolescents: evaluation of a naturalistic inpatient multidisciplinary treatment. *Child and Adolescent Psychiatry and Mental Health, 12* (1), 34.

**Helfrich, C. D., Rose, A. J., Hartmann, C. W., van Bodegom-Vos, L., Graham, I. D., Wood, S. J., ... & Au, D. H.** (2018). How the dual process model of human cognition can inform efforts to de-implement ineffective and harmful clinical practices: A preliminary model of unlearning and substitution. *Journal of Evaluation in Clinical Practice, 24* (1), 198–205.

**Helgeson, V. S.** (2018). Personal projects and psychological well-being: Emerging adults with and without diabetes. *Journal of Pediatric Psychology.* jsy065

**Helgeson, V. S., Swanson, J., Ra, O., Randall, H., & Zhao, Y.** (2015). Links between unmitigated communion, interpersonal behaviors and well-being: A daily diary approach. *Journal of Research in Personality, 57,* 53–60.

**Helle, A. C., DeShong, H. L., Lengel, G. J., Meyer, N. A., Butler, J., & Mullins-Sweatt, S. N.** (2018). Utilizing Five Factor Model facets to conceptualize counterproductive, unethical, and organizational citizenship workplace behaviors. *Personality and Individual Differences, 135,* 113–120.

**Helleman, H. W., & Dreschler, W. A.** (2015). Short-term music-induced hearing loss after sound exposure to discotheque music: The effectiveness of a break in reducing temporary threshold shift. *International Journal of Audiology, 54* (Suppl. 1), S46–S52.

**Helleseter, M. D., Kuhn, P., & Shen, K.** (2018). The age twist in employers' gender requests: Evidence from four job boards. *Journal of Human Resources,* 0416-7836R2.

**Hellmer, K., & Nyström, P.** (2017). Infant acetylcholine, dopamine, and melatonin dysregulation: Neonatal biomarkers and causal factors for ASD and ADHD phenotypes. *Medical Hypotheses, 100,* 64–66.

**Hellmich, N.** (2008, October 9). Think fat just hangs around and does nothing? It doesn't. *USA Today.* http://usatoday30.usatoday.com/news/health/weightloss/2008-10-08-fat-cells_N.htm (accessed March 16, 2016)

**Helsen, K., Goubert, L., Peters, M. L., & Vlaeyen, J. W. S.** (2011). Observational learning and pain-related fear: An experimental study with colored cold pressor tasks. *Journal of Pain, 12* (12), 1230–1239.

**Hem, M. H., Gjerberg, E., Husum, T. L., & Pedersen, R.** (2018). Ethical challenges when using coercion in mental healthcare: A systematic literature review. *Nursing Ethics, 25* (1), 92–110.

**Henderson, M.** (2008, February 18). Welcome to the town that will make you lose weight. *The Times,* http://www.thetimes.co.uk/tto/health/article1881007.ece (accessed April 14, 2016)

**Hendrick, C. E., Cance, J. D., & Maslowsky, J.** (2016). Peer and individual risk factors in adolescence explaining the relationship between girls' pubertal timing and teenage childbearing. *Journal of Youth and Adolescence, 45,* 916–927.

**Hendrick, C., & Hendrick, S. S.** (2006). Styles of romantic love. In R. J. Sternberg & K. Weis (Eds.),

*The new psychology of love* (pp. 149–170). New Haven, CT: Yale University Press.

**Hendrick, C., & Hendrick, S. S.** (2009). Love. In S. Lopez & C. R. Snyder (Eds.), *The Oxford handbook of positive psychology* (2nd ed., pp. 447–454). New York: Oxford University Press.

**Hennessey, B. A.** (2011). Intrinsic motivation and creativity: Have we come full circle? In R. A. Beghetto & J. C. Kaufman (Eds.), *Nurturing creativity in the classroom* (pp. 329–361). New York: Cambridge University Press.

**Henry, J. D., MacLeod, M. S., Phillips, L. H., & Crawford, J. R.** (2004). A meta-analytic review of prospective memory and aging. *Psychology and Aging, 19* (1), 27–39.

**Henson, K. E., Brock, R., Charnock, J., Wickramasinghe, B., Will, O., & Pitman, A.** (2018). Risk of suicide after cancer diagnosis in England. *JAMA Psychiatry.* doi:10.1001/jamapsychiatry.2018.3181

**Hepting, U., & Solle, R.** (1973). Sex-specific differences in color coding. *Archiv fur Psychologie, 125* (2–3), 184–202.

**Herbert, J.** (1988). The physiology of aggression. In J. Groebel & R. Hinde (Eds.), *Aggression and war: The biological and social bases.* New York: Cambridge University Press.

**Hering, E.** (1878). *Zur Lehre vom Lichtsinne* (illustration, 2nd ed.). Wien: C. Gerold's Sohn.

**Herlan, A., Ottenbacher, J., Schneider, J., Riemann, D., & Feige, B.** (2018). Electrodermal activity patterns in sleep stages and their utility for sleep versus wake classification. *Journal of Sleep Research,* e12694.

**Hermes, M., Hagemann, D., Naumann, E., & Walter, C.** (2011). Extraversion and its positive emotional core–further evidence from neuroscience. *Emotion, 11* (2), 367–378.

**Hernandez, R., Kershaw, K. N., Siddique, J., Boehm, J. K., Kubzansky, L. D., Diez-Roux, A., ... & Lloyd-Jones, D. M.** (2015). Optimism and cardiovascular health: Multi-Ethnic Study of Atherosclerosis (MESA). *Health Behavior and Policy Review, 2* (1), 62–73.

**Hernandez-Kane, K. M., & Mahoney, A.** (2018). Sex through a sacred lens: Longitudinal effects of sanctification of marital sexuality. *Journal of Family Psychology, 32* (4), 425–434.

**Herry, C., Bach, D. R., Esposito, F., Di Salle, F., Perrig, W. J., Scheffler, K., Lüthi, A., & Seifritz, E.** (2007). Processing of temporal unpredictability in human and animal amygdala. *Journal of Neuroscience, 27* (2), 5958–5966.

**Hershfield, H., Scheibe, S., Sims, T., & Carstensen, L. L.** (2013). When feeling bad can be good: Mixed emotions benefit physical health across adulthood. *Social Psychological and Personality Science, 4* (1), 54–61.

**Hertwig, R., Hoffrage, U., & the ABC Research Group** (Eds.). (2013). *Simple heuristics in a social world.* New York: Oxford University Press.

**Hertz, U., Kelly, M., Rutledge, R. B., Winston, J., Wright, N., Dolan, R. J., & Bahrami, B.** (2016). Oxytocin effect on collective decision making: A randomized placebo controlled study. *PloS One, 11* (4), e0153352.

**Herzog, D. P., Beckmann, H., Lieb, K., Ryu, S., & Müller, M. B.** (2018). Understanding and predicting antidepressant response: Using animal models to move towards precision psychiatry. *Frontiers in Psychiatry, 9,* 512.

**Herzog, H.** (2006). Forty-two thousand and one Dalmatians: Fads, social contagion, and dog breed popularity. *Society & Animals, 14,* 383–397.

**Hespos, S. J., & van Marle, K.** (2012). Physics for infants: Characterizing the origins of knowledge about objects, substances, and number. *WIREs Cognitive Science, 3* (1), 19–27.

**Hetherington, M. M., & Blundell-Birtill, P.** (2018). The portion size effect and overconsumption: Towards downsizing solutions for children and adolescents. *Nutrition Bulletin, 43* (1), 61–68.

**Heyes, C. J., & Latham, J. R.** (2018). Trans surgeries and cosmetic surgeries: The politics of analogy. *Transgender Studies Quarterly, 5* (2), 174–189.

**Hicks, J. A., Trent, J., Davis, W., & King, L. A.** (2012). Positive affect, meaning in life, and future time perspective: An application of socioemotional selectivity theory. *Psychology and Aging, 27,* 181–189.

**Hicks, S. D., Rajan, A., Wagner, K. E., Barns, S., Carpenter, R., & Middleton, F. A.** (2018). Validation of a salivary RNA test for childhood autism spectrum disorder. *Frontiers in Genetics, 9,* 534.

**Hilgard, E. R.** (1977). *Divided consciousness: Multiple controls in human thought and action.* New York: Wiley.

**Hilgard, E. R.** (1992). Dissociation and theories of hypnosis. In E. Fromm & M. R. Nash (Eds.), *Contemporary hypnosis research.* New York: Guilford.

**Hilgard, J., Engelhardt, C. R., Bartholow, B. D., & Rouder, J. N.** (2017). How much evidence is p >.05? Stimulus pre-testing and null primary outcomes in violent video games research. *Psychology of Popular Media Culture, 6* (4), 361–380.

**Hill, K. P., & Saxon, A. J.** (2018). The role of cannabis legalization in the opioid crisis. *JAMA Internal Medicine, 178,* 679–680.

**Hill, P. L., Turiano, N. A., & Burrow, A. L.** (2018). Early life adversity as a predictor of sense of purpose during adulthood. *International Journal of Behavioral Development, 42* (1), 143–147.

**Himmerich, H., Hotopf, M., Shetty, H., Schmidt, U., Treasure, J., Hayes, R. D., ... & Chang, C. K.** (2018). Psychiatric comorbidity as a risk factor for mortality in people with anorexia nervosa. *European Archives of Psychiatry and Clinical Neuroscience,* 1–9.

**Hinshaw, S. P.** (2018). The development of children when a parent experiences mental disorder: Stigma, communication, and humanization. *Human Development.* doi: 10.1159/000487748

**Hiroeh, U., Appleby, L., Mortensen, P. B., & Dunn, G.** (2001). Death by homicide, suicide, and other unnatural causes in people with mental illness: A population-based study. *The Lancet, 358* (9299), 2110–2112.

**Hirsch, J. K., & Rabon, J. K.** (2015). Optimistic explanatory style and suicide attempt in young adults. *International Journal of Mental Health and Addiction, 13* (6), 675–686.

**Hirschfeld, M. R., & Wittenborn, A. K.** (2016). Emotionally focused family therapy and play therapy for young children whose parents are divorced. *Journal of Divorce and Remarriage, 57* (2), 133–150.

**Hirschmüller, S., Schmukle, S. C., Krause, S., Back, M. D., & Egloff, B.** (2018). Accuracy of self-esteem judgments at zero acquaintance. *Journal of Personality, 86* (2), 308–319.

**Hirst, W., Phelps, E. A., Meksin, R., Vaidya, C. J., Johnson, M. K., Mitchell, K. J., ... & Olsson, A.** (2015). A ten-year follow-up of a study of memory for the attack of September 11, 2001: Flashbulb memories and memories for flashbulb events. *Journal of Experimental Psychology: General, 144* (3), 604–623.

**Hishinuma, E. S., Smith, M. D., McCarthy, K., Lee, M., Goebert, D. A., Sugimoto-Matsuda, J. J., ... & Andrade, J. K.** (2018). Longitudinal prediction of suicide attempts for a diverse adolescent sample of Native Hawaiians, Pacific Peoples, and Asian Americans. *Archives of Suicide Research, 22* (1), 67–90.

**Hisle-Gorman, E., Susi, A., Stokes, T., Gorman, G., Erdie-Lalena, C., & Nylund, C. M.** (2018). Prenatal, perinatal, and neonatal risk factors of autism spectrum disorder. *Pediatric Research, 84,* 190–198.

**Hobson, J. A.** (1999). Dreams. In R. Conlan (Ed.), *States of mind.* New York: Wiley.

**Hobson, J. A.** (2000). Dreams: Physiology. In A. E. Kazdin (Ed.), *Encyclopedia of psychology.* Washington, DC: American Psychological Association.

**Hobson, J. A.** (2002). *Dreaming.* New York: Oxford University Press.

**Hobson, J. A.** (2004). Freud returns? Like a bad dream. *Scientific American, 290* (5), *89.*

**Hobson, J. A., & Friston, K. J.** (2012). Waking and dreaming consciousness: Neurobiological and functional considerations. *Progress in Neurobiology, 98* (1), 82–98.

**Hobson, J. A., & Voss, U.** (2011). A mind to go out of: Reflections on primary and secondary consciousness. *Consciousness and Cognition, 20* (4), 993–997.

**Hobson, J. A., Pace-Schott, E. F., & Stickgold, R.** (2000). Dreaming and the brain. *Behavior and Brain Sciences, 23* (6), 793–842.

**Hoch, J. E., Bommer, W. H., Dulebohn, J. H., & Wu, D.** (2018). Do ethical, authentic, and servant leadership explain variance above and beyond transformational leadership? A meta-analysis. *Journal of Management, 44* (2), 501–529.

**Hockett, C. F.** (1960). The origin of speech. *Scientific American, 203,* 88–96.

**Hodges, A. L., & Holland, A. C.** (2018). Common sexually transmitted infections in women. *Nursing Clinics of North America, 53* (2), 189–202.

**Hodges, T. D., & Clifton, D. O.** (2004). Strengths-based development in practice. In A. Linley & S. Joseph (Eds.), *Positive psychology in practice* (pp. 256–268). Hoboken, NJ: Wiley.

**Hofer, P. D., Wahl, K., Meyer, A. H., Miché, M., Beesdo-Baum, K., Wong, S. F., ... & Lieb, R.** (2018). Obsessive–compulsive disorder and the risk of subsequent mental disorders: A community study of adolescents and young adults. *Depression and Anxiety, 35* (4), 339–345.

**Hoffmann, J., & Charles, A.** (2018). Glutamate and its receptors as therapeutic targets for migraine. *Neurotherapeutics, 15,* 361–370.

**Hogan, R.** (2009). Much ado about nothing: The person–situation debate. *Journal of Research in Personality, 43* (2), 249.

**Holland, J., & Sayal, K.** (2018). Relative age and ADHD symptoms, diagnosis and medication: A systematic review. *European Child & Adolescent Psychiatry,* 1–13.

**Holland, K. J., & Cortina, L. M.** (2016). Sexual harassment: Undermining the well-being of working women. In M. L. Connerly & J. Wu (Eds.), *Handbook on well-being of working women* (pp. 83–101). Amsterdam: Springer Netherlands.

**Holland, K. J., Rabelo, V. C., & Cortina, L. M.** (2017). (Missing) knowledge about sexual assault resources: Undermining military mental health. *Violence and Victims, 32* (1), 60–77.

**Holman, A., & Koenig Kellas, J.** (2018). "Say something instead of nothing": Adolescents' perceptions of memorable conversations about sex-related topics with their parents. *Communication Monographs, 85,* 357–379.

**Holoyda, B. J., & Kellaher, D. C.** (2016). The biological treatment of paraphilic disorders: An updated review. *Current Psychiatry Reports, 18* (2), 1–7.

**Holy, T. E.** (2018). The accessory olfactory system: Innately specialized or microcosm of mammalian circuitry? *Annual Review of Neuroscience, 41,* 501–525.

**Holz, N. E., Boecker, R., Jennen-Steinmetz, C., Buchmann, A. F., Blomeyer, D., Baumeister, S., ... & Laucht, M.** (2016). Positive coping styles and ACC volume: Two related mechanisms for conferring resilience? *Social Cognitive and Affective Neuroscience, 11* (5), 813–820.. doi: 10.1093/scan/nsw005

**Homan, K. J.** (2018). Secure attachment and eudaimonic well-being in late adulthood: The mediating role of self-compassion. *Aging & Mental Health,*

22 (3), 363–370. doi:10.1080/13607863.2016.125 4597

**Hong, K., Nezgovorova, V., Uzunova, G., Schlussel, D., & Hollander, E.** (2018). Pharmacological treatment of body dysmorphic disorder. *Current Neuropharmacology*. doi: 10.2174/1570159X16666180426153940

**Hood, K. B., Shook, N. J., & Belgrave, F. Z.** (2017). "Jimmy cap before you tap": Developing condom use messages for African American women. *The Journal of Sex Research, 54* (4–5), 651–664.

**Hoogman, M., Bralten, J., Hibar, D. P., Mennes, M., Zwiers, M. P., Schweren, L. S., ... & Franke, B.** (2017). Subcortical brain volume differences in participants with attention deficit hyperactivity disorder in children and adults: A cross-sectional mega-analysis. *The Lancet Psychiatry, 4* (4), 310–319.

**Hooper, J., & Teresi, D.** (1993). *The 3-pound universe.* New York: Tarcher/Putnam.

**Hopkinson, M. D., Reavell, J., Lane, D. A., & Mallikarjun, P.** (2018). Cognitive behavioral therapy for depression, anxiety, and stress in caregivers of dementia patients: A systematic review and meta-analysis. *The Gerontologist*. gnx217. doi: 10.1093/geront/gnx217

**Horne, C. M., & Norbury, R.** (2018). Altered resting-state connectivity within default mode network associated with late chronotype. *Journal of Psychiatric Research, 102*, 223–229.

**Horney, K.** (1937). *The neurotic personality of our time.* New York: WW Norton.

**Horney, K.** (1945). *Our inner conflicts.* New York: Norton.

**Horney, K.** (1967). *Feminine psychology: Collected essays, 1922–1937.* New York: Norton.

**Horr, N. K., Braun, C., & Volz, K. G.** (2014). Feeling before knowing why: The role of the orbitofrontal cortex in intuitive judgments—an MEG study. *Cognitive, Affective, and Behavioral Neuroscience, 14* (4), 1271–1285.

**Horry, R., Wright, D. B., & Tredoux, C. G.** (2010). Recognition and context memory for faces from own and other ethnic groups: A remember–know investigation. *Memory & Cognition, 38* (2), 134–141. https://doi.org/10.3758/MC.38.2.134

**Hortensius, R., & de Gelder, B.** (2018). From empathy to apathy: The bystander effect revisited. *Current Directions in Psychological Science, 27* (4), 249–256.

**Horvath, A. O.** (2013). You can't step into the same river twice, but you can stub your toes on the same rock: Psychotherapy outcome from a 50-year perspective. *Psychotherapy, 50* (1), 25–32.

**Horvath, S., & Raj, K.** (2018). DNA methylation-based biomarkers and the epigenetic clock theory of ageing. *Nature Reviews Genetics, 19,* 371–384.

**Hotard, S. R., McFatter, R. M., McWhirter, R. M., & Stegall, M. E.** (1989). Interactive effects of extraversion, neuroticism, and social relationships on subjective well-being. *Journal of Personality and Social Psychology, 57* (2), 321–331.

**Hotez, P. J.** (2018). *Vaccines did not cause Rachel's autism: My journey as a vaccine scientist, pediatrician, and autism dad.* Baltimore: Johns Hopkins University Press.

**House, J. S., Landis, K. R., & Umberson, D.** (1988). Social relationships and health. *Science, 241* (4865), 540–545.

**Houser-Marko, L., & Sheldon, K. M.** (2008). Eyes on the prize or nose to the grindstone? The effects of level of goal evaluation on mood and motivation. *Personality and Social Psychology Bulletin, 34* (11), 1556–1569.

**Houston, K. A., Clifford, B. R., Phillips, L. H., & Memon, A.** (2013). The emotional eyewitness: The effects of emotion on specific aspects of eyewitness recall and recognition performance. *Emotion, 13* (1), 118–128.

**Hovland, C. I., Janis, I. L., & Kelley, H. H.** (1953). *Communication and persuasion: Psychological studies of opinion change.* New Haven, CT: Yale University Press.

**Howard, J.** (2018, August 28). *Rates of three STDs in US reach record high, CDC says.* CNN. https://www.cnn.com/2018/08/28/health/std-rates-united-states-2018-bn/index.html

**Howard, L. H., Festa, C., & Lonsdorf, E. V.** (2018). Through their eyes: The influence of social models on attention and memory in capuchin monkeys (Sapajus apella). *Journal of Comparative Psychology, 132,* 210–219.

**Howes, O., McCutcheon, R., & Stone, J.** (2015). Glutamate and dopamine in schizophrenia: An update for the 21st century. *Journal of Psychopharmacology, 29* (2), 97–115.

**Howes, O., Nour, M., Pepper, F., & Jauhar, S.** (2018). 249. Dopaminergic and glutamatergic function in bipolar disorder and schizophrenia and treatment response: PET and MRS evidence in drug naive patients. *Biological Psychiatry, 83* (9), S100–S101.

**Howland, R. H.** (2012). The use of dopaminergic and stimulant drugs for the treatment of depression. *Journal of Psychosocial Nursing and Mental Health Services, 50* (2), 11–14.

**Howsmon, D. P., Vargason, T., Rubin, R. A., Delhey, L., Tippett, M., Rose, S., ... & Hahn, J.** (2018). Multivariate techniques enable a biochemical classification of children with autism spectrum disorder versus typically-developing peers: A comparison and validation study. *Bioengineering & Translational Medicine*, 2018. doi: 10.1002/btm2.10095

**Hoyer, D., Hannon, J. P., & Martin, G. R.** (2002). Molecular, pharmacological, and functional diversity of 5-HT receptors. *Pharmacology, Biochemistry, and Behavior, 71* (4), 533–554.

**Hoyt, C. L., & Murphy, S. E.** (2016). Managing to clear the air: Stereotype threat, women, and leadership. *Leadership Quarterly, 27,* 387–399.

**Hsiao, S. S., & Gomez-Ramirez, M.** (2013). Neural mechanisms of tactile perception. In R. J. Nelson, S. J. Y. Mizumori, & I. B. Weiner (Eds.), *Handbook of psychology* (2nd ed., vol. 3, pp. 206–239). Hoboken, NJ: Wiley.

**Hsiao, V., Kiwanuka, E., Woo, A. S., & Kwan, D.** (2018). The landscape of transgender surgery in the United States. *Plastic and Reconstructive Surgery-Global Open, 6* (8S), 188.

**Hsueh, J., McCormick, M., Merrillees, C., Chou, P., & Cummings, E. M.** (2018). Marital interactions, family intervention, and disagreements: A daily diary study in a low-income sample. *Family Process, 7,* 359–379.

**Hu, S., & Kuh, G. D.** (2003). Diversity learning experiences and college student learning and development. *Journal of College Student Development, 44* (3), 320–334.

**Hu, Y., Pan, Y., Shi, X., Cai, Q., Li, X., & Cheng, X.** (2018). Inter-brain synchrony and cooperation context in interactive decision making. *Biological Psychology, 133,* 54–62.

**Huang, C. C., & Chang, Y. C.** (2009). The long-term effects of febrile seizures on the hippocampal neuronal plasticity—clinical and experimental evidence. *Brain and Development, 31* (5), 383–387.

**Huang, J., Reinders, A. A., Wang, Y., Xu, T., Zeng, Y. W., Li, K., ... & Dazzan, P.** (2018). Neural correlates of audiovisual sensory integration. *Neuropsychology, 32* (3), 329.

**Huang, Y.** (2016). Downward social comparison increases life-satisfaction in the giving and volunteering context. *Social Indicators Research, 125* (2), 665–676.

**Huang, Y., Li, C., Wu, J., & Lin, Z.** (2018). Online customer reviews and consumer evaluation: The role of review font. *Information & Management, 55* (4), 430–440.

**Hubble, M. A., & Miller, S. D.** (2004). The client: Psychotherapy's missing link for promoting a positive psychology. In A. Linley & S. Joseph (Eds.), *Positive psychology in practice* (pp. 335–353). Hoboken, NJ: Wiley.

**Hubel, D. H., & Wiesel, T. N.** (1963). Receptive fields of cells in striate cortex of very young, visually inexperienced kittens. *Journal of Neurophysiology, 26* (6), 994–1002.

**Huber, E., Webster, J. M., Brewer, A. A., MacLeod, D. I., Wandell, B. A., Boynton, G. M., ... & Fine, I.** (2015). A lack of experience-dependent plasticity after more than a decade of recovered sight. *Psychological Science, 26*(4), 393–401.

**Huchard, E., & Pechouskova, E.** (2014). The major histocompatibility complex and primate behavioral ecology: New tools and future questions. *International Journal of Primatology, 35* (1), 11–31.

**Huckins, L. M., Hatzikotoulas, K., Southam, L., Thornton, L. M., Steinberg, J., Aguilera-McKay, F., ... & Curtis, C.** (2018). Investigation of common, low-frequency and rare genome-wide variation in anorexia nervosa. *Molecular Psychiatry, 23* (5), 1169–1180.

**Hudac, C. M.** (2018). Social priming modulates the neural response to ostracism: A new exploratory approach. *Social Neuroscience*. doi: 10.1080/17470919.2018.1463926.

**Huensch, A., & Tremblay, A.** (2015). Effects of perceptual phonetic training on the perception and production of second language syllable structure. *Journal of Phonetics, 52,* 105–120.

**Huettig, F., Lachmann, T., Reis, A., & Petersson, K. M.** (2018). Distinguishing cause from effect—many deficits associated with developmental dyslexia may be a consequence of reduced and suboptimal reading experience. *Language, Cognition and Neuroscience, 33* (3), 333–350.

**Huft, J., & Jonathan, N.** (2018). An integration of feminism into experiential psychotherapy. *The American Journal of Family Therapy*. doi: 10.1080/01926187.2018.1502640

**Huggins, A. W. F.** (2017). Speech perception and auditory processing. In D. J. Getty & J. H. Howard, Jr. (Eds.), *Auditory and visual pattern recognition* (pp. 97–110). London: Routledge.

**Hui, K., & Lent, R. W.** (2018). The roles of family, culture, and social cognitive variables in the career interests and goals of Asian American college students. *Journal of Counseling Psychology, 65* (1), 98–109.

**Huisingh, C., Owsley, C., Levitan, E. B., Irvin, M. R., Maclennan, P., & McGwin, G.** (2018). Distracted driving and risk of crash or near-crash involvement among older drivers using naturalistic driving data with a case-crossover study design. *Risk, 6,* doi:10.1093/gerona/gly11

**Hull, C.** (1952). *A behavior system: An introduction to behavior theory concerning the individual organism.* Westport, CT: Greenwood Press.

**Hulst, B. M., Zeeuw, P., Bos, D. J., Rijks, Y., Neggers, S. F., & Durston, S.** (2017). Children with ADHD symptoms show decreased activity in ventral striatum during the anticipation of reward, irrespective of ADHD diagnosis. *Journal of Child Psychology and Psychiatry, 58* (2), 206–214.

**Humphries, B., Collins, S., Guillaumie, L., Lemieux, J., Dionne, A., Provencher, L., ... & Lauzier, S.** (2018). Women's beliefs on early adherence to adjuvant endocrine therapy for breast cancer: A theory-based qualitative study to guide the development of community pharmacist interventions. *Pharmacy, 6* (2), 53. doi: 10.3390/pharmacy6020053

**Hung, C. M., Li, Y. C., Chen, H. J., Lu, K., Liang, C. L., Liliang, P. C., ... & Wang, K. W.** (2018). Risk of dementia in patients with primary insomnia: A nationwide population-based case-control study. *BMC Psychiatry, 18* (1), 38.

**Hunsley, J., & Bailey, J. M.** (2001). Whither the Rorschach? An analysis of the evidence. *Psychological Assessment, 13* (4), 472–485.

**Hunt, D.** (2018). "In search of our better selves": Totem transfer narratives and indigenous futurities. *American Indian Culture and Research Journal, 42* (1), 71–90.

**Hunt, H. T.** (2012). A collective unconscious reconsidered: Jung's archetypal imagination in the light of contemporary psychology and social science. *Journal of Analytical Psychology, 57* (1), 76–98.

**Huntjens, R. J. C., Wessel, I., Hermans, D., & van Minnen, A.** (2014). Autobiographical memory specificity in dissociative identity disorder. *Journal of Abnormal Psychology, 123* (2), 419–428.

**Huprich, S. K.** (Ed.). (2013). *Rorschach assessment of the personality disorders.* New York: Routledge.

**Hutchinson, M. R.** (2018). 'Convergence'created psychoneuroimmunology, and is needed again to secure the future of the field. *Brain, Behavior, and Immunity, 71,* 1–2.

**Huttenlocher, P. R.** (1999). Dendritic synaptic development in human cerebral cortex: Time course and critical periods. *Developmental Neuropsychology, 16* (3), 347–349.

**Huuhka, K., Vlikki, M., Tammentie, T., Tuohimaa, K., Björkqvist, M., Alanen, H. M., Leinonen, E., & Kampman, O.** (2012). One-year follow-up after discontinuing maintenance electroconvulsive therapy. *Journal of Electroconvulsive Therapy, 28* (4), 225–228.

**Hyde, J. S.** (2005). The gender similarities hypothesis. *American Psychologist, 60* (6), 581–592.

**Hyde, J. S.** (2006). Gender similarities in mathematics and science. *Science, 314* (5799), 599–600.

**Hyde, J. S.** (2007). New directions in the study of gender similarities and differences. *Current Directions in Psychological Science, 16* (5), 259–263.

**Hyde, J. S.** (2014). Gender similarities and differences. *Annual Review of Psychology* (vol. 65, pp. 373–398). Palo Alto, CA: Annual Reviews.

**Hyde, J. S., Bigler, R. S., Joel, D., Tate, C. C., & van Anders, S. M.** (2018). The future of sex and gender in psychology: Five challenges to the gender binary. *American Psychologist.* doi: 10.1037/amp0000307

**Hyde, J. S., & Else-Quest, N.** (2013). *Half the human experience* (8th ed.). Boston: Cengage.

**Hyman, I. E., Roundhill, R. F., Werner, K., & Rabiroff, C. A.** (2014). Collaboration inflation: Egocentric source monitoring errors following collaborative remembering. *Journal of Applied Research in Memory and Cognition, 3,* 293–299.

**Hyman, R.** (2010). Meta-analysis that conceals more than it reveals: Comment on Storm et al. (2010). *Psychological Bulletin, 136* (4), 486–490.

**Hyung, S., Jung, K., Cho, S. R., & Jeon, N. L.** (2018). The Schwann cell as an active synaptic partner. *ChemPhysChem, 19* (10), 1123–1127.

**Hyvönen, K., Törnroos, K., Salonen, K., Korpela, K., Feldt, T., & Kinnunen, U.** (2018). Profiles of nature exposure and outdoor activities associated with occupational well-being among employees. *Frontiers in Psychology, 9.*

## I

**Iacono, W. G., & Ben-Shakhar, G.** (2018). Current status of forensic lie detection with the comparison question technique: An update of the 2003 National Academy of Sciences report on polygraph testing. *Law and Human Behavior.* doi: 10.1037/lhb0000307 (in press)

**Iao, L. S., Tsang, Y. T., Wong, M. Y., & Ho, H. Y.** (2015). Talking while thinking about another's mind in preschoolers: Evidence of getting Vygotskian about social cognition. *Early Childhood Research Quarterly, 31,* 1–8.

**Ibanez, A., Huepe, D., Gempp, R., Gutiérrez, V., Rivera-Rei, A., & Toledo, M. I.** (2013). Empathy, sex and fluid intelligence as predictors of theory of mind. *Personality and Individual Differences, 54* (5), 616–621.

**Igarashi, H., Levenson, M. R., & Aldwin, C. M.** (2018). The development of wisdom: A social ecological approach. *The Journals of Gerontology: Series B, 73,* 1350–1358.

**Ikeda, B. E., Collins, C. E., Alvaro, F., Marshall, G., & Garg, M. L.** (2006). Wellbeing and nutrition-related side effects in children undergoing chemotherapy. *Nutrition and Dietetics, 63* (4), 227–239.

**Illies, M. Y., & Reiter-Palmon, R.** (2018). The effect of value similarity on mentoring relationships and outcomes. *International Journal of Evidence-based Coaching and Mentoring, 16* (1), 20–34.

**Impett, E. A., Muise, A., & Harasymchuk, C.** (2018). Giving in the bedroom: The costs and benefits of responding to a partner's sexual needs in daily life. *Journal of Social and Personal Relationships.* doi: 10.1177/0265407518787349

**Impett, E. A., Peplau, L. A., & Gable, S. L.** (2005). Approach and avoidance sexual motives: Implications for personal and interpersonal well-being. *Personal Relationships, 12* (4), 465–482.

**Insel, C., & Somerville, L. H.** (2018). Asymmetric neural tracking of gain and loss magnitude during adolescence. *Social Cognitive and Affective Neuroscience, 13* (8), 785–796.

**Institute for Women's Policy Research.** (2018). *The gender wage gap, 2017: Earnings differences by gender, race, and ethnicity. #C473.* Washington, DC: Author.

**Inta, D., & Gass, P.** (2015). Is forebrain neurogenesis a potential repair mechanism after stroke? *Journal of Cerebral Blood Flow & Metabolism, 35,* 1220–1221.

**Irwin, M. R., Wang, M., Campomayor, C. O., Collado-Hidalgo, A., & Cole, S.** (2006). Sleep deprivation and activation of morning levels of cellular and genomic markers of inflammation. *Archives of Internal Medicine, 166* (16), 1756–1762.

**Israel, T.** (2018). Bisexuality: From margin to center. *Psychology of Sexual Orientation and Gender Diversity, 5* (2), 233–242. doi: 10.1037/sgd0000294

**Ivanenko, Y., & Gurfinkel, V. S.** (2018). Human postural control. *Frontiers in Neuroscience, 12,* 171. doi: 10.3389/fnins.2018.00171

**Iyer, V. J., Finch, D. G., & Kalu, C. O.** (2018). Unlocking the locked-in syndrome: capacity evaluation and a multidisciplinary approach to care. *Psychiatric Annals, 48* (9), 448–451.

**Izuma, K.** (2017). The neural bases of social influence on valuation and behavior. In J. Dreher & L. Tremblay, (Eds.), *Decision neuroscience* (pp. 199–209). New York: Academic Press.

**Izurieta Hidalgo, N. A., Oelkers-Ax, R., Nagy, K., Mancke, F., Bohus, M., Herpertz, S. C., & Bertsch, K.** (2016). Time course of facial emotion processing in women with borderline personality disorder: An ERP study. *Journal of Psychiatry and Neuroscience, 41* (1), 16–26.

## J

**Jabbi, M., Nash, T., Kohn, P., Ianni, A., Rubinstein, D., Holroyd, T., ... & Berman, K. F.** (2013). Midbrain presynaptic dopamine tone predicts sustained and transient neural response to emotional salience in humans: fMRI, MEG, and FDOPA PET. *Molecular Psychiatry, 18* (1), 4–6.

**Jablensky, E.** (2000). Epidemiology of schizophrenia: The global burden of disease and disability. *European Archives of Psychiatry and Clinical Neuroscience, 250* (6), 274–285.

**Jablensky, E., Sartorius, N., Ernberg, G., Anker, M., Korten, A., Cooper, J. E., Day, R., & Bertelsen, A.** (1992). Schizophrenia: Manifestations, incidence, and course in different cultures: A World Health Organization 10-country study. *Psychological Medicine Monograph Supplement, 20,* 1–97.

**Jackendoff, R.** (2012). *A user's guide to thought and meaning.* New York: Oxford University Press.

**Jackowska, M., Brown, J., Ronaldson, A., & Steptoe, A.** (2016). The impact of a brief gratitude intervention on subjective well-being, biology and sleep. *Journal of Health Psychology, 21* (10), 2207–2217. doi: 10.1177/1359105315572455

**Jackson, J. C., Jong, J., Bilkey, D., Whitehouse, H., Zollmann, S., McNaughton, C., & Halberstadt, J.** (2018). Synchrony and physiological arousal increase cohesion and cooperation in large naturalistic groups. *Scientific Reports, 8* (1), 127.

**Jackson, L. C., & Greene, B.** (2000). *Psychotherapy with African-American women.* New York: Guilford.

**Jackson, M. L., Hughes, M. E., Croft, R. J., Howard, M. E., Crewther, D., Kennedy, G. A., ... & Johnston, P.** (2011). The effect of sleep deprivation on BOLD activity elicited by a divided attention task. *Brain Imaging and Behavior, 5* (2), 97–108.

**Jacob, Y., Shany, O., Goldin, P., Gross, J., & Hendler, T.** (2018). S36. Reappraisal of personal criticism in social anxiety disorder: A brain network perspective. *Biological Psychiatry, 83* (9), S360–S361.

**Jacobs, T. L., Epel, E. S., Lin, J., Blackburn, E. H., Wolkowitz, O. M., Bridwell, D. A., ... & Saron, C. D.** (2011). Intensive meditation training, immune cell telomerase activity, and psychological mediators. *Psychoneuroendocrinology, 36* (5), 664–681.

**Jaffee, S.** (2018). Promises and pitfalls in the development of biomarkers that can promote early intervention in children at risk. *Journal of Child Psychology and Psychiatry, 59* (2), 97–98.

**Jain, A., Christopher, P., & Appelbaum, P. S.** (2018). Civil commitment for opioid and other substance use disorders: Does it work? *Psychiatric Services, 69* (4), 374–376.

**Jäkel, S., & Dimou, L.** (2017). Glial cells and their function in the adult brain: a journey through the history of their ablation. *Frontiers in Cellular Neuroscience, 11,* 24.

**Jakhetiya, V., Lin, W., Jaiswal, S., Gu, K., & Guntuku, S. C.** (2018). Just Noticeable Difference for natural images using RMS contrast and feed-back mechanism. *Neurocomputing, 275,* 366–376.

**James, W.** (1950). *Principles of psychology.* New York: Dover. (original work published 1890)

**Jamieson, J. P., Hangen, E. J., Lee, H. Y., & Yeager, D. S.** (2018). Capitalizing on appraisal processes to improve affective responses to social stress. *Emotion Review, 10* (1), 30–39.

**Jang, K. L., & Vernon, P. A.** (2018). Genetics. In W.J. Livesly & R. Larstone (Eds.), *Handbook of personality disorders: Theory, research, and treatment* (2nd ed., pp. 235–250) New York: Guilford.

**Jang, K. L., Livesley, W. J., & Vernon, P. A.** (1996). Heritability of the big five personality dimensions and their facets: A twin study. *Journal of Personality, 64* (3), 577–591.

**Janis, I.** (1972). *Victims of groupthink: A psychological study of foreign-policy decisions and fiascos.* Boston: Houghton Mifflin.

**Janis, I. L., & Hovland, C. I.** (1959). An overview of persuasibility research. In C. I. Hovland & I. L. Janis (Eds.), *Personality and persuasibility* (pp. 1–26). New Haven, CT: Yale University Press.

**Jannot, A. S., Ehret, G., & Perneger, T.** (2015). $P < 5 \times 10(-8)$ has emerged as a standard of statistical significance for genome-wide association studies. *Journal of Clinical Epidemiology, 68* (4), 460–465.

**Janowsky, D. S., Addario, D., & Risch, S. C.** (1987). *Psychopharmacology case studies* (2nd ed.). New York: Guilford.

**Jansson-Fröjmark, M., Evander, J., & Alfonsson, S.** (2018). Are sleep hygiene practices related to the incidence, persistence and remission of insomnia? Findings from a prospective community study. *Journal of Behavioral Medicine,* 1–11.

**"Japanese breaks pi memory record."** (2005, July 2). *BBC News.* http://news.bbc.co.uk/2/hi/asia-pacific/4644103.stm (accessed March 4, 2016)

**Japardi, K., Bookheimer, S., Knudsen, K., Ghahremani, D. G., & Bilder, R. M.** (2018). Functional magnetic resonance imaging of divergent and convergent thinking in Big-C creativity. *Neuropsychologia, 118,* 59–67.

**Jaradat, M., & Rahhal, A.** (2015). Obstructive sleep apnea, prevalence, etiology & role of dentist & oral appliances in treatment: Review article. *Open Journal of Stomatology, 5* (7), 187–201.

**Jaradat, Y., Nielsen, M. B., Kristensen, P., Nijem, K., Bjertness, E., & Bast-Pettersen, R.** (2018). Mental distress and job satisfaction in Palestinian nurses exposed to workplace aggression: A cross-sectional study. *The Lancet, 391,* S37.

**Jaramillo, N., Buhi, E. R., Elder, J. P., & Corliss, H. L.** (2017). Associations between sex education and contraceptive use among heterosexually active, adolescent males in the United States. *Journal of Adolescent Health, 60* (5), 534–540.

**Jarrahi, M. H.** (2018). Artificial intelligence and the future of work: Human-AI symbiosis in organizational decision making. *Business Horizons, 61,* 577–586.

**Jaworski, C., Ravichandran, S., Karpinski, A. C., & Singh, S.** (2018). The effects of training satisfaction, employee benefits, and incentives on part-time employees' commitment. *International Journal of Hospitality Management, 74,* 1–12.

**Jeffay, J.** (February 2, 2017). Brave young woman with 'locked in syndrome' can't speak or move after suffering stroke at 21. *The Mirror.* https://www.mirror.co.uk/news/uk-news/brave-young-woman-locked-syndrome-9744127

**Jeffery, A. J., Shackelford, T. K., Zeigler-Hill, V., Vonk, J., & McDonald, M.** (2018). The evolution of human female sexual orientation. *Evolutionary Psychological Science*, 1–16.

**Jeffery, K. J.** (2018). The hippocampus: From memory, to map, to memory map. *Trends in Neurosciences, 41* (2), 64–66.

**Jena, A. B., Barnett, M., & Layton, T. J.** (2018, November 28). The link between August birthdays and A.D.H.D. *The New York Times*, Opinion. https://www.nytimes.com/2018/11/28/opinion/august-birthdays-adhd.html

**Jerath, R., & Beveridge, C.** (2018). Top mysteries of the mind: Insights from the default space model of consciousness. *Frontiers in Human Neuroscience, 12,* 162.

**Jern, P., Johansson, A., Piha, J., Westberg, L., & Santtila, P.** (2015). Antidepressant treatment of premature ejaculation: Discontinuation rates and prevalence of side effects for dapoxetine and paroxetine in a naturalistic setting. *International Journal of Impotence Research, 27* (2), 75–80.

**Jiang, H., Yang, Z., Sun, P., & Xu, M.** (2018). When does social exclusion increase or decrease food self-regulation? The moderating role of time orientation. *Journal of Consumer Behaviour, 17* (1), 34–46.

**Jiang, K., Hong, Y., McKay, P. F., Avery, D. R., Wilson, D. C., & Volpone, S. D.** (2015). Retaining employees through anti-sexual harassment practices: Exploring the mediating role of psychological distress and employee engagement. *Human Resource Management, 54* (1), 1–21.

**Jiang, L., & Johnson, M. J.** (2018). Meaningful work and affective commitment: A moderated mediation model of positive work reflection and work centrality. *Journal of Business and Psychology, 33* (4), 545–558.

**Jimenez, M. E., Wade, R., Schwartz-Soicher, O., Lin, Y., & Reichman, N. E.** (2017). Adverse childhood experiences and ADHD diagnosis at age 9 years in a national urban sample. *Academic Pediatrics, 17* (4), 356–361.

**Jin, K., Houston, J. L., Baillargeon, R., Groh, A. M., & Roisman, G. I.** (2018). Young infants expect an unfamiliar adult to comfort a crying baby: Evidence from a standard violation-of-expectation task and a novel infant-triggered-video task. *Cognitive Psychology, 102,* 1–20.

**Jin, S., Seo, M. G., & Shapiro, D. L.** (2016). Do happy leaders lead better? Affective and attitudinal antecedents of transformational leadership. *Leadership Quarterly, 27* (1), 64–84.

**Job, R. F. S.** (1987). The effect of mood on helping behavior. *Journal of Social Psychology, 127,* 323–328.

**Joel, D.** (2011). Male or female? Brains are intersex. *Frontiers in Integrative Neuroscience, 5,* 57.

**Joel, D., Berman, Z., Tavor, I., Wexler, N., Gaber, O., Stein, Y., ... & Assaf, Y.** (2015). Sex beyond the genitalia: The human brain mosaic. *Proceedings of the National Academy of Sciences of the United States of America, 112,* 15468–15473. doi: 10.1073/pnas.1509654112

**Johansson Nolaker, E., Murray, K., Happé, F., & Charlton, R. A.** (2018). Cognitive and affective associations with an ecologically valid test of theory of mind across the lifespan. *Neuropsychology*, 32, 754–763.

**John, S. G., Cisler, J. M., & Sigel, B. A.** (2017). Emotion regulation mediates the relationship between a history of child abuse and current PTSD/depression severity in adolescent females. *Journal of Family Violence, 32,* 565–575.

**Johnson, E. K., Finlayson, C., Rowell, E. E., Gosiengfiao, Y., Pavone, M. E., Lockart, B., ... & Woodruff, T. K.** (2017). Fertility preservation for pediatric patients: Current state and future possibilities. *The Journal of Urology, 198* (1), 186–194.

**Johnson, I. R., Kopp, B. M., & Petty, R. E.** (2018). Just say no! (and mean it): Meaningful negation as a tool to modify automatic racial attitudes. *Group Processes & Intergroup Relations, 21* (1), 88–110.

**Johnson, J. S., & Newport, E. L.** (1991). Critical period effects on universal properties of language: The status of subjacency in the acquisition of a second language. *Cognition, 39,* 215–258.

**Johnson, M.** (November 12, 2018). Healing 4 Heroes helping veterans' transition with trained service dogs. WTVM, Columbus, Georgia. http://www.wtvm.com/2018/11/12/healing-heroes-helping-veterans-transition-with-trained-service-dogs/

**Johnson, W. D., O'Leary, A., & Flores, S. A.** (2018). Per-partner condom effectiveness against HIV for men who have sex with men. *AIDS, 32* (11), 1499–1505.

**Johnstone, E., Benowitz, N., Cargill, A., Jacob, R., Hinks, L., Day, I., Murphy, M., & Walton, R.** (2006). Determinants of the rate of nicotine metabolism and the effects on smoking behavior. *Clinical Pharmacology and Therapeutics, 80* (4), 319–330.

**Joiner, Jr., T. E.** (2005). *Why people die by suicide.* Cambridge, MA: Harvard University Press.

**Joiner, Jr., T. E., Ribeiro, J. D., & Silva, C.** (2012). Nonsuicidal self-injury, suicidal behavior, and their co-occurrence as viewed through the lens of the interpersonal theory of suicide. *Current Directions in Psychological Science, 21* (5), 342–347.

**Jokela, M.** (2018). Personality as a determinant of health behaviors and chronic diseases: Review of meta-analytic evidence. In C. Ryff and R. F. Krueger (Eds.), *The Oxford handbook of integrative health science* (pp. 317–332). New York: Oxford University Press.

**Jokela, M., Batty, G. D., Nyberg, S. T., Virtanen, M., Nabi, H., Singh-Manoux, A., & Kivimäki, M.** (2013). Personality and all-cause mortality: Individual-participant meta-analysis of 3,947 deaths in 76,150 adults. *American Journal of Epidemiology, 178* (5), 667–675.

**Jones, A., Hannigan, B., Coffey, M., & Simpson, A.** (2018). Traditions of research in community mental health care planning and care coordination: A systematic meta-narrative review of the literature. *PloS One, 13* (6), e0198427.

**Jones, C. R., Simonoff, E., Baird, G., Pickles, A., Marsden, A. J., Tregay, J., ... & Charman, T.** (2018). The association between theory of mind, executive function, and the symptoms of autism spectrum disorder. *Autism Research, 11* (1), 95–109.

**Jones, E. E., & Harris, V. A.** (1967). The attribution of attitudes. *Journal of Experimental Social Psychology, 3,* 1–24.

**Jones, G. R., & George, J. M.** (2007). *Essentials of contemporary management* (2nd ed.). New York: McGraw-Hill.

**Jones, K. A., Crozier, W. E., & Strange, D.** (2017). Believing is seeing: Biased viewing of body-worn camera footage. *Journal of Applied Research in Memory and Cognition, 6* (4), 460–474.

**Jones, S. M., Vijayakumar, S., Dow, S. A., Holt, J. C., Jordan, P. M., & Luebke, A. E.** (2018). Loss of α-calcitonin gene-related peptide (αCGRP) reduces otolith activation timing dynamics and impairs balance. *Frontiers in Molecular Neuroscience, 11,* 289 doi: 10.3389/fnmol.2018.00289

**Jones, S. V., & McCollum, R.** (2018). Subjective memory complaints after electroconvulsive therapy: Systematic review. *BJPsych Bulletin.* doi: 10.1192/bjb.2018.45

**Jordan, K., & Tseris, E.** (2018). Locating, understanding and celebrating disability: Revisiting Erikson's "stages." *Feminism & Psychology, 28* (3), 427–444.

**Joseph, J.** (2006). *The missing gene.* New York: Algora.

**Joseph, J., Breslin, C., & Skinner, H.** (1999). Critical perspectives on the transtheoretical model and stages of change. In J. A. Tucker, D. M. Donovan, & G. A. Marlatt (Eds.), *Changing addictive behavior: Bridging clinical and public health strategies* (pp. 160–190). New York: Guilford.

**Jost, J. T.** (2017). Ideological asymmetries and the essence of political psychology. *Political Psychology, 38,* 167–208.

**Jost, J. T., Sapolsky, R. M., & Nam, H. H.** (2018). Speculations on the evolutionary origins of system justification. *Evolutionary Psychology, 16* (2). doi:10.1474704918765342 (in press)

**Joyal, C. C.** (2018). Controversies in the definition of paraphilia. *The Journal df Sexual Medicine, 15* (10), 1378–1380.

**Judge, T. A., Bono, J. E., Ilies, R., & Gerhardt, M. W.** (2002). Personality and leadership: A qualitative and quantitative review. *Journal of Applied Psychology, 87* (4), 765–780.

**Judge, T. A., Piccolo, R. F., Podsakoff, J. C., & Rich, B. L.** (2010). The relationship between pay satisfaction and job satisfaction. *Journal of Vocational Behavior, 77* (2), 157–167.

**Judge, T. A., Thorson, C. J., Bono, J. E., & Patton, G. K.** (2001). The job satisfaction–job performance relationship: A qualitative and quantitative review. *Psychological Bulletin, 127* (3), 376–407.

**Judge, T. A., & Zapata, C. P.** (2015). The person-situation debate revisited: Effect of situation strength and trait activation on the validity of the big five personality traits in predicting job performance. *Academy of Management Journal, 58* (4), 1149–1179.

**Jung, C.** (1917). *Analytic psychology.* New York: Moffat, Yard.

**Junior, J. B. L., de Mello Bastos, J. M., Samuels, R. I., Carey, R. J., & Carrera, M. P.** (2018). Reversal elimination of morphine conditioned behavior by an anti-dopaminergic post-trial drug treatment during re-consolidation. *Behavioural Brain Research.* doi: 10.1016/j.bbr.2018.08.009

**Jury, M., Smeding, A., Stephens, N. M., Nelson, J. E., Aelenei, C., Darnon, C.** (2017). The experience of low-SES students in higher education: Psychological barriers to success and interventions to reduce social-class inequality. *Journal of Social Issues, 73* (1), 23–41.

## K

**Kabat-Zinn, J.** (2006). *Coming to our senses: Healing ourselves and the world through mindfulness.* New York: Hyperion.

**Kabat-Zinn, J.** (2009, March 18). *This analog life: Reconnecting with what is important in an always uncertain world.* Presentation at the 7th Annual Conference at the Center for Mindful Meditation, Worcester, MA.

**Kabat-Zinn, J., & Davidson, R.** (Eds.). (2012). *The mind's own physician.* Berkeley, CA: New Harbinger.

**Kabat-Zinn, J., Lipworth, L., & Burney, R.** (1985). The clinical use of mindfulness meditation for the self-regulation of chronic pain. *Journal of Behavioral Medicine, 8* (2), 163–190.

**Kabat-Zinn, J., Wheeler, E., Light, T., Skillings, A., Scharf, M. J., Cropley, T. G., Hosmer, D., & Bernhard, J. D.** (1998). Influence of a mindfulness meditation-based stress reduction intervention on rates of skin clearing in patients with moderate to severe psoriasis undergoing phototherapy (UVB) and photochemotherapy (PUVA). *Psychosomatic Medicine, 60* (5), 625–632.

**Kaftan, O. J., & Freund, A. M.** (2018). A motivational life-span perspective on procrastination: The development of delaying goal pursuit across adulthood. *Research in Human Development*, 15.

**Kagan, J.** (2018). *Galen's prophecy: Temperament in human nature*. London: Routledge.

**Kahalon, R., Shnabel, N., & Becker, J. C.** (2018). "Don't bother your pretty little head": Appearance compliments lead to improved mood but impaired cognitive performance. *Psychology of Women Quarterly, 42* (2), 136–150.

**Kahan, D. M., Peters, E., Wittlin, M., Slovic, P., Ouellette, L. L., Braman, D., & Mandel, G.** (2012). The polarizing impact of science literacy and numeracy on perceived climate change risks. *Nature Climate Change, 2* (10), 732–735.

**Kahneman, D.** (2011). *Thinking, fast and slow*. New York: Farrar, Straus, & Giroux.

**Kahneman, D., & Deaton, A.** (2010). High income improves evaluation of life but not emotional well-being. *Proceedings of the National Academy of Sciences, 107,* 16489–16493.

**Kahneman, D., & Klein, G.** (2009). Conditions for intuitive experience: A failure to disagree. *American Psychologist, 64* (6), 515–526.

**Kahneman, D., Knetsch, J. L., & Thaler, R. H.** (1990). Experimental tests of the endowment effect and the cause theorem. *Journal of Political Economy, 98* (6), 1325–1348.

**Kahneman, D., & Tversky, A.** (1984). Choices, values, and frames. *American Psychologist, 39* (4), 341–350.

**Kaiser, R. H., Clegg, R., Goer, F., Pechtel, P., Beltzer, M., Vitaliano, G., ... & Pizzagalli, D. A.** (2018). Childhood stress, grown-up brain networks: Corticolimbic correlates of threat-related early life stress and adult stress response. *Psychological Medicine, 48* (7), 1157–1166.

**Kamin, L. J.** (1968). Attention-like processes in classical conditioning. In M. R. Jones (Ed.), *Miami symposium on the prediction of behavior: Aversive stimuli.* Coral Gables, FL: University of Miami Press.

**Kaminer, Y., Ohannessian, C. M., McKay, J. R., Burke, R. H., & Flannery, K.** (2018). Goal commitment predicts treatment outcome for adolescents with alcohol use disorder. *Addictive Behaviors, 76,* 122–128.

**Kammrath, L. K., & Scholer, A. A.** (2013). Cognitive-affective processing system. In H. A. Tennen, J. M. Suls, & I. B. Weiner (Eds.), *Handbook of psychology* (2nd ed., vol. 5, pp. 161–182). Hoboken, NJ: Wiley.

**Kamps, F. S., Morris, E. J., & Dilks, D. D.** (2019). A face is more than just the eyes, nose, and mouth: fMRI evidence that face-selective cortex represents external features. *NeuroImage, 184,* 90–100.

**Kandel, D., & Kandel, E.** (2015). The gateway hypothesis of substance abuse: Developmental, biological, and societal perspectives. *Acta Paediatrica, 104* (2), 130–137.

**Kandel, E. R., & Schwartz, J. H.** (1982). Molecular biology of learning: Modulation of transmitter release. *Science, 218* (4571), 433–443.

**Kang, S., Vervliet, B., Engelhard, I. M., van Dis, E. A., & Hagenaars, M. A.** (2018). Reduced return of threat expectancy after counterconditioning verus extinction. *Behaviour Research and Therapy, 108,* 78–84.

**Kannan, V. D., & Veazie, P. J.** (2018). Political orientation, political environment, and health behaviors in the United States. *Preventive Medicine, 114,* 95–101.

**Kanwisher, N.** (2006). Neuroscience: What's in a face? *Science, 311* (5761), 617–618.

**Kanwisher, N., & Yovel, G.** (2010). Cortical specialization for face perception in humans. In J. T. Cacioppo & G. G. Berentson (Eds.), *Handbook of neuroscience for the behavioral sciences.* New York: Wiley.

**Kaplan, H. S.** (1974). *The new sex therapy: Active treatment of sexual dysfunctions*. New York: Routledge.

**Kaplan, K. W., Sayegh, M. A., Dowell, J., & Bundy, J.** (2018). Suicidal ideation among Midwestern adolescents: Substance abuse and hopelessness. *Journal of Adolescent Health, 62* (2), S53.

**Kaplan, R. L., Van Damme, I., Levine, L. J., & Loftus, E. F.** (2016). Emotion and false memory. *Emotion Review, 8* (1), 8–13.

**Kapur, N.** (1996). Paradoxical functional facilitation in brain-behaviour research. A critical review. *Brain, 119,* 1775–1790.

**Kapur, S.** (2003). Psychosis as a state of aberrant salience: A framework linking biology, phenomenology, and pharmacology. *American Journal of Psychiatry, 160* (1), 13–23.

**Karas, P., Lee, S., Sheth, S. A., Jimenez-Shahed, J., Goodman, W., & Viswanathan, A.** (2018). Deep brain stimulation for obsessive compulsive disorder: Evolution of surgical stimulation target parallels changing model of dysfunctional brain circuits. *Frontiers in Neuroscience, 12,* 998.

**Karkoulian, S., Assaker, G., & Hallak, R.** (2016). An empirical study of 360-degree feedback, organizational justice, and firm sustainability. *Journal of Business Research, 69* (5), 1962–1867.

**Karlinsky, N., & Frost, M.** (2012, April 27). Real "Beautiful Mind": College dropout became mathematical genius after mugging. *ABC News.* http://abcnews.go.com/blogs/health/2012/04/27/real-beautiful-mind-accidental-genius-draws-complex-math-formulas-photos (accessed February 4, 2016)

**Karremans, J. C., Pronk, T. M., & van der Wal, R. C.** (2015). Executive control and relationship maintenance processes: An empirical overview and theoretical integration. *Social and Personality Psychology Compass, 9* (7), 333–347. doi:10.1111/spc3.12177

**Karriker-Jaffe, K. J., Klinger, J. L., Witbrodt, J., & Kaskutas, L. A.** (2018). Effects of treatment type on alcohol consumption partially mediated by Alcoholics Anonymous attendance. *Substance Use & Misuse, 53* (4), 596–605.

**Karson, C., Duffy, R. A., Eramo, A., Nylander, A. G., & Offord, S. J.** (2016). Long-term outcomes of antipsychotic treatment in patients with first-episode schizophrenia: A systematic review. *Neuropsychiatric Disease and Treatment, 12,* 57–67.

**Kashdan, T. B., Blalock, D. V., Young, K. C., Machell, K. A., Monfort, S. S., McKnight, P. E., & Ferssizidis, P.** (2018). Personality strengths in romantic relationships: Measuring perceptions of benefits and costs and their impact on personal and relational well-being. *Psychological Assessment, 30* (2), 241–258.

**Kaskutas, L. A.** (2009). Alcoholics Anonymous effectiveness: Faith meets science. *Journal of Addictive Diseases, 28* (2), 145–157.

**Kaspersen, S. L., Pape, K., Vie, G. Å., Ose, S. O., Krokstad, S., Gunnell, D., & Bjorngaard, J. H.** (2015). Health and unemployment: 14 years of follow-up on the Norwegian HUNT Study. *European Journal of Public Health, 25* (Suppl. 3), 134–171.

**Kasser, T.** (2017). Integrating psychobiography into psychology's mainstream: Introduction to the special section. *American Psychologist, 72* (5), 430–433.

**Kasser, T., & Ryan, R. M.** (1996). Further examining the American dream: Differential correlates of intrinsic and extrinsic goals. *Personality and Social Psychology Bulletin, 22* (3), 280–287.

**Kasser, T., Ryan, R. M., Couchman, C. E., & Sheldon, K. M.** (2004). Materialistic values: Their causes and consequences. In T. Kasser & A. D. Kanner (Eds.), *Psychology and consumer culture: The struggle for a good life in a materialistic world* (pp. 11–28). Washington, DC: American Psychological Association.

**Kassin, S. M., Redlich, A. D., Alceste, F., & Luke, T. J.** (2018). On the general acceptance of confessions research: Opinions of the scientific community. *American Psychologist, 73* (1), 63–80.

**Katakam, K. K., Sethi, N. J., Jakobsen, J. C., & Gluud, C.** (2018). Great boast, small roast on effects of selective serotonin reuptake inhibitors: response to a critique of our systematic review. *Acta Neuropsychiatrica,* 30, 251–265.

**Kato, I., Franco, P., Groswasser, J., Scaillet, S., Kelmanson, I., Togari, H., & Kahn, A.** (2003). Incomplete arousal processes in infants who were victims of sudden death. *American Journal of Respiratory Critical Care Medicine, 168* (11), 1298–1303.

**Katz-Wise, S. L., & Hyde, J. S.** (2015). Sexual fluidity and related attitudes and beliefs among young adults with a same-gender orientation. *Archives of Sexual Behavior, 44* (5), 1459–1470.

**Kaur, K., Nanut, M. P., Ko, M. W., Safaie, T., Kos, J., & Jewett, A.** (2018). Natural killer cells target and differentiate cancer stem-like cells/undifferentiated tumors: strategies to optimize their growth and expansion for effective cancer immunotherapy. *Current Opinion in Immunology, 51,* 170–180.

**Kawasaka, K.** (2018). Contradictory discourses on sexual normality and national identity in Japanese modernity. *Sexuality & Culture, 22* (2), 593–613.

**Kaye, S. A., White, M. J., & Lewis, I.** (2018). Young females' attention toward road safety images: An ERP study of the revised reinforcement sensitivity theory. *Traffic Injury Prevention, 19* (2), 201–206.

**Kazanis, I.** (2013). Neurogenesis in the adult mammalian brain: How much do we need, how much do we have? *Current Topics in Behavioral Neuroscience, 15,* 3–29.

**Kazdin, A. E., & McWhinney, E.** (2018). Therapeutic alliance, perceived treatment barriers, and therapeutic change in the treatment of children with conduct problems. *Journal of Child and Family Studies, 27* (1), 240–252.

**Ke, F., Whalon, K., & Yun, J.** (2018). Social skill interventions for youth and adults with autism spectrum disorder: A systematic review. *Review of Educational Research, 88* (1), 3–42.

**Keast, R. S. J., Costanzo, A.** (2015). Is fat the sixth taste primary? Evidence and implications. *Flavour, 4,* 5. doi: 10.1186/2044-7248-4-5

**Keehn, J. D.** (2018). *Animal models for psychiatry*. London: Routledge.

**Keenan, G. S., Childs, L., Rogers, P. J., Hetherington, M. M., & Brunstrom, J. M.** (2018). The portion size effect: Women demonstrate an awareness of eating more than intended when served larger than normal portions. *Appetite, 126*, 54–60.

**Keenan, H. T., Clark, A. E., Holubkov, R., Cox, C. S., & Ewing-Cobbs, L.** (2018). Psychosocial and executive function recovery trajectories one year after pediatric traumatic brain injury: The influence of age and injury severity. *Journal of Neurotrauma, 35* (2), 286–296.

**Kehayes, I. L. L., Smith, M. M., Sherry, S. B., Vidovic, V., & Saklofske, D. H.** (2018). Are perfectionism dimensions risk factors for bulimic symptoms? A meta-analysis of longitudinal studies. *Personality and Individual Differences, 138*, 117–125.

**Kekatos, M.** (October 31, 2018). Florida girl, 13, makes 125 superhero capes for premature babies who have to spend Halloween in the NICU. TheDailyMail.Com. https://www.dailymail.co.uk/health/article-6337813/Florida-teenager-13-makes-125-superhero-capes-Halloween-premature-babies.html

**Kell, H. J.** (2018). Unifying vocational psychology's trait and social-cognitive approaches through the cognitive-affective personality system. *Review of General Psychology, 22* (3), 343–353.

**Kellen, D., & Klauer, K. C.** (2018). Elementary signal detection and threshold theory. In Wixted (Ed.), *The Stevens handbook of experimental psychology and cognitive neuroscience: Methodology* (4th ed., vol. 5, pp. 161–201). New York: Wiley.

**Kelley, H. H.** (1973). The processes of causal attribution. *American Psychologist, 28* (2), 107–128.

**Kellner, M., Muhtz, C., Nowack, S., Leichsenring, I., Wiedemann, K., & Yassouridis, A.** (2018). Effects of 35% carbon dioxide (CO2) inhalation in patients with post-traumatic stress disorder (PTSD): A double-blind, randomized, placebo-controlled, cross-over trial. *Journal of Psychiatric Research, 96*, 260–264.

**Kellogg, M. B., Knight, M., Dowling, J. S., & Crawford, S. L.** (2018). Secondary traumatic stress in pediatric nurses. *Journal of Pediatric Nursing, 43*, 97–103.

**Kelly, J. F.** (2013). Alcoholics Anonymous science update: Introduction to the special issue. *Substance Abuse, 34* (1), 1–3.

**Kempermann, G., Gage, F. H., Aigner, L., Song, H., Curtis, M. A., Thuret, S., ... & Gould, E.** (2018). Human adult neurogenesis: Evidence and remaining questions. *Cell Stem Cell, 23* (1), 25–30.

**Kendler, K. S., Gardner, C., & Dick, D. M.** (2011). Predicting alcohol consumption in adolescence from alcohol-specific and general externalizing genetic risk factors, key environmental factors, and their interaction. *Psychological Medicine, 41* (7), 1507–1516.

**Kennedy, B. L., & Most, S. B.** (2015). Affective stimuli capture attention regardless of categorical distinctiveness: An emotion-induced blindness study. *Visual Cognition, 23* (1–2), 105–117.

**Kensinger, E. A., & Choi, E. S.** (2009). When side matters: Hemispheric processing and the visual specificity of emotional memories. *Journal of Experimental Psychology: Learning, Memory, and Cognition, 35* (1), 247–253.

**Kent, R.** (2016). Locked in by labels: A mental illness diagnosis may lead to discrimination, including from health professionals, says Rachel Kent. *Nursing Standard, 30* (19), 26–27.

**Kern, R. M., & Curlette, W. L.** (2015). The individual psychology perspective: Positive psychology, Freud and Adler in Paris, philosophy, neuroticism, and classroom techniques. *Journal of Individual Psychology, 71* (4), 359–361.

**Kernis, M. H.** (2003). Toward a conceptualization of optimal self-esteem. *Psychological Inquiry, 14* (1), 1–26.

**Kerr, J., Rosenberg, D., Millstein, R. A., Bolling, K., Crist, K., Takemoto, M., ... & Buchner, D.** (2018). Cluster randomized controlled trial of a multilevel physical activity intervention for older adults. *International Journal of Behavioral Nutrition and Physical Activity, 15*(1), 32. doi: 10.1186/s12966-018-0658-4

**Kerr, M., Siegle, G. J., & Orsini, J.** (2018). Voluntary arousing negative experiences (VANE): Why we like to be scared. *Emotion*. doi: 10.1037/emo0000470 (in press)

**Kesby, J. P., Eyles, D. W., McGrath, J. J., & Scott, J. G.** (2018). Dopamine, psychosis and schizophrenia: the widening gap between basic and clinical neuroscience. *Translational Psychiatry, 8* (1), 30.

**Kessler, R. M., Hutson, P. H., Herman, B. K., & Potenza, M. N.** (2016). The neurobiological basis of binge-eating disorder. *Neuroscience and Biobehavioral Reviews, 63*, 223–238.

**Kettering, T. L., Fisher, W. W., Kelley, M. E., & LaRue, R. H.** (2018). Sound attenuation and preferred music in the treatment of problem behavior maintained by escape from noise. *Journal of Applied Behavior Analysis, 51*, 687–693.

**Keyes, C. L., Kendler, K. S., Myers, J. M., & Martin, C. C.** (2015). The genetic overlap and distinctiveness of flourishing and the big five personality traits. *Journal of Happiness Studies, 16* (3), 655–668.

**Kezelman, S., Crosby, R. D., Rhodes, P., Hunt, C., Anderson, G., Clarke, S., & Touyz, S.** (2018). Anorexia nervosa, anxiety and the clinical implications of rapid refeeding. *Frontiers in Psychology, 9*, 1097.

**Khajehei, M., & Behroozpour, E.** (2018). Endorphins, oxytocin, sexuality and romantic relationships. *World Journal of Obstetrics and Gynecology, 7* (2), 17–23.

**Khalis, A., & Mikami, A. Y.** (2018). Who's gotta catch 'em all?: Individual differences in Pokèmon Go gameplay behaviors. *Personality and Individual Differences, 124*, 35–38.

**Khalis, A., Mikami, A. Y., & Hudec, K. L.** (2018). Positive peer relationships facilitate adjustment in the transition to university for emerging adults with ADHD symptoms. *Emerging Adulthood, 6* (4), 243–254.

**Khan, Z. H., Karvandian, K., Maghsoudloo, M., & Albareh, H. M.** (2018). The role of opioids and non-opioids in postoperative pain relief: A narrative review. *Archives of Anesthesiology and Critical Care, 4* (1), 430–435.

**Khorashad, B. S., Khazai, B., Roshan, G. M., Hiradfar, M., Afkhamizadeh, M., & van de Grift, T. C.** (2018). Prenatal testosterone and theory of mind development: Findings from disorders of sex development. *Psychoneuroendocrinology, 89*, 250–255.

**Kidd, D. G., Singer, J., Huey, R., & Kerfoot, L.** (2018). The effect of a gearshift interlock on seat belt use by drivers who do not always use a belt and its acceptance among those who do. *Journal of Safety Research, 65*, 39–51.

**Kihlstrom, J.** (2005). Is hypnosis an altered state of consciousness or what?: Comment. *Contemporary Hypnosis, 22* (1), 34–38.

**Kikkert, S., Johansen-Berg, H., Tracey, I., & Makin, T. R.** (2018). Reaffirming the link between chronic phantom limb pain and maintained missing hand representation. *Cortex, 106*, 174–184.

**Kilic, K., Karatas, H., Dönmez-Demir, B., Eren-Kocak, E., Gursoy-Ozdemir, Y., Can, A., ... & Dalkara, T.** (2018). Inadequate brain glycogen or sleep increases spreading depression susceptibility. *Annals of Neurology, 83* (1), 61–73.

**Kilpatrick, D. G.** (2000). *The mental health impact of rape.* Medical University of South Carolina: National Violence Against Women Prevention Research Center. https://mainweb-v.musc.edu/vawprevention/research/mentalimpact.shtml

**Kim, A. Y., & Baik, E. J.** (2019). Glutamate dehydrogenase as a neuroprotective target against neurodegeneration. *Neurochemical Research, 44* (1), 147–153.

**Kim, G. S., Smith, A. K., Nievergelt, C. M., & Uddin, M.** (2018). Neuroepigenetics of post-traumatic stress disorder. *Progress in Molecular Biology and Translational Science, 158*, 227–253.

**Kim, H., Im, J., & Qu, H.** (2018). Exploring antecedents and consequences of job crafting. *International Journal of Hospitality Management, 75*, 18–26.

**Kim, H. J., Yang, G. S., Greenspan, J. D., Downton, K. D., Griffith, K. A., Renn, C. L., Johantgen, M., & Dorsey, S. G.** (2017). Racial and ethnic differences in experimental pain sensitivity: Systematic review and meta-analysis. *Pain, 158* (2), 194–211.

**Kim, S. W., Choi, J. B., Kim, S. J., Kim, K. S., Kim, C. M., Lee, D. H., & Choi, W. S.** (2018). Tolerability and adequate therapeutic dosage of oral clomipramine for the treatment of premature ejaculation: A randomized, double-blind, placebo-controlled, fixed-dose, parallel-grouped clinical study. *International Journal of Impotence Research, 30*, 65–70.

**Kim, S., & Frank, T. D.** (2018). Correlations between hysteretic categorical and continuous judgments of perceptual stimuli supporting a unified dynamical systems approach to perception. *Perception, 47* (1), 44–66.

**Kim, Y., & Ployhart, R. E.** (2018). The strategic value of selection practices: antecedents and consequences of firm-level selection practice usage. *Academy of Management Journal, 61* (1), 46–66.

**King, J. D., Horton, S. E., Hughes, J. L., Eaddy, M., Kennard, B. D., Emslie, G. J., & Stewart, S. M.** (2018). The interpersonal–psychological theory of suicide in adolescents: A preliminary report of changes following treatment. *Suicide and Life-Threatening Behavior, 48* (3), 294–304.

**King, L. A.** (2001). The health benefits of writing about life goals. *Personality and Social Psychology Bulletin, 27*, 798–807.

**King, L. A.** (2003). Measures and meanings: The use of qualitative data in social and personality psychology. In C. Sansone, C. Morf, & A. Panter (Eds.), *The Sage handbook of methods in social psychology* (pp. 173–194). Thousand Oaks, CA: Sage.

**King, L. A., & Geise, A. C.** (2011). Being forgotten: Implications for the experience of meaning in life. *Journal of Social Psychology, 151* (6), 696–709.

**King, L. A., & Hicks, J. A.** (2007). Whatever happened to "what might have been"? Regret, happiness, and maturity. *American Psychologist, 62* (7), 625–636.

**King, L. A., Hicks, J. A., Krull, J., & Del Gaiso, A. K.** (2006). Positive affect and the experience of meaning in life. *Journal of Personality and Social Psychology, 90*, 179–196.

**King, L. A., & Miner, K. N.** (2000). Writing about the perceived benefits of traumatic life events: Implications for physical health. *Personality and Social Psychology Bulletin, 26*, 220–230.

**King, L. A., Scollon, C. K., Ramsey, C. M., & Williams, T.** (2000). Stories of life transition: Happy endings, subjective well-being, and ego development in parents of children with Down syndrome. *Journal of Research in Personality, 34* (4), 509–536.

**King, L. A., & Smith, S. N.** (2005). Happy, mature, and gay: Intimacy, power, and difficult times in coming out stories. *Journal of Research in Personality, 39* (2), 278–298.

**King, L. A., & Trent, J.** (2013). Personality strengths. In H. A. Tennen, J. M. Suls, & I. B. Weiner (Eds.), *Handbook of psychology* (2nd ed., vol. 5, pp. 197–224). Hoboken, NJ: Wiley.

**King, M. L., Manzel, K., Bruss, J., & Tranel, D.** (2018). Neural correlates of improvements in personality and behavior following a neurological event. *Neuropsychologia* (in press)

**Kinnish, K. K., Strassberg, D. S., & Turner, C. M.** (2005). Sex differences in the flexibility of sexual orientation: A multidimensional retrospective assessment. *Archives of Sexual Behavior, 34* (2), 173–183.

**Kinori, M., Schwartzstein, H., Zeid, J. L., Kurup, S. P., & Mets, M. B.** (2018). Congenital lymphocytic choriomeningitis virus–an underdiagnosed fetal teratogen. *Journal of American Association for Pediatric Ophthalmology and Strabismus, 22* (1), 79–81.

**Kinsey, A. C., Martin, C. E., & Pomeroy, W. B.** (1953). *Sexual behavior in the human female.* Philadelphia: Saunders.

**Kinsey, A. C., Pomeroy, W. B., & Martin, C. E.** (1948). *Sexual behavior in the human male.* Philadelphia: Saunders.

**Kinzler, K. D., Dupoux, E., & Spelke, E. S.** (2013). "Native" objects and collaborators: Infants' object choices and acts of giving reflect favor for native over foreign speakers. *Journal of Cognition and Development, 13* (1), 67–81.

**Kippax, S.** (2018). A journey to HIV prevention research: From social psychology to social health via multidisciplinarity. *Journal of Health Psychology, 23* (3), 442–456.

**Kirby, D. B.** (2008). The impact of abstinence and comprehensive sex and STD/HIV education programs on adolescent sexual behavior. *Sexuality Research & Social Policy, 5,* 18–27.

**Kirchhof, J., Petrakova, L., Brinkhoff, A., Benson, S., Schmidt, J., Unteroberdörster, M., ... & Schedlowski, M.** (2018). Learned immunosuppressive placebo responses in renal transplant patients. *Proceedings of the National Academy of Sciences, PNAS, 115* (16), 4223-4227.

**Kirk, H. E., Gray, K., Riby, D. M., & Cornish, K. M.** (2015). Cognitive training as a resolution for early executive function difficulties in children with intellectual disabilities. *Research in Developmental Disabilities, 38,* 145–160.

**Kirschman, L. J., Crespi, E. J., & Warne, R. W.** (2018). Critical disease windows shaped by stress exposure alter allocation trade-offs between development and immunity. *Journal of Animal Ecology, 87* (1), 235–246.

**Kirschner, K. L.** (2018). He's in there somewhere! Reflecting on the past, present, and future of disorders of consciousness. *AJOB Neuroscience, 9,* 73–75.

**Kisely, S., Li, A., Warren, N., & Siskind, D.** (2018). A systematic review and meta-analysis of deep brain stimulation for depression. *Depression and Anxiety, 35* (5), 468–480.

**Kitchener, K. S., King, P. M., & DeLuca, S.** (2006). The development of reflective judgment in adulthood. In C. Hoare (Ed.), *Handbook of adult development and learning.* New York: Oxford University Press.

**Kivimäki, M., Nyberg, S. T., Batty, G. D., Madsen, I. E., & Tabák, A. G.** (2018). Long working hours and risk of venous thromboembolism. *Epidemiology, 29* (5), e42.

**Klaassen, L., Dirksen, C., Boersma, L., Hoving, C., & B-beslist!-group.** (2018). Developing an aftercare decision aid: Assessing health professionals' and patients' preferences. *European Journal of Cancer Care, 27* (2), e12730.

**Klatell, P.** (2012). How big are your dinner plates–and why it matters. EatoutWell.com https://eatouteatwell.com/how-big-are-your-dinner-plates-and-why-it-matters/

**Klein, M., Onnink, M., van Donkelaar, M., Wolfers, T., Harich, B., Shi, Y., ... & Franke, B.** (2017). Brain imaging genetics in ADHD and beyond: Mapping pathways from gene to disorder at different levels of complexity. *Neuroscience & Biobehavioral Reviews, 80,* 115–155.

**Kleinmann, M., & Ingold, P. V.** (2019). Toward a better understanding of assessment centers: A conceptual review. *Annual Review of Organizational Psychology and Organizational Behavior, 6,* 349–372.

**Klemfuss, J. Z., & Ceci, S. J.** (2012a). Legal and psychological perspectives on children's competence to testify in court. *Developmental Review, 32* (3), 268–286.

**Klemfuss, J. Z., & Ceci, S. J.** (2012b). The law and science of children's testimonial competence. In R. Holliday & T. Marche (Eds.), *Child forensic psychology.* New York: Macmillan.

**Klimstra, T. A., Hale, W. W., Raaijmakers, Q. A., Branje, S. J., & Meeus, W. H.** (2009). Maturation of personality in adolescence. *Journal of Personality and Social Psychology, 96* (4), 898–912.

**Klimstra, T. A., Luyckx, K., Hale, W. A., Frijns, T., van Lier, P. A., & Meeus, W. H.** (2010). Short-term fluctuations in identity: Introducing a micro-level approach to identity formation. *Journal of Personality and Social Psychology, 99* (1), 191–202.

**Kline, A. C., Cooper, A. A., Rytwinksi, N. K., & Feeny, N. C.** (2018). Long-term efficacy of psychotherapy for posttraumatic stress disorder: A meta-analysis of randomized controlled trials. *Clinical Psychology Review, 59,* 30–40.

**Kling, S. M., Roe, L. S., Keller, K. L., & Rolls, B. J.** (2016). Double trouble: Portion size and energy density combine to increase preschool children's lunch intake. *Physiology and Behavior, 162,* 18–26.

**Klingseisen, A., & Lyons, D. A.** (2018). Axonal regulation of central nervous system myelination: Structure and function. *The Neuroscientist, 24* (1), 7–21.

**Klosterhalfen, S., Rüttgers, A., Krumrey, E., Otto, B., Stockhorst, U., Riepl, R. L., Probst, T., & Enck, P.** (2000). Pavlovian conditioning of taste aversion using a motion sickness paradigm. *Psychosomatic Medicine, 62* (5), 671–677.

**Klotz, A. C., Bolino, M. C., Song, H., & Stornelli, J.** (2018). Examining the nature, causes, and consequences of profiles of organizational citizenship behavior. *Journal of Organizational Behavior, 39* (5), 629–647.

**Klucharev, V., Hytonen, K., Rijpkema, M., Smidts, A., & Fernandez, G.** (2009). Reinforcement learning signal predicts social conformity. *Neuron, 61* (1), 140–151.

**Klump, K. L., Fowler, N., Mayhall, L., Sisk, C. L., Culbert, K. M., & Burt, S. A.** (2018). Estrogen moderates genetic influences on binge eating during puberty: Disruption of normative processes? *Journal of Abnormal Psychology, 127* (5), 458–470.

**Knafo-Noam, A., Vertsberger, D., & Israel, S.** (2018). Genetic and environmental contributions to children's prosocial behavior: Brief review and new evidence from a reanalysis of experimental twin data. *Current Opinion in Psychology, 20,* 60–65.

**Knapp, S., & VandeCreek, L.** (2000). Recovered memories of childhood abuse: Is there an underlying consensus. *Professional Psychology: Research and Practice, 31* (4), 365–371.

**Knekt, P., Virtala, E., Härkänen, T., Vaarama, M., Lehtonen, J., & Lindfors, O.** (2016). The outcome of short- and long-term psychotherapy 10 years after start of treatment. *Psychological Medicine, 46* (6), 1175–1188.

**Knouse, L. E., Teller, J., & Brooks, M. A.** (2017). Meta-analysis of cognitive–behavioral treatments for adult ADHD. *Journal of Consulting and Clinical Psychology, 85* (7), 737–750.

**Kobasa, S., Maddi, S., & Kahn, S.** (1982). Hardiness and health: A prospective study. *Journal of Personality and Social Psychology, 42* (1), 168–177.

**Kobasa, S. C., Maddi, S. R., Puccetti, M. C., & Zola, M.** (1986). Relative effectiveness of hardiness, exercise, and social support as resources against illness. *Journal of Psychosomatic Research, 29,* 525–533.

**Kobayashi, L. C., & Steptoe, A.** (2018). Social isolation, loneliness, and health behaviors at older ages: Longitudinal cohort study. *Annals of Behavioral Medicine, 52* (7), 582–593.

**Kobylecki, C., Haense, C., Harris, J. M., Stopford, C. L., Segobin, S. H., Jones, M., ... & Herholz, K.** (2018). Functional neuroanatomical associations of working memory in early-onset Alzheimer's disease. *International Journal of Geriatric Psychiatry, 33*(1), 176–184.

**Koch, S. C., Acton, D., & Goulding, M.** (2018). Spinal circuits for touch, pain, and itch. *Annual Review of Physiology, 80,* 189–217.

**Koelsch, S.** (2018). Identifying emotional specificity in complex large-scale brain networks. *Emotion Review, 10* (3), 217–218.

**Koelsch, S., Enge, J., & Jentschke, S.** (2012). Cardiac signatures of personality. *PLoS One, 7* (2), e31441.

**Koenig, K. A., Rao, S. M., Lowe, M. J., Lin, J., Sakaie, K. E., Stone, L., ... & Phillips, M. D.** (2018). The role of the thalamus and hippocampus in episodic memory performance in patients with multiple sclerosis. *Multiple Sclerosis Journal,* 1352458518760716.

**Kohlberg, L.** (1958). *The development of modes of moral thinking and choice in the years 10 to 16.* Unpublished doctoral dissertation, University of Chicago.

**Kohlberg, L.** (1986). A current statement on some theoretical issues. In S. Modgil & C. Modgil (Eds.), *Lawrence Kohlberg.* Philadelphia: Falmer.

**Kohler, P. K., Manhart, L. E., & Lafferty, W. E.** (2008). Abstinence-only and comprehensive sex education and the initiation of sexual activity and teen pregnancy. *Journal of Adolescent Health, 42* (4), 344–351.

**Köhler, W.** (1925). *The mentality of apes.* New York: Harcourt-Brace.

**Kohut, H.** (1977). *Restoration of the self.* New York: International Universities Press.

**Koike, S., Yamaguchi, S., Ojio, Y., Ohta, K., Shimada, T., Watanabe, K., ... & Ando, S.** (2018). A randomised controlled trial of repeated filmed social contact on reducing mental illness-related stigma in young adults. *Epidemiology and Psychiatric Sciences, 27* (2), 199–208.

**Koitabashi, T., Oyaizu, T., & Ouchi, T.** (2009). Low bispectral index values following electroconvulsive therapy associated with memory impairment. *Journal of Anesthesiology, 23* (2), 182–187.

**Kok, B. E., Waugh, C. E., & Fredrickson, B. L.** (2013). Meditation and health: The search for mechanisms of action. *Social and Personality Psychology Compass, 7* (1), 27–39.

**Kong, D. T., & Ho, V. T.** (2016). A self-determination perspective of strengths use at work: Examining its determinant and performance implications. *Journal of Positive Psychology, 11* (1), 15–25.

**Kong, F., Hu, S., Xue, S., Song, Y., & Liu, J.** (2015). Extraversion mediates the relationship between structural variations in the dorsolateral prefrontal cortex and social well-being. *NeuroImage, 105,* 269–275.

**Kong, L. L., Allen, J. J. B., & Glisky, E. L.** (2008). Interidentity memory transfer in dissociative identity disorder. *Journal of Abnormal Psychology, 117* (3), 686–692.

**Koppel, J., & Berntsen, D.** (2016). The reminiscence bump in autobiographical memory and for public events: A comparison across different cueing methods. *Memory, 24* (1), 44–62.

**Kopp-Scheinpflug, C., Sinclair, J. L., & Linden, J. F.** (2018). When sound stops: Offset responses in the auditory system. *Trends in Neurosciences, 41*(10), 712–728.

**Koren, D., Chirinos, J. A., Katz, L. E. L., Mohler, E. R., Gallagher, P. R., Mitchell, G. F., & Marcus, C. L.** (2015). Interrelationships between obesity, obstructive sleep apnea syndrome, and cardiovascular risk in obese adolescents. *International Journal of Obesity, 39* (7), 1086–1093.

**Kornell, N., Klein, P. J., & Rawson, K. A.** (2015). Retrieval attempts enhance learning, but retrieval success (versus failure) does not matter. *Journal of Experimental Psychology: Learning, Memory, and Cognition, 41* (1), 283–290.

**Kornmann, J., Zettler, I., Kammerer, Y., Gerjets, P., & Trautwein, U.** (2015). What characterizes children nominated as gifted by teachers? A closer consideration of working memory and intelligence. *High Ability Studies, 26* (1), 75–92.

**Koster, A., Stenholm, S., & Schrack, J. A.** (2018). The benefits of physical activity for older people. In S.R. Nyman, A. Barker, T. Haines, K. Horton, C. Musselwhite, G. Peeters, C. R. Victor, & J. K. Wolff

(Eds.) *The Palgrave Handbook of Ageing and Physical Activity Promotion* (pp. 43–60). Cham, Switzerland: Palgrave Macmillan.

**Kotter-Grühn, D., & Smith, J.** (2011). When time is running out: Changes in positive future perception and their relationships to changes in well-being in old age. *Psychology and Aging, 26* (2), 381–387.

**Koutsoklenis, A., & Gaitanidis, A.** (2017). Interrogating the effectiveness of educational practices: A critique of evidence-based psychosocial treatments for children diagnosed with attention-deficit/hyperactivity disorder. *Frontiers in Education, 2,* 11.

**Kovjanic, S., Schuh, S. C., Jonas, K., Van Quaquebeke, N., & van Dick, R.** (2012). How do transformational leaders foster positive employee outcomes? A self-determination-based analysis of employees' needs as mediating links. *Journal of Organizational Behavior, 33* (8), 1031–1052.

**Kowalski, R., Limber, S. P., & McCord, A.** (2018). A developmental approach to cyberbullying: Prevalence and protective factors. *Aggression and Violent Behavior.* doi: 10.1016/j.avb.2018.02.009

**Kowialiewski, B., & Majerus, S.** (2018). The non-strategic nature of linguistic long-term memory effects in verbal short-term memory. *Journal of Memory and Language, 101,* 64–83.

**Kozak, A.** (2018). Understanding pseudoscience vulnerability through epistemological development, critical thinking, and science literacy. In A. B. Kaufman & J. C. Kaufman (Eds.), *Pseudoscience: The conspiracy against science* (pp. 223–238). Cambridge, MA: MIT Press.

**Kozlowski, S. W., Mak, S., & Chao, G. T.** (2016). Team-centric leadership: An integrative review. *Annual Review of Organizational Psychology and Organizational Behavior* (vol. 3, pp. 21–64). Palo Alto, CA: Annual Reviews.

**Kragel, P. A., Kano, M., Van Oudenhove, L., Ly, H. G., Dupont, P., Rubio, A., ... & Ceko, M.** (2018). Generalizable representations of pain, cognitive control, and negative emotion in medial frontal cortex. *Nature Neuroscience, 21* (2), 283.

**Krause, N., Hill, P. C., Emmons, R., Pargament, K. I., & Ironson, G.** (2017). Assessing the relationship between religious involvement and health behaviors. *Health Education & Behavior, 44* (2), 278–284.

**Krause-Utz, A., & Elzinga, B.** (2018). Current understanding of the neural mechanisms of dissociation in borderline personality disorder. *Current Behavioral Neuroscience Reports, 5* (1), 113–123.

**Krauss, S. W., Russell, D. W., Kazman, J. B., Russell, C. A., Schuler, E. R., & Deuster, P. A.** (2018). Longitudinal effects of deployment, recency of return, and hardiness on mental health symptoms in US Army combat medics. *Traumatology.* doi: 10.1037/trm0000173

**Krautbauer, K. H., & Drossel, C.** (2018). Cancer-related eating problems. In A. Maragaki & W. T. O'Donohue, (Eds.), Principle-based *stepped care and brief psychotherapy for integrated care settings* (pp. 89–97). Cham: Springer.

**Kress, V. E., Stargell, N. A., Zoldan, C. A., & Paylo, M. J.** (2016). Hoarding disorder: Diagnosis, assessment, and treatment. *Journal of Counseling and Development, 94* (1), 83–90.

**Krieger, I.** (2017). *Counseling transgender and non-binary youth: The essential guide.* London: Jessica Kingsley Publishers.

**Kringelbach, M. L.** (2005). The human orbitofrontal cortex: Linking reward to hedonic experience. *Nature Reviews: Neuroscience, 6,* 691–702.

**Kringelbach, M. L., & Berridge, K. C.** (2015). Motivation and pleasure in the brain. In W. Hofmann & L. F. Nordgren (Eds.), *The psychology of desire* (pp. 129–145). New York: Guilford.

**Kringelbach, M. L., & Berridge, K. C.** (2018). The joyful mind. *Scientific American, 27,* 72–77.

**Kroesbergen, E. H., van't Noordende, J. E., & Kolkman, M. E.** (2014). Training working memory in kindergarten children: Effects on working memory and early numeracy. *Child Neuropsychology, 20* (1), 23–37.

**Kroese, F., Adriaanse, M. A., Evers, C., Anderson, J. H., & De Ridder, D.** (2018). Commentary: Why don't you go to bed on time? A daily diary study on the relationships between chronotype, self-control resources and the phenomenon of bedtime procrastination. *Frontiers in Psychology, 9,* 915.

**Kroger, J., Martinussen, M., & Marcia, J. E.** (2010). Identity change in adolescence and young adulthood: A meta-analysis. *Journal of Adolescence, 33* (5), 683–698.

**Krogsrud, S. K., Fjell, A. M., Tamnes, C. K., Grydeland, H., Mork, L., Due-Tønnessen, P., ... & Walhovd, K. B.** (2016). Changes in white matter microstructure in the developing brain—A longitudinal diffusion tensor imaging study of children from 4 to 11 years of age. *NeuroImage, 124* (Pt. A), 473–486.

**Krok, D.** (2015). The role of meaning in life within the relations of religious coping and psychological well-being. *Journal of Religion and Health, 54* (6), 2292–2308.

**Krouwel, M., Greenfield, S., Farley, A., Ismail, T., & Jolly, K.** (2018). Factors which affect the efficacy of hypnotherapy for IBS: Protocol for a systematic review and meta-regression. *European Journal of Integrative Medicine, 21,* 58–62.

**Krueger, R. F., Markon, K. E., & Bouchard, T. J.** (2003). The extended genotype: The heritability of personality accounts for the heritability of recalled family environments in twins reared apart. *Journal of Personality, 71* (5), 809–833.

**Kruger, J., Blanck, H. M., & Gillespie, C.** (2006). Dietary and physical activity behaviors among adults successful at weight loss maintenance. *International Journal of Behavioral Nutrition and Physical Activity, 3,* 17.

**Kruglanski, A. W., & Webster, D. M.** (2018). Motivated closing of the mind: "Seizing" and "freezing." In A. W. Kruglanski, *The motivated mind* (pp. 68–111). London: Routledge.

**Kruschwitz, J. D., Walter, M., Varikuti, D., Jensen, J., Plichta, M. N., Haddad, L, ... & Walter, H.** (2015). 5-HTTLPR/rs25531 polymorphism and neuroticism are linked by resting state functional connectivity of amygdala and fusiform gyrus. *Brain Structure and Function, 220* (4), 2373–2385.

**Kubota, M., van Haren, N. E., Haijma, S. V., Schnack, H. G., Cahn, W., Pol, H. E. H., & Kahn, R. S.** (2015). Association of IQ changes and progressive brain changes in patients with schizophrenia. *JAMA Psychiatry, 72* (8), 803–812.

**Kubzansky, L. D., Huffman, J. C., Boehm, J. K., Hernandez, R., Kim, E. S., Koga, H. K., ... & Labarthe, D. R.** (2018). Positive psychological well-being and cardiovascular disease: JACC health promotion series. *Journal of the American College of Cardiology, 72* (12), 1382–1396.

**Kuchibhotla, K., & Bathellier, B.** (2018). Neural encoding of sensory and behavioral complexity in the auditory cortex. *Current Opinion in Neurobiology, 52,* 65–71.

**Kuchibhotla, K. V., Gill, J. V., Lindsay, G. W., Papadoyannis, E. S., Field, R. E., Sten, T. A. H., ... & Froemke, R. C.** (2017). Parallel processing by cortical inhibition enables context-dependent behavior. *Nature Neuroscience, 20* (1), 62–71.

**Kudryavtsev, A.** (2018). The availability heuristic and reversals following large stock price changes. *Journal of Behavioral Finance, 19* (2), 159–176.

**Kuehn, K. S., Wagner, A., & Velloza, J.** (2018). Estimating the magnitude of the relation between bullying, e-bullying, and suicidal behaviors among United States youth, 2015. *Crisis: The Journal of Crisis Intervention and Suicide Prevention.* doi: 10.1027/0227-5910/a000544

**Kuehnle, K., & Connell, M.** (2013). Child sexual abuse evaluations. In R. K. Otto & I. B. Weiner (Eds.), *Handbook of psychology* (2nd ed., vol. 11, pp. 579–614). Hoboken, NJ: Wiley.

**Kuhl, P. K.** (1993). Infant speech perception: A window on psycholinguistic development. *International Journal of Psycholinguistics, 9,* 33–56.

**Kuhl, P. K.** (2000). A new view of language acquisition. *Proceedings of the National Academy of Sciences USA, 97* (22), 11850–11857.

**Kuhl, P. K.** (2011). Early language learning and literacy: Neuroscience implications for education. *Mind, Brain, and Education, 5* (3), 128–142.

**Kuhl, P. K.** (2012). Language learning and the developing brain: Cross-cultural studies unravel the effects of biology and culture. *Journal of the Acoustical Society of America, 131* (4), 3207.

**Kuhl, P. K.** (2015). Baby talk. *Scientific American, 313* (5), 64–69.

**Kuhn, D.** (2009). Adolescent thinking. In R. M. Lerner & L. Steinberg (Eds.), *Handbook of adolescent psychology, Vol. 1: Individual bases of adolescent development* (3rd ed., pp. 152–186). Hoboken, NJ: Wiley.

**Kühnel, J., & Sonnentag, S.** (2011). How long do you benefit from vacation? A closer look at the fade-out of vacation effect. *Journal of Organizational Behavior, 32* (1), 125–143.

**Kumar, A., & Epley, N.** (2018). Undervaluing gratitude: Expressers misunderstand the consequences of showing appreciation. *Psychological Science, 29* (9), 1423–1435. doi: 10.1177/0956797618772506

**Kumar, A., Tiwari, A., Gadiyar, A., Gaunkar, R. B., & Kamat, A. K.** (2018). Assessment of readiness to quit tobacco among patients with oral potentially malignant disorders using transtheoretical model. *Journal of Education and Health Promotion, 7,* 9. doi: 10.4103/jehp.jehp_75_17

**Kundu, P., Benson, B. E., Rosen, D., Frangou, S., Leibenluft, E., Luh, W. M., ... & Ernst, M.** (2018). The integration of functional brain activity from adolescence to adulthood. *Journal of Neuroscience, 38* (14), 3559–3570.

**Kuo, S. P., Schwartz, G. W., & Rieke, F.** (2016). Nonlinear spatiotemporal integration by electrical and chemical synapses in the retina. *Neuron, 90,* 320–332.

**Kupfer, D. J.** (2015). Anxiety and DSM-5. *Dialogues in Clinical Neuroscience, 17* (3), 245–246.

**Kupper, N., van den Broek, K., Haagh, E., Van Der Voort, P., Widdershoven, J., & Denollet, J.** (2018). Type D personality affects health-related quality of life in patients with lone atrial fibrillation by increasing symptoms related to sympathetic activation. *Journal of Psychosomatic Research, 115,* 44–52.

**Kurdek, L. A.** (2004). Are gay and lesbian cohabiting couples really different from heterosexual married couples? *Journal of Marriage and Family, 66* (4), 880–900.

**Kurson, R.** (2007). *Crashing through: A true story of risk, adventure, and the man who dared to see.* New York: Random House.

**Kushlev, K., Heintzelman, S. J., Oishi, S., & Diener, E.** (2018). The declining marginal utility of social time for subjective well-being. *Journal of Research in Personality, 74,* 124–140. doi:10.1016/j.jrp.2018.04.004

**Kuyper, P.** (1972). The cocktail party effect. *Audiology, 11,* 277–282.

**Kwan, M. Y., Gordon, K. H., & Minnich, A. M.** (2018). An examination of the relationships between acculturative stress, perceived discrimination, and eating disorder symptoms among ethnic minority college students. *Eating Behaviors, 28,* 25–31.

# L


**L'Episcopo, F., Tirolo, C., Peruzzotti-Jametti, L., Serapide, M. F., Testa, N., Caniglia, S., ... & Marchetti, B.** (2018). Neural stem cell grafts promote astroglia-driven neurorestoration in the aged parkinsonian brain via Wnt/β-Catenin signaling. *STEM CELLS*. doi: 10.1002/stem.2827

**Labouvie-Vief, G.** (1986, August). *Modes of knowing and life-span cognition.* Paper presented at the meeting of the American Psychological Association, Washington, DC.

**Labouvie-Vief, G.** (2006). Emerging structures of adult thought. In J. J. Arnett & J. L. Tanner (Eds.), *Emerging adults in America* (pp. 60–84). Washington, DC: American Psychological Association.

**Laceulle, O. M., van Aken, M. A., Ormel, J., & Nederhof, E.** (2015). Stress-sensitivity and reciprocal associations between stressful events and adolescent temperament. *Personality and Individual Differences, 81,* 76–83.

**Lachman, M. E., Rocke, C., Rosnick, C., & Ryff, C. D.** (2008). Realism and illusion in Americans' temporal views of their life satisfaction: Age differences in reconstructing the past and anticipating the future. *Psychological Science, 19,* 89–97.

**Lacombe-Duncan, A., Newman, P. A., & Baiden, P.** (2018). Human papillomavirus vaccine acceptability and decision-making among adolescent boys and parents: A meta-ethnography of qualitative studies. *Vaccine, 36,* 2545–2558.

**LaCount, P. A., & Hartung, C. M.** (2018). Physical exercise interventions for emerging adults with attention-deficit/hyperactivity disorder (ADHD). *The ADHD Report, 26* (5), 1–11.

**LaFrance, M., & Vial, A. C.** (2016). Gender and nonverbal behavior. In D. Matsumoto, C. H. Hwang, & M. G. Frank (Eds.), *APA handbook of nonverbal communication* (pp. 139–161). Washington, DC: American Psychological Association.

**Laguna, M.** (2013). Self-efficacy, self-esteem, and entrepreneurship among the unemployed. *Journal of Applied Social Psychology, 43* (2), 253–262.

**Lahm, H., Jia, M., Dreßen, M., Puluca, N., Beck, N., Cleuziou, J., ... & Lange, R.** (2018). GWAS analysis reveals previously unknown genomic variants associated with different subgroups of congenital heart disease. *The Thoracic and Cardiovascular Surgeon, 66* (S 01), DGTHG-V315.

**Laible, D. J., & Thompson, R. A.** (2000). Mother–child discourse, attachment security, shared positive affect, and early conscience development. *Child Development, 71* (5), 1424–1440.

**Laible, D. J., & Thompson, R. A.** (2002). Mother–child conflict in the toddler years: Lessons in emotion, morality, and relationships. *Child Development, 73* (4), 1187–1203.

**Laible, D. J., & Thompson, R. A.** (2007). Early socialization: A relationship perspective. In J. E. Grusec & P. D. Hastings (Eds.), *Handbook of socialization.* New York: Guilford.

**Laiglesia, L. M., Lorente-Cebrián, S., Martínez-Fernández, L., Sáinz, N., Prieto-Hontoria, P. L., Burrell, M. A., ... & Moreno-Aliaga, M. J.** (2018). Maresin 1 mitigates liver steatosis in ob/ob and diet-induced obese mice. *International Journal of Obesity, 42* (3), 572.

**Lam, C. B., & McBride-Chang, C. A.** (2007). Resilience in young adulthood: The moderating influences of gender-related personality traits and coping flexibility. *Sex Roles, 56* (3-4), 159–172.

**Lambert, M. J.** (2001). The effectiveness of psychotherapy: What a century of research tells us about the effects of treatment. *Psychotherapeutically speaking–Updates from the Division of Psychotherapy* (29). Washington, DC: American Psychological Association.

**Lambert, M. J.** (2013). Outcome in psychotherapy: The past and important advances. *Psychotherapy, 50* (1), 42–51.

**Lanagan-Leitzel, L. K., & Diller, J. W.** (2018). Teaching psychological critical thinking using popular media. *Scholarship of Teaching and Learning in Psychology, 4* (2), 120–125. doi:10.1037/stl0000112

**Landau, K., & Rohmert, W.** (Eds.). (2017). *Recent developments in job analysis* (Vol. 24). London: Routledge.

**Landgraf, D., Long, J., Der-Avakian, A., Streets, M., & Welsh, D. K.** (2015). Dissociation of learned helplessness and fear conditioning in mice: A mouse model of depression. *PLoS One, 10* (4), e0125892.

**Landgraf, S., & von Treskow, I.** (2017). The seduction script: psychological and cultural norms of interpersonal approaches as markers for sexual aggression and abuse. *Frontiers in Psychology, 7,* 2070.

**Landis, C., & Erlick, D.** (1950). An analysis of the Porteus Maze Test as affected by psychosurgery. *American Journal of Psychology, 63* (4), 557–566.

**Landler, M.** (2012, January 30). From Biden, a vivid account of Bin Laden raid. *New York Times.* http://thecaucus.blogs.nytimes.com/2012/01/30/from-biden-a-vivid-account-of-bin-laden-decision/?_r=0 (accessed April 4, 2016)

**Lane, A., Mikolajczak, M., Treinen, E., Samson, D., Corneille, O., de Timary, P., & Luminet, O.** (2015). Failed replication of oxytocin effects on trust: The envelope task case. *PLoS One, 10* (9), e0137000. doi: 10.1371/journal.pone.0137000

**Lane, S. M., & Schooler, J. W.** (2004). Skimming the surface: Verbal overshadowing of analogical retrieval. *Psychological Science, 15* (11), 715–719.

**Laney, C., & Loftus, E. F.** (2009). Eyewitness memory. In R. N. Kocsis (Ed.), *Applied criminal psychology.* Springfield, IL: Thomas.

**Lange, C. G.** (1922). *The emotions.* Baltimore: Williams & Wilkins.

**Langer, E. J.** (1997). *The power of mindful learning.* Reading, MA: Addison-Wesley.

**Langer, E. J.** (2000). Mindful learning. *Current Directions in Psychological Science, 9* (6), 220–223.

**Langer, E. J.** (2005). *On becoming an artist.* New York: Ballantine.

**Langer, E., Blank, A., & Chanowitz, B.** (1978). The mindlessness of ostensibly thoughtful action: The role of "placebic" information in interpersonal interaction. *Journal of Personality and Social Psychology, 36* (6), 635–642.

**Langer, E. J., & Rodin, J.** (1976). The effects of choice and enhanced personal responsibility for the aged: A field experiment in an institutional setting. *Journal of Personality and Social Psychology, 34* (2), 191–198.

**Langer, J. J.** (1991). *Holocaust testimonies: The ruins of memory.* New Haven, CT: Yale University Press.

**Langlois, J. H., Roggman, L. A., & Musselman, L.** (1994). What is average and what is not average about attractive faces? *Psychological Science, 5* (4), 214–220.

**Långström, N., Rahman, Q., Carlström, E., & Lichtenstein, P.** (2010). Genetic and environmental effects on same-sex sexual behavior: A population study of twins in Sweden. *Archives of Sexual Behavior, 39* (1), 75–80.

**Laposa, J. M., Collimore, K. C., Hawley, L. L., & Rector, N. A.** (2015). Distress tolerance in OCD and anxiety disorders, and its relationship with anxiety sensitivity and intolerance of uncertainty. *Journal of Anxiety Disorders, 33,* 8–14.

**Lapsley, D. K.** (2018). *Moral psychology.* London: Routledge.

**Large, M., Myles, N., Myles, H., Corderoy, A., Weiser, M., Davidson, M., & Ryan, C. J.** (2018). Suicide risk assessment among psychiatric inpatients: A systematic review and meta-analysis of high-risk categories. *Psychological Medicine, 48* (7), 1119–1127.

**Larson, E. L., Murray, M. T., Cohen, B., Simpser, E., Pavia, M., Jackson, O., ... & Saiman, L.** (2018). Behavioral interventions to reduce infections in pediatric long-term care facilities: The Keep It Clean for Kids Trial. *Behavioral Medicine, 44* (2), 141–150.

**Larzabal, C., Tramoni, E., Muratot, S., Thorpe, S. J., & Barbeau, E. J.** (2018). Extremely long-term memory and familiarity after 12 years. *Cognition, 170,* 254–262.

**Larzelere, R. E., Gunnoe, M. L., & Ferguson, C. J.** (2018). Improving causal inferences in meta-analyses of longitudinal studies: Spanking as an illustration. *Child Development.* doi: 10.1111/cdev.13097

**Lashley, K.** (1950). In search of the engram. In *Symposium of the Society for Experimental Biology* (vol. 4). New York: Cambridge University Press.

**Laska, K. M., Gurman, A. S., & Wampold, B. E.** (2014). Expanding the lens of evidence-based practice in psychotherapy: A common factors perspective. *Psychotherapy, 51* (4), 467–481.

**Latham, G. P.** (2019). Perspectives of a practitioner-scientist on organizational psychology/organizational behavior. *Annual Review of Organizational Psychology and Organizational Behavior, 6,* 1–16.

**Latorre, D., Kallweit, U., Armentani, E., Foglierini, M., Mele, F., Cassotta, A., ... & Becher, B.** (2018). T cells in patients with narcolepsy target self-antigens of hypocretin neurons. *Nature, 562,* 63–68.

**Latzman, R. D., Boysen, S. T., & Schapiro, S. J.** (2018). Neuroanatomical correlates of hierarchical personality traits in chimpanzees: Associations with limbic structures. *Personality Neuroscience, 1.*

**Laughlin, C. D.** (2015). Neuroarchaeology. *Time and Mind, 8* (4), 335–349.

**Lavagnino, L., Mwangi, B., Cao, B., Shott, M. E., Soares, J. C., & Frank, G. K.** (2018). Cortical thickness patterns as state biomarker of anorexia nervosa. *International Journal of Eating Disorders, 51* (3), 241–249.

**Lavezzi, A. M., Ottaviani, G., & Matturri, L.** (2015). Developmental alterations of the auditory brainstem centers—Pathogenetic implications in Sudden Infant Death Syndrome. *Journal of the Neurological Sciences, 357* (1-2), 257–263.

**Lavi, K., Jacobson, G. A., Rosenblum, K., & Lüthi, A.** (2018). Encoding of conditioned taste aversion in cortico-amygdala circuits. *Cell Reports, 24* (2), 278–283.

**Lawson, G. M., Hook, C. J., & Farah, M. J.** (2018). A meta-analysis of the relationship between socioeconomic status and executive function performance among children. *Developmental Science, 21* (2), e12529.

**Layland, E. K., Hill, B. J., & Nelson, L. J.** (2018). Freedom to explore the self: How emerging adults use leisure to develop identity. *The Journal of Positive Psychology, 13* (1), 78–91.

**Layton, T. J., Barnett, M. L., Hicks, T. R. & Jena, A. B.** (2018). Attention-deficit/hyperactivity disorder and month of school enrollment. *New England Journal of Medicine, 379,* 2122–2130

**Lazarus, A. A., Beutler, L. E., & Norcross, J. C.** (1992). The future of technical eclecticism. *Psychotherapy, 29* (1), 11–20.

**Lazarus, R. S.** (1991). On the primacy of cognition. *American Psychologist, 39* (2), 124–129.

**Lazarus, R. S.** (1993). Coping theory and research: Past, present, and future. *Psychosomatic Medicine, 55* (3), 234–247.

**Lazarus, R. S.** (2000). Toward better research on stress and coping. *American Psychologist, 55* (6), 665–673.

**Lazarus, R. S.** (2003). Does the positive psychology movement have legs? *Psychological Inquiry, 14,* 93–109.

**Le Bihan, D.** (2016). *Looking inside the brain: The power of neuroimaging.* (T. Lavender Fagan, trans.). Princeton, NJ: Princeton University Press.

**Le Grange, D.** (2016). Elusive etiology of anorexia nervosa: Finding answers in an integrative biopsychosocial approach. *Journal of the American*

*Academy of Child and Adolescent Psychiatry, 55* (1), 12–13.

**Le Texier, T.** (2018). *Histoire d'un mensonge. Enquête sur l'expérience de Stanford.* Paris: Zones (published in French).

**Le, C. P., Nowell, C. J., Kim-Fuchs, C., Botteri, E., Hiller, J. G., Hilmy, I., ... & Sloan, E. K.** (2016). Chronic stress in mice remodels lymph vasculature to promote tumour cell dissemination. *Nature Communications, 7,* 10634.

**Leamy, M., Clarke, E., Le Boutillier, C., Bird, V., Choudhury, R., MacPherson, R., ... & Slade, M..** (2016). Recovery practice in community mental health teams: National survey. *British Journal of Psychiatry, 209* (4), 340–346.

**Leaper, C.** (2013). Gender development. In P. D. Zelazo (Ed.), *The Oxford handbook of developmental psychology* (vol. 2, pp. 326–377). New York: Oxford University Press.

**Leasure, J. L., & Decker, L.** (2009). Social isolation prevents exercise-induced proliferation of hippocampal progenitor cells in female rats. *Hippocampus, 19* (10), 907–912.

**Lebel, C., & Deoni, S.** (2018). The development of brain white matter microstructure. *NeuroImage, 182,* 207–218.

**Lebow, J. L.** (2016). Editorial: Family research and the practice of family therapy. *Family Process, 55* (1), 3–6.

**Lechinger, J., Heib, D. P. J., Gruber, W., Schabus, M., & Klimesch, W.** (2015). Heartbeat-related EEG amplitude and phase modulations from wakefulness to deep sleep: Interactions with sleep spindles and slow oscillations. *Psychophysiology, 52* (11), 1441–1450.

**LeDoux, J. E.** (2009). Emotional coloration of consciousness: How feelings come about. In L. W. Weiskrantz & M. Davis (Eds.), *Frontiers of consciousness.* New York: Oxford University Press.

**LeDoux, J. E.** (2012). Evolution of human emotion: A view through fear. *Progress in Brain Research, 195,* 431–442.

**LeDoux, J. E.** (2013). The slippery slope of fear. *Trends in Cognitive Science, 17* (4), 155–156.

**LeDoux, J., & Daw, N. D.** (2018). Surviving threats: Neural circuit and computational implications of a new taxonomy of defensive behaviour. *Nature Reviews Neuroscience, 19,* 269–282.

**Lee, A. H., & DiGiuseppe, R.** (2018). Anger and aggression treatments: a review of meta-analyses. *Current Opinion in Psychology, 19,* 65–74.

**Lee, B.** (2018). Toward an integrative applied positive psychology. In N. L. Brown, T. Lomas, & F. J. Eiroa-Orosa (Eds.), *The Routledge international handbook of critical positive psychology* (pp. 337–350). New York: Routledge/Taylor & Francis Group.

**Lee, J.** (2018). Passive leadership and sexual harassment: Roles of observed hostility and workplace gender ratio. *Personnel Review, 47* (3), 594–612.

**Lee, J. C., Hall, D. L., & Wood, W.** (2018). Experiential or material purchases? Social class determines purchase happiness. *Psychological Science, 29.* doi: 10.1177/0956797617736386

**Lee, K., Quinn, P. C., Pascalis, O., & Slater, A.** (2013b). Development of face-processing ability in children. In P. D. Zelazo (Ed.), *The Oxford handbook of developmental psychology* (vol. 1, pp. 338–370). New York: Oxford University Press.

**Lee, M. R., Ellingson, J. M., & Sher, K. J.** (2015). Integrating social-contextual and intrapersonal mechanisms of "maturing out": Joint influences of familial-role transitions and personality maturation on problem-drinking reductions. *Alcoholism: Clinical and Experimental Research, 39* (9), 1775–1787.

**Lee, S., Choi, S., & Matejkowski, J.** (2013). Comparison of major depressive disorder onset among foreign-born Asian Americans: Chinese, Filipino, and Vietnamese ethnic groups. *Psychiatry Research, 210* (1), 315–322.

**Lee, T. T., Graham, J. R., & Arbisi, P. A.** (2018). The utility of MMPI-2-RF scale scores in the differential diagnosis of schizophrenia and major depressive disorder. *Journal of Personality Assessment, 100* (3), 305–312.

**Lee, T. Y., Kim, M., Lee, J., & Kwon, J. S.** (2018). T223. Real world effectiveness of antipsychotic drugs in patients with schizophrenia: A 10-years retrospective study. *Schizophrenia Bulletin, 44* (Suppl. 1), S203.

**Legate, N., Ryan, R. M., & Weinstein, N.** (2012). Is coming out always a "good thing"? Exploring the relations of autonomy support, outness, and wellness for lesbian, gay, and bisexual individuals. *Social Psychological and Personality Science, 3* (2), 145–152.

**Leibold, N. K., van den Hove, D. L. A., Esquivel, G., De Cort, K., Goossens, L., Strackx, E., ... & Schruers, K. R. J.** (2015). The brain acid–base homeostasis and serotonin: A perspective on the use of carbon dioxide as human and rodent experimental model of panic. *Progress in Neurobiology, 129,* 58–78.

**Leiter, M. P., Day, A., & Price, L.** (2015). Attachment styles at work: Measurement, collegial relationships, and burnout. *Burnout Research, 2* (1), 25–35.

**Lemmens, L. H. J. M., Arntz, A., Peeters, F. P. M. L., Hollon, S. D., Roefs, A., & Huibers, M. J. H.** (2015). Clinical effectiveness of cognitive therapy v. interpersonal psychotherapy for depression: Results of a randomized controlled trial. *Psychological Medicine, 45* (10), 2095–2110.

**Lemmer, G., & Wagner, U.** (2015). Can we really reduce ethnic prejudice outside the lab? A meta-analysis of direct and indirect contact interventions. *European Journal of Social Psychology, 45* (2), 152–168.

**Lemmon, G., & Wayne, S. J.** (2015). Underlying motives of organizational citizenship behavior: Comparing egoistic and altruistic motivations. *Journal of Leadership and Organizational Studies, 22* (2), 129–148.

**Lenneberg, E. H., Rebelsky, F. G., & Nichols, I. A.** (1965). The vocalization of infants born to deaf and hearing parents. *Human Development, 8,* 23–37.

**Leo, I., Angeli, V., Lunghi, M., Dalla Barba, B., & Simion, F.** (2018). Newborns' face recognition: The role of facial movement. *Infancy, 23* (1), 45–60.

**Lepore, S. J., & Smyth, J. (Eds.).** (2002). *The writing cure.* Washington, DC: American Psychological Association.

**Lerner, B. H.** (2005). Last-ditch medical therapy—Revisiting lobotomy. *New England Journal of Medicine, 353* (2), 119–121.

**Lerner, J. V., Bowers, E. P., Minor, K., Boyd, M. J., Kiely Mueller, M., Schmid, K. L., ... & Lerner, R. M.** (2013). Positive youth development: Processes, philosophies, and programs. In R. M. Lerner, M. A. Easterbrooks, J. Mistry, & I. B. Weiner (Eds.), *Handbook of psychology* (2nd ed., vol. 6, pp. 365–392). Hoboken, NJ: Wiley.

**Leslie, L. M., Snyder, M., & Glomb, T. M.** (2013). Who gives? Multilevel effects of gender and ethnicity on workplace charitable giving. *Journal of Applied Psychology, 98* (1), 49–62.

**Leung, A. K., Maddux, W. W., Galinsky, A. D., & Chiu, C.** (2008). Multicultural experience enhances creativity. *American Psychologist, 63* (3), 169–181.

**Leung, R. C., Pang, E. W., Anagnostou, E., & Taylor, M. J.** (2018). Young adults with autism spectrum disorder show early atypical neural activity during emotional face processing. *Frontiers in Human Neuroscience, 12,* 57.

**Lev, A. I.** (2007). Transgender communities: Developing identity through connection. In K. J. Bieschke, R. M. Perez, & K. A. DeBord (Eds.), *Handbook of counseling and psychotherapy with lesbian, gay, bisexual, and transgender clients* (2nd ed., pp. 147–175). Washington, DC: American Psychological Association.

**Levelink, B., Feron, F. J., Dompeling, E., & van Zeben-van de Aa, D. M.** (2018). Children with ADHD symptoms: Who can do without specialized mental health care? *Journal of Attention Disorders.* doi: 10.1177/1087054718756194

**Levi, O., Shoval-Zuckerman, Y., Fruchter, E., Bibi, A., Bar-Haim, Y. and Wald, I.** (2017), Benefits of a psychodynamic group therapy (PGT) model for treating veterans with PTSD. *Journal of Clinical Psychology, 73,* 1247–1258.

**Levine, F. M., & De Simone, L. L.** (1991). The effects of experimenter gender on pain report in male and female subjects. *Pain, 44* (1), 69–72.

**Levine, S. C., Huttenlocher, J., Taylor, A., & Langrock, A.** (1999). Early sex differences in spatial skill. *Developmental Psychology, 35* (4), 940–949.

**Levy, B. R., Slade, M. D., Kunkel, S. R., & Kasl, S. V.** (2002). Increased longevity by positive self-perceptions of aging. *Journal of Personality and Social Psychology, 83* (2), 261–270.

**Lewis, D. M. G., Al-Shawaf, L., Conroy-Beam, D., Asao, K., & Buss, D. M.** (2017). Evolutionary psychology: A how-to guide. *American Psychologist, 72* (4), 353–373. doi: 10.1037/a0040409

**Lewis, G. J., Dickie, D. A., Cox, S. R., Karama, S., Evans, A. C., Starr, J. M., ... & Deary, I. J.** (2018). Widespread associations between trait conscientiousness and thickness of brain cortical regions. *NeuroImage, 176,* 22–28.

**Lewis, J. D., Evans, A. C., Pruett, J. R., Jr, Botteron, J. N., McKinstry, R. C., Zwaigenbaum, L., .... & Piven, J.** (2017). Infant Brain Imaging Study Network. The emergence of network inefficiencies in infants with autism spectrum disorder. *Biological Psychiatry, 82,* 176–185.

**Lewis, N. A., Jr., & Earl, A.** (2018). Seeing more and eating less: Effects of portion size granularity on the perception and regulation of food consumption. *Journal of Personality and Social Psychology, 114* (5), 786–803. doi: 10.1037/pspp0000183.supp (Supplemental)

**Lewis, V. A., MacGregor, C. A., & Putnam, R. D.** (2013). Religion, networks, and neighborliness: The impact of religious social networks on civic engagement. *Social Science Research, 42* (2), 331–346.

**Lewkowicz, D. J., & Hansen-Tift, A. M.** (2012). Infants deploy selective attention to the mouth of a talking face when learning speech. *Proceedings of the National Academy of Sciences USA, 109* (5), 1431–1436.

**Li, N. P., van Vugt, M., & Colarelli, S. M.** (2018). The evolutionary mismatch hypothesis: Implications for psychological science. *Current Directions in Psychological Science, 27* (1), 38–44.

**Li, Y. I., Starr, L. R., & Wray-Lake, L.** (2018). Insomnia mediates the longitudinal relationship between anxiety and depressive symptoms in a nationally representative sample of adolescents. *Depression and Anxiety, 35* (6), 583–591.

**Liang, B., Williams, L. M., & Siegel, J. A.** (2006). Relational outcomes of childhood sexual trauma in female survivors: A longitudinal study. *Journal of Interpersonal Violence, 21* (1), 42–57.

**Liang, C. S., Chung, C. H., Ho, P. S., Tsai, C. K., & Chien, W. C.** (2018). Superior anti-suicidal effects of electroconvulsive therapy in unipolar disorder and bipolar depression. *Bipolar Disorders, 20* (6), 539–546.

**Lichtstein, D., Ilani, A., Rosen, H., Horesh, N., Singh, S., Buzaglo, N., & Hodes, A.** (2018). Na+, K+-ATPase signaling and bipolar disorder. *International Journal of Molecular Sciences, 19* (8), 2314.

**Lieberman, R., Kranzler, H. R., Levine, E. S., & Covault, J.** (2018). Examining the effects of alcohol on GABAA receptor mRNA expression and function in neural cultures generated from control and alcohol dependent donor induced pluripotent stem cells. *Alcohol, 66,* 45–53.

**Lieblich, A.** (2018). The contribution of narrative approach to post-traumatic growth. *Journal of Applied Arts and Health, 9* (2), 253–262.

**Lievens, F., Lang, J. W., De Fruyt, F., Corstjens, J., Van de Vijver, M., & Bledow, R.** (2018). The predictive power of people's intraindividual variability across situations: Implementing whole trait theory in assessment. *Journal of Applied Psychology, 103,* 753–771.

**Lilienfeld, S. O., Wood, J. M., & Garb, H. N.** (2000). The scientific status of projective techniques. *Psychological Science in the Public Interest, 1* (2), 27–66.

**Lim, M. H., Gleeson, J. F., Alvarez-Jimenez, M., & Penn, D. L.** (2018). Loneliness in psychosis: A systematic review. *Social Psychiatry and Psychiatric Epidemiology, 53,* 221–238.

**Lin, C., Adolphs, R., & Alvarez, R. M.** (2018). Inferring whether officials are corruptible from looking at their faces. *Psychological Science.* doi: 10.1177/0956797618788882

**Lin, C. L., Liu, T. C., Chung, C. H., & Chien, W. C.** (2018). Risk of pneumonia in patients with insomnia: A nationwide population-based retrospective cohort study. *Journal of Infection and Public Health, 11* (2), 270–274.

**Lin, H.-Y., Huang, C.-K., Tai, C.-M., Lin, H.-Y., Kao, Y.-H., Tsai, C.-C., ... & Yen, Y.-C.** (2013). Psychiatric disorders of patients seeking obesity treatment. *BMC Psychiatry, 13* (1), 1–8.

**Lin, P., Li, L., Wang, Y., Zhao, Z., Liu, G., Chen, W., ... & Gao, X.** (2018). Type D personality, but not Type A behavior pattern, is associated with coronary plaque vulnerability. *Psychology, Health & Medicine, 23* (2), 216–223.

**Lin, Y. T., Seo, J., Gao, F., Feldman, H. M., Wen, H. L., Penney, J., ... & Rueda, R.** (2018). APOE4 causes widespread molecular and cellular alterations associated with Alzheimer's disease phenotypes in human iPSC-derived brain cell types. *Neuron, 98,* 1141–1154.e7.

**Linden, W., Lenz, J. W., & Con, A. H.** (2001). Individualized stress management for primary hypertension: A randomized trial. *Archives of Internal Medicine, 161* (8), 1071–1080.

**Lindenberger, U., von Oertzen, T., Ghisletta, P., & Hertzogg, C.** (2011). Cross-sectional age variance extraction: What's change got to do with it? *Psychology and Aging, 26* (1), 34–47.

**Lindwall, M., Cimino, C. R., Gibbons, L. E., Mitchell, M. B., Benitez, A., Brown, C. L., ... & Piccinin, A. M.** (2012). Dynamic associations of change in physical activity and change in cognitive function: Coordinated analyses across four studies with up to 21 years of longitudinal data. *Journal of Aging Research.* doi: 10.1155/2012/493598

**Linebaugh, G., & Roche, T. B.** (2015). Evidence that L2 production training can enhance perception. *Journal of Academic Language and Learning, 9* (1), A1–A17.

**Linehan, M. M.** (2018). Cognitive-behavioral *treatment of borderline personality disorder.* New York: Guilford.

**Linke, S. E., Rutledge, T., Johnson, B. D., Vaccarino, V., Bittner, V., Cornell, C. E., ... & Merz, C. N. B.** (2009). Depressive symptom dimensions and cardiovascular prognosis among women with suspected myocardial ischemia: A report from the NHLBI-sponsored WISE study. *Archives of General Psychiatry, 66* (5), 499–507.

**Linnman, C., Zeidan, M. A., Furtak, S. C., Pitman, R. K., Quirk, G. J., & Milad, M. R.** (2012). Resting amygdala and medial prefrontal metabolism predicts functional activation of the fear extinction circuit. *American Journal of Psychiatry, 169* (4), 415–423.

**Linster, C.** (2018). Cellular and network processes of noradrenergic modulation in the olfactory system. *Brain Research.* doi: 10.1016/j.brainres.2018.03.008

**Lipford, M. C., Ramar, K., Liang, Y. J., Lin, C. W., Chao, Y. T., An, J., ... & Chiang, R. P.** (2015). Serotonin as a possible biomarker in obstructive sleep apnea. *Sleep Medicine Reviews, 28,* 121–128.

**Lipnevich, A. A., Credè, M., Hahn, E., Spinath, F. M., Roberts, R. D., & Preckel, F.** (2017). How distinctive are morningness and eveningness from the Big Five factors of personality? A meta-analytic investigation. *Journal of Personality and Social Psychology, 112* (3), 491–509. doi:10.1037/pspp0000099

**Lippa, R.** (2000). Gender-related traits in gay men, lesbian women, and heterosexual men and women: The virtual identity of homosexual-heterosexual diagnosticity and gender diagnosticity. *Journal of Personality, 68* (5), 899–926.

**Lippa, R.** (2008). The relation between childhood gender nonconformity and adult masculinity-femininity and anxiety in heterosexual and homosexual men and women. *Sex Roles, 59* (9–10), 684–693.

**Lippa, R. A.** (2013). Men and women with bisexual identities show bisexual patterns of sexual attraction to male and female "swimsuit models." *Archives of Sexual Behavior, 42* (2), 187–196.

**Liszkowski, U., Schäffer, M., Carpenter, M., & Tomasello, M.** (2009). Prelinguistic infants, but not chimpanzees, communicate about absent entities. *Psychological Science, 20* (5), 654–660.

**Littell, J. H., & Girvin, H.** (2002). Stages of change: A critique. *Behavior Modification, 26* (2), 223–273.

**Litterer, J.** (2018). *The emergence of systematic management as shown by the literature of management from 1870–1900.* London: Routledge.

**Little, K. Y., Zhang, L., & Cook, E.** (2006). Fluoxetine-induced alterations in human platelet serotonin transporter expression: Serotonin transporter polymorphism effects. *Psychiatry and Neuroscience, 31* (5), 333–339.

**Little, L. M., Dean, E., Tomchek, S., & Dunn, W.** (2018). Sensory processing patterns in autism, attention deficit hyperactivity disorder, and typical development. *Physical & Occupational Therapy in Pediatrics, 38* (3), 243–254.

**Liu, B., Tang, T. L. P., & Yang, K.** (2015). When does public service motivation fuel the job satisfaction fire? The joint moderation of person–organization fit and needs–supplies fit. *Public Management Review, 17* (6), 876–900.

**Liu, C. Y., Huang, W. L., Kao, W. C., & Gau, S. S. F.** (2017). Influence of disruptive behavior disorders on academic performance and school functions of youths with attention-deficit/hyperactivity disorder. *Child Psychiatry & Human Development, 48,* 870–880.

**Liu, D., Costanzo, A., Evans, M. D., Archer, N. S., Nowson, C., Duesing, K., & Keast, R.** (2018). Expression of the candidate fat taste receptors in human fungiform papillae and the association with fat taste function. *British Journal of Nutrition, 120* (1), 64–73.

**Liu, P., Chan, D., Qiu, L., Tov, W., & Tong, V. J. C.** (2018). Effects of cultural tightness–looseness and social network density on expression of positive and negative emotions: A large-scale study of impression management by Facebook users. *Personality and Social Psychology Bulletin,* doi: 10.1177/0146167218770999

**Livesly, W. J., & Larstone, R.** (Eds.). (2018) *Handbook of personality disorders: Theory, research, and treatment,* (2nd ed.). New York: Guilford.

**Llewellyn, S., & Hobson, J. A.** (2015). Not only... but also: REM sleep creates and NREM Stage 2 instantiates landmark junctions in cortical memory networks. *Neurobiology of Learning and Memory, 122,* 69–87.

**Lo Sauro, C., Ravaldi, C., Cabras, P. L., Faravelli, C., & Ricca, V.** (2008). Stress, hypothalamic-pituitary-adrenal axis, and eating disorders. *Neuropsychobiology, 57* (3), 95–115.

**Lo, J. C., Lee, S. M., Lee, X. K., Sasmita, K., Chee, N. I., Tandi, J., ... & Chee, M. W.** (2018). Sustained benefits of delaying school start time on adolescent sleep and well-being. *Sleep, 41* (6), zsy052.

**Loehlin, J. C., & Martin, N. G.** (2018). Personality types: A twin study. *Personality and Individual Differences, 122,* 99–103.

**Loflin, D. C., & Barry, C. T.** (2016). "You can't sit with us": Gender and the differential roles of social intelligence and peer status in adolescent relational aggression. *Personality and Individual Differences, 91,* 22–26.

**Loftus, E. F.** (1975). Leading questions and the eyewitness report. *Cognitive Psychology, 7,* 560–572.

**Loftus, E. F.** (1993). Psychologists in the eyewitness world. *American Psychologist, 48* (5), 550–552.

**Logue, M. W., van Rooij, S. J., Dennis, E. L., Davis, S. L., Hayes, J. P., Stevens, J. S., ... & Korgaonkar, M.** (2018). Smaller hippocampal volume in posttraumatic stress disorder: A multisite ENIGMA-PGC study: Subcortical volumetry results from posttraumatic stress disorder consortia. *Biological Psychiatry, 83* (3), 244–253.

**Lohnas, L. J., Duncan, K., Doyle, W. K., Thesen, T., Devinsky, O., & Davachi, L.** (2018). Time-resolved neural reinstatement and pattern separation during memory decisions in human hippocampus. *Proceedings of the National Academy of Sciences, 115* (31), E7418–E7427.

**Lois, B. H., & Miller, A. L.** (2018). Stopping the nonadherence cycle: The clinical and theoretical basis for dialectical behavior therapy adapted for adolescents with chronic medical illness (DBT-CMI). *Cognitive and Behavioral Practice, 25* (1), 32–43.

**Lokensgard, K. H.** (2014). Blackfoot nation. In D. A. Leeming (Ed.), *Encyclopedia of psychology and religion.* Cham: Springer.

**Lombardo, M., Villari, V., Micali, N., Roy, P., Sousa, S. H., & Lombardo, G.** (2018). Assessment of trans-scleral iontophoresis delivery of lutein to the human retina. *Journal of Biophotonics, 11* (3), e201870132.

**Lømo, T.** (2018). Discovering long-term potentiation (ltp)–recollections and reflections on what came after. *Acta Physiologica, 222*(2), e12921.

**Long, E. C., Aggen, S. H., Gardner, C., & Kendler, K. S.** (2015). Differential parenting and risk for psychopathology: A monozygotic twin difference approach. *Social Psychiatry and Psychiatric Epidemiology, 50* (10), 1569–1576.

**Lopes, A. T., de Aguiar, E., De Souza, A. F., & Oliveira-Santos, T.** (2017). Facial expression recognition with convolutional neural networks: Coping with few data and the training sample order. *Pattern Recognition, 61,* 610–628.

**Lopez, R., Barateau, L., Evangelista, E., & Dauvilliers, Y.** (2017). Depression and hypersomnia: A complex association. *Sleep Medicine Clinics, 12* (3), 395–405.

**Lorant, V., Croux, C., Weich, S., Deliege, D., Mackenbach, J., & Ansseau, M.** (2007). Depression and socioeconomic risk factors: 7-year longitudinal population study. *British Journal of Psychiatry, 190* (4), 293–298.

**Lorenz, K. Z.** (1965). *Evolution and the modification of behavior.* Chicago: University of Chicago Press.

**Loring-Meier, S., & Halpern, D. F.** (1999). Sex differences in visual-spatial working memory: Components of cognitive processing. *Psychonomic Bulletin and Review, 6* (3), 464–471.

**Lovell, B., & Gaszka, S.** (2018). Problem-focused coping mediates the effect of subclinical trauma symptoms in returning service members on psychological distress in their civilian partners. *Traumatology.* doi: 10.1037/trm0000150

**Low, C. A., Stanton, A., & Danoff-Burg, S.** (2006). Expressive disclosure and benefit finding among breast cancer patients: Mechanisms for positive health effects. *Health Psychology, 25,* 181–189.

**Löwenkamp, C., Gärtner, W., Haus, I. D., & Franz, V. H.** (2015). Semantic grasping escapes Weber's law. *Neuropsychologia, 70,* 235–245.

**Lowery-Gionta, E. G., DiBerto, J., Mazzone, C. M., & Kash, T. L.** (2018). GABA neurons of the ventral periaqueductal gray area modulate behaviors associated with anxiety and conditioned fear. *Brain Structure and Function,* 223, 3787–3799.

**Lu, H., Li, Y., Chen, M., Kim, H., & Serikawa, S.** (2018). Brain intelligence: Go beyond artificial intelligence. *Mobile Networks and Applications, 23* (2), 368–375.

**Lu, J., Sherman, D., Devor, M., & Saper, C. B.** (2006). A putative flip-flop switch for control of REM sleep. *Nature, 441,* 589–594.

**Lu, L., Lu, A. C. C., Gursoy, D., & Neale, N. R.** (2016). Work engagement, job satisfaction, and turnover intentions: A comparison between supervisors and line-level employees. *International Journal of Contemporary Hospitality Management, 28* (4), 737–761.

**Lu, Q., Gallagher, M. W., Loh, A., & Young, L.** (2018). Expressive writing intervention improves quality of life among Chinese-American breast cancer survivors: A randomized controlled trial. *Annals of Behavioral Medicine.* doi: 10.1093/abm/kax067

**Lubinski, D., Benbow, C. P., & Kell, H. J.** (2014). Life paths and accomplishments of mathematically precocious males and females four decades later. *Psychological Science, 25,* 2217–2232.

**Lubinski, D., Benbow, C. P., Webb, R. M., & Bleske-Rechek, A.** (2006). Tracking exceptional human capital over two decades. *Psychological Science, 17* (3), 194–199.

**Lubinski, D., Webb, R. M., Morelock, M. J., & Benbow, C. P.** (2001). Top 1 in 10,000: A 10-year follow-up of the profoundly gifted. *Journal of Applied Psychology, 86* (4), 718–729.

**Luborsky, L., Rosenthal, R., Diguer, L., Andrusyna, T. P., Berman, J. S., Levitt, J. T., Seligman, D. A., & Krause, E. D.** (2002). The dodo bird verdict is alive and well—mostly. *Clinical Psychology: Science and Practice, 9* (1), 2–12.

**Lucas, J. W., & Phelan, J. C.** (2018). Influence and social distance consequences across categories of race and mental illness. *Society and Mental Health.* doi: 10.1177/2156869318761125 (in press)

**Lucas, R. E.** (2007). Extraversion. In R. Baumeister & K. Vohs (Eds.), *The encyclopedia of social psychology.* Thousand Oaks, CA: Sage.

**Lucas, R. E.** (2008). Personality and subjective well-being. In M. Eid & R. J. Larsen (Eds.), *The science of subjective well-being* (pp. 171–194). New York: Psychology Press.

**Lucas, R. E., Clark, A. E., Georgellis, Y., & Diener, E.** (2004). Unemployment alters the set-point for life satisfaction. *Psychological Science, 15* (1), 8–13.

**Luciano, M., Gow, A. J., Pattie, A., Bates, T. C., & Deary, I. J.** (2018). The influence of dyslexia candidate genes on reading skill in old age. *Behavior Genetics, 48* (5), 351–360.

**Ludwikowski, W. M., Armstrong, P. I., & Lannin, D. G.** (2018). Explaining gender differences in interests: The roles of instrumentality and expressiveness. *Journal of Career Assessment, 26* (2), 240–257.

**Lueken, U., Krushwitz, J. D., Muehlhan, M., Siegert, J., Hoyer, J., & Wittchen, H.-U.** (2011). How specific is specific phobia? Different neural response patterns in two subtypes of specific phobia. *NeuroImage, 56* (1), 363–372.

**Luhmann, M., Hofmann, W., Eid, M., & Lucas, R. E.** (2012). Subjective well-being and adaptation to life events: A meta-analysis. *Journal of Personality and Social Psychology, 102* (3), 592–615.

**Lumma, A. L., Kok, B. E., & Singer, T.** (2015). Is meditation always relaxing? Investigating heart rate, heart rate variability, experienced effort and likeability during training of three types of meditation. *International Journal of Psychophysiology, 97* (1), 38–45.

**Lund, C.** (2015). Poverty, inequality and mental health in low- and middle-income countries: Time to expand the research and policy agendas. *Epidemiology and Psychiatric Sciences, 24* (2), 97–99.

**Lund, H. G., Reider, B. D., Whiting, A. B., & Prichard, J. R.** (2010). Sleep patterns and predictors of disturbed sleep in a large population of college students. *Journal of Adolescent Health, 46* (2), 124–132.

**Luo, Y., & Baillargeon, R.** (2005). Can a self-propelled box have a goal? Psychological reasoning in 5-month-old infants. *Psychological Science, 16* (8), 601–608.

**Luoto, S., Krams, I., & Rantala, M. J.** (2018). A life history approach to the female sexual orientation spectrum: Evolution, development, causal mechanisms, and health. *Archives of Sexual Behavior,* 1–36.

**Luszczynska, A., Horodyska, K., Zarychta, K., Liszewska, N., Knoll, N., & Scholz, U.** (2016). Planning and self-efficacy interventions encouraging replacing energy-dense foods intake with fruit and vegetable: A longitudinal experimental study. *Psychology and Health, 31* (1), 40–64.

**Luyten, P., & Fonagy, P.** (2016). An integrative, attachment-based approach to the management and treatment of patients with persistent somatic complaints. In J. Hunter & R. Maunder (Eds.), *Improving patient treatment with attachment theory* (pp. 127–144). Switzerland: Springer International Publishing.

**Lykken, D.** (1999). *Happiness: What studies on twins show us about nature, nurture, and the happiness set-point.* New York: Golden Books.

**Lynam, D. R., Caspi, A., Moffitt, T. E., Loeber, R., & Stouthamer-Loeber, M.** (2007). Longitudinal evidence that psychopathy scores in early adolescence predict adult psychopathy. *Journal of Abnormal Psychology, 116* (1), 155–165.

**Lynn, S. J., Green, J. P., Kirsch, I., Capafons, A., Lilienfeld, S. O., Laurence, J. R., & Montgomery, G. H.** (2015). Grounding hypnosis in science: The "new" APA Division 30 definition of hypnosis as a step backward. *American Journal of Clinical Hypnosis, 57* (4), 390–401.

**Lynn, S. J., Laurence, J.-R., & Kirsch, I.** (2015). Hypnosis, suggestion, and suggestibility: An integrative model. *American Journal of Clinical Hypnosis, 57* (3), 314–329.

**Lyubomirsky, S.** (2008). *The how of happiness: A scientific approach to getting the life you want.* New York: Penguin.

**Lyubomirsky, S.** (2011). *The way to happiness: Action plan for a happy life.* Yehuda, Israel: Kinneret.

**Lyubomirsky, S.** (2013). *The myth of happiness.* New York: Penguin.

**Lyubomirsky, S., Boehm, J. K., Kasri, F., & Zehm, K.** (2011a). The cognitive and hedonic costs of dwelling on achievement-related negative experiences: Implications for enduring happiness and unhappiness. *Emotion, 11* (5), 1152–1167.

**Lyubomirsky, S., Dickerhoof, R., Boehm, J. K., & Sheldon, K. M.** (2011b). Becoming happier takes both a will and a proper way: An experimental longitudinal intervention to boost well-being. *Emotion, 11* (2), 391–402.

# M

**Ma, F., Heyman, G. D., Jing, C., Fu, Y., Compton, B. J., Xu, F., & Lee, K.** (2018). Promoting honesty in young children through observational learning. *Journal of Experimental Child Psychology, 167,* 234–245.

**Ma, Y., Shamay-Tsoory, S., Han, S., & Zink, C. F.** (2016). Oxytocin and social adaptation: Insights from neuroimaging studies of healthy and clinical populations. *Trends in Cognitive Sciences, 20* (2), 133–145.

**Maas, M. K., McDaniel, B. T., Feinberg, M. E., & Jones, D. E.** (2018). Division of labor and multiple domains of sexual satisfaction among first-time parents. *Journal of Family Issues, 39* (1), 104–127.

**Maccoby, E. E.** (2002). Gender and group process: A developmental perspective. *Current Directions in Psychological Science, 11,* 54–58.

**Macdonald, J. S. P., & Lavie, N.** (2008). Load induced blindness. *Journal of Experimental Psychology: Human Perception and Performance, 34* (5), 1078–1091.

**MacIntosh, H., Reissing, E. D., & Andruff, H.** (2010). Same-sex marriage in Canada: The impact of legal marriage on the first cohort of gay and lesbian Canadians to wed. *Canadian Journal of Human Sexuality, 19* (3), 79–90.

**Mack, M. L., & Preston, A. R.** (2016). Decisions about the past are guided by reinstatement of specific memories in the hippocampus and perirhinal cortex. *NeuroImage, 127,* 144–157.

**MacKay, K., & Quigley, M.** (2018). Exacerbating inequalities? Health policy and the behavioural sciences. *Health Care Analysis, 26,* 380–397.

**Mackintosh, N. J.** (2018). Cognitive or associative theories of conditioning: Implications of an analysis of blocking. In S. H. Hulse, H. Fowler, & W. K. Honig (Eds.), *Cognitive processes in animal behavior* (pp. 155–175). London: Routledge.

**Macleod, A., Busija, L., & McCabe, M.** (2018). Understanding sexuality in later life: Presenting a new conceptual model to define the sexual experience of older adults. *The American Journal of Geriatric Psychiatry, 26* (3), S124.

**MacPherson, H. A., Weinstein, S. M., & West, A. E.** (2018). Non-suicidal self-injury in pediatric bipolar disorder: Clinical correlates and impact on psychosocial treatment outcomes. *Journal of Abnormal Child Psychology, 46* (4), 857–870.

**Maddi, S.** (1998). Hardiness. In H. S. Friedman (Ed.), *Encyclopedia of mental health* (vol. 3). San Diego: Academic.

**Maddi, S. R., Matthews, M. D., Kelly, D. R., Villarreal, B. J., Gundersen, K. K., & Savino, S. C.** (2017). The continuing role of hardiness and grit on performance and retention in West Point cadets. *Military Psychology, 29* (5), 355–358. doi: 10.1037/mil0000145

**Maddux, W. W., & Galinsky, A. D.** (2009). Cultural borders and mental barriers: The relationship between living abroad and creativity. *Journal of Personality and Social Psychology, 96* (5), 1047–1061. https://doi.org/10.1037/a0014861

**Madhyastha, T. M., Hamaker, E. L., & Gottman, J. M.** (2011). Investigating spousal influence using moment-to-moment affect data from marital conflict. *Journal of Family Psychology, 25* (2), 292–300.

**Madras, B. K.** (2013). History of the discovery of the antipsychotic dopamine d2 receptor: A basis for the dopamine hypothesis of schizophrenia. *Journal of the History of the Neurosciences, 22* (1), 62–78.

**Madsen, T. E., McLean, S., Zhai, W., Linnstaedt, S., Kurz, M. C., Swor, R., ... & O'Neil, B.** (2018). Gender differences in pain experience and treatment after motor vehicle collisions: A secondary analysis of the CRASH Injury Study. *Clinical Therapeutics, 40* (2), 204–213.

**Maeda, U., Shen, B. J., Schwarz, E. R., Farrell, K. A., & Mallon, S.** (2012). Self-efficacy mediates the association of social support and depression with treatment adherence in heart failure patients. *International Journal of Behavioral Medicine, 20* (1), 88–96.

**Magee, C., & Biesanz, J. C.** (2018). Toward understanding the relationship between personality and well-being states and traits. *Journal of Personality*. doi: 10.1111/jopy.12389

**Maglione, D., Caputi, M., Moretti, B., & Scaini, S.** (2018). Psychopathological consequences of maltreatment among children and adolescents: A systematic review of the G x E literature. *Research in Developmental Disabilities, 82,* 53–66.

**Maguire, E. A., Gadian, D. G., Johnsrude, I. S., Good, C. D., Ashburner, J., Frackowiak, R. S. J., & Frith, C. D.** (2000). Navigation-related structural change in the hippocampi of taxi drivers. *Proceedings of the National Academy of Sciences USA, 97* (8), 4398–4403.

**Mahar, M., & Cavalli, V.** (2018). Intrinsic mechanisms of neuronal axon regeneration. *Nature Reviews Neuroscience*, 19, 323–337.

**Maier, N. R. F.** (1931). Reasoning in humans. *Journal of Comparative Psychology, 12* (2), 181–194.

**Makarova, E., Aeschlimann, B., & Herzog, W.** (2016). Why is the pipeline leaking? Experiences of young women in STEM vocational education and training and their adjustment strategies. *Empirical Research in Vocational Education and Training, 8* (1), 1. doi: 10.1186/s40461-016-0027-y

**Makrygianni, M. K., Gena, A., Katoudi, S., & Galanis, P.** (2018). The effectiveness of applied behavior analytic interventions for children with autism spectrum disorder: A meta-analytic study. *Research in Autism Spectrum Disorders, 51,* 18–31.

**Malamuth, N. M., Addison, T., & Koss, M.** (2000). Pornography and sexual aggression: Are there reliable effects and can we understand them? *Annual Review of Sex Research, 11,* 26–91.

**Malesza, M., & Kaczmarek, M. C.** (2018). The convergent validity between self- and peer-ratings of the Dark Triad personality. *Current Psychology*, 1–8.

**Malhi, G. S., Das, P., Outhred, T., Irwin, L., Morris, G., Hamilton, A., ... & Mannie, Z.** (2018). Understanding suicide: Focusing on its mechanisms through a lithium lens. *Journal of Affective Disorders, 241,* 338–347.

**Malkani, R. G., Abbott, S. M., Reid, K. J., & Zee, P. C.** (2018). Diagnostic and treatment challenges of sighted non–24-hour sleep-wake disorder. *Journal of Clinical Sleep Medicine, 14* (4), 603–613.

**Malón, A.** (2012). Pedophilia: A diagnosis in search of a disorder. *Archives of Sexual Behavior, 41* (5), 1083–1097.

**Mamarde, A., Navkhare, P., Singam, A., & Kanoje, A.** (2013). Recurrent dissociative fugue. *Indian Journal of Psychological Medicine, 35* (4), 400–401.

**Mancke, F., Schmitt, R., Winter, D., Niedtfeld, I., Herpertz, S. C., & Schmahl, C.** (2018). Assessing the marks of change: How psychotherapy alters the brain structure in women with borderline personality disorder. *Journal of Psychiatry & Neuroscience: JPN, 43* (3), 171–181.

**Mandler, G.** (1980). Recognizing: The judgment of previous occurrence. *Psychological Review, 87* (3), 252–271.

**Manini, T. M., Everhart, J. E., Patel, K. V., Schoeller, D. A., Colbert, L. H., Visser, M., ... & Harris, T. B.** (2006). Daily activity energy expenditure and mortality among older adults. *Journal of the American Medical Association, 296* (2), 171–179.

**Mann, J. J., Sublette, M. E., Oquendo, M., Ogden, T., Zanderigo, F., Miller, J., & Galfalvy, H.** (2018). 53. Neurotransmitter and neural circuitry correlates of suicide risk. *Biological Psychiatry, 83* (9), S21–S22.

**Mannino, D. M.** (2015). Smoking and emphysema: Looking beyond the cigarette. *CHEST Journal, 148* (5), 1126–1127.

**Manookin, M. B., Patterson, S. S., & Linehan, C. M.** (2018). Neural mechanisms mediating motion sensitivity in parasol ganglion cells of the primate retina. *Neuron, 97* (6), 1327–1340.

**Manrique, H. M., Völter, C. J. & Call, J.** (2013). Repeated innovation in great apes. *Animal Behaviour, 85* (1), 195–202.

**Manstead, A. S.** (2018). The psychology of social class: How socioeconomic status impacts thought, feelings, and behaviour. *British Journal of Social Psychology, 57* (2), 267–291.

**Mantsch, J. R., & Twining, R. C.** (2018). Kappa counterconditioning of cocaine cues. *Neuropsychopharmacology, 43* (7), 1469.

**Manzouri, A., & Savic, I.** (2018). Cerebral sex dimorphism and sexual orientation. *Human brain mapping, 39* (3), 1175–1186.

**Marazziti, D., Corsi, M., Baroni, G., Consoli, M., & Catena-Dell'Osso, M.** (2012). Latest advancements in the pharmacological treatment of binge eating disorder. *European Review for Medical and Pharmacological Science, 16* (15), 2102–2107.

**Marcar, V. L., & Jäncke, L.** (2018). Stimuli to differentiate the neural response at successive stages of visual processing using the VEP from human visual cortex. *Journal of Neuroscience Methods, 293,* 199–209.

**March, D. S., Gaertner, L., & Olson, M. A.** (2018). On the prioritized processing of threat in a dual implicit process model of evaluation. *Psychological Inquiry, 29* (1), 1–13.

**Marchant, N. J., Campbell, E. J., Pelloux, Y., Bossert, J. M., & Shaham, Y.** (2019). Context-induced relapse after extinction versus punishment: Similarities and differences. *Psychopharmacology, 236* (1), 439–448.

**Marchi, M., Provitera, V., Nolano, M., Romano, M., Maccora, S., D'Amato, I., ... & Lauria, G.** (2018). A novel SCN9A splicing mutation in a compound heterozygous girl with congenital insensitivity to pain, hyposmia and hypogeusia. *Journal of the Peripheral Nervous System, 23* (3), 202–206.

**Marcia, J. E.** (1980). Ego identity development. In J. Adelson (Ed.), *Handbook of adolescent psychology.* New York: Wiley.

**Marcia, J. E.** (2002). Identity and psychosocial development in adulthood. *Identity, 2* (1), 7–28.

**Marcovitch, S., O'Brien, M., Calkins, S. D., Leerkes, E. M., Weaver, J. M., & Levine, D. W.** (2015). A longitudinal assessment of the relation between executive function and theory of mind at 3, 4, and 5 years. *Cognitive Development, 33,* 40–55.

**Margolis, M. F.** (2018). *From politics to the pews: How partisanship and the political environment shape religious identity*. Chicago: University of Chicago Press.

**Marien, H., Custers, R., & Aarts, H.** (2018). Understanding the formation of human habits: An analysis of mechanisms of habitual behaviour. In B. Verplanken (Ed.), *The psychology of habit* (pp. 51–69). Cham: Springer.

**Marini, R. P., Wachtman, L. M. Tardif, S. D., Mansfield, K., & Fox, G.** (Eds.) (2018). *The common marmoset in captivity and biomedical research.* Cambridge: Academic Press.

**Marinova, S. V., Cao, X., & Park, H.** (2018). Constructive organizational values climate and organizational citizenship behaviors: A configurational view. *Journal of Management, 45,* 2045–2071.

**Marioni, R. E., Harris, S. E., Zhang, Q., McRae, A. F., Hagenaars, S. P., Hill, W. D., ... & Goate, A. M.** (2018). GWAS on family history of Alzheimer's disease. *Translational psychiatry, 8.*

**Markett, S., Montag, C., & Reuter, M.** (2018). Network neuroscience and personality. *Personality Neuroscience*, doi: 10.1017/pen.2018.12

**Markey, P. M., Markey, C. N., & French, J. E.** (2015). Violent video games and real-world violence: Rhetoric versus data. *Psychology of Popular Media Culture, 4* (4), 277.

**Markström, U., Svensson, B., Bergmark, M., Hansson, L., & Bejerholm, U.** (2018). What influences a sustainable implementation of evidence-based interventions in community mental health services? Development and pilot testing of a tool for mapping core components. *Journal of Mental Health, 27* (5), 395–401.

**Marmor, J.** (Ed.) (2018). *Modern psychoanalysis: New directions and perspectives*. London: Routledge. (original work published 1995)

**Marrazzo, J. M., Coffey, P., & Bingham, A.** (2005). Sexual practices, risk perception, and knowledge of bacterial vaginosis among lesbian and bisexual women. *Perspectives on Sexual and Reproductive Health, 37* (1), 6–12.

**Marsh, A. A.** (2019). The caring continuum: Evolved hormonal and proximal mechanisms explain prosocial and antisocial extremes. *Annual Review of Psychology, 70,* 347–371.

**Marsh, E. J., & Roediger, H. L.** (2013). Episodic and autobiographical memory. In A. F. Healy, R. W. Proctor, & I. B. Weiner (Eds.), *Handbook of psychology* (2nd ed., vol. 4, pp. 472–494). Hoboken, NJ: Wiley.

**Marshall, D. S.** (1971). Sexual behavior in Mangaia. In D. S. Marshall & R. C. Suggs (Eds.), *Human sexual behavior: Variations in the ethnographic spectrum* (pp. 103–162). New York: Basic.

**Marshall, K.** (2018). Encouraging resilience in the science curriculum. *School Science Review, 99* (369), 108–115.

**Martin, C. L., Cook, R. E., & Andrews, N. C.** (2017). Reviving androgyny: A modern day perspective on flexibility of gender identity and behavior. *Sex Roles, 76* (9-10), 592–603.

**Martin, C. L., & Ruble, D. N.** (2010). Patterns of gender development. *Annual Review of Psychology* (vol. 61, pp. 353-381). Palo Alto, CA: Annual Reviews.

**Martin, G., Nakata, V., Nakata, M., & Day, A.** (2017). Promoting the persistence of Indigenous students through teaching at the Cultural Interface. *Studies in Higher Education, 42* (7), 1158–1173.

**Martin, R. L., Bauer, B. W., Ramsey, K. L., Green, B. A., Capron, D. W., & Anestis, M. D.** (2018). How distress tolerance mediates the relationship between posttraumatic stress disorder and the interpersonal theory of suicide constructs in a US military sample. *Suicide and Life-Threatening Behavior*. doi: 10.1111/sltb.12523

**Martin, R. M.** (2019). Influence of biological sex, trait gender, and state gender on pain threshold, pain tolerance, and ratings of pain severity. *Personality and Individual Differences, 138,* 183–187.

**Martínez-Amorós, E., Cardoner, N., Soria, V., Gálvez, V., Menchón, J. M., & Urretavizcaya, M.** (2012). Long-term treatment strategies in major depression: A 2-year prospective naturalistic follow-up. *Journal of Electroconvulsive Therapy, 28* (2), 92–97.

**Martins, M. D., Gingras, B., Puig-Waldmueller, E., & Fitch, W. T.** (2017). Cognitive representation of "musical fractals": Processing hierarchy and recursion in the auditory domain. *Cognition, 161,* 31–45.

**Marx, R. F., & Didziulis, V.** (2009, February 27). A life, interrupted. *New York Times.* www.nytimes

.com/2009/03/01/nyregion/thecity/01miss.html?pagewanted=all (accessed January 5, 2015)
**Mashour, G. A., & Hudetz, A. G.** (2017). Bottom-up and top-down mechanisms of general anesthetics modulate different dimensions of consciousness. *Frontiers in Neural Circuits, 11.* doi: 10.3389/fncir.2017.0004444
**Maslow, A. H.** (1954). *Motivation and personality.* New York: Harper & Row.
**Maslow, A. H.** (1971). *The farther reaches of human nature.* New York: Viking.
**Mason, T. B., Lavender, J. M., Wonderlich, S. A., Crosby, R. D., Engel, S. G., Mitchell, J. E., ... & Peterson, C. B.** (2018). Examining a momentary mediation model of appearance-related stress, anxiety, and eating disorder behaviors in adult anorexia nervosa. *Eating and Weight Disorders: Studies on Anorexia, Bulimia and Obesity, 23* (5), 637–644.
**Massimini, F., & Delle Fave, A.** (2000). Individual development in bio-cultural perspective. *American Psychologist, 55* (1), 24–33.
**Massing-Schaffer, M., Helms, S. W., Rudolph, K. D., Slavich, G. M., Hastings, P. D., Giletta, M., ... & Prinstein, M. J.** (2018). Preliminary associations among relational victimization, targeted rejection, and suicidality in adolescents: A prospective study. *Journal of Clinical Child & Adolescent Psychology.* doi: 10.1080/15374416.2018.1469093
**Masten, A. S.** (2015). *Ordinary magic: Resilience in development.* New York: Guilford.
**Masten, A. S.** (2018). Adult resilience after child abuse. *Nature Human Behaviour, 2* (4), 244.
**Masters, W. H., & Johnson, V. E.** (1966). *Human sexual response.* Boston: Little, Brown.
**Masterton, R. B., Bitterman, M. E., Campbell, C. B. G., & Hotton, N.** (Eds.). (2018). *Evolution of brain and behavior in vertebrates.* Routledge.
**Mateos-Romero, L., & del Mar Salinas-Jiménez, M.** (2018). Labor mismatches: Effects on wages and on job satisfaction in 17 OECD countries. *Social Indicators Research.* doi: 10.1007/s11205-017-1830-y (in press)
**Matos, A. P., Ferreira, J. A., & Haase, R. F.** (2012). Television and aggression: A test of a mediated model with a sample of Portuguese students. *Journal of Social Psychology, 152,* 75–91.
**Matsick, J. L., & Rubin, J. D.** (2018). Bisexual prejudice among lesbian and gay people: Examining the roles of gender and perceived sexual orientation. *Psychology of Sexual Orientation and Gender Diversity, 5* (2), 143.
**Matsumoto, D., & Juang, L.** (2017). *Culture and psychology* (6th ed.). Boston: Cengage.
**Mattarozzi, K., Colonnello, V., Russo, P. M., & Todorov, A.** (2018). Person information facilitates memory for face identity. *Psychological Research,* 1–8.
**Mattek, A. M., Wolford, G. L., & Whalen, P. J.** (2017). A mathematical model captures the structure of subjective affect. *Perspectives on Psychological Science, 12* (3), 508–526.
**Matthews, K. A., Gump, B. B., Harris, K. F., Haney, T. L., & Barefoot, J. C.** (2004). Hostile behaviors predict cardiovascular mortality among men enrolled in the Multiple Risk Factor Intervention Trial. *Circulation, 109* (1), 66–70.
**Matthews, R. A., Bulger, C. A., & Barnes-Farrell, J. L.** (2010). Work social supports, role stressors, and work–family conflict: The moderating effect of age. *Journal of Vocational Behavior, 76* (1), 78–90.
**Matud, M. P., Bethencourt, J. M., & Ibáñez, I.** (2014). Relevance of gender roles in life satisfaction in adult people. *Personality and Individual Differences, 70,* 206–211.
**Mavrides, N., & Nemeroff, C.** (2013). Treatment of depression in cardiovascular disease. *Depression and Anxiety, 30,* 328–341.
**May, M.** (2003, August 25). "The trees were a deeper green than I imagined, and so tall." *The Guardian.* https://www.theguardian.com/science/2003/aug/26/genetics.g2 (accessed February 29, 2016)
**May, T., & Williams, K.** (2018). Brief report: Gender and age of diagnosis time trends in children with autism using Australian Medicare data. *Journal of Autism and Developmental Disorders, 48,* 4056–4062.
**Mayer, J. D., Salovey, P., Caruso, D. R., & Cherkassky, L.** (2011). Emotional intelligence. In R. J. Sternberg & S. B. Kaufman (Eds.), *Handbook of intelligence.* New York: Cambridge University Press.
**Mayersohn, M.** (October 18, 2018). The computer chauffeur is creeping closer. *New York Times,* F6.
**Mayhew, A. J., Pigeyre, M., Couturier, J., & Meyre, D.** (2018). An evolutionary genetic perspective of eating disorders. *Neuroendocrinology, 106* (3), 292–306.
**Maylea, C., Jorgensen, A., Matta, S., Ogilvie, K., & Wallin, P.** (2018). Consumers' experiences of mental health advance statements. *Laws, 7* (2), 22. doi: 10.3390/laws7020022
**Mazei, J., Hüffmeier, J., Freund, P. A., Stuhlmacher, A. F., Bilke, L., & Hertel, G.** (2015). A meta-analysis on gender differences in negotiation outcomes and their moderators. *Psychological Bulletin, 141* (1), 85–104.
**McAbee, S. T., & Oswald, F. L.** (2013). The criterion-related validity of personality measures for predicting GPA: A meta-analytic validity comparison. *Psychological Assessment, 25* (2), 532–544.
**McAdams, D. P.** (1989). *Intimacy: The need to be close.* New York: Doubleday.
**McAdams, D. P.** (2001). The psychology of life stories. *Review of General Psychology, 5* (2), 100–122.
**McAdams, D. P.** (2006). *The redemptive self: Stories Americans live by.* New York: Oxford University Press.
**McAdams, D. P.** (2009). *The person* (5th ed.). New York: Wiley.
**McAdams, D. P.** (2013). How actors, agents, and authors find meaning in life. In K. D. Markman, T. Proulx, & M. J. Lindberg (Eds.), *The psychology of meaning.* Washington, DC: American Psychological Association.
**McAdams, D. P.** (2018). "I am what survives me": Generativity and the self. In J. A. Frey & C. Vogler (Eds.), *Self-transcendence and virtue* (pp. 251–273). London: Routledge.
**McAdams, D. P.** (2018). Narrative identity: What is it? What does it do? How do you measure it? *Imagination, Cognition and Personality, 37* (3), 359–372.
**McAdams, D. P., & Bryant, F. B.** (1987). Intimacy motivation and subjective mental health in a nationwide sample. *Journal of Personality, 55* (3), 395–413.
**McAdams, D. P., & Guo, J.** (2015). Narrating the generative life. *Psychological Science, 26* (4), 475–483.
**McAleavey, A. A., Youn, S. J., Xiao, H., Castonguay, L. G., Hayes, J. A., & Locke, B. D.** (2017). Effectiveness of routine psychotherapy: Method matters. *Psychotherapy Research.* doi: 10.1080/10503307.2017.1395921
**McAleese, K. E., Walker, L., Colloby, S. J., Taylor, J. P., Thomas, A. J., DeCarli, C., & Attems, J.** (2018). Cortical tau pathology: a major player in fibre-specific white matter reductions in Alzheimer's disease? *Brain, 141*(6), e44.
**McCabe, J., Tanner, A. E., & Heiman, J. R.** (2010). The impact of gender expectations on meanings of sex and sexuality: Results from a cognitive interview study. *Sex Roles, 62* (3), 252–263.
**McCarthy, M. J., Wei, H., Nievergelt, C. M., Stautland, A., Maihofer, A. X., Welsh, D. K., ... & Andreasson, O. A.** (2018). Chronotype and cellular circadian rhythms predict the clinical response to lithium maintenance treatment in patients with bipolar disorder. *Neuropsychopharmacology,* 1.
**McCarthy, M. M.** (2018). Intersection of schizophrenia genetics and placental complications. *Nature Medicine, 24* (6), 707–708.
**McCaul, M. E., & Wand, G. S.** (2018). Detecting deception in our research participants: Are your participants who you think they are? *Alcoholism: Clinical and Experimental Research, 42* (2), 230–237.
**McCauley, E., Berk, M. S., Asarnow, J. R., Adrian, M., Cohen, J., Korslund, K., ... & Linehan, M. M.** (2018). Efficacy of dialectical behavior therapy for adolescents at high risk for suicide: A randomized clinical trial. *JAMA Psychiatry* 75 (8), 777–785.
**McClelland, J. L.** (2011). Memory as a constructive process: The parallel-distributed processing approach. In S. Nalbantian, P. Matthews, & J. L. McClelland (Eds.), *The memory process.* Cambridge, MA: MIT Press.
**McClelland, J. L., Botvinick, M. M., Noelle, D. C., Plaut, D. C., Rogers, T. T., Seidenberg, M. S., & Smith, L. B.** (2010). Letting structure emerge: Connectionist and dynamical systems approaches to cognition. *Trends in Cognitive Science, 14* (8), 348–356.
**McClernon, F. J., Conklin, C. A., Kozink, R. V., Adcock, R. A., Sweitzer, M. M., Addicott, M. A., ... & DeVito, A. M.** (2015). Hippocampal and insular response to smoking-related environments: Neuroimaging evidence for drug-context effects in nicotine dependence. *Neuropsychopharmacology, 41* (3), 877–885.
**McClure, E., Feinstein, L., Ferrando-Martinez, S., Leal, M., Galea, S., & Aiello, A. E.** (2018). The Great Recession and immune function. *RSF: The Russell Sage Foundation Journal of the Social Sciences, 4,* 62–81. doi: 10.7758/RSF.2018.4.4.04
**McCombs, B. L.** (2013). Educational psychology and educational transformation. In W. M. Reynolds, G. F. Miller, & I. B. Weiner (Eds.), *Handbook of psychology* (2nd ed., vol. 7, pp. 493–534). Hoboken, NJ: Wiley.
**McCoy, K., McCoy, M., Callis-Duehl, K., & Levey, D.** (2018). What kind of person becomes a scientist? *Science Scope, 41* (8), 72–77.
**McCrae, R. R., & Sutin, A. R.** (2009). Openness to experience. In M. R. Leary & R. H. Hoyle (Eds.), *Handbook of individual differences in social behavior* (pp. 257–273). New York: Guilford.
**McCuen-Wurst, C., Ruggieri, M., & Allison, K. C.** (2018). Disordered eating and obesity: Associations between binge-eating disorder, night-eating syndrome, and weight-related comorbidities. *Annals of the New York Academy of Sciences, 1411* (1), 96–105.
**McDaniel, M. A., & Einstein, G. O.** (2007). *Prospective memory: An overview and synthesis of an emerging field.* Thousand Oaks, CA: Sage.
**McDermott, R., & Hatemi, P. K.** (2018). To go forward, we must look back: The importance of evolutionary psychology for understanding modern politics. *Evolutionary Psychology, 16*(2). doi: 10.1474704918764506 (in press)
**McDonald, N. M., & Perdue, K. L.** (2018). The infant brain in the social world: Moving toward interactive social neuroscience with functional near-infrared spectroscopy. *Neuroscience and Biobehavioral Reviews, 87,* 38–49.
**McDonald, P.** (2012). Workplace sexual harassment 30 years on: A review of the literature. *International Journal of Management Reviews, 14* (1), 1–17.
**McDonald, R. J., & White, N. M.** (2013). A triple dissociation of memory systems: Hippocampus, amygdala, & dorsal striatum. *Behavioral Neuroscience, 127* (6), 835–853.
**McDowell, C. P., Dishman, R. K., Hallgren, M., MacDonncha, C., & Herring, M. P.** (2018). Associations of physical activity and depression: Results from the Irish Longitudinal Study on Ageing. *Experimental Gerontology, 112,* 68–75.
**McElroy, S. L., Mori, N., Guerdjikova, A. I., & Keck Jr, P. E.** (2018). Would glucagon-like peptide-1 receptor agonists have efficacy in binge eating disorder and

bulimia nervosa? A review of the current literature. *Medical Hypotheses, 111,* 90–93.

**McEwen, B. S., & Karatsoreos, I. N.** (2015). Sleep deprivation and circadian disruption: Stress, allostasis, and allostatic load. *Sleep Medicine Clinics, 10* (1), 1–10.

**McGinnis, D.** (2018). Resilience, life events, and well-being during midlife: Examining resilience subgroups. *Journal of Adult Development, 25,* 198–221.

**McGinty, J., Haque, M. S., & Upthegrove, R.** (2018). Depression during first episode psychosis and subsequent suicide risk: A systematic review and meta-analysis of longitudinal studies. *Schizophrenia Research, 195,* 58–66.

**McGregor, D. M.** (1960). *The human side of enterprise.* New York: McGraw-Hill.

**McGuire, W. J.** (2003). Doing psychology my way. In R. J. Sternberg (Ed.), *Psychologists defying the crowd: Stories of those who battled the establishment and won* (pp. 119–137). Washington, DC: American Psychological Association.

**McGuire, W. J., & Papageorgis, D.** (1961). The relative efficacy of various types of prior belief-defense in producing immunity against persuasion. *Journal of Abnormal Social Psychology, 62,* 327–337.

**McIntosh, D. E., Dixon, F. A., & Pierson, E. F.** (2018). The use of intelligence tests in the identification of giftedness. In D. P. Flanagan & E. M. McDonough (Eds.), *Contemporary intellectual assessment: Theories, tests, and issues* (4th ed., pp. 587–607). New York: Guilford.

**McIntosh, W. D., Harlow, T. F., & Martin, L. L.** (1995). Linkers and nonlinkers: Goal beliefs as a moderator of the effects of everyday hassles on rumination, depression, and physical complaints. *Journal of Applied Social Psychology, 25* (14), 1231–1244.

**McKay, K. M., Imel, Z. E., & Wampold, B. E.** (2006). Psychiatrist effects in the psychopharmacological treatment of depression. *Journal of Affective Disorders, 92* (2–3), 287–290.

**McKinley, S., Patrick, C., & Verona, E.** (2018). Antisocial personality disorder: Neurophysiological mechanisms and distinct subtypes. *Current Behavioral Neuroscience Reports, 5* (1), 72–80.

**McKone, E., Crookes, K., & Kanwisher, N.** (2010). The cognitive and neural development of face recognition in humans. In M. Gazzaniga (Ed.), *The cognitive neurosciences* (4th ed.). New York: Cambridge University Press.

**McLafferty, M., O'Neill, S., Murphy, S., Ferry, F., & Bunting, B.** (2018). The moderating impact of childhood adversity profiles and conflict on psychological health and suicidal behaviour in the Northern Ireland population. *Psychiatry Research, 262,* 213–220.

**McLean, B., & Elkind, P.** (2004). *The smartest guys in the room: The amazing rise and scandalous fall of Enron.* New York: Penguin Group.

**McMahon, D. M., Burch, J. B., Wirth, M. D., Youngstedt, S. D., Hardin, J. W., Hurley, T. G., ... & Burgess, S.** (2018). Persistence of social jet-lag and sleep disruption in healthy young adults. *Chronobiology International, 35* (3), 312–328.

**McMillan, C., Felmlee, D., & Osgood, D. W.** (2018). Peer influence, friend selection, and gender: How network processes shape adolescent smoking, drinking, and delinquency. *Social Networks, 55,* 86–96.

**McNamara, T. P.** (2013). Semantic memory and priming. In A. F. Healy, R. W. Proctor, & I. B. Weiner (Eds.), *Handbook of psychology* (2nd ed., vol. 4, pp. 449–471). Hoboken, NJ: Wiley.

**McNaughton, N., & Corr, P. J.** (2008). The neuropsychology of fear and anxiety: A foundation for reinforcement sensitivity theory. In P. J. Corr (Ed.), *The reinforcement sensitivity theory of personality* (pp. 44–94). New York: Cambridge University Press.

**McNaughton, N., & Smillie, L. D.** (2018). Some meta-theoretical principles for personality neuroscience. *Personality Neuroscience.* doi: 10.1017/pen.2018.9

**McNicholas, P. J., Floyd, R. G., Woods, I. J., Singh, L. J., Manguno, M. S., & Maki, K. E.** (2017). State special education criteria for identifying intellectual disability: A review following revised diagnostic criteria and Rosa's Law. *School Psychology Quarterly,* doi:10.1037/spq0000208

**McNiel, J. M., Lowman, J. C., & Fleeson, W.** (2010). The effect of state extraversion on four types of affect. *European Journal of Personality, 24* (1), 18–35.

**McNulty, J. K.** (2011). The dark side of forgiveness: The tendency to forgive predicts continued psychological and physical aggression in marriage. *Personality and Social Psychology Bulletin, 37,* 770–783.

**McNulty, J. K., Wenner, C. A., & Fisher, T. D.** (2016). Longitudinal associations among relationship satisfaction, sexual satisfaction, and frequency of sex in early marriage. *Archives of Sexual Behavior, 45* (1), 85–97.

**McPherson, E., Park, B., & Ito, T. A.** (2018). The role of prototype matching in science pursuits: Perceptions of scientists that are inaccurate and diverge from self-perceptions predict reduced interest in a science career. *Personality and Social Psychology Bulletin, 44* (6), 881–898.

**McRae, K., Hughes, B., Chopra, S., Gabrieli, J. D. E., Gross, J. J., & Ochsner, K. N.** (2010). The neural bases of distraction and reappraisal. *Journal of Cognitive Neuroscience, 22* (2), 248–262.

**Meade, A. W., Pappalardo, G., Braddy, P. W., & Fleenor, J. W.** (2018). Rapid response measurement: Development of a faking-resistant assessment method for personality. *Organizational Research Methods.* (in press)

**Meade, M. E., Wammes, J. D., & Fernandes, M. A.** (2018). Drawing as an encoding tool: Memorial benefits in younger and older adults. *Experimental Aging Research, 44,* 369–396.

**Mecocci, P., Boccardi, V., Cecchetti, R., Bastiani, P., Scamosci, M., Ruggiero, C., & Baroni, M.** (2018). A long journey into aging, brain aging, and Alzheimer's disease following the oxidative stress tracks. *Journal of Alzheimer's Disease, 62* (3), 1319–1335.

**Medalia, A., Beck, A. T., & Grant, P. M.** (2018). Cognitive therapies for psychosis: Advances and challenges. *Schizophrenia Research.* doi: 10.1016/j.schres.2018.05.021

**Medin, D., Ojalehto, B., Marin, A., & Bang, M.** (2017). Systems of (non-) diversity. *Nature Human Behaviour, 1* (5), 0088.

**Meehan, K. B., Cain, N. M., Roche, M. J., Clarkin, J. F., & De Panfilis, C.** (2018). Rejection sensitivity and interpersonal behavior in daily life. *Personality and Individual Differences, 126,* 109–115.

**Mehr, S. A., & Spelke, E. S.** (2018). Shared musical knowledge in 11-month-old infants. *Developmental Science, 21* (2), 1–7.

**Mehta, D., Voisey, J., Bruenig, D., Harvey, W., Morris, C. P., Lawford, B., & Young, R. M.** (2018). Transcriptome analysis reveals novel genes and immune networks dysregulated in veterans with PTSD. *Brain, Behavior, and Immunity, 74,* 133–142.

**Meir Drexler, S., & Wolf, O. T.** (2018). Behavioral disruption of memory reconsolidation: From bench to bedside and back again. *Behavioral Neuroscience, 132* (1), 13.

**Meisel, S. N., Colder, C. R., Bowker, J. C., & Hussong, A. M.** (2018). A longitudinal examination of mediational pathways linking chronic victimization and exclusion to adolescent alcohol use. *Developmental Psychology, 54* (9), 1795–1807.

**Melara, R. D., Ruglass, L. M., Fertuck, E. A., & Hien, D. A.** (2018). Regulation of threat in post-traumatic stress disorder: Associations between inhibitory control and dissociative symptoms. *Biological Psychology, 133,* 89–98.

**Melby-Lervåg, M., & Hulme, C.** (2016). There is no convincing evidence that working memory training is effective: A reply to Au et al. (2014) and Karbach and Verhaeghen (2014). *Psychonomic Bulletin and Review, 23* (1), 324–330.

**Melendez-Torres, G. J., Sutcliffe, K., Burchett, H. E., Rees, R., Richardson, M., & Thomas, J.** (2018). Weight management programmes: Re-analysis of a systematic review to identify pathways to effectiveness. *Health Expectations.* doi: 10.1111/hex.12667

**Mellers, B., Stone, E., Atanasov, P., Rohrbaugh, N., Metz, S. E., Ungar, L., ... & Tetlock, P.** (2015). The psychology of intelligence analysis: Drivers of prediction accuracy in world politics. *Journal of Experimental Psychology: Applied, 21* (1), 1–14.

**Mellman, T. A., Bell, K. A., Abu-Bader, S. H., & Kobayashi, I.** (2018). Neighborhood stress and autonomic nervous system activity during sleep. *Sleep, 41* (6), zsy059. doi: 10.1093/sleep/zsy059

**Mello, J., & Garcia-Marques, T.** (2018). The attractiveness-positivity link: Let's contextualize it. *The Journal of Social Psychology, 158,* 639–645.

**Melton, L.** (2005). How brain power can help you cheat old age. *New Scientist, 25,* 30–32.

**Meltzer, A. L., Makhanova, A., Hicks, L. L., French, J. E., McNulty, J. K., & Bradbury, T. N.** (2017). Quantifying the sexual afterglow: The lingering benefits of sex and their implications for pair-bonded relationships. *Psychological Science, 28* (5), 587–598.

**Meltzer, L.** (Ed.). (2018). *Executive function in education: From theory to practice.* New York: Guilford.

**Memel, M., Woolverton, C. B., Bourassa, K., & Glisky, E. L.** (2018). Working memory predicts subsequent episodic memory decline during healthy cognitive aging: Evidence from a cross-lagged panel design. *Aging, Neuropsychology, and Cognition.* doi: 10.1080/13825585.2018.1521507

**Mendes, N., Hanus, D., & Call, J.** (2007). Raising the level: Orangutans use water as a tool. *Biology Letters, 3* (5), 453–455.

**Mendoza, J.** (2018). Food intake and addictive-like eating behaviors: Time to think about the circadian clock(s). *Neuroscience & Biobehavioral Reviews.* doi: 10.1016/j.neubiorev.2018.07.003 (in press)

**Menges, C.** (2016). Toward improving the effectiveness of formal mentoring programs matching by personality matters. *Group and Organization Management, 41* (1), 98–129.

**Menn, L., & Stoel-Gammon, C.** (2009). Phonological development: Learning sounds and sound patterns. In J. Berko Gleason & N. Ratner (Eds.), *The development of language* (7th ed.). Boston: Allyn & Bacon.

**Mercer, C. H., Bailey, J. V., Johnson, A. M., Erens, B., Wellings, K., Fenton, K. A., & Copas, A. J.** (2007). Women who report having sex with women: British national probability data on prevalence, sexual behaviors, and health outcomes. *American Journal of Public Health, 97* (6), 1126–1133.

**Mercer, D. A., Ditto, B., Lavoie, K. L., Campbell, T., Arsenault, A., & Bacon, S. L.** (2018). Health locus of control is associated with physical activity and other health behaviors in cardiac patients. *Journal of Cardiopulmonary Rehabilitation and Prevention, 38* (6), 394–399.

**Mertes, H.** (2017). The role of anticipated decision regret and the patient's best interest in sterilisation and medically assisted reproduction. *Journal of Medical Ethics, 43* (5), 314–318. doi:10.1136/medethics-2016-103551

**Mesman, J., & Groeneveld, M. G.** (2018). Gendered parenting in early childhood: Subtle but unmistakable if you know where to look. *Child Development Perspectives, 12* (1), 22–27.

**Mesquita, B.** (2002). Emotions as dynamic cultural phenomena. In R. J. Davidson, K. R. Scherer, & H. H. Goldsmith (Eds.), *Handbook of affective sciences.* New York: Oxford University Press.

**Messenger, J. C.** (1971). Sex and repression in an Irish folk community. In D. S. Marshall & R. C. Suggs (Eds.), *Human sexual behavior.* New York: Basic.

**Metcalfe, J., & Mischel, W.** (1999). A hot/cool system analysis of delay of gratification: Dynamics of will power. *Psychological Review, 106* (1), 3–19.

**Mettler, F. A.** (Ed.). (1952). *Psychosurgical problems.* Oxford, UK: Blakiston.

**Meuret, A. E., Ritz, T., Wilhelm, F. H., Roth, W. T., & Rosenfield, D.** (2018). Hypoventilation therapy alleviates panic by repeated induction of dyspnea. *Biological Psychiatry: Cognitive Neuroscience and Neuroimaging, 3* (6), 539–545.

**Meyer, B., Schermuly, C. C., & Kauffeld, S. (**2016). That's not my place: The interacting effects of faultlines, subgroup size, and social competence on social loafing behaviour in work groups. *European Journal of Work and Organizational Psychology, 25* (1), 31–49.

**Meyer, E. C., La, H. B., DeBeer, B. B., Kimbrel, N. A., Gulliver, S. B., & Morissette, S. B.** (2018). Psychological inflexibility predicts PTSD symptom severity in war veterans after accounting for established PTSD risk factors and personality. *Psychological Trauma: Theory, Research, Practice and Policy*. doi: 10.1037/tra0000358

**Meyer, J. P., Becker, T. E., & Vandenberghe, C.** (2004). Employee commitment and motivation: A conceptual analysis and integrative model. *Journal of Applied Psychology, 89* (6), 991–1007.

**Meyer-Bahlburg, H. F. L.** (1998). Gender assignment in intersexuality. *Journal of Psychology and Human Sexuality, 10* (2), 1–21.

**Meyer-Bahlburg, H. F.** (2005). Gender identity outcome in female-raised 46, XY persons with penile agenesis, cloacal exstrophy of the bladder, or penile ablation. *Archives of Sexual Behavior, 34* (4), 423–438.

**Meyer-Bahlburg, H. F.** (2010). From mental disorder to iatrogenic hypogonadism: Dilemmas in conceptualizing gender identity variants as psychiatric conditions. *Archives of Sexual Behavior, 39* (2), 461–476.

**Meyer-Bahlburg, H. F., Baratz Dalke, K., Berenbaum, S. A., Cohen-Kettenis, P. T., Hines, M., & Schober, J. M.** (2016). Gender assignment, reassignment, and outcome in disorders of sex development: Update of the 2005 Consensus Conference. *Hormone Research in Paediatrics, 85* (2), 112–118.

**Meynhardt, T., Brieger, S. A., & Hermann, C.** (2018). Organizational public value and employee life satisfaction: The mediating roles of work engagement and organizational citizenship behavior. *The International Journal of Human Resource Management*, 1–34.

**Michalski, D., Kohout, J., Wicherski, M., & Hart, B.** (2011). 2009 Doctorate Employment Survey (Table 3). https://www.apa.org/workforce/publications/09-doc-empl/report.pdf

**Michel, M.** (2017). A role for the anterior insular cortex in the global neuronal workspace model of consciousness. *Consciousness and Cognition, 49*, 333–346.

**Miczek, K. A., DeBold, J. F., Hwa, L. S., Newman, E. L., & Almeida, R. M.** (2015). Alcohol and violence: Neuropeptidergic modulation of monoamine systems. *Annals of the New York Academy of Sciences, 1349* (1), 96–118.

**Miech, R. A., Johnston, L. D., O'Malley, P. M., Bachman, J. G., Schulenberg, J. E., & Patrick, M. E.** (2018). *Monitoring the Future national survey results on drug use, 1975–2017: Volume I, Secondary school students.* Ann Arbor: Institute for Social Research, University of Michigan.

**Mihelicova, M., Brown, M., & Shuman, V.** (2018). Trauma-informed care for individuals with serious mental illness: An avenue for community psychology's involvement in community mental health. *American Journal of Community Psychology, 61* (1-2), 141–152.

**Mihura, J. L., Bombel, G., Dumitrascu, N., Roy, M., & Meadows, E. A.** (2018). Why we need a formal systematic approach to validating psychological tests: the case of the Rorschach comprehensive system. *Journal of Personality Assessment*. doi: 10.1080/00223891.2018.1458315

**Mikolajczyk, T., Ciobanu, I., Badea, D. I., Iliescu, A., Pizzamiglio, S., Schauer, T., ... & Berteanu, M.** (2018). Advanced technology for gait rehabilitation: An overview. *Advances in Mechanical Engineering, 10* (7), 1687814018783627.

**Milgram, S.** (1965). Some conditions of obedience and disobedience to authority. *Human Relations, 18,* 56–76.

**Milgram, S.** (1974). *Obedience to authority.* New York: Harper & Row.

**Miller, A. G.** (2004). What can the Milgram obedience experiments tell us about the Holocaust? Generalizing from the social psychology laboratory. In A. G. Miller (Ed.), *The social psychology of good and evil* (pp. 193–239). New York: Guilford.

**Miller, D. J., Vachon, D. D., & Lynam, D. R.** (2009). Neuroticism, negative affect, and negative affect instability: Establishing convergent and discriminant validity using ecological momentary assessment. *Personality and Individual Differences, 47,* 873–877.

**Miller, G. A.** (1956). The magical number seven, plus or minus two: Some limits on our capacity for information processing. *Psychological Review, 63* (2), 81–97.

**Miller, J. G., Kahle, S., & Hastings, P. D.** (2015). Roots and benefits of costly giving: Children who are more altruistic have greater autonomic flexibility and less family wealth. *Psychological Science, 26* (7), 1038–1045.

**Miller, J. J., Fletcher, K., & Kabat-Zinn, J.** (1995). Three-year follow-up and clinical implications of a mindfulness meditation-based stress reduction intervention in the treatment of anxiety disorders. *General Hospital Psychiatry, 17* (3), 192–200.

**Miller, P. H.** (2011). Piaget's theory: Past, present, and future. In U. Goswami (Ed.), Wiley-Blackwell *handbook of childhood cognitive development* (2nd ed.). New York: Wiley-Blackwell.

**Miller, R. R., & Grace, R. C.** (2013). Conditioning and learning. In A. F. Healy, R. W. Proctor, & I. B. Weiner (Eds.), *Handbook of psychology* (2nd ed., vol. 4, pp. 357–392). Hoboken, NJ: Wiley.

**Miller, S. D., Hubble, M. A., Chow, D. L., & Seidel, J. A.** (2013). The outcome of psychotherapy: Yesterday, today, and tomorrow. *Psychotherapy, 50* (1), 88–97.

**Miner-Rubino, K., Twenge, J. M., & Fredrickson, B. L.** (2002). Trait self-objectification in women: Affective and personality correlates. *Journal of Research in Personality, 36* (2), 147–172.

**Minges, K. E., & Redeker, N. S.** (2016). Delayed school start times and adolescent sleep: A systematic review of the experimental evidence. *Sleep Medicine Reviews, 28*, 82–91.

**Minifie, J., Bell, J., & Zhang, Y.** (2018). Recruiting at campus job fairs: Matching candidate to individual industry requirements. *Journal of Behavioral and Applied Management, 18* (1), 3751.

**Mischel, W.** (2004). Toward an integrative science of the person. *Annual Review of Psychology* (vol. 55, pp. 1–22). Palo Alto, CA: Annual Reviews.

**Mischel, W.** (2009). From *Personality and Assessment* (1968) to personality science, 2009. *Journal of Research in Personality, 43* (2), 282–290.

**Mischel, W., Ayduk, O., Berman, M. G., Casey, B. J., Gotlib, I. H., Jonides, J., ... & Shoda, Y.** (2011). "Willpower" over the life span: Decomposing self-regulation. *Social Cognitive and Affective Neuroscience, 6* (2), 252–256.

**Mischel, W., Shoda, Y., & Peake, P. K.** (1988). The nature of adolescent competencies predicted by preschool delay of gratification. *Journal of Personality and Social Psychology, 54*(4), 687–696. doi: 10.1037/0022-3514.54.4.687

**Mischel, W., Shoda, Y., & Rodriguez, M. L.** (1989). Delay of gratification in children. *Science, 244* (4907), 933–938. doi: 10.1126/science.2658056

**Miskowiak, K. W., Macoveanu, J., Jørgensen, M. B., Ott, C. V., Støttrup, M. M., Jensen, H. M., ... & Kessing, L. V.** (2018). Effect of electroconvulsive therapy on neural response to affective pictures: A randomized, sham-controlled fMRI study. *European Neuropsychopharmacology, 28* (8), 915–924.

**Miss, F. M., & Burkart, J. M.** (2018). Corepresentation during joint action in marmoset monkeys. *Psychological Science, 29*, 984–995.

**Mistry, J., Contreras, M., & Dutta, R.** (2013). Culture and child development. In R. M. Lerner, M. A. Easterbrooks, J. Mistry, & I. B. Weiner (Eds.), *Handbook of psychology* (2nd ed., vol. 6, pp. 265–286). Hoboken, NJ: Wiley.

**Mitchell, D. B., Kelly, C. L., & Brown, A. S.** (2018). Replication and extension of long-term implicit memory: Perceptual priming but conceptual cessation. *Consciousness and Cognition, 58*, 1–9.

**Mitchell, M. B., Cimino, C. R., Benitez, A., Brown, C. L., Gibbons, L. E., Kennison, R. F., ... & Piccinin, A. M.** (2012). Cognitively stimulating activities: Effects on cognition across four studies with up to 21 years of longitudinal data. *Journal of Aging Research.* doi: 10.1155/2012/461592

**Mitchell, S.** (2014, January 31). Can Ambien really cause sleep-driving and sleep-eating? *Consumer Reports.* http://www.consumerreports.org/cro/news/2014/01/can-ambien-and-other-sleeping-pills-cause-sleep-driving-and-sleep-eating/index.htm (accessed March 20, 2016)

**Mizutani, S., Ekuni, D., Yamane-Takeuchi, M., Azuma, T., Taniguchi-Tabata, A., Tomofuji, T., ... & Morita, M.** (2018). Type D personality and periodontal disease in university students: A prospective cohort study. *Journal of Health Psychology, 23* (5), 754–762.

**Mlecnik, B., Galon, J., & Bindea, G.** (2018). Comprehensive functional analysis of large lists of genes and proteins. *Journal of Proteomics, 171*, 2–10.

**Moberg, P. J., Richman, M. J., Roalf, D. R., Morse, C. L., Graefe, A. C., Brennan, L., ... & Gur, R. C.** (2018). Neurocognitive functioning in patients with 22q11. 2 Deletion Syndrome: A meta-analytic review. *Behavior Genetics, 48*, 259–270.

**Mock, S., & Boerner, K.** (2010). Sense making and benefit finding among patients with amyotrophic lateral sclerosis and their primary caregivers. *Journal of Health Psychology, 15* (1), 115–121.

**Mock, S. E., & Eibach, R. P.** (2011). Stability and change in sexual orientation identity over a 10-year period in adulthood. *Archives of Sexual Behavior, 41* (3), 641–648.

**Modecki, K. L.** (2016). Do risks matter? Variable and person-centered approaches to adolescents' problem behavior. *Journal of Applied Developmental Psychology, 42*, 8–20.

**Moffitt, T. E., Arseneault, L., Belsky, D., Dickson, N., Hancox, R. J., Harrington, H., ... & Caspi, A.** (2011). A gradient of childhood self-control predicts health, wealth, and public safety. *Proceedings of the National Academy of Sciences USA, 108* (7), 2693–2698.

**Mogan, R., Fischer, R., & Bulbulia, J. A.** (2017). To be in synchrony or not? A meta-analysis of synchrony's effects on behavior, perception, cognition and affect. *Journal of Experimental Social Psychology, 72*, 13–20.

**Mogorovich, G., & Caltabiano, N. J.** (2018). Therapeutic alliance and anorexia nervosa treatment outcomes: Experiences of young people and their families. *Community Mental Health Journal, 54* (8), 1259–1265.

**Moholdt, T., Lavie, C. J., & Nauman, J.** (2018). Sustained physical activity, not weight loss, associated with improved survival in coronary heart disease. *Journal of the American College of Cardiology, 71* (10), 1094–1101.

**Moieni, M., Irwin, M. R., Haltom, K. E. B., Jevtic, I., Meyer, M. L., Breen, E. C., Cole, S. W., & Eisenberger, N. I.** (2018). Exploring the role of gratitude and support-giving on inflammatory outcomes. *Emotion.* doi: 10.1037/emo0000472 (in press)

**Mojica, A.** (March, 29, 2018). Hero who stopped Tennessee church shooter receives high national honor. https://fox17.com/news/local/hero-who-stopped-tennessee-church-shooter-receives-national-honor

**Monaco, J., Rocchi, L., Ginatempo, F., D'Angelo, E., & Rothwell, J. C.** (2018). Cerebellar theta-burst stimulation impairs memory consolidation in eyeblink classical conditioning. *Neural Plasticity.* (in press)

**Money, J., Hampson, J. G., & Hampson, J. L.** (1955). Hermaphroditism: Recommendations concerning assignment of sex, change of sex, and psychological management. *Bulletin of Johns Hopkins Hospital, 97* (4), 284–300.

**Money, J., & Tucker P.** (1975). *Sexual signatures: On being a man or woman.* Boston: Little Brown.

**Mongrain, M., Barnes, C., Barnhart, R., & Zalan, L. B.** (2018). Acts of kindness reduce depression in individuals low on agreeableness. *Translational Issues in Psychological Science, 4* (3), 323–334.

**Montanaro, E. A., Kershaw, T. S., & Bryan, A. D.** (2018). Dismantling the theory of planned behavior: Evaluating the relative effectiveness of attempts to uniquely change attitudes, norms, and perceived behavioral control. *Journal of Behavioral Medicine.* doi: 10.1007/s10865-018-9923-x

**Monteiro, P., & Feng, G.** (2016). Learning from animal models of obsessive-compulsive disorder. *Biological Psychiatry, 79* (1), 7–16.

**Monteleone, A. M., Castellini, G., Volpe, U., Ricca, V., Lelli, L., Monteleone, P., & Maj, M.** (2018). Neuroendocrinology and brain imaging of reward in eating disorders: A possible key to the treatment of anorexia nervosa and bulimia nervosa. *Progress in Neuro-psychopharmacology and Biological Psychiatry, 80,* 132–142.

**Moody, C. T., Baker, B. L., & Blacher, J.** (2018). Contribution of parenting to complex syntax development in preschool children with developmental delays or typical development. *Journal of Intellectual Disability Research, 62,* 604–616.

**Moody, L. N., Tegge, A. N., Poe, L. M., Koffarnus, M. N., & Bickel, W. K.** (2018). To drink or to drink less? Distinguishing between effects of implementation intentions on decisions to drink and how much to drink in treatment-seeking individuals with alcohol use disorder. *Addictive Behaviors, 83,* 64–71.

**Moore, D. J., Fazeli, P. L., Moore, R. C., Woods, S. P., Letendre, S. L., Jeste, D. V., & Grant, I.** (2018). Positive psychological factors are linked to successful cognitive aging among older persons living with HIV/AIDS. *AIDS and Behavior, 22* (5), 1551–1561.

**Moore, J.** (2017). John B. Watson's classical S–R behaviorism. *Journal of Mind and Behavior, 38* (1), 1–34.

**Moore, S. A., & Zoellner, L. A.** (2012). The effects of expressive and experiential suppression on memory accuracy and memory distortion in women with and without PTSD. *Journal of Experimental Psychopathology, 3* (3), 368–392.

**Moradi, B., & Huang, Y.** (2008). Objectification theory and psychology of women: A decade of advances and future directions. *Psychology of Women Quarterly, 32* (4), 377–398.

**Morales Knight, L. F., & Hope, D. A.** (2012). Correlates of same-sex attractions and behaviors among self-identified heterosexual university students. *Archives of Sexual Behavior, 41* (5), 1199–1208.

**Moran, R. J., Kishida, K. T., Lohrenz, T., Saez, I., Laxton, A. W., Witcher, M. R., ... & Montague, P. R.** (2018). The protective action encoding of serotonin transients in the human brain. *Neuropsychopharmacology, 43* (6), 1425–1435.

**Morawski, J. G., & Bayer, B. M.** (2013). Social psychology. In D. K. Freedheim & I. B. Weiner (Eds.), *Handbook of psychology* (2nd ed., vol. 1, pp. 248–278). Hoboken, NJ: Wiley.

**Moreau, D.** (2015). Brains and brawn: Complex motor activities to maximize cognitive enhancement. *Educational Psychology Review, 27* (3), 475–482.

**Moreno, O., & Cardemil, E.** (2018). The role of religious attendance on mental health among Mexican populations: A contribution toward the discussion of the immigrant health paradox. *American Journal of Orthopsychiatry, 88* (1), 10.

**Morey, C. C.** (2018). The case against specialized visual-spatial short-term memory. *Psychological Bulletin, 144,* 849–883. doi: 10.1037/bul0000155

**Morgan, A. J., Reavley, N. J., Ross, A., San Too, L., & Jorm, A. F.** (2018). Interventions to reduce stigma towards people with severe mental illness: Systematic review and meta-analysis. *Journal of Psychiatric Research, 103,* 120–133.

**Morgan, C. D., & Murray, H. A.** (1935). A method of investigating fantasies: The Thematic Apperception Test. *Archives of Neurology and Psychiatry, 34,* 289–306.

**Morgan, H.** (2012). "To paint the portrait of a bird": Analytic work from the perspective of a "developmental" Jungian. *Journal of Analytical Psychology, 57* (1), 40–56.

**Morgan, T. J. H., Uomini, N. T., Rendell, L. E., Chouinard-Thuly, L., Street, S. E., Lewis, H. M., ... & Laland, K. N.** (2015). Experimental evidence for the co-evolution of hominin tool-making teaching and language. *Nature Communications, 6* (6029). doi: 10.1038/ncomms7029

**Morikawa, Y., Mizuno, Y., Harada, E., Katoh, D., Kashiwagi, Y., Morita, S., ... & Yasue, H.** (2013). Aerobic interval exercise training in the afternoon reduces attacks of coronary spastic angina in conjunction with improvement in endothelial function, oxidative stress, and inflammation. *Coronary Artery Disease, 24* (3), 177–182. doi: 10.1097/MCA.0b013e32835cbef5

**Morimoto, Y., Shimada-Sugimoto, M., Otowa, T., Yoshida, S., Kinoshita, A., Mishima, H., ... & Kurotaki, N.** (2018). Whole-exome sequencing and gene-based rare variant association tests suggest that PLA2G4E might be a risk gene for panic disorder. *Translational Psychiatry, 8* (1), 41.

**Morin, A. S., Meyer, J. P., Bélanger, É., Boudrias, J., Gagné, M., & Parker, P. D.** (2016). Longitudinal associations between employees' beliefs about the quality of the change management process, affective commitment to change and psychological empowerment. *Human Relations, 69* (3), 839–867.

**Morisaki, R., Bon, C., & Levitt, J. O.** (2016). The use of an imagery mnemonic to teach the Krebs cycle. *Biochemistry and Molecular Biology Education.* doi: 10.1002/bmb

**Moro, S. S., & Harris, L. R.** (2018). Vestibular-somatosensory interactions affect the perceived timing of tactile stimuli. *Experimental Brain Research, 236,* 2877–2885.

**Morowitz, H. J.** (2018). *The mind, the brain and complex adaptive systems.* London: Routledge.

**Morra, S.** (2015). How do subvocal rehearsal and general attentional resources contribute to verbal short-term memory span? *Frontiers in Psychology, 6,* 145.

**Morris, A. S., Squeglia, L. M., Jacobus, J., & Silk, J. S.** (2018). Adolescent brain development: Implications for understanding risk and resilience processes through neuroimaging research. *Journal of Research on Adolescence, 28* (1), 4–9.

**Morrison, A. S., & Heimberg, R. G.** (2013). Social anxiety and social anxiety disorder. *Annual Review of Clinical Psychology* (vol. 9, pp. 249–274). Palo Alto, CA: Annual Reviews.

**Mortimer, J. A., Snowdon, D. A., & Markesbery, W. R.** (2009). The effect of APOE-epsilon4 on dementia is mediated by Alzheimer neuropathology. *Alzheimer Disease and Associated Disorders, 23,* 152–157.

**Morton, J.** (2017). Interidentity amnesia in dissociative identity disorder. *Cognitive Neuropsychiatry, 22,* 315–330.

**Moscovici, S.** (1985). Social influence and conformity. In G. Lindzey & E. Aronson (Eds.), *Handbook of social psychology* (3rd ed., vol. 2). New York: Random House.

**Moscovitch, M., Cabeza, R., Winocur, G., & Nadel, L.** (2016). Episodic memory and beyond: The hippocampus and neocortex in transformation. *Annual Review of Psychology* (vol. 67, pp. 105–134). Palo Alto, CA: Annual Reviews.

**Mosher, W. D., Chandra, A., & Jones, J.** (2005). Sexual behavior and selected health measures: Men and women 15–44 years of age, United States, 2002. *Advance data from vital and health statistics, no. 362.* http://www.cdc.gov/nchs/data/ad/ad362.pdf (accessed March 22, 2016)

**Moskowitz, J. T.** (2003). Positive affect predicts lower risk of AIDS mortality. *Psychosomatic Medicine, 65* (4), 620–626.

**Moss, C., Dhillo, W. S., Frost, G., & Hickson, M.** (2012). Gastrointestinal hormones: The regulation of appetite and the anorexia of aging. *Journal of Human Nutrition and Dietetics, 25* (1), 3–15.

**Mostofsky, E., Maclure, M., Sherwood, J. B., Tofler, G. H., Muller, J. E., & Mittleman, M. A.** (2012). Risk of acute myocardial infarction after the death of a significant person in one's life: The determinants of myocardial infarction onset study. *Circulation, 125* (3), 491–496.

**Mounteney, J., Griffiths, P., Bo, A., Cunningham, A., Matias, J., & Pirona, A.** (2018). Nine reasons why Ecstasy is not quite what it used to be. *International Journal of Drug Policy, 51,* 36–41.

**Mowen, T. J., & Schroeder, R. D.** (2018). Maternal parenting style and delinquency by race and the moderating effect of structural disadvantage. *Youth & Society, 50* (2), 139–159.

**Mowlem, F. D., Rosenqvist, M. A., Martin, J., Lichtenstein, P., Asherson, P., & Larsson, H.** (2018). Sex differences in predicting ADHD clinical diagnosis and pharmacological treatment. *European Child & Adolescent Psychiatry,* 1–9.

**Mowrey, W. B., Lipton, R. B., Katz, M. J., Ramratan, W. S., Loewenstein, D. A., Zimmerman, M. E., & Buschke, H.** (2018). Memory binding test predicts incident dementia: Results from the Einstein Aging Study. *Journal of Alzheimer's Disease, 62* (1), 293–304.

**Moyle, P., & Hackston, J.** (2018). Personality assessment for employee development: Ivory tower or real world? *Journal of Personality Assessment, 100,* 507–517.

**Mroczek, B., Kurpas, D., Gronowska, M., Kotwas, A., & Karakiewicz, B.** (2013). Psychosexual needs and sexual behaviors of nursing care home residents. *Archives of Gerontology and Geriatrics, 57* (1), 32–38.

**Mroczek, D. K., & Spiro, A.** (2005). Change in life satisfaction during adulthood: Findings from the Veterans Affairs normative aging study. *Journal of Personality and Social Psychology, 88* (1), 189–202.

**Mueller, P. A., & Oppenheimer, D. M.** (2014). The pen is mightier than the keyboard: Advantages of longhand over laptop note taking. *Psychological Science, 25,* 1159–1168.

**Muhle, R. A., Reed, H. E., Stratigos, K. A., & Veenstra-VanderWeele, J.** (2018). The emerging clinical neuroscience of autism spectrum disorder: A review. *JAMA Psychiatry, 75* (5), 514–523.

**Muise, A., Schimmack, U., & Impett, E. A.** (2016). Sexual frequency predicts greater well-being, but more is not always better. *Social Psychological and Personality Science, 7* (4), 295–302.

**Mulder, R. T.** (2012). Cultural aspects of personality disorder. In T. Widiger (Ed.), *The Oxford handbook of personality disorders.* New York: Oxford University Press.

**Mulkens, S., de Vos, C., de Graaff, A., & Waller, G.** (2018). To deliver or not to deliver cognitive behavioral therapy for eating disorders: Replication and extension of our understanding of why therapists fail to do what they should do. *Behaviour Research and Therapy, 106,* 57–63.

**Mullen, N. W., Maxwell, H., & Bédard, M.** (2015). Decreasing driver speeding with feedback and a token economy. *Transportation Research Part F: Traffic Psychology and Behaviour, 28,* 77–85.

**Müller, C., Nicoletti, C., Omlin, S., Brink, M., & Läubli, T.** (2015). Relationship between sleep stages and nocturnal trapezius muscle activity. *Journal of Electromyography and Kinesiology, 25* (3), 457–462.

**Müller, G., Wellmann, J., Hartwig, S., Greiser, K. H., Moebus, S., Jöckel, K. H., ... & DIAB-CORE Consortium.** (2015). Association of neighbourhood unemployment rate with incident Type 2 diabetes mellitus in five German regions. *Diabetic Medicine, 32* (8), 1017–1022.

**Müller, R. A., & Fishman, I.** (2018). Brain connectivity and neuroimaging of social networks in autism. *Trends in Cognitive Sciences, 22* (12), 1103–1116.

**Müller, S., & Moshagen, M.** (2018). Overclaiming shares processes with the hindsight bias. *Personality and Individual Differences, 134,* 298–300.

**Mullin, A. S., Hilsenroth, M. J., Gold, J., & Farber, B. A.** (2018). Facets of object representation: Process and outcome over the course of psychodynamic psychotherapy. *Journal of Personality Assessment, 100* (2), 145–155.

**Mullis, I. V. S., Marting, M. O., Gonzales, E. J., & Kennedy, A. M.** (2003). *PIRLS 2001 International Report: IEA's study of reading literacy achievement in primary schools.* Chestnut Hill, MA: Boston College.

**Munder, T., Flückiger, C., Leichsenring, F., Abbass, A. A., Hilsenroth, M. J., Luyten, P., ... & Wampold, B. E.** (2018). Is psychotherapy effective? A reanalysis of treatments for depression. *Epidemiology and Psychiatric Sciences,* 1-7.

**Munoz-Rubke, F., Olson, D., Will, R., & James, K. H.** (2018). Functional fixedness in tool use: Learning modality, limitations and individual differences. *Acta Psychologica, 190,* 11–26.

**Muris, P., & Merckelbach, H.** (2012). Specific phobia: Phenomenology, epidemiology, and etiology. In T. E. Davis, T. H. Ollendick, & L.-G. Öst (Eds.), *Intensive one-session treatment of specific phobias.* New York: Springer.

**Murphy, D. L., Moya, P. R., Fox, M. A., Rubenstein, L. M., Wendland, J. R., & Timpano, K. R.** (2013). Anxiety and affective disorder comorbidity related to serotonin and other neurotransmitter systems: Obsessive-compulsive disorder as an example of overlapping clinical and genetic heterogeneity. *Philosophical Transactions of the Royal Society of London: Series B: Biological Sciences, 368* (1615), 20120435.

**Murphy, G., & Greene, C. M.** (2015). High perceptual load causes inattentional blindness and deafness in drivers. *Visual Cognition, 23* (7), 810–814.

**Murphy, N. A., Hall, J. A., Ruben, M. A., Frauendorfer, D., Schmid Mast, M., Johnson, K. E., & Nguyen, L.** (2018). Predictive validity of thin-slice nonverbal behavior from social interactions. *Personality and Social Psychology Bulletin,* 0146167218802834.

**Murphy-Baum, B. L., & Awatramani, G. B.** (2018). An old neuron learns new tricks: Redefining motion processing in the primate retina. *Neuron, 97,* 1205–1208.

**Murray, M.** (2013, April 11). NBC/ WSJ poll: 53 percent support gay marriage. *NBC News.* http://firstread.nbcnews.com/_news/2013/04/11/17708688-nbcwsj-poll-53-percent-support-gay-marriage?lite (accessed March 22, 2016)

**Murru, A., & Carpiniello, B.** (2018). Duration of untreated illness as a key to early intervention in schizophrenia: A review. *Neuroscience Letters, 669,* 59–67.

**Mustoe, A., Taylor, J. H., & French, J. A.** (2018). Oxytocin structure and function in New World monkeys: From pharmacology to behavior. *Integrative Zoology.*

**Mwendwa, D. T., Ali, M. K., Sims, R. C., Madhere, S., Levy, S. A., Callender, C. O., & Campbell, A. L.** (2013). Psychometric properties of the Cook Medley Hostility Scale and its association with inflammatory markers in African Americans. *Psychology, Health, and Medicine, 18* (4), 431–444.

**Myers, N. L.** (2010). Culture, stress, and recovery from schizophrenia: Lessons from the field for global mental health. *Culture, Medicine, and Psychiatry, 34* (3), 500–528.

**Myrick, A. C., Webermann, A. R., Loewenstein, R. J., Lanius, R., Putnam, F. W., & Brand, B. L.** (2017). Six-year follow-up of the treatment of patients with dissociative disorders study. *European Journal of Psychotraumatology, 8* (1), Article 1344080.

## N

**Naaijen, J., Zwiers, M. P., Forde, N. J., Williams, S. C., Durston, S., Brandeis, D., ... & Buitelaar, J. K.** (2018). Striatal structure and its association with N-Acetylaspartate and glutamate in autism spectrum disorder and obsessive compulsive disorder. *European Neuropsychopharmacology, 28* (1), 118–129.

**Nadler, A.** (2019). From help giving to helping relations: Belongingness and independence in social interactions. In K. Deaux & M. Snyder (Eds.), *The Oxford handbook of personality and social psychology* (2nd ed., pp. 465–488). New York: Oxford University Press.

**Nagaraja, A. S., Armaiz-Pena, G. N., Lutgendorf, S. K., & Sood, A. K.** (2013). Why stress is BAD for cancer patients. *Journal of Clinical Investigation, 123* (2), 558–560.

**Nagata, J. M., Garber, A. K., Tabler, J. L., Murray, S. B., & Bibbins-Domingo, K.** (2018). Differential risk factors for unhealthy weight control behaviors by sex and weight status among US adolescents. *Journal of Adolescent Health, 63* (3), 335–341.

**Nagl, M., Jacobi, C., Paul, M., Beesdo-Baum, K., Höfler, M., Lieb, R., & Wittchen, H. U.** (2016). Prevalence, incidence, and natural course of anorexia and bulimia nervosa among adolescents and young adults. *European Child and Adolescent Psychiatry, 25* (8), 903–918.

**Nakajima, S.** (2018). Extinction of running-based taste aversion in rats (Rattus norvegicus). *International Journal of Comparative Psychology, 31.*

**Nam, M. J., & Cho, Y. M.** (2018). The effect of basic psychological needs and wisdom on successful aging in the elderly. *Korean Journal of Adult Nursing, 30* (1), 70–78.

**Nanda, S.** (2008). Cross-cultural issues. In D. L. Rowland & L. Incrocci (Eds.), *Handbook of sexual and gender identity disorders* (pp. 457–485). Hoboken, NJ: Wiley.

**Narvaez, D., Wang, L., & Cheng, Y.** (2016). The evolved developmental niche in childhood: Relation to adult psychopathology and morality. *Applied Developmental Science.* doi: 10.1080/10888691.2015.1128835

**Nasser, J.** (2013) Empirically supported treatments and efficacy trials: What steps do we still need to take? *Journal of Contemporary Psychotherapy, 43* (3), 141–149.

**National Aeronautics and Space Administration (NASA).** (2018). *Scientific consensus: Earth's climate is warming.* Pasadena, CA: Earth Science Communications Team, NASA Jet Propulsion Laboratory. https://climate.nasa.gov/scientific-consensus/

**National Center for PTSD.** (2018). PTSD: National Center for PTSD. https://www.ptsd.va.gov/

**National Federation of the Blind.** (2018). *Blindness statistics.* https://nfb.org/blindness-statistics downloaded 10/28/18

**National Institute Alcohol Abuse and Alcoholism (NIAAA).** (2018). *Alcohol facts and statistics.* https://www.niaaa.nih.gov/alcohol-health/overview-alcohol-consumption/alcohol-facts-and-statistics

**National Institute of Mental Health (NIMH).** (2016). *Eating disorders. National Institutes of Health.* http://www.nimh.nih.gov/health/topics/eating-disorders/index.shtml (accessed February 21, 2016)

**National Institute of Mental Health (NIMH).** (2016). Schizophrenia. *National Institutes of Health.* http://www.nimh.nih.gov/health/topics/schizophrenia/index.shtml (accessed April 8, 2016)

**National Institute of Mental Health (NIMH).** (2018). Depression. https://www.nimh.nih.gov/health/topics/depression/index.shtml

**National Institute of Mental Health (NIMH).** (2018, May). Suicide. https://www.nimh.nih.gov/health/statistics/suicide.shtml#part_154969

**National Institute on Deafness and Other Communication Disorders.** (2017). *Cochlear implants.* https://www.nidcd.nih.gov/health/cochlear-implants (accessed November 8, 2018)

**National Institute on Drug Abuse (NIDA).** (2016, June). *Fentanyl.* https://www.drugabuse.gov/publications/drugfacts/fentanyl

**National Institute on Drug Abuse (NIDA).** (2017, September). *Overdose death rates.* https://www.drugabuse.gov/related-topics/trends-statistics/overdose-death-rates

**National Institutes of Health (NIH).** (October 30, 2018). What was the Human Genome Project and why has it been important? https://ghr.nlm.nih.gov/primer/hgp/description

**National Science Foundation** (2017). Women, minorities, and persons with disabilities in science and engineering: 2017. (Special Report NSF 17-310). Arlington, VA: National Center for Science and Engineering Statistics.

**National Sleep Foundation.** (2007, March 6). Stressed-out *American women have no time for sleep: Stay-at-home mothers most likely to sleep poorly.* Washington, DC: Author.

**Naumann, L. P., Vazire, S., Rentfrow, P. J., & Gosling, S. D.** (2009). Personality judgments based on physical appearance. *Personality and Social Psychology Bulletin, 35* (12), 1661-1671.

**Naumova, E., Ivanova, M. Pawelec, G., Constantinescu, I., Bogunia-Kubik, K., Lange, A., ... & Middleton, D.** (2013). 16th IHIW: Immunogenetics of aging. *International Journal of Immunogenetics, 40* (1), 77-81.

**Needham, A., Barrett, T., & Peterman, K.** (2002). A pick-me-up for infants' exploratory skills: Early simulated experiences reaching for objects using "sticky mittens" enhances young infants' object exploration skills. *Infant Behavior and Development, 25* (3), 279–295.

**Negru-Subtirica, O., Tiganasu, A., Dezutter, J., & Luyckx, K.** (2017). A cultural take on the links between religiosity, identity, and meaning in life in religious emerging adults. *British Journal of Developmental Psychology, 35* (1), 106–126.

**Neligan, A.** (2018). Why we sleep? A manifesto in defence of sleep. *Brain, 141* (6), 1884–1886.

**Nelis, S. M., Thom, J. M., Jones, I. R., Hindle, J. V., & Clare, L.** (2018). Goal-setting to promote a healthier lifestyle in later life: Qualitative evaluation of the AgeWell trial. *Clinical Gerontologist, 41* (4), 335–345.

**Nelson, D. W., & Sim, E. K.** (2014). Positive affect facilitates social problem solving. *Journal of Applied Social Psychology, 44* (10), 635–642.

**Nerstad, C. G., Dysvik, A., Kuvaas, B., & Buch, R.** (2018). Negative and positive synergies: On employee development practices, motivational climate, and employee outcomes. *Human Resource Management, 57* (5), 1285–1302.

**Neumann, E.** (2015). *The great mother: An analysis of the archetype.* Princeton, NJ: Princeton University Press.

**Neville, H. J.** (2006). Different profiles of plasticity within human cognition. In Y. Munakata & M. H. Johnson (Eds.), *Attention and performance.* Oxford, UK: Oxford University Press.

**Newcombe, N. S.** (2002). The nativist-empiricist controversy. *Psychological Science, 13* (5), 395–401.

**Newirth, J.** (2018). *From sign to symbol: Transformational processes in psychoanalysis, psychotherapy, and psychology.* Lanham, MD: Lexington Books.

**Newman, E., Jernigan, T. L., Lisdahl, K. M., Tamm, L., Tapert, S. F., Potkin, S. G., ... & Group, M. N.** (2016). Go/No Go task performance predicts cortical thickness in the caudal inferior frontal gyrus in young adults with and without ADHD. *Brain Imaging and Behavior, 10* (3), 880–892.

**Newsom, J. T., Shaw, B. A., August, K. J., & Strath, S. J.** (2018). Physical activity–related social control and social support in older adults: Cognitive and emotional pathways to physical activity. *Journal of Health Psychology, 23* (11), 1389–1404.

**Nezlek, J. B., Krejtz, I., Rusanowska, M., & Holas, P.** (2018). Within-person relationships among daily gratitude, well-being, stress, and positive experiences. *Journal of Happiness Studies*, 1-16.

**Nezu, A. M., Nezu, C. M., Felgoise, S. H., & Greenberg, L. M.** (2013). Psychological oncology. In A. M. Nezu, C. Maguth Nezu, P. A. Geller, & I. B. Weiner (Eds.), *Handbook of psychology* (2nd ed., vol. 9, pp. 271–291). Hoboken, NJ: Wiley.

**Ng, W., & Diener, E.** (2018). Affluence and subjective well-being: Does income inequality moderate their associations? *Applied Research in Quality of Life,* 1–16.

**Nguyen, T., & Sin, B.** (2015). A case of an older adult patient and drugs associated with serotonin syndrome. *Consultant Pharmacist, 30* (8), 455–458.

**Nicholson, C.** (2008). Scanning sexuality. *Nature Reviews: Neuroscience, 9,* 582.

**Nickel, K., Joos, A., Tebartz van Elst, L., Matthis, J., Holovics, L., Endres, D., ... & Maier, S.** (2018). Recovery of cortical volume and thickness after remission from acute anorexia nervosa. *International Journal of Eating Disorders.* doi: 10.1002/eat.22918

**Nickel, L. B., Roberts, B. W., & Chernyshenko, O. S.** (2018). No evidence of a curvilinear relation between conscientiousness and relationship, work, and health outcomes. *Journal of Personality and Social Psychology.* doi: 10.1037/pspp0000176 (in press)

**Nickels, N., Kubicki, K., & Maestripieri, D.** (2017). Sex differences in the effects of psychosocial stress on cooperative and prosocial behavior: Evidence for 'flight or fight' in males and 'tend and befriend' in females. *Adaptive Human Behavior and Physiology, 3* (2), 171–183.

**Nickerson, R. S., & Adams, M. J.** (1979). Long-term memory for a common object. *Cognitive Psychology, 11* (3), 287–307.

**NIDA.** (2018). How does marijuana produce its effects? https://www.drugabuse.gov/publications/research-reports/marijuana/how-does-marijuana-produce-its-effects

**Nienhuis, J. B., Owen, J., Valentine, J. C., Winkeljohn Black, S., Halford, T. C., Parazak, S. E., ... & Hilsenroth, M.** (2018). Therapeutic alliance, empathy, and genuineness in individual adult psychotherapy: A meta-analytic review. *Psychotherapy Research, 28* (4), 593–605.

**Nies, V. J. M., Struik, D., Wolfs, M. G. M., Rensen, S. S., Szalowska, E., Unmehopa, U. A., ... & Greve, J. W.** (2018). TUB gene expression in hypothalamus and adipose tissue and its association with obesity in humans. *International Journal of Obesity, 42* (3), 376–383.

**Nikandrou, I., & Tsachouridi, I.** (2015). Towards a better understanding of the "buffering effects" of organizational virtuousness' perceptions on employee outcomes. *Management Decision, 53* (8), 1823–1842.

**Nilsson, N. C., Serafin, S., Steinicke, F., & Nordahl, R.** (2018). Natural walking in virtual reality: A review. *Computers in Entertainment (CIE), 16* (2), 8.

**Ninio, A., & Snow, C. E.** (2018). *Pragmatic development.* London: Routledge.

**Nisbett, R. E.** (1987). Lay trait theory: Its nature, origins, and utility. In N. E. Grunberg, R. E. Nisbett, J. Rodin, & J. E. Singer (Eds.), *A distinctive approach to psychological research: The influence of Stanley Schachter.* Hillsdale, NJ: Erlbaum.

**Nisbett, R. E. & Cohen, D.** (2018). *Culture of honor: The psychology of violence in the South.* New York: Routledge.

**Nisbett, R. E., Aronson, J., Blair, C., Dickens, W., Flynn, J., Halpern, D. F., & Turkheimer, E.** (2012). Intelligence: New findings and theoretical developments. *American Psychologist, 67* (2), 130–159.

**Nisbett, R. E., & Ross, L.** (1980). *Human inference.* Upper Saddle River, NJ: Prentice-Hall.

**Nishida, A., Miyaoka, T., Inagaki, T., & Horiguchi, J.** (2009). New approaches to antidepressant drug design: Cytokine-regulated pathways. *Current Pharmaceutical Design, 15* (14), 1683-1687.

**Nishino, H., Watanabe, H., Kamimura, I., Yokohari, F., & Mizunami, M.** (2015). Coarse topographic organization of pheromone-sensitive afferents from different antennal surfaces in the American cockroach. *Neuroscience Letters, 595,* 35–40.

**Nixon, J., & Braithwaite, G. R.** (2018). What do aircraft accident investigators do and what makes them good at it? Developing a competency framework for investigators using grounded theory. *Safety science, 103,* 153–161.

**Nobili, A., Glazebrook, C., & Arcelus, J.** (2018). Quality of life of treatment-seeking transgender adults: A systematic review and meta-analysis. *Reviews in Endocrine and Metabolic Disorders, 19* (3), 199–220.

**Nock, M. K., Millner, A. J., Joiner, T. E., Gutierrez, P. M., Han, G., Hwang, I., ... & Stein, M. B.** (2018). Risk factors for the transition from suicide ideation to suicide attempt: Results from the Army Study to Assess Risk and Resilience in Servicemembers (Army STARRS). *Journal of Abnormal Psychology, 127* (2), 139–149.

**Noel, J. P., Wallace, M., & Blake, R.** (2015). Cognitive neuroscience: Integration of sight and sound outside of awareness? *Current Biology, 25* (4), R157–R159.

**Nokia, M. S., Lensu, S., Ahtiainen, J. P., Johansson, P. P., Koch, L. G., Britton, S. L., & Kainulainen, H.** (2016). Physical exercise increases adult hippocampal neurogenesis in male rats provided it is aerobic and sustained. *Journal of Physiology, 594,* 1355–1373.

**Nolan, J. M., Hanley, B. G., DiVietri, T. P., & Harvey, N. A.** (2018). She who teaches learns: Performance benefits of a jigsaw activity in a college classroom. *Scholarship of Teaching and Learning in Psychology, 4* (2), 93–104.

**Norcross, J. C., Campbell, L. M., Grohol, J. M., Santrock, J. W., Selagea, F., & Sommer, R.** (2013). Self-help *that works: Evidence-based resources for the public and professionals* (4th ed.). New York: Oxford University Press.

**Norcross, J. C., Loberg, K., & Norcross, J.** (2012). *Changeology: 5 steps to realizing your goals and resolutions.* New York: Simon & Schuster.

**Nordstrom, B. R., Gao, Y., Glenn, A. L., Peskin, M., Rudo-Hutt, A. S., Schug, R. A., ... & Raine, A.** (2011). Neurocriminology. *Advances in Genetics, 75,* 255–283.

**Northoff, G.** (2018). What is the unconscious? A novel taxonomy of psychoanalytic, psychological, neuroscientific, and philosophical concepts. In H. Boeker, P. Hartwich, & G. Northoff (Eds.), *Neuropsychodynamic Psychiatry* (pp. 117–136). Cham: Springer.

**Northouse, P. G.** (2018). *Leadership: Theory and practice* (8th ed.) London: Sage.

**Nosek, B. A., & Errington, T. M.** (2017). Reproducibility in cancer biology: Making sense of replications. *Elife, 6,* e23383.

**Noyes-Grosser, D. M., Elbaum, B., Wu, Y., Siegenthaler, K. M., Cavalari, R. S., Gillis, J. M., & Romanczyk, R. G.** (2018). Early intervention outcomes for toddlers with autism spectrum disorder and their families. *Infants & Young Children, 31* (3), 177–199.

**Nuccitelli, C., Valentini, A., Caletti, M. T., Caselli, C., Mazzella, N., Forlani, G., & Marchesini, G.** (2018). Sense of coherence, self-esteem, and health locus of control in subjects with type 1 diabetes mellitus with/without satisfactory metabolic control. *Journal of Endocrinological Investigation, 41*(3), 307–314.

**Nulman, I., Shulman, T., & Liu, F.** (2018). Fetal alcohol spectrum disorder. In W. Slikker, M.G. Paule, & C. Wang (Eds.). *Handbook of developmental neurotoxicology* (2nd ed., pp. 427–437). New York: Academic Press.

**Numan, M., & Young, L. J.** (2016). Neural mechanisms of mother–infant bonding and pair bonding: Similarities, differences, and broader implications. *Hormones and Behavior, 77,* 98–112.

**Numbers, K. T., Barnier, A. J., Harris, C. B., & Meade, M. L.** (2018). Ageing stereotypes influence the transmission of false memories in the social contagion paradigm. *Memory.* (in press)

**Nummenmaa, L., Hari, R., Hietanen, J. K., & Glerean, E.** (2018). Maps of subjective feelings. *Proceedings of the National Academy of Sciences, 115* (37), 9198–9203.

**Nyberg, L., & Pudas, S.** (2019). Successful memory aging. *Annual Review of Psychology, 70,* 219–243.

**Nyer, M., Nauphal, M., Roberg, R., & Streeter, C.** (2018). Applications of yoga in psychiatry: What we know. *Focus, 16* (1), 12–18.

**Nylander, L., Axmon, A., Björne, P., Ahlström, G., & Gillberg, C.** (2018). Older adults with autism spectrum disorders in Sweden: A register study of diagnoses, psychiatric care utilization and psychotropic medication of 601 individuals. *Journal of Autism and Developmental Disorders, 48,* 3076–3085.

## O

**O'Connor, D. B., Conner, M., Jones, F., McMillan, B., & Ferguson, E.** (2009). Exploring the benefits of conscientiousness: An investigation of the role of daily stressors and health behaviors. *Annals of Behavioral Medicine, 37* (2), 184–196.

**O'Connor, K. M., & Gladstone, E.** (2018). Beauty and social capital: Being attractive shapes social networks. *Social Networks, 52,* 42–47.

**O'Dell, K. R., Masters, K. S., Spielmans, G. I., & Maisto, S. A.** (2011). Does type-D personality predict outcomes among patients with cardiovascular disease? A meta-analytic review. *Journal of Psychosomatic Research, 71* (4), 199–206.

**O'Donnell, M., Nelson, L. D., Ackermann, E., Aczel, B., Akhtar, A., Aldrovandi, S., ... & Balatekin, N.** (2018). Registered Replication Report: Dijksterhuis and van Knippenberg (1998). *Perspectives on Psychological Science, 13*(2), 268–294.

**O'Loughlin, J. I., Basson, R., & Brotto, L. A.** (2018). Women with hypoactive sexual desire disorder versus sexual interest/arousal disorder: An empirical test of

with low and high resistance to peer influence. *Social Neuroscience, 3* (3-4), 303-316.

**Pavletic, A.** (2017). Safety, science, or both? Deceptive healthy volunteers: psychiatric conditions uncovered by objective methods of screening. *Psychosomatics, 58*(6), 657-663.

**Pavlov, I. P.** (1927). *Conditioned reflexes* (G. V. Anrep, trans.). New York: Dover.

**Paz-Alonso, P. M., Oliver, M., Lerma-Usabiaga, G., Caballero-Gaudes, C., Quiñones, I., Suárez-Coalla, P., ... & Carreiras, M.** (2018). Neural correlates of phonological, orthographic and semantic reading processing in dyslexia. *NeuroImage: Clinical, 20*, 433-447.

**Peachman, R. R.** (January 31, 2017). Raising a transgender child. *New York Times*, D4.

**Pedersen, S., Sniehotta, F. F., Sainsbury, K., Evans, E. H., Marques, M. M., Stubbs, R. J., ... & Lähteenmäki, L.** (2018). The complexity of self-regulating food intake in weight loss maintenance. A qualitative study among short-and long-term weight loss maintainers. *Social Science & Medicine, 208*, 18-24.

**Peets, K., & Hodges, E. V.** (2018). Authenticity in friendships and well-being in adolescence. *Social Development, 27* (1), 140-153.

**Peira, N., Ziaei, M., & Persson, J.** (2016). Age differences in brain systems supporting transient and sustained processes involved in prospective memory and working memory. *NeuroImage, 125*, 745-755.

**Pejic, T., Hermann, A., Vaitl, D., & Stark, R.** (2013). Social anxiety modulates amygdala activation during social conditioning. *Social Cognitive Affective Neuroscience, 8* (3), 267-276.

**Pekala, R. J.** (2015). Hypnosis as a "state of consciousness": How quantifying the mind can help us better understand hypnosis. *American Journal of Clinical Hypnosis, 57* (4), 402-424.

**Pelham, W. E., Smith, B. H., Evans, S. W., Bukstein, O., Gnagy, E. M., Greiner, A. R., & Sibley, M. H.** (2017). The effectiveness of short-and long-acting stimulant medications for adolescents with ADHD in a naturalistic secondary school setting. *Journal of Attention Disorders, 21* (1), 40-45.

**Pelleymounter, M. A., Cullen, M. J., Baker, M. B., Hecht, R., Winters, D., Boone, T., & Collins, F.** (1995). Effects of the obese gene product on body weight regulation in ob/ob mice. *Science, 269* (5223), 540-543.

**Pelt, D. H., van der Linden, D., & Born, M. P.** (2018). How emotional intelligence might get you the job: The relationship between trait emotional intelligence and faking on personality tests. *Human Performance, 31* (1), 33-54.

**Penedo, F. J., Molton, I., Dahn, J. R., Shen, B. J., Kinsigner, D., Traeger, L., Siegel, S., Schneiderman, N., & Antoni, M.** (2006). A randomized clinical trial of group-based cognitive-behavioral stress management in localized prostate cancer: Development of stress management skills improves quality of life and benefit finding. *Annals of Behavioral Medicine, 31* (3), 261-270.

**Penfield, W.** (1947). Some observations on the cerebral cortex of man. *Proceedings of the Royal Society of London: Series B: Biological Sciences, 134* (876), 329-347.

**Peng, L., Zeng, L. L., Liu, Q., Wang, L., Qin, J., Xu, H., ... & Hu, D.** (2018). Functional connectivity changes in the entorhinal cortex of taxi drivers. *Brain and Behavior, 8*(9), e01022.

**Penn Medicine** (June 5, 2018). *1 in 4 Americans develop insomnia each year.* https://www.pennmedicine.org/news/news-releases/2018/june/1-in-4-americans-develop-insomnia-each-year

**Pennebaker, J. W.** (2016). Expressive writing. In R. Sternberg, S. Fiske, & D. Foss (Eds.), *Scientists making a difference: The greatest living behavioral and brain scientists talk about their most important contributions.* NY: Cambridge University Press.

**Pennebaker, J. W., & Evans, J. F.** (2014). *Expressive writing: Words that heal.* Enumclaw, WA: Idyll Arbor.

**Pennebaker, J. W., & O'Heeron, R. C.** (1984). Confiding in others and illness rate among spouses of suicide and accidental-death victims. *Journal of Abnormal Psychology, 93,* 473-476.

**Pennebaker, J. W., & Smyth, J.** (2016). Opening up by writing it down: The healing power of expressive writing (3rd ed.). New York: Guilford.

**Pennefather, J., Hieneman, M., Raulston, T. J., & Caraway, N.** (2018). Evaluation of an online training program to improve family routines, parental well-being, and the behavior of children with autism. *Research in Autism Spectrum Disorders, 54*, 21-26.

**Pennycook, G., De Neys, W., Evans, J. S. B., Stanovich, K. E., & Thompson, V. A.** (2018). The mythical dual-process typology. *Trends in Cognitive Sciences.* doi: 10.1016/j.tics.2018.04.008

**Pennycook, G., Fugelsang, J. A., & Koehler, D. J.** (2015). What makes us think? A three-stage dual-process model of analytic engagement. *Cognitive Psychology, 80*, 34-72.

**Peplau, L. A., Spalding, L. R., Conley, T. D., & Veniegas, R. C.** (1999). The development of sexual orientation in women. *Annual Review of Sex Research, 10* (1), 70-99.

**Pepping, C. A., Lyons, A., & Morris, E. M.** (2018). Affirmative LGBT psychotherapy: Outcomes of a therapist training protocol. *Psychotherapy, 55* (1), 52-62.

**Perera, F. P., Wheelock, K., Wang, Y., Tang, D., Margolis, A. E., Badia, G., ... & Herbstman, J. B.** (2018). Combined effects of prenatal exposure to polycyclic aromatic hydrocarbons and material hardship on child ADHD behavior problems. *Environmental Research, 160*, 506-513.

**Perez, I. J., Cabrerizo, F. J., Alonso, S., Dong, Y. C., Chiclana, F., & Herrera-Viedma, E.** (2018). On dynamic consensus processes in group decision making problems. *Information Sciences, 459*, 20-35.

**Pérez-Pérez, B., Cristóbal-Narváez, P., Sheinbaum, T., Kwapil, T. R., Ballespí, S., Peña, E., ... & Barrantes-Vidal, N.** (2018). Interaction between FKBP5 variability and recent life events in the anxiety spectrum: Evidence for the differential susceptibility model. *PloS One, 13* (2), e0193044.

**Perfumi, S. C., Bagnoli, F., Caudek, C., & Guazzini, A.** (2018). Deindividuation effects on normative and informational social influence within computer-mediated-communication. *Computers in Human Behavior, 92*, 230-237.

**Perkins, D.** (1994, September). Creativity by design. *Educational Leadership,* 18-25.

**Pesce, N. L.** (October 12, 2018) Why the International Day of the Girl Child matters more than ever. *MarketWatch.* https://www.marketwatch.com/story/why-the-international-day-of-the-girl-child-matters-more-than-ever-2018-10-12

**Pešlová, E., Mareček, R., Shaw, D. J., Kašpárek, T., Pail, M., & Brázdil, M.** (2018). Hippocampal involvement in nonpathological déjà vu: Subfield vulnerability rather than temporal lobe epilepsy equivalent. *Brain and Behavior,* e00996. doi: 10.1002/brb3.996

**Pessoa, L.** (2018). Embracing integration and complexity: Placing emotion within a science of brain and behaviour. *Cognition and Emotion.* doi: 10.1080/02699931.2018.1520079

**Peteranderl, S., & Oberauer, K.** (2018). Serial recall of colors: Two models of memory for serial order applied to continuous visual stimuli. *Memory & Cognition, 46*(1), 1-16.

**Petersen, J. L., & Hyde, J. S.** (2010). A meta-analytic review of research on gender differences in sexuality, 1973-2007. *Psychological Bulletin, 136* (1), 21-38.

**Peters-Scheffer, N., Didden, R., & Lang, R.** (2016). Intellectual disability. In J. L. Matson (Ed.), *Comorbid conditions among children with autism spectrum disorders* (pp. 283-300). Switzerland: Springer International Publishing.

**Petrelli, B., Weinberg, J., & Hicks, G. G.** (2018). Effects of prenatal alcohol exposure (PAE): Insights into FASD using mouse models of PAE. *Biochemistry and Cell Biology, 96* (2), 131-147.

**Petrie, K. J., Pressman, S. D., Pennebaker, J. W., Øverland, S., Tell, G. S., & Sivertsen, B.** (2018). Which aspects of positive affect are related to mortality? Results from a general population longitudinal study. *Annals of Behavioral Medicine, 52* (7), 571-581.

**Petschner, P., Tamasi, V., Adori, C., Kirilly, E., Ando, R. D., Tothfalusi, L., & Bagdy, G.** (2018). Gene expression analysis indicates reduced memory and cognitive functions in the hippocampus and increase in synaptic reorganization in the frontal cortex 3 weeks after MDMA administration in Dark Agouti rats. *BMC Genomics, 19* (1), 580.

**Pettersson, E. T., & Turkheimer, E.** (2013). Approach temperament, anger, and evaluation: Resolving a paradox. *Journal of Personality and Social Psychology, 105* (2), 285-300.

**Petticrew, M., Bell, R., & Hunter, D.** (2002). Influence of psychological coping on survival and recurrence in people with cancer: Systematic review. *British Medical Journal, 325* (7372), 1066-1069.

**Pettigrew, T. F.** (2019). The intertwined histories of personality and social psychology. In K. Deaux & M. Snyder (Eds.), *The Oxford handbook of personality and social psychology, 2nd edition.* (pp. 11-34). New York: Oxford University Press.

**Pettigrew, T. F., & Tropp, L. R.** (2006). A meta-analytic test of intergroup contact theory. *Journal of Personality and Social Psychology, 90* (5), 751- 783.

**Petty, R. E.** (2018). *Attitudes and persuasion: Classic and contemporary approaches.* London: Routledge.

**Petty, R. E., & Cacioppo, J. T.** (1986). The elaboration likelihood of persuasion. In L. Berkowitz (Ed.), *Advances in experimental social psychology* (vol. 19). New York: Academic.

**Pew Research Center.** (2015, July 29). Changing attitudes on gay marriage. *PewForum.org.* http://www.pewforum.org/2015/07/29/graphics-slideshow-changing-attitudes-on-gay-marriage/ (accessed March 22, 2016)

**Pezdek, K.** (2003). Event memory and autobiographical memory for the events of September 11, 2001. *Applied Cognitive Psychology, 17,* 1033-1045.

**Pezdek, K.** (2012). Fallible eyewitness memory and identification. In B. L. Cutler (Ed.), *Conviction of the innocent: Lessons from psychological research* (pp. 105-124). Washington, DC: American Psychological Association.

**Pezzuti, L., Artistico, D., Chirumbolo, A., Picone, L., & Dowd, S. M.** (2014). The relevance of logical thinking and cognitive style to everyday problem solving among older adults. *Learning and Individual Differences, 36,* 218-223.

**Pfafflin, F.** (2010). Understanding transgendered phenomena. In S. B. Levine, C. B. Risen, & S. E. Althof (Eds.), *Handbook of clinical sexuality for mental health professionals* (2nd ed., pp. 425-447). New York: Routledge.

**Pfeffer, J.** (2016). Why the assholes are winning: Money trumps all. *Journal of Management Studies, 53* (4), 663-669.

**Pfundmair, M., Rimpel, A., Duffy, K., & Zwarg, C.** (2018). Oxytocin blurs the self-other distinction implicitly but not explicitly. *Hormones and Behavior, 98,* 115-120.

**Phelan, S., Hill, J. O., Lang, W., Dibello, J. R., Wing, R. R.** (2003). Recovery from relapse among successful weight maintainers. *American Journal of Clinical Nutrition, 78* (6), 1079-1084.

**Philip, B., Valyear, K., Cirstea, C., & Frey, S.** (2017). Reorganization of primary somatosensory cortex after upper limb amputation may lack functional significance. *Archives of Physical Medicine and Rehabilitation, 98*(10), e103.

**Philipp-Wiegmann, F., Rösler, M., Clasen, O., Zinnow, T., Retz-Junginger, P., & Retz, W.** (2018). ADHD modulates the course of delinquency: A 15-year follow-up study of young incarcerated man. *European Archives of Psychiatry and Clinical Neuroscience, 268* (4), 391–399.

**Phillips, K. A., Osborne, R. H., Giles, G. G., Dite, G. S., Apicella, C., Hopper, J. L., & Milne, R. L.** (2008). Psychosocial factors and survival of young women with breast cancer: A population-based prospective cohort study. *Journal of Clinical Oncology, 26* (28), 4666–4671.

**Piaget, J.** (1952). *The origins of intelligence in children.* New York: Oxford University Press.

**Pica, G., Chernikova, M., Pierro, A., Giannini, A. M., & Kruglanski, A.** (2018). Retrieval-Induced Forgetting as Motivated Cognition. *Frontiers in Psychology, 9,* 2030.

**Picchioni, D., Schmidt, K. C., McWhirter, K. K., Loutaev, I., Pavletic, A. J., Speer, A. M., ... & Morrow, A. S.** (2018). Rates of cerebral protein synthesis in primary visual cortex during sleep-dependent memory consolidation, a study in human subjects. *Sleep, 41* (7), zsy088.

**Piccinini, G., & Schulz, A. W.** (2018). The ways of altruism. *Evolutionary Psychological Science,* 1–13.

**Picerni, E., Santarcangelo, E. L., Laricchiuta, D., Cutuli, D., Petrosini, L., Spalletta, G., & Piras, F.** (2018). Cerebellar structural variations in subjects with different hypnotizability. *The Cerebellum,* 1–10.

**Piché, M. E., Poirier, P., Lemieux, I., & Després, J. P.** (2018). Overview of epidemiology and contribution of obesity and body fat distribution to cardiovascular disease: an update. *Progress in Cardiovascular Diseases, 61,* 103–113.

**Piedimonte, A., & Benedetti, F.** (2015). Words and drugs: Same mechanisms of action? *Journal of Contemporary Psychotherapy.* doi: 10.1007/s10879-015-9321-4

**Pietri, E. S., Johnson, I. R., Ozgumus, E., & Young, A. I.** (2018). Maybe she is relatable: Increasing women's awareness of gender bias encourages their identification with women scientists. *Psychology of Women Quarterly, 42* (2), 192–219.

**Piff, P. K., Kraus, M. W., & Keltner, D.** (2018). Unpacking the inequality paradox: The psychological roots of inequality and social class. *Advances in Experimental Social Psychology, 57,* 53–124.

**Pike, K. M., Yamamiya, Y., & Konishi, H.** (2011). Eating disorders in Japan: Cultural context, clinical features, and future directions. In R. H. Striegel-Moore, S. A. Wonderlich, B. T. Walsh, & J. E. Mitchell (Eds.), *Developing an evidence-based classification of eating disorders: Scientific findings for DSM-5* (pp. 335–349). Washington, DC: American Psychiatric Association.

**Pillai, A., Howell, K. R., Ahmed, A. O., Weinberg, D., Allen, K. M., Bruggermann, J., ... & Weickert, T. W.** (2016). Association of serum VEGF levels with prefrontal cortex volume in schizophrenia. *Molecular Psychiatry, 21* (5), 686–692.

**Pillemer, D. B.** (1998). *Momentous events: Vivid memories.* Cambridge, MA: Harvard University Press.

**Pillinger, T., D'Ambrosio, E., McCutcheon, R., & Howes, O.** (2018). Is psychosis a multisystem disorder? A meta-review of central nervous system, immune, cardiometabolic, and endocrine alterations in first-episode psychosis and perspective on potential models. *Molecular Psychiatry.* (in press)

**Pinciotti, C. M., & Orcutt, H. K.** (2018). Rape aggression defense: Unique self-efficacy benefits for survivors of sexual trauma. *Violence Against Women, 24* (5), 528–544.

**Pinck, A. S., & Sonnentag, S.** (2018). Leader mindfulness and employee well-being: The mediating role of transformational leadership. *Mindfulness, 9* (3), 884–896.

**Pinedo, M., Zemore, S., & Rogers, S.** (2018). Understanding barriers to specialty substance abuse treatment among Latinos. *Journal of Substance Abuse Treatment, 94,* 1–8.

**Pinel, E. C.** (2018). Existential isolation and I-sharing: Interpersonal and intergroup implications. *Current Opinion in Psychology, 23,* 84–87.

**Piolino, P., Desgranges, B., Clarys, D., Guillery-Girard, B., Taconnat, L., Isingrini, M., & Eustache, F.** (2006). Autobiographical memory, autonoetic consciousness, and self-perspective in aging. *Psychology and Aging, 21* (3), 510–525.

**Piotrowski, C.** (2015). Projective techniques usage worldwide: A review of applied settings 1995–2015. *Journal of the Indian Academy of Applied Psychology, 41* (3), 9–19.

**Pitcher, D., Goldhaber, T., Duchaine, B., Walsh, V., & Kanswisher, N.** (2012). Two critical and functionally distinct stages of face and body perception. *Journal of Neuroscience, 32* (45), 15877–15885.

**Pittig, A., Treanor, M., LeBeau, R. T., & Craske, M. G.** (2018). The role of associative fear and avoidance learning in anxiety disorders: Gaps and directions for future research. *Neuroscience & Biobehavioral Reviews, 88,* 117–140.

**Pittman, T.** (August 5, 2016). Mom creates sightseeing bucket list for daughter losing her vision. *Huffington Post.* https://www.today.com/parents/mom-creates-sightseeing-bucket-list-daughter-losing-her-vision-t101720

**Plack, C. J.** (2018). *The sense of hearing.* London: Routledge.

**Plaza-Zabala, A., Martin-Garcia, E., de Lecea, L., Maldonado, R., & Berrendero, F.** (2010). Hypocretins regulate the anxiogenic-like effects of nicotine and induce reinstatement of nicotine-seeking behavior. *Journal of Neuroscience, 30* (6), 2300–2310.

**Plomin, R., & von Stumm, S.** (2018). The new genetics of intelligence. *Nature Reviews Genetics, 19,* 148–159.

**Pluess, M., Belsky, J., Way, B. M., & Taylor, S. E.** (2010). 5-HTTLPR moderates effects of current life events on neuroticism: Differential susceptibility to environmental influences. *Progress in Neuro-Psychopharmacology and Biological Psychiatry, 34* (6), 1070–1074.

**Podina, I. R., & Fodor, L. A.** (2018). Critical review and meta-analysis of multicomponent behavioral e-health interventions for weight loss. *Health Psychology, 37* (6), 501–515. doi: 10.1037/hea0000623

**Podsakoff, P. M., MacKenzie, S. B., & Podsakoff, N. P.** (Eds.). (2018). *The Oxford handbook of organizational citizenship behavior.* New York: Oxford University Press.

**Poehlmann-Tynan, J., Vigna, A. B., Weymouth, L. A., Gerstein, E. D., Burnson, C., Zabransky, M., Lee, P., & Zahn-Waxler, C.** (2016). A pilot study of contemplative practices with economically disadvantaged preschoolers: Children's empathic and self-regulatory behaviors. *Mindfulness, 7* (1), 46–58.

**Pohl, R. F., Bayen, U. J., Arnold, N., Auer, T. S., & Martin, C.** (2019). Age differences in processes underlying hindsight bias: A lifespan study. *Journal of Cognition and Development, 19* (3), 278–300.

**Polanczyk, G. V., Salum, G. A., Sugaya, L. S., Caye, A., & Rohde, L. A.** (2015). Annual research review: A meta-analysis of the worldwide prevalence of mental disorders in children and adolescents. *Journal of Child Psychology and Psychiatry, 56* (3), 345–365.

**Polverino, A., Grimaldi, M., Sorrentino, P., Jacini, F., D'Ursi, A. M., & Sorrentino, G.** (2018). Effects of acetylcholine on β-amyloid-induced cPLA2 activation in the TB neuroectodermal cell line: Implications for the pathogenesis of Alzheimer's disease. *Cellular and Molecular Neurobiology, 38* (4), 817–826.

**Pomerantz, E. M., Saxon, J. L., & Oishi, S.** (2000). The psychological trade-offs of goal investment. *Journal of Personality and Social Psychology, 79* (4), 617–630.

**Pompili, M., Amador, X. F., Girardi, P., Harkavy-Friedman, J., Harrow, M., Kaplan, K., ... & Tatarelli, R.** (2007). Suicide risk in schizophrenia: Learning from the past to change the future. *Annals of General Psychiatry, 6,* 10.

**Ponseti, J., Bruhn, D., Nolting, J., Gerwinn, H., Pohl, A., Stirn, A., ... & Jansen, O.** (2018a). Decoding pedophilia: Increased anterior insula response to infant animal pictures. Frontiers in Human Neuroscience, 11, 645.

**Ponseti, J., Dähnke, K., Fischermeier, L., Gerwinn, H., Kluth, A., Müller, J., ... & Stirn, A.** (2018b). Sexual responses are facilitated by high-order contextual cues in females but not in males. *Evolutionary Psychology, 16* (1), 1474704918761103.

**Popat, S., & Winslade, W.** (2015). While you were sleepwalking: Science and neurobiology of sleep disorders & the enigma of legal responsibility of violence during parasomnia. *Neuroethics, 8* (2), 203–214.

**Porcerelli, J. H., Cramer, P., Porcerelli, D. J., & Arterbery, V. E.** (2017). Defense mechanisms and utilization in cancer patients undergoing radiation therapy: A pilot study. *The Journal of Nervous and Mental Disease, 205* (6), 466–470.

**Portnoy, J., & Farrington, D. P.** (2015). Resting heart rate and antisocial behavior: An updated systematic review and meta-analysis. *Aggression and Violent Behavior, 22,* 33–45.

**Portnuff, C. D., Fligor, B. J., & Arehart, K. H.** (2011). Teenage use of portable listening devices: A hazard to hearing? *Journal of the American Academy of Audiology, 22* (10), 663–677.

**Posada, G., Trumbell, J., Noblega, M., Plata, S., Peña, P., Carbonell, O. A., & Lu, T.** (2015). Maternal sensitivity and child secure base use in early childhood: Studies in different cultural contexts. *Child Development, 87* (1), 297–311.

**Posner, M. I., & Rothbart, M. K.** (2018). Temperament and brain networks of attention. *Philosophical Transactions of the Royal Society, B, 373*(1744), 20170254.

**Post, R. M.** (2018). The new news about lithium: An underutilized treatment in the United States. *Neuropsychopharmacology, 43* (5), 1174.

**Potter, N. N.** (2012). Mad, bad, or virtuous? The moral, cultural, and pathologizing features of deviance. *Theory & Psychology, 22,* 23–45.

**Powell, D., Pacula, R. L., & Jacobson, M.** (2018). Do medical marijuana laws reduce addictions and deaths related to pain killers? *Journal of Health Economics, 58,* 29–42.

**Powell, D. M., Spencer, M. B., & Petrie, K. J.** (2011). Automated collection of fatigue ratings at the top of descent: A practical commercial airline tool. *Aviation, Space, and Environmental Science, 82* (11), 1037–1041.

**Powell, L. J., Kosakowski, H. L., & Saxe, R.** (2018). Social origins of cortical face areas. *Trends in Cognitive Sciences, 22* (9), P752–P763.

**Powers, R.** (2017). *No one cares about crazy people.* New York: Hachette.

**Prather, A. A., Epel, E. S., Parra, E. P., Coccia, M., Puterman, E., Aiello, A. E., & Dhabhar, F. S.** (2018). Associations between chronic caregiving stress and T cell markers implicated in immunosenescence. *Brain, Behavior, and Immunity, 73,* 546–549.

**Prat-Ortega, G., & de la Rocha, J.** (2018). Selective attention: A plausible mechanism underlying confirmation bias. *Current Biology, 28* (19), R1151–R1154.

**Pratscher, S., Wood, P., King, L. A., & Bettencourt, B. A.** (2018). Interpersonal mindfulness: Scale development and initial construct validation. *Mindfulness.* (in press)

Pratt, M. W., & Matsuba, M. K. (2018). *The life story, domains of identity, and personality development in emerging adulthood: Integrating narrative and traditional approaches.* New York: Oxford University Press.

Prebble, S. C., Addis, D. R., & Tippett, L. J. (2013). Autobiographical memory and sense of self. *Psychological Bulletin, 139* (4), 815–840.

Prendergast, B. J., & Zucker, I. (2018). Social behavior: Developmental timing defies puberty. *Current Biology, 28* (9), R553–R555.

Prescott, J., Kraft, P., Chasman, D. I., Savage, S. A., Mirabello, L., Berndt, S. I., ... & De Vivo, I. (2011). Genome-wide association study of relative telomere length. *PLoS One, 6* (5), e19635.

Pressman, S. D., & Cohen, S. (2012). Positive emotion word use and longevity in famous deceased psychologists. *Health Psychology, 31,* 297–305.

Pressman, S. D., & Cross, M. P. (2018). Moving beyond a one-size-fits-all view of positive affect in health research. *Current Directions in Psychological Science, 27* (5), 339–344.

Pressman, S. D., Gallagher, M. W., & Lopez, S. J. (2013). Is the emotion–health connection a "first-world problem"? *Psychological Science, 24* (4), 544–549.

Pressman, S. D., Jenkins, B. N., & Moskowitz, J. T. (2018). Positive affect and health: What do we know and where next should we go? *Annual Review of Psychology*, 70. doi: 10.1146/annurev-psych-010418-102955

Price, D. D., Finniss, D. G., & Benedetti, F. (2008). A comprehensive review of the placebo effect. *Annual Review of Psychology* (vol. 59, pp. 565–590). Palo Alto, CA: Annual Reviews.

Prichard, A., Cook, P. G., Spivak, M., Chhibber, R., & Berns, G. S. (2018). Awake fMRI reveals brain regions for novel word detection in dogs. *Frontiers in Neuroscience, 12,* 737.

Prince, J. (2018). Substance use disorder and suicide attempt among people who report compromised health. *Substance Use & Misuse, 53* (1), 9–15.

Prochaska, J. O., & Norcross, J. C. (2018). *Systems of psychotherapy: A transtheoretical analysis.* New York: Oxford University Press.

Prochaska, J. O., Redding, C. A., & Evers, K. E. (2015). The transtheoretical model and stages of change. In K. Glanz, B. K. Rimer, K. Viswanath (Eds.), *Health behavior: Theory, research, and practice* (5th ed., pp. 125–148). San Francisco, CA: Jossey-Bass.

Prochazkova, E., Prochazkova, L., Giffin, M. R., Scholte, H. S., De Dreu, C. K., & Kret, M. E. (2018). Pupil mimicry promotes trust through the theory-of-mind network. *Proceedings of the National Academy of Sciences*, 201803916. PNAS published ahead of print July 16, 2018. doi: 10.1073/pnas.1803916115

Protzko, J. (2017). Raising IQ among school-aged children: Five meta-analyses and a review of randomized controlled trials. *Developmental Review, 46,* 81–101.

Protzko, J., Aronson, J., & Blair, C. (2013). How to make a young child smarter: Evidence from the Database of Raising Intelligence. *Perspectives on Psychological Science, 8* (1), 25–40.

Provençal, N., Booij, L., & Tremblay, R. E. (2015). The developmental origins of chronic physical aggression: Biological pathways triggered by early life adversity. *Journal of Experimental Biology, 218* (1), 123–133.

Provenzo, E. F. (2002). *Teaching, learning, and schooling in American culture: A critical perspective.* Boston: Allyn & Bacon.

Pucci, M., Di Bonaventura, M. V. M., Wille-Bille, A., Fernández, M. S., Maccarrone, M., Pautassi, R. M., ... & D'Addario, C. (2018). Environmental stressors and alcoholism development: focus on molecular targets and their epigenetic regulation. *Neuroscience & Biobehavioral Reviews.* doi: 10.1016/j.neubiorev.2018.07.004

Puckett, J. A., Cleary, P., Rossman, K., Mustanski, B., & Newcomb, M. E. (2018). Barriers to gender-affirming care for transgender and gender nonconforming individuals. *Sexuality Research and Social Policy, 15* (1), 48–59.

Pulakos, E. D., Mueller-Hanson, R. & Arad, S. (2019). The evolution of performance management: Searching for value. *Annual Review of Organizational Psychology and Organizational Behavior, 6.* (in press)

Puller, C., Manookin, M. B., Neitz, J., Rieke, F., & Neitz, M. (2015). Broad thorny ganglion cells: A candidate for visual pursuit error signaling in the primate retina. *Journal of Neuroscience, 35* (13), 5397–5408.

Purdy, J. (2013). Chronic physical illness: A psychophysiological approach for chronic physical illness. *Yale Journal of Biology and Medicine, 86* (1), 15–28.

Puschmann, S., Baillet, S., & Zatorre, R. J. (2018). Musicians at the cocktail party: Neural substrates of musical training during selective listening in multi-speaker situations. *Cerebral Cortex.* (in press)

Pushkarskaya, H., Tolin, D. F., Henick, D., Levy, I., & Pittenger, C. (2018). Unbending mind: Individuals with hoarding disorder do not modify decision strategy in response to feedback under risk. *Psychiatry Research, 259,* 506–513.

Puterman, E., Weiss, J., Lin, J., Schilf, S., Slusher, A., Johansen, K. L., & Epel, E. S. (2018). Aerobic exercise lengthens telomeres and reduces stress in family caregivers: A randomized controlled trial-Curt Richter Award Paper 2018. *Psychoneuroendocrinology.* doi: 10.1016/j.psyneuen.2018.08.002

Puts, D. (2016). Human sexual selection. *Current Opinion in Psychology, 7,* 28–32.

Putz, Á., Kocsor, F., & Bereczkei, T. (2018). Beauty stereotypes affect the generalization of behavioral traits associated with previously seen faces. *Personality and Individual Differences, 131,* 7–14.

Pyne, J. M., Fischer, E. P., Mittal, D., & Owen, R. (2018). A patient-centered antipsychotic medication adherence intervention: Results from a randomized controlled trial. *The Journal of Nervous and Mental Disease, 206* (2), 142–148.

## Q

Qasim, A., Mayhew, A. J., Ehtesham, S., Alyass, A., Volckmar, A. L., Herpertz, S., ... & Meyre, D. (2018). Gain-of-function variants in the melanocortin 4 receptor gene confer susceptibility to binge eating disorder in subjects with obesity: A systematic review and meta-analysis. *Obesity Reviews.* doi: 10.1111/obr.12761

Quas, J. A., Castro, A., Bryce, C. I., & Granger, D. A. (2018). Stress physiology and memory for emotional information: Moderation by individual differences in pubertal hormones. *Developmental Psychology, 54* (9), 1606–1620.

Quidé, Y., Andersson, F., & El-Hage, W. (2018). S26. Smaller hippocampal volume predicts the development of posttraumatic stress disorder following sexual assault in females. *Biological Psychiatry, 83* (9), S356–S357.

## R

Rabeyron, T. (2014). Retro-priming, priming, and double testing: Psi and replication in a test–retest design. *Frontiers in Human Neuroscience, 8,* 154. doi: 10.3389/fnhum.2014.00154

Racey, D. N., Fox, J., Berry, V. L., Blockley, K. V., Longridge, R. A., Simmons, J. L., ... & Ford, T. J. (2018). Mindfulness-based cognitive therapy for young people and their carers: A mixed-method feasibility study. *Mindfulness, 9* (4), 1063–1075.

Racine, M., Tousignant-Laflamme, Y., Kloda, L. A., Dion, D., Dupuis, G., & Choinière, M. (2012a). A systematic literature review of 10 years of research on sex/gender and experimental pain perception—Part 1: Are there really differences between women and men? *Pain, 153* (3), 602–618.

Racine, M., Tousignant-Laflamme, Y., Kloda, L. A., Dion, D., Dupuis, G., & Choinière, M. (2012b). A systematic literature review of 10 years of research on sex/gender and pain perception—Part 2: Do biopsychosocial factors alter pain sensitivity differently in women and men? *Pain, 153* (3), 619–635.

Radulovic, J., Lee, R., & Ortony, A. (2018). State-dependent memory: Neurobiological advances and prospects for translation to dissociative amnesia. *Frontiers in Behavioral Neuroscience, 12,* 259.

Rafful, C., Orozco, R., Rangel, G., Davidson, P., Werb, D., Beletsky, L., & Strathdee, S. A. (2018). Increased non-fatal overdose risk associated with involuntary drug treatment in a longitudinal study with people who inject drugs. *Addiction, 113* (6), 1056–1063.

Ragins, B. R., Cotton, J. L., & Miller, J. S. (2000). Marginal mentoring: The effects of type of mentor, quality of relationship, and program design on work and career attitudes. *Academy of Management Journal, 43* (6), 1177–1194.

Rahman, Q., & Wilson, G. D. (2003). Sexual orientation and the 2nd to 4th finger length ratio: Evidence for organising effects of sex hormones or developmental instability? *Psychoneuroendocrinology, 28* (3), 288–303.

Rai, A. (2018). Job crafting intervention: Fostering individual job redesign for sustainable organisation. *Industrial and Commercial Training, 50* (4), 200–208.

Rai, S., Gurung, D., Kaiser, B. N., Sikkema, K. J., Dhakal, M., Bhardwaj, A., ... & Kohrt, B. A. (2018). A service user co-facilitated intervention to reduce mental illness stigma among primary healthcare workers: Utilizing perspectives of family members and caregivers. *Families, Systems, & Health, 36* (2), 198.

Raifman, J., & Sherman, S. G. (2018). US guidelines that empower women to prevent HIV with preexposure prophylaxis. *Sexually Transmitted Diseases, 45* (6), e38–e39.

Raine, A. (2018a). Antisocial personality as a neurodevelopmental disorder. *Annual Review of Clinical Psychology* (vol. 14, pp. 259–289). Palo Alto, CA: Annual Reviews.

Raine, A. (2018b). The neuromoral theory of antisocial, violent, and psychopathic behavior. *Psychiatry Research.* doi: 10.1016/j.psychres.2018.11.025

Raine, A., Venables, P. H., & Williams, M. (1990). Relationships between N1, P300 and CNV recorded at age 15 and criminal behavior at age 24. *Psychophysiology, 27* (5), 567–574.

Ram, N., Morelli, S., Lindberg, C., & Carstensen, L. L. (2008). From static to dynamic: The ongoing dialectic about human development. In K. W. Schaie & R. P. Abeles (Eds.), *Social structures and aging individuals.* Mahwah, NJ: Erlbaum.

Ramachandran, V. S. (2000, May 31). Mirror neurons and imitation learning as the driving force behind "the great leap forward" in human evolution. *EDGE.* https://edge.org/conversation/mirror-neurons-and-imitation-learning-as-the-driving-force-behind-the-great-leap-forward-in-human-evolution (accessed February 1, 2016)

Ramírez-Esparza, N., Gosling, S. D., Benet-Martínez, V., Potter, J. P., & Pennebaker, J. W. (2006). Do bilinguals have two personalities? A special case of cultural frame switching. *Journal of Research in Personality, 40* (2), 99–120.

Ramos, P., Batistuzzo, M., Shavitt, R., Simionato, A., Diniz, J., & Bazán, P. (2018). S19. Memory processes and fear conditioning: Preliminary results. *Biological Psychiatry, 83* (9), S354.

Ramsey, J. L., Langlois, J. H., Hoss, R. A., Rubenstein, A. J., & Griffin, A. M. (2004). Origins of a stereotype: Categorization of facial attractiveness by

6-month-old infants. *Developmental Science, 7* (2), 201–211.

**Ramus, F., Altarelli, I., Jednoróg, K., Zhao, J., & di Covella, L. S.** (2018). Neuroanatomy of developmental dyslexia: Pitfalls and promise. *Neuroscience and Biobehavioral Reviews, 84,* 434–452.

**Randel, A. E., Galvin, B. M., Shore, L. M., Ehrhart, K. H., Chung, B. G., Dean, M. A., & Kedharnath, U.** (2018). Inclusive leadership: Realizing positive outcomes through belongingness and being valued for uniqueness. *Human Resource Management Review, 28* (2), 190–203.

**Ranjit, Y. S., Snyder, L. B., Hamilton, M. A., & Rimal, R. N.** (2017). Self-determination theory and risk behavior in a collectivistic society: Preventing reckless driving in urban Nepal. *Journal of Health Communication, 22*(8), 672–681.

**Rankin, L. C., & Artis, D.** (2018). Beyond host defense: Emerging functions of the immune system in regulating complex tissue physiology. *Cell, 173* (3), 554–567.

**Rapaport, D.** (1967). On the psychoanalytic theory of thinking. In M. M. Gill (Ed.), *The collected papers of David Rapaport.* New York: Basic.

**Rash, B. G., Micali, N., Huttner, A. J., Morozov, Y. M., Horvath, T. L., & Rakic, P.** (2018). Metabolic regulation and glucose sensitivity of cortical radial glial cells. *Proceedings of the National Academy of Sciences, 115* (40), 10142–10147.

**Rathunde, K., & Csikszentmihalyi, M.** (2006). The developing person: An experiential perspective. In W. Damon & R. Lerner (Eds.), *Handbook of child psychology* (6th ed.). New York: Wiley.

**Rattan, A., Savani, K., Chugh, D., & Dweck, C. S.** (2015). Leveraging mindsets to promote academic achievement policy recommendations. *Perspectives on Psychological Science, 10* (6), 721–726.

**Ravizza, S. M., Uitvlugt, M. G., & Fenn, K. M.** (2017). The negative effects of laptop internet use during class. *Neuroscience Letters, 637,* 44–49.

**Raw, R. K., Wilkie, R. M., Culmer, P. R., & Mon-Williams, M.** (2012). Reduced motor asymmetry in older adults when manually tracing paths. *Experimental Brain Research, 217* (1), 35–41.

**Ray, D. G., Gomillion, S., Pintea, A. I., & Hamlin, I.** (2018). On being forgotten: Memory and forgetting serve as signals of interpersonal importance. *Journal of Personality and Social Psychology, 116,* 259–276.

**Reb, J., Chaturvedi, S., Narayanan, J., & Kudesia, R. S.** (2018). Leader mindfulness and employee performance: A sequential mediation model of lmx quality, interpersonal justice, and employee stress. *Journal of Business Ethics.* doi: 10.1007/s10551-018-3927-x

**Reb, J., & Choi, E.** (2014). Mindfulness in organizations. In N. N. Singh (Ed.), *Psychology of meditation* (pp. 279–309). Hauppauge, NY: Nova Science Publishers. Retrieved from http://proxy.mul.missouri.edu/login?url=http://search.ebscohost.com/login.aspx?direct=true&AuthType=ip,cookie,url,uid&db=psyh&AN=2014-13600-013&site=ehost-live&scope=site

**Recksiedler, C., Loter, K., Klaas, H. S., Hollstein, B., & Perrig-Chiello, P.** (2018). Social dimensions of personal growth following widowhood: A three-wave study. *Gerontology, 64* (4), 344–360.

**Record, R. A., Harrington, N. G., Helme, D. W., & Savage, M. W.** (2018). Using the theory of planned behavior to guide focus group development of messages aimed at increasing compliance with a tobacco-free policy. *American Journal of Health Promotion, 32*(1), 143–152.

**Redick, T. S., Shipstead, Z., Wiemers, E. A., Melby-Lervag, M., & Hulme, C.** (2015). What's working in working memory training? An educational perspective. *Educational Psychology Review, 27* (4), 617–633.

**Redman, L. M., Smith, S. R., Burton, J. H., Martin, C. K., Il'yasova, D., & Ravussin, E.** (2018). Metabolic slowing and reduced oxidative damage with sustained caloric restriction support the rate of living and oxidative damage theories of aging. *Cell Metabolism, 27* (4), 805–815.

**Reed, S. K.** (2010). *Thinking visually.* New York: Psychology Press.

**Rees, G., & Garcia, J. R.** (2017). An investigation into the solitary and interpersonal aspects of sexual object fetishism: A mixed-methods approach. *Psychology & Sexuality, 8* (4), 252–267.

**Reese, B. M., Haydon, A. A., Herring, A. H., & Halpern, C. T.** (2013). The association between sequences of sexual initiation and the likelihood of teenage pregnancy. *Journal of Adolescent Health, 52* (2), 228–233.

**Reeve, C. L., & Charles, J. E.** (2008). Survey of opinions on the primacy of *g* and social consequences of ability testing: A comparison of expert and non-expert views. *Intelligence, 36* (6), 681–688.

**Reich, R. R., Cummings, J. R., Greenbaum, P. E., Moltisanti, A. J., & Goldman, M. S.** (2015). The temporal "pulse" of drinking: Tracking 5 years of binge drinking in emerging adults. *Journal of Abnormal Psychology, 124* (3), 635–647.

**Reichborn-Kjennerud, T., Czajkowski, N., Ystrom, E., Orstavik, R., Aggen, S. H., Tambs, K., ... & Kendler, K. S.** (2015). A longitudinal twin study of borderline and antisocial personality disorder traits in early to middle adulthood. *Psychological Medicine, 45* (14), 3121–3131.

**Reid, A. M., Guzick, A. G., Fernandez, A. G., Deacon, B., McNamara, J. P., Geffken, G. R., ... & Striley, C. W.** (2018). Exposure therapy for youth with anxiety: Utilization rates and predictors of implementation in a sample of practicing clinicians from across the United States. *Journal of Anxiety Disorders, 58,* 8–17.

**Reiersen, A. M.** (2018). New evidence of genetic overlap between atypical sensory reactivity and autistic traits: Implications for future research. *Journal of the American Academy of Child & Adolescent Psychiatry, 57* (2), 84–85.

**Reinders, A. A. T. S., Chalavi, S., Schlumpf, Y. R., Vissia, E. M., Nijenhuis, E. R. S., Jäncke, L., ... & Ecker, C.** (2018). Neurodevelopmental origins of abnormal cortical morphology in dissociative identity disorder. *Acta Psychiatrica Scandinavica, 137* (2), 157–170.

**Reinhold, M., Bürkner, P.-C. & Holling, H.** (2018). Effects of expressive writing on depressive symptoms–A meta-analysis. *Clinical Psychology: Science and Practice, 25* (1), e12224. doi: 10.1111/cpsp.12224

**Reisner, S. L., Mimiaga, M. J., Skeer, M., & Mayer, K. H.** (2009). Beyond anal sex: Sexual practices associated with HIV risk reduction among men who have sex with men in Boston, Massachusetts. *AIDS Patient Care and STDs, 23* (7), 545–550.

**Reiss, P. T.** (2018). Cross-sectional versus longitudinal designs for function estimation, with an application to cerebral cortex development. *Statistics in Medicine, 37* (11), 1895–1909.

**Rendell, P. G., & Craik, F. I. M.** (2000). Virtual week and actual week: Age-related differences in prospective memory. *Applied Cognitive Psychology, 14* (7), S43–S62.

**Reniers, R. L., Corcoran, R., Völlm, B. A., Mashru, A., Howard, R., & Liddle, P. F.** (2012). Moral decision-making, ToM, empathy, and the mode default network. *Biological Psychology, 90* (3), 202–210.

**Rennels, J. L., Kayl, A. J., Langlois, J. H., Davis, R. E., & Orlewicz, M.** (2016). Asymmetries in infants' attention toward and categorization of male faces: The potential role of experience. *Journal of Experimental Child Psychology, 142,* 137–157.

**Renteria, R., Baltz, E. T., & Gremel, C. M.** (2018). Chronic alcohol exposure disrupts top-down control over basal ganglia action selection to produce habits. *Nature Communications, 9* (1), 211.

**Repacholi, B. M., Meltzoff, A. N., Toub, T. S., & Ruba, A. L.** (2016). Infants' generalizations about other people's emotions: Foundations for trait-like attributions. *Developmental Psychology, 52* (3), 364.

**Rescorla, R. A.** (1966). Predictability and number of pairings in Pavlovian fear conditioning. *Psychonomic Science, 4* (11), 383–384.

**Rescorla, R. A.** (1988). Pavlovian conditioning: It's not what you think it is. *American Psychologist, 43* (3), 151–160.

**Rescorla, R. A.** (2003). Contemporary study of Pavlovian conditioning. *Spanish Journal of Psychology, 6* (2), 185–195.

**Rescorla, R. A.** (2004). Spontaneous recovery varies inversely with the training-extinction interval. *Learning and Behavior, 32* (4), 401–408.

**Rescorla, R. A.** (2005). Spontaneous recovery of excitation but not inhibition. *Journal of Experimental Psychology: Animal Behavior Processes, 31* (3), 277–288.

**Rescorla, R. A.** (2006a). Stimulus generalization of excitation and inhibition. *Quarterly Journal of Experimental Psychology, 59* (1), 53–67.

**Rescorla, R. A.** (2006b). Spontaneous recovery from overexpectation. *Learning and Behavior, 34* (1), 13–20.

**Rescorla, R. A.** (2006c). Deepened extinction from compound stimulus presentation. *Journal of Experimental Psychology: Animal Behavior Processes, 32* (2), 135–144.

**Rescorla, R. A.** (2009). A theory of Pavlovian conditioning: Variations in the effectiveness of reinforcement and nonreinforcement. In D. Shanks (Ed.), *Psychology of learning.* Thousand Oaks, CA: Sage.

**Resnick, B.** (2018, June 13). The most famous psychological studies are often wrong. Textbooks need to catch up. *Vox.com.* https://www.vox.com/2018/6/13/17449118/stanford-prison-experiment-fraud-psychology-replication

**Reuter, A. R., Abram, S. V., MacDonald III, A. W., Rustichini, A., & DeYoung, C. G.** (2018). The goal priority network as a neural substrate of Conscientiousness. *Human Brain Mapping, 39* (9), 3574–3585. doi: 10.1002/hbm.24195

**Reyes, S., Tajiri, N., & Borlongan, C. V.** (2015). Developments in intracerebral stem cell grafts. *Expert Review of Neurotherapeutics, 15* (4), 381–393.

**Reynolds, J. P., Webb, T. L., Benn, Y., Chang, B. P., & Sheeran, P.** (2018). Feeling bad about progress does not lead people to want to change their health behaviour. *Psychology & Health, 33* (2), 275–291.

**Reynolds, P. D., & Helfers, R. C.** (2018). Differences in perceptions of organizational fairness based on job characteristics among police officers. *American Journal of Criminal Justice, 43* (2), 371–388.

**Reznik, S. J., & Allen, J. J.** (2018). Frontal asymmetry as a mediator and moderator of emotion: An updated review. *Psychophysiology, 55* (1), e12965.

**Reznik, S. J., Nusslock, R., Pornpattananangkul, N., Abramson, L. Y., Coan, J. A., & Harmon-Jones, E.** (2017). Laboratory-induced learned helplessness attenuates approach motivation as indexed by posterior versus frontal theta activity. *Cognitive, Affective, & Behavioral Neuroscience, 17* (4), 904–916.

**Ribeiro, J. D., Huang, X., Fox, K. R., & Franklin, J. C.** (2018). Depression and hopelessness as risk factors for suicide ideation, attempts and death: Meta-analysis of longitudinal studies. *The British Journal of Psychiatry, 212* (5), 279–286.

**Ribeiro, M. P., Moreira, D., Coelho, R., Pereira, A., & Almeida, F.** (2018). Gender identity. *Advances in Social Sciences Research Journal, 5* (10).

**Rice, C. E., Maierhofer, C., Fields, K. S., Ervin, M., Lanza, S. T., & Turner, A. N.** (2016). Beyond anal sex: Sexual practices of men who have sex with men and associations with HIV and other sexually transmitted infections. *Journal of Sexual Medicine, 13* (3), 374–382.

**Richardson, G. A., & Day, N. L.** (2018). Longitudinal studies of the effects of prenatal cocaine exposure on development and behavior. In W. Slikker, M.G. Paule, & C. Wang (Eds.), *Handbook of developmental neurotoxicology* (2nd ed., pp. 379–388). New York: Academic Press.

**Rieger, G., Linsenmeier, J. A. W., & Bailey, J. M.** (2009). Childhood gender nonconformity remains a robust and neutral correlate of sexual orientation: Reply to Hegarty (2009). *Developmental Psychology, 45* (4), 901–903.

**Rieger, G., Linsenmeier, J. A. W., Gygax, L., & Bailey, J. M.** (2008). Sexual orientation and childhood gender nonconformity: Evidence from home videos. *Developmental Psychology, 44* (1), 46–58.

**Riek, B. M., & DeWit, C. C.** (2018). Differences and similarities in forgiveness seeking across childhood and adolescence. *Personality and Social Psychology Bulletin, 44* (8), 1119–1132. doi: 10.1177/0146167218760797

**Rifkin, W. J., Kantar, R. S., Ali-Khan, S., Plana, N. M., Diaz-Siso, J. R., Tsakiris, M., & Rodriguez, E. D.** (2018). DDS facial disfigurement and identity: A review of the literature and implications for facial transplantation. *AMA Journal of Ethics, 20,* 309–323.

**Rigby, C. S., & Ryan, R. M.** (2018). Self-determination theory in human resource development: New directions and practical considerations. *Advances in Developing Human Resources, 20* (2), 133–147.

**Riketta, M.** (2002). Attitudinal organizational commitment and job performance: A meta-analysis. *Journal of Organizational Behavior, 23* (3), 257–266.

**Riley, S. M., Michael, S. C., & Mahoney, J. T.** (2017). Human capital matters: Market valuation of firm investments in training and the role of complementary assets. *Strategic Management Journal, 38* (9), 1895–1914.

**Rimmele, U., Davachi, L., & Phelps, E. A.** (2012). Memory for time and place contributes to enhanced confidence in memories for emotional events. *Emotion, 12* (4), 834–846.

**Rinderu, M. I., Bushman, B. J., & Van Lange, P. A.** (2018). Climate, aggression, and violence (CLASH): A cultural-evolutionary approach. *Current Opinion in Psychology, 19,* 113–118.

**Ripp, I., zur Nieden, A. N., Blankenagel, S., Franzmeier, N., Lundström, J. N., & Freiherr, J.** (2018). Multisensory integration processing during olfactory-visual stimulation—An fMRI graph theoretical network analysis. *Human Brain Mapping.* doi: 10.1002/hbm.24206

**Riske, L., Thomas, R. K., Baker, G. B., & Dursun, S. M.** (2017). Lactate in the brain: An update on its relevance to brain energy, neurons, glia and panic disorder. *Therapeutic Advances in Psychopharmacology, 7* (2), 85–89.

**Risley, T. R., & Hart, B.** (2006). Promoting early language development. In N. F. Watt, C. Ayoub, R. H. Bradley, J. E. Puma, & W. A. LeBoeuf (Eds.), *The crisis in youth mental health: Critical issues and effective programs: Vol. 4: Early intervention programs and policies* (pp. 83–88). Westport, CT: Praeger.

**Ristow, I., Li, M., Colic, L., Marr, V., Födisch, C., von Düring, F., ... & Beier, K.** (2018). Pedophilic sex offenders are characterised by reduced GABA concentration in dorsal anterior cingulate cortex. *NeuroImage: Clinical, 18,* 335–341.

**Ritchey, A. J., & Ruback, R. B.** (2018). Predicting lynching atrocity: The situational norms of lynchings in Georgia. *Personality and Social Psychology Bulletin, 44* (5), 619–637.

**Ritskes, R., Ritskes-Hoitinga, M., Stodkilde-Jorgensen, H., Baerentsen, K., & Hartman, T.** (2003). MRI scanning during Zen meditation: The picture of enlightenment? *Constructivism in the Human Sciences, 8* (1), 85–90.

**Riva-Posse, P., Choi, K. S., Holtzheimer, P. E., Crowell, A. L., Garlow, S. J., Rajendra, J. K., ... & Mayberg, H. S.** (2018). A connectomic approach for subcallosal cingulate deep brain stimulation surgery: Prospective targeting in treatment-resistant depression. *Molecular Psychiatry, 23* (4), 843.

**Rivas-Grajales, A. M., Mouradian, P., Papadimitriou, G., Lee, E., Kubicki, M., Makris, N., & Camprodon, J. A.** (2018). S141. Electroconvulsive therapy leads to plastic changes in the medial forebrain bundle associated with improvement in anhedonia and depression severity. *Biological Psychiatry, 83* (9), S402–S403.

**Roberts, B. W.** (2018). A revised sociogenomic model of personality traits. *Journal of Personality, 86* (1), 23–35.

**Roberts, B. W., & Mroczek, D.** (2008). Personality trait change in adulthood. *Current Directions in Psychological Science, 17* (1), 31–35.

**Roberts, B. W., Walton, K. E., & Viechtbauer, W.** (2006). Patterns of mean level change in personality traits across the life course: A meta-analysis of longitudinal studies. *Psychological Bulletin, 132* (1), 1–25.

**Roberts, C. A., Quednow, B. B., Montgomery, C., & Parrott, A. C.** (2018). MDMA and brain activity during neurocognitive performance: An overview of neuroimaging studies with abstinent 'Ecstasy' users. *Neuroscience & Biobehavioral Reviews, 84,* 470–482.

**Roberts, D., Calman, L., Large, P., Appleton, L., Grande, G., Lloyd-Williams, M., & Walshe, C.** (2018). A revised model for coping with advanced cancer: Mapping concepts from a longitudinal qualitative study of patients and carers coping with advanced cancer onto Folkman and Greer's theoretical model of appraisal and coping. Psycho-oncology, *27* (1), 229–235.

**Roberts, G., Quach, J., Gold, L., Anderson, P., Rickards F., Mensah, F., Ainley, J., Gathercole, S., & Wake, M.** (2011). Can improving working memory prevent academic difficulties? A school based randomized controlled trial. *BMC Pediatrics, 11,* 57.

**Roberts, H., & Hickey, M.** (2016). Managing the menopause: An update. *Maturitas, 86,* 53–58.

**Roberts, K., Miller, M., & Azrael, D.** (2018). Honor-related suicide in the United States: A study of national violent death reporting system data. *Archives of Suicide Research.* doi: 10.1080/13811118.2017.1411299.

**Roberts, R. M., Tarescavage, A. M., Ben-Porath, Y. S., & Roberts, M. D.** (2018). Predicting postprobationary job performance of police officers using CPI and MMPI-2-RF test data obtained during preemployment psychological screening. *Journal of Personality Assessment.* doi: 10.1080/00223891.2018.1423990 (in press)

**Roberts, T. A., Calogero, R. M., & Gervais, S. J.** (2018). Objectification theory: Continuing contributions to feminist psychology. In C. B. Travis, J. W. White, A. Rutherford, W. S. Williams, S. L. Cook, & K. F. Wyche (Eds.), *APA handbook of the psychology of women: History, theory, and battlegrounds* (pp. 249–271). Washington, DC: American Psychological Association.

**Robertson, C. E., & Baron-Cohen, S.** (2017). Sensory perception in autism. *Nature Reviews Neuroscience, 18,* 671–684.

**Robertson, S. C., & Swickert, R. J.** (2018). The stories we tell: How age, gender, and forgiveness affect the emotional content of autobiographical narratives. *Aging & Mental Health, 22*(4), 535-543. doi: 10.1080/13607863.2016.1269149

**Robinson, S., & Leach, J.** (2018). Fighting for our lives: The psychobiology of surviving an emergency. In P. M. Murphy (Ed.), *The Routledge international handbook of psychobiology* (pp. 37–60). London: Routledge.

**Robinson-Morral, E. J., Hendrickson, C., Gilbert, S., Myers, T., Simpson, K., & Loignon, A. C.** (2018). Practical considerations for conducting job analysis linkage exercises. *Journal of Personnel Psychology, 17,* 12–21.

**Roche, M., Haar, J. M., & Luthans, F.** (2014). The role of mindfulness and psychological capital on the well-being of leaders. *Journal of Occupational Health Psychology, 19* (4), 476–489. doi: 10.1037/a0037183

**Rodin, J.** (1984, December). Interview: A sense of control. *Psychology Today,* 38–45.

**Rodriguez, C. M., Pu, D. F., & Foiles, A. R.** (2018). Cognitive-affective pathways to child depressive and anxious symptoms: Role of children's discipline attributions. *Child Psychiatry & Human Development,* 1–9.

**Roediger, H. L., & McDermott, K. B.** (1995). Creating false memories: Remembering words not presented in lists. *Journal of Experimental Psychology: Learning, Memory, and Cognition, 21* (4), 803–814.

**Roehm, M. L.** (2016). An exploration of flashbulb memory. *Journal of Consumer Psychology, 26* (1), 1–16.

**Roelfs, D., Shor, E., Davidson, K. W., & Schwartz, J. E.** (2011). Losing life and livelihood: A systematic review and meta-analysis of unemployment and all-cause mortality. *Social Science and Medicine, 72* (6), 840–854.

**Roepke, A. M., Tsukayama, E., Forgeard, M., Blackie, L., & Jayawickreme, E.** (2018). Randomized controlled trial of SecondStory, an intervention targeting posttraumatic growth, with bereaved adults. *Journal of Consulting and Clinical Psychology, 86* (6), 518.

**Roffwarg, H. P., Muzio, J. N., & Dement, W. C.** (1966, 29 April). Ontogenetic development of human dream-sleep cycle. *Science, 152*(3722), 604–619.

**Rogers, C. R.** (1961). *On becoming a person.* Boston: Houghton Mifflin.

**Rogers, C. R.** (1980). *A way of being.* Boston: Houghton Mifflin.

**Rogers, K.** (2018, November 11). How service dogs are helping disabled veterans cope with post-war stress. CNBC. https://www.cnbc.com/2018/11/10/disabled-veterans-get-help-from-nonprofit-that-trains-service-dogs.html

**Rogers, K. H., Le, M. T., Buckels, E. E., Kim, M., & Biesanz, J. C.** (2018). Dispositional malevolence and impression formation: Dark Tetrad associations with accuracy and positivity in first impressions. *Journal of Personality.* doi: 10.1111/jopy.12374

**Rohleder, P., Braathen, S. H., Carew, M. T., Chiwaula, M., Hunt, X., & Swartz, L.** (2018). Creative collaboration on a disability and sexuality participatory action research project: A reflective diary account. *Qualitative Research in Psychology.* doi: 10.1080/14780887.2018.1499837

**Rohr, C. S., Dreyer, F. R., Aderka, I. M., Margulies, D. S., Frisch, S., Villringer, A., & Okon-Singer, H.** (2015). Individual differences in common factors of emotional traits and executive functions predict functional connectivity of the amygdala. *NeuroImage, 120,* 154-163.

**Rohrer, D., & Pashler, H.** (2012). Learning styles: Where's the evidence? *Medical Education, 46* (7), 634–635.

**Rohrer, D., Pashler, H., & Harris, C. R.** (2015). Do subtle reminders of money change people's political views? *Journal of Experimental Psychology: General, 144* (4), e73.

**Rohrer, J. M., Egloff, B., & Schmukle, S. C.** (2015). Examining the effects of birth order on personality. *Proceedings of the National Academy of Sciences USA, 112* (46), 14224–14229.

**Roiser, J. P., Stephan, K. E., den Ouden, H. E. M., Friston, K. J., & Joyce, E. M.** (2010). Adaptive and aberrant reward prediction signals in the human brain. *NeuroImage, 50* (2), 657–664.

**Rolan, E. P., Schmitt, S. A., Purpura, D. J., & Nichols, D. L.** (2018). Sibling presence, executive function, and the role of parenting. *Infant and Child Development,* e2091.

**Rolls, E. T.** (2015). Limbic systems for emotion and for memory, but no single limbic system. *Cortex, 62,* 119–157.

**Romain, A. J., Horwath, C., & Bernard, P.** (2018). Prediction of physical activity level using processes of change from the transtheoretical model: Experiential, behavioral, or an interaction effect? *American Journal of Health Promotion, 32* (1), 16–23.

**Roman, C. G., Klein, H. J., & Wolff, K. T.** (2017). Quasi-experimental designs for community-level public health violence reduction interventions: A case study in the challenges of selecting the counterfactual. *Journal of Experimental Criminology.* doi: 10.1007/s11292-017-9308-0

**Romero, A. J., Piña-Watson, B., & Toomey, R. B.** (2018). When is bicultural stress associated with loss of hope and depressive symptoms? Variation by ethnic identity status among Mexican descent youth. *Journal of Latina/o Psychology, 6* (1), 49.

**Romo, D. L., Garnett, C., Younger, A. P., Soren, K., Stockwell, M. S., Catallozzi, M., & Neu, N.** (2016). Understanding adolescent social media use: Association with sexual risk and parental monitoring factors that can influence protection. *Journal of Adolescent Health, 58* (2), S16–S17.

**Roquet, R. F., Seo, D.-o., Jones, C. E., & Monfils, M.-H.** (2018). Differential effects of predictable vs. unpredictable aversive experience early in development on fear memory and learning in adulthood. *Behavioral Neuroscience, 132* (1), 57–65. doi: 10.1037/bne0000228

**Rosa-Salva, O., Hernik, M., Broseghini, A., & Vallortigara, G.** (2018). Visually-naïve chicks prefer agents that move as if constrained by a bilateral body-plan. *Cognition, 173,* 106–114.

**Rose, N. S., & Craik, F. I.** (2012). A processing approach to the working memory/long-term memory distinction: Evidence from the levels-of-processing span task. *Journal of Experimental Psychology: Learning, Memory, and Cognition, 38* (4), 1019–1029.

**Rose, N. S., Craik, F. I., & Buchsbaum, B. R.** (2015). Levels of processing in working memory: Differential involvement of frontotemporal networks. *Journal of Cognitive Neuroscience, 27* (3), 522–532.

**Roselli, C. E.** (2018). Neurobiology of gender identity and sexual orientation. *Journal of Neuroendocrinology, 30* (7), e12562.

**Rosellini, A. J., Street, A. E., Ursano, R. J., Chiu, W. T., Heeringa, S. G., Monahan, J., ... & Kessler, R. C.** (2017). Sexual assault victimization and mental health treatment, suicide attempts, and career outcomes among women in the US Army. *American Journal of Public Health, 107* (5), 732–739.

**Roseman, I. J., & Smith, C. A.** (2009). Appraisal theory: Overview, assumptions, varieties, controversies. In K. R. Scherer, A. Schorr, & T. Johnstone (Eds.), *Appraisal processes in emotion: Theory, methods, research* (pp. 3–19). Oxford, UK: Oxford University Press.

**Rosen, K., & Garety, P.** (2005). Predicting recovery from schizophrenia: A retrospective comparison of characteristics at onset of people with single and multiple episodes. *Schizophrenia Bulletin, 31* (3), 735–750.

**Rosen, M. G.** (2018). How bizarre? A pluralist approach to dream content. *Consciousness and Cognition, 62,* 148–162.

**Rosenbaum, B., Harder, S., Knudsen, P., Køster, A., Lajer, M., Lindhardt, A., Valbak, K., & Winther, G.** (2012). Supportive psychodynamic psychotherapy versus treatment as usual for first-episode psychosis: Two-year outcome. *Psychiatry: Interpersonal and Biological Processes, 75* (4), 331–341.

**Rosenbaum, S., Tiedemann, A., Sherrington, C., Curtis, J., & Ward, P. B.** (2014). Physical activity interventions for people with mental illness: A systematic review and meta-analysis. *Journal of Clinical Psychiatry, 75* (9), 964–974.

**Rosenberg, L., Rosenberg, M., Sharp, S., Thomas, C. R., Humphries, H. F., Holzer III, C. E., ... & Meyer III, W. J.** (2018). Does acute propranolol treatment prevent posttraumatic stress disorder, anxiety, and depression in children with burns? *Journal of Child and Adolescent Psychopharmacology, 28* (2), 117–123.

**Rosenhan, D. L.** (1973). On being sane in insane places. *Science, 179* (4070), 250–258.

**Rosenson, R. S., Brewer Jr, H. B., Barter, P. J., Björkegren, J. L., Chapman, M. J., Gaudet, D., ... & Tardif, J. C.** (2018). HDL and atherosclerotic cardiovascular disease: Genetic insights into complex biology. *Nature Reviews Cardiology, 15* (1), 9–19.

**Rosenström, T., & Jokela, M.** (2017). A parsimonious explanation of the resilient, undercontrolled, and overcontrolled personality types. *European Journal of Personality, 31* (6), 658–668. doi: 10.1002/per.2117

**Rosenthal, L., Carroll-Scott, A., Earnshaw, V. A., Santilli, A., & Ickovics, J. R.** (2012). The importance of full-time work for urban adults' mental and physical health. *Social Science and Medicine, 75* (9), 1692–1696.

**Rosenthal, R.** (1966). *Experimenter effects in behavioral research.* New York: Appleton-Century-Crofts.

**Rosenthal, R., & Jacobson, L.** (1968). *Pygmalion in the classroom: Teacher expectation and student intellectual development.* New York: Holt, Rinehart & Winston.

**Ross, B. M., & Barnes, D. M.** (2018). Self-determination theory with application to employee health settings. *Workplace Health & Safety,* 2165079917749863.

**Ross, C. A., Keyes, B. B., Yan, H., Wang, Z., Zou, Z., Xu, Y., ... & Xiao, Z.** (2008). A cross-cultural test of the trauma model of dissociation. *Journal of Trauma & Dissociation, 9* (1), 35–49.

**Rossi, E. L.** (2009). The psychosocial genomics of therapeutic hypnosis, psychotherapy, and rehabilitation. *American Journal of Clinical Hypnosis, 51* (3), 281–298.

**Rostalski, T., Muehlan, H., & Schmidt, S.** (2018). Momentary affect and the optimism-health relationship: An ambulatory assessment study. *European Journal of Health Psychology, 25* (1), 9–17. doi:10.1027/2512-8442/a000003

**Roten, R. G.** (2007). DSM-IV and the taxonomy of roles: How can the taxonomy of roles complement the DSM-IV to create a more holistic diagnostic tool? *The Arts in Psychotherapy, 34* (1), 53–68.

**Rotge, J.-Y., Dilharreguy, B., Aouizerate, B., Martin-Guehl, C., Guehl, D., Jaafari, N., ... & Burbaud, P.** (2009). Inverse relationship between thalamic and orbitofrontal volumes in obsessive-compulsive disorder. *Progress in Neuro-Psychopharmacology and Biological Psychiatry, 33* (4), 682–687.

**Rothbart, M. K., & Gartstein, M. A.** (2008). Temperament. In M. M. Haith & J. B. Benson (Eds.), *Encyclopedia of infant and early childhood development.* London: Elsevier.

**Rouder, J. N., Morey, R. D., & Province, J. M.** (2013). A Bayes factor meta-analysis of recent extrasensory perception experiments: Comment on Storm, Tressoldi, and Di Risio (2010). *Psychological Bulletin, 139* (1), 241–247.

**Rouel, M., Stevenson, R. J., & Smith, E.** (2018). Predicting contamination aversion using implicit and explicit measures of disgust and threat overestimation. *Behaviour Change, 35* (1), 22–38.

**Roughgarden, J., Oishi, M., & Akçay, E.** (2006). Reproductive social behavior: Cooperative games to replace sexual selection. *Science, 311* (5763), 965–968.

**Rowe, P., & Guerin, B.** (2018). Contextualizing the mental health of metal youth: A community for social protection, identity, and musical empowerment. *Journal of Community Psychology, 46* (4), 429–441.

**Rowland, A. S., Skipper, B. J., Rabiner, D. L., Qeadan, F., Campbell, R. A., Naftel, A. J., & Umbach, D. M.** (2018). Attention-deficit/hyperactivity disorder (ADHD): Interaction between socioeconomic status and parental history of ADHD determines prevalence. *Journal of Child Psychology and Psychiatry, 59* (3), 213–222.

**Roy, B., Riley, C., & Sinha, R.** (2018). Emotion regulation moderates the association between chronic stress and cardiovascular disease risk in humans: a cross-sectional study. *Stress,* 1–8. doi: 10.1080/10253890.2018.1490724

**Rubenstein, E., Wiggins, L. D., Schieve, L. A., Bradley, C., DiGuiseppi, C., Moody, E., ... & Pence, B. W.** (2018). Associations between parental broader autism phenotype and child autism spectrum disorder phenotype in the Study to Explore Early Development. *Autism.* doi: 10.1177/1362361317753563

**Rubia, K.** (2018). Cognitive neuroscience of attention deficit hyperactivity disorder (ADHD) and its clinical translation. *Frontiers in Human Neuroscience, 12,* 100.

**Rubington, E., & Weinberg, M.** (2015). *Deviance: The interactionist perspective.* New York: Routledge.

**Rubino, C., Avery, D. R., McKay, P. F., Moore, B. L., Wilson, D. C., Van Driel, M. S., ... & McDonald, D. P.** (2018). And justice for all: How organizational justice climate deters sexual harassment. *Personnel Psychology, 71* (4), 519–544.

**Rubio-Fernández, P., & Geurts, B.** (2013). How to pass the false-belief task before your fourth birthday. *Psychological Science, 24,* 27–33.

**Ruocco, S., Gordon, J., & McLean, L. A.** (2016). Effectiveness of a school-based early intervention CBT group programme for children with anxiety aged 5–7 years. *Advances in School Mental Health Promotion, 9* (1), 29–49.

**Rusbult, C. E., Agnew, C. R., & Arriaga, X. B.** (2012). The investment model of commitment processes. In P. A. M. Van Lange, A. W. Kruglanski, & E. T. Higgins (Eds.), *Handbook of theories of social psychology.* Thousand Oaks, CA: Sage.

**Rusbult, C. E., Finkel, E. J., & Kumashiro, M.** (2009). The Michelangelo phenomenon. *Current Directions in Psychological Science, 18* (6), 305–309.

**Russell, D. W., Clavél, F. D., Cutrona, C. E., Abraham, W. T., & Burzette, R. G.** (2018). Neighborhood racial discrimination and the development of major depression. *Journal of Abnormal Psychology, 127* (2), 150–159.

**Russell, J. L.** (2018). High school teachers' perceptions of giftedness, gifted education, and talent development. *Journal of Advanced Academics.* doi: 10.1177/1932202X18775658

**Russo, S. J., Dietz, D. M., Dumitriu, D., Morrison, J. H., Malenka, R. C., & Nestler, E. J.** (2010). The addicted synapse: Mechanisms of synaptic and structural plasticity in nucleus accumbens. *Trends in Neuroscience, 33* (6), 267–276.

**Rusz, D., Bijleveld, E., & Kompier, M.** (2018). *Striving for solid science: Preregistration and direct replication in experimental psychology.* Los Angeles, CA: Sage. doi: 10.4135/9781526439987

**Rutherford, A., Whitton, A. E., Ironside, M. L., Jensen, J. E., Du, F., Farabaugh, A., ... & Pizzagalli, D. A.** (2018). F87. Rostral anterior cingulate glutamate levels are linked to abnormal high-frequency resting-state functional connectivity in bipolar disorder. *Biological Psychiatry, 83* (9), S271.

**Ruzich, E., Allison, C., Smith, P., Ring, H., Auyeung, B., & Baron-Cohen, S.** (2017). The Autism-Spectrum Quotient in siblings of people with autism. *Autism Research, 10* (2), 289–297.

**Ryan, A., Duignan, S., Kenny, D., & McMahon, C. J.** (2018). Decision making in paediatric cardiology. Are we prone to heuristics, biases and traps? *Pediatric Cardiology, 39* (1), 160–167.

**Ryan, R. M., & Deci, E. L.** (2017). Self-determination *theory: Basic psychological needs in motivation, development, and wellness.* New York: Guilford.

**Ryan, W. S., & Ryan, R. M.** (2018). Toward a social psychology of authenticity: Exploring within-person variation in autonomy, congruence, and genuineness using self-determination theory. *Review of General Psychology*. doi: 10.1037/gpr0000162

**Rydberg, J. A.** (2017). Research and clinical issues in trauma and dissociation: Ethical and logical fallacies, myths, misreports, and misrepresentations. *European Journal of Trauma & Dissociation, 1*, 89–99.

**Ryff, C. D.** (2018). Well-being with soul: Science in pursuit of human potential. *Perspectives on Psychological Science, 13* (2), 242–248.

**Ryff, C. D., Singer, B. H., & Love, G. D.** (2004). Positive health: Connecting well-being with biology. *Philosophical Transactions of the Royal Society of London, 359* (1449), 1383–1394.

## S

**Saab, M. M., Reidy, M., Hegarty, J., O'Mahony, M., Murphy, M., Von Wagner, C., & Drummond, F. J.** (2018). Men's information-seeking behavior regarding cancer risk and screening: A meta-narrative systematic review. Psycho-oncology, *27* (2), 410–419.

**Saad, G.** (2017). On the method of evolutionary psychology and its applicability to consumer research. *Journal of Marketing Research, 54* (3), 464–477.

**Sabeti, S., Al-Darsani, Z., Mander, B. A., Corrada, M. M., & Kawas, C. H.** (2018). Sleep, hippocampal volume, and cognition in adults over 90 years old. *Aging Clinical and Experimental Research, 30* (11), 1307–1318.

**Sachs, J.** (2009). Communication development in infancy. In J. Berko Gleason & N. Ratner (Eds.), *The development of language* (7th ed.). Boston: Allyn & Bacon.

**Sackett, P. R., Walmsley, P. T., Koch, A. J., Beatty, A. S., & Kuncel, N. R.** (2016). Predictor content matters for knowledge testing: Evidence supporting content validation. *Human Performance, 29* (1), 54–71.

**Sacks, O.** (2006, June 19). Stereo Sue. *The New Yorker*, 64–73.

**Saddoris, M. P., Siletti, K. A., Stansfield, K. J., & Bercum, M. F.** (2018). Heterogeneous dopamine signals support distinct features of motivated actions: Implications for learning and addiction. *Learning & Memory, 25* (9), 416–424.

**Saeed, S., Arslan, M., & Froguel, P.** (2018). Genetics of obesity in consanguineous populations: Toward precision medicine and the discovery of novel obesity genes. *Obesity, 26* (3), 474–484.

**Safren, S. A., Blashill, A. J., Lee, J. S., O'Cleirigh, C., Tomassili, J., Biello, K. B., ... & Mayer, K. H.** (2018). Condom-use self-efficacy as a mediator between syndemics and condomless sex in men who have sex with men (MSM). *Health Psychology, 37*(9), 820–827.

**Sahakyan, L., & Malmberg, K. J.** (2018). Divided attention during encoding causes separate memory traces to be encoded for repeated events. *Journal of Memory and Language, 101*, 153–161.

**Sahib, A. K., Erb, M., Marquetand, J., Martin, P., Elshahabi, A., Klamer, S., ... & Focke, N. K.** (2018). Evaluating the impact of fast-fMRI on dynamic functional connectivity in an event-based paradigm. *PloS One, 13* (1), e0190480.

**Sahly, J., Shaffer, T. W., Erdberg, P., & O'Toole, S.** (2011). Rorschach intercoder reliability for protocol-level comprehensive system variables in an international sample. *Journal of Personality Assessment, 93* (6), 592–596.

**Saitz, R., Heeren, T. C., Zha, W., & Hingson, R.** (2018). Transitions to and from at-risk alcohol use in adults in the United States. *Journal of Substance Use, 24*, 41–46.

**Sakai, K.** (2018). Single unit activity of periaqueductal gray and deep mesencephalic nucleus neurons involved in sleep stage switching in the mouse. *European Journal of Neuroscience, 47* (9), 1110–1126.

**Salisbury, L. A., Nyce, J. D., Hannum, C. D., Sheldrick, R. C., & Perrin, E. C.** (2018). Sensitivity and specificity of 2 autism screeners among referred children between 16 and 48 months of age. *Journal of Developmental & Behavioral Pediatrics, 39* (3), 254–258.

**Salmon, C. A., & Hehman, J. A.** (2018). Second to fourth digit ratio (2D: 4D), tomboyism, and temperament. *Personality and Individual Differences, 123*, 131–134.

**Salthouse, T. A.** (1994). The nature of the influence of speed on adult age differences in cognition. *Developmental Psychology, 30* (2), 240–259.

**Salthouse, T. A.** (2012). Consequences of age-related cognitive declines. *Annual Review of Psychology* (vol. 63, pp. 201–226). Palo Alto, CA: Annual Reviews.

**Salvatore, J. E., Han, S., Farris, S. P., Mignogna, K. M., Miles, M. F., & Agrawal, A.** (2018). Beyond genome-wide significance: Integrative approaches to the interpretation and extension of GWAS findings for alcohol use disorder. *Addiction Biology*. doi: 10.1111/adb.12591

**Sampaio, D. G., & Grant, J. E.** (2018). Body-focused repetitive behaviors and the dermatology patient. *Clinics in Dermatology, 36* (6), 723–727.

**Sandberg, J. G., & Knestel, A.** (2011). The experience of learning emotionally focused couples therapy. *Journal of Marital and Family Therapy, 37* (4), 393–410.

**Sandvik, A. M., Bartone, P. T., Hystad, S. W., Phillips, T. M., Thayer, J. F., & Johnsen, B. H.** (2013). Psychological hardiness predicts neuroimmunological responses to stress. *Psychology, Health, and Medicine, 18* (6), 705–713.

**Sapolsky, R. M.** (2004). *Why zebras don't get ulcers* (3rd ed.). New York: Henry Holt.

**Sar, V., Akyuz, G., & Dogan, O.** (2007). Prevalence of dissociative disorders among women in the general population. *Psychiatry Research, 149* (1–3), 169–176.

**Sârbescu, P., & Boncu, A.** (2018). The resilient, the restraint and the restless: Personality types based on the Alternative Five-Factor Model. *Personality and Individual Differences, 134*, 81–87.

**Sarkar, U., Ali, S., & Whooley, M. A.** (2009). Self-efficacy as a marker of cardiac function and predictor of heart failure hospitalization and mortality in patients with stable coronary heart disease: Findings from the Heart and Soul Study. *Health Psychology, 28* (2), 166–173.

**Sarvet, A. L., Wall, M. M., Fink, D. S., Greene, E., Le, A., Boustead, A. E., Pacula, R. L., Keyes, K. M., Cerda, M., Galea, S., & Hasin, D. S.** (2018) Medical marijuana laws and adolescent marijuana use in the United States: A systematic review and meta-analysis. *Addiction*, doi: 10.1111/add.14136.

**Sasaki, S., Yoshioka, E., Saijo, Y., Bannai, A., Kita, T., Tamakoshi, A., & Kishi, R.** (2018). A prospective cohort study of insomnia and chronic kidney disease in Japanese workers. *Sleep and Breathing, 22* (1), 257–265.

**Satpute, A. B., Kragel, P. A., Barrett, L. F., Wager, T. D., & Bianciardi, M.** (2018). Deconstructing arousal into wakeful, autonomic and affective varieties. *Neuroscience Letters*. doi: 10.1016/j.neulet.2018.01.042

**Sattler, C., Toro, P., Schönknecht, P., & Schröder, J.** (2012). Cognitive activity, education and socioeconomic status as preventive factors for mild cognitive impairment and Alzheimer's disease. *Psychiatry Research, 196* (1), 90–95.

**Sau, K., & Saha, P.** (2018). Segmentation of the ventricle from CT scan brain image: Active contour model. *Advances in Computational Sciences and Technology, 11* (1), 57–68.

**Sauce, B., & Matzel, L. D.** (2018). The paradox of intelligence: Heritability and malleability coexist in hidden gene-environment interplay. *Psychological Bulletin, 144* (1), 26–47.

**Savage, J., & Yancey, C.** (2008). The effects of media violence exposure on criminal aggression: A meta-analysis. *Criminal Justice and Behavior, 35* (6), 772–791.

**Savage, K., Firth, J., Stough, C., & Sarris, J.** (2018). GABA-modulating phytomedicines for anxiety: A systematic review of preclinical and clinical evidence. *Phytotherapy Research, 32* (1), 3–18.

**Saw, G., Chang, C. N., & Chan, H. Y.** (2018). Cross-sectional and longitudinal disparities in STEM career aspirations at the intersection of gender, race/ethnicity, and socioeconomic status. *Educational Researcher, 47* (8), 525–531.

**Sayal, K., Prasad, V., Daley, D., Ford, T., & Coghill, D.** (2018). ADHD in children and young people: Prevalence, care pathways, and service provision. *The Lancet Psychiatry, 5* (2), 175–186.

**Sayer, N. A., Noorbaloochi, S., Frazier, P. A., Pennebaker, J. W., Orazem, R. J., Schnurr, P. P., ... & Litz, B. T.** (2015). Randomized controlled trial of online expressive writing to address readjustment difficulties among US Afghanistan and Iraq war veterans. *Journal of Traumatic Stress, 28* (5), 381–390.

**Scaini, G., Quevedo, J., Velligan, D., Roberts, D. L., Raventos, H., & Walss-Bass, C.** (2018). Second generation antipsychotic-induced mitochondrial alterations: Implications for increased risk of metabolic syndrome in patients with schizophrenia. *European Neuropsychopharmacology, 28* (3), 369–380.

**Schachter, H. L.** (2018). Labor at the Taylor Society: Scientific management and a proactive approach to increase diversity for effective problem solving. *Journal of Management History, 24* (1), 7–19.

**Schachter, S., & Singer, J. E.** (1962). Cognitive, social, and physiological determinants of emotional state. *Psychological Review, 69* (5), 379–399.

**Schacter, D. L.** (2001). *The seven sins of memory.* Boston: Houghton Mifflin.

**Schaie, K. W.** (1994). The life course of adult intellectual abilities. *American Psychologist, 49* (4), 304–313.

**Schaie, K. W.** (2006). Intelligence. In R. Schultz (Ed.), *Encyclopedia of aging* (4th ed.). New York: Springer.

**Schaie, K. W.** (2007). Generational differences: The age–cohort period model. In J. E. Birren & K. W. Schaie (Eds.), *Encyclopedia of gerontology.* Oxford, UK: Elsevier.

**Schaie, K. W.** (2010). Adult intellectual abilities. *Corsini encyclopedia of psychology.* New York: Wiley.

**Schaie, K. W.** (2012). *Developmental influences on adult intellectual development: The Seattle Longitudinal Study* (2nd ed.). New York: Oxford University Press.

**Schank, R., & Abelson, R.** (1977). *Scripts, plans, goals, and understanding.* Mahwah, NJ: Erlbaum.

**Schaumberg, K., Zerwas, S., Goodman, E., Yilmaz, Z., Bulik, C. M., & Micali, N.** (2019). Anxiety disorder symptoms at age 10 predict eating disorder symptoms and diagnoses in adolescence. *Journal of Child Psychology and Psychiatry, 60*, 686–696. doi: 10.1111/jcpp.12984

**Scherbaum, C., Dickson, M., Larson, E., Bellenger, B., Yusko, K., & Goldstein, H.** (2018). Creating test score bands for assessments involving ratings using a generalizability theory approach to reliability estimation. *Personnel Assessment and Decisions, 4* (1), 1.

**Scherer, K. R.** (2018). Attribution theory: A lively legacy. *Motivation Science, 4* (1), 15–16.

**Schermer, J. A., & Goffin, R. D.** (2018). A tale of two general factors of personality in relation to intelligence and validity measures. *Personality and Individual Differences, 124*, 111–116.

**Schieffelin, B., & Ochs, E.** (Eds.). (1986). *Language socialization across cultures.* Cambridge, UK: Cambridge University Press.

**Schirmer, A.** (2013). Sex differences in emotion. In J. Armony & P. Vuilleumier (Eds.), *The Cambridge handbook of human affective neuroscience* (pp. 591–610). New York: Cambridge University Press.

**Schkade, D. A., & Kahneman, D.** (1998). Does living in California make people happy? A focusing illusion in judgments of life satisfaction. *Psychological Science, 9* (5), 340–346.

**Schlaug, G.** (2018). Even when right is all that's left: There are still more options for recovery from aphasia. *Annals of Neurology, 83* (4), 661–663.

**Schmidt, A. M., Beck, J. W., & Gillespie, J. Z.** (2013). Motivation. In N. W. Schmitt, S. Highhouse, & I. B. Weiner (Eds.), *Handbook of psychology* (2nd ed., vol. 12, pp. 311–340). Hoboken, NJ: Wiley.

**Schmidt, M. H.** (2014). The energy allocation function of sleep: A unifying theory of sleep, torpor, and continuous wakefulness. *Neuroscience and Biobehavioral Reviews, 47,* 122–153.

**Schmidt, N. B., & Koselka, M.** (2000). Gender differences in patients with panic disorder: Evaluating cognitive mediation of phobic avoidance. *Cognitive Therapy and Research, 24* (5), 533–550.

**Schmitter, A.** (2017). "I've got a little list": Classification, explanation, and the focal passions in Descartes and Hobbes. In A. Cohen & R. Stern (Eds.), *Thinking about the emotions: A philosophical history* (pp. 109–129). New York, NY: Oxford University Press.

**Schneck, N., Miller, J. M., Delorenzo, C., Kikuchi, T., Sublette, M. E., Oquendo, M. A., Mann, J. J., & Parsey, R. V.** (2016). Relationship of the serotonin transporter gene promoter polymorphism (5-HTTLPR) genotype and serotonin transporter binding to neural processing of negative emotional stimuli. *Journal of Affective Disorders, 190,* 494–498.

**Schneegans, S., & Bays, P. M.** (2017). Neural architecture for feature binding in visual working memory. *Journal of Neuroscience, 3493,* 16. doi: 10.1523/JNEUROSCI.3493-16.2017

**Schneider, D., Harknett, K., & Stimpson, M.** (2018). What explains the decline in first marriage in the united states? Evidence from the panel study of income dynamics, 1969 to 2013. *Journal of Marriage and Family, 80* (4), 791–811.

**Schneider, I., Kugel, H., Redlich, R., Grotegerd, D., Bürger, C., Bürkner, P. C., ... & Schröder, N.** (2018). Association of serotonin transporter gene AluJb methylation with major depression, amygdala responsiveness, 5-HTTLPR/rs25531 polymorphism, and stress. *Neuropsychopharmacology, 43* (6), 1308–1316.

**Schneiderman, I., Zagoory-Sharon, O., Leckman, J. F., & Feldman, R.** (2012). Oxytocin during the initial stages of romantic attachment: Relations to couples' interactive reciprocity. *Psychoneuroendocrinology, 37* (8), 1277–1285.

**Schnohr, P., O'Keefe, J. H., Holtermann, A., Lavie, C. J., Lange, P., Boje, G., & Marott, J. L.** (2018). Various leisure-time physical activities associated with widely divergent life expectancies: The Copenhagen City Heart Study. *Mayo Clinic Proceedings.* doi: 10.1016/j.mayocp.2018.06.025

**Schoenfeld, E. A., Loving, T. J., Pope, M. T., Huston, T. L., & Štulhofer, A.** (2017). Does sex really matter? Examining the connections between spouses' nonsexual behaviors, sexual frequency, sexual satisfaction, and marital satisfaction. *Archives of Sexual Behavior, 46* (2), 489–501.

**Schomerus, G., Stolzenburg, S., Freitag, S., Speerforck, S., Janowitz, D., Evans-Lacko, S., ... & Schmidt, S.** (2018). Stigma as a barrier to recognizing personal mental illness and seeking help: A prospective study among untreated persons with mental illness. *European Archives of Psychiatry and Clinical Neuroscience,* 1–11.

**Schon, K., Parker, A., & Woods, C. G.** (2018). Congenital insensitivity to pain overview. In M. P. Adam (Ed.), *GeneReviews* (online). Seattle: University of Washington. https://www.ncbi.nlm.nih.gov/books/NBK481553/

**Schönke, M., Björnholm, M., Chibalin, A. V., Zierath, J. R., & Deshmukh, A. S.** (2018). Proteomics analysis of skeletal muscle from leptin-deficient ob/ob mice reveals adaptive remodeling of metabolic characteristics and fiber type composition. *Proteomics, 18* (5–6), 1700375.

**Schooler, J. W.** (2002). Re-representing consciousness: Dissociations between experience and metaconsciousness. *Trends in Cognitive Sciences, 6* (8), 339–344.

**Schooler, J. W., Ambadar, Z., & Bendiksen, M.** (1997). A cognitive corroborative case study approach for investigating discovered memories of sexual abuse. In J. D. Read & D. S. Lindsay (Eds.), *Recollections of trauma: Scientific evidence and clinical practice.* (pp. 379–387). New York, NY: Plenum Press.

**Schooler, J. W., Ariely, D., & Loewenstein, G.** (2003). The explicit pursuit and assessment of happiness can be self-defeating. In I. Brocas & J. Carrillo (Eds.), *The psychology of economic decisions.* Oxford, UK: Oxford University Press.

**Schooler, J. W., Baumgart, S., & Franklin, M.** (2018). Entertaining without endorsing: The case for the scientific investigation of anomalous cognition. *Psychology of Consciousness: Theory, Research, and Practice, 5* (1), 63–77.

**Schooler, J. W., & Eich, E.** (2000). Memory for emotional events. In E. Tulving & F. I. M. Craik (Eds.), *The Oxford handbook of memory* (pp. 379–392). New York: Oxford University Press.

**Schoppmann, J., Schneider, S., & Seehagen, S.** (2018). Wait and see: Observational learning of distraction as an emotion regulation strategy in 22-month-old toddlers. *Journal of Abnormal Child Psychology,* 1–13.

**Schrantee, A., Tamminga, H. G., Bouziane, C., Bottelier, M. A., Bron, E. E., Mutsaerts, H. J. M., ... & Reneman, L.** (2016). Age-dependent effects of methylphenidate on the human dopaminergic system in young vs adult patients with attention-deficit/hyperactivity disorder: A randomized clinical trial. *JAMA Psychiatry, 73* (9), 955–962.

**Schredl, M.** (2010). Nightmare frequency and nightmare topics in a representative German sample. *European Archives of Psychiatry and Clinical Neuroscience, 260* (8), 565–570.

**Schredl, M.** (2018). *Researching dreams: The fundamentals.* New York: Palgrave Macmillan.

**Schulenberg, J. E., Johnston, L. D., O'Malley, P. M., Bachman, J. G., Miech, R. A., & Patrick, M. E.** (2018). *Monitoring the Future national survey results on drug use, 1975–2017: Volume II, college students and adults ages 19–55.* Ann Arbor: Institute for Social Research, University of Michigan.

**Schüler, J., Brandstätter, V., Wegner, M., & Baumann, N.** (2015). Testing the convergent and discriminant validity of three implicit motive measures: PSE, OMT, and MMG. *Motivation and Emotion, 39* (6), 839–857.

**Schultheiss, O. C., & Brunstein, J. C.** (2005). An implicit motive perspective on competence. In A. J. Elliot & C. S. Dweck (Eds.), *Handbook of competence and motivation* (pp. 31–51). New York: Guilford.

**Schultz, P. W., Nolan, J. M., Cialdini, R. B., Goldstein, N. J., & Griskevicius, V.** (2018). The constructive, destructive, and reconstructive power of social norms: Reprise. *Perspectives on Psychological Science, 13* (2), 249–254.

**Schultz, W. T., & Lawrence, S.** (2017). Psychobiography: Theory and method. *American Psychologist, 72* (5), 434–445.

**Schulze, L., Schmahl, C., & Niedtfeld, I.** (2016). Neural correlates of disturbed emotion processing in borderline personality disorder: A multi-modal meta-analysis. *Biological Psychiatry 79,* 97–106.

**Schulz-Stübner, S., Krings, T., Meister, I. G., Rex, S., Thron, A., & Rossaint, R.** (2004). Clinical hypnosis modulates functional magnetic resonance imaging signal intensities and pain perception in a thermal stimulation paradigm. *Regional Anesthesia and Pain Medicine, 29* (6), 549–556.

**Schunk, D. H.** (2012). *Learning theories: An educational perspective* (6th ed.). Upper Saddle River, NJ: Pearson.

**Schutte, N. S., & Malouff, J. M.** (2016). General and realm-specific self-efficacy: Connections to life functioning. *Current Psychology, 35,* 361–369.

**Schwartz, B. L., & Metcalfe, J.** (2011). Tip-of-the-tongue (TOT) states: Retrieval, behavior, and experience. *Memory and Cognition, 39* (5), 737–749.

**Schwarz, N.** (2018). Of fluency, beauty, and truth. In J. Proust & M. Fortier (Eds.), *Metacognitive diversity: An interdisciplinary approach.* New York: Oxford University Press.

**Schyns, B. & Schilling, J.** (2013). How bad are the effects of bad leaders? A meta-analysis of destructive leadership and its outcomes. *Leadership Quarterly, 24* (1), 138–158.

**Scott, D., Tan, C., Yanagi, M., & Tamminga, C. A.** (2018). F190. Hippocampal subfield activity may mediate aspects of psychosis. *Biological Psychiatry, 83* (9), S312–S313.

**Scott, J. G., Ross, C. A., Dorahy, M. J., Read, J., & Schäfer, I.** (2018). Childhood trauma in psychotic and dissociative disorders. In A. Moskowitz, M. J. Dorahy, & I. Schafer (Eds). *Psychosis, trauma and dissociation: Evolving perspectives on severe psychopathology* (2nd ed., pp. 141–157). New York: Wiley-Blackwell.

**Scott, M. N., Hunter, S. J., Joseph, R. M., O'Shea, T. M., Hooper, S. R., Allred, E. N., Leviton, A., & Kuban, K.** (2017). Neurocognitive correlates of attention-deficit/hyperactivity disorder symptoms in children born at extremely low gestational age. *Journal of Developmental & Behavioral Pediatrics, 38* (4), 249–259.

**Scott, R. B., Samaha, J., Chrisley, R., & Dienes, Z.** (2018). Prevailing theories of consciousness are challenged by novel cross-modal associations acquired between subliminal stimuli. *Cognition, 175,* 169–185.

**Scott-Sheldon, L. A. J., & Johnson, B. T.** (2006). Eroticizing creates safer sex: A research synthesis. *Journal of Primary Prevention, 27* (6), 619–640.

**Seabrook, R. C., Ward, L. M., Reed, L., Manago, A., Giaccardi, S., & Lippman, J. R.** (2016). Our scripted sexuality: The development and validation of a measure of the heterosexual script and its relation to television consumption. *Emerging Adulthood, 1* (18).

**Sebastian, C. L., McCrory, E. J., Cecil, C. A., Lockwood, P. L., De Brito, S. A., Fontaine, N. M., & Viding, E.** (2012). Neural responses to affective and cognitive theory of mind in children with conduct problems and varying levels of callous-unemotional traits. *Archives of General Psychiatry, 69* (8), 814–822.

**Seelye, A., Mattek, N., Howieson, D., Riley, T., Wild, K., & Kaye, J.** (2015). The impact of sleep on neuropsychological performance in cognitively intact older adults using a novel in-home sensor-based sleep assessment approach. *Clinical Neuropsychologist, 29* (1), 53–66.

**Segerstrale, U., & Molnár, P.** (Eds.). (2018). *Nonverbal communication: Where nature meets culture.* London: Routledge.

**Segerstrom, S. C., & Sephton, S. E.** (2010). Optimistic expectations and cell-mediated immunity: The role of positive affect. *Psychological Science, 21* (3), 448–455.

**Segrin, C., McNelis, M., & Pavlich, C. A.** (2018). Indirect effects of loneliness on substance use through stress. *Health Communication, 33* (5), 513–518.

**Seifert, M., Brockner, J., Bianchi, E. C., & Moon, H.** (2016). How workplace fairness affects employee commitment. *MIT Sloan Management Review, 57* (2), 15–17.

**Seixas, A., Ferreira, T., Silva, M. V., & Rodrigues, M. A.** (2018). The impact of shift work on burnout syndrome, depression, anxiety and stress: A case study in the metalworking industry. *International Journal of Occupational and Environmental Safety, 2* (1), 1–8.

**Sekeres, M. J., Winocur, G., & Moscovitch, M.** (2018). The hippocampus and related neocortical structures in memory transformation. *Neuroscience Letters, 680,* 39–53.

**Seli, P., Carriere, J. S., Wammes, J. D., Risko, E. F., Schacter, D. L., & Smilek, D.** (2018). On the clock: Evidence for the rapid and strategic modulation of mind wandering. *Psychological Science, 29* (8), 1247.

**Seligman, M. E. P.** (1970). On the generality of the laws of learning. *Psychological Review, 77* (5), 406–418.

**Seligman, M. E. P.** (1994). *What you can change and what you can't.* New York: Knopf.

**Seligman, M. E. P., & Csikszentmihalyi, M.** (2000). Positive psychology: An introduction. *American Psychologist, 55,* 5–14.

**Seligman, M. E. P., & Maier, S. F.** (1967). Failure to escape traumatic shock. *Journal of Experimental Psychology, 74* (1), 1–9.

**Seligman, M. E. P., Rosellini, R. A., & Kozak, M. J.** (1975). Learned helplessness in the rat: Time course, immunization, and reversibility. *Journal of Comparative and Physiological Psychology, 88* (2), 542–547.

**Sellbom, M., & Wygant, D. B.** (2018). *Forensic applications of the MMPI-2-RF: A casebook.* Minneapolis: University of Minnesota Press.

**Selye, H.** (1974). *Stress without distress.* Philadelphia: Saunders.

**Selye, H.** (1983). The stress concept: Past, present, and future. In C. I. Cooper (Ed.), *Stress research.* New York: Wiley.

**Serdarevic, F., Jansen, P. R., Ghassabian, A., White, T., Jaddoe, V. W., Posthuma, D., & Tiemeier, H.** (2018). Association of genetic risk for schizophrenia and bipolar disorder with infant neuromotor development. *JAMA Psychiatry, 75* (1), 96–98.

**Serrano-Villar, M., & Calzada, E. J.** (2016). Ethnic identity: Evidence of protective effects for young, Latino children. *Journal of Applied Developmental Psychology, 42,* 21–30.

**Sestan-Pesa, M., & Horvath, T. L.** (2016). Metabolism and mental illness. *Trends in Molecular Medicine, 22* (2), 174–185.

**Seto, M. C.** (2017). The puzzle of male chronophilias. *Archives of Sexual Behavior, 46,* 3–22.

**Seto, M. C.** (2018). *Pedophilia and sexual offending against children: Theory, assessment, and intervention* (2nd ed.). Washington, DC: American Psychological Association.

**Settles, R. E., Fischer, S., Cyders, M. A., Combs, J. L., Gunn, R. L., & Smith, G. T.** (2012). Negative urgency: A personality predictor of externalizing behavior characterized by neuroticism, low conscientiousness, and disagreeableness. *Journal of Abnormal Psychology, 121* (1), 160–172.

**Sexton, J. E., Cox, J. J., Zhao, J., & Wood, J. N.** (2018). The genetics of pain: Implications for therapeutics. *Annual Review of Pharmacology and Toxicology, 58,* 123–142.

**Shadrina, M., Bondarenko, E. A., & Slominsky, P. A.** (2018). Genetics factors in major depression disease. *Frontiers in Psychiatry, 9,* 334.

**Shaharabani, R., Ram-On, M., Talmon, Y., & Beck, R.** (2018). Pathological transitions in myelin membranes driven by environmental and multiple sclerosis conditions. *Proceedings of the National Academy of Sciences, 115* (44), 11156–11161.

**Shakeshaft, N. G., Trzaskowski, M., McMillan, A., Krapohl, E., Simpson, M. A., Reichenberg, A., Cederloff, M., Larsson, H., Lichtenstein, P., & Plomin, R.** (2015). Thinking positively: The genetics of high intelligence. *Intelligence, 48,* 123–132.

**Shallice, T., & Cipolotti, L.** (2018). The prefrontal cortex and neurological impairments of active thought. *Annual Review of Psychology, 69,* 157–180.

**Shamay-Tsoory, S., & Lamm, C.** (2018). The neuroscience of empathy: From past to present and future. *Neuropsychologia, 116,* 1–4.

**Shariff, A. F., & Tracy, J. L.** (2011). What are emotion expressions for? *Current Directions in Psychological Science, 20* (6), 395–399.

**Sharma, R., Meurk, C., Bell, S., Ford, P., & Gartner, C.** (2018). Australian mental health care practitioners' practices and attitudes for encouraging smoking cessation and tobacco harm reduction in smokers with severe mental illness. *International Journal of Mental Health Nursing, 27* (1), 247–257.

**Sharma, S., Powers, A., Bradley, B., & Ressler, K. J.** (2016). Gene x environment determinants of stress- and anxiety-related disorders. *Annual Review of Psychology* (vol. 67, pp. 239–261). Palo Alto, CA: Annual Reviews.

**Sharp, E. S., Reynolds, C. A., Pedersen, N. L., & Gatz, M.** (2010). Cognitive engagement and cognitive aging: Is openness protective? *Psychology and Aging, 25* (1), 60–73.

**Sharples, J. M., Oliver, S., Oxman, A. D., Mahtani, K. R., Chalmers, I., Collins, K., ... & Hoffman, T.** (2018). Critical thinking: A core skill within education and healthcare. *Profession, 18* (19), 19.

**Shaw, P., Eckstrand, K., Sharp, W., Blumenthal, J., Lerch, J. P., Greenstein, D., ... & Rapoport, J. L.** (2007). Attention-deficit/hyperactivity disorder is characterized by a delay in cortical maturation. *Proceedings of the National Academy of Sciences, 104* (49), 19649–19654.

**Shay, J. W.** (2018). Telomeres and aging. *Current Opinion in Cell Biology, 52,* 1–7.

**Shearer, J., Papanikolaou, N., Meiser-Stedman, R., McKinnon, A., Dalgleish, T., Smith, P., ... & Byford, S.** (2018). Cost-effectiveness of cognitive therapy as an early intervention for post-traumatic stress disorder in children and adolescents: a trial based evaluation and model. *Journal of Child Psychology and Psychiatry, 59* (7), 773–780.

**Shedler, J.** (2018). Where is the evidence for "evidence-based" therapy? *Psychiatric Clinics of North America, 41* (2), 319–329.

**Sheldon, K. M.** (2002). The self-concordance model of healthy goal-striving: When personal goals correctly represent the person. In E. L. Deci & R. M. Ryan (Eds.), *Handbook of self-determination research* (pp. 65–86). Rochester, NY: University of Rochester Press.

**Sheldon, K. M., & Lyubomirsky, S.** (2007). Is it possible to become happier? (And if so, how?). *Social and Personality Psychology Compass, 1* (1), 129–145.

**Sheldon, K. M., & Lyubomirsky, S.** (2012). The challenge of staying happier: Testing the happiness adaptation model. *Personality and Social Psychology Bulletin, 38* (5), 670–680.

**Shelton, R. C., Osuntokun, O., Heinloth, A. N., & Corya, S. A.** (2010). Therapeutic options for treatment-resistant depression. *CNS Drugs, 24* (2), 131–161.

**Sheremata, S. L., Somers, D. C., & Shomstein, S.** (2018). Visual short-term memory activity in parietal lobe reflects cognitive processes beyond attentional selection. *Journal of Neuroscience, 38* (6), 1511–1519.

**Sherif, M., Harvey, O. J., White, B. J., Hood, W. R., & Sherif, C. W.** (1961). *Intergroup cooperation and competition: The Robbers Cave experiment.* Norman: University of Oklahoma Press.

**Sherman, R. A., Nave, C., & Funder, D. C.** (2010). Situational similarity and personality predict behavioral consistency. *Journal of Personality and Social Psychology, 99* (2), 330–343.

**Shetty, A. K., Rao, M. S., & Hattiangady, B.** (2008). Behavior of hippocampal stem/progenitor cells following grafting into the injured hippocampus. *Journal of Neuroscience Research, 86* (14), 3062–3074.

**Shi, J., Hu, P., Lai, K. K., & Chen, G.** (2018). Determinants of users' information dissemination behavior on social networking sites: An elaboration likelihood model perspective. *Internet Research, 28* (2), 393–418.

**Shi, Y., Liang, D., Bao, Y., An, R., Wallace, M. S., & Grant, I.** (2019). Recreational marijuana legalization and prescription opioids received by Medicaid enrollees. *Drug and Alcohol Dependence, 194,* 13–19.

**Shier, M. L., Nicholas, D. B., Graham, J. R., & Young, A.** (2018). Preventing workplace violence in human services workplaces: Organizational dynamics to support positive interpersonal interactions among colleagues. *Human Service Organizations: Management, Leadership & Governance, 42* (1), 4–18.

**Shih, I. F., Paul, K., Haan, M., Yu, Y., & Ritz, B.** (2018). Physical activity modifies the influence of apolipoprotein E $\varepsilon$4 allele and type 2 diabetes on dementia and cognitive impairment among older Mexican Americans. *Alzheimer's & Dementia, 14* (1), 1–9.

**Shilo, R., Weinsdörfer, A., Rakoczy, H., & Diesendruck, G.** (2018). The out-group homogeneity effect across development: A cross-cultural investigation. *Child Development.* doi: 10.1111/cdev.13082

**Shim, E. J., Hahm, B. J., Go, D. J., Lee, K. M., Noh, H. L., Park, S. H., & Song, Y. W.** (2018). Modeling quality of life in patients with rheumatic diseases: The role of pain catastrophizing, fear-avoidance beliefs, physical disability, and depression. *Disability and Rehabilitation, 40* (13), 1509–1516.

**Shiota, M. N., Campos, B., Oveis, C., Hertenstein, M. J., Simon-Thomas, E., & Keltner, D.** (2017). Beyond happiness: Building a science of discrete positive emotions. *American Psychologist, 72* (7), 617–643.

**Shirayama, Y., Ishima, T., Oda, Y., Okamura, N., Iyo, M., & Hashimoto, K.** (2015). Opposite roles for neuropeptide S in the nucleus accumbens and bed nucleus of the *stria terminalis* in learned helplessness rats. *Behavioural Brain Research, 291,* 67–71.

**Shockley, K. M., & Allen, T. D.** (2018). It's not what I expected: The association between dual-earner couples' met expectations for the division of paid and family labor and well-being. *Journal of Vocational Behavior, 104,* 240–260.

**Shoda, Y., Wilson, N. L., Chen, J., Gilmore, A. K., & Smith, R. E.** (2013). Cognitive-affective processing system analysis of intra-individual dynamics in collaborative therapeutic assessment: Translating basic theory and research into clinical applications. *Journal of Personality, 81* (6), 554–568.

**Shokri-Kojori, E., Wang, G. J., Wiers, C. E., Demiral, S. B., Guo, M., Kim, S. W., ... & Miller, G.** (2018). $\beta$-Amyloid accumulation in the human brain after one night of sleep deprivation. *Proceedings of the National Academy of Sciences, 115* (17), 4483–4488.

**Shor, E., & Roelfs, D. J.** (2013). The longevity effects of religious and nonreligious participation: A meta-analysis and meta-regression. *Journal for the Scientific Study of Religion, 52* (1), 120–145.

**Showers, C. J., Ditzfeld, C. P., & Zeigler-Hill, V.** (2015). Self-concept structure and the quality of self-knowledge. *Journal of Personality, 83* (5), 535–551.

**Shrout, P. E., & Rodgers, J. L.** (2018). Psychology, science, and knowledge construction: Broadening perspectives from the replication crisis. *Annual Review of Psychology, 69,* 487–510.

**Shu, L. L., Gino, F., & Bazerman, M. H.** (2011). Dishonest deed, clear conscience: When cheating leads to moral disengagement and motivated forgetting. *Personality and Social Psychology Bulletin, 37* (3), 330–349.

**Shukla, P., & Rishi, P.** (2018). Health locus of control, psychosocial/spiritual well-being and death anxiety among advanced-stage cancer patients. *Psychological Studies, 63* (2), 200–207.

**Shulman, J. L., Gotta, G., & Green, R.** (2012). Will marriage matter? Effects of marriage anticipated by same-sex couples. *Journal of Family Issues, 33* (2), 158–181.

**Sidtis, D., & Sidtis, J. J.** (2018). The affective nature of formulaic language: A right-hemisphere subcortical process. *Frontiers in Neurology, 9,* 573.

**Sieber, W. J., Rodin, J., Larson, L., Ortega, S., & Cummings, N.** (1992). Modulation of human natural killer cell activity by exposure to uncontrollable stress. *Brain, Behavior, and Immunity, 6* (2), 141–156.

**Siegel, J. M.** (2005). Clues to the functions of mammalian sleep. *Nature, 437* (7063), 1264–1271.

**Siegel, M. H.** (2018). *Preventing and managing violence in organizations: Workplace violence, targeted violence, and active shooters.* Boca Raton: CRC Press.

**Siegel, S.** (1988). State dependent learning and morphine tolerance. *Behavioral Neuroscience, 102* (2), 228–232.

**Siegler, I. C., Bosworth, H. B., Davey, A., & Elias, M. F.** (2013a). Disease, health, and aging in the first decade of the 21st century. In R. M. Lerner, M. A. Easterbrooks, J. Mistry, & I. B. Weiner (Eds.), *Handbook of psychology* (2nd ed., vol. 6, pp. 437–450). Hoboken, NJ: Wiley.

**Siegler, I. C., Elias, M. F., Brummett, B. H., & Bosworth, H. B.** (2013b). Adult development and aging. In A. M. Nezu, C. Maguth Nezu, P. A. Geller, & I. B. Weiner (Eds.), *Handbook of psychology* (2nd ed., vol. 9, pp. 459–476). Hoboken, NJ: Wiley.

**Sifferlin, A.** (2017, December 1). The 25 Best Inventions of 2017: Glasses that give sight to the blind. *Time.* http://time.com/5023212/best-inventions-of-2017/

**Sikorskii, A., Given, C., Given, B., Jeon, S., & McCorkle, R.** (2006). Testing the effects of treatment complications on a cognitive-behavioral intervention for reducing symptom severity. *Journal of Pain and Symptom Management, 32* (2), 129–139.

**Silver, N., & Hovick, S. R.** (2018). A schema of denial: The influence of rape myth acceptance on beliefs, attitudes, and processing of affirmative consent campaign messages. *Journal of Health Communication, 23,* 505–513.

**Simcock, G., & Hayne, H.** (2002). Breaking the barrier? Children fail to translate their preverbal memories into language. *Psychological Science, 13*(3), 225–231.

**Simola, S. K., Barling, J., & Turner, N.** (2010). Transformational leadership and leader moral orientation: Contrasting an ethic of justice and an ethic of care. *Leadership Quarterly, 21* (1), 179–188.

**Simon, A.** (April 25, 2018). Stroke victim paralyzed from the neck down writes a book using only her eyes. *The Independent.* https://www.independent.co.uk/life-style/stroke-victim-paralysed-writes-book-eyes-mia-austin-locked-in-syndrome-a8321381.html

**Simon, H. A.** (1969). *The sciences of the artificial.* Cambridge, MA: MIT Press.

**Simone, A. N., Marks, D. J., Bédard, A. C., & Halperin, J. M.** (2017). Low working memory rather than ADHD symptoms predicts poor academic achievement in school-aged children. *Journal of Abnormal Child Psychology.* doi: 10.1007/s10802-017-0288-3

**Simons, D. J., & Chabris, C. F.** (1999). Gorillas in our midst: Sustained inattentional blindness for dynamic events. *Perception, 28* (9), 1059–1074.

**Simons, D. J., & Chabris, C. F.** (2011). What people believe about how memory works: A representative survey of the U.S. population. *PLoS One, 6* (8), e22757.

**Simonton, D. K.** (2016). Defining creativity: Don't we also need to define what is not creative? *Journal of Creative Behavior.* doi: 10.1002/jocb.137

**Sindhu, P., Kumar, S., Iqbal, B., Ali, J., & Baboota, S.** (2018). Duloxetine loaded-microemulsion system to improve behavioral activities by upregulating serotonin and norepinephrine in brain for the treatment of depression. *Journal of Psychiatric Research, 99,* 83–95.

**Singer, J. A., & Conway, M. A.** (2011). Reconsidering therapeutic action: Loewald, cognitive neuroscience, and the integration of memory's duality. *International Journal of Psychoanalysis, 92* (5), 1183–1207.

**Singer, J. A., Singer, B. F., & Berry, M.** (2013). A meaning-based intervention for addiction: Using narrative therapy to treat alcohol abuse. In J. Hicks & C. Routledge (Eds.), *The experience of meaning in life.* New York: Springer.

**Singh, R., Wegener, D. T., Sankaran, K., Bhullar, N., Ang, K. Q., Chia, P. J., ... & Chen, F.** (2017). Attitude similarity and attraction: Validation, positive affect, and trust as sequential mediators. *Personal Relationships, 24* (1), 203–222.

**Sinnapah, S., Cadelis, G., Waltz, X., Lamarre, Y., & Connes, P.** (2015). Overweight explains the increased red blood cell aggregation in patients with obstructive sleep apnea. *Clinical Hemorheology and Microcirculation, 59* (1), 17–26.

**Sio, U. N., & Ormerod, T. C.** (2015). Incubation and cueing effects in problem-solving: Set aside the difficult problems but focus on the easy ones. *Thinking & Reasoning, 21* (1), 113–129.

**Siow, E., Leung, D. Y. P., Wong, E. M. L., Lam, W. H., & Lo, S. M.** (2018). Do depressive symptoms moderate the effects of exercise self-efficacy on physical activity among patients with coronary heart disease? *Journal of Cardiovascular Nursing, 33* (4), E26–E34.

**Sitzmann, T., & Weinhardt, J. M.** (2018). Training engagement theory: A multilevel perspective on the effectiveness of work-related training. *Journal of Management, 44* (2), 732–756.

**Sivacek, J., & Crano, W. D.** (1982). Vested interest as a moderator of attitude-behavior consistency. *Journal of Personality and Social Psychology, 43* (2), 210–221.

**Sjöwall, D., Bohlin, G., Rydell, A. M., & Thorell, L. B.** (2017). Neuropsychological deficits in preschool as predictors of ADHD symptoms and academic achievement in late adolescence. *Child Neuropsychology, 23* (1), 111–128.

**Skinner, B. F.** (1938). *The behavior of organisms: An experimental analysis.* New York: Appleton-Century-Crofts.

**Skinner, B. F.** (1957). *Verbal behavior.* New York: Appleton-Century-Crofts.

**Skolin, I., Wahlin, Y. B., Broman, D. A., Koivisto Hursti, U., Vikström Larssen, M., & Hernell, O.** (2006). Altered food intake and taste perception in children with cancer after start of chemotherapy: Perspectives of children, parents, and nurses. *Supportive Care in Cancer, 14* (4), 369–378.

**Slade, E., Keeney, E., Mavranezouli, I., Dias, S., Fou, L., Stockton, S., ... & Fairburn, C. G.** (2018). Treatments for bulimia nervosa: A network meta-analysis. *Psychological Medicine, 48,* 2629–2636.

**Slater, A., Field, T., & Hernandez-Reif, M.** (2007). The development of the senses. In A. Slater & M. Lewis (Eds.), *Introduction to infant development* (2nd ed.). New York: Oxford University Press.

**Slavin, R. E.** (2006). Translating research into widespread practice: The case of success for all. In M. A. Constas & R. J. Sternberg (Eds.), *Translating theory and research into educational practice: Developments in content domains, large-scale reform, and intellectual capacity* (pp. 113–126). Mahwah, NJ: Erlbaum.

**Sloan, D. M., & Marx, B. P.** (2018). Maximizing outcomes associated with expressive writing. *Clinical Psychology: Science and Practice, 25* (1), e12231.

**Smalarz, L., & Wells, G. L.** (2013). Eyewitness certainty as a system variable. In B. L. Cutler (Ed.), *Reform of eyewitness identification procedures* (pp. 161–177). Washington, DC: American Psychological Association.

**Smallheer, B. A., Vollman, M., & Dietrich, M. S.** (2018). Learned helplessness and depressive symptoms following myocardial infarction. *Clinical Nursing Research, 27* (5), 597–616.

**Smallwood, J., & Schooler, J. W.** (2015). The science of mind wandering: Empirically navigating the stream of consciousness. *Annual Review of Psychology* (vol. 66, pp. 487–518). Palo Alto, CA: Annual Reviews.

**Smit, F., Willemse, G., Koopmanschap, M., Onrust, S., Cuijpers, P., & Beekman, A.** (2006). Cost-effectiveness of preventing depression in primary care patients: Randomized trial. *British Journal of Psychiatry, 188,* 330–336.

**Smith, C. P.** (Ed.). (1992). *Thematic content analysis for motivation and personality research.* New York: Cambridge University Press.

**Smith, D.** (2004, February 7). Love that dare not squeak its name. *New York Times.* http://www.nytimes.com/2004/02/07/arts/love-that-dare-not-squeak-its-name.html (accessed March 22, 2016)

**Smith, K. E., Mason, T. B., Peterson, C. B., & Pearson, C. M.** (2018). Relationships between eating disorder-specific and transdiagnostic risk factors for binge eating: An integrative moderated mediation model of emotion regulation, anticipatory reward, and expectancy. *Eating Behaviors, 31,* 131–136.

**Smith, M. C., Bibi, U., & Sheard, D. E.** (2003). Evidence for the differential impact of time and emotion on personal and event memories for September 11, 2001. *Applied Cognitive Psychology, 17,* 1047–1055.

**Smith, M. L., Yang, L. H., Huang, D., Pike, K. M., Yuan, C., & Wang, Z.** (2018). Measuring internalized stigma of mental illness among Chinese outpatients with mood disorders. *International Journal of Culture and Mental Health.* doi: 10.1080/17542863.2018.1442484

**Smith, R. E., Horn, S. S., & Bayen, U. J.** (2012). Prospective memory in young and older adults: The effects of ongoing task load. *Neuropsychology, Development, and Cognition: Aging, Neuropsychology, and Cognition, 19* (4), 495–514.

**Smith, S. J., Axelton, A. M., & Saucier, D. A.** (2009). The effects of contact on sexual prejudice: A meta-analysis. *Sex Roles, 61* (3), 178–191.

**Smith, S. K., Kuhn, E., O'Donnell, J., Koontz, B. F., Nelson, N., Molloy, K., ... & Hoffman, J.** (2018). Cancer distress coach: Pilot study of a mobile app for managing posttraumatic stress. Psycho-oncology, *27* (1), 350–353.

**Smith-Spark, J. H., Zięcik, A. P., & Sterling, C.** (2016). Time-based prospective memory in adults with developmental dyslexia. *Research in Developmental Disabilities, 49–50,* 34–46.

**Smyth, J.** (1998). Written emotional expression: Effect sizes, outcome types, and moderating variables. *Journal of Consulting and Clinical Psychology, 66,* 174–184.

**Snell, R. S., & Wong, Y. L.** (2007). Differentiating good soldiers from good actors. *Journal of Management Studies, 44* (6), 883–909.

**Snippe, E., Jeronimus, B. F., aan het Rot, M., Bos, E. H., de Jonge, P., & Wichers, M.** (2018). The reciprocity of prosocial behavior and positive affect in daily life. *Journal of Personality, 86* (2), 139–146.

**Snowdon, D. A.** (2003). Healthy aging and dementia: Findings from the Nun Study. *Annals of Internal Medicine, 139* (5, Pt. 2), 450–454.

**Snowdon, D. A.** (2007, April). *Aging with grace: Findings from the Nun Study.* Paper presented at the 22nd annual Alzheimer's regional conference, Seattle.

**Snyder, C. R., & Lopez, S. J.** (Eds.). (2007). *Positive psychology: The scientific and practical explorations of human strengths.* Thousand Oaks, CA: Sage.

**Snyder, J. A., Scherer, H. L., & Fisher, B. S.** (2012). Social organization and social ties: Their effects on sexual harassment victimization in the workplace. *Work, 42* (1), 137–150.

**Soares, M. S., Paiva, W. S., Guertzenstein, E. Z., Amorim, R. L., Bernardo, L. S., Pereira, J. F., Fonoff, E. T., & Teixeira, M. J.** (2013). Psychosurgery for schizophrenia: History and perspectives. *Neuropsychiatric Disease and Treatment, 9,* 509–515.

**Sobol-Kwapinska, M.** (2016). Calm down—It's only neuroticism. Time perspectives as moderators and mediators of the relationship between neuroticism and well-being. *Personality and Individual Differences, 94,* 64–71.

**Söderkvist, S., Ohlén, K., & Dimberg, U.** (2018). How the experience of emotion is modulated by facial feedback. *Journal of Nonverbal Behavior, 42*(1), 129–151.

**Sokolowski, M., Wasserman, J., & Wasserman, D.** (2018). Gene-level associations in suicide attempter families show overrepresentation of synaptic genes and genes differentially expressed in brain development. *American Journal of Medical Genetics Part B: Neuropsychiatric Genetics.* doi: 10.1002/ajmg.b.32694

**Solmi, M., Pigato, G., Kane, J. M., & Correll, C. U.** (2018). Clinical risk factors for the development of tardive dyskinesia. *Journal of the Neurological Sciences, 389,* 21–27.

**Solomon, A.** (2012, December 22). Anatomy of a murder-suicide. *New York Times Sunday Review.* http://www.nytimes.com/2012/12/23/opinion/sunday/anatomy-of-a-murder-suicide.html?_r=0 (accessed April 10, 2016)

**Sommer, V., & Vasey, P. L. (Eds.).** (2006). *Homosexual behaviour in animals: An evolutionary perspective.* New York: Cambridge University Press.

**Sommerfeld, C. G., Weiner, D. J., Nowalk, A., & Larkin, A.** (2018). Hypersensitivity pneumonitis and acute respiratory distress syndrome from e-cigarette use. *Pediatrics, 141,* http://pediatrics.aappublications.org/content/141/6/e20163927

**Song, J., Bergen, S. E., Di Florio, A., Karlsson, R., Charney, A., Ruderfer, D. M., ... & Belliveau, R. A.** (2015). Genome-wide association study identifies SESTD1 as a novel risk gene for lithium-responsive bipolar disorder. *Molecular Psychiatry.* http://www.nature.com/mp/journal/vaop/ncurrent/full/mp2015165a.html (accessed April 12, 2016)

**Song, J., Ying, Y., Wang, W., Liu, X., Xu, X., Wei, X., & Ruan, X.** (2018). The role of P2X7R/ERK signaling in dorsal root ganglia satellite glial cells in the development of chronic postsurgical pain induced by skin/muscle incision and retraction (SMIR). *Brain, Behavior, and Immunity, 69,* 180–189.

**Song, S.** (2006, March 19). Mind over medicine. *Time.* http://content.time.com/time/magazine/article/0,9171,1174707,00.html (accessed February 29, 2016)

**Sonne, J. W. H., & Gash, D. M.** (2018). Psychopathy to altruism: Neurobiology of the selfish-selfless spectrum. *Frontiers in Psychology, 9,* 575.

**Sonnentag, S., & Fritz, C.** (2015). Recovery from job stress: The stressor-detachment model as an integrative framework. *Journal of Organizational Behavior, 36* (S1), S72–S103.

**Sontag-Padilla, L. M., Dorn, L. D., Tissot, A., Susman, E. J., Beers, S. R., & Rose, S. R.** (2012). Executive functioning, cortisol reactivity, and symptoms of psychopathology in girls with premature adrenarche. *Development and Psychopathology, 24* (1), 211–223.

**Sony, M., & Mekoth, N.** (2016). The relationship between emotional intelligence, frontline employee adaptability, job satisfaction, and job performance. *Journal of Retailing and Consumer Services, 30,* 20–32.

**Soriano, E. C., Perndorfer, C., Otto, A. K., Siegel, S. D., & Laurenceau, J. P.** (2018). Does sharing good news buffer fear of bad news? A daily diary study of fear of cancer recurrence in couples approaching the first mammogram post-diagnosis. Psycho-Oncology. doi: 10.1002/pon.4813

**Sorrentino, R., Brown, A., Berard, B., & Peretti, K.** (2018). Sex offenders: General information and treatment. *Psychiatric Annals, 48* (2), 120–128.

**Sortheix, F. M., & Schwartz, S. H.** (2017). Values that underlie and undermine well-being: Variability across countries. *European Journal of Personality, 31* (2), 187–201.

**South, S. C., & Krueger, R. F.** (2008). And interactionist on genetic and environmental contributions to personality. *Social and Personality Psychology Compass, 2* (2), 929–948.

**Southwick, S. M., & Charney, D. S.** (2018). *Resilience: The science of mastering life's greatest challenges* (2nd ed.). Cambridge: Cambridge University Press.

**Spalding, K. N.** (2018). The role of the medial prefrontal cortex in the generalization of conditioned fear. *Neuropsychology, 32* (1), 1.

**Spanhel, K., Wagner, K., Geiger, M. J., Ofer, I., Schulze-Bonhage, A., & Metternich, B.** (2018). Flashbulb memories: Is the amygdala central? An investigation of patients with amygdalar damage. *Neuropsychologia, 111,* 163–171.

**Spann, M. N., Sourander, A., Surcel, H. M., Hinkka-Yli-Salomäki, S., & Brown, A. S.** (2017). Prenatal toxoplasmosis antibody and childhood autism. *Autism Research, 10* (5), 769–777.

**Spanos, N. P.** (1996). *Multiple identities and false memories: A sociocognitive perspective.* Washington, DC: American Psychological Association.

**Sparrow, B., Liu, J., & Wegner, D. M.** (2011). Google effects on memory: Cognitive consequences of having information at our fingertips. *Science, 333* (6043), 776–778.

**Spätgens, T., & Schoonen, R.** (2018). The semantic network, lexical access, and reading comprehension in monolingual and bilingual children: An individual differences study. *Applied Psycholinguistics, 39* (1), 225–256.

**Speakman, J. R., Loos, R. J. F., O'Rahilly, S., Hirschhorn, J. N., & Allison, D. B.** (2018). GWAS for BMI: A treasure trove of fundamental insights into the genetic basis of obesity. *International Journal of Obesity, 42,* 1524–1531.

**Spearman, C.** (1904). "General intelligence" objectively determined and measured. *American Journal of Psychology, 15,* 201–293.

**Spelke, E. S., & Kinzler, K. D.** (2007). Core knowledge. *Developmental Science, 10* (1), 89–96.

**Spence, C., & Wang, Q. J.** (2018). On the meaning (s) of perceived complexity in the chemical senses. *Chemical Senses, 43* (7), 451–461.

**Spence, K. W.** (1938). Gradual versus sudden solution of discrimination problems by chimpanzees. *Journal of Comparative Psychology, 25,* 213–224.

**Spencer, J. P., Blumberg, M. S., McMurray, B., Robinson, S. R., Samuelson, L. K., & Tomblin, J. B.** (2009). Short arms and talking eggs: Why we should no longer abide the nativist-empiricist debate. *Child Development Perspective, 3* (2), 79–87.

**Spencer, S. J., Logel, C., & Davies, P. G.** (2016). Stereotype threat. *Annual Review of Psychology* (vol. 67, pp. 415–437). Palo Alto, CA: Annual Reviews.

**Spencer, S. J., Steele, C. M., & Quinn, D. M.** (1999). Stereotype threat and women's math performance. *Journal of Experimental Social Psychology, 35* (1), 4–28.

**Spengler, M., Roberts, B. W., Lüdtke, O., Martin, R., & Brunner, M.** (2016). The kind of student you were in elementary school predicts mortality. *Journal of Personality, 84.* doi: 10.1111/jopy.12180

**Sperdin, H. F., Spierer, L., Becker, R., Michel, C. M., & Landis, T.** (2015). Submillisecond unmasked subliminal visual stimuli evoke electrical brain responses. *Human Brain Mapping, 36* (4), 1470–1483.

**Sperling, G.** (1960). The information available in brief presentations. *Psychological Monographs, 74* (11), 1–29.

**Sperry, R. W.** (1968). Hemisphere deconnection and unity in conscious awareness. *American Psychologist, 23* (10), 723–733.

**Sperry, R. W.** (1974). Lateral specialization in surgically separated hemispheres. In F. O. Schmitt & F. G. Worden (Eds.), *The neurosciences: Third study program* (vol. 3, pp. 5–19). Cambridge, MA: MIT Press.

**Spiegel, D.** (2006). Editorial: Recognizing traumatic dissociation. *American Journal of Psychiatry, 163* (4), 566–568.

**Spielberger, C. D.** (2004, August). *Type A behavior, anger-hostility, and heart disease.* Paper presented at the 28th International Congress of Psychology, Beijing, China.

**Sprich, S. E., Safren, S. A., Finkelstein, D., Remmert, J. E., & Hammerness, P.** (2016). A randomized controlled trial of cognitive behavioral therapy for ADHD in medication-treated adolescents. *Journal of Child Psychology and Psychiatry, 57* (11), 1218–1226.

**Sprott, R. A., & Benoit Hadcock, B.** (2018). Bisexuality, pansexuality, queer identity, and kink identity. *Sexual and Relationship Therapy, 33* (1–2), 214–232.

**Squire, L. R.** (1990, June). *Memory and brain systems.* Paper presented at the meeting of the American Psychological Society, Dallas.

**Squire, L. R.** (2004). Memory systems of the brain: A brief history and current perspective. *Neurobiology of Learning and Memory, 82,* 171–177.

**Squire, L. R.** (2007). Memory systems as a biological concept. In H. L. Roediger, Y. Dudai, & S. Fitzpatrick (Eds.), *Science of memory: Concepts.* New York: Oxford University Press.

**Sriram, N., & Greenwald, A. G.** (2009). The Brief Implicit Association Test. *Experimental Psychology, 56* (4), 283–204.

**Srivastava, A. K., Bulte, C. A., Shats, I., Walczak, P., & Bulte, J. W.** (2016). Co-transplantation of syngeneic mesenchymal stem cells improves survival of allogeneic glial-restricted precursors in mouse brain. *Experimental Neurology, 275* (Pt. 1), 154–161.

**Sroufe, L. A., Coffino, B., & Carlson, E. A.** (2010). Conceptualizing the role of early experience: Lessons from the Minnesota Longitudinal Study. *Developmental Review, 30* (1), 36–51.

**Stallen, M., De Dreu, C. K., Shalvi, S., Smidts, A., & Sanfey, A. G.** (2012). The herding hormone: Oxytocin stimulates in-group conformity. *Psychological Science, 23* (11), 1288–1292.

**Stanley, C. T., Petscher, Y., & Catts, H.** (2018). A longitudinal investigation of direct and indirect links between reading skills in kindergarten and reading comprehension in tenth grade. *Reading and Writing, 31* (1), 133–153.

**Stanley, I. H., Hom, M. A., & Joiner, T. E.** (2018). Modifying mental health help-seeking stigma among undergraduates with untreated psychiatric disorders: A pilot randomized trial of a novel cognitive bias modification intervention. *Behaviour Research and Therapy, 103*, 33–42.

**Stanley, I. H., Yancey, J. R., Patrick, C. J., & Joiner, T. E.** (2018). A distinct configuration of MMPI-2-RF scales RCd and RC9/ACT is associated with suicide attempt risk among suicide ideators in a psychiatric outpatient sample. *Psychological Assessment, 30* (9), 124912-54.

**Stanley, J. T., & Isaacowitz, D. M.** (2012). Socioemotional perspectives on adult development. In S. K. Whitbourne & M. Sliwinski (Eds.), Wiley-Blackwell *handbook of adult development.* New York: Wiley-Blackwell.

**Stanovich, K. E.** (2018). Miserliness in human cognition: the interaction of detection, override and mindware. *Thinking & Reasoning.* doi: 10.1080/13546783.2018.1459314 (in press)

**Stanton, K., Ellickson-Larew, S., & Watson, D.** (2016). Development and validation of a measure of online deception and intimacy. *Personality and Individual Differences, 88*, 187–196.

**Staresina, B. P., Gray, J. C., & Davachi, L.** (2009). Event congruency enhances episodic memory encoding through semantic elaboration and relational binding. *Cerebral Cortex, 19* (5), 1198–1207.

**Starrett, M. J., & Ekstrom, A. D.** (2018). Perspective: Assessing the flexible acquisition, integration, and deployment of human spatial representations and information. *Frontiers in Human Neuroscience, 12.*

**Stassart, R., Möbius, W., Nave, K. A., & Edgar, J. M.** (2018). The axon-myelin unit in development and degenerative disease. *Frontiers in Neuroscience, 12*, 467. doi: 10.3389/fnins.2018.00467

**Staudinger, U. M., & Gluck, J.** (2011). Psychological wisdom research. *Annual Review of Psychology* (vol. 62, pp. 215–241). Palo Alto, CA: Annual Reviews.

**Stavrova, O.** (2015). Religion, self-rated health, and mortality: Whether religiosity delays death depends on the cultural context. *Social Psychological and Personality Science, 6* (8), 911–922.

**Staw, B. M., Bell, N. E., & Clausen, J. A.** (1986). The dispositional approach to job attitudes: A lifetime longitudinal test. *Administrative Science Quarterly, 31* (1), 56–77.

**Steblay, N., Dysart, J., & Wells, G. L.** (2011). Seventy-two tests of the sequential lineup superiority effect: A meta-analysis and policy discussion. *Psychology, Public Policy, and Law, 17* (1), 99–139.

**Steel, P., Svartdal, F., Thundiyil, T., & Brothen, T.** (2018a). Examining procrastination across multiple goal stages: A longitudinal study of temporal motivation theory. *Frontiers in Psychology, 9*, 327.

**Steel, P., Taras, V., Uggerslev, K., & Bosco, F.** (2018b). The happy culture: A theoretical, meta-analytic, and empirical review of the relationship between culture and wealth and subjective well-being. *Personality and Social Psychology Review, 22* (2), 128–169.

**Steele, C. M., & Aronson, J.** (1995). Stereotype threat and the intellectual test performance of African Americans. *Journal of Personality and Social Psychology, 69* (5), 797–811.

**Steels, L., & Brooks, R.** (2018). *The artificial life route to artificial intelligence: Building embodied, situated agents.* London: Routledge.

**Steenen, S. A., van Wijk, A. J., van der Heijden, G. J., van Westrhenen, R., de Lange, J., & de Jongh, A.** (2016). Propranolol for the treatment of anxiety disorders: Systematic review and meta-analysis. *Journal of Psychopharmacology, 30* (2), 128–139.

**Steensma, T. D., & Cohen-Kettenis, P. T.** (2018). A critical commentary on follow-up studies and "desistence" theories about transgender and gender non-conforming children. *International Journal of Transgenderism*, 1–6. doi: 10.1080/0092623X.2018.1437580

**Steensma, T. D., Cohen-Kettenis, P. T., & Zucker, K. J.** (2018). Evidence for a change in the sex ratio of children referred for gender dysphoria: Data from the Center of Expertise on Gender Dysphoria in Amsterdam (1988–2016). *Journal of Sex & Marital Therapy.* doi: 10.1080/0092623X.2018.1437580

**Steensma, T. D., & Wensing-Kruger, A.** (2018). Gender dysphoria. In T. H. Ollendick, S. W. White, & B. A. White (Eds.), *The Oxford handbook of clinical child and adolescent psychology.* (pp. 398–412). New York: Oxford University Press.

**Steg, L.** (2015). Environmental psychology and sustainable consumption. In L. A. Reisch & J. Thøgersen (Eds.), *Handbook of research on sustainable consumption* (pp. 70–83). Northampton, MA: Edward Elgar Publishing.

**Stegen, A., & Wankier, J.** (2018). Generating gratitude in the workplace to improve faculty job satisfaction. *Journal of Nursing Education, 57* (6), 375–378.

**Steger, M. F.** (2012). Meaning in life. In S. J. Lopez & C. R. Snyder (Eds.), *The Oxford handbook of positive psychology* (2nd ed.). New York: Oxford University Press.

**Steger, M. F., Frazier, P., Oishi, S., & Kaler, M.** (2006). The meaning in life questionnaire: Assessing the presence of and search for meaning in life. *Journal of Counseling Psychology, 53* (1), 80–93.

**Stein, G. L., Supple, A. J., Huq, N., Dunbar, A. S., & Prinstein, M. J.** (2016). A longitudinal examination of perceived discrimination and depressive symptoms in ethnic minority youth: The roles of attributional style, positive ethnic/racial affect, and emotional reactivity. *Developmental Psychology, 52* (2), 259–271.

**Stein, J.** (2018). What is developmental dyslexia? *Brain Sciences, 8*, 26.

**Stein, R.** (2003, September 2). Blinded by the light. *The Age.* http://www.theage.com.au/articles/2003/09/01/1062403448264.html (accessed February 19, 2016)

**Steinberg, L.** (2012). Adolescent risk-taking: A social neuroscience perspective. In E. Amsel & J. Smetana (Eds.), *Adolescent vulnerabilities and opportunities: Constructivist developmental perspectives.* New York: Cambridge University Press.

**Steinberg, L.** (2013). How should the science of adolescent brain development inform legal policy? In J. Bhabha (Ed.), *Coming of age: A new framework for adolescent rights.* Philadelphia: University of Pennsylvania Press.

**Steinhausen, H. C., Jakobsen, H., Meyer, A., Jørgensen, P. M., & Lieb, R.** (2016). Family aggregation and risk factors in phobic disorders over three generations in a nationwide study. *PloS One, 11* (1), e0146591.

**Steinke, J., & Tavarez, P. M. P.** (2018). Cultural representations of gender and STEM: Portrayals of female STEM characters in popular films, 2002–2014. *International Journal of Gender, Science and Technology, 9* (3), 244–277.

**Stenholm, S., Head, J., Kivimäki, M., Magnusson Hanson, L. L., Pentti, J., Rod, N. H., ... & Vahtera, J.** (2018). Sleep duration and sleep disturbances as predictors of healthy and chronic disease-free life expectancy between ages 50 and 75: A pooled analysis of three cohorts. *The Journals of Gerontology: Series A, 74* (2), 204–210.

**Stenhouse, N., Myers, T., Vraga, E., Kotcher, J., Beall, L., & Maibach, E.** (2018). The potential role of actively open-minded thinking in preventing motivated reasoning about controversial science. *Journal of Environmental Psychology, 57*, 17–24.

**Stephan, Y., Sutin, A. R., Kornadt, A., Caudroit, J., & Terracciano, A.** (2018). Higher IQ in adolescence is related to a younger subjective age in later life: Findings from the Wisconsin Longitudinal Study. *Intelligence, 69*, 195–199.

**Stephens, N. M., Townsend, S. S. M., Hamedani, M. G., Destin, M., & Manzo, V.** (2015). A difference-education intervention equips first-generation college students to thrive in the face of stressful college situations. *Psychological Science, 26* (10), 1556–1566.

**Stern, B. L., Caligor, E., Hörz-Sagstetter, S., & Clarkin, J. F.** (2018). An object-relations based model for the assessment of borderline psychopathology. *Psychiatric Clinics, 41* (4), 595–611.

**Stern, Y., Alexander, G. E., Prohovnik, I., & Mayeux, R.** (1992). Inverse relationship between education and parietotemporal perfusion deficit in Alzheimer's disease. *Annals of Neurology, 32* (3), 371–375.

**Stern, Y., Scarmeas, N., & Habeck, C.** (2004). Imaging cognitive reserve. *International Journal of Psychology, 39* (1), 18–26.

**Sternberg, R. J.** (2018). The triarchic theory of successful intelligence. In D. P. Flanagan & E. M. McDonough (Eds.), *Contemporary intellectual assessment: Theories, tests, and issues* (4th ed., pp. 174–193). New York: Guilford.

**Sternberg, R. J., & Sternberg, K.** (Eds.). (2018). *The new psychology of love.* New York: Cambridge University Press.

**Sterponi, L.** (2010). Learning communicative competence. In D. F. Lancy, J. Bock, & S. Gaskins (Eds.), *The anthropology of learning in childhood* (pp. 235–259). Walnut Creek, CA: AltaMira.

**Stevelink, R., Abramovic, L., Verkooijen, S., Begemann, M. J., Sommer, I. E., Boks, M. P., ... & Vinkers, C. H.** (2018). Childhood abuse and white matter integrity in bipolar disorder patients and healthy controls. *European Neuropsychopharmacology, 28*, 807–817.

**Stevens, J. S., & Hamann, S.** (2012). Sex differences in brain activation to emotional stimuli: A meta-analysis of neuroimaging studies. *Neuropsychologia, 50* (7), 1578–1593.

**Stevens, L., & Woodruff, C. C.** (Eds.) (2018). *The neuroscience of empathy, compassion, and self-compassion.* Cambridge, MA: Academic Press.

**Stevens, M. C., Pearlson, G. D., Calhoun, V. D., & Bessette, K. L.** (2018). Functional neuroimaging evidence for distinct neurobiological pathways in attention-deficit/hyperactivity disorder. *Biological Psychiatry: Cognitive Neuroscience and Neuroimaging, 3* (8), 675–685.

**Stevenson, T. J., Alward, B. A., Ebling, F. J., Fernald, R. D., Kelly, A., & Ophir, A. G.** (2018). The value of comparative animal research: Krogh's principle facilitates scientific discoveries. *Policy Insights from the Behavioral and Brain Sciences, 5* (1), 118–125.

**Stewart, G. L., Dustin, S. L., Barrick, M. R., & Darnold, T. C.** (2008). Handshake in employment interviews. *Journal of Applied Psychology, 93* (5), 1139–1146.

**Stewart, R. E., Chambless, D. L., & Stirman, S. W.** (2018). Decision making and the use of evidence-based practice: Is the three-legged stool balanced? *Practice Innovations, 3* (1), 56–67.

**Stickgold, R.** (2001). Watching the sleeping brain watch us: Sensory processing during sleep. *Trends in Neurosciences, 24* (6), 307–309.

**Stirling, J. D.** (2002). *Introducing neuropsychology.* East Sussex, UK: Psychology Press.

**Stirrups, R.** (2018). The storm and stress in the adolescent brain. *The Lancet Neurology, 17* (5), 404.

**Stoet, G., & Geary, D. C.** (2018). The gender-equality paradox in science, technology, engineering, and mathematics education. *Psychological Science, 29* (4), 581–593.

**Stokes, A., Collins, J. M., Grant, B. F., Scamuffa, R. F., Hsiao, C. W., Johnston, S. S., ... & Preston, S. H.** (2018). Obesity progression between young adulthood and midlife and incident diabetes: A retrospective cohort study of US adults. *Diabetes Care*, dc172336.

**Stone, A. A., Schwartz, J. E., Broderick, J. E., & Deaton, A.** (2010). A snapshot of the age distribution of psychological well-being in the United States. *Proceedings of the National Academy of Sciences USA, 107* (22), 9985–9990.

**Stone, J.** (2002). Battling doubt by avoiding practice: The effects of stereotype threat on self-handicapping in white athletes. *Personality and Social Psychology Bulletin, 28* (12), 1667–1678.

**Stoner, J.** (1961). *A comparison of individual and group decisions, including risk.* Unpublished master's thesis, School of Industrial Management, MIT.

**Stoodley, C. J., & Schmahmann, J. D.** (2018). Functional topography of the human cerebellum. *Handbook of Clinical Neurology, 154,* 59–70.

**Störmer, V. S., & Alvarez, G. A.** (2016). Attention alters perceived attractiveness. *Psychological Science, 27,* 563–571.

**Strahan, E., Spencer, S. J., & Zanna, M. P.** (2002). Subliminal priming and persuasion: Striking while the iron is hot. *Journal of Experimental Social Psychology, 38,* 556–568.

**Strand, R. C., & Eldevik, S.** (2018). Improvements in problem behavior in a child with autism spectrum diagnosis through synthesized analysis and treatment: A replication in an EIBI home program. *Behavioral Interventions, 33* (1), 102–111.

**Strauss, A. Y., Huppert, J. D., Simpson, H. B., & Foa, E. B.** (2018). What matters more? Common or specific factors in cognitive behavioral therapy for OCD: Therapeutic alliance and expectations as predictors of treatment outcome. *Behaviour Research and Therapy, 105,* 43–51.

**Strawn, J. R., Geracioti, L., Rajdev, N., Clemenza, K., & Levine, A.** (2018). Pharmacotherapy for generalized anxiety disorder in adult and pediatric patients: an evidence-based treatment review. *Expert Opinion on Pharmacotherapy, 19* (10), 1057–1070.

**Strawn, J. R., Vollmer, L. L., McMurray, K. M., Mills, J. A., Mossman, S. A., Varney, S. T., ... & Sah, R.** (2018). Acid-sensing T cell death associated gene-8 receptor expression in panic disorder. *Brain, Behavior, and Immunity, 67,* 36–41.

**Strike, P. C., Magid, K., Whitehead, D. L., Brydon, L., Bhattacharyya, M. R., & Steptoe, A.** (2006). Pathophysiological processes underlying emotional triggering of acute cardiac events. *Proceedings of the National Academy of Sciences USA, 103* (11), 4322–4327.

**Stripp, T. K., Jorgensen, M. B., & Olsen, N. V.** (2018). Anaesthesia for electroconvulsive therapy—new tricks for old drugs: A systematic review. *Acta Neuropsychiatrica, 30* (2), 61–69.

**Stritof, S.** (2018, August 4). Estimated median age of first marriage by gender, 1890–2015. *The Spruce.* https://www.thespruce.com/estimated-median-age-marriage-2303878

**Strobbe, D., & Campanella, M.** (2018). Anxiolytic therapy: A paradigm of successful mitochondrial pharmacology. *Trends in Pharmacological Sciences, 39* (5), 437–439.

**Stroebe, W.** (2018). The task of social psychology is to explain behavior not just to observe it. *Social Psychological Bulletin, 13* (2), Article e26131. doi: 10.5964/spb.v13i2.26131

**Stroop, J. R.** (1935). Studies of interference in serial verbal reactions. *Journal of Experimental Psychology, 18,* 643–662.

**Strosahl, K. D., & Robinson, P. J.** (2018). Adapting empirically supported treatments in the era of integrated care: A roadmap for success. *Clinical Psychology: Science and Practice, 25* (3), e12246.

**Stuart, S., Schultz, J., & Ashen, C.** (2018). A new community-based model for training in evidence-based psychotherapy practice. *Community Mental Health Journal, 54,* 912–920.

**Stulhofer, A., Busko, V., & Landripet, I.** (2010). Pornography, sexual socialization, and satisfaction among young men. *Archives of Sexual Behavior, 39* (1), 168–178.

**Stürmer, T., Hasselbach, P., & Amelang, M.** (2006). Personality, lifestyle, and risk of cardiovascular disease and cancer: Follow-up of population-based cohort. *British Medical Journal, 332* (7554), 1359–1362.

**Su, C. S., & Lu, P. H.** (2018). A study of the factors influencing customers' impulse buying behavior in restaurants. *Advances in Hospitality and Tourism Research (AHTR), 6* (1), 47–67.

**Sue, D., Sue, D. W., Sue, D. M., & Sue, S.** (2014). *Essentials of understanding abnormal psychology* (2nd ed.). Boston: Cengage.

**Suinn, R. M.** (1984). *Fundamentals of abnormal psychology.* Chicago: Nelson-Hall.

**Sullivan, H. S.** (1953). *The interpersonal theory of psychiatry.* New York: Norton.

**Sullivan, P. F., Neale, M. C. & Kendler, K. S.** (2000). Genetic epidemiology of major depression: Review and meta-analysis. *American Journal of Psychiatry, 157,* 1552–1562

**Suls, J., & Swain, A.** (1998). Type A–Type B personalities. In H. S. Friedman (Ed.), *Encyclopedia of mental health* (vol. 3). San Diego: Academic.

**Sun, D.** (2016). Endogenous neurogenic cell response in the mature mammalian brain following traumatic injury. *Experimental Neurology, 275* (Pt. 3), 405–410.

**Sun, M., Feng, W., Wang, F., Li, P., Li, Z., Li, M., ... & Tse, L. A.** (2018). Meta-analysis on shift work and risks of specific obesity types. *Obesity Reviews, 19* (1), 28–40.

**Sun, N., Lu, H., & Qu, C.** (2018). Sex differences in extinction to negative stimuli: Event-related brain potentials. *Medicine, 97* (17), e0503.

**Sun, N., Wu, Y., Nanba, K., Sbiera, S., Kircher, S., Kunzke, T., ... & Fassnacht, M.** (2018). High-resolution tissue mass spectrometry imaging reveals a refined functional anatomy of the human adult adrenal gland. *Endocrinology, 159* (3), 1511–1524.

**Supekar, K., Kochalka, J., Schaer, M., Wakeman, H., Qin, S., Padmanabhan, A., & Menon, V.** (2018). Deficits in mesolimbic reward pathway underlie social interaction impairments in children with autism. *Brain, 141* (9), 2795–2805.

**Surís, A., Holliday, R., & North, C. S.** (2016). The evolution of the classification of psychiatric disorders. *Behavioral Sciences, 6* (1), 5–15.

**Sutin, A. R., Stephan, Y., & Terracciano, A.** (2018). Facets of conscientiousness and objective markers of health status. *Psychology & Health, 33,* 1100–1115.

**Swami, V., Barron, D., & Furnham, A.** (2018). Exposure to natural environments, and photographs of natural environments, promotes more positive body image. *Body Image, 24,* 82–94.

**Swanson, S. A., Saito, N., Borges, G., Benjet, C., Aguilar-Gaxiola, S., Medina-Mora, M. E., & Breslau, J.** (2012). Change in binge eating and binge eating disorder associated with migration from Mexico to the U.S. *Journal of Psychiatric Research, 46* (1), 31–37.

**Swider, B. W., Barrick, M. R., & Harris, T. B.** (2016). Initial impressions: What they are, what they are not, and how they influence structured interview outcomes. *Journal of Applied Psychology, 101,* 625–638.

**Swift, J. K., Callahan, J. L., Cooper, M., & Parkin, S. R.** (2018). The impact of accommodating client preference in psychotherapy: A meta-analysis. *Journal of Clinical Psychology, 74* (11), 1924–1937.

**Swinbourne, R., Miller, J., Smart, D., Dulson, D. K., & Gill, N.** (2018). The effects of sleep extension on sleep, performance, immunity and physical stress in rugby players. *Sports, 6* (2), 42.

**Syrek, C. J., Weigelt, O., Kühnel, J., & de Bloom, J.** (2018). All I want for Christmas is recovery–changes in employee affective well-being before and after vacation. *Work & Stress, 32,* 313–333. doi: 10.1080/02678373.2018.1427816

# T

**Taciak, P. P., Lysenko, N., & Mazurek, A. P.** (2018). Drugs which influence serotonin transporter and serotonergic receptors: Pharmacological and clinical properties in the treatment of depression. *Pharmacological Reports, 70* (1), 37–46.

**Taga, K. A., Markey, C. N., & Friedman, H. S.** (2006). A longitudinal investigation of associations between boys' pubertal timing and adult behavioral health and well-being. *Journal of Youth and Adolescence, 35* (3), 401–411.

**Taillieu, T. L., Afifi, T. O., Turner, S., Cheung, K., Fortier, J., Zamorski, M., & Sareen, J.** (2018). Risk factors, clinical presentations, and functional impairments for generalized anxiety disorder in military personnel and the general population in Canada. *The Canadian Journal of Psychiatry* doi: 10.1177/0706743717752878

**Tajfel, H.** (1978). The achievement of group differentiation. In H. Tajfel (Ed.), *Differentiation between social groups.* London: Academic.

**Takano, T., Nakamura, K., & Watanabe, M.** (2002). Urban residential environments and senior citizens' longevity in mega-city areas: The importance of walkable green space. *Journal of Epidemiology and Community Health, 56* (12), 913–916.

**Talsma, K., Schüz, B., Schwarzer, R., & Norris, K.** (2018). I believe, therefore I achieve (and vice versa): A meta-analytic cross-lagged panel analysis of self-efficacy and academic performance. *Learning and Individual Differences, 61,* 136–150.

**Tamir, D. I., & Thornton, M. A.** (2018). Modeling the predictive social mind. *Trends in Cognitive Sciences, 22,* 201–212.

**Tamm, L., Denton, C. A., Epstein, J. N., Schatschneider, C., Taylor, H., Arnold, L. E., ... & Vaughn, A.** (2017). Comparing treatments for children with ADHD and word reading difficulties: A randomized clinical trial. *Journal of Consulting and Clinical Psychology, 85* (5), 434–446.

**Tanabe, S., & Yamashita, T.** (2018). The role of immune cells in brain development and neurodevelopmental diseases. *International Immunology, 30* (10), 437–444.

**Tang, N. K., Lereya, S. T., Boulton, H., Miller, M. A., Wolke, D., & Cappuccio, F. P.** (2015). Nonpharmacological treatments of insomnia for long-term painful conditions: A systematic review and meta-analysis of patient-reported outcomes in randomized controlled trials. *Sleep, 38* (11), 1751–1764.

**Tang, Y. Y., Hölzel, B. K., & Posner, M. I.** (2015). The neuroscience of mindfulness meditation. *Nature Reviews: Neuroscience, 16* (4), 213–225.

**Tangney, J. P., Boone, A. L., & Baumeister, R. F.** (2018). High self-control predicts good adjustment, less pathology, better grades, and interpersonal success. In R.F. Baumeister, (Ed.), Self-regulation *and self-control* (pp. 181–220). London: Routledge.

**Tangolo, A. E.** (2018). *Psychodynamic psychotherapy with transactional analysis: Theory and narration of a living experience.* London: Routledge.

**Tanida, Y., Nakayama, M., & Saito, S.** (2018). The interaction between temporal grouping and phonotactic chunking in short-term serial order memory for novel verbal sequences. *Memory,* 1–12.

**Tanner, J. M., Whitehouse, R. H., Takaishi, M.** (1966). Standards from birth to maturity for height, weight, height velocity, and weight velocity: British children, 1965. Part I. *Archives of Diseases in Childhood, 41,* 454–471.

**Tarescavage, A. M., Scheman, J., & Ben-Porath, Y. S.** (2018). Prospective comparison of the Minnesota Multiphasic Personality Inventory-2 (MMPI-2) and MMPI-2-Restructured Form (MMPI-2-RF) in predicting treatment outcomes among patients with chronic low back pain. *Journal of Clinical Psychology in Medical Settings, 25* (1), 66–79.

**Tarokh, L., & Carskadon, M. A.** (2010). Developmental changes in the human sleep EEG during early adolescence. *Sleep, 33* (6), 801–809.

**Tarter, R. E., Vanyukov, M., Kirisci, L., Reynolds, M., & Clark, D. B.** (2006). Predictors of marijuana use in adolescents before and after illicit drug use: Examination of the gateway hypothesis. *American Journal of Psychiatry, 163* (12), 2134–2140.

**Tatalovich, R., & Wendell, D. G.** (2018). Expanding the scope and content of morality policy research: lessons from Moral Foundations Theory. *Policy Sciences, 51,* 565–579.

**Tavassoli, T., Miller, L. J., Schoen, S. A., Brout, J. J., Sullivan, J., & Baron-Cohen, S.** (2018). Sensory reactivity, empathizing and systemizing in autism spectrum conditions and sensory processing disorder. *Developmental Cognitive Neuroscience, 29,* 72–77.

**Tay, C., Ang, S., & Van Dyne, L.** (2006). Personality, biographical characteristics, and job interview success: A longitudinal study of the mediating effects of self-efficacy and the moderating effects of internal locus of causality. *Journal of Applied Psychology, 91* (2), 446–454.

**Taylor, B. J., & Hasler, B. P.** (2018). Chronotype and mental health: Recent advances. *Current Psychiatry Reports, 20* (8), 59.

**Taylor, F. W.** (1911). *Scientific management.* New York: Harper & Row.

**Taylor, N. C., Seedall, R. B., Robinson, W. D., & Bradford, K.** (2018). The systemic interaction of attachment on psychophysiological arousal in couple conflict. *Journal of Marital and Family Therapy, 44* (1), 46–60.

**Taylor, R. J., Chatters, L. M., Lincoln, K. D., & Woodward, A. T.** (2017). Church-based exchanges of informal social support among African Americans. *Race and Social Problems, 9*(1), 53–62.

**Taylor, S. E.** (2011). Tend and befriend theory. In A. M. van Lange, A. W. Kruglanski, & E. T. Higgins (Eds.), *Handbook of theories of social psychology* (vol. 2). Thousand Oaks, CA: Sage.

**te Nijenhuis, J., Willigers, D., Dragt, J., & van der Flier, H.** (2016). The effects of language bias and cultural bias estimated using the method of correlated vectors on a large database of IQ comparisons between native Dutch and ethnic minority immigrants from non-Western countries. *Intelligence, 54,* 117–135.

**Tekampe, J., van Middendorp, H., Sweep, F. C., Roerink, S. H., Hermus, A. R., & Evers, A. W.** (2018). Human pharmacological conditioning of the immune and endocrine system: Challenges and opportunities. *International Review of Neurobiology 138,* 61–80.

**Temple Newhook, J., Pyne, J., Winters, K., Feder, S., Holmes, C., Tosh, J., ... & Pickett, S.** (2018). A critical commentary on follow-up studies and "desistance" theories about transgender and gender-nonconforming children. *International Journal of Transgenderism, 19,* 212–224.

**Tenbergen, G., Wittfoth, M., Frieling, H., Ponseti, J., Walter, M., Beier, K. M., ... Kruger, T. H. C.** (2015). The neurobiology and psychology of pedophilia: Recent advances and challenges. *Frontiers in Human Neuroscience, 9.*

**Tennie, C., Call, J., & Tomasello, M.** (2010). Evidence for emulation in chimpanzees in social settings using the floating peanut task. *PLoS One, 5* (5), e10544.

**Teoh, J. S., Wong, M. Y. Y., Vijayaraghavan, T., & Neumann, B.** (2018). Bridging the gap: Axonal fusion drives rapid functional recovery of the nervous system. *Neural Regeneration Research, 13* (4), 591–594.

**Tepper, B. J., Dimotakis, N., Lambert, L. S., Koopman, J., Matta, F. K., Man Park, H., & Goo, W.** (2018). Examining follower responses to transformational leadership from a dynamic, person–environment fit perspective. *Academy of Management Journal, 61* (4), 1343–1368.

**Tepper, B. J., Duffy, M. K., Hoobler, J., & Ensley, M. D.** (2004). Moderators of the relationships between coworkers' organizational citizenship behavior and fellow employees' attitudes. *Journal of Applied Psychology, 89* (3), 455–465.

**Terman, L.** (1925). *Genetic studies of genius: Vol. 1: Mental and physical traits of a thousand gifted children.* Stanford, CA: Stanford University Press.

**Testa, M., Parks, K. A., Hoffman, J. H., Crane, C. A., Leonard, K. E., & Shyhalla, K.** (2015). Do drinking episodes contribute to sexual aggression perpetration in college men? *Journal of Studies on Alcohol and Drugs, 76* (4), 507–515.

**Tetreault, C., Bates, E. A., & Bolam, L. T.** (2018). How dark personalities perpetrate partner and general aggression in Sweden and the United Kingdom. *Journal of Interpersonal Violence.* doi: 10.1177/0886260518793992

**Thapar, A., & Cooper, M.** (2016). Attention-deficit hyperactivity disorder. *Lancet, 387,* 1240–1250.

**Thatcher, A., Waterson, P., Todd, A., & Moray, N.** (2018). State of science: Ergonomics and global issues. *Ergonomics, 61,* 197–213.

**Thielen, J. W., Hong, D., Rohani Rankouhi, S., Wiltfang, J., Fernández, G., Norris, D. G., & Tendolkar, I.** (2018). The increase in medial prefrontal glutamate/glutamine concentration during memory encoding is associated with better memory performance and stronger functional connectivity in the human medial prefrontal–thalamus–hippocampus network. *Human Brain Mapping, 39*(6), 2381–2390.

**Thielmann, I., & Hilbig, B. E.** (2018). Is it all about the money? A re-analysis of the link between Honesty-Humility and Dictator Game giving. *Journal of Research in Personality, 76,* 1–5.

**Thigpen, C. H., & Cleckley, H. M.** (1957). *The three faces of Eve.* New York. McGraw-Hill.

**Thomas, M. S. C., & Johnson, M. H.** (2008). New advances in understanding sensitive periods in brain development. *Current Directions in Psychological Science, 17* (1), 1–5.

**Thomas, M., Tyers, P., Lazic, S. E., Caldwell, M. A., Barker, R. A., Beazley, L., & Ziman, M.** (2009). Graft outcomes influences by co-expression of Pax7 in graft and host tissue. *Journal of Anatomy, 214* (3), 396–405.

**Thompson, A. E.** (2015). Medical marijuana. *Journal of the American Medical Association, 313* (24), 2508.

**Thompson, A. K., Cote, R., Sniffen, J., & Brangaccio, J. A.** (2018). Operant conditioning of the tibialis anterior motor evoked potential in people with and without chronic incomplete spinal cord injury. *Journal of Neurophysiology,* 15, 669–683.

**Thompson, A., McEvoy, P. M., & Lipp, O. V.** (2018). Enhancing extinction learning: Occasional presentations of the unconditioned stimulus during extinction eliminate spontaneous recovery, but not necessarily reacquisition of fear. *Behaviour Research and Therapy, 108,* 29–39.

**Thompson, R. A.** (2013a). Attachment theory and research: Precis and prospect. In P. D. Zelazo (Ed.), *The Oxford handbook of developmental psychology* (vol. 2, pp. 191–216). New York: Oxford University Press.

**Thompson, R. A.** (2013b). Socialization of emotion regulation in the family. In J. Gross (Ed.), *Handbook of emotion regulation* (2nd ed.). New York: Guilford.

**Thompson, R. A.** (2013c). Relationships, regulation, and development. In R. M. Lerner (Ed.), *Handbook of child psychology* (7th ed.). New York: Wiley.

**Thompson, T.** (2013). Autism research and services for young children: History, progress, and challenges. *Journal of Applied Research on Intellectual Disabilities, 26* (2), 1–27.

**Thorbecke, C.** (July 4, 2018). After wife gets amnesia in accident, couple dates all over again to build back their bond. Good Morning America. ABC News. https://abcnews.go.com/GMA/Family/wife-amnesia-accident-couple-dates-build-back-bond/story?id=55574758

**Thorell, L. B., Sjöwall, D., Diamatopoulou, S., Rydell, A. M., & Bohlin, G.** (2017). Emotional functioning, ADHD symptoms, and peer problems: A longitudinal investigation of children age 6–9.5 years. *Infant and Child Development, 26* (4), E2008.

**Thorndike, E. L.** (1898). Animal intelligence: An experimental study of the associative processes in animals. *Psychological Review,* monograph supplements, no. 8. New York: Macmillan.

**Thornicroft, G., Brohan, E., Rose, D., Sartorius, N., & Leese, M.** (2009). Global pattern of experienced and anticipated discrimination against people with schizophrenia: A cross-sectional survey. *The Lancet, 373* (9661), 408–415.

**Thornton, L. M., Munn-Chernoff, M. A., Baker, J. H., Juréus, A., Parker, R., Henders, A. K., ... & Kirk, K. M.** (2018). The anorexia nervosa genetics initiative (ANGI): Overview and methods. *Contemporary Clinical Trials, 74,* 61–69.

**Thow, M. E., Summers, M. J., Saunders, N. L., Summers, J. J., Ritchie, K., & Vickers, J. C.** (2018). Further education improves cognitive reserve and triggers improvement in selective cognitive functions in older adults: The Tasmanian Healthy Brain Project. *Alzheimer's & Dementia: Diagnosis, Assessment & Disease Monitoring, 10,* 22–30.

**Tian, X., Zarate, J. M., & Poeppel, D.** (2016). Mental imagery of speech implicates two mechanisms of perceptual reactivation. *Cortex, 77,* 1–12.

**Tichko, P., & Skoe, E.** (2018). Musical experience, sensorineural auditory processing, and reading subskills in adults. *Brain Sciences, 8* (5). doi: 10.3390/brainsci8050077

**Tikhomirov, A. A., & Spangler, W. D.** (2010). Neo-charismatic leadership and the fate of mergers and acquisitions: An institutional model of CEO leadership. *Journal of Leadership and Organizational Studies, 17* (1), 44–60.

***Time* staff.** (2017, December 1). The 25 best inventions of 2017. http://time.com/5023212/best-inventions-of-2017/

**Timimi, S.** (2017). Non-diagnostic based approaches to helping children who could be labelled ADHD and their families. *International Journal of Qualitative Studies on Health and Well-being, 12* (Suppl. 1). doi: 10.1080/17482631.2017.1298270.

**Timmers, A. D., Bossio, J. A., & Chivers, M. L.** (2018). Disgust, sexual cues, and the prophylaxis hypothesis. *Evolutionary Psychological Science, 4* (2), 179–190.

**Timmons, L., & Ekas, N. V.** (2018). Giving thanks: Findings from a gratitude intervention with mothers of children with autism spectrum disorder. *Research in Autism Spectrum Disorders, 49,* 13–24.

**Timulak, L.** (2018). Humanistic-experiential therapies in the treatment of generalised anxiety: A perspective. *Counselling and Psychotherapy Research, 18* (3), 233–236.

**Tinaz, S., Chow, C., Kuo, P. H., Krupinski, E. A., Blumenfeld, H., Louis, E. D., & Zubal, G.** (2018). Semiquantitative analysis of dopamine transporter scans in patients with Parkinson disease. *Clinical Nuclear Medicine, 43* (1), e1–e7.

**Tinbergen, N.** (1969). *The study of instinct.* New York: Oxford University Press.

**Tindle, H., Belnap, B. H., Houck, P. R., Mazumdar, S., Scheier, M. F., Matthews, K. A., He, F., & Rollman, B. L.** (2012). Optimism, response to treatment of depression, and rehospitalization after coronary artery bypass graft surgery. *Psychosomatic Medicine, 74* (2), 200–207.

**Titova, O. E., Hogenkamp, P. S., Jacobsson, J. A., Feldman, I., Schiöth, H. B., & Benedict, C.** (2015). Associations of self-reported sleep disturbance and duration with academic failure in community-dwelling Swedish adolescents: Sleep and academic performance at school. *Sleep Medicine, 16* (1), 87–93.

**Tochkov, K., & Williams, N.** (2018). Patient or prisoner? Forced treatment for the severely mentally ill:

Life-long implications for patients who have been treated against their will. *Ethical Human Psychology and Psychiatry, 20* (1), 56–68.

**Todorov, A., Mandisodza, A. N., Goren, A., & Hall, C. C.** (2005). Inferences of competence from faces predict election outcomes. *Science, 308* (5728), 1623–1626.

**Tolman, E. C.** (1932). *Purposive behavior in animals and man*. New York: Appleton-Century-Crofts.

**Tolman, E. C., & Honzik, C. H.** (1930). Degrees of hunger, reward and non-reward, and maze performance in rats. *University of California Publications in Psychology, 4,* 241–256.

**Tomasetti, C. & Vogelstein, B.** (2015). Variation in cancer risk among tissues can be explained by the number of stem cell divisions. *Science, 347* (6217), 78–81.

**Tomé-Pires, C., & Miró, J.** (2012). Hypnosis for the management of chronic and cancer procedure-related pain in children. *International Journal of Clinical and Experimental Hypnosis, 60* (4), 432–457.

**Tomko, R. L., Trull, T. J., Wood, P. K., & Sher, K. J.** (2013). Characteristics of borderline personality disorder in a community sample: Comorbidity, treatment utilization, and general functioning. *Journal of Personality Disorders, 28* (5), 734–750.

**Tong, F., Nakayama, K., Moscovitch, M., Weinrib, O., & Kanwisher, N.** (2000). Response properties of the human fusiform face area. *Cognitive Neuropsychology, 17* (1-2-3), 257–279.

**Toplak, M. E., West, R. F., & Stanovich, K. E.** (2011). The Cognitive Reflection Test as a predictor of performance on heuristics-and-biases tasks. *Memory and Cognition, 39,* 1275–1289.

**Torvik, F. A., Welander-Vatn, A., Ystrom, E., Knudsen, G. P., Czajkowski, N., Kendler, K. S., & Reichborn-Kjennerud, T.** (2016). Longitudinal associations between social anxiety disorder and avoidant personality disorder: A twin study. *Journal of Abnormal Psychology, 125* (1), 114–124.

**Toschi, N., Riccelli, R., Indovina, I., Terracciano, A., & Passamonti, L.** (2018). Functional connectome of the five-factor model of personality. *Personality Neuroscience*. doi: 10.1017/pen.2017.2

**Tov, W., Nai, Z. L., & Lee, H. W.** (2016). Extraversion and agreeableness: Divergent routes to daily satisfaction with social relationships. *Journal of Personality, 84* (1), 121–134.

**Traczyk, J., Sobkow, A., Fulawka, K., Kus, J., Petrova, D., & Garcia-Retamero, R.** (2018). Numerate decision makers don't use more effortful strategies unless it pays: A process tracing investigation of skilled and adaptive strategy selection in risky decision making. *Judgment and Decision Making, 13* (4), 372–381.

**Træen, B., Štulhofer, A., Janssen, E., Carvalheira, A. A., Hald, G. M., Lange, T., & Graham, C.** (2018). Sexual activity and sexual satisfaction among older adults in four European countries. *Archives of Sexual Behavior*, 1–15.

**Trantham-Davidson, H., & Chandler, L. J.** (2015). Alcohol-induced alterations in dopamine modulation of prefrontal activity. *Alcohol, 49* (8), 773–779.

**Tremblay, R. E., Vitaro, F., & Côté, S. M.** (2018). Developmental origins of chronic physical aggression: A bio-psycho-social model for the next generation of preventive interventions. *Annual Review of Psychology, 69,* 383–407.

**Trent, J., Lavelock, C., & King, L. A.** (2013). Processing fluency, positive affect, and judgments of meaning in life. *Journal of Positive Psychology, 8* (2), 135–139.

**Trentham, C. E., Hensley, C., & Policastro, C.** (2018). Recurrent childhood animal cruelty and its link to recurrent adult interpersonal violence. *International Journal of Offender Therapy and Comparative Criminology, 62* (8), 2345–2356.

**Triandis, H. C.** (2018). *Individualism and collectivism*. London: Routledge.

**Tropp, L. R., & Molina, L. E.** (2019). Intergroup processes: From prejudice to positive relations between groups. In K. Deaux & M. Snyder (Eds.), *The Oxford handbook of personality and social psychology* (2nd ed., pp. 621–644). New York: Oxford University Press.

**Trotman, G. P., Williams, S. E., Quinton, M. L., & van Zanten, J. J. V.** (2018). Challenge and threat states: Examining cardiovascular, cognitive and affective responses to two distinct laboratory stress tasks. *International Journal of Psychophysiology, 126,* 42–51.

**Trull, T. J.** (2018). Ambulatory assessment of borderline personality disorder. *Psychopathology, 51* (2), 137–140.

**Trull, T. J., & Brown, W. C.** (2013). Borderline personality disorder: A five-factor model perspective. In T. A. Widiger & P. T. Costa (Eds.), *Personality disorders and the five-factor model of personality* (3rd ed., pp. 119–132). Washington, DC: American Psychological Association.

**Trull, T. J., Carpenter, R. W., & Widiger, T. A.** (2013). Personality disorders. In G. Stricker, T. A. Widiger, & I. B. Weiner (Eds.), *Handbook of psychology* (2nd ed., vol. 8, pp. 94–120). Hoboken, NJ: Wiley.

**Trundt, K. M., Keith, T. Z., Caemmerer, J. M., & Smith, L. V.** (2018). Testing for construct bias in the differential ability scales: A comparison among African American, Asian, Hispanic, and Caucasian children. *Journal of Psychoeducational Assessment, 36* (7), 670–683.

**Trus, M., Galdikiene, N., Balciunas, S., Green, P., Helminen, M., & Suominen, T.** (2018). Connection between organizational culture and climate and empowerment: The perspective of nurse managers. *Nursing & Health Sciences*. doi: 10.1111/nhs.12549

**Tryon, R. C.** (1940). Genetic differences in maze-learning ability in rats. *39th Yearbook, National Society for the Study of Education.* Chicago: University of Chicago Press.

**Tsai, A. C.** (2015). Home foreclosure, health, and mental health: A systematic review of individual, aggregate, and contextual associations. *PLoS One, 10,* e0123182.

**Tsuchiya, N., Wilke, M., Frässle, S., & Lamme, V. A. F.** (2015). No-report paradigms: Extracting the true neural correlates of consciousness. *Trends in Cognitive Sciences, 19* (12), 757–770.

**Tu, K. M., Erath, S. A., & El-Sheikh, M.** (2015). Peer victimization and adolescent adjustment: The moderating role of sleep. *Journal of Abnormal Child Psychology, 43* (8), 1447–1457.

**Tu, M. H., Bono, J. E., Shum, C., & LaMontagne, L.** (2018). Breaking the cycle: The effects of role model performance and ideal leadership self-concepts on abusive supervision spillover. *Journal of Applied Psychology, 103* (7), 689–702.

**Tu, Y., Park, J., Ahlfors, S. P., Khan, S., Egorova, N., Lang, C., ... & Kong, J.** (2019). A neural mechanism of direct and observational conditioning for placebo and nocebo responses. *NeuroImage, 184,* 954–963.

**Tucker, J. S., Edelen, M. O., Go, M. H., Pollard, M. S., Green, Jr., H. D., & Kennedy, D. P.** (2012). Resisting smoking when a best friend smokes: Do intrapersonal and contextual factors matter? *Journal of Research on Adolescence, 22* (1), 113–122.

**Tugade, M. M., Fredrickson, B. L., & Feldman Barrett, L.** (2004). Psychological resilience and positive emotional granularity: Examining the benefits of positive emotions on coping and health. *Journal of Personality, 72* (6), 1161–1190.

**Tully, P. J., Sardinha, A., & Nardi, A. E.** (2017). A new CBT model of panic attack treatment in comorbid heart diseases (PATCHD): How to calm an anxious heart and mind. *Cognitive and Behavioral Practice, 24* (3), 329–341.

**Tulving, E.** (1972). Episodic and semantic memory. In E. Tulving & W. Donaldson (Eds.), *Origins of memory.* San Diego: Academic.

**Tulving, E.** (1983). *Elements of episodic memory.* New York: Oxford University Press.

**Tulving, E.** (1989). Remembering and knowing the past. *American Scientist, 77* (4), 361–367.

**Tulving, E.** (2000). Concepts of memory. In E. Tulving & F. I. M. Craik (Eds.), *Oxford handbook of memory*. New York: Oxford University Press.

**Tural, U., & Iosifescu, D. V.** (2018). The prevalence of mitral valve prolapse in panic disorder: A meta-analysis. *Psychosomatics*. doi: 10.1016/j.psym.2018.10.002

**Turiano, N. A., Chapman, B. P., Gruenewald, T. L., & Mroczek, D. K.** (2015). Personality and the leading behavioral contributors of mortality. *Health Psychology, 34* (1), 51–60.

**Turiano, N. A., Pitzer, L., Armour, C., Karlamangla, A., Ryff, C. D., & Mroczek, D. K.** (2012). Personality trait level and change as predictors of health outcomes: Findings from a national study of Americans (MIDUS). *Journals of Gerontology: B: Psychological Sciences and Social Sciences, 67* (1), 4–12.

**Turkewitz, J.** (September 21, 2017). 'The pills are everywhere': The opioid crisis and its youngest victims. *New York Times*, p. A15.

**Turkheimer, E.** (2011). Genetics and human agency: Comment on Dar-Nimrod and Heine. *Psychological Bulletin, 137* (5), 825–828.

**Turkheimer, E., Haley, A., Waldron, M., D'Onofrio, B., & Gottesman, I. I.** (2003). Socioeconomic status modifies heritability of IQ in young children. *Psychological Science, 14* (6), 623–628.

**Turner, D., & Briken, P.** (2018). Treatment of paraphilic disorders in sexual offenders or men with a risk of sexual offending with luteinizing hormone-releasing hormone agonists: An updated systematic review. *The Journal of Sexual Medicine, 15* (1), 77–93.

**Turner, I. N., Foster, J. D., & Webster, G. D.** (2019). The Dark Triad's inverse relations with cognitive and emotional empathy: High-powered tests with multiple measures. *Personality and Individual Differences, 139,* 1–6.

**Turner, S.** (2018). Memory for trauma. In A. Alayarian (Ed.), *Resilience, Suffering and Creativity* (pp. 29–44). London: Routledge.

**Turowetz, J., & Hollander, M. M.** (2018). From "ridiculous" to "glad to have helped": Debriefing news delivery and improved reactions to science in Milgram's "obedience" experiments. *Social Psychology Quarterly, 81* (1), 71–93.

**Tversky, A., & Kahneman, J.** (1974). Judgment under uncertainty: Heuristics and biases. *Science, 185* (4157), 1124–1131.

**Tversky, A., & Liberman, V.** (2018). *Critical thinking: Statistical reasoning and intuitive judgment.* New York: Columbia University Press.

**Twenge, J. M., Sherman, R. A., & Wells, B. E.** (2017). Declines in sexual frequency among American adults, 1989–2014. *Archives of Sexual Behavior, 46* (8), 2389–2401.

**Tziner, A., & Rabenu, E.** (2018). Ways to improve the performance appraisal system. 1: Rater training. In *Improving performance appraisal at work*. Northampton, MA: Edward Elgar Publishing.

**Tzourio-Mazoyer, N., Crivello, F., & Mazoyer, B.** (2018). Is the planum temporale surface area a marker of hemispheric or regional language lateralization? *Brain Structure and Function, 223* (3), 1217–1228.

## U

**Uchida, M., Spencer, T. J., Faraone, S. V., & Biederman, J.** (2018). Adult outcome of ADHD: An overview of results from the MGH longitudinal family studies of pediatrically and psychiatrically referred youth with and without ADHD of both sexes. *Journal of Attention Disorders, 22* (6), 523–534.

**Udo, T., & Grilo, C. M.** (2018). Prevalence and correlates of DSM-5–defined eating disorders in a nationally representative sample of US adults. *Biological Psychiatry, 84,* 345–354.

**Uher, J.** (2015). Developing "personality" taxonomies: Metatheoretical and methodological rationales underlying selection approaches, methods of data generation, and reduction principles. *Integrative Psychological and Behavioral Science, 49* (4), 531–589.

**Uher, R., & Rutter, M.** (2012). Classification of feeding and eating disorders: Review of evidence and proposals for ICD-11. *World Psychiatry, 11* (2), 80–92.

**Uhl-Bien, M., & Arena, M.** (2018). Leadership for organizational adaptability: A theoretical synthesis and integrative framework. *The Leadership Quarterly, 29* (1), 89–104.

**Uleman, J. S. & Sarribay, S. A.** (2019). Initial impressions of others. In K. Deaux & M. Snyder (Eds.), *The Oxford handbook of personality and social psychology* (2nd ed., pp. 415–438). New York: Oxford University Press.

**Ullman, A. D.** (1952). "Antabuse" in the treatment of alcoholism. *Psychological Bulletin, 49* (5), 557–558.

**Ulrich, R. S., Simons, R. F., Losito, B. F., Fiorito, E., Miles, M. A., & Zelson, M.** (1991). Stress recovery during exposure to natural and urban environments. *Journal of Environmental Psychology, 11* (3), 201–230.

**Underhill, K., Montgomery, P., & Operario, D.** (2007). Sexual abstinence programs to prevent HIV infection in high-income countries. *British Medical Journal, 335* (7613), 248.

**Undurraga, J., & Baldessarini, R. J.** (2012). Randomized, placebo-controlled trials of antidepressants for acute major depression: Thirty-year meta-analytic review. *Neuropsychopharmacology, 37* (4), 851–864.

**University of Western Ontario.** (2018, June 12). Researchers map brain of blind patient who can see motion. *Science Daily.* www.sciencedaily.com/releases/2018/06/180612105716.htm (accessed October 30, 2018)

**Unkelbach, C.** (2007). Reversing the truth effect: Learning the interpretation of processing fluency in judgments of truth. *Journal of Experimental Psychology: Learning, Memory, and Cognition, 33* (1), 219–230.

**UNODC**. (2018). *Drug use.* https://www.unodc.org/unodc/en/data-and-analysis/statistics/drug-use.html

**Unsworth, N., Brewer, G. A., & Spillers, G. J.** (2011). Variation in working memory capacity and episodic memory: Examining the importance of encoding specificity. *Psychonomic Bulletin and Review, 18* (6), 1113–1118.

**Urbina, S.** (2011). Tests of intelligence. In R. J. Sternberg & S. B. Kaufman (Eds.), *Handbook of intelligence.* New York: Cambridge University Press.

**Urquhart, J. A., & O'Connor, A. R.** (2014). The awareness of novelty for strangely familiar words: A laboratory analogue of the déjà vu experience. *PeerJ, 2,* e666.

**Urquhart, J. A., Sivakumaran, M. H., MacFarlane, J. A., & O'Connor, A. R.** (2018). fMRI evidence supporting the role of memory conflict in the déjà vu experience. *Memory*, 1–12. doi: 10.1080/09658211.2018.1524496

**Urry, H. L., Nitschke, J. B., Dolski, I., Jackson, D. C., Dalton, K. M., Mueller, C. J., Rosenkranz, M. A., Ryff, C. D., Singer, B. H., & Davidson, R. J.** (2004). Making a life worth living: Neural correlates of well-being. *Psychological Science, 15* (6), 367–372.

## V

**Vaillant, G.** (2003). A 60-year follow-up of alcoholic men. *Addiction, 98,* 1043–1051.

**Vakil, E., Wasserman, A., & Tibon, R.** (2018). Development of perceptual and conceptual memory in explicit and implicit memory systems. *Journal of Applied Developmental Psychology, 57,* 16–23.

**Valente, T. W.** (2017). Social network studies in public health. *Annual Review of Public Health* (vol. 38). Palo Alto, CA: Annual Reviews.

**Valentine, S., & Fleischman, G.** (2018). From schoolyard to workplace: The impact of bullying on sales and business employees' Machiavellianism, job satisfaction, and perceived importance of an ethical issue. *Human Resource Management, 57* (1), 293–305.

**Valentino, R. J., & Volkow, N.** (2018). Untangling the complexity of opioid receptor function. *Neuropsychopharmacology, 43,* 2514–2520. doi: 10.1038/s41386-018-0225-3

**Valko, M., Jomova, K., Rhodes, C. J., Kuča, K., & Musílek, K.** (2016). Redox-and non-redox-metal-induced formation of free radicals and their role in human disease. *Archives of Toxicology, 90* (1), 1–37.

**Valtorta, N. K., Kanaan, M., Gilbody, S., & Hanratty, B.** (2018). Loneliness, social isolation and risk of cardiovascular disease in the English Longitudinal Study of Ageing. *European Journal of Preventive Cardiology, 25* (13), 1387–1396.

**Valvano, A. K., Rollock, M. J., Hudson, W. H., Goodworth, M. C. R., Lopez, E., & Stepleman, L.** (2018). Sexual communication, sexual satisfaction, and relationship quality in people with multiple sclerosis. *Rehabilitation Psychology, 63* (2), 267–275.

**Van Bavel, J., Schwartz, C. R., & Esteve, A.** (2018). The reversal of the gender gap in education and its consequences for family life. *Annual Review of Sociology, 44,* 341–360.

**Van Beusekom, G., Bos, H. M., Kuyper, L., Overbeek, G., & Sandfort, T. G.** (2018). Gender nonconformity and mental health among lesbian, gay, and bisexual adults: Homophobic stigmatization and internalized homophobia as mediators. *Journal of Health Psychology, 23* (9), 1211–1222.

**Van Cappellen, P., Rice, E. L., Catalino, L. I., & Fredrickson, B. L.** (2018). Positive affective processes underlie positive health behaviour change. *Psychology & Health, 33* (1), 77–97. doi:10.1080/08870446.2017.1320798

**Van Dam, N. T., van Vugt, M. K., Vago, D. R., Schmalzl, L., Saron, C. D., Olendzki, A., ... & Fox, K. C.** (2018). Mind the hype: A critical evaluation and prescriptive agenda for research on mindfulness and meditation. *Perspectives on Psychological Science, 13* (1), 36–61.

**van den Berk-Clark, C., Secrest, S., Walls, J., Hallberg, E., Lustman, P. J., Schneider, F. D., & Scherrer, J. F.** (2018). Association between posttraumatic stress disorder and lack of exercise, poor diet, obesity, and co-occurring smoking: A systematic review and meta-analysis. *Health Psychology, 37* (5), 407–416.

**van der Doef, S., & Reinders, J.** (2018). Stepwise sexual development of adolescents: The Dutch approach to sexuality education. *Nature Reviews Urology, 15,* 133–134.

**van der Geest, V., Blokland, A., & Bijleveld, C.** (2009). Delinquent development in a sample of high-risk youth: Shape, content, and predictors of delinquent trajectories from age 12 to 32. *Journal of Research in Crime and Delinquency, 46* (2), 111–143.

**Van der Graaff, J., Carlo, G., Crocetti, E., Koot, H. M., & Branje, S.** (2018). Prosocial behavior in adolescence: Gender differences in development and links with empathy. *Journal of Youth and Adolescence, 47* (5), 1086–1099.

**van der Merwe, C., Jahanshad, N., Cheung, J. W., Mufford, M., Groenewold, N. A., Koen, N., ... & Hibar, D. P.** (2019). Concordance of genetic variation that increases risk for anxiety disorders and posttraumatic stress disorders and that influences their underlying neurocircuitry. *Journal of Affective Disorders, 245,* 885–896.

**Van Ede, F., Chekroud, S. R., Stokes, M. G., & Nobre, A. C.** (2018). Decoding the influence of anticipatory states on visual perception in the presence of temporal distractors. *Nature Communications, 9* (1), 1449.

**van Eerde, W., & Klingsieck, K. B.** (2018). Overcoming procrastination? A meta-analysis of intervention studies. *Educational Research Review, 25,* 73–85.

**van Hecke, O., Hocking, L. J., Torrance, N., Campbell, A., Padmanabhan, S., Porteous, D. J., ... & Smith, B. H.** (2017). Chronic pain, depression and cardiovascular disease linked through a shared genetic predisposition: Analysis of a family-based cohort and twin study. *PloS One, 12* (2), e0170653.

**van Hulzen, K. J., Scholz, C. J., Franke, B., Ripke, S., Klein, M., McQuillin, A., ... & Lesch, K. P.** (2017). Genetic overlap between attention-deficit/hyperactivity disorder and bipolar disorder: evidence from genome-wide association study meta-analysis. *Biological Psychiatry, 82* (9), 634–641.

**Van Iddekinge, C. H., Aguinis, H., Mackey, J. D., & DeOrtentiis, P. S.** (2018). A meta-analysis of the interactive, additive, and relative effects of cognitive ability and motivation on performance. *Journal of Management, 44* (1), 249–279.

**Van Lange, P. A. M., Rusbult, C. E., Drigotas, S. M., & Arriaga, X. B.** (1997). Willingness to sacrifice in close relationships. *Journal of Personality and Social Psychology, 72* (6), 1373–1395.

**van Leeuwen, W. M., Sallinen, M., Virkkala, J., Lindholm, H., Hirvonen, A., Hublin, C., ... & Härmä, M.** (2018). Physiological and autonomic stress responses after prolonged sleep restriction and subsequent recovery sleep in healthy young men. *Sleep and Biological Rhythms, 16* (1), 45–54.

**Van Orden, K. A., Smith, P. N., Chen, T., & Conwell, Y.** (2016). A case-controlled examination of the interpersonal theory of suicide in the second half of life. *Archives of Suicide Research, 20* (3), 323–335.

**Van Riper, M.** (2007). Families of children with Down syndrome: Responding to "a change in plans" with resilience. *Journal of Pediatric Nursing, 22* (2), 116–128.

**van Setten, E. R., Maurits, N. M., & Maassen, B. A.** (2018). N1 lateralization and dyslexia: An event-related potential study in children with a familial risk of dyslexia. *Dyslexia*. doi: 10.1002/dys.1604

**van Steensel, F. J. A., & Bögels, S. M.** (2015). CBT for anxiety disorders in children with and without autism spectrum disorders. *Journal of Consulting and Clinical Psychology, 83* (3), 512–523.

**van Vianen, A. E. M.** (2018). Person–environment fit: A review of its basic tenets. *Annual Review of Organizational Psychology and Organizational Behavior, 5,* 75–101.

**van Vliet, I. M., van Well, E. P. L., Bruggeman, R., á Campo, J., Hijman, R., van Megen, H. J. G. M., van Balkom, A. J. L. M., & van Rijen, P. C.** (2013). An evaluation of irreversible psychosurgical treatment of patients with obsessive-compulsive disorder in the Netherlands, 2001–2008. *Journal of Nervous and Mental Disease, 201* (3), 226–228.

**Vandello, J. A., Cohen, D., Grandon, R., & Franiuk, R.** (2009). Stand by your man: Indirect prescriptions for honorable violence and feminine loyalty in Canada, Chile, and the United States. *Journal of Cross-Cultural Psychology, 40* (1), 81–104.

**Vandenberghe, C., & Panaccio, A.** (2015). Delving into the motivational bases of continuance commitment: Locus of control and empowerment as predictors of perceived sacrifice and few alternatives. *European Journal of Work and Organizational Psychology, 24* (1), 1–14.

**VanderWeele, T. J.** (2017). Religion and health in Europe: Cultures, countries, context. *European Journal of Epidemiology, 32* (10), 857–861.

**Vanlangendonck, F., Takashima, A., Willems, R. M., & Hagoort, P.** (2018). Distinguishable memory retrieval networks for collaboratively and non-collaboratively learned information. *Neuropsychologia, 111,* 123–132.

**Vansteenkiste, M., Aelterman, N., De Muynck, G. J., Haerens, L., Patall, E., & Reeve, J.** (2018). Fostering personal meaning and self-relevance: A self-determination theory perspective on internalization. *The Journal of Experimental Education, 86* (1), 30–49.

**Varkevisser, R. D. M., van Stralen, M. M., Kroeze, W., Ket, J. C. F., & Steenhuis, I. H. M.** (2018). Determinants of weight loss maintenance: A systematic review. *Obesity Reviews.* doi: 10.1111/obr.12772

**Vasquez, B. P., Tomaszczyk, J. C., Sharma, B., Colella, B., & Green, R. E.** (2018). Longitudinal recovery of executive control functions after moderate-severe traumatic brain injury: Examining trajectories of variability and ex-Gaussian parameters. *Neurorehabilitation and Neural Repair, 32* (3), 191–199.

**Vásquez-Amézquita, M., Leongómez, J. D., Seto, M. C., Bonilla, F. M., Rodríguez-Padilla, A., & Salvador, A.** (2018). No relation between digit ratio (2D: 4D) and visual attention patterns to sexually preferred and non-preferred stimuli. *Personality and Individual Differences, 120,* 151–158.

**Vastano, R., Deschrijver, E., Pozzo, T., & Brass, M.** (2018). Temporal binding effect in the action observation domain: Evidence from an action-based somatosensory paradigm. *Consciousness and Cognition, 60,* 1–8.

**Vaughn, S., Bos, C. S., & Schumm, J. S.** (2003). *Teaching exceptional, diverse, and at-risk students in the general education classroom* (3rd ed.). Boston: Allyn & Bacon.

**Vavatzanidis, N. K., Mürbe, D., Friederici, A. D., & Hahne, A.** (2018). Establishing a mental lexicon with cochlear implants: An ERP study with young children. *Scientific Reports, 8* (1), 910.

**Vayshenker, B. A., DeLuca, J., Bustle, T., & Yanos, P.** (2018). "As soon as people hear that word...": associative stigma among clinicians working with people with serious mental illness. *Journal of Public Mental Health, 17* (1), 20–28.

**Vazquez, J., Hall, S. C., Witkowska, H. E., & Greco, M. A.** (2008). Rapid alterations in cortical protein profiles underlie spontaneous sleep and wake bouts. *Journal of Cellular Biochemistry, 105* (6), 1472–1484.

**Vega, V., & Malamuth, N. M.** (2007). Predicting sexual aggression: The role of pornography in the context of general and specific risk factors. *Aggressive Behavior, 33* (2), 104–117.

**Veiga-Fernandes, H., & Artis, D.** (2018). Neuronal–immune system cross-talk in homeostasis. *Science, 359* (6383), 1465–1466.

**Vella, E. J., Kamarck, T. W., Flory, J. D., & Manuck, S.** (2012). Hostile mood and social strain during daily life: A test of the transactional model. *Annals of Behavioral Medicine, 44* (3), 341–352.

**Venz, L., Pundt, A., & Sonnentag, S.** (2018). What matters for work engagement? A diary study on resources and the benefits of selective optimization with compensation for state work engagement. *Journal of Organizational Behavior, 39* (1), 26–38.

**Verhagen, M., Lodder, G. M., & Baumeister, R. F.** (2018). Unmet belongingness needs but not high belongingness needs alone predict adverse well-being: A response surface modeling approach. *Journal of Personality, 86* (3), 498–507.

**Verkhratsky, A., Bush, N. A. O., Nedergaard, M., & Butt, A.** (2018). The special case of human astrocytes. *Neuroglia, 1,* 21–29. doi:10.3390/neuroglia1010004

**Verkuyten, M.** (2018). *The social psychology of ethnic identity.* London: Routledge.

**Vernetti, A., Senju, A., Charman, T., Johnson, M. H., Gliga, T., & BASIS Team.** (2018). Simulating interaction: Using gaze-contingent eye-tracking to measure the reward value of social signals in toddlers with and without autism. *Developmental Cognitive Neuroscience, 29,* 21–29.

**Vernon, L., Modecki, K. L., & Barber, B. L.** (2018). Mobile phones in the bedroom: Trajectories of sleep habits and subsequent adolescent psychosocial development. *Child Development, 89*(1), 66–77.

**Verosky, S. C., Porter, J., Martinez, J. E., & Todorov, A.** (2018). Robust effects of affective person learning on evaluation of faces. *Journal of Personality and Social Psychology, 114* (4), 516–528.

**Verriotis, M., Jones, L., Whitehead, K., Laudiano-Dray, M., Panayotidis, I., Patel, H., ... & Fitzgerald, M.** (2018). The distribution of pain activity across the human neonatal brain is sex dependent. *NeuroImage, 178,* 69–77.

**Verschuere, B., Crombez, G., De Clercq, A., & Koster, E. H. W.** (2005). Psychopathic traits and autonomic responding to concealed information in a prison sample. *Psychophysiology, 42* (2), 239–245.

**Verwijk, E., Comijs, H. C., Kok, R. M., Spaans, H., Stek, M. L., & Scherder, E. J. A.** (2012). Neurocognitive effects after brief pulse and ultrabrief pulse unilateral electroconvulsive therapy for major depression: A review. *Journal of Affective Disorders, 140* (3), 233–243.

**Victor, D.** (2017, February 17). As Jewish institutions endure attacks, Muslims pledge financial aid. *New York Times,* A16. https://www.nytimes.com/2017/02/27/us/muslims-give-money-to-jewish-institutions-that-are-attacked.html

**Victor, D.** (2017, March 28). Indian-Americans reward man who intervened in Kansas shooting. *New York Times,* https://www.nytimes.com/2017/03/28/us/kansas-shooting-india-immigrants-ian-grillot.html

**Vidal, F.** (2018). Phenomenology of the locked-in syndrome: An overview and some suggestions. *Neuroethics.* doi: 10.1007/s12152-018-9388-1

**Vinen, Z., Clark, M., Paynter, J., & Dissanayake, C.** (2018). School-age outcomes of children with autism spectrum disorder who received community-based early interventions. *Journal of Autism and Developmental Disorders, 48* (5), 1673–1683.

**Visser, S., van der Molen, H. F., Sluiter, J. K., & Frings-Dresen, M. H.** (2018). The process evaluation of two alternative participatory ergonomics intervention strategies for construction companies. *Ergonomics, 61,* 1156–1172.

**Vitaliano, P. P., Fitzpatrick, A. L., Williams, L. E., Montano, M. A., & Russo, J. E.** (2018). Demographic-specific rates for life events in the cardiovascular health study and comparisons with other studies. *Innovation in Aging, 2* (1). doi: 10.1093/geroni/igy005

**Vitulano, N., Di Marco Bernadino, A., Re, A., Riccioni, G., Perna, F., Mormile, F., Valente, S., & Belloci, F.** (2013). Obstructive sleep apnea and heart disease: The biomarkers point of view. *Frontiers in Bioscience, 5,* 588–599.

**Vize, C. E., Miller, J. D., & Lynam, D. R.** (2018). FFM facets and their relations with different forms of antisocial behavior: An expanded meta-analysis. *Journal of Criminal Justice, 57,* 67–75.

**Vogels, E. A., & O'Sullivan, L. F.** (2018). Porn, peers, and performing oral sex: The mediating role of peer norms on pornography's influence regarding oral sex. *Media Psychology, 21* (4), 669–699.

**Vogt, T. M., Mullooly, J. P., Ernst, D., Pople, C. R., & Hollis, J. F.** (1992). Social networks as predictors of ischemic heart disease, cancer, stroke, and hypertension. *Journal of Clinical Epidemiology, 45* (6), 659–666.

**Vohs, J. L., Leonhardt, B. L., James, A. V., Francis, M. M., Breier, A., Mehdiyoun, N., ... & Lysaker, P. H.** (2018). Metacognitive reflection and insight therapy for early psychosis: A preliminary study of a novel integrative psychotherapy. *Schizophrenia Research, 195,* 428–433.

**Volkow, N. D., Compton, W. M., & Wargo, E. M.** (2017). The risks of marijuana use during pregnancy. *JAMA, 317* (2), 129–130.

**Volz, L. J., Hillyard, S. A., Miller, M. B., & Gazzaniga, M. S.** (2018). Unifying control over the body: consciousness and cross-cueing in split-brain patients. *Brain, 141* (3), e15.

**von Békésy, G.** (1960). Vibratory patterns of the basilar membrane. In E. G. Wever (Ed.), *Experiments in hearing* (pp. 404–429). New York: McGraw-Hill.

**von Dawans, B., Ditzen, B., Trueg, A., Fischbacher, U., & Heinrichs, M.** (2019). Effects of acute stress on social behavior in women. *Psychoneuroendocrinology, 99,* 137–144.

**Von Der Heide, R., Vyas, G., & Olson, I. R.** (2014). The social network-network: Size is predicted by brain structure and function in the amygdala and paralimbic regions. *Social Cognitive and Affective Neuroscience, 9* (12), 1962–1972.

**von Helmholtz, H.** (1852). On the theory of compound colours. *Philosophical Magazine, 4,* 519–534.

**von Neumann, J.** (1958). *The computer and the brain.* New Haven, CT: Yale University Press.

**Voracek, M., Pietschnig, J., Nader, I. W., & Stieger, S.** (2011). Digit ratio (2D:4D) and sex-role orientation: Further evidence and meta-analysis. *Personality and Individual Differences, 51* (4), 417–422.

**Vouloumanos, A., & Curtin, S.** (2014). Foundational tuning: How infants' attention to speech predicts language development. *Cognitive Science, 38* (8), 1675–1686.

**Vuillermot, S., Weber, L., Feldon, J., & Meyer, U.** (2010). A longitudinal examination of the neurodevelopmental impact of prenatal immune activation in mice reveals primary defects in dopaminergic development relevant to schizophrenia. *Journal of Neuroscience, 30* (4), 1270–1287.

**Vyas, N. S., Buchsbaum, M. S., Lehrer, D. S., Merrill, B. M., DeCastro, A., Doninger, N. A., ... & Mukherjee, J.** (2018). D2/D3 dopamine receptor binding with [F-18] fallypride correlates of executive function in medication-naïve patients with schizophrenia. *Schizophrenia Research, 192,* 442–456.

**Vygotsky, L. S.** (1962). *Thought and language.* Cambridge, MA: MIT Press.

## W

**Wabnegger, A., Schwab, D., & Schienle, A.** (2018). Aversive aftertaste changes visual food cue reactivity: An fMRI study on cross-modal perception. *Neuroscience Letters, 673,* 56–60.

**Wacker, J.** (2018). Effects of positive emotion, extraversion, and dopamine on cognitive stability-flexibility and frontal EEG asymmetry. *Psychophysiology, 55* (1), e12727.

**Wacker, J., & Smillie, L. D.** (2015). Trait extraversion and dopamine function. *Social and Personality Psychology Compass, 9* (6), 225–238.

**Wade, N. G., Cornish, M. A., Tucker, J. R., Worthington, E. J., Sandage, S. J., & Rye, M. S.** (2018). Promoting forgiveness: Characteristics of the treatment, the clients, and their interaction. *Journal of Counseling Psychology, 65* (3), 358–371. doi:10.1037/cou0000260

**Wagenaar, K., & Baars, J.** (2012). Family and family therapy in the Netherlands. *International Review of Psychiatry, 24* (2), 144–148.

**Wagner, A. D., Schacter, D. L., Rotte, M., Koutstaal, B., Maril, A., Dale, A. M., Rosen, B. R., & Buckner, R. L.** (1998). Building memories: Remembering and forgetting of verbal experiences as predicted by brain activity. *Science, 281* (5380), 1185–1187.

**Wagner, F. B., Mignardot, J., Le Goff-Mignardot, C. G., Demesmaeker, R., Komi, S., ... & Courtine, G.** (2018). Targeted neurotechnologies restore walking in humans with spinal cord injury. *Nature, 563* (7729), 65. doi: 10.1038/s41593-018-0262-6

**Wagner, N. J., Hastings, P. D., & Rubin, K. H.** (2018). Callous-unemotional traits and autonomic functioning in toddlerhood interact to predict externalizing behaviors in preschool. *Journal of Abnormal Child Psychology, 46* (7), 1439–1450.

**Wahlstrom, D., Raiford, S. E., Breaux, K. C. Zhu, J., & Weiss, L. G.** (2018). The Wechsler Preschool and Primary Scales of Intelligence—4th ed., Wechsler Intelligence Scale for Children—5th ed., and Wechsler Individual Achievement Test—3rd ed. In D. P. Flanagan & E. M. McDonough (Eds.), *Contemporary intellectual assessment: Theories, tests, and issues* (4th ed., pp. 245–282). New York: Guilford.

**Wai, J., Lubinski, D., & Benbow, C. P.** (2005). Creativity and occupational accomplishments among intellectually precocious youths: An age 13 to age 33 longitudinal study. *Journal of Educational Psychology, 97* (3), 484–492.

**Wainright, J. L., & Patterson, C. J.** (2008). Peer relations among adolescents with female same-sex parents. *Developmental Psychology, 44* (1), 117–126.

**Waite, B., & Morote, E. S.** (2018). Hiring practices, uses of social media, and teacher retention differences. In S. M. Perry (Ed.), *Maximizing social science research through publicly accessible data sets* (pp. 275–292). Hershey, PA: IGI Global.

**Wakefield, J. C.** (2016). Diagnostic issues and controversies in DSM-5: Return of the false positives problem. *Annual Review of Clinical Psychology* (vol. 12, pp. 105–132). Palo Alto, CA: Annual Reviews.

**Walder, D. J., Ospina, L., Daly, M., Statucka, M., & Raparia, E.** (2012). Early neurodevelopment and psychosis risk: Role of neurohormones and biological sex in modulating genetic, prenatal, and sensory processing factors in brain development. In X. Anastassion-Hadjicharalambous (Ed.), *Psychosis: Causes, diagnosis and treatment.* Hauppauge, NY: Nova Science.

**Waldhauser, G. T., Braun, V., & Hanslmayr, S.** (2016). Episodic memory retrieval functionally relies on very rapid reactivation of sensory information. *Journal of Neuroscience, 36* (1), 251–260.

**Walker, L. E. A.** (2009). *The battered woman syndrome* (3rd ed.). New York: Springer.

**Wallace, L. E., Anthony, R., End, C. M., & Way, B. M.** (2018). Does religion stave off the grave? Religious affiliation in one's obituary and longevity. *Social Psychological and Personality Science*, 1948550618779820.

**Waller, R., & Hyde, L. W.** (2018). Callous-unemotional behaviors in early childhood: The development of empathy and prosociality gone awry. *Current Opinion in Psychology, 20,* 11–16.

**Wallis, A., Miskovic-Wheatley, J., Madden, S., Rhodes, P., Crosby, R. D., Cao, L., & Touyz, S.** (2018). Family functioning and relationship quality for adolescents in family-based treatment with severe anorexia nervosa compared with non-clinical adolescents. *European Eating Disorders Review, 26* (1), 29–37.

**Walters, K. J., Simons, J. S., & Simons, R. M.** (2018). Self-control demands and alcohol-related problems: Within-and between-person associations. *Psychology of Addictive Behaviors, 32* (6), 573–582.

**Wampold, B. E.** (2001). *The great psychotherapy debate: Models, methods, and findings.* Mahwah, NJ: Erlbaum.

**Wampold, B. E.** (2013). The good, the bad, and the ugly: A 50-year perspective on the outcome problem. *Psychotherapy, 50* (1), 16–24.

**Wampold, B. E., & Brown, G. S.** (2005). Estimating variability in outcomes attributable to therapists: A naturalistic study of outcomes of managed care. *Journal of Consulting and Clinical Psychology, 73* (5), 914–923.

**Wang, B., & Bukuan, S.** (2015). Timing matters: Negative emotion elicited 5 min but not 30 min or 45 min after learning enhances consolidation of internal-monitoring source memory. *Acta Psychologica, 157,* 56–64.

**Wang, J., Gong, J., Li, L., Chen, Y., Liu, L., Gu, H., ... & Song, R.** (2018). Neurexin gene family variants as risk factors for autism spectrum disorder. *Autism Research, 11* (1), 37–43.

**Wang, J. L., Hsieh, H. F., Assari, S., Gaskin, J., & Rost, D. H.** (2018). The protective effects of social support and engagement coping strategy on the relationship between perceived discrimination and psychological distress among Chinese migrant children. *Youth & Society, 50* (5), 593–614.

**Wang, J. M., Hartl, A. C., Laursen, B., & Rubin, K. H.** (2017). The high costs of low agreeableness: Low agreeableness exacerbates interpersonal consequences of rejection sensitivity in U.S. and Chinese adolescents. *Journal of Research in Personality, 67,* 36–43.

**Wang, L., & Chen, Q.** (2018). Experiencing sweet taste affects romantic semantic processing. *Current Psychology.* doi: 10.1007/s12144-018-9877-8

**Wang, L., He, J. L., & Zhang, X. H.** (2013). The efficacy of massage on preterm infants: A meta-analysis. *American Journal of Perinatology, 30* (9), 731–738.

**Wang, M., Rieger, M. O., & Hens, T.** (2016). The impact of culture on loss aversion. *Journal of Behavioral Decision Making.* doi: 10.1002/bdm.1941

**Wang, R.** (2015). L. S. Vygotsky and education. *British Journal of Educational Studies, 63* (1), 112–114.

**Wang, S. M., Chang, J. C., Weng, S. C., Yeh, M. K., & Lee, C. S.** (2018). Risk of suicide within 1 year of cancer diagnosis. *International Journal of Cancer, 142* (10), 1986–1993.

**Wang, W., Feng, J., Ji, C., Mu, X., Ma, Q., Fan, Y., ... & Zhu, F.** (2017). Increased methylation of glucocorticoid receptor gene promoter 1F in peripheral blood of patients with generalized anxiety disorder. *Journal of Psychiatric Research, 91,* 18–25.

**Wang, Z., Xu, H., & Liu, Y.** (2018). Servant leadership as a driver of employee service performance: Test of a trickle-down model and its boundary conditions. *Human Relations, 71* (9), 1179–1203. doi: 10.1177/0018726717738320

**Waninger, S., Berka, C., Meghdadi, A., Karic, M. S., Stevens, K., Aguero, C., ... & Verma, A.** (2018). Event-related potentials during sustained attention and memory tasks: Utility as biomarkers for mild cognitive impairment. *Alzheimer's & Dementia: Diagnosis, Assessment & Disease Monitoring, 10,* 452–460.

**Wannan, C. M., Bartholomeusz, C. F., Cropley, V. L., Van Rheenen, T. E., Panayiotou, A., Brewer, W. J., ... & McGorry, P.** (2018). Deterioration of visuospatial associative memory following a first psychotic episode: a long-term follow-up study. *Psychological Medicine, 48* (1), 132–141.

**Wannemüller, A., Moser, D., Kumsta, R., Jöhren, H. P., & Margraf, J.** (2018). The return of fear: variation of the serotonin transporter gene predicts outcome of a highly standardized exposure-based one-session fear treatment. *Psychotherapy and psychosomatics, 87* (2), 95–104.

**Ward, J., Ipser, A., Phanvanova, E., Brown, P., Bunte, I., & Simner, J.** (2018). The prevalence and cognitive profile of sequence-space synaesthesia. *Consciousness and Cognition, 61,* 79–93.

**Ward, J., Schnakenberg, P., & Banissy, M. J.** (2018). The relationship between mirror-touch synaesthesia and empathy: New evidence and a new screening tool. *Cognitive Neuropsychology,* 1–19.

**Ward, S. J., & King, L. A.** (2018). Religion and moral self-image: The contributions of prosocial behavior, socially desirable responding, and personality. *Personality and Individual Differences, 131,* 222–231. doi: 10.1016/j.paid.2018.04.028

**Ward, S. J., & King, L. A.** (2019). Exploring the place of financial status in the good life: Income and meaning in life. *Journal of Positive Psychology, 14* (3), 312–323. doi: 10.1080/17439760.2017.1402075

**Ward-Fear, G., Thomas, J., Webb, J. K., Pearson, D. J., & Shine, R.** (2017). Eliciting conditioned taste aversion in lizards: Live toxic prey are more effective than scent and taste cues alone. *Integrative Zoology, 12* (2), 112–120.

**Warnecke, R. B., Morera, O., Turner, L., Mermelstein, R., Johnson, T. P., Parsons, J., Crittenden, K., Freels, S., & Flay, B.** (2001). Changes in self-efficacy and readiness for smoking cessation among women with high school or less education. *Journal of Health and Social Behavior, 42* (1), 97–109.

**Warner, L. M., Stadler, G., Lüscher, J., Knoll, N., Ochsner, S., Hornung, R., & Scholz, U.** (2018). Day-to-day mastery and self-efficacy changes during a smoking quit attempt: Two studies. *British Journal of Health Psychology, 23* (2), 371–386.

**Warner, L. R., Settles, I. H., & Shields, S. A.** (2018). Intersectionality theory in the psychology of women. In C. B. Travis, J. W. White, A. Rutherford, W. S. Williams, S. L. Cook, & K. F. Wyche (Eds.), *APA handbooks in psychology series. APA handbook of the psychology of women: History, theory, and battlegrounds* (pp. 521–539). Washington, DC: American Psychological Association.

**Wasylyshyn, N., Hemenway Falk, B., Garcia, J. O., Cascio, C. N., O'Donnell, M. B., Bingham, C. R., ... & Falk, E. B.** (2018). Global brain dynamics during social exclusion predict subsequent behavioral conformity. *Social Cognitive and Affective Neuroscience, 13* (2), 182–191.

**Watanabe, H., & Mizunami, M.** (2007). Pavlov's cockroach: Classical conditioning of salivation in an insect. *PloS One, 6,* e529.

**Watanabe, T., Ishiguro, S., Aoki, A., Ueda, M., Hayashi, Y., Akiyama, K., ... & Shimoda, K.** (2017). Genetic polymorphism of 1019C/G (rs6295) promoter of serotonin 1A receptor and catechol-O-methyltransferase in panic disorder. *Psychiatry Investigation, 14* (1), 86–92.

**Watson, A., El-Deredy, W., Bentley, D. E., Vogt, B. A., & Jones, A. K.** (2006). Categories of placebo response in the absence of site-specific stimulation of analgesia. *Pain, 126* (1–3), 115–122.

**Watson, D., & Clark, L. A.** (1997). Extraversion and its positive emotional core. In R. Hogan, J. A. Johnson, & S. R., Briggs (Eds.), *Handbook of personality psychology* (pp. 767–793). San Diego: Academic Press.

**Watson, D., Clark, L. A., & Tellegen, A.** (1988). Development and validation of brief measures of positive and negative affect: The PANAS scales. *Journal of Personality and Social Psychology, 54* (6), 1063–1070. doi: 10.1037/0022-3514.54.6.1063

**Watson, D., & Naragon, K.** (2009). Positive affectivity: The disposition to experience positive emotional states. In S. J. Lopez & C. R. Snyder (Eds.), *The Oxford handbook of positive psychology* (2nd ed., pp. 207–215). New York: Oxford University Press.

**Watson, D., & Stanton, K.** (2017). Emotion blends and mixed emotions in the hierarchical structure of affect. *Emotion Review, 9* (2), 99–104.

**Watson, D., Stasik, S. M., Ellickson-Larew, S., & Stanton, K.** (2015). Extraversion and psychopathology: A facet-level analysis. *Journal of Abnormal Psychology, 124* (2), 432–446.

**Watson, J. B., & Rayner, R.** (1920). Conditioned emotional reactions. *Journal of Experimental Psychology, 3* (1), 1–14.

**Watson, M.** (2015). Listening to the Wherewho: A lived experience of schizophrenia. *Schizophrenia Bulletin, 41* (1), 6–8.

**Watson, M., Homewood, J., Haviland, J., & Bliss, J. M.** (2005). Influence of psychological response on breast cancer survival: A 10-year follow-up of a population-based cohort. *European Journal of Cancer, 41* (12), 1710–1714.

**Watson, S. J., & Milfont, T. L.** (2017). A short-term longitudinal examination of the associations between self-control, delay of gratification and temporal considerations. *Personality and Individual Differences, 106,* 57–60.

**Watts, T. M., Holmes, L., Raines, J., Orbell, S., & Rieger, G.** (2018). Finger length ratios of identical twins with discordant sexual orientations. *Archives of Sexual Behavior, 47* (8), 2435–2444.

**Watts, T. W., Duncan, G. J., & Quan, H.** (2018). Revisiting the marshmallow test: A conceptual replication investigating links between early delay

**Woo, J., Min, J. O., Kang, D. S., Kim, Y. S., Jung, G. H., Park, H. J., … & Kim, H. G.** (2018). Control of motor coordination by astrocytic tonic GABA release through modulation of excitation/inhibition balance in cerebellum. *Proceedings of the National Academy of Sciences, 115,* 5004–5009.

**Wood, A. M., Froh, J. J., & Geraghty, A. W.** (2010). Gratitude and well-being: A review and theoretical integration. *Clinical Psychology Review, 30* (7), 890–905.

**Wood, D., Crapnell, T., Lau, L., Bennett, A., Lotstein, D., Ferris, M., & Kuo, A.** (2018). Emerging adulthood as a critical stage in the life course. In N. Halfon, C.B. Forrest, R. M. Lerner, & E. M. Faustman (Eds.), *Handbook of life course health development* (pp. 123–143). Cham: Springer.

**Wood, R. L., & Liossi, C.** (2006). Neuropsychological and neurobehavioral correlates of aggression following traumatic brain injury. *Journal of Neuropsychiatry and Clinical Neurosciences, 18* (3), 333–341.

**Woodhead, E. L., Northrop, L., & Edelstein, B.** (2016). Stress, social support, and burnout among long-term care nursing staff. *Journal of Applied Gerontology, 35* (1), 84–105.

**Woods, K. N., Stroebel, S. S., O'Keefe, S. L., Griffee, K., Harper-Dorton, K. V., Beard, K. W., … & Lawhon, M.** (2018). Conditioning by orgasm produced by heterosexual oral sex during the critical period. *Sexual Addiction & Compulsivity, 25* (1), 96–119.

**Woods, S. A., Mustafa, M. J., Anderson, N., & Sayer, B.** (2018). Innovative work behavior and personality traits: Examining the moderating effects of organizational tenure. *Journal of Managerial Psychology, 33* (1), 29–42.

**Woolf, C. J.** (2018). Pain amplification—A perspective on the how, why, when, and where of central sensitization. *Journal of Applied Biobehavioral Research,* e12124.

**Woolfolk, A.** (2013). *Educational psychology* (12th ed.). Upper Saddle River, NJ: Pearson.

**Woolley, K., & Fishbach, A.** (2018). It's about time: Earlier rewards increase intrinsic motivation. *Journal of Personality and Social Psychology, 114* (6), 877–890. doi: 10.1037/pspa0000116

**World Health Organization.** (2018a). *Information sheet on opioid overdose.* http://www.who.int/substance_abuse/information-sheet/en/

**World Health Organization.** (2018b). *Tobacco: Key facts.* http://www.who.int/news-room/fact-sheets/detail/tobacco

**World Population Review** (2018). Suicide rate by country 2018. http://worldpopulationreview.com/countries/suicide-rate-by-country/

**Worthington, R. L., Navarro, R. L., Savoy, H. B., & Hampton, D.** (2008). Development, reliability, and validity of the Measure of Sexual Identity Exploration and Commitment (MoSIEC). *Developmental Psychology, 44* (1), 22–33.

**Wrangham, R. W.** (2018). Two types of aggression in human evolution. *Proceedings of the National Academy of Sciences, 115* (2), 245–253.

**Wray, N. R., Ripke, S., Mattheisen, M., Trzaskowski, M., Byrne, E. M., Abdellaoui, A., … & Bacanu, S. A.** (2018). Genome-wide association analyses identify 44 risk variants and refine the genetic architecture of major depression. *Nature Genetics, 50* (5), 668–681.

**Wright, B. R., Wallace, M., Wisnesky, A. S., Donnelly, C. M., Missari, S., & Zozula, C.** (2015). Religion, race, and discrimination: A field experiment of how American churches welcome newcomers. *Journal for the Scientific Study of Religion, 54* (2), 185–204.

**Wright, R. G.** (2008). Sex offender post-incarceration sanctions: Are there any limits? *Criminal and Civil Confinement, 34* (1), 17–50.

**Wright, S.** (2018). De-pathologization of consensual BDSM. *The Journal of Sexual Medicine, 15* (5), 622–624.

**Wrzesniewski, A.** (2003). Finding positive meaning in work. In K. S. Cameron, J. E. Dutton, & R. E. Quinn (Eds.), *Positive organizational scholarship: Foundations of a new discipline* (pp. 296–308). San Francisco: Berrett-Koehler.

**Wrzesniewski, A., Dutton, J. E., & Debebe, G.** (2003). Interpersonal sense-making and the meaning of work. In R. M. Kramer, M. Roderick, & B. M. Staw (Eds.). *Research in organizational behavior: An annual series of analytical essays and critical reviews* (vol. 25, pp. 93–135). Oxford, UK: Elsevier.

**Wrzesniewski, A., McCauley, C. I., Rozin, P., & Schwartz, B.** (1997). Jobs, careers, and callings: People's relations to their work. *Journal of Research in Personality, 31* (1), 21–33.

**Wrzus, C., Hanel, M., Wagner, J., & Neyer, F. J.** (2012). Social network changes and life events across the lifespan: A meta-analysis. *Psychological Bulletin, 139* (1), 53–80.

**Wu, H., Luo, Y., & Feng, C.** (2016). Neural signatures of social conformity: A coordinate-based activation likelihood estimation meta-analysis of functional brain imaging studies. *Neuroscience & Biobehavioral Reviews, 71,* 101–111.

**Wu, K., Chen, C., Moyzis, R. K., Nuno, M., Yu, Z., & Greenberger, E.** (2018). More than skin deep: Major histocompatibility complex (MHC)-based attraction among Asian American speed-daters. *Evolution and Human Behavior.*

**Wynn, T., & Coolidge, F. L.** (2010). Beyond symbolism and language. *Current Anthropology, 51* (Suppl. 1), S5–S16.

**Wynn, T., Coolidge, F. L., & Bright, M.** (2009). Hohlenstein-Stadel and the evolution of human conceptual thought. *Cambridge Archaeological Journal, 19* (1), 73–83.

## X

**Xiao, N. G., Quinn, P. C., Liu, S., Ge, L., Pascalis, O., & Lee, K.** (2015). Eye tracking reveals a crucial role for facial motion in recognition of faces by infants. *Developmental Psychology, 51* (6), 744–757.

**Xiao, X., Dupuis-Roy, N., Jiang, J., Du, X., Zhang, M., & Zhang, Q.** (2018). The neural basis of taste-visual modal conflict control in appetitive and aversive gustatory context. *Neuroscience, 372,* 154–160.

**Xiong, A., & Proctor, R. W.** (2018). Information processing: The language and analytical tools for cognitive psychology in the information age. *Frontiers in Psychology, 9.*

**Xu, H., Huang, W., Wang, Y., Sun, W., Tang, J., Li, D., … & Fan, X.** (2013). The function of BMP4 during neurogenesis in the adult hippocampus in Alzheimer's disease. *Ageing Research and Reviews, 12* (1), 157–164.

**Xuan, Z., Blanchette, J. G., Nelson, T. F., Nguyen, T. H., Hadland, S. E., Oussayef, N. L., Heeren, T. C., & Naimi, T. S.** (2015). Youth drinking in the United States: Relationships with alcohol policies and adult drinking. *Pediatrics, 136* (1), 18–27.

## Y

**Yalom, I. D., & Leszcz, M.** (2006). *Theory and practice of group psychotherapy* (5th ed.). New York: Basic.

**Yam, M., Loh, Y., Tan, C., Khadijah Adam, S., Abdul Manan, N., & Basir, R.** (2018). General pathways of pain sensation and the major neurotransmitters involved in pain regulation. *International Journal of Molecular Sciences, 19* (8), 2164.

**Yang, H., Yang, S., Ceci, S. J., & Isen, A. M.** (2015). Positive affect facilitates the effect of a warning on false memory in the DRM paradigm. *Journal of Positive Psychology, 10* (3), 196–206.

**Yang, L. Q., & Caughlin, D. E.** (2017). Aggression-preventive supervisor behavior: Implications for workplace climate and employee outcomes. *Journal of Occupational Health Psychology, 22* (1), 1–18.

**Yang, X., Lau, J. T., Wang, Z., Ma, Y. L., & Lau, M. C.** (2018). The mediation roles of discrepancy stress and self-esteem between masculine role discrepancy and mental health problems. *Journal of Affective Disorders, 235,* 513–520.

**Yang, Y.** (2008). Social inequalities in happiness in the United States, 1972–2004: An age-period cohort analysis. *American Sociological Review, 73,* 204–226.

**Yang, Y., Zhang, Y., & Sheldon, K. M.** (2018). Self-determined motivation for studying abroad predicts lower culture shock and greater well-being among international students: The mediating role of basic psychological needs satisfaction. *International Journal of Intercultural Relations, 63,* 95–104.

**Yanos, P. T.** (2018). *Written-off: Mental health stigma and the loss of human potential.* Cambridge, England: Cambridge University Press.

**Yao, Y. H., Locke, E. A., & Jamal, M.** (2018). On a combined theory of pay level satisfaction. *Journal of Organizational Behavior, 39* (4), 448–461.

**Ybarra, M. L., Rosario, M., Saewyc, E., & Goodenow, C.** (2016). Sexual behaviors and partner characteristics by sexual identity among adolescent girls. *Journal of Adolescent Health, 58* (3), 310–316.

**Yen, C. F., Chen, C. C., Lee, Y., Tang, T. C., Ko, C. H., & Yen, J. Y.** (2009). Association between quality of life and self-stigma, insight, and adverse effects of medication in patients with depressive disorders. *Depression and Anxiety, 26* (11), 1033–1039.

**Yerkes, R. M. & Dodson, J. D.** (1908). The relationship of strength of stimulus to rapidity of habit formation. *Journal of Comparative Neurology and Psychology, 18,* 459–482.

**Yilmaz, Z., Halvorsen, M., Bryois, J., Yu, D., Thornton, L. M., Zerwas, S., … & Erdman, L.** (2018). Examination of the shared genetic basis of anorexia nervosa and obsessive-compulsive disorder. *Molecular Psychiatry,* 1.

**Yip, B. H. K., Bai, D., Mahjani, B., Klei, L., Pawitan, Y., Hultman, C. M., … & Reichenberg, A.** (2018). Heritable variation, with little or no maternal effect, accounts for recurrence risk to autism spectrum disorder in Sweden. *Biological Psychiatry, 83*(7), 589–597.

**Yip, T.** (2018). Ethnic/racial identity—A double-edged sword? Associations with discrimination and psychological outcomes. *Current Directions in Psychological Science, 27* (3), 170–175.

**Yonelinas, A. P., & Ritchey, M.** (2015). The slow forgetting of emotional episodic memories: An emotional binding account. *Trends in Cognitive Sciences, 19* (5), 259–267.

**Yoon, J. S., Anders Ericsson, K., & Donatelli, D.** (2018). Effects of 30 Years of Disuse on Exceptional Memory Performance. *Cognitive Science.* doi: 10.1111/cogs.12562

**Yost, W. A.** (2018). Auditory motion parallax. *Proceedings of the National Academy of Sciences, 115* (16), 3998–4000.

**Youdim, M. B.** (2018). Monoamine oxidase inhibitors, and iron chelators in depressive illness and neurodegenerative diseases. *Journal of Neural Transmission, 125* (11), 1719–1733.

**Youman, M., Mather, N., Act, R. E. A. D., & Act, D.** (2018). Dyslexia laws in the US: A 2018 update. *Perspectives on Language and Literacy, 44* (2), 37–41.

**Younan, D., Li, L., Tuvblad, C., Wu, J., Lurmann, F., Franklin, M., … & Chen, J. C.** (2018). Long-term ambient temperature and externalizing behaviors in adolescents. *American Journal of Epidemiology, 187,* 1931–1941. doi: 10.1093/aje/kwy104

**Young, D. A., Inslicht, S. S., Metzler, T. J., Neylan, T. C., & Ross, J. A.** (2018). The effects of early trauma and the FKBP5 gene on PTSD and the

## C

# D

## E



## F

## G

## H

## I



## J

## K

## N



## O

## P

## S

## T

## U



## V

## X



## Y



## Z

# SUBJECT INDEX

Note: Page references in **bold** refer to definitions. Page references followed by "*f*" refer to figures.

# D

## F



## G

## J



## K



## L



## M

## N



## O

## P

# Q



# R

## S

## U



## V



## W



## X



## Y



## Z